The VCL Hierarchy: Components (continued)

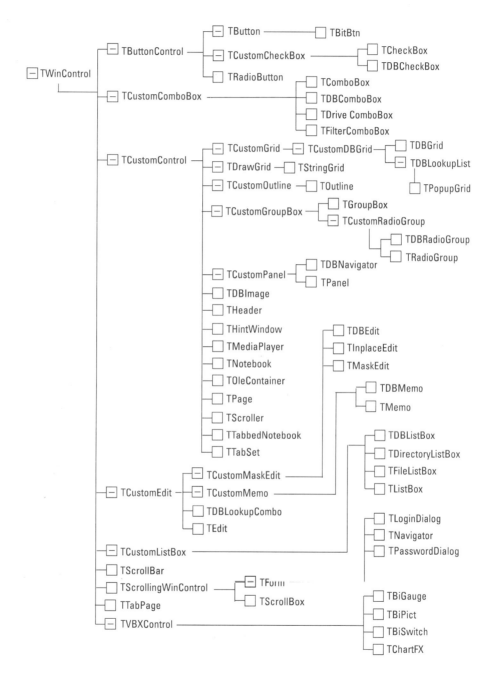

See Chapter 6 for details of the VCL hierarchy

Mastering Delphi™

Marco Cantù

SYBEX®

San Francisco • Paris • Düsseldorf • Soest

Acquisitions Manager: Kristine Plachy
Developmental Editor: Jane Reh
Editors: Marilyn Smith, Dusty Bernard
Project Editor: Valerie Potter
Technical Editor: Danny Thorpe
Book Designer: Suzanne Albertson
Technical Artist: Dan Schiff
Desktop Publisher: Ann Dunn
Production Assistant: Reneé Avalos
Indexer: Nancy Guenther
Cover Designer: Design Site
Cover Photographer: Mark Johann

Library of Congress Card Number: 95-68657
ISBN: 0-7821-1739-2

Manufactured in the United States of America
10 9 8 7 6 5 4 3

To my wife Lella, with all of my love

ACKNOWLEDGMENTS

I spent almost a year working on this book, and many things happened in that period of time. Many people got involved with my work and my life, and it is not easy to find the right words to thank all of them.

Probably the first thank you goes to Borland programmers and managers, because they built a great product. The thanks go in particular to Zack Urlocker (who showed me an early demo of the product and always kept in contact with me), David Intersimone (who really helped me a lot in several ways, since we met many years ago), Paul Gross, and Ian Robinson. I would also like to extend my thanks to all of Borland's Delphi team, including the people I've been in contact with and those I've never met.

By the way (and this is the first tip in the book), you can see a list of the names of the Borland developers by opening Delphi's About box and pressing the T-E-A-M keys while holding down the Alt key. You can get the names of the R&D team members by pressing Alt and typing D-E-V-E-L-O-P-E-R-S, or press Alt and A-N-D for a funny picture (with some animation) of Anders Heïlsberg, Delphi's chief technical engineer.

The book actually owes a lot to Nan Borreson of Borland, who first suggested that I have a look at the product and write about it. At that time, other people pushed the idea of a book about Delphi, including Steve Guty (the editor of my previous books) and Bruce Eckel, a friend and an author of great C++ books. In the last year, Bruce and I spent some time discussing Delphi while wandering in such different places as the small streets of Venice or the woods north of San Francisco.

Then Sybex came in. Many people at the company got involved with the book, and I do not even know all of them. My first thanks go to Gary Masters, for his initial support and continuous assistance, to Barbara Gordon, to Kristine Plachy, and to Jane Reh, the only person at Sybex I actually met in person. Jane was probably my greatest supporter and helped me to see things from the right perspective.

An invaluable help came from the editors, who endured understanding my drafts of the text and keeping such a huge book consistent. So thanks a lot to Marilyn Smith, Dusty Bernard, and Valerie Potter, who coordinated the whole process, and to the production team of Ann Dunn and Reneé Avalos, who were helpful, patient, and professional. Other people I was in contact with are Judy Jigarjian, Veronica Eddy, and Celeste Grinage. Thanks to all of you, and those I haven't mentioned, too.

While working on the book, I started my own company after quitting my consulting job at Mondadori Informatica, where I learned a lot about Windows programming from Stefano Maruzzi. So, thanks a lot to Stefano, his wife Antonella, Claudio Galletti, Giovanni Librando (for introducing me to Visual Basic and helping me to understand why Delphi is better), Andrea Provaglio, and also to Elena, Mariella, and all of the other people working there. I still write regularly for a magazine they publish, *PCProfessionale* (the Italian edition of Ziff-Davis' *PC Magazine*). This magazine actually published my first Delphi reviews and articles, thanks to Giorgio Panzeri (who still thinks I can deliver articles on time) and Roberto Mazzoni.

Of course, they are not the only people in the Italian programmers community I worked with. A very special thank you goes to Marco Miotti, who was the Delphi and C++ product manager at Borland Italia before the office was closed, to Ernesto Franchini, and to other people working for Borland in Italy and in France. I would also like to thank all the people who attended my programming courses over the years, and many other programmers I've met and worked with.

Some friends and magazine editors looked at portions of the book, or just examples and ideas for it, and provided some invaluable feedback. The magazine editors include J.D. Hildebrand of *Windows Tech Journal*, Tim Gooch of *Delphi Developers Journal*, and Jerry Coffrey of *Delphi Informant*. Other people on the staff of these magazines got involved, too, revising articles I've submitted. Thanks a lot to all of you, also because of the help you give to the Delphi programmer community.

Other comments came from Norm McIntosh, who so kindly hosted me at his home in San Francisco the last time I was there and showed me some real-life Delphi projects. The OLE chapter was reviewed by OLE expert (and book writer) Bryan Waters, who suggested some changes. Many suggestions also came from people *living* on CompuServe forums, mainly the Delphi forum (GO DELPHI), but also some others, including magazine-related forums and the Italian forum (GO ITALFOR). The help you get from many people on CompuServe is great, and many *TeamB* members do an incredible job supporting Borland products. I've decided not to list any of their names individually, because the thanks go to the whole group, and I did not want to mention some of them and forget others. I also owe them some excuses for not being very helpful myself, but having to make international phone calls to connect to CompuServe (until an Italian node was finally opened) made me somewhat conservative regarding my on-line time.

Other invaluable comments came from Steve Tendon, co-author of my first C++ book, who read the whole manuscript, made many suggestions, and helped me in particular with writing an example involving Borland Paradox for Windows. Speaking of other books and co-authors, I still owe a thank you to Bob Arnson and to Dan Horn.

At Borland, Scott Frolich reviewed the table of contents, which helped shape the book. Danny Thorpe, also at Borland, did incredibly great work as this book's technical editor, finding many errors, suggesting improvements, revealing features I was not aware of, bashing me on silly mistakes, explaining things to me, adding notes to the text, and providing many insights. The quality of the book owes quite a lot to Danny, more than any other person, so thank you very much.

Another thank you goes to all the people and companies who contributed material for the companion CD-ROM. Some of them endured a lot of work for the almost instant deadlines I gave them. Many people are doing a great job supporting Delphi, and those people and companies are among them. Some of them also do it for free, and in this case, the thank you is double.

Besides those involved with my work and the book, I want to thank other people, capable of keeping up with my little free time and tough deadlines, and helping me while I was writing. First of all my wife, Lella, who never stopped supporting me in any possible way. Many of her plans, particularly for holidays and weekends, had to change because of the book, and things were really hectic at times.

She also improved my self-confidence when things were not working out as planned and forced me to stop working from time to time. For this same reason, I have to thank many of our friends, who supported my brain health, inviting us to their homes, to eat a pizza, or to see a film. I don't know if I would have ever reached the end of the book without those breaks.

The list of the friends is quite long, and includes Sandro and Monica, Stefano and Elena, Marco and Laura, Chiara, Luca and Elena, Chiara and Daniele, and Laura, to name just a few. There are also many others who have worked with me in local political movements and in other groups. Our parents, brothers, sisters, and their families were very supportive, too. It was nice to spend some of our limited free time with them and our five nephews, Matteo, Andrea, Giacomo, Stefano, and Andrea; playing with them helped me to relax.

Finally, I would like to thank all of the people, many unknown, who enjoy life and help in building a better world. If I never stop believing in the future, it is because of them.

CONTENTS AT A GLANCE

TABLE OF CONTENTS

PART IV   Creating Components and Libraries

APPENDICES

INTRODUCTION

Last year, I went to a conference in San Jose, California and was in a hotel room with Michael Himan and Zack Urlocker (both working for Borland at that time). After some chatting about compilers, Borland, languages, and similar topics, Michael asked me for my wish list of features for the next version of Borland C++. I spoke for some time about tools that could make Windows programming much simpler. He replied, "We have what you ask, only it's not based on C++." Zack moved to a keyboard and showed me what was to be known as Delphi. I was astonished, but at that time I could not really realize how great a job Borland was doing.

My first thought was that Pascal was striking back. Although at that time I earned most of my living from C++, this made me happy. Pascal had been my first serious programming language—the one used at the University for the first projects—and at that time, Pascal actually meant Turbo Pascal.

The more I delved into this programming language and the Delphi environment, the more I liked it, and the more I wanted to write this book. Writing articles and books, discussing object-oriented programming languages, and teaching Windows programming had been my job for some years, and Delphi was the natural next step in this direction.

If you have opened this book, you probably already know about this product, so I won't spend time here describing what Delphi is. As you read the book, you'll see what I like in Delphi and why. Here I'll just give you an overview of Delphi's key elements.

Delphi? Great!

There are many programming environments you can work with, but Delphi is outstanding for a number of reasons. Here are my top ten reasons to use Delphi, in reverse order:

10. Previous Borland Pascal and C++ compilers

9. The third-party components and tools

8. The editor, the debugger, the browser, and the other tools

7. The library source code availability

6. The form-based and object-oriented approach

5. A fast compiler

4. The database support

3. The close integration with Windows programming

2. Delphi's component technology

1. The Object Pascal language

If you want to know the details about each of these points, this book is for you.

Becoming a Delphi Master (Reading This Book)

Provided that Delphi is a great tool, it is also a complex programming environment that involves many different elements. This book will help you master Delphi programming, including the Object Pascal language, Delphi components (both using the existing ones and developing new components), the database support, and the key elements of Windows programming.

You do not need an in-depth knowledge of any of these topics to read this book. Having some familiarity with Delphi will help you a lot, particularly after the introductory chapters.

What this book does require is a knowledge of the basics of programming, using any language and with any operating system or environment. You should have an idea of what variables and functions are and what the term *loop* means. If you've never written a program line in your life, this might not be the book for you right now. First, read a book that provides an introduction to programming using Delphi, and then read this book.

If you already program in Delphi, or have some experience in a similar environment, you'll find this book very useful. After the first few chapters, you'll probably start learning things you didn't know, even if you have been programming in Delphi for months.

The Structure of the Book

The book is divided into four parts. The first part, Visual Programming and Language, introduces beginners to Delphi programming and also provides some tips for more experienced users. The focus in the first three chapters is on the Delphi development environment, and just a few examples are presented. This part goes on to discuss the Object Pascal language, from a brief overview of Pascal to the object-oriented features of the language. The final chapter in this part examines the key elements of Delphi's Visual Component Library (VCL).

The second part, Using Components, explores the use of Delphi components and forms to build Windows applications. It covers standard components, graphic components, menus, mouse input, graphical output, MDI (Multiple Document Interface), database programming, and many other topics. The chapters include both Delphi-specific topics and related Windows programming ideas.

The third part, Advanced Delphi Programming, discusses some advanced Windows programming techniques, such as memory handling, using resources, printing support, file handling, Dynamic Data Exchange (DDE), and Object Linking and Embedding (OLE). The chapters in this part provide more advanced examples and suggestions for further exploration of Delphi tools, to help you acquire a solid knowledge of the Windows environment.

The fourth part, Creating Components and Libraries, covers Delphi components and dynamic link library (DLL) development. Writing components, which is more difficult than using them, constitutes a key element of Delphi programming.

The book has two appendices, which are both quick introductions to programming concepts. Appendix A deals with OOP (object-oriented programming), and Appendix B covers SQL (Structured Query Language).

Other elements you'll find throughout this book are Notes, Tips, and Warnings. Notes present information related to the topic being discussed, such as some advanced features you don't need to know much about or references to differences between Windows 3.1 and Windows 95 (so that you can get ready for the new version of the operating system). Tips are extra information that you may find interesting or useful. If there is a possibility of something going wrong or a problem to be avoided, you'll find that information in a Warning.

How to Read This Book

This book focuses on examples. After the presentation of each concept and each Delphi component, there is usually one example (or more than one), to let you see how the feature can be used. Most of the examples are quite simple and focus on a single feature. More complex examples are often built step-by-step, with intermediate steps including some solutions that do not work well.

In this book, I've tried to skip reference material almost completely. You'll see just a few tables listing the meanings of different parameters of a procedure. A list of parameters of a function is presented only in a couple of cases where the original Delphi documentation is not correct. I've always thought that adding a lot of reference material is an easy way to increase the size of the book, and to make it obsolete as soon as the software changes slightly.

I suggest that you read this book with the Delphi Help files at hand, to have reference material readily available. Also, if you read it somewhere near a computer, you can test and run the programs immediately, and follow instructions as you come to them. However, I've done my best to allow you to read the book far away from a computer if you prefer (I'll let you choose your favorite place). Screen images and the key portions of the listings should help in this direction.

Even if you tend to read books from cover to cover, considering the size of this book and the various topics it covers, you might follow one of these paths for reading the book:

- If you are quite new to the whole subject, you might want to read the first two parts, skipping some of the more advanced constructs of the language. Also read the two appendices, which introduce OOP and SQL. Then reread the chapters about the language and using components, and move along only when you are familiar with the information there.

- If you consider yourself a good programmer, but not a Delphi expert, read the book straight through. You can skip the sections that introduce Windows topics if you are familiar with the API of the system.

- If you are an experienced Delphi programmer and you don't have much time, you can focus on the language chapters, then start from Chapter 9 and read forward from there. You'll probably spend most of your time on the advanced parts of the book, but keep in mind that not all of the examples in the earlier chapters are simple. For example, Chapter 10 includes an example of a clone of the Windows' MineSweeper game.

Conventions Used in This Book

The book uses a few conventions to make it more readable. Some elements of the language, such as the keywords and the names of constant values, appear in a different, "program" font, as in "the for keyword." Direct calls of Windows API functions also appear in program font to distinguish them from similarly named Delphi methods. Delphi data types, component names, method names, and property names are in the regular font used for the text (you can easily spot them by their mixed capitalization).

In capitalizing and formatting the source code, I've tried to remain consistent with the most common conventions, but you'll notice that I have my preferences. Code formatting is a topic of much debate, as is any subject that involves personal taste and habits more than fixed rules.

The text contains code fragments and partial or full listings. You'll be able to find all of the listings on the companion disk (actually, a companion CD). To make it simple to locate the examples on the disk, each chapter has its own directory, and each sample has its own subdirectory. The names of these subdirectories reflect the names of the examples, as indicated in this book.

The Companion CD

The main reason for the companion CD is to hold the source code of the examples in the book. Since there are more than 200 examples and I wanted to provide the ready-to-use executable files, the choice of a CD as the medium is justified. Also, with the examples on a CD, you don't need to copy all of the files onto your hard disk. You can just open the source files, run the executable files to see their effect, and then copy the examples you want to modify onto your hard disk. On the CD, you'll find a browser application, CDVIEW.EXE (a variation of an example built in Chapter 14), which can be used to look at the source code and run the executable files directly.

I've compiled and executed each of the examples on different computers, and done my best to keep the disk listings consistent with those in the text.

In some cases, the name of an example's project file does not match the name of the directory containing it, particularly for those examples with multiple versions. In these cases, the name of the example mentioned in the text refers to the directory name, not to the project name. Since there is a single Delphi project in each directory, it should be quite simple to find a particular example.

Requirements for the Executable Files

There are a few requirements for running some of the executable files. The database examples (in Chapters 17 and 18) require the proper database aliases, which are automatically set up by Delphi. You also need to have the Delphi sample databases installed (this installation takes place when you install the Delphi samples).

To run the examples in the chapter devoted to client/server applications (Chapter 18), you do not need the Client-Server version of Delphi, but one of the examples requires building a table with another example first. Some examples in the chapter about multimedia applications (Chapter 26) require a sound board, others require one of the Windows video extensions, and for one example, you need a CD driver capable of playing an audio CD.

Third-Party Tools

The companion CD holds much more than the source code of the book examples. You'll find many third-party tools, including a number of Delphi components. Some of them are in demo versions, others are shareware, and others are public domain versions. Of course, you'll need to register the demo and shareware components (and the other shareware tools) if you use them to build programs.

The CD contains a variety of Delphi-related tools, ranging from installation programs, to resource editors, to table viewers. The selection includes only tools that are strictly Delphi-related, and most of them are written in Delphi, too.

The CD also contains some electronic Delphi magazines, provided as Windows Help files or Acrobat files (the Acrobat reader is included, in case you don't have it). I hope you'll enjoy these magazines, subscribe to them, and support the vendors of Delphi-related tools in general.

Components and tools are available both in compressed and uncompressed formats. In the latter case, I've also installed some of the tools, so that you can see them running compiled samples and looking at some files from the CD, before you decide whether to install them. Note that some of the preinstalled versions might have some minor problems if executed from the CD, so I suggest that you install them if you want to study them in detail.

Again, you can use the CDVIEW program to browse through the add-on tools. Every directory has a README.TXT file, which is automatically loaded by CDVIEW as soon as you reach a new directory.

How to Contact the Author

If you find any problems in the text or examples in this book, or if you have specific questions, I would be happy to hear from you. You can reach me directly via electronic mail (see the address below).

If you have some more general questions and you have a CompuServe account, you can address them to me in the DELPHI forum or in the SYBEX forum. I'll reply to them, but others might help you at the same time (probably sooner).

I would definitely like to hear from you. Besides reporting errors and problems, give me your unbiased opinion of the book or tell me which example you liked best and which you found most useless. Suggestions for future editions are also appreciated.

To reach me, my e-mail address on CompuServe is **100273,2610**. From the Internet, that becomes **100273.2610@compuserve.com**. Considering that I live in Italy, this is an effective way to keep in touch. (I also frequently attend programmers and computer conferences in the United States and around the world.)

I hope you'll enjoy reading this book, as I've enjoyed writing it.

PART I

Visual Programming and Language

CHAPTER

ONE

A Form Is a Window

- Form creation

- Components and properties

- Program compilation

- Events and code

- Delphi as a two-way tool

In this chapter, we will build our first MS Windows application with Delphi. As the name suggests, Windows applications are usually based on windows. So, how are we going to create our first window? We'll do it by using a form.

As the chapter's title says, in fact, a form really is a window in disguise. There is no real difference between the two concepts, at least from a general point of view. Focusing more sharply, you will find differences: A form is always a window, but the reverse doesn't hold true.

Some Delphi components are windows, too. A push button is a window. A list box is a window. So, to avoid any confusion, I'll use the term *form* to indicate the main window of an application or a similar window; I'll use the term *window* in the broader sense.

Creating Your First Form

Even though you have probably already created at least a simple application in Delphi, I'm going to show you the process again, to highlight some interesting points.

Creating a form is probably one of the easiest operations in the system: You only need to open Delphi, and it will automatically create a new, empty form for you, as you can see in Figure 1.1. That's all there is to it.

If you have another project open, you can choose the New Project command from the File menu, which will close the old project automatically (you might be asked if you want to save some of the files). When you select the New Project command, the system might create a new blank project for you or ask you to select a standard template. The choice depends on a setting in the Environment Options, which I'll discuss in the next chapter. If you must choose a template, select Blank Project.

Believe it or not, you already have a working application. You can run it, using the proper toolbar icon or menu command, and it will result in a standard MS Windows program. Delphi creates a stand-alone executable file that you can easily move to another machine. In fact, no run-time libraries are needed. Of course, this application won't be very useful, since it has a single empty window with no capabilities.

FIGURE 1.1:

The empty form created when you open the Delphi environment

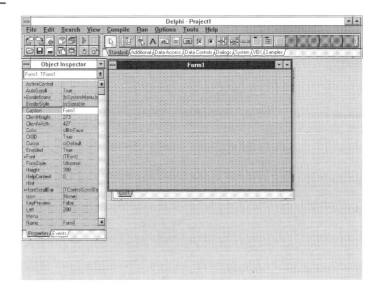

Adding a Title

Before we actually run the application, let's make a quick change. The title of the form is *Form1*. For a user, the title of the main window stands for the name of the application. So we should change *Form1* to something more meaningful.

When you first open Delphi, the Object Inspector window should appear on the left side of the form (see Figure 1.1). If not, open it by choosing the Object Inspector command from the View menu. In the Object Inspector window, you can see a list of the properties of the form (the Object Inspector shows the properties of the selected component). At the bottom of the list, you can see a tab labeled Properties. The other tab is labeled Events, which you can choose to switch to a list of events that can take place in the form, or in the selected component.

We can change the title of the form simply by changing the Caption property, which is selected by default. (The properties are listed in alphabetical order, so it's quite easy to find the ones you want to change.) Type in a new Caption for the form. While you type, you can see the title of the form change accordingly. If you type *Hello*, the title of the form changes immediately, as you can see in Figure 1.2.

FIGURE 1.2:

The form with a new title

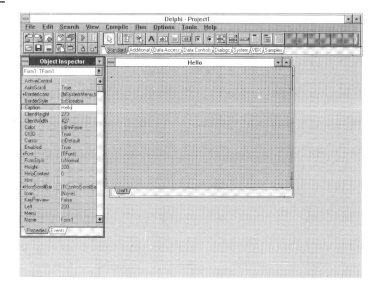

As an alternative, you can modify the internal name of the form by changing its Name property. If you have not entered a new Caption, the new value of the Name property will be used for the Caption property, too.

Although we haven't done much work, we have built a full-blown application, with a system menu and the default minimize and maximize buttons. You can resize the form by dragging its borders, move it by dragging its caption, maximize it to full-screen size, or reduce it to an icon. It works, but again, it's not very useful.

If you do minimize the window, you'll see that something isn't right. Instead of showing the caption of the form as the icon caption, it shows the name of the project, something like *Project1*. We can fix this by giving a name to the project. This can be done by saving the project to disk with a new name.

Saving the Form

Select the Save Project or Save Project As command from the File menu, and Delphi will ask you to give a name to the source code file associated with the form, and then to give a name to the project file. Since I like the name of the project to match the caption of the form (*Hello*), I've named the form source file HELLO_F .PAS (see Figure 1.3), which stands for Hello Form. I've given the project file the name HELLO.DPR (see Figure 1.4).

FIGURE 1.3:

When you save a project, you need to name the Pascal source file first.

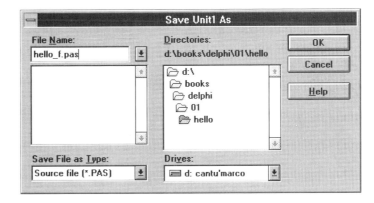

FIGURE 1.4:

After you name the source file, name the project file. If the project file name matches the form's caption, when you minimize its window, the name won't change.

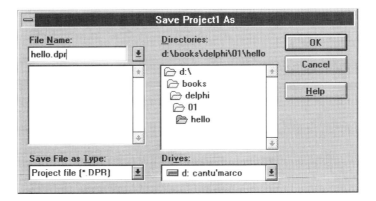

Unfortunately, we cannot use the same name for the project and the form; they must be unique Delphi names. Adding an underscore and the letter f (_f) after the form name is a solution, but then you have only 6 characters remaining for the name. You could use a totally different name, or simply call it Mainform. However, I dislike this approach because you will end up with a number of forms (in different projects) that all have the same name, which can become confusing.

Both files have been placed in a HELLO subdirectory of directory 01 (which stands for Chapter 1). This is the way I'll save source files throughout the book, and you should follow this approach to find the code of the examples on the companion disk.

When you use matching names for the project file and the title of the form, the caption of the form and the caption of the icon (when the form is minimized) will be the same. The same holds for the name displayed by the MS Windows Task Manager (just press the Ctrl and Esc keys at the same time to test this). This is the default behavior for an MS Windows 3.1 application.

Most of the sample programs in Delphi do not use this matching names approach. This means that when you minimize the main window, the name of the icon is different from the caption of the form. The same happens for the name listed in the Windows Task Manager, which also shows the name of the project and not the caption of the form. This can be quite confusing, particularly if the two names are really different.

The advantage of this approach is that it is probably going to be similar to the behavior of Windows 95 applications, which use a TaskBar instead of the icons and the Task Manager. In any case, you are free to change the name of a Delphi project both at design-time and at run-time. For example, you might copy the name of the form into the name of the project at run-time.

As an alternative, you can add a title to the application using the Application page of the Project Options dialog box (choose Project from the Options pull-down menu, go to the Application page, and fill in the Title field). In fact, Delphi will use the name of the executable file as the application title only if such a title hasn't been defined.

Both approaches can also be used to solve another problem: the project name cannot have more than 8 characters, since it is a file name and we are still in the DOS world. But the Caption property of the form and the application title can be much longer.

Using Components

Now it's time to start placing something useful in our Hello form. Forms can be described as component containers. Each form can host a number of components or controls. You can choose a component from the multipage palette above the form, in the Delphi window:

To complete our example, choose the Button component from the Standard page of the Components palette. Just click on this component, move the mouse cursor to the form, press the left mouse button to set the upper-left corner of the button, and drag the mouse to set the button's size. Now your form should look like Figure 1.5.

FIGURE 1.5:

Adding a button to the Hello form

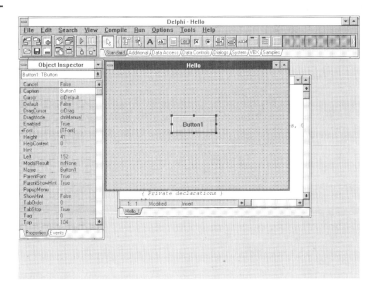

Our form will have only one button, so we'll center it in the form. You can probably do this by hand, moving the button to the center, but I'm not that good at it. Fortunately, I have help from Borland. When you choose the Alignment Palette option from the View menu, a toolbox with alignment icons appears:

This toolbox makes a number of operations easy. It includes buttons to align controls or to center them in the form. Using the two buttons in the third column, you can place the button in the center of the form.

Consider that although we've placed the button in the center, as soon as you run the program, you can resize the form. Then the button won't be in the middle anymore. So we can say that the button is in the center of the form only at startup. Later on, we'll see how to make the button remain in the middle after the form is resized, by adding some code. For now, our first priority is to change the label shown inside the button.

Changing Properties

Like the form, the button has a Caption property that we can use to change its label, which is the text displayed inside the button. As a better alternative, we can change the Name of the button. The Name is a kind of internal property—a property used only in the code of the program. However, as I mentioned earlier, if you change the Name of a button before changing its Caption, the Caption property will have the same text as the Name property.

Changing the Name property is usually a good choice, and you should generally make this operation early in the development cycle, before you write much code. However, you often need to change the Caption property, too. There are at least two reasons for this.

The first reason to have a Caption different from the Name is that it's a good habit to have the word *Button* in the Name of the component, but it's not that nice to see it in the button's text. In the code, it's better to refer to *HelloButton* than to *Hello*, since *Hello* can refer to a form or any other kind of component. At the same time, a caption such as *Say hello* is certainly better than *HelloButton*.

The second reason is that captions should be descriptive, and therefore they often use two or more words, as in *Say hello*. If you try to use this text as the Name property, however, Delphi will show an error message, such as the one in Figure 1.6.

The name is an internal property, and it is used as the name of a variable referring to the component. Therefore, for the Name property, you must follow the rules

FIGURE 1.6:

The error message shown when you try to use a space in the Name property of a component

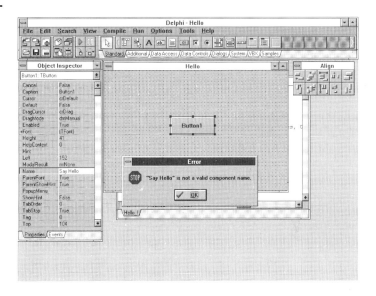

for naming an identifier in the Pascal language:

- An identifier is a sequence of letters, digits, or underscore characters of any length (although only the first 63 characters are significant).

- The first character of an identifier cannot be a number; it must be a letter or the underscore character.

- No spaces are allowed in an identifier.

- Identifiers are not case-sensitive, but usually each of the words in an identifier begins with a capital letter, as in HelloButton. But hellobutton, HELLOBUTTON, and helloButton refer to this same identifier.

Here is a summary of the changes we have made to the properties of the button and form. I'll usually show you the structure of the form as it appears once it has been converted in a readable format (I'll describe how to convert a form into text later in the chapter). Usually, I won't show you the entire textual description of a form, which is often quite long, but only its key elements. I won't include the lines describing the position of the components, their sizes, or some less important default values. I will also use bold text to highlight the names of the elements (following the object keyword):

```
object Form1: TForm1
  Caption = 'Hello'
  OnClick = FormClick
  object HelloButton: TButton
    Caption = 'Say hello'
    OnClick = HelloButtonClick
  end
end
```

This description shows some attributes of the components and the events they respond to. We will see the code for these events in the following sections.

If you run this program now, you will see that the button works properly. In fact, if you press the mouse button on it, it will be pushed, and when you release the mouse button, the on-screen button will be released. The only problem is that when you press the button, you might expect something to happen. Me, too.

Responding to Events

When you press the mouse button on a form, or on a component, MS Windows informs your application of the event by sending it a message. Ignoring Windows behavior, at least for the moment, you should be aware of the fact that Delphi responds by receiving an *event notification* and calling a proper *event-response method*. As a programmer, you can provide several of these methods, both for the form itself and for the components you have placed in the form (in our case, the button).

Delphi defines a number of different events for each kind of component. The list of the events for a form is different from the list of the events for a button, although some events are common to both components. You can determine the events available for a form or a component by viewing the Events page of the Object Inspector while that element is selected.

Here are the operations necessary to display a hello message when the button is pressed:

- Select the button, in the form or in the Object Inspector using the Object Selector (the combo box just below the title of the Object Inspector).

- Select the Events page.

- Double-click with the left mouse button in the white area on the right side of the OnClick event. A new method name will appear:

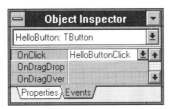

Delphi creates a procedure named HelloButtonClick in the code of the form, and opens the source code file in that position, as shown in Figure 1.7. Instead of following the steps above, you can accomplish the same task by just double-clicking on the button in the form.

This operation invokes the *default action* for the component. The default action for a button is to add a procedure to respond to the click event. Even if you are not sure that you want to use the default action, you can use the double-click method. If you end up adding a new procedure you don't need, just leave it empty. Empty method bodies generated by Delphi will be removed as soon as you save the project. In other words, if you don't put any code in them, they simply go away.

FIGURE 1.7:

The edit window after you have created a procedure to handle the click of the Hello button

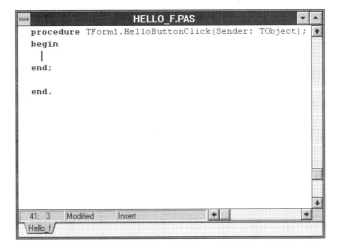

> **TIP**
>
> When you want to remove an event-response method you have written from the source code of a Delphi application, you could delete all of the references to it. However, a better way is to delete all of the code from the corresponding procedure, leaving only the declaration and the `begin` and `end` keywords. The text should be the same as what Delphi automatically generated when you first decided to handle the method. When you save a project, Delphi removes any empty methods from the source code and from the form description (including the reference to them in the Events page of the Object Inspector).

Now we can start typing some instructions between the `begin` and the `end` keywords delimiting the code of the procedure. If you do not know the Object Pascal language, don't worry. We will explore its most important features in Chapters 4 and 5. Writing code is usually so simple that you don't need to be an expert in the language to start to work with Delphi.

For the moment, type the following code. You should type only the line at the middle (shown in bold typeface), but I've included the whole source code of the procedure to let you know where you need to add the new code in the editor:

```
procedure TForm1.HelloButtonClick(Sender: TObject);
begin
  MessageDlg ('Hello, guys', mtInformation, [mbOK], 0);
end;
```

The code is very simple. There is only a call to a function, MessageDlg, to display a small message dialog box. The function has four parameters. You can see the details about this function by clicking on its name in the edit window and pressing the F1 key. This brings up the Help information. Here is a summary of the description in the Help system:

- The first parameter is the string you want to display: the message.

- The second parameter is the type of message box. You can choose `mtWarning`, `mtError`, `mtInformation`, or `mtConfirmation`. For each type of message, the corresponding caption is used and a proper icon is displayed at the side of the text.

- The third parameter is a set of values indicating the buttons you want to use. You can choose mbYes, mbNo, mbOK, mbCancel, or mbHelp. Since this is a set of values, you can have more than one of these values. Always use the proper set notation with square brackets ([and]) to denote the set, even if you have only one value, as in the example. (Chapter 4 discusses Pascal sets.)

- The fourth parameter is the *help context*, a number indicating which page of the Help system should be invoked if the user presses the F1 key. We will usually write 0, since we don't care to include the help, at least for the moment.

The function also has a return value, which I've just ignored, using it as if it were a procedure. In any case, it's important to know that the function returns an identifier of the button that the user clicked to close the message box.

NOTE Programmers who are not familiar with the Pascal language, particularly programmers who use C/C++, might be confused by the phrase "The function also has a return value, which I've just ignored, using it as if it were a procedure." In Pascal, there are two different keywords to define procedures and functions. The only difference between functions and procedures is that only functions have a type, or return value. Procedures have no return value, although they can have parameters passed by reference (var parameters) which allow a sort of return value. One enhancement over previous versions of Borland's Pascal compiler products is that Delphi allows you to ignore the return value of a function, using it as a procedure, as in the example here.

After you have written this line of code, you should be able to run the program. When you click on the button, you'll obtain the message box shown in Figure 1.8.

Every time the user clicks the left mouse button on the push button of the form, a message is displayed. What if the mouse is pressed outside that area? Nothing happens. Of course, we can add some new code to handle this event. We only need to add an OnClick event to the form itself.

To accomplish this, move to the Events page of the Object Inspector and select the form. Then double-click at the right side of the OnClick event, and you'll end up in

FIGURE 1.8:

The message box displayed when
you press the Say hello button

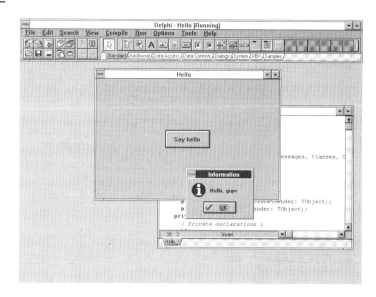

the proper position of the edit window. Now add a new call to the MessageDlg
function, as in the following code:

```
procedure TForm1.FormClick(Sender: TObject);
begin
  MessageDlg ('You have clicked outside of the button',
    mtWarning, [mbOK], 0);
end;
```

Notice that I've written the code on two lines, instead of one. The Pascal compiler
completely ignores new lines, white spaces, tab spaces, and similar formatting
characters. Program statements are separated by semicolons (;), not by starting to
write code on a new line.

WARNING   There is one case in which Delphi doesn't completely ignore line
breaks. Strings cannot extend across multiple lines. In some cases, you
can split a very long string into two different strings, written on two
lines, and merge them using the + operator.

With this new version of the program, if the user clicks on the button, the hello message is displayed (Figure 1.8), but if he or she misses the button, a warning message appears, as in Figure 1.9.

FIGURE 1.9:

The message displayed when you click in the form outside the button

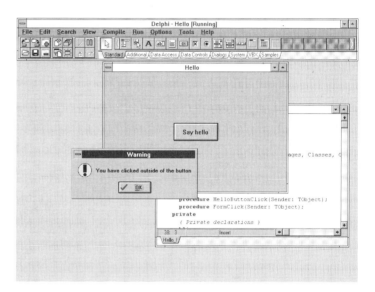

Compiling and Running a Program

Before we make any further changes to our HELLO program, let's stop for a moment to consider what goes on when you run the application. When you click on the run button on the toolbar or select the corresponding menu command (Run from the Run menu), Delphi does the following:

- Compiles the source code file describing the form
- Compiles the project file
- Builds the executable (EXE) file linking the proper libraries (as specified)
- Runs the EXE file, usually in debug mode

The key point is that when you ask Delphi to run your application, it compiles it. As I've already mentioned, the executable file you obtain is a stand-alone program. You can easily run it from the MS Windows File Manager or Program Manager, and even move it to a different computer.

Because it's a compiled program, it is also extremely fast, with speed comparable to a C or C++ compiled program. Delphi compiled code runs much faster (on average, 10 or 20 times faster) than the equivalent code in interpreted environments such as Visual Basic, PowerBuilder, Paradox, and dBASE.

Some users cannot believe that Delphi generates real executable code, because when you run a small program, its main window appears immediately, as in an interpreted environment. To see for yourself, try this: Open the Environment Options dialog box, move to the Preferences page, and turn on the Show Compile Progress option. Now select the Build All command from the Run menu. You'll see a dialog box with the compilation status. You'll find that this takes just a few seconds, or even less on a fast machine.

The Pascal compiler embedded in Delphi works very quickly, in the tradition of Borland's Turbo Pascal compilers, and is really much faster than any C++ compiler for a number of technical reasons. One reason is that the language definition is much simpler. Another is that the Pascal compilers and linkers have less work to do to include libraries or other compiled source files in a program.

Changing Properties at Run-Time

After this short digression, we are ready to finish the HELLO application, building a new version of the program, HELLO2. If you want to save the current version of the program without overwriting it, you can copy all of the source files in a new subdirectory. If you use the Save Project As command on the File menu, the new project will refer to, and modify, the source files of the older version.

In this book (as well as on the companion disk), you will find multiple versions for some complex examples, built step-by-step. This makes it easier to understand the various steps and to test what doesn't work well in the intermediate versions. Along this line, the current example, has two versions: HELLO and HELLO2.

NOTE The different version names for the example refer to different subdirectories where the files are stored on the companion disk. I refer to the new example as HELLO2 because this is the name of the directory hosting it, not the name of this project file.

We now want to try to change some properties at run-time. For example, we might change the text of the HelloButton from *Say hello* to *Say hello again* after the first time a user clicks on it. This is really simple. You only need to change the code of the Hello-ButtonClick procedure as follows (new code is in boldface):

```
procedure TForm1.HelloButtonClick(Sender: TObject);
begin
  MessageDlg ('Hello, guys', mtInformation, [mbOK], 0);
  HelloButton.Caption := 'Say Hello Again';
end;
```

NOTE The Pascal language uses the := operator to express an assignment, and the = operator to test for equality. At the beginning, this can be confusing for programmers coming from other languages. For example in C and C++, the assignment operator is =, and the equality is tested with = =. After a while, you'll get used to it. In the meantime, if you happen to use = instead of :=, you'll get an error from the compiler.

A property such as Caption can be changed at run-time very easily, using an assignment statement. Figure 1.10 shows the result of this operation.

Not every property can be changed at run-time, and some can be changed *only* at run-time. You can easily spot this last group: They are not listed in the Object Inspector, but they appear in the Help file. Some run-time properties are defined as *read-only*, which means that you can access their value but cannot change it. If you have any doubt, the Help file describes each property, indicating if it can be used at run-time.

FIGURE 1.10:

The new caption of the button, after the change. Notice that the button is not in the middle of the form, because it has been resized—a problem we will solve soon.

Adding Code to the Program

Our program is almost finished, but we still have a problem to resolve, which will require some real coding. As I mentioned before, the button starts in the middle of the form but will not remain there when you resize the form. This problem can be solved in two radically different ways.

One solution is to change the border of the form to a thin frame, so that the form cannot be resized at run-time. Just move to the BorderStyle property of the form, and choose bsSingle (for border style single) instead of bsSizeable in the combo box on the right. The result will be the form shown in Figure 1.11. As you can see in that figure, the Size command on the system menu is automatically disabled.

The other approach is to write some code to move the button to the center of the form each time the form is resized. This is exactly what we are going to do next. Why have I chosen this second approach? Just to start showing you some code. You might start having the idea that programming with Delphi is just a matter of select-ing options and visual elements. This is certainly a main method, but there comes a time when you need to write code.

When you want to add some code to a program, the first question you need to ask yourself is: Where? In an event-driven environment, the code is always executed in response to an event. When a form is resized, an event takes place: OnResize.

Select the form in the Object Inspector and double-click to the right of the name of this event in the Events page. A new procedure is added to the source file of the

FIGURE 1.11:

The non-resizable form with a fixed border, and its system menu with the Size command disabled

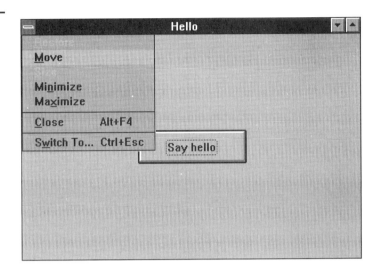

form. Now you need to type some code, as follows:

```
procedure TForm1.FormResize(Sender: TObject);
begin
  HelloButton.Top :=
    Form1.ClientHeight div 2 -
    HelloButton.Height div 2;
  HelloButton.Left :=
    Form1.ClientWidth div 2 -
    HelloButton.Width div 2;
end;
```

The meaning of this code should be quite straightforward. The Top and Left properties of the button—that is, the position of its top-left corner—should be set considering:

- The center of the frame, which is computed by dividing the height and the width of the internal area of the frame by 2. The internal area is its client area, indicated by the ClientWidth and ClientHeight properties. If you use the Height and Width properties instead, you will reference the center of the whole window. Here, we really need the center of the internal portion of the window. The height and width of the whole window and the internal area do not match, because the top border of the frame contains the caption.

- The height and the width of the button itself, since the top-left corner of the button should not be placed in the center of the form, but in the center minus half the height and half the width of the button itself.

This final version of the example works quite well, as you can see in Figure 1.12. This figure includes a couple of versions of the form, with different sizes. By the way, this figure is a real snapshot of the screen. Once you have created a Windows application, you can run several copies of it at the same time by using the File Manager or Program Manager. The Delphi environment can run only one copy of a program. Why? Because when you run a program within Delphi, you really start its debugger, and it cannot debug two programs at the same time—not even two copies of the same program.

FIGURE 1.12:

With the last version of the program, the Hello button always remains in the center of the form.

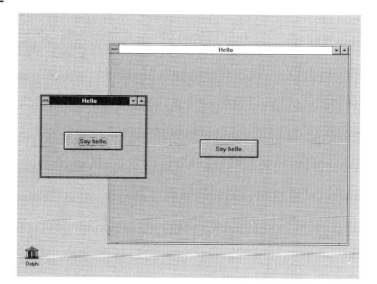

A Two-Way Tool

In the HELLO example, we have written three small portions of code, to respond to three different events. Each portion of code was part of a different method. But where does the code we write end up? The whole source code of a form is written in a single Pascal language source file, the one we've named HELLO_F.PAS. This file evolves and grows not only when you code the response of some events, but also as you add components to the form. The properties of these components are stored together with the properties of the form in a second file, named HELLO_F.DFM.

Delphi can be defined as a two-way tool, since everything you do in the visual environment ends up in some code. Nothing is hidden away and inaccessible. You have the complete code, and although some of it might be fairly complex, you can edit everything. Of course, it is easier to use only the visual tools, at least until you are an expert Delphi programmer.

The term *two-way tool* means also that you are free to change the code that has been produced, and then go back to the visual tools. This is true as long as you follow some simple rules.

Looking at the Source Code

Although you might not be able to understand everything in the source code of a program, let's take a look at what Delphi has generated during the operations we have done previously. Every action has an effect— in the Pascal code, in the code of the form, or in both.

When you start a new, blank project, the empty form has some code associated with it, such as in Listing 1.1.

The file, named Unit1, uses a number of units and defines a new data type (a class) and a new variable (an object instance). The class is named TForm1, and it is derived from TForm. The global variable is Form1, of the new type TForm1.

NOTE   *Units* are the modules into which a Pascal program is divided. When you start a new project, you have a program and a unit. Each time you add a form to a Delphi program, you add a new unit. Units are then compiled separately and linked into the main program. From a different point of view, units are the Pascal code source files indicated by the PAS extension.

LISTING 1.1: Code associated with a new, blank project in Delphi

```
unit Unit1;

interface

uses
  SysUtils, WinTypes, WinProcs, Messages, Classes,
  Graphics, Controls, Forms, Dialogs;

type
  TForm1 = class(TForm)
  private
    { Private declarations }
  public
    { Public declarations }
  end;

var
  Form1: TForm1;

implementation

{$R *.DFM}

end.
```

If you rename the files as suggested in the example, the code changes slightly, since the name of the unit must reflect the name of the file. If you name the file HELLO_F.PAS, the code begins with:

```
unit Hello_f;
```

As soon as you start adding new components, the form class declaration in the source code changes. For example, when you add a button to the form, the portion of the source code defining the new data type becomes (the new line is in boldface):

```
type
  TForm1 = class(TForm)
    Button1: TButton;
  private
    { Private declarations }
  public
    { Public declarations }
  end;
```

Now if you change the button's Name property (using the Object Inspector) to
HelloButton, the code changes slightly again:

```
type
  TForm1 = class(TForm)
    HelloButton: TButton;
  private
    { Private declarations }
  public
    { Public declarations }
  end;
```

Setting properties other than the name has no effect in the source code. The properties of the form and its components are stored in a separate form description file
(with a DFM extension).

Adding new event handlers has the biggest impact on the code. Each time you define a new handler for an event, a line is added to the data type definition of the
form, an empty method body is added in the implementation part, and some information is stored in the form description file, too. Listing 1.2 shows the complete
Pascal source code of the HELLO example (not the second version, HELLO2):

It is worth noting that there is a single file for the whole code of the form, not just
small fragments. Of course, this source code is only a partial description of the
form. The source code determines *how* the form and its components react to events.
The form description (the DFM file) stores the properties of the form and its components, including descriptions of the components in the form, where they are located on the form's display surface, and a host of other information about the
form's state. In general, source code provides the actions of the system, and properties provide the state of the system.

The Textual Description
of the Form

As I've just mentioned, along with the PAS file containing the source code, there is
another file describing the form, its properties, its components, and the properties
of the components. This is the DFM file, a binary file which isn't readable with an
editor.

LISTING 1.2:   The file HELLO_F.PAS, with the complete source code of the first
version of the HELLO example

```
unit Hello_f;

interface

uses
  SysUtils, WinTypes, WinProcs, Messages, Classes, Graphics,
  Controls, Forms, Dialogs, StdCtrls;

type
  TForm1 = class(TForm)
    HelloButton: TButton;
    procedure HelloButtonClick(Sender: TObject);
    procedure FormClick(Sender: TObject);
  private
    { Private declarations }
  public
    { Public declarations }
  end;

var
  Form1: TForm1;

implementation

{$R *.DFM}

procedure TForm1.HelloButtonClick(Sender: TObject);
begin
  MessageDlg ('Hello, guys', mtInformation, [mbOK], 0);
end;

procedure TForm1.FormClick(Sender: TObject);
begin
  MessageDlg ('You have clicked outside of the button',
    mtWarning, [mbOK], 0);
end;

end.
```

However, if you load this file in the Delphi code editor, it will be converted into a
textual description. This might give the false impression that the DFM file is indeed
a text file. For performance reasons, Borland has preferred to save the binary version, and has provided tools that allow for easy conversion to and from text. The
simplest of these tools is the editor itself. In Figure 1.13, you can see the two representations of the file when loaded in two different editors.

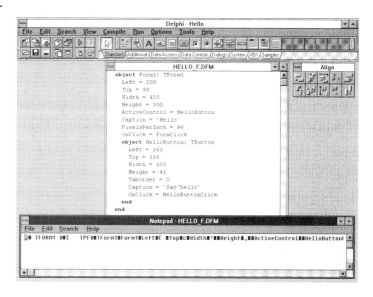

The DFM file holds a binary code that can be converted with the Delphi editor.

To understand what is stored in the DFM file, look at Listing 1.3, which shows the textual description of the form of the first version of the HELLO example. This is exactly the code produced by Delphi after a conversion of the form binary file, with boldface characters added to highlight the different portions of the text. You can compare this code with the short one I used before to indicate the key features and properties of the form and its components. As I mentioned earlier, I usually will show you a shorter version of the textual description of forms.

As you can see in this listing, the textual description of a form describes a number of objects (in this case, two) at different levels. The Form1 object contains the Hello-Button object, as you can infer from the indentation of the text. Each object has a number of properties and some methods connected to events (in this case, OnClick).

If you use the Delphi editor to view the textual description of a form, you are requested by the system to save the form first, to avoid having two representations of the same file you can work on. In fact, you can *edit* the textual description of the form, although this should be done with extreme care. As soon as you save the file, it will be turned back into a binary file, with a sort of compile process.

LISTING 1.3: The complete textual description of the form of the HELLO example, in the source file HELLO_F.DFM

```
object Form1: TForm1
  Left = 200
  Top = 99
  Width = 435
  Height = 300
  ActiveControl = HelloButton
  Caption = 'Hello'
  Font.Color = clWindowText
  Font.Height = -13
  Font.Name = 'System'
  Font.Style = []
  PixelsPerInch = 96
  OnClick = FormClick
  TextHeight = 16
  object HelloButton: TButton
    Left = 161
    Top = 116
    Width = 105
    Height = 41
    Caption = 'Say hello'
    TabOrder = 0
    OnClick = HelloButtonClick
  end
end
```

If something goes wrong in this compilation, or if you've made incorrect changes, you risk losing the contents of your DFM file, which means you will need to rebuild it from scratch. This is true, of course, only if you do not know what you are doing. An expert Delphi programmer might work on the text of a form for a number of reasons.

For big projects, the textual description of the form is a powerful documenting tool, an important form of backup (in case someone plays with the form, you can understand what has gone wrong by comparing the two textual versions), and a good version-handling tool. For these reasons, Borland has documented how to convert forms, using a couple of specific functions, and third-party tools for Delphi will probably take advantage of this capability. As we will see in the next chapter, the conversion is also applied when you cut or copy components from a form.

The Project File

In addition to the two files describing the form (PAS and DFM), there is a third file that is vital to rebuild the application. This is the Delphi project file (DPR). This file is built automatically, and you seldom need to change it, particularly for small programs. If you do need to change the behavior of a project, there are basically two ways: You can use the Delphi Project Manager (see Figure 1.14) and some options of the environment, or you can edit the project file directly.

FIGURE 1.14:

The Delphi Project Manager allows you to add units to the project, thus changing the contents of the project source file.

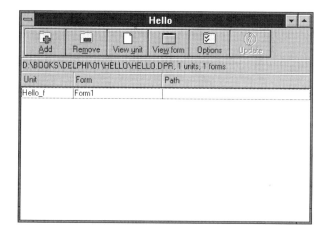

This project file is really a Pascal language source file, describing the overall structure of the program and its startup code:

```
program Hello;

uses
  Forms,
  Hello_f in 'HELLO F.PAS' {Form1};

{$R *.RES}

begin
  Application.CreateForm(TForm1, Form1);
  Application.Run;
end.
```

You can see this file by selecting the Select unit from list button on the SpeedBar (or the equivalent command on the View menu: Units). Here are the two Delphi Speed-Bar buttons you can use to view the list of units (on the left) or the list of forms (on the right):

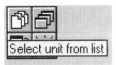

When you use one of these commands, a dialog box with the list of the source files of the project (or a list with the forms) appears. You can choose the project file (named HELLO in the example), or any other file you are interested in seeing.

Again, you should not edit this file unless you know what you are doing. You can find more details on this code in Chapter 19, where I discuss the use of the application object. Some basic information about how to manage a project without editing its source file manually is provided in Chapter 2.

Summary

In this chapter, we have created a simple program, added a button to it, and handled some basic events, such as a click with the mouse or a resize operation. We have also seen how to name files, projects, forms, and components, and how this affects the source code of the program.

Before we can look into more complex examples, however, we need to explore the Delphi development environment and study the Object Pascal language. These are the topics of the next few chapters.

The example in this chapter should have given you the impression that Delphi is really easy to use. Now the book starts to show you that there are some complex elements behind the scenes. You'll see that Delphi is a very powerful tool, even though you can use it to write programs very easily and quickly.

CHAPTER

TWO

2

Highlights of the Delphi Environment

- Delphi Help and Tutors

- Delphi menus and SpeedBars

- Form design tools

- The Delphi editor

- Project management

- Compiled program tools

- Delphi source files

In a visual programming tool such as Delphi, the role of the environment is certainly important, at times even more important than the programming language used by its compiler or interpreter. This is a good reason to spend some time reading the Delphi *User's Guide* manual, as well as this chapter. Even if the main features of this environment are intuitive, it is a mistake to skip the manual (or this chapter) altogether.

In this chapter, I won't discuss all of the features of Delphi or list all of its menu commands. The focus here is to give you the overall picture and help you to explore some of the environment traits that are not obvious.

Different Versions of Delphi

Before delving into the details of the Delphi programming environment, let's take a side step to underline two key ideas. First, there isn't a single version of Delphi. Although the basic version (the Desktop edition) has a hefty number of features, some advanced elements have been left out. These advanced features are part of the Client-Server edition. This Client-Server version includes the SQL Links that allow your applications to access data on a remote SQL database server, an SQL-enabled version of ReportSmith, and a Visual Query Builder property editor.

Both editions include the Local Interbase Server, for developing full SQL applications even if you don't have a network or remote host. The Client-Server version also includes the source code of the Run-Time Libraries (RTL) and of the Visual Component Library (VCL). The source code is available separately, as is the stand-alone debugger, Turbo Debugger for Windows.

Only a small section of this book, in Chapter 18, describes features not available in the basic version. You should be aware, however, some Delphi menus can have slight differences between the two editions.

The second idea to keep in mind is that there are a number of ways to customize the Delphi environment. You can change the buttons of the SpeedBar, attach new commands to the Tools menu, hide some of the windows or elements, and resize and move all of them. I'll try to use a standard user interface (as it comes out of the box), although I have my preferences and they will probably be reflected in some of the screenshots I'll show you in this chapter and throughout the whole book.

2

Another set of changes in the user interface takes place when you install some of Delphi's available tools and extensions. For example, if you add a version control system to the environment (such as PVCS Version Management from Intersolv), a new pull-down menu, Workgroups, appears in the menu bar.

Asking for Help

Now we can really start our tour. The first element of the environment we'll explore is the Help system. Since I'm not going to describe 100 percent of Delphi's components, objects, and methods, you will want to complement the information provided in the book with the reference material present in the Help files.

There are basically two ways to invoke the Help system: select the proper command in the Help pull-down menu, or choose an element of the Delphi interface or a token in the source code and press the F1 key.

TIP

When you press the F1 key, Delphi doesn't search for an exact match in the Help Search list. Instead, it tries to guess what you are asking. For example, if you press F1 when the text cursor is on the name of the Button1 component in the source code, the Delphi Help system automatically opens the description of the TButton class, since this is what you are probably looking for. This technique doesn't work in every case, just with simple, automatically generated names.

Note that there isn't a single Help file in Delphi. Most of the time, you'll invoke Delphi Help, but this file is complemented by the MS Windows API Help and the Component Writer's Help. These three Help files have a common search engine you activate by choosing the Help Topic Search command, or by pressing the Search All button in the Help window. The Search button in the Help window relates only to the current Help file.

You can find almost everything in the Help system, but you need to know what to search for. Usually this is obvious, but at times it is not. Spending some time just playing with the Help system will probably help you to understand the structure of these files and to learn how to find the information you need. Along with the three main Help files, there are a number of other files related to specific topics, such as Creating Windows Help, or tools, such as WinSight Help.

The Help files provide a lot of information, both for beginner and expert programmers, but they are especially valuable as a reference tool. They list all of the methods and properties for each component, the parameters of each method or function, and similar details, which are particularly important while you are writing code.

You can also merge third-party Help files into the Delphi Help system, using the HelpInst utility program.

The Role of Interactive Tutors

The first time you use Delphi (something you might have done a long time ago by now), the Help system might be confusing because you do not know where to start. In fact, the starting point of your Delphi exploration should not be in the Help system, but in the Interactive Tutors (see Figure 2.1).

FIGURE 2.1:

Delphi Interactive Tutors in action

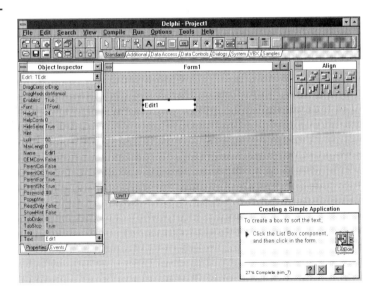

If you haven't run these on-line lessons introducing the key Delphi features, you should do so immediately (choose the Interactive Tutors command from the Help menu). They'll help you to understand the Delphi terminology and guide you in writing your first simple programs. Even experienced Delphi programmers will probably enjoy these Tutors, although they probably won't learn much.

The idea of the Tutors is really great, since they can guide you step-by-step, pointing you toward the solution of the simple problems presented and checking if your actions are correct. (I've wondered if I could have used similar tutors for the lessons covered in this book, but I still prefer good, old-fashioned paper for complex examples.)

Now that I'm sure you've looked at the Interactive Tutors, let's continue with our exploration of the Delphi environment.

Delphi Menus and Commands

There are basically three ways to issue a command in the Delphi environment:

- Use the menu.
- Use the SpeedBar (or toolbar).
- Use a SpeedMenu (one of the local menus activated by pressing the right mouse button).

Using the Menus

The Delphi menus offer many commands. I have no intention of boring you with a detailed description of the menu structure. For this type of information, you can refer to your *User's Guide* or the Help file. In the following sections, I'll present some suggestions on the use of some of the menu commands. Other suggestions will follow in the rest of the chapter. Of course, these hints will probably be more useful for beginners than for experienced users.

The File Menu

The starting point of this analysis is the File pull-down menu. This menu is somewhat complex, because it contains commands that operate on projects and commands that operate on files. Okay, I know that both are files, so this is the proper menu, but every time I open this menu, I need to think twice about what I'm doing.

The commands related to projects are the first five (New Project, Open Project, Save Project, Save Project As, and Close Project), Add File, Remove File, and the list of the last projects you have used are at the end of the menu. The Add File menu command can be used to add an existing file to the current project; other commands can be used to add new files (New Form and New Unit).

Some of the New commands (particularly New Project and New Form, but also New Component) invoke galleries of Experts or templates. I won't discuss this topic here, because the next chapter is devoted to these galleries.

Another strange command is Print. If you are editing the source code and select this command, the printer will output this text. If you are working on a form and select Print from the File menu, the printer will receive the graphical representation of the form. This is certainly nice, but can be confusing, particularly if you are working on other Delphi windows. Fortunately, two different print options dialog boxes are displayed (see Figure 2.2), so that you can check that the operation is correct.

FIGURE 2.2:

The two Delphi print options dialog boxes

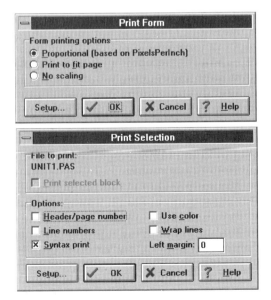

2

The Edit Menu

The Edit menu has some typical operations, such as the Undo and Redo features, and the Cut, Copy, and Paste commands, plus some specific commands for form or editor windows. The important thing to notice is that the standard features of the Edit menu work both with text and with form components.

Of course, you can copy and paste some text in the editor, or you can copy and paste components in one form, or from a form to another one. You can even copy and paste to a different parent window of the same form, as a panel or a group box.

TIP
When you copy and paste a component from two different containers, the coordinates of the component will be maintained. This means that if you copy a control from the middle of a form to a small panel, the component will be placed outside the visible area. To avoid this problem, a common technique is to drag the component near the top-left corner of the source before cutting or copying it, so it will appear near the top-left corner of the destination container. Another alternative is to paste the control in the editor, change its coordinates, and then copy and paste it into the proper form.

What you might not have noticed is that you can also copy components from the form to the editor and vice versa. Delphi places components in the clipboard after converting them to their textual description, as you can see in Figure 2.3. You can edit this text properly and then paste it back into the form as a new component.

For example, if you place a button on a form, copy it, then paste it to an editor (which can be Delphi's own source code editor or any word processor), you'll get the following description:

```
object Button1: TButton
  Left = 56
  Top = 48
  Width = 161
  Height = 57
  TabOrder = 0
  Caption = 'Button1'
end
```

FIGURE 2.3:

FIGURE 2.3:

Delphi copies the textual representation of components to the clipboard (as you can see in the Clipboard Viewer on the right), so that they are available to any editor.

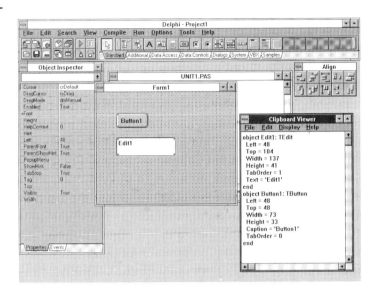

Now, if you change the name of the object, caption, or position, or add a new property, these changes can be copied and pasted back to a form. Here are some sample changes:

```
object MyButton: TButton
  Left = 200
  Top = 200
  Width = 180
  Height = 60
  TabOrder = 0
  Caption = 'My Button'
  Font.Name = 'Arial'
end
```

Pasting this code into the form will create a button in the specified position with the caption *My Button* in an Arial font. Figure 2.4 shows the result.

If you want to make use of this technique, you need to know how to edit the textual representation of a component properly. However, during this operation, Delphi can solve some minor problems and conflicts between properties of the component. You can understand what goes on by copying the component back to the editor.

FIGURE 2.4:

You can paste the textual description of a component into a form.

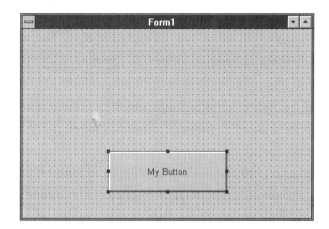

This is what you get if you copy the previous button again:

```
object MyButton: TButton
  Left = 200
  Top = 200
  Width = 180
  Height = 60
  TabOrder = 1
  Caption = 'My Button'
  Font.Height = -13
  Font.Name = 'Arial'
  ParentFont = False
end
```

As you can see, two lines have been added automatically: changing the height of the font and setting the ParentFont property to False. Of course, if you write something completely wrong, such as:

```
object Button3: TButton
  Left = 100
  Eight = 60
end
```

When you paste it into the form, Delphi will show an error indicating what has gone wrong (just a spelling error), as you can see in Figure 2.5.

FIGURE 2.5:
An error message is displayed when you try to paste a component with a property that doesn't exist or is misspelled.

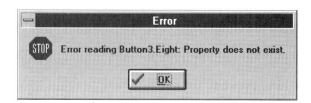

You can select several components and copy them all at once, either to another form or to a text editor. This might be useful when you need to work on a series of similar components. You can copy one to the editor, replicate it a number of times, then paste the whole group into the form again.

Along with the typical commands on the Edit menu, Delphi includes a number of other commands, which are mostly related to forms. The specific operations for forms can also be accessed through the form SpeedMenu (the local menu you can invoke with the right mouse button). These will be covered later in the chapter.

The Search Menu

The Search menu has some standard commands, too, such as Search and Replace. Other commands are not so simple to understand. The Incremental Search command is one of them. When you select this command, instead of showing a dialog box where you can enter the text you want to find, Delphi moves to the editor. There, you can type the text you want to search for directly in the editor message area, as you can see in Figure 2.6.

When you type the first letter, the editor will move to the first word starting with that letter. (But if your search text isn't found, the letters you typed won't even be displayed in the editor message area.) If this is not the word you are looking for, keep typing; the cursor will continue to jump to the next word that begins with those letters.

Although this command might look strange at first, it is very effective and extremely fast, particularly if you are typing and invoke it with a shortcut key (Ctrl-E if you are using the standard editor shortcut).

The Go to Line Number and Show Last Compile Error commands are quite intuitive. The Find Error command might seem strange at first. It is not used to search

FIGURE 2.6:

An example of using the Incremental Search command

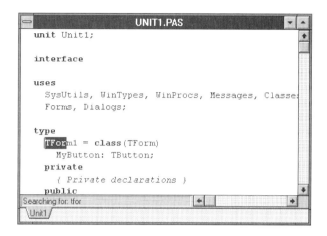

for a compiler error but to find a run-time error. When you are running a stand-alone program, and you hit a very bad error, Delphi displays an internal address number (that is, the *logical* address of the compiled code). You can enter this value in the Find Error dialog box to have Delphi recompile the program, looking for the specific address. When it finds the address, Delphi shows the corresponding source code line.

The last command on the Search menu, Browse Symbol, invokes the Browser, a tool you can use to explore a compiled program, looking at many details. To understand the output of the Browser, you need an in-depth understanding of the Object Pascal language and of the Visual Components Library (VCL). For this reason, the use of the Browser will be discussed in Chapter 20.

The View Menu

The View pull-down menu combines the features you usually find in View and Window menus. The Window menu in not present in Delphi, since it is not an MDI application.

Most of the View commands can be used to display one of the windows of the Delphi environment, such as the Project Manager, the Breakpoints list, or the Components list. These windows are not related. Some are used during debugging; others when you are writing the code. In Figure 2.7, you can see some of these views, or

FIGURE 2.7:

Some of the Delphi windows you can open with the View menu commands. The ones on the right are related to the debug phase; the ones on the left to the development phase.

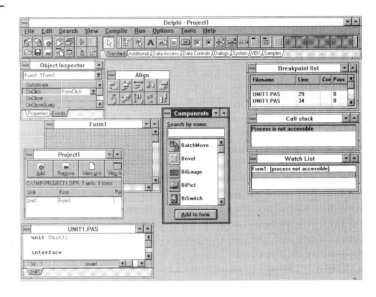

windows, related to the first group of commands on the menu. Most of these will be described later in this chapter.

The next commands on the View menu are important, which is why the Toggle, Units, and Forms commands are also available on the default SpeedBar. Toggle is used to move between the form you are working on and its source code. If you use a source code window big enough to hold a reasonable amount of text, you'll use this command often. As an alternative, you can place the two windows (the editor and the form) so that a portion of the one below is always visible. With this arrangement, you can click on it with the mouse to move it to the front.

The last two commands on the View menu can be used to hide the SpeedBar or the Components palette, although this is a good way to make Delphi look silly and uncomfortable. I know that everyone has his or her own taste, so every customizable option will make some people happy. However, working on forms without the Component palette is certainly not easy. If you remove both elements, the Delphi main window is reduced to a bare menu. (Now where is the option to hide the menus? This would reduce Delphi to a caption!)

The Compile Menu

The next pull-down menu, Compile, is probably the simplest. The Compile command builds or updates the application executable file, checking which source files have changed. With Build All, you can ask Delphi to compile every source file of the project, even if it has not been changed since the last compilation.

If you just want to know whether the syntax of the code you've written is correct, but you do not want to build the program—maybe this is still an unfinished module—you can use the Syntax Check command.

The last command on the Compile menu, Information, displays some details about the last compilation you've made. Figure 2.8 shows the information related to the compilation of the last program presented in Chapter 1, HELLO2.

TIP

The Compile command can be used only when you have loaded a project in the editor. If no project is active and you load a Pascal source file, you cannot compile it. However, if you load the source file as if it were a project, that will do the trick. Simply select the Open Project command or button, select the *.PAS filter, and load a file. Now you can compile it, building a DCU (Delphi Compiled Unit) or an executable file.

FIGURE 2.8:

The information about the compilation of HELLO2

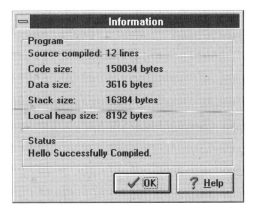

The Run Menu

The Run menu could have been named Debug as well. Most of the commands are related to debugging, including the Run command itself. As I've mentioned before, when you run a program within the Delphi environment, you execute it under the integrated debugger. The Run command, and the corresponding SpeedBar icon, are among the most commonly used commands, since Delphi automatically recompiles a program before running it—at least if the source code has changed.

The following command, Parameters, can be used to pass some parameters on the command line to the program you are going to run. (We will see an example of its use in Chapter 19.) The remaining commands are all used during debugging, to execute the program step-by-step, set breakpoints, inspect the values of variables and objects, and so on.

The Options Menu

The name of the Options menu describes the use of its commands. You can set options for the project you are working on (Project) and configure the Delphi environment (the other commands). You can set general options (Environment), add new commands to the Tools menu, add new templates or Experts to the Gallery, and change the VCL library by installing new components.

The Tools Menu

The Tools menu simply lists a number of external programs and tools, just to make it easier to run them. Some tools will already be present in this pull-down menu, depending on your version of Delphi. You can easily add new applications to this menu by using the Tools command on the Options menu. As you can see in Figure 2.9, besides simply running a program, you can pass some parameters to it. Simple parameter lists can be passed directly on the command line, while complex ones can be built using the Transfer Macros in the lower part of the Tool Properties dialog box.

I usually add certain applications to the Tools menu. One of them is WinSight, which is part of the Delphi package; many others are programmer tools I use often.

The Help Menu

As often happens, our tour of the menu system ends with Help. This can be used to get information about the Delphi environment, its language, and the MS Windows API. The Help menu also provides access to the Interactive Tutors.

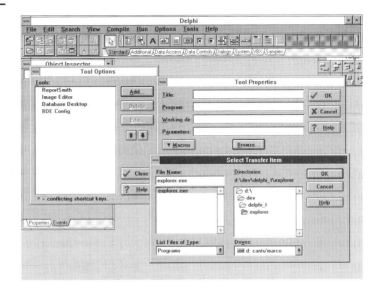

FIGURE 2.9:

It is easy to add new applications to the Tools menu.

The SpeedBar

After you have used Delphi for a while, you'll realize that you frequently use only a small number of commands. Some of these commands are probably already available on the SpeedBar (Borland's name for its toolbars); some are not. If the commands you use a lot are not there, it's time to customize the SpeedBar so that it really helps you to use Delphi more efficiently.

> **TIP**
>
> An alternative to using the SpeedBar is to use shortcut keys. Although you must remember some key combinations to use them, shortcut keys let you invoke commands very quickly, particularly when you are writing code and your fingers are already on the keyboard.

You can easily resize the SpeedBar, by dragging the thick line between it and the Components palette.

The other operations you can do with the SpeedBar (besides removing it) are to add, remove, or replace the icons, by using the Configure command of the

SpeedBar's own SpeedMenu (see Figure 2.10, near the upper-left corner). This operation invokes the SpeedBar Editor (shown in Figure 2.10), one of the Delphi tools with the best user interface, at least in my opinion.

FIGURE 2.10:

The SpeedBar Editor and the SpeedBar local menu used to run it

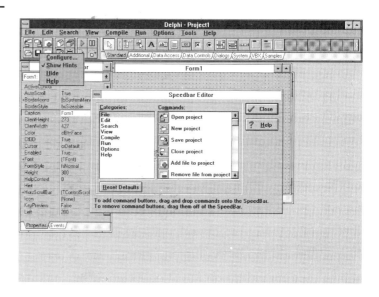

To add an icon to the SpeedBar, you simply need to find it under the proper category, or pull-down menu, and drag it to the bar. In the same way, you can drag an icon away from the SpeedBar, or simply move it to another location. During these operations, you can easily leave some space between groups of icons, to make them easier to remember and select. In Figure 2.11, you can see a series of consecutive changes to the SpeedBar, from the Delphi original one to a very peculiar layout.

In this figure, you can see almost all of the Delphi SpeedBar buttons. There is no "best way" to arrange a SpeedBar. My SpeedBar changes quite often, depending on the kind of work I'm doing (debugging a single big program, writing a number of small ones, and so on).

When the SpeedBar has become so confused that you are at a loss, you can use the SpeedBar Editor's Reset Defaults button to restore the original Delphi SpeedBar.

2

Change after change—the SpeedBar can lose debug support, add copy and paste operations, and change its original layout.

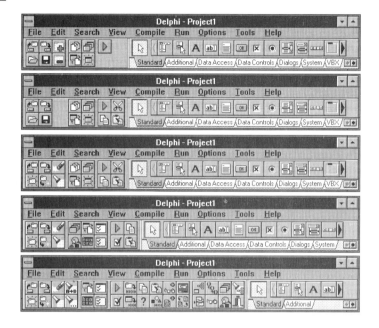

The SpeedMenus

Although Delphi has a good number of menu items, not all of the commands are available though the pull-down menus. At times, you need to use SpeedMenus (local menus) for specific windows or window areas. To activate a SpeedMenu, press the right mouse button over a certain element of the user interface, or press the Alt and F10 keys.

Even if you have other alternatives, using a SpeedMenu is usually faster, because you don't need to move the mouse up to the menu bar and select two levels of menus. It's also often easier, since SpeedMenu commands are related to the current window. Figure 2.12 shows examples of the Component palette, Object Inspector, and Code Editor SpeedMenus.

Here is a list of the elements of the Delphi environment that have an associated SpeedMenu:

- On the main window: the SpeedBar (see Figure 2.10) and the Component palette (see Figure 2.12).

FIGURE 2.12:

The Component palette, Object
Inspector, and Code Editor
SpeedMenus

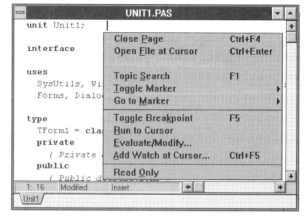

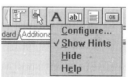

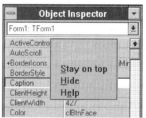

- Among the more common windows: the Form Designer (see the following section about working with forms), the Object Inspector, and Code Editor (both in Figure 2.12).

- Among other windows: the Project Manager, the Menu Designer, the Alignment palette, the Breakpoint List, the Call Stack, the Watch List, and the ObjectBrowser.

Some of the SpeedMenu commands are described later in this chapter. Every time there is a choice, I tend to use the SpeedMenu commands, so I'll usually refer you to them rather than to the corresponding commands of the pull-down menus.

Working with Forms

The design of forms is the core of the visual development in the Delphi environment. Every component you place on a form or any property you set, is stored in a file describing the form (a DFM file) and also has some effect on the source code associated with the form (the PAS file).

When you start a new, blank project, Delphi creates an empty form, and you can start working with it. You can also start with an existing form (using the various templates available), or add new forms to a project. A project (an application) can have any number of forms. There is virtually no limit.

When you are working with a form, you can operate on its properties, on one of its components, or on several components at a time. To select the form or a component, you can simply click on it or use the Object Selector (the combo box in the Object Inspector), where you can always see the name and type of the selected item. You can select more than one component by pressing the Shift key and clicking on the component with the left mouse button.

TIP   Even when a component covers the whole surface of the form, you can still select the form with the mouse. Just press the Shift key while you click on the selected component. Using the keyboard, you can press the Esc key to select the parent of the current component.

Once you are working on a form, the SpeedMenu (see Figure 2.13) has a number of useful features.

You can bring a component to front or send it to back, thus accessing a temporarily hidden component. When you have selected more than one component, you can align or size them. Most of the options in the Alignment dialog box are also on the Alignment palette, as you can see in Figure 2.14.

From the SpeedMenu, you can also open two dialog boxes to set the tab order of the visual controls and the creation order of the nonvisual controls. Last, but not least, you can use the Save as Template command to add the form you are working on to a list of forms available for use in other projects.

FIGURE 2.13:

The Form Designer SpeedMenu

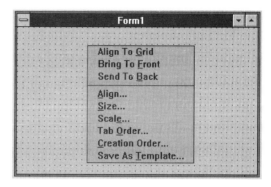

FIGURE 2.14:

The Alignment dialog box and the Alignment palette

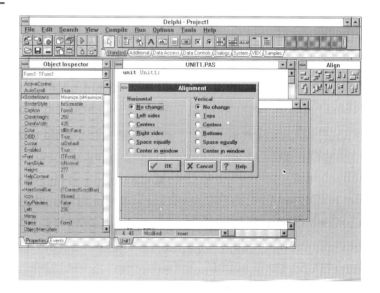

Along with specific SpeedMenu commands, you can set some form options by using the Environment command on the Options menu and choosing the Preferences page (see Figure 2.15). The options related to forms are listed under the Form Designer heading (grid activation and size). When you activate the grid, you can move components on the form only at fixed positions (separated by the number of pixels of the grid size), and size them only at fixed intervals. Without a grid, you will rarely be able to align two components manually (using the mouse).

FIGURE 2.15:

The Preferences page of the Environment Options dialog box

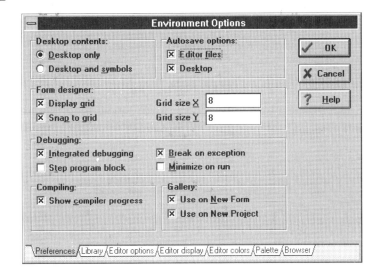

There are two alternatives to using the mouse to set the position of a component:

- Set the value for the Left and Top properties.
- Use the arrow keys while holding down the Ctrl key.

Using the Ctrl-arrow key method is particularly useful for fine-tuning an element's position. (The Snap to Grid option works only for mouse operations.) Similarly, by pressing the arrow keys while you hold down the Shift key, you can fine-tune the size of a component.

Along with the commands described so far, a form's SpeedMenu offers other commands when particular components are selected. In some cases, these menu commands are an alternative to the selection of a property for a component. In some cases, they contain particularly useful commands. Here are the other commands you may see on the SpeedMenu of a form:

- The Query Builder command is available when the query component (one of the database components) is selected, but only in the Client-Server edition of Delphi, which includes the Visual Query Builder tool.

- The Fields Editor command and the Define Parameters command are available for query and table components.

- The Execute command is present when a BatchMove component is selected.

- The Edit Report component loads ReportSmith and is available for Report components.

- The Next Page and Previous Page commands are present when a NoteBook or TabbedNoteBook component is selected. These commands are used to change to another page.

The Components Palette

When you want to add a new component to the form you are working on, you can click on a component in one of the pages of the Components palette, then click on the form to place the new component. On the form, you can press the left mouse button and drag the mouse to set the position and size of the component at once, or just click, to let Delphi use a default size.

Each page of the palette has a number of components, indicated by an icon, and a name, which appears as a "fly-by" hint (just move the mouse on the icon and wait for a second):

These names are the official names of components, and they are the names I'll use in the book to refer to components.

If you need to place a number of components of the same kind into a form, click on the Components palette while pressing the Shift key to activate a component. Then, every time you click on the form, Delphi adds a new component of that kind. To stop this operation, simply click on the standard selector (the arrow icon) on the left side of the Components palette.

What if you have decided to hide the Components palette? There is another way to add components to a form: select Components List from the View menu, select a component in the list or type its name in the edit window marked Search by Name, then click on the Add to Form button. This technique might be handy when you are using a mouseless computer (or laptop), or when you have installed so many components that you cannot remember where they are on the palette.

Of course, you can completely rearrange the components in the various pages of the palette, adding new elements or just moving them from page to page. I suggest that you wait until you have become well acquainted with the Delphi environment before you make any changes to the Components palette. If you do want to rearrange the components on the various pages, select Environment from the Options menu, and choose the Palette page (see Figure 2.16). In this dialog box, you can simply drag a component from the Components list box to the Pages list box to move that component to a different page.

WARNING It's not a good idea to move components too often. If you do, you'll probably waste time trying to locate them afterwards.

FIGURE 2.16:

The Palette page of the Environment Options dialog box

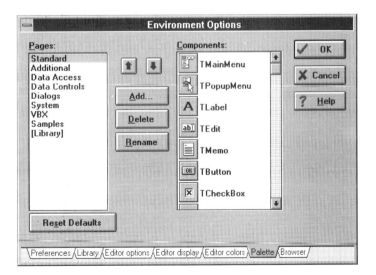

The Object Inspector

When you are designing a form, to set the property of a component (or the form itself), you use the Object Inspector. Its window lists the properties of the selected element and their values in two resizable columns. An Object Selector at the top of the Object Inspector indicates the current component and its data type, and this selector can be used to change the current selection.

It is important to notice that the Object Inspector doesn't list all of the properties of a component. It includes only the properties that can be set at design-time. As mentioned in Chapter 1, other properties are accessible only at run-time. To know about all the different properties of a component, refer to the Help files.

An interesting feature of the Object Inspector is that the right column allows the correct editing for the data type of the property. Depending on the property, you will be able to select a string, insert a number, enter a value, or choose from a list of options:

When a property allows only two values, such as True and False, you can toggle the value by double-clicking on it with the left mouse button. If there are many values available, a double-click will select the next one in the list. If you double-click a number of times, all the values will appear, but it is easier to select a multiple-choice value using the small combo box. For some properties, such as Color, you can either enter a value or select an element from the list.

When an option is particularly complex, the Object Inspector has special editors you can activate by pressing the small button with three dots:

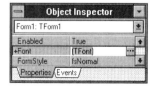

In some cases, such as with string lists, the special editors are the only way to select a property. Other times, the special editors provide an alternative way to expand a property, such as the Font property. And sometimes, you may want to use an editor simply because it's easier than trying to write a long string in a limited space, such as when you are specifying file filters.

At times, you can either set a property as a whole, or explode its subfields and set them independently. This behavior is available in two different cases: with sets and classes. When a property is a set, you can either edit it inside the square brackets, as if it were a string, or explode the property in a series of Boolean values, one for each possible value of the set:

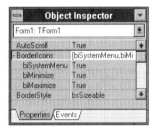

The difference between sets and multiple-choice properties is that with sets you can select many elements at the same time, but with multiple choices you can select only one value. This difference depends on the use of two different kinds of data type constructors of the Pascal language: set and enumeration (see Chapter 4).

When a property is a class, you can explode it to set a value for each of the fields. Here is an example for a Font property:

Each of the fields of the record has its own behavior in the Object Inspector. The name of the font can be entered or selected in a list, the style is a set that can be further exploded, and so on.

You will use the Object Inspector often. It should always be visible when you are editing a form, but it can also be useful to look at the names of components and properties while you are writing code. For this reason, the Object Inspector's SpeedMenu has a Stay on Top command, which keeps the Object Inspector window in front of the Form Designer and the editor.

The Alignment Palette

The last tool related to form design is the Alignment palette. You can open this palette with the View menu's Alignment Palette command. As an alternative, you can choose the components you want to align, and then issue the Align command from the SpeedMenu of the form.

The Alignment palette features a number of commands to position the various controls, center them, space them equally, and so on. To see the effect of each button, simply move the mouse over the window and look at the fly-by hints. When I'm designing complex forms, I position the Alignment palette on the far side of the screen, and make sure it always stays in sight by using the Stay on Top command of its SpeedMenu, as you can see in Figure 2.17.

Writing Code

When you have designed a form in Delphi, you usually need to write some code to respond to some of its events, as we did in Chapter 1. Every time you work on an event, Delphi opens the editor with the source file related to the form. You can easily jump back and forth between the Form Designer and the editor with the related source code by pressing the Toggle Form Unit button on the SpeedBar.

The Delphi editor allows you to work on several source code files at once, using a "notebook with tabs" metaphor (see Figure 2.18). Each page of the notebook corresponds to a different file. You can work on units related to forms, independent units of Pascal code, project files, and even open the form description files in textual format.

FIGURE 2.17:

The far-right position of the Alignment palette, and its SpeedMenu

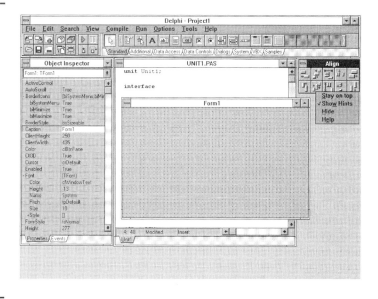

FIGURE 2.18:

The editor with several source code files loaded

```
unit Hello_f;

interface

uses
   SysUtils, WinTypes, WinProcs, Messages, Classes,
   Forms, Dialogs, StdCtrls;

type
   TForm1 = class(TForm)
      HelloButton: TButton;
      procedure HelloButtonClick(Sender: TObject);
      procedure FormClick(Sender: TObject);
      procedure FormResize(Sender: TObject);
   private
```

When you work with the editor, you should probably expand its window, so that you can see as many full lines of code as possible. A good solution is to size the editor so that it and the Object Inspector are the only windows that appear on the screen. With this approach, the Inspector is visible both when you work on the form and when you write code. When you are working on stand-alone units, you might also want to maximize the editor window.

There are a number of options available for the editor environment, mostly located in the Editor Options, Editor Display, and Editor Colors pages of the Environment Options dialog box. In the Preferences page, you can set the editor files Autosave feature. Saving the source code files each time you run the program can save the day when your program happens to crash the whole system (something not so rare).

The other three pages of editor options can be used to set the default editor settings (choosing among different standard keystroke mappings), syntax highlighting features, and font. Most of these options are fairly simple to understand. Again, I recommend that you wait until you are better acquainted with the Delphi system before changing any of these settings.

Managing Projects

The next important thing in Delphi is to manage project files. In Chapter 1, we saw that you can open a project file in the editor and edit it. However, there are simpler ways to change some of the features of a project. You can use a specific Project Manager window and the options related to a project.

The Project Manager

When a project is loaded, choose the Project Manager command from the View menu to open a project window. The window lists all of the forms and units that make up the current project. In Figure 2.19, you can see an example of such a window, related to a project with two different forms. When you select a source file, the Project Manager window displays the name of the corresponding files and their time/date stamps.

The Project Manager's SpeedMenu allows you to perform a number of operations on the project, such as adding new or existing files, removing files, viewing a source code file or a form, and saving the project as a template. Most of these commands are also available in the SpeedBar of this window (not the main Delphi SpeedBar).

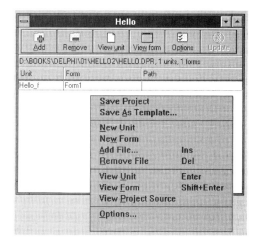

FIGURE 2.19:

The Project Manager window with its SpeedMenu

Setting Project Options

From the Project Manager (or from the Options menu), you can invoke the Project Options. The first page of the Project Options, named Forms, is shown in Figure 2.20. It lists the forms that should be created automatically at program startup (the default behavior) and the forms that are created manually by the program. You can easily move a form from one list to the other.

The Application page is used to set the name of the application, the name of its Help file, and the icon of the program. Other Project Options choices relate to the Delphi compiler and linker.

NOTE There are two ways to set compiler options. One is to use the Compiler page of the Project Options, the other is to set or remove individual options in the source code with the {$X+} or {$X-} commands, where X is the option you want to set. This second approach is more flexible, since it allows you to change an option only for a specific source code file, or even for just a few lines of code.

FIGURE 2.20:

The Forms page of the Project
Options

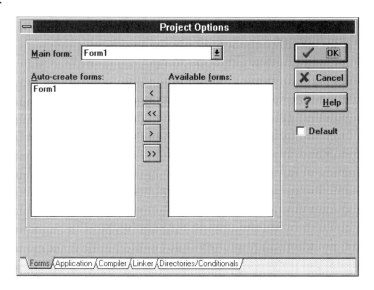

All of the Project Options are saved automatically with the project, but in a separate file with an OPT extension. Do not delete this file if you have changed any of the default options.

Compiling a Project

There are several ways to compile a project. If you run it (by pressing F9 or clicking on the SpeedBar icon), Delphi will compile it first. When Delphi compiles a project, it only compiles the files that have changed. If you select the Compile menu's Build All command, instead, every file is compiled, even if it has not changed. This second command is seldom used, since Delphi can usually determine which files have changed and compile them as required. Since Delphi looks at the time/date stamp of source files and intermediate files to know when they were last compiled, the Build All command might be useful when the clock of the PC doesn't work properly, when you have moved files from a computer to another, or when you change project-wide compiler options.

A source code file, eventually with the related form, is indicated with the name of the unit. The source code file is turned into a Delphi compiled unit, a file with the same name as the Pascal source file and the DCU extension. For example, UNIT1.PAS is compiled into UNIT1.DCU.

The compiled units that constitute the project are merged (or linked) into the executable file when the project itself is compiled. You can better understand the compilation steps and follow what happens during this operation if you enable the Show Compiler Progress option. This option is on the Preferences page of the Environment Options dialog box, under the Compiling heading (see Figure 2.15, shown earlier). Although this slows down the compilation a bit, the Compile window lets you see which source files are compiled each time you run the program. You can see an example of this window in Figure 2.21.

Once the project is compiled, you can see some information about the last compilation by choosing the Information command from the Compile menu (see Figure 2.8, earlier in the chapter). Along with the compilation status, the Information dialog box displays the number of compiled lines and the size of the code, data, stack, and heap (see Chapter 20 for a description of memory handling and of the role of the stack and the heap in an MS Windows application).

FIGURE 2.21:

A compiler progress window

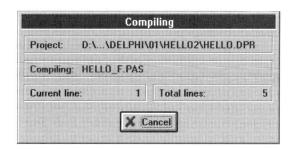

Exploring a Compiled Program

Delphi provides a number of tools you can use to explore a compiled program, including the debugger and the Browser. The following sections provide a brief introducton to these tools, which we'll cover in detail in Chapter 20.

The Integrated Debugger

Delphi has an integrated debugger, which has a huge number of features. However, it is also possible to buy a more powerful stand-alone debugger, called Turbo Debugger. For 90 percent of your debugging tasks, the integrated debugger works well enough. The Turbo Debugger package might be useful in special cases, such as when you need to use a debugger that is not itself an MS Windows application.

You don't need to do much to use the integrated debugger. In fact, each time you run a program from Delphi, it is executed in the debugger. This means that you can set a breakpoint to stop the program when it reaches a set line of code.

For example, open the HELLO2 example we created in Chapter 1 and double-click on the button in the form to jump to the related code. Now set a breakpoint by clicking on the space between the left window border and the text, by choosing the Toggle Breakpoint SpeedMenu command, or by pressing the F5 key.

The editor will highlight the breakpoint as shown in Figure 2.22. Now you can run the program as usual, but each time you press the button, the debugger halts the program, showing you the corresponding line of code. You can execute this and the following lines one at a time (that is, step-by-step), look at the code of the functions called by the code, or continue running the program.

FIGURE 2.22:

Breakpoints in source code are clearly visible.

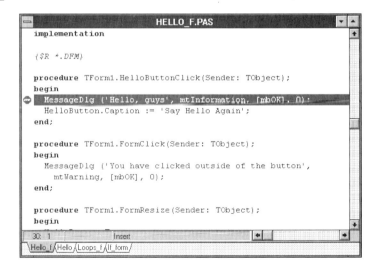

```
HELLO_F.PAS
implementation

{$R *.DFM}

procedure TForm1.HelloButtonClick(Sender: TObject);
begin
  MessageDlg ('Hello, guys', mtInformation, [mbOK], 0);
  HelloButton.Caption := 'Say Hello Again';
end;

procedure TForm1.FormClick(Sender: TObject);
begin
  MessageDlg ('You have clicked outside of the button',
    mtWarning, [mbOK], 0);
end;

procedure TForm1.FormResize(Sender: TObject);
begin
```

30: 1   Insert

Hello_f / Hello / Loops_f / If_form /

When a program is stopped, you can inspect its status in detail. You can look at the value of a variable (with the Evaluate command), set a watch on its value (to see when it changes), or even view the function calls on the stack.

For example, you can set a watch on the HelloButton.Caption property, then step though the program and see when it changes. You can see this watch and the dialog box used to set it in Figure 2.23.

FIGURE 2.23:

The watch and the dialog box used to set it

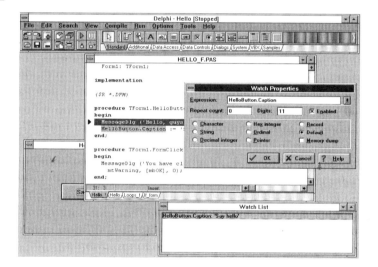

The Object Browser

When you have compiled a program (even if you are not running or debugging it), you can run the Object Browser to explore your program (see Figure 2.24). This tool allows you to see all of the classes defined by the program (or by the units used directly and indirectly by the program), all the global names and variables, and so on. For every class, the Object Browser shows the list of properties, methods, and variables—both local and inherited, private and public.

But the features of the Object Browser won't mean much to you until you understand the object-oriented capabilities of the Object Pascal language used by Delphi. We'll get to the details in Chapter 20, after we've covered the information you need for this understanding.

FIGURE 2.24:

Delphi Object Browser

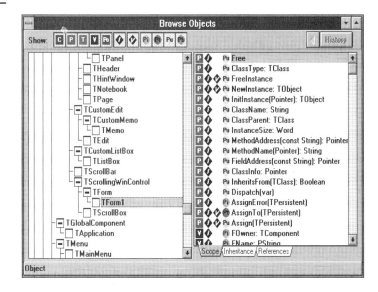

Additional Tools

Delphi provides many more tools for your programming efforts. For example, the Menu Designer is a visual tool used to create the structure of a menu. There are also the various Experts, used to generate the structure of an application or a new form.

Other tools are stand-alone applications related to the development of an MS Windows application. These include the Bitmap Editor and the stand-alone debugger, Turbo Debugger, which is separately available from Borland. Other external tools actually included in Delphi are ReportSmith, a report generator; the Database Desktop, a tool to create and manage databases; WinSight, a *spy* program that lets you see the Windows message flow; and WinSpector, a postmortem debugger similar to Microsoft's Dr. Watson.

A programmer can use even more tools to cover weak areas of Delphi. For example, you can use a resource editor (such as Borland's Resource Workshop), a tool to generate Help files more easily, and other technical Windows utilities, including more advanced spying programs. (*Spying* or *API spying* are common names for these programs, simply because the first of them was a program actually named Spy, present in the original Microsoft Software Development Kit for Windows.)

Most of the tools included in Delphi will be discussed in the book. Here is a short list of references:

- The Experts are covered in Chapter 3.
- The Menu Designer is described in Chapter 8.
- The Bitmap Editor is used in several chapters, starting with Chapter 10.
- Database tools are the topics of Chapters 17 and 18.
- WinSight is discussed in Chapter 21.
- Report building is described in Chapter 22.

The Files Produced by the System

As you have seen, Delphi produces a number of files for you, and you should be aware of how it names these files. There are basically two elements that have an impact on how files are named:

- The names you give to a project and its forms
- The predefined extensions used by Delphi for the files you write and those generated by the system

Table 2.1 lists the extensions of the files you'll find in the directory where a Delphi project resides. The table also shows when these files are created and their importance for future compilations.

Most of these files are very short (see Figure 2.25), including the source and backup files, the project files, the options, and the desktop file. The compiled units are slightly bigger, and the executable file is often the biggest file of the directory, unless there are files with debugging information, such as the DSM file.

The DSM file holds Browser information to allow the use of the Object Browser, even when you have changed the source code (but always after a successful compilation). This can be particularly useful when the program doesn't compile any more. These files can easily become quite big, and you can turn off their creation by checking Desktop Only instead of Desktop and Symbols in the Preferences page of

TABLE 2.1: The Delphi File Extensions

Extension	File Type	Creation Time	Required to Recompile	Description
BMP, ICO	Graphical files	Development (Image Editor)	No, but they might be required at run-time	Bitmaps and icons are usually included in the code, but you won't delete them. They are used for button or list box glyphs, image components, and so on.
DCU	Delphi compiled unit	Compilation	No, but if the source has not changed, they speed up a rebuild process	These object files are the result of the compilation of a PAS file (and the corresponding form).
~DF	Graphical form backup	Development	No	This is the backup file of the form's DFM file.
DFM	Delphi graphical form file	Development	Yes	This is the binary file with the description of the properties of a form and of the controls it hosts. The file is converted to a textual format automatically when you load it in Delphi editor.
~DP	Project backup	Development	No	This file is generated automatically when a new version of a project file is saved. It is a copy of the older version of the file.
DPR	Delphi project file	Development	Yes	In Delphi, the project file is in Pascal source code. It lists all of the elements of a project and provides some initialization code.
DSK	Desktop settings	Development	No	This file contains information about the position of the Delphi windows, the files open in the editor, and other desktop settings, including some environment options.

TABLE 2.1: The Delphi File Extensions (continued)

Exten-sion	File Type	Creation Time	Required to Recompile	Description
DSM	Object Browser Data	Compilation (only if option is set)	No, used by the Browser	This file stores all the Browser information, and can be used to access this information without recompiling the project (or when you cannot recompile it because of an error).
EXE	Compiled executable file	Compilation	No	This is the result of your efforts: the executable file of your application. It includes all of the compiled units, resources, and forms.
OPT	Project options	Development	Required only if special options have been set	This is a text file, similar to an MS Windows INI file, with the current settings for the project options.
~PA	Unit backup	Development	No	This file stores a backup copy of a PAS file of a unit. It is generated automatically by Delphi.
PAS	Unit source code	Development	Yes	This file contains the source code of a Pascal unit, which can be the source code of a form, or a stand-alone source file. Contains the definition of the class for the form and the code of its event handlers.
RES	Compiled resource file	Development	Yes	The binary file associated with the project and containing by default its icon. You can add other resources to this file or other files of this type to the project.

FIGURE 2.25:

The files produced by working with and compiling the HELLO2 example, as seen by the File Manager

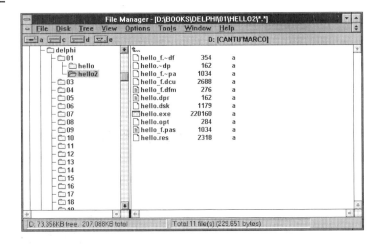

the Environment Options dialog box (see Figure 2.5, shown earlier). This will also reduce the compile/link time.

The great advantage of Delphi over other visual programming environments is that most of the source code files are plain ASCII text files. We have already explored Pascal source code, project code, and form description files at the end of Chapter 1. Now let's take a minute to look at the structure of options and desktop files. Both these files use a structure similar to MS Windows INI files, where each section is indicated by a name enclosed in square brackets. For example, this is a fragment of the HELLO.OPT file of the HELLO2 example:

```
[Linker]
MapFile=0
LinkBuffer=0
DebugInfo-0
OptimizeExe=0
StackSize=16384
HeapSize=8192

[Directories]
OutputDir=
SearchPath=
Conditionals=

[Parameters]
RunParams=
```

The rest of the code of this file (the portion I've omitted) is a long list of compiler options. The same structure is used by the desktop files, which are usually much longer. It is worth looking at what is stored in these files to understand their role.

In short, a desktop file lists Delphi windows, indicating their position and status. For example, this is the description of the main window:

```
[MainWindow]
Create=1
Visible=1
State=0
Left=-2
Top=0
Width=800
Height=97
```

These are some of the sections related to other windows:

```
[PropertyInspector]
[AlignmentPalette]
[ProjectManager]
[WatchWindow]
[BreakpointWindow]
[CallStackWindow]
[Components]
[EditWindow0]
```

The desktop file also contains a number of history lists (lists of files of a certain kind, which are available in the open dialog boxes), and an indication of the current breakpoints, watches, active modules, closed modules, and forms.

Summary

This chapter presented a short overview of the Delphi programming environment, including a number of tips and suggestions. Getting used to a new programming environment takes some time, particularly if it is a complex one. I could write a book with the details of the Delphi programming environment, but I think that a book describing how to actually write programs is more useful and interesting.

A good way to learn about the Delphi environment is to use the Help system. Look up information about the environment elements, windows, and commands. Spend some time just browsing through the Help files. Of course, the best way to learn how the Delphi environment works is to use it to write programs. That's what Delphi is about.

Now we can move on to an introduction to two important features of the Delphi environment we have only mentioned: Templates and Experts.

CHAPTER

THREE

3

Templates and Experts

- Delphi's Browse Gallery

- Application and form templates

- The Database Form Expert

- The Application Expert

- The Dialog Expert

- The Component Expert

When you start working on a new application, or simply a new form, you have two choices: You can start from scratch with a blank application or form, or you can choose a predefined model from the Browse Gallery. If you decide to pick a model from the Browse Gallery, you have two alternatives: You can use a predefined template, or you can use one of the available Experts, which provides the proper parameters.

What is the difference between Delphi's templates and Experts? A template is like a fixed snapshot. Instead of starting from scratch, with a template, you load some previously saved files, corresponding to a form or a whole application. An Expert is a code generator. The Expert asks you a number of questions, and it uses the results to create some basic code, following standard guidelines.

In both cases, you start working on a project or a form that already has some code and components. Usually, the code generated by these tools can be compiled immediately, and it makes up the basic structure on which you can build your program.

The intention of this short chapter is to make you aware of the existence of Experts and templates and the fact that they are easy to use. We won't study the code they generate, since this will be the topic of many examples in the book. From a programming standpoint, the Experts are really useful. The pitfall is that you might be tempted to use them, without trying to understand what they do. For this reason, I will often introduce the Expert-generated code only after describing the steps you need to obtain the same effect *manually*.

The Project Browse Gallery

Each time you create a new project in Delphi, the Browse Gallery dialog box appears. If you don't see it, and a blank, new project is created immediately instead, you should set the Environment Options so that this dialog box does appear. Select Environment from the Options menu, then go to the Preferences page and put a check in the Use on New Project check box in the Gallery group.

The Browse Gallery dialog box allows you to select from a number of templates or Experts, as you can see in Figure 3.1. For projects, Delphi has four predefined application templates and a single standard application Expert. You can create new application templates quite easily, as we will see in a moment. You can also buy application Experts and templates from third-party developers.

FIGURE 3.1:

The Browse Gallery with application templates

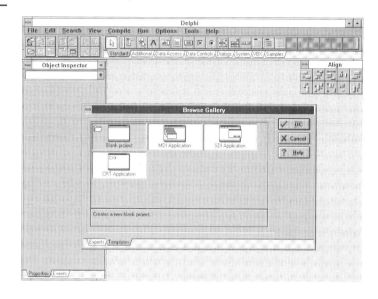

When you select a new template, for example the SDI Application template, Delphi asks you to enter the name of an existing or a new directory. If you indicate a new directory, Delphi will create it automatically (see Figure 3.2).

FIGURE 3.2:

The dialog box used to select a directory for the files of the template you have chosen. Notice that you can indicate a new directory, as I've done here.

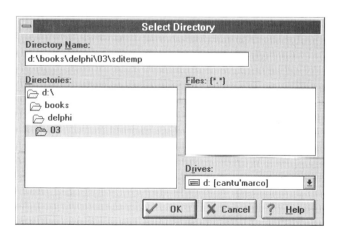

TIP

This is a welcome addition to the standard behavior of Delphi. When you save a file, you must place it in an existing directory. Only when you create a new project with a wizard or template can you create a new directory within Delphi. Of course, when the Save As dialog box is open, and you can't find a proper directory, you can always move to File Manager and create a new one, then come back to the dialog box and use it. However, having a direct way to define one is handy.

After you have generated an SDI application based on the template, you can customize it, giving it a proper title, removing or adding new components, and writing some code. Notice, however, that some interesting components are already there, and that there is even some ready-to-use code to make those components work properly. The menu of the application, and also its toolbar, can be used to open some dialog boxes. File Open and File Save dialog boxes are wrapped up in components that are added to the form by the template; the About box is defined by the template as a second form.

In the example, I've decided to make just a few limited changes, and run the application. I've entered a new title for the main form and some text for the labels of the About box (the property to use is Caption in both cases). The result is the application shown in Figure 3.3 (you can find it on the companion disk as SDITEMP).

Choosing a Project Template

Delphi's four preinstalled application templates are simple application schemes, with the following capabilities:

- The Blank Project is not really a template, but an elegant way to say "No thanks." It simply creates a project with an empty (blank) form in it. This is certainly not the most effective way to start a new application, but I've used it as a default starting point to build most of the examples in the book. This choice is selected automatically with the New Project command on the File menu when the Project Browse Gallery option is not selected.

- The MDI Application template defines the main elements of a Multiple Document Interface (MDI) program. It defines a main form for the MDI frame window, with a menu, a status bar, and a toolbar. It also defines a second form

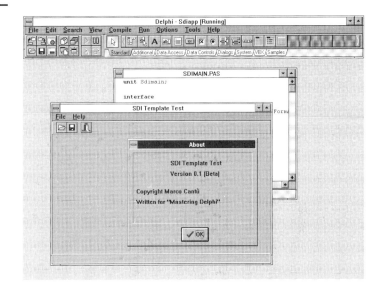

FIGURE 3.3:

The output of the application generated by the SDI template, after just a bit of customization

that can be used at run-time to create a number of child windows. We will explore the use of this template in Chapter 15.

- The SDI Application template defines a main form with the standard attributes of a modern user interface, including a toolbar and a status bar. This template also generates a typical About box. We will see the details of this template when we focus on the use of toolbars and status bars, in Chapter 11.

- The CRT Application template generates an application which can barely be defined as a Delphi program. In fact, it makes no use of forms and components, but only uses a terminal window (or CRT window) where you can direct the output of typical DOS procedures, such as Writeln. This template is described in the following section.

The CRT Application Template

The CRT Application template can be useful when you are writing small test applications, also called "quick-and-dirty" programs. At times, this is done to study features of the Pascal language (something I've avoided doing in the book, since Delphi programming is the topic). Other times, it is used to make a partial porting to MS Windows of an existing DOS Pascal program. I've said *partial* porting because even if the application will run in a window, it won't seem like a real MS Windows native program.

As its code suggests, the CRT Application template is based on a predefined WinCrt unit, which was already present in earlier versions of Borland Pascal compilers (see Delphi on-line help for a list of supported functions and procedures). Listing 3.1 shows the code generated by the template.

LISTING 3.1: Code generated by the CRT Application template

```
program CrtApp;

uses WinCrt;

begin
  Writeln('Delphi');
end.
```

Before running it, let's make a quick change in its body (the portion between the begin and end reserved words). These changes are shown in Listing 3.2

LISTING 3.2: Modified code for the CRT Application template

```
program CrtApp;

uses WinCrt;

begin
  Writeln;
  Writeln('"Mastering Delphi"');
  Writeln('WinCrt template example');
  Writeln;
  Writeln('This is almost Hello World program');
end.
```

This program leaves a blank space, outputs a message on two lines, and then writes a last line after another empty one. You can see the result of this program in Figure 3.4. It was really easy, but the result is not very satisfactory. I think that the two HELLO programs in Chapter 1, although simple, are better (or at least more Windows-like).

FIGURE 3.4:

The output of the modified version of the CRT Application generated by the standard template (the final code is in Listing 3.2)

> **TIP**   Along with building a brand new application, the WinCrt unit can be used as a side element of an existing application. It is quite common to use this or similar approaches to provide some custom tracing capability for debugging an application. I'll show you an example of this approach in Chapter 20.

Adding New Application Templates

Just as it is easy to use an existing template to build an application, it is also simple to add a new template to Delphi's Browse Gallery. When you have a working application you want to use as a starting point for further development, or two or more similar programs, you can save the current status to a template, then paste it back.

As an example, the following steps describe how you can save the slightly modified version of the default SDI template (shown earlier) as a template. This example is just to demonstrate the process. (It's not a real-world example, since the code is far too simple and similar to the existing template.) Here are the required steps:

1. Open the modified SDITEMP example (or any other project you are working on).

2. Open the Project Manager (using the corresponding command of the View menu), select its SpeedMenu, and choose Save as Template.

3. In the Save Project Template dialog box, enter a name, a title, and a description for the new project template (see Figure 3.5). You can also choose a bitmap to indicate the new template or accept the default image.

4. Press the OK button, and the new template is added to the Delphi Browse Gallery.

FIGURE 3.5:

The Save Project Template dialog box, used to define the name and descriptions of a new template

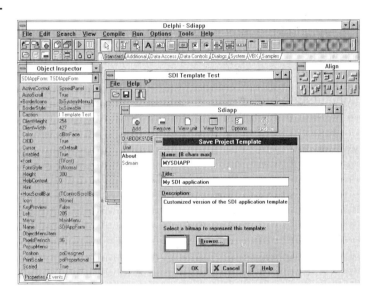

Now, each time you create a new project, the Browse Gallery will include your custom template, as you can see in Figure 3.6. If you later discover that the template is not useful any more, you can remove it. Just select the Gallery command from the Options menu, and move to the proper page of the dialog box.

You can use a project template to make a copy of an existing project so that you can continue to work on it after saving the original version. However, there is a simpler way to accomplish this: copy the source files to a new directory and open the new project.

FIGURE 3.6:

The Browse Gallery for projects, after I have added the custom template

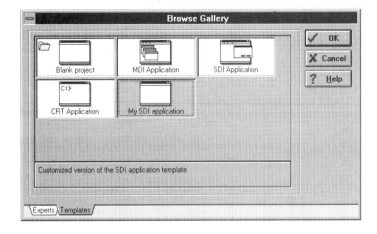

If you do copy the source files, do *not* copy the DSK file, indicating the position of the windows on the screen. The DSK file holds a list of files open in the editor, using an absolute path. This means that as soon as you open the new project and start working on it, you are actually editing the source code files of the older project, but you compile the files of the new version, since the project manager stores relative paths. This will certainly surprise you when the changes you make in the code or in the form seem to have no effect. Simply deleting the DSK file, or not copying it in the first place, avoids this problem.

The Gallery Options

An important element of Delphi's Browse Gallery is the use of the defaults. In this dialog box, the project-related pages have a Default Project button. You can use this button to select the project that will be used by default. This project will be active in the Browse Gallery for new projects, if the Gallery is active (that is, if the Gallery is used for new projects, as determined in the Preferences page of the Environment Options). If the Gallery is not active, the default project will be used automatically for every new project.

The form-related pages have two different buttons, Default Main Form and Default New Form (see Figure 3.7). The second button simply indicates the form used by default when a new form is created. The first button is particularly important, because it determines the main form of a new blank project.

FIGURE 3.7:

The Form Templates page of the
Gallery Options dialog box

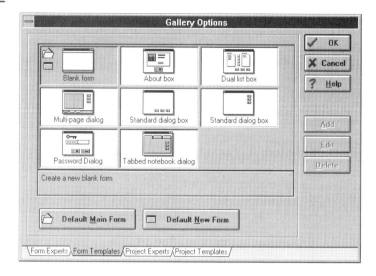

This means that the term *blank project* is really misleading. A new blank project can actually have a complex default form! This option should probably be renamed Default Form Project, or something similar.

The current default form, like the current default project, is indicated by a small glyph added to its bitmap. To make things clearer, this is the same glyph that appears in the button used to set the default.

Special Tip: A Really Blank Project

When you choose the Blank Project template, you are not really selecting a template; it is only a default option. The fact that the default form is used can be a tough problem, particularly when you have selected a special form as default project form. To solve this problem, you can add a *Really Blank Project* template to the Gallery.

The steps required to accomplish this are simple. First check that the blank form is used as the default project form. Then create a new blank project, and add this project to the templates, naming it "Really Blank Project," or something similar.

When you select this project from the Browse Gallery, you gain two advantages, and a slight disadvantage. The advantages are that you know a blank form will always be used, regardless of the project default form, and that you can specify a new directory for the project, where the template files will be copied. The disadvantage is that you cannot name the files, and you need to use the Save As command for both the project and the unit, thus duplicating files in your working directory.

Using Form Templates in an Application

As you can see in Figure 3.7, Delphi provides more form templates than application templates. Predefined form templates are simple, with a limited amount of code. But they can provide a fast way to start working on a new form or dialog box.

The Predefined Form Templates

Here is a short list of the predefined form templates available in Delphi:

- About box, the same simple About dialog box used by the SDI Application template.

- Dual list box, a form with two different list boxes, allowing a user to select a number of elements and move them to the other list by pressing a button. Along with the components in the form, this template has a good amount of not-so-simple Pascal code.

- Multi-page dialog, a dialog box with a notebook, a tab set, and some buttons. The only existing code is used to connect the notebook pages with the tabs. The use of these components is covered in Chapter 13.

- Two different Standard dialog boxes, with the buttons on the right or on the bottom of the form, and no code.

- Password dialog, a dialog box with a simple edit box with the options required to input a password, and no code.

- Tabbed notebook dialog, another multipage dialog box, which uses the new notebook style introduced by Microsoft. The use of this component is also covered in Chapter 13.

Notice that the Browse Gallery for forms is displayed only when you add a new form to an existing project, or when you create a form by itself, without an open project. Opening only a form is rarely done, since you cannot compile a form that is not part of a project, unless you select its source code file as if it were a project (to do this, select the Open Project command or button, select the *.PAS filter, and load a file).

To create a new project based on one of these forms, select the form as the default in the Gallery Options, as described in the previous section, and then create a new blank project that will use it.

Adding New Form Templates to the List

Just as you can add new template projects to the Browse Gallery, you can also add new form templates. Simply move to the form, press the right mouse button over it, and select the Save As Template command from the SpeedMenu.

In the dialog box that appears (see Figure 3.8), you can choose which form of the current project should become a new template, and set the name, title, description, and bitmap, as usual. Once you have set this element and clicked the OK button, the form is added to the Form Templates page of the Browse Gallery.

FIGURE 3.8:

Saving a form as a template

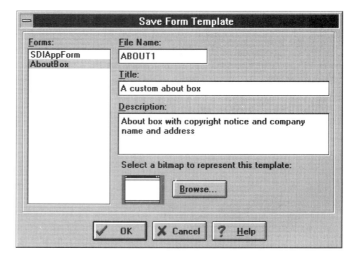

This approach is suggested if you have a complex form to make available to other applications and other programmers. However, you can use a more manual approach instead, by copying the files that describe the form and the corresponding unit. The real difference it that the Browse Gallery allows you to build a complete catalog of forms that can be reused.

Delphi Experts

The difference between a template and an Expert is that the template is a ready-to-use form or project, while an Expert allows you to enter a number of options and provides an internal schema to produce the code corresponding to your choices.

The most important predefined expert is the Database Form Expert, but there are also Application, Dialog, and Component Experts. You can also buy add-on Experts from third-party tool providers, or even write your own Experts.

The Database Form Expert

The Database Form Expert is probably the single most interesting tool in Delphi. In this section, I'll show you a short example of its use, so that you can get an idea of its power, but I won't describe the details of what goes on. Refer to Chapter 17 for an introduction to database programming.

In this example, we'll build a database program using some of the data already available in Delphi. First, note that to start the Database Form Expert for a new project, you need to select it as default form for a new project in the Gallery Options dialog box. Remember also to remove this option for future projects not based on this template (unless you decide to use the Really Blank Project approach, described earlier in this chapter).

An alternative is to create a new project first, then use the Expert to define a new form (maybe calling it from the Help menu directly), and remove the older form from the project. The selection of the new form generated by the Expert as the main form can be accomplished using an option of the Expert itself, displayed at the end.

As soon as you start the Database Form Expert, you will be presented with a number of choices, which depend on the options you choose at each step. The first page, shown in Figure 3.9, lets you choose between a simple or a master detail form, and

FIGURE 3.9:

The first page of the Database Form
Expert

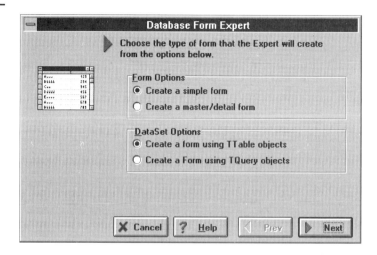

between the use of tables or queries. Leave the selections as they are by default, and
move on by clicking the Next button.

In the following page, shown in Figure 3.10, you choose an existing database table
to work on. In the Drive or Alias Name combo box, there should be a DBDEMOS
alias. After you select this option, a number of Delphi demo database tables appear
in the list. Choose the first, ANIMALS.DBF.

FIGURE 3.10:

The selection of a table in the
Database Form Expert

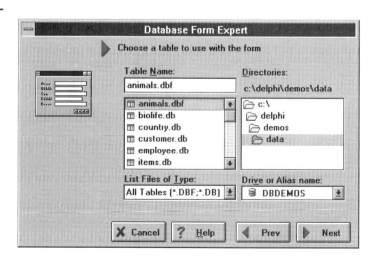

3

In the third page, you can choose the fields of the selected database table that you want to consider. To build this first example, choose all of the fields by clicking the >> button. Another step, and you can choose from various layouts. If you choose Vertical, the following page will ask you the position of the labels. The default option, Left, might do. After another step, we are at the end. Leave the Generate a Main Form check box selected, and click the Create button.

Give proper names to the code and project files, and you can now compile and run the application. The result, shown in Figure 3.11, is a working database application, allowing you to navigate among many records using the buttons. Notice that the application even has a graphical field, displaying a bitmap with the current animal.

As you can see in Figure 3.11, this output is far from adequate. The image area is too small, and the positioning of the other fields may not be satisfactory. Of course, you can easily move and resize the various components placed on the form at design-time. To make this easier, you can select the Table component (the one in the upper-left corner of the form) and toggle its Active property. Then the data of the table's first record will be displayed at design-time. This is helpful because it allows you to see an example of the length of the field's text and the size of the image. You can see an example of how the form can be improved in Figure 3.12.

FIGURE 3.11:

The output of the Expert-generated database program

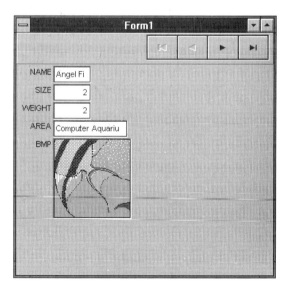

FIGURE 3.12:

The customized form of the example generated by the Database Form Expert. Notice that when you activate the Table component, the data of the database table is also visible at design-time.

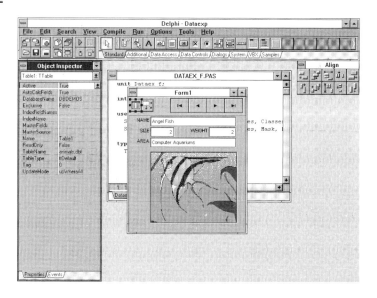

Note that the Database Form Expert generates almost no code. The capabilities of the resulting programs depend on the power of the database-related components available in Delphi. But since we have not yet discussed these components, I won't show you the textual description of the properties of this form. (If you are interested, you can look to the files of the companion disk for this project, DATAEXP.)

The Application Expert

Another important Expert in Delphi is the Application Expert. You can activate it from the Browse Gallery when you create a new project. The Application Expert allows you to create the skeleton of a number of different kinds of applications, depending on the options you select.

The first page of this Expert (see Figure 3.13) allows you to select some standard pull-down menus: File, Edit, Window, and Help. If you choose the File menu, the second page will ask you to enter the file extensions the program should consider. You enter both a description of the file, such as *Text file (*.txt)*, and the extension, *txt*. You can have several extensions, each with its own description. These values will be used by the default File Open and File Save dialog boxes that the Application

FIGURE 3.13:

The first page of the Application Expert

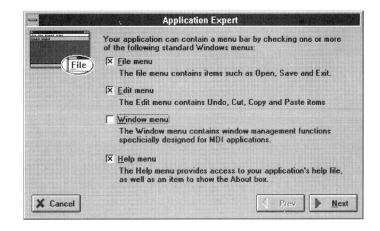

Expert will add to the program if you select file support (that is, if you check the File menu option on the first page).

Then, if you have selected any of the pull-down menus, the Application Expert displays a nice visual tool you can use to build a toolbar. Unfortunately, this tool is not available by itself. As you can see in Figure 3.14, you simply select one of the pull-down menus, and a number of standard buttons corresponding to the typical menu items of this pull-down menu appear (but only if the menu has been selected on the first page of the Expert).

FIGURE 3.14:

One of the pages of the Application Expert is a visual tool you can use to build a toolbar with predefined buttons.

To add a new button, select one of them in the graphical list box on the right, and push the Insert button. The new toolbar button will be added in the position of the small triangular cursor. You can move this cursor by clicking on one of the elements already added to the toolbar. Notice that the cursor also indicates the button you want to remove from the toolbar.

When the toolbar is finished, you can move to the last page (see Figure 3.15). Here you can set many more options, such as choosing MDI support, adding a status bar, and enabling hints. You can also give a name to the new application and specify a directory for the source files. The name of the application is limited to eight characters, because this is the name used for the application project file. The directory for the application should be an existing directory. If you want to create a new one, choose the Browse button, and enter its path; the dialog box will prompt you if you want to create the new directory.

FIGURE 3.15:

The final page of the Application Expert

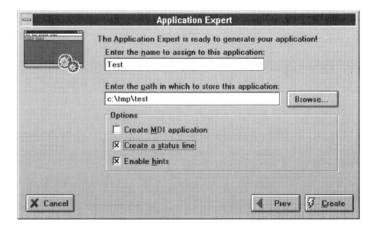

Although it is somewhat bare and it has room for improvement, the Delphi Application Expert can be much more useful than the predefined application templates for building the first version of an application. The biggest advantage is that you can define your own toolbar with this Expert, which allows you to choose from a number of buttons. Another advantage is that the Application Expert generates more code (and more comments) than the corresponding templates do.

The disadvantage of this Expert is that it generates an application with a single form. Its MDI support is limited, because no child form is defined, and an SDI application has no About box.

The Dialog Expert

Delphi's Dialog Expert is a simple Expert provided as a demo with its own source code. From the code of this Expert, you can learn how to built other Experts of your own.

However, you can still use the Dialog Expert as a tool to build three different kinds of dialog boxes:

- Simple dialog boxes
- Multiple-page dialog boxes using a Microsoft-style tabbed notebook
- Multiple-page dialog boxes based on Borland-style tabs

If you choose the simple dialog box, the Expert will jump to the third page, where you can choose the button layout. If you choose either of the multiple-page dialog boxes, an intermediate page will appear to let you input some strings for the text of the tabs. You can see the three pages of the Dialog Expert in Figure 3.16.

This Expert is an alternative to the corresponding form templates of the Browse Gallery. Its advantage is that the Expert allows you to input the names of the tabs. When you use a multiple-page dialog box template, you must add the names in a second pass.

We will explore dialog boxes in general and this Expert in particular in Chapter 12.

The Component Expert

The Component Expert is far more simple than the other Experts. It can be used to define a new custom component. When you start the Component Expert, it asks you to enter the name of the new class that you want to define, the parent component, and the page of the Components palette you want to add the component to (see Figure 3.17). After you fill in these entries, you get a source code file with some predefined code, particularly to accomplish the registration of the component.

FIGURE 3.16:

The three pages of the Dialog Expert
dialog box

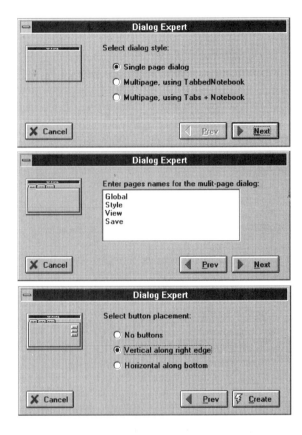

FIGURE 3.17:

The simple options of the
Component Expert

The support here is extremely limited, but to understand even the simple code generated by this Expert, you need to understand the basic elements of the Object Pascal language. I'll discuss component creation in Chapter 27.

Summary

In this short chapter, we have seen how you can start the development of an application not from scratch, but by using some code generated (or copied) by the system. The choices are:

- Use one of the few predefined application templates.
- Use one of the available form templates.
- Use the Database Form Expert to build the core of a database application.
- Use the Application Expert and the Dialog Expert as an alternative to the corresponding templates, for a fast start on development.
- Use the Component Expert to start the development of a new Delphi component.

In the rest of the book, I'll use these templates and Experts from time to time, but not very often. With the exception of the Database Form Expert, these tools let you build very simple applications, which you can often put together yourself in seconds once you are an experienced Delphi programmer.

For beginners, Experts and templates provide a quick start in code development. But you are not going to *remain* a beginner, are you? So we need to restart our exploration of Delphi from scratch, studying the Object Pascal language and exploring the use of the VCL (Visual Component Library) components. This is what we will do in the following chapters.

CHAPTER

FOUR

The Pascal Language

4

- Predefined and user-defined data types

- Pascal string handling

- Coding style

- Conditional statements and loops

- Procedures and functions

Dr. Nicklaus Wirth designed the Pascal language back in 1972 in Geneva, Switzerland. (That's about 300 miles from my home town, by the way.) The Pascal language, named after the French philosopher Blaise Pascal, has some distinctive characteristics. It was designed to be a learning tool, but it was found to be so powerful that it became a widespread programming language. In part, this is due to Borland and its world-famous Turbo Pascal series of compilers, introduced in 1985. The Turbo Pascal compiler made the language even more popular, particularly on the PC platform, due to a proper mix of simplicity and power.

When Pascal was designed, few programming languages existed (among them FORTRAN, COBOL, and BASIC). The key idea of the new language was order, managed through a strong concept of data type.

This book is not about Pascal, and it doesn't include a detailed discussion of the ideas behind this programming language. A specific book on Pascal might be what you need if you have never written a program in your life. However, if you know the basic programming concepts, but are not sure how they are implemented in Pascal, this chapter is for you.

Even if you have already used the Pascal language, perhaps during a programming course (something quite common in Europe but not so common in the United States), you should read this chapter. All of the examples are implemented using the Delphi environment. What you probably do not know much about is the object-oriented extensions of Object Pascal, which are available in Delphi. New Object Pascal extensions are the topic of the next chapter.

Pascal Data Types

The original Pascal language was based on some simple notions, which have now become quite common in programming languages. The first is the notion of *data type*. The type determines the values a variable can have (and the internal representation of these values) and the operations that can be accomplished on that variable. The notion of type in Pascal is stronger than in C, where the arithmetic data types are almost interchangeable, and much stronger than in the original versions of BASIC, which had no similar notion.

Here are some sample data declarations:

```
var
  Value: Integer;
  Correct: Boolean;
  A, B: Char;
```

The var keyword can be used in several places in the code, such as at the beginning of the code for a function. After var comes a list of variable names, followed by a colon and the name of the data type. You can write more than one variable name on a single line, as in the last line of the code above.

Once you have defined a variable of a given type, you can make on it only the operations supported by its data type. For example, you can use the Boolean value in a test and the integer value in a numerical expression. You cannot do the reverse, as is possible with the C language.

Using simple assignments, we can write the following code:

```
Value := 10;
Correct := True;
```

But the next statement is not correct, because the two variables have different data types:

```
Value := Correct;
```

If you try to compile this code, Delphi issues a Type Mismatch error. Usually, errors like this are programming errors, because it does not make sense to assign a True or False value to an integer. You should not blame Delphi for these errors. It only warns you that there is something wrong in the code.

Of course, it is often possible to convert the value of a variable of a type into one of a different type. In some cases, this conversion is automatic, but usually you need to call a specific system procedure that changes the internal representation of the data.

Predefined Data Types

There are several predefined data types, which can be divided into three different groups: ordinal types, real types, and strings. We'll discuss ordinal and real types in the following sections. Strings are covered later in this chapter.

Ordinal Types

Ordinal types have the notion of order. This not only relates to the fact that you can compare two values to see which is higher, but that you can also ask for the following or preceding value of a given value or compute the lowest or highest value.

The three most important predefined ordinal types are integer, Boolean, and character. However, there are a number of other related types that have the same meaning but a different internal representation and range of values.

Here is a complete list of the ordinal types:

- Integer, ShortInt, LongInt, Byte, Word
- Boolean, ByteBool, WordBool, LongBool
- Char

The various integer types correspond to different internal representations. Some of them are needed for MS Windows programming, as is the case with the different Boolean types.

The RANGE Example

To give you an idea of the different ranges of some of the ordinal types, I've written a simple Delphi program, named RANGE. You can try to rebuild it, or simply open the project on the companion disk, compile the program, and run it. The results are shown in Figure 4.1.

FIGURE 4.1:
The RANGE example displays some information about ordinal data types (integers in this screen).

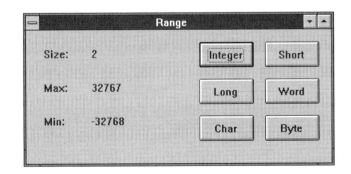

The RANGE program is based on a simple form, which has six buttons and six labels, as you can see in Listing 4.1. If you compare this description with the output of Figure 4.1, you might be puzzled by the number of labels. Each piece of text in the form is actually made of two labels: one with the description (for example, *Size*) and one with the value, which is generated by the program.

LISTING 4.1: The textual description of the form of the RANGE example

```
object Form1: TForm1
  Caption = 'Range'
  object SizeLabel: TLabel
  end
  object MaxLabel: TLabel
  end
  object MinLabel: TLabel
  end
  object Label4: TLabel
    Caption = 'Size:'
  end
  object Label5: TLabel
    Caption = 'Max:'
  end
  object Label6: TLabel
    Caption = 'Min:'
  end
  object IntButton: TButton
    Caption = 'Integer'
    OnClick = IntButtonClick
  end
  object ShortButton: TButton
    Caption = 'Short'
    OnClick = ShortButtonClick
  end
  object LongButton: TButton
    Caption = 'Long'
    OnClick = LongButtonClick
  end
  object WordButton: TButton
    Caption = 'Word'
    OnClick = WordButtonClick
  end
  object CharButton: TButton
    Caption = 'Char'
    OnClick = CharButtonClick
  end
  object ByteButton: TButton
    Caption = 'Byte'
    OnClick = ByteButtonClick
  end
end
```

4

Every time you press one of the buttons on the right, the program updates the three labels. These labels hold the number of bytes of the representation of the data type, and the maximum value and minimum value the data type can store. Each button has its own OnClick event-response method, but the code used to compute the three values is slightly different from button to button. For example, here is the source code of the OnClick event for the integer button (IntButton):

```
procedure TForm1.IntButtonClick(Sender: TObject);
var
  Number: Integer;
begin
  Number := 34;
  SizeLabel.Caption := IntToStr (SizeOf (Number));
  MaxLabel.Caption := IntToStr (High (Number));
  MinLabel.Caption := IntToStr (Low (Number));
end;
```

If you have some experience with Delphi programming, you can examine the source code of the program to understand how it works. For beginners, it's enough to notice the use of three functions: SizeOf, High, and Low. The results of the last two functions are ordinals of the same kind (in this case, integers), so they are first translated into strings using the IntToStr function, then copied to the three labels.

When the same code is applied to characters, the High and Low functions return characters themselves, so you cannot turn them into strings as we have done before. You can use another function, Ord, to compute the ordinal index of the value. In practice, the ordinal index of a character is the numerical value of the character. If you look in the code, you can see the following lines:

```
procedure TForm1.CharButtonClick(Sender: TObject);
var
  Number: Char;
begin
  Number := 'x';
  SizeLabel.Caption := IntToStr (SizeOf (Number));
  MaxLabel.Caption := IntToStr (Ord (High (Number)));
  MinLabel.Caption := IntToStr (Ord (Low (Number)));
end;
```

Figure 4.2 shows the result of the execution of this code. I won't show you the other methods, because they are very similar to the two procedures above. The only real difference is in the data type of the Number local variable.

```
-a100
in al,61
and al,fc
04  xor al,2
out 61,al
mov cx,140
BBloop  16f
jmp 104

30
1f 110
1E.
```

FIGURE 4.2:

The form of the RANGE example when you press the Char button

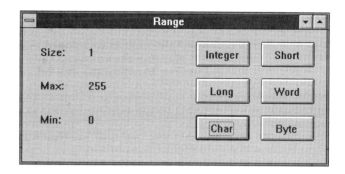

The size of integers varies depending on the CPU and operating system you are using. In MS Windows 3.1, integers are typically two bytes wide. In Windows 95, integers are four bytes wide. This means that if you recompile this application in a (future) Delphi edition for Windows 95, the results will change. This is common to all Delphi applications; however, it isn't a problem, as long as you don't make any assumptions about the size of integers. Instead, use system functions, such as SizeOf, High, and Low, to access to this information.

The result of integer calculations will not change when you move to a 32-bit environment, so you can use this data type without any problems. In fact, this change is interesting because, by using the native CPU integer sizes, you obtain the most programming power for integer computations. A real bonus you get for free is the ability to recompile your programs in a (future) 32-bit version of Delphi.

There are some system routines—routines defined in the Pascal language and in the Delphi system unit—working on ordinal types, as you can see in Table 4.1. C++ programmers should notice that the two versions of the Inc procedure, with one or two parameters, correspond to the ++ and += operators (the same holds for Dec).

Real Types

Real types represent floating-point numbers in various formats. The smallest storage size is given by Single numbers. Then there are Real numbers, Double numbers, and Extended numbers. There is also a strange data type, Comp, which describes integers too long to be considered ordinals.

TABLE 4.1: System Routines for Ordinal Types

Routine	Purpose
Dec	Decrements the variable passed as parameter, by one or by the value of the eventual second parameter.
Inc	Increments the variable passed as parameter, by one or by the specified value.
Odd	Returns True if the argument is an odd number.
Pred	Returns the value before the argument in the order determined by the data type, the predecessor.
Succ	Returns the value after the argument, the successor.
Ord	Returns a number indicating the order of the argument within the set of values of the data type.
Low	Returns the lowest value in the range of the ordinal type passed as parameter.
High	Returns the highest value in the range of the ordinal data type.

We cannot build a program similar to RANGE with real data types, because we cannot use the High and Low functions or the Ord function on real type variables. Real types represent (in theory) an infinite set of numbers; ordinal types represent a fixed set of values. For this reason, it makes sense to ask the order of the w character in the char data type, but it makes no sense at all to ask the order of 7143.1562 in the real data type.

Although you can indeed know if a real number has a higher value than another one, it makes no sense to ask how many real numbers exist before a given number (this is the meaning of the Ord function). The same discussion can be extended to other functions available only for ordinal types.

Real types are used almost exclusively in programs involving math formulas, and they usually have a limited role in the user interface portion of the code (the Windows side). Of course, a large number of applications involve real number math formulas. Examples are design software (CAD), image processing (ray tracing, rendering, and photo editing), image compression and decompression (JPEG and MPEG algorithms), and simulation and modeling software. Delphi itself uses real types in the TDateTime data type. This is a floating-point type, which is the only type that has a wide enough range of values to store days, months, years, hours, minutes, and seconds, down to millisecond resolution in a single variable.

Fortunately, the existence of so many different numeric data types makes Object Pascal a complete language for those involved in mathematics. If you are interested in this aspect, you can look at the arithmetic functions provided by the Delphi in the system unit (for example, see the Delphi Help topic named Arithmetic Routines).

Specific Windows Types

The predefined data types we have seen so far are part of the Pascal language. Delphi also includes other data types defined by MS Windows. These data types are not an integral part of the language, but they are part of Windows libraries.

4

> **NOTE** Windows types are not exactly predefined data types, since they are not directly understood by the compiler. However, they are simple data types, so I decided to discuss them here.

Among Windows data types, two simple and commonly used types are handles and color references. The names of these data types are, respectively, THandle and TColorRef. The first is just a redefinition of the Word data type, the second of the LongInt type.

A color reference is simply a number describing a color. There are some predefined constants with values of colors, such as clRed, or with Windows standard colors, such as clWindow (the default color for the surface of a window). Besides using these constants, you can choose any kind of color by setting the amount of red, green, and blue of any TColorRef value by using the RGB function or by accessing the representation of the color directly.

Handle data types are not understandable values. In Windows, a handle is a number referring to an internal data structure of the system. For example, when you work with a window, the system gives you a *handle to the window*, or hwnd. The system informs you that the window you are working with is window number 142, for example. From that point on, your application can ask the system to operate on window number 142—moving it, resizing it, reducing it to an icon, and so on.

In other words, a handle is an internal code you can use to refer to a specific element handled by the system, including windows, bitmaps, icons, memory blocks, cursors, fonts, menus, and so on. In Delphi, you seldom need to use handles directly, since they are hidden inside forms, bitmaps, and other Delphi objects. They become useful when you want to call an MS Windows API function that is not supported by Delphi.

Typecasting and Type Conversions

As we have seen, you cannot assign a variable to another one of a different type. In case you need to do this, there are two choices.

The first choice is *typecasting*, which uses a simple functional notation, with the name of the destination data type:

```
var
  N: Integer;
  C: Char;
  B: Boolean;

begin
  N := Integer ('X');
  C := Char (N);
  B := Boolean (0);
  ...
```

You can generally typecast between data types having the same size. It is usually safe to typecast between ordinal types, or between real types, but you can also typecast between pointer types (and also objects) as long as you know what you are doing. Casting, however, is generally a dangerous programming practice, because it allows you to access a value as if it represented something else. Since the internal representation of data types and objects generally do not match, you risk hard-to-track errors. For this reason, you should avoid typecasting, or use the safe techniques for typecasting between objects offered by run-time type methods, which we will see in the next chapter.

The second choice is to use a type-conversion routine. The routines for the various types of conversions are summarized in Table 4.2. Some of these routines work on the data types that we'll discuss in the following sections.

TABLE 4.2: System Routines for Type Conversion

Routine	Purpose
Chr	Converts an ordinal number into a character.
Ord	Converts an ordinal-type value into the number indicating its order.
Round	Converts a real-type value into an integer-type value, rounding its value.
Trunc	Converts a real-type value into an integer-type value, truncating its value.
IntToStr	Converts a number into a string.
IntToHex	Converts a number into a string with its hexadecimal representation.
StrToInt	Converts a string into a number, raising an exception if the string is not correct (see Chapter 5 for a description of exceptions in Object Pascal).
StrToIntDef	Converts a string into a number, using a default value if the string is not correct.
Val	Converts a string into a number.
Str	Converts a number into a string, using formatting parameters.
StrPas	Converts a null-terminated string into a Pascal-style string.
StrPCopy	Converts (copies) a Pascal-style string into a null-terminated string.
StrPLCopy	Converts (copies) a portion of a Pascal-style string into a null-terminated string.

4

User-Defined Data Types

Along with the notion of type, one of the great ideas introduced by the Pascal language is the capability to define new data types in a program. This is something that was not commonly available in earlier programming languages. Besides using the predefined data types, programmers can define their own data types by means of type constructors, such as subranges, arrays, records, enumerations, pointers, and sets. The most important user-defined data type is the class, which will be discussed in the next chapter.

These types can be given a name for later use or applied to a variable directly. When you give a name to a type, you must provide a specific section in the code, such as the following:

```
type
  {subrange definition:}
  Uppercase = 'A'..'Z';
```

```
{array definition:}
Temperatures = array [1..24] of Integer;

{record definition:}
Date = record
  Month: Byte;
  Day: Byte;
  Year: Integer;
end;

{enumerated type definition:}
Colors = (Red, Yellow, Green, Cyan, Blue, Violet);

{set definition:}
Letters = set of Char;
```

Similar type definition constructs can be used directly to define a variable without an explicit type definition, as in:

```
var:
  DecemberTemperature: array [1..31] of Byte;
  ColorCode: array [Red..Violet] of Word;
  Palette: set of Colors;
```

WARNING In general, you should avoid using *unnamed* types as in the code above, because you cannot pass them as parameters to subroutines, or declare other variables of the same type. Get used to defining a data type each time you need a complex variable, and you won't regret the time you spent for it.

But what do these type definitions mean? Most of you probably already know, but I'll provide some short descriptions for those of you who are not familiar with Pascal type constructs. I'll also try to underline the differences from the same constructs in other programming languages, so you might be interested in reading the following sections even if you are familiar with type definitions.

Subranges

A subrange type defines a range of values within the range of another type (hence the name *subrange*). You can define a subrange of integers, from 1 to 10 or from 100 to 1000. Or you can define a subrange of characters, as in:

```
type
   Uppercase = 'A'..'Z';
```

Figure 4.3 illustrates the subrange above. In the definition of a subrange, you don't need to specify the name of the base type. You just need to supply two constants of that type. Both the original type and the subrange type are ordinal types.

FIGURE 4.3:

A representation of a subrange

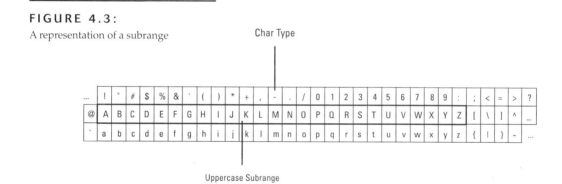

When you have defined a subrange, you can legally assign it a value within that range. This is valid:

```
UppLetter := 'F';
```

But this is not:

```
UppLetter := 'e';
```

Enumerations

Enumerated types constitute another user-defined ordinal type. Instead of indicating a range of an existing type, in an enumeration, you list all of the possible values for the type. An enumeration is a list of values. Here are some examples:

```
type
   Colors = (Red, Yellow, Green, Cyan, Blue, Violet);
   Suit = (Club, Diamond, Heart, Spade);
```

Each value in the list has an associated *ordinality*, starting with zero. When you apply the Ord function to a value of an enumerated type, you get this zero-based value. For example, Ord (Diamonds) returns 1. Enumerations are limited to an 8-bit representation. This means that an enumeration can have at most 256 different values.

In Delphi, there are several properties that have an enumerated value. For example, the style of the border of a form is defined as follows:

```
type
   TFormBorderStyle = (bsNone, bsSingle, bsSizeable, bsDialog);
```

When the value of a property is an enumeration, you usually can choose from the list of values displayed in the Object Inspector:

Sets

A set type indicates the power set of an ordinal type, quite often an enumeration, since the base type cannot have more than 256 possible values in its range. Each set can contain none, one, more than one, or all the values within the range of the ordinal type (see Figure 4.4).

Here is an example of a set, graphically shown in Figure 4.4:

```
type
   Letters = set of Uppercase;
```

Now I can define a variable of this type and assign to it some values of the original type. To indicate some values in a set, you write a comma-separated list, enclosed within square brackets. When you have defined a variable such as:

```
var
   MyLetters: Letters;
```

FIGURE 4.4:

A representation of a set

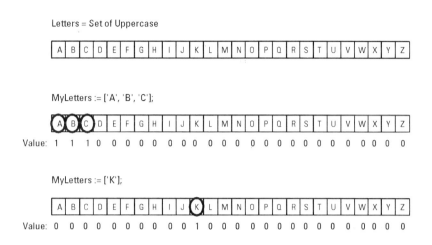

you can set its value with the following statements (respectively assigning several values, a single value, and an empty value):

```
MyLetters := ['A', 'B', 'C'];
MyLetters := ['K'];
MyLetters := [];
```

In Delphi, sets are often used to indicate nonexclusive flags. For example, the following two lines declare an enumeration of possible icons for the border of a window and the corresponding set:

```
type
  TBorderIcon = (biSystemMenu, biMinimize, biMaximize);
  TBorderIcons = set of TBorderIcon;
```

In fact, a window can have none of these icons, one icon, two icons, or all of them. When working with the Object Inspector, you can provide the values of a set either by writing the proper list between square brackets or by expanding the selection and toggling on and off the presence of each value:

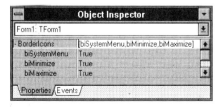

Arrays

An array defines a fixed number of elements of one specific type (see Figure 4.5). For example, you can define a *group* of 24 integers with this code:

```
type
   DayTemperatures = array [1..24] of Integer;
```

In the array definition, you need to use two constants of an ordinal type to specify the valid indexes of the array. Since you specify both the upper and the lower index of the array, the indexes don't need to be zero-based, as is necessary in C/C++ and other programming languages.

In the former case, you can set the value of a DayTemp variable of the DayTemperatures type as follows:

```
DayTemp [1] := 34;
DayTemp [2] := 32;
...
DayTemp [24] := 36;
```

FIGURE 4.5:

A representation of an array

DayTemperatures = Array [1..24] of Integer;

An array can have more than one dimension, as in the following examples:

```
type
  MonthTemperatures = array [1..24, 1..31] of Integer;
  YearTemperatures = array [1..24, 1..31, January..December]
    of Integer;
```

These arrays are built on the same core types. So you can declare them using the preceding data types, such as in:

```
type
  MonthTemps = array [1..31] of DayTemps;
  YearTemps = array [Jan..Dec] of MonthTemps;
```

This declaration inverts the order of the indexes as presented above, but it also allows assignment of whole blocks between variables. For example, the following copies January's temperatures to February:

```
ThisYear[Feb] := ThisYear[Jan];
```

You can also define zero-based arrays—arrays with the lower bound set to zero. Generally, the use of more logical bounds is an advantage, since you don't need to use the index 2 to access the third item, and so on. If you need to work on an array, you can always test its bounds by using the standard Low and High functions.

NOTE Using Low and High when operating on arrays is highly recommended, especially in loops, since it makes the code independent of the range of the array. You can later change the declared range of the array indices, and the code that uses Low and High will still work. Code that is hard-coded for an array's range would not work. Low and High make your code easier to maintain and more reliable. Incidentally, there is no run-time overhead for using Low and High. They are resolved at compile-time into constant expressions, not actual function calls.

Records

A record type defines a fixed collection of elements of different types. Each element, or field, has its own type. The definition of a record type lists all these fields, giving each a name you'll use later to access it. Here is an example of the definition of a record type (see also Figure 4.6), a variable of that type, and the use of this variable:

```
type
  Date = record
    Year: Integer;
    Month: Byte;
    Day: Byte;
  end;

var
  BirthDay: Date;

begin
  BirthDay.Year := 1995;
  BirthDay.Month := 2;
  BirthDay.Day := 14;
  ...
```

FIGURE 4.6:

A representation of a record

Date = Record
  Year: Integer;
  Month: Byte;
  Day: Byte;

Year :	Integer
Month:	Byte
Day:	Byte

The record type is important because it is similar to the class type, which we will discuss in the next chapter. In fact, classes and objects can be considered an extension of the record type.

Records can also have a variant part; that is, multiple fields can be mapped to the same memory area, even if they have a different data type. Alternatively, you can use these variant fields or groups of fields to access the same memory location within a record, but considering those values from different perspectives. The effect you obtain is similar to that of typecasting, and this is actually the most common reason variant records were used in the past, when the Pascal language allowed no explicit typecasting. The use of variant records is not type-safe and is not a recommended programming practice, particularly for beginners.

Pointers

A pointer type defines a variable that holds the memory address of yet another variable of a certain data type. So a pointer variable indirectly refers to a value, as you can see in Figure 4.7. The definition of a pointer type uses a special character, the caret (^).

```
type
    PointerToInt = ^Integer;
```

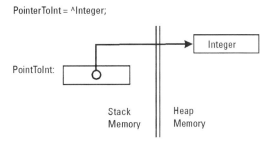

Once you have defined a pointer variable, you can assign to it the address of another variable of the same type, using the @ operator, or create a new variable on the heap with the New procedure. If a pointer has no value, you can assign to it nil. You can test if a pointer is nil to see if it currently refers to a value. This is often used, because dereferencing an invalid pointer causes a general protection fault.

The fact that pointers are seldom necessary in Delphi is an interesting advantage of this environment. Understanding pointers is important for advanced programming and if you want to understand the Delphi object model, which uses pointers "behind the scenes." However, you can probably write even the most complex Delphi applications without using any *explicit* pointers at all.

> **NOTE**
>
> You use pointers often in Delphi, but behind the scenes. Every object instance is really an implicit pointer or reference to its actual data. However, this is completely transparent to the programmer, who uses object variables just like any other data type. We will see some more details about the Delphi object reference model in the next chapter.

Files

Another Pascal-specific type constructor is the file type. Files are related to input/output, and they will be discussed in more detail in Chapter 23. In short, you can define a new file data type as follows:

```
type
    IntFile = file of Integer
```

Then you can open a physical file associated with this structure, and write values (integers) to it or read the current values. The use of files in Pascal is quite straightforward, but in Delphi there are also some components that are capable of storing or loading their contents to or from a file. There is some serialization support and there is also database support. We will discuss these issues in Chapters 17 and 23.

Pascal Strings

String handling is a complex issue in the MS Windows versions of the Pascal language. In fact, the Pascal language has one way of handling strings, while Windows has its own way, borrowed from the C language.

In Pascal, a string type is a sequence of characters with a length counter that can change dynamically. Each string has a fixed size (which by default is 255), although it usually holds fewer characters. An example is:

```
var
  Name: string;
  Title: string [50];
```

Name is a string of 255 characters. Title holds a maximum of 50 characters.

As you can see from the use of brackets, strings are similar to arrays. In fact, a string is almost an array of characters. This is demonstrated by the fact that you can write:

```
FirstChar := Name [1];
```

to access the first character of the Name string. There are a number of functions you can use to operate on strings, as you can see in Table 4.3. In particular, using Pascal strings, you can easily add two strings using the plus sign:

```
FinalString := FirstString + ' ' + SecondString;
```

This expression merges the two strings, adding a blank character (a space) between them.

TABLE 4.3: System Routines for Pascal Strings

AssignStr	CompareStr	CompareText	Concat	Copy
Delete	DisposeStr	Format	FormatBuf	FormatStr
Insert	IntToHex	IntToStr	Length	LowerCase
NewStr	Pos	Str	StrToInt	StrToIntDef
UpperCase	Val			

C-like Character Arrays

As an alternative, to the string type, you can use zero-based character arrays to store *null-terminated* strings. A *null-terminated* string is a sequence of characters followed by a byte set to zero (or null). Character arrays are typical of the C language, and they are used extensively by MS Windows API functions. You declare a character array as follows:

```
var
  Name: array[0..50] of Char;
```

However, there is a second way to use character arrays. If the language *extended syntax* is enabled (which happens by default), a zero-based character array is compatible with PChar, a pointer to a character. You might wonder why this compatibility would be necessary. The short answer is that many MS Windows API functions require PChar parameters, so this compatibility rule allows you to pass declared character arrays, eventually fill them with a value, and then pass them as parameters to these API functions.

Although many Windows functions have a PChar parameter, in most cases, declaring PChar and passing it to those functions generates a bad error. By writing such code, you end up passing a null pointer (that is, an uninitialized pointer) to the function, which will cause an error inside Windows code when the system tries to read or write the string. This error usually results in a system unrecoverable application error message.

In general, before passing a pointer to a Windows function, you should allocate memory for it. In the case of strings, the easiest technique is to declare an array of characters instead of a pointer, and pass that array to the function. Again, this is possible because of the type-compatibility rules for zero-based character arrays and for PChars. This compatibility rule corresponds to the standard behavior of the C language.

There are a number of functions that work on null-terminated strings, too. However, at the beginning it is probably better to stay with the Pascal strings, which are much easier to manage. In Delphi, you'll need to use null-terminated strings only to interact with the MS Windows API directly.

In case you need to do this, there are a couple of conversion functions which might come in handy. StrPas converts a null-terminated string into a Pascal string. StrPCopy makes the reverse conversion. Null-terminated strings have a broader set of system functions and procedures (see Table 4.4), but they are generally more complex to use.

TABLE 4.4: System Routines for Null-Terminated Strings

StrAlloc	StrBufSize	StrCat	StrComp	StrCopy
StrDispose	StrECopy	StrEnd	StrLCat	StrIComp
StrLComp	StrLCopy	StrFmt	StrLen	StrLFmt
StrLIComp	StrLower	StrMove	StrNew	StrPas
StrPCopy	StrPLCopy	StrPos	StrScan	StrRScan
StrUpper				

Coding Style

Before we start to write actual Pascal language statements, it is important to highlight a couple of elements of Pascal coding style. The question I'm addressing is: Besides the syntax rules, how do you write the code? There isn't a single answer to this question, since personal taste can dictate different styles. However, there are some principles you need to know regarding comments, uppercase, spaces, and the so-called "pretty-printing."

Comments

In Pascal, comments are enclosed in either braces or parentheses followed by a star:

```
{this is a comment}
(* this is another comment *)
```

The first form is shorter and more commonly used. The second form is often preferred in Europe due to the lack of the brace symbol on many European keyboards (including the one I currently use). Of course, one can get used to typing Alt-123 and Alt-125 to obtain the proper symbol, but having an alternative is better.

Having two different forms of comments can be helpful to make nested comments. If you want to comment out several lines of source code, to disable them, and these lines contain some real comments, you cannot use the same comment identifier:

```
{
  ... code
  ... code
  {comment, creating problems,
  since the following close brace is related
  to the first open brace above}
  ... code
  ... code
}
```

With a second comment identifier, you can write the following code, which is correct:

```
(*
  ... code
  ... code
  {this comment is OK}
```

```
... code
... code
*)
```

This approach might be familiar to C++ programmers, who use two different kinds of comments: /* and //.

Note that if the open brace or parenthesis-star is followed by the dollar character ($), it becomes a compiler directive, as in:

```
{$X+}
```

NOTE Actually, {$*nnnn*} directives are still comments. `{$X+ This is a comment}` is legal. It's both a valid directive and a comment, although "sane" programmers will probably tend to separate directives and comments.

Use of Uppercase

Unlike in other languages, the Pascal compiler ignores the case of the characters. Therefore, the identifiers `Myname`, `MyName`, `myname`, `myName`, and `MYNAME` are all exactly equivalent. This is definitely positive, since in case-sensitive languages, many syntax errors are due to incorrect capitalization.

There are a couple of subtle drawbacks, however. First, you must be aware that these identifiers really are the same, so you must avoid trying to use them as different elements. Second, you should try to be consistent in the use of uppercase letters, to improve the readability of the code.

A common approach is to capitalize only the first letter of each identifier. When an identifier is made up of several consecutive words (you cannot insert a space in an identifier), every first letter of a word should be capitalized, as in:

```
MyLongIdentifier
MyVeryLongAndAlmostStupidIdentifier
```

A consistent use of the cases isn't enforced by the compiler, but it is a good habit to get into.

White Spaces

Other elements completely ignored by the compiler are the amount of spaces, new lines, and tab spaces you add to the source code. All these elements are collectively known as white spaces. White spaces are used only to improve code readability; they do not affect the compilation.

Unlike BASIC, Pascal allows you to write a statement in several lines of code, splitting a long instruction on two or more lines. The drawback (at least for many BASIC programmers) of allowing statements on more than one line is the presence of the semicolon to indicate the end of a statement, or more precisely, to separate a statement from the next one. Remember that the only restriction in splitting programming statements on different lines is that you cannot have a newline character in string literals.

Again, there are no fixed rules on the use of spaces and multiple-line statements, just some rules of the thumb:

- The Delphi editor has a vertical line you can place after 60 or 70 characters. If you use this line and try to avoid surpassing this limit, your source code will look better when you print it on paper. Long lines can be broken automatically at any position, even in the middle of a word, when you print them.

- When a function or procedure has several parameters, it is common practice to place the parameters on different lines.

- You can leave a line completely white (blank) before a comment or to divide a long piece of code in smaller portions. Even this simple idea can improve the readability of the code, both on screen and when you print it.

- Use white spaces to separate the parameters of a function call, and maybe even a space before the initial open parenthesis. Separate operands of an expression. I know that some programmers will disagree with these ideas, but I insist: Spaces are free, you don't pay for them. (Okay, I know that they use up disk space, and modem time when you upload or download a file, but they can be compressed fairly well.)

The last suggestion on the use of white spaces relates to the typical Pascal language-formatting style, known as pretty-printing.

Pretty-Printing

Source-code formatting in Pascal usually follows a standard approach, known as pretty-printing. Its rule is simple: Each time you need to write a compound statement, indent it two spaces to the right of the rest of the current statement. A compound statement inside another compound statement is indented four spaces, and so on:

```
if ... then
  statement;

if ... then
begin
  statement1;
  statement2;
end;

if ... then
begin
  if ... then
    statement1
  statement2;
end;
```

A similar indented format is often used for lists of variables or data types, as in the code fragments of this chapter, and to continue a statement from the previous line:

```
type
  Letters = set of Char;

var
  Name: string;

very long source code statement going on in the
  following line, and indented two or four spaces;
```

Of course, any such convention is just a suggestion to make the code more readable to other programmers, and it is completely ignored by the compiler.

I won't give you a detailed coverage of pretty-printing rules here, but I've tried to use them consistently in all of the samples and code fragments in this book. Delphi source code, manuals, and help examples use a similar formatting style.

NOTE

Some programmers and authors follow different conventions for source-code formatting. For example, some insist on not using a line for a `begin` or `end` statement. Packing more text in a single line, you might be able to see more lines of code in the editor window. I've never liked this approach, since I prefer to waste a line with only an open or closed parenthesis, even in C++. For readability of code, both in an editor and on paper, I tend to leave a number of white spaces before and after operators, before the parameters of procedures, and so on. This is just my personal taste. You should follow your own habits, at least if they are not too bad!

Syntax Highlighting

To make it easier to read and write Pascal code, the Delphi editor has a feature named *color syntax highlighting*. Depending on the meaning in the Pascal language of the words you type in the editor, they are displayed using different colors. By default, keywords are in bold, strings and comments are in color, and so on.

Reserved words, comments, and strings are probably the three elements that benefit most from this feature. You can see at a glance a misspelled keyword, a string not properly terminated, and the length of a multiple-line comment.

You can easily customize the syntax highlight settings using the Editor Colors page of the Environment Options dialog box (see Figure 4.8). If you work by yourself, choose the colors you like. If you work closely with other programmers, you should all agree on a standard color scheme. I find that working on a computer with a different syntax coloring than the one I am used to is really difficult.

Pascal Statements

Once you have defined some identifiers, you can use them in statements and in the expressions that are part of some statements. In Pascal, there are several different statements and expressions. Let's look at expressions and operators first.

FIGURE 4.8:

The dialog box used to set the color
syntax highlighting

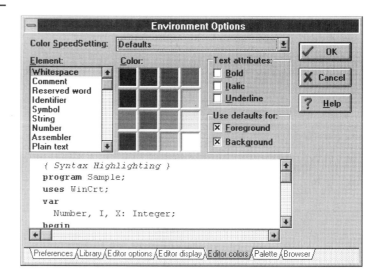

Expressions and Operators

There isn't a general rule for building expressions, since they mainly depend on the operators being used, and Pascal has a number of operators. There are logical, arithmetic, Boolean, relational, and set operators, plus some others. Expressions can be used to determine the value to assign to a variable, to compute the parameter of a function or procedure, or to test for a condition. Expressions can include function calls, too. Every time you are performing an operation on the value of an identifier, rather than using an identifier by itself, that is an expression.

> **NOTE**
> Expressions are common to most programming languages. An *expression* is any valid combination of constants, variables, literal values, operators, and function results. Expressions are read-only. You can use the result of an expression but not assign a value to it. In other words, an expression can appear on the right side of an assignment, but not on the left side (that is, expressions cannot be used as l-values). Expressions can also be passed to value parameters of procedures and functions, but not to reference (`var`) parameters (which require an *l-value*).

If you have ever written a program in your life, you already know what an expression is. Here, I'll highlight specific elements of Pascal operators. You can see a list of the operators of the language, grouped by precedence, in Table 4.5.

TABLE 4.5: Pascal Language Operators, Grouped by Precedence

Operator	Purpose
Unary Operators (Highest Precedence)	
@	Address of (returns a pointer)
not	Boolean or bitwise not
Multiplicative and Bitwise Operators	
*	Arithmetic multiplication or set intersection
/	Real-type division
div	Integer-type division
mod	Modulus (the remainder of integer division)
as	Type-safe typecast (RTTI)
and	Boolean and bitwise and
shl	Bitwise left shift
shr	Bitwise right shift
Additive Operators	
+	Addition, set union, string concatenation, positive value, or offset addition
−	Subtraction, set difference, negative value, or offset subtraction
or	Boolean or bitwise or
xor	Boolean or bitwise exclusive or
Relational and Comparison Operators (Lowest Precedence)	
=	Test if equal
<>	Test if not equal
<	Test if less than
>	Test if greater than
<=	Test if less or equal or subset of a set
>=	Test if greater or equal or superset of a set
in	Test if member of
is	Test if type compatible (RTTI)

Notice that some of the common operators have different meanings with different data types. For example, the + operator can be used to add two numbers, concatenate two strings, make the union of two sets, and even add an offset to a PChar. However, you cannot add two characters, as is possible in C.

Another strange operator is div. In Pascal, you can divide any two numbers (real or integers) with the / operator, and you'll invariably get a real type result. If you need to divide two integers and want an integer result, use the div operator. (By the way, div is faster than /.)

Set Operators

The set operators include:

- Set union (+)
- Difference (-)
- Intersection (*)
- Set membership test (in)
- Relational operators

To add an element to a set, you can make the union of the set with another one that has only the element you need. Here's a Delphi example related to font styles:

```
Style := Style + [fsBold];
Style := Style + [fsBold, fsItalic] - [fsUnderline];
```

As an alternative, you can use the standard Include and Exclude procedures, which are much more efficient (but cannot be used with component properties of the set type, because they require an I = value parameter):

```
Include (Style, fsBold);
```

Simple and Compound Statements

A Pascal statement is simple when it doesn't contain any other statements. Examples of simple statements are assign statements and procedure statements.

Simple statements are separated by a semicolon:

```
X := Y + Z; {assignment}
Randomize; {procedure call}
```

As I mentioned in Chapter 1, assignments in Pascal use the odd operator := (odd for programmers who are used to other languages, of course). The = operator, which is used for assignments in other languages, is used to test for equality in Pascal.

4

NOTE   By using two different symbols for an assignment and an equality test, the Pascal compiler can translate source code faster, because it doesn't need to examine the context in which the operator is used to determine its meaning. The use of different operators also makes the code easier for us to read.

Usually, statements are part of a compound statement, marked by begin and end brackets. A compound statement can appear in place of a generic Pascal statement. Here is an example:

```
begin
  A := B;
  C := A * 2;
end;
```

The semicolon after the last statement before the end isn't required, as in:

```
begin
  A := B;
  C := A * 2
end;
```

Both versions are correct. The first version has a useless (but harmless) semicolon. This semicolon is, in fact, a null statement; that is, a statement with no code. (Notice that, at times, null statements can be used inside loops or in other particular cases.)

Pascal Conditional Statements

A conditional statement is used to execute one or none of the statements that compose it. There are two basic flavors of conditional statements: `if` statements and `case` statements.

If Statements

The `if` statement can be used to execute a statement only if a certain condition is met (`if-then`), or to choose between two different statements (`if-then-else`). The condition is described with a Boolean expression.

We'll go through a simple Delphi example to show you how to write simple conditional statements. The example includes some components that we haven't gotten to yet, but I think you can get the basic idea.

First, create a new blank application, and put two check boxes and four buttons in the form, as shown in Figure 4.9.

FIGURE 4.9:

The form of the IF_TEST application

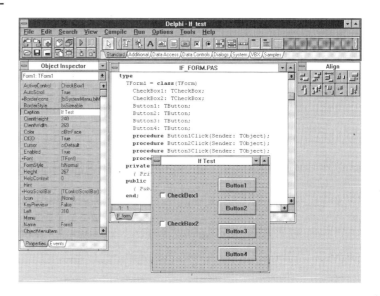

Do not change the names of buttons or check boxes, but do double-click on each of the buttons to add an OnClick event handler. Here's a simple `if` statement for the first button:

```
procedure TForm1.Button1Click(Sender: TObject);
begin
  {simple if statement}
  if CheckBox1.Checked then
    ShowMessage ('CheckBox1 is checked')
end;
```

When you click the button, if the first check box has a check mark in it, the program will show a simple message in a small window (see Figure 4.10). I've used the ShowMessage function because it is the simplest Delphi function you can use to display a short message to the user, although the output of the MessageDlg function I've used in past examples is much better looking.

FIGURE 4.10:

The message displayed when the check mark is checked

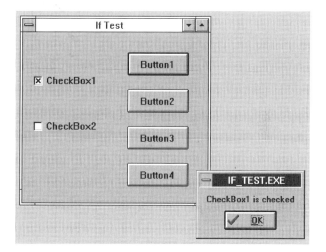

If you click the button and nothing happens, it means the check box was not checked. In general, it is better to make this more explicit, as with this code for the second button, which uses an `if-then-else` statement.

```
procedure TForm1.Button2Click(Sender: TObject);
begin
  {if-then-else statement}
```

```
  if CheckBox2.Checked then
    ShowMessage ('CheckBox2 is checked')
  else
    ShowMessage ('CheckBox2 is NOT checked');
end;
```

Notice that you cannot have a semicolon after the first statement and before the else keyword, or the compiler will issue a syntax error.

If statements can be quite complex. The condition can be turned into a series of conditions, or the if statement can nest a second if statement. The last two buttons of the IF_TEST example demonstrate these cases.

```
procedure TForm1.Button3Click(Sender: TObject);
begin
  {statement with a double condition}
  if CheckBox1.Checked and CheckBox2.Checked then
    ShowMessage ('Both check boxes are checked')
end;

procedure TForm1.Button4Click(Sender: TObject);
begin
  {compound if statement}
  if CheckBox1.Checked then
  if CheckBox2.Checked then
    ShowMessage ('CheckBox1 and 2 are checked')
  else
    ShowMessage ('Only CheckBox2 is checked')
  else
    ShowMessage ('Checkbox1 is not checked, who cares for Checkbox2?')
end;
```

Look at the code carefully and run the program to see if you understand everything. When you have doubts about a programming construct, writing a very simple program such as this can help you learn a lot. You can add more check boxes and increase the complexity of this small example, making any test you like.

Case Statements

If your if statements become very complex, you can replace them with case statements. A case statement consists of an expression, used to select a value, and a list of possible values or ranges of values. These values are constants, and they must be unique and of an ordinal type. Eventually, there can be an `else` statement that is executed if none of the labels correspond to the value of the selector. Here are two simple examples:

```
case Number of
  1: Text := 'One';
  2: Text := 'Two';
  3: Text := 'Three';
end;

case MyChar of
  '+' := Text := 'Plus sign';
  '-' := Text := 'Minus sign';
  '0'..'9': Text := 'Number';
  'a'..'z': Text := 'Lowercase character';
  'A'..'Z': Text := 'Uppercase character';
else
  Text := 'Unknown character';
```

Pascal Loops

The Pascal language has the typical repetitive statements of most programming languages, including `for`, `while`, and `repeat` statements.

For Statements

The `for` loop in Pascal is strictly based on a counter, which can be either increased or decreased each time the loop is executed. Here is a simple example of a `for` loop used to add the first ten integer numbers.

```
K := 0;
for I := 1 to 10 do
  K :- K + I;
```

This same `for` statement could have been written using a reverse counter:

```
K := 0;
for I := 10 downto 1 do
  K := K + I;
```

The for loop in Pascal is less flexible than in C, but it is simpler and much easier to understand. If you want to test for a more complex condition, or to provide a customized counter, you need to use one of the other two repetitive statements instead of for.

While and Repeat Statements

The difference between the while-do loop and the repeat-until loop is that the code of the repeat statement is always executed at least once. You can easily understand why by looking at a simple example:

```
while I < 100 and J < 100 do
begin
  {use I and J to compute something... }
  I := I + 1;
  J := J + 1;
end;

repeat
  {use I and J to compute something... }
  I := I + 1;
  J := J + 1;
until I < 100 and J < 100;
```

If the initial value of I or J is greater than 100, the statements inside the repeat-until loop are executed anyway.

To explore the details of loops, let's look at a small Delphi example. This example, called LOOPS, highlights the difference between a loop with a fixed counter and a loop with an almost random counter.

Start with a new blank project, and place a list box and two buttons on the main form, as shown in Figure 4.11. Listing 4.2 shows the textual description of this form.

Now we can add some code to the OnClick events of the two buttons. The first button has a simple for loop to display a list of numbers, as you can see in Figure 4.12.

FIGURE 4.11:

The form of the LOOPS example at design-time

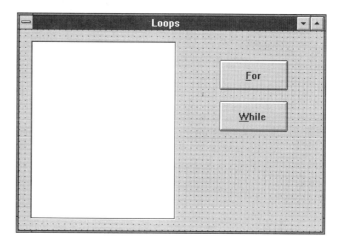

FIGURE 4.12:

Each time you press the For button, the list box is filled with consecutive numbers

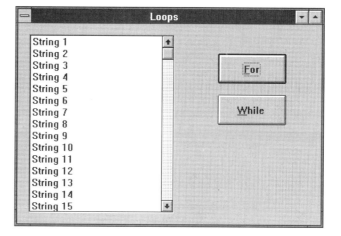

LISTING 4.2: The textual description of the form of the LOOPS example

```
object Form1: TForm1
  ActiveControl = ListBox1
  Caption = 'Loops'
  object ListBox1: TListBox
    ItemHeight = 16
  end
  object Button1: TButton
    Caption = '&For'
    OnClick = Button1Click
  end
  object Button2: TButton
    Caption = '&While'
    OnClick = Button2Click
  end
end
```

Before executing this loop, which adds a number of strings to the Items property of the list box, you need to clear the contents of the list box itself:

```
procedure TForm1.Button1Click(Sender: TObject);
var
  I: Integer;
begin
  ListBox1.Items.Clear;
  for I := 1 to 20 do
  Listbox1.Items.Add ('String ' + IntToStr (I));
end;
```

The code associated with the second button is slightly more complex. In this case, there is a while loop based on a counter, which is increased randomly. To accomplish this, I've called the Randomize procedure, which resets the random-number generator, and the Random function with a range value of 100. The result of this function is a number between 0 and 99, chosen randomly.

```
procedure TForm1.Button2Click(Sender: TObject);
var
  I: Integer;
begin
  ListBox1.Items.Clear;
  Randomize;
  I := 0;
  while I < 1000 do
```

```
begin
  I := I + Random (100);
  Listbox1.Items.Add ('Random Number: ' + IntToStr (I));
  end;
end;
```

Each time you click the second button, the numbers are different, because they depend on the random-number generator. Two examples are shown in Figure 4.13.

FIGURE 4.13:
The contents of the list box of the LOOPS example changes from time to time when you press the While button

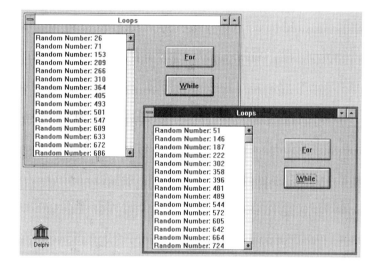

The With Statement

The last kind of Pascal statement I'll focus on is the `with` statement, which is peculiar to this programming language and very useful in Delphi programming. The `with` statement is nothing but shorthand. When you need to refer to a record (or an object), instead of repeating its name every time, you can use a `with` statement. For example, for the discussion of records, I wrote this code:

```
type
  Date = record
    Year: Integer;
    Month: Byte;
    Day: Byte;
  end;
```

```
var
  BirthDay: Date;

begin
  BirthDay.Year := 1995;
  BirthDay.Month := 2;
  BirthDay.Day := 14;
  ...
```

I can improve the final part of this code, using a with statement, as follows:

```
begin
  with BirthDay do
  begin
    Year := 1995;
    Month := 2;
    Day := 14;
  end;
  ...
```

This approach can be used in Delphi programs to refer to components. For example, we can rewrite the final part of the last example, LOOPS, using a with statement to access the items in the list box:

```
procedure TForm1.Button2Click(Sender: TObject);
var
  I: Integer;
begin
  with ListBox1.Items do
  begin
    Clear;
    Randomize;
    I := 0;
    while I < 1000 do
    begin
      I := I + Random (100);
      Add ('Random Number: ' + IntToStr (I));
    end;
  end;
end;
```

When you work with components or classes in general, the with statement allows you to save some code, particularly for nested fields. For example, suppose that you need to change the width and the color of the drawing pen for a form. You can write:

```
Form1.Canvas.Pen.Width := 2;
Form1.Canvas.Pen.Color := clRed;
```

But it is certainly easier to write:

```
with Form1.Canvas.Pen do
begin
  Width := 2;
  Color := clRed;
end;
```

When you are writing complex code, the `with` statement can be effective, but it has a drawback. It can make the code less readable, particularly when you are working with different objects that have similar or corresponding properties. Consider this code:

```
with Form1.Canvas.Pen do
  Width := 2;
  Color := clRed;
```

It changes the width of the pen and the color of the current object, maybe a form. In fact, the indentation above is inconsistent with the rules I've suggested. The statement changing the color should be aligned with the initial `with` statement.

Considering this kind of drawback, and the aim of this book, which is to show you how programs work, I've decided to use `with` statements sparingly, in favor of readability. However, I suggest that you do use them often in your code, particularly if you are not a good typist.

Pascal Procedures and Functions

Another important idea underlined by the Pascal language is the concept of the subroutine. In Pascal, subroutines can assume two different forms: procedures and functions. The only real difference between the two constructs is that functions have a return value, while procedures haven't got one. Here are the definitions of a procedure and two versions of the same function, using a slightly different syntax:

```
procedure Hello;
begin
  ShowMessage ('Hello world!');
end;

function Double (Value: Integer) : Integer;
begin
  Double := Value * 2;
end

{or, as an alternative:}
function Double2 (Value: Integer) : Integer;
begin
  Result := Value * 2;
end
```

Once these subroutines have been defined, you can call them as follows:

```
Hello;
X := Double (Y);
Hello;
Z := Double2 (X);
```

This approach is different from that of the C language, which only has functions (although some C functions do not have a return value). It is also different from the original BASIC, where you needed to use GOSUB statements. Modern BASIC dialects have introduced an approach similar to the Pascal language.

NOTE In the last version of its Pascal compiler, Borland introduced the option of not using the return value of a function (something that was previously compulsory). Now you can freely call a function and ignore its result; that is, use a function as if it were a procedure. This is particularly useful when you call some of the functions of the MS Windows API.

Reference Parameters

Both procedures and functions allow parameter passing by value and by reference. Passing a parameter by reference means that its value is not copied on the stack in the formal parameter of the subroutine (avoiding a copy often means that the program saves some time). Instead, the program refers to the original value also in the code of the subroutine. This allows the procedure or function to change the value of the parameter. Parameter passing by reference is expressed by the var keyword.

This technique is available in most programming languages. It isn't present in C, but has been introduced in C++, where you use the & operator. In Visual Basic it is based on the ByVal keyword. Here is an example:

```
procedure DoubleTheValue (var Value: Integer);
begin
  Value := Value * 2;
end
```

In this case, the parameter is used both to pass a value to the procedure and to return a new value to the calling code.

What Is a Method?

If you have already worked with Delphi, read the manuals, or stepped through the Interactive Tutors, you have probably heard the term *method*. A method is a special kind of function or procedure that is related to a data type, a class.

In Delphi, every time we handle an event or message, we need to define a method, which can be either a function or a procedure. For this reason, the term *method* is used to indicate functions and procedures in general, although this is not always the case. Strictly speaking, only the subroutines related to a class are methods.

We have already seen a number of methods in the examples in this and the previous chapters. Here is an empty method automatically added by Delphi to the source code of a form:

```
procedure TForm1.Button1Click(Sender: TObject);
begin
  {here goes your code}
end;
```

We will discuss methods in more detail in the next chapter.

Forward Declarations

When you need to use an identifier (of any kind), the compiler must have already seen some sort of declaration, to know what the identifier refers to. For this reason, you usually provide a full declaration before using any subroutine. However, there are cases in which this is not possible. If procedure A calls procedure B, and procedure B calls procedure A, when you start writing the code, you will need to call a subroutine the compiler still doesn't know.

If you want to declare the existence of a procedure or function with a certain name and given parameters, without providing its actual code, you can write the procedure or function followed by the forward keyword:

```
procedure Hello; forward;
```

Later on, the code should provide a full definition of the procedure, but this can be called even before it is fully defined. Here is a silly example, just to give you the idea:

```
procedure Hello; forward;

procedure DoubleHello;
begin
  Hello;
  Hello;
end;

procedure Hello;
begin
  ShowMessage ('Hello world!');
end;
```

This approach allows you to write mutual recursion: DoubleHello calls Hello, but Hello might call DoubleHello, too, provided that there is a condition to terminate this recursion.

Although a forward procedure declaration is not very common in Delphi, there is another similar case, which is much more frequent. Every time you see the declaration of a method inside a class type that was automatically generated by Delphi (as you added an event to a form or its components), this is a forward declaration, although the specific keyword is not used. Here is an excerpt of the source code of an earlier example:

```
type
  TForm1 = class(TForm)
    ListBox1: TListBox;
    Button1: TButton;
    procedure Button1Click(Sender: TObject);
    ...
  end;
```

To sum things up, when you need to call a subroutine that is still not fully defined, you can write a forward declaration, define the procedure (or method) in the type definition of a class, or place it in the interface portion of a unit. Since we have not discussed units yet, we won't go into this third approach here. You'll find more on this topic in the next chapter.

External Declarations

Another special kind of procedure declaration is the external declaration. Originally used to link the Pascal code to external functions written in assembly language, the external directive is used in MS Windows programming to call functions from a DLL (a dynamic link library). In Delphi, there are a number of such declarations in the WinProcs unit:

```
function LineTo; external 'GDI' index 19;
```

This declaration means that the code of the function LineTo is stored in the GDI dynamic library (one of the most important MS Windows system libraries) and has an index of 19. You seldom need to write similar declarations, since they are already listed in the WinProcs unit (see Figure 4.14), which is automatically included in the uses statement at the beginning of the code for any form generated by Delphi.

NOTE The only reason you might need to write this external declaration code is to call undocumented MS Windows functions. If you are interested, in Chapter 12, there is an example that includes a call to an undocumented function.

FIGURE 4.14:

An excerpt of the WinProcs unit
with the external declaration of the
Windows API functions

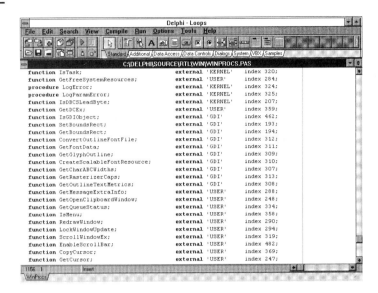

Near and Far Declarations

Borland Pascal has two different ways to handle procedure or function calls: the near model and the far model. The default near calls are more efficient, but they can be called only within a compiled module. Far procedures are slower but have no restrictions, and they are commonly used in MS Windows programming. These two models were not invented by Borland; they depend on Intel architecture and the MS Windows operating system.

Usually, you do not need to decide which model to choose, because Delphi can select the correct one for you. In some cases, however, you need to use the far directive to change the default behavior. This happens in MS Windows DLL programming, but also when you work with procedural types, as we will see in the next section.

Procedural Types

Another strange feature of the Object Pascal is the presence of procedural types. This is really an advanced language topic, which only a few Delphi programmers will use regularly. However, since we will discuss related topics in later chapters, and procedural types constitute the first step in understanding events in Delphi, I've decided to devote a section to them here. If you are a novice programmer, you can skip this section for now, and come back to it when you're ready.

In the standard version of the Pascal language, procedures can be defined and called. Period. In Borland Object Pascal extensions, there is the notion of procedural type (which is similar to the C language concept of function pointer). The declaration of a procedural type indicates the list of parameters, and eventually the return type in the case of a function. For example, you can declare the type "procedure with an integer parameter" as:

4

```
type
   IntProc = procedure (var Num: Integer);
```

Notice that the parameter can simply be an Integer. The name Num can be regarded as a comment, and has no special meaning or effect. This procedural type is compatible with procedures that have exactly the same parameters (or the same function signature, using the C jargon). Here is an example:

```
procedure DoubleTheValue (var Value: Integer); far;
begin
   Value := Value * 2;
end;
```

The only special feature is that the procedure or function should be declared with the far directive as in the example above, or compiled with the {$F+} flag.

You can declare variables of procedure types or pass procedures as parameters. Given the preceding type and procedure declarations, you can write this code:

```
var
   IP: IntProc;
   X: Integer;
begin
   IP := DoubleTheValue;
   X := 5;
   IP (X);
end;
```

This code has the same effect as the following shorter version:

```
var
   X: Integer;
begin
   X := 5;
```

```
        DoubleTheValue (X);
    end;
```

So why use it? In some cases, being able to decide which function to call and actually calling it at a different time can be useful. It is possible to build a complex example showing this approach. However, since it might be too complex this early in the book, I prefer to let you explore a fairly simple one, named PROCTYPE. This example is more complex than those we have seen so far, to make the situation a little more realistic.

For this example, create a blank project and place two radio buttons, a push button, and two labels in the form, as you can see in Figure 4.15. Listing 4.3 shows some of the details of the form.

FIGURE 4.15:
The form of the PROCTYPE example

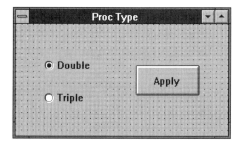

LISTING 4.3: The textual description of the form of the PROCTYPE example}

```
object Form1: TForm1
  ActiveControl = ApplyButton
  Caption = 'Proc Type'
  OnCreate = FormCreate
  object ApplyButton: TButton
    Caption = 'Apply'
    OnClick = ApplyButtonClick
  end
  object DoubleRadioButton: TRadioButton
    Caption = 'Double'
    Checked = True
    OnClick = DoubleRadioButtonClick
  end
  object TripleRadioButton: TRadioButton
    Caption = 'Triple'
    OnClick = TripleRadioButtonClick
  end
end
```

This example is based on two procedures. One procedure is used to double the value of a variable. This procedure is slightly different from the version I've already used in this section. The other procedure is to triple the value.

```
procedure DoubleTheValue (var Value: Integer); far;
begin
  Value := Value * 2;
  ShowMessage ('Value doubled: ' + IntToStr (Value));
end;

procedure TripleTheValue (var Value: Integer); far;
begin
  Value := Value * 3;
  ShowMessage ('Value tripled: ' + IntToStr (Value));
end;
```

Both procedures display what is going on, to let us know that they have been called. This is a simple debugging feature you can use to test whether or when a certain portion of code is executed, instead of adding a breakpoint in it.

Each time a user presses the Apply button, one of the two functions is executed, depending on the status of the radio buttons. When you have two radio buttons, only one of them can be selected at a time. This code could have been implemented by testing the value of the radio buttons inside the code for the OnClick event of the Apply push button. Instead, I've used a longer but interesting approach, to demonstrate the use of procedure types. Each time a user clicks on one of the two radio buttons, one of the procedures is stored in a variable. For example:

```
procedure TForm1.DoubleRadioButtonClick(Sender: TObject);
begin
  IP := DoubleTheValue;
end;
```

When the user presses the push button, the stored procedure is executed:

```
procedure TForm1.ApplyButtonClick(Sender: TObject);
begin
  IP (X);
end;
```

To allow three different functions to access the IP and X variables, they cannot be declared locally (inside one of the methods) but should be visible to the whole form. A solution to this problem is to place these variables inside the form declaration, as you can see in the complete source code of the example in Listing 4.4.

LISTING 4.4: The source code of the PROCTYPE example

```pascal
unit Proc_f;

interface

uses
  SysUtils, WinTypes, WinProcs, Messages, Classes, Graphics, Controls,
  Forms, Dialogs, StdCtrls;

type
  {procedure type definition}
  IntProc = procedure (var Num: Integer);

  TForm1 = class(TForm)
    ApplyButton: TButton;
    DoubleRadioButton: TRadioButton;
    TripleRadioButton: TRadioButton;
    procedure FormCreate(Sender: TObject);
    procedure ApplyButtonClick(Sender: TObject);
    procedure DoubleRadioButtonClick(Sender: TObject);
    procedure TripleRadioButtonClick(Sender: TObject);
  private
    { Private declarations }
    IP: IntProc;
    X: Integer;
  public
    { Public declarations }
  end;

var
  Form1: TForm1;

implementation

{$R *.DFM}

{procedures of the IntProc type}
procedure DoubleTheValue (var Value: Integer); far;
begin
  Value := Value * 2;
  ShowMessage ('Value doubled: ' + IntToStr (Value));
end;

procedure TripleTheValue (var Value: Integer); far;
begin
  Value := Value * 3;
  ShowMessage ('Value tripled: ' + IntToStr (Value));
end;

{initialization code}
procedure TForm1.FormCreate(Sender: TObject);
```

LISTING 4.4: The source code of the PROCTYPE example (continued)

```
begin
  IP := DoubleTheValue;
  X := 2;
end;

{push button OnClick event}
procedure TForm1.ApplyButtonClick(Sender: TObject);
begin
  IP (X);
end;

{Radio buttons OnClick events}
procedure TForm1.DoubleRadioButtonClick(Sender: TObject);
begin
  IP := DoubleTheValue;
end;

procedure TForm1.TripleRadioButtonClick(Sender: TObject);
begin
  IP := TripleTheValue;
end;

end.
```

We will see exactly what this means in the next chapter, but for the moment, you need to modify the code generated by Delphi for the class type above, and add the definition of the procedure type we have seen before. To initialize these two variables with suitable values, we can add the OnCreate event to the form. Notice that since the value of X is initialized once, and then always increased, it can easily overflow the typical integers limit.

Summary

In this chapter, we have seen an overview of the basic elements of the Object Pascal language. This chapter can be considered a review of the notions of standard Pascal, plus an introduction to some advanced features.

What we have still not seen are the object-oriented capabilities of the language, which will be detailed in the next chapter. We also still have not considered the division of a program in units and other Pascal programming techniques, which we'll get to soon.

As I mentioned, this chapter was intended for people who have some programming experience, either with Pascal or another programming language. I haven't tried to explain how to use a `for` loop or write a conditional expression for an `if` statement. If these things are not clear to you, before you get started with Delphi, you should read a basic Pascal language text, or spend some time with the Delphi Help files.

This doesn't mean that you need to understand these topics perfectly. I'll show you a huge number of examples in the book, and most of them will also highlight features of the Pascal language. If you keep on reading, you will learn more about the topics we have discussed in this chapter.

CHAPTER

FIVE

Object Pascal as an OOP Language

5

- **Object Pascal classes and objects**

- **The Object Pascal object model**

- **Object instance creation**

- **Information hiding**

- **Delphi units**

- **The self keyword**

- **Class methods and method pointers**

Using existing data types, defining new ones, and writing code in small blocks (subroutines) are the essence of traditional Pascal programming. But modern Pascal versions allow a completely different approach: object-oriented programming (OOP). OOP languages are based on three fundamental concepts: classes, inheritance, and polymorphism (or late binding). These three features are available in Object Pascal, too, and will be described in the first part of this chapter.

Earlier Turbo Pascal and Borland Pascal compilers used a slightly different object-oriented extension of the Pascal language. Therefore, reading this chapter should be useful for everyone, including long-time Turbo Pascal programmers. Of course, some of the topics covered here won't be new to Pascal programmers—they serve as introductory material for the less experienced OOP readers.

As you read this material, keep in mind that you can start to write code in Delphi without knowing all of the details of the language. For example, you don't need to understand some of OOP's advanced features, such as exception handling. As you create a new form, add new components, and handle events, most of the related code is automatically prepared for you by Delphi. But knowing the details of the language and its implementation will help you to understand precisely what goes on and to truly master Delphi. From another point of view, you don't need to understand OOP, virtual methods, or polymorphism to create a complete Delphi application. However, you do need to understand these concepts to design new components.

Introducing Classes and Objects

Class and *object* are two common terms. However, since they are often misused, let's be sure that we agree on their definitions.

A class is a user-defined data type, which has a state, a representation, and some operations or behavior. A class has some internal data and some methods, in the form of procedures or functions. A class usually describes the generic characteristics and behavior of a number of very similar objects. Classes are used by the programmer to arrange the source code, and by the compiler to generate the application.

An object is an instance of a class or, using other words, a variable of the data type defined by the class. Objects are *real* entities. When the program runs, objects take up some memory for their internal representation.

The relationship between object and class is the same as the one that exists between variable and type. Unfortunately, in some languages or environments, this difference is not clear. To increase the confusion, earlier versions of the Borland Pascal compiler used the keyword `object` to define classes. For this reason, long-time Pascal programmers tend to use the term *object* instead of class to denote a type, and the term *object instance* to indicate the real objects.

Delphi has introduced a new object model, based on the new keyword `class`, but the older model is still available for compatibility. I'll explain some of the technical elements behind this new object model in a later section of this chapter. For the moment, however, I'll focus on the concept of class and its syntax.

5

To declare a new class data type in Object Pascal, use the following syntax:

```
type
  MyNewClass = class
  end;
```

Of course, this code is not very useful, because the class does not have any data or operations. We can start adding some data as follows:

```
type
  Date = class
    Month, Day, Year: Integer;
  end;
```

This declaration is similar to that of a record. In fact, we can declare an object and access its three fields with a standard notation:

```
var
  ADay: Date;

begin
  ... {something is missing here}
  ADay.Month := 7;
  ADay.Day := 12;
  ADay.Year := 1984;
end;
```

Things start to get interesting when we put in some methods—functions or procedures—to add operations to the class:

```
type
  Date = class
    Month, Day, Year: Integer;
    procedure SetValue(m, d, y: Integer);
    function LeapYear: Boolean;
  end;
```

The function and the procedure should be supplied in the code, indicating that they are part of the Date class. To accomplish this, Object Pascal uses the dot notation again, but in a slightly different way. The syntax is ClassName.Method:

```
procedure Date.SetValue(m, d, y: Integer);
begin
  Month := m;
  Day := d;
  Year := y;
end;

function Date.LeapYear: Boolean;
begin
  if (Year mod 4 <> 0) then
    LeapYear := False
  else
    if (Year mod 100 <> 0) then
      LeapYear := True
    else
    if (Year mod 400 <> 0) then
      LeapYear := False
    else
      LeapYear := True;
end;
```

Once these methods have been written, they can be called as follows:

```
var
  Day: Date;
  Leap: Boolean;

begin
  ... {something is still missing here}
  Day.SetValue (10, 10, 1994);
  Leap := Day.LeapYear;
end;
```

The notation used is nothing strange, but it is powerful. We can write complex functions (such as LeapYear) and then access this value for every Date object as if it were a primitive data type. Notice that `Day.LeapYear` is a notation similar to `Day.Year`, although its meaning is completely different. The first expression stands for a direct data access, the second for a function call.

> **NOTE** By the way, the option to use the same notation for different operations is a very interesting feature Object Pascal shares with other OOP languages. C++, on the other hand, uses a different syntax notation for data access and function calls, which is not so nice (I know, this is just "syntactic sugar," not a real difference). From a theoretical point of view, using the same notation means that you can remove a public field from your class, and replace it with a function computing the corresponding value. The source code eventually using this field or method requires no changes at all.

Although the code shown here is correct, it won't work as is. To use the new Object Pascal object model, we need to create an instance of an object before we can use it. This is described in the next section.

The Delphi Object Model

The object-oriented extensions of the previous versions of the Borland Pascal language were based on the `object` keyword. In the new version, this has been replaced by the `class` keyword.

Both the `object` and `class` keywords are used to define a new data type, a new class. Both support `private`, `protected`, and `public` methods and fields (as described later in the chapter). Both allow inheritance. They are really very similar. So why did Borland introduce the new keyword?

The reason is that although the code you write in the two cases is almost the same, the behavior of the compiled code is different. The new `class` keyword indicates a new object model, which we can describe as a reference model.

The basic idea is that each variable of a class type, such as Day in the code fragment above, does not hold the value of the object. Rather, it contains a reference, or a pointer, to indicate the memory location where the object has been stored. You can see a scheme of the situation in Figure 5.1.

FIGURE 5.1:

A graphical representation of the Object Pascal reference model

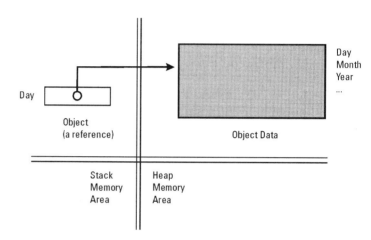

The reference object model is powerful, yet easier to use than other models. Other OOP languages use similar models, notably Eiffel. In my opinion, adopting a reference object model was one of the best design decisions of Delphi development.

The only problem with this approach is that when you declare a variable, writing:

```
var
   Day: Date;
```

You do not create an object, but only a place to keep a reference to an object—a sort of pointer. Object instances must be created manually, at least for the objects of the classes you define. Component instances are built automatically.

To create an instance of an object, we can call its Create method, which is a constructor (a special procedure used to allocate memory for new objects and initialize them):

```
var
   ADay: Date;
```

```
begin
  Day := Date.Create;
  ADay.Month := 7;
  ADay.Day := 12;
  ADay.Year := 1984;
end;
```

Where does Create come from? It is a constructor of the class TObject, from which all the other classes inherit (subclassing, or inheritance, will be discussed later in this chapter). Writing this:

```
type
  Date = class
```

equals writing this:

```
type
  Date = class (TObject)
```

Of course, once you have created an object, you need to dispose of it. This can be accomplished by calling the Free method. The following is an example of the correct (although useless) code used to create, use, and dispose of an object:

```
begin
  ADay := Date.Create;
  ADay.Month := 7;
  ADay.Day := 12;
  ADay.Year := 1984;
  ADay.Free;
end;
```

As long as you allocate memory for an object (and free the memory when you're finished), the reference object model works without any glitches. You can assign an object to another, pass an object as parameter to a function, and perform any other operation.

The First Delphi Example with Classes

After all this discussion, without any hands-on examples, it is time to go back to Delphi. The idea is to collect the Date class code we have written so far and write a simple program using it. This way, we can make sure that it works correctly, including the delicate point of object initialization.

The LEAPYEAR example has a simple form with two buttons, as you can see in Figure 5.2 and in the textual description in Listing 5.1.

Each time one of the buttons is pressed, a Date object is set and tested to see whether 1995 (or 1996) is a leap year. Here is the code of the OnClick event for one of the buttons:

```
procedure TForm1.Button1995Click(Sender: TObject);
begin
  ADay.SetValue (1, 1, 1995);
  if ADay.LeapYear then
    ShowMessage ('Leap Year')
  else
    ShowMessage ('Non Leap Year')
end;
```

FIGURE 5.2:
The LEAPYEAR form

LISTING 5.1: The textual description of the LEAPYEAR form

```
object form1: TForm1
  Caption = 'Leap Year'
  OnCreate = FormCreate
  OnDestroy = FormDestroy
  object Button1995: TButton
    Caption = '1995'
    OnClick = Button1995Click
  end
  object Button1996: TButton
    Caption = '1996'
    OnClick = Button1996Click
  end
end
```

The object ADay is a variable defined as:

```
var
  ADay: Date;
```

This object should be created before the button is pressed. A common approach is to use the OnCreate event of the form to create an instance of the object:

```
procedure TForm1.FormCreate(Sender: TObject);
begin
  ADay := Date.Create;
end;
```

This method is executed before a user can press the button, and even before the form and its components are displayed on the screen. The opposite holds for the OnDestroy event, which is executed after the form is hidden from view. We can use this method to free the memory used by the object:

```
procedure TForm1.FormDestroy(Sender: TObject);
begin
  ADay.Free;
end;
```

You can see the complete code of the form in this example in Listing 5.2. When you press one of the buttons, the proper message is displayed, as you can see in Figure 5.3.

FIGURE 5.3:

The result of pressing the 1996 button of the LEAPYEAR example

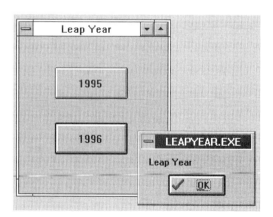

LISTING 5.2: The source code of the form of the LEAPYEAR example

```
unit Leapy_f;

interface

uses
  SysUtils, WinTypes, WinProcs, Messages, Classes, Graphics,
  Controls, Forms, Dialogs, StdCtrls;

type
  TForm1 = class(TForm)
    Button1995: TButton;
    Button1996: TButton;
    procedure FormCreate(Sender: TObject);
    procedure FormDestroy(Sender: TObject);
    procedure Button1995Click(Sender: TObject);
    procedure Button1996Click(Sender: TObject);
  private
    { Private declarations }
  public
    { Public declarations }
  end;

  {new data type, a Date}
  Date = class
    Month, Day, Year: Integer;
    procedure SetValue(m, d, y: Integer);
    function LeapYear: Boolean;
  end;

var
  Form1: TForm1;
  {new "global" object of class Date}
  ADay: Date;

implementation

{$R *.DFM}

procedure Date.SetValue(m, d, y: Integer);
begin
  Month := m;
  Day := d;
  Year := y;
end;

function Date.LeapYear: Boolean;
begin
  if (Year mod 4 <> 0) then
    LeapYear := False
  else
    if (Year mod 100 <> 0) then
```

LISTING 5.2: The source code of the form of the LEAPYEAR example (continued)

```
      LeapYear := True
    else
    if (Year mod 400 <> 0) then

      LeapYear := False
    else
      LeapYear := True;
end;

procedure TForm1.FormCreate(Sender: TObject);
begin
  ADay := Date.Create;
end;

procedure TForm1.FormDestroy(Sender: TObject);
begin
  ADay.Free;
end;

procedure TForm1.Button1995Click(Sender: TObject);
begin
  ADay.SetValue (1, 1, 1995);
  if ADay.LeapYear then
    ShowMessage ('Leap Year')
  else
    ShowMessage ('Non Leap Year')
end;

procedure TForm1.Button1996Click(Sender: TObject);
begin
  ADay.SetValue (1, 1, 1996);
  if ADay.LeapYear then
    ShowMessage ('Leap Year')
  else
    ShowMessage ('Non Leap Year')
end;

end.
```

If you alter the code of this example, remember that the captions of the buttons have no direct relationship with the code. If you change the caption of the button, nothing will happen. You should also change the third parameter of the corresponding call to the SetValue procedure to try out different years.

While you are exploring the code of this example, make the following test. Comment out the code used to create an instance of the object:

```
procedure TForm1.FormCreate(Sender: TObject);
begin
  {ADay := Date.Create;}
end;
```

If you recompile the project now, you won't get an error. However, when you run the program, as soon as you press one of the buttons, an exception is raised by the system (indicating that you have accessed an invalid pointer), as you can see in Figure 5.4.

FIGURE 5.4:

The exception error message displayed if you forget to create an instance of the object

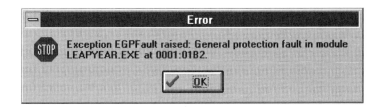

Declaring a Constructor

To allocate the memory for the object, we call the Create method. However, before we can actually use the object, we often need to initialize the object. To accomplish this, we can add a constructor to the class. We can either provide a customized version of the Create method, or define a constructor with any other name.

A constructor is a special procedure, because Delphi automatically allocates memory for the object you apply the constructor to. Adding a constructor to the class solves any run-time error due to a missing or an incorrect initialization. These errors are usually hard to find, so you should use preventive techniques to avoid them in the first place. One such technique is the use of constructors.

To add a constructor to the Date class, write this code:

```
Date = class
  Month, Day, Year: Integer;
  constructor Init (m, d, y: Integer);
  procedure SetValue(m, d, y: Integer);
```

```
    function LeapYear: Boolean;
  end;
```

I've chosen the name Init for the constructor, but any other name will do. The important element is the presence of the constructor keyword instead of the procedure keyword. Then we write the code of the constructor:

```
constructor Date.Init (m, d, y: Integer);
begin
  Month := m;
  Day := d;
  Year := y;
end;
```

Once this is done, we can change the initialization code of the LEAPYEAR example, to allocate memory for the ADay object and set an initial value at the same time:

```
procedure TForm1.FormCreate(Sender: TObject);
begin
  ADay := Date.Init (1, 1, 1900);
end;
```

NOTE   For the complete code of the LEAP2 example, see the companion disk. The entire listing isn't included in the book because it is so similar to the LEAPYEAR example already presented in Listing 5.2.

Classes and Information Hiding

A class can have any amount of data and any number of methods. However, for a good object-oriented approach, data should be hidden, or *encapsulated,* inside the class using it. When you access a date, for example, it makes no sense to change the value of the day by itself. In fact, changing the value of the day may result in an invalid date, such as February 30.

Using methods to access the internal representation of an object limits the risk of generating erroneous situations, and allows the class writer to modify the internal representation in a future version.

The concept of encapsulation is quite simple: Just think of a class as a black box with a small visible portion (see Figure 5.5). The visible portion, called the *class interface*, allows other parts of a program to access and use the objects of that class. However, when you use the objects, most of their code is hidden. You seldom know which internal data the object has, and usually have no way to access it directly. Of course, you are supposed to use methods to access the data, which is shielded from unauthorized access. This is the object-oriented approach to a classical programming theory known as *information hiding*.

FIGURE 5.5:

A graphical representation of the information hiding of a class

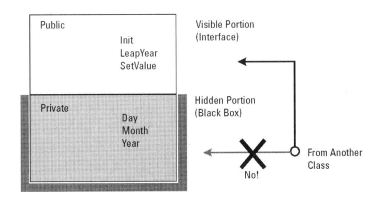

In theory, this should be nothing new for a Pascal programmer, since OOP follows the same ideas of order, type definition, and safety that are promoted by the Pascal language.

In Object Pascal, there are two different constructs involved with encapsulation, protection, and variables access: classes and units. Associated with classes are some special access-specifier keywords, which are discussed in the next section.

Private, Protected, and Public

Object Pascal has borrowed the C++ language's three access specifiers: `private`, `protected`, and `public`. A fourth one, `published`, will be discussed in the next section.

- The `private` keyword denotes fields and methods of a class that are not accessible outside the unit (the source code file) declaring the class. This is slightly different from C++, where the private portion of a class cannot be accessed even by other classes defined in the same module or source code file.

- The `public` specifier denotes methods and fields that are freely accessible from any other portion of the code of a program, as well as in the unit in which they are defined.

- The `protected` keyword is used to indicate partially protected methods and fields. Protected elements can be accessed by the current class and all its descendent classes, but not by users of this class (code that creates instances of this class).

Generally, the fields (the data) of a class should be private. Methods (the code) are usually public. However, this is not always the case. Methods can be private or protected if they are needed only internally to perform some computations. Fields can be public when you want an easy and direct access, and you are fairly sure that their type definition is not going to change. As an example, consider this new version of the Date class:

```
type
  Date = class

  private
    Month, Day, Year: Integer;

  public
    procedure SetValue(m, d, y: Integer);
    function LeapYear: Boolean;
    function GetText: string;
    procedure Increase;

  protected
    function DaysInMonth: Integer;
  end;
```

In this version, the fields are now declared to be `private`, and there are some new methods. The first, GetText, is a function that returns a string with the date. This is the only way we have to retrieve the value of the `private` data. We might think of adding other functions, named GetDay, GetMonth, and GetYear, which simply return the corresponding private data, but similar direct data-access functions are not always needed.

The second new method is the Increase procedure, which increases the date by one day. This is far from simple, since you need to consider the different lengths of the various months, as well as leap and non-leap years.

To simplify this (and other methods I'll add), I've written a function that returns the number of days in the current month, DaysInMonth. This function is not part of the public interface of this class. It doesn't make much sense to ask a specific Date object for the number of days in its current month without knowing which month it refers to. So, I had two choices: declare the function as `private` or declare it as `protected`. I decided to use the `protected` keyword because I might later define a new class that would inherit from Date and need access to this function.

Public and Published

Along with the `public`, `protected`, and `private` directives, you can use a fourth one, called `published`, in a class declaration. A published field or method is not only available at run-time, but also at design-time. In fact, every component in the Delphi Components palette has a published interface that is used by some Delphi tools, in particular the Object Inspector. This interface is accessible through some advanced techniques, which are part of run-time type information (RTTI) that is stored in objects.

For this reason, a regular use of published fields is much more important when you write a component than when you write the code of an application. Usually, the published part of a component does not contain any fields or methods, but has a new element of the language: properties. Chapter 27 focuses on component writing and related Object Pascal language elements.

Besides the case of components, when Delphi generates a form, it places the definitions of its components and methods in the first portion of its definition, before the `public` and `private` keywords. These fields and methods of the initial portion of the class are `published`. This is the default when no special keyword is added before an element of a class.

By the way, the methods assigned to any event property must be published methods, and the fields corresponding to your components in the form must be published in order for them to be automatically initialized.

Classes and Units

Delphi applications, like most Pascal programs, make intensive use of *units*. Units, in fact, are the basis of the modularity in the language. In Delphi applications, every form has a corresponding unit behind it. The reverse is not true, however; units do not need to have forms.

The concept of unit is simple. A unit has an `interface` section declaring what is visible to other units, an `implementation` section with the real code, and other hidden declarations. Finally, the unit can have an optional `initialization` section with some startup code, to be executed when the program using this unit is loaded into memory.

In previous versions of Borland Pascal language, the initialization section of a unit was marked with `begin` and `end` keywords. The new `initialization` keyword was introduced to make it easier for Delphi to manage your source code. Delphi still supports the use of `begin` to mark the start of the initialization section of a unit for backward-compatibility, but you should get into the habit of using the new `initialization` keyword instead.

The general structure of a unit is the following (with the `interface` and `implementation` keywords in bold to highlight these two main portions of the unit):

```
unit unitName;

interface
```

```
{other units we need to refer to}
uses A, B, C;

{exported type definition}
type
  newType = TypeDefinition;

{list of exported functions and procedures}
procedure MyProc;

implementation

{all the exported functions must be coded}

procedure MyProc;
{code of procedure MyProc follows}

initialization
  {optional initialization part}
end.
```

The uses clause at the beginning of the interface section indicates which other units we need to access from the current one. These units must be present in the project directory or in a directory in the search path.

The interface of the unit can declare a number of different elements, including procedures, functions, global variables, and data types. This last element is probably the most used in an object-oriented approach and in Delphi applications.

You can easily place a class in a unit, and this is probably the right thing to do. Delphi does this automatically each time you create a form. Do you remember the code generated for a new form in Chapter 1? Here is it again:

```
unit Unit1;

interface

uses
  SysUtils, WinTypes, WinProcs, Messages, Classes, Graphics, Controls,
  Forms, Dialogs;

type
  TForm1 = class(TForm)
  private
    { Private declarations }
```

```
public
  { Public declarations }
end;

var
  Form1: TForm1;

implementation

{$R *.DFM}

end.
```

The only elements exported by this unit are the definition of a new data type, TForm1, and a global variable of this type, Form1. Notice the presence of the `private` and `public` keywords, and the inclusion of the form description file with the $R compiler directive.

Placing forms in units is certainly not the only use for units in Delphi. You can continue to have traditional units, listing functions and procedures, and you can have units with classes that do not refer to forms or other visual elements. To create a new unit that is not related to a form, select the New Unit command from the File menu. Here is the code automatically generated in this case:

```
unit Unit2;

interface

implementation

end.
```

Quite bare, isn't it? Delphi is a visual environment, so when you write nonvisual code, it cannot be of much help. To show you an example of a full-scale unit, I've further developed the Date class. Placing this class in a unit will make it available to any application, as we will investigate soon. Before we delve into this, however, we should consider some details related to class interfaces, scope, and encapsulation in units.

The Interface of a Class

When you declare a new class type and place it in a unit, you write in the interface of the unit what is known as the *interface* of a class (that is, its declaration). The interface of a class contains the declaration of its data, its fields, and the forward declaration of its methods. The data declaration is needed to determine the size of the objects of that class. The method declaration is usually placed in the implementation portion of the unit.

Note also that it is even possible to make a forward declaration of a class:

```
type
  MyClass = class;
```

You cannot really start using a class without its full declaration, but you can use this new data type as field of another class or as parameter of a method of another class. Consider this example of two related classes:

```
type
  THusband = class;
  TWife = class
    Husband: THusband;
    ...
    end;
  THusband = class
    Wife: TWife;
    ...
    end;
```

In other OOP languages (including C++), similar code would be illegal. In Object Pascal, it is legal, thanks to the object reference semantic. In fact, we can place a partially defined object (that is, an object of a class having only a forward reference) in another class, only because the compiler knows how much memory the object will take. In fact, every object takes up the space required for a reference or pointer. It isn't strange that in C++, writing similar code is possible only if you use explicit pointers.

Units and Scope

In Pascal, units are the key to encapsulation and visibility (or scope), and they are probably even more important than the `private` and `public` keywords of a class. In fact, the effect of the `private` keyword is related to the scope of the unit containing the class.

The scope of an identifier (such as a variable, procedure, function, or a data type) defines the portion of the code in which the identifier is accessible. The basic rule is that an identifier is meaningful only within its scope; that is, only within the block in which it is declared. You cannot use an identifier outside its scope.

Here are some examples. If you declare a variable within the block defining a procedure, you cannot use this variable outside that procedure. The scope of the identifier spans the whole procedure, including nested blocks (unless an identifier with the same name in the nested blocks hides the outer definition).

If you declare an identifier in the implementation portion of a unit, you cannot use it outside the unit, but you can use it in any block and procedure defined within the unit. If you declare an identifier in the interface portion of the unit, its scope extends to any other unit that uses the one declaring it. Any identifier declared in the interface of a unit is indicated by the term *global*; all other identifiers are said to be *local*.

For this reason, declaring a type in the interface portion of a unit makes it accessible from the whole program. Variables of form classes are declared in the same way, so that you can refer to a form (and its public fields and methods) from the code of any other form.

Encapsulating Changes

One of the key ideas of encapsulation is to reduce the number of global variables used by a program. A global variable can be accessed from every portion of a program. For this reason, a change in a global variable has effects on the whole program.

On the other hand, when you change the representation of a field of a class, you only need to change the code of some methods of that class, and nothing else. For this reason, we can say that information hiding refers to "encapsulating changes."

Let me clarify this idea with an example. In LEAPYEAR, I added a Date object to the var declarations of the unit interface, as you can see in Listing 5.2 (shown earlier). This object can be accessed from any other portion of this unit, but also from any other unit of the application, because it has been declared in the interface portion of the unit. (See the next section for a detailed description of units.)

In our small program, this is fine. However, in a complex application, developed by several programmers, other units might use this object. In this case, changing the Date object's name or the way it is used could ruin the whole program.

To avoid this situation, I could have declared the Date object inside the class describing the new form:

```
type
  {new data type, a Date}
  Date = class
    Month, Day, Year: Integer;
    constructor Init (m, d, y: Integer);
    procedure SetValue(m, d, y: Integer);
    function LeapYear: Boolean;
  end;

  TForm1 = class(TForm)
    Button1995: TButton;
    Button1996: TButton;
    procedure FormCreate(Sender: TObject);
    procedure FormDestroy(Sender: TObject);
    procedure Button1995Click(Sender: TObject);
    procedure Button1996Click(Sender: TObject);
  private
    { Private declarations }
    ADay: Date;
  public
    { Public declarations }
  end;

var
  Form1: TForm1;
```

If I add it as a private field, the Date object won't be accessible from outside the unit, unless I provide a proper method to do so. And if I write a method, and later on I decide to change the meaning or the representation of the object, I can just change the code of the method accordingly, without any effect on the rest of the program's code.

Of course, declaring the three fields of the Date class as private will improve the encapsulation performed by the program, and make it more object-oriented. To accomplish this, however, we need to add some methods to the class, to be able to access the private fields.

A Date Unit

Throughout this chapter, we have developed a couple of examples with simple versions of a Date class. The final version of this class will have some more functions, and we will place it in a unit. This is the interface of the class:

```
type
  Date = class
    private
    Month, Day, Year: Integer;
  public
    constructor Init (m, d, y: Integer);
    procedure SetValue (m, d, y: Integer);
    function LeapYear: Boolean;
    procedure Increase;
    procedure Decrease;
    procedure Add (NumberOfDays: Integer);
    procedure Subtract (NumberOfDays: Integer);
    function GetText: string;
  protected
    function DaysInMonth: Integer;
  end;
```

The aim of the new methods is quite easy to understand. Decrease changes the value of the date to the day before. Add and Subtract change the date by adding or subtracting the number of days passed as parameter, instead of a single day. For example, if the value of the current object is 3/11/1995, adding 10 days makes it 3/21/1995.

Listing 5.3 shows the full source code listing of the Dates unit. (You can find this code in the companion disk as part of the VIEWDATE example used to test it.) Browsing though the listing, you'll notice some new functions (Str, Inc, and Dec), a strange case statement (in the method DaysInMonth), and a demonstration of the use of strings as arrays of characters (in the function GetText).

To test this unit, we can create a new example. The new form will have a caption to display a date and four buttons, which can be used to modify the date. You can see the main form of the VIEWDATE example in Figure 5.6 and its description in Listing 5.4.

LISTING 5.3: The full source code listing of the Dates unit

```pascal
unit Dates;

interface

type
  Date = class
  private
    Month, Day, Year: Integer;
  public
    constructor Init (m, d, y: Integer);
    procedure SetValue (m, d, y: Integer);
    function LeapYear: Boolean;
    procedure Increase;
    procedure Decrease;
    procedure Add (NumberOfDays: Integer);
    procedure Subtract (NumberOfDays: Integer);
    function GetText: string;
  protected
    function DaysInMonth: Integer;
  end;

implementation

constructor Date.Init (m, d, y: Integer);
begin
  Month := m;
  Day := d;
  Year := y;
end;

procedure Date.SetValue (m, d, y: Integer);
begin
  Month := m;
  Day := d;
  Year := y;
end;

function Date.LeapYear: Boolean;
begin
  {compute leap years, considering "exceptions"}
  if (Year mod 4 <> 0) then
    LeapYear := False
  else
    if (Year mod 100 <> 0) then
      LeapYear := True
    else
    if (Year mod 400 <> 0) then
      LeapYear := False
```

LISTING 5.3: The full source code listing of the Dates unit (continued)

```
if (Year mod 400 = 0) then
     LeapYear := True
   else
   if (Year mod 100 = 0) then
     LeapYear := False
   else
     LeapYear := True;
end;

function Date.DaysInMonth: Integer;
begin
  case Month of
    1, 3, 5, 7, 8, 10, 12:
      DaysInMonth := 31;
    4, 6, 9, 11:
      DaysInMonth := 30;
    2:
      if (LeapYear) then
        DaysInMonth := 29
      else
        DaysInMonth := 28;
  end;
end;

procedure Date.Increase;
begin
  {if this day is not the last of the month}
  if (Day < DaysInMonth) then
    Inc (Day)  {increase the value by 1}
  else
  {if it is not in December}
    if (Month < 12) then
      begin
        {Day 1 of next month}
        Inc (Month);
        Day := 1;
      end
    else
      begin
        {else it is next year New Year's Day}
        Inc (Year);
        Month := 1;
        Day := 1;
      end;
end;

procedure Date.Decrease;
{exactly the reverse of the Increase method}
begin
  if (Day > 1) then
    Dec (Day)  {decrease the value by 1}
```

LISTING 5.3: The full source code listing of the Dates unit (continued)

```
else
{it is the first of a month}
  if (Month > 1) then
    begin
      {assign last day of previous month}
      Dec (Month);
      Day := DaysInMOnth;
    end
  else
  {it is the first of January}
    begin
      {assign last day of previous year}
      Dec (Year);
      Month := 12;
      Day := DaysInMonth;
    end;
end;

function Date.GetText: string;
var
  {temporary substrings}
  m, d, y: string;
begin
  {writes Month to string m, using two characters}
  str (Month:2, m);
  {if first character is blank, replace it with a zero}
  if Month < 10 then
    m[1] := '0';
  {make the same for the day}
  str (Day:2, d);
  if Day < 10 then
    d[1] := '0';
  {convert the year to a four-digits string}
  str (Year:4, y);
  {add the substrings}
  GetText :=  m + '.' + d + '.' + y;
end;

procedure Date.Add (NumberOfDays: Integer);
var
  n: Integer;
begin
  {increase the day n times}
  for n:=1 to NumberOfDays do
    Increase;
end;
```

LISTING 5.3: The full source code listing of the Dates unit (continued)

```
procedure Date.Subtract (NumberOfDays: Integer);
var
  n: Integer;
begin
  {decrease the day n times}
  for n:=1 to NumberOfDays do
    Decrease;
end;

end.
```

LISTING 5.4: The textual description of the form of the VIEWDATE example

```
object DateForm: TDateForm
  Caption = 'Dates'
  OnCreate = FormCreate
  OnDestroy = FormDestroy
  object DateLabel: TLabel
    Alignment = taCenter
    AutoSize = False
    Caption = 'date'
    Font.Color = clBlack
    Font.Height = -27
    Font.Name = 'Arial'
    Font.Style = [fsBold]
    ParentFont = False
  end
  object IncreaseButton: TButton
    Caption = '&Increase'
    OnClick = IncreaseButtonClick
  end
  object DecreaseButton: TButton
    Caption = '&Decrease'
    OnClick = DecreaseButtonClick
  end
  object Add10Button: TButton
    Caption = '&Add 10'
    OnClick = Add10ButtonClick
  end
  object Subtract10Button: TButton
    Caption = '&Subtract 10'
    OnClick = Subtract10ButtonClick
  end
end
```

5

FIGURE 5.6:

The form of the VIEWDATE example

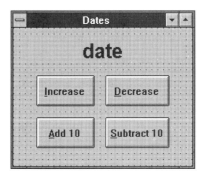

To make this work, we need to create an instance of the Date class, initialize this object, and then show its textual description in the caption of the label:

```
TheDay := Date.Init(2, 14, 1995);
DateLabel.Caption := TheDay.GetText;
```

Figure 5.7 shows the result of this code.

FIGURE 5.7:

The output of the VIEWDATE example at startup

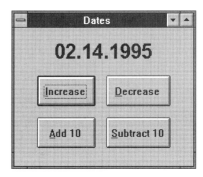

TheDay is a private field of the TDateForm data type. It was automatically named by Delphi when we changed the Name property of the form to DateForm. You can see its definition in Listing 5.5.

LISTING 5.5: The source code of the VIEWDATE main form

```
unit Date_f;

interface

uses
  SysUtils, WinTypes, WinProcs, Messages, Classes, Graphics,
  Controls, Forms, Dialogs, Dates, StdCtrls;

type
  TDateForm = class(TForm)
    DateLabel: TLabel;
    IncreaseButton: TButton;
    DecreaseButton: TButton;
    Add10Button: TButton;
    Subtract10Button: TButton;
    procedure IncreaseButtonClick(Sender: TObject);
    procedure FormCreate(Sender: TObject);
    procedure DecreaseButtonClick(Sender: TObject);
    procedure Add10ButtonClick(Sender: TObject);
    procedure Subtract10ButtonClick(Sender: TObject);
    procedure FormDestroy(Sender: TObject);

  private
    TheDay: Date;

  public
    { Public declarations }
  end;

var
  DateForm: TDateForm;

implementation

{$R *.DFM}

procedure TDateForm.FormCreate(Sender: TObject);
begin
  TheDay := Date.Init(2, 14, 1995);
  {that's the day Delphi was officially presented}
  DateLabel.Caption := TheDay.GetText;
end;

procedure TDateForm.IncreaseButtonClick(Sender: TObject);
begin
  TheDay.Increase;
  DateLabel.Caption := TheDay.GetText;
end;
```

LISTING 5.5: The source code of the VIEWDATE main form (continued)

```pascal
procedure TDateForm.DecreaseButtonClick(Sender: TObject);
begin
  TheDay.Decrease;
  DateLabel.Caption := TheDay.GetText;
end;

procedure TDateForm.Add10ButtonClick(Sender: TObject);
begin
  TheDay.Add(10);
  DateLabel.Caption := TheDay.GetText;
end;

procedure TDateForm.Subtract10ButtonClick(Sender: TObject);
begin
  TheDay.Subtract(10);
  DateLabel.Caption := TheDay.GetText;
end;

procedure TDateForm.FormDestroy(Sender: TObject);
begin
  TheDay.Free;
end;

end.
```

When one of the four buttons is pressed, you need to apply the corresponding method to the TheDay object, then display the new value of the date in the label. Here is an example:

```pascal
TheDay.Increase;
DateLabel.Caption := TheDay.GetText;
```

TIP

As you can see in Figures 5.6 and 5.7, the four buttons of the form have the first letter underlined, which means that those characters can be used as shortcut keys. To obtain this effect, just add the & character in front of the letter in the caption of the button, as you can see in Listing 5.4. Pressing a shortcut key is a quick way to change the date. When you hold down one of the four underlined keys, the date will change rapidly.

If it still isn't clear to you how the program works, refer to its full source code in Listing 5.5, and try to change it. For example, you can add new buttons to increase or decrease the date by a higher number of days. Try to add a Next Year button—one that will also work with leap years.

Units and Programs

A Delphi application is made of two different kinds of source code files. There are one or more units and one program file.

The units can be considered as secondary files, which are referred to by the main part of the application, the program. In theory, this is true. In practice, the program file is usually an automatically generated file with a limited role. It simply needs to start up the program running the main form. As we have already seen in Chapters 1 and 2, the code of the program file, or Delphi project file (DPR), can be edited either manually or by using the Project Manager and some of the Project Options.

The structure of the program file is usually much simpler than the structure of the units. For example, here is the code of the VIEWDATE program:

```
program Viewdate;

uses
  Forms,
  Date_f in 'DATE_F.PAS' {DateForm},
  Dates in 'DATES.PAS';

begin
  Application.CreateForm(TDateForm, DateForm);
  Application.Run;
end.
```

As you can see, there is simply a `uses` section and the main code of the application, enclosed by the `begin` and `end` keywords. The program's `uses` statement is particularly important, because it is used to manage the compilation and linking of the application.

Advanced Topics Relating to Methods and Classes

Some other advanced features are not used often in Delphi applications, but you probably should be aware of them. The structure of Delphi and of the VCL relies on some of these elements. If you are new to object-oriented programming concepts, you might want to skip this section altogether and continue with the section titled "Inheriting from Existing Types." Later, when you are more confident with the basic OOP concepts, you can return to this section.

The advanced topics relate to concept of class and its methods. We will discuss the use of self, the definition of class methods, and the use of method pointers.

The Self Keyword

The self keyword refers to an implicit parameter automatically passed to any method when it is called. Self can be defined as a pointer to the current object (the current instance of the class) and is used by the language to refer to the fields of that specific object inside a method.

In fact, when you declare five objects of the same class, each time you apply a method to one of the objects, the method should operate only on its own data and not affect the other objects.

Here is a method we have already encountered:

```
procedure Date.SetValue(m, d, y: Integer);
begin
  Month := m;
  Day := d;
  Year := y;
end;
```

In a method like this, Month really refers to the Month field of the current object, something you might express (those of you who know how to use pointers) as:

```
Self^.Month := m;
```

If you have ever used an object-oriented programming language, you should already have met the concept of self, maybe with a different name, such as this in C++. Self is rarely used directly by programmers, but it is a fundamental language construct used by the compiler. At times, `self` is used to resolve name conflicts and to make tricky code more readable.

All you really need to know about `self` is that the presence of this hidden parameter is what makes a method different from a procedure that is not related to a class. The technical implementation of a call to a method differs from that of the call of generic subroutines. Methods have an extra hidden parameter, `self`. But since everything is behind the scenes, you do not need to know much about how `self` works.

Class Methods and Class Data

When you add a field to a class, you really add this field to each object instance of that class. Each instance has its own independent representation (referred to by the `self` pointer). In same cases, however, it might be useful to have a field that is shared by all the objects of a class.

Other object-oriented programming languages have formal constructs to express this, such as C++'s `static`. In Object Pascal, this is not needed, because the encapsulation is always provided at the unit level. For this reason, if you simply add a variable in the implementation portion of a unit, it behaves as a class variable—a single memory location shared by all of the objects of a class.

If you need to access this value from outside the unit, you might use a method of the class. However, this forces you to apply this method to one of the instances of the class. An alternative solution is to declare a class method. A class method is a method that cannot access the data of any single object, but can be called by referring to a class rather than to a particular instance. A class method is a method related to the whole class, not its objects, its instances. Technically, a class method is a method that does not have the `self` parameter.

Class methods are present in several object-oriented languages, and they are implemented in C++ using `static` member functions. To declare a class method in Object Pascal, you simply add the `class` keyword in front of the `function` or `procedure`:

```
type
  MyClass
    ...
    class function ClassMeanValue: Integer;
    ...
  end;
```

The use of class methods is not very common in Object Pascal, because you can obtain the same effect by adding a procedure or function to a unit declaring a class. A difference is that you can have two class methods with the same name in a complex application, but you cannot have two functions or procedures with the same name. The class methods, like any other method, are in the scope of the class. Object-oriented purists will definitely prefer the use of a class method over a procedure unrelated to a class. Class methods can also be virtual, so they can be overridden and used polymorphically (concepts which we'll discuss later in this chapter).

Class data is used to maintain general information related to the class, such as the number of objects created or a list of these objects. In these cases, class methods can return the number of objects in the class or offer a way to navigate the list of objects.

Method Pointers

Another addition to the Object Pascal language is the method pointer. A method pointer is like a procedural type, but refers to an object method. Technically, a method pointer type implies the idea of a procedural type that has the `self` parameter. In other words, a method pointer stores two addresses: the address of the method body code and the address of the object instance data, which will show up as `self` inside the method body.

The declaration of a method pointer type is similar to that of a procedural type, except that it has the keywords `of object` at the end of the declaration:

```
type
  IntProceduralType = procedure (Num: Integer);
  IntMethodPointer = procedure (Num: Integer) of object;
```

When you have declared a method pointer, such as the one above, you can have a field type of this kind in an object:

```
type
  MyClass = class
    Value: Integer;
    Operation: IntMethodPointer;
  end;
```

Similar to a variable of a procedural type, this field can be assigned any other type-compatible method; that is, any other method of the same kind and with the same parameters. For example, you can declare another class having a method with the same integer parameter:

```
type
  AnotherClass = class
    X: Integer;
    procedure Add (N: Integer);
  end;
```

If you now declare a couple of objects of the two classes, such as:

```
var
  MyObject: MyClass;
  AnotherObject: AnotherClass;
```

You can then make a similar assignment:

```
MyObject.Operation := AnotherObject.Add;
```

At first glance, the goal of this overly complicated technique may not be clear, but this is one of the cornerstones of Delphi component technology. The secret is in the word *delegation*. If someone has built an object that has some method pointers, you are free to change the behavior of such prebuilt objects simply by assigning a new method to them.

Does this sound familiar? It really should. When you add an OnClick event to a button, Delphi does exactly this. The button has a method pointer, named OnClick, and you can directly or indirectly assign a method of the form to it. When a user clicks on the button, this method is executed, even if you have defined it inside another class (typically, in the form).

This is the same code as above with different class, method, and parameter names, and it is a portion of the code actually used by Delphi. Here are the new declarations:

```
type
  TNotifyEvent = procedure (Sender: TObject) of object;

  MyButton = class
    FOnClick: TNotifyEvent;
  end;

  TForm1 = class (TForm)
    procedure OnButton1Click (Sender: TObject);
    Button1: MyButton;
  end;
```

```
var
  Form1: TForm1;
```

Now inside a procedure, you can write:

```
MyButton.FOnClick := Form1.OnButton1Click;
```

Although you can make this code work as it is written, you'll usually assign a new value, not directly to the method pointer but to the property wrapping it up:

```
MyButton.OnClick := Form1.OnButton1Click;
```

A property of the Events page of the Object Inspector, in fact, is nothing more than a property of a method pointer type. We will discuss this again in the next chapter.

Class References

Another strange construct of Object Pascal is the definition of class references. A class reference is not an object, or a reference to an object, but a reference to the class type. A class reference is indeed a type, and you can declare variables of that type.

```
type
  MyClass = class
    ...
  end;

  MyClassRef = class of MyClass;

var
  AnObject: MyClass;
  AClassRef: MyClassRef;
```

You may wonder what class references are used for. You can use a class reference in any expression where the use of a data type is legal. Of course, there are not many, but the few cases are interesting. In general, class references allow you to manipulate a data type at run-time.

What is the use of this? Being able to manipulate a data type at run-time is a fundamental element of the Delphi environment itself. When you add a new component to a form by selecting it from the Components palette, you select a data type and create an object of that data type. Or, at least, this is what Delphi does for you behind the scenes.

To give you a better idea of how class references work, I built a simple example, named CLASSREF.

The form of this example is quite simple, as you can see in Figure 5.8. It just has three radio buttons in the upper portion. When you select one of these radio buttons and click on the form, you'll be able to create new components of the three types indicated by the button labels: radio buttons, push buttons, and edit boxes.

FIGURE 5.8:
The CLASSREF form

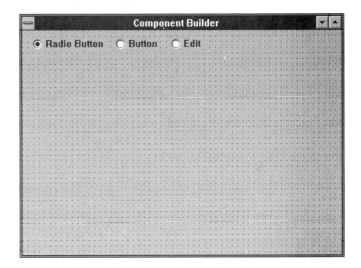

To make this program run properly, you need to change the names of the three components of the form, as you can see in the description of the form in Listing 5.6.

For this program to work, the form for this example must have a class reference field. You should declare a new class reference type first:

```
type
  CRefType = class of TControl;
```

Then you can declare a new field for the form:

```
private
  ClassRef: CRefType;
```

LISTING 5.6: The textual description of the form of the CLASSREF example

```
object Form1: TForm1
  ActiveControl = RadioButtonRadio
  Caption = 'Component Builder'
  OnCreate = FormCreate
  OnMouseDown = FormMouseDown
  object RadioButtonRadio: TRadioButton
    Caption = 'Radio Button'
    Checked = True
    OnClick = RadioButtonRadioClick
  end
  object RadioButtonButton: TRadioButton
    Caption = 'Button'
    OnClick = RadioButtonButtonClick
  end
  object RadioButtonEdit: TRadioButton
    Caption = 'Edit'
    OnClick = RadioButtonEditClick
  end
end
```

This field can be used to store a data type when one of the radio buttons is clicked:

```
ClassRef := TButton;
```

The other two methods, and the initialization method, FormCreate, have a similar code, as you can see in the complete source code in Listing 5.7.

LISTING 5.7: The listing of the form of the CLASSREF example

```
unit Cref_f;

interface

uses
  SysUtils, WinTypes, WinProcs, Messages, Classes, Graphics,
  Controls, Forms, Dialogs, StdCtrls;

type
  CRefType = class of TControl;
  TForm1 = class(TForm)
    RadioButtonRadio: TRadioButton;
    RadioButtonButton: TRadioButton;
    RadioButtonEdit: TRadioButton;
    procedure RadioButtonRadioClick(Sender: TObject);
    procedure RadioButtonButtonClick(Sender: TObject);
    procedure RadioButtonEditClick(Sender: TObject);
    procedure FormCreate(Sender: TObject);
    procedure FormMouseDown(Sender: TObject;
```

LISTING 5.7: The listing of the form of the CLASSREF example (continued)

```
      Button: TMouseButton;
      Shift: TShiftState; X, Y: Integer);
  private
    ClassRef: CRefType;
    Counter: Integer;
  public
    { Public declarations }
  end;

var
  Form1: TForm1;

implementation

{$R *.DFM}

procedure TForm1.RadioButtonRadioClick(Sender: TObject);
begin
  ClassRef := TRadioButton;
end;

procedure TForm1.RadioButtonButtonClick(Sender: TObject);
begin
  ClassRef := TButton;
end;

procedure TForm1.RadioButtonEditClick(Sender: TObject);
begin
  ClassRef := TEdit;
end;

procedure TForm1.FormCreate(Sender: TObject);
begin
  ClassRef := TRadioButton;
end;

procedure TForm1.FormMouseDown(Sender: TObject;
  Button: TMouseButton; Shift: TShiftState; X, Y: Integer);
var
  MyObj: TControl;
  MyName: String;
begin
  MyObj := ClassRef.Create (self);
  MyObj.Parent := self;
  MyObj.Left := X;
  MyObj.Top := Y;
  Inc (Counter);
  MyName := ClassRef.ClassName + IntToStr (Counter);
  Delete (MyName, 1, 1);
  MyObj.Name := MyName;
  MyObj.Visible := True;
end;

end.
```

The interesting part of the code is executed when the user clicks on the form. Instead of using the OnClick event, I've chosen the OnButtonDown event of the form, to give the position of the mouse-click.

The first line of the code for this method is the key. It creates a new object of the data type stored in the class reference field:

```
MyObj := ClassRef.Create (self);
```

Now you can set the value of the Parent property, the position of the new component, give it a name, and make it visible. Notice in particular the code used to build the name, which will also be used as the control's caption. To mimic Delphi's default naming convention, I've taken the name of the class with the expression:

```
ClassRef.ClassName
```

(The meaning of this method will be described in the next chapter.)

Then I've added a number and removed the initial letter of the string. For the first radio button, the basic string is TRadioButton, plus the 1 at the end, and minus the T at the beginning of the class name; that is, RadioButton1. Sound familiar?

You can see two examples of the output of this program in Figure 5.9. Notice, however, that the naming is not the same as that used by Delphi. Delphi uses a separate

FIGURE 5.9:

Two examples of the output of the CLASSREF program, in two different windows

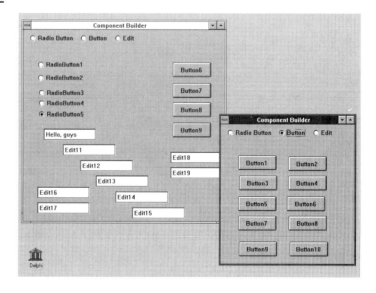

counter for each type of control; I've used a single counter for all of the components. If you place a radio button, a push button and an edit box in a form, their names will be RadioButton1, Button2, and Edit3.

> **NOTE** Class references imply an idea similar to the concept of *meta-class* available in other programming languages. In Object Pascal, however, a class reference is not a class, but only a type pointer. Therefore, the analogy with meta-classes can be somewhat confusing.

5

Inheriting from Existing Types

It is quite common to need a slightly different version of an existing class. For example, you might need to add a new method or change an existing one slightly. You can do this easily by modifying the original code, unless you are already using the same class in another unit of your program. In that case, making changes can create problems for the other unit. You should avoid modifications that can affect other units, particularly in big applications.

A typical alternative is to make a copy of the original type definition, change its code to support the new features, and give a new name to the type. This might work, but it also might create problems, such as duplicate code and bugs. Because it results in two completely different data types, this approach cannot help you to take advantage of the similarities among different types, as we will see later.

In short, Object Pascal allows you to define a new type directly from an existing one. This technique is known as *inheritance* (or *subclassing*, or *derivation*) and is one of the fundamental elements of object-oriented programming languages. To inherit from an existing type, you only need to indicate that type at the beginning of the class declaration. This is done by Delphi each time you create a new form:

```
type
  TForm1 = class(TForm)
  end;
```

This simple definition indicates that the TForm1 class inherits all the methods, fields, and other elements of the TForm class. You can apply to an object of the

TForm1 type each public method of the TForm class. If you look up TForm in the Help file, you'll see that this class has a number of methods. TForm, in turn, inherits some of its methods from another class, and so on, up to the TObject class. (For an introduction to the hierarchy of classes of Delphi, see the next chapter, which includes information about the Visual Components Library, or VCL.)

As a simple example of inheritance, we can change the previous program slightly, deriving a new class and modifying one of its functions, GetText. (You can find this code in the companion disk in the DATES.PAS file of the VIEWD2 example.)

```
type
  NewDate = class (Date)
  public
    function GetText: string;
  end;
```

In this example, NewDate is derived from Date. It is common to say that Date is an *ancestor* class (or a *parent* class) of NewDate and that NewDate is a *descendent* class (or a *child* class) of Date. Other times, you might hear the typical C++ terms of *base* class (that is, the ancestor) and *derived* class (the descendent). Other object-oriented programming languages use different terms to denote inheritance and the classes involved. Unfortunately, there isn't a common jargon for all object-oriented languages—or better, for object-oriented *programmers*.

The new GetText function uses a constant array of month names, defined in the implementation section of the unit, to output the description of the date:

```
{definition of the month names}
const
  MonthNames: array [1..12] of string =
    ('January', 'February', 'March', 'April', 'May', 'June',
    'July', 'August', 'September', 'October', 'November', 'December');

{method of the descendent class}
function NewDate.GetText: string;
var
  d, y: string;
begin
  str(Day:2, d);
  str(Year:4, y);
  GetText := MonthNames[Month] + ' ' + d + ', ' + y;
end;
```

Note that this code works only if it is written in the same unit as the Date class, since we access `private` fields of the ancestor class. If we decided to place the descendent class in a new unit, we would need to either declare the three fields as `protected` or add three simple methods to read their values.

Once we have defined the new class, we simply need to use this new data type to define the NewDate object and to call its constructor (the new code is in bold):

```
type
  TDateForm = class(TForm)
    ...
  private
    TheDay: NewDate;
    ...

procedure TDateForm.FormCreate(Sender: TObject);
begin
  TheDay := NewDate.Init(2, 14, 1995);
  DateLabel.Caption := TheDay.GetText;
end;
```

Without any other changes, the new VIEWD2 example will work properly. The NewDate class has inherited methods to increase the date, add a number of days, and so on. At the same time, to call the new version of the GetText method, we don't need to change the source code. Therefore, the source code of the events remains exactly the same, although its meaning changes considerably, as the new output demonstrates (see Figure 5.10).

FIGURE 5.10:
An example of the output of the VIEWD2 program

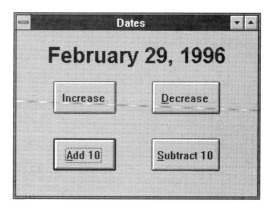

Inheritance and Type Compatibility

Pascal is a strictly typed language. This means that you cannot assign an integer value to a Boolean variable or similar items, at least not without making a hard type cast, which can result in meaningless data. The rule is that two values are compatible only if they are of the same data type. However, there is an important exception to this rule in the case of class types. If you declare a class, such as Animal, and derive from it a new class, say Dog, you can assign an object of type Dog to a variable of type Animal. That is because a dog is an animal!

So, although this might surprise you, the following constructor calls are both legal:

```
var
  MyAnimal, MyAnimal2: Animal;
begin
  MyAnimal := Animal.Create;
  MyAnimal2 := Dog.Create;
  ...
```

As a general rule, you can use an object of a descendent class each time an object of an ancestor class is expected. However, the reverse is not legal; you cannot use an object of an ancestor class when an object of a descendent class is expected. In short:

```
MyAnimal := MyDog; { This is OK }
MyDog := MyAnimal; { This is an error!!! }
```

I'll show you how you can use this feature in a complete example, ANIMAL1, which we will extend later. The two classes are defined as follows (in the ANIM.PAS unit):

```
type
  Animal = class
    public
    constructor Create;
    function GetKind: string;
  private
    Kind: string;
  end;

  Dog = class (Animal)
  public
    constructor Create;
  end;
```

The two Create functions simply set the value of kind, which is returned by the Get-Kind function:

```
constructor Animal.Create;
begin
  Kind := 'An animal';
end;

function Animal.GetKind: string;
begin
  GetKind := Kind;
end;

constructor Dog.Create;
begin
  Kind := 'A dog';
end;
```

To show an example of the use of these classes, I've built a simple form with two radio buttons, a push button, and a label (see the form in Figure 5.11 and its description in Listing 5.8).

FIGURE 5.11:

The ANIMAL1 form

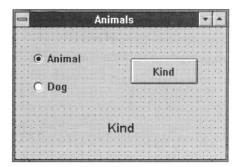

LISTING 5.8: The textual description of the form of the ANIMAL1 example

```
object FormAnimals: TFormAnimals
  Caption = 'Animals'
  OnCreate = FormCreate
  OnDestroy = FormDestroy
  object KindLabel: TLabel
    Alignment = taCenter
    AutoSize = False
    Caption = 'Kind'
    Font.Color = clBlack
    Font.Height = -16
    Font.Name = 'Arial'
    Font.Style = [fsBold]
    ParentFont = False
  end
  object KindButton: TButton
    Caption = 'Kind'
    OnClick = KindButtonClick
  end
  object AnimalRadioButton: TRadioButton
    Caption = 'Animal'
    Checked = True
    OnClick = AnimalRadioButtonClick
  end
  object DogRadioButton: TRadioButton
    Caption = 'Dog'
    OnClick = DogRadioButtonClick
  end
end
```

The form has some fields, which store the values of an animal, a dog, and a generic object, MyAnimal:

```
type
  TFormAnimals = class(TForm)
    ...
  private
    MyAnimal: Animal;
    AnAnimal: Animal;
    ADog: Dog;
  public
    { Public declarations }
  end;
```

The instances of these objects are created and initialized when the form is created (see the FormCreate method in Listing 5.9). The two radio buttons serve to change the object associated with the generic MyAnimal:

```
MyAnimal := ADog;
```

LISTING 5.9: The source code of the form of the ANIMAL1 example

```
unit Anim_f;

interface

uses
  SysUtils, WinTypes, WinProcs, Messages, Classes, Graphics,
  Controls, Forms, Dialogs, StdCtrls, Anim;

type
  TFormAnimals = class(TForm)
    KindLabel: TLabel;
    KindButton: TButton;
    AnimalRadioButton: TRadioButton;
    DogRadioButton: TRadioButton;
    procedure FormCreate(Sender: TObject);
    procedure FormDestroy(Sender: TObject);
    procedure KindButtonClick(Sender: TObject);
    procedure AnimalRadioButtonClick(Sender: TObject);
    procedure DogRadioButtonClick(Sender: TObject);
  private
    MyAnimal: Animal;
    AnAnimal: Animal;
    ADog: Dog;
  public
    { Public declarations }
  end;

var
  FormAnimals: TFormAnimals;

implementation

{$R *.DFM}

procedure TFormAnimals.FormCreate(Sender: TObject);
begin
  AnAnimal := Animal.Create;
  ADog := Dog.Create;
  MyAnimal := AnAnimal;
end;

procedure TFormAnimals.FormDestroy(Sender: TObject);
```

LISTING 5.9: The source code of the form of the ANIMAL1 example (continued)

```
begin
  AnAnimal.Free;
  ADog.Free;
end;

procedure TFormAnimals.KindButtonClick(Sender: TObject);
begin
  KindLabel.Caption := MyAnimal.GetKind;
end;

procedure TFormAnimals.AnimalRadioButtonClick(Sender: TObject);
begin
  MyAnimal := AnAnimal;
end;

procedure TFormAnimals.DogRadioButtonClick(Sender: TObject);
begin
  MyAnimal := ADog;
end;

end.
```

The Kind button calls the GetKind method for the current animal, and displays the result in the label:

```
LabelKind.Caption := MyAnimal.GetKind;
```

This is shown in Figure 5.12.

The two *real* objects are destroyed in the FormDestroy method. See Listing 5.9 for the full source code listing of the form unit.

FIGURE 5.12:

The output of the ANIMAL1 program when the Dog button is selected

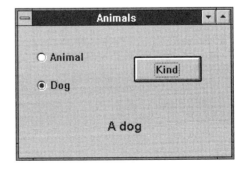

Virtual and Dynamic Methods

Pascal functions and procedures are usually based on *static binding*. This means that a method call is resolved by the compiler and the linker. They replace the call with a call to the specific memory location where the function or procedure resides (which is known as the address of the function).

Object-oriented programming languages, including Object Pascal, allow the use of another form of binding, known as *dynamic binding* or *late binding*. In this case, the actual address of the method to be called is determined at run-time.

The advantage of this approach is known as *polymorphism*. Suppose that a class and its subclass (let's say Animal and Dog) both define a method, and this method has dynamic binding. Now you can apply this method to a generic variable, such as MyAnimal, which at run-time can either refer to an object of class Animal or to an object of class Dog. In this case, the actual method to call is determined at run-time, depending on the class of the current object.

The basic idea of polymorphism is that you write the call to a method, but the code actually called depends on the type of the object, which can be determined only at run-time because of the type-compatibility rule discussed in the previous section. The following ANIMAL2 example extends ANIMAL1 and demonstrates this technique.

In the new version of the example, the Animal and the Dog classes have a new method, Verse (to get the sound made by the selected animal). This method is defined as virtual in the definition in the Animal function and is later overridden in the definition in the Dog class. This is accomplished by the use of the override and virtual keywords:

```
type
  Animal = class
    public
    constructor Create;
    function GetKind: string;
    function Verse: string; virtual;
    private
    Kind: string;
  end;
```

```
Dog = class (Animal)
public
  constructor Create;
  function Verse: string; override;
end;
```

Of course, the two methods should be implemented. Here is a simple approach:

```
function Animal.Verse: string;
begin
  Verse := 'Verse of the animal';
end;

function Dog.Verse: string;
begin
  Verse := 'Arf Arf';
end;
```

Now what is the effect of this call if you write this code:

```
MyAnimal.Verse;
```

It depends. If the MyAnimal variable currently refers to an object of the Animal class, it will call the method Animal.Verse (shorthand used to indicate the Verse method of the Animal class). If it refers to an object of the Dog class, it will call the method Dog.Verse instead. This happens only because the function is virtual, and so it has dynamic binding.

The call to `MyAnimal.Verse` will work for an object instance of any descendent of the Animal class, even classes that are defined after or outside the scope of this method call. The compiler doesn't need to know about all the descendents in order to make the call compatible with them; only the base ancestor class is needed.

In other words, this call to `MyAnimal.Verse` is compatible with all future Animal classes that haven't been created yet. This is the key technical reason that leads to the assumption that object-oriented programming languages favor reusability. You can write some code that uses the classes of a hierarchy without any knowledge of the actual classes of the hierarchy itself. In other words, the hierarchy—and the program—is still extensible, even when you've written thousands of lines of code using it. Of course, there is one condition: the ancestor classes of the hierarchy need to be designed very carefully.

The Delphi program used to demonstrate the use of these new classes has a form that is similar to that of the previous example (compare the new Figure 5.13 with Figure 5.11). The new button has the label Verse. The old KindButton and the old KindLabel have been replaced by a VerseButton and a VerseLabel.

```
procedure TFormAnimals.VerseButtonClick(Sender: TObject);
begin
  VerseLabel.Caption := MyAnimal.Verse;
end;
```

FIGURE 5.13:
The modified form of the ANIMAL2 example

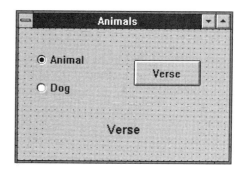

In Figure 5.14, you can see an example of the output of this program. If you compare it with the previous version, you may very well say, "So what?" The output and the behavior of the two programs are similar, but something behind the scenes is really different.

FIGURE 5.14:
The output of ANIMAL2

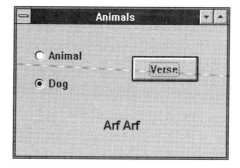

In ANIMAL1, there was a call to a function, GetKind, which simply returned the value of a field. In ANIMAL2, there is a single call, MyAnimal.Verse, that sometimes refers to a method of a class and other times refers to a method of another class. This is an interesting and powerful technique. The same compiled code calls one of two functions depending on the actual type of an object at run-time.

To appreciate this fully, consider that the two or more methods can be complex and completely different from each other. Virtual methods can also be called by other methods of the same class, and they can call other virtual or static methods.

Overriding Virtual and Static Methods

As we have seen before, to override a virtual method in a descendent class, you need to use the override keyword. Notice, however, that this can take place only if the method was defined as virtual in the ancestor class. Otherwise, if it was a static method, there is no way to make it dynamic, other than by changing the code of the ancestor class (if this is possible).

The rules are simple:

- A method defined as static remains static in every subclass.
- A method defined as virtual remains virtual.

There is no way to change this, because of the way the compiler generates the code for virtual methods.

To override a static method, you simply add a method to a subclass having the same parameters as the original one, without any further specifications. To override a virtual method, you must specify the override keyword.

```
type
  MyClass = class
    procedure One; virtual;
    procedure Two; {static method}
  end;
  MySubClass = class(MyClass)
    procedure One; override;
    procedure Two;
  end;
```

There are typically two different approaches to overriding a method. One is to re-place the method of the ancestor class with a new version. The other is to add some more code to the existing method. This can be accomplished by using the `inherited` keyword to call the same method of the ancestor class. For example, you can write:

```
procedure MySubClass.One;
begin
  {new code}
  ...
  {call older version, procedure MyClass.One}
  inherited;
end;
```

You might wonder why you need to use the `override` keyword. In other lan-guages, when you redefine a method in a subclass, you automatically override the original one. The reason this approach is taken is that if you add a method in a sub-class, and later Borland happens to add a method with the same name in a new ver-sion of the base class, your code will continue to work, although it will ignore the new method. Thus, the `override` keyword makes Object Pascal code more resilient and tolerant of changes. Changes made (with or without your knowledge) to the class you inherit from are much less likely to break your descendent code than in other programming languages.

Virtual versus Dynamic Methods

In Delphi, there are basically two different ways to use *late binding* with a method. You can declare the method as virtual, as we have seen before, or declare it as dy-namic. The syntax of these two keywords is exactly the same, and the result of their use is also the same. What is different is the internal mechanism used by the com-piler to implement *dynamic binding*.

Virtual methods are based on a virtual method table (VMT), also known as *vtable* (from the C++ jargon). A virtual method table is a collection of method addresses. For a call to a virtual method, the compiler generates code to jump to an address stored in the *nth* slot in the object's virtual method table. The *nth* is determined by the compiler to correspond to the virtual method indicated in the source code.

Virtual method tables allow a fast execution of the method calls. Their main draw-back is that they require an entry for each virtual method for each descendent class, even if the method is not overridden in the descendent. At times, this has the effect of propagating virtual method table entries (even for methods that aren't overridden) throughout your class hierarchy. This will require a lot of memory just to store the same method address a number of times.

Dynamic method calls, on the other hand, are dispatched using a unique code indicating the method. The search for the corresponding function is generally slower than the simple one-step table lookup for virtual methods. The advantage is that dynamic method entries only propagate in descendents when the descendents override the method. For large or deep object hierarchies, using dynamic methods instead of virtual methods can result in significant memory savings, and causes just a minimal speed penalty.

From a programmer's perspective, the difference between these two approaches lies only in a different internal representation, and slightly different speed or memory usage. Beside this, virtual and dynamic methods are the same.

Here is a general rule of thumb: If the method is going to be overridden by nearly every descendent, make it virtual. If the method is not going to be overridden very often, but still needs late binding for flexibility, make it dynamic, especially if there will be a lot of descendent classes. If the method is going to be called a lot (such as hundreds of times per second), make it virtual. Otherwise, make it dynamic. Of course, this assumes that you have already decided the method must be late-bound. Nonvirtual methods are the fastest form of method dispatch.

Message Handlers

In the past, a form of dynamic methods was used to handle Windows messages. Now this can be accomplished using yet another directive, message, to define message-handling methods. These methods must be procedures (they have no return value) with a single var parameter. They are followed by the message directive plus an index, which is the number of the Windows message they refer to. For example:

```
type
  TForm1 = class(TForm)
    procedure WMMinMax (var Message: TMessage);
    message WM_GETMINMAXINFO;
  end;
```

The name of the procedure and the type of the parameters are up to you, although there are a number of predefined record types for the various Windows messages.

This technique can be extremely useful for long-time MS Windows programmers, who know all about Windows messages and API functions.

The ability to handle messages and call functions as you do when you are programming with the C language may horrify some programmers and delight others. But in Delphi, when writing Windows applications, you will seldom need to use message methods. When you are working with components in Delphi, most of your code will be in message methods (because components typically must work more closely with the Windows API and respond directly to Windows messages). In some examples of the book, I'll handle Windows messages directly in a form, mainly to let you see how simple this is.

Abstract Methods

The `abstract` keyword is used to declare methods that will be defined only in subclasses of the current class. The abstract directive fully defines the method; it is not a forward declaration. If you try to provide a definition for the method, the compiler will complain.

In Object Pascal, you can create instances of classes that have abstract methods. (Note that C++ uses an opposite approach. In C++, you cannot create instances of abstract classes—classes that have pure virtual functions.)

If you happen to call an abstract method, Delphi will issue a run-time error and terminate your application. Unlike most run-time errors, the "Call to abstract method" run-time error does not raise an exception that your program can trap. Calling an abstract method (a method which has no implementation) is considered a severe programmer error, worthy of a fatal exit.

```
type
  AbstractClass = class
    function F: Integer; virtual; abstract;
  end;
```

You might wonder why you would want to use abstract methods. The reason lies in the use of polymorphism. If class Animal has the abstract method Verse, every subclass can redefine it. The advantage is that you can now use a generic Animal object to refer to each animal defined by a subclass, and invoke this method. If this method was not present in the interface of the Animal class, the call would not have been allowed by the compiler, which performs static type checking.

The next example, ANIMAL3, demonstrates the use of abstract methods and some other features of polymorphism, I've written a new version of the Anim unit, declaring three classes: Animal, Dog, and Cat. You can see the complete source code of this unit in Listing 5.10.

LISTING 5.10: The third version of the Anim unit, part of the ANIMAL3 example

```
unit Anim;

interface

type
  Animal = class
    public
    constructor Create;
    function GetKind: string;
    function Verse: string; virtual; abstract;
    private
    Kind: string;
  end;

  Dog = class (Animal)
  public
    constructor Create;
    function Verse: string; override;
    function Eat: string; virtual;
  end;

  Cat = class (Animal)
  public
    constructor Create;
    function Verse: string; override;
    function Eat: string; virtual;
  end;

implementation

constructor Animal.Create;
begin
  Kind := 'An animal';
end;

function Animal.GetKind: string;
begin
  GetKind := Kind;
end;

constructor Dog.Create;
begin
  Kind := 'A dog';
end;
```

LISTING 5.10: The third version of the Anim unit, part of the ANIMAL3
example (continued)

```
function Dog.Verse: string;
begin
  Verse := 'Arf Arf';
end;

function Dog.Eat: string;
begin
  Eat := 'A bone, please!';
end;

constructor Cat.Create;
begin
  Kind := 'A cat';
end;

function Cat.Verse: string;
begin
  Verse := 'Mieow';
end;

function Cat.Eat: string;
begin
  Eat := 'A mouse, please!';
end;

end.
```

The most interesting portion is the definition of the class Animal, which includes a
virtual abstract method, Verse. It is also important to notice that each derived class
overrides this definition and adds a new virtual method, Eat.

What are the implications of these two different approaches? To call the Verse function, we can simply write the same code as in the previous version of the program:

```
VerseLabel.Caption := MyAnimal.Verse;
```

How can we call the Eat method? We cannot apply it to an object of the Animal
class. The statement:

```
VerseLabel.Caption := MyAnimal.Eat;
```

generates the compiler error:

```
Field identifier expected
```

To solve this problem, you can use RTTI to cast the Animal object to a Cat or Dog object, but without the proper cast, the program will raise an exception. We will see an example of this approach later on, but it is far from simple. Adding the method definition in the Animal class is a typical solution for the problem, and the presence of the abstract keyword favors this choice.

To test our three new classes, we can modify the form of the previous version slightly (see Figure 5.13 for the old version; Figure 5.15 for the new one).

FIGURE 5.15:

The third version of the form used to test the Anim unit

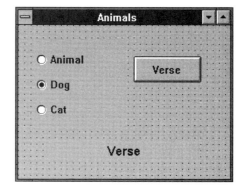

Along with adding the required code, I've made some other changes. The two previous versions of the program created an object of each type at the beginning, then assigned the existing objects to the MyAnimal variable when the user selected one of the radio buttons. Now only one object exists at a time. Before creating a new Animal object the previous one is destroyed; for example:

```
MyAnimal.Free;
MyAnimal := Dog.Create;
```

You can see the full source code of the form in Listing 5.11. When you run this program, the label displays the sound of the dog or the sound of the cat (see Figure 5.16), or you experience a bad run-time error that will stop your application.

LISTING 5.11: The full source code of the form of the ANIMAL3 example

```
unit Anim_f;

interface

uses
  SysUtils, WinTypes, WinProcs, Messages, Classes, Graphics,
  Controls, Forms, Dialogs, StdCtrls, Anim;

type
  TFormAnimals = class(TForm)
    VerseLabel: TLabel;
    VerseButton: TButton;
    AnimalRadioButton: TRadioButton;
    DogRadioButton: TRadioButton;
    CatRadioButton: TRadioButton;
    procedure FormCreate(Sender: TObject);
    procedure FormDestroy(Sender: TObject);
    procedure VerseButtonClick(Sender: TObject);
    procedure AnimalRadioButtonClick(Sender: TObject);
    procedure DogRadioButtonClick(Sender: TObject);
    procedure CatRadioButtonClick(Sender: TObject);
  private
    MyAnimal: Animal;
  public
    { Public declarations }
  end;

var
  FormAnimals: TFormAnimals;

implementation

{$R *.DFM}

procedure TFormAnimals.FormCreate(Sender: TObject);
begin
  MyAnimal := Dog.Create;
end;

procedure TFormAnimals.FormDestroy(Sender: TObject);
begin
  MyAnimal.Free;
end;

procedure TFormAnimals.VerseButtonClick(Sender: TObject);
begin
  VerseLabel.Caption := MyAnimal.Verse;
end;

procedure TFormAnimals.AnimalRadioButtonClick(Sender: TObject);
begin
```

LISTING 5.11: The full source code of the form of the ANIMAL3 example (continued)

```
  MyAnimal.Free;
  MyAnimal := Animal.Create;
end;

procedure TFormAnimals.DogRadioButtonClick(Sender: TObject);
begin
  MyAnimal.Free;
  MyAnimal := Dog.Create;
end;

procedure TFormAnimals.CatRadioButtonClick(Sender: TObject);
begin
  MyAnimal.Free;
  MyAnimal := Cat.Create;
end;

end.
```

FIGURE 5.16:

The output of ANIMAL3, when the Cat button is selected

Run-Time Type Information

The Object Pascal type-compatibility rule for descendent classes allows you to use a descendent class where an ancestor class is expected. As I mentioned earlier, the reverse is not possible. Now suppose that the Dog class has an Eat function, which is not present in the Animal class.

If the variable MyAnimal refers to a dog, it should be possible to call the function. But if you try, and the variable is referring to another class, the result is an error. We could cause a nasty run-time error (or worse, a subtle memory overwrite problem) by making an explicit typecast, since the compiler cannot determine if the value will be correct during execution.

To solve the problem, we can use some techniques based on RTTI. In short, each object knows its type and its inheritance, and we can ask for this information with the is operator. The parameters of is are an object and a type:

```
if MyAnimal is Dog then ...
```

The is expression evaluates as True only if the MyAnimal object is currently referring to an object of type Dog, or a type descendent from Dog. This means that if you test if a Dog object is of type Animal, the test will succeed. In other words, this expression evaluates as True if you can safely assign the object (MyAnimal) to a variable of the data type (Dog).

Now that you know for sure that the animal is a dog, you can make a safe typecast (or type conversion). You can accomplish this direct cast by writing:

```
if MyAnimal is Dog then
  MyDog := Dog (MyAnimal);
```

This same operation can be accomplished directly by the second RTTI operator, as. We can write:

```
MyDog := MyAnimal as Dog;
Text := MyDog.Eat;
```

If we want to call the Eat function, we might also use another notation, shorter but more difficult to read:

```
(MyAnimal as Dog).Eat;
```

The result of the expression is an object of Dog class data type, so you can apply to it any method of that class.

The difference between the traditional cast and the use of the as cast is that the second one raises an exception if the type of the object is not compatible with the type you are trying to cast it to. The exception raised is EInvalidCast (exceptions will be described in the next section).

To avoid this exception, use the is operator and, if it succeeds, make a plain typecast:

```
if MyAnimal is Dog then
  (Dog (MyAnimal) ).Eat;
```

Both run-time type operators are very useful in Delphi because you often want to write generic code that can be used with a number of components of the same type or even of different types. When a component is passed as a parameter to an event-response method, a generic data type is used (TObject), so you often need to cast it back to the original component type.

```
procedure TForm1.Click(Sender: TObject);
begin
  if Sender is TButton then ...
end;
```

This is a common technique in Delphi, and I'll use it in a number of examples throughout the book. Besides its use with is and as expressions, the term RTTI refers to a number of operations you can do on any class or object, such as asking for the class name or the size of an instance. We will discuss this topic in the next chapter, where we will see the definition of the default ancestor of any class, TObject.

The two RTTI operators, is and as, are extremely powerful, and you might think of using them as a standard programming construct. Although they are indeed powerful, you should probably limit their use to special cases.

When you need to solve a complex problem involving several classes, try using polymorphism first. Only in special cases, where polymorphism alone cannot be applied, should you try using the RTTI operators to complement it. Do not use RTTI instead of polymorphism. This is both bad programming practice and results in slower programs. RTTI, in fact, has a high negative impact on performance, since it must walk the hierarchy of classes to see if the typecast is correct. As we have seen, virtual method calls require just a memory lookup, which is much faster.

Handling Exceptions

The last interesting feature of Object Pascal we will cover in this chapter is exception handling. The syntax and semantics of Object Pascal's exception handling are similar to the C++ language. The implementation (machine code) of Pascal's exception handling is radically different (and far simpler) than C++.

The idea of exceptions is to make programs more robust, by adding the capability of handling software or hardware errors. A program can survive such errors or terminate gracefully, allowing the user to save data before exiting.

There are several alternative ways to cope with errors, including extensive testing of function return codes. However testing each time and for each function to see if something wrong has happened is boring and error-prone. Function-result error codes are problematic because each call to a subroutine must be checked for an error situation, and if such a situation exists, the current routine must be cleaned up and the error condition reported to the caller of the current routine. Each function in the call chain is responsible for passing the error information on to the next, a sort of fire brigade. If one routine in the call chain neglects to pass on the error information, your code will not be informed of errors, thus breaking down the whole process.

Exceptions solve this problem by removing the reporting mechanism, the fire brigade, from your normal code. If a particular body of code is not interested in error conditions, it doesn't need to do anything to ensure that error reporting works smoothly. Exceptions enable you to write more compact code that is less cluttered by fire brigade maintenance chores unrelated to the actual programming objective. Exceptions also allow you to separate the code that discovers an error condition from the code that reports the error condition.

Exceptions are a plus also because they define a uniform and universal (within your program) error-reporting mechanism, which is used by Delphi too. During run-time, Delphi raises exceptions when something goes wrong. If your code has been written properly, it can acknowledge the problem and try to solve it; otherwise, the exception is passed to its calling code, and so on. Eventually, if nobody handles the exception, Delphi handles it, by displaying a standard error message and trying to continue the program.

The whole mechanism is based on four keywords:

- `try`, delimits the beginning of a protected block of code.
- `except`, delimits the end of a protected block of code, and introduces the exception-handling statements, with the form:

  ```
  on {exception type} do {statement}
  ```

- `finally`, indicates an optional block used to free resources allocated in the `try` block, before the exception is handled; this block is terminated by the `end` keyword.

- `raise`, the statement used to raise an exception. Most exceptions you'll encounter in your Delphi programming will be raised by the system, but you can also raise exceptions in your own code when it discovers invalid or inconsistent data at run-time. The `raise` keyword can also be used inside a handler to re-raise an exception; that is, to propagate it to the next handler.

Here is the example of a simple protected block:

```
function Divide (A, B: Integer); Integer;
begin
  try
    {the following statement is protected because it
      can generate an error if B equals 0}
    Divide := A div B;
  except
    on EDivByZero do
      Divide := 0;
end;
```

In the exception-handling statement, we catch the EDivByZero exception, which is an exception defined by Delphi. There are a number of these exceptions referring to run-time problems (such as a division by zero or a wrong dynamic cast), to Windows resource problems (such as out-of-memory errors), or to component errors (such as a wrong index). However, programmers can define their own exceptions. Simply create a new subclass of the existing exception classes:

```
type
  EArrayFull = class (Exception);
```

When you add a new element in your array and it is already full (probably due to an error in the logic of the program), you can raise the corresponding exception, by creating an object of this class:

```
if MyArray.Full then
  raise EArrayFull.Create ('Array full');
```

This Create method has a string parameter to describe the exception. You don't need to worry about destroying the object you have created for the exception, since it will be deleted automatically by the exception handler.

There is another keyword involved in exception handling, but one that is used infrequently: the at keyword. It can be used in a `raise` statement, to indicate which machine code location should be indicated as the one causing the exception. The syntax is:

```
raise [object] at [location]
```

For example, in the SYSUTILS.PAS source code, you can see the expression:

```
raise OutOfMemory at ReturnAddr
```

It will seem like the error was encountered in the code calling this procedure, and not in the procedure itself; that is, in the location returned by the system Return-Addr function. This will let the run-time module think that the exception was indeed raised by the caller function. Of course, this kind of code makes sense only in special cases related to the system.

An Example of the Use of Exceptions

The code presented in this example and the previous Divide function are part of a sample program you can experiment with to test exceptions. The program is named EXCEPT, and it is based on the simple form shown in Figure 5.17. I did not include the textual description, because it is so simple. There are just the buttons, each with an intuitive name and an OnClick event handler.

FIGURE 5.17:

The form of the EXCEPT example in the Delphi environment

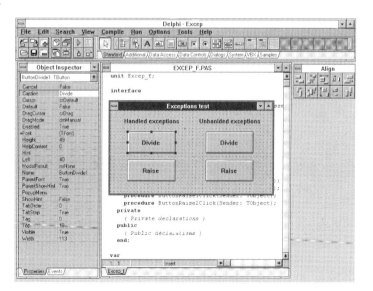

Each time a user presses one of the buttons, an exception is generated, either by making a division by zero or by an explicit `raise` statement. The two events of the two buttons on the left have the proper exception-handling code. But those on the right do not bother with handling exceptions.

WARNING When you run a program in the debugger, the debugger will stop the program by default when an exception is encountered. This is certainly positive, since you'll know where the exception took place and can see the call of the handler step by step. However, this behavior will confuse the execution of this specific test program. In fact, even if the exception is properly handled by the code, the debugger will stop the program execution. Then moving step-by-step through the code, you can see how it is handled. If you just want to let the program run when the exception is properly handled, run the program from File Manager, or temporarily disable the Break on Exception debugging feature in the Environment Options.

The first Divide button calls the Divide function, in a slightly different version than the one described earlier:

```
procedure TForm1.ButtonDivide1Click(Sender: TObject);
begin
  Divide (10, 0);
end;

{protected version of the div operator}
function Divide (A, B: Integer): Integer;
begin
  try
    {the following statement is protected because it
      can generate an error if B equals 0}
    Divide := A div B;
  except
    on EDivByZero do
    begin
      Divide := 0;
      MessageDlg ('Divide by zero corrected', mtError, [mbOK], 0);
    end;
```

```
    on E: Exception do
    begin
      Divide := 0;
      MessageDlg (E.Message, mtError, [mbOK], 0);
    end;
  end;
end;
```

This code generates an exception, which is trapped immediately. Notice that there are two different exception handlers after the same try block. You can have any number of these handlers, which are evaluated in sequence. For this reason, you need to place the broader handlers (the handlers of the ancestor exception classes) at the end.

In fact, using a hierarchy of exceptions, a handler is called also for the subclasses of the type it refers to, as any procedure will do. This is polymorphism in action again. But keep in mind that using a handler for every exception, such as the one above, is not usually a good choice. It is better to leave unknown exceptions to Delphi. The default exception handler in VCL displays the error-message text of the exception class in a message box, then resumes normal operation of the program.

 Another important element is that you can use the exception object you receive in the handler. In the example above, I've written something like:

```
on E: Exception do
  MessageDlg (E.Message, mtError, [mbOK], 0);
```

The object E of class Exception receives the value of the exception object passed by the raise statement. When you work with exceptions, remember this rule: You raise an exception creating an object and handle it indicating its type. This has an important benefit, because, as we have seen, when you handle a type of exception, you really handle the exception of the type you specify plus each descendent type.

For this reason, Delphi defines a hierarchy of exceptions, and you can choose to handle each specific type of exception in a different way, or handle groups of them together. (Refer to the next chapter for graphs of the hierarchy of the classes Delphi defines for exceptions.)

A message box (see Figure 5.18, on the left) is displayed only because we generate it in the code, with the MessageDlg call. On the other hand, if we simply make a division by zero, Delphi will handle this exception, displaying a standard message box (see Figure 5.18, on the right).

FIGURE 5.18:

Two Divide buttons of the EXCEPT example raise exceptions and handle them directly (on the left) or leave them to Delphi (on the right).

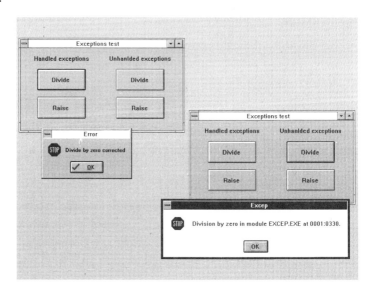

This happens when you press the second Divide button, executing the following code:

```
procedure TForm1.ButtonDivide2Click(Sender: TObject);
var
  A, B, C: Integer;
begin
  A := 10;
  B := 0;
  {generates an exception, which is not handled by us}
  C := A div B;
end;
```

The other two buttons are even simpler. They call a function which invariably raises an exception. Again, the first button handles it, without even showing a message box to the user, and the second button doesn't seem to care. When the user presses the first Raise button, nothing seems to happen. This is exactly what is meant by handling an exception!

```
{fake procedure: the array is always full}
procedure AddToArray (N: Integer);
```

```
begin
  raise EArrayFull.Create ('Array full');
end;

procedure TForm1.ButtonRaise1Click(Sender: TObject);
begin
  try
    {this procedure raises an exception}
    AddToArray (24);
  except
    {simply ignores the exception}
    on EArrayFull do; {do nothing}
  end;
end;

procedure TForm1.ButtonRaise2Click(Sender: TObject);
begin
  {unguarded call}
  AddToArray (24);
end;
```

Exceptions and the Stack

When you raise an exception, what happens to your function call stack? The program starts searching for a handler among the functions already on the stack. This means that the program exits from existing functions and does not execute the remaining statements.

To understand how this works, you can either use the debugger or add a number of simple message boxes in the code, to be informed when a certain source code statement is executed. In the next example, EXCEPT2, I've followed this second approach.

For example, when you press the Raise2 button in the EXCEPT form, an exception is raised and not handled, so that the final part of the code will never be executed:

```
procedure TForm1.ButtonRaise2Click(Sender: TObject);
begin
  {unguarded call}
  AddToArray (24);
  ShowMessage ('Program never gets here');
end;
```

Notice that this method calls the AddToArray procedure, which raises the exception. The final code of this procedure is not executed either:

```
procedure AddToArray (N: Integer);
begin
  raise EArrayFull.Create ('Array full');
  ShowMessage ('Program never gets here');
end;
```

If you run the EXCEPT program, you'll never see these messages, unless you comment the raise statement (I suggest that you do comment it, so that you can see the difference between when the exception is raised and when it is not).

NOTE   Technically, there are two different ways to handle exceptions in different programming languages or environments. In Object Pascal (or in C++), run-time unwinds the stack to reach a handler, and then continues with the code after the handler. Other systems use resumption instead. This means that after the handler is found, the code restarts from the exact position were the error occurred. However, this approach is not very safe, since there is a good chance that a new error will take place again in the same code. Seeing a number of system error messages in a row is something that can really bother users.

When the exception is handled, the flow starts again after the handler, and not after the code that raises the exception. Consider this modified method:

```
procedure TForm1.ButtonRaise1Click(Sender: TObject);
begin
  try
    {this procedure raises an exception}
    AddToArray (24);
    ShowMessage ('Program never gets here');
  except
    {simply ignores the exception}
    on EArrayFull do
      ShowMessage ('Handle the exception');
  end;
  ShowMessage ('Exception has already been handled');
end;
```

The last ShowMessage call will be executed right after the second one, while the first is always ignored. I suggest that you run the program, change its code, and play with it. (You can find its complete source code on the companion disk, as EXCEPT2.)

The Finally Block

There is a fourth keyword for exception handling that I've mentioned but haven't used so far, finally. A finally block is used to perform some action (usually cleanup) in the event of an exception, and in the event of normal execution. The code in the finally block will always be executed as execution leaves the associated try block, whether that departure is by normal program flow or by exception.

Consider this function:

```
function ComputeBits (A, B: Integer): Integer;
var
  Bmp: TBitmap;
begin
  try
    Bmp := TBitmap.Create;
    {compute bits ...}
    ComputeBits := A div B;
    Bmp.Free;
  except
    on EDivByZero do
    begin
      ComputeBits := 0;
      MessageDlg ('Error in ComputeBits', mtError, [mbOK], 0);
    end;
  end;
```

This code is fundamentally flawed. When B is zero and the exception is raised, the statement used to free the bitmap won't be executed at all. The program jumps from the code generating the exception to the corresponding handler, skipping statements in between.

One might think of placing the resource deallocation code at the end of the function, after the try block, but if an exception is raised and not handled, the try block won't be executed. The solution to the problem is to use the finally statement:

```
function ComputeBits (A, B: Integer): Integer;
var
  Bmp: TBitmap;begin
```

```
  Bmp := TBitmap.Create;
  try

    {compute bits ...}
    ComputeBits := A div B;
  finally
    Bmp.Free;
  end;
end;
```

When this code is run, the Free method of the bitmap is always called, whether an exception occurs (of any sort) or not. The drawback to this version of the function is that we want to handle the exception, too. Strangely enough, this is not possible. A `try` block can be followed by either `except` or `finally`, but not both at the same time. The solution? Use two nested `try` blocks. Give the internal one a `finally` statement, and give the external one an except statement or vice versa, as the situation requires:

```
function ComputeBits (A, B: Integer): Integer;
var
  Bmp: TBitmap;
begin
  Bmp := TBitmap.Create;
  try try
    {compute bits ...}
    ComputeBits := A div B;
  finally
    Bmp.Free;
    end;
  except
    on EDivByZero do
    begin
      {handle or re-raise the exception to inform the caller program}
    end;
  end;
end;
```

To demonstrate that this code works as I've described, I've written an extended version of the above function in a simple Delphi example. The new example is called EXCEPT3, and it has just two buttons (see the output in Figure 5.19, when a user clicks on the first button). Its code contains two versions of the fake ComputeBits function, one similar to the last version above and the other having only the `finally` block. I've added a number of message boxes to both functions so that you are informed of the allocation and deallocation of the bitmap, and of the flow of execution.

FIGURE 5.19:

The three steps of the output of the EXCEPT3 program. Notice the order of the three messages.

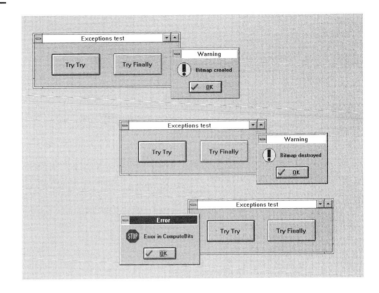

In particular, instead of handling the exception (in the first version of ComputeBits) I simply re-raise it, after changing the text of its message:

```
except
  on E: EDivByZero do
  begin
    E.Message := 'Error in ComputeBits';
    raise;
  end;
```

The *must* for a programmer is to protect blocks with the `finally` statement, to avoid resource or memory leaks in case an exception is raised. Handling the exception is probably less important, since Delphi can survive most of them. The difference between the two versions is that in the first one, the program customizes the error message, using the code I've just shown.

The form is simple, so I'll skip the description of its structure. The final code of the form, including the two versions of the ComputeBits function, is shown in Listing 5.12. To understand this program, run it, see what it does, and try to change its behavior. As an alternative, look at Figure 5.19, which shows the three messages displayed when a user presses the Try Try button.

LISTING 5.12: The complete listing of the EXCEPT2 example

```
unit Excep_f;

interface

uses SysUtils, WinTypes, WinProcs, Messages, Classes, Graphics,
  Controls, Forms, Dialogs, StdCtrls;

type
  TForm1 = class(TForm)
    Button1: TButton;
    Button2: TButton;
    procedure Button1Click(Sender: TObject);
    procedure Button2Click(Sender: TObject);
  private
    { Private declarations }
  public
    { Public declarations }
  end;

var
  Form1: TForm1;

implementation

{$R *.DFM}

function ComputeBits (A, B: Integer): Integer;
var
  Bmp: TBitmap;
begin
  try try
    Bmp := TBitmap.Create;
    MessageDlg ('Bit map created', mtWarning, [mbOK], 0);
    {compute bits ...}
    ComputeBits := A div B;
  finally
    Bmp.Free;
    MessageDlg ('Bit map destroyed', mtWarning, [mbOK], 0);
    end;
  except
    on EDivByZero do
    begin
      ComputeBits := 0;
      MessageDlg ('Error in ComputeBits', mtError, [mbOK], 0);
    end;
  end;
end;
```

LISTING 5.12: The complete listing of the EXCEPT2 example (continued)

```
function ComputeBits2 (A, B: Integer): Integer;
var
  Bmp: TBitmap;
begin
  try
    Bmp := TBitmap.Create;
    MessageDlg ('Bit map created', mtWarning, [mbOK], 0);
    {compute bits ...}
    ComputeBits2 := A div B;
  finally
    Bmp.Free;
    MessageDlg ('Bit map destroyed', mtWarning, [mbOK], 0);
  end;
end;

procedure TForm1.Button1Click(Sender: TObject);
begin
  ComputeBits (10, 0);
end;

procedure TForm1.Button2Click(Sender: TObject);
begin
  ComputeBits2 (10, 0);
end;

end.
```

5

WARNING If you change this code, and the new version doesn't properly free the bitmap, you might experience some memory problems or Windows resource leaks.

Summary

In this chapter, we have discussed object-oriented programming in Object Pascal. We have considered the definition of classes, the use of methods, encapsulation, subclassing, the definition of units, run-time type information, and exception handling. Certainly this is quite a lot for a single chapter, and if you have never heard about OOP, the information presented here may be too concise.

If you want to familiarize yourself with object-oriented programming, spend some time with a book fully devoted to this subject, one that also includes some theory. To become a fluent Delphi programmer, the ideas presented in this chapter should be enough. If they are too hard to grasp, particularly the more advanced topics, such as class references, don't let that stop you. Go on reading, and come back to this chapter later on.

CHAPTER

SIX

The Visual Component Library

- The Delphi hierarchy of classes

- Delphi components and objects

- An overview of Delphi properties

- Component methods and events

- Types of Delphi collections

6

We have seen that the Delphi language has a number of ready-to-use, standard routines. But there is a larger and much more important set of classes. These are component classes, related to the user interface, and general-purpose classes. The use of the component classes, and other classes related to MS Windows, is the subject of the next chapters of the book. In this chapter, we'll focus on the Delphi class library. We'll discuss the structure of the Delphi hierarchy of classes, review some key concepts of their use, and look at an overview of some general-purpose classes.

The Delphi system library is called the Visual Component Library, or VCL for short, although it includes more than components. This chapter is short but delves into some intricacies of the VCL. If you would like to skip the VCL details for now, and continue with more information about the use of the Delphi components, you can go directly to the next chapter.

The Conceptual Foundation

At the heart of Delphi is a hierarchy of classes. Since every class in the system is a subclass of the TObject data type, the whole hierarchy has a single root. This allows you to use TObject as a replacement for any data type in the system. For example, event-response methods usually have a Sender parameter of type TObject. This simply means that the sender can be of any class, since every class is derived from TObject.

The typical drawback of a similar approach is that to work on the object, you need to know its data type. One way to solve this problem is by using the RTTI (run-time type information) features of the language, which are represented by the is and as keywords. RTTI and the exceptions generated when a type conversion fails make it safe to use this approach to express a generic type.

Since there isn't a specific Object Pascal syntax to write *generic* classes, known also as *template* classes in C++ jargon, the use of the TObject type and RTTI is generally accepted. To be honest, I don't miss C++ templates, because Object Pascal's approach is much easier and equally as powerful. I know this is often regarded as an unsafe approach, because of the required type conversions, but by using RTTI and *controlled* casts, we can avoid any problems. We will discuss generic classes later in this chapter, when we focus on some container classes of the VCL.

Since the TObject class is the "mother of all classes," let's take a quick look at its definition in the Delphi source code (see Listing 6.1).

LISTING 6.1: The definition of the TObject class in Delphi source code

```
type
  TObject = class;
  TClass = class of TObject;
  TObject = class
    constructor Create;
    destructor Destroy; virtual;
    procedure Free;
    class function NewInstance: TObject; virtual;
    procedure FreeInstance; virtual;
    class procedure InitInstance(Instance: Pointer):
TObject;
    function ClassType: TClass;
    class function ClassName: string;
    class function ClassParent: TClass;
    class function ClassInfo: Pointer;
    class function InstanceSize: Word;
    class function InheritsForm(AClass: TClass): Boolean;
    procedure DefaultHandler(var Message); virtual;
    procedure Dispatch(var Message);
    class function MethodAddress(const Name: string):
Pointer;
    class function MethodName(Address: Pointer): string;
    function FieldAddress(const Name: string): Pointer;
  end;
```

The code in Listing 6.1 defines two data types: the class TObject and the class reference TClass. The TObject class lists a number of methods that you can use on any object, including objects that you have defined yourself (that do not contain these methods). Most of the methods of the TObject class are often used by the system, and they become particularly useful if you need to write a tool to extend the Delphi programming environment. For example, debugger and browser tools use this kind of information extensively.

Some of the TObject methods might have a role when writing generic Windows applications. For example, the ClassName method returns a string with the name of the class. You can apply this method both to an object (an instance) and to a class (a data type), because it is a class method. Suppose that you have defined a Date class and a Day object of that class. The following statements have the same effect:

```
text := Day.ClassName;
text := Date.ClassName;
```

There are occasions to use the name of a class, but it might also be useful to retrieve a class reference to the class itself or to its base class. This can be done with the Class-Type and ClassParent methods. Once you have a class reference, you can use it as if it were an object; for example, to call the ClassName method.

Another method that might be useful is InstanceSize, which returns the size of an object. Although you might think that you can use the SizeOf function for this information, that function actually returns the size of an object reference—a pointer—instead of the size of the object.

To illustrate the use of some of the methods of the TObject class, and of every class in the system, I've written a small example, called OBJUSE. To rebuild it, place a button and a list box in the form of a new, blank application. See Figure 6.1 for the form for this example, and Listing 6.2 for the textual description of the form.

FIGURE 6.1:

The form of the OBJUSE example

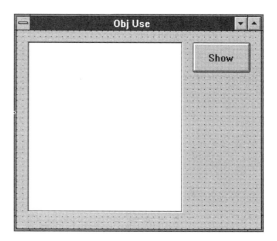

When the user clicks on the button, the following code is executed:

```
procedure TForm1.ShowButtonClick(Sender: TObject);
var
  Day: Date;
begin
  {create an instance and show some information}
  Day := Date.Init (6, 1, 1995);
  ListBox1.Items.Add ('Class name: ' + Day.ClassName);
```

```
ListBox1.Items.Add ('Parent class name: ' +
  Day.ClassParent.ClassName);
ListBox1.Items.Add ('Instance size: ' +
  IntToStr (Day.InstanceSize));
ListBox1.Items.Add ('Size of object: ' +
  IntToStr (SizeOf (Day)));

{leave a blank line}
ListBox1.Items.Add (' ');

{show the same information about the form}
ListBox1.Items.Add ('Class name: ' + ClassName);
ListBox1.Items.Add ('Parent class name: ' +
  ClassParent.ClassName);
ListBox1.Items.Add ('Instance size: ' +
  IntToStr (InstanceSize));
ListBox1.Items.Add ('Size of object: ' +
  IntToStr (SizeOf (self)));

{free memory}
Day.Free;

{disable the button, to avoid a second click}
ShowButton.Enabled := False;
end;
```

When you run this program, the list box will contain the name of the class of the Day object, the name of its parent class, the size of its instance, and the size of the object itself, as shown in Figure 6.2.

LISTING 6.2: The textual description of the form of the OBJUSE example

```
object Form1: TForm1
  ActiveControl = ShowButton
  Caption = 'Obj Use'
  object ShowButton: TButton
    Caption = 'Show'
    OnClick = ShowButtonClick
  end
  object ListBox1: TListBox
    ItemHeight = 16
  end
end
```

FIGURE 6.2:

The output of the OBJUSE example

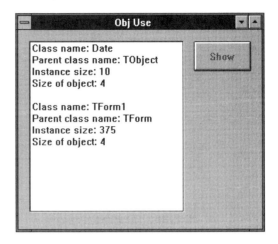

The second part of the program shows the same information for the form object. Since we are writing a method of its class, TForm1, we can call this method directly, or we can use self as the parameter of the SizeOf function. Notice that when you call SizeOf for an object, it always returns 4, which is not the size of the object, but of its reference (that is, a far pointer).

The VCL Hierarchy

The VCL defines a number of subclasses of TObject. Many of these classes are actually subclasses of other subclasses, forming a complex hierarchy. Unless you are interested in developing new components, you'll use only the *terminal* classes of this hierarchy—the leaf nodes of the hierarchy tree—which are fully documented in the Delphi Help system.

Components

Components are the central elements of Delphi applications. When you write a program, you basically choose a number of components and define their interactions. That's all there is to most of Delphi programming.

There are different kinds of components in Delphi. Most of the components are included in the Components palette, but some of them (including TForm and TApplication) are not.

Technically, components are subclasses of the TComponent class (see Figure 6.3). As such, they can be manipulated visually, as you set their properties at design-time.

We will use most of the Delphi components in the examples throughout this book. I'll try to present the components in logical groups, to cover related topics in each chapter. My logical groups only partially match the pages of the Components palette. From a technical point of view, there are common names to indicate groups of components. These groups indicate components with a similar internal structure and relationship to Windows elements. These technical groups reflect each component's position in the hierarchy and its use. You can see a representation of these groups in Figure 6.4.

Controls can be defined as visual components. You can place a control on a form at design-time and see how it looks, and you can see controls on the form at run-time. Controls account for most components, and the terms are often used as synonyms — although there are components that are not controls.

Windowed controls are visual components based on a window. From a technical point of view, this means that the controls have a windows handle. From a user perspective, windowed controls can receive the input focus and can contain other controls. This is the biggest group of components.

Nonwindowed controls are visual components that are not based on a window. Therefore, they have no handle, cannot receive the focus, and cannot contain other controls. Examples of nonwindowed controls are the Label and the TSpeedButton component. There are just a few controls in this group, but they are critical to minimizing the use of system resources, particularly for components used often and in number, such as labels or toolbar buttons.

Components can be visual or nonvisual. *Nonvisual* components are the components that are not controls. At design-time, a nonvisual component appears on the form as a little icon. At run-time, some of these components are visible (for example, the standard dialog boxes), and others are invisible (for example, some database connections). In other words, nonvisual components are not visible themselves at run-time, but often manage something that is visual, such as a dialog box.

FIGURE 6.3A:

The first part of the VCL hierarchy: Components

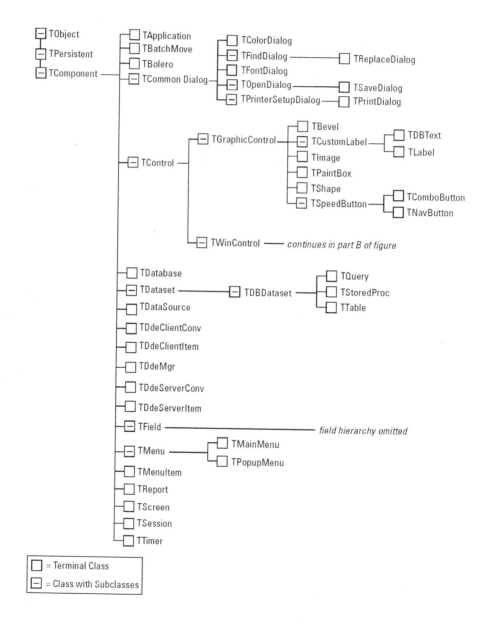

FIGURE 6.3B:

The first part of the VCL hierarchy: Components (continued)

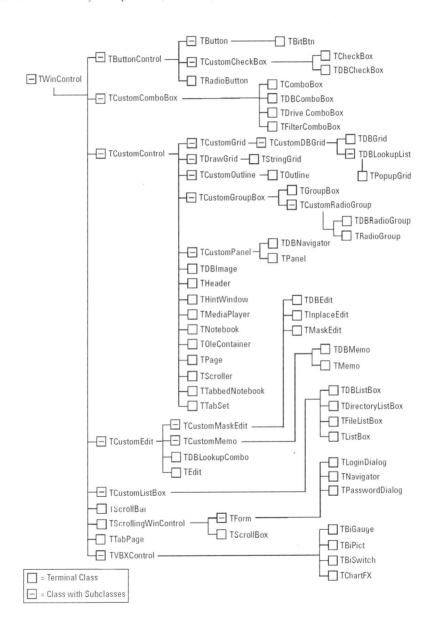

FIGURE 6.4:

A graphical representation of the groups of components

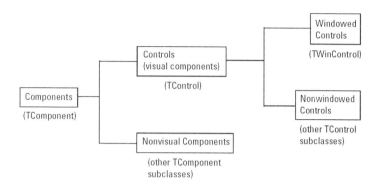

> **TIP**
>
> To set the order of creation and of activation of the components on a form, you can change the creation order of nonvisual components and the tab order of windowed controls. To accomplish this, use the corresponding commands in the SpeedBar menu of the Form Designer, as I'll show you in an example in the next chapter.

Objects

Although the VCL is basically a collection of components, there are other classes that do not fit in this category. You can see some of these classes (only the most important ones) in the hierarchy shown in Figure 6.5.

All the noncomponent classes are often indicated by the term *objects*, although this is not a precise definition. There are mainly two uses of these classes. Generally, noncomponent classes define the data type of component properties, such as the Picture property of an image component (which is a TGraphic object) or the Items property of a list box (which is a TStrings object).

The second use of noncomponent classes is a direct use. In the Delphi code you write, you can allocate and manipulate objects of these classes. You might do this for a number of reasons, including to store a copy of the value of a property in memory and modify it while it does not relate to any component, to store a list of values,

FIGURE 6.5:

The second part of the VCL hierarchy: Objects

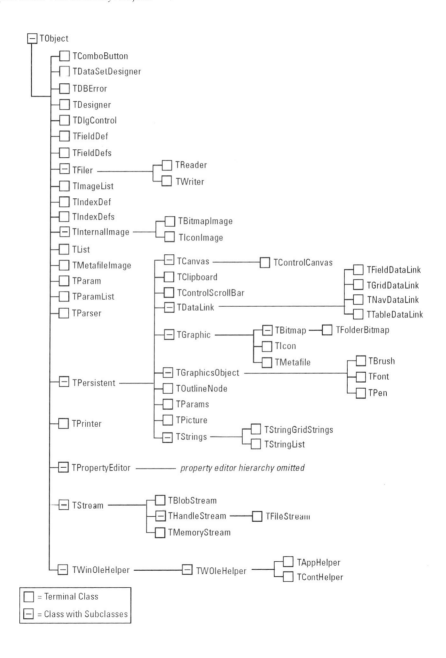

to write complex algorithms, and so on. You'll see several examples in the book that show how to use noncomponent classes directly.

There are several groups of noncomponent classes in the VCL:

- **Graphic objects:** TBitmap, TBrush, TCanvas, TFont, TGraphic, TGraphicsObject, TIcon, TMetafile, TPen, and TPicture.

- **Stream/file objects:** TBlobStream, TFileStream, THandleStream, TIniFile, TMemoryStream, TFiler, TReader, and TWriter.

- **Collections:** TList, TStrings, and TStringList.

We will focus on collections in a later section of this chapter. Graphic and stream objects are described throughout the following chapters, in the discussions of the components that use them and in other sections where they are relevant.

Exceptions

The third main part of the VCL classes is made up of the exception classes. We have already discussed exception handling in Chapter 5, so we won't repeat the details here. You can see the hierarchy of the exception classes in Figure 6.6.

All the exception classes are subclasses of Exception, which is defined as follows:

```
Exception = class(TObject)
public
  constructor Create(const Msg: string);
  constructor CreateFmt(const Msg: string;
    const Args: array of const);
  constructor CreateRes(Ident: Word);
  constructor CreateResFmt(Ident: Word;
    const Args: array of const);
  destructor Destroy; override;
  property Message: string;
  property MessagePtr: PString;
end;
```

Two things are worth noticing in this definition:

- The various constructors, with their parameters of string, the resource identifier of a string, and so on

- The Message property, which can be used to access the message defined in the constructor

6

FIGURE 6.6:

The third part of the VCL hierarchy: Exceptions

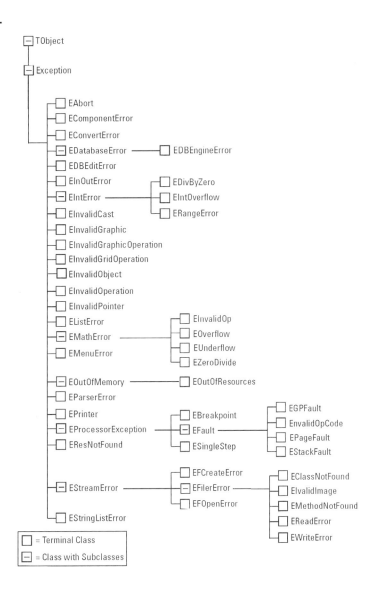

To see how these elements are used, turn back to the examples of exception handling at the end of Chapter 5. More examples are presented in the rest of the book, whenever resource allocation is involved.

Using Components and Objects

Once you have added a component to your application, or defined a new object, you need to set its status and its behavior. There are a number of ways to interact with objects in Delphi, and in some cases, you can accomplish the same task in different ways. Each class defined by the VCL has some properties you can read or set, some methods you can call, and some events you can handle. An overview of these elements of the VCL classes is presented in the following sections.

Keep in mind that there are basically two ways to create an object in Delphi. You can define a new instance by adding a new component to a form, or you can create an object dynamically. We have already seen an interesting example of the definition of run-time objects in Chapter 5 (the CLASSREF example).

To recap the related information, you simply need to define an object, allocate its instance (calling the Create constructor), and set the Parent property. From this point on, you can act on the object, just as if it were defined at design-time. In any form method, you can create a new button by writing:

```
MyButton := TButton.Create (self);
MyButton.Parent := self;
MyButton.Left := 100;
MyButton.Top := 200;
MyButton.Visible := True;
```

Notice that if you add a statement to define the Name property of MyButton, you cannot run this code twice. It will raise an exception, because the value of the Name property, if present, must be unique among all the components of a form. If you really want to add a name, you can use a counter to add a unique number to the name, as I've done in the CLASSREF example (in Chapter 5), and as Delphi's Form Designer does.

There are no limits to the components you can create. Every component you can use at design-time, even forms, can also be created at run-time. Well, there actually are limits, imposed by the computer memory and MS Windows resources, but they do not depend on Delphi and might be raised in future versions of the Microsoft operating environment.

NOTE Besides being a visual programming environment, Delphi allows a programmer to create the visual components. When you create a component, usually subclassing an existing one, you define its properties, methods, and events. You also need to add some code for the visual editing of your controls, such as property editors, and so on. Creating a component is not as difficult as it might seem at first, but it does require an in-depth understanding of Windows programming. Unfortunately, the Delphi environment offers limited help in this area. Chapter 27 provides an introduction to component creation.

6

Properties

Properties are class attributes that determine the status of an object, such as its position and its appearance, and also its behavior. To know the value of a property at design-time, or to change it, you can use the Object Inspector. At run-time, you can access a property by reading or writing it with some simple code.

The Object Inspector lists only the design-time properties of a component, and the run-time properties are not included. For a complete list of properties, refer to the Delphi Help files.

Usually, you can either set a property, indicating a new value, or read its current value. However, there are read-only properties, and (a few) write-only properties. Both read-only and write-only properties are usually available only at run-time.

To summarize, along with the properties listed in the Object Inspector (design-time), there are other properties (run-time), some of which can only be read (read-only) or can only be written (write-only). The description of each property in the Help file tells which kind of property it is.

From a technical point of view, the distinction between design-time properties and run-time properties is merely that design-time properties are declared in a published section of the class declaration. Anything that is not declared in a published section is by definition not available at design-time—it is run-time only.

WARNING When you write the code, you might be lead to think that properties are similar to data fields. This is not true. Every time you read the value of a property or change it, a method might be called. Some properties map directly to data fields, particularly when you read their value. When you change the value of a property, you generally end up calling a method. It is important to realize this, since some of these methods take some time to execute. They also can produce a number of side effects, often including a (slow) repainting of the component on the screen. Although property side effects are seldom documented, you should be aware that they exist, particularly when you are trying to optimize your code.

Note that you can usually assign a value to a property or read it, and even use properties in expressions, but you cannot always pass a property as a parameter to a procedure or method. This is because a property is not a memory location, so it cannot be used as a var parameter (or reference parameter).

Not all of the VCL classes have properties. Properties are present in components and in other subclasses of the TPersistent class, because properties usually can be streamed and saved to a file (persistency is covered in detail in Chapter 23).

Although each component has its own set of properties, you might have already noticed that some properties are common to all of them. Table 6.1 lists some of the common properties along with short descriptions.

Since there is inheritance among components, it is interesting to see in which ancestor classes the most common properties are introduced. Study the source code, and see Figure 6.7 for an overview of the properties introduced by the topmost classes of the VCL hierarchy.

We will use most of these properties in examples throughout the book. The following sections provide basic descriptions of the most common properties. I know that this is a slight violation of the rule of the book not to provide reference material

TABLE 6.1: Some Properties Available for Most Components

Property	Available for	Description
Align	All controls	Determines how the control is aligned in its parent control area
BoundsRect	All controls	Indicates the bounding rectangle of the control
Caption	All controls	The caption of the control
ComponentCount	All components	The number of components owned by the current one
ComponentIndex	All components	Indicates the position of the component in the list of components of the owner
Components	All components	An array of the components owned by the current one
ControlCount	All controls	The number of controls that are the child of the current one
Controls	All controls	An array of controls that are the child of the current one
Color	Many objects and components	Indicates the color of the surface, of the background, or the current color
Ctrl3D	Most components	Determines whether the control has a three-dimensional look
Cursor	All controls	The cursor used when the mouse pointer is over the control
DragCursor	Most controls	The cursor used to indicate that the control accepts dragging
DragMode	Most controls	Determines the drag-and-drop behavior of the control as the starting component for a dragging operation
Enabled	All controls and some other components	Determines whether the control is active or is inactive (or grayed)
Font	All controls	Determines the font of the text displayed inside the component
Handle	All controls	The handle of the window, used by the system
Height	All controls and some other components	The vertical size of the control
HelpContext	All controls and the dialog box components	A context number used to call context-sensitive help automatically

6

TABLE 6.1: Some Properties Available for Most Components (continued)

Property	Available for	Description
Hint	All controls	The string used to display fly-by hints for the control
Left	All controls	The horizontal coordinate of the upper-left corner of the component
Name	All components	The unique name of the component, which can be used in the source code
Owner	All components	Indicates the owner component
Parent	All controls	Indicates the parent control
ParentFont	All controls	Determines if the component should use its own Font property or that of the parent component
ParentShowHint	All controls	Determines if the component should use its own ShowHint property or that of the parent control
PopupMenu	All controls	Indicates the pop-up menu to use when the user clicks on the control with the left mouse button
ShowHint	All controls	Determines if hints are enabled
Showing	All controls	Determines if the control is currently showing on the screen; that is, visible, when its parent control is showing
TabOrder	All controls (except TForm)	Determines the tab order in the parent control
TabStop	All controls (except TForm)	Determines if the user can tab to this control
Tag	All components	A long integer available to store custom data
Top	All controls	The vertical coordinate of the upper-left corner of the component
Visible	All controls and some other components	Determines if the control is visible (see also the Showing property)
Width	All controls and some other components	The horizontal size of the control

FIGURE 6.7:

The properties introduced by the topmost classes of the VCL hierarchy, and available in all of the subclasses

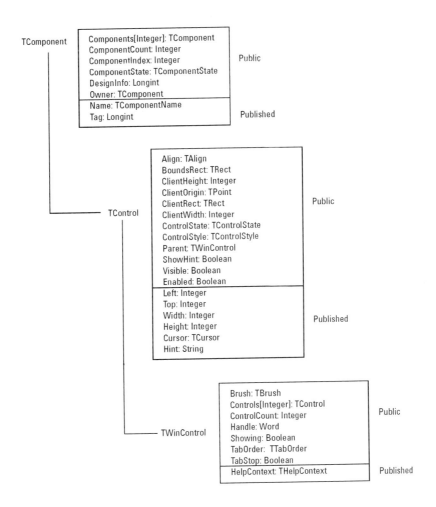

directly, but to my defense, I can say that the following descriptions don't mimic the Help reference. They are intended to give you some general guidelines and hints for using the more common properties.

The Name Property

As I've already mentioned, every component in Delphi can have a name. If you do give a component a name, the name must be unique within the owner component, generally a form. This means that an application can have two different forms that each have a component with the same name.

There are two important elements related to the Name property of the components. First, as I mentioned in Chapter 1, if you set the Name property of a control before changing its Caption property, the new name is copied to the caption. That is, if the name and the caption are identical, then changing the name will also change the caption.

Second, Delphi uses the name of the component to create the default name of the methods related to its events. If you have a Button1 component, its OnClick event is connected to a Button1Click method, unless you specify a different name. If you later change the name of the component, Delphi will modify the names of the related methods accordingly. For example, if you change the name of the button to MyButton, the method automatically becomes MyButtonClick.

Properties Related to Component Size and Position

Other important properties, common to most components, are those related to their size and position. The position of a component is determined by its Left and Top properties, and its size (available only for controls) is determined by the Height and Width properties.

An important feature of the position of a component, like any other coordinate in Windows, is that it always relates to the client area of its parent component (which is the component indicated by its Parent property). For a form, the client area is the surface included within its borders (but without the borders themselves). (It would have been messy to work in screen coordinates, although there are some ready-to-use methods that convert the coordinates between the form and the screen and vice versa.)

Note, however, that the same holds true for panels and other *container* components. If you place a panel in a form, and a button in a panel, the coordinates of the button relate to the panel, and not to the form. In fact, in this case, the parent component of the button is the panel.

The Enabled, Visible, and Showing Properties

There are two basic properties you can use to let the user interact with an existing component. The simplest is the Enabled property. When a component is disabled (when Enabled is set to False), there is usually some visual hint to specify this state to the user. At design-time, the disabled property does not always have an effect, but at run-time, disabled components are generally grayed, as you can see in Figures 6.8 and 6.9.

If you want to check to see how the disabled elements behave, you can run a program used to generate the two figures, named DISABLED (on the companion disk).

6

FIGURE 6.8:

The user interface of some common controls at design-time when they are enabled (on the left) and disabled (on the right)

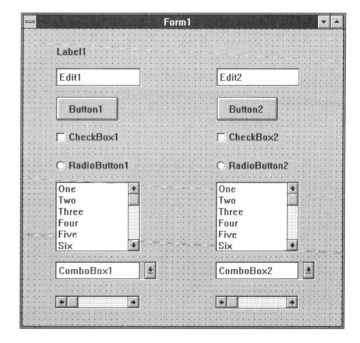

FIGURE 6.9:

The user interface with the same controls of Figure 6.8 at run-time

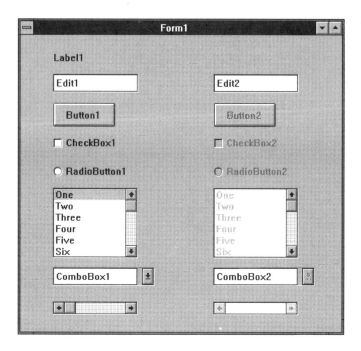

TIP

To disable all of the controls in the right column, you can simply select all of them and toggle the Enabled property of all the selected components at the same time.

If you want to take a more radical approach, you can completely hide a component, either by using the corresponding method or by setting its Visible property to False. Notice however, that reading the status of the Visible property does not tell you if the control is actually visible. In fact, if the container of a control is hidden, even if the control is set to Visible, you cannot see it. For this reason, there is another property, Showing, which is a run-time and read-only property. You can read the value of Showing to know if the control is really visible to the user; that is, if it is visible, its parent control is visible, the parent control of the parent control is visible, and so on.

The Tag Property

The Tag property is a strange one, because it has no effect at all. It is merely an extra memory location, present in each component class, where you can store custom values. The kind of information stored and the way it is used are completely up to you.

It is often useful to have an extra memory location to attach information to a component, without needing to define your component class. Technically speaking, the Tag property stores a long integer, which can be a number by itself or the number of the entry of an array or list corresponding to an object. Using typecasting, in the Tag property, you can store a pointer, an object, or anything else that is four bytes wide. This allows a programmer to associate virtually anything with the component using its tag.

NOTE   Experienced MS Windows programmers might find a relationship between the Tag property of Delphi components and the extra bytes attached to windows. Both elements can be used to associate some user-defined information with a predefined structure, but the similarities end soon. Using Delphi's Tag property is much easier than using extra bytes, and is also a lot faster than digging up the Windows extra bytes.

Properties Related to Color and Font

Two properties often used to customize the user interface of a component are Color and Font. There are several properties related to the color. The Color property itself usually refers to the background color of the component. Also, there is the Color attribute of fonts and many other graphic elements.

Many components also have a ParentColor and a ParentFont property, indicating whether the control should use the current font and color of the parent component, usually the form. You can use these properties to change the font of each control of a form by setting only the Font property of the form itself.

Notice that when you set a font, either by entering values for the attributes of the property in the Object Inspector or by using the standard font selection dialog box, you can choose one of the fonts installed in the system.

The fact that Delphi allows you to use all the fonts installed on your system has both advantages and drawbacks. The main advantage is that if you have a number of nice fonts installed, your program can use all of them. The drawback is that these fonts might not be available on the computers of the users of your application.

If your program uses a font that your user doesn't have, Windows will select some other font to use in its place. In some cases, they might see just plain fonts when running the program. At times, the nice output of a program can be ruined by the font substitution. For this reason, you should probably rely only on the MS Windows standard fonts (System, Arial, Times New Roman, and so on). The alternative is to ship some fonts with your application.

When you set the value of a color, you have a number of options. The type of this property is TColor. This type allows you to choose a value from a series of predefined constants or to enter a value directly.

You can specify the name of a color, using one of the *clXXX* constants, to try to use the closest matching color in the system palette. The following are the possible values:

- clAqua
- clBlack
- clBlue
- clDkGray
- clFuchsia
- clGray
- clGreen
- clLime
- clLtGray
- clMaroon
- clNavy
- clOlive
- clPurple
- clRed

- clSilver
- clTeal
- clWhite
- clYellow

As an alternative, you can use one of the colors used by Windows for system elements, such as the background of a window, a highlighted menu, the active caption, and so on. You can see a list of these values, along with a short description, in Table 6.2.

TABLE 6.2: Colors Used by MS Windows for System Elements

Name	Applies To
clActiveBorder	Border color of the active window
clActiveCaption	Color of the title bar of the active window
clAppWorkSpace	Color of the application work space
clBackground	Color of your Windows background
clBtnFace	Color of a button face
clBtnHighlight	Color of the highlighting on a button
clBtnShadow	Color of a shadow cast by a button
clBtnText	Color of text on a button
clCaptionText	Color of the text on the title bar of the active window
clGrayText	Color of text that is dimmed
clHighlight	Background color of selected text
clHightlightText	Color of selected text
clInactiveBorder	Border color of inactive windows
clInactiveCaption	Color of the title bar of inactive windows
clInactiveCaptionText	Color of the text on the title bar of an inactive window
clMenu	Background color of menus
clMenuText	Color of text on menus
clWindow	Background color of windows
clWindowFrame	Color of window frames
clWindowText	Color of text in windows

6

Another option is to specify TColor as a number (a four-byte hexadecimal value) instead of using a predefined value. If you use this approach, you should know that the low three bytes of this number represent RGB color intensities for blue, green, and red, respectively. For example, $00FF0000 corresponds to a pure blue color, $0000FF00 to green, $000000FF to red, $00000000 to black, and $00FFFFFF to white. Specifying intermediate values, you can obtain any of the 16 million possible colors.

Instead of using these hexadecimal values directly, I suggest that you use the RGB function, which has three parameters ranging from 0 to 255, the first for the amount of red, the second for the amount of green, and the last for the amount of blue. Using RGB makes the programs slightly more readable than using a single hexadecimal constant.

NOTE RGB is *almost* a Windows API function. It is defined by the Windows related units, and not by Delphi units, but a similar function does not exist in the Windows API. In C, there is a macro that has the same name and effect, so this is a welcome addition to the Pascal interface to Windows.

The highest-order byte of the TColor type is used to indicate which palette should be searched for the closest matching color, but this is far too advanced a topic to discuss here. It is also used by sophisticated imaging programs to carry transparency information for each display element on the screen.

Regarding palettes and color matching, just notice that sometimes the color is matched by MS Windows using the closest available solid color, at least in video modes that use a palette. This is always the case with fonts, lines, and so on.

Other times, MS Windows uses a dithering technique to mimic the requested color by drawing a tight pattern of pixels with the available colors. In 16-color adapters (VGA), but also at higher resolution, you often end up seeing confused patterns of pixels of different colors, and not the color you had in mind.

Component Methods

Component methods are just like any other methods. There are procedures and functions related to an object you can call to perform the corresponding action. As I already mentioned, you can often use methods to accomplish the same effect as reading or writing a property.

Usually, the code is easier to read and to understand when you use properties. However, not all of the methods actually have corresponding properties. Most of them are procedures, which actually execute an action, instead of reading or writing a value.

Again, there are some methods available in all of the components, other methods that are shared only by controls (visual components), and so on. Table 6.3 lists some common component methods.

6

TABLE 6.3: Some Methods Available for Most Components or Controls

Method	Available For	Description
BeginDrag	All controls	Starts manual dragging
BringToFront	All controls	Puts the component in front of all others
CanFocus	All controls	Determines if the control can receive the focus
ClientToScreen	All controls	Translates screen coordinates
ContainsControl	All windowed controls	Determines if a certain control is contained by the current one
Create	All objects and components	Creates a new instance
Destroy	All objects and components	Destroys the instance (if you have used Create to build the object, it is better to use the Free method instead of Destroy)
Dragging	All controls	Indicates if the controls are being dragged
EndDrag	All controls	Manually terminates dragging
FindComponent	All components	Returns the component in the Components array property having a given name
Focused	All windowed controls	Determines if the control has the focus

TABLE 6.3: Some Methods Available for Most Components or Controls (continued)

Method	Available For	Description
Free	All objects and components (not suggested for forms)	Deletes the instance and its associated memory (forms should use the Release method instead)
GetTextBuf	All controls	Retrieves the text or caption of the control
GetTextLen	All controls	Returns the length of the text or caption of the control
HandleAllocated	All controls	Returns True if the handle of the control exists
HandleNeeded	All controls	Creates a handle if one doesn't already exist
Hide	All controls	Makes the control not visible
InsertComponent	All components	Adds a new element to the list of owned components
InsertControl	All controls	Adds a new element to the list of controls that are the child of the current one
Invalidate	All controls	Forces a repaint of the control
RemoveComponent	All components	Removes a component from the Components list
ScaleBy	All controls	Scales the control a given percentage
ScreenToClient	All controls	Translates screen coordinates
ScrollBy	All controls	Scrolls the contents of the control
SendToBack	All controls	Puts the component behind all the others
SetBounds	All controls	Changes the position and the size of the control (faster than accessing the related properties one by one)
SetFocus	All controls	Gives the input focus to the control
SetTextBuf	All controls	Sets the control text or caption
Show	All controls	Makes the control visible
Update	All controls	Immediately repaints the control, but only if a repaint operation has been requested (that is, after a call to the Invalidate method)

Component Events

When a user takes an action on a component, such as clicking on it, the component generates an event. Other times, events are generated by the system, as a response to a method call or a property change on that component (or even on a different one). For example, if you set the focus on a component, the component currently having the focus loses it, triggering the corresponding event.

Technically, Delphi events are triggered when a corresponding Windows message is received, although the events do not match the messages on a one-to-one basis. Delphi events tend to be higher level than Windows messages, as is the case in the mouse-dragging area (there are no specific mouse-dragging events in Windows).

Just as there is a set of properties common to all components, so there are some events that are available for all components. Table 6.4 provides short descriptions of these events.

6

Delegation Is the Key

From a theoretical point of view, an event is the result of a message sent to a window, and this window (or the corresponding component) is allowed to respond to the message. Following this approach, to handle the click event of a button, we need to subclass the TButton class and add the new event handler.

In practice, creating a new class is too complex to be a reasonable solution. In Delphi, the event handler of a component usually is a method of the form that holds that component, not of the component itself. In other words, the component delegates its owner to handle its events.

Events Are Properties

Another important concept is that events are properties. This means that you can handle an event of a component, but also assign a method to it (or check the currently assigned method). This is exactly what happens when you handle an event for a component: a new method is added to the owner form, and this method is assigned to the proper event property.

TABLE 6.4: Some Events Available for Most Components

Event	Available For	Description
OnChange	Many objects and components	Occurs when the object (or its content) changes
OnClick	Many controls	Occurs when the left mouse button is clicked over the component
OnDblClick	Many controls	Occurs when the user double-clicks with the mouse over the component
OnDragDrop	Many controls	Occurs when a dragging operation terminates over the component
OnDragOver	Many controls	Occurs when the user is dragging over the component
OnEndDrag	Many controls	Occurs when the dragging terminates, and is sent to the component that started the dragging operation
OnEnter	All windowed controls	Occurs when the component is activated; that is, the component receives the focus
OnExit	All windowed controls	Occurs when the component loses the focus
OnKeyDown	Many controls	Occurs when the user presses a key of the keyboard, and is sent to the component having the focus
OnKeyPress	Many controls	Occurs when the user presses a key, and is sent to the component having the focus
OnKeyUp	Many controls	Occurs when the user releases a key, and is sent to the component having the focus
OnMouseDown	Many controls	Occurs when the user presses one of the mouse buttons, and is generally sent to the component under the mouse cursor
OnMouseMove	Many controls	Occurs when the user moves the mouse over a component
OnMouseUp	Many controls	Occurs when the user releases one of the mouse buttons

For this reason, it is possible for several events to share the same event handler, but also to change an event handler at run-time, as I mentioned in Chapter 5 (in the section titled "Method Pointers").

Using Delphi Collections

Among the various objects (that is, the noncomponent classes), an important group is collections. There are basically three different collection classes:

- TList defines a list of objects of any class. The list actually stores pointers to the objects. A list is far more flexible than an array, since it can be expanded and reduced at run-time.

- TStrings is an abstract class to represent all forms of string lists, regardless of what their storage implementations are. This class defines a list of strings, without providing proper storage. For this reason, TStrings objects are used only as properties of components capable of storing the strings themselves, such as a list box.

- TStringList defines a list of strings with their own storage. You can use this class to define your own lists of strings in a program.

6

NOTE   TListbox actually uses a TStringList object when it needs to store strings while its window handle is invalid or a TStrings object when it relates to a MS Windows list box control, which stores its own strings. Making all string list properties use the same abstract type allows you to copy data between different string lists, copying the actual strings between components and not just assigning string list pointers.

All these lists have a number of methods and properties. You can operate on lists using the array notation, [and], both to read and to change elements. There are other properties, including a Count property, as well as typical access methods, such as Add, Insert, Delete, Remove, and Search methods (for example, IndexOf, First, and Last).

Notice that TStringList and TStrings objects have both a list of strings and a list of objects associated with the strings. This opens up a number of different uses for these classes. For example, you can use them for dictionaries of associated objects or to store bitmaps or other elements to be used in a list box.

The two classes of lists of strings also have some ready-to-use methods to store or load their contents to or from a text file. To iterate on a list, you can use a simple for loop based on its index, as if it were an array (or, as an alternative, use the List property). Here is how you can operate on each of the objects of type MyClass stored in AList:

```
for Index := 0 to AList.Count - 1 do
  with AList[Index] as MyClass do
  begin
    {operate on the object}
  end;
```

The VCL Source Code

In this chapter, we have just scratched the surface of the VCL. To learn more about the library classes—the components—just go on reading the book. Of course, you can also use the Delphi Help system, which includes a complete reference to the properties, events, and methods of every component, together with the description of the most common tasks and operations.

If you really want to delve into the details and study the implementation of the components, there is another path to explore: the VCL source code. This is included in the Client/Server edition of Delphi, but is also available as a separate purchase for owners of the Delphi Desktop edition.

Delphi comes with the source code of the run-time library (RTL) and the VCL library. Only the source code of a couple of components, TTabSet and TTabbedNotebook, is not present for copyright reasons. These components are available on request to registered owners of the VCL source code package. You can freely peruse the VCL source code if you want to understand what goes on in detail.

However, do not take this approach to learn how to *use* components. Looking at the source code is useful for learning how to write new components and how to extend existing ones. Before you attempt this, you should be fluent in Delphi programming, and also in MS Windows programming, with a complete knowledge of the API of the environment.

If you want to spend some time browsing through Delphi source code, consider using some tool, instead of loading the files in an editor. To let other tools see the VCL source code, you need to set its path (usually C:\DELPHI\SOURCE\VCL) for the Search Path option in the Directories page of the Project Options. By rebuilding the project, it will be compiled using the source code, which takes some more time.

The advantage is that now you can use the integrated debugger to trace the execution both through your code and the VCL source code. Another tool you can use is the Browser, which indicates where in the source code each class is defined and referenced, and allows you to open the editor on the proper file (and the right line) with a click of the left mouse button.

Summary

As we have seen in this chapter, Delphi includes a full-scale class library that is just as complete as Borland's OWL or Microsoft's MFC C++ class libraries. Delphi VCL, of course, is much more component-oriented, and it encapsulates the behavior of the operating system in a hierarchy of higher-level classes than the C++ libraries do.

As you can tell from the length of this chapter, a great advantage of VCL and of Delphi is that you are not required to know the structure of the hierarchy of classes to use the components. You only need a clear understanding of the leaf nodes of the tree; that is, the components you are going to use. You really don't need a deeper knowledge of the VCL internals to use components; this knowledge is only necessary to write new components or modify existing ones.

Another reason that this chapter is short is that I've discussed components in general, without providing real examples. The following chapters are devoted to exploring most of the Delphi predefined components.

PART II

Using Components

CHAPTER

SEVEN

A Tour of the Basic Components

- Clicking a button or another component

- Adding colored text to a form

- Dragging from one component to another

- Accepting input from the user

- Creating a simple editor

- Making a choice with radio buttons and list boxes

- Allowing multiple selections

- Choosing a value in a range

After an introduction to the use of the environment and an overview of the Object Pascal language and the Visual Component Library, we are ready to delve into the most important part of the book: the use of components. This is really what Delphi is about. Visual programming using components is the key feature of this development environment.

The system comes with a number of ready-to-use components. I will not describe every component in detail, examining each of its properties and methods. If you need this information, you can find it easily in the Help system. The aim of Part III of this book is to show you how to use some of the features offered by the Delphi predefined components to build applications. In fact, this chapter and those following will be based heavily on sample programs. These examples tend to be quite simple—although I've tried to make them meaningful—to focus on only a couple of features at a time. In future chapters, I'll try to show you some more complex examples.

I'll start by focusing on a number of basic components, all present in the Standard page of the Delphi Components palette. However, I'm not going to describe all the components of this page. My approach will be to discuss, in each chapter, logically related components, ignoring the order suggested by the pages of the Components palette.

Windows' Own Components

You might have asked yourself where the idea of using components for Windows programming came from. The answer is simple: Windows itself has some components, usually called controls. A *control* is technically a predefined window with a specific behavior, some properties, and some methods. These controls are not as simple to use in a program as Delphi components, but they were the first step in this direction. The second step was probably Visual Basic controls, and the third step is the Delphi components.

Windows 3.1 has six kinds of predefined controls, generally used inside dialog boxes. They are buttons (push buttons, check boxes, and radio buttons), static labels, edit fields, list boxes, combo boxes, and scroll bars. There is also a seventh kind of predefined window in the system, used to build MDI applications, and some others that are not documented.

These controls are the basic components of each Windows application, regardless of the programming language used to write it, and are very well known by every Windows user. Delphi literally wraps these Windows predefined controls in some of its basic components—the components discussed in this chapter.

NOTE Windows 95 will have new kinds of standard controls, including graphical list boxes, more powerful text editors, and notebooks with tabs. Most of these controls, or very similar ones, are already available in Delphi.

Clicking a Button

In the first part of this book, we built small applications based on a button. Clicking that button caused a "Hello" message to appear on the screen. The only other operation that program performed was moving the button so that it always appeared in the middle of the form.

Now we are going to build another form, with several buttons, and change some of their properties at run-time; clicking a button will usually change a property of another button.

To rebuild the BUTTONS program, I suggest you follow the instructions closely at first and then make any changes you want. Of course, you can read the description in the book and then work on the source files on the companion disk.

The BUTTONS Example

First, open a new project and give it a name by saving it to disk. I've given the name BUTTON_F.PAS to the unit describing the form and the name BUTTONS.DPR to the project.

Now you can create a number of buttons, let's say six. Instead of selecting the component, dragging it to the form, and then selecting it again and repeating the operation, you can take a shortcut. Simply select the component by clicking on the Components palette while holding down the Shift key. The component will remain selected, as indicated by a little border around it. Now you can create a number of instances of that component.

Even if you use the grid behind the form, you might need to use the Edit Align command to arrange the buttons properly.

Remember that to select all six buttons at a time, you can either drag a rectangle around them or select them in turn, holding down the Shift key. In this case, it's probably better to select a column of three buttons at a time and arrange them as shown in Figure 7.1.

Now that we have a form with six buttons, we can start to set their properties. First of all, we can give the form a name (ButtonsForm) and a caption (Buttons). The next step is to set the text, or captions, of the buttons. Usually, a button's caption describes the action performed when a user clicks on it. We want to follow this rule, adding the number of the button at the beginning of each caption. So if the first button disables button number four (which is the one on the same row), we can name it *1: Disable 4*. Following the same rule, we can create captions for buttons 2 and 4, which copy their font to another button, and button 5, which hides button 2. See the captions and other properties of these components in Listing 7.1. We can use the last two buttons (numbered 3 and 6) to enlarge or shrink button 6.

FIGURE 7.1:

The six aligned buttons used to build the example

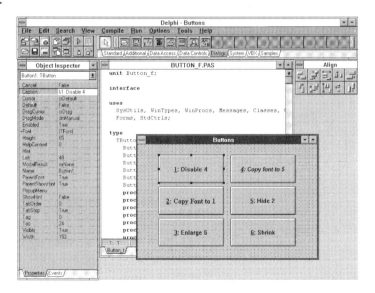

LISTING 7.1: The design-time properties of the components of the BUTTONS example, as indicated in the textual description of its main form

```
object ButtonsForm: TButtonsForm
  ActiveControl = Button1
  Caption = 'Buttons'
  OnCreate = FormCreate
  object Button1: TButton
    Caption = '&1: Disable 4'
    TabOrder = 0
    OnClick = Button1Click
  end
  object Button2: TButton
    Caption = '&2: Copy Font to 1'
    Font.Color = clBlack
    Font.Height = -16
    Font.Name = 'Times New Roman'
    Font.Style = [fsBold]
    ParentFont = False
    TabOrder = 1
    OnClick = Button2Click
  end
  object Button3: TButton
    Caption = '&3: Enlarge 6'
    Font.Color = clBlack
    Font.Height = -13
    Font.Name = 'System'
    Font.Style = [fsBold]
    ParentFont = False
    TabOrder = 2
    OnClick = Button3Click
  end
  object Button4: TButton
    Caption = '&4: Copy font to 5'
    Font.Color = clBlack
    Font.Height = -13
    Font.Name = 'Arial'
    Font.Style = [fsBold, fsItalic]
    ParentFont = False
    TabOrder = 3
    OnClick = Button4Click
  end
  object Button5: TButton
    Caption = '&5: Hide 2'
    TabOrder = 4
    OnClick = Button5Click
  end
  object Button6: TButton
    Caption = '&6: Shrink'
    TabOrder = 5
    OnClick = Button6Click
  end
end
```

7

TIP   Notice that every button has an underlined shortcut key, in this case the number of the button. Simply by placing an ampersand (&) character in front of each caption, we can create buttons that can be used with the keyboard. Just press a number below 7, and one of the buttons will be selected, although you won't see it pressed and released.

The final step, of course, is to write the code to provide the desired behavior. We want to handle the OnClick property of each button. The easiest code is that of buttons 2 and 4. Here is one of them:

```
Button1.Font := Button2.Font;
```

To implement the disable and the hide operations, we need a Boolean variable to store the current status; in fact, the same button is also used for the reverse operation. When one of these two buttons is clicked, it should change the status of the other button, change its own title to indicate the new action, and set the value of the Boolean variable (see Figure 7.2 for an example and Listing 7.2 for the actual code).

FIGURE 7.2:

In the BUTTONS form, you can hide or disable some buttons.

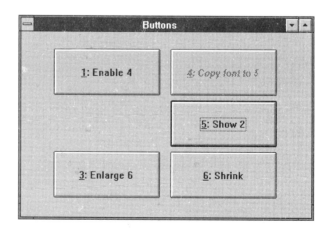

To compile this code, you need to declare the variable Disabled in the form's private data and add a statement to give it a startup value in the OnCreate event of the form.

LISTING 7.2: The complete source code listing of the BUTTONS example

```
unit Button_f;

interface

uses
  SysUtils, WinTypes, WinProcs, Messages, Classes, Graphics,
  Controls, Forms, StdCtrls;

type
  TButtonsForm = class(TForm)
    Button1: TButton;
    Button2: TButton;
    Button3: TButton;
    Button4: TButton;
    Button5: TButton;
    Button6: TButton;
    procedure Button2Click(Sender: TObject);
    procedure Button4Click(Sender: TObject);
    procedure Button3Click(Sender: TObject);
    procedure Button1Click(Sender: TObject);
    procedure FormCreate(Sender: TObject);
    procedure Button5Click(Sender: TObject);
    procedure Button6Click(Sender: TObject);
  private
    { Private declarations }
    Disabled: Boolean;
    Hidden: Boolean;
  public
    { Public declarations }
  end;

var
  ButtonsForm: TButtonsForm;

implementation

{$R *.DFM}

procedure TButtonsForm.Button2Click(Sender: TObject);
begin
  Button1.Font := Button2.Font;
end;

procedure TButtonsForm.Button4Click(Sender: TObject);
begin
  Button5.Font := Button4.Font;
end;
```

LISTING 7.2: The complete source code listing of the BUTTONS example (continued)

```
procedure TButtonsForm.Button3Click(Sender: TObject);
begin
  Button6.Height := Button6.Height + 3;
  Button6.Width := Button6.Width + 3;
end;

procedure TButtonsForm.Button1Click(Sender: TObject);
begin
  if Disabled then
  begin
    Button4.Enabled := True;
    Button1.Caption := '&1: Disable 4';
    Disabled := False;
  end
  else
  begin
    Button4.Enabled := False;
    Button1.Caption := '&1: Enable 4';
    Disabled := True;
  end;
end;

procedure TButtonsForm.FormCreate(Sender: TObject);
begin
  Disabled := False;
  Hidden := False;
end;

procedure TButtonsForm.Button5Click(Sender: TObject);
begin
  if Hidden then
  begin
    Button2.Visible := True;
    Button5.Caption := '&5: Hide 2';
    Hidden := False;
  end
  else
  begin
    Button2.Visible := False;
    Button5.Caption := '&5: Show 2';
    Hidden := True;
  end;
end;

procedure TButtonsForm.Button6Click(Sender: TObject);
begin
  Button6.Height := Button6.Height - 3;
  Button6.Width := Button6.Width - 3;
end;

end.
```

The last two buttons have *unconstrained* code. This means that you can shrink button 6 so much that it will eventually disappear completely (in Figure 7.3 you can see the button reduced to a minimum size). It would have been quite easy, in any case, to check the current size of the button and prevent its reduction or enlargement by more than a certain value. If you haven't already done it, you can take a look at the complete source code of the example in Listing 7.2.

FIGURE 7.3:

The shrink function is unlimited, so the button might eventually disappear completely.

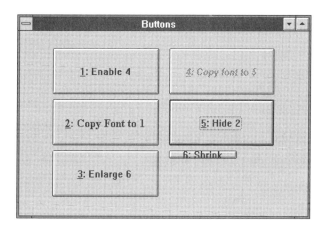

Clicking the Mouse on a Component

Up to now we have based the examples on the OnClick event of buttons. Almost every component has a similar click event. But what exactly is a click? And how is it related to other events, such as OnMouseDown and OnMouseUp?

First, consider the click. At first sight you might think that to generate a click, a user has to press and release the left mouse button on the control. This is certainly true, but the situation is more complex: when the user clicks the left mouse button on a button component, the component is graphically pressed, too. However, if the user moves the cursor (holding down the left mouse button) outside the button surface, this button will be released. If the user now releases the left mouse button outside the button area, no effect—no click—takes place. On the other hand, if the user places the cursor back on the button, it will be *pressed* again, and when the mouse button is released, the click will occur. If this is not clear, experiment with a button; any button in any Windows application will do.

Now to the second question. In Windows, the behavior just described is typical of buttons, although Delphi has extended it to most components, as well as to forms. In any case, the system generates more basic events—one each time a mouse button is pressed, and another each time a button is released. In Delphi, these events are called MouseDown and MouseUp.

Since the mouse has more than one button, these same events are generated when the user presses either the left mouse button or the right mouse button (or even the middle mouse button if your input device has one and the driver you have installed handles it).

Since you might want different actions to occur depending on the mouse button that has been pressed or released, these event handlers include a parameter indicating which button was pressed. These methods also include another parameter, indicating whether some special key (such as Shift or Ctrl) has been pressed and, finally, two more values indicating the x and y positions where the action took place. The method corresponding to this event for a form is:

```
procedure TForm1.FormMouseDown(
   Sender: TObject;
   Button: TMouseButton;
   Shift: TShiftState;
   X, Y: Integer);
```

Most of the time, we do not need such a detailed view, and handling the mouse-click event is probably more appropriate. In Chapter 9, I'll show you a more detailed example of mouse input.

Adding Colored Text to a Form

Now that you have played with buttons for a while, it's time to move to a new component, labels. *Labels* are just text, or comments, written in a form. Usually, the user doesn't interact with a label at all—or at least not directly. It doesn't make much sense to click on a label.

We use labels to provide descriptions of other components, particularly edit fields and list or combo boxes, because they have no titles. If you open a dialog box in any Windows application, you'll probably see some text. These are *static controls* (in Windows terms) or *labels* (in Delphi terms).

> **NOTE** Windows implements labels as windows of the static class. Delphi, instead, implements labels as non-windowed components. This is very important since it allows you to speed up form creation and save some Windows resources.

Besides using labels for descriptions, we can use instances of this component to improve and add some color to the user interface of our application. This is what we are going to do in the next example, LABEL_CO. The basic idea of this application is to test a couple of properties of the label component at run-time. Specifically, we want to alter the color of the label, the color of its font, and the alignment of the text.

The LABEL_CO Example

The first thing to do is to place a big label in the form and enter some text. Write something long. I suggest you set the WordWrap property to True, to have several lines of text, and the AutoSize property to False, to allow the label to be resized freely. It might also be a good idea to select a large font, to choose a color for the font, and to select a color for the label.

To change some of the properties of the label at run-time, we can use some buttons. We need a couple to change the colors and three more to select the alignment—left, center, or right. The resulting form is shown in Figure 7.4 and the corresponding textual description in Listing 7.3.

Now it's time to write some code. The click methods for the three alignment buttons are very simple. The program has to change the alignment of the label, as in:

```
Label1.Alignment := taLeftJustify;
```

The other two methods should use the values `taCenter` and `taRightJustify` instead of `taLeftJustify`. You can find the names of these three choices in the Alignment property of the label, in the Object Inspector.

FIGURE 7.4:

The form of the colored label
example

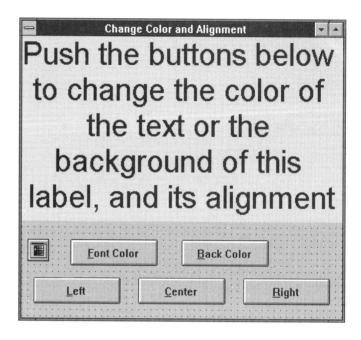

Writing some code to change the color is a little more complex. In fact, we can provide a new value for the color, maybe choosing it from a list with a series of possible
values. We might solve this problem, for example, by declaring an array of colors,
entering a number of values, and then selecting a different element of the array each
time. However, I'll apply a different and more professional solution, which needs
even less code: using the Windows standard dialog box to select a color.

The Standard Color Dialog Box

To use the standard Color dialog box, move to the Dialogs page of the Delphi Components palette. Select the ColorDialog component and place it anywhere on the
form. The position has no effect since at run-time this component is not visible inside the form. (A more detailed presentation of these standard dialog boxes will be
presented in Chapter 12, although I'll use them often before.)

LISTING 7.3: The textual description of the form of the LABEL_CO example

```
object ColorTextForm: TColorTextForm
  Caption = 'Change Color and Alignment'
  object Label1: TLabel
    Alignment = taCenter
    AutoSize = False
    Caption = 'Push the buttons below to change the color of the text or
the background of this label, and its alignment'
    Color = clYellow
    Font.Color = clNavy
    Font.Height = -40
    Font.Name = 'Arial'
    ParentColor = False
    ParentFont = False
    WordWrap = True
  end
  object FontColorButton: TButton
    Caption = '&Font Color'
    OnClick = FontColorButtonClick
  end
  object BackColorButton: TButton
    Caption = '&Back Color'
    OnClick = BackColorButtonClick
  end
  object AlignLeftButton: TButton
    Caption = '&Left'
    OnClick = AlignLeftButtonClick
  end
  object CenterButton: TButton
    Caption = '&Center'
    OnClick = CenterButtonClick
  end
  object RightButton: TButton
    Caption = '&Right'
    OnClick = RightButtonClick
  end
  object ColorDialog1: TColorDialog
    Color = clBlack
    Options = []
  end
end
```

7

Now we can use the component, writing the following code:

```
ColorDialog1.Color := Label1.Color;
ColorDialog1.Execute;
Label1.Color := ColorDialog1.Color;
```

The three lines have the following meanings: with the first, we select, as the color of the label, the current color displayed by the dialog box; with the second, we run the dialog box; with the third, the color selected by the user in the dialog box is copied back to the label. You can see the dialog box in action in Figure 7.5. This dialog box can also be expanded by clicking on the Define Custom Colors button.

FIGURE 7.5:

The dialog box used to select the color of the label and its text (in this case, the user is changing the color of the text)

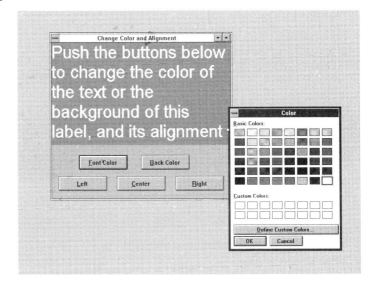

To change the color of the label's text, we have to write a similar piece of code, referring this time to the `Label1.Font.Color` property. You can see the complete source code of this example in Listing 7.4

LISTING 7.4: The source code of the LABEL_CO example

```
unit Label_f;

interface

uses
  SysUtils, WinTypes, WinProcs, Messages, Classes, Graphics,
  Controls, Forms, Dialogs, StdCtrls;

type
  TColorTextForm = class(TForm)
    Label1: TLabel;
    FontColorButton: TButton;
    BackColorButton: TButton;
    AlignLeftButton: TButton;
    CenterButton: TButton;
    RightButton: TButton;
    ColorDialog1: TColorDialog;
    procedure FontColorButtonClick(Sender: TObject);
    procedure BackColorButtonClick(Sender: TObject);
    procedure AlignLeftButtonClick(Sender: TObject);
    procedure CenterButtonClick(Sender: TObject);
    procedure RightButtonClick(Sender: TObject);
  private

  public

  end;

var
  ColorTextForm: TColorTextForm;

implementation

{$R *.DFM}

procedure TColorTextForm.FontColorButtonClick(Sender: TObject);
begin
  ColorDialog1.Color := Label1.Font.Color;
  ColorDialog1.Execute;
  Label1.Font.Color := ColorDialog1.Color;
end;

procedure TColorTextForm.BackColorButtonClick(Sender: TObject);
begin
  ColorDialog1.Color := Label1.Color;
  ColorDialog1.Execute;
  Label1.Color := ColorDialog1.Color;
end;
```

LISTING 7.4: The source code of the LABEL_CO example (continued)

```
procedure TColorTextForm.AlignLeftButtonClick(Sender: TObject);
begin
  Label1.Alignment := taLeftJustify;
end;

procedure TColorTextForm.CenterButtonClick(Sender: TObject);
begin
  Label1.Alignment := taCenter;
end;

procedure TColorTextForm.RightButtonClick(Sender: TObject);
begin
  Label1.Alignment := taRightJustify;
end;

end.
```

Dragging from One Component to Another

Before I introduce you to another component, I would like to devote a section to a particular technique, *dragging*. The dragging operation is quite simple and is increasingly common in Windows. In Delphi, you usually perform this operation by pressing the mouse button on one component and releasing it on another component. When this operation occurs, you can provide some code, usually for copying a property, a value, or something else to the destination component.

As an example, consider the form in Figure 7.6. There are four color labels, with the name of each color as text, and a destination label, with some descriptive text. The aim of this example, named DRAGGING, is to be able to drag the color from one of the labels on the left to the big one, changing its color accordingly.

After preparing the labels by supplying the proper values for the names and caption, as well as a corresponding color (the list of values is shown in Listing 7.5), you have to enable dragging. You can do this by selecting the value dmAutomatic for the DragMode property of the four labels on the left and responding to a couple of events in the destination label.

FIGURE 7.6:

The form for the DRAGGING example

LISTING 7.5: The properties of the components of the DRAGGING example

7

```
object DraggingForm: TDraggingForm
  Caption = 'Dragging'
  object RedLabel: TLabel
    Alignment = taCenter
    AutoSize = False
    Caption = 'Red'
    Color = clRed
    DragMode = dmAutomatic
    Font.Color = clBlack
    Font.Height = -16
    Font.Name = 'Arial'
    Font.Style = [fsBold]
    ParentColor = False
    ParentFont = False
  end
  object AquaLabel: TLabel
    Alignment = taCenter
    AutoSize = False
    Caption = 'Aqua'
    Color = clAqua
    DragMode = dmAutomatic
    {Font and Parent properties as above}
  end
  object GreenLabel: TLabel
    Alignment = taCenter
    AutoSize = False
    Caption = 'Green'
    Color = clGreen
```

LISTING 7.5 : The properties of the components of the DRAGGING example (continued)

```
      DragMode = dmAutomatic
      {Font and Parent properties as above}
    end
    object YellowLabel: TLabel
      Alignment = taCenter
      AutoSize = False
      Caption = 'Yellow'
      Color = clYellow
      DragMode = dmAutomatic
      {Font and Parent properties as above}
    end
    object Label5: TLabel
      AutoSize = False
      Caption = 'Drag colors here to change the color'
      Font.Color = clBlack
      Font.Height = -32
      Font.Name = 'Arial'
      ParentFont = False
      OnDragDrop = Label5DragDrop
      OnDragOver = Label5DragOver
    end
end
```

> **NOTE**   As an alternative to automatic dragging, you might choose a manual dragging approach, based on the use of the BeginDrag and EndDrag methods. This technique will be shown in the NODES example in Chapter 10. Other examples in the book will show you how to handle dragging manually, simply by providing a handler for events related to moving the mouse and pressing and releasing mouse buttons.

The Code for the DRAGGING Example

The first event I want to consider is OnDragOver, which is called each time you are dragging and move the cursor over a component. This event indicates that the component accepts dragging. Usually, the event takes place after a determination of whether the Source component (the one that originated the dragging operation) is of a specific type:

```
procedure TDraggingForm.Label5DragOver(
  Sender, Source: TObject;
  X, Y: Integer; State: TDragState;
  var Accept: Boolean);
begin
  Accept := Source is TLabel;
end;
```

This code accepts the dragging operation, activating the corresponding cursor, only if the source object is really a label object. Notice the use of the is RTTI operator.

The second method we have to write corresponds to the OnDragDrop event:

```
procedure TDraggingForm.Label5DragDrop(
  Sender, Source: TObject;
  X, Y: Integer);
begin
  Label7.Color := (Source as TLabel).Color;
end;
```

To read the value of the Color property from the Source object, we need to cast this object to the proper data type, in this case TLabel. We have to perform a type conversion—technically speaking, a type downcast (a typecast from a base class to a derived class, down through the hierarchy). A type downcast is not always type safe. In fact, the idea behind this cast is that we receive the parameter Source of type TObject, which is really a label, and want to use it as a TLabel object, where TLabel is a class derived by TObject. However, in general, we face the risk of downcasting to TLabel an object that wasn't originally a label but, say, a button. When we start using the button as a label, we might have run-time errors.

In any case, using the as typecast, a type check is performed. Had the type of the Source object not been TLabel, an exception would have been raised.

In this particular case, however, we haven't much to worry about. In fact, the On-DragDrop event is received only when the Accept parameter of the OnDragOver method is set to True, and we make this only if the Source object really is a TLabel.

Accepting Input from the User

We have seen a number of ways a user can interact with the application we write: mouse clicks, mouse dragging, and so on. However, these examples involved only the mouse. What about the keyboard? We know that the user can use the keyboard instead of the mouse to select a button by pressing the key corresponding to the underlined letter of the caption (if any).

Aside from some particular cases, Windows can handle keyboard input directly. Defining handlers for keyboard-related events isn't a common operation, anyway. In fact, the system provides a ready-to-use control to build edit fields. Delphi has a slightly different approach, with two components, Edit and Memo.

An Edit component allows a single line of text and has some specific properties, such as one that allows only a limited number of characters or one that shows asterisks instead of the actual characters of the text (a useful technique for entering a password). A Memo component, as we will see later, can host several lines of text.

Our first example of the Edit component, named FOCUS, will stress a feature common to many controls, the focus. In Windows, it's fairly simple to determine which is the active main window: it is in front of the other windows, and the title bar is a different color (blue, by default). It is not as easy to determine which window (or component) has the *input* focus. If the user presses a key, what is going to receive the corresponding input message? It can be the active window, but it can also be one of its controls or subwindows. Consider a form with several edit fields. Only one has the focus at a given time. You can move the focus by using the Tab key or by clicking with the mouse on another component.

Handling the Input Focus

What's important for our example is that each time a component receives or loses the focus, it receives a corresponding event indicating that the user either has reached (OnEnter) or has left (OnExit) the component. So we can add some methods to the form to take control over the focus and display this information in a label. Other labels indicate the meaning of the edit fields (First name, Last name, and Password). You can see the values of the components' properties in Listing 7.6 and the form used for this example in Figure 7.7.

LISTING 7.6: The textual description of the form for the FOCUS example, including the
values of the TabOrder properties

```
object FocusForm: TFocusForm
  ActiveControl = FirstNameEdit
  Caption = 'Focus'
  object Label1: TLabel
    Caption = '&First name:'
    FocusControl = FirstNameEdit
  end
  object Label2: TLabel
    Caption = '&Last name:'
    FocusControl = LastNameEdit
  end
  object Label3: TLabel
    Caption = '&Password:'
    FocusControl = PasswordEdit
  end
  object ActionLabel: TLabel
    Caption = 'ActionLabel'
    Font.Color = clBlack
    Font.Height = -16
    Font.Name = 'Arial'
    Font.Style = [fsItalic]
    ParentFont = False
  end
  object FirstNameEdit: TEdit
    TabOrder = 0
    OnEnter = FirstNameEditEnter
  end
  object LastNameEdit: TEdit
    TabOrder = 1
    OnEnter = LastNameEditEnter
  end
  object PasswordEdit: TEdit
    TabOrder = 2
    OnEnter = PasswordEditEnter
    PasswordChar = '*'
  end
  object CopyButton: TButton
    TabOrder = 3
    OnEnter = CopyButtonEnter
    Caption = '&Copy Last Name to Title'
    OnClick = CopyButtonClick
  end
end
```

FIGURE 7.7:

The form of the FOCUS example

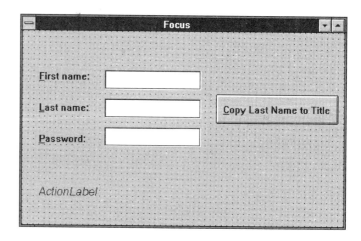

The form contains some edit boxes, as well as a button we can use to copy the text of the LastNameEdit to the form's caption. This is just a sample of how to use the text that has been entered. As you can see in the following code, it's a good idea to test whether some text has really been entered by the user or if the edit field is still empty:

```
procedure TFocusForm.CopyButtonClick(Sender: TObject);
begin
  if (LastNameEdit.Text <> '') then
    FocusForm.Caption := LastNameEdit.Text;
end;
```

Now to the most interesting part of the program. We can write a comment in the ActionLabel each time the focus is moved to a different control, as in Figure 7.8. To accomplish this, we need four methods, one for each of the Edit components and one for the button, referring to the OnEnter event. Here is their complete code:

```
procedure TFocusForm.FirstNameEditGotFocus(Sender: TObject);
begin
  ActionLabel.Caption := 'Entering the first name...';
end;


procedure TFocusForm.LastNameEditGotFocus(Sender: TObject);
begin
  ActionLabel.Caption := 'Entering the last name...';
end;
```

```
procedure TFocusForm.PasswordEditGotFocus(Sender: TObject);
begin
  ActionLabel.Caption := 'Entering the password...';
end;

procedure TFocusForm.CopyButtonGotFocus(Sender: TObject);
begin
  ActionLabel.Caption := 'Pressing the copy button...';
end;
```

FIGURE 7.8:

One of the messages shown when the FOCUS program is running. Notice the form's new caption.

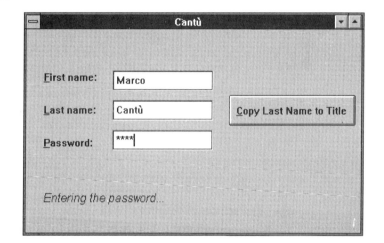

You can test this program with the mouse or use the keyboard. If you press the Tab key, the input focus cycles among the Edit components and the button, without involving the labels. To have a proper sequence, you can change the TabOrder property of the windowed component.

You can change this order either by entering a proper value for this property in the Object Inspector or (much better and easier) by using the Edit Tab Order dialog box, which can be called using the Tab Order command on the form's SpeedMenu. If you open this dialog box for the FOCUS example, you can see the output shown in Figure 7.9.

FIGURE 7.9:

The Edit Tab Order dialog box for the main form of the FOCUS example

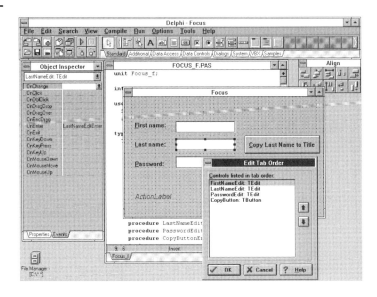

A second way to select a component is to use a shortcut key. It is easy to place a shortcut key on the button, but how can you jump directly to an edit? It isn't possible, but there is an indirect way. You can add the shortcut key—the ampersand (&)—to the label before the Edit component, then set the FocusControl property of the label, selecting the corresponding Edit component. You can see the values of these components in the textual description of the form shown earlier in Listing 7.6.

Entering Numbers

We saw in the previous example that it is very easy to use an Edit component to ask the user to input some text, although it must be limited to a single line. In general, it's quite common to ask the user to input a number, too. To accomplish this, you can use the MaskEdit component (in the Additional page of the Components palette), but in the following example, I'll try to use an Edit component and then convert the input string into an integer, using the standard Pascal `val` procedure.

This sounds good, but what if the user types a letter when a number is expected? Of course, the `val` procedure returns an error code, so we can use it to test whether the user has really entered a number. The second question is, when can we perform this test? Maybe when the value of the edit box changes, when the component loses the focus, or when the user clicks a particular button, such as the OK button in a dialog box. As you'll see, not all of these techniques work well.

There is another, radically different, solution to the problem of having only numerical input in an edit box. You can look at the input stream to the edit box and stop any nonnumerical input. This technique is not foolproof (a user can always paste some text into an edit box), but it works quite well and is easy to implement. Of course, you can improve it by combining it with one of the other techniques.

The next example, NUMBERS, shows just some of these techniques so you can compare them easily. Before you start working on it, however, remember that this is not the best way to handle numerical input; Delphi provides the MaskEdit component, as mentioned earlier. We will see an example of advanced input in Chapter 10.

First of all, build a form with five edit fields and five corresponding labels. As you can see in Figure 7.10, the labels describe either which kind of check is made by the corresponding Edit component or when the check is made. The form also has a button to check the contents of the first edit field.

Since the elements of this form have no particular properties, let's look directly to the code. The contents of the first edit box are checked when the button on the right is pressed. First of all, the text is converted into a number, using the val procedure, which eventually returns an error code:

```
val (Edit1.Text, Number, Code);
```

FIGURE 7.10:
The form of the NUMBERS example. The edit fields should accept only numbers as input.

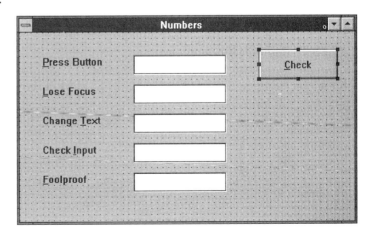

Depending on the value of the code, a message is shown to the user:

```
if Code <> 0 then
begin
  Edit1.SetFocus;
  MessageDlg ('Not a number in the first edit',
    mtError, [mbOK], 0);
end
else
  MessageDlg ('OK, in the first edit there is a number',
    mtInformation, [mbOK], 0);
```

If an error occurs, the application moves the focus back to the edit field before show-ing the error message to the user, thus inviting the user to correct the value. Of course, in this case a user can ignore this suggestion and move to another edit field.

WARNING   It is extremely important to move the focus to the edit box at the proper moment. If you exchange the order of the MessageDlg and SetFocus calls in the code segment above, the program won't behave as it should. Typically, you won't be able to move the focus correctly to the other edit boxes. This is not very intuitive (or well documented), but the order of these two calls really makes a lot of difference.

The same kind of check is made on the second edit field when it loses the focus, as you can see in Listing 7.7. In this case, the message is displayed automatically, but only if an error occurs (see Figure 7.11). Why bother the user if everything is fine?

The code is somewhat different from that of the first edit field; it makes no reference to the Edit2 component but always refers to the generic Sender control, making a safe typecast. This code is a little more complex to write, but we will be able to use it again for a different component. Aside from the name, in fact, it has no reference at all to the second Edit component, and the name is…just a name, so it's not that important. Also, the code related to the third and fourth edit boxes has no direct ref-erences to them.

The third Edit component makes a similar test each time its content changes. Al-though we have checked the input on different occasions—using different events—the three functions are very similar to each other. The idea is to check the string

FIGURE 7.11:

The error displayed when the second edit loses the focus and the user has entered letters

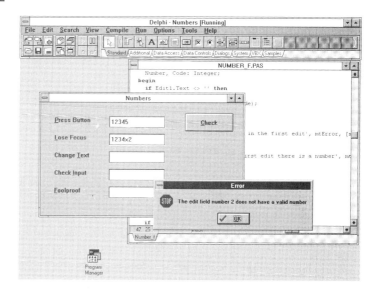

LISTING 7.7: The complete source code for the NUMBERS example

```
unit Number_f;

interface

uses
  SysUtils, WinTypes, WinProcs, Messages, Classes, Graphics,
  Controls, Forms, Dialogs, StdCtrls;

type
  TNumbersForm = class(TForm)
    Label1: TLabel;
    Edit1: TEdit;
    Label2: TLabel;
    Edit2: TEdit;
    Label3: TLabel;
    Edit3: TEdit;
    Label5: TLabel;
    Edit5: TEdit;
    Label4: TLabel;
    Edit4: TEdit;
    CheckButton: TButton;
    procedure CheckButtonClick(Sender: TObject);
    procedure Edit2Exit(Sender: TObject);
    procedure Edit3Change(Sender: TObject);
    procedure Edit4KeyPress(Sender: TObject; var Key: Char);
```

LISTING 7.7: The complete source code for the NUMBERS example (continued)

```
  private
    { Private declarations }
  public
    { Public declarations }
  end;

var
  NumbersForm: TNumbersForm;

implementation

{$R *.DFM}

procedure TNumbersForm.CheckButtonClick(Sender: TObject);
var
  Number, Code: Integer;
begin
  if Edit1.Text <> '' then
  begin
    val (Edit1.Text, Number, Code);
    if Code <> 0 then
    begin
      Edit1.SetFocus;
      MessageDlg ('Not a number in the first edit',
        mtError, [mbOK], 0);
    end
    else
      MessageDlg ('OK, in the first edit there is a number',
        mtInformation, [mbOK], 0);
  end;
end;

procedure TNumbersForm.Edit2Exit(Sender: TObject);
var
  Number, Code: Integer;
begin
  if (Sender as TEdit).Text <> '' then
  begin
    val ((Sender as TEdit).Text, Number, Code);
    if Code <> 0 then
    begin
      (Sender as TEdit).SetFocus;
      MessageDlg ('The edit field number ' +
        IntToStr ((Sender as TEdit).Tag) +
        ' does not have a valid number',
        mtError, [mbOK], 0);
    end
  end;
end;
```

LISTING 7.7: The complete source code for the NUMBERS example (continued)

```
procedure TNumbersForm.Edit3Change(Sender: TObject);
var
  Number, Code: Integer;
begin
  if (Sender as TEdit).Text <> '' then
  begin
    val ((Sender as TEdit).Text, Number, Code);
    if Code <> 0 then

    MessageDlg ('The edit field number ' +
        IntToStr ((Sender as TEdit).Tag) +
        ' does not have a valid number',
        mtError, [mbOK], 0);
  end;
end;

procedure TNumbersForm.Edit4KeyPress(Sender: TObject;
  var Key: Char);
begin
  {check if the key is a number or backspace}
  if not (key in ['0'..'9', #8]) then
  begin
    Key := #0;
    MessageBeep ($FFFF);
    {this hexadecimal value is -1 as integer,
    or 65535 as word}
  end;
end;

end.
```

once the user has entered it. For the fourth Edit component, instead, I want to show you a completely different technique: We are going to make a check *before* the Edit even knows that a key has been pressed.

The Edit component has an event, OnKeyPress, that corresponds to the action of the user. We can provide a method for this event and test whether the character is a number or the Backspace key (which has a numerical value of 8). If not, we change the value of the key to Null so it won't be processed by the edit control and produce a little warning sound using the MessageBeep function of the Windows API, as you can see in Listing 7.7.

TIP   The parameter of the `MessageBeep` function needs some explanation. If you look it up in the Windows API reference—just press the F1 key while the cursor is on the name of the function—its description indicates that the value of −1 should be used to produce a short beep (other values involve the installed sound board, so I won't consider them). However, if you write −1 in the code, the Object Pascal compiler will flag an error. In fact, −1 is a negative value, and the parameter is a Word—that is, an unsigned integer. It turns out that you can obtain the same value with the hexadecimal number FFFF, which is 64K minus 1, or 65,535. Using either of these values will do, but you can also write -1 and cast this value to the Word data type. Notice also that there are other values you can use in this API function to produce sounds, as we will see in Chapter 26.

The code of the fourth Edit component that I have written and that you saw in Listing 7.7 accepts only numbers for input, but it is not foolproof. A user can copy some text to the clipboard and paste it into this Edit control, avoiding any check. To solve this problem, we might think of adding a check on the change of the contents, as in the third edit field, or a check on the contents when the user leaves the edit field, as in the second component. This is the reason for the fifth, Foolproof edit field: it uses the OnKeyPress event of the fourth edit field, the OnChange method of the third, and the OnExit event of the second, thus requiring no new code.

To reuse an existing method for a new event, just select the Events page of the Object Inspector, move to the component, and instead of double-clicking to the left of the event name, select the button in the combo box at the right. A list of names of old methods compatible with the current event—having the same number of parameters—will be displayed:

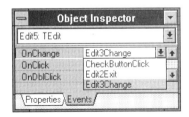

If you select the proper methods, the fifth component will combine the features of the third and the fourth. This is possible because I took care in writing these methods, avoiding any reference to the control they were related to.

The technique I used was to refer to the generic Sender parameter and cast it to the proper data type, which in this case was TButton. As long as you connect a method of this kind to a component of the same kind, no problem should arise. Otherwise, you should make a number of type checks (using the is operator), which will probably make the code more complex to read. My suggestion is to share code only between controls of the same kind.

Notice also that to tell the user which edit box has incorrect text, I've added to each Edit component a value for the Tag property. Every edit box has a tag with its number, from 1 to 5. You can see how the Tag property is defined in the textual description in Listing 7.7 (and see how it is used in the complete source code of Listing 7.8).

LISTING 7.8:   The textual description of the form for the NUMBERS example. Notice the use of the edit fields' Tag property and the labels' FocusControl property.

7

```
object NumbersForm: TNumbersForm
  ActiveControl = Edit1
  Caption = 'Numbers'
  object Label1: TLabel
    Caption = '&Press Button'
    FocusControl = Edit1
  end
  object Label2: TLabel
    Caption = '&Loose Focus'
    FocusControl = Edit2
  end
  object Label3: TLabel
    Caption = 'Change &Text'
    FocusControl = Edit3
  end
  object Label5: TLabel
    Caption = '&Foolproof'
    FocusControl = Edit5
  end
  object Label4: TLabel
    Caption = 'Check &Input'
    FocusControl = Edit4
  end
  object Edit1: TEdit
    Tag = 1
    TabOrder = 0
  end
```

LISTING 7.8: The textual description of the form for the NUMBERS example (continued)

```
  object Edit2: TEdit
    Tag = 2
    TabOrder = 1
    OnExit = Edit2Exit
  end
  object Edit3: TEdit
    Tag = 3
    TabOrder = 2
    OnChange = Edit3Change
  end
  object Edit4: TEdit
    Tag = 4
    TabOrder = 3
    OnKeyPress = Edit4KeyPress
  end
  object Edit5: TEdit
    Tag = 5
    TabOrder = 4
    OnChange = Edit3Change
    OnExit = Edit2Exit
    OnKeyPress = Edit4KeyPress
  end
  object CheckButton: TButton
    Caption = '&Check'
    TabOrder = 5
    OnClick = CheckButtonClick
  end
end
```

Creating a Simple Editor

Edit components can handle a limited amount of text, and only on a single line. If you need something similar to an Edit field but more powerful, you should use the Memo component. A Memo component is like an Edit component, but it can span several lines, contain scroll bars to move though the text, and host up to 32K of text. (The idea for the Memo and its name probably come from the database world, in which a table, instead of storing some text, can refer to an external text file, usually called a memo.)

NOTE   Some Delphi documentation mentions a higher limit for the text of the Edit component, 256K. This is simply not true. The Delphi Memo component is based on Windows' edit control, which cannot host more than 32K, at least in Windows 3.1. The 32-bit versions of the Microsoft operating environment (Windows NT and Windows 95) overcome this limitation.

The easiest thing we can use a Memo for is as an Editor, and this is what I'm going to show you in the next example, NOTES. The idea is to implement an Editor covering all of the window (or form) hosting it, to resemble Windows' own Notepad. The only other option we will implement is to give the user the option of choosing the font for the editor.

Both parts are very easy to implement. Create a new project, and place in it a Memo component (from the Standard page of the Components palette). Delete its text, and place it at the coordinates –1, –1 so its border is not visible. As an alternative, you can remove the border and set the Alignment property to `alClient`.

If you have problems doing this operation by dragging the component, you can use the Object Inspector and set the Left and Top properties to –1. Also add both scroll bars, horizontal and vertical, selecting the value `ssBoth` for the memo's ScrollBars property. You can see the complete description of the form in Listing 7.9 and its structure at design-time in Figure 7.12.

LISTING 7.9:   The textual description of the form for the NOTES example

```
object NotesForm: TNotesForm
  Caption = 'Notes'
  OnResize = FormResize
  object Memo1: TMemo
    Left = -1
    Top = -1
    ScrollBars = ssBoth
    OnDblClick = Memo1DblClick
  end
  object FontDialog1: TFontDialog
  end
end
```

FIGURE 7.12:

The form of the NOTES program

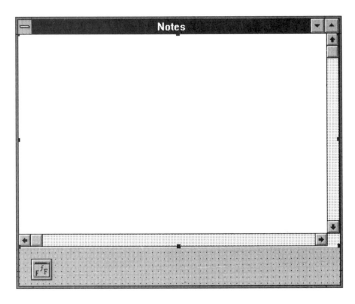

Now we can add some code to size the Memo component so it fills the whole client area of the form each time the form is resized (the event is OnResize):

```
procedure TNotesForm.FormResize(Sender: TObject);
begin
  Memo1.Width := NotesForm.ClientWidth + 1;
  Memo1.Height := NotesForm.ClientHeight + 1;
end;
```

Be aware that you do not need to size the Memo properly at the beginning because when the form is created, it receives a resize message from the system, which determines the Delphi OnResize event. Actually, this code is almost useless because most Delphi components, including the Memo component, have an Alignment property that can be used to make Delphi resize the component automatically. If you set the Alignment property of the Memo to alClient, the component will be resized each time the size of the form changes. The memo will always cover the whole client area, with an effect very close to the one we just coded.

The Font Dialog Box

The second portion of the program involves the font. In the same way we used the standard Color dialog box in a previous example, we can use the standard Font selection dialog box provided by Windows. Just move to the Dialogs page of the Components palette and select the FontDialog component. Place it anywhere on the form, and add the following code when the user double-clicks inside the Memo:

```
procedure TNotesForm.Memo1DblClick(Sender: TObject);
begin
  FontDialog1.Font := Memo1.Font;
  FontDialog1.Execute;
  Memo1.Font := FontDialog1.Font;
end;
```

This code copies the current font to the corresponding Dialog property so it will be selected by default. Then it executes the dialog box (see Figure 7.13). At the end, the Font property will contain the font the user selected, which the third line of the above code copies back to the Memo, activating it.

FIGURE 7.13:

The Font dialog box for the NOTES program

This program is more powerful than it appears at first glance. For example, it allows copy and paste operations using the keyboard—this means you can copy text from your favorite word processor—and can handle the color of the font. Why not use it to place a big and colorful message on your screen?

Selecting a Choice

There are two standard Windows controls that allow the user to choose different options. The first is the check box. A *check box* corresponds to an option that can be selected freely, although at times a check box can be disabled. The second control is the radio button. A *radio button* corresponds to an exclusive selection. For example, if you see two radio buttons with the labels *A* and *B*, you can select A or select B, but not both of them at the same time. The other characteristic of a multiple choice is that you *must* choose one of the selections.

If the difference between check boxes and radio buttons is still not clear, an example might help you. In Figure 7.14, you see the form used as a basis for the CHOICE example. There are three check boxes, to select the style Bold, Italic, or Underlined, and three radio buttons, to choose a font (Times New Roman, Arial, or Courier). There is also a memo field with some text to show the effect of the user selections immediately.

FIGURE 7.14:
The form of the CHOICE example

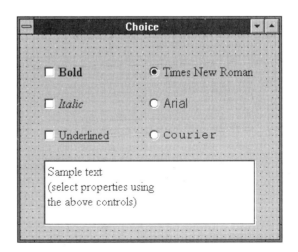

The difference between the use of the check boxes and the radio buttons should be obvious: the text might be bold and italic at the same time, but it cannot be Arial and Courier at once. A user must choose only one font (and cannot choose none) but can select each of the styles independently from the other two (including no style at all). You can see the complete textual description of the form in Listing 7.10.

LISTING 7.10: The textual description of the form for the CHOICE example

```
object Form1: TForm1
  Caption = 'Choice'
  object CheckBold: TCheckBox
    Caption = 'Bold'
    Font.Color = clWindowText
    Font.Height = -16
    Font.Name = 'Times New Roman'
    Font.Style = [fsBold]
    OnClick = CheckBoldClick
  end
  object CheckItalic: TCheckBox
    Caption = 'Italic'
    Font.Color = clWindowText
    Font.Height = -16
    Font.Name = 'Times New Roman'
    Font.Style = [fsItalic]
    OnClick = CheckItalicClick
  end
  object CheckUnderlined: TCheckBox
    Caption = 'Underlined'
    Font.Color = clWindowText
    Font.Height = -16
    Font.Name = 'Times New Roman'
    Font.Style = [fsUnderline]
    OnClick = CheckUnderlinedClick
  end
  object RadioTimes: TRadioButton
    Caption = 'Times New Roman'
    Checked = True
    Font.Color = clWindowText
    Font.Height = -16
    Font.Name = 'Times New Roman'
    Font.Style = []
    OnClick = RadioTimesClick
  end
  object RadioArial: TRadioButton
    Caption = 'Arial'
    Font.Color = clWindowText
    Font.Height = -16
    Font.Name = 'Arial'
    Font.Style = []
    OnClick = RadioArialClick
  end
```

7

LISTING 7.10 : The textual description of the form for the CHOICE example (continued)

```
object RadioCourier: TRadioButton
   Caption = 'Courier'
   Font.Color = clWindowText
   Font.Height = -16
   Font.Name = 'Courier New'
   Font.Style = []
   OnClick = RadioCourierClick
 end
 object Memo1: TMemo
   Font.Color = clBlack
   Font.Height = -16
   Font.Name = 'Times New Roman'
   Font.Style = []
   Lines.Strings = (
     'Sample text'
     '(select properties using '
     'the above controls)')
 end
end
```

This program requires some simple code. In short, each time the user clicks on a component, we have to create a corresponding action. For the text styles, we have to look at the Check property of the control and add or remove the corresponding element from the memo's Font property Style set (as you can see in Figure 7.15).

FIGURE 7.15:

The output of the CHOICE example

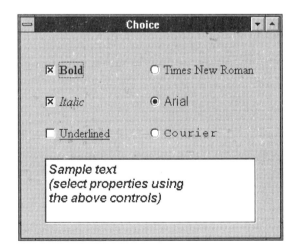

The three check boxes have similar code for their OnClick events (see Listing 7.11). The basic code for the radio buttons is even simpler since you cannot deselect a radio button by clicking on it.

LISTING 7.11: The complete source code for the CHOICE example

```
unit Choice_f;

interface

uses
  SysUtils, WinTypes, WinProcs, Messages, Classes, Graphics,
  Controls, Forms, Dialogs, StdCtrls;

type
  TForm1 = class(TForm)
    CheckBold: TCheckBox;
    CheckItalic: TCheckBox;
    CheckUnderlined: TCheckBox;
    RadioTimes: TRadioButton;
    RadioArial: TRadioButton;
    RadioCourier: TRadioButton;
    Memo1: TMemo;
    procedure CheckBoldClick(Sender: TObject);
    procedure CheckItalicClick(Sender: TObject);
    procedure CheckUnderlinedClick(Sender: TObject);
    procedure RadioTimesClick(Sender: TObject);
    procedure RadioArialClick(Sender: TObject);
    procedure RadioCourierClick(Sender: TObject);
  private
    { Private declarations }
  public
    { Public declarations }
  end;

var
  Form1: TForm1;

implementation

{$R *.DFM}

procedure TForm1.CheckBoldClick(Sender: TObject);
begin
  if CheckBold.Checked then
    Memo1.Font.Style := Memo1.Font.Style + [fsBold]
  else
    Memo1.Font.Style := Memo1.Font.Style - [fsBold];
end;
```

LISTING 7.11: The complete source code for the CHOICE example (continued)

```
procedure TForm1.CheckItalicClick(Sender: TObject);
begin
  if CheckItalic.Checked then
    Memo1.Font.Style := Memo1.Font.Style + [fsItalic]
  else
    Memo1.Font.Style := Memo1.Font.Style - [fsItalic];
end;

procedure TForm1.CheckUnderlinedClick(Sender: TObject);
begin
  if CheckUnderlined.Checked then
    Memo1.Font.Style := Memo1.Font.Style + [fsUnderline]
  else
    Memo1.Font.Style := Memo1.Font.Style - [fsUnderline];
end;

procedure TForm1.RadioTimesClick(Sender: TObject);
begin
  Memo1.Font.Name := 'Times New Roman';
end;

procedure TForm1.RadioArialClick(Sender: TObject);
begin
  Memo1.Font.Name := 'Arial';
end;

procedure TForm1.RadioCourierClick(Sender: TObject);
begin
  Memo1.Font.Name := 'Courier';
end;

end.
```

Grouping Radio Buttons

Radio buttons represent exclusive choices. However, a form might contain several groups of radio buttons. Windows cannot determine by itself how the various radio buttons relate to each other. The solution, both in Windows and in Delphi, is to place the related radio buttons inside a container component. The standard Windows user interface uses a group box control to hold the radio buttons together, both functionally and visually. In Delphi, this control is implemented in the Group-Box component. However, Delphi has a second, similar component that can be used specifically for radio buttons—the RadioGroup component. A RadioGroup is a group box with some radio button clones painted inside it.

For the moment, however, I'll follow the traditional approach. Using the radio group is probably easier than using the group box, but I want to show you the code you can write to work with controls that have been placed inside another control. The fact that you have some controls inside another control is also a good reason *not* to follow this approach in real programs, because you end up with more windows on the screen (wasting some system resources) and with slightly slower code.

The rules for building a group box with radio buttons are very simple: Place the GroupBox component in the form, then place the radio buttons in the group box. The GroupBox component contains other controls and is one of the container components used most often, together with the Panel component. If you disable or hide the group box, all the controls inside it will be disabled or hidden.

You can continue handling the individual radio buttons, but you might as well navigate though the array of controls owned by the group box. The name of this property is Controls. Another property, ControlCount, holds the number of elements. These two properties can be accessed only at run-time.

NOTE

In Delphi, there are some components that are also component containers: the GroupBox, the Panel, the Notebook, and the TabbedNotebook (that is, if you do not consider the TForm component). When you use these controls, you can add other components inside them. In this case, the container is the parent of the components (as indicated by the Parent property), while the form is their owner. You can use the Controls property of a form or group box to navigate the child controls, and you can use the Components property of the form to navigate all the owned components, regardless of their parent.

The PHRASES Example

I spent some time figuring out an example for this section; then I had an idea. If you've ever tried to learn a foreign language, there is some chance you spent some time repeating the same silly and useless phrases over and over. Probably the most typical, when you learn English, is the infamous *The book is on the table*. The aim of this example is to create a tool to build such phrases by choosing among different available options. A look at the form in Figure 7.16 will probably make the idea clearer.

FIGURE 7.16:

The form of the PHRASES1 example

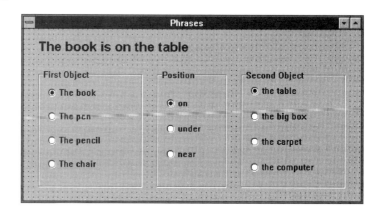

The form for this example, named PHRASES1, is quite complex. If you rebuild it, remember that you must place the GroupBox components first and the radio buttons later. After doing this, you have to enter a proper caption for each element, as you can see in Figure 7.16 and in the textual description of the form in Listing 7.12. Remember that you also need to add a label, select a large font for it, and enter text corresponding to the radio buttons that are checked at design-time. This is an important point: when you place some radio buttons in a form (or in a group box), remember to check one of the elements at design-time. One radio button in each group should always be checked. Listing 7.12 presents the textual description of the form, reduced to a bare minimum (much more so than usual). Although the properties of the components of this form are very simple, it is important to have a look at this description, because you can see the effect in this text of the group boxes *parenting* the radio buttons.

LISTING 7.12: The textual description of the form for the PHRASES1 example. Notice that the group boxes are the Parent components of the radio buttons, as the indentation demonstrates.

```
object Form1: TForm1
  Caption = 'Phrases'
  object Label1: TLabel
    Caption = 'The book is on the table'
    Font.Color = clBlack
    Font.Height = -21
    Font.Name = 'Arial'
    Font.Style = [fsBold]
  end
```

LISTING 7.12 : The textual description of the form for the PHRASES1 example (continued)

```
object GroupBox1: TGroupBox
  Caption = 'First Object'
  object RadioBook: TRadioButton
    Caption = 'The book'
    Checked = True
  end
  object RadioPen: TRadioButton
    Caption = 'The pen'
  end
  object RadioPencil: TRadioButton
    Caption = 'The pencil'
  end
  object RadioChair: TRadioButton
    Caption = 'The chair'
  end
end
object GroupBox2: TGroupBox
  Caption = 'Position'
  object RadioOn: TRadioButton
    Caption = 'on'
    Checked = True
  end
  object RadioUnder: TRadioButton
    Caption = 'under'
  end
  object RadioNear: TRadioButton
    Caption = 'near'
  end
end
object GroupBox3: TGroupBox
  Caption = 'Second Object'
  object RadioTable: TRadioButton
    Caption = 'the table'
    Checked = True
  end
  object RadioBox: TRadioButton
    Caption = 'the big box'
  end
  object RadioCarpet: TRadioButton
    Caption = 'the carpet'
  end
  object RadioComputer: TRadioButton
    Caption = 'the computer'
  end
end
end
```

7

Now we have to write some code so that when the user clicks on the radio buttons, the phrase changes accordingly (see Figure 7.17). There are different alternatives. One is to follow the same approach as the last example, providing a method for each button's OnClick event. Then we need to store the various portions of the phrase in some of the form's variables, change the portion corresponding to that button, and rebuild the whole phrase.

FIGURE 7.17:

The output of the PHRASES1 example

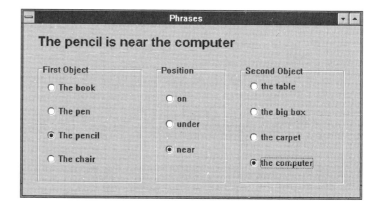

An alternative solution is to write a single method that looks at which buttons are currently checked and builds the corresponding phrase. This single method must be connected to the OnClick event of every radio button. This is simple to accomplish: select each of the radio buttons on the form (clicking on each one while you hold down the Shift key) and enter the name of the method in the Object Inspector (see Figure 7.18). Notice that in Listing 7.12, I've omitted all the method names (that is, the same name repeated a number of times).

Since the method used to compute the new phrase doesn't refer to a specific control, you might name it yourself, simply entering a name in the second column of the Object Inspector next to the OnClick event. In Listing 7.13, you can see the code of this single complex method.

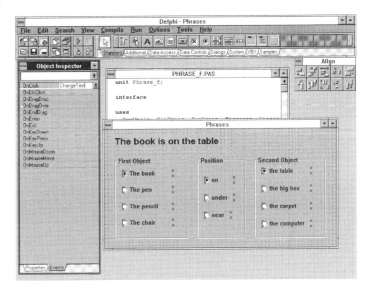

FIGURE 7.18:
Adding a method for the OnClick event of each radio button

The ChangeText method starts building an empty string, then adds to it the various pieces, including the verb (*is*) and some blank spaces. To determine which control in a group box is checked, the procedure scans these controls in a for loop. The for loop ranges from 0 to the number of controls minus 1, because the Controls array is zero based, and tests whether the Checked property of the radio button is True. A cast is required to perform this operation—we cannot use the Checked property on a generic control. When the checked radio button has been found, the program simply copies its caption to the string. At this point, the for loop might terminate, but since only one radio button is checked at a time, it is safe to let it reach its natural end—testing all the elements. The same operation is repeated three times because there are three group boxes to examine.

Of course, in a form based on the RadioGroup component, a similar method would have been much simpler. This control, in fact, has an ItemIndex property indicating which radio button is selected and an Items property with a list of the text of the fake radio buttons. Overall, using a radio group is very similar to using a list box, aside from the obvious differences in the user interface of the two components.

LISTING 7.13: The source code for the ChangeText method in the PHRASES1 example

```
procedure TForm1.ChangeText(Sender: TObject);
var
  Phrase: String;
  I: Integer;
begin
  Phrase := '';
  {look at which radio button is selected
    and add its text to the phrase}
  for I:=0 to GroupBox1.ControlCount - 1 do
    if (GroupBox1.Controls[I] as TRadioButton).Checked then
      Phrase := Phrase +
        (GroupBox1.Controls[I] as TRadioButton).Caption;

  {add the verb and blank spaces}
  Phrase := Phrase + ' is ';
  {repeat the operation on the second group box}
  for I:=0 to GroupBox2.ControlCount - 1 do
    if (GroupBox2.Controls[I] as TRadioButton).Checked then
      Phrase := Phrase +
        (GroupBox2.Controls[I] as TRadioButton).Caption;

  {add another blank space}
  Phrase := Phrase + ' ';
  {works on the third group}
  for I:=0 to GroupBox3.ControlCount - 1 do
    if (GroupBox3.Controls[I] as TRadioButton).Checked then
      Phrase := Phrase +
        (GroupBox3.Controls[I] as TRadioButton).Caption;

  {display the phrase in the label}
  Label1.Caption := Phrase;
end;
```

A List with Many Choices

If you want to add many selections, radio buttons are not appropriate, unless you create a really big form. The usual number of radio buttons is in the range between 2 and 5 or 6. Another problem is that although you can disable a radio button, the elements of a group are usually fixed. Radio buttons are not very flexible.

When these problems occur, there is a solution: use a list box. A *list box* can host a large number of choices (up to 32K elements) in a small space and can contain a scroll bar to show on screen only a limited portion of the whole selection. Another advantage of a list box is that you can easily add new items to it or remove some of the current items. List boxes are extremely flexible and powerful.

Another important feature is that by using the ListBox component, you can choose between a single selection—a behavior similar to a group of radio buttons—and a multiple selection—similar to a group of check boxes. The next version of this example will have a multiple-selection list box.

For the moment, though, let's focus on a single-selection list box. We might use a couple of these components to change the PHRASE1 example slightly. Instead of having a number of radio buttons to select the first and second objects of the phrase, we can use two list boxes. Besides allowing us to have a larger number of items, the advantage is that we can allow the user to insert new objects in the list and prevent selection of the same object twice, to avoid a phrase such as *The book is on the book.* As you might imagine, this example is really much more complicated than the previous one and will require some fairly complex code.

The Form for PHRASES2

As usual, the first step is to build a form (see Figure 7.19). You can start with the form from the last example and remove the two group boxes on the sides and replace them with two list boxes. The radio buttons inside the group boxes will be deleted automatically.

FIGURE 7.19:

The form of the second version of the PHRASES example

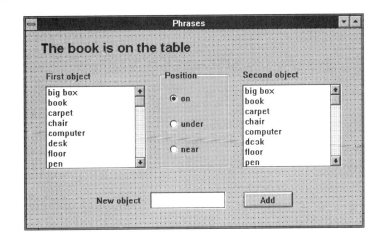

Now, add some strings to the Items property of both list boxes, as shown in Figure 7.20. For the example to work properly, the two list boxes should have the same strings; you can copy and paste them from the Items property of one list box to the same property of the other one.

FIGURE 7.20:

Adding some strings to a list box

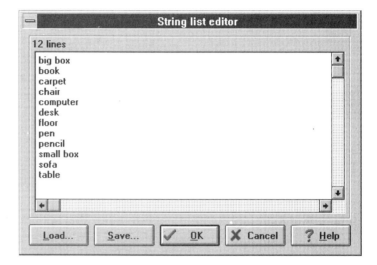

To improve the usability of the program, you might sort the strings in the list boxes, setting their Sorted property to True. Remember also to add a couple of labels above the list boxes, to describe their contents.

In the lower part of the form (see Figure 7.19 again), I've also added an edit field, with its label, and a button. As we will see later, when a user presses the button, the text in the Edit control is added to both list boxes. This operation will take place only if the text of the edit box is not empty and the string is not already present in the list boxes. In the textual description of the form (see Listing 7.14) is the summary of the components' properties.

LISTING 7.14: The textual description of the form for the PHRASES2 example

```
object Form1: TForm1
  Caption = 'Phrases'
  OnCreate = FormCreate
  object Label1: TLabel
    Caption = 'The book is on the table'
    Font.Color = clBlack
    Font.Height = -21
    Font.Name = 'Arial'
    Font.Style = [fsBold]
  end
  object Label2: TLabel
    Caption = 'First object'
  end
  object Label3: TLabel
    Caption = 'Second object'
  end
  object Label4: TLabel
    Caption = 'New object'
  end
  object GroupBox2: TGroupBox
    Caption = 'Position'
    TabOrder = 0
    object RadioOn: TRadioButton
      Caption = 'on'
      Checked = True
      OnClick = ChangeText
    end
    object RadioUnder: TRadioButton
      Caption = 'under'
      OnClick = ChangeText
    end
    object RadioNear: TRadioButton
      Caption = 'near'
      OnClick = ChangeText
    end
  end
  object ListBox1: TListBox
    ItemHeight = 16
    Items.Strings = (
      'big box'
      'book'
      'carpet'
      'chair'
      'computer'
      'desk'
      'floor'
      'pen'
      'pencil'
      'small box'
      'sofa'
      'table')
```

7

LISTING 7.14: The textual description of the form for the PHRASES2 example (continued)

```
      Sorted = True
      OnClick = ChangeText
   end
   object ListBox2: TListBox
      ItemHeight = 16
      Items.Strings = (...) {as above}
      Sorted = True
      OnClick = ChangeText
   end
   object EditNew: TEdit
   end
   object ButtonAdd: TButton
      Caption = 'Add'
      OnClick = ButtonAddClick
   end
end
```

Working with the List Boxes

Once you have built this or a similar form, you can start writing some code. The first thing to do is to provide a new ChangeText procedure, connected with the OnClick event of the radio buttons of the group box and of the two list boxes. This procedure is simpler than in the previous version of the example. In fact, to retrieve the selected text from the list box, you only need to get the number of the item selected (stored in the run-time property ItemIndex) and then retrieve the string at the corresponding position of the Item array. You can accomplish the two operations at the same time by writing:

```
ListBox1.Items [ListBox1.ItemIndex]
```

Here is the code for the procedure (which is not present on the companion disk because it is replaced by another version that I'll show you in a moment):

```
procedure TForm1.ChangeText(Sender: TObject);
var
  Phrase: String;
  I: Integer;
begin
  Phrase := 'The ';
  Phrase := Phrase + ListBox1.Items [ListBox1.ItemIndex];
  Phrase := Phrase + ' is ';
```

```
{looks at which radio button is selected
  and adds its text to the phrase}
for I:=0 to GroupBox2.ControlCount - 1 do
  if (GroupBox2.Controls[I] as TRadioButton).Checked then
    Phrase := Phrase +
      (GroupBox2.Controls[I] as TRadioButton).Caption;

Phrase := Phrase + ' the ';
Phrase := Phrase + ListBox2.Items [ListBox2.ItemIndex];

Label1.Caption := Phrase;
end;
```

This program, however, won't work properly because, at the beginning, no item is selected in either list box. To solve this problem, we can add a method for the form's OnCreate event. In its code, we can look for the two default strings, "book" and "table," and select them. You should do this operation in two steps. First, you need to look for the string's index in the array of strings, with the IndexOf method. Then you can use that value as the index of the currently selected item:

```
procedure TForm1.FormCreate(Sender: TObject);
var
  N : Integer;
begin
  N := ListBox1.Items.IndexOf ('book');
  ListBox1.ItemIndex := N;
  N := ListBox2.Items.IndexOf ('table');
  ListBox2.ItemIndex := N;
end;
```

Removing a Selected String from the Other List Box

Once this part of the program works, we have two more problems to solve: we must remove the selected string from the other list box to avoid using the same term twice in a phrase, as already described, and we must write the code for the click event on the button.

The first problem is more complex, but I'll address it immediately since the solution of the second problem will be based partially on the code already written for the first one. Our aim is to delete from a list box the item currently selected in the other list box. This is easy to code. The problem is that once the selection changes, we have to restore the previous items, or our list boxes will rapidly become empty. A good solution is to store the two currently selected strings for the two list boxes in two variables of the form String1 and String2 (see the complete source code in Listing 7.15).

LISTING 7.15: The complete source code for the PHRASES2 example

```
unit Phrase_f;

interface

uses
  SysUtils, WinTypes, WinProcs, Messages, Classes,
  Graphics, Controls, Forms, Dialogs, StdCtrls;

type
  TForm1 = class(TForm)
    GroupBox2: TGroupBox;
    RadioOn: TRadioButton;
    RadioUnder: TRadioButton;
    RadioNear: TRadioButton;
    Label1: TLabel;
    ListBox1: TListBox;
    ListBox2: TListBox;
    Label2: TLabel;
    Label3: TLabel;
    Label4: TLabel;
    EditNew: TEdit;
    ButtonAdd: TButton;
    procedure ChangeText(Sender: TObject);
    procedure FormCreate(Sender: TObject);
    procedure ButtonAddClick(Sender: TObject);
  private
    { Private declarations }
    String1, String2: String;
  public
    { Public declarations }
  end;

var
  Form1: TForm1;

implementation

{$R *.DFM}

procedure TForm1.ChangeText(Sender: TObject);
var
  Phrase, TmpStr: String;
  I: integer;
```

LISTING 7.15: The complete source code for the PHRASES2 example (continued)

```
begin
  {delete the selected item from the other list box}
  if Sender is TListBox then
  begin
    TmpStr := ListBox1.Items [ListBox1.ItemIndex];
    if TmpStr <> String1 then
    begin
      ListBox2.Items.Add (String1);
      ListBox2.Items.Delete (ListBox2.Items.IndexOf (TmpStr));
      ListBox2.ItemIndex := ListBox2.Items.IndexOf (String2);
      String1 := TmpStr;
    end;
    TmpStr := ListBox2.Items [ListBox2.ItemIndex];
    if TmpStr <> String2 then
    begin
      ListBox1.Items.Add (String2);
      ListBox1.Items.Delete (ListBox1.Items.IndexOf (TmpStr));
      ListBox1.ItemIndex := ListBox1.Items.IndexOf (String1);
      String2 := TmpStr;
    end;
  end;

  {build the phrase}
  Phrase := 'The ' + String1 + ' is ';

  {look at which radio button is selected
  and add its text to the phrase}
  for I:=0 to GroupBox2.ControlCount - 1 do
    if (GroupBox2.Controls[I] as TRadioButton).Checked then
      Phrase := Phrase +
        (GroupBox2.Controls[I] as TRadioButton).Caption;

  Phrase := Phrase + ' the ' + String2;
  Label1.Caption := Phrase;
end;

procedure TForm1.FormCreate(Sender: TObject);
var
  N : Integer;
begin
  String1 := 'book';
  String2 := 'table';

  {delete the selected string from the other list box
  to avoid a double selection}
  ListBox2.Items.Delete (ListBox2.Items.IndexOf (String1));
  ListBox1.Items.Delete (ListBox1.Items.IndexOf (String2));

  {selects the two strings in their respective list boxes}
  N := ListBox1.Items.IndexOf (String1);
  ListBox1.ItemIndex := N;
```

7

LISTING 7.15: The complete source code for the PHRASES2 example (continued)

```
  N := ListBox2.Items.IndexOf (String2);
  ListBox2.ItemIndex := N;
end;

procedure TForm1.ButtonAddClick(Sender: TObject);
begin
  {if there is a string in the edit control and
    the string is not already present in one of the lists}
  if (EditNew.Text <> '') and
    (ListBox1.Items.IndexOf(EditNew.Text) < 0) and
    (ListBox2.Items.IndexOf(EditNew.Text) < 0) then
  begin
    {add the string to both list boxes}
    ListBox1.Items.Add (EditNew.Text);
    ListBox2.Items.Add (EditNew.Text);

    {re-selects the current items properly}
    ListBox1.ItemIndex := ListBox1.Items.IndexOf (String1);
    ListBox2.ItemIndex := ListBox2.Items.IndexOf (String2);
  end
  else
  MessageDlg (
    'The edit control is empty or contains a string' +
    ' which is already present',
    mtError, [mbOK], 0);
end;

end.
```

Now we have to change the code executed at startup and the code executed each time a new selection is made. In the FormCreate method, we need to store the initial value of the two strings and remove them from the other list box; the first string should be removed from the second list box, and vice versa. Since the Delete methods of the TStrings class require the index, we again have to use the IndexOf function to determine it. The code to select the string should be executed after the deletion because removing an element before the one currently selected will alter the selection. The fact is that the selection is just a number referring to a string, not the reverse, as it should probably be. By the way, this doesn't depend on Delphi implementation but on the behavior of list boxes in Windows.

The final version of the code executed at startup produces the effects shown in Figure 7.21. Things get complicated when a new item is selected in one of the list boxes.

The ChangeText procedure has some new code at the beginning, executed only if the click took place on one of the list boxes (remember that the code is also associated with the group box):

```
if Sender is TListBox then ...
```

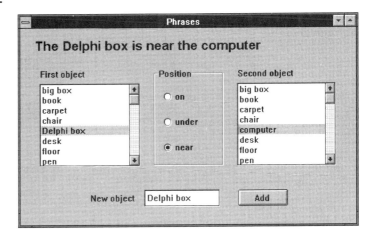

For each string, we have to check whether the selected item has changed and, in this case:

- Add the previously selected string to the other list box.
- Delete the new string from the other list box.

You can see an example of how the list box contents change by comparing Figure 7.21 with Figure 7.22.

It's easy to make errors in this code since the two list boxes are used at the same time. I made a number of errors the first time I wrote this example, partly because I copied portions of code, forgetting to correct all the references.

Here is a detailed description of the operations, referring to a new selection in the first list box (the full source code is in Listing 7.15). The procedure stores the selected element of the first list box in the temporary string TmpStr:

```
TmpStr := ListBox1.Items [ListBox1.ItemIndex];
```

FIGURE 7.22:

When you select a new phrase, the contents of the list boxes change.

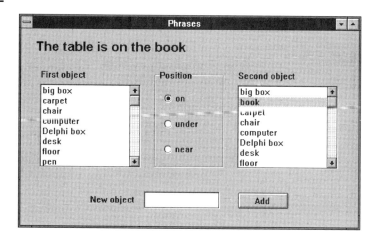

If this is different from the older selection, String1, four operations take place:

```
if TmpStr <> String1 then
begin
  {1.} ListBox2.Items.Add (String1);
  {2.} ListBox2.Items.Delete (ListBox2.Items.IndexOf (TmpStr));
  {3.} ListBox2.ItemIndex := ListBox2.Items.IndexOf (String2);
  {4.} String1 := TmpStr;
end;
```

This is what the operations do:

1. The previously selected string, String1, is added to the other list box, ListBox2.

2. The new selection, TmpStr, is removed from the other list box.

3. The selected string of the other list box, String2, is reselected in case its position has changed because of the two preceding operations.

4. Once the two lists contain the correct elements, we can store the new value in String1 and use it later on to build the phrase.

The same happens for the other list box a few lines later. Notice that we can avoid having to access the list boxes again to build the phrase, since String1 and String2 already contain the values we need, as you can see in the final version of the code in Listing 7.15 (shown earlier).

Implementing the OnClick event for the Add button is quite simple. The only precautions we have to take are to test whether there is actually some text in the edit box or if it is empty and to check whether the string is already present in one of the two list boxes. Checking only one of the list boxes will miss a correspondence between the text of the edit box and the item currently selected in the other list box.

To make this check, we can ask the new string's index; if it is not present in the list—if there is no match —the value –1 will be returned. Otherwise, the IndexOf function returns the correct index, starting with 0 for the first element. In technical terms, we can say that the function returns the *zero-based* index of the element, or the error code –1 if it is not found.

In the final part of this method's code, we need to reselect the current item of the list box since the position of the selected item might change. This happens if the new item is inserted before the one that is currently selected—that is, if it has a lower sort order.

Allowing Multiple Selections

There is a basic choice that determines how a list box works. A list box can allow the selection of a single element or the selection of a number of elements. The actual choice is determined by the value of the list box's Multiple property. As the name implies, setting Multiple to True allows multiple selections.

There are really two different kinds of multiple selections in Windows and in Delphi list boxes; one is called *multiple selection* and the other *extended selection*. This second choice is determined by the ExtendedSelect property.

If setting up a multiple-selection list box is very simple, the problems start to appear when you have to write the code. Accessing the selected item of a single-selection list box is simple. The ItemIndex property holds the index of the selected item, and the selected string can be retrieved with a simple expression, such as:

```
ListBox2.Items[ListBox2.ItemIndex];
```

In a multiple-selection list box, on the other hand, we do not know how many items are selected, or even whether there is any item selected. In fact, a user can click on an item to select it, drag the cursor to select a number of consecutive items in the list, or click the mouse button on an item while holding down the Ctrl key to toggle the selection of a single item without affecting the others. Using this last option, a user can even deselect all the items in a list box.

From a program, we can retrieve information on the currently selected items by examining the Selected array. This array of Boolean values has the same number of entries as the list box. Each entry indicates whether the corresponding item is selected, as shown in the schema of Figure 7.23.

FIGURE 7.23:

A schema of the relationship between the Selected and Items properties in a multiple-selection list box

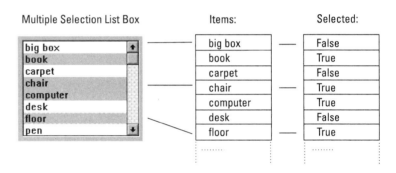

For example, to know how many items are selected in a list box, we need to scan the Selected array, usually with a `for` loop ranging from 0 to the number of items in the list minus one:

```
SelectCount := 0;
for ListItem := 0 to ListBox1.Items.Count - 1 do
  if ListBox1.Selected[ListItem] then
    Inc (SelectCount);
```

The Third Version of PHRASES

With this information, we can build a new version of the PHRASES example, allowing a user to select several items in the first list box. The only difference between the form of this new version and that of the last one is the value of the MultiSelect property in the first list box:

```
object ListBox1: TListBox
  MultiSelect = True
end
```

In addition, the label at the top of the form has been enlarged, enabling the Word-Wrap property and disabling the AutoSize property, to accommodate longer phrases. Since the example's code is complex enough, I've removed the portion used to delete from a list box the item selected in the other list box. In the case of multiple selections, this would have been really complicated.

The main problem we face is building the different phrases correctly. The basic idea is to scan the Selected array each time and add each of the selected objects to the phrase. However, we need to place an *and* before the last object, omitting the comma if there are only two. Moreover, we need to decide between singular and plural (*is* or *are*) and provide some default text if no element is selected.

As you can see from Table 7.1 (and in Figure 7.24), building these phrases is not simple. In fact, if we store the phrase *The book and the computer*, when we need to add a third item, we must go back and change it.

TABLE 7.1: Possible Combinations of Phrases

Items Selected	SelectCount	Phrase
(none)	0	Nothing is…
book	1	The book is…
book, computer	2	The book and the computer are…
book, computer, pen	3	The book, the computer, and the pen are…
book, computer, pen, small box	4	The book, the computer, the pen, and the small box are…

An alternative idea is to create two different phrases, one good if no other elements will be added, the other prepared to host future objects (without the *and*). In the code, the TmpStr1 string is the tentative final statement, while TmpStr2 is the temporary string used to add a further element. At the end of the loop, TmpStr1 holds the correct value.

FIGURE 7.24:

An example of the output of the PHRASES3 program

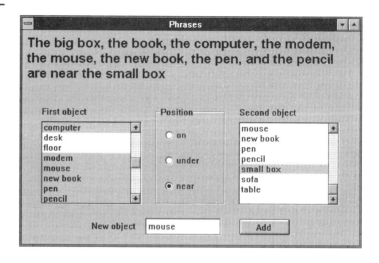

Notice when scanning a sorted list box that the objects are always added to the resulting string in alphabetical order, not in the order in which they were selected.

You can study this idea as it has been implemented in the new version of the ChangeText method, in Listing 7.16. If things are still not clear, look at Table 7.2, which describes step-by-step how the strings are built.

TABLE 7.2: The Process of Building the Strings Step-by-Step

Items Selected	Steps	TmpStr1 (tentative final statement)	TmpStr2 (temporary statement)
book	1	book	book
+ computer	2	book and the computer	book, the computer
+ pen	3	book, the computer, and the pen	book, the computer, the pen
+ small box	4	book, the computer, the pen, and the small box	book, the computer, the pen, the small box

LISTING 7.16: The source code for the new version of the ChangeText, included in the complete listing of the PHRASES3 example

```pascal
procedure TForm1.ChangeText(Sender: TObject);
var
  Phrase, TmpStr1, TmpStr2: String;
  SelectCount, ListItem, GroupItem: Integer;
begin
  SelectCount := 0;
  {look at each item of the multiple-selection list box}
  for ListItem := 0 to ListBox1.Items.Count - 1 do
    if ListBox1.Selected [ListItem] then
    begin
      {if the item is selected increase the count}
      Inc (SelectCount);
      if SelectCount = 1 then
      begin
        {store the string of the first selection}
        TmpStr1 := ListBox1.Items.Strings [ListItem];
        TmpStr2 := TmpStr1;
      end;
      if SelectCount = 2 then
      begin
        {add the string of the second selection}
        TmpStr1 := TmpStr1 + ' and the ' +
          ListBox1.Items.Strings [ListItem];
        TmpStr2 := TmpStr2 + ', the ' +
          ListBox1.Items.Strings [ListItem];
      end;
      if SelectCount > 2 then
      begin
        {add the string of the further selection}
        TmpStr1 := TmpStr2 + ', and the ' +
          ListBox1.Items.Strings [ListItem];

        TmpStr2 := TmpStr2 + ', the ' +
          ListBox1.Items.Strings [ListItem];
      end;
    end;

  {build the first part of the phrase}
  if SelectCount > 0 then
    Phrase := 'The ' + TmpStr1
  else
    Phrase := 'Nothing';

  if SelectCount <= 1 then
    Phrase := Phrase + ' is '
  else
    Phrase := Phrase + ' are ';
```

LISTING 7.16: The source code for the new version of the ChangeText, included in the complete listing of the PHRASES3 example (continued)

```
{look at which radio button is selected
  and add its text to the phrase}
for GroupItem:=0 to GroupBox2.ControlCount - 1 do
  if (GroupBox2.Controls [GroupItem] as TRadioButton).Checked then
    Phrase := Phrase +
      (GroupBox2.Controls [GroupItem] as TRadioButton).Caption;

{add the text of the second list box}
Phrase := Phrase + ' the ' +
  ListBox2.Items [ListBox2.ItemIndex];

Label1.Caption := Phrase;
end;
```

The other procedures of the program change only slightly. The FormCreate method is simplified because we do not need to delete the selected item from the other list box. The Add method is simplified because both list boxes always have the same items and because the multiple-selection list box creates no problems if you add a new element.

An alternative solution to handle the status of multiple-selection list boxes is to look at the value of the ItemIndex property, which holds the number of the item of the list having the focus. If a user clicks on several items while holding down the Ctrl key, each time a click event takes place, you know which of the items have been selected or deselected—you can easily determine which of the two operations took place by looking at the value of the Selected array for that index. The problem is that if the user selects a number of elements by dragging the mouse, this method won't work. You need to intercept the dragging events, and this is considerably more complex than the technique described earlier.

Many Lists, Little Space

List boxes have a problem: they take up a lot of screen space. Another problem is that they offer a fixed selection. That is, a user can choose only among the items in the list box, and he or she cannot make a choice that was not foreseen.

You can solve both these problems by using a ComboBox control. A *combo box* is similar to an edit box, and you can often enter some text in it. It is also similar to a list box since pressing the arrow at the end of the control displays a list box below it. Even the name of the control suggests that it is a combination of two other controls, an Edit and a ListBox.

However, the behavior of a ComboBox component might change a lot, depending on the value of its Style property. Here is a short description of the various styles:

- The `csDropDown` style defines a typical combo box, which allows direct editing and displays a list box on request.

- The `csDropDownList` style defines a combo box that does not allow editing. By pressing a key, the user selects the first word starting with that letter in the list.

- The `csSimple` style defines a combo box that always displays the list box below it. This version of the control allows direct editing.

- The `csOwnerDrawFixed` and `csOwnerDrawVariable` styles define combo boxes based on an owner-draw list—that is, a list not containing simple strings but, instead, any graphics determined by the program.

If this is not clear, you can run the COMBOS example that I'll describe in a moment. As you can see in Figure 7.25 and better appreciate by testing the program, there are three combo boxes having three different styles: drop-down, drop-down list, and simple.

FIGURE 7.25:

The output of the COMBOS example, with the three basic types of combo boxes

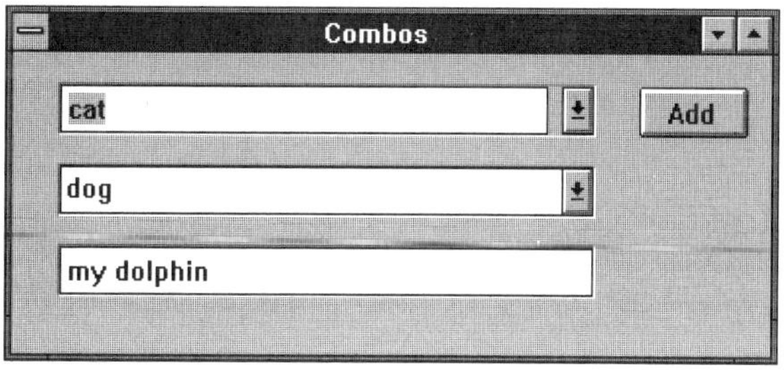

This program is very simple, as you can see from the textual description of its form in Listing 7.17. Each of the combo boxes has the same basic strings—the names of more than 20 different animals—omitted in the description.

The first combo box contains an Add button. If the user presses the button, the text entered in the combo box (if any) is added to its list, provided it is not already present. This is the code associated with the OnClick event of the button:

```
procedure TForm1.ButtonAddClick(Sender: TObject);
begin
  with ComboBox1 do
    if (Text <> '') and (Items.IndexOf (Text) < 0) then
      Items.Add (Text);
end;
```

LISTING 7.17: The textual description of the form for the COMBOS example, without the full lists of items of the combo boxes

```
object Form1: TForm1
  Caption = 'Combos'
  object ComboBox1: TComboBox
    ItemHeight = 16
    Items.Strings = (
      'ant'
      'beetle'
      'bull'
      ...)
    Sorted = True
  end
  object ComboBox2: TComboBox
    Style = csDropDownList
    ItemHeight = 16
    Items.Strings = (...)
    Sorted = True
  end
  object ComboBox3: TComboBox
    Style = csSimple
    ItemHeight = 16
    Items.Strings = (...)
    Sorted = True
    OnKeyPress = ComboBox3KeyPress
  end
  object ButtonAdd: TButton
    Caption = 'Add'
    OnClick = ButtonAddClick
  end
end
```

You can use the second combo box to experiment with the automatic lookup technique. If you press a key, the first of the names in the list starting with that letter will be selected. By pressing the up and down arrow keys, you can further navigate in the list without opening it. This navigation technique of using initial letters and arrows can be used with each of the combo boxes.

The third list box is a variation of the first. Instead of adding the new element when the Add button is pressed, that action is performed when the user presses the Enter key. To test for this event, we can write a method for the combo box's OnKeyPress event and check whether the key is the Enter key, which has the numeric code 13. The remaining statements are similar to those of the button's OnClick event.

```
procedure TForm1.ComboBox3KeyPress(Sender: TObject;
  var Key: Char);
begin
  {if the user presses the Enter key}
  if key = chr (13) then
    with ComboBox3 do
      if (Text <> '') and (Items.IndexOf (Text) < 0) then
        Items.Add (Text);
end;
```

Choosing a Value in a Range

The last basic component I want to explore in this chapter is the scroll bar. Scroll bars are usually associated with other components, such as list boxes and memo fields, or are associated directly with forms. Notice, however, that when a scroll bar is associated with another component, it is really a portion of that component—one of its properties—and there is little relationship to the ScrollBar component itself. Forms having a scroll bar have no ScrollBar component. A portion of their border is used to display that graphical element. Forms with scroll bars will be discussed in Chapter 13.

Direct usage of the ScrollBar component is quite rare. However, there are cases in which it can play a role. The typical example is to allow a user to choose a numerical value in a range. Instead of entering the value, he or she can drag the scroll bar thumb or click on the scroll bar to set the value, which is probably displayed somewhere else on the screen. Scroll bars have no text. (An alternative solution in Delphi is to use the SpinButton or SpinEdit component, both located in the Samples page of the Components palette.)

Most Windows programming books describe scroll bars using the example of selecting a color. This book makes no exception to the rule. But if you've seen one of the original Windows examples, you'll notice something very interesting: using Delphi, you can build this example in half the time and by writing a minimal amount of code.

The Scroll Color Example

The SCROLLC example—the name stands for scroll color—has a simple form with three scroll bars and three corresponding labels, as you can see in Figure 7.26. Each of the scroll bars refers to one of the three fundamental colors, which in Windows are red, green, and blue (RGB). Each of the labels displays the name of the corresponding color and the current value.

FIGURE 7.26:

The form for the SCROLLC example

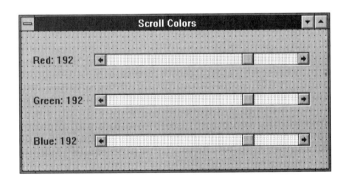

The scroll bars have a number of peculiar properties. You can use Min and Max to determine the range of possible values; Position holds the current position; and the LargeChange and SmallChange properties indicate the increment caused by clicking on the bar or on the arrow at the end of the bar, respectively. You can see a graphical description of these properties, with the values used in the example, in Figure 7.27.

FIGURE 7.27:

A graphical description of some properties of a scroll bar (the values are borrowed from the SCROLLC example)

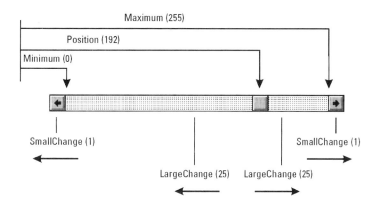

In the SCROLLC example, the value of each bar ranges from 0 to 255, the initial value is 192, and the changes are 1 and 25. The range is determined by the fact that each color is a byte, with 256 possible values. The value of 192 has been chosen for the position because with settings of 192 for red, 192 for green, and 192 for blue, you get the typical light gray, which is the default value for the color of the form. Listing 7.18 provides the textual description of the form for the example.

As I mentioned earlier, the code for this example is very simple. When one of the scroll bars changes (the OnScroll event), the program has to update the label and update the form's color (see Figure 7.28):

```
LabelRed.Caption := 'Red: ' + IntToStr(ScrollPos);
FormScroll.Color := RGB (ScrollBarRed.Position,
  ScrollBarGreen.Position, ScrollBarBlue.Position);
```

You need to copy this code only three times, once for each scroll bar, and correct the label and its value, as you can see in the complete source code in Listing 7.19. The second statement always remains the same. It is based on a Windows function, RGB, which takes three values in the range 0–255 and creates a 32-bit value with the code of the corresponding color.

LISTING 7.18: The textual description of the form for the SCROLLC example

```
object FormScroll: TFormScroll
  Caption = 'Scroll Colors'
  object LabelRed: TLabel
    Caption = 'Red: 192'
  end
  object LabelGreen: TLabel
    Caption = 'Green: 102'
  end
  object LabelBlue: TLabel
    Caption = 'Blue: 192'
  end
  object ScrollBarRed: TScrollBar
    LargeChange = 25
    Max = 255
    Position = 192
    OnScroll = ScrollBarRedScroll
  end
  object ScrollBarGreen: TScrollBar
    LargeChange = 25
    Max = 255
    Position = 192
    OnScroll = ScrollBarGreenScroll
  end
  object ScrollBarBlue: TScrollBar
    LargeChange = 25
    Max = 255
    Position = 192
    OnScroll = ScrollBarBlueScroll
  end
end
```

FIGURE 7.28:

The output of the SCROLLC example

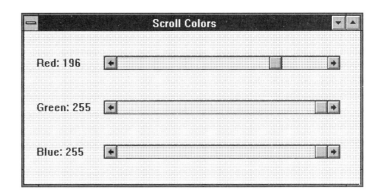

LISTING 7.19: The complete listing for the SCROLLC example

```
unit Scroll_f;

interface

uses
  SysUtils, WinTypes, WinProcs, Messages, Classes,
  Graphics, Controls, Forms, Dialogs, StdCtrls;

type
  TFormScroll = class(TForm)
    ScrollBarRed: TScrollBar;
    ScrollBarGreen: TScrollBar;
    ScrollBarBlue: TScrollBar;
    LabelRed: TLabel;
    LabelGreen: TLabel;
    LabelBlue: TLabel;
    procedure ScrollBarRedScroll(Sender: TObject;
      ScrollCode: TScrollCode; var ScrollPos: Integer);
    procedure ScrollBarGreenScroll(Sender: TObject;
      ScrollCode: TScrollCode; var ScrollPos: Integer);
    procedure ScrollBarBlueScroll(Sender: TObject;
      ScrollCode: TScrollCode; var ScrollPos: Integer);
  private
    { Private declarations }
  public
    { Public declarations }
  end;

var
  FormScroll: TFormScroll;

implementation

{$R *.DFM}

procedure TFormScroll.ScrollBarRedScroll(Sender: TObject;
  ScrollCode: TScrollCode; var ScrollPos: Integer);
begin
  LabelRed.Caption := 'Red: ' + IntToStr(ScrollPos);
  FormScroll.Color := RGB (ScrollBarRed.Position,
    ScrollBarGreen.Position, ScrollBarBlue.Position);
end;

procedure TFormScroll.ScrollBarGreenScroll(Sender: TObject;
  ScrollCode: TScrollCode; var ScrollPos: Integer);
begin
  LabelGreen.Caption := 'Green: ' + IntToStr(ScrollPos);
  FormScroll.Color := RGB (ScrollBarRed.Position,
    ScrollBarGreen.Position, ScrollBarBlue.Position);
end;
```

7

LISTING 7.19: The complete listing for the SCROLLC example (continued)

```
procedure TFormScroll.ScrollBarBlueScroll(Sender: TObject;
  ScrollCode: TScrollCode; var ScrollPos: Integer);
begin
  LabelBlue.Caption := 'Blue: ' + IntToStr(ScrollPos);
  FormScroll.Color := RGB (ScrollBarRed.Position,
    ScrollBarGreen.Position, ScrollBarBlue.Position);
end;

end.
```

It is interesting to note that the OnScroll event has three parameters: the sender, the kind of event (ScrollCode), and the final position of the thumb (ScrollPos). This type of event can be used for very precise control of the user's actions. Its value indicates whether the user is dragging the thumb (`scTrack`, `scPosition`, and `scEndScroll`), whether he or she has clicked on the arrows or on the bar in one of the two directions (`scLineUp`, `scLineDown`, `scPageUp`, and `scPageDown`), and if the user is trying to scroll out of the range (`scTop` and `scBottom`).

Summary

In this chapter, we have started to explore some of the basic components available in Delphi. These components correspond to the standard Windows controls and are extremely common in applications (with the exception of the stand-alone scroll bars).

The user interface for these controls can be easily improved using the (default) three-dimensional look, and many Windows users will be comfortable using them. Of course, when you start adding more advanced Delphi components to an application, you can easily build more complex and colorful user interfaces and more powerful programs.

We will explore some of the advanced components in future chapters, but the next two are devoted to specific and important topics: the use of menus and a detailed description of forms. After these two in-depth discussions, we will move back to the use of other components, including the graphical versions of list boxes, edit boxes allowing specific data entries, grids, and more.

CHAPTER

EIGHT

Creating and Handling Menus

- The structure of a menu

- Checking, disabling, and modifying menus at run-time

- The Menu Designer

- Menu templates

- A custom menu check mark

- The NOTES example

- Pop-up menus

8

The programs we have built so far have lacked one of the most important user-interface elements of any Windows application: the menu bar. Although our forms have a system menu, it has a very limited use. The menu bar, on the other hand, is a central element in the development of a program. The user can press buttons, drag the mouse, and select options, but usually, most of the complex tasks involve using a menu command. Consider the application you use and the number-of-menu-commands issue, including those invoked by an accelerator key, such as Ctrl-Ins or Ctrl-C, which replace the Edit Copy command in most applications.

Menus are so important that almost any real Windows application has at least one. In fact, an application can also have several menus that change at run-time (more on this later). The Borland programmers who created Delphi also considered them very important; the menu components are in the Standard page of the Components palette.

The Structure of a Menu

Before delving into ideas and examples on the use of menus in Delphi, let me recap some general information on menus and their structure.

Usually, a menu has two levels. A menu bar contains the names of the pull-down menus. Each pull-down menu contains a number of items. You can see this standard situation in Figure 8.1.

However, the menu structure is very flexible. It is possible to place a menu item directly in the menu bar and to place a pull-down menu inside another pull-down menu. You should always avoid the first situation because users tend to select the elements of the menu bar to explore the structure of the menu. They do not expect to issue a command this way. If, for some reason, you really need to place a command in the menu bar, at least place an exclamation mark after it:

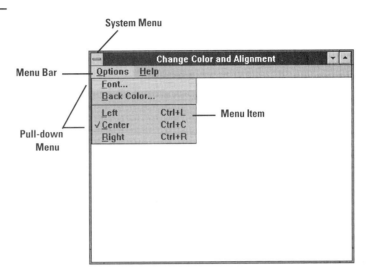

FIGURE 8.1:

The standard structure of a menu

This is a standard hint, but most users have never seen it, so it's better to avoid the whole situation altogether. There is nothing negative in having a pull-down menu with a single menu item.

Having a pull-down menu inside another pull-down menu, or a second-level pull-down, is far more common, and Windows in this case provides a default visual clue, a small triangular glyph at the right of the menu:

Many applications use this technique, but only for seldom-used commands. In fact, selecting a menu item in a second-level pull-down takes more time and can become tedious. Many times, instead of having a second-level pull-down, you can simply group a number of options in the original pull-down and place two separators, one before and one after the group.

Once I used a shareware program with four levels of pull-down menus. I often ended up clicking a lot of times before I could find the proper pull-down. For every wrong choice, I had to start again from the menu bar. The situation was so negative that I soon removed the program from my hard disk, although it was quite useful.

You can see a similar situation in Figure 8.2, or you can test it directly using the LEV-ELS example on the disk. Since it is a demonstration of what you should avoid, I won't list the structure of the menu here. As an exercise, you can try to rebuild a correct menu structure having the same commands (or better, rebuild the original menu structure I've scrambled to produce this example).

FIGURE 8.2:

The multilevel menu of the LEVELS example

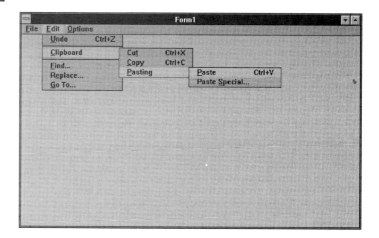

Different Roles of Menu Items

Now let's turn our attention to menu items, regardless of their position in the menu structure. There are three fundamental kinds of menu items:

- *Commands* are menu items used to give a command, to execute an action. They provide no visual clue.

- *State-setters* are menu items used to toggle an option on and off, to change the state of a particular element. When they have two states, these commands usually have a check mark on the left when they are active. In this case, selecting the command produces the opposite action.

- *Dialog items* are menu items causing a dialog box to appear. The real difference between these and the other menu items is that a user should be able to explore the possible effects of the corresponding dialog box and eventually abort them by choosing the Cancel button in the dialog box. These commands should have a visual clue, consisting of three dots after the text. This is not compulsory from a technical point of view—you write the text of the menu item—but it is so common that you just cannot ignore this guideline.

Changing Menu Items at Run-Time

It is important to notice that menu items can change at run-time. The structure of a menu can change in a number of ways, as I'll describe later in this chapter, but some important changes apply to individual items. For example, when a menu command cannot or should not be selected, it is usually grayed. In this case, the user has no way to issue that command.

Another visual change is the use of the check mark, which applications can toggle on and off easily. At times, to implement a state-setter menu item, you can change the text of the menu item altogether, which might result in an easier interface.

I'll describe what I mean with an example. Suppose an application has a List Visible command. If you select it, a list box will probably appear. Now, if you look at the menu, there should be a check mark near the item. This means that if you select the List Visible command now, the list box will disappear. When the check mark is present, the command you issue has the opposite effect of its textual description.

As an alternative, you might use two different captions for the two states of the item, such as Show List and Hide List. No user will have any doubt about the effect of choosing commands like these. The same technique can be applied to commands having three or more states, although this is rare.

Editing a Menu with the Menu Designer

Delphi includes a special editor for menus, the Menu Designer. To invoke this tool, place a menu component on a form and click on it, as shown in Figure 8.3. Don't worry too much about the position of the menu component on the form, since it doesn't affect the result; the menu is always placed properly, below the form's caption.

FIGURE 8.3:

The Menu Designer at startup

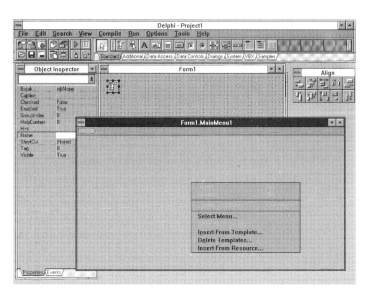

NOTE

To be more precise, the form displays, below its caption, the menu indicated in its Menu property, which is set by default as soon as you create the first main menu component of the form. If the form has more than one main menu component, this property should be set manually and can be changed both at design-time and at run-time.

My convention is to place the icon of the menu component in the upper-left corner of the form, to make it easy to spot it, but this is only a personal convention. As you know, a number of components in Delphi provide no visual clue at design-time. They are just displayed as an icon. Of course, you won't see these icons at run-time. Some of them will correspond to certain visual elements, such as menus, but most of them won't. By the way, since you have defined the structure of the menu with the Menu Designer, the menu will appear on the form below the caption at design-time, too.

The Menu Designer is really powerful: it allows you to create a menu simply by writing the text of the commands, to move the items or pull-down menus by dragging them around, and to set the properties of the items easily. It is also very flexible, allowing you to place a command directly in the menu bar (this happens each time you do not write any element in the corresponding pull-down menu) or to create second-level pull-down menus. To accomplish this, you have to select the Create Submenu command on the Menu Designer's SpeedMenu (the local menu invoked with the right mouse button).

Another very important feature is the ability to create a menu from a template. You can easily define new templates of your own: simply create a menu, and use the Save As Template command on the SpeedMenu to add it to the list. This makes sense in particular if you need to have a similar menu in two applications or in two different forms of the same application. This last case, however, is not common, since there are a number of techniques you can use to merge the menus of two different forms of an application. Some examples of menu merging will be described in Chapter 12 (for multiple forms) and Chapter 15 (for MDI applications).

The Standard Structure of a Menu

If you've used Windows applications for some time, you have certainly noticed that the structure of an application's menu is not an invention of its programmers. There are a number of standard Windows guidelines describing how to arrange the commands in a menu. However, you can infer most of the rules by looking at the menu of some of the best-selling applications.

An application's menu bar should start with a File pull-down, followed by Edit, View, and some other specific commands. The final part of the sequence includes Options, Tools, and Window (only for MDI applications) and always terminates with Help. Each of these pull-down menus has a standard layout, although the actual items depend on the specific applications. The File menu, for example, usually has commands such as New, Open, Save, Save As, Print, Print Setup, and Exit.

Menu Shortcuts

A common feature of menu items is that they contain an underlined letter. This letter, which is often the first letter of the text, can be used to select the menu using the keyboard. Pressing the Alt key plus another key selects the corresponding pull-down menu. By pressing a second key and holding down the Alt key, you issue a command.

Of course, each element of the menu bar should have a different underlined character. The same is true for the menu items on a specific pull-down menu. Obviously, menu items on different pull-down menus can have the same underlined letter; otherwise, we would end up with the ridiculous limit of about 50 menu commands (26 letters, 10 numbers, and certain other keys).

To determine the underlined key, you simply place an ampersand (&) before it, as in *&File* or *Save &As*.... You can also place the ampersand in the middle of a word.

Menu items have another standard feature: shortcut keys. When you see the shorthand description of a key or key combination beside a menu item, it means you can press those keys to give that command. Although giving menu commands with the mouse is easier, it tends to be somewhat slow, particularly for keyboard-intensive applications, since you have to move one of your hands from the keyboard to the mouse. Pressing the Alt key and the underlined letter might be faster, but it still requires two operations. Using a shortcut key usually involves pressing a special key and a key at the same time (such as Ctrl-C). Windows doesn't even display the corresponding pull-down menu, and this results in a faster operation.

In Delphi, associating a shortcut key with a menu item (pull-down menus cannot have a shortcut key) is easy. You need only select a value for the ShortCut property, choosing one of the standard combinations: Ctrl or Shift plus almost any key.

Using the Predefined Menu Templates

To let you start developing an application's menu following the standard guidelines, Delphi contains some predefined menu templates. The templates include two different File pull-down menus, an Edit menu (including OLE commands), a Window menu, and two Help menus. There is also a complete MDI menu bar template, which has the same four menu categories.

Using these standard templates brings you some advantages. First of all, it is faster to reuse an existing menu than to build one from scratch. Second, the menu template follows the standard Windows guidelines for naming menu commands, for using the proper shortcuts, and so on. Of course, using these menus makes sense in a file-based application. But if the program you are writing doesn't handle files, has no editing capabilities, and is not MDI, you'll end up using only the template Help pull-down menu.

Responding to Menu Commands

For MENU_ONE, the first example with menus, I've chosen one of the simplest applications, LABEL_CO, from the last chapter. You can see its original form in Figure 7.4 in Chapter 7. The new version of the form is still simpler: I've removed all the buttons and added a menu bar instead. This menu bar has only two pull-down menus, one with the various options and the other a Help menu with the About menu item. You can see the menu bar in the Menu Designer in Figure 8.4.

FIGURE 8.4:

The menu bar of the MENU_ONE application

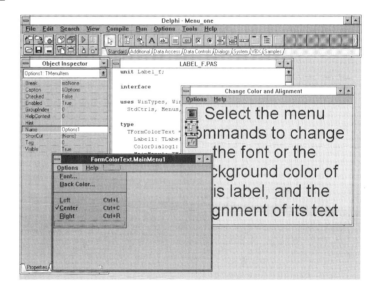

To add the separator in the Options pull-down, you simply insert a hyphen as the text of the command. Do not alter the Break property. Except for rare situations, the Break property will make a mess of your menu. You are better off forgetting the existence of this property.

Of course, the Break property has its uses, or it would not have been added to the component. You can better understand it if I use its real name, *NewLine* or *NewColumn.* If an item on the menu bar has the MenuBarBreak (or *NewLine*) value, this item will be displayed in a second or subsequent *line.* If a menu item has a the MenuBreak (or *NewColumn*) value, this item will be added to a second or subsequent *column* of the pull-down. You can get an idea of these effects by looking at Figure 8.5, which demonstrates why I've suggested that you forget this property. In rare cases, however, it might be useful.

FIGURE 8.5:

An example of the use of the Break property. The main menu is displayed on two lines, and the Edit pull-down menu in two columns.

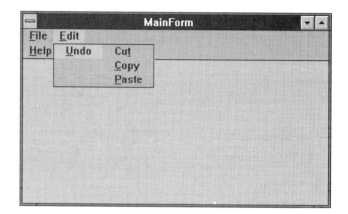

The Code Generated by the Menu Designer

Once you have built this menu, take a look at the list of components displayed by the Object Inspector and reported in Listing 8.1. As you can see, there is a separate component for each menu item, one for each pull-down menu, and, surprisingly, even one for each separator.

Delphi builds the names of these components automatically when you insert the menu item's label. The rules are simple:

- Any blank or special character (including the ampersand and the hyphen) is removed.

- If there are no characters left, a letter is added (*N*).

- A number is added at the end of the name (1 if this is the first menu item with this name, a higher number if not).

LISTING 8.1: The structure of the menu bar of the MENU_ONE example, as it appears in the textual description of the form

```
object MainMenu1: TMainMenu
  Left = 8
  Top = 40
  object Options1: TMenuItem
    Caption = '&Options'
    object Font1: TMenuItem
      Caption = '&Font...'
      OnClick = Font1Click
    end
    object BackColor1: TMenuItem
      Caption = '&Back Color...'
      OnClick = BackColor1Click
    end
    object N1: TMenuItem
      Caption = '-'
    end
    object Left1: TMenuItem
      Caption = '&Left'
      OnClick = Left1Click
      ShortCutText = 'Ctrl+L'
    end
    object Center1: TMenuItem
      Caption = '&Center'
      Checked = True
      OnClick = Center1Click
      ShortCutText = 'Ctrl+C'
    end
    object Right1: TMenuItem
      Caption = '&Right'
      OnClick = Right1Click
      ShortCutText = 'Ctrl+R'
    end
  end
  object Help1: TMenuItem
    Caption = '&Help'
    object About1: TMenuItem
      Caption = '&About...'
      OnClick = About1Click
    end
  end
end
```

To respond to menu commands, you need to define a method for the OnClick event of each menu item. The OnClick event of the pull-down menus is used only in special cases—for example, to check whether the menu items below should be disabled. The OnClick event of the separators is useless.

337

> **TIP**
>
> Once you have defined a menu for a form and it is displayed below the caption, you can add a new method for the OnClick event of a menu command simply by selecting it in the menu bar. If a handler is already present, Delphi will show you the corresponding portion of the source code; otherwise, a new method is added to the form.

The Code of the MENU_ONE Example

Here is the code I've written to complete the MENU_ONE example. Before we look at the code, notice that the label should automatically resize itself when a user changes the dimensions of the form. For this reason, you have to set its Align property to alClient.

The two menu commands involving dialog boxes should set the startup value and then retrieve the final value only if the user has selected the OK button (that is, if the Execute function returns True):

```
procedure TFormColorText.Font1Click(Sender: TObject);
begin
  with FontDialog1 do
  begin
    Font := Label1.Font;
    if Execute then
      Label1.Font := Font;
  end;
end;

procedure TFormColorText.BackColor1Click(Sender: TObject);
begin
  with ColorDialog1 do
  begin
    Color := Label1.Color;
    if Execute then
      Label1.Color := Color;
  end;
end;
```

Three more menu commands are used to change the alignment of the text in the label. A first-draft version of their code is shown here:

```
procedure TFormColorText.Left1Click(Sender: TObject);
begin
  Label1.Alignment := taLeftJustify;
end;

procedure TFormColorText.Center1Click(Sender: TObject);
begin
  Label1.Alignment := taCenter;
end;

procedure TFormColorText.Right1Click(Sender: TObject);
begin
  Label1.Alignment := taRightJustify;
end;
```

This works fine, but the resulting application doesn't follow the standard guidelines. Each time you have a series of choices in a menu, the selected choice should have a check mark beside it. To accomplish this, you need to create two different operations. First of all, you have to place a check mark near the default choice, Center, changing the value of the menu item's Check property in the Object Inspector. Second, you should correct the code so that each time the selection changes, the check mark is properly set (as shown in Figure 8.6):

```
procedure TFormColorText.Left1Click(Sender: TObject);
begin
  Label1.Alignment := taLeftJustify;
  Left1.Checked := True;
  Center1.Checked := False;
  Right1.Checked := False;
end;
```

The other two functions are similar. You might as well copy the source code of the last three statements, paste this text twice in the other two functions, and correct the values of the three Checked properties so that each time one of them is set to True.

FIGURE 8.6:

The check mark in the pull-down
menu of the MENU_ONE example
indicates the current selection.

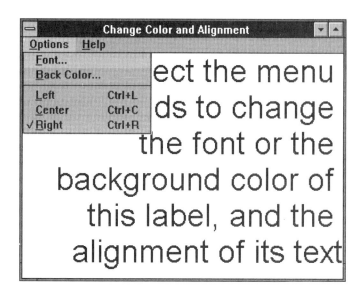

FIGURE 8.6:

The check mark in the pull-down menu of the MENU_ONE example indicates the current selection.

Checking and Disabling Menus

You can perform a number of operations in Windows to change the structure of the menu at run-time. For the moment, we will focus only on changes involving single menu items.

Changing Menu Items

Three properties are commonly used to modify a menu item. We used the Checked property in the example above to add or remove a check mark beside the menu item. The Enabled property can be used to gray a menu item so it cannot be selected by a user. The last property of this group is the Caption, the text of the menu item. By changing the text of a menu item, you indicate to the user that the program has a different status.

I'll try to show you the use of these properties with a simple example, named CHANGE because its menu changes a lot. The form of this example is shown in

Figure 8.7 and described in Listing 8.2, in terms of its main elements. Notice, in particular, the menu.

FIGURE 8.7:

The form of the CHANGE example

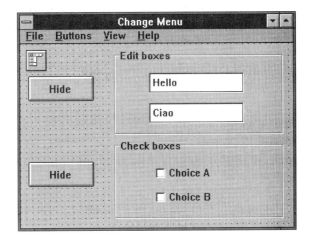

FIGURE 8.7:

The form of the CHANGE example

LISTING 8.2: The textual description of the form of the CHANGE example

8

```
object Form1: TForm1
  ActiveControl = Button1
  Caption = 'Change Menu'
  Menu = MainMenu1
  object Button1: TButton
    Caption = 'Hide'
    OnClick = EditBoxes1Click
  end
  object Button2: TButton
    Caption = 'Hide'
    OnClick = CheckBoxes1Click
  end
  object GroupBox1: TGroupBox
    Caption = 'Edit boxes'
    object Edit1: TEdit
      Text = 'Hello'
    end
    object Edit2: TEdit
      Text = 'Ciao'
    end
  end
```

LISTING 8.2: The textual description of the form of the CHANGE example (continued)

```
object GroupBox2: TGroupBox
  Caption = 'Check boxes'
  object CheckBox1: TCheckBox
    Caption = 'Choice A'
  end
  object CheckBox2: TCheckBox
    Caption = 'Choice B'
  end
end
object MainMenu1: TMainMenu
  object File1: TMenuItem
    Caption = '&File'
    object Exit1: TMenuItem
      Caption = 'E&xit'
      OnClick = Exit1Click
    end
  
    t Buttons1: TMenuItem
     ption = '&Buttons'
    ject EnableFirst1: TMenuItem
      Caption = 'Disable &First'
      Enabled = False
      OnClick = EnableFirst1Click
    end
    object EnableSecond1: TMenuItem
      Caption = 'Disable &Second'
      OnClick = EnableSecond1Click
    end
  end
  object View1: TMenuItem
    Caption = '&View'
    object EditBoxes1: TMenuItem
      Caption = '&Edit boxes'
      Checked = True
      OnClick = EditBoxes1Click
    end
    object CheckBoxes1: TMenuItem
      Caption = '&Check boxes'
      Checked = True
      OnClick = CheckBoxes1Click
    end
  end
  object Help1: TMenuItem
    Caption = '&Help'
    object About1: TMenuItem
      Caption = '&About...'
      OnClick = About1Click
    end
  end
end
end
```

As you can see, the form has two group boxes and two buttons. The first group box contains two edit boxes; the second, two check boxes. The components inside the group boxes are not really used by the example. However, you can use the two buttons to hide or display each of the two group boxes, together with the controls they contain.

The same action can be accomplished with two menu commands, View Edit Boxes and View Check Boxes. Each time you select one of these two menu commands or press one of the two buttons, three different actions take place. First, the group box is either shown or hidden; second, the text of the button changes from *Hide* to *Show* or vice versa; third, a check mark is added or removed from the corresponding menu item (see Figure 8.8). Here is the code of one of the two methods, which is connected to both the menu-command click and the button click events:

```
procedure TForm1.EditBoxes1Click(Sender: TObject);
begin
  {toggle status and menu check mark}
  GroupBox1.Visible := not GroupBox1.Visible;
  EditBoxes1.Checked := not EditBoxes1.Checked;
  {change the text of the button}
  if GroupBox1.Visible then
    Button1.Caption := 'Hide'
  else
    Button1.Caption := 'Show';
end;
```

FIGURE 8.8:

When you hide one of the groups, the button text changes and the corresponding menu item is unchecked.

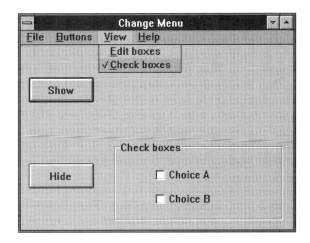

343

The other two menu commands are more complex, although they do not require much more code. The basic idea is that the two enable/disable menu items should change the text to describe the operation they are going to perform, enabling or disabling one of the two buttons of the form. This can be accomplished with a method such as:

```
procedure TForm1.EnableFirst1Click(Sender: TObject);
begin
  if Button1.Enabled then
  begin
    Button1.Enabled := False;
    EnableFirst1.Caption := 'Enable &First';
  end
  else
  begin
    Button1.Enabled := True;
    EnableFirst1.Caption := 'Disable &First';
  end;
end;
```

Things get a bit more convoluted because there is a rule determining the order of the operations you can perform with these commands: The second button can be enabled only if the first one is enabled. The buttons can both be enabled or they can both be disabled. The third choice is to have the first button enabled and the second disabled. Sound confusing? Consider the enable/disable options as two consecutive events having a priority. If B follows A, you can select nothing, only A, or both A and B. B alone is not allowed.

To accomplish this, when both buttons are enabled, we disable the first menu command, preventing the user from enabling only the first button. When both buttons are disabled, we disable the second menu command, preventing the user from enabling only the second button (see Figure 8.9).

The source code I've written to accomplish this is probably much simpler than you would expect:

```
procedure TForm1.EnableFirst1Click(Sender: TObject);
begin
  if Button1.Enabled then
  begin
    Button1.Enabled := False;
    EnableFirst1.Caption := 'Enable &First';
    EnableSecond1.Enabled := False;
```

```
        end
      else
      begin
        Button1.Enabled := True;
        EnableFirst1.Caption := 'Disable &First';
        EnableSecond1.Enabled := True;
      end;
    end;

    procedure TForm1.EnableSecond1Click(Sender: TObject);
    begin
    begin
      if Button2.Enabled then
      begin
        Button2.Enabled := False;
        EnableSecond1.Caption := 'Enable &Second';
        EnableFirst1.Enabled := True;
      end
      else
      begin
        Button2.Enabled := True;
        EnableSecond1.Caption := 'Disable &Second';
        EnableFirst1.Enabled := False;
      end;
    end;
```

8

FIGURE 8.9:

When both buttons are disabled, you can enable only the first one.

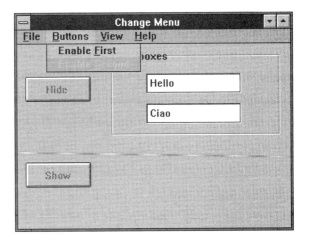

At the beginning of this section, I mentioned three common operations on a menu item: adding a check mark, disabling the command, and changing its text. In theory, there is a fourth operation: removing the menu item, or making it invisible. This is easily accomplished by changing the value of the Visible property to False.

However, I suggest you avoid this operation. If you remove a menu item, an inexperienced user of your application may lose some time trying to find it in the various pull-down menus. The user might try to remember where the item was and what exactly its name was. It is much more common to disable a menu item so the user can see where is it and realize that it is temporarily not available.

Changing Pull-Down Menus

You can use the Visible property to change pull-down menus. You can choose between a disabled pull-down or an invisible pull-down since there are applications using both approaches, but the second choice is more common.

Study the second version of the CHANGE example, CHANGES2, which has a couple of new menu items used to gray or hide other pull-down menus. The menu bar of the form at design-time (see Figure 8.10) can be different from the one at run-time (see Figure 8.11).

FIGURE 8.10:
The form of the CHANGE2 program at design-time

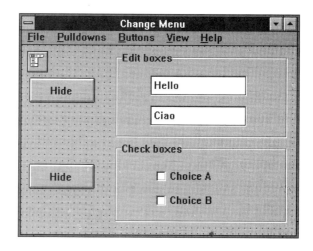

FIGURE 8.11:

The form of the CHANGE2 example at run-time, with some pull-down menus disabled or hidden

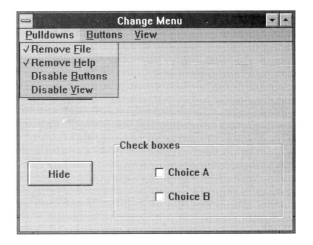

In Figure 8.11, the File and the Help pull-down menus have been removed, and the other two pull-down menus are still enabled, as you can see by looking at the check marks next to the items on the Pulldowns menu. The four commands of this menu, in fact, are associated with the four similar methods, which operate both on other pull-downs and on the check mark of the menu item itself. Here are two of them:

```
procedure TForm1.RemoveFile1Click(Sender: TObject);
begin
  {toggle status and check mark}
  File1.Visible := not File1.Visible;
  RemoveFile1.Checked := not RemoveFile1.Checked;
end;

procedure TForm1.DisableButtons1Click(Sender: TObject);
begin
  {toggle status and check mark}
  Buttons1.Enabled := not Buttons1.Enabled;
  DisableButtons1.Checked := not DisableButtons1.Checked;
end;
```

8

Changing the Menu Structure at Run-Time

The run-time changes on menu items and pull-down menus we've seen so far were all based on the direct manipulation of some properties. These components, however, also have some interesting methods, such as AppendTo, AtInsert, AtRemove, and so on, that you can use to make further changes.

The basic idea is that each object of the TMenuItem class—which Delphi uses for both menu items and pull-down menus—holds a list of menu items. Each of these items has the same structure, in a kind of *recursive* way. The properties you can use to explore the structure of an existing menu are Items, the array of menu items, and ItemsSize, the number of elements, which is 0 for a menu item and has a positive value for a pull-down menu.

Adding new menu items, or entire pull-down menus, to a menu is fairly easy. Slightly more complex is the handling of the commands related to the new menu items. Basically, you need to have a specific message-response method in your code, and you can assign it to the new menu item by setting its OnClick property. As an alternative, you can have a single method used for several OnClick events and use its Sender parameter to determine which menu command the user issued.

If you don't like this approach, there are a couple of good alternatives:

- Create a large menu with all the items you need, then hide all the items and pull-down menus you do not want at the beginning. To add a new command you need only unhide it. This solution is a follow-up on what we have done up to now.

- Create several menus, possibly with common elements, and exchange them as required. This approach is demonstrated in the next section.

> **NOTE** Besides the run-time changes on a menu's structure I've listed so far, which are all directly available in Delphi, consider that there are a number of operations you can perform on menus using the Windows API. In fact, there are several API functions referring to menus. The menu is a typical no-limit area of the system, although you should avoid the more uncommon operations. An example of the direct use of a Windows API function is described later in this chapter.

Short and Long Menus

A typical example of a form having two menus is the use of two different sets of menus (long and short menus) for two different kinds of users, expert and inexperienced. This technique was common in major Windows applications for some years and has since been replaced by other approaches, such as letting each user redefine the whole structure of the menu.

The idea is simple and its implementation straightforward:

1. Prepare the full menu of the application, adding only a Short menu command.

2. Add this menu to the Delphi menu template.

3. Place a second MainMenu component on the form, and copy its structure from the template.

4. In the second menu, remove the items corresponding to advanced features and change the Short menu item into a Long menu item.

5. In the Menu property of the form, set the MainMenu component you want to use when the application starts, choosing one of the two available. Notice that this operation has an effect on the form at design-time, too.

6. Write the code for the Short and Long commands so that when they are selected, the menu changes.

If you follow these steps, you'll end up with an application similar to TWOMENUS (see Figure 8.12), which has two different MainMenu components, with a bunch of useless menu items, plus the Short and Long commands. You can see the complete structure of the two menus in Figures 8.13 and 8.14. Notice in particular where I've placed the ampersand to avoid replicated underlined letters in menu items.

FIGURE 8.12:

The form of the TWOMENUS example

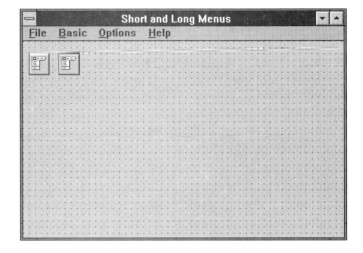

FIGURE 8.13:

The long menu of the TWOMENUS example

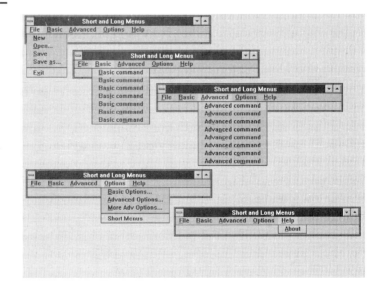

FIGURE 8.14:

The short menu of the TWOMENUS example

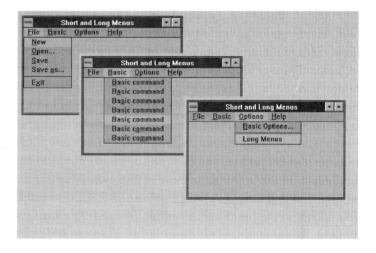

The application does nothing apart from changing the main menu, with the following code. Selecting any other menu command has no effect.

```
procedure TForm1.ShortMenus1Click(Sender: TObject);
begin
  {activate short menu}
  Form1.Menu := MainMenu2;
end;

procedure TForm1.LongMenus1Click(Sender: TObject);
begin
  {activate long menu}
  Form1.Menu := MainMenu1;
end;
```

Customizing the Menu Check Mark

As I've mentioned before, there are a number of common and less common ways to customize a menu in Windows. In this section, I'm going to show you how you can customize the check mark used by a menu item, with two bitmaps of your own. This example, NEWCHECK, involves using bitmaps and calling a Windows API function.

First of all, I have to explain why we need two bitmaps, not just one. If you look at a menu item, it can have either a check mark or nothing. In general, however, Windows uses two different bitmaps for the checked and unchecked menu item.

I've prepared two bitmaps, of 16 x 14 pixels, using the Delphi Image Editor (see Figure 8.15). You can easily run this program from the Tools menu, but you can prepare the bitmaps with any other editor, including Windows' Paintbrush. The bitmaps should be stored in two BMP files in the same directory as the project.

The NEWCHECK program has a very simple form (see Figure 8.16), with just two components, a MainMenu and a label. The menu has a single command, Toggle, which changes the text of the label from ON to OFF and changes the check mark, too. The textual description of this form is presented in Listing 8.3.

When this menu command is selected, the program executes the usual code to check the menu item:

```
procedure TForm1.Toggle1Click(Sender: TObject);
begin
  Toggle1.Checked := not Toggle1.Checked;
  if Toggle1.Checked then
    Label1.Caption := 'ON'
  else
    Label1.Caption := 'OFF';
end;
```

FIGURE 8.15:

One of the two new check marks in the Delphi Image Editor

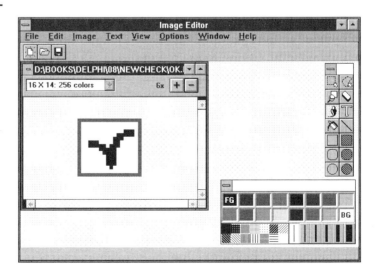

FIGURE 8.16:

The form of the NEWCHECK
example in Delphi

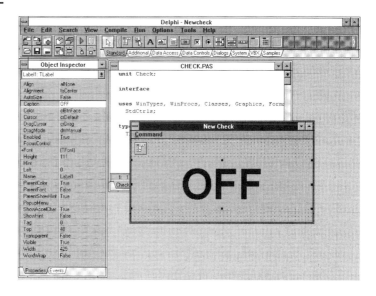

LISTING 8.3: The textual description of the form of the NEWCHECK example

```
object Form1: TForm1
  Caption = 'New Check'
  Menu = MainMenu1
  OnCreate = FormCreate
  OnDestroy = FormDestroy
  object Label1: TLabel
    Alignment = taCenter
    AutoSize = False
    Caption = 'OFF'
    Font.Color = clBlack
    Font.Height = -96
    Font.Name = 'Arial'
    Font.Style = [fsBold]
  end
  object MainMenu1: TMainMenu
    object Command1: TMenuItem
      Caption = '&Command'
      OnClick = Command1Click
      object Toggle1: TMenuItem
        Caption = '&Toggle'
        OnClick = Toggle1Click
      end
    end
  end
end
```

8

The most important portion of the code of this example is the call of the `SetMenu-ItemBitmaps` Windows API function. This function has a number of parameters:

```
function SetMenuItemBitmaps (Menu: HMenu;
  Position, Flags: Word;
  BitmapUnchecked, BitmapChecked: HBitmap): Bool;
```

The first parameter is the pull-down menu we refer to, the second is the position of the menu item in that pull-down menu, the third is a flag that determines how to interpret the previous parameter (Position), and the last two parameters indicate the bitmaps that should be used. Notice that this function changes the check mark bitmaps only for a specific menu item. (You can look up a detailed description of the function in the Help related to the Windows API, directly available from the Delphi Help menu or by pressing the F1 key after you have selected the name of the function in the code.)

Here is the code you can use in Delphi to call the function, and Figure 8.17 is an example of its effect:

```
SetMenuItemBitmaps (Command1.Handle, Toggle1.Command,
  MF_BYCOMMAND, Bmp2.Handle, Bmp1.Handle);
```

This call uses two bitmap variables that are defined inside the code and the names of some components (Command1 and Toggle1, already described in the textual description of the form in Listing 8.3). The code above shows that it is usually very easy to pass the handle of an element to a Windows function—just use its Handle property.

FIGURE 8.17:

The NEWCHECK example at run-time. Notice the new OFF check mark (usually, it is blank).

At first I thought this function could be called when the form was created, after the two bitmaps had been loaded from the file, but I've found out that is not true. Delphi changes the default Windows behavior somewhat.

The solution I've found is to execute this call each time the pull-down menu is selected—that is, on the OnClick event of the pull-down.

The only thing left is to load the bitmaps. You need to declare two variables of the TBitmap class, create an instance of the two objects, and then load the bitmaps from the two BMP files. This is done once, when the form is created.

The two bitmaps should also be destroyed when the program terminates, as you can see in the complete source code of the example, shown in Listing 8.4. Notice that to run this program, you need to have the two BMP files in the same directory as the executable file. The bitmaps, in fact, are loaded at run-time and are not embedded by Delphi in the EXE file.

LISTING 8.4: The complete source code of the NEWCHECK example

```
unit Check;

interface

uses
  WinTypes, WinProcs, Classes, Graphics, Forms,
  Controls, Menus, StdCtrls;

type
  TForm1 = class(TForm)
    MainMenu1: TMainMenu;
    Command1: TMenuItem;
    Toggle1: TMenuItem;
    Label1: TLabel;
    procedure FormCreate(Sender: TObject);
    procedure Toggle1Click(Sender: TObject);
    procedure Command1Click(Sender: TObject);
    procedure FormDestroy(Sender: TObject);
  private
    Bmp1, Bmp2: TBitmap;
  public
    { Public declarations }
  end;

var
  Form1: TForm1;

implementation
```

LISTING 8.4: The complete source code of the NEWCHECK example (continued)

```
{$R *.DFM}

procedure TForm1.FormCreate(Sender: TObject);
begin
  Bmp1 := TBitmap.Create;
  Bmp2 := TBitmap.Create;
  Bmp1.LoadFromFile ('ok.bmp');
  Bmp2.LoadFromFile ('no.bmp');
end;

procedure TForm1.Toggle1Click(Sender: TObject);
begin
  Toggle1.Checked := not Toggle1.Checked;
  if Toggle1.Checked then
    Label1.Caption := 'ON'
  else
    Label1.Caption := 'OFF';
end;

procedure TForm1.Command1Click(Sender: TObject);
begin
  {Windows API call}
  SetMenuItemBitmaps (Command1.Handle, Toggle1.Command,
    MF_BYCOMMAND, Bmp2.Handle, Bmp1.Handle);
end;

procedure TForm1.FormDestroy(Sender: TObject);
begin
  Bmp1.Free;
  Bmp2.Free;
end;

end.
```

NOTE You can include a bitmap in the resources of an application and in its executable file in order to be able to ship the application in a single file. This process, however, is slightly more complex, so I've decided not to use it for the moment. Later chapters (starting with Chapter 10) include examples of the use of resources to store a bitmap. Chapter 21 is devoted to Windows resources.

The Menu of the NOTES Program

Now that we know how to write a complex menu, disable and check menu items, and so on, we are ready to build the menu of a full-fledged application. Do you remember the NOTES example of the last chapter? You could use it to write text and change the font. That was all. Now we want to add a menu to it and implement a number of features, including a complex scheme to open and save text files. In fact, we want to be able to ask the user to save any modified file before opening a new one, to avoid losing any changes. Sounds like a professional application, doesn't it?

First of all, we need to build the menu, following the standard. The menu's structure is shown in Listing 8.5, together with the complete textual description of the form.

LISTING 8.5: The menu of the NOTES2 application and the textual description of the form

```
object NotesForm: TNotesForm
  Caption = 'Notes - (Untitled)'
  Menu = MainMenu1
  OnCloseQuery = FormCloseQuery
  OnCreate = FormCreate
  OnResize = FormResize
  object Memo1: TMemo
    Left = -1
    Top = -1
    ScrollBars = ssBoth
    OnChange = Memo1Change
  end
  object FontDialog1: TFontDialog
    Font.Height = -13
    Font.Name = 'System'
  end
  object MainMenu1: TMainMenu
    object File1: TMenuItem
      Caption = '&File'
      object New1: TMenuItem
        Caption = '&New'
        OnClick = New1Click
      end
      object N1: TMenuItem
        Caption = '-'
      end
      object Open1: TMenuItem
        Caption = '&Open'
        OnClick = Open1Click
      end
```

LISTING 8.5: The menu of the NOTES2 application and the textual description of the form (continued)

```
      object Save1: TMenuItem
        Caption = '&Save'
        OnClick = Save1Click
      end
      object Saveas1: TMenuItem
        Caption = 'Save &as...'
        OnClick = Saveas1Click
      end
      object N2: TMenuItem
        Caption = '-'
      end
      object Print1: TMenuItem
        Caption = '&Print...'
        Enabled = False
      end
      object Printsetup1: TMenuItem
        Caption = 'P&rint Setup'
        Enabled = False
      end
      object N3: TMenuItem
        Caption = '-'
      end
      object Exit1: TMenuItem
        Caption = 'E&xit'
        OnClick = Exit1Click
      end
    end
    object Edit1: TMenuItem
      Caption = '&Edit'
      object Cut2: TMenuItem
        Caption = 'Cu&t'
        Enabled = False
      end
      object Copy1: TMenuItem
        Caption = '&Copy'
        Enabled = False
      end
      object Paste1: TMenuItem
        Caption = '&Paste'
        Enabled = False
      end
    end
    object Text1: TMenuItem
      Caption = '&Text'
      object AlignLeft1: TMenuItem
        Caption = 'Align &Left'
        Checked = True
        OnClick = AlignLeft1Click
      end
```

LISTING 8.5: The menu of the NOTES2 application and the textual description of the form (continued)

```
object AlignRight1: TMenuItem
  Caption = 'Align &Right'
  OnClick = AlignRight1Click
end
object Center1: TMenuItem
  Caption = '&Center'
  OnClick = Center1Click
end
object N4: TMenuItem
  Caption = '-'
end
object WordWrap1: TMenuItem
  Caption = '&Word Wrap'
  OnClick = WordWrap1Click
end
object ReadOnly1: TMenuItem
  Caption = 'Read &Only'
  OnClick = ReadOnly1Click
end
end
object Options1: TMenuItem
  Caption = '&Options'
  object SetFont1: TMenuItem
    Caption = '&Font...'
    OnClick = SetFont1Click
  end
  object BackColor1: TMenuItem
    Caption = 'Back &Color...'
    OnClick = BackColor1Click
  end
  object N5: TMenuItem
    Caption = '-'
  end
  object Countchars1: TMenuItem
    Caption = 'Count chars'
    OnClick = Countchars1Click
  end
end
object Help1: TMenuItem
  Caption = '&Help'
  object AboutNotes1: TMenuItem
    Caption = '&About Notes...'
    OnClick = AboutNotes1Click
  end
end
end
object ColorDialog1: TColorDialog
  Color = clBlack
  Options = []
end
```

LISTING 8.5: The menu of the NOTES2 application and the textual description of the form (continued)

```
object OpenDialog1: TOpenDialog
  Filter = 'Text Files (*.txt)|*.txt|
    Pascal files (*.pas)|*.pas|
    Windows ini files (*.ini)|*.ini|
    All files (*.*)|*.*'
  Options = [ofHideReadOnly, ofPathMustExist,
    ofFileMustExist, ofShareAware]
end
object SaveDialog1: TSaveDialog
  Filter = ... {same as above}
  Options = [ofOverwritePrompt, ofHideReadOnly,
    ofPathMustExist]
end
end
```

Now we want to implement most of the commands of the NOTES2 program. Those referring to printing and to accessing the clipboard will be implemented in Chapters 22 and 24, respectively.

As in the NOTES example in Chapter 5, the Memo component, which is the only visual component of the form, is resized to fill the whole form (see Listing 8.6 for the full Pascal code of this example). Some of the properties of the memo are set by corresponding menu items. You can change the color of the background of the text, change the font (and color) of the text, align the text to the left or right, or center it. As the text alignment changes, a check mark is added to the menu beside the current selection.

Activating the word-wrap features of the Memo component is slightly more complex, as you can see in the code. In fact, when the text beyond the visible end of a line moves automatically to a new line, the horizontal scroll bar becomes useless and is removed. Setting the Read-Only property, instead, is very simple.

An interesting feature we can add to the program is a method to count the number of characters in the text and display it in a message box. The core of the method is the call to the memo's GetTextLen function. This number is extracted and immediately turned into a string with the statement:

```
Str(Memo1.GetTextLen, text);
```

LISTING 8.6: The complete source code of the NOTES2 example

```
unit Notes_f;

interface

uses WinTypes, WinProcs, Classes, Graphics, Forms, Controls,
  Menus, StdCtrls, Dialogs;

type
  TNotesForm = class(TForm)
    Memo1: TMemo;
    FontDialog1: TFontDialog;
    MainMenu1: TMainMenu;
    {menu item objects omitted}
    ColorDialog1: TColorDialog;
    OpenDialog1: TOpenDialog;
    SaveDialog1: TSaveDialog;
    procedure FormResize(Sender: TObject);
    procedure BackColor1Click(Sender: TObject);
    procedure Font1Click(Sender: TObject);
    procedure New1Click(Sender: TObject);
    procedure Exit1Click(Sender: TObject);
    procedure AlignLeft1Click(Sender: TObject);
    procedure AlignRight1Click(Sender: TObject);
    procedure Center1Click(Sender: TObject);
    procedure WordWrap1Click(Sender: TObject);
    procedure ReadOnly1Click(Sender: TObject);
    procedure Countchars1Click(Sender: TObject);
    procedure AboutNotes1Click(Sender: TObject);
    procedure Open1Click(Sender: TObject);
    procedure FormCreate(Sender: TObject);
    procedure Save1Click(Sender: TObject);
    procedure Saveas1Click(Sender: TObject);
    procedure FormCloseQuery(Sender: TObject;
      var CanClose: Boolean);
    procedure Memo1Change(Sender: TObject);
  private
    { Private declarations }
    filename: string;
    modified: Bool;
  public
    { Public declarations }
    function SaveChanges: Boolean;
    function Save: Boolean;
    function SaveAs: Boolean;
  end;

var
  NotesForm: TNotesForm;

implementation
```

LISTING 8.6: The complete source code of the NOTES2 example (continued)

```
{$R *.DFM}

procedure TNotesForm.FormResize(Sender: TObject);
begin
  Memo1.Width := NotesForm.ClientWidth + 1;
  Memo1.Height := NotesForm.ClientHeight + 1;
end;

procedure TNotesForm.BackColor1Click(Sender: TObject);
begin
  ColorDialog1.Color := Memo1.Color;
  if ColorDialog1.Execute then
    Memo1.Color := ColorDialog1.Color;
end;

procedure TNotesForm.Font1Click(Sender: TObject);
begin
  FontDialog1.Font := Memo1.Font;
  if FontDialog1.Execute then
    Memo1.Font := FontDialog1.Font;
end;

procedure TNotesForm.AlignLeft1Click(Sender: TObject);
begin
  Memo1.Alignment := taLeftJustify;
  AlignLeft1.Checked := True;
  AlignRight1.Checked := False;
  Center1.Checked := False;
end;

procedure TNotesForm.AlignRight1Click(Sender: TObject);
begin
  Memo1.Alignment := taRightJustify;
  AlignLeft1.Checked := False;
  AlignRight1.Checked := True;
  Center1.Checked := False;
end;

procedure TNotesForm.Center1Click(Sender: TObject);
begin
  Memo1.Alignment := taCenter;
  AlignLeft1.Checked := False;
  AlignRight1.Checked := False;
  Center1.Checked := True;
end;

procedure TNotesForm.WordWrap1Click(Sender: TObject);
begin
  if Memo1.WordWrap then
  begin
    Memo1.WordWrap := False;
```

LISTING 8.6: The complete source code of the NOTES2 example (continued)

```
      WordWrap1.Checked := False;
      Memo1.ScrollBars := ssBoth;
    end
    else
    begin
      Memo1.WordWrap := True;
      WordWrap1.Checked := True;
      Memo1.ScrollBars := ssVertical;
    end;
end;

procedure TNotesForm.ReadOnly1Click(Sender: TObject);
begin
  Memo1.ReadOnly := NOT Memo1.ReadOnly;
  ReadOnly1.Checked := NOT ReadOnly1.Checked;
end;

procedure TNotesForm.Countchars1Click(Sender: TObject);
var
  text: string;
begin
  Str(Memo1.GetTextLen, text);
  MessageDlg ('The text has ' + text + ' characters',
    mtInformation, [mbOK], 0);
end;

procedure TNotesForm.AboutNotes1Click(Sender: TObject);
begin
  MessageDlg ('The notes program has been written with ' +
    'Delphi for the book Mastering Delphi by Marco Cantù',
    mtInformation, [mbOK], 0);
end;

procedure TNotesForm.FormCreate(Sender: TObject);
begin
  filename := '';
  modified := False;
end;

procedure TNotesForm.Memo1Change(Sender: TObject);
begin
  modified := True;
end;

procedure TNotesForm.New1Click(Sender: TObject);
begin
  if not modified or SaveChanges then
  begin
    Memo1.Text := '';
    modified := False;
    filename := '';
```

LISTING 8.6: The complete source code of the NOTES2 example (continued)

```
      NotesForm.Caption := 'Notes - [Untitled]';
    end;
  end;

function TNotesForm.SaveChanges: Boolean;
{return value False means you need to skip current operation}
var
  code: Integer;
begin
  SaveChanges := True;
  code := MessageDlg ('The document ' + filename +
    ' has changed. Do you want to save the changes?',
    mtConfirmation, mbYesNoCancel, 0);
  if (code = IDYES) then
    SaveChanges := Save;
  if (code = IDCANCEL) then
    SaveChanges := False;
end;

function TNotesForm.Save: Boolean;
{return False if the SaveAs operation has been aborted}
begin
  if filename = '' then
    Save := SaveAs
  else
  begin
    modified := False;
    Memo1.Lines.SaveToFile(filename);
    Save := True;
  end;
end;

function TNotesForm.SaveAs: Boolean;
{return False if the dialog box has been 'cancelled'}
begin
  SaveDialog1.FileName := filename;
  if SaveDialog1.Execute then
  begin
    filename := SaveDialog1.FileName;
    Memo1.Lines.SaveToFile(filename);
    modified := False;
    NotesForm.Caption := 'Notes - ' + filename;
    SaveAs := True;
  end
  else
    SaveAs := False;
end;
```

LISTING 8.6: The complete source code of the NOTES2 example (continued)

```
procedure TNotesForm.Save1Click(Sender: TObject);
begin
  if modified then
    Save;
end;

procedure TNotesForm.Saveas1Click(Sender: TObject);
begin
  SaveAs;
end;

procedure TNotesForm.Open1Click(Sender: TObject);
begin
  if not modified or SaveChanges then
    if OpenDialog1.Execute then
    begin
      filename := OpenDialog1.FileName;
      Memo1.Lines.LoadFromFile(filename);
      modified := False;
      NotesForm.Caption := 'Notes - ' + filename;
    end;
end;

procedure TNotesForm.FormCloseQuery(Sender: TObject;
  var CanClose: Boolean);
begin
  if modified then
    if SaveChanges then
      CanClose := True
    else
      CanClose := False
  else
    CanClose := True;
end;

procedure TNotesForm.Exit1Click(Sender: TObject);
begin
  NotesForm.Close;
end;

end.
```

Loading and Saving Files

As I mentioned at the beginning of the description of the NOTES example, the most complex part is the implementation of the File pull-down menu commands. The commands are New, Open, Save, and Save As. In each case, we need to track whether the current file has changed, saving the file only if it has. We should ask the user to save the file each time he or she creates a new file, loads an existing one, or exits from the application.

To accomplish this, I've added two fields and three methods to the class describing the form of the application:

```
private
  { Private declarations }
  filename: string;
  modified: Boolean;
public
  { Public declarations }
  function SaveChanges: Boolean;
  function Save: Boolean;
  function SaveAs: Boolean;
```

The `filename` string and the modified flag are set when the form is created and changed when a new file is loaded or the user gives a new name to a file with the Save As command. The flag's value changes as soon as you type new characters in the memo.

When a new file is created, the program checks whether the text has been modified. If it has, it calls the SaveChanges function, which asks the user whether to save the changes, lose them, or skip the current operation. If the creation of a new file is confirmed, some simple operations take place, including using *Untitled* instead of the file name in the form's caption.

NOTE The expression `if not modified or SaveChanges then` requires some explanation. By default, Pascal performs what is called *short-circuit evaluation* of complex conditional expressions. The idea is simple. If the expression `not modified` is true, we are sure that the whole `or` expression is going to be true. The evaluation of the second expression becomes useless. In this particular case, the second expression is a function call, and the function is called only if `modified` is True. This behavior of `or` and `and` expressions can be changed by setting a compiler option. In Delphi, this option is called Complete Boolean Eval. You can find it on the Compiler page of the Project Options dialog box.

The message box of the SaveChanges function has three options (see Figure 8.18). If the user selects the Cancel button, the function returns False. If the user selects the No button, nothing happens (the file is not saved) and the function returns True. If the user selects the Yes button, the file is saved and the function returns True.

FIGURE 8.18:

The message box displayed when the text of the memo has been changed and has not been saved

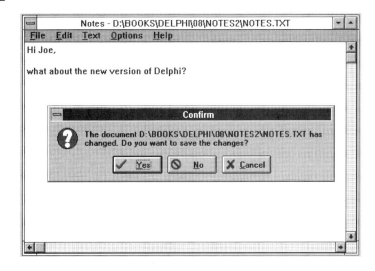

To actually save the file, another function is invoked, Save. In the first version of the program, I just called the Save1Click method to respond to the selection of the Save command. In fact, this method should simply save the file if it already has a proper file name or ask the user to enter a name, maybe using the SaveAs1Click method. The problem is that with a similar implementation, when the user selects Cancel in the Save As dialog box, there is no way to report the problem to the calling function.

To solve this problem, I've added the two Save and SaveAs functions, both of which return a Boolean value. The two corresponding menu commands are implemented by calling these two functions. The SaveAs function is based on the use of a SaveDialog component (see Figure 8.19), which will be used several times and described in more detail in Chapter 12, along with all the other common dialog boxes.

As you can see in Listing 8.6, opening a file is much simpler. Before loading a new file, the program checks whether the current file has changed, asking the user to save it with the SaveChanges function, as before. The Open1Click method is based

FIGURE 8.19:

The standard Save As dialog box in the NOTES2 program. Notice the available filters.

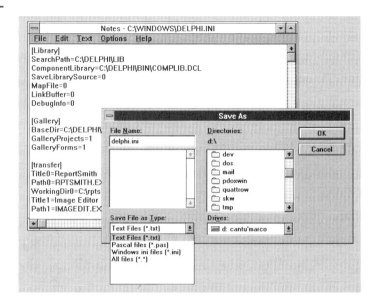

on the OpenDialog component, another default dialog box provided by Windows and supported by Delphi.

The only issue I want to discuss now is that both this and the SaveDialog component of the NotesForm have a particular value for their Filter property:

```
Text Files (*.txt)|*.txt|Pascal files (*.pas)|*.pas|
Windows ini files (*.ini)|*.ini|All files (*.*)|*.*
```

This string (which should be written on a single line) contains four pairs of substrings, separated by the | symbol. Each pair has a description of the type of file which will appear in the List Files of Type combo box in the File Open dialog box, or the corresponding Save File as Type combo box of the File Save dialog box (as shown in Figure 8.19), and the filter to be applied to the files in the directory, such as *.txt.

However, to set the filters in Delphi, you can simply invoke the editor of this property, which displays a list with two columns (see Figure 8.20). Again, more details on this topic will be presented in Chapter 12.

FIGURE 8.20:

The Filter Editor of the Filter property of the standard dialog box components

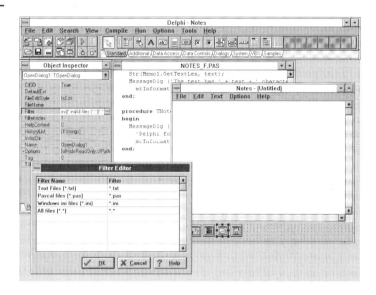

The last two methods of the source code refer to closing the form. The FormClose-Query method is called each time the user tries to close the form, terminating the program. We can make this happen in various ways—by double-clicking on the system menu icon, selecting the system menu's Close command, pressing the Alt and F4 keys, or calling the Close method in the code, as in the File Exit command.

In FormCloseQuery, you can decide whether or not to actually close the application by setting the CanClose parameter, which is passed by reference. Again, if the current file has been modified, we call the SaveChanges function. This time, however, the implementation uses two different `if` statements instead of the short-circuit evaluation technique.

Pop-Up Menus (and the Right Mouse Button)

It is becoming increasingly common to see applications that have special local menus you activate by clicking the right mouse button. The menu that is displayed—a pop-up menu, in Windows terms—usually depends on the position of the mouse click. These menus tend to be easy to use since they group only the few commands related to the element that is currently selected. They are also usually faster to use than full-blown menus because you don't need to move the mouse up to the menu bar and then down again to go on working.

Borland has used pop-up menus in many applications and named them *Speed-Menus,* although other software houses use them as well, with different names. Delphi and other programming environments use them a lot. Therefore, your next great application should use them, too.

In Delphi, there are basically two ways to use pop-up menus, using the corresponding component. You can let Delphi handle them automatically or choose a manual technique. I'll explore both approaches, starting with the first, which is the simplest one.

If you want to add a pop-up menu to a form, you need to perform a few simple operations:

1. Create a PopupMenu component.

2. Add some menu items to the component.

3. Select the component as the value of the form's PopupMenu property.

That's all. Of course, you should also add some handlers for the OnClick events of the local menu's various menu items, as you do with an ordinary menu.

The LOCAL Example

To show you how to create a local menu, I've built an example that is an extension of the DRAGGING example in Chapter 5. The new example is named LOCAL1. I've added a PopupMenu1 component to the form (see Figure 8.21), with the following structure:

```
object PopupMenu1: TPopupMenu
    object BackgroundColor1: TMenuItem
      Caption = '&Background Color...'
      OnClick = BackgroundColor1Click
    end
    object N1: TMenuItem
      Caption = '-'
    end
```

```
object About1: TMenuItem
  Caption = '&About...'
  OnClick = About1Click
end
end
```

This pop-up menu is connected to the form setting the PopupMenu property of the form itself. Once this is done, running the program and clicking the right mouse button on the surface of the form displays the local menu (see Figure 8.22).

The source code for the pop-up menu commands is very simple:

```
procedure TDraggingForm.BackgroundColor1Click(Sender: TObject);
begin
  ColorDialog1.Color := Color;
  if ColorDialog1.Execute then
    Color := ColorDialog1.Color;
end;

procedure TDraggingForm.About1Click(Sender: TObject);
begin
  MessageDlg ('Example of the use of a pop-up menu, ' +
    'from the book "Mastering Delphi"',
    mtInformation, [mbOK], 0);
end;
```

FIGURE 8.21:

The form of the LOCAL1 example

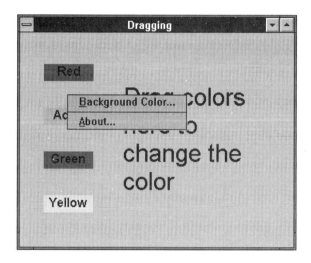

To make things slightly more complex, I've added a second pop-up menu to the
form, attached to the big label on the right, Label5. To connect a local menu to a specific component, you simply need to set its PopupMenu property. The structure of
this second pop-up menu is more complex since it has two pull-down menus, each
with several commands, as shown in Listing 8.7.

The code associated with the commands of this pop-up menu is quite simple (see
Listing 8.8 for the complete source code). The four methods related to the first
group of commands of the Colors pull-down menu just select a color:

```
Label5.Color := clRed;
```

The other two methods also involve colors. The Transparent command selects the
color of the parent form as the current color, setting the value of the ParentColor
property to True.

LISTING 8.7: The textual description of the second pop-up menu of the LOCAL1 example

```
object PopupMenu2: TPopupMenu
  OnPopup = PopupMenu2Popup
  object Colors1: TMenuItem
    Caption = '&Colors'
    object Red1: TMenuItem
      Caption = '&Red'
      OnClick = Red1Click
    end
    object Aqua1: TMenuItem
      Caption = '&Aqua'
      OnClick = Aqua1Click
    end
    object Green1: TMenuItem
      Caption = '&Green'
      OnClick = Green1Click
    end
    object Yellow1: TMenuItem
      Caption = '&Yellow'
      OnClick = Yellow1Click
    end
    object N2: TMenuItem
      Caption = '-'
    end
    object Transparent1: TMenuItem
      Caption = '&Transparent'
      OnClick = Transparent1Click
    end
    object Userdefined1: TMenuItem
      Caption = '&User defined...'
      OnClick = Userdefined1Click
    end
  end
  object Alignment1: TMenuItem
    Caption = '&Alignment'
    object Left1: TMenuItem
      Caption = '&Left'
      Checked = True
      OnClick - Left1Click
    end
    object Center1: TMenuItem
      Caption = '&Center'
      OnClick = Center1Click
    end
    object Right1: TMenuItem
      Caption = '&Right'
      OnClick = Right1Click
    end
  end
end
```

LISTING 8.8: The full Pascal source code of the form of the LOCAL1 example

```pascal
unit Drag_f;

interface

uses
  WinTypes, WinProcs, Classes, Graphics, Forms,
  Controls, StdCtrls, Menus, Dialogs;

type
  TDraggingForm = class(TForm)
    RedLabel: TLabel;
    AquaLabel: TLabel;
    GreenLabel: TLabel;
    YellowLabel: TLabel;
    Label5: TLabel;
    PopupMenu1: TPopupMenu;
    BackgroundColor1: TMenuItem;
    N1: TMenuItem;
    About1: TMenuItem;
    ColorDialog1: TColorDialog;
    PopupMenu2: TPopupMenu;
    Colors1: TMenuItem;
    Red1: TMenuItem;
    Aqua1: TMenuItem;
    Green1: TMenuItem;
    Yellow1: TMenuItem;
    Alignment1: TMenuItem;
    Left1: TMenuItem;
    Right1: TMenuItem;
    Center1: TMenuItem;
    N2: TMenuItem;
    Transparent1: TMenuItem;
    Userdefined1: TMenuItem;
    procedure Label5DragDrop(Sender, Source: TObject;
      X, Y: Integer);
    procedure Label5DragOver(Sender, Source: TObject;
      X, Y: Integer; State: TDragState; var Accept: Boolean);
    procedure BackgroundColor1Click(Sender: TObject);
    procedure About1Click(Sender: TObject);
    procedure Red1Click(Sender: TObject);
    procedure Aqua1Click(Sender: TObject);
    procedure Green1Click(Sender: TObject);
    procedure Yellow1Click(Sender: TObject);
    procedure Transparent1Click(Sender: TObject);
    procedure Left1Click(Sender: TObject);
    procedure Center1Click(Sender: TObject);
    procedure Right1Click(Sender: TObject);
    procedure PopupMenu2Popup(Sender: TObject);
    procedure Userdefined1Click(Sender: TObject);
  private
    { Private declarations }
```

LISTING 8.8: The full Pascal source code of the form of the LOCAL1 example
(continued)

```pascal
public
  { Public declarations }
end;

var
  DraggingForm: TDraggingForm;

implementation

{$R *.DFM}

procedure TDraggingForm.Label5DragDrop(Sender, Source: TObject;
  X, Y: Integer);
begin
  Label5.Color := (Source as TLabel).Color;
end;

procedure TDraggingForm.Label5DragOver(Sender, Source: TObject;
  X, Y: Integer; State: TDragState; var Accept: Boolean);
begin
  Accept := Source is TLabel;
end;

procedure TDraggingForm.BackgroundColor1Click(Sender: TObject);
begin
  ColorDialog1.Color := Color;
  if ColorDialog1.Execute then
    Color := ColorDialog1.Color;
end;

procedure TDraggingForm.About1Click(Sender: TObject);
begin
  MessageDlg ('Example of the use of a pop-up menu, ' +
    'from the book "Mastering Delphi"',
    mtInformation, [mbOk], 0);
end;

procedure TDraggingForm.Red1Click(Sender: TObject);
begin
  Label5.Color := clRed;
end;

procedure TDraggingForm.Aqua1Click(Sender: TObject);
begin
  Label5.Color := clAqua;
end;

procedure TDraggingForm.Green1Click(Sender: TObject);
begin
  Label5.Color := clGreen;
end;
```

LISTING 8.8: The full Pascal source code of the form of the LOCAL1 example
(continued)

```pascal
procedure TDraggingForm.Yellow1Click(Sender: TObject);
begin
  Label5.Color := clYellow;
end;

procedure TDraggingForm.Transparent1Click(Sender: TObject);
begin
  Label5.ParentColor := True;
end;

procedure TDraggingForm.Userdefined1Click(Sender: TObject);
begin
  ColorDialog1.Color := Label5.Color;
  if ColorDialog1.Execute then
    Label5.Color := ColorDialog1.Color;
end;

procedure TDraggingForm.Left1Click(Sender: TObject);
begin
  Label5.Alignment := taLeftJustify;
  Left1.Checked := True;
  Center1.Checked := False;
  Right1.Checked := False;
end;

procedure TDraggingForm.Center1Click(Sender: TObject);
begin
  Label5.Alignment := taCenter;
  Left1.Checked := False;
  Center1.Checked := True;
  Right1.Checked := False;
end;

procedure TDraggingForm.Right1Click(Sender: TObject);
begin
  Label5.Alignment := taRightJustify;
  Left1.Checked := False;
  Center1.Checked := False;
  Right1.Checked := True;
end;

procedure TDraggingForm.PopupMenu2Popup(Sender: TObject);
var
  Counter: Integer;
begin
  {un-checks all menu items}
  with Colors1 do
    for Counter := 0 to Count - 1 do
      Items[Counter].Checked := False;
  {checks the proper item}
```

LISTING 8.8: The full Pascal source code of the form of the LOCAL1 example (continued)

```
  if Label5.Color = clRed then
    Red1.Checked := True
  else if Label5.Color = clAqua then
    Aqua1.Checked := True
  else if Label5.Color = clGreen then
    Green1.Checked := True
  else if Label5.Color = clYellow then
    Yellow1.Checked := True
  else if Label5.ParentColor = True then
    Transparent1.Checked := True
  else
    Userdefined1.Checked := True;
end;

end.
```

NOTE The components of a form usually borrow some properties from the form. This is indicated by specific properties, such as ParentColor or ParentFont. When these properties are set to True, the current value of the component's property is ignored, and the value of the form is used instead. Usually, this is not a problem since as soon as you set a property of the component (for example, the font), the corresponding property indicating the use of the parent attribute (ParentFont) is automatically set to False.

The last command of the pull-down menu, User Defined, presents the Color Selection dialog box to the user. The three commands of the pop-up menu's second pull-down change the alignment of the text of the big label and add a check mark near the current selection, deselecting the other two menu items, as in Figure 8.23. A pop-up menu, in fact, can use all the features of a main menu and can have checked, disabled, or hidden items, and more.

The checked Alignment pull-down menu of the second pop-up in the example

Changing a Pop-up Menu When It Is Activated

Why not use the same technique to display a check mark near the selected color? It is possible, but it's not a very good solution. In fact, there are six menu items to consider, and the color can also change when a user drags it from one of the labels on the left of the form. For this reason, and to have the opportunity to show you another technique, I've followed a different approach.

Each time a pop-up menu is displayed, the OnPopup event is sent to your application. In the code of the corresponding method, you can place the check mark on the current selection of the color, independently from the action used to set it.

The procedure's code (shown in Listing 8.8) requires some explanation. At the beginning, the menu items are all unchecked by using a for loop on the Items array of the Colors1 menu. The counter of the loop starts at 0 and stops at Count –1. The advantage of this loop is that it operates on all the menu items, regardless of their number.

The second element to look at is the use of a series of nested else if statements. In fact, you cannot use a case statement with the Color property, because its value is a long, not an integer.

Handling Pop-Up Menus Manually

Up to now, we have seen how to use an automatic pop-up menu. As an alternative, you can turn the AutoPopup property to False and use the pop-up menu's Popup method to display it on the screen. This procedure requires two parameters, the x and y values of the position where the menu is going to be displayed. The problem is that you need to supply the screen coordinates of the point, not the client coordinates, which are the usual coordinates related to the form's client area.

As an example, I've taken an existing application with a menu—MENU_ONE, described at the beginning of this chapter—and added a peculiar pop-up menu. The idea is that there are two different pop-up menus, one to change the colors and the other to change the alignment of the text. Each time the user clicks the right mouse button on the caption, one of the two pop-up menus is displayed. In real applications, you'll probably have to decide which menu to display depending on the status of some variable. Here, I've followed a simple (and somewhat dumb) rule: Each time the right mouse button is clicked, the pop-up menu changes. Again, my aim is to show you how to do this in the simplest possible way, not to build complex and unmanageable examples.

Here is the description of the first pop-up menu, extracted by the textual representation of the form (the example is LOCAL2):

```
object PopupMenu1: TPopupMenu
  AutoPopup = False
  object Font2: TMenuItem
    Caption = '&Font...'
    OnClick = Font1Click
  end
  object BackColor2: TMenuItem
    Caption = '&Back Color...'
    OnClick = BackColor1Click
  end
end
```

The second pop-up menu is shown in Figure 8.24. These pop-up menus have been built by copying the main menu to a template and then pasting from it. The only change I've made is to remove the shortcut keys, since they make no sense in a pop-up menu.

FIGURE 8.24:

The second pop-up menu of the LOCAL2 example in the Delphi Menu Designer

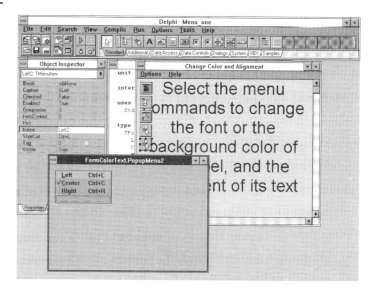

When the user clicks the right mouse button over the label, which takes up the whole surface of the form, a method displays one of the two menus (see the source code in Listing 8.9). In this procedure, you first have to check which mouse button was clicked:

```
if Button = mbRight then
```

The second step is to translate the coordinate of the position of the mouse click from client coordinates—the x and y parameters of the mouse events are in the client co-ordinate system, having their origin in the top-left corner of the form—to screen co-ordinates, using the ClientToScreen method. Screen coordinates are required by the PopupMenu component's Popup method. The menu commands of these two pop-up menus reuse the methods of the corresponding menu items of the main menu.

LISTING 8.9: The source code of the OnMouseDown event of the LOCAL2
example, used to display one of the two pop-up menus

```
procedure TFormColorText.Label1MouseDown(Sender: TObject;
  Button: TMouseButton; Shift: TShiftState; X, Y: Integer);
var
  ClientPoint, ScreenPoint: TPoint;
begin
  {if the right mouse button has been pressed}
  if Button = mbRight then
  begin
    {convert coordinates}
    ClientPoint.X := X;
    ClientPoint.Y := Y;
    ScreenPoint := ClientToScreen (ClientPoint);
    {show one of the two menus, alterning them}
    Inc (ClickCount);
    if Odd (ClickCount) then
      PopupMenu1.Popup (ScreenPoint.X, ScreenPoint.Y)
    else
    begin
      {set the checkmark as in the main menu}
      Left2.Checked := Left1.Checked;
      Center2.Checked := Center1.Checked;
      Right2.Checked := Right1.Checked;
      PopupMenu2.Popup (ScreenPoint.X, ScreenPoint.Y);
    end;
  end;
end;
```

Summary

In this chapter, we have seen how to create a main menu or a pop-up menu in Delphi. These are the key elements:

- When defining a menu, follow the standard guidelines for the names of the pull-down menus and of the menu items and for their ordering.

- Remember to use shortcut keys and the ampersand properly, but use them a lot, to allow the user to access the menu by using the keyboard.

- Check menu items, disable them, and change the structure of a menu at will; Delphi and Windows offer a number of choices for changing a menu at run-time.

- Use local menus whenever possible, as most large applications do.

You can explore in other directions, as well. For example, you can create a menu dynamically (at run-time) or copy portions of a menu to another menu. We will see some further examples on the use of the menu, particularly in Chapter 12, when we will explore menu-merging techniques, the problems related to the use of menus in dialog boxes, a custom use of the system menu, and other related topics.

But first, in the next chapter, we will start exploring in detail a key element of Delphi programming: forms.

CHAPTER

NINE

Back to the Form

- The hidden application window

- Form styles and topmost forms

- Border styles and icons

- Form positioning and scaling

- Form creation

- Mouse input

- How to draw and paint on a form

9

If you've read the book up to this point, you should now be able to use Delphi's basic components and to create and use menus. So I suppose it's time to turn our attention to the central element of the development in Delphi: the form. We have used forms since the first chapter, but I've never described to you in detail what you can do with a form, which properties you can use, or which methods of the TForm component are particularly interesting.

In this chapter, we'll look at some of the properties and styles of forms and at their size and position. We'll also devote some time to input and output on a form. Let me start this chapter with a general, theoretical discussion on forms and windows.

Forms versus Windows

Do you remember the title of the first chapter of this book? It was "A Form Is a Window," and at the beginning of the text I explained that there is a sort of correspondence between the forms we create in Delphi and the Windows windows. Now it's time to look into the details of this correspondence.

In Windows, most of the elements of the user interface are windows. For this reason, in Delphi most of the components are also windows—most of them, but not all; there are some very interesting exceptions. Of course, this is not what a user perceives. To make things clearer, study the following definitions carefully. Then we can make some further observations.

- From a user standpoint, a window is a portion of the screen surrounded by a border, having a caption and usually a system menu, that can be moved on the screen, closed, and at times also minimized and maximized. Windows move on the screen or inside other windows, as in MDI applications—think of the familiar look of the Program Manager. These user windows can be divided into two general categories: main windows and dialog boxes.

- Technically speaking, a window is an entry in an internal memory area of the Windows system, often corresponding to an element visible on the screen, that has some associated code. One of the Windows system libraries contains a list of all the windows that have been built by every application and assigns to each of them a unique number (usually known as a *handle*). Some of these windows are perceived as such by the users (see the first definition above), others have the role of controls or visual components, others are temporarily created by the system (for example, to show a pull-down menu), and still others are created by the application but remain hidden from the user.

The common denominator of all windows is that they are known by the Windows system and refer to a function for their behavior: each time an event takes place in the system, the function associated with the corresponding window is called.

> **NOTE**
>
> The area of the Windows system listing all the windows that have been built is limited. Building too many windows reduces the so-called *system resources,* as you can see from the Program Manager About box. Once there are too many windows in the system (counting all the controls and hidden windows, as well), you cannot create one more window, something that will block most applications. The obvious solution is to close one or more applications to free some system space. However, some applications give the user ambiguous messages, such as `There is not enough memory to ...'`. This refers not to the overall memory of your computer but to the limited portion of memory the system uses for this special purpose. As you might imagine from this discussion, the more windows you build, the worse the situation becomes. This is why, in Delphi, there are a number of non-windowed components, including labels. This approach lets you save a lot of this system memory without having to worry about or even know about it. We will see some details about system resources in Chapter 20, and also write a program to monitor them.

With these general definitions in mind, we can now move back to Delphi and try to understand the role of forms. Forms represent windows from a user standpoint and can be used to build main windows, MDI windows, and dialog boxes. Their behavior depends mostly on their code, but also on a couple of very important properties I'll discuss in a moment.

Many other components are based on windows, but only forms define windows from a user point of view. The other windowed components, or controls, can be defined as windows only according to the second, technical definition.

Take as an example the first application we built in Chapter 1, HELLO. Using the WinSight tool that comes with Delphi, you can see the list of the windows created by the application, as shown in Figure 9.1 (for more details on WinSight and the information it can deliver, see Chapter 20). These include the following windows:

- A main window, the form, with the title *Hello*. It is an overlapped window of class TForm1.

- A child window, the button inside the form, with the title *Say Hello*. This is a child window of class TButton.

- A hidden main window, the application window, entitled *Hello*. This is a pop-up window of class TApplication.

- An extra hint pop-up window (hints are covered in Chapter 11).

Notice that the names in brackets in WinSight, which are internal names of the system, correspond to the names of the classes of the Delphi components.

FIGURE 9.1:

The windows of the HELLO application as they appear in WinSight

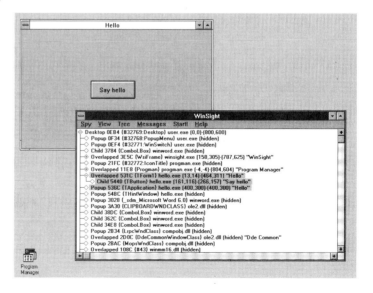

Overlapped, Pop-Up, and Child Windows

To understand the role of the various windows of this program, we need to look at some technical elements related to the Windows environment. These are not simple ideas, but I think they are worth knowing.

Each window you create has one of three general styles that determine its behavior. These styles are overlapped, pop-up, and child. *Overlapped* windows are main windows of the application, which behave as you would probably expect. *Pop-up* windows are often used for dialog boxes and message boxes and can be considered a leftover from older versions of the system. In fact, in Windows 1.0, the windows were not overlapped but tiled, and only the pop-up windows could cover other windows. Pop-up windows are generally very similar to overlapped windows.

The third group, *child* windows, was originally used for controls inside a dialog box. You can use this style for any window that cannot move outside the client area of the parent window. The obvious extension is to use child windows to build MDI applications, but, as we will see in Chapter 12, Microsoft added a fix-up technique to allow this behavior, which is not automatic.

It is important to note that, technically speaking, only child windows can have a parent. Any other window, however, can have an owner. An *owner* is a window that has a continuous message exchange with the windows it owns—for example, when the window is reduced to an icon, when it is activated, and so on. Usually a parent is also the owner, but it forces its child to live inside its client area. The child windows use not screen coordinates but instead the client area coordinates of their parent window; they borrow pixels not from the screen to display themselves but from their parent window.

In Delphi, forms are all overlapped windows, even the dialog boxes, and the windowed components (the controls) you place inside a form are all owned by the form. However, their parent can be either the form or one of the special *container* components, such as the GroupBox or the Panel. When you place a radio button inside a group box, the group box is its parent, but the form is its owner.

What about pop-up windows? In Delphi, they are used only for the hidden application window.

The Application Is a Window

From the analysis of the WinSight information, you might have noticed something very strange: the application is a window! When I first noticed this I was astonished, because the forms work so well they appear to be the main windows of the application. Instead, forms are connected to an owner, the application window. This window is hidden from sight unless you minimize the form.

What are the role and effect of this hidden main window? The role of the application object is to provide some startup code before you create any form, or even before you decide which form to create. The application's initialization code usually looks like this:

```
begin
  Application.CreateForm(TForm1, Form1);
  Application.Run;
end.
```

The window related to the Application object—the application window—serves to keep together all the windows of an application. The fact that all the top-level forms of a program have this hidden owner window, for example, is fundamental when the application is activated.

In fact, when the windows of your program are behind other windows, clicking on one window in your application will bring all of your application's windows to the front. In other words, the hidden application window is used to connect the different forms of the application.

The Application object, which is an instance of one of the few components not present in the Components palette, has some properties, including the name of the executable file and the title of the application. The title usually is the name of the executable file without the extension.

When you work with the form, you do not see the application's title. However, Windows contains this name in its internal list of main windows (erroneously called the task list). When you open the Task Manager (by pressing Ctrl-Esc or double-clicking on the background), the application title appears in the list instead of the caption of the main form. The same name appears when you scan the running application with the Alt-Tab keys. Again, the application's title is used when the application is minimized.

If you don't like this discrepancy between the two titles, you can change the application's title at design-time, in the Application page of the Project Options dialog box. At run-time, you can copy the form's caption to the title of the application with this code:

```
Application.Title := Form1.Caption;
```

> **NOTE** The presence of the hidden application window causes some other strange behaviors in Delphi. For example, Delphi applications do not tile or cascade properly. These odd behaviors were actually introduced by Microsoft with Visual Basic. The structure of Delphi applications follows the Visual Basic approach.

The application window is hidden in most applications, but it has some interesting uses. For this reason, all of Chapter 19 is devoted to this topic.

Setting Form Styles

Among the properties of a form, two of them determine the fundamental rules of its behavior: FormStyle and BorderStyle. The first of these two special properties allows you to choose between a normal SDI form—*SDI* stands for *Single Document Interface*—and one of the windows that make up an MDI application. The values of FormStyle are:

- `fsNormal`: The form is a normal SDI window or a dialog box.
- `fsMDIChild`: The form is an MDI child window.
- `fsMDIForm`: The form is an MDI parent window—that is, the frame window of the MDI application.
- `fsStayOnTop`: The form is an SDI window, but it always remains on top of all other windows except for any that also happen to have a similar topmost style.

Since an application following the Multiple Document Interface standard needs windows of two different kinds (frame and child), two values of the FormStyle property are involved. To build an MDI application, you can use the standard application template or look at Chapter 15, which focuses on the MDI in detail. For now, though, it might be interesting to explore the use of the fsStayOnTop style.

Creating Topmost Forms

To create a topmost form, you need only set the FormStyle property, as indicated above. However, what is the behavior of a topmost form?

In Windows 3.1, there are two standard applications that can have topmost windows: Clock and WinHelp. In these programs, when you select a specific menu command, the main window receives the Topmost style and always remains in front of every other window, including the active one. You can try to use these applications to understand the behavior of topmost windows, or look at Figure 9.2 for a similar example with the TOP application, which I'll discuss in a moment.

FIGURE 9.2:

The main window of the TOP application is always on top of the active window (notice the color of the title bars).

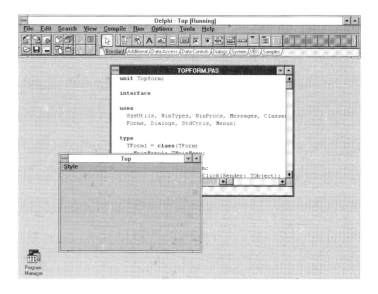

Before we look at an example, however, consider that topmost windows can be useful, but they can also be very disappointing. When a topmost window is maximized, activating another application (for example, with the Alt-Tab keys) has almost no effect. My advice is to use topmost windows sparingly.

TIP

Notice this difference between Delphi topmost windows and typical Windows topmost windows: when they are minimized, their icon doesn't remain in front of the active window. The reason for this difference is obvious if you consider that the icon is really another window, the application window. Again, Delphi behavior follows the Visual Basic approach. In any case, I tend to like this solution more than the plain Windows topmost style.

Building a topmost window is very easy. I've decided to create an example, TOP, that also allows a user to toggle the Topmost attribute on and off.

The form of the example has only a menu component, as you can see in the textual description of Listing 9.1. As you can see in the code, the Topmost style is set at design-time. When the user selects the Stay on Top command from the Style menu, this style is toggled, together with the check mark beside the menu item:

```
procedure TForm1.Stayontop1Click(Sender: TObject);
begin
  if FormStyle = fsStayOnTop then
  begin
    FormStyle := fsNormal;
    StayOnTop1.Checked := False;
  end
  else
  begin
    FormStyle := fsStayOnTop;
    StayOnTop1.Checked := True;
  end;
end;
```

When you run this program, you can notice some flickering when the topmost style is set or removed. This occurs because Delphi has to destroy and re-create the (same) window each time you toggle the value of the Topmost property.

LISTING 9.1: The textual description of the simple form of the TOP example

```
object Form1: TForm1
  Caption = 'Top'
  FormStyle = fsStayOnTop
  Menu = MainMenu1
  object MainMenu1: TMainMenu
    object Style1: TMenuItem
      Caption = '&Style'
      object Stayontop1: TMenuItem
        Caption = '&Stay on top'
        Checked = True
        OnClick = Stayontop1Click
      end
    end
  end
end
```

Avoiding Topmost Flickering

To avoid the negative effect of topmost flickering, we can forget for a second what we know about Delphi and this form property and ask ourselves how we could have toggled the Topmost attribute using the Windows API. There are a number of techniques. The Topmost attribute is technically an extended Windows style (ws_ex_Topmost). In regard to a style, we can use the SetWindowLong API function, which allows a programmer to change at run-time a number of window attributes. This function, however, is very complex and also requires some type conversions.

A second (and better) approach is to use the SetWindowPos API function, which has seven parameters but in our case is easy to use. In fact, there are some flags we can use to toggle the Topmost property, and we can ignore most of the parameters.

To make a window the topmost window, we can write

```
SetWindowPos (Handle, hwnd_TopMost, 0, 0, 0, 0,
  swp_NoMove or swpNoSize);
```

NOTE `SetWindowPos` is a strange function. It requires the handle of the window you want to operate on, the handle of a second window or a special flag, two position-related parameters (x and y), two size parameters (cx and cy, the width and the height), and some flags. The strange thing is that you can use the flags to indicate which of the parameters make sense and should be used. For example, if you write `swp_NoMove`, the third and fourth parameters will be ignored (for this reason, I've just written some zeros).

For the opposite effect, removing the topmost style, simply replace `hwnd_TopMost` with `hwnd_NoTopMost` in the code above. The new version of the example is named TOP2. Its form is the same as the previous one, aside from the fact that the Topmost property is not enabled at first. Here is the code for the new version of the Stayon-top1Click method:

```
procedure TForm1.Stayontop1Click(Sender: TObject);
begin
  if StayOnTop1.Checked then
  begin
    SetWindowPos (Handle, hwnd_NoTopMost,
      0, 0, 0, 0,
      swp_NoMove or swp_NoSize);
    StayOnTop1.Checked := False;
  end
  else
  begin
    SetWindowPos (Handle, hwnd_TopMost,
      0, 0, 0, 0,
      swp_NoMove or swp_NoSize);
    StayOnTop1.Checked := True;
  end;
end;
```

Notice that this time I've decided to test the status of the menu item's check mark to determine the current status of the form. In fact, the FormStyle always remains normal, even when the Topmost style of the form has been set. Remember that some properties of Delphi components duplicate information available in Windows and do not retrieve it every time you access it. This is always true for properties not having a direct correspondence in the system, such as a form's style.

If you experiment with TOP and TOP2, you'll notice that the second version has no flickering at all. Although Delphi is a great environment, at times, if you know what you are doing, you can bypass undesired behavior by using a direct call to the Windows API.

With this said, you might wonder why Borland hasn't followed this approach. Well, there are a number of very good reasons. The technique based on the `SetWindow-Pos` API shown above works only in some circumstances. When your application is made up of several windows or when your topmost window opens a message box or dialog box, the system does not handle the focus and activation of the windows properly. Basically, there are problems in Windows with the ownership of topmost windows. Delphi, with its solution, bypasses these problems.

To sum up, if you have just a single window, you can use the approach shown above; otherwise, I suggest you stay with the Delphi solution. Better yet, consider setting the Topmost flag at design-time and avoid toggling it whenever possible.

The Border Style

The second basic property of a form I want to focus on is BorderStyle. This property refers to a visual element of the form, but it has a much more profound influence on the behavior of the window.

The BorderStyle property of a form has four possible values, as you can see in Figure 9.3:

- `fsSizeable`: The form has a standard thick border that a user can drag to resize it. This is the default style.

- `fsDialog`: The form has a standard dialog box border, which is thick but not resizable. A form with this style behaves like a dialog box—it really *is* a dialog box.

- `fsSingle`: The form has a thin border and cannot be resized; it is also known as a *fixed* border.

- `fsNone`: The form has no border nor any of the traditional elements (caption, minimize and maximize buttons, system menu).

FIGURE 9.3:

Sample forms with the four different border styles, created by the BORDERS example

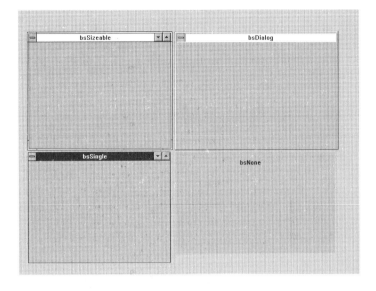

Setting the BorderStyle property at design-time produces no visible effect. There are good reasons for this. How could you resize the form with the mouse if it were turned into a dialog box? When you run the application, though, the form will have the border you requested.

Several component properties do not take effect at design-time because this would prevent you from working on them while developing the program. For example, setting its Visible property to False at design-time does not hide a component, because this would prevent you from working with it. Hidden windows, in fact, can receive no messages.

The Effect of the BorderStyle Property

At design-time, the form is always shown with the default value of BorderStyle, `fsSizeable`. This corresponds to a Windows style known as *thick frame.* The fact is that when a main window has a thick frame around it—two lines separated by a couple of pixels, or the number of pixels defined in WIN.INI—a user can resize it by dragging its border. This is made clear by the special *resize* cursors (with the shape of a double-pointer arrow) displayed when the user moves the mouse on this thick window border.

A second important choice for this property is `fsDialog`. If you select it, the form uses as its border the typical dialog box frame—a thick frame made up of a single thick line that doesn't allow resizing. See Figure 9.3 for the visual differences between these two kinds of thick frames (as well as the other borders). In addition to this graphical element, what I would like to underline here is that if you select the `fsDialog` value, the form becomes a dialog box. This involves a number of changes. For example, the items on its system menu are different, and if the form has a menu, the VCL will ignore it (along with the BorderIcons property) because Windows doesn't support these things on dialog boxes.

When are you supposed to use this kind of frame? There are basically two possibilities: when you are actually building a dialog box (see Chapter 12) or when you want to use a dialog box as the application's main window. In this case, which is quite common, the only suggestion I have is to remember that the menu won't be displayed at all.

NOTE   The menu in Windows 3.1 (and in earlier versions) conflicts with the typical border style of the dialog boxes. Chapter 12 discusses this problem further and provides a number of possible solutions.

We can give two more values to the BorderStyle property: `fsSingle` and `fsNone`. The first value can be used to create a main nonresizeable window. Many applications based on windows with controls (such as data-entry forms) and many games use this value simply because resizing these forms make no sense. Enlarging a form to see an empty area or reducing its size to lose the visibility of some components often doesn't help a program's user (although Delphi's automatic scroll bars partially solve the last problem). The last value, `fsNone`, is used only in very special situations and inside other forms. You'll never see an application with a main window with no border and caption (except as an example to show you that this makes no sense).

The BORDERS Example

To test the effect and behavior of the different values of the BorderStyle property, I've written a simple program. You saw its output in Figure 9.3. However, I suggest you run this example and experiment with it for a while to help you understand all the differences in the four forms.

In case you want to rebuild this program instead of using the version available on the companion disk, here are some suggestions for what you can do. Open a new project and create three more blank forms. Set the BorderStyle property of each of the four forms using a different value, and copy it in the title (or in a label, for the form without a border). Then set the Visible property of each form to True.

The last thing you have to do is to place the forms in a proper position on the screen, as shown in Figure 9.4. Comparing this screen snapshot to the previous one, you can also see that at design-time, the border style of the forms is ignored.

The Border Icons

Another important element of a form is the presence of icons on its border. By default, a form has in its caption a system menu, a minimize box, and a maximize box.

FIGURE 9.4:

The forms of the BORDERS example at design-time

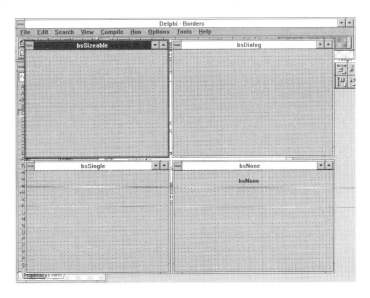

You can set different options using the BorderIcons property, a setting that can be expanded in the Object Inspector as follows:

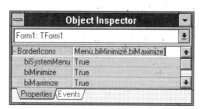

Again, I've written a simple program to show you the behavior of a form with different border icons and to show you how to change this property at run-time. The form of this example is very simple (see Listing 9.2): it has only a menu, with a pull-down having three menu items, one for each of the possible elements of the set of border icons.

LISTING 9.2: The textual description of the form of the BICONS example

```
object Form1: TForm1
  Caption = 'Toggle Border Icons'
  Menu = MainMenu1
  object MainMenu1: TMainMenu
    object BorderIcons1: TMenuItem
      Caption = '&Border Icons'
      object SystemMenu1: TMenuItem
        Caption = '&System Menu'
        Checked = True
        OnClick = SetIcons
      end
      object MinimizeBox1: TMenuItem
        Caption = '&Minimize Box'
        Checked = True
        OnClick = SetIcons
      end
      object MaximizeBox1: TMenuItem
        Caption = 'M&aximize Box'
        Checked = True
        OnClick = SetIcons
      end
    end
  end
end
```

Each time you select one of the menu commands, its check mark and the corresponding border icon are toggled. This could be accomplished by writing three methods, one for each menu command, but I've decided to use a different approach. I've written a single method, connected with the three commands (as you can see in the textual description of the form in Listing 9.2), that reads the check marks on the menu items to determine the value of the BorderIcons property. This code represents a good exercise in working with sets:

```
procedure TForm1.SetIcons(Sender: TObject);
var
  BorIco: TBorderIcons;
begin
  (Sender as TMenuItem).Checked :=
    not (Sender as TMenuItem).Checked;
  if SystemMenu1.Checked then
    BorIco := [biSystemMenu]
  else
    BorIco := [];
  if MaximizeBox1.Checked then
    Include (BorIco, biMaximize);
  if MinimizeBox1.Checked then
    Include (BorIco, biMinimize);
  BorderIcons := BorIco;
end;
```

By running the BICONS example, you can easily set and remove the various visual elements of the form's border. Notice that when you remove one of the two icons used to resize the form, the corresponding items of the system menu are automatically disabled, as you can see in Figure 9.5. This is standard behavior for any Windows application.

Forms in Different Screen Resolutions

When you create forms with a number of components, it is common to make the form nonresizable to avoid having some of the components fall outside the visible portions of the form. This is not a big problem, because Delphi automatically adds scroll bars to the form so you can reach every control easily (form scrolling is one of the subjects of Chapter 13).

FIGURE 9.5:

The system menu of the BICONS example reflects the presence or absence of the form's minimize or maximize button.

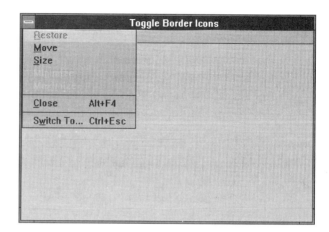

Be aware of this problem when you create a big form: if you build a form on a high-resolution screen, it might be bigger than the available screen size. This is a pity, and it is more common that you might expect. If you can, never build a form larger than 640 x 480 pixels.

If you have to build a bigger form and using scroll bars is not a solution, Delphi has some nice scaling features. There are two basic techniques:

- The form's ScaleBy method allows you to scale the form and each of its components. You can use this method at startup after you've determined the screen resolution, or it can be used in response to a specific request by the user, by means of a command you can add to the form's menu.

- The PixelsPerInch and Scaled properties allow Delphi to resize an application automatically when the application is run with a different screen resolution. Of course, you can change the values of these properties manually, as described in the next section, and let the system scale the form only when you want. To make the form scale its window, be sure to also set the AutoScroll property to False. Otherwise, the contents of the form will be scaled, but the form border itself will not.

Manual Form Scaling

Each time you want to scale a form, including its components, you can use the ScaleBy method, which has two integer parameters, a multiplier and a divisor—a fraction. You can apply the same method to a single component. For example, with the statement:

```
ScaleBy (3, 4);
```

the size of the current form is divided by 4 and multiplied by 3; that is, the form is reduced to three-quarters of its original size. Generally, it is easier to use percentage values. The same statement can be written as:

```
ScaleBy (75, 100);
```

When you scale a form, all the proportions are maintained, but if you go below or above certain limits, the text strings can alter their proportions slightly. Notice that if you reduce the size of a form too much, most of the components will become unusable or even disappear completely. The problem is that in Windows, components can be placed and sized only in whole pixels, while scaling almost always involves multiplying by fractional numbers. So any fractional portion of a component's origin or size will be truncated.

This means that form scaling is a degenerative process. If you scale the same form down 30 percent and up 30 percent over and over, you will see the form's components creep toward the top-left corner of the form, as truncation errors accumulate.

To avoid similar problems, you should let a user perform only a limited number of scaling operations, or re-create the form from scratch before each new scaling so round-off errors do not accumulate.

WARNING If you apply the ScaleBy method to a form, the form won't actually be scaled. Only the components inside the form will change their size. As I mentioned before, to overcome this problem, you should disable the form's AutoScroll property. What is the relationship between scaling and scrolling? My guess is that if scrolling is enabled, the component can be moved outside the form's visible area without many problems; otherwise, the form is resized, too.

I've built a simple example, SCALE, to show how you can scale a form manually, responding to a request by the user.

The form of this application (see Figure 9.6) has two buttons, a label, and a component we have not yet used, the SpinEdit. A SpinEdit (located on the Samples page of the Components palette) is an edit box with a sort of scroll bar having only the two arrows at the ends. You can input a number in the edit box, or you can press one of the two buttons to change the current value by a fixed increment or decrement.

FIGURE 9.6:

The form of the SCALE example

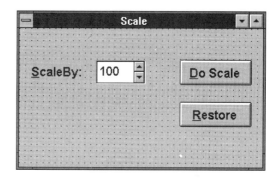

In the SCALE example, the value of the SpinEdit can range from 50 to 200. See the properties of this and the other components in the textual description of the form in Listing 9.3 (and notice again the value of the AutoScroll property, which is required to make this program work properly, as described in the warning above). When you press the ScaleButton, the current input value is used to determine the scaling percentage of the form:

```
procedure TForm1.ScaleButtonClick(Sender: TObject);
begin
  AmountScaled := SpinEdit1.Value;
  ScaleBy (AmountScaled, 100);
  ScaleButton.Enabled := False;
  RestoreButton.Enabled := True;
end;
```

LISTING 9.3: The textual description of the form of the SCALE example, including the properties of the SpinEdit component

```
object Form1: TForm1
  ActiveControl = ScaleButton
  AutoScroll = False
  Caption = 'Scale'
  Font.Color = clBlack
  Font.Height = -16
  Font.Name = 'Arial'
  Font.Style = [fsBold]
  TextHeight = 19
  object Label1: TLabel
    Caption = '&ScaleBy:'
    FocusControl = SpinEdit1
  end
  object ScaleButton: TButton
    Caption = '&Do Scale'
    OnClick = ScaleButtonClick
  end
  object RestoreButton: TButton
    Caption = '&Restore'
    Enabled = False
    OnClick = RestoreButtonClick
  end
  object SpinEdit1: TSpinEdit
    Increment = 5
    MaxValue = 200
    MinValue = 50
    Value = 100
  end
end
```

9

This method stores the current input value in the form's AmountScaled private field and enables the Restore button, disabling the one that was pressed. Later on, when the user presses the Restore button, the opposite scaling takes place, and the Scale button is restored:

```
procedure TForm1.RestoreButtonClick(Sender: TObject);
begin
  ScaleBy (100, AmountScaled);
  ScaleButton.Enabled := True;
  RestoreButton.Enabled := False;
end;
```

In Figure 9.7, you can see the results of applying the maximum possible scaling the SpinEdit allows, 50 percent and 200 percent. If you use higher or lower values,

FIGURE 9.7:

The form of the SCALE example after a scaling with the extreme values the SpinEdit can allow

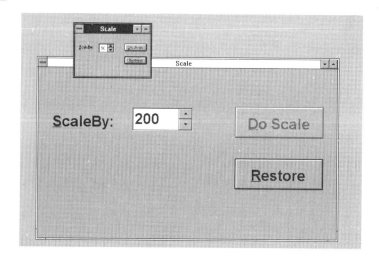

the application doesn't behave properly, and it cannot be restored exactly. By the way, even when you use *these* values, the SpinEdit cannot always restore its two arrow bitmaps properly. If you reduce the form by 50 percent and restore it, the two arrows will become bigger.

> **TIP**
>
> If you want to scale the text of the form properly, including the captions of components, the items in list boxes, and so on, you should use True Type fonts exclusively. The system font and other bitmapped fonts do not scale well. The font issue is important because the size of many components depends on that of their captions, and if the caption does not scale well, the component might not work properly. For this reason, in the SCALE example I've used an Arial font.

Automatic Form Scaling

Instead of playing with the ScaleBy method, you can ask Delphi to do the work for you. When Delphi starts, it asks the system the screen resolution and stores the value in the PixelsPerInch property of a the Screen object, a special global object of the VCL, available in any application. At design-time, the PixelsPerInch value of the screen, which is a read-only property, is copied to any form of the application. Delphi then uses the value of PixelsPerInch, if the Scaled property is set to True, to resize the form when the application starts.

Therefore, the same application running at a different screen resolution automatically scales itself, without any specific code. You can also manually set a different value for this property at design-time so that the form automatically scales when it is executed.

> **NOTE** Both this scaling and that performed by the ScaleBy method operate on components by changing the size of the font. The size of each control (or windowed component), in fact, depends on the font it uses. For example, the value of the form's PixelsPerInch property (the design-time value) is compared to the system value (indicated by the corresponding property of the Screen object), and the result is used to change the font. However, to improve the accuracy of this code, even the final height of the text is compared to the design-time value, and its size is eventually adjusted if they do not match. It is important to note that scaling is not done according to screen size or resolution but according to font size. Even at the same screen resolution, different machines can be set up with different-sized system fonts, and therefore Delphi will activate form scaling. For example, at the 800 x 600 screen resolution, using small fonts, the PixelPerInch ratio is 96; using large fonts, it is 120.

9

Setting the Form's Position and Size

If you don't set specific values for the PixelsPerInch property, you might expect your form to appear on the screen as you designed it. This is the default behavior, but you can modify it by setting some more properties.

One of them is the Position property, which can assume the values indicated by the Object Inspector:

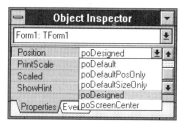

This property indicates the initial position of the form on the screen when it is first created and has no meaning when the form is active. Some of its choices depend on a feature of the Windows environment: using a specific flag, Windows can position new windows using a standard arrangement, which follows the cascade layout. Here are the possible values of the property:

- poDesigned: The form appears in the same position and at the same size you designed it. The properties that determine this attribute are Left, Top, Height, and Width, although you usually set them by dragging the caption or the form's borders.

- poDefault: Windows determines the form's position and size by using a cascade layout, ignoring the design-time attributes completely. If you run the application a number of times in a row, each time its form moves down and to the right of the screen, and if it is resizable, it is reduced from time to time (see Figure 9.8). After a number of windows have been created, the original position is used again.

- poDefaultPosOnly: The form uses the size you determined at design-time, but Windows chooses its position on the screen, again using the same algorithm.

- poDefaultSizeOnly: The form is displayed in the design position, but Windows determines its size. The right border of the form is always near the right side of the screen, and the bottom border of the form is always near the bottom of the screen, regardless of the form's position.

- poScreenCenter: The form is always displayed in the center of the screen, with the size you set at design-time.

WARNING   If you do develop a Delphi application using a high-resolution video mode, be careful not to leave the Position property of your forms set to poDefault. Otherwise, if the forms you design in Delphi tend to place them in the right portion of the screen, and a user runs your application at a lower-resolution video mode, the forms will be completely off-screen—not a nice effect.

FIGURE 9.8:

The default layout of windows in the system, with the poDefault position (using the form of the next example, POSITION)

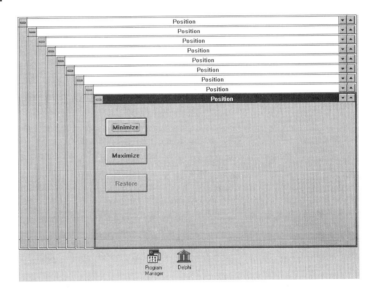

The second parameter that affects the initial size and position of a window is its state. You can use the WindowState property at design-time to display a maximized or minimized window at startup. This property, in fact, can have only three values, as you can see in the Object Inspector:

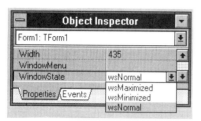

The meaning of this property is really intuitive. If you set a minimized window state, it will be displayed as an icon; if you set a maximized window state, it will be displayed full screen. Notice that if you change the default values of the border icons or set a fixed-size border for the form, it is always displayed as required by the WindowState property. In other words, if you set this property to wsMaximized, it will be displayed full screen even if it has a dialog border, and a dialog box usually cannot be maximized.

Of course, you can maximize or minimize a window at run-time, too. Simply change the value of the WindowState property. This is exactly what happens in the example I've written, which demonstrates both the default position of a form, as determined by the system, and the use of the WindowState property at run-time.

The POSITION example has a simple form with three buttons, as you can see in the textual description of Listing 9.4 and in the output of Figures 9.8 and 9.9. When the user presses one of the three buttons, a simple statement is executed, such as:

```
procedure TForm1.MinimizeButtonClick(Sender: TObject);
begin
  WindowState := wsMinimized;
end;
```

The other two buttons have similar code, with the Restore button setting the property to wsNormal. Of course, there are some limits in the use of these buttons. If a window is maximized, pressing the maximize button again has no effect, so we can disable it. Simple? Not at all. If you disable the maximize button when it is pressed and enable it again when the Restore button is pressed, the use of the maximize button of the form's border will mess things up. We need a different approach.

LISTING 9.4: The textual description of the form of the POSITION example

```
object Form1: TForm1
  ActiveControl = MinimizeButton
  Caption = 'Position'
  Position = poDefault
  OnResize = FormResize
  object MinimizeButton: TButton
    Caption = '&Minimize'
    TabOrder = 0
    OnClick = MinimizeButtonClick
  end
  object MaximizeButton: TButton
    Caption = 'Ma&ximize'
    TabOrder = 1
    OnClick = MaximizeButtonClick
  end
  object RestoreButton: TButton
    Caption = '&Restore'
    TabOrder = 2
    OnClick = RestoreButtonClick
  end
end
```

FIGURE 9.9:

The maximized form of the POSITION example. Notice the status of the buttons.

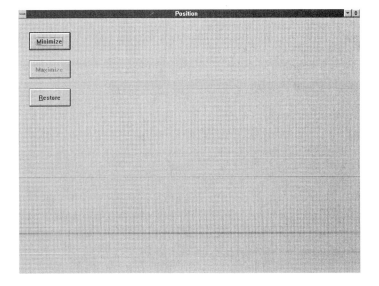

Since we are in an event-based system, we should look for an event. In our example, we can use the OnResize event, which is called each time the form is resized, and this happens when we maximize, minimize, or restore it. Here is the code I've written for this event:

```
procedure TForm1.FormResize(Sender: TObject);
begin
  if WindowState = wsMaximized then
  begin
    MaximizeButton.Enabled := False;
    RestoreButton.Enabled := True;
  end
  else
  begin
    MaximizeButton.Enabled := True;
    RestoreButton.Enabled := False;
  end
end;
```

Notice that the minimized state is completely ignored. Since in this case the buttons are not visible at all, changing their state would be silly. Notice that this code also works when the application starts. The buttons are all enabled at design-time, but since the WindowState is wsNormal, the Restore button is automatically disabled (see Figure 9.8). As you maximize the form, the Enabled properties of the last two buttons are reversed (as you can see in Figure 9.9).

The Size of a Form and Its Client Area

At design-time, there are two ways to set the size of a form: setting the value of the Width and Height properties or dragging its borders. At run-time, if the form has a resizable border, the user can resize it, and in any case, the program can resize it by changing the value of the two-dimensional properties.

However, if you look at a form's properties, you can see that there are two properties referring to its width and two referring to its height:

- Height is the height of the form, including the borders.
- Width is the width of the form, including the borders.

- ClientHeight is the height of the internal area of the form, excluding the borders, the caption, and the menu bar.

- ClientWidth is the width of the internal area of the form, excluding its borders.

Two of these properties refer to the client area of the form, which is its internal portion, the one gray by default. It is the area you can use to place components on the form, to create output, and to receive user input.

NOTE   In Windows, it is also possible to create output and receive input from the non-client area of the form—that is, its border. Painting on the border and getting input when you click on it is really a complex issue. If you are interested in this issue, look in the help at the description of such Windows messages as wm_NCPaint, wm_NCCalcSize, and wm_NCHitTest and the series of non-client messages related to the mouse input, such as wm_NCLButtonDown. The difficulty of this approach is in combining your code with the default Windows behavior. Notice, however, that Delphi lets you process these low-level Windows messages without any problem, something that most visual programming environments do not allow at all.

Since you might be interested in having a certain available area, at times it makes sense to set the *client* size of a form instead of its global size. This is straightforward since as you set one of the two client properties, the corresponding form property changes accordingly. When you modify the value of ClientHeight, the value of Height immediately changes.

The Maximum and Minimum Size of a Form

When you choose a resizable border for a form, users can generally resize the form as they like and also maximize it at full screen. Windows informs you that the form's size has changed with the wm_Size message, which generates the OnResize event. OnResize takes place after the size of the form has already been changed.

Modifying the size again in this event, if the user has reduced or enlarged the form too much, is silly. A preventive approach is better suited to this problem.

Before I show you how to set the possible maximum and minimum sizes of a window, let me recap a couple of ideas. First of all, if you want a window of a fixed size, you should avoid a resizable border and choose instead the fixed border or the dialog one. Second, if some of the controls go out of the border and the AutoScroll property is set to True, Delphi automatically adds the scroll bars to the form so you can reach them anyway.

Nonetheless, it is often useful to set a limit on the form size, particularly the minimum size. Delphi does not include a property to set this value, but you can easily handle the proper Windows message in the form to obtain this effect.

The message we can use is wm_GetMinMaxInfo. The parameter of the corresponding method should be of the type TWMGetMinMaxInfo (the types of the message's parameters are defined in the Messages unit). This structure contains a field that is a pointer to the MinMaxInfo structure, defined in the WinTypes unit as:

```
type
  PMinMaxInfo = ^TMinMaxInfo;
  TMinMaxInfo = record
    ptReserved: TPoint;
    ptMaxSize: TPoint;
    ptMaxPosition: TPoint;
    ptMinTrackSize: TPoint;
    ptMaxTrackSize: TPoint;
  end;
```

The fields of this structure are complex, but only because it is a very powerful tool:

- ptReserved is an undocumented field, reserved for Windows' internal use.

- ptMaxSize is a point holding, in the x field, the maximized width of the window, and in the y field, its maximized height.

- ptMaxPosition is a point indicating the position of the window (that is, its top-left corner) when it is maximized.

- ptMinTrackSize indicates the minimum width and height of the window when a user resizes it.

- ptMaxTrackSize specifies the maximum width and height of the window.

When you receive this message, this structure has some default values, so you need to change only the fields you are interested in. In the MINMAX example, I've decided to fix both the minimum and the maximum *tracking* size of the window and disable its maximize button. In fact, in my opinion, letting the user maximize the window without making it full screen (see Figure 9.10) makes sense only in a few cases. By the way, an example of one of these few cases is the Delphi main window.

FIGURE 9.10:

The strange-looking maximized window of the MINMAX example (before disabling the maximize button), which doesn't cover the whole surface of the screen

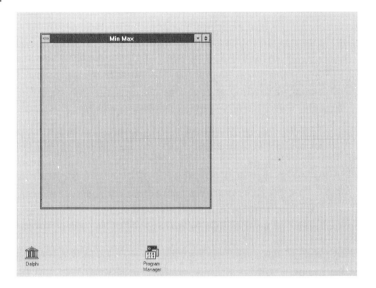

The form of the MINMAX example is so simple, I won't even list its properties. In fact, it has no components at all. The only change you have to make from the default is to disable the `biMaximize` border icon:

9

413

To handle windows size tracking you have to add a message response procedure and write some code. In the type definition of the TForm1 class, you have to define the new procedure as:

```
type
  TForm1 = class(TForm)
  public
    procedure GetMinMax (var MinMaxMessage: TWMGetMinMaxInfo);
      message wm_GetMinMaxInfo;
  end;
```

Notice the `message` directive, which connects the procedure directly with the Windows message. The second step is to write the code of this procedure (see Listing 9.5), setting the proper values in the structure pointed to by the MinMaxInfo field of the MinMaxMessage parameter. To make it easy to access a number of fields of this structure, we can use a complex `with` statement, which uses the structure pointed to by the MinMaxInfo pointer:

```
with MinMaxMessage.MinMaxInfo^ do
```

Inside this `with` statement you can easily access the various fields, as you can see in Listing 9.5. The effect of this code is simple: a user cannot reduce the window below a certain limit or enlarge it too much. I haven't provided a figure to show this since I cannot show in a screen snapshot that the window's border cannot be moved beyond a certain position. You should run this program and test it.

LISTING 9.5: The source code of the GetMinMax method of the MINMAX example

```
procedure TForm1.GetMinMax (
  var MinMaxMessage: TWMGetMinMaxInfo);
begin
  with MinMaxMessage.MinMaxInfo^ do
  begin
    ptMinTrackSize.x := 200;
    ptMinTrackSize.y := 200;
    ptMaxTrackSize.x := 400;
    ptMaxTrackSize.y := 400;
  end;
end;
```

Automatic Form Creation

Up to now we have ignored the issue of form creation. We know that when the form is created, we receive the OnCreate event and can change or test some of the form's properties. But the form is invariably created. The statement responsible for this is in the project source code:

```
begin
  Application.CreateForm(TForm1, Form1);
  Application.Run;
end.
```

To skip the automatic form creation, you can either modify this code or, better, use the Forms page of the Project Options dialog box (see Figure 9.11). In this dialog box, you can decide whether or not the form is automatically created. If you disable the automatic creation, the project's initialization code becomes:

```
begin
  Application.Run;
end.
```

FIGURE 9.11:

The Forms page of the Delphi Project Options dialog box

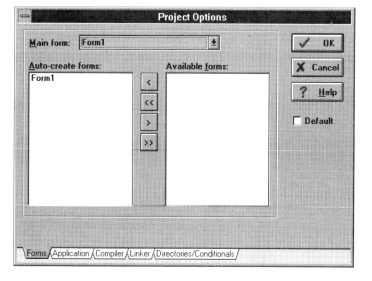

If you now run this program, nothing happens, and it terminates immediately because no main window is created. So, what is the effect of the call to the application's CreateForm method? It creates a new instance of the class passed as the first parameter and assigns it to the variable passed as the second parameter.

Something else happens behind the scenes. When CreateForm is called, if there is currently no main form, the current form is assigned to the application's MainForm property. For this reason, the form indicated as *Main form* in the dialog box shown in Figure 9.11 corresponds to the first call to the application's CreateForm method (that is, when several forms are created at startup).

Since up to now, the examples in this book, have used only one form, this topic is not too important. We will discuss it again in Chapter 12, which introduces projects with multiple forms. In that chapter, we will see that if you disable the automatic creation of secondary forms, you will have to write code to create that form on demand. For example, when the user selects a menu command, you can create the form first and then display it.

The same holds for form closing. If you have a single form, closing the main form closes the application. If you want to perform this operation from the program's code, simply call the form's Close method.

Closing a Form

When you close the form using the method just described or by usual means (Alt-F4, the system menu, and so on), the OnCloseQuery event is called. In this event, you can ask the user to confirm the action, particularly if there is unsaved data in the form. I used this approach in the NOTES example in the preceding chapter. Just as a reminder, you can write the following code:

```
procedure TForm1.FormCloseQuery(Sender: TObject;
  var CanClose: Boolean);
begin
  if MessageDlg ('Are you sure you want to exit?',
      mtConfirmation, [mbYes, mbNo], 0) = idNo then
    CanClose := False;
end;
```

You can find this code in the simple CLOSE example, which has a form with a button to close it (you can see the result of the call of the previous method in Figure 9.12). If OnCloseQuery indicates that the form should still be closed, the OnClose event is called. This method is generally used to deallocate objects related to the form and free the corresponding memory, but it is also another chance to avoid closing the application. The method, in fact, has an Action parameter passed by reference. You can assign the following values to this parameter:

- `caNone`: The form is not allowed to close.

- `caHide`: The form is not closed, just hidden. This makes sense if there are other forms in the application; otherwise, the program terminates.

- `caFree`: The form is closed, freeing its memory, and the application eventually terminates if this was the main form.

FIGURE 9.12:

The close confirmation dialog box of the CLOSE example

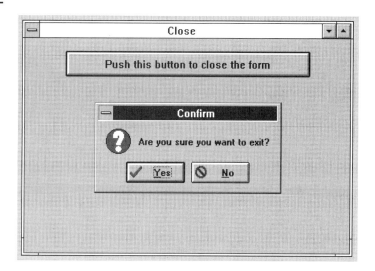

In the CLOSE example, I've written a method for the OnClose event, too. This procedure asks users once again if they really want to exit (see Figure 9.13):

```
procedure TForm1.FormClose(Sender: TObject;
  var Action: TCloseAction);
begin
  if MessageDlg ('Are you REALLY SURE you want to exit?' +
      Chr(13) + '(This is your last chance to remain with us!)',
      mtConfirmation, [mbYes, mbNo], 0) = idNo then
```

```
        Action := caNone
    else
        Action := caFree;
end;
```

FIGURE 9.13:

The second, redundant, close confirmation of the CLOSE program

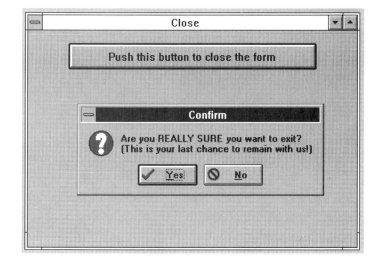

I've written this second request just to demonstrate to you that there are two possible solutions to the "stop closing" problem. Be sure never to write something similar, or your application's users will get really angry.

When you build applications with a single main form, handling the OnClose event is not a particular problem. As you add other forms to a program, they are often created at startup by the project code and destroyed only when the program terminates. In this case, the default close action, which corresponds to hiding the form, makes sense. However, when you create forms dynamically, maybe because you need several forms of the same kind in a single program, you should also take care of deleting a form when it is closed, eventually using the caFree value as the closing action (more on this topic in the chapters dealing with multiple forms, particularly Chapters 12 and 15).

> **TIP**
>
> In the first parameter of the MessageDlg call, in the code above, I've used the Chr(13) function call to add a newline character in the string. As you can see in Figure 9.13, the effect of this special character is to move the following portion of the string to a new line. If you try removing it and run the program again, the first line of the message box will be much longer than the second one, producing an unpleasant effect. As an alternative to the Char(13) expression, you can use the #13 character and concatenate it automatically in a string by writing the expression `First line'#13'Second line.`

Having discussed some special capabilities of forms, I'll now move to a very important topic, input and output. If you decide to make limited use of components, you might write complex programs as well, receiving input from the mouse (and eventually the keyboard) and drawing directly on the surface of the form.

Getting Mouse Input

When a user presses one of the mouse buttons over a form (or over a component, by the way), Windows sends the application some messages. Delphi defines some events to write code in response to these messages. The two basic events are as follows:

- OnMouseDown is received when one of the mouse buttons is pressed.

- OnMouseUp is received when one of the buttons is released.

Another fundamental system message is related to mouse movement. The event is OnMouseMove. Although it should be easy to understand the meaning of the three messages down, up, and move, the question that might arise is, how do they relate to the OnClick event we have often used up to now?

We have often used the OnClick event for components, but it is also available for the form. Its general meaning is that the left mouse button has been pressed and released on the same window or component. However, between these two actions, the cursor might have been moved outside the area of the window or component, while the left mouse button was held down. If you press the mouse button at a certain position and then move it away and release it, no click is involved. In this case, the window receives *only* a down message, some move messages, and an up message.

Another difference is that the click event relates only to the left mouse button. Most of the mouse types connected to a Windows PC have two mouse buttons, and at times even three. Usually we refer to these buttons as the left mouse button, which is the most used; the right mouse button; and the middle mouse button.

The Role of Mouse Buttons

The left mouse button is *the* mouse button. It is used to select elements on screen, to give menu commands, to click buttons, to select and move elements (*dragging*), to select and activate (usually with a double-click), and so on.

The right mouse button is often used for local pop-up menus. I first saw it in an old version of a drawing program; then Borland started to use it heavily and spread the technique. Delphi has automatic support for SpeedMenus, as we saw in the last chapter.

The middle button is seldom used because most users either don't even have it or don't have a proper software driver. Some CAD programs use the middle button. If you want to support it, it should be optional, or else you should be ready to provide your customers with a free three-button mouse and the corresponding driver (this makes sense only if your package is expensive, of course).

Using Windows without a Mouse

While I am on this topic, consider the following statement: a user should always be able to use any Windows application without the mouse. This is not an option; it is a Windows programming rule. Of course, it might be easier to use an application with a mouse, but it should never be compulsory. In fact, there are users who for several reasons might not have a mouse connected to their system, such as travelers with a small laptop and no space, workers in industrial environments, and bank clerks with a number of other peripherals around.

There is another reason, already mentioned in this chapter in respect to the menu, to support the keyboard: using the mouse is nice, but it tends to be slower. If you are a touch typist, you won't use the mouse to drag a word of text; you'll use short-cut keys to copy and paste it, without moving your hands from the keyboard.

For all these reasons, you should always set up a proper tab order for a form's components, remember to add keys for buttons and menu items for keyboard selection, use shortcut keys on menu commands, and so on. An exception to this rule might be a graphics program. However, be aware that you can use a program such as Paintbrush without the mouse—although I don't recommend this experience.

The Mouse Events

Since I'm going to build a graphics program, too, I will focus only on the use of the mouse. The first event we need to consider for the first minimal version of the SHAPES program is OnMouseDown. The related method has a number of parameters, as shown in the following declaration:

```
procedure TShapesForm.FormMouseDown (
Sender: TObject;
Button: TMouseButton;
Shift: TShiftState;
X, Y: Integer);
```

In addition to the usual Sender parameter, there are four more:

- Button indicates which of the three mouse buttons has been pressed. Possible values are `mbRight`, `mbLeft`, and `mbCenter`. These are exclusive values because the purpose of this parameter is to determine which button generated the click message.

- Shift indicates which *mouse-related keys* were pressed when the event occurred. These mouse-related keys are Alt, Ctrl, and Shift, plus the mouse buttons themselves. This parameter is of a set type since several keys might be pressed at the same time. This means you should test for a condition using the `in` expression, not test for equality.

- *X* and *Y* indicate the coordinates of the position of the mouse, in *client area* coordinates. The origin of the x and y axes of these coordinates is the upper-left corner of the client area of the window receiving the event, not the upper-left corner of the whole window (for components, at times the client area corresponds to the surface of the whole window).

We can start writing our example, SHAPES1, with a simple MouseDown method. As you can see from the class name, the form of this example, which has no components, has been renamed ShapesForm:

```
procedure TShapesForm.FormMouseDown(
  Sender: TObject; Button: TMouseButton;
  Shift: TShiftState; X, Y: Integer);
begin
  if Button = mbLeft then
      Canvas.Ellipse (X-10, Y-10, X+10, Y+10);
end;
```

If the user presses the left mouse button, the program draws a circle on the surface of the form, using as its center the position of the mouse. To draw the circle, we have to use the Ellipse procedure since neither Windows nor Delphi has a function to draw a circle. The Ellipse method requires four parameters representing the opposite sides of the bounding rectangle, as shown in Figure 9.14.

FIGURE 9.14:

The bounding rectangle of an ellipse

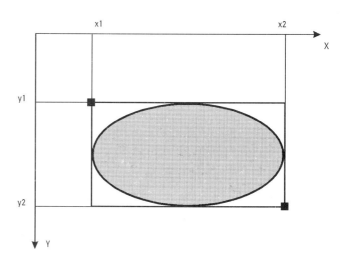

To draw on the form, we use a very special property, Canvas. A Canvas object has two distinctive features: it holds a collection of drawing tools (such as a pen, a brush, and a font) and it has a number of drawing methods, which use the current tools. More on the canvas in the next section.

Before we look into the problems of painting, let me add a couple of new features to the bare program. First of all, I want to allow the user to draw shapes of different forms depending on the keys pressed with the left mouse button. You can accomplish this by checking the value of the procedure's third parameter, corresponding to the OnMouseDown event:

```
procedure TShapesForm.FormMouseDown(
   Sender: TObject; Button: TMouseButton;
   Shift: TShiftState; X, Y: Integer);
begin
   if Button = mbLeft then
      if ssShift in Shift then
         Canvas.Rectangle (X-10, Y-10, X+10, Y+10)
      else
         Canvas.Ellipse (X-10, Y-10, X+10, Y+10);
end;
```

Now, if the user presses the Shift key and the left mouse button, the program draws a small square instead of a small circle (see Figure 9.15). You might further customize this example by drawing lines or rectangles with rounded corners. In Table 9.1, you can see a partial list of drawing methods of the TCanvas class.

FIGURE 9.15:

The output of the SHAPES1 example

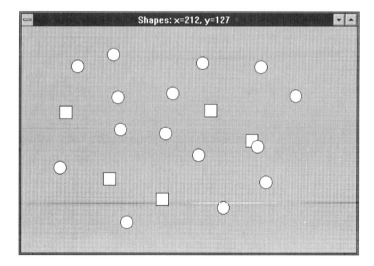

NOTE

Experienced Windows programmers should notice that the canvas technically represents a device context. The methods of the TCanvas class are similar to the Windows API functions having an hdc (a handle to a device context) as the first parameter, or to the member functions of the TDC (or CDC) class for OWL (or MFC) programmers. By the way, you can extract the hdc from a Canvas object by accessing its Handle property. The Handle property, in fact, refers to the handle of the current element: a window handle for a form, a device context handle for a canvas, a bitmap handle for a bitmap, and so on.

TABLE 9.1: The Sample Table for the Programming Series

Method	Description
LineTo	Draws a straight line from the current position to the point passed as a parameter
PolyLine	Draws a number of lines, connecting the points passed as parameters
Arc	Draws a curved line, a portion of an ellipse
Chord	Draws a line connecting two points on the perimeter of an ellipse
Rectangle	Draws a rectangle (or a square)
RoundRect	Draws a rectangle with rounded corners
FillRect	Fills a rectangle with color
Ellipse	Draws an ellipse (or circle) enclosed in the rectangle indicated by the parameters
Pie	Draws a pie slice
Polygon	Draws a polygon defined by an array of points
FloodFill	Fills a surface delimited by an existing border of a given color, or fills an area of pixels all of a given color with a new color
Draw	Outputs graphics and bitmaps
StretchDraw	Outputs graphics and bitmaps, stretching them
CopyRect	Duplicates a portion of the surface of a canvas

To end the first version of the SHAPES program, we can add a new feature. I want to show the position of the mouse in client-area coordinates to allow more precise drawings. As soon as the mouse moves over the form, the OnMouseMove event is sent to our program. By providing a method for this event, we can transform the x and y values we receive as parameters into a string and display it. Since our application has no status bar (at least for the moment) and no labels, we can use the form's caption for the output (see the title of the window in Figure 9.15):

```
procedure TShapesForm.FormMouseMove(Sender: TObject;
  Shift: TShiftState; X, Y: Integer);
begin
  Caption := Format ('Shapes: x=%d, y=%d', [X, Y]);
```

In this code, I've used the Format system function to build a string converting several integer values. The Format function takes as parameters a string, with some placeholders indicated by the % symbol, and a list of corresponding values enclosed in square brackets. The letters and numbers following the % symbol indicate the parameter's data type and eventually some formatting information. You can find details about formatting codes in the Delphi Help file under "Format Strings."

The effect of the statement above corresponds to:

```
Caption := 'Shapes: x=' + IntToStr (X) +
  ', y=' + IntToStr (Y);end;
```

The version I've used in the code is more efficient and uses less stack space than the statement above, based on two IntToStr calls and three different concatenations.

9

Now our drawing program is slightly more interesting. But the real advantage is that you can use this example to understand how the mouse works. Make this test: run the program and resize the windows on the desktop so that the form of the SHAPES program is behind another window and inactive, but with the title visible. Now move the mouse over the form, and you'll see that the coordinates change. This means that the MouseMove event is sent to the application even if its window is not active, and it proves what I have already mentioned: mouse messages are always directed to the window under the mouse, with only a few exceptions.

Drawing on the Form

Using SHAPES1, you can draw a number of circles and squares on the surface of the form, as shown earlier in Figure 9.15. This seems to work fairly well, but it doesn't. There are several related problems. If you cover your form with another window, the shapes will disappear (see Figure 9.16). If you reduce the size of the form, the shapes outside the new smaller surface will disappear, too; and if you enlarge the form again, they won't reappear.

Why does this happen? It depends on Windows' default behavior. As you draw on a window, Windows does *not* store the resulting bitmap. When the window is covered, its contents are usually lost.

Why doesn't Windows store the contents of each window in a bitmap? The answer is simple: to spare memory. A color bitmap for a 300 x 400 image at 256 colors requires about 120 KB. By increasing the color count or the number of pixels, you can easily have full-screen bitmaps of about 1 MB and reach 4 MB of memory for a 1280 x 1024 resolution at 16 million colors. If storing the bitmap was the default choice, running half a dozen simple applications will require at least 8 MB of memory, if not 16 MB.

FIGURE 9.16:

The output of SHAPES1 can get lost when another window covers the form. Also, part of the output was ruined when I moved the Program Manager window over the middle of the form.

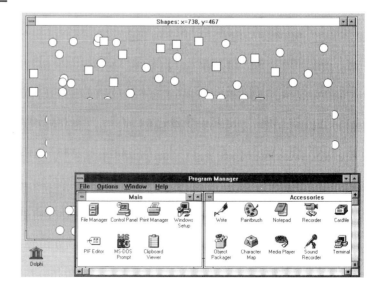

There are some techniques in both Windows and Delphi to save the contents of a form in a bitmap. In Windows, these techniques require some coding; in Delphi, they require the use of the proper components. In this chapter, focusing on forms and on direct output, I'll follow the usual Windows drawing technique, based on painting, which is the focus of the next section. In the next chapter I'll show you how to use the Image component to store the current output of a form in a bitmap.

The Drawing Tools

For the moment, let me improve the application by playing with the drawing tools available in a canvas. Here is a list of the these drawing tools (or *GDI tools,* from the Graphics Device Interface, one of the Windows system libraries) of a canvas:

- The Brush property determines the color of the enclosed surfaces. The brush is used to fill closed shapes, such as circles or rectangles. The properties of a brush are its color, its style, and eventually its bitmap. Brush styles are shown in Figure 9.17.

FIGURE 9.17:

The sample output of the various brush styles available in Delphi and Windows

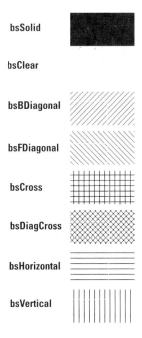

bsSolid

bsClear

bsBDiagonal

bsFDiagonal

bsCross

bsDiagCross

bsHorizontal

bsVertical

9

- The Pen property determines the color and size of the lines and of the borders of the shapes. The properties of a pen are its color, its size if it is a solid line, or other styles, including a number of dotted and dashed lines (1 pixel in size). Pen styles are listed in Table 9.2 and shown in Figure 9.18.

- The Font property determines the font used to write text in the form, using the TextOut method of the canvas. A font has a name, a size, a style, a color, and so on.

TABLE 9.2: Pen Styles

Pen Style	Description	Windows PS Flag*
psSolid	The pen draws a continuous line	PS_SOLID
psDash	The pen draws a dashed line (a series of short dashes)	PS_DASH
psDot	The pen draws a dotted line (a series of dots)	PS_DOT
psDashDot	The pen draws a line alternating dashes and dots	PS_DASHDOT
psDashDotDot	The pen draws a line alternating a dash and two dots	PS_DASHDOTDOT
psClear	The pen draws lines made up of no visible marks	PS_CLEAR (not shown in figure)
psInsideFrame	The pen draws lines inside the frame of closed shapes instead of right on the border. The difference becomes visible when the line is thick	PS_INSIDEFRAME (not shown in figure)

*See Figure 9.18

Brushes, pens, fonts, forms, and most other components have a Color property, but to change the color of an element properly, you should know how Windows treats the color. In theory, Windows uses 24-bit RGB colors. This means you can use 256 different values for each of the three basic colors (red, green, and blue), obtaining an impressive number of different shades.

The reality is that you or the users of your programs might have a video adapter which cannot display such a variety of colors, although this is increasingly less frequent. In this case, Windows uses either a technique called *dithering,* which basically consists of using a number of pixels of the available colors to simulate the requested one, or approximates the color, using the nearest one.

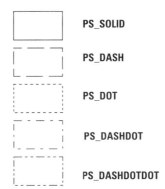

FIGURE 9.18:

The sample output of the various pen styles available in Delphi and in Windows (see Table 9.2 for the simple correspondence between Delphi and Windows styles)

NOTE

When Windows runs with a poor video adapter, dithering takes place for the background color of a form or component and for the color of a brush. Pens and fonts, instead, use a different technique. They use only *pure* colors—that is, colors that are directly available for the currently installed video driver. If you ask for a color that is not available, instead of using dithering, Windows chooses the nearest pure color. Of course, my suggestion is to ignore this, buy a higher-resolution video adapter, and suggest that your users do the same. (By the way, this is usually a good technique for losing some of your users!)

In terms of pens, you can read (but not change) the current pen position with the PenPos property. The pen position determines the starting point of the next line the program will draw, using the LineTo method. To change it, you can use the canvas's MoveTo method.

Other properties of the canvas affect lines and colors, too. Interesting examples are CopyMode and ScaleMode. Another property you can manipulate directly to change the output is the array of pixels, which you can use to access (read) or change (write) any individual point on the surface of the form.

Drawing Shapes

Now we want to improve the SHAPES application. We need to add a menu to choose the color of the shapes and of their borders—that is, the color of the pen and the brush, respectively—and the size of the shape and of its border. In Listing 9.6 you can see the textual description of the menu of the SHAPES2 example, together with the other components of the form.

LISTING 9.6: The textual description of the form of the SHAPES2 example

```
object ShapesForm: TShapesForm
  Caption = 'Shapes'
  Menu = MainMenu1
  Position = poDefault
  OnCreate = FormCreate
  OnMouseDown = FormMouseDown
  OnMouseMove = FormMouseMove
  object MainMenu1: TMainMenu
    object File1: TMenuItem
      Caption = '&File'
      object New1: TMenuItem
        Caption = '&New'
        OnClick = New1Click
      end
      object N1: TMenuItem
        Caption = '-'
      end
      object Exit1: TMenuItem
        Caption = '&Exit'
        OnClick = Exit1Click
      end
    end
    object Colors1: TMenuItem
      Caption = '&Colors'
      object PenColor1: TMenuItem
        Caption = '&Pen Color...'
        OnClick = PenColor1Click
      end
      object BrushColor1: TMenuItem
        Caption = '&Brush Color...'
        OnClick = BrushColor1Click
      end
    end
    object Size1: TMenuItem
      Caption = '&Size'
      object IncreasePenSize1: TMenuItem
        Caption = '&Increase Pen Size'
        OnClick = IncreasePenSize1Click
      end
```

LISTING 9.6: The textual description of the form of the SHAPES2 example (continued)

```
      object DecreasePenSize1: TMenuItem
        Caption = '&Decrease Pen Size'
        Enabled = False
        OnClick = DecreasePenSize1Click
      end
      object N2: TMenuItem
        Caption = '-'
      end
      object IncreaseShapeSize1: TMenuItem
        Caption = 'I&ncrease Shape Size'
        OnClick = IncreaseShapeSize1Click
      end
      object DecreaseShapeSize1: TMenuItem
        Caption = 'D&ecrease Shape Size'
        Enabled = False
        OnClick = DecreaseShapeSize1Click
      end
    end
    object Help1: TMenuItem
      Caption = '&Help'
      object AboutShapes1: TMenuItem
        Caption = '&About Shapes...'
        OnClick = AboutShapes1Click
      end
    end
  end
  object ColorDialog1: TColorDialog
    Color = clBlack
    Options = []
  end
end
```

The code needed to implement these commands is quite simple, although some-what longer than usual (see Listing 9.7). The form initializes and stores only the cur-rent radius of the circle (used also as the value of half of the side of the square—that is, the *radius* of the square) since all the other values are saved in properties of the canvas. To change the colors, I've used the standard Color dialog box. When setting the size of the border and of the shape, I disabled the menu items to avoid negative values. If you want, you can add similar checks to avoid too-large values.

LISTING 9.7: The complete source code of SHAPES_F.PAS, in the second version of
the example, SHAPES2

```pascal
unit Shapes_f;

interface

uses
  WinTypes, WinProcs, Classes, Graphics,
  Forms, Controls, Menus, Dialogs, SysUtils;

type
  TShapesForm = class(TForm)
    MainMenu1: TMainMenu;
    ColorDialog1: TColorDialog;
    File1: TMenuItem;
    New1: TMenuItem;
    N1: TMenuItem;
    Exit1: TMenuItem;
    Colors1: TMenuItem;
    PenColor1: TMenuItem;
    BrushColor1: TMenuItem;
    Size1: TMenuItem;
    IncreasePenSize1: TMenuItem;
    DecreasePenSize1: TMenuItem;
    N2: TMenuItem;
    IncreaseShapeSize1: TMenuItem;
    DecreaseShapeSize1: TMenuItem;
    Help1: TMenuItem;
    AboutShapes1: TMenuItem;
    procedure FormMouseDown(Sender: TObject;
      Button: TMouseButton;
      Shift: TShiftState; X, Y: Integer);
    procedure PenColor1Click(Sender: TObject);
    procedure BrushColor1Click(Sender: TObject);
    procedure IncreasePenSize1Click(Sender: TObject);
    procedure DecreasePenSize1Click(Sender: TObject);
    procedure IncreaseShapeSize1Click(Sender: TObject);
    procedure DecreaseShapeSize1Click(Sender: TObject);
    procedure FormCreate(Sender: TObject);
    procedure FormMouseMove(Sender: TObject;
      Shift: TShiftState; X, Y: Integer);
    procedure AboutShapes1Click(Sender: TObject);
    procedure Exit1Click(Sender: TObject);
    procedure New1Click(Sender: TObject);
  private
    { Private declarations }
    Radius: Integer;
  public
    { Public declarations }
  end;
```

LISTING 9.7: The complete source code of SHAPES_F.PAS, in the second version of
the example, SHAPES2 (continued)

```
var
  ShapesForm: TShapesForm;

implementation

{$R *.DFM}

procedure TShapesForm.FormMouseDown(Sender: TObject;
  Button: TMouseButton;
  Shift: TShiftState; X, Y: Integer);
begin
  {draw a form in x:y, using the curent radius}
  if Button = mbLeft then
    if ssShift in Shift then
      Canvas.Rectangle (X-Radius, Y-Radius, X+Radius, Y+Radius)
    else
      Canvas.Ellipse (X-Radius, Y-Radius, X+Radius, Y+Radius);
end;

procedure TShapesForm.PenColor1Click(Sender: TObject);
begin
  {select a new color for the pen}
  ColorDialog1.Color := Canvas.Pen.Color;
  ColorDialog1.Execute;
  Canvas.Pen.Color := ColorDialog1.Color;
end;

procedure TShapesForm.BrushColor1Click(Sender: TObject);
begin
  {select a new color for the brush}
  ColorDialog1.Color := Canvas.Brush.Color;
  ColorDialog1.Execute;
  Canvas.Brush.Color := ColorDialog1.Color;
end;

procedure TShapesForm.IncreasePenSize1Click(Sender: TObject);
begin
  {increase the size of the pen}
  Canvas.Pen.Width := Canvas.Pen.Width + 2;
  DecreasePenSize1.Enabled := True;
end;

procedure TShapesForm.DecreasePenSize1Click(Sender: TObject);
begin
  {decrease the size of the pen,
  avoiding letting it go below zero}
  Canvas.Pen.Width := Canvas.Pen.Width - 2;
  if Canvas.Pen.Width < 3 then
    DecreasePenSize1.Enabled := False;
end;
```

9

LISTING 9.7: The complete source code of SHAPES_F.PAS, in the second version of the example, SHAPES2 (continued)

```pascal
procedure TShapesForm.IncreaseShapeSize1Click(Sender: TObject);
begin
  {increase radius, a private field of the form}
  Radius := Radius + 5;
  DecreaseShapeSize1.Enabled := True;
end;

procedure TShapesForm.DecreaseShapeSize1Click(Sender: TObject);
begin
  {decrease the radius, but not below the limit}
  Radius := Radius - 5;
  if Radius < 10 then
    DecreaseShapeSize1.Enabled := False;
end;

procedure TShapesForm.FormCreate(Sender: TObject);
begin
  {initial value}
  Radius := 5;
end;

procedure TShapesForm.FormMouseMove(Sender: TObject;
  Shift: TShiftState; X, Y: Integer);
begin
  {display the position of the mouse in the caption}
  Caption := Format ('Shapes: x=%d, y=%d', [X, Y]);
end;

procedure TShapesForm.AboutShapes1Click(Sender: TObject);
begin
  {show a message box}
  MessageDlg ('Shape application (v. 2.0)' +
    Chr(13) + '"Mastering Delphi", Marco Cantù',
    mtInformation, [mbOK], 0);
end;

procedure TShapesForm.Exit1Click(Sender: TObject);
begin
  {close the form and the application}
  Close;
end;

procedure TShapesForm.New1Click(Sender: TObject);
begin
  {repaint the surface}
  Refresh;
end;

end.
```

The only really interesting aspect of the code is the method the program uses to clear the surface of the form when the File New command is called:

```
procedure TShapesForm.New1Click(Sender: TObject);
begin
  {repaint the surface}
  Refresh;
end;
```

Refresh repaints the whole surface of the window, erasing its contents (see Figure 9.19). The effect, of course, is that you lose any previous output since it was not stored. This program, in fact, has the same big problem of the previous version. If you move another window over this form or reduce its size, you lose its contents. We need a way to store the contents and repaint the window on request.

FIGURE 9.19:

The output of the SHAPES2 program is improved over the last version, but it is still flawed, as you can see in the right portion of the window.

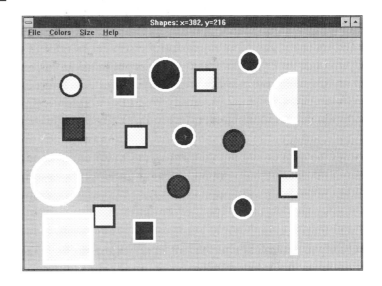

NOTE

Curiously enough, the contents of the form are also erased if you open the Color dialog box to its maximum extent (by pressing the Define Custom Colors button), but it remains on screen if you open only the basic version of the dialog box. In fact, when small areas are covered (by menus, message boxes, or small dialog boxes), Windows actually saves the bitmap of the corresponding area of the form being covered. When these elements become too big, however, Windows doesn't save the surface and later asks the program to redraw the area. For Windows experts, this is the effect of the `cs_SaveBits` class style.

Drawing and Painting in Windows

It's time to face the problems related to drawing and painting in Windows. Want do I mean by these two terms?

- *Drawing* is what we have done up to now in the Shape application. You access the form's canvas and call some of its methods. Since the image is not saved, the form can lose part or all of its contents, as shown earlier in Figures 9.16 and 9.19. The output might change because the image is not saved and the application doesn't know how to redraw it.

- *Painting* is what we will do to let the application repaint its whole surface under any of the possible conditions. If we provide a method to redraw the contents of the form and this method is automatically called when a portion of the form has been hidden and needs repainting, we will be able to re-create the output properly.

Painting is the common approach in handling output in Windows, aside from particular graphics-oriented programs that store the form's whole image in a bitmap (as I'll describe in the next chapter). The approach used to implement painting has a very descriptive name: *store and paint*. In fact, when the user presses the mouse buttons or performs any other operation, we need to store the position and other elements; then, in the painting method, we use this information to actually paint the corresponding image.

Since this approach takes two steps, we must be able to execute these two operations in a row, asking the system to repaint the window—without waiting for a portion of the window to become invalid because some another window has been placed above it. You can use several methods (which can be applied to both forms and controls) to invoke repainting; the first two correspond to the Windows API functions, while the latter two have been introduced by Delphi:

- The Invalidate method informs Windows that the entire surface of the form should be repainted. The most important thing is that Invalidate does *not* enforce a painting operation. Windows simply stores the request and will respond to it only after the current procedure has been completely executed and as soon as there are no other events pending in the system. Windows deliberately delays the painting operation since it is one of the most time-consuming operations. At times, with this delay, it is possible to paint the form only after a number of changes have taken place, avoiding a number of consecutive calls to the (slow) paint method.

- The Update method asks Windows to update the contents of the form, repainting it immediately. However, remember that this operation will take place only if there is an *invalid area.* This happens if the Invalidate method has just been called or as the result of an operation by the user. If there is no invalid area, a call to Update has no effect at all. For this reason, it is common to see a call to Update just after a call to Invalidate. This is exactly what is done by the two new Delphi methods, Repaint and Refresh.

- The Repaint method calls Paint.

- The Refresh method calls Paint, too.

A call to Repaint or Refresh corresponds to these calls:

```
Invalidate;
Update;
```

The documentation and the Help file of the first official version of Delphi state that the difference between Repaint and Refresh lies in the fact that the first method doesn't erase the surface of the form before repainting it. However, this is *not* true. The Refresh method is identical to Repaint and can be considered obsolete. This means you should avoid using it. Contrary to what the documentation says, to avoid erasing the form's background, you need to set the `csOpaque` flag in the undocumented ControlStyle property of the form (or of the component you want to use).

When you need to ask the form for a repaint operation, you should generally call Invalidate, following the standard Windows approach. This is particularly important when you need to request this operation very often, because if Windows takes too much time to update the screen, the requests for repaint can be accumulated into a simple repaint action. The `wm_Paint` message, in Windows, is a sort of low-priority message. To be more precise, if a request for repaint is pending but other messages are waiting, the other messages are handled before the system actually performs the paint action.

On the other hand, if you call Repaint several times, the screen must be repainted each time before Windows can process other messages, and since paint operations are slow, this can actually make your application less responsive. There are times, however, when you want the application to repaint a surface as quickly as possible. In these less-frequent cases, calling Repaint is the way to go.

As the number of shapes to display on the window grows, there is another useful technique. Instead of invalidating, erasing, and repainting the whole surface of the form, you might consider doing the same operation for only a smaller portion of it. To accomplish this, Delphi offers no specific support, but you can call a function of the Windows API, `InvalidateRect`:

```
procedure InvalidateRect(Wnd: HWnd;
  Rect: PRect; Erase: Bool);
```

The three parameters indicate the handle of the windows (that is, the Handle property of the form), the rectangle you want to repaint, and a flag indicating whether or not you want to erase the area before repainting it. You can see an example of the use of this function in the SHAPES4 example at the end of this chapter.

Painting a Single Shape

Do you remember the first version of the SHAPES example? It was the one capable of drawing simple circles and squares, with no support for color or other frills. I've implemented it again using the *store and draw* technique because I thought it was better to write a simple program with this approach than to start with a complex one.

When the user presses the left mouse button, we need to store three values: the two coordinates of the center of the shape and a Boolean indicating whether the shape is a circle or a square (see the code of the method in the Listing 9.8). The values are stored in the Center and Circle fields of the form (respectively a TPoint and a Boolean). At the end of the FormMouseDown method, there is a call to Refresh, which indirectly calls FormPaint, the method associated with the OnPaint event. This procedure draws a shape, using the current values.

LISTING 9.8: The source code listing of the form of the SHAPES3 example

```
unit Shapes_f;

interface

uses
  WinTypes, WinProcs, Classes, Graphics,
  Forms, Controls, SysUtils;

type
  TShapesForm = class(TForm)
    procedure FormMouseDown(Sender: TObject;
      Button: TMouseButton;
      Shift: TShiftState; X, Y: Integer);
    procedure FormMouseMove(Sender: TObject;
      Shift: TShiftState; X, Y: Integer);
    procedure FormPaint(Sender: TObject);
    procedure FormCreate(Sender: TObject);
  private
    Center: TPoint;
    Circle: Boolean;
  public
    { Public declarations }
  end;

var
  ShapesForm: TShapesForm;

implementation

{$R *.DFM}

procedure TShapesForm.FormMouseDown(Sender: TObject;
  Button: TMouseButton;
  Shift: TShiftState; X, Y: Integer);
begin
  {store the value of the center}
  Center.X := X;
  Center.Y := Y;
  {store the kind of shape}
```

9

LISTING 9.8: The source code listing of the form of the SHAPES3 example (continued)

```
  if Button = mbLeft then
    if ssShift in Shift then
      Circle := False
    else
      Circle := True;
  {ask to repaint the form}
  Refresh;
end;

procedure TShapesForm.FormMouseMove(Sender: TObject;
  Shift: TShiftState; X, Y: Integer);
begin
  {copy the mouse coordinates to the title}
  Caption := Format ('Shapes: x=%d, y=%d', [X, Y]);
end;

procedure TShapesForm.FormPaint(Sender: TObject);
begin
  {paint one of the two shapes, using the stored values}
  if Circle then
    Canvas.Ellipse(Center.X-10, Center.Y-10,
      Center.X+10, Center.Y+10)
  else
    Canvas.Rectangle(Center.X-10, Center.Y-10,
      Center.X+10, Center.Y+10);
end;

procedure TShapesForm.FormCreate(Sender: TObject);
begin
  {initialization, out of the form surface}
  Circle := True;
  Center.X := -100;
  Center.Y := -100;
end;

end.
```

The values of the private fields are set at the beginning, setting the center's coordinates at a negative offset, so that at the beginning, the shape is not visible. In fact, the OnPaint method is also executed at startup.

As you can see in Figure 9.20 and experience by running the program, SHAPES3 allows you to draw only one shape at a time. As soon as you draw a second shape, the first one is erased. Had we set the special csOpaque flag (see the preceding section), this wouldn't have happened. However, it would probably have been worse;

FIGURE 9.20:

The output of the SHAPES3 example: one shape

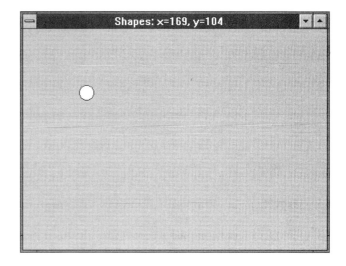

in fact, if you had painted a number of shapes and hidden the window, all the shapes except the last one would have been erased.

This last version of the SHAPES program we have build is probably the most robust. Although it is not by any means the best, you might easily paste its code with that of version 2 to allow a user to choose the colors and sizes of the single shape.

We can improve this program (or the modified version I've just suggested) by storing not only the last shape, but a number of them, and not only the position and type, but also the color, size, and all the other attributes we need to repaint them properly.

Painting a Number of Shapes

There is a simple solution in Delphi to the problem of storing a number of elements: use a TList object. This is what I've done in SHAPES4, which is a mix of the second and third versions of the program, plus the support for a number of shapes. In particular, the new version uses the same form and the same menu structure as the SHAPES2 example.

The program defines a custom ShapeData data type to store the attributes of a single shape:

```
ShapeData = class (TObject)
   Circle: Boolean;
   X, Y, Size, PenSize: Integer;
   PenColor, BrushColor: TColor;
end;
```

The form has a TList object data member, named ShapesList, which is initialized in the OnCreate event (see the complete source code in Listing 9.9). A new object is added to the list each time the user creates a new shape by pressing the left mouse button:

```
Shape := ShapeData.Create;
{... store the values ...}
ShapesList.Add (Shape);
Repaint;
```

LISTING 9.9: The complete source code of the SHAPES4 example

```
unit Shapes_f;

interface

uses
  WinTypes, WinProcs, Classes, Graphics, Forms,
  Controls, Menus, Dialogs, SysUtils;

type
  ShapeData = class (TObject)
    Circle: Boolean;
    X, Y, Size, PenSize: Integer;
    PenColor, BrushColor: TColor;
  end;

  TShapesForm = class(TForm)
    MainMenu1: TMainMenu;
    ColorDialog1: TColorDialog;
    File1: TMenuItem;
    New1: TMenuItem;
    N1: TMenuItem;
    Exit1: TMenuItem;
    Colors1: TMenuItem;
    PenColor1: TMenuItem;
    BrushColor1: TMenuItem;
    BackGroundColor1: TMenuItem;
    Size1: TMenuItem;
    IncreasePenSize1: TMenuItem;[
    DecreasePenSize1: TMenuItem;
```

LISTING 9.9: The complete source code of the SHAPES4 example (continued)

```
    N2: TMenuItem;
    IncreaseShapeSize1: TMenuItem;
    DecreaseShapeSize1: TMenuItem;
    Help1: TMenuItem;
    AboutShapes1: TMenuItem;
    procedure FormMouseDown(Sender: TObject;
      Button: TMouseButton;
      Shift: TShiftState; X, Y: Integer);
    procedure PenColor1Click(Sender: TObject);
    procedure BrushColor1Click(Sender: TObject);
    procedure BackGroundColor1Click(Sender: TObject);
    procedure IncreasePenSize1Click(Sender: TObject);
    procedure DecreasePenSize1Click(Sender: TObject);
    procedure IncreaseShapeSize1Click(Sender: TObject);
    procedure DecreaseShapeSize1Click(Sender: TObject);
    procedure FormCreate(Sender: TObject);
    procedure FormMouseMove(Sender: TObject;
      Shift: TShiftState; X, Y: Integer);
    procedure AboutShapes1Click(Sender: TObject);
    procedure Exit1Click(Sender: TObject);
    procedure New1Click(Sender: TObject);
    procedure FormPaint(Sender: TObject);
    procedure FormCloseQuery(Sender: TObject;
      var CanClose: Boolean);
  private
    { Private declarations }
    Radius: Integer;
    ShapesList: TList;
  public
    { Public declarations }
  end;

var
  ShapesForm: TShapesForm;

implementation

{$R *.DFM}

procedure TShapesForm.FormMouseDown(Sender: TObject;
  Button: TMouseButton;
  Shift: TShiftState; X, Y: Integer);
var
  Shape: ShapeData;
  InvRect: TRect;
begin
  if Button = mbLeft then
  begin
    Shape := ShapeData.Create;
    if (ssShift in Shift) then
      Shape.Circle := False
```

LISTING 9.9: The complete source code of the SHAPES4 example (continued)

```
      else
        Shape.Circle := True;
      Shape.X := X;
      Shape.Y := Y;
      Shape.Size := Radius;
      Shape.PenSize := Canvas.Pen.Width;
      Shape.PenColor := Canvas.Pen.Color;
      Shape.BrushColor := Canvas.Brush.Color;
      ShapesList.Add (Shape);

      {two versions of the code required to repaint
      the form with the new shape}

      {standard code:}
      Repaint;

      {optimized code:}
  {   InvRect := Rect (X-Radius-Shape.PenSize,
        Y-Radius-Shape.PenSize, X+Radius+Shape.PenSize,
        Y+Radius+Shape.PenSize);
      InvalidateRect (Handle, @InvRect, False);  }
    end;
end;

procedure TShapesForm.PenColor1Click(Sender: TObject);
begin
  {select a new color for the pen}
  ColorDialog1.Color := Canvas.Pen.Color;
  ColorDialog1.Execute;
  Canvas.Pen.Color := ColorDialog1.Color;
end;

procedure TShapesForm.BrushColor1Click(Sender: TObject);
begin
  {select a new color for the brush}
  ColorDialog1.Color := Canvas.Brush.Color;
  ColorDialog1.Execute;
  Canvas.Brush.Color := ColorDialog1.Color;
end;

procedure TShapesForm.BackGroundColor1Click(Sender: TObject);
begin
  {select a new color for the background of the form}
  ColorDialog1.Color := Color;
  ColorDialog1.Execute;
  Color := ColorDialog1.Color;
end;

procedure TShapesForm.IncreasePenSize1Click(Sender: TObject);
begin
  {increase the size of the pen}
  Canvas.Pen.Width := Canvas.Pen.Width + 2;
```

LISTING 9.9: The complete source code of the SHAPES4 example (continued)

```
    DecreasePenSize1.Enabled := True;
end;

procedure TShapesForm.DecreasePenSize1Click(Sender: TObject);
begin
  {decrease the size of the pen,
  avoiding letting it go below zero}
  Canvas.Pen.Width := Canvas.Pen.Width - 2;
  if Canvas.Pen.Width < 3 then
    DecreasePenSize1.Enabled := False;
end;

procedure TShapesForm.IncreaseShapeSize1Click(Sender: TObject);
begin
  {increase radius, a private field of the form}
  Radius := Radius + 5;
  DecreaseShapeSize1.Enabled := True;
end;

procedure TShapesForm.DecreaseShapeSize1Click(Sender: TObject);
begin
  {decrease the radius, but not below the limit}
  Radius := Radius - 5;
  if Radius < 10 then
    DecreaseShapeSize1.Enabled := False;
end;

procedure TShapesForm.FormCreate(Sender: TObject);
begin
  {initialization and creation of the list}
  Radius := 5;
  ShapesList := TList.Create;
end;

procedure TShapesForm.FormMouseMove(Sender: TObject;
  Shift: TShiftState; X, Y: Integer);
begin
  {copy the mouse coordinates to the title}
  Caption := Format ('Shapes: x=%d, y=%d', [X, Y]);
end;

procedure TShapesForm.AboutShapes1Click(Sender: TObject);
begin
  {show a message box}
  MessageDlg ('Shape application (v. 4.0)' +
    Chr(13) + '"Mastering Delphi", Marco Cantù',
    mtInformation, [mbOK], 0);
end;

procedure TShapesForm.Exit1Click(Sender: TObject);
begin
  {close the form and the application}
```

9

LISTING 9.9: The complete source code of the SHAPES4 example (continued)

```
  Close;
end;

procedure TShapesForm.New1Click(Sender: TObject);
begin
  {repaint the surface, after removing the elements
  from the list box, if there is any element and the
  user confirms his request}
  if ShapesList.Count > 0 then
    if MessageDlg ('Are you sure you want to delete '
      + 'all the shapes?',
      mtConfirmation, [mbYes, mbNo], 0) = idYes then
    begin
      ShapesList.Clear;
      Refresh;
    end;
end;

procedure TShapesForm.FormPaint(Sender: TObject);
var
  I: Integer;
  CurShape: ShapeData;
begin
  {repaint each shape of the list, using the stored values}
  for I := 0 to ShapesList.Count - 1 do
  begin
    CurShape := ShapesList.Items [I];
    with CurShape do
    begin
      Canvas.Pen.Color := PenColor;
      Canvas.Pen.Width := PenSize;
      Canvas.Brush.Color := BrushColor;
      if Circle then
        Canvas.Ellipse (X-Size, Y-Size, X+Size, Y+Size)
      else
        Canvas.Rectangle (X-Size, Y-Size, X+Size, Y+Size);
    end;
  end;
end;

procedure TShapesForm.FormCloseQuery(Sender: TObject;
  var CanClose: Boolean);
begin
  {ask the user to confirm closing}
  if MessageDlg ('Are you sure you want to exit?',
      mtConfirmation, [mbYes, mbNo], 0) = idNo then
    CanClose := False;
end;

end.
```

In the method corresponding to the OnPaint event, all the shapes currently stored in the list are painted:

```
for I := 0 to ShapesList.Count - 1 do
begin
  CurShape := ShapesList.Items [I];
  with CurShape do
  {...paint the shape...}
end
```

The other methods of the ShapeForm class are simple. The program asks the user to confirm some operations, such as exiting from the program or removing all the shapes from the list (with the File New command), but you should easily understand the corresponding code.

This time, the output looks great (see Figure 9.21), and whatever happens to the window, the shapes are always repainted in the proper position.

FIGURE 9.21:

The output of the SHAPES4 example

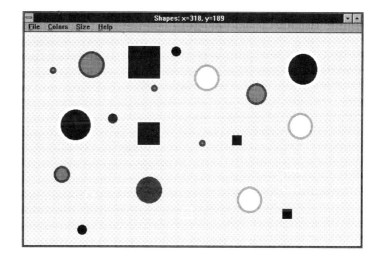

The only drawback is that when you have a number of shapes on the form, if you add a new shape, the program takes some time to redisplay them all, and the drawing tends to flicker. To solve this problem, or at least to reduce its effect, you can use a call to the `InvalidateRect` API function, instead of the Repaint method, in the FormMouseDown procedure:

```
InvRect := Rect (X-Radius-Shape.PenSize,
  Y-Radius-Shape.PenSize, X+Radius+Shape.PenSize,
  Y+Radius+Shape.PenSize);
InvalidateRect (Handle, @InvRect, False);
```

This code is already present in Listing 9.9 and in the source code of the example on the companion disk, but it is commented. You need only uncomment it (by removing the two braces) and comment or delete the Repaint call instead. I suggest you experiment with the two versions of the example to get an idea of why calling `InvalidateRect` at times is really a great benefit to a slow program.

The key idea is that if Repaint or Invalidate is called, the surface of the form is erased, and then each shape is repainted. When there are many shapes, this makes the display flicker.

Invalidating only a small portion of the window, instead, makes any flicker less noticeable. In this case, the invalidated area is erased, too, but it is smaller (so if there is any flickering, it involves only that area), and Windows can redraw it more quickly. In fact, paint operations are limited by a clipping rectangle, which usually has the size of the form but in this case is limited to the invalidated area. Windows automatically skips every output operation outside the clipping rectangle, avoiding any time-consuming output operation.

To be more precise, I should have used the term *clipping region* instead of *clipping rectangle* because this area can have any complex form. If you want more details, you can see the description of the `InvalidateRegion` and `CreateRegion` API functions in the Windows Help file.

TIP

The area you invalidate with the `InvalidateRect` call should be big enough for the last shape, including its eventual thick border (unless the pen style is `psInsideFrame`). For this reason, I've added the size of the pen, although half the size of the pen would have probably been enough.

Delphi Output Components

We have made four versions of the SHAPES example, using almost no components, aside from a standard color selection dialog box. As an alternative, we could have used two Delphi components: the PaintBox and the Shape. What are these two components for?

- You use the PaintBox component when you need to paint on a certain area of a form and that area might move on the form. For example, the PaintBox is useful for painting on a dialog box without the risk of mixing the area for the output with the area for the controls. The PaintBox might fit within other controls of a form, such as a toolbar or a status bar, and avoid any confusion or overlapping of the output. In the SHAPES example, using this component made no sense since we always worked on the whole surface of the form.

- You use the Shape component to paint shapes on the screen, exactly as we have done up to now. We could indeed use the Shape component instead of our manual output, but I really wanted to show you how to accomplish some direct output operations. Our approach was not much more complex than the one Delphi suggests. Using the Shape component would have been useful to extend the example, allowing a user to drag shapes on the screen, remove them, and work on them in a number of other ways. You can see an example of the use of the Shape component in the MDIDEMO4 example in Chapter 15.

9

Summary

Since Chapter 1 we have seen that a form is a window, but until this chapter we had not explored any of a form's properties. Now we know how to handle the size and position of a form, how to resize it, how to get mouse input, and how to paint on the surface of the form.

I've also mentioned the existence of two global objects, Application and Screen, which will be further explored in Chapter 19.

Other chapters in the book will describe other topics strictly related to forms. In particular, Chapters 11 through 15 cover the use of toolbars and status bars; building a dialog box and an application with multiple forms; scrolling forms; forms with multiple pages; splitting forms; and building MDI applications. As you can see from this list, forms play a central role in Delphi programming, and we still have to explore a number of topics related to them.

Before going on to these topics, however, in the next chapter I'll show you how to use a number of other components, including the graphical components mentioned in the last section of this chapter, and many other graphical components, including buttons, list boxes, and grids. Now, who told you that you could learn Delphi programming in two days? To master Delphi, you probably need some more time (and to read the rest of this book!).

CHAPTER

TEN

Graphical Components

- Bitmap buttons

- Animated buttons

- An image viewer

- Drawing over a bitmap

- The Mines game

- Font and color selection grids

- The MaskEdit component

10

In addition to the basic controls borrowed from Windows, Delphi sports a number of more powerful components having a modern user interface. Some of these controls are the graphical versions of traditional ones, such as graphical buttons or list boxes; others are brand-new elements. We will start exploring some of these advanced controls in this chapter, and we will continue for several more chapters. Most of the components described in this chapter are located in the Additional page of Delphi's Components palette, others in the Samples page.

We saw in the last chapter that it is easy to draw on the surface of a form. The same operation is possible for other components, too. However, we have also seen that the Windows painting model is far from simple. For this reason, having ready-to-use graphical controls is a big advantage over the traditional approach. You can improve your application's user interface with a very limited effort by using graphical buttons, grids, and outlines and adding, at the same time, powerful capabilities to the application in almost no time. This is true also for a particular nongraphical component we will discuss at the end of the chapter—an edit field with a mask.

Improving the User Interface with Graphics

The user interface of Windows applications before Windows 3.1 came out was very different. Independent of the new release and at the same time, a number of techniques to improve the user interface became common, including toolbars, graphical buttons, graphical list boxes, and so on. The Windows API did not directly support these elements, and they required a lot of coding. However, articles in magazines and tutorials in conferences started spreading the word, and it became much easier to find documentation on how to build one of these nice graphical windows.

Now things are changing again. The new version of the operating environment, Windows 95, includes a number of improved graphical components, and Delphi has a number of them readily available. I'll briefly describe some of these controls and use them in some examples, as usual.

Before we start looking at the code, however, consider that while some graphics can improve a program and make it seem more professional, too many colors and too many graphics can be counterproductive. The user interface of Windows and of the application running in this environment follow specific rules, defined by Microsoft and known as *Windows Style Guides*. Without referring to this document, you can easily understand what these rules dictate by looking at the mainstream Windows applications.

Slight differences from the rules can improve a program, but diverging too much from the standard might add a negative feeling to it. If an application behaves differently from the others, a user might conclude that it behaves wrongly. Of course, you can write a manual to explain the details of your choices, but how many users will read your manual before they start using the program?

An important point, however, is that the *standard* for a user interface is a moving target. Each time someone (read Microsoft) writes down the details, a new application with a new feature comes out, thus changing the standard.

Consider this example. A couple of years ago, there were no toolbars. Then some toolbars with big buttons containing text and graphics were introduced. The following standard was to have smaller buttons, and maybe several lines of them. A couple of months later, every application allowed users to change the buttons on the toolbar. More time passed, and an application without *tool tips* (the yellow *hint* messages that appear when the cursor remains for some time over a button) was considered old. Other waves are coming, including dockable toolbars (that is, toolbars you can drag to different positions on the screen), an increased use of color, and many more.

A Bitmap in a Button

One of the simplest and most common improvements to an application's user interface is to make the buttons more colorful and, at the same time, more intuitive. Several years ago, Borland started to place bitmaps in buttons to highlight their meanings. For example, OK buttons have a green check mark on them, and Cancel buttons have a red cross.

10

Delphi offers two kinds of graphical buttons:

- The BitBtn (bitmap button) component usually has some graphics and some text, as did the old Borland buttons. The behavior of BitBtn buttons is similar to the TButton components—that is, they implement push buttons. You can choose one of the typical Borland buttons with a corresponding return value for these buttons in a modal form or dialog box.

- The SpeedButton component allows both graphics and text, but you'll often use it with only a glyph. As the name implies, speed buttons are mainly used in toolbars. Their behavior can mimic push buttons, check boxes with an off and an on state, and even radio buttons. They also allow you to use different glyphs for the various states.

The key technical difference between the BitBtn component and the SpeedButton component is that the first is based on a Windows button, using the owner-drawn technique to paint on its surface, and the second is a graphical component, not based on a window (it has no window handle). For this reason, speed buttons make a more limited use of system resources, which is particularly important when you need many buttons.

In this section, I'll focus on bitmap buttons, leaving the speed buttons for the next chapter, which is entirely devoted to SpeedBars (or toolbars) and status bars.

Once you have created an object with the BitBtn component, you can simply use the Kind property to select a default text, glyph, and return value. The available choices are the values of the TBitBtnKind enumeration:

```
TBitBtnKind = (bkCustom, bkOK, bkCancel, bkHelp, bkYes,
    bkNo, bkClose, bkAbort, bkRetry, bkIgnore, bkAll);
```

If you select a custom button, you have to supply the button's caption and its glyph; otherwise, a default glyph and caption are shown.

Other properties let you arrange the position of text and graphics (Layout), set the space between them (Spacing), and choose between the Windows 3.1 or the new shadowing styles (Style).

NOTE   The Style property of bitmap buttons, and of speed buttons as well, determines whether the button's three-dimensional effect should mimic the typical Windows 3.1 behavior or the new Windows 95 user interface. To look at the differences between the two styles, try setting them in a sample program. In a real application, the best solution is probably to leave the default value of the property, bsAutoDetect, so that the program automatically uses the style of the hosting environment. Using this choice, the bitmap buttons will always have the same user interface as the other normal buttons, which is certainly a recommended approach.

Another important concept is the idea of transparent color. When you prepare a bitmap for a button or other graphical components, the color found in the bottom-left corner pixel of the bitmap is considered the transparent color. For this reason, many applications and Delphi itself use bitmaps with a dark yellow background (the clOlive color), a color seldom used in the bitmap itself.

This value determines which color of the glyph should be considered transparent and replaced by the button's background color. If you use this approach, the system will be able to use the default colors (light gray, dark gray, and so on) for the various states of the button, always integrating your bitmap seamlessly.

A Car in a Button

To experiment with graphical buttons, we'll build a simple and almost useless example, CARS, having a number of bitmap buttons with different behaviors (see Figure 10.1). The program is going to have a *two-state* button that changes its text and its image each time it is pressed. It will also have a group of three buttons, only one of which is active at a time. The last two buttons are simpler. One of them, however, has its text and its caption reversed, for symmetry.

Besides the bitmap buttons, the form contains a label, an Image component, and a Bevel component. We have never used these two components, so I'll describe

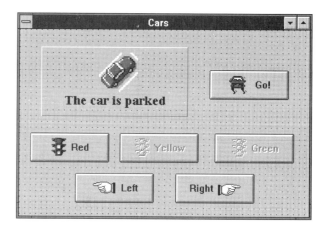

them briefly (and then move back to the example):

- You can use the Image component to display images on the background of
  the form, eventually behind other components. To load the bitmap for an image from a file or to store it in a new file, you simply call the LoadFromFile
  and SaveToFile methods of the component's Picture property. You can
  choose to show the image in its original size or stretch it to the size of the
  component. Since Image components support only click events, they can be
  considered almost static elements. Later in this chapter, we'll use this component again to build an image viewer.

- The Bevel component defines a 3D effect you can use to make some of the
  form's controls stand out or to group them. It defines *beveled* boxes, frames or
  lines (see its Shape property) that can be either lowered or raised, as described by the Style property. Bevels have no events at all, so their only use is
  to improve the user interface. As we will see in detail in the next chapter,
  there is another component, Panel, that is similar to a bevel but with much
  more functionality. Along with TPanel's extra capabilities comes additional
  resource overhead, so do not use a panel when a bevel is enough.

As you can see in Figure 10.1 and Listing 10.1, the form of the CARS example has
a number of bitmap buttons, plus a bevel in the upper-left portion, with an image
and a label inside. When the Left or Right button is pressed, the image is moved to

LISTING 10.1: The textual description of the form of the CARS example

```
object CarsForm: TCarsForm
  ActiveControl = CarButton
  Caption = 'Cars'
  OnCreate = FormCreate
  OnDestroy = FormDestroy
  object CarLabel: TLabel
    Alignment = taCenter
    AutoSize = False
    Caption = 'The car is parked'
    Font.Color = clBlack
    Font.Height = -19
    Font.Name = 'Times New Roman'
    Font.Style = [fsBold]
    ParentFont = False
  end
  object Bevel1: TBevel
    Style = bsRaised
  end
  object CarImage: TImage
    Picture.Data = ... {omitted}
    Stretch = True
  end
  object CarButton: TBitBtn
    Caption = 'Go!'
    Default = True
    OnClick = CarButtonClick
    Glyph.Data = ... {omitted}
    Spacing = 12
  end
  object GreenButton: TBitBtn
    Caption = 'Green'
    Enabled = False
    OnClick = GreenButtonClick
    Glyph.Data = ... {omitted}
  end
  object RightButton: TBitBtn
    Caption = 'Right'
    OnClick = RightButtonClick
    Glyph.Data = ... {omitted}
    Layout = blGlyphRight
  end
  object RedButton: TBitBtn
    Caption = 'Red'
    OnClick = RedButtonClick
    Glyph.Data = ... {omitted}
  end
  object LeftButton: TBitBtn
    Caption = 'Left'
    OnClick = LeftButtonClick
    Glyph.Data = ... {omitted}
  end
```

10

```
  object YellowButton: TBitBtn
    Caption = 'Yellow'
    Enabled = False
    OnClick = YellowButtonClick
    Glyph.Data = ... {omitted}
  end
end
```

the left or right until it bounces against the form's border (or almost the border, since some pixels are left). As you can see in Figure 10.2, this is far from good since the limit should be set on the border of the bevel. This simple change is left to you as an exercise.

When each of the three buttons with the traffic-light bitmaps is pressed, the code simply disables the button and enables another one, following a round-robin approach: the green button follows the red button, the yellow button follows the green button, and the red button follows the yellow button.

If you look at the code in Listing 10.2, you will notice that there is a call to the Set-Focus method of the GreenButton object before the control is disabled. By disabling the button, it loses the focus anyway, but it will move almost randomly to other buttons, with a nasty flash effect. Instead, if the SetFocus method is called before the button is disabled, we can decide which button is going to receive the focus.

FIGURE 10.2 :

The image of the car can be moved without limit; notice the status of the various buttons, different from those in Figure 10.1 (showing the form at design-time).

LISTING 10.2: The complete source code of the form of the CARS example

```
unit Cars_f;

interface

uses
  WinTypes, WinProcs, Classes, Graphics, Forms,
  Controls, Buttons, StdCtrls, ExtCtrls, Dialogs;

type
  TCarsForm = class(TForm)
    CarButton: TBitBtn;
    GreenButton: TBitBtn;
    RightButton: TBitBtn;
    RedButton: TBitBtn;
    LeftButton: TBitBtn;
    YellowButton: TBitBtn;
    CarImage: TImage;
    CarLabel: TLabel;
    Bevel1: TBevel;
    procedure CarButtonClick(Sender: TObject);
    procedure FormCreate(Sender: TObject);
    procedure FormDestroy(Sender: TObject);
    procedure RedButtonClick(Sender: TObject);
    procedure YellowButtonClick(Sender: TObject);
    procedure GreenButtonClick(Sender: TObject);
    procedure LeftButtonClick(Sender: TObject);
    procedure RightButtonClick(Sender: TObject);

  private
    CarStopped: Boolean;
    Car1Bmp, Car2Bmp: TBitmap;
  public
    { Public declarations }
  end;

var
  CarsForm: TCarsForm;

implementation

{$R *.DFM}

procedure TCarsForm.CarButtonClick(Sender: TObject);
begin
  {a car should not start if the light is red}
  if CarStopped then
    if RedButton.Enabled then
      MessageDlg ('No turn on red, please!',
        mtWarning, [mbOK], 0)
```

LISTING 10.2: The complete source code of the form of the CARS example (continued)

```
    else
    {if was stopped and it is not red}
      begin
        {change the bitmaps and captions}
        CarButton.Glyph := Car1Bmp;
        CarButton.Caption := 'Stop';
        CarImage.Picture.Graphic := Car2Bmp;
        CarLabel.Caption := 'The car is on the road';
        CarStopped := False;
      end
  else
  {if it was moving, regardless of the lights}
    begin
      {change the bitmaps and captions}
      CarButton.Glyph := Car2Bmp;
      CarButton.Caption := 'Go!';
      CarImage.Picture.Graphic := Car1Bmp;
      CarLabel.Caption := 'The car is parked';
      CarStopped := True;
    end;
end;

procedure TCarsForm.FormCreate(Sender: TObject);
begin
  {set the flag and load the two bitmaps of the car}
  CarStopped := True;
  Car1Bmp := TBitmap.Create;
  Car2Bmp := TBitmap.Create;
  Car1Bmp.LoadFromFile ('cars.bmp');
  Car2Bmp.LoadFromFile ('cars2.bmp');
end;

procedure TCarsForm.FormDestroy(Sender: TObject);
begin
  {delete the two TBitmap objects}
  Car1Bmp.Free;
  Car2Bmp.Free;
end;

procedure TCarsForm.RedButtonClick(Sender: TObject);
begin
  {after the red, green}
  GreenButton.Enabled := True;
  GreenButton.SetFocus;
  RedButton.Enabled := False;
end;

procedure TCarsForm.YellowButtonClick(Sender: TObject);
begin
  {after the yellow, red}
```

LISTING 10.2: The complete source code of the form of the CARS example (continued)

```
  RedButton.Enabled := True;
  RedButton.SetFocus;
  YellowButton.Enabled := False;
end;

procedure TCarsForm.GreenButtonClick(Sender: TObject);
begin
  {after the green, yellow}
  YellowButton.Enabled := True;
  YellowButton.SetFocus;
  GreenButton.Enabled := False;
end;

procedure TCarsForm.LeftButtonClick(Sender: TObject);
begin
  {move the car, but not outside the area of the form}
  RightButton.Enabled := True;
  CarImage.Left := CarImage.Left - 10;
  {when the left border of the image is less than ten
  pixels from the left border of the form, which is at 0}
  if CarImage.Left < 10 then
  begin
    RightButton.SetFocus;
    LeftButton.Enabled := False;
  end;
end;

procedure TCarsForm.RightButtonClick(Sender: TObject);
begin
  {move the car, but not outside the area of the form}
  LeftButton.Enabled := True;
  CarImage.Left := CarImage.Left + 10;
  {when the right border of the image is less than
  ten pixels from the left border of the form}
  if CarImage.Left + CarImage.Width > ClientWidth - 10 then
  begin
    LeftButton.SetFocus;
    RightButton.Enabled := False;
  end;
end;

end.
```

10

The advantage of moving the focus is that if you press the button by pressing the spacebar, you can tap the spacebar a number of times and see the active state moving from button to button, together with the focus. The same happens with the Left and Right buttons. If you press the spacebar repeatedly, the image will bounce against the border and then move back since the focus is set on the button corresponding to the opposite direction.

The most complex piece of code of the example is that of the button with the car picture on it. The effect of a click on this button is to change the glyph and the caption of the button itself, the picture of the Image component, and the caption of the label below it. The code also sets the value of a private Boolean field of the form CarStopped to keep track of the current status.

To avoid loading a bitmap for the image and one for the button each time, with a statement such as:

```
CarButton.Glyph.LoadFromFile ('cars2.bmp');
```

I've decided to add to the form two bitmap objects, storing the two graphical images. The form has three fields:

```
private
  CarStopped: Boolean;
  Car1Bmp, Car2Bmp: TBitmap;
```

These private fields are initialized when the form is created:

```
procedure TCarsForm.FormCreate(Sender: TObject);
begin
  {set the flag and load the two bitmaps of the car}
  CarStopped := True;
  Car1Bmp := TBitmap.Create;
  Car2Bmp := TBitmap.Create;
  Car1Bmp.LoadFromFile ('cars.bmp');
  Car2Bmp.LoadFromFile ('cars2.bmp')
end;
```

After this initialization, we can use the two bitmap objects to set a value for the image and the graphical button. Of course, there are two alternative versions, which depend on the value of the CarStopped flag. There is also a special case: if the car is not moving and the red light is on—that is, the RedButton is enabled—you cannot go. A warning message is displayed, and nothing happens (see Figure 10.3).

FIGURE 10.3:

The message displayed by the CARS program when the user presses the Go button and the red light is on

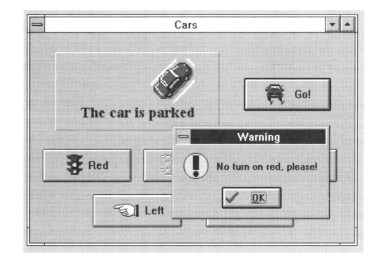

An Animated Bitmap in a Button

As you saw in the previous example, bitmap buttons are easy to use and can produce better-looking applications than the standard push buttons (the Button component). To further improve the visual effect of a button, we can also think of *animating* the button. There are basically two kinds of animated buttons—buttons that change their glyph slightly when they are pressed and buttons having a moving image, regardless of the current operation. I'll show you a simple example of each kind, FIRE and WORLD. Each of these examples will have a couple of slightly different versions.

A Two-State Button

The first example, FIRE, has a very simple form, containing only a bitmap button. This button has the caption *Fire* and is connected to a glyph representing a cannon, as shown in Figure 10.4 (see the textual description of the form in Listing 10.3). Imagine such a button as part of a game program.

FIGURE 10.4:

The default glyph of the bitmap button of the FIRE example

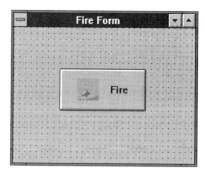

LISTING 10.3: The textual description of the simple form of the FIRE example

```
object Form1: TForm1
  ActiveControl = BitBtnFire
  Caption = 'Fire Form'
  object BitBtnFire: TBitBtn
    Caption = 'Fire'
    OnClick = BitBtnFireClick
    OnMouseDown = BitBtnFireMouseDown
    OnMouseUp = BitBtnFireMouseUp
    Glyph.Data = ...
    Spacing = 15
  end
end
```

As the button is pressed, the glyph changes to show a firing cannon, as you can see in Figure 10.5. As soon as the button is released, the default glyph is loaded again. In between, the program shows the user a message if that user really presses the button. In fact, a user might press the button and then move the mouse away and release it. In this case, the OnClick event doesn't take place, but the bitmap is temporarily changed anyway.

To write this program, we need to handle three of the button's events: OnMouse-Down, OnMouseUp, and OnMouseClick. The code of the three procedures is extremely simple:

```
procedure TForm1.BitBtnFireMouseDown(Sender: TObject;
  Button: TMouseButton;
  Shift: TShiftState; X, Y: Integer);
```

```
begin
  {load firing cannon bitmap}
  BitBtnFire.Glyph.LoadFromFile ('fire2.bmp');
end;

procedure TForm1.BitBtnFireMouseUp(Sender: TObject;
  Button: TMouseButton;
  Shift: TShiftState; X, Y: Integer);
begin
  {load default cannon bitmap}
  BitBtnFire.Glyph.LoadFromFile ('fire.bmp');
end;

procedure TForm1.BitBtnFireClick(Sender: TObject);
begin
  MessageDlg ('Boom!', mtWarning, [mbOk], 0);
end;
```

FIGURE 10.5:

The image displayed when the button is pressed, and the "Boom" message

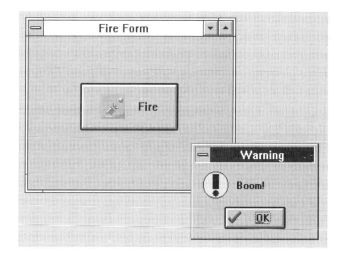

When you press the left mouse button over the bitmap button, the bitmap button is pressed. If you then move the mouse cursor away from the button, holding down the mouse button, the bitmap button is released, but it doesn't get an OnMouseUp event, so the firing cannon remains there. If you later release the left mouse button outside the surface of the bitmap button, it receives the OnMouseUp event anyway.

Windows, follows this rule: All mouse events are sent to the window or component behind the cursor. So how can we send a mouse event to the button if we release it outside its surface? This behavior depends on the *mouse capture.* A window can decide to capture all of the following input of the mouse, independently of the current window below the cursor. This is the default behavior of all the buttons in Windows when they are pressed. So we can state the rule above more correctly as: All mouse events are sent to the window or component behind the cursor or to the window, if any, that has captured the mouse input.

TIP   You can capture the mouse using the Windows API SetCapture function and later stop this operation with ReleaseCapture. Capturing the mouse can be very interesting in some applications but is an extremely dangerous behavior. In fact, while the mouse is *captive,* you cannot activate another application of the system. To understand what I mean, try this: press a push button (any button, including the minimize or maximize button, will do), hold it down, and try to use the Alt and Tab keys to move to another application. You'll discover that while the button is pressed, most system commands are disabled. This is not a bug. It should be this way; otherwise, you would send mouse messages to a window behind the one in front, a nasty situation. For this reason, consider capturing the mouse only for a very short amount of time, usually while a mouse button is pressed, to avoid halting the whole system.

Many Images in a Bitmap

In the FIRE example, I have used a manual approach. I loaded two bitmaps and changed the value of the Glyph property when I wanted to change the image. The BitBtn component, however, can also handle a number of bitmaps automatically. You can prepare a single bitmap that contains a number of images (or glyphs) and set this number as the value of the NumGlyph property. All sub-bitmaps must have the same size since the overall bitmap is divided into equal parts.

If you provide more than one glyph in the bitmap, they are used according to the following rules:

- The first bitmap is used for the released button, the default position.
- The second bitmap is used for the disabled button.
- The third bitmap is used when the button is clicked.
- The fourth bitmap is used when the button remains down, such as in buttons behaving as check boxes.

Usually you provide a single glyph and the others are automatically computed from it, with simple graphical changes. However, it is easy to provide a second, a third, and a fourth customized picture. If you do not provide all four bitmaps, the missing ones will be computed automatically from the first one. However, only the last or the last two bitmaps can be missing. You can't specify a normal and a pressed image without including the disabled bitmap between them.

In our example, the new version of FIRE (named FIRE2), we really need the first and third glyphs of the bitmap but are obliged to add the second bitmap, too. To see how this third glyph (the second of the bitmap) can be used, I've added a check box to disable the bitmap button (see Listing 10.4 for the textual description of the form of FIRE2).

LISTING 10.4: The textual description of the form of FIRE2

```
object Form1: TForm1
  ActiveControl = BitBtnFire
  Caption = 'Fire Form'
  object BitBtnFire: TBitBtn
    Caption = 'Fire'
    OnClick = BitBtnFireClick
    Glyph.Data = ...
    NumGlyphs = 3
    Spacing = 15
  end
  object CheckBox1: TCheckBox
    Caption = 'Enable Bitmap Button'
    OnClick = CheckBox1Click
  end
end
```

10

To build the new version of the program, I've prepared a bitmap of 32 x 96 pixels (see Figure 10.6) and used it for the Glyph property of the bitmap. To my surprise, the NumGlyphs property was *automatically* set to 3 since the bitmap is three times wider than it is high. Then I removed most of the program's code, added the new check box, and wrote a line of code for its OnClick property, as you can see in Listing 10.5.

FIGURE 10.6:

The bitmap with three images of the FIRE2 example, as seen in the Delphi Image Editor

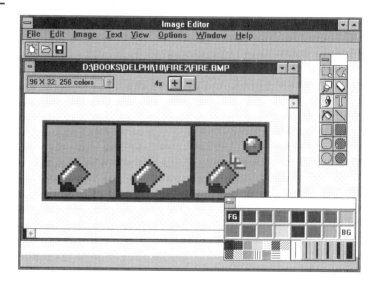

That's it. When you run the program, you can disable the bitmap button by using the check box (see Figure 10.7) or by pressing the bitmap button to see the cannon fire and the resulting message (see Figure 10.8). If you compare Figure 10.8, showing FIRE2, with Figure 10.5, showing FIRE, you will notice a remarkable difference. In the first version, the image with the firing cannon remained on the button until the message box was closed. Now the image is shown only while the button is pressed. As soon as you move outside the surface of the button or release the button after having pressed it (activating the message box), the standard glyph is displayed.

LISTING 10.5: The source code of the FIRE2 example

```pascal
unit Fire_f;

interface

uses
  WinTypes, WinProcs, Classes, Graphics, Forms,
  Controls, Buttons, Dialogs, StdCtrls;

type
  TForm1 = class(TForm)
    BitBtnFire: TBitBtn;
    CheckBox1: TCheckBox;
    procedure BitBtnFireClick(Sender: TObject);
    procedure CheckBox1Click(Sender: TObject);
  private
    { Private declarations }
  public
    { Public declarations }
  end;

var
  Form1: TForm1;

implementation

{$R *.DFM}

procedure TForm1.BitBtnFireClick(Sender: TObject);
begin
  MessageDlg ('Boom!', mtWarning, [mbOk], 0);
end;

procedure TForm1.CheckBox1Click(Sender: TObject);
begin
  BitBtnFire.Enabled := not BitBtnFire.Enabled;
end;

end.
```

10

FIGURE 10.7:

The enabled and disabled bitmap buttons of the FIRE2 example, in two different copies of the application

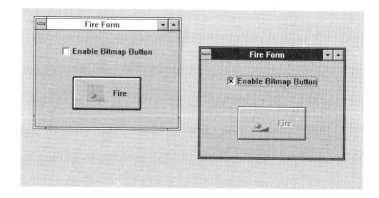

FIGURE 10.8:

If you press the bitmap button in FIRE2, the program displays the message box, but only after it has restored the original glyph.

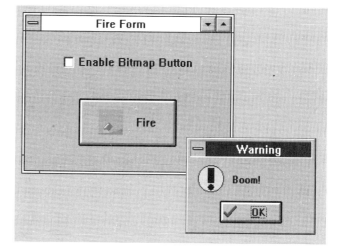

TIP

To test the difference between the two versions of the program, you can try to run FIRE and FIRE2 at the same time, but this is not as simple as it appears at first. If you open the Windows File Manager and run both executable files, the second one will not work properly and will probably complain about missing files or display incorrect bitmaps. The fact is that in Windows, you cannot run two programs having the same name! The second program you run uses the code of the first copy, which is already in memory, but having a different directory, it might not work properly. The quick and dirty solution to this problem is simple: rename one of the two executable files, and they will run side by side without a glitch. The real solution is to rename one of the projects and recompile it. At times, in fact, Windows can do strange things when the module name of a program does not match the name of its executable file.

The Rotating World

The second example, WORLD, has a button featuring the earth, which slowly rotates, showing the various continents. You can see some samples in Figure 10.9, but, of course, you should run the program to see its output since it cannot be captured in a static figure.

10

FIGURE 10.9:

Some examples of the running WORLD program

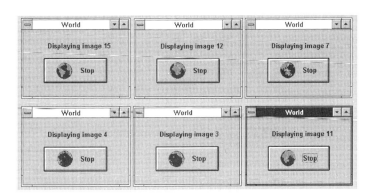

In the previous example, the image changed when the button was pressed. Now the image changes by itself, automatically. This occurs thanks to the presence of a Timer component, which receives a message at fixed time intervals. For a detailed discussion of timers and related topics, see Chapter 19.

This timer is started and stopped by pressing the bitmap button with the world image. The button has a *Start* caption, which changes to *Stop* when the timer is active. So by pressing the button, you start or stop the animation:

```
procedure TWorldForm.WorldButtonClick(Sender: TObject);
begin
  if Timer1.Enabled then
    begin
      Timer1.Enabled := False;
      WorldButton.Caption := 'Start';
    end
  else
    begin
      Timer1.Enabled := True;
      WorldButton.Caption := 'Stop';
    end;
end;
```

As you can see in Figure 10.9, a label above the button indicates which of the images is being displayed (see Listing 10.6 for the complete textual description of the form). I added the label as a debugging tool when I started writing this program, but then I decided to leave it there. You might replace it with information on time zones or something else.

Each time the timer message is received, the image and label change:

```
procedure TWorldForm.Timer1Timer(Sender: TObject);
begin
  Count := (Count mod 16) + 1;
  Label1.Caption := 'Displaying image ' + IntToStr (Count);
  WorldButton.Glyph.LoadFromFile (
    'w' + IntToStr (Count) + '.bmp');
end;
```

Count is a field of the form that is initialized to 1 in the FormCreate method. At each timer interval, Count is increased modulus 16 and then converted into a string when it is used. The modulus operation returns the remainder of the division between integers. This means that the resulting value is always in the range 1–16. The reason for this limit is simple: I had 16 bitmaps of the earth to display. Naming the

LISTING 10.6: The textual description of the form of the WORLD example

```
object WorldForm: TWorldForm
  ActiveControl = WorldButton
  Caption = 'World'
  OnCreate = FormCreate
  object Label1: TLabel
    Caption = 'Displaying image 1'
    Font.Color = clBlack
    Font.Height = -13
    Font.Name = 'Arial'
    Font.Style = [fsBold]
  end
  object WorldButton: TBitBtn
    Caption = 'Start'
    Font.Height = -13
    Font.Name = 'Arial'
    Font.Style = [fsBold]
    OnClick = WorldButtonClick
    Glyph.Data = ...
    Spacing = 15
  end
  object Timer1: TTimer
    Enabled = False
    Interval = 500
    OnTimer = Timer1Timer
  end
end
```

bitmap files W1.BMP, W2.BMP, and so on, makes it easy for the program to access them, building the string with the name at run-time. The string is:

```
'w' + IntToStr (Count)  + '.bmp'
```

10

A List of Bitmaps, the Use of Resources, and a Paintbox

The WORLD program works, but it is very slow, for a couple of reasons. First of all, at each time interval, it needs to read a file from the disk, and although a disk cache can make this faster, it is certainly not the most efficient solution. Besides reading the file from disk, the program has to create and destroy Windows bitmap objects, and this takes some time, too.

The second problem is due to updating the image: when you change the button's bitmap, the component has some flickering that results from a screen repainting with no image.

To solve the first problem (and to show you a different approach to handling bitmaps), I've added to the form of the second version of the example, WORLD2, a TList object, storing a list of bitmaps. All the bitmaps are loaded when the program starts and destroyed when it terminates. At each timer interval, the program shows, in the bitmap button, one of the list's bitmaps. You can see how this is done by looking at the complete source file in Listing 10.7, although you might prefer to continue reading in order to understand all the other changes to the code.

LISTING 10.7: The complete source code of the WORLD2 example, based on a list of bitmaps, using resources, and smoothing the image's transition with a paintbox

```
unit World_f;

interface

uses
  WinTypes, WinProcs, Classes, Graphics, Forms, Controls,
  Buttons, StdCtrls, ExtCtrls, SysUtils;

type
  TWorldForm = class(TForm)
    WorldButton: TBitBtn;
    Timer1: TTimer;
    Label1: TLabel;
    PaintBox1: TPaintBox;
    procedure WorldButtonClick(Sender: TObject);
    procedure Timer1Timer(Sender: TObject);
    procedure FormCreate(Sender: TObject);
    procedure FormDestroy(Sender: TObject);
    procedure WorldButtonMouseDown(Sender: TObject;
      Button: TMouseButton; Shift: TShiftState; X, Y: Integer);
  private
    Count: Integer;
    ImageList: TList;
  public
    { Public declarations }
  end;

var
  WorldForm: TWorldForm;

implementation
```

LISTING 10.7: The complete source code of the WORLD2 example (continued)

```
{$R *.DFM}

procedure TWorldForm.WorldButtonClick(Sender: TObject);
begin
  if Timer1.Enabled then
    begin
      Timer1.Enablod := False;
      WorldButton.Caption := 'Start';
      {copy the current image to the button}
      WorldButton.Glyph.Assign (ImageList.Items[Count-1]);
    end
  else
    begin
      Timer1.Enabled := True;
      WorldButton.Caption := 'Stop';
    end;
end;

procedure TWorldForm.Timer1Timer(Sender: TObject);
var
  NumberName: string;
begin
  Count := (Count mod 16) + 1;
  str (Count, NumberName);
  Label1.Caption := 'Displaying image ' + NumberName;

  {draw the current bitmap in the canvas placed over
  the bitmap button}
  PaintBox1.Canvas.Draw (WorldButton.Margin + 2,
    WorldButton.Margin + 2, ImageList.Items[Count-1]);
end;

procedure TWorldForm.FormCreate(Sender: TObject);
var
  I: Integer;
  Bmp: TBitmap;
  Name: array [0..10] of Char;
begin
  Count := 1;

  {load the bitmaps from the resources of the
  application to the list of TBitmap objects}
  ImageList := TList.Create;
  for I := 1 to 16 do
  begin
    Bmp := TBitmap.Create;
    StrPCopy (Name, 'W' + IntToStr (I));
    {load the bitmap from the resources:
    LoadBitmap is a Windows API function}
    Bmp.Handle := LoadBitmap (HInstance, Name);
    ImageList.Add (Bmp);
  end;
```

10

LISTING 10.7: The complete source code of the WORLD2 example (continued)

```
  {change the parent of the paintbox, placing it inside
  the button instead of inside the form}
  PaintBox1.Parent := WorldButton;
end;

procedure TWorldForm.FormDestroy(Sender: TObject);
var
  I: Integer;
begin
  {free each element of the list and the list itself}
  for I := 0 to 15 do
    ImageList.Delete (0);
  ImageList.Free;
end;

procedure TWorldForm.WorldButtonMouseDown(Sender: TObject;
  Button: TMouseButton; Shift: TShiftState; X, Y: Integer);
begin
  {copy the current image to the button}
  WorldButton.Glyph.Assign (ImageList.Items[Count-1]);
end;

end.
```

By using a list, we avoid loading a file each time we need to display a bitmap, but we still need to have all the files with the images in the directory with the executable file. A solution to this problem is to move the bitmaps from independent files to the application's resource file. This is easier to do than to explain.

Resources are graphical or textual data connected to a Windows program. The most important resources in Delphi include bitmaps, icons, fonts, string tables, and the images of the forms. (Note that an application's resources have nothing to do with free system resources—the two uses of the term are completely unrelated!) We will discuss resources in Chapter 21.

NOTE   There are basically three reasons for resources in Windows applications. The first is that some of them refer to graphical elements and require proper editors; the second and more important reason is that resources are handled in memory in a special way (see Chapter 20 for more information on memory in Windows); the third is that to localize a Windows application, you usually translate the text of the resources in a different language, without changing the source code.

To use the resources instead of the bitmap files, we need first of all to copy the bitmap to the resource file. Although this is a tedious operation, you can use the Delphi Image editor to open the WORLD.RES file of the example and create new bitmap resources. Now you can open each of the bitmap files and perform a copy-and-paste operation to the bitmap in the resource file. (Of course, the final resource file is available on the companion disk.)

As a better alternative, you can write a resource script (an RC file) listing the names of the bitmap file and the names of the corresponding resources. This is a sample of the text of this file (which can be written with any editor):

```
W1   BITMAP   'W1.BMP'
W2   BITMAP   'W2.BMP'
W3   BITMAP   'W3.BMP'
...
```

Once you have prepared the RC file, you can compile it into a RES file using the resource compiler included in Delphi (the BRCC command-line application). See Chapter 21 for details on compilation of resource files.

10

Once you have properly defined the resources of the application, you need to load the bitmaps from the resources. Delphi components do not support this operation directly, but you can easily accomplish it using the Windows API LoadBitmap function. This function requires two parameters: a handle to the application, known as HInstance, which is available in Delphi as a global variable; and a string with the name of the resource. Of course, you need to pass a PChar string, not a Pascal string, so a conversion might be required (if you decide to use Pascal strings to define the text in the first place):

```
StrPCopy (Name, 'W' + IntToStr (I));
Bmp.Handle := LoadBitmap (HInstance, Name);
```

One problem remains to be solved: how can we obtain a smooth transition from an image of the world to the following one? I tried to work it out using the TBmpBtn class, but there were many obstacles. After a while, I figured out a completely different solution: why not paint the bitmaps in a canvas using the Draw method? Unluckily, the bitmap button's canvas is not directly available, so I added a new component, PaintBox, to the form. Again, things weren't working. You cannot place the paintbox inside the button; you can place it only inside the form. Even if you place it over the button, Delphi will connect the paintbox to the form, thus hiding it behind the button. The paintbox, in fact, is not a window. It uses the one of its parent control—in this case, the form. The solution? Very easy, once you think about it: change the parent of the paintbox at run-time, by writing:

```
PaintBox1.Parent := WorldButton;
```

If you originally placed the paintbox near the top-left corner of the form, it will appear near the top-left corner of the button.

Here is the definition of the paintbox in the textual description of the form (the other elements are similar to those of the first version of the WORLD example, shown in Listing 10.6):

```
object PaintBox1: TPaintBox
  Left = 0
  Top = 0
  Width = 60
  Height = 60
end
```

Once the paintbox is properly set, you can simply write

```
PaintBox1.Canvas.Draw (
  WorldButton.Margin + 2,
  WorldButton.Margin + 2,
  ImageList.Items[Count-1]);
```

This code copies the bitmap to the surface of the paintbox—that is, the surface of its parent component, the bitmap button. The position I've copied the bitmap to depends on the margin from the borders of the button to the bitmap, plus some border. Margin is a property that I set at design-time to a value of 2 since its default value is –1, meaning that the bitmap is placed in the center of the button. However, I should have written much more code to compute the bitmap's top-left corner this way.

You can see the complete source code of this example in Listing 10.7 (shown earlier in this section).

An Image Viewer

The Image component I briefly described earlier in this chapter is usually considered to be an image viewer. In fact, you can easily load into it a bitmap file (BMP), an icon (ICO), or a Windows metafile (WMF). Bitmap and icon files are well-known formats. Windows metafiles, however, are not so common. They are a collection of graphical commands, similar to a list of GDI function calls that need to be executed to rebuild an image. Metafiles are usually referred to as vector graphics and are similar to the graphics file formats used for clip-art libraries.

NOTE

To produce a Windows metafile, a program should call GDI functions, redirecting their output to the file. Later on, this metafile can be *played* or executed to call the corresponding functions, thus producing a graph. The advantage of metafiles is the limited amount of storage required compared to other graphical formats, and the device independence of their output. Metafiles, however, are not commonly used in Windows 3.1 because not all the GDI primitives are implemented and there are compatibility problems. For this reason, Delphi has limited support for metafiles. Microsoft includes full support for metafiles in the Win32 API (that is, both Windows 95 and Windows NT), improving the support and solving compatibility problems for 32 bit-applications.

10

To build a full-blown image viewer program, IMAGEV, around the Image component we need only a form with an image filling the whole client area, a simple menu, and an OpenDialog component. You can see the structure of the menu and the properties of the components of the form in Listing 10.8.

LISTING 10.8: The textual description of the form of the IMAGEV example

```
object ViewerForm: TViewerForm
  Caption = 'Image Viewer'
  Menu = MainMenu1
  object Image1: TImage
    Align = alClient
  end
  object MainMenu1: TMainMenu
    object File1: TMenuItem
      Caption = '&File'
      object Open1: TMenuItem
        Caption = '&Open'
        OnClick = Open1Click
      end
      object N1: TMenuItem
        Caption = '-'
      end
      object Exit1: TMenuItem
        Caption = '&Exit'
        OnClick = Exit1Click
      end
    end
    object Options1: TMenuItem
      Caption = '&Options'
      object Stretch1: TMenuItem
        Caption = '&Stretch'
        OnClick = Stretch1Click
      end
      object Center1: TMenuItem
        Caption = '&Center'
        OnClick = Center1Click
      end
    end
    object Help1: TMenuItem
      Caption = '&Help'
      object AboutImageViewer1: TMenuItem
        Caption = '&About Image Viewer...'
        OnClick = AboutImageViewer1Click
      end
    end
  end
  object OpenDialog1: TOpenDialog
    Filter = 'Bitmap (*.bmp)|*.bmp|
      Icon (*.ico)|*.ico|Metafile (*.wmf)|*.wmf'
    Options = [ofHideReadOnly, ofPathMustExist, ofFileMustExist]
    Left = 56
    Top = 16
  end
end
```

Surprisingly, this application requires very little coding, at least for a first basic version. The Exit and About commands are simple, and the Open command has the following code:

```
procedure TViewerForm.Open1Click(Sender: TObject);
begin
  if OpenDialog1.Execute then
  begin
    Image1.Picture.LoadFromFile (OpenDialog1.FileName);
    Caption := 'Image Viewer - ' + OpenDialog1.FileName;
  end;
end;
```

The fourth and the fifth menu commands, Stretch and Center, simply toggle the component's Stretch property (see Figure 10.10 for the result) or Center property and add a check mark to themselves:

```
procedure TViewerForm.Stretch1Click(Sender: TObject);
begin
  Image1.Stretch := not Image1.Stretch;
  Stretch1.Checked := Image1.Stretch;
end;

procedure TViewerForm.Center1Click(Sender: TObject);
begin
  Image1.Center := not Image1.Center;
  Center1.Checked := Image1.Center;
end;
```

FIGURE 10.10:

The IMAGEV program displaying the regular and stretched versions of the bitmap used in the FIRE2 example

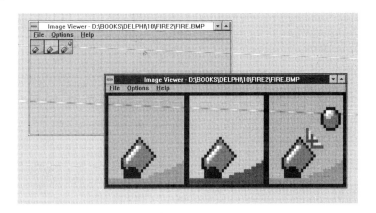

10

Consider in any case that not all the images can be properly stretched. Stretching applies only to bitmaps, and not all of them, depending on the color palette used. Several black-and-white or 256-color bitmaps cannot be stretched properly, particularly when they are reduced (see Figure 10.11 for an example of very bad stretching, applied to one of the 256-color bitmaps shipped with Delphi).

Besides this problem, the application has some other drawbacks. If you select a file without the proper extension, you'll get an exception error. At debug-time, this will stop the program and jump you back to the Code Editor window, but if you run the program by itself, the behavior of the exception handler provided by the system is good enough: the wrong image file is not loaded and the program can safely continue.

Another problem is that if you load a large image, the viewer has no scroll bars. You can maximize the viewer window, but this might not be enough. The Image components do not handle them automatically, but the form can do it. I'll further extend this example to include scroll bars in Chapter 13.

Drawing in a Bitmap

In the last chapter, I mentioned that by using an Image component, you can draw images directly in a bitmap. Instead of drawing on the surface of a window, you draw in a bitmap in memory; then the bitmap is copied to the surface of the

FIGURE 10.11:

At times, stretching a bitmap with IMAGEV produces an ugly effect

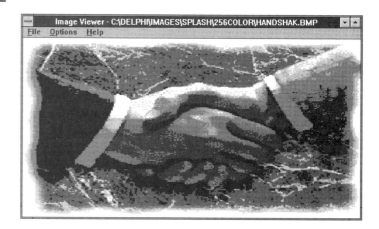

window. The advantage is that instead of having to repaint the image each time an OnPaint event occurs, the component copies the bitmap back to video.

Technically, a TBitmap object has its own canvas. By drawing on this canvas, you can change the contents of the bitmap. As an alternative, you can work on the canvas of an Image component connected to the bitmap you want to change.

You might think of choosing this approach instead of the typical painting approach if one or more of the following conditions are true:

- The program has to support freehand drawing or very complex graphics (such as fractal images).

- The program should be very fast in drawing a number of images.

- You and your users have a lot of RAM or are going to use only a few applications.

- You are a lazy programmer.

The last point is interesting because painting generally requires more code than drawing, although it allows more flexibility. In a graphics program, for example, if you use painting, you have to store the location and colors of each shape. On the other hand, you can easily change the color of an existing shape or move it. These operations are very difficult with the painting approach and may cause the area behind an image to be lost. If you are working on a complex graphical application, you should probably choose a mix of the two approaches.

For casual graphics programmers, the choice between the two approaches involves a typical speed-versus-memory decision: painting requires less memory; storing the bitmap is faster.

10

Drawing Shapes

After this general introduction about the use of the Image component to paint on a bitmap in Delphi, I'm going to show you an example. What better than a new version of the SHAPES series of examples of the last chapter?

The idea is simple. I've taken version 2 of the SHAPES example, the one having colored shapes but still no support to save them—that is, with drawing but without painting. Then I placed an Image component on its form, covering the whole client area, and I redirected all the output operations to the canvas of this Image component.

In the example SHAPES5, I've also added some new menu items to save the image to a file and to load an existing bitmap. To accomplish this, I've added to the form a couple of default dialog components, OpenDialog and SaveDialog. You can see the complete description of the form and of the properties of its components in Listing 10.9.

LISTING 10.9: The textual description of the form of the SHAPES5 example

```
object ShapesForm: TShapesForm
  Caption = 'Shapes'
  Color = clWhite
  Menu = MainMenu1
  Position = poDefaultPosOnly
  OnCreate = FormCreate
  object Image1: TImage
    Align = alClient
    OnMouseDown = Image1MouseDown
    OnMouseMove = Image1MouseMove
  end
  object MainMenu1: TMainMenu
    object File1: TMenuItem
      Caption = '&File'
      object New1: TMenuItem
        Caption = '&New'
        OnClick = New1Click
      end
      object Load1: TMenuItem
        Caption = '&Load...'
        OnClick = Load1Click
      end
      object Saveas1: TMenuItem
        Caption = 'Save &as...'
        OnClick = Saveas1Click
      end
      object N1: TMenuItem
        Caption = '-'
      end
      object Exit1: TMenuItem
        Caption = '&Exit'
        OnClick = Exit1Click
      end
    end
    object Colors1: TMenuItem
      Caption = '&Colors'
      object PenColor1: TMenuItem
        Caption = '&Pen Color...'
```

LISTING 10.9: The textual description of the form of the SHAPES5 example (continued)

```
        OnClick = PenColor1Click
      end
      object BrushColor1: TMenuItem
        Caption = '&Brush Color...'
        OnClick = BrushColor1Click
      end
    end
    object Size1: TMenuItem
      Caption = '&Size'
      object IncreasePenSize1: TMenuItem
        Caption = '&Increase Pen Size'
        OnClick = IncreasePenSize1Click
      end
      object DecreasePenSize1: TMenuItem
        Caption = '&Decrease Pen Size'
        Enabled = False
        OnClick = DecreasePenSize1Click
      end
      object N2: TMenuItem
        Caption = '-'
      end
      object IncreaseShapeSize1: TMenuItem
        Caption = 'I&ncrease Shape Size'
        OnClick = IncreaseShapeSize1Click
      end
      object DecreaseShapeSize1: TMenuItem
        Caption = 'D&ecrease Shape Size'
        Enabled = False
        OnClick = DecreaseShapeSize1Click
      end
    end
    object Help1: TMenuItem
      Caption = '&Help'
      object AboutShapes1: TMenuItem
        Caption = '&About Shapes...'
        OnClick = AboutShapes1Click
      end
    end
  end
  object ColorDialog1: TColorDialog
    Color = clBlack
    Options = []
  end
  object SaveDialog1: TSaveDialog
    DefaultExt = 'BMP'
    FileName = 'shapes.bmp'
    Filter = 'Bitmap file (*.bmp)|*.bmp'
    Options = [ofOverwritePrompt, ofHideReadOnly,
      ofPathMustExist, ofFileMustExist]
  end
```

10

LISTING 10.9: The textual description of the form of the SHAPES5 example (continued)

```
object OpenDialog1: TOpenDialog
  DefaultExt = 'BMP'
  Filter = 'Bitmap files (*.bmp)|*.bmp'
  Options = [ofHideReadOnly, ofPathMustExist,
    ofFileMustExist, ofShareAware]
  end
end
```

One of the properties I had to change was the background color of the form. In fact, when you perform the first graphical operation on the image, it creates a bitmap, which has a white background by default. If the form has a gray background, each time the window is repainted, some flickering occurs. For this reason, I've chosen a white background for the form, too.

The code of this example is still quite simple, considering the number of operations and menu commands. The drawing portion is linear and very close to SHAPES2, except that the mouse events now relate to the image instead of to the form, and that the canvas of the image is used. To avoid overly complex file support, I decided to implement File Load and File Save As commands, and not handle Save and the problems related to changes. To add this support, you should merge the code of this example with that of the NOTES2 example of Chapter 8.

You can look at the source file with the complete listing (see Listing 10.10), but I'll describe here two small code excerpts, which need some comments. The first is the code of the File New menu item, which calls the FillArea method to paint a big white rectangle over the whole bitmap:

```
Area := Rect (0, 0, Image1.Picture.Width,
  Image1.Picture.Height);
Image1.Canvas.Brush.Color := clWhite;
Image1.Canvas.FillRect (Area);
```

Of course, the code should also save the original color and restore it later on. The same happens in the File Load command response method. When you load a new bitmap, in fact, the Image component creates a new canvas, with the default

LISTING 10.10: The fifth version of the file SHAPE_F.PAS, with the complete listing of the form unit

```
unit Shapes_f;

interface

uses WinTypes, WinProcs, Classes, Graphics, Forms, Controls,
   Menus, Dialogs, ExtCtrls, SysUtils;

type
  TShapesForm = class(TForm)
    MainMenu1: TMainMenu;
    ColorDialog1: TColorDialog;
    File1: TMenuItem;
    New1: TMenuItem;
    N1: TMenuItem;
    Exit1: TMenuItem;
    Colors1: TMenuItem;
    PenColor1: TMenuItem;
    BrushColor1: TMenuItem;
    Size1: TMenuItem;
    IncreasePenSize1: TMenuItem;
    DecreasePenSize1: TMenuItem;
    N2: TMenuItem;
    IncreaseShapeSize1: TMenuItem;
    DecreaseShapeSize1: TMenuItem;
    Help1: TMenuItem;
    AboutShapes1: TMenuItem;
    Image1: TImage;
    Saveas1: TMenuItem;
    SaveDialog1: TSaveDialog;
    Load1: TMenuItem;
    OpenDialog1: TOpenDialog;
    procedure PenColor1Click(Sender: TObject);
    procedure BrushColor1Click(Sender: TObject);
    procedure IncreasePenSize1Click(Sender: TObject);
    procedure DecreasePenSize1Click(Sender: TObject);
    procedure IncreaseShapeSize1Click(Sender: TObject);
    procedure DecreaseShapeSize1Click(Sender: TObject);
    procedure FormCreate(Sender: TObject);
    procedure AboutShapes1Click(Sender: TObject);
    procedure Exit1Click(Sender: TObject);
    procedure New1Click(Sender: TObject);
procedure Image1MouseDown(Sender: TObject;
      Button: TMouseButton;
      Shift: TShiftState; X, Y: Integer);
procedure Image1MouseMove(Sender: TObject;
      Shift: TShiftState;
      X, Y: Integer);
    procedure Saveas1Click(Sender: TObject);
    procedure Load1Click(Sender: TObject);
```

10

LISTING 10.10: The fifth version of the file SHAPE_F.PAS, with the complete listing of the form unit (continued)

```
private
  { Private declarations }
  Radius: Integer;
public
  { Public declarations }
end;

var
  ShapesForm: TShapesForm;

implementation

{$R *.DFM}

procedure TShapesForm.PenColor1Click(Sender: TObject);
begin
  {select a new color for the pen}
  ColorDialog1.Color := Image1.Canvas.Pen.Color;
  ColorDialog1.Execute;
  Image1.Canvas.Pen.Color := ColorDialog1.Color;
end;

procedure TShapesForm.BrushColor1Click(Sender: TObject);
begin
  {select a new color for the brush}
  ColorDialog1.Color := Image1.Canvas.Brush.Color;
  ColorDialog1.Execute;
  Image1.Canvas.Brush.Color := ColorDialog1.Color;
end;

procedure TShapesForm.IncreasePenSize1Click(Sender: TObject);
begin
  {increase the size of the pen}
  Image1.Canvas.Pen.Width := Image1.Canvas.Pen.Width + 2;
  DecreasePenSize1.Enabled := True;
end;

procedure TShapesForm.DecreasePenSize1Click(Sender: TObject);
begin
  {decrease the size of the pen,
  avoiding letting it go below zero}
  Image1.Canvas.Pen.Width := Image1.Canvas.Pen.Width - 2;
  if Image1.Canvas.Pen.Width < 3 then
    DecreasePenSize1.Enabled := False;
end;

procedure TShapesForm.IncreaseShapeSize1Click(Sender: TObject);
begin
  {increase radius, a private field of the form}
  Radius := Radius + 5;
```

LISTING 10.10: The fifth version of the file SHAPE_F.PAS, with the complete listing of the form unit (continued)

```
    DecreaseShapeSize1.Enabled := True;
end;

procedure TShapesForm.DecreaseShapeSize1Click(Sender: TObject);
begin
  {decrease the radius, but not below the limit}
  Radius := Radius - 5;
  if Radius < 10 then
    DecreaseShapeSize1.Enabled := False;
end;

procedure TShapesForm.FormCreate(Sender: TObject);
begin
  {initial value}
  Radius := 5;
end;

procedure TShapesForm.AboutShapes1Click(Sender: TObject);
begin
  {show a message box}
  MessageDlg ('Shape application (v. 5.0)' +
    Chr(13) + '"Mastering Delphi", Marco Cantù',
    mtInformation, [mbOK], 0);
end;

procedure TShapesForm.Exit1Click(Sender: TObject);
begin
  {close the form and the application}
  Close;
end;

procedure TShapesForm.New1Click(Sender: TObject);
var
  Area: TRect;
  OldColor: TColor;
begin
  if MessageDlg ('Are you sure you want to cover ' +
    'the current image?',
    mtConfirmation, [mbYes, mbNo], 0) = idYes then
  begin
    {repaint the surface, covering the whole area,
    and resetting the old brush}
    Area := Rect (0, 0, Image1.Picture.Width,
      Image1.Picture.Height);
    OldColor := Image1.Canvas.Brush.Color;
    Image1.Canvas.Brush.Color := clWhite;
    Image1.Canvas.FillRect (Area);
    Image1.Canvas.Brush.Color := OldColor;
  end
end;
```

10

LISTING 10.10:   The fifth version of the file SHAPE_F.PAS, with the complete listing of the form unit (continued)

```pascal
procedure TShapesForm.Image1MouseDown(Sender: TObject;
  Button: TMouseButton; Shift: TShiftState; X, Y: Integer);
begin
  {draw a form in x:y, using the current radius}
  if Button = mbLeft then
    if ssShift in Shift then
      Image1.Canvas.Rectangle (X-Radius, Y-Radius,
        X+Radius, Y+Radius)
    else
      Image1.Canvas.Ellipse (X-Radius, Y-Radius,
        X+Radius, Y+Radius);
end;

procedure TShapesForm.Image1MouseMove(Sender: TObject;
  Shift: TShiftState; X, Y: Integer);
begin
  {display the position of the mouse in the caption}
  ShapesForm.Caption := 'Shapes: x=' + IntToStr (X)
    + ', y=' + IntToStr (Y);
end;

procedure TShapesForm.Saveas1Click(Sender: TObject);
begin
  if SaveDialog1.Execute then
    Image1.Picture.SaveToFile (SaveDialog1.Filename);
end;

procedure TShapesForm.Load1Click(Sender: TObject);
var
  PenCol, BrushCol: TColor;
  PenSize: Integer;
begin
  if OpenDialog1.Execute then
  begin
    PenCol := Image1.Canvas.Pen.Color;
    BrushCol := Image1.Canvas.Brush.Color;
    PenSize := Image1.Canvas.Pen.Width;
    Image1.Picture.LoadFromFile (OpenDialog1.Filename);
    Image1.Canvas.Pen.Color := PenCol;
    Image1.Canvas.Brush.Color := BrushCol;
    Image1.Canvas.Pen.Width := PenSize;
  end;
end;

end.
```

attribute. For this reason, the program saves the pen's colors and size and copies them later to the new canvas:

```
PenCol := Image1.Canvas.Pen.Color;
BrushCol := Image1.Canvas.Brush.Color;
PenSize := Image1.Canvas.Pen.Width;
Image1.Picture.LoadFromFile (OpenDialog1.Filename);
Image1.Canvas.Pen.Color := PenCol;
Image1.Canvas.Brush.Color := BrushCol;
Image1.Canvas.Pen.Width := PenSize;
```

SHAPES5 is an interesting program, with bare but working file support (see Figure 10.12), although its graphical capabilities are limited. The real problem is that the Image component creates a bitmap of its own size. When you increase the size of the window, the Image component is resized, but not the bitmap in memory. Therefore, you cannot draw on the right and bottom areas of the window.

FIGURE 10.12:

The SHAPES5 example has limited but working file support: you can load an existing bitmap, draw shapes over it, and save it to disk.

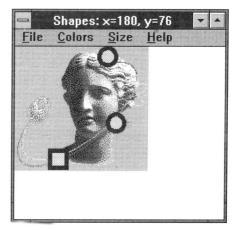

There are a number of possible solutions: use the Windows wm_GetMinMaxInfo message to set the maximum size of the form (as shown in Chapter 9), use a fixed border, visually mark the *drawing area* on the screen, and so on. However, I've decided to leave the program as is since it does its job of demonstrating how to draw in a bitmap well enough. The second reason is that this is already the fifth version of the SHAPES program. It seems better to move to another topic and to a different example.

The Outline of the Book

It has become common to see Windows applications with graphical list boxes, particularly lists of files. To draw in a list box in Windows, you have to declare it as owner-drawn and provide some painting code. In Delphi, you can indeed have an owner-drawn list box, but for the most common situations, there are easier and better alternatives. The graphical version of the list box is the Outline component, and there are also two customized versions, the FileListBox and DirectoryListBox components.

The Outline component has two features: it allows you to add a bitmap before the text of the items of the list and to build a graphical hierarchy of items. To create a simple list of elements, you only need to add them to the Lines property and provide a specific bitmap in the PictureLeaf property.

The use of the outline makes particular sense when you have hierarchical information to display. I've taken as an example the draft of the table of contents of this book, and I've built the BOOKOUT example with it.

WARNING   When I started writing the example, my intention was to call it OUTLINE. However, had I done so, the Pascal compiler would not have been able to refer properly to the Outline unit of the system since it is *hidden* by the program file. The moral of this story is that you should avoid duplicate identifiers in general, but especially unit and module names.

The Styles of the Outline

Before looking at the example, let me describe some of the properties and styles of the Outline component. The Lines property holds the contents of the control at design-time. At run-time, you can access the same information using the Items property. When you enter the text of the outline or read it from a text file, notice that you can leave either a space or a tab in front of an item's text to indicate its level of indentation. You can see a portion of the text of the example in the String List editor in Figure 10.13.

FIGURE 10.13:

The items of the outline of the BOOKOUT example in the String List editor

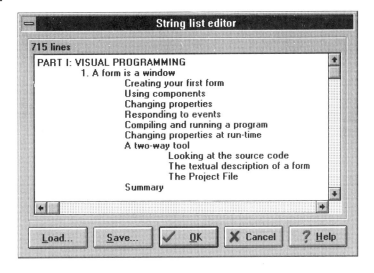

> **TIP**
>
> When you are using the Delphi String List editor, by pressing the Tab key you move the focus to one of the buttons below instead of entering a tab in the text. To enter a tab in front of an item, use Ctrl-Tab instead of pressing only the Tab key.

Once you have defined the outline's text, you can set its style. The OutlineStyle property has six possible values, shown in the six samples of Figure 10.14:

10

- osPictureText defines an outline with the open picture (specified in Picture-Open) for the expanded nodes, the closed picture (specified in PictureClosed) for the collapsed nodes, or the leaf picture (specified in PictureLeaf) for the items without further subitems.

- osPlusMinusPictureText defines an outline as osPictureText, also with the plus picture (specified in PicturePlus) and a minus picture (specified in PictureMinus) for items you can expand or collapse.

- osPlusMinusText defines an outline having only the plus and minus pictures and missing the other three graphical elements (open, closed, item).

- osText defines an outline having only text, with no glyphs.

- `osTreePictureText` defines an outline as `osPictureText`, having in addition some lines to highlight the tree of items and the different indentation levels.

- `osTreeText` defines an outline having only the graphical tree and the text, with no bitmaps.

FIGURE 10.14:

The effect of the use of the six values of the OutlineStyle property on the BOOKOUT example (on the top, from the left: picture text, plus/minus picture text, plus/minus text; on the bottom: text, tree picture text, tree text)

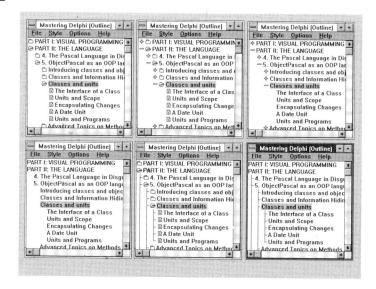

Each of these versions of the outline shows the text with the proper indentation. A second relevant property is Options, which you can use to:

- Define the presence of a tree root (`ooDrawTreeRoot`), as you can see in Figure 10.15.

- Choose the activation of a focus rectangle (`ooDrawFocusRect`).

- Stretch the standard bitmaps (`ooStretchBitmap`) to fit in the size of the item, which depends on the height of the component's font. If you don't set this property, the bitmaps are displayed as they are, eventually cutting out a portion or leaving some border around them. When you select a big font or big bitmaps, this option can come handy.

FIGURE 10.15:
You can add a tree root diagram to outlines with the tree picture text (on the left) or tree text (on the right) style

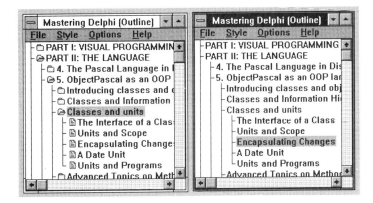

The last property that determines the outline's global behavior is its Style, which can be osStandard or osOwnerDraw. In the latter case, you have to define the height of the elements (ItemHeight) and draw each of them, both graphics and text.

> **NOTE** The same owner-drawn style I mentioned for the outlines is also available for list boxes, combo boxes, and other standard Windows elements.

Building a Flexible Outline

Having seen the main elements of an Outline component, we can write an example to see how it can be used. Our example, named BOOKOUT will allow you to test the different styles of the outline, which can be activated by means of the application's menu.

The simple form of the BOOKOUT example contains an outline, filling the form's whole client area, and a menu, with the structure you can see in Listing 10.11 (I've removed the value of the outline's Lines property, which is quite complex). The code of the application is simple, too. It contains only commands to toggle on and off some styles of the outline, with the proper check marks beside the selected menu items.

LISTING 10.11: The textual description of the form of the BOOKOUT example, with the structure of its menu

```
object Form1: TForm1
  Caption = 'Mastering Delphi (Outline)'
  Menu = MainMenu1
  object Outline1: TOutline
    Lines.Nodes = (...) {omitted}
    Options = []
    Align = alClient
    TabOrder = 0
    BorderStyle = bsNone
    ItemSeparator = '\'
  end
  object MainMenu1: TMainMenu
    object File1: TMenuItem
      Caption = '&File'
      object Exit1: TMenuItem
        Caption = 'E&xit'
        OnClick = Exit1Click
      end
    end
    object Style1: TMenuItem
      Caption = '&Style'
      object PictureText1: TMenuItem
        Caption = '&Picture Text'
        OnClick = PictureText1Click
      end
      object PlusMinusPictureText1: TMenuItem
        Caption = 'P&lus Minus Picture Text'
        OnClick = PlusMinusPictureText1Click
      end
      object PlusMinusText1: TMenuItem
        Caption = 'Plus &Minus Text'
        OnClick = PlusMinusText1Click
      end
      object Text1: TMenuItem
        Caption = '&Text'
        OnClick = Text1Click
      end
      object TreePictureText1: TMenuItem
        Caption = 'T&ree Picture Text'
        Checked = True
        OnClick = TreePictureText1Click
      end
      object TreeText1: TMenuItem
        Caption = 'Tr&ee Text'
        OnClick = TreeText1Click
      end
    end
    object Options1: TMenuItem
      Caption = '&Options'
      object DrawTreeRoot1: TMenuItem
```

LISTING 10.11: The textual description of the form of the BOOKOUT example (continued)

```
          Caption = '&Draw Tree Root'
          OnClick = DrawTreeRoot1Click
        end
        object DrawFocusRect1: TMenuItem
          Caption = 'Draw Focus &Rect'
          OnClick = DrawFocusRect1Click
        end
        object StretchBitmaps1: TMenuItem
          Caption = '&Stretch Bitmaps'
          OnClick = StretchBitmaps1Click
        end
        object N1: TMenuItem
          Caption = '-'
        end
        object Font1: TMenuItem
          Caption = '&Font...'
          OnClick = Font1Click
        end
      end
      object Help1: TMenuItem
        Caption = '&Help'
        object About1: TMenuItem
          Caption = '&About...'
          OnClick = About1Click
        end
      end
    end
    object FontDialog1: TFontDialog
      Font.Color = clWindowText
      Font.Height = -13
      Font.Name = 'System'
      Font.Style = []
    end
end
```

10

The menu items of the Style menu are mutually exclusive. This means that when you select and check an item, all the other items should be unchecked. For this reason, I've added a RemoveStyleChecks private method to the form (see the full source code in Listing 10.12), which is called every time one of this menu's commands is selected.

LISTING 10.12 : The complete listing of the BOOKOUT example

```
unit Outli_f;

interface

uses
  SysUtils, WinTypes, WinProcs, Messages, Classes,
  Graphics, Controls, Forms, Dialogs, Menus, Grids,
  Outline, ExtCtrls;

type
  TForm1 = class(TForm)
    Outline1: TOutline;
    MainMenu1: TMainMenu;
    Style1: TMenuItem;
    PictureText1: TMenuItem;
    PlusMinusPictureText1: TMenuItem;
    PlusMinusText1: TMenuItem;
    Text1: TMenuItem;
    TreePictureText1: TMenuItem;
    TreeText1: TMenuItem;
    Options1: TMenuItem;
    DrawTreeRoot1: TMenuItem;
    DrawFocusRect1: TMenuItem;
    StretchBitmaps1: TMenuItem;
    Help1: TMenuItem;
    About1: TMenuItem;
    File1: TMenuItem;
    Exit1: TMenuItem;
    N1: TMenuItem;
    Font1: TMenuItem;
    FontDialog1: TFontDialog;
    procedure Exit1Click(Sender: TObject);
    procedure PictureText1Click(Sender: TObject);
    procedure PlusMinusPictureText1Click(Sender: TObject);
    procedure PlusMinusText1Click(Sender: TObject);
    procedure Text1Click(Sender: TObject);
    procedure TreePictureText1Click(Sender: TObject);
    procedure TreeText1Click(Sender: TObject);
    procedure DrawTreeRoot1Click(Sender: TObject);
    procedure DrawFocusRect1Click(Sender: TObject);
    procedure StretchBitmaps1Click(Sender: TObject);
    procedure Font1Click(Sender: TObject);
    procedure About1Click(Sender: TObject);
  private
    { Private declarations }
    procedure RemoveStyleChecks;
  public
    { Public declarations }
  end;
```

LISTING 10.12: The complete listing of the BOOKOUT example (continued)

```
var
  Form1: TForm1;

implementation

{$R *.DFM}

procedure TForm1.Exit1Click(Sender: TObject);
begin
  Close;
end;

procedure TForm1.RemoveStyleChecks;
begin
  PictureText1.Checked := False;
  PlusMinusPictureText1.Checked := False;
  PlusMinusText1.Checked := False;
  Text1.Checked := False;
  TreePictureText1.Checked := False;
  TreeText1.Checked := False;
end;

procedure TForm1.PictureText1Click(Sender: TObject);
begin
  Outline1.OutlineStyle := osPictureText;
  RemoveStyleChecks;
  PictureText1.Checked := True;
end;

procedure TForm1.PlusMinusPictureText1Click(Sender: TObject);
begin
  Outline1.OutlineStyle := osPlusMinusPictureText;
  RemoveStyleChecks;
  PlusMinusPictureText1.Checked := True;
end;

procedure TForm1.PlusMinusText1Click(Sender: TObject);
begin
  Outline1.OutlineStyle := osPlusMinusText;
  RemoveStyleChecks;
  PlusMinusText1.Checked := True;
end;

procedure TForm1.Text1Click(Sender: TObject);
begin
  Outline1.OutlineStyle := osText;
  RemoveStyleChecks;
  Text1.Checked := True;
end;
```

10

LISTING 10.12 : The complete listing of the BOOKOUT example (continued)

```
procedure TForm1.TreePictureText1Click(Sender: TObject);
begin
  Outline1.OutlineStyle := osTreePictureText;
  RemoveStyleChecks;
  TreePictureText1.Checked := True;
end;

procedure TForm1.TreeText1Click(Sender: TObject);
begin
  Outline1.OutlineStyle := osTreeText;
  RemoveStyleChecks;
  TreeText1.Checked := True;
end;

procedure TForm1.DrawTreeRoot1Click(Sender: TObject);
begin
  if ooDrawTreeRoot in Outline1.Options then
    Outline1.Options := Outline1.Options - [ooDrawTreeRoot]
  else
    Outline1.Options := Outline1.Options + [ooDrawTreeRoot];
  DrawTreeRoot1.Checked := not DrawTreeRoot1.Checked;
end;

procedure TForm1.DrawFocusRect1Click(Sender: TObject);
begin
  if ooDrawFocusRect in Outline1.Options then
    Outline1.Options := Outline1.Options - [ooDrawFocusRect]
  else
    Outline1.Options := Outline1.Options + [ooDrawFocusRect];
  DrawFocusRect1.Checked := not DrawFocusRect1.Checked;
end;

procedure TForm1.StretchBitmaps1Click(Sender: TObject);
begin
  if ooStretchBitmaps in Outline1.Options then
    Outline1.Options := Outline1.Options - [ooStretchBitmaps]
  else
    Outline1.Options := Outline1.Options + [ooStretchBitmaps];
  StretchBitmaps1.Checked := not StretchBitmaps1.Checked;
end;

procedure TForm1.Font1Click(Sender: TObject);
begin
  FontDialog1.Font := Outline1.Font;
  if FontDialog1.Execute then
    Outline1.Font := FontDialog1.Font;
end;
```

LISTING 10.12: The complete listing of the BOOKOUT example (continued)

```
procedure TForm1.About1Click(Sender: TObject);
begin
  MessageDlg ('Outline of the book: "Mastering Delphi"' +
    Chr(13) + 'Author: Marco Cantù',
    mtInformation, [mbOk], 0);
end;

end.
```

The Options menu, instead, has nonexclusive options, so each menu item is checked and unchecked independently of the other two. This menu has also a Font command, to change the outline's font. I've added this command so you can see the effect of the bitmap stretching (see Figure 10.16).

FIGURE 10.16:

An example of BOOKOUT with a big, fancy font and the stretched bitmaps

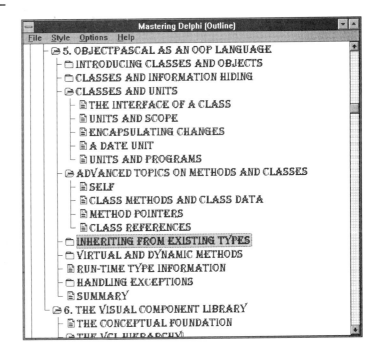

10

The Nodes of the Outline

At the core of the Outline component is a list of TOutlineNode objects. Each of these objects has some text, possibly some data, and a bunch of other properties. For example, Level indicates the level of indentation of an item, and FullPath indicates the name, including all the parent items. For an advanced use of the Outline component, study the class of the nodes in detail. Instead of boring you with a list of all the operations you can do on an outline, I will show you a slightly more advanced example of the use of this component.

The example, named NODES, is a kind of geography test. The main form of the program (see Figure 10.17) has two graphical list boxes. The list on the left contains a number of countries, states, and country organizations (such as the European Community or NAFTA). Of course, this is not a full list: if you live in a state or country that is not present, please add it to the list. The list on the right contains just two entries, America and Europe (again, you can expand this by adding more continents).

The aim of the program is to drag items from the left outline to the proper position in the hierarchy on the right (see Figure 10.18). To accomplish this, you need to select an element in the left outline and drag it over the parent node in the right outline. For example, you can select Brazil and drag it over America.

FIGURE 10.17:

The form of the NODES program at design-time

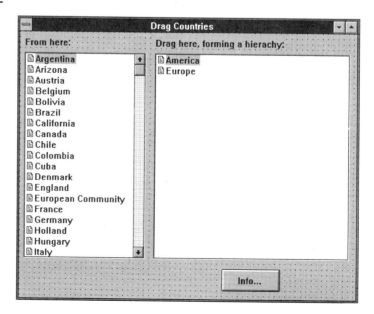

FIGURE 10.18:

The aim of the NODES program is to drag items properly to the hierarchy on the right.

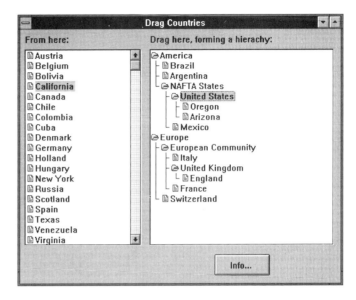

Other elements should be dragged to a lower level. For example, England should be placed under United Kingdom, which should go under European Community, which should be under Europe. When you have done this, you can get information on an item by pressing the Info button below the list. This information includes the full path of the item, as you can see in Figure 10.19.

If we want to build the example, the form is quite simple: just two Outline components, two labels, and a button. The two outlines have no special attributes. I've only removed the root node and added the text of the items. Notice that automatic dragging has not been enabled. I decided to use manual dragging instead.

10

TIP

If you select automatic dragging for a list box or similar component, your code should handle the selection of elements. To allow a user to both select items and drag them, you have to use manual dragging, calling the BeginDrag method and passing to it the False parameter. In this case, dragging is not started immediately, and a click properly selects a new item.

FIGURE 10.19:

The information about the England item, including its full path

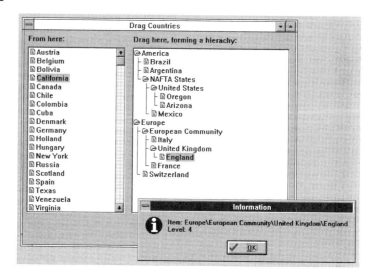

Handling the dragging manually is easy, as you can see from the source code in Listing 10.13. When the user presses the left mouse button over the first Outline component (if it is not empty), the program calls the BeginDrag method. As soon as the button is released, the program calls the EndDrag method. The second Outline component defines two handlers for the OnDragOver and OnDragDrop events.

LISTING 10.13: The full listing of the NODES example

```
unit Nodes_f;

interface

uses
  SysUtils, WinTypes, WinProcs, Messages, Classes, Graphics,
  Controls, Forms, Dialogs, StdCtrls, Grids, Outline;

type
  TForm1 = class(TForm)
    Outline1: TOutline;
    Outline2: TOutline;
    Label1: TLabel;
    Label2: TLabel;
    ButtonInfo: TButton;
    procedure Outline2DragOver(Sender, Source: TObject;
      X, Y: Integer;
```

LISTING 10.13: The full listing of the NODES example (continued)

```
        State: TDragState; var Accept: Boolean);
      procedure Outline1MouseDown(Sender: TObject;
        Button: TMouseButton;
        Shift: TShiftState; X, Y: Integer);
      procedure Outline1MouseUp(Sender: TObject;
        Button: TMouseButton;
        Shift: TShiftState; X, Y: Integer);
      procedure Outline2DragDrop(Sender, Source: TObject;
        X, Y: Integer);
      procedure ButtonInfoClick(Sender: TObject);
    private
      { Private declarations }
    public
      { Public declarations }
    end;

var
  Form1: TForm1;

implementation

{$R *.DFM}

procedure TForm1.Outline2DragOver(Sender, Source: TObject;
  X, Y: Integer; State: TDragState; var Accept: Boolean);
begin
  if Sender is TOutline then
    Accept := True;
end;

procedure TForm1.Outline1MouseDown(Sender: TObject;
  Button: TMouseButton;
  Shift: TShiftState; X, Y: Integer);
begin
  if (Outline1.ItemCount > 0) and (Button = mbLeft) then
    OutLine1.BeginDrag (False);
end;

procedure TForm1.Outline1MouseUp(Sender: TObject;
  Button: TMouseButton;
  Shift: TShiftState; X, Y: Integer);
begin
  OutLine1.EndDrag (True);
end;

procedure TForm1.Outline2DragDrop(Sender, Source: TObject;
  X, Y: Integer);
var
  Current: Integer;
begin
  Current := Outline2.GetItem (X, Y);
```

10

LISTING 10.13: The full listing of the NODES example (continued)

```
    Outline2.AddChild (Current, Outline1.Lines[Outline1.SelectedItem - 1]);
    Outline2.Items [Current].Expanded := True;
    Outline1.Delete (Outline1.SelectedItem);
end;

procedure TForm1.ButtonInfoClick(Sender: TObject);
var
  Node: TOutlineNode;
  Text: string;
begin
  Node := Outline2.Items [Outline2.SelectedItem];
  Text := 'Item: ' + Node.FullPath + Chr (13) +
    'Level: ' + IntToStr (Node.Level);
  if Node.HasItems then
    Text := Text + ' * Has sub-items';
  if Node.Expanded then
    Text := Text + ' and is expanded';
  MessageDlg (Text, mtInformation, [mbOk], 0);
end;

end.
```

This last method, the heart of the program, is quite complex. When the user drags a new element, the program first determines the item of the destination outline on which the element was dropped, using the GetItem function and the coordinates passed by the event. Then the program selects this item as the outline's current item—that is, the item that will be affected by the following call to the Add method:

```
    Outline2.Add (Outline1.Lines[Outline1.SelectedItem - 1], nil);
```

This statement adds to the second outline the text of the selected item of the first outline. The –1 is needed because the Lines array is zero-based, while the items are numbered starting from 1. It is possible to extract the text of the item directly from the Lines array only because the items of the source list have no indentation. The Lines value for an indented item, in fact, might have a tab character at the beginning. Windows displays this as a vertical line.

After the element is copied to the destination outline, it should be deleted from the source outline, and its new parent node should be expanded to show the new element.

The only other complex method is the one that computes the string to display as information about the item. This string includes the item's full path, its level, and whether it is an intermediate node (see Figures 10.19 and 10.20).

The information displayed by the NODES program about an intermediate node; compare it with Figure 10.19, which displays information about a terminal node (a leaf).

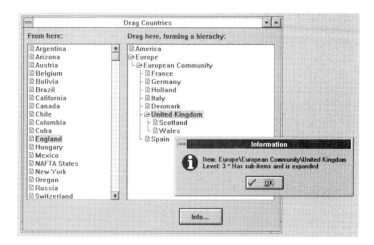

Building Grids

Another interesting group of Delphi graphical components is represented by grids. The system contains four different grid components: a grid of strings, one of images, a database grid, and a grid of colors. The first two kinds of grids are particularly useful since they allow you to represent a lot of information and let the user navigate it. Of course, grids are extremely important in database programming. We will use the DBGrid component a lot in Chapters 17 and 18, which are devoted to databases and client-server programming, respectively.

The DrawGrid and StringGrid components are closely related. In fact, the TStringGrid class is a subclass of TDrawGrid. What is the use of these grids? Basically, you can store some values, either in the strings related to the StringGrid or in other data structures, and then display each of the values, using specific criteria. While grids of strings can almost be used as they are since they already provide even editing capabilities, the grids of generic drawings usually require more coding.

Grids, in fact, define display organization, not storage. The only grids that store the data they display are the StringGrid and Outline components. All other grids are just viewers, not containers.

The basic structure of a grid includes some fixed columns and rows (as you can see in Figure 10.21), which indicate the non-scrollable region of the grid. Grids are among the most complex components available in Delphi, as indicated by the high number of properties and methods they have. There is a plethora of options and properties for grids, controlling both their appearance and their behavior.

FIGURE 10.21:

When you place a new grid component on a form, it contains a fixed row and a fixed column by default.

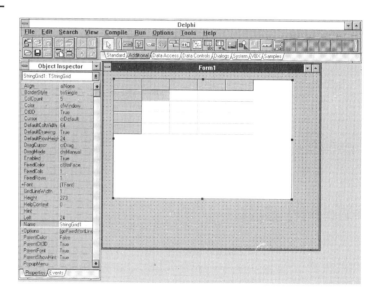

Regarding the user interface, the grid can have lines of different sizes or even have no lines. You can set the size of each column or row independently of the others because the RowSize, ColWidth, and RowHeight properties are arrays.

Regarding user actions, you can let the user resize the columns and the rows (goColSizing and goRowSizing), drag entire columns and rows to a new position (goRowMoving and goColumnMoving), select automatic editing, and allow range selections. Since users can perform a number of operations on grids with the proper options, there are also a number of events related to grids. Here are some events specifically used by grids:

```
OnColumnMoved
OnDrawCell
OnGetEditText
OnRowMoved
OnSelectCell
OnSetEditText
OnTopLeftChanged
```

The most important is probably OnDrawCell. In response to this event, a program has to paint a certain cell of the grid. Only string grids can automatically display their contents. The DrawGrid, in fact, doesn't have support for storing data. It is simply a tool for arranging a portion of the screen to display information in a regular format. It is a simple tool but, at the same time, a powerful one. Methods like CellRect, which returns the rectangle corresponding to the area of a cell, or Mouse-ToCell, which returns the cell in a specific location, are a joy to use, considering that they handle resizable rows and columns and scrollable grids.

What can you use a grid for? Building a spreadsheet is probably the first idea that comes to mind, but I have chosen not to follow this. I suspect there will be a nice spreadsheet add-on for Delphi, although using a string grid allowing only numerical input is easy. Add a simple formula translator, and most of the work is done.

I've decided to use the two grids to build two examples, presented in the next two sections. The StringGrid creates a program that shows the fonts installed in the system, and the DrawGrid creates a program that emulates the Windows Minesweeper game. Yes, a game; Delphi is good for games, too (although the game I've built is not very efficient during screen redrawing). The fact that you can build Windows games in Delphi should not be underestimated, even if your business is completely different. Games and other entertainment programs, in fact, demand more in terms of system and development tools than any other category of software, databases included. So being good for games means that Delphi is a very good development environment.

After the Minesweeper clone comes a simple example of the use of another, completely different grid, the ColorGrid.

10

A Grid of Fonts

If you place a StringGrid component on a form and set its options properly, you have a full working editor of strings arranged in a grid, with no programming at all. So to make the example more interesting, I've decided to draw each cell of the grid with a different font, varying both its size and its type. You can see the result of this program, FONTGRID, in Figure 10.22.

The form of this program is very simple (see Listing 10.14 for the textual description of the form). You need only place a grid component on a form, align it with the client area, set a few properties and options, and let the program do the rest. The number of columns and rows and their size, in fact, are computed at run-time. The important properties you need to set are DefaultDrawing, which should be False to let us paint the grid as we like, and Options.

As usually happens in Delphi, the simpler the form is, the more complex the code, at least when you are building a non-trivial application. This example follows that rule, although it has only two methods, one to initialize the grid at startup and the other to draw the items. The editing, in fact, has not been customized and takes place using the system font.

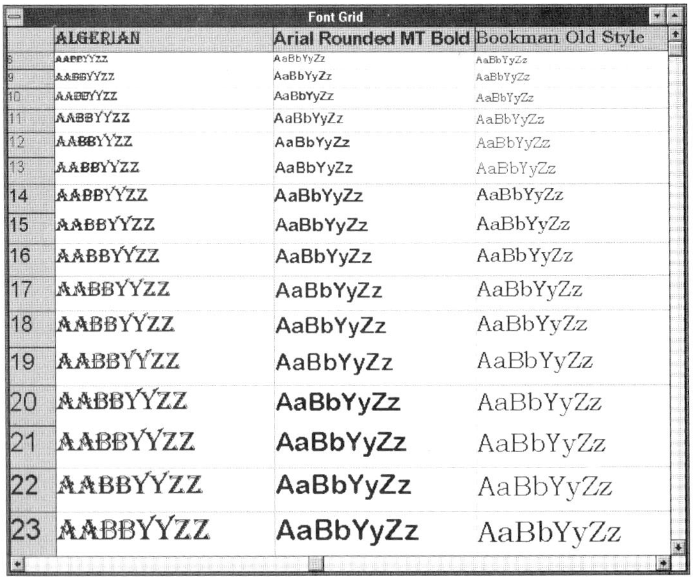

FIGURE 10.22:

An example of the output of the FONTGRID example

LISTING 10.14: The textual description of the form of the FONTGRID example

```
object Form1: TForm1
  ActiveControl = StringGrid1
  Caption = 'Font Grid'
  OnCreate = FormCreate
  object StringGrid1: TStringGrid
    Left = 0
    Top = 0
    Align = alClient
    ColCount = 20
    DefaultColWidth = 200
    DefaultDrawing = False
    Options = [goFixedHorzLine, goFixedVertLine,
      goHorzLine, goVertLine, goDrawFocusSelected,
      goColSizing, goColMoving, goEditing]
    RowCount = 20
    OnDrawCell = StringGrid1DrawCell
  end
end
```

The first of the two methods (see Listing 10.15 for the complete source code) is FormCreate. At the beginning, this method uses the global Screen object to access the fonts installed in the system.

> **TIP**
>
> The Screen global variable holds an object of type TScreen, which holds a number of pieces of information about the attributes of the screen, the fonts installed in the system, and the forms of the current application. Chapter 19 contains a specific section about the Screen object.

The grid has a column for each font, plus a fixed column. The name of each column is copied from the Screen object to the first row of each column (which has a zero index):

```
StringGrid1.ColCount := Screen.Fonts.Count + 1;
...
StringGrid1.Cells [I, 0] :=
  Screen.Fonts.Strings [I-1];
```

LISTING 10.15: The complete listing of the FONTGRID example

```pascal
unit Grid_f;

interface

uses
  SysUtils, WinTypes, WinProcs, Messages, Classes, Graphics,
   Controls, Forms, Dialogs, StdCtrls, Buttons, ExtCtrls, Grids;

type
  TForm1 = class(TForm)
    StringGrid1: TStringGrid;
    procedure FormCreate(Sender: TObject);
    procedure StringGrid1DrawCell(Sender: TObject;
      Col, Row: LongInt;
      Rect: TRect; State: TGridDrawState);
  private
    { Private declarations }
  public
    { Public declarations }
  end;

var
  Form1: TForm1;

implementation

{$R *.DFM}

procedure TForm1.FormCreate(Sender: TObject);
var
  I, J: Integer;
begin
  {the number of columns equals the number of fonts plus
  1 for the first fixed column, which has a size of 20}
  StringGrid1.ColCount := Screen.Fonts.Count + 1;
  StringGrid1.ColWidths [0] := 50;

  for I := 1 to Screen.Fonts.Count do
  begin
    {write the name of the font in the first row}
    StringGrid1.Cells [I, 0] := Screen.Fonts.Strings [I-1];

    {compute maximum required size of column,
    getting the width of the text with the biggest
    size of the font of the column}
    StringGrid1.Canvas.Font.Name := StringGrid1.Cells [I, 0];
    StringGrid1.Canvas.Font.Size := 32;
    StringGrid1.ColWidths [I] :=
      StringGrid1.Canvas.TextWidth ('AaBbYyZz');
  end;
```

LISTING 10.15: The complete listing of the FONTGRID example (continued)

```
  {defines the number of columns}
  StringGrid1.RowCount := 26;
  for I := 1 to 25 do
  begin
    {write the number in the first column}
    StringGrid1.Cells [0, I] := IntToStr (I+7);
    {set an increasing height for the rows}
    StringGrid1.RowHeights [I] := 15 + I*2;
    {insert default text}
    for J := 1 to StringGrid1.ColCount do
      StringGrid1.Cells [J, I] := 'AaBbYyZz'
  end;
  StringGrid1.RowHeights [0] := 25;
end;

procedure TForm1.StringGrid1DrawCell(Sender: TObject;
  Col, Row: Longint; Rect: TRect; State: TGridDrawState);
begin
  {select a font, depending on the column}
  if Col = 0 then
    StringGrid1.Canvas.Font.Name := 'Arial'
  else
    StringGrid1.Canvas.Font.Name := StringGrid1.Cells [Col, 0];

  {select the size of the font, depending on the row}
  if Row = 0 then
    StringGrid1.Canvas.Font.Size := 14
  else
    StringGrid1.Canvas.Font.Size := Row + 7;

  {select the background color}
  if gdSelected in State then
    StringGrid1.Canvas.Brush.Color := clHighlight
  else if gdFixed in State then
    StringGrid1.Canvas.Brush.Color := clBtnFace
  else
    StringGrid1.Canvas.Brush.Color := clWindow;

  {output the text}
  StringGrid1.Canvas.TextRect (Rect, Rect.Left, Rect.Top,
    StringGrid1.Cells [Col, Row]);

  {draw the focus}
  if gdFocused in State then
    StringGrid1.Canvas.DrawFocusRect (Rect);

end;

end.
```

10

The width of each column is computed by evaluating the space occupied by the custom string of text *AaBbYyZz*, using the font of the column (written in the first row) and the biggest size used by the program (32). To compute the space required by the text, you can apply the TextWidth and TextHeight methods to a canvas having the proper font selected:

```
StringGrid1.Canvas.Font.Name :=
  StringGrid1.Cells [I, 0];
StringGrid1.Canvas.Font.Size := 32;
StringGrid1.ColWidths [I] :=
  StringGrid1.Canvas.TextWidth ('AaBbYyZz');
```

The rows, instead, are always 26 and have an increasing height, computed with the approximate formula 15 + I*2. In fact, computing the highest text means checking the height of the text in each column, certainly too complex an operation. The approximate formula works well enough, as you can see in Figures 10.22 and 10.23 and by running the program. In the first cell of each row, the program writes the size of the font.

The last operation is to store the test string "AaBbYyZz" in each non-fixed cell of the grid. To accomplish this, the program uses a nested `for` loop. Expect to use nested `for` loops often when working with grids.

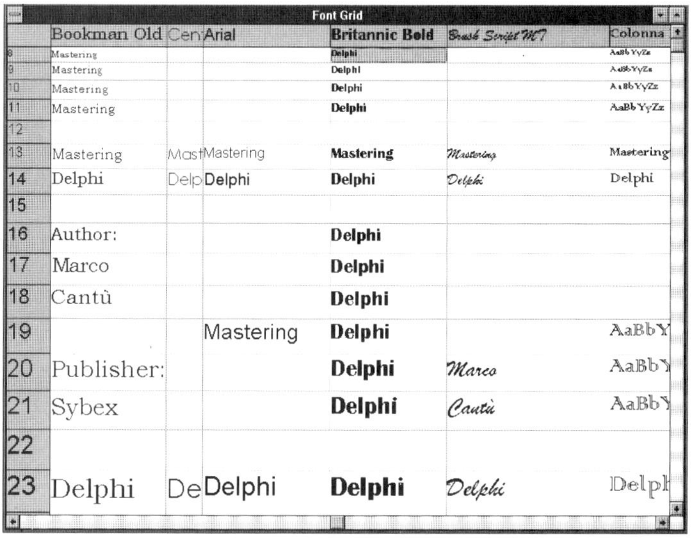

FIGURE 10.23:

A second example of the output of the FONTGRID program. Notice that a user can move columns, resize them, and enter new text for each of the non-fixed cells.

Now we can study the second method, StringGrid1DrawCell, which corresponds to the grid's OnDrawCell event. This method has a number of parameters:

```
procedure TForm1.StringGrid1DrawCell(Sender: TObject;
  Col, Row: Longint; Rect: TRect; State: TGridDrawState);
```

- *Sender* is the Sender object, as usual.

- *Col* and *Row* refer to the cell we are currently painting.

- *Rect* is the area of the cell we are going to paint. We can access its top-left corner using the corresponding fields of the TRect structure.

- *State* is the state of the cell, a set of three flags, which can be active at the same time: gdSelected (the cell is selected), gdFocused (the cell has the input focus), and gdFixed (the cell is in the fixed area, which usually has a different background color). Knowing the state of the cell is important because this usually affects its output.

The DrawCell method paints the text of the corresponding element of the grid, with the font used by the column and the size used for the row. The font's name is retrieved by the first row of the same column:

```
StringGrid1.Canvas.Font.Name :=
  StringGrid1.Cells [Col, 0];
```

The size is calculated with this line:

```
StringGrid1.Canvas.Font.Size := Row + 7;
```

The fixed columns (indicated by the number 0) use some default values. Having set the font and its size, the program selects a color for the background for the possible states of the cell: selected, fixed, or normal (that is, no special style). The value of the style's gdFocused flag is used a few lines later to draw the typical focus rectangle—a rectangle with a thin dotted line. The two calls that perform some real output are this one and the call to draw the text of the string corresponding to the grid's cell:

```
StringGrid1.Canvas.TextRect (Rect, Rect.Left, Rect.Top,
    StringGrid1.Cells [Col, Row]);
if gdFocused in State then
    StringGrid1.Canvas.DrawFocusRect (Rect);
```

10

TIP
To draw the text in the grid's cell, I've used the TextRect method of the canvas instead of the more common TextOut method. The reason is that TextRect clips the output to the given rectangle, preventing drawing outside this area. This is particularly important in the case of grids because the output of a cell should not cross its borders. Since we are painting on the canvas of the whole grid, when we are drawing a cell, we can end up corrupting the contents of neighboring cells, too.

As a final observation, notice that when you decide to draw the contents of a grid's cell (or that of an item of an owner-drawn list, by the way), you should not only draw the default image, you should provide a different output for the selected item, properly draw the focus, and so on.

Mines in a Grid

The grid of strings uses the Cells array to store the values of the elements and also has an Objects property to store custom data for each cell. The DrawGrid component, instead, doesn't have a predefined storage. For this reason, in the next example, I'm going to define a two-dimensional array to store the value of the grid's cells, or better, of the playing field.

As I mentioned before, the MINES example is a clone of the Minesweeper application in Windows 3.1. If you have never played this game, I suggest you try it and read its rules in the Help file since I'll give only a concise description. When the program starts, it displays an empty field, where there are some hidden mines (see Figure 10.24). By clicking the left mouse button, you test whether or not there is a mine in that position of the grid. If you find a mine, it explodes, and the game is over: you have lost.

If there is no mine, the program indicates in the cell the number of mines in the eight other cells surrounding it. Knowing the number of mines near the cell, you have a good hint for the following turn. To help you further on, when a cell has zero mines in the surrounding area, the number of mines for these cells is automatically displayed, and if one of them has zero surrounding mines, the process is repeated. So if you are lucky, with a single click you might uncover a good number of mines (see Figure 10.25).

The MINES program at startup: the field is empty.

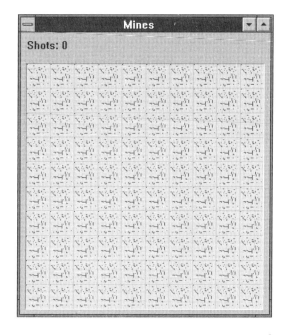

FIGURE 10.25:
The MINES program after a single lucky click: a group of cells with no mines is displayed at once.

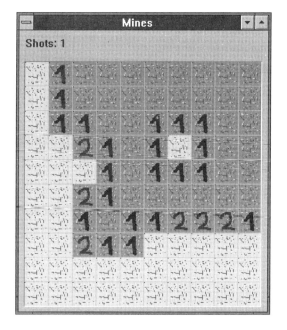

10

When you think you have found a mine, simply click on the cell with the right mouse button, positioning a flag. The program ignores whether or not the flag is in the proper position; it is only a hint for your future attempts. If you later change your mind, you can again click the right mouse button on the cell, to remove the flag. When you have placed a flag on each of the mines, you have won, and the game terminates.

Those are the rules of the game. Now we have to implement it, using a DrawGrid as a starting point. You can see the properties of the grid, along with those of the form, in Listing 10.16. There is nothing special to say, aside from the fact that the grid is fixed and cannot be resized or modified in any way at run-time. In fact, it has square cells of 30 x 30 pixels, which will be used to display bitmaps of the same size.

LISTING 10.16: The textual description of the simple form of the MINES example

```
object Form1: TForm1
  Width = 334
  Height = 383
  Caption = 'Mines'
  OnCreate = FormCreate
  OnDestroy = FormDestroy
  object Label1: TLabel
    Caption = 'Shots: 0'
  end
  object DrawGrid1: TDrawGrid
    Width = 309
    Height = 309
    BorderStyle = bsNone
    ColCount = 10
    DefaultColWidth = 30
    DefaultRowHeight = 30
    DefaultDrawing = False
    FixedCols = 0
    FixedRows = 0
    Options = [goFixedVertLine, goFixedHorzLine,
      goVertLine, goHorzLine]
    RowCount = 10
    ScrollBars = ssNone
    OnDrawCell = DrawGrid1DrawCell
    OnMouseUp = DrawGrid1MouseUp
  end
end
```

The code of this program is complex, and it is not easy to find a starting point to describe it. For this reason, I've added more comments than usual to the code so you can browse through it to understand what it does. Nonetheless, I'll describe its most important element, highlighting the key methods and algorithms used and trying to follow its logical flow.

First of all, the program's data is stored in two arrays (declared as private fields of the form):

```
Display: array [0 .. NItems - 1, 0 .. NItems -1] of Boolean;
Map: array [0 .. NItems - 1, 0 .. NItems -1] of Char;
```

The first is an array of Boolean values that indicates whether the items should be displayed or remain hidden. Notice that the number of rows and columns of this array is NItems. You can freely change this constant but should resize the grid accordingly.

The second array, Map, holds the positions of the mines and flags and the numbers of the surrounding mines. It uses character codes instead of a proper enumeration data type, for the advantage of using the digits 0–8 to indicate the number of mines around the cell. Here is a list of the codes:

- *'M': Mine* indicates the position of a mine that the user still has not found.

- *'K': Known mine* indicates the position of a mine already found by the user and having a flag.

- *'W': Wrong mine* indicates a position where the user has set a flag but where there is no mine.

- *From '0' to '8': Number of mines* indicates the number of mines in the surrounding cells.

The first method I'll explore is FormCreate, executed at startup (see Listing 10.17 for the complete source code). This method initializes a number of fields of the form class, fills the two arrays with default values (using two nested for loops) and then sets the mines in the grid. For the number of times defined in a constant (that is, the number of mines), the program adds a new mine in a random position. However, if there was already a mine, the loop should be executed once more since the final number of mines in the Map array should equal the requested one. If not, the program will never terminate since it tests when the number of mines found equals the number of mines added to the grid. This is the code of the loop, which can be executed more than NMines times, thanks to the statement that decrements the loop counter:

```
Randomize;
for I := 1 to NMines do
begin
  X := Random (NItems);
  Y := Random (NItems);
  {if there isn't a mine}
  if not (Map [X, Y] = 'M') then
    {add a mine}
    Map [X, Y] := 'M'
  else
    {else, repeat the loop}
    Dec (I);
end;
```

LISTING 10.17: The complete source code of the MINES example, probably one of the most complex Pascal listings of the book up to this point

```
unit Mines_f;

interface

uses
  SysUtils, WinTypes, WinProcs, Messages, Classes, Graphics,
  Controls, Forms, Dialogs, Grids, StdCtrls;

{constant values used by the program; if you change the
number of items, you should resize the grid accordingly}
const NItems = 10;  {items on each side of the 'square' grid}
const NMines = 12;  {number of mines in the grid}

{character codes use to describe the contents
of the cells of the grid:
  'M': Mine
  'K': Known mine
  'W': Wrong mine
  '0'..'8': Number of mines}

type
  TForm1 = class(TForm)
    DrawGrid1: TDrawGrid;
    Label1: TLabel;
    procedure FormCreate(Sender: TObject);
    procedure DrawGrid1MouseUp(Sender: TObject;
      Button: TMouseButton;
      Shift: TShiftState; X, Y: Integer);
```

LISTING 10.17: The complete source code of the MINES example (continued)

```
    procedure DrawGrid1DrawCell(Sender: TObject;
      Col, Row: Longint;
      Rect: TRect; State: TGridDrawState);
    procedure FormDestroy(Sender: TObject);
  private
    Playing: Boolean;      {still playing or terminated}
    Bmp: TBitmap;          {temporary bitmap}
    LastBmp: Char;         {code of the temporary bitmap}
    Shots,                 {number of shots}
    MinesFound: Integer;   {mines really found}

    {Boolean array indicating visible elements}
    Display: array [0 .. NItems - 1, 0 .. NItems -1] of Boolean;

    {map with the codes for the cells (see above for the codes)}
    Map: array [0 .. NItems - 1, 0 .. NItems -1] of Char;

    {compute the number of mines surrounding the given cell}
    procedure ComputeMines (X, Y: Integer);

    {display items near a visible zero-cell,
    using a recursive call}
    procedure FloodZeros (X, Y: Integer);

  public
    { Public declarations }
  end;

var
  Form1: TForm1;

implementation

{$R *.DFM}
{$R BITMAPS.RES}

procedure TForm1.FormCreate(Sender: TObject);
var
  I, J, X, Y: Integer;
begin
  {initializations}
  Randomize;
  Playing := True;
  Shots := 0;
  MinesFound := 0;
  Bmp := TBitmap.Create;
  LastBmp := ' ';

  {empty the two arrays}
  for I := 0 to NItems - 1 do
```

LISTING 10.17: The complete source code of the MINES example (continued)

```
      for J := 0 to NItems - 1 do
      begin
        Map [I, J] := ' ';
        Display [I, J] := False;
      end;

  {place 'NMines' non-overlapping mines}
  for I := 1 to NMines do
  begin
    X := Random (NItems);
    Y := Random (NItems);
    {if there isn't a mine}
    if not (Map [X, Y] = 'M') then
      {add a mine}
      Map [X, Y] := 'M'
    else
      {else, repeat the loop}
      Dec (I);
  end;

  {compute the number of surrounding mines in
  every location not having a mine}
  for I := 0 to NItems - 1 do
    for J := 0 to NItems - 1 do
      if not (Map [I, J] = 'M') then
        ComputeMines (I, J);
end;

{compute the number of mines surrounding the given cell}
procedure TForm1.ComputeMines (X, Y: Integer);
var
  Col, Row: Integer;
  Total : Char;
begin
  Total := '0';
  {for every contiguous cell...}
  for Col := X - 1 to X + 1 do
    for Row := Y -1 to Y + 1 do
      {excluding those out of the borders...}
      if (Col >= 0) and (Col < NItems) and
          (Row >= 0) and (Row < NItems) then
        {if there is a mine, hidden or known,
        increase the total surrounding mines}
        if (Map [Col, Row] = 'M') or
            (Map [Col, Row] = 'K') then
          Inc (Total);
  {store the total number of
  surrounding mines in the map}
  Map [X, Y] := Total;
end;
```

LISTING 10.17: The complete source code of the MINES example (continued)

```
{display items near a visible zero-cell,
using a recursive call}
procedure TForm1.FloodZeros (X, Y: Integer);
var
  Col, Row: Integer;
  MyRect: TRect;
begin
  {double-check that we are on a zero}
  if Map [X, Y] = '0' then
    {for every contiguous cell...}
    for Col := X - 1 to X + 1 do
      for Row := Y -1 to Y + 1 do
        {excluding out of borders and the item itself...}
        if (Col >= 0) and (Col < NItems) and
          (Row >= 0) and (Row < NItems) and
          not ( (Col = X) and (Row = Y) )then
        begin
          {display the element, and if it is a zero,
          repeat the operation; the code seems redundant
          but the program needs to avoid infinite
          recursion with great care}
          if (Map [Col, Row] = '0') and
              (Display [Col, Row] = False) then
          begin
            {if the cell is still hidden and there is a zero
            display it, then make the flood the zeros
            near the cell}
            Display [Col, Row] := True;
            FloodZeros (Col, Row);
          end
          else
            {if it is not a zero, display it}
            Display [Col, Row] := True;
          {compute the area of the cell, and invalidate it}
          MyRect := DrawGrid1.CellRect (Col, Row);
          InvalidateRect (DrawGrid1.Handle, @MyRect, False);
        end
end;

procedure TForm1.DrawGrid1MouseUp(Sender: TObject; Button: TMouseButton;
  Shift: TShiftState; X, Y: Integer);
var
  Col, Row: LongInt;
  MyRect: TRect;
begin
  {get the current column and grid}
  DrawGrid1.MouseToCell (X, Y, Col, Row);
  {if game has ended, beep and ignore the action}
  if not Playing then
    MessageBeep ($FFFF)
```

10

LISTING 10.17: The complete source code of the MINES example (continued)

```
else if Button = mbLeft then
begin
  {left mouse button click: shot}
  Inc (Shots);
  Label1.Caption := 'Shots: ' + IntToStr (Shots);

  {if there is a mine, end the game, else display the cell}
  if (Map [Col, Row] = 'M') or (Map [Col, Row] = 'K') then
  {mine found...}
  begin
    MessageDlg ('B O O M !' + Chr(13) +
      'You have found a mine', mtError, [mbOK], 0);
    {end the game and redisplay the grid}
    Playing := False;
    DrawGrid1.Repaint;
  end
  else
  {not a mine...}
  begin
    {show location}
    Display [Col, Row] := True;
    {if the click was on a 0, then show near elements}
    if Map [Col, Row] = '0' then
      FloodZeros (Col, Row);
  end;
end
else
begin
  {right mouse button click: mine?}
  case Map [Col, Row] of
    {if there is a mine, turn code to K, known mine,
    display the cell, increment points}
    'M': begin
      Map [Col, Row] := 'K';
      Display [Col, Row] := True;
      Inc (MinesFound);
      {if all mines have been found, the game ends}
      if MinesFound = NMines then
      begin
        MessageDlg ('You have won. Congratulations!',
          mtInformation, [mbOK], 0);
        Playing := False;
        DrawGrid1.Repaint;
      end
    end;
    {if there was a known mine, the 'hidden' mine
    is restored and the points decremented}
    'K': begin
      Map [Col, Row] := 'M';
      Display [Col, Row] := False;
```

LISTING 10.17: The complete source code of the MINES example (continued)

```
        Dec (MinesFound);
      end;
      {if there was a number, set W, wrong mine}
      '0'..'8': begin
        Map [Col, Row] := 'W';
        Display [Col, Row] := True;
      end;
      {if there was a wrong mine, restore the
      number computing it again}
      'W': begin
        ComputeMines (Col, Row);
        Display [Col, Row] := False;
      end;
    end;
  end;
  {redraw the cell of the grid}
  MyRect := DrawGrid1.CellRect (Col, Row);
  InvalidateRect (DrawGrid1.Handle, @MyRect, False);
end;

procedure TForm1.DrawGrid1DrawCell(Sender: TObject;
  Col, Row: Longint;
  Rect: TRect; State: TGridDrawState);
var
  Code: Char;
  Name: Array [0..10] of Char;
begin
  {extract the code and check its value}
  Code := Map [Col, Row];

  {if the cell is visible}
  if Display [Col, Row] then
  begin
    {if the code corresponds to that of the 'cached' bitmap,
    use it, else load the new bitmap}
    if not (Code = LastBmp) then
    begin
      StrPCopy (Name, 'M' + Code);
      Bmp.Handle := LoadBitmap (HInstance, Name);
      LastBmp := Code;
    end;
    DrawGrid1.Canvas.Draw (Rect.Left, Rect.Top, Bmp);
  end
  else
  {the cell is not visible: show the default bitmap,
  using the cache mechanism again}
  begin
    if not (LastBmp = 'U') then      {'U': unfefined}
    begin
      Bmp.Handle := LoadBitmap (HInstance, 'UNDEF');
```

10

LISTING 10.17: The complete source code of the MINES example (continued)

```
      LastBmp := 'U';
    end;
    DrawGrid1.Canvas.Draw (Rect.Left, Rect.Top, Bmp);
  end;

  {if the game is done, show the mines that were not found
  using the cache again}
  if (not Playing) and (Code = 'M') then
  begin
    if not (Code = LastBmp) then
    begin
      StrPCopy (Name, 'M' + Code);
      Bmp.Handle := LoadBitmap (HInstance, Name);
      LastBmp := Code;
    end;
    DrawGrid1.Canvas.Draw (Rect.Left, Rect.Top, Bmp);
  end;
end;

procedure TForm1.FormDestroy(Sender: TObject);
begin
  Bmp.Free;
end;

end.
```

The last portion of the initialization code is the computation of the number of sur-rounding mines for each cell not having a mine in itself. This is accomplished by calling the ComputeMines procedure for each cell. The code of this function is fairly complex since it has to consider the special cases of the mines near a border of the grid. At the end of the code (which you can study in the listing or simply ignore if you like), the digit with the number of mines is stored in the Map array.

The next logical procedure is DrawGrid1MouseUp, called when the mouse button is released over a cell (using the mouse-down event, there were some problems with the focus, so I decided on the mouse-up event). This method first computes the cell on which the mouse has been clicked, with a call to the grid's MouseToCell method. Then there are three alternative portions of code: a small one when the game has ended, and the other two for the two mouse buttons.

When the left mouse button is pressed, the program checks whether there is a mine (hidden or not), and in this case it displays a message and terminates the program (see Figure 10.26):

```
if (Map [Col, Row] = 'M') or (Map [Col, Row] = 'K') then
begin
  MessageDlg ('B O O M !' + Chr(13) +
    'You have found a mine', mtError, [mbOK], 0);
  Playing := False;
  DrawGrid1.Repaint;
end
```

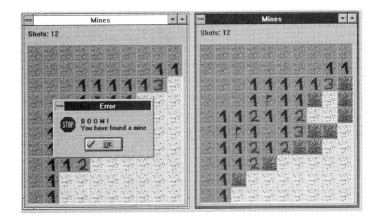

FIGURE 10.26:

Ouch! You have stepped on a mine (on the left is the error message, and on the right the blown-up mines displayed as soon as you close the message box).

Notice the last call, which is used to repaint the whole grid. When the game is done, in fact, the mines still hidden are displayed to the user. If there is no mine, the program sets the Display value for the cell to True, and if there is a 0, it starts the FloodZeros procedure. This method displays the eight items near a visible cell having a value of 0, repeating the operation over and over if one of the surrounding cells also has a value of 0. This recursive call is complex because you have to provide a way to terminate it. If there are two cells, one near the other, having a value of 0, each one is in the surrounding area of the other one, so they might continue forever to ask the other cell to display itself and its surrounding cells. Again, the code is complex; you can either study it or skip it altogether since the focus of this book is on Delphi programming, not on writing complex algorithms in Object Pascal.

If the right mouse button was pressed, the program changes the status of a cell from 'M' (Hidden mine) to 'K' (Known mine) and vice versa, or from a number to 'W' (Wrong mine) and the opposite. If all the mines have been found, the program terminates with a congratulation message (see Figure 10.27).

FIGURE 10.27:

The program terminates when all the flags have been set, although there might still be some cells covered.

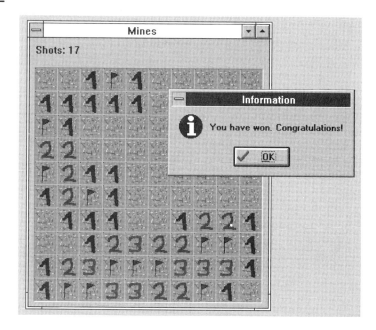

A very important piece of code is at the end of the OnMouseUp event response method. Each time the user clicks on a cell and its contents change, that cell should be repainted. If you ask to repaint the whole grid, the program will be slower. For this reason, I've used the Windows API function InvalidateRect, as I already did once before (in Chapter 9):

```
MyRect := DrawGrid1.CellRect (Col, Row);
InvalidateRect (DrawGrid1.Handle, @MyRect, False);
```

The last important method is DrawGrid1DrawCell. We already used this painting procedure in the last example, so you should remember that it is called for each cell that needs repainting. Fundamentally, this method extracts the code corresponding to the cell, which shows a corresponding bitmap, loaded from a file.

I've prepared a bitmap for each of the images in a new resource file, included in the form's code with the directive:

```
{$R BITMAPS.RES}
```

The reason is that when using resources, the code tends to be faster than when using separate files, and again, we end up with a single executable file to distribute. The bitmaps have names corresponding to the code in the grid, with a character ('M') in front since the '0' name would have been invalid. The bitmaps can be loaded and drawn in the cell with this code:

```
StrPCopy (Name, 'M' + Code);
Bmp.Handle := LoadBitmap (HInstance, Name);
DrawGrid1.Canvas.Draw (Rect.Left, Rect.Top, Bmp);
```

Of course, this takes place only if the cell is visible, if Display is True. Otherwise, a default undefined bitmap is displayed (the bitmap name is UNDEF). Loading the bitmaps from the resources each time seems slow, so the program could have stored all the bitmaps in a list in memory, as I did in the WORLD2 example earlier in this chapter. However, this time, I've decided to use a different, although slightly less efficient, approach: a cache. This makes sense because we already use resources instead of files to speed up things.

The bitmap cache of MINES is small since it has just one element, but its presence speeds up the program considerably. The program stores the last bitmap it has used, and its code; then, each time it has to draw a new item, if the code is the same, it uses the cached bitmap. Here is the new version of the code above:

```
if not (Code = LastBmp) then
begin
  StrPCopy (Name, 'M' + Code);
  Bmp.Handle := LoadBitmap (HInstance, Name);
  LastBmp := Code;
end;
DrawGrid1.Canvas.Draw (Rect.Left, Rect.Top, Bmp);
```

Increasing the size of this cache will certainly improve its speed. You can consider a list of bitmaps as a big cache, but this is probably useless since some bitmaps (those with high numbers) are seldom used.

As you can see, some improvements can be made to speed up the program. At the same time, much can be done to improve its user interface. You could add a menu, allowing a user to start a new match (currently you have to restart the program) and

10

change the number of mines and the size of the grid. If you have understood this version of the program, I think you'll be able to improve it considerably.

Choosing Colors

The last example on grids is much simpler than the previous ones. It uses the Color-Grid, a component of the Samples page of the Components palette. This component hasn't much in common with the other grids, and its use is straightforward.

A ColorGrid has a number of cells, each with a color, and uses the left and right mouse clicks to select two colors, namely a foreground color with the left mouse button and a background color with the right mouse button. Two properties, Fore-groundIndex and BackgroundIndex, hold the values of the current colors, which the user automatically changes by clicking, but only if they are active.

The only other peculiar property is the GridOrdering, which indicates the structure of the grid—the number of lines and rows. Since the color grid always has 16 colors, you can choose a vertical or horizontal line, two lines of 8 colors, or a 4×4 square grid.

I've built a simple example, COL_GRID, which has a grid and a text label, using the colors indicated in the grid (see Figure 10.28). The form of the example is described in Listing 10.18. Its source code is just two lines. Each time a user clicks on the grid, the two colors are copied to the label:

```
procedure TForm1.ColorGrid1Change(Sender: TObject);
begin
  Label1.Color := ColorGrid1.BackgroundColor;
  Label1.Font.Color := ColorGrid1.ForegroundColor;
end;
```

Towards Sophisticated Input Schemes

In this final section, the focus is on a peculiar component, although it is somewhat unrelated to the other topics of the chapter, which has focused on graphical components. I simply felt the MaskEdit component was too important not to show an example of its use.

FIGURE 10.28:

The COL_GRID example at run-time

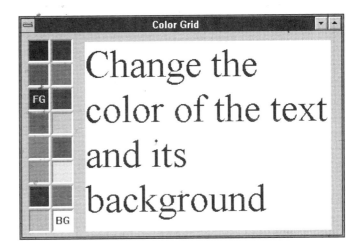

LISTING 10.18: The textual description of the form of the COL_GRID example

```
object Form1: TForm1
  ActiveControl = ColorGrid1
  Caption = 'Color Grid'
  object Label1: TLabel
    AutoSize = False
    Caption = 'Change the color of the text and its background'
    Font.Color = clWindowText
    Font.Height = -53
    Font.Name = 'Times New Roman'
  end
  object ColorGrid1: TColorGrid
    Ctl3D = True
    GridOrdering = go2x8
    BackgroundIndex = 7
    OnChange = ColorGrid1Change
  end
end
```

10

At the same time, this component is easy to use and well documented, so I won't give you too much detail. First of all, a mask edit is an edit control, with all the corresponding properties and methods. In addition, the MaskEdit component has a special EditMask property, holding a string. If you open the corresponding property editor (by pressing the small button in the Object Inspector), you can easily define a string making up the mask or copy one of the predefined codes (see Figure 10.29).

FIGURE 10.29:

The editor of the EditMask property
of the MaskEdit component

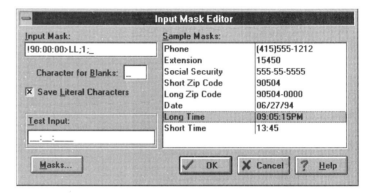

Notice that the Input Mask editor allows you to enter a mask but also asks you to indicate a character to be used as a placeholder for the input and to decide whether to save the literals present in the mask, together with the final string. For example, you can choose to have the parentheses around the area code of a phone number only as an input hint or to save them with the string holding the resulting number. These two entries in the Input Mask editor correspond to the last portion of the mask, made of two more fields (separated, by default, with semicolons).

For more default input masks, you can press the Masks button, which allows you to open a mask file (see Figure 10.30). The predefined files hold standard codes grouped by country. For example, if you open the Italian group, you can find the taxpayer number (or *fiscal code*, which is used for everything, like the social security number in the U.S.). This code is a complex mix of letters and numbers (including the consonants of the name, the birth date, an area code, and more), as its mask demonstrates:

    LLLLLL00L00L000L

FIGURE 10.30:

Delphi's predefined groups of masks are divided by country.

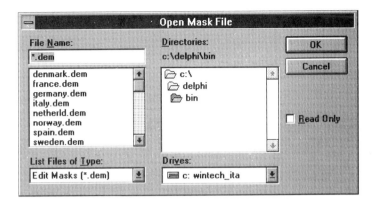

In this kind of code, *L* stands for a letter and *0* for a number. These are required codes, but other characters can be present or not. I suggest that you study the description of the EditMask property, which shows in detail how to build a mask. A summary of these codes is present in the following MASK1 example (you can see them in Listing 10.19).

LISTING 10.19: The textual description of the form of the MASK1 example

```
object Form1: TForm1
  Caption = 'Mask1'
  OnCreate = FormCreate
  object Label1: TLabel
    Caption = 'Edit with a mask:'
  end
  object Label2: TLabel
    Caption = 'Mask of the edit:'
  end
  object Label3: TLabel
    Caption = 'Instructions:'
  end
  object MaskEdit1: TMaskEdit
    EditMask - '!90:00:00>||;1;_'
    MaxLength = 10
    Text = '  :  :   '
  end
  object Edit1: TEdit
    OnChange = Edit1Change
  end
  object ListBox1: TListBox
    Items.Strings = (
```

LISTING 10.19: The textual description of the form of the MASK1 example (continued)

```
            'Alphabetic character possible (l)'
            'Alphabetic character required (L)'
            'Alphanumeric character posible (a)'
            'Alphanumeric character required (A)'
            'Blank (you can set this value) (_)'
            'Character possible (c)'
            'Character required (C)'
            'Lowercase on (>)'
            'Mask fields separator (;)'
            'Next char is interpreted as literal (\)'
            'No case checking (<>)'
            'Numeric character or sign possible (#)'
            'Numeric character possible (9)'
            'Numeric character required (0)'
            'Skip leading blanks (!)'
            'Standard system separator (/)'
            'Standard system separator (:)'
            'Uppercase on (<)')
        Sorted = True
    end
end
```

After you have reviewed the description, you can play with the MASK1 sample program, where you can both input a mask and enter text in the associated Mask-Edit component (see Figure 10.31 for an example of the output of this program). The form of MASK1 simply includes a MaskEdit and an Edit component (see Listing 10.19 for the textual description). The second is used to edit the EditMask property of the first one. To accomplish this, I've just written a couple of lines of code, to copy the text of the property into the edit box at the beginning (OnCreate event) and make the reverse action each time the plain edit box changes (Edit1Change):

```
procedure TForm1.FormCreate(Sender: TObject);
begin
  Edit1.Text := MaskEdit1.EditMask;
end;

procedure TForm1.Edit1Change(Sender: TObject);
begin
  MaskEdit1.EditMask := Edit1.Text;
end;
```

An example of the output of the
MASK1 program

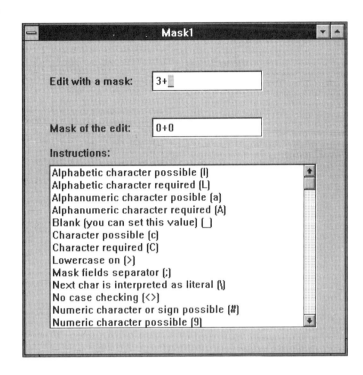

As you can see in Figure 10.31, the form also has a list box with the description of the most important codes used to build the mask. You can see these codes in Listing 10.19.

Summary

In this chapter, we have explored a number of different Delphi components, including outlines, grids, and bitmap buttons. Of course, there are other components of this kind, including those of the Sample pages of the Components palette. You can also create or buy new components and add them to Delphi. We will explore this topic briefly at the end of the book.

What is important is that when components are well documented, using them is usually fairly simple. There is nothing to understand, aside from the meanings of the properties and methods. What is required of a great Delphi programmer is a good knowledge of the basics and some imagination in mixing different components on a form to build an application.

It is just with such imagination that Delphi programmers can easily build toolbars and status bars out of the existing components, as we will do in the next chapter. And it is with our imagination that we will be able to build splitters (in Chapter 14) or figure out strange uses for the Notebook component (in Chapter 13). These are some of the topics of the next chapters, together with some foundation for applications with multiple forms and dialog boxes (in Chapter 12).

CHAPTER

ELEVEN

A Toolbar and a Status Bar

- How to use a TPanel to build a toolbar

- Toolbar buttons

- A combo box in a toolbar

- How to drag a toolbar around the form

- Hints and the status bar

- The bars of the Delphi SDI template

One of the distinctive features of many Windows applications is the presence of a toolbar at the top of the window and a status bar at its bottom. The toolbar might have a variety of names, such as SpeedBar or control bar, depending on the application's producer. Some of these names are also trademarks, although I find this really strange.

Whatever name you give it, a toolbar usually hosts a number of small buttons you can press with a mouse click to give commands or to toggle options on and off. At times, a toolbar can also host a combo box, an edit box, or some other control. The toolbars of the last generation of big applications usually can be moved to the left or right of the window, or even taken away and used as a *toolbox*, a small floating window with an array of buttons.

A status bar, instead, usually has one or more areas with a textual description of the current status of the program. You might have an area for coordinates; to show the selected font; or to display hints on what to do next, error messages, and so on. What should go in a status bar really depends on the application.

After we have seen the key ideas behind toolbars and status bars, we will use Delphi's default SDI application template to build an application automatically with these elements.

Grouping Controls with Panels

To create a toolbar or status bar in Delphi, you can use the Panel component, adding a number of buttons or other panels inside it. A panel can be considered a tool to divide the client area of a frame into different portions and to group other components.

Although a panel can have its own text, it rarely does. Instead, panels can make good use of their three-dimensional aspect to improve the look of the application. In this respect, a panel is similar to a bevel, although this last component has a less important role and much less functionality. From a graphical point of view, a panel can be described as a *double-bevel* since it has two elements of this kind you can play with (see the properties BevelInner and BevelOuter). Combined with the different values for the BevelWidth, this allows for a variety of effects, as shown in Figure 11.1.

FIGURE 11.1:

Some of the graphical effects of a panel (with the corresponding values for the Bevel and Width properties)

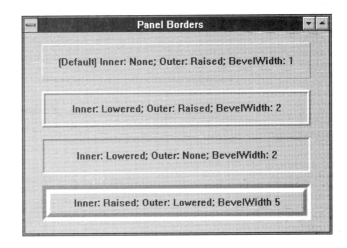

(This figure is the output of the PAN_BORD example, which is available on the companion disk as a test but is not discussed in the text.)

Usually, when you create a panel, you place it in a particular area of the form, changing the value of the Align property. For a typical toolbar, use the value alTop, and for a status bar, use alBottom. You might also choose vertical panels, although they are less common. Besides other common properties, the Panel component can handle hints; Hint and ShowHints are the two most relevant properties. *Hints* are short messages displayed near the cursor when the user moves the mouse over a toolbar button; they will be discussed later in this chapter.

NOTE Hints are not available only in panels. Every form can have hints for some or all of the components it hosts. We will see an example of a plain form with a hint later in this chapter.

Of course, a form can have several toolbars and change the active one easily. In this case, a good suggestion is to define a variable in the form referring to the current toolbar so you can easily access its properties.

Building a Toolbar

To build a typical toolbar, you simply need to place a panel at the top of the frame and place a number of SpeedButton components in it (see Figure 11.2). A *speed button* is similar to a bitmap button, a component described in the last chapter. Like bitmap buttons, speed buttons can have a caption and a glyph, although usually they have only the graphical element.

FIGURE 11.2:

To build a toolbar, you simply place a graphical button on a panel.

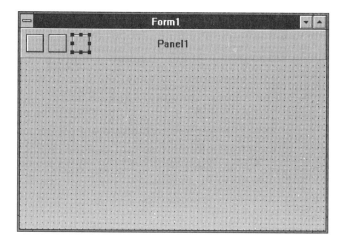

The main difference is in the behavior. Bitmap buttons are like push buttons (that is, the Button component) and are mainly used inside dialog boxes. Speed buttons can behave like push buttons, check boxes, or radio buttons, and they can have different bitmaps for various situations.

If you simply select the SpeedButton component and place an instance in the panel—the toolbar—you end up with a graphical push button. You can select a bitmap for it or type in a caption, although the first solution is more common. A toolbar's push buttons tend to be quite small, around 20 x 20 pixels: you cannot usually write much text in such a limited space. A glyph, on the other hand, can be meaningful even if it is small. Consider, in any case, that 20 x 20-pixel glyphs on a high-resolution screen can be quite small.

A Simple Toolbar

Once you have added a speed button, you might simply write some code for its On-Click event. This is the default operation you obtain by double-clicking on it in the form. In the TOOLBAR example, I've prepared a musical note glyph and added the following code to the button:

```
procedure TToolbarForm.SpeedButtonNoteClick(Sender: TObject);
begin
  MessageBeep($FFFF);
end;
```

Now we can add a group of speed buttons that will work like radio buttons. Just place some more speed buttons on the panel, select all of them, and give their GroupIndex properties the same value. All the buttons having the same GroupIndex become mutually exclusive selections, similar to radio buttons. One of these buttons should always be selected, so remember to set the Down property to True for one of them at design-time or as soon as the program starts.

As an alternative, you can have mutually exclusive buttons that can all be *up*. This means you can click on the selected button and deselect it. You can choose this behavior by setting the AllowAllUp property for all the buttons of the group to True (the default is False). In this case, of course, at startup the buttons can all be in the up position.

As an example of the two approaches, you can add two different groups of speed buttons to the panel (or toolbar). In the TOOLBAR example (see the form in Figure 11.3 and its textual description in Listing 11.1), I've added three exclusive buttons to determine the alignment of a label's text and three more buttons to determine its style. The idea is that one of the alignment buttons should always be selected since the text must always have an alignment. The methods corresponding to the three OnClick events of these buttons have the following structure:

```
procedure TToolbarForm.SpeedButtonLeftClick(Sender: TObject);
begin
  Label1.Alignment := taLeftJustify;
end;
```

FIGURE 11.3:

The form of the TOOLBAR example

LISTING 11.1: The textual description of the form of the TOOLBAR example

```
object ToolbarForm: TToolbarForm
  ActiveControl = Panel1
  Caption = 'Toolbar'
  object Label1: TLabel
    Align = alClient
    AutoSize = False
    Caption = 'A caption with some sample text ...'
    Font.Color = clBlack
    Font.Height = -16
    Font.Name = 'Arial'
    Font.Style = []
    ParentFont = False
    WordWrap = True
  end
  object Panel1: TPanel
    Height = 30
    Align = alTop
    object SpeedButtonNote: TSpeedButton
      Left = 8
      Top = 2
      Width = 25
      Height = 25
      Glyph.Data = {omitted}
      OnClick = SpeedButtonNoteClick
    end
    object SpeedButtonLeft: TSpeedButton
      Left = 40
      {Top, Width, and Height as above,
      for each button of the toolbar}
```

LISTING 11.1:   The textual description of the form of the TOOLBAR example (continued)

```
        GroupIndex = 1
        Down = True
        OnClick = SpeedButtonLeftClick
      end
      object SpeedButtonCenter: TSpeedButton
        Left = 64
        GroupIndex = 1
        OnClick = SpeedButtonCenterClick
      end
      object SpeedButtonRight: TSpeedButton
        Left = 88
        GroupIndex = 1
        OnClick = SpeedButtonRightClick
      end
      object SpeedButtonBold: TSpeedButton
        Left = 120
        AllowAllUp = True
        GroupIndex = 2
        OnClick = SpeedButtonBoldClick
      end
      object SpeedButtonItalic: TSpeedButton
        Left = 144
        AllowAllUp = True
        GroupIndex = 2
        OnClick = SpeedButtonItalicClick
      end
      object SpeedButtonUnderline: TSpeedButton
        Left = 168
        AllowAllUp = True
        GroupIndex = 2
        OnClick = SpeedButtonUnderlineClick
      end
      object SpeedButtonBig: TSpeedButton
        Left = 200
        AllowAllUp = True
        GroupIndex = 3
        OnClick = SpeedButtonBigClick
      end
    end
end
```

On the other hand, the three style speed buttons (those of the second group) can all be off since the text can be *normal,* as shown in Figure 11.4. This use of the styles is far from perfect since they are not usually considered exclusive selections—you can have **bold *italic*** text, but I've decided to part from the common behavior for this example.

FIGURE 11.4:

An example of the output of the
TOOLBAR example

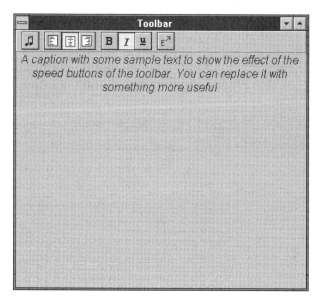

The problem in this portion of the code is that you cannot simply select the style
when the button is pressed. You also have to deselect it, resetting the normal
style, when the button is released. In the methods responding to the click events
of these speed buttons, we have to write something similar to:

```
procedure TToolbarForm.SpeedButtonBoldClick(Sender: TObject);
begin
  if SpeedButtonBold.Down then
    Label1.Font.Style := [fsBold]
  else
    Label1.Font.Style := [];
end;
```

I could have used three different speed buttons behaving as check boxes instead of
this second group of buttons since the three attributes are not really exclusive. But
how do you add a speed button that works as a check box to the toolbar? Is there a
special property? If you look at the properties of the SpeedButton component,
you'll find nothing. In fact, the solution is already at hand: a check box is a group
with only one item that allows all the buttons to be deselected.

In practice, add a new speed button, give it a specific value for the GroupIndex property (different from the indexes of the other groups), and choose True for the AllowAllUp property. That's all you need to have a fully working check box. The code corresponding to this last speed button is simple:

```
procedure TToolbarForm.SpeedButtonBigClick(Sender: TObject);
begin
  if SpeedButtonBig.Down then
    Label1.Font.Size := 24
  else
    Label1.Font.Size := 12;
end;
```

As you press this button, it remains down (see Figure 11.5); when you press it again, it is released. I suggest you test the example to check the behavior of the various buttons and groups of buttons. Look also at its complete source code in Listing 11.2.

FIGURE 11.5:

The last speed button behaves like a check box; compare this situation with the one in Figure 11.4 to see the difference.

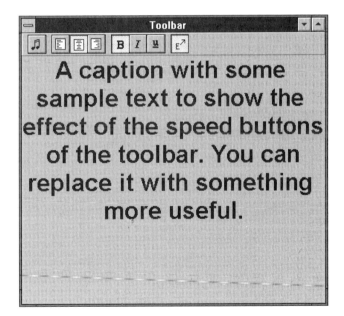

LISTING 11.2: The source code of the TOOLBAR example

```
unit Tool_f;

interface

uses
  WinTypes, WinProcs, Classes, Graphics, Forms,
  Controls, Menus, Buttons, StdCtrls, ExtCtrls;

type
  TToolbarForm = class(TForm)
    Panel1: TPanel;
    SpeedButtonNote: TSpeedButton;
    SpeedButtonBig: TSpeedButton;
    SpeedButtonBold: TSpeedButton;
    SpeedButtonItalic: TSpeedButton;
    SpeedButtonUnderline: TSpeedButton;
    SpeedButtonLeft: TSpeedButton;
    SpeedButtonCenter: TSpeedButton;
    SpeedButtonRight: TSpeedButton;
    Label1: TLabel;
    procedure SpeedButtonNoteClick(Sender: TObject);
    procedure SpeedButtonLeftClick(Sender: TObject);
    procedure SpeedButtonCenterClick(Sender: TObject);
    procedure SpeedButtonRightClick(Sender: TObject);
    procedure SpeedButtonBoldClick(Sender: TObject);
    procedure SpeedButtonItalicClick(Sender: TObject);
    procedure SpeedButtonUnderlineClick(Sender: TObject);
    procedure SpeedButtonBigClick(Sender: TObject);
  private
    { Private declarations }
  public
    { Public declarations }
  end;

var
  ToolbarForm: TToolbarForm;

implementation

{$R *.DFM}

procedure TToolbarForm.SpeedButtonNoteClick(Sender: TObject);
begin
  MessageBeep($FFFF);
end;

procedure TToolbarForm.SpeedButtonLeftClick(Sender: TObject);
begin
  Label1.Alignment := taLeftJustify;
end;
```

LISTING 11.2: The source code of the TOOLBAR example (continued)

```
procedure TToolbarForm.SpeedButtonCenterClick(Sender: TObject);
begin
  Label1.Alignment := taCenter;
end;

procedure TToolbarForm.SpeedButtonRightClick(
  Sender: TObject);
begin
  Label1.Alignment := taRightJustify;
end;

procedure TToolbarForm.SpeedButtonBoldClick(
  Sender: TObject);
begin
  if SpeedButtonBold.Down then
    Label1.Font.Style := [fsBold]
  else
    Label1.Font.Style := [];
end;

procedure TToolbarForm.SpeedButtonItalicClick(
  Sender: TObject);
begin
  if SpeedButtonItalic.Down then
    Label1.Font.Style := [fsItalic]
  else
    Label1.Font.Style := [];
end;

procedure TToolbarForm.SpeedButtonUnderlineClick(
  Sender: TObject);
begin
  if SpeedButtonUnderline.Down then
    Label1.Font.Style := [fsUnderline]
  else
    Label1.Font.Style := [];
end;

procedure TToolbarForm.SpeedButtonBigClick(
  Sender: TObject);
begin
  if SpeedButtonBig.Down then
    Label1.Font.Size := 24
  else
    Label1.Font.Size := 12;
end;

end.
```

Enabling and Disabling Toolbar Buttons

This simple example has more-or-less standard behavior. Every button has its own glyph, which is used both for selected and deselected check boxes or radio buttons. However, each speed button can have a number of different glyphs (that is, different bitmaps) without requiring you to change the bitmap manually. We saw the differences between these two approaches in the two versions of the FIRE example in the last chapter.

To make some tests on this topic, I've prepared a second version of the toolbar example, TOOLBAR2. In this example, I've added a menu with some menu items that can be used to disable some of the speed buttons or even hide the whole toolbar (see Listing 11.3 for a description of the new elements in this version of the form).

LISTING 11.3: The textual description of the form of the TOOLBAR2 example, also containing a menu (components already present in Listing 11.1 have been omitted)

```
object ToolbarForm: TToolbarForm
  ActiveControl = Panel1
  Caption = 'Toolbar'
  Menu = MainMenu1
  object Label1: TLabel
    {as in TOOLBAR}
  object Panel1: TPanel
    {as in TOOLBAR}
  object MainMenu1: TMainMenu
    object File1: TMenuItem
      Caption = '&File'
      object Exit1: TMenuItem
        Caption = 'E&xit'
        OnClick = Exit1Click
      end
    end
    object Toolbar1: TMenuItem
      Caption = '&Toolbar'
      object Visible1: TMenuItem
        Caption = '&Visible'
        Checked = True
        OnClick = Visible1Click
      end
      object DisableSound1: TMenuItem
        Caption = 'Disable &Sound'
        OnClick = DisableSound1Click
      end
```

LISTING 11.3 : The textual description of the form of the TOOLBAR2 example
(continued)

```
    object DisableStyles1: TMenuItem
      Caption = 'Disable S&tyles'
      OnClick = DisableStyles1Click
    end
    object DisableSize1: TMenuItem
      Caption = 'Disable Si&ze'
      OnClick = DisableSize1Click
    end
  end
  object Help1: TMenuItem
    Caption = '&Help'
    object AboutToolbar1: TMenuItem
      Caption = '&About Toolbar...'
      OnClick = AboutToolbar1Click
    end
  end
end
end
```

The Toolbar pull-down menu contains a command to hide the whole toolbar. It calls
the following method:

```
procedure TToolbarForm.Visible1Click(Sender: TObject);
begin
  {hide or display the toolbar, setting the menu item check mark}
  Panel1.Visible := not Panel1.Visible;
  Visible1.Checked := not Visible1.Checked;
end;
```

This code toggles the value of two Boolean properties, one to accomplish the required action and the second to add or remove the check mark beside the menu
item. Two similar statements are also present in the commands used to disable or
enable specific speed buttons:

```
procedure TToolbarForm.DisableSound1Click(Sender: TObject);
begin
  {disable or enable button and set menu check mark}
  SpeedButtonNote.Enabled := not SpeedButtonNote.Enabled;
  DisableSound1.Checked := not DisableSound1.Checked;
end;
```

When you disable one of these speed buttons, Delphi automatically paints a grayed
version of the bitmap you have supplied, as you can see by comparing Figure 11.6

FIGURE 11.6:

The output of the TOOLBAR2 example, with some disabled toolbar buttons

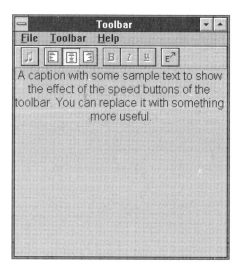

with one of the figures of the previous version of the example (such as Figure 11.4).

In this example, Delphi generates three versions of the bitmaps: normal, pressed, and disabled. However, I've decided to supply a custom version of the glyphs of the last button, preparing the bitmap shown in Figure 11.7, with four different portions. For this button, I just needed two glyphs, one for the normal button and one for the pressed button, but I had to provide two more glyphs for the other states because the Stay Down glyph is the fourth. By preparing more glyphs, I was able to animate the button: if you run the program and press the button, the bitmap will change immediately and will later change again, after the click event.

This program is nice, but a minor problem shows up. If you select one of the three font style buttons, disable them using the corresponding menu command, and enable them again, the button that was originally pressed will be repainted as if it were up (not down). The problem is in the transition between the disabled and the down state. Everything works (the button is really pressed), but the wrong image is displayed on the screen. To correct this problem, you might force an update of the button glyph by toggling it up and down:

```
SpeedButtonBold.Down := False;
SpeedButtonBold.Down := True;
```

FIGURE 11.7:

The bitmap used for the last speed button of the toolbar in the TOOLBAR2 example

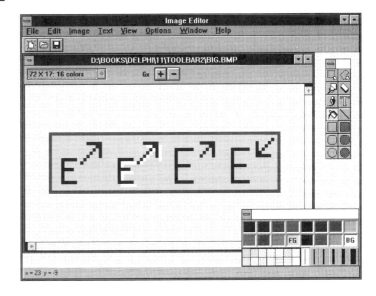

Of course, this code should be executed only if the button is currently selected. You should write the same code for the other two buttons and add it to the form's DisableStyles1Click method:

```
procedure TToolbarForm.DisableStyles1Click(Sender: TObject);
begin
  {disable or enable buttons and set menu text properly}
  if SpeedButtonBold.Enabled then
  begin
    SpeedButtonBold.Enabled := False;
    SpeedButtonItalic.Enabled := False;
    SpeedButtonUnderline.Enabled := False;
    DisableStyles1.Checked := True;
  end
  else
  begin
    SpeedButtonBold.Enabled := True;
    SpeedButtonItalic.Enabled := True;
    SpeedButtonUnderline.Enabled := True;
```

```
{FIX: toggle the down button to repaint
it with the proper attributes}
with SpeedButtonItalic do
  if Down then
  begin
    Down := False;
    Down := True;
  end;
with SpeedButtonBold do
  if Down then
  begin
    Down := False;
    Down := True;
  end;
with SpeedButtonUnderline do
  if Down then
  begin
    Down := False;
    Down := True;
  end;

  DisableStyles1.Checked := False;
end;
```

This problem also shows up in the future versions of these example (such as TOOL-BAR3, COMBOBAR, and DRAGTOOL), but I've decided not to correct it in every example because it is a minor glitch.

NOTE   In the TOOLBAR example, I've used gray-scale bitmaps, but you can make intensive use of color in speed buttons. In the last year, this has become common in all major applications, but Windows 95 seems to move away from color. The Borland BWCC colorful buttons have actually received a lot of criticism for being unprofessional. Actually, too much color can be confusing, and having no speed buttons is probably better than having confusing ones, but I won't like living in a gray world. Maybe those who suggest avoiding colors in toolbar buttons have a closet full of gray suits.

Adding Hints to the Toolbar

Another element, which is becoming quite common in toolbars and speed bars, is the presence of a hint, also called *balloon help*—some text that briefly describes the speed button under the cursor. This text is usually displayed in a yellow box after the mouse cursor has remained steady over a button for a set amount of time.

To add hints to an application's toolbar, simply set the ShowHints property of the panel used as the toolbar to True. You can also change the default value of the HintColor and HintPause properties and, optionally, add a specific text for the hint of the toolbar itself (Hint property).

The toolbar, however, usually has no hint. It shows the hints of the buttons or other elements it contains. In this example, TOOLBAR3, I've added a proper value for the Hint property of the various speed buttons, as you can see in the textual description of the form in Listing 11.4.

LISTING 11.4: Excerpts of the textual description of the form of TOOLBAR3

```
object ToolbarForm: TToolbarForm
  Caption = 'Toolbar'
  Menu = MainMenu1
  object Label1: TLabel
    {omitted}
  object Panel1: TPanel
    Align = alTop
    ParentShowHint = False
    ShowHint = True
    object SpeedButtonNote: TSpeedButton
      Hint = 'Play Note'
    end
    object SpeedButtonLeft: TSpeedButton
      Hint = 'Left Align'
      GroupIndex = 1
      Down = True
    end
    object SpeedButtonCenter: TSpeedButton
      Hint = 'Center'
      GroupIndex = 1
    end
    object SpeedButtonRight: TSpeedButton
      Hint = 'Right Align'
      GroupIndex = 1
    end
    object SpeedButtonBold: TSpeedButton
      Hint = 'Bold'
```

LISTING 11.4 : Excerpts of the textual description of the form of TOOLBAR3 (continued)

```
      AllowAllUp = True
      GroupIndex = 2
    end
    object SpeedButtonItalic: TSpeedButton
      Hint = 'Italic'
      AllowAllUp = True
      GroupIndex = 2
    end
    object SpeedButtonUnderline: TSpeedButton
      Hint = 'Underlined'
      AllowAllUp = True
      GroupIndex = 2
    end
    object SpeedButtonBig: TSpeedButton
      Hint = 'Expand'
      OnClick = SpeedButtonBigClick
    end
  end
  object MainMenu1: TMainMenu
    {omitted...}
  end
end
```

Without our writing any code, the new version of the programs works very well and makes the example look much more professional (see Figure 11.8). However, we can still do something to improve the program. The last button has a hint, *Expand,* which is appropriate only when the button is not pressed. When it is down, the hint should become *Shrink* or something similar. We can accomplish this by adding two lines of code to the SpeedButtonBigClick method, to change the hint each time its status changes:

```
procedure TToolbarForm.SpeedButtonBigClick(Sender: TObject);
begin
  if SpeedButtonBig.Down then
  begin
    Label1.Font.Size := 24;
    SpeedButtonBig.Hint := 'Shrink';
  end
  else
```

```
begin
  Label1.Font.Size := 12;
  SpeedButtonBig.Hint := 'Expand';
  end;
end;
```

FIGURE 11.8:

The output of the TOOLBAR3 example, with the fly-by hints

As you have seen, there was almost no coding involved in adding the hints. I've added some code only to support *context-sensitive hints*, hints with text that changes depending on the status of the speed button.

Adding Hints to a Form

As we have added hints to an application's toolbar, we can add hints to forms, or to the components of a form, without the need to add a panel. I'll show you a simple example of adding fly-by hints to an existing program, PHRASES3. The new version, PHRASES4, shows hints when you move over the components hosted by the form, as you can see in Figure 11.9.

FIGURE 11.9:

The output of the PHRASES4 example, with a hint

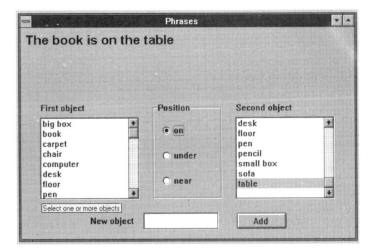

As you can see in the figure and if you run the program, the hints are usually displayed below the component, which is okay for the buttons of a toolbar but not always the best solution for the components of a form. If you add a hint to the form itself, it will be displayed below the window. If you add it to the label at the top, it will be shown far away from its text because the surface of the label, at least at the beginning, has enough space to show three lines. I suggest you try adding these hints, to see their effect.

Another negative effect takes place inside the group box holding the radio buttons. When you add the hint to the group, by default, each of the radio buttons borrows the same text, which is really a good idea. The problem is that if you move the mouse cursor over the group box, the hint window will jump up and down (from below the group to below a button). To solve this problem, you can simply disable the hints for the radio button so that the hint of text and the position of the hint of the group will also be used when you are on the buttons.

Customizing the Hints

We have seen that it is easy to add hint support to a toolbar or a form. It is also easy to customize the way hints are displayed. The simplest thing you can do is change the value of the HintColor and HintPause properties of the Application object. The first defines the background color of the hint window, usually yellow, and the second the amount of time the cursor should remain on a component before hints are displayed.

To obtain more control over their display, you can customize hints even further by assigning a method to the application's OnShowHint event. You cannot do this with the Object Inspector since the Application object doesn't show up in the list. Instead, you need to add a new method to the form manually and then assign it to the OnHint property of the Application object at startup (for example, when the form is created).

The method you have to define has some interesting parameters, such as a string with the text of the hint, a Boolean flag for its activation, and further information:

```
TShowHintEvent = procedure (
  var HintStr: string;
  var CanShow: Boolean;
  var HintInfo: THintInfo) of object;
```

Each of the parameters is passed by reference, so you have a chance to change it. The last parameter is a structure, with the indication of the control, the position of the hint, its color, and other information:

```
THintInfo = record
  HintControl: TControl;
  HintPos: TPoint;
  HintMaxWidth: Integer;
  HintColor: TColor;
  CursorRect: TRect;
  CursorPos: TPoint;
end;
```

Again, you can modify the values of this structure, for example, to change the position of the hint window before it is displayed.

Adding Features to a Toolbar

The TOOLBAR example we built in three steps contained a standard toolbar, although it had buttons with different behaviors, changing bitmaps, and hints. We can extend this example in two directions. The first is to add some new features to the toolbar panel, such as a combo box, a pop-up menu, and so on. The second is to implement a *dockable* or *draggable* toolbar—a toolbar you can position on any side of the form at run-time.

A Combo Box in a Toolbar

The first extension of TOOLBAR3 is the COMBOBAR example, which has a combo box in its toolbar. There are a number of common applications using combo boxes in toolbars to show lists of styles, fonts, font sizes, and so on. Our program is along the same lines, but it follows a slightly different approach: it uses a combo box to let the user choose a font and a spin edit box for setting the font size. You can see an example of this program's form at run-time in Figure 11.10.

FIGURE 11.10:

The COMBOBAR example at run-time

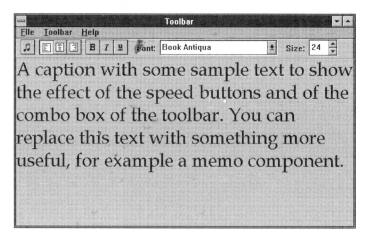

The form of this example is similar to that of the previous version, TOOLBAR3. I've removed the size speed button and added a combo box and a spin edit control, each with its own label. The two new components and their labels have a proper message in the Hint property. Having removed the size button, I had to delete the menu item used to disable it, its code, and the code related to the click on the button itself.

The form has another component, a pop-up menu, connected with the panel and having almost the same menu commands as the menu bar's Toolbar pull-down. You can see the textual description of the new version of the form in Listing 11.5. To make this new pop-up menu work without much effort, I simply connected the

LISTING 11.5: The new elements in the textual description of the form of the
COMBOBAR example

```
object ToolbarForm: TToolbarForm
  Caption = 'Toolbar'
  Menu = MainMenu1
  OnCreate = FormCreate
  object Label1: TLabel...
  object Panel1: TPanel
    Align = alTop
    PopupMenu = PopupMenu1
    ShowHint = True
    object SpeedButtonNote: TSpeedButton...
    object SpeedButtonLeft: TSpeedButton...
    object SpeedButtonCenter: TSpeedButton...
    object SpeedButtonRight: TSpeedButton...
    object SpeedButtonBold: TSpeedButton...
    object SpeedButtonItalic: TSpeedButton...
    object SpeedButtonUnderline: TSpeedButton...
    object Label2: TLabel
      Hint = 'Select Font'
      Caption = 'Font:'
    end
    object Label3: TLabel
      Hint = 'Font Size'
      Caption = 'Size:'
    end
    object ComboBox1: TComboBox
      Hint = 'Select Font'
      Style = csDropDownList
      OnChange = ComboBox1Change
    end
    object SpinEdit1: TSpinEdit
      Hint = 'Font Size'
      Increment = 2
      MaxLength = 2
      MaxValue = 72
      MinValue = 8
      Value = 12
      OnChange = SpinEdit1Change
    end
  end
  object MainMenu1: TMainMenu
    object File1: TMenuItem...
    object Toolbar1: TMenuItem
      Caption = '&Toolbar'
      object Visible1: TMenuItem
        Caption = '&Visible'
        Checked = True
        OnClick = Visible1Click
      end
      object DisableSound1: TMenuItem
        Caption = 'Disable &Sound'
```

LISTING 11.5: The new elements in the textual description of the form of the COMBOBAR example (continued)

```
        OnClick = DisableSound1Click
      end
      object DisableStyles1: TMenuItem
        Caption = 'Disable S&tyles'
        OnClick = DisableStyles1Click
      end
    end
    object Help1: TMenuItem...
  end
  object PopupMenu1: TPopupMenu
    OnPopup = PopupMenu1Popup
    object Hide1: TMenuItem
      Caption = 'Hide SpeedBar'
      OnClick = Visible1Click
    end
    object N1: TMenuItem
      Caption = '-'
    end
    object DisableSound2: TMenuItem
      Caption = 'Disable &Sound'
      OnClick = DisableSound1Click
    end
    object DisableStyles2: TMenuItem
      Caption = 'Disable S&tyles'
      OnClick = DisableStyles1Click
    end
  end
end
```

OnClick events of its items with the methods of the corresponding items of the main menu, using the Object Inspector.

The original methods associated with these commands add and remove the check marks only from the items of the Toolbar pull-down, not from the items of the pop-up menu. I could have changed these methods to operate also on the items of the pop-up menu, but I decided to follow a different approach. When the pop-up menu is going to be displayed, I copy to its items the current check marks of the corresponding items of the main menu (see Figure 11.11):

```
procedure TToolbarForm.PopupMenu1Popup(Sender: TObject);
begin
  DisableSound2.Checked := DisableSound1.Checked;
  DisableStyles2.Checked := DisableStyles1.Checked;
end;
```

FIGURE 11.11:

The pop-up menu of the toolbar of the COMBOBAR example has the same check marks as the corresponding items of the main menu.

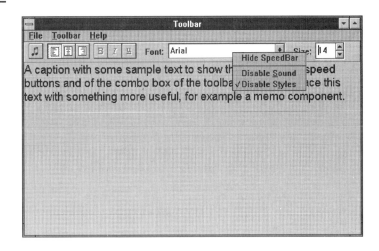

The rest of the new code of the example refers to the new components placed on the toolbar. The combo box is filled when the application starts, copying once more the names of the current fonts from the Screen object (as happened in the FONTGRID example in Chapter 10):

```
procedure TToolbarForm.FormCreate(Sender: TObject);
var
  I: Integer;
begin
  for I := 1 to Screen.Fonts.Count do
    {copy the name of the font in the combo box}
    ComboBox1.Items.Add (Screen.Fonts.Strings [I-1]);
  {select the current font}
  ComboBox1.ItemIndex :=
    ComboBox1.Items.IndexOf (Label1.Font.Name);
end;
```

Notice the last statement of the method, used to select the current font of the label into the combo box. When a new element of the combo box is selected, the reverse action takes place: the text of the current item of the combo box is copied to the name of the label's font:

```
procedure TToolbarForm.ComboBox1Change(Sender: TObject);
begin
  Label1.Font.Name :=
```

```
        ComboBox1.Items [ComboBox1.ItemIndex];
    end;
```

Something similar takes place for the spin edit control. You can access the current value of the spin edit by using its Value property and copy it to the Size field of the label's Font property. You might think this a safe operation to do each time the contents of the spin edit box change, since its limits have been set to 8 and 72 (using the MinValue and MaxValue properties). This is not true. The limits of a spin edit control affect only the scrolling operations, but a user can type in a new value, which has no limit, aside from the fact that this edit box accepts only two input characters (as indicated by its MaxLength property).

Even worse, when the user replaces the current text with something else, for a moment there will be no text in the control, and if you access the Value property while the spin edit box has no text, an exception occurs. In fact, the code behind the Value property tries to convert the current text to a number, but if there is no text, it fails. The solution? We should test whether the spin edit box really has some text before we can safely access its value:

```
procedure TToolbarForm.SpinEdit1Change(Sender: TObject);
begin
  if not (SpinEdit1.Text = '') then
    Label1.Font.Size := SpinEdit1.Value;
end;
```

If you consider only the toolbar of this example (see Figure 11.12), it seems almost that of a professional application. Of course, the rest of the program (which has only a bare label) isn't up to this level, but you can mix this code with that of an example, such as NOTES2 in Chapter 8, to obtain a nice editor.

A Toolbar You Can Drag

Another improvement to the TOOLBAR3 example is to allow the user to drag the toolbar to a different area of the screen. Some Windows applications have toolbars that can be placed only below the menu or at the bottom of the window, others allow vertical bars, and some even have the choice of turning the toolbar into a toolbox—that is, a small floating window. In the following example, DRAGTOOL, I'm going to explore only the first two choices: moving a toolbar to the bottom and turning it into a vertical bar.

11

The toolbar of the COMBOBAR example has a combo box to select a font (but also hints and a local menu) like many commercial applications.

To accomplish this, the panel used as the toolbar should support automatic dragging, and the label should accept dragging when certain conditions are met. So first of all, set the DragMode property of Panel1 to `dmAutomatic`, and then add an On-DragOver event method to the label covering the form and check the position of the bar (Listing 11.6 shows the changes to the textual description of the form of the DRAGTOOL example, compared with that of the TOOLBAR3 example).

The first version of the example contained a new enumerated data type, indicating the possible positions of the toolbar:

```
type
    TBarPosition = (bpTop, bpBottom, bpLeft, bpRight, bpNone);
```

LISTING 11.6: The changes in the textual description of the form of the DRAGTOOL example

```
object ToolbarForm: TToolbarForm
  object Label1: TLabel
    ...
    OnDragDrop = Label1DragDrop
    OnDragOver = Label1DragOver
  end
  object Panel1: TPanel
    DragMode = dmAutomatic
    ...
  end
  object MainMenu1: TMainMenu
    ...
  end
end
```

In the final version, however, I based the code directly on the TAlign data type defined by the VCL as:

```
TAlign = (alNone, alTop, alBottom,
  alLeft, alRight, alClient);
```

As we will see, using the TAlign data type directly allows us to write less code. This data type is the return value of a GetBarPos function, which returns the different code depending on the value of the X and Y parameters, which represent form coordinates:

```
function TToolbarForm.GetBarPos (X, Y: Integer): TAlign;
begin
  if X < DragSize then
    GetBarPos := alLeft
  else if Y < DragSize then
    GetBarPos := alTop
  else if X > ClientWidth - DragSize then
    GetBarPos := alRight
  else if Y > ClientHeight - DragSize then
    GetBarPos := alBottom
  else
    GetBarPos := alNone;
end;
```

In this code, DragSize is a constant defined by the program that should be less than the height (or width) of the toolbar. Once this function is defined, the DragOver event has very simple coding:

```
procedure TToolbarForm.Label1DragOver(Sender, Source: TObject;
  X, Y: Integer; State: TDragState; var Accept: Boolean);
begin
  if GetBarPos (X + Label1.Left, Y + Label1.Top) = alNone then
    Accept := False
  else
    Accept := True;
end;
```

Notice that the parameters passed to the GetBarPos function are converted from label coordinates to form coordinates by adding the difference between the two origins. Once the dragging ends, we have to move the toolbar to the new position. This is the interesting part of the program, but it is probably easier than you might imagine.

Let me start with a simple case. What is the code you have to write to move the toolbar from the top to the bottom of the form (see Figure 11.13)? You should

FIGURE 11.13:

In the DRAGTOOL example, a user can drag the toolbar to the bottom of the form.

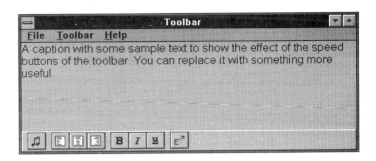

change only the value of the Align property of the panel:

```
Panel1.Align := alBottom;
```

Notice that we can simply ignore the form's other components only because there is a label aligned with the client area; that is, it covers the whole area of the form, excluding the rectangle taken up by the toolbar. To restore Panel1 to the top, the reverse action is required. When you move the toolbar to another location, a similar action should be performed, using the return value of the GetBarPos function directly:

```
ReqPos := GetBarPos (X + Label1.Left, Y + Label1.Top);
Panel1.Align := ReqPos;
```

Had I used a custom enumerated type, such as TBarPosition above, I would need to use a case statement instead of the simpler code above:

```
ReqPos := GetBarPos (X + Label1.Left, Y + Label1.Top);
case ReqPos of
  bpBottom: Panel1.Align := alBottom;
  bpTop: Panel1.Align := alTop;
  bpLeft: Panel1.Align := alLeft;
  bpRight: Panel1.Align := alRight;
end;
```

In turning the panel into a vertical one, the problem is not in the panel itself but in the speed buttons it hosts. We need to move each of the buttons to a new location or they won't be visible, aside from the first one. Again, this seems more complex than it is.

To move a button from the horizontal bar to the vertical bar, you can simply exchange its Top coordinate with its Left coordinate. If you think about it twice and look at Figure 11.14, you should understand why. Luckily, to move the buttons back to a horizontal bar, we have to perform exactly the same operation again. Here is the code of the RotateSpeedbar procedure:

```
procedure TToolbarForm.RotateSpeedbar;
var
  I, X, Y: Integer;
begin
  for I := 0 to Panel1.ControlCount - 1 do
  begin
    {reverse X and Y}
    X := Panel1.Controls [I].Top;
    Y := Panel1.Controls [I].Left;
    Panel1.Controls [I].Top := Y;
    Panel1.Controls [I].Left := X;
  end;
end;
```

FIGURE 11.14:

Four copies of the DRAGTOOL example, with the toolbar in the four possible positions

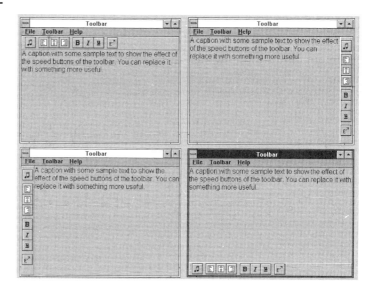

The method inverts the *X* and *Y* values for each of the controls of the bar, scanning the Controls array ControlCount times.

Of course, this code works well only for *square* controls. If you have a combo box on the toolbar, it will fail. When should you call this method? Only when the old and the new toolbar are one vertical and the other horizontal, or vice versa:

```
if ( (ReqPos in [alTop, alBottom]) and
     (BarPos in [alLeft, alRight]) ) or
   ( (ReqPos in [alLeft, alRight]) and
     (BarPos in [alTop, alBottom]) ) then
   RotateSpeedbar;
```

In this `if` test, BarPos is the current position of the toolbar. With this code, we can now move the SpeedBar to each of the four sides of the form, as you can see in Figure 11.14. I've omitted only minor details, but you can look them up in the complete listing of this program, in Listing 11.7.

LISTING 11.7: The main elements of the source code of the DRAGTOOL example (code already present in earlier versions has been omitted)

```
unit Tool_f;

interface

uses
  SysUtils, WinTypes, WinProcs, Messages, Classes, Graphics,
  Controls, Forms, Dialogs, StdCtrls, Menus, Buttons, ExtCtrls;

type
  TToolbarForm = class(TForm)
    Panel1: TPanel;
    {...omitted speed buttons and menu items...}
    Label1: TLabel;
    MainMenu1: TMainMenu;
    procedure SpeedButtonNoteClick(Sender: TObject);
    procedure SpeedButtonLeftClick(Sender: TObject);
    procedure SpeedButtonCenterClick(Sender: TObject);
    procedure SpeedButtonRightClick(Sender: TObject);
    procedure SpeedButtonBoldClick(Sender: TObject);
    procedure SpeedButtonItalicClick(Sender: TObject);
    procedure SpeedButtonUnderlineClick(Sender: TObject);
    procedure SpeedButtonBigClick(Sender: TObject);
    procedure Exit1Click(Sender: TObject);
    procedure Visible1Click(Sender: TObject);
    procedure DisableSound1Click(Sender: TObject);
    procedure DisableStyles1Click(Sender: TObject);
    procedure AboutToolbar1Click(Sender: TObject);
    procedure DisableSize1Click(Sender: TObject);
    procedure Label1DragOver(Sender, Source:
      TObject; X, Y: Integer;
      State: TDragState; var Accept: Boolean);
```

LISTING 11.7: The main elements of the source code of the DRAGTOOL example
(continued)

```
    procedure Label1DragDrop(Sender, Source:
      TObject; X, Y: Integer);
    procedure FormCreate(Sender: TObject);
  private
    BarPos: TAlign;
    PanelSize: Integer;
    function GetBarPos (X, Y: Integer): TAlign;
    procedure RotateSpeedbar;
  end;

var
  ToolbarForm: TToolbarForm;

implementation

{$R *.DFM}

const DragSize = 20;

{...menu command handlers omitted...}

function TToolbarForm.GetBarPos (X, Y: Integer): TAlign;
begin
  if X < DragSize then
    GetBarPos := alLeft
  else if Y < DragSize then
    GetBarPos := alTop
  else if X > ClientWidth - DragSize then
    GetBarPos := alRight
  else if Y > ClientHeight - DragSize then
    GetBarPos := alBottom
  else
    GetBarPos := alNone;
end;

procedure TToolbarForm.Label1DragOver(
  Sender, Source: TObject; X, Y: Integer;
  State: TDragState; var Accept: Boolean);
begin
  if GetBarPos (X + Label1.Left, Y + Label1.Top)
      = alNone then
    Accept := False
  else
    Accept := True;
end;

procedure TToolbarForm.Label1DragDrop(
  Sender, Source: TObject; X, Y: Integer);
var
  ReqPos: TAlign;
```

LISTING 11.7: The main elements of the source code of the DRAGTOOL example
(continued)

```
begin
  ReqPos := GetBarPos (X + Label1.Left, Y + Label1.Top);
  Panel1.Align := ReqPos;
  if ( (ReqPos in [alTop, alBottom]) and
       (BarPos in [alLeft, alRight]) ) or
     ( (ReqPos in [alLeft, alRight]) and
       (BarPos in [alTop, alBottom]) ) then
    RotateSpeedbar;
  BarPos := ReqPos;
end;

procedure TToolbarForm.RotateSpeedbar;
var
  I, X, Y: Integer;
begin
  for I := 0 to Panel1.ControlCount - 1 do
  begin
    {reverse X and Y}
    X := Panel1.Controls [I].Top;
    Y := Panel1.Controls [I].Left;
    Panel1.Controls [I].Top := Y;
    Panel1.Controls [I].Left := X;
  end;
end;

procedure TToolbarForm.FormCreate(Sender: TObject);
begin
  BarPos := alTop;
  PanelSize := Panel1.Height;
end;

end.
```

Creating a Status Bar

Building a status bar is probably even simpler than building a toolbar. Again, you can use a Panel component, place it on the form, usually aligned at the bottom, and define a proper three-dimensional effect.

There are a number of uses for a status bar. The most common is to display information about the menu item currently selected by the user. Besides this, a status bar often displays status information about the program (hence the name). For example, you might display the position of the cursor in a graphical application, the current line of text in a word processor, the status of the lock keys, the time and date, or other information.

Menu Hints in the Status Bar

Besides the panel with the role of status bar, the STATUS1 example has a main menu. When the user moves to the menu to select an element, the program displays a description of the current command in the status bar, as you can see in Figure 11.15.

FIGURE 11.15:

The simple status bar of the STATUS1 example displays a description of the current menu item.

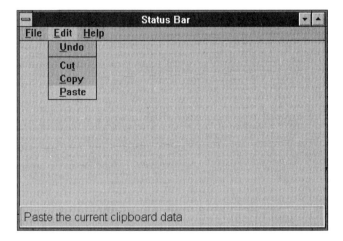

To obtain this effect, you need to take two steps. First, input a string as a Hint property of each item or pull-down of the main menu, as you can see in the textual description of the form in Listing 11.8.

Second, write some code to handle the application's OnHint event. Again, you need to add a new method to the form manually and then assign it to the OnHint property of the Application object at startup (for example, when the form is created). In the form's interface, you can add the following definition:

```
procedure ShowHint(Sender: TObject);
```

LISTING 11.8: The textual description of the form of the STATUS1 example, including a menu with hints

```
object Form1: TForm1
  Caption = 'Status Bar'
  Menu = MainMenu1
  OnCreate = FormCreate
  object Panel1: TPanel
    Align = alBottom
    Alignment = taLeftJustify
    BevelInner = bvLowered
    Font.Color = clBlack
    Font.Height = -16
    Font.Name = 'Arial'
    Font.Style = []
  end
  object MainMenu1: TMainMenu
    object File1: TMenuItem
      Caption = '&File'
      Hint = 'Operations on files'
      object New1: TMenuItem
        Caption = '&New...'
        Hint = 'Create a new file'
      end
      object Open1: TMenuItem
        Caption = '&Open...'
        Hint = 'Open an existing file'
      end
      object Save1: TMenuItem
        Caption = '&Save'
        Hint = 'Save the current file'
      end
      object Saveas1: TMenuItem
        Caption = 'Save &as...'
        Hint = 'Save the file with a new name'
      end
      object N1: TMenuItem
        Caption = '-'
      end
      object Exit1: TMenuItem
        Caption = 'E&xit'
        Hint = 'Terminate the application'
      end
    end
    object Edit1: TMenuItem
      Caption = '&Edit'
      Hint = 'Operations on the text'
      object Undo1: TMenuItem
        Caption = '&Undo'
        Hint = 'Reverse the last action'
      end
```

LISTING 11.8: The textual description of the form of the STATUS1 example,
including a menu with hints (continued)

```
      object N2: TMenuItem
        Caption = '-'
      end
      object Cut1: TMenuItem
        Caption = 'Cu&t'
        Hint = 'Delete the selection, moving it to the clipboard'
      end
      object Copy1: TMenuItem
        Caption = '&Copy'
        Hint = 'Make a copy of the current selection
          to the clipboard'
      end
      object Paste1: TMenuItem
        Caption = '&Paste'
        Hint = 'Paste the current clipboard data'
      end
    end
    object Help1: TMenuItem
      Caption = '&Help'
      Hint = 'Access information about the program'
      object About1: TMenuItem
        Caption = 'About...'
        Hint = 'Display the About Box'
      end
    end
  end
end
```

This procedure should copy the current value of the application's Hint property, which temporarily contains a copy of the hint of the selected item to the status bar (or Panel1). You can see its code in the short Listing 11.9.

Speed Button Hints in the Status Bar

We can easily extend this application by adding a toolbar to it and providing a way to display a description of the speed buttons when the mouse moves over them. As you should remember, the Hint property of the speed buttons is already used to display the yellow fly-by hints near the buttons. How can we use the same property for two different strings? Strangely enough, this problem has a direct solution: write a simple string divided in two portions by a separator, the | character. For

LISTING 11.9: The source code of the STATUS1 example

```
unit Status_f;

interface

uses
  SysUtils, WinTypes, WinProcs, Messages, Classes, Graphics,
  Controls, Forms, Dialogs, Menus, ExtCtrls;

type
  TForm1 = class(TForm)
    Panel1: TPanel;
    MainMenu1: TMainMenu;
      {...I've removed the definitions of
      the menu item objects...}
    procedure FormCreate(Sender: TObject);
  private
    { Private declarations }
  public
    { Public declarations }
    procedure ShowHint(Sender: TObject);
  end;

var
  Form1: TForm1;

implementation

{$R *.DFM}

procedure TForm1.FormCreate(Sender: TObject);
begin
  Application.OnHint := ShowHint;
end;

procedure TForm1.ShowHint(Sender: TObject);
begin
  Panel1.Caption := ' ' + Application.Hint;
end;

end.
```

example, you might enter, as the value of the Hint property:

```
Help|Activate the help of the application
```

The first portion of the string, "Help", is used by fly-by hints, the second portion by the status bar. This takes place automatically when you have written the code described in the first version of the status bar.

When the hint of a control is made up of two strings, you can use the GetShortHint and GetLongHint methods to extract the first (short) and second (long) substrings from the string you pass as a parameter, which is usually the value of the Hint property.

For example, in STATUS2, I copied the form of STATUS1 and its code; then I pasted the toolbar of an older application. Without changing the code, but only properly setting the value of the Hint property of the graphical buttons, you can produce a form with the nice effect of showing both hints, as you can see in Figure 11.16.

Aside from showing hints and status messages, the STATUS2 example doesn't work at all, so do not even try to use it, except for testing the hints.

To build the example above, I copied a group of components from one application to another. This is quite simple, as I mentioned in Chapter 2. Open the source example, select a number of components (in this case, the panel and some of the speed buttons it contains), copy them to the clipboard, and then move to the destination form and paste them in.

FIGURE 11.16:

The output of STATUS2, with speed buttons having both a fly-by hint and a status bar description

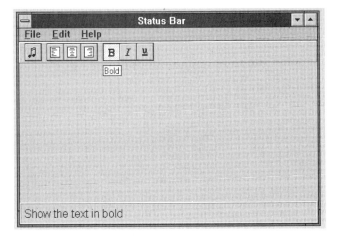

Status Bars the Hard Way

We have seen that if you simply assign a proper message to the application's On-Hint event, the status bar works properly. But what happens behind the scenes when you select a menu item command? In short, each time a user changes the menu selection, Windows sends the form a wm_MenuSelect message. By intercepting this message, you might circumvent the use of Delphi hints and make some custom actions, although 99 percent of the time, the default behavior is good enough. So there is a good chance you don't care about this problem, and since I'll have to use some low-level code, you might well decide to skip this short section.

To show you how this works and to delve into complex Windows behavior, I've written a simple application that has a very poor output but proves a point: you can interact with the menu without using hints.

The form of this example, STATUS_H (the *H* stands for *handmade*) contains only a panel at the bottom and a main menu. Also, its code is short (although not simple). You need to define a new method inside the form's class:

```
public
    procedure WMMenuSelect (var Msg: TWMMenuSelect);
      message wm_MenuSelect;
```

The parameter of this method is the message itself. Each Windows message has its own structure, and you can find all these definitions in the file MESSAGES.PAS. Here is the one we need:

```
TWMMenuSelect = record
  Msg: TMsgParam;
  IDItem: Word;
  MenuFlag: Word;
  Menu: HMENU;
  Result: LongInt;
end;
```

We receive the item's identifier (a numeric code), the menu's handle, and a menu flag, which can assume one or more of these values:

MF_BITMAP	MF_CHECKED	MF_DISABLED
MF_GRAYED	MF_MOUSESELECT	MF_OWNERDRAW
MF_POPUP	MF_SEPARATOR	MF_SYSMENU

To keep the example simple, I decided to output, in the status bar, the identifier of the menu item and its text. To retrieve the string from the menu, I've used the GetMenuString API function, which copies text of the menu corresponding to a certain identifier to a buffer, a character array. You can see a detailed description of this API function in the Help file.

```
procedure TForm1.WMMenuSelect (var Msg: TWMMenuSelect);
var
  Text: array [0..50] of char;
begin
  {notice that the following test uses a binary and}
  if (Msg.MenuFlag and MF_SEPARATOR) = 0 then
  begin
    GetMenuString (Msg.Menu, Msg.IDItem, Text,
      SizeOf (Text), MF_BYCOMMAND);
    Panel1.Caption := IntToStr (Msg.IDItem) +
      ': ' + StrPas(Text);
  end;
end;
```

By running this program, you can see the output shown in Figure 11.17, which is somewhat strange since the underscore characters of the menu commands are copied to the status bar. This problem has another problem within it: when you stop working with the menu, the last message remains in the panel. To solve this problem, we should add two more lines at the end of the previous method, to intercept this special circumstance:

```
if Msg.Menu = 0 then
    Panel1.Caption := 'Ready';
```

The SDI Template

In some of the examples in this chapter, we have built quite complex toolbars, but if you need a simple one, or the startup code for a complex one, you can create a project based on the Delphi SDI application template. When this project is generated, the application's main form has both a working toolbar and a working status bar (see Figure 11.18).

11

FIGURE 11.17:

The output of the STATUS_H example

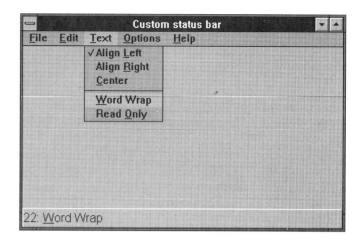

FIGURE 11.18:

The form of an application generated with the SDI template, and the bitmap of one of its buttons (on the right)

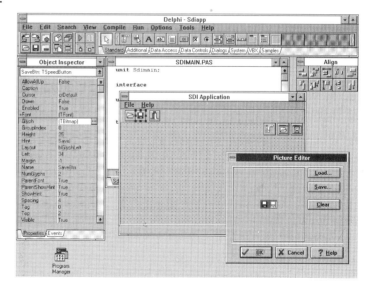

The bitmaps used for the toolbar are colorful and provide two glyphs (as you can see on the right side of Figure 11.18). Besides a number of components with some predefined properties and a standard menu bar, the template contains some code to handle the status bar (and to run the About box and the file-related dialog boxes).

This code is almost the same as the STATUS1 example above, with the definition of a custom ShowHint method and its association with the application's OnHint event:

```
procedure TSDIAppForm.ShowHint(Sender: TObject);
begin
  StatusBar.Caption := Application.Hint;
end;

procedure TSDIAppForm.FormCreate(Sender: TObject);
begin
  Application.OnHint := ShowHint;
end;
```

The behavior of the toolbar, instead, is completely defined by the properties of its components and requires no Pascal code. Of course, there are a number of ways to customize this application, including making the toolbar (or status bar) optional or draggable or adding other components to them.

Summary

In this chapter, we have examined a specific topic: the definition of a toolbar and a status bar for simple SDI applications. We have seen that although there are predefined components for these elements in Delphi, it is easy to build them using the Panel component.

Panels are indeed powerful, because they can contain other components and you can easily manipulate both the panel as a whole and the individual controls it holds.

You can consider this chapter as the first step toward professional applications. We will take other steps in the following chapters, but our programs now are similar to some best-selling Windows applications, which may be very important for our own clients.

Now that the elements of the main form of our programs are properly set up, we can consider adding secondary forms and dialog boxes. This is the topic of the next chapter.

CHAPTER

TWELVE

12

Multiple Forms and Dialog Boxes

- Modal and modeless forms

- How to merge form menus

- Modal and modeless dialog boxes

- Predefined dialog boxes

- A dialog box as main window

- Extensible dialog boxes

- An About box with hidden credits

Up to this point, the programs in this book have been made up of a single form. Although it is possible to build fully functional applications with one form and a number of components, it is far more common to have more than one form. Usually, applications have a main window, some floating toolboxes or palettes, and a number of dialog boxes that can be invoked though menu commands or command buttons. More complex applications might have an MDI structure—a frame window with a number of child windows inside its client area. The development of MDI applications will be discussed in Chapter 15. This chapter focuses on applications having more than one form or having dialog boxes.

Dialog boxes are not a new subject. We have already used a number of default dialog boxes, to select colors, fonts, and files, and some message boxes, obtained with the MessageDlg function. In this chapter, you will see how you can define your own dialog boxes.

Dialog Boxes versus Forms

Before presenting examples of applications with multiple forms and applications with user-defined dialog boxes, let me begin with a general description of these two alternatives and their differences.

We have already seen a correspondence between forms in Delphi and Windows as perceived by the user (see the definitions in the section "Forms versus Windows" in Chapter 9). Since dialog boxes are a particular kind of window, you can expect dialog boxes in Delphi to be based on forms, too. This is, indeed, the case. Once we have added a second form to a program, we can display it as a form or as a dialog box. Something slightly different might take place behind the scenes in Delphi and in Windows, but it won't matter to us.

When you write a program, there is really no big difference between a dialog box and a second form, aside from the border and other user-interface elements you can customize.

What users usually associate with the idea of a dialog box is the concept of a modal window. A *modal window* is a window that takes the focus and must be closed before users move back to the main window. This is true for message boxes and usually for dialog boxes, as well. However, you can also have nonmodal—or *modeless*—dialog boxes. So if you think that dialog boxes are just modal forms, you are on the

12

right track, but your description is not precise. In Delphi (as in Windows), you can have modeless dialog boxes and modal forms.

We have to consider two different elements:

- The form's border and its user interface determine whether it looks like a dialog box, maybe with the new three-dimensional effect.

- The use of two different functions (Show or ShowModal) to create the second form determines its behavior (modeless or modal).

By combining these two elements, we can build any kind of secondary form. This is what we will do in this chapter.

Adding a Second Form to a Program

Now we are ready to delve into an example. We will add a second form to an application to experiment with modeless forms. I won't show you how to create a modal form now, simply because this is what dialog boxes are for.

The example, PHONES, is simple: the main form (Form1) has a list of phone numbers; the secondary form (Form2) has a list of e-mail addresses. (Of course, to build this program, I've just invented a list of names and nonexistent phone numbers and e-mail addresses. Any resemblance to existing people or references is unintentional.)

NOTE   To add a second form to an application, you simply press the New Form button on the Delphi toolbar. If the corresponding option is set, you'll be prompted to choose a form template or Expert. In most of the examples in this chapter, we will start with a blank main form and one or more blank secondary forms.

You can see the two forms in Figure 12.1 and their detailed textual descriptions in Listings 12.1 and 12.2. If you have two forms in a project, you can use the Select Form or the Select Unit button of the toolbar to navigate through them.

FIGURE 12.1:

The two forms of the PHONES example at run-time

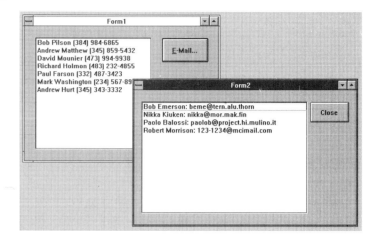

LISTING 12.1: The textual description of the first form of the PHONES example (UNIT1.DFM)

```
object Form1: TForm1
  ActiveControl = ListBox1
  Caption = 'Form1'
  object ListBox1: TListBox
    Items.Strings = (...)
  end
  object Button1: TButton
    Caption = '&E-Mail...'
    OnClick = Button1Click
  end
end
```

LISTING 12.2: The textual description of the second form of the PHONES example (UNIT2.DFM)

```
object Form2: TForm2
  ActiveControl = ListBox1
  Caption = 'Form2'
  object ListBox1: TListBox
    Items.Strings = (...)
  end
  object CloseButton: TButton
    Caption = 'Close'
    OnClick = CloseButtonClick
  end
end
```

You can also choose which form is the main one and which forms should be automatically created at startup using the Forms page of the Project Options dialog box (see Figure 12.2).

FIGURE 12.2:
The Forms options of the PHONES project

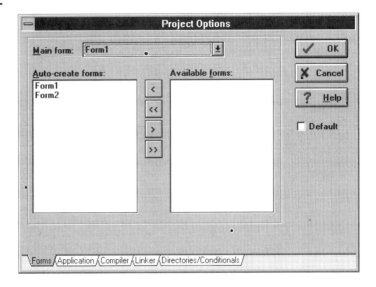

Once you have prepared the two forms, you need to add some code to the program to make them work properly. In both forms, I've added a button. In the first form, the button is used to show the second window, and in the second form, it is used to close itself. In fact, you can close the second form and continue with the first one. The opposite is not possible: as soon as you close the main form of a Delphi application, the program terminates.

To run the second form when the user presses Button1, you should write this simple code:

```
procedure TForm1.Button1Click(Sender: TObject);
begin
  Form2.Show;
end;
```

If you use the Show function, the second form will be displayed as modeless, so you can move back to the first one while the second is still visible. Notice that the code simply displays the form; it doesn't create it. In fact, the form is created by the project file, as indicated in the Forms page of the Project Options dialog box. If you look at the project file's code, you can see that both forms are included (*used*) and that both are created, using the application's CreateForm method. The first form being created becomes the application's main form:

```
program Phones;

uses
  Forms,
  Unit1 in 'UNIT1.PAS' {Form1},
  Unit2 in 'UNIT2.PAS' {Form2};

begin
  Application.CreateForm(TForm1, Form1);
  Application.CreateForm(TForm2, Form2);
  Application.Run;
end.
```

To compile the code of the first form, you need to include the unit containing the second form (in this case, Unit2) in its uses statement, the list of units at the beginning of the code:

```
unit Unit1;

interface

uses
  WinTypes, WinProcs, Classes, Graphics, Forms,
  Controls, StdCtrls, Unit2;

type
  TForm1 = class(TForm)
  ...
```

To close the second form, you might use its system menu or click on the Close button, calling the following method:

```
procedure TForm2.CloseButtonClick(Sender: TObject);
begin
  Close;
end;
```

Modal and Modeless Forms

As you saw in the previous section, adding a second form to a program (and a third, and so on) is really simple, so let's try something more complex. I would like to expand this example into a generic one allowing a user to open a number of modal or modeless forms.

The main form of the MODES program is shown in Figure 12.3, and its description is in Listing 12.3. It has two buttons, used to create modal and modeless forms. Once you have added two new forms to the project—I've named them ModalForm and ModelessForm—you can write the following methods, corresponding to the two OnClick events of the two buttons:

```
procedure TMainAppForm.ModalButtonClick(Sender: TObject);
var
  Modal: TModalForm;
begin
  Modal := TModalForm.Create (self);
  Modal.ShowModal;
  Modal.Free;
end;

procedure TMainAppForm.ModelessButtonClick(Sender: TObject);
var
  NonModal: TModelessForm;
begin
  NonModal := TModelessForm.Create (self);
  NonModal.Show;
end;
```

FIGURE 12.3:

The main form of the MODES project

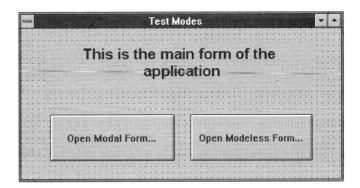

LISTING 12.3: The textual description of the MainAppForm of the MODES example

```
object MainAppForm: TMainAppForm
  ActiveControl = ModalButton
  Caption = 'Test Modes'
object Label1: TLabel
    Alignment = taCenter
    AutoSize = False
    Caption = 'This is the main form of the application'
    Font.Color = clBlack
    Font.Height = -21
    Font.Name = 'Arial'
    Font.Style = [fsBold]
  end
  object ModalButton: TButton
    Caption = 'Open Modal Form...'
    OnClick = ModalButtonClick
  end
  object ModelessButton: TButton
    Caption = 'Open Modeless Form...'
    OnClick = ModelessButtonClick
  end
end
```

When the modal form is created and executed by means of ShowModal, it remains active until you close it. This means that the call to the ShowModal function does not return until the form is closed. During this time, the application's main form remains *partially disabled.* You cannot click the two buttons or interact with the form in any way. Once the modal form has been closed, the ShowModal function terminates and the code deletes the object from memory.

The behavior of the modeless form is different. The Show procedure—notice that this is a procedure, while ShowModal is a function—returns immediately. Of course, we cannot delete the object from memory since the corresponding window is currently on the screen. We can, instead, press the Modeless button again to create a second modeless form, then a third form, a fourth, and so on. There is practically no limit. The objects corresponding to these modeless forms will be destroyed by the main form when it is closed—that is, the form that was passed as a parameter to the Create method of the objects. This is far from perfect, but it won't create many problems.

The main form can display secondary forms. What can you do with these forms? They both have a Close button, as you can see in Figure 12.4. The two Close buttons are connected with a simple method that calls the Close procedure.

FIGURE 12.4:

The modal and modeless forms of the MODES program at run-time

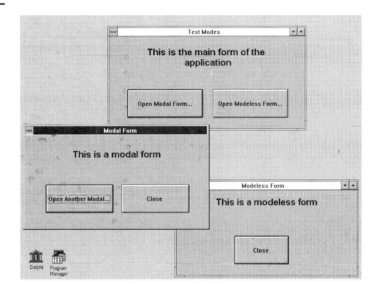

The modal form also has a second button, to create another *nested* modal form (see Figure 12.5). The OnClick method for this button has the following code:

```
procedure TModalForm.Modal2ButtonClick(Sender: TObject);
var
  AnotherModal: TModalForm;
begin
  AnotherModal := TModalForm.Create (self);
  AnotherModal.ShowModal;
  AnotherModal.Free;
end;
```

If you look at this code, you might suppose you can create an unlimited number of nested modal forms. However, this is not true. Modal forms consume some space on the stack, and with default settings, once you have created 10 or 12 modal forms, the application's stack will be full. Creating one more form will crash the application! For this reason, I've imposed a limit on the number of modeless forms you can

FIGURE 12.5:

Nested modal forms in the MODES
program

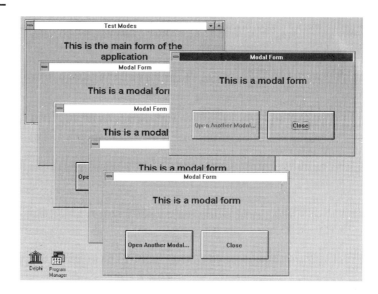

create, using a global variable of the unit. This implies setting the number to 1 in the main form when the first modal form is built and then increasing and decreasing this number each time a new modal form is created. You can see how this is done in the complete source code of the application, shown in Listings 12.4, 12.5, and 12.6.

Notice that each time you create a form object in your code, you can remove the code that Delphi automatically generates to define an object for the form and initialize it. If you look at the source code for this example, you'll see that I've commented this code, adding a *to be removed* indication. You should certainly avoid creating such useless objects. Before you do this, however, remember to remove automatic form creation, using the Forms page of the Project Options dialog box, as shown in Figure 12.6.

LISTING 12.4: The listing of the main form of the MODES example

```pascal
unit Mainform;

interface

uses
  WinTypes, WinProcs, Classes, Graphics, Forms,
  Controls, Modal, Modeless, StdCtrls;

type
  TMainAppForm = class(TForm)
    Label1: TLabel;
    ModalButton: TButton;
    ModelessButton: TButton;
    procedure ModalButtonClick(Sender: TObject);
    procedure ModelessButtonClick(Sender: TObject);
  private
    { Private declarations }
  public
    { Public declarations }
  end;

var
  MainAppForm: TMainAppForm;

implementation

{$R *.DFM}

procedure TMainAppForm.ModalButtonClick(Sender: TObject);
var
  Modal: TModalForm;
begin
  ModalNumber := 1;
  Modal := TModalForm.Create (self);
  Modal.ShowModal;
  Modal.Free;
end;

procedure TMainAppForm.ModelessButtonClick(Sender: TObject);
var
  NonModal: TModelessForm;
begin
  NonModal := TModelessForm.Create (self);
  NonModal.Show;
end;

end.
```

LISTING 12.5: The listing of the modal form of the MODES example

```
unit Modal;

interface

uses WinTypes, WinProcs, Classes, Graphics, Forms,
  Controls, StdCtrls;

type
  TModalForm = class(TForm)
    Label1: TLabel;
    Modal2Button: TButton;
    CloseButton: TButton;
    procedure CloseButtonClick(Sender: TObject);
    procedure Modal2ButtonClick(Sender: TObject);
    procedure FormCreate(Sender: TObject);
  private
    { Private declarations }
  public
    { Public declarations }
  end;

var
{to be removed:
  ModalForm: TModalForm;}

  ModalNumber: Integer;

implementation

{$R *.DFM}

procedure TModalForm.CloseButtonClick(Sender: TObject);
begin
  Dec (ModalNumber);
  Close;
end;

procedure TModalForm.Modal2ButtonClick(Sender: TObject);
var
  AnotherModal: TModalForm;
begin
  if ModalNumber < 5 then
  begin
    Inc (ModalNumber);
    AnotherModal := TModalForm.Create (self);
    AnotherModal.ShowModal;
    AnotherModal.Free;
  end;
end;
```

LISTING 12.5: The listing of the modal form of the MODES example (continued)

```pascal
procedure TModalForm.FormCreate(Sender: TObject);
begin
  if ModalNumber = 5 then
    Modal2Button.Enabled := False;
end;

end.
```

LISTING 12.6: The listing of the modeless form of the MODES example

```pascal
unit Modeless;

interface

uses WinTypes, WinProcs, Classes, Graphics, Forms, Controls,
  StdCtrls;

type
  TModelessForm = class(TForm)
    Label1: TLabel;
    CloseButton: TButton;
    procedure CloseButtonClick(Sender: TObject);
  private
    { Private declarations }
  public
    { Public declarations }
  end;

{to be removed:
var
  ModelessForm: TModelessForm;}

implementation

{$R *.DFM}

procedure TModelessForm.CloseButtonClick(Sender: TObject);
begin
  Close;
end;

end.
```

FIGURE 12.6:

In the MODES program, only the main form is automatically created, as you can see in the Forms page of the Project Options dialog box.

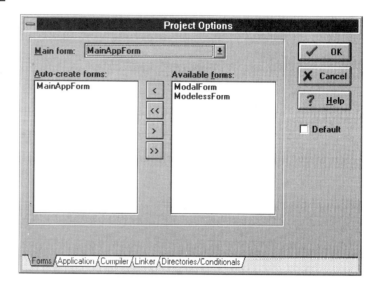

Two Forms, Two Menus

Now we can go back to our PHONES example and try to add a menu to the forms, building PHONES2. The easiest thing to do is to add a menu to each of them. I've used the menu structures present in the form descriptions of Listings 12.7 and 12.8.

LISTING 12.7: The textual description of the first form of the PHONES2 example

```
object Form1: TForm1
  ActiveControl = ListBox1
  Caption = 'Phone Numbers'
  Menu = MainMenu1
  object ListBox1: TListBox
    Items.Strings = (
      'Bob Pilson (384) 984-6865'
      'Andrew Matthew (345) 859-5432'
      ...)
  end
  object MainMenu1: TMainMenu
    object File1: TMenuItem
      Caption = '&File'
      object New1: TMenuItem
        Caption = '&New'
        Enabled = False
      end
```

LISTING 12.7:   The textual description of the first form of the PHONES2 example
(continued)

```
      object Open1: TMenuItem
        Caption = '&Open...'
        Enabled = False
      end
      object Save1: TMenuItem
        Caption = '&Save'
        Enabled = False
      end
      object Saveas1: TMenuItem
        Caption = 'Save &as...'
        Enabled = False
      end
      object N1: TMenuItem
        Caption = '-'
      end
      object Exit1: TMenuItem
        Caption = 'E&xit'
        OnClick = Exit1Click
      end
    end
    object Email1: TMenuItem
      Caption = '&E-Mail'
      object ShowModal1: TMenuItem
        Caption = '&Show Modal...'
        OnClick = ShowModal1Click
      end
      object ShowModeless1: TMenuItem
        Caption = 'S&how Modeless...'
        OnClick = ShowModeless1Click
      end
      object CloseModeless1: TMenuItem
        Caption = '&Close Modeless'
        Enabled = False
        OnClick = CloseModeless1Click
      end
    end
    object Help1: TMenuItem
      Caption = '&Help'
      object AboutPhones1: TMenuItem
        Caption = '&About Phones...'
        Enabled = False
      end
    end
  end
end
```

LISTING 12.8: The textual description of the second form of the PHONES2 example

```
object Form2: TForm2
  ActiveControl = ListBox1
  Caption = 'E-mail addresses'
  Menu = MainMenu1
  OnClose = FormClose
  object ListBox1: TListBox
    Items.Strings = (
      'Bob Emerson: beme@tern.alu.thorn'
      'Nikka Kiuken: nikka@mor.mak.fin'
      ...)
  end
  object MainMenu1: TMainMenu
    object EMail1: TMenuItem
      Caption = '&E-Mail File'
      object Open1: TMenuItem
        Caption = '&Open...'
        Enabled = False
      end
      object Save1: TMenuItem
        Caption = '&Save'
        Enabled = False
      end
      object Saveas1: TMenuItem
        Caption = 'Save &as...'
        Enabled = False
      end
      object N1: TMenuItem
        Caption = '-'
      end
      object Close1: TMenuItem
        Caption = '&Close'
        OnClick = Close1Click
      end
    end
  end
end
```

By running this application, we end up with the forms shown in Figure 12.7. To show that this approach works with both a modal and a modeless form, I've added to the older version of the program the code to create the second form as either modal or modeless, using the first two menu items of the E-Mail pull-down menu.

FIGURE 12.7:

The forms of the PHONES2 program at run-time; the second form can be executed as modal.

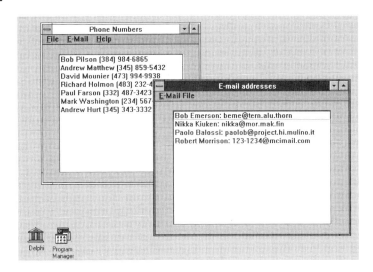

To show the form, you need only apply either the ShowModal or Show method to it, as in:

```
procedure TForm1.ShowModal1Click(Sender: TObject);
begin
  Form2.ShowModal;
end;
```

In fact, the forms of this program are both created by the project's code at startup. When the program shows the second form as modal, the main form's menu is automatically disabled, together with the form itself, but when the form is displayed as modeless, you should disable it manually. Since there is only one form, trying to show it twice won't be a good choice.

```
procedure TForm1.ShowModeless1Click(Sender: TObject);
begin
  ShowModal1.Enabled := False;
  ShowModeless1.Enabled := False;
  Form1.CloseModeless1.Enabled := True;
  Form2.Show;
end;
```

When the form is displayed, the first two items of this pull-down menu are disabled and the third is enabled (it was disabled at design-time), as shown in Figure 12.8.

FIGURE 12.8:

The disabled menu items of the main form of the PHONES2 example, when the second is executed as modeless

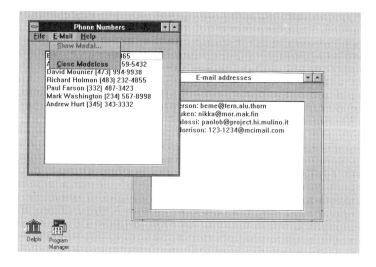

Notice that in the figure the menu items have different colors because the first is currently selected (although it is grayed). When you select this last menu item, the modeless form is closed:

```
procedure TForm1.CloseModeless1Click(Sender: TObject);
begin
  Form2.Close;
end;
```

So what happens to the menu items? Shouldn't we re-enable them in the above method? We might do so, but the program won't work properly. In fact, there are a number of ways to close the second modeless form, including its own Close menu command. Instead of repeating the code to enable the menu items in a number of places, you can write it in the second form's OnClose event:

```
procedure TForm2.FormClose(Sender: TObject;
  var Action: TCloseAction);
begin
  Form1.ShowModal1.Enabled := True;
  Form1.ShowModeless1.Enabled := True;
  Form1.CloseModeless1.Enabled := False;
end;
```

Notice that this method of the second form refers to the first one; that is, it needs to access to some properties of the TForm1 class. For this reason, you need to add a uses statement referring to the proper module in the implementation section of the unit (see the complete source code of the two forms in Listings 12.9 and 12.10). In fact, adding this module to the uses statement of the interface, at the beginning of the unit, would cause a circular reference.

LISTING 12.9: The complete source code of the first unit of the PHONES2 example, corresponding to the main form

```
unit Unit1;

interface

uses
  WinTypes, WinProcs, Classes, Graphics, Forms,
  Controls, Unit2, Menus, StdCtrls;

type
  TForm1 = class(TForm)
    ListBox1: TListBox;
    MainMenu1: TMainMenu;
    {menu items have been removed}
    procedure ShowModal1Click(Sender: TObject);
    procedure ShowModeless1Click(Sender: TObject);
    procedure CloseModeless1Click(Sender: TObject);
    procedure Exit1Click(Sender: TObject);
  private
    { Private declarations }
  public
    { Public declarations }
  end;

var
  Form1: TForm1;

implementation

{$R *.DFM}

procedure TForm1.ShowModal1Click(Sender: TObject);
begin
  Form2.ShowModal;
end;

procedure TForm1.ShowModeless1Click(Sender: TObject);
begin
  ShowModal1.Enabled := False;
  ShowModeless1.Enabled := False;
  Form1.CloseModeless1.Enabled := True;
```

LISTING 12.9: The complete source code of the first unit of the PHONES2 example, corresponding to the main form (continued)

```
   Form2.Show;
end;


procedure TForm1.CloseModeless1Click(Sender: TObject);
begin
   Form2.Close;
end;

procedure TForm1.Exit1Click(Sender: TObject);
begin
   Close;
end;

end.
```

LISTING 12.10: The complete source code of the second unit of the PHONES2 example, corresponding to the secondary form

```
unit Unit2;

interface

uses
   WinTypes, WinProcs, Classes, Graphics, Forms,
   Controls, Menus, StdCtrls;

type
   TForm2 = class(TForm)
     ListBox1: TListBox;
     MainMenu1: TMainMenu;
     {menu items have been removed}
     procedure Close1Click(Sender: TObject);
     procedure FormClose(Sender: TObject;
       var Action: TCloseAction);
   private
     { Private declarations }
   public
     { Public declarations }
   end;

var
   Form2: TForm2;

implementation

{$R *.DFM}
```

LISTING 12.10: The complete source code of the second unit of the PHONES2
example, corresponding to the secondary form (continued)

```
uses Unit1;

procedure TForm2.Close1Click(Sender: TObject);
begin
  Close;
end;

procedure TForm2.FormClose(Sender: TObject;
  var Action: TCloseAction);
begin
  Form1.ShowModal1.Enabled := True;
  Form1.ShowModeless1.Enabled := True;
  Form1.CloseModeless1.Enabled := False;
end;

end.
```

NOTE   If Unit1 uses Unit2, Unit2 cannot use Unit1, at least not in its public interface (this problem is known as *circular reference*). In the implementation portion, instead, a unit can refer to any other unit, including those from which it is used.

This example demonstrates that on the whole, handling modal forms is usually easier than handling modeless forms since you do not need to change the behavior of the main window. In fact, the main form cannot be accessed when the modal form is open, and you don't need to keep track of the open or closed forms, as you do with modeless forms.

Merging Form Menus

In the preceding version of the PHONES program, each of the two forms had its own menu bar. Delphi, however, supports a technique to merge the menu bars of two or more forms automatically.

This is the idea: the application's main window has a menu bar, as usual. The other forms have a menu bar with the AutoMerge property enabled, so their menu bar won't be displayed in the form but will be merged with the one of the main window, according to the rules you indicate. You can see this behavior in Figure 12.9.

FIGURE 12.9:

The two menu bars of the PHONES3 example and how they are merged

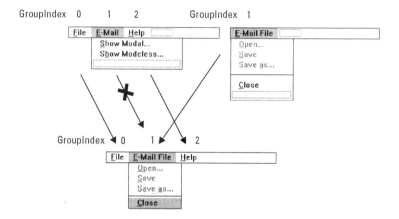

These are the rules for menu merging: Each menu item and pull-down menu has a GroupIndex property. When menu bars are merged, the pull-down menus, and eventually the specific items, are arranged as follows:

- If two elements of the different menu bars have the same GroupIndex, those of the original menu are removed.

- Elements are ordered for ascending GroupIndex values.

For example, in Figure 12.9, you can see how the menus of the two forms of the PHONES3 example are merged. The pull-down menus of the main form have indexes 0, 1, and 2. The only pull-down has an index 1, so it replaces the pull-down with the corresponding index of the main form's menu.

Consider, however, that menu merging makes sense only for modeless forms. If you display the second form as modal, you cannot access the main window's menu bar, so Delphi doesn't perform any merging.

Using menu merging is extremely simple, at least at first glance. If you open PHONES2 again, set the AutoMerge property of the second form's main menu to True, and set proper values for the GroupIndex properties, as indicated in the following table, the program will almost work:

Form	Pull-Down Menu	GroupIndex
Form1	File	0
	E-Mail	1
	Help	2
Form2	E-Mail File	1

In fact, though, there are two problems: first, when the form is displayed as modal, its menu is not accessible; second, when the modeless form is closed, the main form's original menu is not restored.

We can solve the first problem easily by adding a statement to set the value of the AutoMerge property of the second form's menu dynamically. The second problem, though, is tough. The menu is not restored, because the second form is not destroyed, only hidden!

The solution to this problem is to change the approach completely in handling the second form. Instead of creating this object when the application starts, we should create and destroy it each time it should be shown or hidden. This requires a number of simple changes in the source code. First of all, you need to disable the automatic form creation using the Forms page of the Project Options dialog box.

To show the form as modal, we have to create it, set its properties, and later destroy it:

```
procedure TForm1.ShowModal1Click(Sender: TObject);
begin
  Form2 := TForm2.Create (Self);
  Form2.MainMenu1.AutoMerge := False;
  Form2.ShowModal;
  Form2.Free;
end;
```

The approach used for the modeless activation is slightly different. The form is created but not destroyed:

```
procedure TForm1.ShowModeless1Click(Sender: TObject);
begin
  Form2 := TForm2.Create (Self);
  Form2.MainMenu1.AutoMerge := True;
  Form2.Show;
end;
```

Notice that from the previous version, I've removed the code used to disable some menu items, since the whole pull-down menu is completely hidden. For this reason, I've also removed the last item, Close.

The modeless form is destroyed when it is closed if you set the Action parameter of the OnClose event to `caFree`:

```
procedure TForm2.FormClose(Sender: TObject;
  var Action: TCloseAction);
begin
  Action := caFree;
end;
```

The rest of the code is the same as in PHONES2, although there isn't much left after the changes we have made. In Figure 12.10 you can see the final output of this program, with the merged menu bar, as already indicated in the schema of Figure 12.9.

FIGURE 12.10:

The merged menus of the two forms of the PHONES3 example

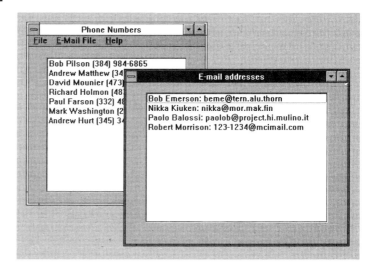

Creating a Dialog Box

I stated earlier in this chapter that a dialog box is not very different from other forms. There is a very simple trick to building a dialog box instead of a form. Just select the `bsDialog` value for the form's BorderStyle property.

With this simple change, the interface of the form becomes dialog box-like (see Figure 12.11), with the new three-dimensional effect, the proper system menu, and no minimize or maximize boxes. Of course, such a form has the typical dialog box thick border, which is nonresizable (see Chapter 9, and in particular Figure 9.3, for a comparison of the border styles).

Once you have built a dialog box form, you can display it as a modal or modeless window using the two usual Show methods (the procedure Show and the function ShowModal). Modal dialog boxes, however, are more common than modeless ones. This is exactly the reverse of forms: modal forms should generally be avoided since a user won't expect them. See the following table for the complete schema of the various combinations of styles:

Window Type	Modal	Modeless
Form	Never	Usual, in SDI applications
Dialog box	Most common kind of second form	Used, but not very common

Consider, in any case, that this table lacks an important element, the use of MDI forms, which will be discussed in Chapter 15. As we will see, using the MDI is currently the most common way to have several forms in an application, although in the near future, many applications might follow an SDI approach instead. Delphi is a good example of this new approach. In both cases, MDI and SDI, having a second modeless form can be very useful for holding palettes or special toolboxes.

Sometimes, an alternative to the use of a second form is to build multipage forms, a new kind of user interface that is spreading rapidly among Windows applications. You can do this easily using Delphi's Notebook and TabbedNotebook components, as we'll see in Chapter 13.

Modal Dialog Boxes

Since modal dialog boxes are more common than modeless ones, I'll concentrate on them first. As an example, we'll build a typical options dialog box. The main form of this example, named DIALOG1, has two labels, and you can use the dialog box to hide or show these two labels. You can see the main form and the dialog box at run-time in Figure 12.11.

FIGURE 12.11:

The main form and the dialog box of the DIALOG1 example

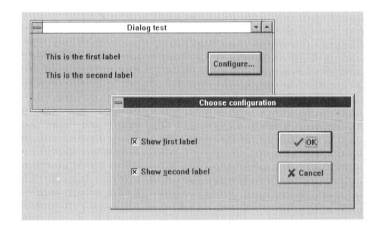

The dialog box also has two standard bitmap buttons, with the default glyphs for OK and Cancel. Using these default buttons is usually a good idea because you can set a single property (Kind) instead of a number of them (including the text, the glyph, the return value, and others). As a consequence, and an important one, you get a standard user interface.

You can see the whole list of the components of the two forms, the main form and the dialog, and their most interesting properties in Listings 12.11 and 12.12, respectively.

Now we can look at the code. After you have included the unit describing the dialog box form in the code of the main form, you can write the following:

```
procedure TForm1.ConfigureButtonClick(Sender: TObject);
begin
  ConfigureDialog.ShowModal;
end;
```

LISTING 12.11: The textual description of the main form of the DIALOG1 example

```
object Form1: TForm1
  ActiveControl = ConfigureButton
  Caption = 'Dialog test'
  object Label1: TLabel
    Caption = 'This is the first label'
  end
  object Label2: TLabel
    Caption = 'This is the second label'
  end
  object ConfigureButton: TButton
    Caption = 'Configure...'
    OnClick = ConfigureButtonClick
  end
end
```

LISTING 12.12: The textual description of the dialog box of the DIALOG1 example

```
object ConfigureDialog: TConfigureDialog
  ActiveControl = BitBtn1
  BorderStyle = bsDialog
  Caption = 'Choose configuration'
  object BitBtn1: TBitBtn
    Kind = bkOK
    NumGlyphs = 2
  end
  object BitBtn2: TBitBtn
    Kind = bkCancel
    NumGlyphs = 2
  end
  object CheckBox1: TCheckBox
    Caption = 'Show &first label'
    State = cbChecked
  end
  object CheckBox2: TCheckBox
    Caption = 'Show &second label'
    State = cbChecked
  end
end
```

Although this code displays the dialog box, it is not very useful. In fact, we do not respond to any actions the user might have taken in the dialog box. This is a better alternative:

```
procedure TForm1.ConfigureButtonClick(Sender: TObject);
begin
  ConfigureDialog.ShowModal;
  Label1.Visible := ConfigureDialog.CheckBox1.Checked;
  Label2.Visible := ConfigureDialog.CheckBox2.Checked;
end;
```

Each time the dialog box is executed, the status of the two check boxes is used to determine which of the labels should be visible. However, this code has at least one bad bug. If the user terminates the dialog box by pressing the Cancel button, the values are considered, anyway. So we need to make the two assignments only if the return value of the ShowModal function (that is, the modal result) is mrOk:

```
procedure TForm1.ConfigureButtonClick(Sender: TObject);
begin
  if ConfigureDialog.ShowModal = mrOk then
  begin
    Label1.Visible := ConfigureDialog.CheckBox1.Checked;
    Label2.Visible := ConfigureDialog.CheckBox2.Checked;
  end;
end;
```

However, something is still wrong. If you open the dialog box, set some options, and press Cancel, the new values are not considered; but the next time you open the dialog box, you'll see the options you set before pressing the Cancel button, not the currently active options.

As a final step, we need to set up the dialog box properly each time it is executed. Here is the final code of the DIALOG1 example:

```
procedure TForm1.ConfigureButtonClick(Sender: TObject);
begin

  {copy current values to the dialog box}
  ConfigureDialog.CheckBox1.Checked := Label1.Visible;
  ConfigureDialog.CheckBox2.Checked := Label2.Visible;

  if ConfigureDialog.ShowModal = mrOk then
  begin
```

```
      {copy new dialog box values in the main form only if OK}
      Label1.Visible := ConfigureDialog.CheckBox1.Checked;
      Label2.Visible := ConfigureDialog.CheckBox2.Checked;
    end;
  end;
```

This is one of the approaches you can follow when you run a modal dialog box. The steps are:

1. Set the initial values each time you run the dialog box.

2. Show the dialog box.

3. If the OK button has been pressed, copy the new values back to the form.

Of course, this is not the only possible technique. As an alternative, you can set up the values of the dialog box only the first time, store the current values each time you run it, and reset the values to the current ones when the user quits the dialog box with the Cancel button. In our example, we could have written

```
procedure TForm1.ConfigureButtonClick(Sender: TObject);
var
  old1, old2: Boolean;
begin
  {store the old values of the dialog box}
  old1 := ConfigureDialog.CheckBox1.Checked;
  old2 := ConfigureDialog.CheckBox2.Checked;

  if (ConfigureDialog.ShowModal = mrOk) then
  begin
    {set the new values in the form}
    Label1.Visible := ConfigureDialog.CheckBox1.Checked;
    Label2.Visible := ConfigureDialog.CheckBox2.Checked;
  end
  else
  begin
    {restore the old values of the dialog box}
    ConfigureDialog.CheckBox1.Checked := old1;
    ConfigureDialog.CheckBox2.Checked := old2;
  end;
end;
```

The advantage here is that the code that saves and restores the old values can be moved into the code of the dialog box. This is useful if there are several places in the code where you can show the same dialog box. As an alternative approach, all the code can be moved to the dialog box itself, and the code of the OnClick method of the dialog box's OK button should copy the proper values to some fields of the main form.

By the way, what happens when the user presses the OK or Cancel button? The code should close the dialog box, returning the proper value to the application.

You can indicate the return value by setting the ModalResult property of the button the user clicks to terminate the dialog box. As a side effect, when you assign a value to this property, in fact, the modal dialog box is automatically closed. Notice that the ModalResult value becomes exactly the return value of the ShowModal method that was used to show the modal dialog box.

So that we don't need to code this by hand, each button component, including bitmap buttons, has a ModalResult property. If you do not handle a button's OnClick event, it automatically uses its ModalResult value to set the corresponding property of its parent form.

A Modeless Dialog Box

The second example of dialog boxes shows a more complex modal dialog box that uses the standard approach, as well as a modeless dialog box.

The main form of the DIALOG2 example has five labels with names (see Figure 12.12). If the user clicks on a name, its color turns to red; if the user double-clicks on it, the program displays a modal dialog box with a list of names to choose from (see Figure 12.12 again). If the user clicks on the Style button, a modeless dialog box appears, allowing the user to change the font style of the main form's labels (see Figure 12.13).

On the whole, this program is based on three forms: a main form and two dialog boxes. The five labels of the main form are connected to two methods, one for the OnClick event and the second for the OnDoubleClick event. The first method turns the last label a user has clicked on to red, resetting all the others to black. Notice that a single method is associated with each of the labels (as you can see in the textual description of the form in Listing 12.13). Here is the code of this method:

```
procedure TForm1.LabelClick(Sender: TObject);
begin
  if Sender is TLabel then
  begin
```

```
      {set the color of all the labels to black}
      Label1.Font.Color := clBlack;
      Label2.Font.Color := clBlack;
      Label3.Font.Color := clBlack;
      Label4.Font.Color := clBlack;
      Label5.Font.Color := clBlack;
      {set the color of the clicked label to red}
      (Sender as TLabel).Font.Color := clRed;
    end;
  end;
```

FIGURE 12.12:

The main form of the DIALOG2 example with the modal dialog box that appears when the user double-clicks on one of the labels

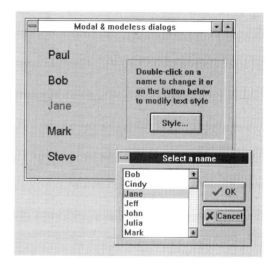

FIGURE 12.13:

The modeless dialog box used to set the style of the text of the labels; notice the names of the buttons: Apply and Close.

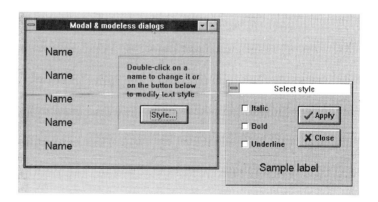

LISTING 12.13: The textual description of the main form of the DIALOG2 example (MAIN.DFM)

```
object Form1: TForm1
  ActiveControl = StyleButton
  Caption = 'Modal & modeless dialogs'
  object Bevel1: TBevel
    Left = 168
    Top = 44
    Width = 169
    Height = 133
  end
  object Label1: TLabel
    Caption = 'Name'
    Font.Color = clBlack
    Font.Height = -19
    Font.Name = 'Arial'
    OnClick = LabelClick
    OnDblClick = LabelDoubleClick
  end
  object Label2: TLabel
    Caption = 'Name'
    {same font as above}
    OnClick = LabelClick
    OnDblClick = LabelDoubleClick
  end
  object Label3: TLabel
    {same as above}
    OnClick = LabelClick
    OnDblClick = LabelDoubleClick
  end
  object Label4: TLabel
    {same as above}
    OnClick = LabelClick
    OnDblClick = LabelDoubleClick
  end
  object Label5: TLabel
    {same as above}
    OnClick = LabelClick
    OnDblClick = LabelDoubleClick
  end
  object Label6: TLabel
    Caption = 'Double-click on a name...'
  end
  object StyleButton: TButton
    Left = 208
    Top = 132
    Width = 89
    Height = 33
    TabOrder = 0
    Caption = 'Style...'
    OnClick = StyleButtonClick
  end
end
```

The second method common to all of the labels, and related to the OnDoubleClick event, shows the modal dialog box after the user selects the label's current caption in the list box of the dialog itself. If the user closes the dialog box by pressing the OK button and an item of the list is selected, the selection is copied back to the label's caption:

```
procedure TForm1.LabelDoubleClick(Sender: TObject);
begin
  if Sender is TLabel then
    with ListDial.Listbox1 do
    begin
      {select the current name in the list box}
      ItemIndex := Items.IndexOf ((Sender as TLabel).Caption);

      {show the modal dialog box, checking the return value}
      if (ListDial.ShowModal = mrOk)
          and (ItemIndex >= 0) then
        {copy the selected item to the label}
        (Sender As TLabel).Caption := Items [ItemIndex];
    end;
end;
```

Notice that all the code used to customize the modal dialog box is in the LabelDouble-Click method of the main form. The dialog has no added code, although the main form can access some of its components (for the textual description of the form, see Listing 12.14).

The modeless dialog box, instead, has a lot of coding behind it. (Its textual description is in Listing 12.15.) The main form simply runs it when the Style button is clicked (notice that the button caption ends with three dots to indicate that when it is pressed, the program will open a dialog box):

```
procedure TForm1.StyleButtonClick(Sender: TObject);
begin
  {run modeless dialog}
  StyleDial.Show;
end;
```

You can see the dialog box running in Figure 12.13. Notice the names of the two buttons, Apply and Close, which usually replace the OK and Cancel buttons in a modeless dialog box. At times, you can find a Cancel button that works as a Close button, but the OK button in a modeless dialog usually has no meaning at

LISTING 12.14: The textual description of the modal dialog box of the DIALOG2
example (LIST_D.DFM)

```
object ListDial: TListDial
  ActiveControl = ListBox1
  BorderStyle = bsDialog
  Caption = 'Select a name'
  ClientHeight = 130
  ClientWidth = 223
  object ListBox1: TListBox
    IntegralHeight = True
    ItemHeight = 16
    Items.Strings = (
      'Bob'
      'Cindy'
      'Jane'
      'Jeff'
      'John'
      ...)
    Sorted = True
  end
  object BitBtn1: TBitBtn
    Kind = bkOK
  end
  object BitBtn2: TBitBtn
    Kind = bkCancel
  end
end
```

all. Instead, there might be one or more buttons that perform specific actions on the main window, such as Apply, Change Style, Replace, Delete, and so on.

If the user clicks on one of the check boxes of this modeless dialog box, the style of the sample label's text at the bottom changes accordingly. You accomplish this by adding or removing the specific flag to or from the set indicating the style, as in:

```
LabelSample.Font.Style :=
  LabelSample.Font.Style + [fsItalic];
```

You can see the complete code of these methods in Listing 12.16. When the user selects the Apply button, instead of the values of the check boxes being checked, the style of the sample label is directly copied to each of the form's labels.

12

LISTING 12.15: The textual description of the modeless dialog box of the DIALOG2 example (.DFM)

```
object StyleDial: TStyleDial
  ActiveControl = ApplyBitBtn
  BorderStyle = bsDialog
  Caption = 'Select style'
  ClientHeight = 159
  ClientWidth = 226
  object LabelSample: TLabel
    Alignment = taCenter
    AutoSize = False
    Caption = 'Sample label'
    Font.Height = -19
    Font.Name = 'Arial'
  end
  object ApplyBitBtn: TBitBtn
    Caption = 'Apply'
    Default = True
    ModalResult = 1
    OnClick = ApplyBitBtnClick
    Glyph.Data = {...}
  end
  object CloseBitBtn: TBitBtn
    Cancel = True
    Caption = 'Close'
    ModalResult = 2
    OnClick = CloseBitBtnClick
    Glyph.Data = {...}
  end
  object ItalicCheckBox: TCheckBox
    Caption = 'Italic'
    OnClick = ItalicCheckBoxClick
  end
  object BoldCheckBox: TCheckBox
    Caption = 'Bold'
    OnClick = BoldCheckBoxClick
  end
  object UnderlineCheckBox: TCheckBox
    Caption = 'Underline'
    OnClick = UnderlineCheckBoxClick
  end
end
```

LISTING 12.16: The complete listing of the modal dialog box of the DIALOG2
example (STYLE_D.PAS)

```
unit Style_d;

interface

uses
  WinTypes, WinProcs, Classes, Graphics, Forms,
  Controls, Buttons, StdCtrls;

type
  TStyleDial = class(TForm)
    ApplyBitBtn: TBitBtn;
    CloseBitBtn: TBitBtn;
    ItalicCheckBox: TCheckBox;
    BoldCheckBox: TCheckBox;
    UnderlineCheckBox: TCheckBox;
    LabelSample: TLabel;
    procedure ApplyBitBtnClick(Sender: TObject);
    procedure CloseBitBtnClick(Sender: TObject);
    procedure ItalicCheckBoxClick(Sender: TObject);
    procedure BoldCheckBoxClick(Sender: TObject);
    procedure UnderlineCheckBoxClick(Sender: TObject);
  private
    { Private declarations }
  public
    { Public declarations }
  end;

var
  StyleDial: TStyleDial;

implementation

{$R *.DFM}

{allow access to the main form}
uses Main;

procedure TStyleDial.ApplyBitBtnClick(Sender: TObject);
begin
  {copy the style from the sample label of the dialog box
  to the five labels of the main form}
  Form1.Label1.Font.Style := LabelSample.Font.Style;
  Form1.Label2.Font.Style := LabelSample.Font.Style;
  Form1.Label3.Font.Style := LabelSample.Font.Style;
  Form1.Label4.Font.Style := LabelSample.Font.Style;
  Form1.Label5.Font.Style := LabelSample.Font.Style;
end;
```

LISTING 12.16: The complete listing of the modal dialog box of the DIALOG2 example (continued)

```
procedure TStyleDial.CloseBitBtnClick(Sender: TObject);
begin
  Close;
end;

procedure TStyleDial.ItalicCheckBoxClick(Sender: TObject);
begin
  if ItalicCheckBox.Checked then
    LabelSample.Font.Style := LabelSample.Font.Style + [fsItalic]
  else
    LabelSample.Font.Style := LabelSample.Font.Style - [fsItalic];
end;

procedure TStyleDial.BoldCheckBoxClick(Sender: TObject);
begin
  if BoldCheckBox.Checked then
    LabelSample.Font.Style := LabelSample.Font.Style + [fsBold]
  else
    LabelSample.Font.Style := LabelSample.Font.Style - [fsBold];
end;

procedure TStyleDial.UnderlineCheckBoxClick(Sender: TObject);
begin
  if UnderlineCheckBox.Checked then
    LabelSample.Font.Style :=
      LabelSample.Font.Style + [fsUnderline]
  else
    LabelSample.Font.Style :=
      LabelSample.Font.Style - [fsUnderline];
end;

end.
```

For this reason, the implementation of the Style dialog box should be able to access the interface of the main form's unit. Again, we need to indicate the proper uses clause in the implementation part to avoid a circular dependency. Notice that when the user clicks on the Apply button, the dialog box is not closed. Only the Close button has this effect.

Using Predefined Dialog Boxes

Besides building your own dialog boxes, Delphi allows you to use some default dialog boxes of different kinds. Some are predefined by Windows, others are simple dialog boxes (such as message boxes) displayed by a Delphi method, and still others are among the Delphi template forms.

Windows Common Dialogs

The Delphi Components palette contains a page of dialog boxes. Each of these dialog boxes—known as *Windows common dialogs*—is defined in the library COMMDLG.DLL, which first appeared in Windows 3.1.

I have already used some of these dialog boxes in several examples in the previous chapters, so you are probably already familiar with them. Basically, you need to put the corresponding component on a form, set some of its properties, run the dialog box (with the Execute method), and retrieve the properties that have been set while running it.

Here we will build a kind of test program, COMMDLG1, to highlight some of the features of the common dialog boxes. In fact, by setting some of the properties and options, you can obtain very different versions of the same dialog box, altering its behavior and its user interface more than you might expect.

The program can display each of the common dialog boxes (see Figures 12.14 and 12.15), although some of them have no real effect. Some of the properties of the controls are set at design-time, as you can see in the textual description of Listing 12.17. Other properties are set at run-time, so we can experiment with different values without having to declare multiple objects.

The only common dialog box for which there are two copies is the Font dialog box, to allow one of the two copies to have an associated OnApply event. A Font dialog box with the Apply button behaves almost like a modeless dialog box, but it isn't. The Find and Replace dialog boxes are really modeless.

FIGURE 12.14:

One of the versions of the Color common dialog box displayed by the COMMDLG1 example

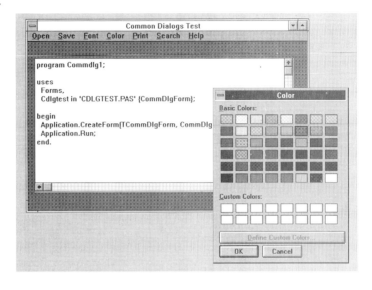

FIGURE 12.15:

The Font selection dialog box with the Apply button

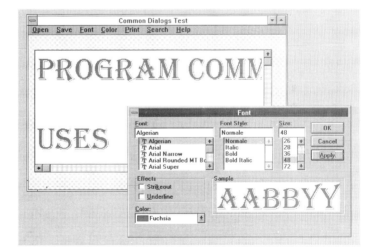

LISTING 12.17: The textual description of the form of the COMMDLG1 example

```
object CommDlgForm: TCommDlgForm
  Caption = 'Common Dialogs Test'
  Menu = MainMenu1
  object Memo1: TMemo
    ScrollBars = ssBoth
  end
  object OpenDialog1: TOpenDialog
  end
  object SaveDialog1: TSaveDialog
  end
  object FontDialog1: TFontDialog
    Font.Color = clWindowText
    Font.Height = -13
    Font.Name = 'System'
    Font.Style = []
    MinFontSize = 0
    MaxFontSize = 0
  end
  object ColorDialog1: TColorDialog
    Ctl3D = True
  end
  object MainMenu1: TMainMenu
    object Open1: TMenuItem
      Caption = '&Open'
      object TextFiles1: TMenuItem
        Caption = 'Existing &Text Files...'
        OnClick = TextFiles1Click
      end
      object Anynewfile1: TMenuItem
        Caption = '&Any file...'
        OnClick = Anynewfile1Click
      end
      object MultipleSelection1: TMenuItem
        Caption = '&Multiple Selection...'
        OnClick = MultipleSelection1Click
      end
    end
    object Save1: TMenuItem
      Caption = '&Save'
      object TextFile1: TMenuItem
        Caption = '&Text File...'
        OnClick = TextFile1Click
      end
      object AnyFile1: TMenuItem
        Caption = '&Any File...'
        OnClick = AnyFile1Click
      end
    end
    object Font1: TMenuItem
      Caption = '&Font'
      object OnlyTrueType1: TMenuItem
```

LISTING 12.17: The textual description of the form of the COMMDLG1 example
(continued)

```
        Caption = 'Only &TrueType...'
        OnClick = OnlyTrueType1Click
      end
      object NoEffects1: TMenuItem
        Caption = 'No &Effects...'
        OnClick = NoEffects1Click
      end
      object NoStyle1: TMenuItem
        Caption = 'No &Style...'
        OnClick = NoStyle1Click
      end
      object Apply1: TMenuItem
        Caption = '&Apply...'
        OnClick = Apply1Click
      end
    end
    object Color1: TMenuItem
      Caption = '&Color'
      object Standard1: TMenuItem
        Caption = '&Standard...'
        OnClick = Standard1Click
      end
      object FullOpen1: TMenuItem
        Caption = '&Full Open...'
        OnClick = FullOpen1Click
      end
      object NoFullOpen1: TMenuItem
        Caption = '&No Full Open...'
        OnClick = NoFullOpen1Click
      end
    end
    object Print1: TMenuItem
      Caption = '&Print'
      object Print2: TMenuItem
        Caption = '&Print...'
        OnClick = Print2Click
      end
      object PrinterSetup1: TMenuItem
        Caption = 'Printer &Setup...'
        OnClick = PrinterSetup1Click
      end
    end
    object Search1: TMenuItem
      Caption = '&Search'
      object Search2: TMenuItem
        Caption = '&Search...'
        OnClick = Search2Click
      end
      object Replace1: TMenuItem
        Caption = '&Replace...'
```

12

LISTING 12.17: The textual description of the form of the COMMDLG1 example (continued)

```
      OnClick = Replace1Click
    end
  end
  object Help1: TMenuItem
    Caption = '&Help'
    object AboutCommonDialogsTest1: TMenuItem
      Caption = 'About Common Dialogs Test...'
      OnClick = AboutCommonDialogsTest1Click
    end
  end
end
object FontDialog2: TFontDialog
  Font.Color = clWindowText
  Font.Height = -13
  Font.Name = 'System'
  Font.Style = []
  MinFontSize = 0
  MaxFontSize = 0
  OnApply = FontDialog2Apply
end
object PrintDialog1: TPrintDialog
  MinPage = 1
  MaxPage = 100
  Options = [poPrintToFile, poPageNums, poSelection, poWarning]
  PrintToFile = True
end
object PrinterSetupDialog1: TPrinterSetupDialog
end
object FindDialog1: TFindDialog
  OnFind = FindDialog1Find
end
object ReplaceDialog1: TReplaceDialog
end
end
```

You can see the choices this program offers by looking at its code (see Listing 12.18) or, even better, by running it. I'll just highlight a couple of points. The first is the use of the Apply button in the second Font dialog box (see Figure 12.15). The code associated with this button is:

```
procedure TCommDlgForm.FontDialog2Apply(
    Sender: TObject; Wnd: Word);
begin
  Memo1.Font := FontDialog2.Font;
end;
```

LISTING 12.18: The source code of the COMMDLG1 example

```
unit Cdlgtest;

interface

uses
  WinTypes, WinProcs, Classes, Graphics, Forms, Controls,
  Menus, StdCtrls, Dialogs;

type
  TCommDlgForm = class(TForm)
    OpenDialog1: TOpenDialog;
    SaveDialog1: TSaveDialog;
    FontDialog1: TFontDialog;
    ColorDialog1: TColorDialog;
    MainMenu1: TMainMenu;
    {menu items...}
    Memo1: TMemo;
    FontDialog2: TFontDialog;
    PrintDialog1: TPrintDialog;
    PrinterSetupDialog1: TPrinterSetupDialog;
    FindDialog1: TFindDialog;
    ReplaceDialog1: TReplaceDialog;
    procedure TextFiles1Click(Sender: TObject);
    procedure Anynewfile1Click(Sender: TObject);
    procedure MultipleSelection1Click(Sender: TObject);
    procedure TextFile1Click(Sender: TObject);
    procedure AnyFile1Click(Sender: TObject);
    procedure OnlyTrueType1Click(Sender: TObject);
    procedure NoEffects1Click(Sender: TObject);
    procedure NoStyle1Click(Sender: TObject);
    procedure FontDialog2Apply(Sender: TObject; Wnd: Word);
    procedure Apply1Click(Sender: TObject);
    procedure Standard1Click(Sender: TObject);
    procedure FullOpen1Click(Sender: TObject);
    procedure NoFullOpen1Click(Sender: TObject);
    procedure AboutCommonDialogsTest1Click(Sender: TObject);
    procedure Print2Click(Sender: TObject);
    procedure PrinterSetup1Click(Sender: TObject);
    procedure Search2Click(Sender: TObject);
    procedure Replace1Click(Sender: TObject);
    procedure FindDialog1Find(Sender: TObject);
    procedure ReplaceDialog1Replace(Sender: TObject);
    procedure ReplaceDialog1Find(Sender: TObject);
  private
    { Private declarations }
  public
    { Public declarations }
  end;
```

LISTING 12.18: The source code of the COMMDLG1 example (continued)

```
var
  CommDlgForm: TCommDlgForm;

implementation

{$R *.DFM}

procedure TCommDlgForm.TextFiles1Click(Sender: TObject);
begin
  with OpenDialog1 do
  begin
    Filter := 'Text File (*.txt)|*.txt';
    DefaultExt := 'txt';
    Filename := '';
    Options := [ofHideReadOnly, ofFileMustExist,
      ofPathMustExist];
    if Execute then
      if ofExtensionDifferent in Options then
        MessageDlg ('Not a file with the .TXT extension',
          mtError, [mbOK], 0)
      else
        Memo1.Lines.LoadFromFile (FileName);
  end;
end;

procedure TCommDlgForm.Anynewfile1Click(Sender: TObject);
begin
  with OpenDialog1 do
  begin
    Filter := 'Any File (*.*)|*.*';
    FileName := '';
    Options := [];
    if Execute then
      Memo1.Lines.LoadFromFile (FileName);
  end;
end;

procedure TCommDlgForm.MultipleSelection1Click(Sender: TObject);
var
  i: Integer;
begin
  with OpenDialog1 do
  begin
    Filter := 'Text File (*.txt)|*.txt|Any File (*.*)|*.*';
    Filename := '';
    Options := [ofAllowMultiSelect, ofPathMustExist,
      ofCreatePrompt];
    if Execute then
      for i := 0 to Files.Count - 1 do
        if MessageDlg ('Open file ' + Files.Strings [i] + '?',
          mtConfirmation, [mbYes, mbNo], 0) = IDYES then
```

12

```
            Memo1.Lines.LoadFromFile (Files.Strings [i]);
      end;
end;

procedure TCommDlgForm.TextFile1Click(Sender: TObject);
begin
  with SaveDialog1 do
  begin
    Filter := 'Text File (*.txt)|*.txt';
    DefaultExt := 'txt';
    Filename := '';
    Options := [ofHideReadOnly, ofPathMustExist];
    if Execute then
      if ofExtensionDifferent in Options then
        MessageDlg ('Not a txt extension', mtError, [mbOK], 0)
      else
        Memo1.Lines.SaveToFile (FileName);
  end;
end;

procedure TCommDlgForm.AnyFile1Click(Sender: TObject);
begin
  with SaveDialog1 do
  begin
    Filter := 'Any File (*.*)|*.*';
    Filename := '';
    Options := [ofPathMustExist];
    if Execute then
      Memo1.Lines.SaveToFile (FileName);
  end;
end;

procedure TCommDlgForm.OnlyTrueType1Click(Sender: TObject);
begin
  with FontDialog1 do
  begin
    Options := [fdEffects, fdTrueTypeOnly, fdForceFontExist];
    if Execute then
      Memo1.Font := Font;
  end;
end;

procedure TCommDlgForm.NoEffects1Click(Sender: TObject);
begin
  with FontDialog1 do
  begin
    Options := [fdForceFontExist];
    if Execute then
      Memo1.Font := Font;
  end;
end;
```

LISTING 12.18: The source code of the COMMDLG1 example (continued)

```
procedure TCommDlgForm.NoStyle1Click(Sender: TObject);
begin
  with FontDialog1 do
  begin
    Options := [fdEffects, fdNoOEMFonts, fdNoStyleSel,
        fdNoSizeSel, fdForceFontExist];
    if Execute then
      Memo1.Font := Font;
  end;
end;

procedure TCommDlgForm.FontDialog2Apply(
  Sender: TObject; Wnd: Word);
begin
  Memo1.Font := FontDialog2.Font;
end;

procedure TCommDlgForm.Apply1Click(Sender: TObject);
begin
  with FontDialog2 do
  begin
    Options := [fdEffects, fdForceFontExist];
    Execute;
  end;
end;

procedure TCommDlgForm.Standard1Click(Sender: TObject);
begin
  with ColorDialog1 do
  begin
    Options := [];
    if Execute then
      CommDlgForm.Color := Color;
  end;
end;

procedure TCommDlgForm.FullOpen1Click(Sender: TObject);
begin
  with ColorDialog1 do
  begin
    Options := [cdFullOpen];
    {ColorDialog1.Left := 80;}
    if Execute then
      CommDlgForm.Color := Color;
  end;
end;

procedure TCommDlgForm.NoFullOpen1Click(Sender: TObject);
begin
  with ColorDialog1 do
  begin
    Options := [cdPreventFullOpen];
```

LISTING 12.18: The source code of the COMMDLG1 example (continued)

```
    if Execute then
      CommDlgForm.Color := Color;
  end;
end;

procedure TCommDlgForm.AboutCommonDialogsTest1Click(
  Sender: TObject);
begin
  MessageDlg ('The ''Common Dialogs Test'' application' +
    ' has been written' + Chr(13) +
    'for the book "Mastering Delphi" by Marco Cantù',
    mtInformation, [mbOk], 0);
end;

procedure TCommDlgForm.Print2Click(Sender: TObject);
begin
  PrintDialog1.Execute;
end;

procedure TCommDlgForm.PrinterSetup1Click(Sender: TObject);
begin
  PrinterSetupDialog1.Execute;
end;

procedure TCommDlgForm.Search2Click(Sender: TObject);
begin
  FindDialog1.Execute;
end;

procedure TCommDlgForm.Replace1Click(Sender: TObject);
begin
  ReplaceDialog1.Execute;
end;

procedure TCommDlgForm.FindDialog1Find(Sender: TObject);
var
  FoundPos: Integer;      {Substring position/String found}
  Before: Integer;        {Text in previous lines}
  I: Integer;             {Loop counter}
begin
  {search the string}
  Before := 0;
  for I := 0 to Memo1.Lines.Count - 1 do
  begin
    FoundPos := Pos (FindDialog1.FindText, Memo1.Lines[I]);
    if FoundPos > 0 then
      break
    else
      Before := Before + Length (Memo1.Lines[I]) + 2;
  end;
  if FoundPos > 0 then
```

12

LISTING 12.18: The source code of the COMMDLG1 example (continued)

```
  begin
    {activate the component, and select the text}
    BringToFront;
    ActiveControl := Memo1;
    Memo1.SelStart := Before + FoundPos - 1;
    Memo1.SelLength := Length(FindDialog1.FindText);
  end
  else
  begin
    MessageDlg ('Text not found', mtInformation, [mbOK], 0);
  end;
end;

procedure TCommDlgForm.ReplaceDialog1Replace(Sender: TObject);
var
  FoundPos: Integer;      {Substring position/String found}
  Before: Integer;        {Text in previous lines}
  I: Integer;             {Loop counter}
begin
  {search the string}
  Before := 0;
  for I := 0 to Memo1.Lines.Count - 1 do
  begin
    FoundPos := Pos (ReplaceDialog1.FindText, Memo1.Lines[I]);
    if FoundPos > 0 then
      break
    else
      Before := Before + Length (Memo1.Lines[I]) + 2;
  end;
  if FoundPos > 0 then
  begin
    {activate the component, and select the text}
    BringToFront;
    ActiveControl := Memo1;
    Memo1.SelStart := Before + FoundPos - 1;
    Memo1.SelLength := Length (ReplaceDialog1.FindText);
    Memo1.SelText := ReplaceDialog1.ReplaceText;
  end
  else
  begin
    MessageDlg ('Text not found', mtInformation, [mbOK], 0);
  end;
end;

procedure TCommDlgForm.ReplaceDialog1Find(Sender: TObject);
begin
  FindDialog1.FindText := ReplaceDialog1.FindText;
  FindDialog1Find (Sender);
end;

end.
```

Notice that there is no flag to add the Apply button to the dialog box; you need only specify a handler for the event, as I've done above. Consider also that the button is part of the dialog box, but its event handler is written in the program's main form. This is really useful since we can change the behavior of the dialog box without having to customize the component.

Another interesting behavior is that of the Color selection dialog box. You can open only the basic portion of the dialog box (see Figure 12.14) and let the user expand it by clicking on a button; display it already fully open (see Figure 12.16); or open only the first part, preventing the user from expanding it.

FIGURE 12.16:

The fully expanded version of the Color selection dialog box

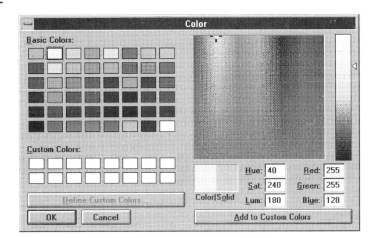

The Open dialog box has a strange feature, too. In the final version, you can select multiple files; then the program asks you to confirm the open operation for each of them. Of course, having a single memo as a viewer, at the end of the operation you'll see only the last file opened.

Finally, notice that I've implemented a bare version of the Find and Replace methods (they just find or replace the first occurrence of the given text, although it wouldn't be very difficult to improve their code). These methods are connected to the buttons of the two dialog boxes, as in the case of the Apply button in the Font dialog box. (By the way, you can find a more complete example of search-and-re-place commands in the Delphi TEXTEDIT demo program, available in the \DEL-PHI\DEMOS\TEXTEDIT directory.)

As you can see in the source code, the FindDialog1Find method looks for the code, scanning each line of the memo. This is the only way we have of performing a string search with the Pos function, which works for Pascal strings up to 255 characters. Of course, there are other solutions, including the use of one of the functions for a null-terminated string.

The find operation for the Replace dialog box is so similar that I could simply call it after an assignment. The best solution would probably have been to write a single Find method to be called to implement the code of the Replace routine, as well.

Other variations in the behavior of these dialog boxes include the presence of a Help button, of optional check boxes, and even of optional portions of the dialog box itself. You can usually choose between a normal and 3D effect, ask users to confirm their choice (particularly in the file-related dialog boxes), and so on. Since I'm probably already boring you, I'll stop here. However, I suggest you explore this subject, first by studying the details of the example and then by adding further customized versions of the common dialog boxes.

Message Boxes Parade

Another set of predefined dialog boxes is the group of Delphi message boxes and input boxes. There are basically six Delphi procedures and functions you can use to display simple dialog boxes:

- MessageDlg shows a customizable message box, with one or more buttons and usually a bitmap. We have used this message box quite often in the past examples.

- MessageDlgPos is similar to MessageDlg. The difference is that the message box is displayed in a given position, not in the center of the screen.

- ShowMessage displays a simpler message box, with the application name as the caption, and just an OK button.

- ShowMessagePos is the same, aside from the fact that you indicate the position of the message box.

- InputBox asks the user to input a string. You provide the caption, the query, and a default string.

- InputQuery asks the user to input a string. The only difference between this and InputBox is in the syntax. Input Query has a Boolean return value that indicates whether the user has pressed the OK or Cancel button.

The first two message boxes are more complex and have a higher number of parameters, including a set of buttons, the type of message box, a help context code (useful if there is a Help button), and eventually the position.

The MessageDlg and MessageDlgPos functions can display different types of message boxes. If you use the `mtWarning` parameter, a program displays a message box with a yellow exclamation point, indicating to the user that there are some risks to consider (such as deleting a file, or not saving it):

Using `mtError`, Delphi shows a message box with a red stop sign to indicate that something went wrong in the program or in the output from the user:

With `mtInformation` we get a message box with a blue *i*, used to display generic information to the user:

The `mtConfirmation` flag generates a message box with a green question mark, typically used together with Yes and No buttons:

Finally, the `mtCustom` flag displays a message box with no bitmap, which uses as its caption the name of the application's executable file:

I've taken all of these images from the following MBPARADE example. In fact, to let you see the various choices of message boxes available in Delphi, I've written another sample program, with a similar approach to the preceding COMMDLG1 example. In this example, MBPARADE, you have a high number of choices (radio buttons, check boxes, edit boxes, and spin edit controls) to set before you press one of the buttons that display a message box. You can get an idea of the program by looking at its form in Figure 12.17.

For a MessageDlg box, you can choose the style of the message box, its buttons (adding, in addition, the Help button), and the message. The two positional functions also use the values of the two spin edit controls. What's interesting is that if you choose a custom type and only the OK button, the MessageDlg box degrades to a ShowMessage box.

The input boxes use only the values in the three edit boxes in the second half of the form. Aside from the fact that the code used to execute them is different, their output is exactly the same (see Figure 12.18):

```
EditValue.Text := InputBox (EditCaption.Text,
    EditPrompt.Text, EditValue.Text);
```

```
Text := EditValue.Text;
if InputQuery (EditCaption.Text, EditPrompt.Text, Text) then
  EditValue.Text := Text;
```

Having said this, I think you can easily understand the rest of the source code by looking at Listing 12.19. To understand what goes on, refer to the simplified textual description of the form in Listing 12.20.

12

FIGURE 12.17:

A message box displayed in a specified position with the MessageDlgPos function. Notice the correspondence between the parameters on the main form and the resulting message box.

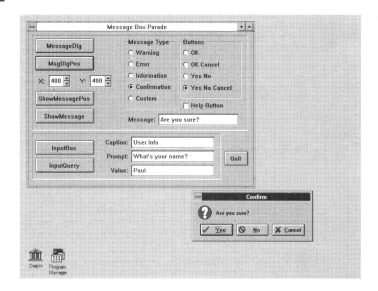

FIGURE 12.18:

The InputQuery message box

LISTING 12.19: The source code of the MBPARADE example

```
unit Mb_f;

interface

uses
  SysUtils, WinTypes, WinProcs, Messages, Classes,
  Graphics, Controls,  Forms, Dialogs, StdCtrls, ExtCtrls,
  Spin, Buttons;

type
  TForm1 = class(TForm)
    ButtonMessageDlg: TButton;
    ButtonShowMessage: TButton;
    ButtonShowMessagePos: TButton;
    GroupBox1: TGroupBox;
    RadioWarning: TRadioButton;
    RadioError: TRadioButton;
    RadioInformation: TRadioButton;
    RadioConfirmation: TRadioButton;
    Bevel1: TBevel;
    Edit1: TEdit;
    Label1: TLabel;
    RadioCustom: TRadioButton;
    GroupBox2: TGroupBox;
    RadioOK: TRadioButton;
    RadioOKCancel: TRadioButton;
    RadioYesNo: TRadioButton;
    RadioYesNoCancel: TRadioButton;
    CheckHelp: TCheckBox;
    ButtonMsgDlgPos: TButton;
    SpinY: TSpinEdit;
    SpinX: TSpinEdit;
    Label2: TLabel;
    Label3: TLabel;
    ButtonInputBox: TButton;
    ButtonInputQuery: TButton;
    Bevel2: TBevel;
    EditCaption: TEdit;
    EditPrompt: TEdit;
    EditValue: TEdit;
    Label4: TLabel;
    Label5: TLabel;
    Label6: TLabel;
    ButtonQuit: TButton;
    procedure ButtonMessageDlgClick(Sender: TObject);
    procedure RadioWarningClick(Sender: TObject);
    procedure RadioErrorClick(Sender: TObject);
    procedure RadioInformationClick(Sender: TObject);
    procedure RadioConfirmationClick(Sender: TObject);
    procedure RadioCustomClick(Sender: TObject)
```

LISTING 12.19: The source code of the MBPARADE example (continued)

```
    procedure FormCreate(Sender: TObject);
    procedure RadioOKClick(Sender: TObject);
    procedure RadioOKCancelClick(Sender: TObject);
    procedure RadioYesNoClick(Sender: TObject);
    procedure RadioYesNoCancelClick(Sender: TObject);
    procedure ButtonMsgDlgPosClick(Sender: TObject);
    procedure ButtonShowMessageClick(Sender: TObject);
    procedure ButtonShowMessagePosClick(Sender: TObject);
    procedure ButtonInputBoxClick(Sender: TObject);
    procedure ButtonInputQueryClick(Sender: TObject);
    procedure ButtonQuitClick(Sender: TObject);
  private
    { Private declarations }
    MsgDlgType: TMsgDlgType;
    MsgButtons: TMsgDlgButtons;
  public
    { Public declarations }
  end;

var
  Form1: TForm1;

implementation

{$R *.DFM}

procedure TForm1.FormCreate(Sender: TObject);
begin
  MsgDlgType := mtWarning;
  MsgButtons := [mbOk];
end;

procedure TForm1.ButtonMessageDlgClick(Sender: TObject);
begin
  if CheckHelp.Checked then
    Include (MsgButtons, mbHelp);
  MessageDlg (Edit1.Text, MsgDlgType, MsgButtons, 0);
end;

procedure TForm1.RadioWarningClick(Sender: TObject);
begin
  MsgDlgType := mtWarning;
end;

procedure TForm1.RadioErrorClick(Sender: TObject);
begin
  MsgDlgType := mtError;
end;
```

12

LISTING 12.19: The source code of the MBPARADE example (continued)

```
procedure TForm1.RadioInformationClick(Sender: TObject);
begin
  MsgDlgType := mtInformation;
end;

procedure TForm1.RadioConfirmationClick(Sender: TObject);
begin
  MsgDlgType := mtConfirmation;
end;

procedure TForm1.RadioCustomClick(Sender: TObject);
begin
  MsgDlgType := mtCustom;
end;

procedure TForm1.RadioOKClick(Sender: TObject);
begin
  MsgButtons := [mbOk];
end;

procedure TForm1.RadioOKCancelClick(Sender: TObject);
begin
  MsgButtons := mbOkCancel;
end;

procedure TForm1.RadioYesNoClick(Sender: TObject);
begin
  MsgButtons := [mbYes, mbNo];
end;

procedure TForm1.RadioYesNoCancelClick(Sender: TObject);
begin
    MsgButtons := mbYesNoCancel;
end;

procedure TForm1.ButtonMsgDlgPosClick(Sender: TObject);
begin
  if CheckHelp.Checked then
    Include (MsgButtons, mbHelp);
  MessageDlgPos (Edit1.Text, MsgDlgType, MsgButtons,
    0, SpinX.Value, SpinY.Value);
end;

procedure TForm1.ButtonShowMessageClick(Sender: TObject);
begin
  ShowMessage (Edit1.Text);
end;

procedure TForm1.ButtonShowMessagePosClick(Sender: TObject);
begin
  ShowMessagePos (Edit1.Text, SpinX.Value, SpinY.Value);
end;
```

LISTING 12.19: The source code of the MBPARADE example (continued)

```
procedure TForm1.ButtonInputBoxClick(Sender: TObject);
begin
  EditValue.Text := InputBox (EditCaption.Text,
    EditPrompt.Text, EditValue.Text);
end;

procedure TForm1.ButtonInputQueryClick(Sender: TObject);
var
  Text: String;
begin
  Text := EditValue.Text;
  if InputQuery (EditCaption.Text, EditPrompt.Text, Text) then
    EditValue.Text := Text;
end;

procedure TForm1.ButtonQuitClick(Sender: TObject);
begin
  Close;
end;

end.
```

LISTING 12.20: The simplified textual description of the MBPARADE form (only a few components are described)

```
object Form1: TForm1
  Caption = 'Message Box Parade'
  OnCreate = FormCreate
  object ButtonMessageDlg: TButton
    Caption = 'MessageDlg'
    Default = True
    OnClick = ButtonMessageDlgClick
  end
  object ButtonShowMessage: TButton...
  object ButtonShowMessagePos: TButton...
  object GroupBox1: TGroupBox
    Caption = 'Message Type'
    object RadioWarning: TRadioButton
      Caption = 'Warning'
      Checked = True
      OnClick = RadioWarningClick
    end
    object RadioError: TRadioButton...
    object RadioInformation: TRadioButton...
    object RadioConfirmation: TRadioButton...
    object RadioCustom: TRadioButton...
  end
```

LISTING 12.20:   The simplified textual description of the MBPARADE form
(continued)

```
object Edit1: TEdit
  Text = 'Hello'
end
object GroupBox2: TGroupBox
  Caption = 'Buttons'
  object RadioOK: TRadioButton
    TabStop = True
    Caption = 'OK'
    Checked = True
    OnClick = RadioOKClick
  end
  object RadioOKCancel: TRadioButton...
  object RadioYesNo: TRadioButton...
  object RadioYesNoCancel: TRadioButton...
end
object CheckHelp: TCheckBox
  Caption = 'Help Button'
end
object ButtonMsgDlgPos: TButton...
object SpinY: TSpinEdit
  Increment = 10
  MaxLength = 3
  MaxValue = 400
  MinValue = 1
  Value = 100
end
object SpinX: TSpinEdit
  {as above, beside:}
  MaxValue = 500
end
object ButtonInputBox: TButton...
object ButtonInputQuery: TButton...
object EditCaption: TEdit
  Text = 'User Info'
end
object EditPrompt: TEdit
  Text = 'What'#39's your name?'
end
object EditValue: TEdit
  Text = 'Paul'
end
object ButtonQuit: TButton...
end
```

12

Customizing the Message Boxes   Delphi message boxes have some default elements that might not suit your needs. What if you do not want the glyph displayed? What if you want to use the new button style? The behavior of these message boxes depends on some constants in the DIALOGS unit that defines them:

```
const
  MsgDlgMinWidth = 150;
  MsgDlgMinHeight = 55;
  MsgDlgButtonStyle: TButtonStyle = bsAutoDetect;
  MsgDlgGlyphs: Boolean = True;
  MsgDlgBtnSize: TPoint = (X: 77; Y: 27);
```

What if you want to change one of these values? A useful suggestion is to change the value in the unit's source code and recompile it, adding the new version to the Delphi library.

However, since some of these constants are typed constants and they are in the unit's interface, you can simply access them and change their value at run-time. Remember, in fact, that the value of a typed constant in Pascal is not always…constant.

For example, in the BIGMB example, I've written the following code:

```
procedure TForm1.BitBtn1Click(Sender: TObject);
begin
  MsgDlgButtonStyle := bsNew;
  MsgDlgGlyphs := False;
  MsgDlgBtnSize := Point (300, 200);
  MessageDlg ('Strange button, isn''t it?',
    mtInformation, [mbOK], 0);
end;
```

Executing it produces a message box with a very big button that uses the new 3D style and has no glyph (see Figure 12.19).

Delphi Template Dialog Boxes

Another source of standard dialog boxes is the Form Gallery, which has a number of predefined templates. For example, there is a default dialog box you can use to ask for a password in input, as we saw in Chapter 3, or a standard About box.

FIGURE 12.19:

The message box with a big button produced by the BIGMB example

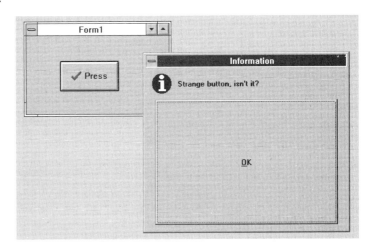

In my opinion, however, even more important are the message box schemes, such as the two standard dialog boxes with buttons arranged below or on the right of the form (see Figure 12.20) and the multipage dialog boxes. The idea behind templates is to provide a starting point for the design of the form, as well as a little predefined code.

12

FIGURE 12.20:
An example of a template-generated dialog box, the standard dialog box with the buttons on the right

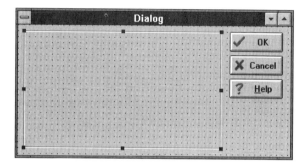

The same approach can be further extended. If you plan to use similar dialog boxes in different applications, you can store them in templates and later reuse both their design and their code. This might be particularly important in an environment with many programmers, some of whom might become template and component builders for the rest of the group.

The Dialog Expert (Single Page)

As an alternative to predefined templates, you can use the simple Dialog Expert tool (or even the Database Form Expert, turning the form into a dialog box afterward). The Dialog Expert can be considered more a learning tool for programmers who want to learn about building add-on Experts than a tool for end users. However, it works, why not use it?

As I mentioned in Chapter 3, when you run the Dialog Expert, you have three choices (see Figure 12.21): a single-page dialog box or a multipage dialog box using two different techniques. Since multipage forms are the topic of the next chapter, for the moment I'll discuss only the single-page dialog boxes, although there isn't much to say.

When you have chosen this option, the Dialog Expert only asks you the position of the buttons, if any. Notice that the form you build this way is slightly different from the standard dialog box built using the templates (as you can see by comparing Figure 12.21 with Figure 12.20).

FIGURE 12.21:

You can use the Dialog Expert to build a simple dialog box. Here are the two steps and the result.

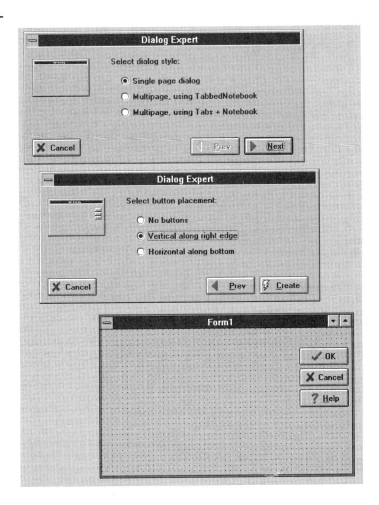

A Dialog Box as a Main Window

12

When the aim of the main form of an application is to host a number of components, you might want to disable the default resizing feature, selecting the bsFixed value for the form's BorderStyle property. An interesting alternative to a fixed-size main form is a dialog box. The use of a dialog box as the main window of an application is quite common, particularly for simple programs. Using Delphi, it's easy to create such a dialog box. You only need to set the BorderStyle property of the main (or only) form of the application to bsDialog.

You can see the result of this operation in Figure 12.22, where a new version of the first example of the PHONE series uses a dialog box as the main form. Compare it to the same form in Figure 12.1. The same change to the style of the border takes place for the secondary form. There is no other new code at all, only a change in the BorderStyle property of the two forms, as you can see in the MAINDLG1 example on the companion disk.

FIGURE 12.22:

A dialog box as a main window

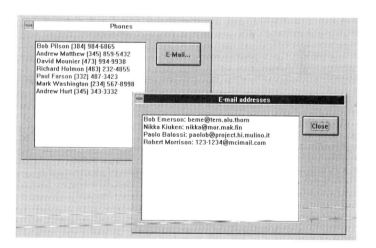

This change was simple, and you can change many other programs in a similar way. Not all of them, however. In fact, a problem arises, and not a minor one: a dialog box cannot have a menu. To be more precise, a dialog box with the typical dialog border does not paint its menu properly. This is basically a Windows problem (nothing to do with Delphi).

To avoid worse problems, if you add a menu to a form with the dialog border, Delphi simply ignores the existence of the menu. With a trick based on the call of two Windows API functions, we can indeed bypass the limitations imposed by Delphi and build a dialog box with a menu not properly painted, as you can see in Figure 12.23.

How have I accomplished this silly effect? Simply with two lines of code, used to set the form's menu using the SetMenu API call:

```
procedure TForm1.FormCreate(Sender: TObject);
begin
  SetMenu (Form1.Handle, MainMenu1.Handle);
  DrawMenuBar (Form1.Handle);
end;
```

You can test how badly this program behaves using the MAINDLG2 example, which is the same program as MAINDLG1 with a simple (and not working) menu added. Basically, the drawing on the screen replacing the regular menu bar depends on the image present on the screen when the form is first painted.

The output is really very bad, so what I've shown you above is an example of what you should avoid. The Delphi solution—better no menu than a wrong one—is nice,

FIGURE 12.23:

Windows does not properly paint the menu of a dialog box

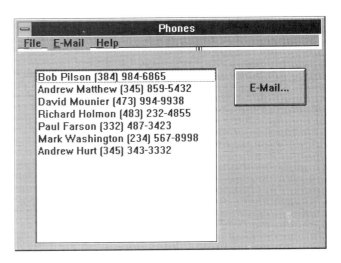

but it is not really a solution. I'll try to show you how to solve—or, better, circumvent—this problem in the next section. Note only that this glitch affects every dialog box, but it becomes a problem only when you use a dialog box as a main form. No user, in fact, will expect to find a menu in a secondary dialog box.

How to Add a Menu to a Dialog Box

In Windows, a dialog box with a menu must not use the `ds_ModalFrame` style because "the menu is not painted properly when this style is specified." This is stated in the Windows API documentation. So in Windows, you can create dialog boxes without the typical border and add a menu to them. However, they won't look like a dialog boxes.

NOTE This problem affected each version of Windows up to and including Windows 3.1 (and Windows for Workgroups 3.11). The new version of the operating environment, Windows 95, shouldn't have this problem anymore, making this section of the book obsolete. The same happens in Windows NT 3.5.

In Delphi, you simply choose between a form and a dialog box by selecting the proper frame. Therefore, by default, you should use a dialog frame only when the form has no menu. To summarize some of the ideas on menus described in the preceding sections, the following table presents a scheme of how you can use menus in secondary forms and dialog boxes:

Type of Form	Modal	Modeless
Secondary Form	Its own menu	Its own menu or menu merging
Dialog Box	None (or a fake menu)	No menu or menu merging

If we want to add a menu to a dialog, particularly when it is used as a main window, we must devise some strategy to solve the output problem of Figure 12.23.

Here are some choices:

- Use no menu at all.

- Add the menu commands to the system menu. This is not too difficult, but since it is not common, your application's users might take some time to discover how to reach these menu commands. By the way, handling the system menu in Delphi is not very easy.

- Use a pop-up menu instead. This is even better but users still might not immediately get used to this approach. This and the previous solution can be merged to increase the chances that a user will find the menu.

- Use a status bar with local menus. This is not standard but might work.

- Build a fake menu. If a fake menu has exactly the same look and feel as the Windows menus, this is the perfect solution. But I imagine you already suspect this is not very easy, and you are right. No good solution comes for free. But as I'll show you in an example, it is probably easier than you think.

The easiest solution is to replace the standard menu with a pop-up menu. Once you have changed a form's style to a dialog box, you can open its menu in the Menu Builder, save the whole structure as a temporary template, delete the main menu, create a new pop-up menu, and use the temporary template to rebuild it. Once you have the menu, you only need to select it in the form's PopupMenu property, as you can see in Figure 12.24.

Using the System Menu

A second solution is to add the menu commands of the pop-up menu to the system menu. Just proceed as before, creating a pop-up menu (you can see the description of the form in Listing 12.21), and then write this code to add its items to the system menu when the form is created:

```
procedure TForm1.FormCreate(Sender: TObject);
begin
  AppendMenu (GetSystemMenu (Handle, FALSE),
    MF_SEPARATOR, 0, '');
  AppendMenu (GetSystemMenu (Handle, FALSE),
    MF_POPUP, PopupMenu1.Handle, 'Menu');
end;
```

FIGURE 12.24:

A pop-up menu can replace the standard menu for a dialog box, as in DLGMENU1.

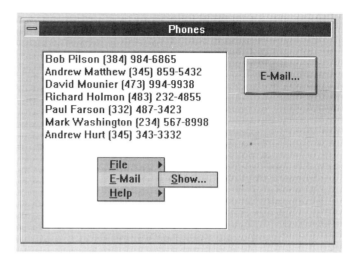

LISTING 12.21: The textual description of the main form of the DLGMENU1 example

```
object Form1: TForm1
  BorderStyle = bsDialog
  Caption = 'Phones'
  PopupMenu = PopupMenu1
  OnCreate = FormCreate
  object ListBox1: TListBox
    Items.Strings = (...)
  end
  object Button1: TButton
    Caption = 'E-Mail...'
    OnClick = Button1Click
  end
  object PopupMenu1: TPopupMenu
    {as in Listing 12.7 -- here in short:}
    object File1: TMenuItem
      object New1: TMenuItem
      object Open1: TMenuItem
      object Save1: TMenuItem
      object Saveas1: TMenuItem
      object N1: TMenuItem
      object Exit1: TMenuItem
    object EMail1: TMenuItem
      object Show1: TMenuItem
    object Help1: TMenuItem
      object AboutPhones1: TMenuItem
  end
end
```

This OnCreate method contains two calls to the Windows API AppendMenu function and two calls to the GetSystemMenu API function. The first appends a menu item to the end of the menu passed as a parameter. In this case, the parameter is the system menu—that is, the return value of the other API function.

With the second statement, I've added the whole pop-up menu to an item named *Menu*, thus building a second-level pull-down:

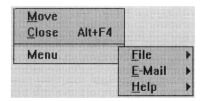

As a better alternative, you can add any of the pull-down menus of the pop-up menu to the system menu, using this code:

```
procedure TForm1.FormCreate(Sender: TObject);
var
  StrTemp: array [0..50] of Char;
begin
  {add a separator to the system menu}
  AppendMenu (GetSystemMenu (Handle, FALSE),
    MF_SEPARATOR, 0, '');

{add pop-up items to the system menu}
  AppendMenu (GetSystemMenu (Handle, FALSE),
    MF_POPUP, File1.Handle, StrPCopy (StrTemp, File1.Caption));
  AppendMenu (GetSystemMenu (Handle, FALSE),
    MF_POPUP, EMail1.Handle, StrPCopy (StrTemp, EMail1.Caption));
  AppendMenu (GetSystemMenu (Handle, FALSE),
    MF_POPUP, Help1.Handle, StrPCopy (StrTemp, Help1.Caption));
end;
```

In this case, each element of the pop-up is separately added to the system menu, using its caption as the new caption:

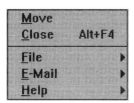

The only problem with the above code is the data-type conversion from the Pascal string returned by the Caption property to the PChar string required by the Append-Menu API function. Once you have added the menu items to the system menu, using one of the two approaches, you need to handle them. In fact, Delphi doesn't automatically call the events related to the OnClick events of these system menu commands.

We must handle the commands of the system menu (see Figure 12.25) using the Windows wm_SysCommand message, and if they are indeed commands related to menu items we have added ourselves, we must activate their OnClick event. To accomplish this, we must manually add a new message-response method to the form class:

```
type
  TForm1 = class(TForm)
    ...
  public
    procedure WMSysCommand (var Msg: TMessage);
      message wm_SysCommand;
end;
```

The code of this procedure is not very complex. Its core is the call to the FindItem method of the TMenu class (and subclasses):

```
procedure TForm1.WMSysCommand (var Msg: TMessage);
var
  Item: TMenuItem;
begin
  Item := PopupMenu1.FindItem (Msg.WParam, fkCommand);
  if not (Item = nil) then
    Item.Click;
  inherited;
end;
```

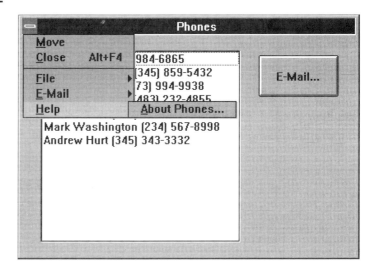

The WParam field of the message passed to the WMSysCommand procedure holds the command of the menu item being called, as it happens, in the corresponding WMCommand procedure, related to the items of the menu bar. Besides using this value to search for the corresponding TMenuItem object, you can simply test whether this code corresponds to a certain value. This is particularly true if you want to handle one of the predefined menu items of the system menu that have special codes for this identifier, such as sc_Close, sc_Minimize, sc_Maximize, and so on. For more information, you can see the description of the wm_SysCommand message in Delphi's Windows API help.

Once you have written this code, you can provide a method for each menu item, as usual. You can later decide whether you want to let the user select the pop-up menu or leave it hidden (that is, not connect it to the form's PopupMenu property). The full source code of the DLGMENU1 example is in Listing 12.22.

LISTING 12.22: The full listing of the main form of the DLGMENU1 example

```
unit Unit1;

interface

uses WinTypes, WinProcs, Classes, Graphics, Forms, Controls,
  Unit2, Menus, StdCtrls, Messages, SysUtils, Dialogs;

type
  TForm1 = class(TForm)
    ListBox1: TListBox;
    Button1: TButton;
    PopupMenu1: TPopupMenu;
    File1: TMenuItem;
    Exit1: TMenuItem;
    N1: TMenuItem;
    Saveas1: TMenuItem;
    Save1: TMenuItem;
    Open1: TMenuItem;
    New1: TMenuItem;
    EMail1: TMenuItem;
    Show1: TMenuItem;
    Help1: TMenuItem;
    AboutPhones1: TMenuItem;
    procedure Button1Click(Sender: TObject);
    procedure Show1Click(Sender: TObject);
    procedure FormCreate(Sender: TObject);
    procedure Exit1Click(Sender: TObject);
    procedure AboutPhones1Click(Sender: TObject);

  private
    { Private declarations }
  public
    procedure WMSysCommand (var Msg: TMessage);
      message wm_SysCommand;

    { Public declarations }
  end;

var
  Form1: TForm1;

implementation

{$R *.DFM}

procedure TForm1.Button1Click(Sender: TObject);
begin
  Form2.ShowModal;
end;
```

LISTING 12.22: The full listing of the main form of the DLGMENU1 example (continued)

```
procedure TForm1.FormCreate(Sender: TObject);
var
  StrTemp: array [0..50] of Char;
begin
  {add a separator to the system menu}
  AppendMenu (GetSystemMenu (Handle, FALSE),
    MF_SEPARATOR, 0, '');

  {add pop-up to the system menu, first version: }
{   AppendMenu (GetSystemMenu (Handle, FALSE),
    MF_POPUP, PopupMenu1.Handle, 'Menu');        }

  {add pop-up items to the system menu, second version:}
  AppendMenu (GetSystemMenu (Handle, FALSE),
    MF_POPUP, File1.Handle, StrPCopy (StrTemp, File1.Caption));
  AppendMenu (GetSystemMenu (Handle, FALSE),
    MF_POPUP, EMail1.Handle, StrPCopy (StrTemp, EMail1.Caption));
  AppendMenu (GetSystemMenu (Handle, FALSE),
    MF_POPUP, Help1.Handle, StrPCopy (StrTemp, Help1.Caption));
end;

procedure TForm1.WMSysCommand (var Msg: TMessage);
var
  Item: TMenuItem;
begin
  Item := PopupMenu1.FindItem (Msg.WParam, fkCommand);
  if not (Item = nil) then
    Item.Click;
  inherited;
end;

procedure TForm1.Show1Click(Sender: TObject);
begin
  Form2.ShowModal;
end;

procedure TForm1.Exit1Click(Sender: TObject);
begin
  MessageBeep ($FFFF);
end;

procedure TForm1.AboutPhones1Click(Sender: TObject);
begin
  MessageDlg ('DLGMENU1, featuring the system menu' +
    Chr(13) + 'Written by Marco Cantù, for "Mastering Delphi"',
    mtInformation, [mbOk], 0);
end;

end.
```

Building a Fake Menu

The last solution to the problems of menus in dialog boxes is to build a fake menu. There are probably several approaches to this problem. I'll just describe one of them, without devoting too much attention to some of its details and without even trying to make this example work in every case and condition.

My aim is only to show you that building a fake menu is possible and to sketch the solution. Notice that this approach can be used to solve other similar problems and that I'll be able to show you some programming techniques (such as the selection of system colors) used elsewhere in the book. Consider this an experiment, silly as it might sound, to fix a Windows problem in Delphi. Since this is not a full solution, I'll just give you some hints on the code in the text and let you refer to the example on the companion disk for the full implementation.

The basic procedure I've followed to build a fake menu bar in the DLGMENU2 example is to create some controls with the text of the various pull-down menus (that is, to build a fake menu bar) and then some pop-up menus that are displayed (as though they were pull-down menus) when you click on one of the elements of the menu bar.

I placed three small panels in the upper part of the frame and a rectangular shape under them. Then I wrote the proper text in the panels (including the ampersands and a couple of leading spaces), removed all the bevels, aligned the text to the left, and changed the background color to clMenu, the color of the menu. For the text, you should use the clMenuText color. In Figure 12.26, you can see the result of this effort in the form at design-time. Study the textual description in Listing 12.23 for a better understanding of the details.

Once this is done, you have to play with the sizes of the various components and their positions for a while to mimic a standard menu bar, at best. Some problems arise from the fact that the dialog uses a thick frame and the three-dimensional look: you have to guess at how to place a menu and which borders it is going to have. At run-time, the results are not bad: in Figure 12.27, you can see a dialog box with a menu bar!

FIGURE 12.26:

The form of the DLGMENU2 example at design-time with the fake menu

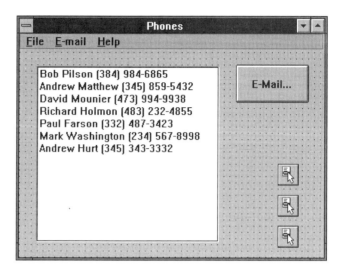

LISTING 12.23: The textual description of the main form of the DLGMENU2 example

```
object Form1: TForm1
  BorderStyle = bsDialog
  Caption = 'Phones'
  object ListBox1: TListBox
    Items.Strings = (...)
  end
  object Button1: TButton
    Caption = 'E-Mail...'
    OnClick = Button1Click
  end
  object Shape1: TShape
    Left = 0
    Top = 0
    Width = 404
    Height = 20
    Brush.Color = clMenu
    Pen.Color = clGray
    Shape = stRectangle
  end
  object Panel1: TPanel
    Left = 1
    Top = 1
    Width = 40
    Height = 18
    Alignment = taLeftJustify
    BevelOuter = bvNone
    Caption = '  &File    '
```

LISTING 12.23: The textual description of the main form of the DLGMENU2 example
(continued)

```
    Color = clMenu
    Ctl3D = False
    Font.Color = clMenuText
    Font.Height = -13
    Font.Name = 'System'
    ParentCtl3D = False
    ParentFont = False
    PopupMenu = PopupMenu1
    OnMouseDown = Panel1MouseDown
  end
  object Panel2: TPanel
    Left = 40
    Top = 1
    Width = 57
    Height = 18
    Caption = '   &E-mail   '
    {other properties as above...}
    PopupMenu = PopupMenu2
    OnMouseDown = Panel2MouseDown
  end
  object Panel3: TPanel
    Left = 96
    Top = 1
    Width = 57
    Height = 18
    {other properties as above...}
    Caption = '   &Help'
    PopupMenu = PopupMenu3
    OnMouseDown = Panel3MouseDown
  end
  object PopupMenu1: TPopupMenu
    object New2: TMenuItem
    object Open2: TMenuItem
    object Save2: TMenuItem
    object Saveas2: TMenuItem
    object N2: TMenuItem
    object Exit2: TMenuItem
  end
  object PopupMenu2: TPopupMenu
    object Show1: TMenuItem
  end
  object PopupMenu3: TPopupMenu
    object AboutPhones1: TMenuItem
  end
end
```

FIGURE 12.27:

At last we have done it: a dialog box
with a menu bar which almost
works.

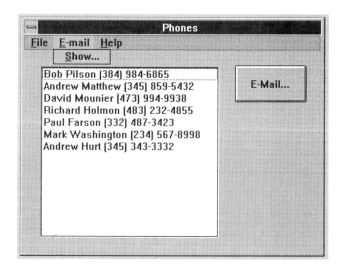

Once the menu is in place, we need to make it work properly. The idea is that when a user selects the element of the menu bar (that is, one of the small panels), a pulldown menu clone should appear. If we create three pop-up menus and then display them in the proper position, just below the menu bar, we have something similar to standard pull-down menus.

The behavior of this fake menu is not precise; you need to click on the menu items to highlight them, not just move the mouse from the menu bar to the items. But it is close enough to what we need.

Listing 12.24 presents the code used to show a fake pull-down menu when the mouse is pressed on one of the panels.

At the beginning of this code, we turn the color of the selected panel to the system highlight color. The original menu colors are set once the pop-up is removed. The remaining code computes the position of the pop-up menu so that it is just below the panel and in the same horizontal position and then converts the point from client coordinates to screen coordinates. Client coordinates start from the upper-left corner of the client area of the window—in this case, the dialog box. We need this conversion because the pop-up method used to display the menu has two parameters in screen coordinates, with an origin in the upper-left corner of the screen. The

LISTING 12.24: The Panel1MouseDown method of the DLGMENU2 example

```
procedure TForm1.Panel1MouseDown(Sender: TObject;
  Button: TMouseButton;
  Shift: TShiftState; X, Y: Integer);
var
  ClientPt, ScreenPt: TPoint;
begin
  Panel1.Color := clHighlight;
  Panel1.Font.Color := clHighLightText;
  ClientPt.x := Panel1.Left;
  ClientPt.y := Panel1.Height + Panel1.Top;
  screenPt := ClientToScreen (ClientPt);
  PopupMenu1.Popup (ScreenPt.x, ScreenPt.y);
  Panel1.Color := clMenu;
  Panel1.Font.Color := clMenuText;
end;
```

ClientToScreen function performs the conversion. (For further details refer to the full source code on the companion disk.)

As I mentioned earlier in this chapter, this example features a far-from-perfect menu, but it is good enough for its purpose. Improving it is a problem because when the pop-up menu is displayed, it captures the mouse input, so the other panels of the fake menu bar cannot receive mouse move messages. The solution, probably, is to subclass the TPopupMenu control, building a specific component.

Extensible Dialog Boxes

Some dialog boxes display a number of components to the user. At times, you can divide them into logical pages, which Delphi supports through the Notebook and TabbedNotebook components (discussed in Chapter 13). At other times, some of the dialog box controls can be temporarily hidden to help first-time users of an application.

There are basically two approaches for displaying advanced information only when the user asks for it: build a secondary dialog box, displayed when the user presses a button with an Advanced... label on it, or increase the size of the dialog box to host new controls when the user presses a More button. The second approach is certainly more interesting but requires a little more care. I'll use it to extend the first example on dialog boxes (DIALOG1) and build the MORE example.

First of all, we need to extend the dialog box with new controls: a More button and a whole new portion of the form. You can compare the new dialog box in Figure 12.28 with the old dialog box in Figure 12.11. Once you have added the new controls, you need to resize the dialog box so that the new elements are outside its visible surface.

Now we need to add some code to the application to handle the two new check boxes (this code is simple, and you can look it up in Listing 12.25) and the code to resize the form when a user clicks on the More button. To prepare the resize effect, we need a couple of integers (named OldHeight and NewHeight) to store the two different heights of the form. We can set up their values when the form is created (see Listing 12.26).

Each time the dialog box is activated (FormActivate), we have to reset its height, disable the hidden components (to avoid letting the user move to them using the Tab key), and enable the More button. This code is required so that each time the dialog box is displayed (remember that is it never destroyed, just hidden), it starts in the small configuration.

FIGURE 12.28:

The two forms of the MORE example. Notice the extensible dialog box with the More button; two more components of this form are outside the visible area.

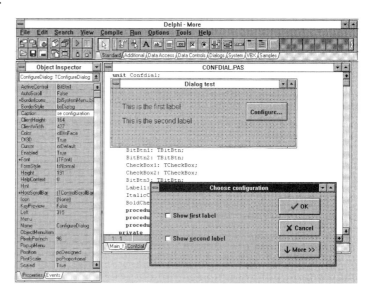

12

LISTING 12.25: The source code of the main form of the MORE example

```
unit Main_f;

interface

uses
  WinTypes, WinProcs, Classes, Graphics, Forms,
  Controls, ConfDial, StdCtrls;

type
  TForm1 = class(TForm)
    ConfigureButton: TButton;
    Label1: TLabel;
    Label2: TLabel;
    procedure ConfigureButtonClick(Sender: TObject);
  private
  public
  end;

var
  Form1: TForm1;

implementation

{$R *.DFM}

procedure TForm1.ConfigureButtonClick(Sender: TObject);
begin
  ConfigureDialog.CheckBox1.Checked := Label1.Visible;
  ConfigureDialog.CheckBox2.Checked := Label2.Visible;
  if (fsItalic in Label1.Font.Style) then
    ConfigureDialog.ItalicCheckBox.Checked := True
  else
    ConfigureDialog.ItalicCheckBox.Checked := False;
  if (fsBold in Label1.Font.Style) then
    ConfigureDialog.BoldCheckBox.Checked := True
  else
    ConfigureDialog.BoldCheckBox.Checked := False;
  if (ConfigureDialog.ShowModal = mrOk) then
    begin
      Label1.Visible := ConfigureDialog.CheckBox1.Checked;
      Label2.Visible := ConfigureDialog.CheckBox2.Checked;

      {compute the style of the first label}
      if ConfigureDialog.BoldCheckBox.Checked then
        Label1.Font.Style := [fsBold]
      else
        Label1.Font.Style := [];
      if ConfigureDialog.ItalicCheckBox.Checked then
        Label1.Font.Style := Label1.Font.Style + [fsItalic];
```

LISTING 12.25: The source code of the main form of the MORE example (continued)

```
      {copy the style to the other label}
      Label2.Font.Style := Label1.Font.Style;
    end;
end;

end.
```

LISTING 12.26: The source code of the extensible dialog box of the MORE example

```
unit Confdial;

interface

uses
  WinTypes, WinProcs, Classes, Graphics, Forms,
  Controls, Buttons, StdCtrls;

type
  TConfigureDialog = class(TForm)
    BitBtn1: TBitBtn;
    BitBtn2: TBitBtn;
    CheckBox1: TCheckBox;
    CheckBox2: TCheckBox;
    BitBtn3: TBitBtn;
    Label1: TLabel;
    ItalicCheckBox: TCheckBox;
    BoldCheckBox: TCheckBox;
    procedure BitBtn3Click(Sender: TObject);
    procedure FormCreate(Sender: TObject);
    procedure FormActivate(Sender: TObject);
  private
    { Private declarations }
  public
    OldHeight, NewHeight: Integer;
  end;

var
  ConfigureDialog: TConfigureDialog;

implementation

{$R *.DFM}

procedure TConfigureDialog.BitBtn3Click(Sender: TObject);
var
  I: Integer;
begin
  BitBtn3.Enabled := False;
```

12

```
  BoldCheckBox.Enabled := True;
  ItalicCheckBox.Enabled := True;
  for I := Height to NewHeight do
  begin
    Height := I;
    Update;
  end;
end;

procedure TConfigureDialog.FormCreate(Sender: TObject);
begin
  OldHeight := Height;
  NewHeight := 316;
end;

procedure TConfigureDialog.FormActivate(Sender: TObject);
begin
  Height := OldHeight;
  BitBtn3.Enabled := True;
  BoldCheckBox.Enabled := False;
  ItalicCheckBox.Enabled := False;
end;

end.
```

The real dialog box resizing takes place when the More button is pressed. Here is a first version:

```
  procedure TConfigureDialog.BitBtn3Click(Sender: TObject);
  begin
    BitBtn3.Enabled := False;
    BoldCheckBox.Enabled := True;
    ItalicCheckBox.Enabled := True;
    Height := NewHeight;
  end;
```

The result it produces is shown in Figure 12.29, where you can see the dialog box before and after the resizing operation. If you want a more spectacular effect, you might increase the height a pixel at a time instead of setting the final value at once. If you write a for loop, increase the height, and repaint the form each time to make the new controls appear, you get a nice effect, only a little slower. Of course, you

FIGURE 12.29:

The dialog box of the MORE example, as it starts and when it is resized when the More button is pressed

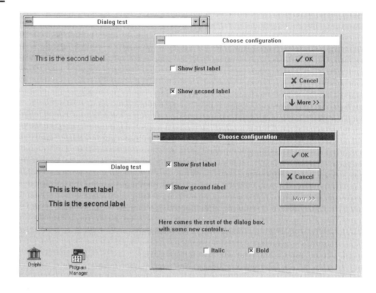

could increase the speed by changing the way the loop counter is increased:

```
for I := Height to NewHeight do
begin
  Height := I;
  Update;
end;
```

An About Box with Hidden Credits

Windows applications usually have an About box, where you can see information such as the version of the product, a copyright notice, and so on. The simplest way to build an About box is to use the MessageDlg function. In this case, you can show only a limited amount of text and no special graphics.

Therefore, the usual method for creating an About box is to use a simple dialog box, such as the one generated with one of the Delphi default templates. I say *simple* because when you have prepared its layout—the form—you seldom need much code.

12

Some code might be required to display system information, such as the version of Windows or the amount of free memory, or some user information, such as the registered user name.

Calling an Undocumented API Function

Another alternative is to use the standard dialog box of many Windows applications. If you select the About box of Program Manager, File Manager, or Paintbrush, you can see that they all use the same dialog box. This is a system dialog box hidden away in a Windows 3.1 library, SHELL.DLL. Can we use this standard dialog box, too? Yes, but we need to call an undocumented Windows function.

As you probably know, the code of Windows is stored in a number of dynamic link libraries (DLLs). Windows applications perform most of their tasks by calling these functions. Most of the functions of these libraries are described in detail in the Windows API documentation, including the Help file present in Delphi. However, the behavior and the parameters of some of these functions have never been described by Microsoft. As a consequence, programmers refer to them as *undocumented* functions. How do you find the documentation of these functions, in case you need them? There are books devoted to this subject, as well as magazine articles and a number of other sources. Consider, however, this danger in calling an undocumented function: there is a chance that in the next version of Windows, it will disappear or have different parameters, thus halting your program. There is no guarantee that the program will also work properly in Windows 95.

In Delphi, you seldom need to call Windows API functions directly, so calling an undocumented function is rare. To call an undocumented function, you need to declare its name and parameters and indicate where the function's code is located. To accomplish this, you need to add to the function declaration the `external` keyword, followed by the name of the library and its index (a number associated with the function in the library):

```
function ShellAbout (HwndOwner: Hwnd; AppName,
  MoreInfo: PChar; Icon: HIcon): Bool;
  far; external 'SHELL' index 22;
```

Here is a short description of the parameters (you won't find this function listed in the Windows API help—it wouldn't be an undocumented function, if you could):

- The handle of a window (the Handle field stores this information for the form)

- The title of the application

- An additional string, usually with copyright information

- The handle of an icon that can be used instead of the standard one, which is displayed when you pass 0 as the fourth parameter

This function is called in the SHABOUT example when the user presses the only button of the main form. The OnClick method retrieves the form's caption and converts this string into a PChar string, to enable it to be passed as the application title:

```
procedure TForm1.Button1Click(Sender: TObject);
var
  Title: array [0..100] of Char;
begin
  StrPCopy (Title, Caption);
  ShellAbout (Handle, Title, 'Copyright Marco Cantù', 0);
end;
```

Running this code results in the dialog box of Figure 12.30. As you can see, the string *Copyright Marco Cantù* I've passed to the function as parameter appears in the standard dialog box, under the standard Microsoft copyright message.

Notice that the system dialog box of SHELL.DLL has a hidden feature, which you are probably aware of. If you double-click on the Windows icon while holding down the Ctrl and Shift keys, close the dialog box, and repeat this operation, an animated flag will again appear. If you close the dialog box and repeat the process once more, an animation presents you with the names of the Microsoft programmers involved in the Windows project. Of course, this also works with the system dialog box of the program you have just built (see Figure 12.31) and this is probably a good reason to choose a different kind of About box!

Building a Custom Hidden Screen

In general, many applications follow a similar approach, hiding some credit screens behind the About box. Can you provide a custom credit screen in your application?

FIGURE 12.30:

The main form of the SHABOUT program and the standard About box it displays when you call an undocumented Windows function

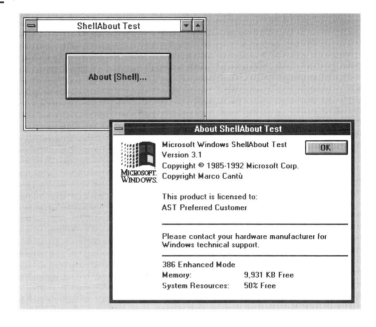

FIGURE 12.31:

The About box of the SHABOUT example with Bill Gates presenting the Windows authors.

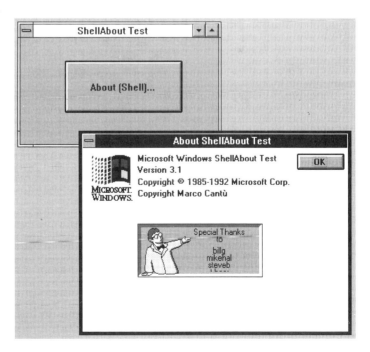

You might do this for a number of reasons. If you work in a big company, this might be your way to prove that you worked on that project, which might help in finding a new job (but only if the project was successful). At times, a hidden About box can be fun to see, with fireworks and similar effects, and they sometimes also provide a good occasion for making jokes about your competitors.

Another more serious reason is that a hidden credit screen can be used to demonstrate who wrote the program, as a sort of legal copyright. By the way, Delphi includes a nice series of hidden screens, as I mentioned in the introduction of the book.

I've written a simple example, showing how you might implement a hidden screen. As you can see in Figure 12.32, the dialog box has a Panel component with two Label components inside its surface. The panel might contain any number of components, to display graphics and text. Some of the strings might even be computed at run-time. The only added feature required to show the hidden credits is a Paintbox component covering the form's whole area.

FIGURE 12.32:

The About box of the CREDITS example at design-time

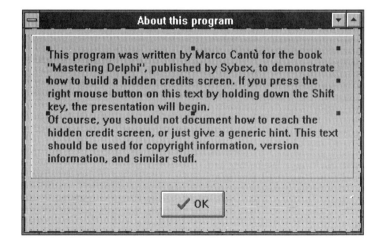

When the user makes a specific complex action (in this case, a click on the upper label with the right mouse button while holding down the Shift key), the panel is hidden and something appears on the screen. A simple solution is to have some text painted on the surface of the form—that is, on its canvas:

```
if (Button = mbRight) and (ssShift in Shift) then
begin
  Panel1.Visible := False;
  PaintBox1.Canvas.Font.Name := 'Arial';
  PaintBox1.Canvas.Font.Size := 20;
  PaintBox1.Canvas.TextOut (40, 50, 'Author: Marco Cantù');
  PaintBox1.Canvas.TextOut (40, 100, 'Version 1.0');
end;
```

To build a more spectacular hidden screen, we might scroll some text in a for loop, as you can see in the source code of the About box in Listing 12.27.

LISTING 12.27: The full source code of the About box with hidden credits, in the CREDITS example

```
unit About;

interface

uses WinTypes, WinProcs, Classes, Graphics, Forms,
  Controls, Buttons, StdCtrls, ExtCtrls;

type
  TAboutBox = class(TForm)
    BitBtn1: TBitBtn;
    Panel1: TPanel;
    Label1: TLabel;
    Label2: TLabel;
    PaintBox1: TPaintBox;
    procedure Label1MouseDown(Sender: TObject;
      Button: TMouseButton;
      Shift: TShiftState; X, Y: Integer);
  private
    { Private declarations }
  public
    { Public declarations }
  end;

var
  AboutBox: TAboutBox;

implementation

{$R *.DFM}
```

LISTING 12.27: The full source code of the About box with hidden credits, in the
CREDITS example (continued)

```
procedure TAboutBox.Label1MouseDown(Sender: TObject;
  Button: TMouseButton;
  Shift: TShiftState; X, Y: Integer);
var
  I: Integer;
begin
  if (Button = mbRight) and (ssShift in Shift) then
  begin
    Panel1.Visible := False;
    for I := 0 to 600 do
      with PaintBox1.Canvas do
      begin
        Font.Name := 'Arial';
        Font.Size := 20;
        TextOut (40, 100-I, 'CREDITS example from:');
        TextOut (40, 150-I, '');
        TextOut (40, 200-I, '"Mastering Delphi"');
        TextOut (40, 250-I, '');
        TextOut (40, 300-I, 'Author: Marco Cantù');
        TextOut (40, 350-I, 'Publisher: Sybex');
        TextOut (40, 400-I, '');
        TextOut (40, 450-I, 'Dedicated with love');
        TextOut (40, 500-I, 'to my wife, Lella');
        {let other applications work}
        Application.ProcessMessages;
      end;
    Panel1.Visible := True;
  end;
end;

end.
```

The result of this code is shown in Figure 12.33, although you should run it to see
the text move. Now that I've suggested this idea to you, do not spend more time
preparing astounding hidden credit screens than writing the rest of the code of
your applications. Although you can save some time by programming with Delphi,
there are probably better ways to use that time!

You need to consider another aspect of the preceding example. We have written
some code to draw on the surface of a dialog box. Although it is not very common,
dialog boxes can have graphical output and respond to mouse input the same as
any other form. In fact, a dialog box *is a form*.

FIGURE 12.33:

The hidden credits of the About box of the CREDITS example

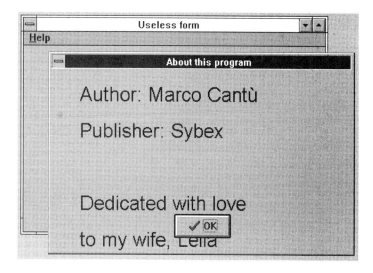

Summary

In this chapter, we have explored many ways to build applications having more than one form. We have seen how you can create a secondary modal or modeless form or a dialog box. The most important point to remember is that in Delphi, dialog boxes are just plain forms with a special border and a couple of other attributes—nothing more.

sBesides the basic examples, we have delved into some advanced topics, such as dynamically building a number of forms, calling undocumented API functions, and creating hidden screens. Another enhancement, the use of the increasingly widespread notebook metaphor, will be one of the topics of the next chapter. Other topics in Chapter 13 include the use of the TabSet component and form scrolling.

CHAPTER

THIRTEEN

13

Scrolling and Multipage Forms

- Scroll bar handling

- Borland-style notebooks with tabs

- Microsoft-style notebooks with tabs

- Tabs without a notebook

- A notebook without tabs

In the beginning, the user interface of MS Windows applications was very simple. Over the years, the most widespread applications and the system itself introduced new features and elements to improve it. For example, to improve ease of use, toolbars and status bars were added.

Another leading idea has been to mimic common metaphors, based on tools we use every day. One such idea was to imitate the behavior of a notebook with tabs to move among the various pages or areas. Delphi has a number of such examples. Tabs are used in Options dialog boxes, in the editor, in the Object Inspector, and in the Components palette.

Many applications have similar approaches in their dialog boxes. Some applications, including leading spreadsheets, even use the notebook metaphor for their main windows. The use of notebooks and tabs has become so important that Microsoft has added direct system support for them in Windows 95.

But before delving into notebooks and multipage forms, we will discuss a simpler but effective technique to use when you need to cram several components in a form: scrolling.

When Forms Are Too Big

When you build a simple application, a single form might hold all of the components you need. As the application grows, you need to squeeze in the components, increase the size of the form, or add new forms. If you reduce the space occupied by the components, you might add some capability to resize them at run-time, eventually splitting the form in different areas. If you choose to increase the size of the form, you might use scroll bars to let the user move around in a form that is bigger than the screen.

Finally, if you choose to add a new form, there are basically three approaches:

- Create secondary forms and dialog boxes, as described in Chapter 12.

- Use Delphi's Notebook component to create forms with multiple pages, as described in this chapter.

- Follow the typical Windows MDI approach, which will be the focus of Chapter 14.

Multipage forms have been introduced in dialog boxes in several Windows applications. Of course, there are several versions of this approach. Microsoft WinWord 2.0 used a graphical list box to select a page. Quattro Pro for Windows uses lateral tabs to change the page of its dialog boxes, and it introduced the notebook metaphor for its main window to build a three-dimensional spreadsheet. The latest generation of Microsoft applications has introduced a new kind of notebook approach for dialog boxes, with tabs above the pages. This probably will become a standard of Windows, because, as I already mentioned, it is going to be directly supported by a new Windows 95 custom control.

13

Delphi has a specific Notebook component, which can be combined with a Tab component to simplify changing pages. This is not compulsory, however. The Notebook component can be used in conjunction with other elements, as we will see later in this chapter.

WARNING   You should avoid making forms that host controls too big. Windows that do not scroll should fit on the screen. This might seem quite obvious, but sometimes it is not. If you develop an application using a high-resolution video driver, you might encounter problems when you move your program to a lower-resolution video PC (although Delphi has some techniques to automatically resize forms on a different video adapter).

Scrolling a Form

Adding a scroll bar to a form is simple. In fact, there is nothing to do. If you place a number of components in a big form, then reduce its size, a scroll bar will be added to the form automatically, as long as you haven't changed the value of the AutoScroll property, which by default is set to True.

Along with AutoScroll, forms have two properties, HorzScrollBar and VertScrollBar, which can be used to set several properties of the two TFormScrollBar objects associated with the form. The Visible property indicates whether the scroll bar is present, the Position property determines the initial status of the scroll thumb, and the Increment property gives the effect of a click on one of the arrows at the ends of the scroll bar. The most important property, however, is Range.

The Range property of a scroll bar determines the virtual size of the form in one direction, not the actual range of values of the scroll bar. At first, this might be somewhat confusing. Here is an example to clarify how the Range property works. Suppose that you need a form with a number of components, and so the form needs to be 1000 pixels wide. We can use this value to set the virtual range of the form, changing the range of the horizontal scroll bar. See Figure 13.1 for an illustration of the virtual size of a form implied by the range of a scroll bar. If the width of the client area of the form is smaller than 1000 pixels, a scroll bar will appear. Now you can start using it at design-time to add new components in the "hidden" portion of the form.

FIGURE 13.1:

A representation of the virtual size of a form implied by the range of a scroll bar

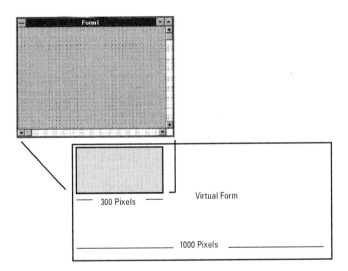

The Position property of the scroll bar ranges from 0 to 1000 minus the current size of the client area. In fact, if the client area of the form is 300 pixels wide, you can scroll 700 pixels to see the far end of the form (the thousandth pixel). See Figure 13.2 for an illustration of this situation.

FIGURE 13.2:

The range of values of the Position property of a scroll bar

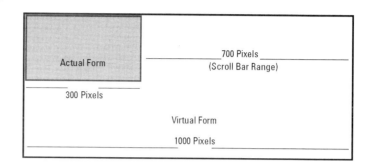

The Scroll Testing Example

As an example, look at the SCROLL1 listing, which has the properties I've just described (that is, a value of 1000 for the range of the horizontal scroll bar). The form of this example has been filled with a number of useless list boxes, as you can see in the reduced textual description of the form in Listing 13.1, containing the properties related to the position and the size of each component.

The interesting part of the example is the presence of a toolbox window displaying the status of the form and of its horizontal scroll bar, as you can see in Figure 13.3. This second form has four labels, two with fixed text and two with the actual output. You can see this in Listing 13.2, which shows the textual description of the Status form. Besides this, the Status form has a single-line border, no minimize or maximize button, and is a topmost window (but you cannot see these elements in the design-time version of the form, because their effect is visible only at run-time). You should also set its Visible property to True, to have its window automatically displayed at startup.

There isn't much code in this program. The aim of the program is to update the values in the toolbox each time the form is resized or it is scrolled (as you can see in Figure 13.4).

LISTING 13.1: The textual description of the main form of the SCROLL1 example

```
object Form1: TForm1
  Width = 440
  Height = 357
  Caption = 'Scrolling Form'
  OnResize = FormResize
  object ListBox1: TListBox
    Left = 44
    Top = 112
    Width = 137
    Height = 193
  end
  object ListBox2: TListBox
    Left = 196
    Top = 80
    Width = 137
    Height = 201
  end
  object ListBox3: TListBox
    Left = 348
    Top = 32
    Width = 137
    Height = 233
  end
  object ListBox4: TListBox
    Left = 504
    Top = 32
    Width = 153
    Height = 249
  end
  object ListBox5: TListBox
    Left = 680
    Top = 32
    Width = 129
    Height = 241
  end
  object ListBox6: TListBox
    Left = 832
    Top = 32
    Width = 145
    Height = 201
  end
end
```

FIGURE 13.3:

The two forms of the SCROLL1 example at design-time

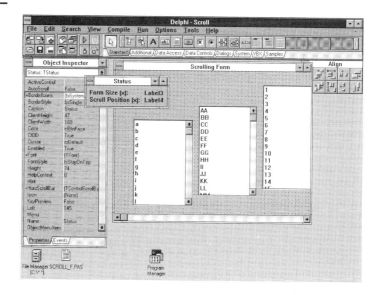

LISTING 13.2: The textual description of the Status form of the SCROLL1 example

```
object Status: TStatus
  BorderIcons = [biSystemMenu]
  BorderStyle = bsSingle
  Caption = 'Status'
  FormStyle = fsStayOnTop
  Visible = True
  object Label1: TLabel
    Caption = 'Form Size (x):'
  end
  object Label2: TLabel
    Caption = 'Scroll Position (x):'
  end
  object Label3: TLabel
    Caption = 'Label3' {used for the output}
  end
  object Label4: TLabel
    Caption = 'Label4' {used for the output}
  end
end
```

FIGURE 13.4:

The output of the SCROLL1 example

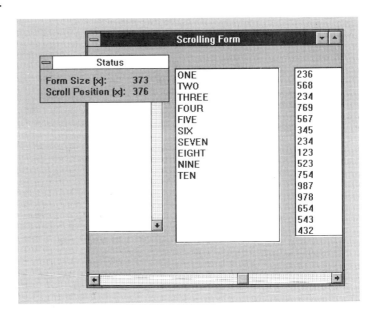

The first part is extremely simple. You can handle the OnResize event of the form, and simply copy a couple of values to the two labels. Notice that the labels are part of another form, so you need to prefix them with the name of the form instance, Status:

```
procedure TForm1.FormResize(Sender: TObject);
begin
  Status.Label3.Caption :=
    IntToStr(ClientWidth);
  Status.Label4.Caption :=
    IntToStr(HorzScrollBar.Position);
end;
```

To compile this code, you need to include the unit with the definition of the second form (in my code, STATUS_F) in the compilation of the unit of the main form.

If we wanted to change the output each time the user scrolls the contents of the form, we could not use a Delphi event handler, because there isn't an OnScroll event for forms (although there is one for stand-alone ScrollBar components). Not having this event makes sense, because Delphi forms handle scroll bars automatically in a powerful way. In comparison, in MS Windows, scroll bars are extremely low-level elements, requiring a lot of coding.

Handling the scroll event makes sense only in special cases, such as in the program I'm building, which is a sort of exploration program.

13

NOTE   What I really like in Delphi is that handling a Windows message that is not supported by the environment requires simply one more line of code. I know that we have already seen this technique in earlier chapters, and that I have already told you how much I like this feature, but I've never seen something so nice in any other visual environment.

Here is the code we need to write. First, add a method declaration to the class, related to Windows horizontal scroll message (wm_HScroll):

```
type
  TForm1 = class(TForm)
    ...
  public
    procedure FormScroll (var ScrollData: TWMScroll);
      message wm_HScroll;
  end;
```

Then write the code of this procedure, which is similar to the code of FormResize:

```
procedure TForm1.FormScroll (var ScrollData: TWMScroll);
begin
  Status.Label3.Caption := IntToStr(ClientWidth);
  Status.Label4.Caption := IntToStr(HorzScrollBar.Position);
  inherited;
end;
```

The only important thing you need to add is the call to `inherited`, which activates the method related to the same message in the base class form. Notice that `inherited` for virtual methods calls the method of the base class we are overriding, which has the same name of the current method, which in this case, calls the method connected with the same message. Without this line of code, the form won't have its default scrolling behavior; that is, it won't scroll at all.

Automatic Scrolling

The use of the Range property of the scroll bar can seem strange until you start to use it consistently. When you think twice about it, you'll start to understand the advantages of this approach.

First of all, the scroll bar is automatically removed from the form when the client area of the form is big enough to accommodate the virtual size. When you reduce the size of the form, the scroll bar is added again.

This becomes particularly interesting when the AutoScroll property of the form is set to True. In this case, the extreme positions of the rightmost and lower controls are automatically copied into the Range properties of the form's two scroll bars. Automatic scrolling works well in Delphi.

In the last example, the virtual size of the form is set to the right border of the last list box. This was defined with the following attributes:

```
object ListBox6: TListBox
  Left = 832
  Width = 145
```

Therefore, the horizontal virtual size of the form is 977 (which is the sum of the two above values). This number is automatically copied into the Range field of the HScrollBar property of the form, as you can see when you explore the attributes of the form at design-time with the Object Inspector.

Another test you can do is the following. Run the program, and move the scroll thumb to the rightmost position. When you add the size of the form and the position of the thumb, you'll always get 977, the virtual coordinate of the rightmost pixel of the form. You can see an example of this behavior in Figure 13.5.

Scrolling an Image

An advantage of the way automatic scrolling works in Delphi is that if the size of a single big component hosted by a form changes, scroll bars are added or removed automatically. A good example is the use of the Image component. If you load a new picture in the component, and its AutoSize property is set to True, the component automatically sizes itself, and the form eventually adds or removes the scroll bars.

An example will probably help clarify how image scrolling works. Do you remember the image viewer we built in Chapter 10? Its form showed a bitmap loaded from

FIGURE 13.5:

Totaling the size of the form and the position of the thumb always results in the same number.

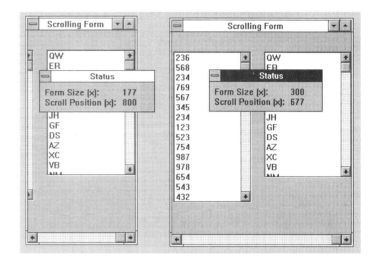

a file, either stretching it to fit the size of the form or leaving it in its original size. The problem is that when the original size is too big to fit in the form, part of the bitmap remains hidden.

The solution to this problem is simple. We can set the AutoSize property of the Image component and disable its alignment with the client area (which is in contrast with the other property, since both can affect the size of the component). You should also set a small initial size for the image (as you can see in the textual description of the form in Listing 13.3).

You don't need to make any adjustments when you load a new bitmap, because the size of the Image component is automatically set for you by the system. Simply write:

```
procedure TViewerForm.Open1Click(Sender: TObject);
begin
  if OpenDialog1.Execute then
    Image1.Picture.LoadFromFile (OpenDialog1.FileName);
end;
```

You can see in Figure 13.6 that scroll bars are actually added to the form. The figure shows two different copies of the program. The difference between the copy of the program on the left and the one on the right is that the first has an image smaller

LISTING 13.3: The textual description of the form of the IMAGEV2 example

```
object ViewerForm: TViewerForm
  Caption = 'Image Viewer'
  Menu = MainMenu1
  object Image1: TImage
    Left = 0
    Top = 0
    Width = 17
    Height = 17
    AutoSize = True
  end
  object MainMenu1: TMainMenu
    {short version}
    object File1: TMenuItem
      object Open1: TMenuItem
      object N1: TMenuItem {separator}
      object Exit1: TMenuItem
    end
    object Options1: TMenuItem
      object Stretch1: TMenuItem
    end
    object Help1: TMenuItem
      object AboutImageViewer1: TMenuItem
    end
  end
  object OpenDialog1: TOpenDialog
    Filter = 'Bitmap (*.bmp)|*.bmp|Icon (*.ico)|*.ico|
      Metafile (*.wmf)|*.wmf'
    Options = [ofHideReadOnly, ofPathMustExist,
      ofFileMustExist]
  end
end
```

than its client area, so no scroll bars were added. When you load a larger image in the program, two scroll bars will automatically appear, as in the example on the right in Figure 13.6.

Some more coding is required to disable the scroll bars and change the alignment of the image when the Stretch menu command is selected, and restore them when this feature is disabled. Again, we do not act directly on the scroll bars themselves, but simply change the alignment of the panel, its Stretch property, and eventually

FIGURE 13.6:

In the IMAGEV2 example, the scroll bars are added automatically to the form when the whole bitmap cannot fit into the client area of the form displayed.

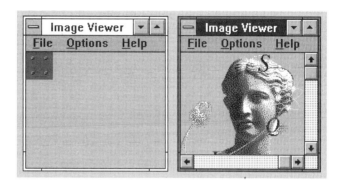

compute manually the new size, using the size of picture currently loaded (this code mimics the effect of the AutoSize property, which works only when a new file is loaded):

```
procedure TViewerForm.Stretch1Click(Sender: TObject);
begin
  Image1.Stretch := not Image1.Stretch;
  Stretch1.Checked := Image1.Stretch;
  if Image1.Stretch then
    Image1.Align := alClient
  else
  begin
    Image1.Align := alNone;
    Image1.Height := Image1.Picture.Height;
    Image1.Width := Image1.Picture.Width;
  end;
end;
```

Scrolling and Form Coordinates

As we have seen in the examples presented in the two previous sections, forms can automatically scroll their components. But what happens if you paint directly on the surface of the form? Some problems arise, but their solution is at hand.

Suppose that we want to draw some lines on the virtual surface of a form, as shown in Figure 13.7. Since you probably do not own a video capable of displaying 2000 pixels on each axis, you can create a smaller form, add two scroll bars, and set their

Range properly, as I've done in the SCROLL2 example (see the textual description of the form in Listing 13.4).

FIGURE 13.7:

The lines to draw on the virtual surface of the form

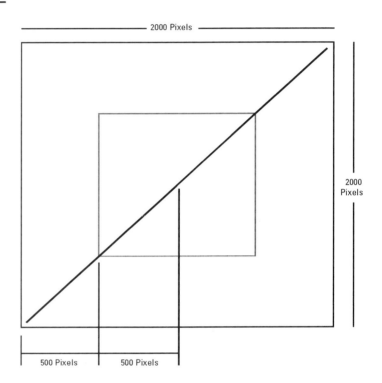

LISTING 13.4: The textual description of the simple form of the SCROLL2 example

```
object Form1: TForm1
  Caption = 'Form1'
  HorzScrollBar.Range = 2000
  VertScrollBar.Range = 2000
  ClientHeight = 336
  ClientWidth = 472
  OnPaint = FormPaint
end
```

If we simply draw the lines using the virtual coordinates of the form, the image won't display properly. In fact, in the OnPaint response method, we need to compute the virtual coordinates ourselves. Fortunately, this is easy, since we know that the *x* and *y* virtual coordinate of the top-left corner of the client area corresponds to the current positions of the two scroll bars:

```
{compute virtual origin}
X1 := HorzScrollBar.Position;
Y1 := VertScrollBar.Position;
...
{use virtual origin}
Canvas.MoveTo (30 - X1, 30 - Y1);
Canvas.LineTo (1970 - X1, 1970 - Y1);
```

You can see the complete source code of the SCROLL2 form, including the FormPaint method in Listing 13.5, and an example of the output of the program in Figure 13.8. Try using the program and changing the drawing functions, but remember to always use coordinates relative to the virtual origin of the form by subtracting the virtual coordinates X1 and Y1 (which refer to the scroll bar position).

You might also try to use plain coordinates to see what happens. You'll find that the output of the program is not correct—it won't scroll; the same image will always remain in the same position, regardless of scrolling operations.

FIGURE 13.8:

An example of the output of the SCROLL2 example

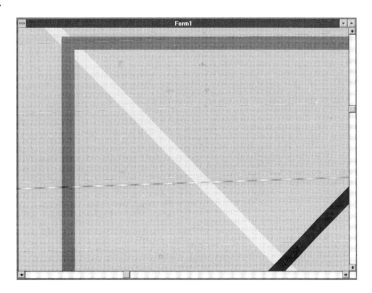

LISTING 13.5: The complete source code of the SCROLL2 example

```
unit Scroll_f;

interface

uses
  WinTypes, WinProcs, Classes, Graphics, Forms,
  Controls, StdCtrls;

type
  TForm1 = class(TForm)
    procedure FormPaint(Sender: TObject);
  end;

var
  Form1: TForm1;

implementation

{$R *.DFM}

procedure TForm1.FormPaint(Sender: TObject);
var
  X1, Y1: Integer;
begin
  X1 := HorzScrollBar.Position;
  Y1 := VertScrollBar.Position;

  {draw a yellow line}
  Canvas.Pen.Width := 30;
  Canvas.Pen.Color := clYellow;
  Canvas.MoveTo (30-X1, 30-Y1);
  Canvas.LineTo (1970-X1, 1970-Y1);

  {draw a blue line}
  Canvas.Pen.Color := clNavy;
  Canvas.MoveTo (30-X1, 1970-Y1);
  Canvas.LineTo (1970-X1, 30-Y1);

  {draw a fuchsia square}
  Canvas.Pen.Color := clFuchsia;
  Canvas.Brush.Style := bsClear;
  Canvas.Rectangle (500-X1, 500-Y1, 1500-X1, 1500-Y1);
end;

end.
```

Building Notebooks with Delphi

There are two different ways to build a notebook with a tab to change the current page. The first is to use a Notebook component together with a Tab component. The second is to use the TabbedNotebook component, which provides the same behavior in a single control.

13

The main difference between the two approaches is in the user interfaces of these components, as you can see in Figure 13.9. In general, the Tab component has a Borland user interface, as is used in the Delphi environment. The TabbedNotebook component has a Microsoft user interface, which is used by several applications and is probably a future standard in Windows 95.

FIGURE 13.9:

The user interface of the two kinds of notebooks with tabs available in Delphi. The top form uses the Notebook and Tab components; the bottom form uses the single TabbedNotebook component.

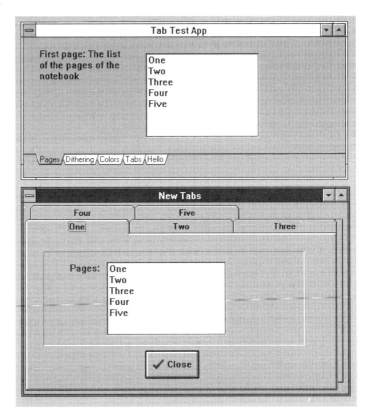

A Notebook with a Tab Set

The standard approach in Delphi is to use the two separate components. To test the basic behavior of the Notebook and the Tab, you can generate a new dialog box. Open the Form Browse Gallery and choose either the Multi-page Dialog template or the Dialog Expert. If you use the Dialog Expert, you can enter the names of the pages of the dialog box directly, as you can see in Figure 13.10.

FIGURE 13.10:

With the Dialog Expert, you can enter the names of the pages of a multipage dialog box directly.

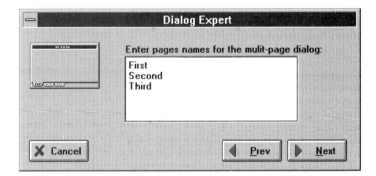

To describe these components in detail, I've written a simple example, named TAB1, without using the Dialog Expert. Its form is the top one in the examples of the different notebook with tabs styles shown earlier in Figure 13.9.

To create this form, you can place a Notebook component on the form and select `alTop` for its Align property. Then place a TabSet component on the form and align it with the top or with the remaining client area.

Now you can name the pages of the notebook, by selecting the Pages property and entering some values in the corresponding editor. The next step is to prepare the tabs, by entering some strings for the Tabs property.

It might be a good idea to use the same names for the pages of the notebook and for the tabs of the TabSet component. However, the names you use for the TabSet component are not particularly important, since it is usually easier to refer to pages and tabs by number than by name. The important thing is that the tabs themselves must have meaningful names, because they are visible. The names of the pages of the notebook, on the other hand, are not displayed on the screen (unless you write some code to do this). But keep in mind that you *must* enter names for both components to set the number of elements—tabs or pages—that you want.

To connect the notebook to the tab set, you need to write at least one line of code, in response to the OnChange event of the TabSet component. This is precisely the code that is present in the Multi-page Dialog template:

13

```
procedure TForm1.TabSet1Change(Sender: TObject;
  NewTab: Integer; var AllowChange: Boolean);
begin
  Notebook1.PageIndex := NewTab;
end;
```

> **WARNING**
> In the OnChange response method, you should use the NewTab parameter and *not* the current index of the tab, because this field contains the older value, the one before the click took place. In fact, the OnChange method can even be used to prohibit the page change, by setting the AllowChange parameter, which is passed by reference, to False.

As an alternative, you can activate the pages by using their names instead of their index. This works only if the names of the pages match those of the tabs:

```
procedure TForm1.TabSet1Change(Sender: TObject;
  NewTab: Integer; var AllowChange: Boolean);
begin
  Notebook1.ActivePage := TabSet1.Tabs [NewTab];
end;
```

To make this program work, we need to add some components to the various pages. At design-time, you can work on the pages of the notebook by changing the value of its PageIndex property. As soon as you enter a new value for this property in the Object Inspector, the visible page of the notebook changes accordingly. This works, but it is not very fast. A better alternative is to select the notebook in the Form Designer, and activate the SpeedMenu. In this particular case, you'll see two new commands, Next Page and Previous Page, which can be used to move through the pages of the notebook.

In the example, since we are working with a notebook and a tab set for the first time, I decided to fill the pages with some controls we can use to change the properties of these two components. You can see all of the pages (at design-time) in Figure 13.11 and the textual description of the form in Listing 13.6. In Figure 13.11, notice that when you change the notebook page at design-time, the corresponding tab is not selected. The two components work together only at run-time.

LISTING 13.6: The textual description of the form of the TAB1 example

```
object Form1: TForm1
  Caption = 'Tab Test App'
  OnCreate = FormCreate
  object Notebook1: TNotebook
    Align = alTop
    object TPage
      Caption = 'One'
      object Label1: TLabel
        Caption = 'First page...'
      end
      object ListBox1: TListBox
        OnClick = ListBox1Click
      end
    end
    object TPage
      Caption = 'Two'
      object Label2: TLabel
        Caption = 'Second page...'
      end
      object GroupBox1: TGroupBox
        Caption = 'Dithering'
        object RadioButton1: TRadioButton
          Caption = 'On'
          OnClick = RadioButton1Click
        end
        object RadioButton2: TRadioButton
          Caption = 'Off'
          Checked = True
          OnClick = RadioButton2Click
        end
      end
    end
    object TPage
      Caption = 'Three'
      object Label3: TLabel
        Caption = 'Third page...'
      end
      object ColorGrid1: TColorGrid
        GridOrdering = go8x2
        ForegroundIndex = 15
```

LISTING 13.6: The textual description of the form of the TAB1 example (continued)

```
        BackgroundIndex = 7
        OnChange = ColorGrid1Change
      end
    end
    object TPage
      Caption = 'Four'
      object Label4: TLabel
        Caption = 'Fourth page...'
      end
      object Memo1: TMemo
      end
      object ChangeButton: TButton
        Caption = 'Change'
        OnClick = ChangeButtonClick
      end
    end
    object TPage
      Caption = 'Five'
      object Label5: TLabel
        Caption = 'Fifth page'
      end
      object Label6: TLabel
        Caption = 'Hello !'
        Font.Color = clRed
        Font.Height = -96
        Font.Name = 'Times New Roman'
        Font.Style = [fsBold]
      end
    end
  end
  object TabSet1: TTabSet
    Align = alTop
    DitherBackground = False
    Font.Color = clBlack
    Font.Height = -11
    Font.Name = 'MS Sans Serif'
    TabHeight = 22
    Tabs.Strings = (
      'Pages'
      'Dithering'
      'Colors'
      'Tabs'
      'Hello')
    OnChange = TabSet1Change
  end
end
```

FIGURE 13.11:

The five pages of the notebook of the TAB1 example

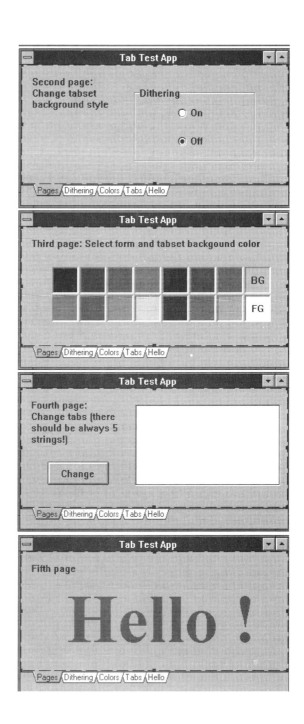

The first page (which, by the way, is page 0) holds a list box with the names of the pages. This list box is filled at run-time, when the form is created, with the names of the pages of the notebook:

```
ListBox1.Items := Notebook1.Pages;
```

In the example, clicking on one of these page names in the list box is an alternate way to move through the notebook. As we change the active page of the notebook, we must remember to select the proper tab as well, since the page and tab index synchronization is not automatic:

```
Notebook1.PageIndex := ListBox1.ItemIndex;
TabSet1.TabIndex := ListBox1.ItemIndex;
```

The second page has a two radio buttons to activate or disable the dithering effect of the background of the TabSet control (see the source code in Listing 13.7). The third page contains a ColorGrid component you can use to select the background color of the form, used also for the notebook. Therefore, it might be a good idea to use it for the background of the tab set and for the active tab, too. The important idea is that to provide the proper three-dimensional effect, the color of the active tab should always match the color of the notebook, so that it seems like an extension of its surface (see Figure 13.12). The second color, the foreground color, is used for the inactive tabs.

LISTING 13.7: The complete source code of the TAB1 example

```
unit Main_f;

interface

uses
  WinTypes, WinProcs, Classes, Graphics, Forms, Controls,
  Tabs, ColorGrd, StdCtrls, ExtCtrls, Dialogs;

type
  TForm1 = class(TForm)
    Notebook1: TNotebook;
    TabSet1: TTabSet;
    Label1: TLabel;
    ListBox1: TListBox;
    Label2: TLabel;
    GroupBox1: TGroupBox;
    RadioButton1: TRadioButton;
    RadioButton2: TRadioButton;
    Label3: TLabel;
    ColorGrid1: TColorGrid;
```

LISTING 13.7: The complete source code of the TAB1 example (continued)

```
    Label4: TLabel;
    Memo1: TMemo;
    Label5: TLabel;
    Label6: TLabel;
    ChangeButton: TButton;
    procedure TabSet1Change(Sender: TObject;
      NewTab: Integer; var AllowChange: Boolean);
    procedure FormCreate(Sender: TObject);
    procedure RadioButton1Click(Sender: TObject);
    procedure RadioButton2Click(Sender: TObject);
    procedure ColorGrid1Change(Sender: TObject);
    procedure ChangeButtonClick(Sender: TObject);
    procedure ListBox1Click(Sender: TObject);
  private
    { Private declarations }
  public
    { Public declarations }
  end;

var
  Form1: TForm1;

implementation

{$R *.DFM}

procedure TForm1.TabSet1Change(Sender: TObject;
  NewTab: Integer; var AllowChange: Boolean);
begin
  Notebook1.PageIndex := NewTab;
end;

procedure TForm1.FormCreate(Sender: TObject);
begin
  ListBox1.Items := Notebook1.Pages;
  Memo1.Lines := TabSet1.Tabs;
end;

procedure TForm1.RadioButton1Click(Sender: TObject);
begin
  TabSet1.DitherBackground := True;
end;

procedure TForm1.RadioButton2Click(Sender: TObject);
begin
  TabSet1.DitherBackground := False;
end;

procedure TForm1.ColorGrid1Change(Sender: TObject);
```

LISTING 13.7: The complete source code of the TAB1 example (continued)

```
begin
  Form1.Color := ColorGrid1.BackgroundColor;
                 TabSet1.BackgroundColor := ColorGrid1.BackgroundColor;
  TabSet1.SelectedColor := ColorGrid1.BackgroundColor;
  TabSet1.UnselectedColor := ColorGrid1.ForegroundColor;
end;

procedure TForm1.ChangeButtonClick(Sender: TObject);
begin
  if (Memo1.Lines.Count <> 5) then
    MessageDlg ('Not 5 lines!', mtError, [mbOk], 0)
  else
    TabSet1.Tabs := Memo1.Lines;
end;

procedure TForm1.ListBox1Click(Sender: TObject);
begin
  Notebook1.PageIndex := ListBox1.ItemIndex;
  TabSet1.TabIndex := ListBox1.ItemIndex;
end;

end.
```

FIGURE 13.12:

An example of the new colors and the dithering effect you can set for the notebook and the tab of the TAB1 example

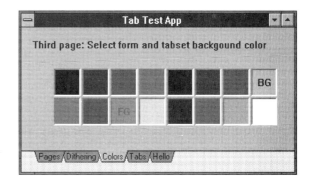

The fourth page is one of the more interesting pages; it allows a user to change the text of the tabs. It contains a memo field, which is initialized with the names of the tabs in the form OnCreate event, together with the list box of the first page.

You should add the new line to the FormCreate method:

```
Memo1.Lines := TabSet1.Tabs;
```

For example, you could use this page to write longer and more descriptive names for the pages. You can even use very long names for the tabs. The TabSet component is capable of adding two "mini" scroll buttons to move among the tabs when they do not fit into the width of the Tab control, as shown in Figure 13.13. This might also happen if you reduce the size of the form at run-time.

FIGURE 13.13:

When the text of the tabs is too long, two miniature scroll buttons are added to the tab control.

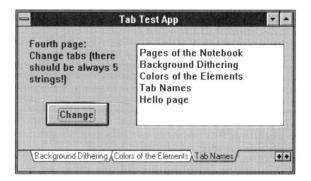

When the Change button is clicked, the program checks to see if there are five lines of text in the memo. Only in this case does it use the lines as text for the tabs. Without this check, it would be possible to change the number of the tabs, so that they no longer match the pages of the notebook (unless you change the notebook pages, too). If the number of notebook pages does not match the number of tabs, selecting a tab might have no effect, other than the tab itself being selected. (This is quite unpleasant, but at least it doesn't crash the program.)

The last page of the notebook has only some text, and no code.

This example highlights two interesting points:

- You are not limited to the use of tabs to change the page of a notebook. The list box on the first page that we have used for this purpose could be placed outside the notebook and used as a page selector, as we will do in the next section.

- It is quite simple to edit the text of the tabs. An instructive example in this direction is Quattro Pro for Windows, which allows users to customize the text of the tabs used to change the active page of the spreadsheet and to refer to that new text in formulas.

Changing the Page of a Notebook

The example we have just finished can be further extended in a number of directions, particularly in providing alternative ways to change the page of the notebook. The technique we'll try first is to add a list box, similar to the one on the first page of the notebook, and make it always visible in the window. Then all you need to do is click on this list box to change to another page. The second addition will be a menu to select the page. The following sections outline some guidelines you can follow to build the TAB2 example from the TAB1 example.

Using a List Box

We can add a new list box on the left or right side of the form. To accomplish this, we need to resize the various components, disable their top alignment, and choose a fixed border for the frame, so that it cannot be resized. Do not choose the dialog border, because we want to be able to add a menu bar later on. You can see an example of the final form in Figure 13.14, and some excerpts of its textual description (without repeating the elements in common with the previous example) in Listing 13.8.

FIGURE 13.14:

The modified form of the TAB2 example at design-time

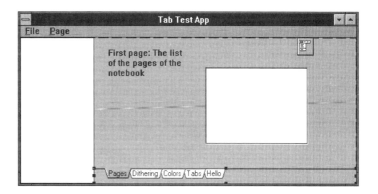

LISTING 13.8: Excerpts of the description of the main form of the TAB2 example, without the description of the components already present in TAB1

```
object Form1: TForm1
  BorderStyle = bsSingle
  Caption = 'Tab Test App'
  Menu = MainMenu1
  OnCreate = FormCreate
  object Notebook1: TNotebook
    {the same as above: see Listing 13.6}
  end
  object TabSet1: TTabSet
    {the same as above: see Listing 13.6}
  end
  object ListBox2: TListBox
    Align = alLeft
    Ctl3D = False
    OnClick = ListBox1Click
  end
  object MainMenu1: TMainMenu
    object File1: TMenuItem
      Caption = '&File'
      object Exit1: TMenuItem
        Caption = 'E&xit'
        OnClick = Exit1Click
      end
    end
    object Page1: TMenuItem
      Caption = '&Page'
      object One: TMenuItem
        Caption = '&One'
        OnClick = MenuPage
      end
      object Two: TMenuItem
        Caption = '&Two'
        GroupIndex = 1
        OnClick = MenuPage
      end
      object Three: TMenuItem
        Caption = 'T&hree'
        GroupIndex = 1
        OnClick = MenuPage
      end
      object Four: TMenuItem
        Caption = '&Four'
        GroupIndex = 1
        OnClick = MenuPage
      end
```

LISTING 13.8: Excerpts of the description of the main form of the TAB2 example (continued)

```
      object Five: TMenuItem
        Caption = 'F&ive'
        GroupIndex = 1
        OnClick = MenuPage
      end
    end
  end
end
```

At program startup, we can initialize the new list box with the same text as the labels of the TabSet component. The code of the FormCreate method becomes:

```
procedure TForm1.FormCreate(Sender: TObject);
begin
  ListBox1.Items := Notebook1.Pages;
  ListBox2.Items := TabSet1.Tabs;                {new line}
  ListBox2.ItemIndex := TabSet1.TabIndex;  {new line}
  Memo1.Lines := TabSet1.Tabs;
end;
```

We can handle when the user clicks on an element of the new list box (ListBox2) by writing a code fragment similar to the one used for the first list box. Copying and pasting might be the way to go, but remember to change the list box numbers. Even better, we can write a single version of the code to act with both list boxes, and connect it with the click event of both of them:

```
procedure TForm1.ListBox1Click(Sender: TObject);
{works with both list boxes}
begin
  Notebook1.PageIndex := (Sender as TListBox).ItemIndex;
  TabSet1.TabIndex := (Sender as TListBox).ItemIndex;
end;
```

With this code, when the list box selection changes, we select a new page and activate the proper tab. You can see an example in Figure 13.15. However, for consistency,

FIGURE 13.15:
The TAB2 program shows the selected page both in the tab and in the list box on the left (both controls can be used to change the page, too).

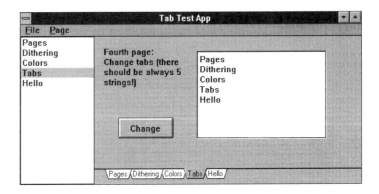

we need to also alter the list box selection when the user changes the page by clicking on one of the tabs:

```
procedure TForm1.TabSet1Change(Sender: TObject;
  NewTab: Integer; var AllowChange: Boolean);
begin
  Notebook1.PageIndex := NewTab;
  ListBox2.ItemIndex := NewTab;              {new line}
end;
```

Using The Menu

The second technique is to add a pull-down menu to select the various pages. You can see the structure of this menu in Listing 13.8 (in the previous section). The On-Click event for each menu item is associated with a single function, MenuPage, which is based on a simple trick: the name of each menu item corresponds to the name of a page of the notebook. This simplifies the code quite a bit:

```
procedure TForm1.MenuPage(Sender: TObject);
begin
  Notebook1.ActivePage := (Sender as TMenuItem).Name;
  TabSet1.TabIndex := Notebook1.PageIndex;
  ListBox2.ItemIndex := Notebook1.PageIndex;
  CheckCurrentPage;
end;
```

This approach also makes the program easily extensible, because you don't need to write new code or change it when new pages and the corresponding menu items are added.

Only the first statement above contains real code. The other two are needed to change the list box and tab selections according to the new page (using the number). The last statement invokes a procedure I've defined, named CheckCurrentPage. This method places a check mark on the menu item corresponding to the currently selected page, as shown in Figure 13.16. It removes the check mark from every menu item, then enables the one corresponding to the current page with a case statement:

```
procedure TForm1.CheckCurrentPage;
var
  I: Integer;
begin
  One.Checked := False;
  Two.Checked := False;
  Three.Checked := False;
  Four.Checked := False;
  Five.Checked := False;
  case Notebook1.PageIndex of
    0: One.Checked := True;
    1: Two.Checked := True;
    2: Three.Checked := True;
    3: Four.Checked := True;
    4: Five.Checked := True;
  end;
end;
```

The code is placed in a stand-alone procedure because we need to call it each time the active page changes. The CheckCurrentPage method is called at the end of the methods ListBox1Click, TabSet1Change, and FormCreate.

Of course, you will seldom need three different ways to select the page of a notebook, as I've included in the TAB2 example, but a couple of choices might be useful to satisfy the tastes of different users. The aim of this example was to show you some alternatives. More are coming after the following section.

FIGURE 13.16:

The active page of the notebook is indicated with a check mark in the Page pull-down menu.

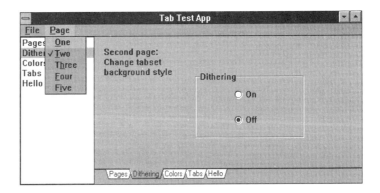

Tabbed Notebooks

A radical alternative to the use of the TabSet and the Notebook components is the use of the TabbedNotebook component. As I've already mentioned, this component has the joined functionality of the other two controls, but it has a different user interface. Here are the differences:

- The TabSet control has downward-pointing tabs; the TabbedNotebook component has upward-pointing tabs.

- The tabs of the TabSet control are big enough to hold the text of the tab; the TabbedNotebook tabs use a fixed amount of space, determined by the width of the controls and the value of its TabsPerRow property.

- When there are too many tabs, two miniature scroll buttons appear near the tabs of the TabSet; the TabbedNotebook uses the typical multiple-row approach.

- The TabbedNotebook user interface is going to be the standard Windows 95 user interface.

- When there are many tabs, the TabSet component gets the two miniature scroll buttons, making the selection of the page a bit slower. The TabbedNotebook component switches to a multi-row format, which takes up some of the client area of the form, leaving you less space for your work. Also, if you have never used multi-row tabs, you'll find that they are not very intuitive.

The example I've built to show the use of the new style tabs (which I personally don't like as much as the Borland style), named NEWTABS, is similar to—although somewhat simpler than—the TAB1 example shown earlier. (In fact, I've used the output of a version of this program, slightly different than the final one, and the output of the TAB1 example in the comparison shown earlier in Figure 13.9.)

As you can see in Figure 13.17, the first page has a list box with the names of the pages, and a second element, a Close button.

The Close button should be present on every page of the notebook, but we want to avoid copying it. Instead, it can be displayed on each page of the notebook at once. To accomplish this, place the button on the form, not on the notebook, then move it over the notebook. When you use this trick, the parent of the component is the form, so it will be displayed in front of each page of the notebook.

In some cases, there is another step to take. To be able to place the button on the form, the form should be visible. You should enlarge the form, after disabling the alignment of the notebook, then perform the Close button operation described in the preceding paragraph, then resize the form again to its proper dimensions.

Notice that in the example I've placed the button in the bottom-center of the form, and selected a non-resizable dialog border for it.

The other pages of the notebook in the NEWTABS example allow you to change the font of the tab captions and the number of tabs per row. The last two pages are almost empty. You can see the complete description of the main form in Listing 13.9.

FIGURE 13.17:

The first page of the NEWTABS form at design-time

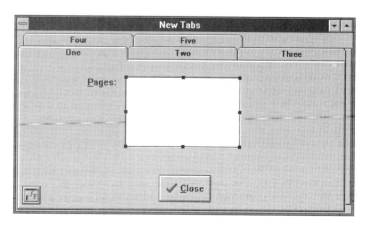

LISTING 13.9: The textual description of the form of the NEWTABS example

```
object Form1: TForm1
  BorderStyle = bsDialog
  Caption = 'New Tabs'
  OnCreate = FormCreate
  object TabbedNotebook1: TTabbedNotebook
    Align = alClient
    TabFont.Color = clBlack
    TabFont.Height = -12
    TabFont.Name = 'MS Sans Serif'
    TabFont.Style = [fsBold]
    object TTabPage
      Caption = 'One'
      object Label1: TLabel
        Caption = '&Pages:'
        FocusControl = ListBoxPages
      end
      object ListBoxPages: TListBox
        OnClick = ListBoxPagesClick
      end
    end
    object TTabPage
      Caption = 'Two'
      object Label3: TLabel
        Caption = 'Tab font:'
      end
      object LabelFont: TLabel
        AutoSize = False
        Caption = 'Label Font'
      end
      object ButtonChangeFont: TButton
        Caption = 'C&hange Font...'
        OnClick = ButtonChangeFontClick
      end
    end
    object TTabPage
      Caption = 'Three'
      object Label4: TLabel
        Caption = 'Number of tabs on each line:'
      end
      object SpinEdit1: TSpinEdit
        MaxValue = 8
        MinValue = 3
        Value = 3
      end
      object ButtonChangeNTabs: TButton
        Caption = 'C&hange'
        OnClick = ButtonChangeNTabsClick
      end
    end
  end
```

LISTING 13.9: The textual description of the form of the NEWTABS example (continued)

```
    object TTabPage
      Caption = 'Four'
      object Label2: TLabel
        Caption = 'Page four...'
        Font.Color = clYellow
        Font.Height = -80
        Font.Name = 'Times New Roman'
      end
    end
    object TTabPage
      Caption = 'Five'
      object Label5: TLabel
        Caption = 'Enter you name:'
      end
      object Edit1: TEdit
        Text = 'John Lee'
      end
    end
  end
  object BitBtn1: TBitBtn
    Caption = '&Close'
    Default = True
    OnClick = BitBtn1Click
    Glyph.Data = {...}
    NumGlyphs = 2
  end
  object FontDialog1: TFontDialog
    Font.Color = clWindowText
    Font.Height = -13
    Font.Name = 'System'
    Font.Style = []
  end
end
```

The code of this example is fairly simple. In fact, the TabbedNotebook component handles page changing automatically. This means that we don't need to change the active page each time the user clicks on a tab, as is the case in the TAB1 and TAB2 examples.

Again, however, we can implement more than one technique to change the page. For example, we can fill the list box of the first page with the names of the pages (that is, the strings that appear in the tabs), and then move to another page when the user clicks on the corresponding element in the list box.

To change the page in the tabbed notebook, we can use the SetTabFocus method, which requires the zero-based index of the new page as a parameter. Since the list box has a zero-based ItemIndex property, indicating the selected item, we can simply write:

```
TabbedNotebook1.SetTabFocus (ListBoxPages.ItemIndex);
```

As a precaution, we can avoid this operation when there are no items selected in the list box, although this should never happen. The other two pages of the notebook can be used to change the font and arrangement of the tabs. You can see examples of the effects of these options in Figures 13.18 and 13.19.

FIGURE 13.18:

The NEWTABS window with a bigger font and more tabs per row; notice the text and the font of the label.

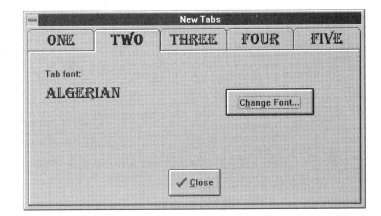

FIGURE 13.19:

The NEWTABS window with a small font and even more tabs per row than in Figure 13.18

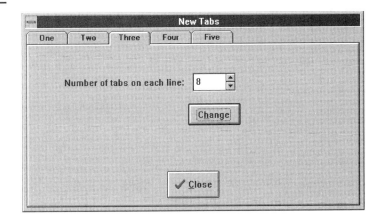

To change the font when the user clicks on the corresponding button, you can simply use a FontDialog component, and use the selected value to change the font of the tabs:

```
if FontDialog1.Execute then
  begin
    TabbedNotebook1.TabFont := FontDialog1.Font;
    ...
```

13

As you can see in the complete source code in Listing 13.10, the program also changes the Caption and Font properties of the label.

LISTING 13.10: The source code of the NEWTABS example

```
unit Newt_f;

interface

uses
  SysUtils, WinTypes, WinProcs, Messages, Classes, Graphics,
  Controls, Forms, Dialogs, StdCtrls, Buttons, TabNotbk,
  Spin, ExtCtrls;

type
  TForm1 = class(TForm)
    TabbedNotebook1: TTabbedNotebook;
    ListBoxPages: TListBox;
    Label1: TLabel;
    Label3: TLabel;
    LabelFont: TLabel;
    ButtonChangeFont: TButton;
    FontDialog1: TFontDialog;
    SpinEdit1: TSpinEdit;
    Label4: TLabel;
    ButtonChangeNTabs: TButton;
    Label2: TLabel;
    Label5: TLabel;
    Edit1: TEdit;
    BitBtn1: TBitBtn;
    procedure BitBtn1Click(Sender: TObject);
    procedure FormCreate(Sender: TObject);
    procedure ButtonChangeFontClick(Sender: TObject);
    procedure ButtonChangeNTabsClick(Sender: TObject);
    procedure ListBoxPagesClick(Sender: TObject);
  private
    { Private declarations }
  public
    { Public declarations }
  end;
```

LISTING 13.10: The source code of the NEWTABS example (continued)

```
var
  Form1: TForm1;

implementation

{$R *.DFM}

procedure TForm1.BitBtn1Click(Sender: TObject);
begin
  Close;
end;


procedure TForm1.FormCreate(Sender: TObject);
begin
  ListBoxPages.Items := TabbedNotebook1.Pages;
  LabelFont.Caption := TabbedNotebook1.TabFont.Name;
  LabelFont.Font := TabbedNotebook1.TabFont;
  FontDialog1.Font := TabbedNotebook1.TabFont;
end;

procedure TForm1.ButtonChangeFontClick(Sender: TObject);
begin
  if FontDialog1.Execute then
  begin
    TabbedNotebook1.TabFont := FontDialog1.Font;
    LabelFont.Caption := TabbedNotebook1.TabFont.Name;
    LabelFont.Font := TabbedNotebook1.TabFont;
  end;
end;

procedure TForm1.ButtonChangeNTabsClick(Sender: TObject);
begin
  TabbedNotebook1.TabsPerRow := SpinEdit1.Value;
  TabbedNotebook1.PageIndex := 2;
end;

procedure TForm1.ListBoxPagesClick(Sender: TObject);
begin
  if ListBoxPages.ItemIndex >= 0 then
    TabbedNotebook1.PageIndex := ListBoxPages.ItemIndex;
end;

end.
```

For the last operation—changing the number of tabs per row—I've simply added a SpinEdit component and a button (as you can see in Figure 13.19). The code is simple. When the user clicks the button, the value of the SpinEdit component is used as the new number of tabs per row:

```
TabbedNotebook1.TabsPerRow := SpinEdit1.Value;
```

Overall, the source code of this example is fairly simple, as you can see in Listing 13.10.

If you like the Microsoft-style user interface of tabbed notebooks, or just need to use it because it is more standard, Delphi provides a good implementation (waiting for Windows 95, when this will become a standard element). As a side effect, writing the code is slightly easier, because you don't need to synchronize the Tab and Notebook components. However, when you use the Borland-style user interface, having two different components to handle is actually more of an advantage than a disadvantage, because you obtain far more flexibility, as the following section will demonstrate. The TabbedNotebook component is also less efficient with resources than the TabSet and Notebook pair.

Notebooks without Tabs and Tabs without Notebooks

The Notebook and Tab components naturally fit with each other. To combine the two, you need only one line of code, like the one at the beginning of the TAB1 example. You can also easily customize these two components and change their behavior.

However, this is not the only choice. As the title of this section suggests, you can write applications with tabs but without a notebook, or with notebooks but without tabs. Here are some examples, some of which will be fully implemented in the following sections.

Tabs alone can be used in a multipage editor (such as the editor in Delphi), in a multipage bitmap viewer, to select a disk drive in a file viewer, in a three-dimensional spreadsheet, or to select a form in a multiple-form program. Delphi uses tabs to select pages in the Component palette, too.

A notebook can be used without tabs if you replace it with a list box or a menu (as shown in the TAB2 example). As an alternative, you can use an outline component instead of a list, obtaining an effect similar to Delphi's multiple-page Options dialog box. It is not difficult to mimic this behavior.

Another alternative to the use of a TabSet component is to add buttons to navigate through the notebook, as demonstrated by the next example. There are basically two ways to use buttons for navigation:

- Add a row of buttons with commands such as First, Next, Previous, and Last. The Windows Help uses a similar toolbar for navigation.

- Add specific buttons in the various pages of the notebook to move to other relevant pages. This solution is similar to the use of hyperlinks, and you can use specific portions of the text or of an image instead of push buttons to launch the move.

A Presentation in a Notebook

Our first example of a notebook without a tab is called NOTEONLY, which has a row of buttons as well as some buttons in the pages to give specific navigation commands. The four buttons in the row at the bottom of the form are placed on a panel, so that the notebook can take up the rest of the client area of the form, as you can see in Figure 13.20.

FIGURE 13.20:

The cover page of the NOTEONLY example, a presentation of Italy, at design-time

Probably the best way to understand this example is to use it a bit. It is a presentation about traveling in Italy (I thought it might be interesting to many people around the world, although I've written just minimal information about the places).

Each page usually has a button to move to the next step, but at times you have two or more choices, as shown in the graph that illustrates the flow of the presentation in Figure 13.21.

You can see some of the pages of this application in Figure 13.22. The key elements of its textual description are shown in Listing 13.11.

The buttons used to move from one page to another are simple. Their code looks like this:

```
procedure TForm1.ButtonGoClick(Sender: TObject);
begin
  Notebook1.PageIndex := 2;
end;
```

FIGURE 13.21:

The flow of the control of the presentation about Italy

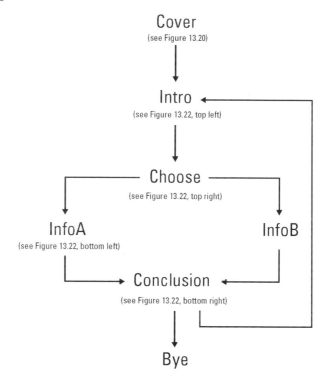

FIGURE 13.22:

Some of the pages of the notebook of the NOTEONLY example, featuring a presentation of Italy, at run-time

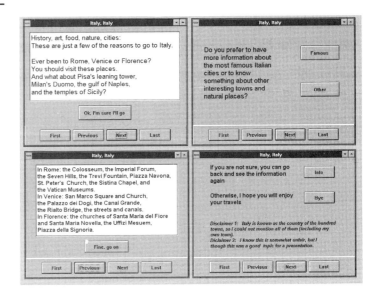

LISTING 13.11: The key elements of the textual description of the NOTEONLY example

```
object Form1: TForm1
  Caption = 'Italy, Italy'
  object Notebook1: TNotebook
    Align = alClient
    object TPage
      Caption = 'Cover'
      object Label1: TLabel
        Caption = 'Travel to Italy'
        Font.Color = clFuchsia
        Font.Name = 'Arial'
        Font.Style = [fsBold]
      end
      object ButtonStart: TButton
        Caption = 'Start'
        OnClick = ButtonStartClick
      end
    end
    object TPage
      Caption = 'Intro'
      object Memo1: TMemo
        Lines.Strings = (
          'History, art, food, nature, cities: '
          'These are just a few of the reasons to go to Italy.'
          '...')
```

LISTING 13.11: The key elements of the textual description of the NOTEONLY example (continued)

```
      ReadOnly = True
    end
    object ButtonGo: TButton
      Caption = 'Ok, I''m sure I''ll go'
      OnClick = ButtonGoClick
    end
  end
  object TPage
    Caption = 'Choose'
    object Label2: TLabel
      Caption = 'Do you prefer to have ... '
    end
    object ButtonFamous: TButton
      Caption = 'Famous'
      OnClick = ButtonFamousClick
    end
    object ButtonOther: TButton
      Caption = 'Other'
      OnClick = ButtonOtherClick
    end
  end
  object TPage
    Caption = 'InfoA'
    object Memo2: TMemo
      Lines.Strings = (
        'In Rome: the Colosseum, the Imperial Forum, '
        'the Seven Hills, the Trevi Fountain, Piazza Navona, '
        'St. Peter'#39's  Church, the Sistina Chapel, and '
        'the Vatican Museums.'
        '... ')
      ReadOnly = True
    end
    object ButtonFine: TButton
      Caption = 'Fine, go on'
      OnClick = ButtonFineClick
    end
  end
  object TPage
    Caption = 'InfoB'
    object Memo3: TMemo
      Lines.Strings = (
        'Milan: the Duomo and the Scala Theater'
        'Naples: the gulf and the Vesuvium'
        '... ')
      ReadOnly = True
    end
    object ButtonFine2: TButton
      Caption = 'Fine, go on'
      OnClick = ButtonFineClick
    end
  end
```

13

LISTING 13.11: The key elements of the textual description of the NOTEONLY example (continued)

```
      object TPage
        Caption = 'Conclusion'
        object Label3: TLabel...
        object Label4: TLabel...
        object Label5: TLabel...
        object Label6: TLabel...
        object ButtonInfo: TButton
          Caption = 'Info'
          OnClick = ButtonInfoClick
        end
        object ButtonBye: TButton
          Caption = 'Bye'
          OnClick = ButtonByeClick
        end
      end
      object TPage
        Caption = 'Bye'
        object Label7: TLabel...
        object Label8: TLabel...
      end
    end
    object Panel1: TPanel
      Align = alBottom
      ShowHint = True
      object ButtonFirst: TButton
        Hint = 'Jump to first page'
        Caption = 'First'
        Enabled = False
        OnClick = ButtonFirstClick
      end
      object ButtonPrevious: TButton
        Hint = 'Move to previous page'
        Caption = 'Previous'
        Enabled = False
        OnClick = ButtonPreviousClick
      end
      object ButtonNext: TButton
        Hint = 'Move to next page'
        Caption = 'Next'
        OnClick = ButtonNextClick
      end
      object ButtonLast: TButton
        Hint = 'Jump to last page'
        Caption = 'Last'
        OnClick = ButtonLastClick
      end
    end
end
```

Besides specific buttons to jump directly to a certain page, you can browse through the notebook using the four buttons in the bottom row. These buttons need a similar method for their OnClick events:

```
procedure TForm1.ButtonFirstClick(Sender: TObject);
begin
  Notebook1.PageIndex := 0;
end;

procedure TForm1.ButtonPreviousClick(Sender: TObject);
begin
  if Notebook1.PageIndex > 0 then
    Notebook1.PageIndex := Notebook1.PageIndex - 1;
end;
```

Some more coding is required to disable the useless buttons of the panel, as you can see in the code in Listing 13.11. For example, after a user clicks on the First button, you should disable the first two buttons (since the user is already at the first page and there are no previous pages) and enable the other two buttons in case they had been disabled. The first method above becomes:

```
procedure TForm1.ButtonFirstClick(Sender: TObject);
begin
  Notebook1.PageIndex := 0;
  ButtonFirst.Enabled := False;
  ButtonPrevious.Enabled := False;
  ButtonNext.Enabled := True;
  ButtonLast.Enabled := True;
end;
```

Even more complex is the case of the Next and the Previous buttons. You should check if the notebook has reached the first or the last page, and disable or enable the various buttons accordingly. The code for the method associated with these buttons is slightly redundant, since we don't check to determine the situation before the button was clicked. For example, instead of always enabling a button, we might add a test to enable it only if it was previously disabled. This code is rarely worth the effort, since the test might take the same amount of time as the useless operation.

Another idea might be to store a couple of Boolean values you can set to True when the user has reached the first or the last page. For example, you need to disable the Last button only if the user is currently on the last page.

The problem here is that we also need to enable and disable some of the buttons on the button row when the navigational buttons of the various pages of the notebook are clicked, to avoid inconsistent behavior. You can see the complete source code in Listing 13.12.

LISTING 13.12: The source code of the NOTEONLY example

```
unit Italy;

interface

uses
  WinTypes, WinProcs, Classes, Graphics, Forms,
  Controls, Menus, StdCtrls, ExtCtrls;

type
  TForm1 = class(TForm)
    Notebook1: TNotebook;
    Panel1: TPanel;
    ButtonFirst: TButton;
    ButtonPrevious: TButton;
    ButtonNext: TButton;
    ButtonLast: TButton;
    ButtonGo: TButton;
    ButtonFamous: TButton;
    ButtonOther: TButton;
    ButtonFine: TButton;
    ButtonFine2: TButton;
    ButtonInfo: TButton;
    ButtonBye: TButton;
    ButtonStart: TButton;
    {some memo and label components have been removed}
    procedure ButtonStartClick(Sender: TObject);
    procedure ButtonGoClick(Sender: TObject);
    procedure ButtonFamousClick(Sender: TObject);
    procedure ButtonOtherClick(Sender: TObject);
    procedure ButtonFineClick(Sender: TObject);
    procedure ButtonInfoClick(Sender: TObject);
    procedure ButtonByeClick(Sender: TObject);
    procedure ButtonFirstClick(Sender: TObject);
    procedure ButtonPreviousClick(Sender: TObject);
    procedure ButtonNextClick(Sender: TObject);
    procedure ButtonLastClick(Sender: TObject);
  private
    { Private declarations }
  public
    { Public declarations }
  end;
```

```
var
  Form1: TForm1;

implementation

{$R *.DFM}

procedure TForm1.ButtonStartClick(Sender: TObject);
begin
  Notebook1.PageIndex := 1;
  ButtonFirst.Enabled := True;
  ButtonPrevious.Enabled := True;
end;

procedure TForm1.ButtonGoClick(Sender: TObject);
begin
  Notebook1.PageIndex := 2;
end;

procedure TForm1.ButtonFamousClick(Sender: TObject);
begin
  Notebook1.PageIndex := 3;
end;

procedure TForm1.ButtonOtherClick(Sender: TObject);
begin
  Notebook1.PageIndex := 4;
end;

procedure TForm1.ButtonFineClick(Sender: TObject);
begin
  Notebook1.PageIndex := 5;
end;

procedure TForm1.ButtonInfoClick(Sender: TObject);
begin
  Notebook1.PageIndex := 2;
end;

procedure TForm1.ButtonByeClick(Sender: TObject);
begin
  Notebook1.PageIndex := 6;
  ButtonLast.Enabled := False;
  ButtonNext.Enabled := False;
end;

procedure TForm1.ButtonFirstClick(Sender: TObject);
begin
  Notebook1.PageIndex := 0;
  ButtonFirst.Enabled := False;
  ButtonPrevious.Enabled := False;
```

13

LISTING 13.12: The source code of the NOTEONLY example (continued)

```
  ButtonNext.Enabled := True;
  ButtonLast.Enabled := True;
end;

procedure TForm1.ButtonPreviousClick(Sender: TObject);
begin
  if Notebook1.PageIndex > 0 then
    Notebook1.PageIndex := Notebook1.PageIndex - 1;
  if Notebook1.PageIndex = 0 then
    begin
      ButtonFirst.Enabled := False;
      ButtonPrevious.Enabled := False;
    end
  else
    begin
      ButtonFirst.Enabled := True;
      ButtonPrevious.Enabled := True;
    end;
  ButtonNext.Enabled := True;
  ButtonLast.Enabled := True;
end;

procedure TForm1.ButtonNextClick(Sender: TObject);
begin
  if Notebook1.PageIndex < 6 then
    Notebook1.PageIndex := Notebook1.PageIndex + 1;
  if Notebook1.PageIndex = 6 then
    begin
      ButtonNext.Enabled := False;
      ButtonLast.Enabled := False;
    end
  else
    begin
      ButtonNext.Enabled := True;
      ButtonLast.Enabled := True;
    end;
  ButtonFirst.Enabled := True;
  ButtonPrevious.Enabled := True;
end;

procedure TForm1.ButtonLastClick(Sender: TObject);
begin
  Notebook1.PageIndex := 6;
  ButtonFirst.Enabled := True;
  ButtonPrevious.Enabled := True;
  ButtonNext.Enabled := False;
  ButtonLast.Enabled := False;
end;

end.
```

An Image Viewer with Tabs

Now that we've gone through an example of a notebook without tabs, we are ready to explore the opposite situation: a tab set that is not attached to a notebook. Often, you'll find another component connected to a tab set. For example, you might attach a tab set to a panel, an image, one of the various kinds of grids, or other types of components.

In our next example, we want to display a bitmap in an Image component. The image that appears depends on the selection in the tab set below it (see Figure 13.23 for an example of the running program). This is a simple example. The form has a Tab-Set component aligned at the bottom and an Image component covering the remaining portion of the client area. The other two components are a main menu and a File Open dialog box that allows multiple selections (see Figure 13.24). Listing 13.13 shows the textual description of the most important properties of the form's elements.

At the beginning, the tab set has only a fake tab, describing the situation ("No file selected"), as you can see in Figure 13.24. When the user selects the Open command from the File menu, the dialog box is displayed. The user can select a number of files, and the array of strings with the names of the files (the Files property of the File Open dialog box) is used as the text for the tabs (the Tabs property of TabSet1):

```
procedure TForm1.Open1Click(Sender: TObject);
begin
  if OpenDialog1.Execute then
    TabSet1.Tabs := OpenDialog1.Files;
end;
```

FIGURE 13.23:

An example of the interface of the bitmap viewer in the TABONLY1 example (at run-time)

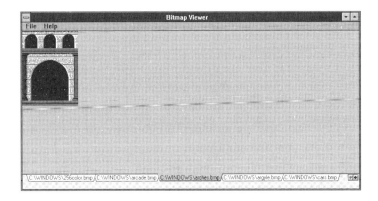

FIGURE 13.24:

The TABONLY1 form at design-time

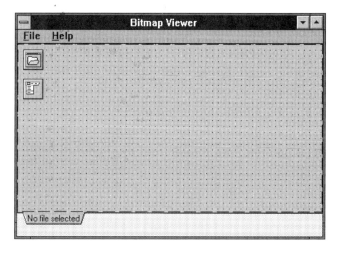

Once the tabs display file names of some bitmaps, you simply need to load in the image file corresponding to the current tab, each time the selection changes:

```
procedure TForm1.TabSet1Change(Sender: TObject;
  NewTab: Integer; var AllowChange: Boolean);
begin
  Image1.Picture.LoadFromFile (TabSet1.Tabs [NewTab]);
end;
```

Add two methods to handle the Exit and About menu commands, and the program is finished. The significant code is in the two procedures above, so I haven't included the listing here.

This example works, but not very well. One of the problems is related to the fact that the file names and the path names have different capitalization and that displaying the whole path makes the tabs very big, so that the program can display only a few of them at a time. To correct this problem, the program should access every string of the array and convert it to uppercase, or even define a set of hidden temporary strings, so that the path name can be removed from the tabs.

Another problem is that if you select a file that doesn't contain a bitmap, an error will occur. However, the program will warn the user with a standard exception, ignore the file, and continue its execution.

LISTING 13.13: The textual description of the TABONLY1 example

```
object Form1: TForm1
  Caption = 'Bitmap Viewer'
  Menu = MainMenu1
  object Image1: TImage
    Align = alClient
  end
  object TabSet1: TTabSet
    Align = alBottom
    Font.Height = -11
    Font.Name = 'MS Sans Serif'
    Tabs.Strings = (
      'No file selected')
    OnChange = TabSet1Change
  end
  object OpenDialog1: TOpenDialog
    Filter = 'Bitmpas (*.bmp)|*.bmp'
    Options = [ofHideReadOnly, ofAllowMultiSelect,
      ofFileMustExist]
  end
  object MainMenu1: TMainMenu
    object File1: TMenuItem
      Caption = '&File'
      object Open1: TMenuItem
        Caption = '&Open...'
        OnClick = Open1Click
      end
      object N1: TMenuItem
        Caption = '-'
      end
      object Exit1: TMenuItem
        Caption = 'E&xit'
        OnClick = Exit1Click
      end
    end
    object Help1: TMenuItem
      Caption = '&Help'
      object About1: TMenuItem
        Caption = '&About...'
        OnClick = About1Click
      end
    end
  end
end
```

13

The last problem involves usability. This program is not very suitable for browsing the hard disk looking for a bitmap, because you need to open the File Open dialog box over and over again. A better idea is to have a list of directories directly on the form and allow the user to browse through it. This is easy to do in Delphi, since there is a DirectoryListBox component readily available. By using some advanced system components and only a few lines of code, we can build a full-fledged image browser.

An Image Browser with Tabs

To build the TABONLY2 example—the image browser—in a new form, place a DriveComboBox and a DirectoryListBox below it, as shown in Figure 13.25. On the right of the form, place the same two components we used in the previous example: an Image and a TabSet. I've also added a Bevel component behind them, to improve the user interface of the form.

FIGURE 13.25:

The form of the TABONLY2 example at design-time

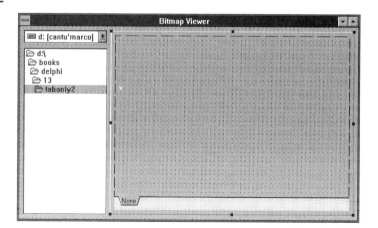

The idea of this program is that as the user selects a new directory, the tabs should immediately display the names of bitmap files of that directory. First, we need to connect the combo box with the names of the drives and with the directory list box, so that each change in the combo box is reflected in the other component. This can be easily done by setting the DirList property of the DriveComboBox.

The second step is to load the names of the bitmap files in the tabs each time the selection in the directory list box changes. We might do this manually, by accessing DOS functions, or we can use another component to solve the problem. The latter solution is more Delphi-oriented, and also much easier, so I've chosen to follow it.

Just place a FileListBox component on the form, and reduce its size so that it will be invisible, place it behind another component, or simply set its Visible property to False. Then change the value of the Mask property of the file list box to *.bmp, as you can see in the overall description of the form in Listing 13.14.

LISTING 13.14: The textual description of the form of the TABONLY2 example, including a hidden component

```
object Form1: TForm1
  ActiveControl = DirectoryListBox1
  BorderStyle = bsDialog
  Caption = 'Bitmap Viewer'
  object Bevel1: TBevel
    Left = 168
    Top = 8
    Width = 449
    Height = 329
    Style = bsRaised
  end
  object Image1: TImage
    Left = 176
    Top = 16
    Width = 433
    Height = 289
  end
  object DirectoryListBox1: TDirectoryListBox
    Left = 8
    Top = 40
    Width = 153
    Height = 297
    FileList = FileListBox1
    OnChange = DirectoryListBox1Change
  end
  object DriveComboBox1: TDriveComboBox
    Left = 8
    Top = 8
    Width = 153
    Height = 22
    DirList = DirectoryListBox1
  end
  object TabSet1: TTabSet
    Left = 176
    Top = 304
    Width = 433
    Height = 25
```

LISTING 13.14: The textual description of the form of the TABONLY2 example, including a hidden component (continued)

```
      Font.Color = clWindowText
      Font.Height = -11
      Font.Name = 'MS Sans Serif'
      Tabs.Strings = ('None')
      OnChange = TabSet1Change
    end
    object FileListBox1: TFileListBox
      Mask = '*.bmp'
      Visible = False
    end
end
```

Now add a method for the OnChange event of the directory list box, and write the following code:

```
procedure TForm1.DirectoryListBox1Change(Sender: TObject);
begin
  with FileListBox1 do
    if Items.Count = 0 then
    begin
      TabSet1.Tabs.Clear;
      Image1.Visible := False;
      TabSet1.Tabs.Add ('None');
    end
    else
    begin
      Image1.Visible := True;
      TabSet1.Tabs := FileListBox1.Items;
    end;
  end;
```

Using this method, each time the user selects a new directory (or a new disk), the directory shown in the file list box changes. Then, if there are some items in this directory, the array of strings is copied to the tab set. As an alternative, the *None* string is added to an empty tab set, and the image with the old bitmap is temporarily hidden.

When the tabs display the names of the files, we can use the simple statement of the earlier example to load the corresponding bitmap in the picture of the Image component:

```
procedure TForm1.TabSet1Change(Sender: TObject; NewTab: Integer;
  var AllowChange: Boolean);
begin
  if TabSet1.Tabs [NewTab] <> 'None' then
    Image1.Picture.LoadFromFile (TabSet1.Tabs [NewTab]);
end;
```

The result of our limited effort is a nice-looking form, as you can see in Figure 13.26.

FIGURE 13.26:

The bitmap viewer of the TABONLY2 example

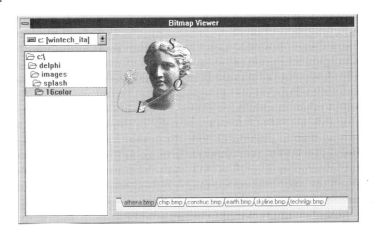

A Multipage Toolbar

The last example of this chapter defines a notebook with tabs used to build a multipage toolbar. Building a multipage toolbar, in general, is easy. You only need to place a panel with some SpeedBar buttons on each page of a small notebook, and add a tab below it. As an alternative, you might do the reverse: place a notebook and a tab in a panel, and add the SpeedBar buttons on the various pages. As a third alternative, you can do without the panel, and simply place the buttons on the notebook pages.

I've used the third alternative in the simple MULTIBAR example. You can see one of the pages of the notebook in Figure 13.27. If you look at the figure, you'll notice something strange: the tab is empty.

I decided not to enter the text for the tabs of the TabSet component, but to simply copy the names of the pages into the tabs of the notebook at run-time:

```
procedure TForm1.FormCreate(Sender: TObject);
begin
  TabSet1.Tabs := Notebook1.Pages;
end;
```

Of course, to make the tabs work properly, you should also connect them to the notebook as usual:

```
procedure TForm1.TabSet1Change(Sender: TObject;
  NewTab: Integer; var AllowChange: Boolean);
begin
  Notebook1.PageIndex := NewTab;
end;
```

You can see an example of the toolbar at run-time in Figure 13.28. Notice that the tabs of this example mimic the names of possible pull-down menus. A better solution might be to provide two or three toolbars corresponding to different environment situations (file editing, folder handling, other tools, and so on). The program might automatically change the toolbar page when you change the context, but the user is still free to select a different page of the toolbar.

FIGURE 13.28:

Some of the pages of the toolbar of the MULTIBAR example

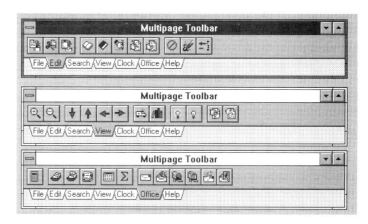

NOTE I've borrowed all of the bitmaps for the examples in this chapter from the Delphi Image Library, a collection of graphic files usually available in the C:\DELPHI\IMAGES directory and its subdirectories.

To fully understand how this example was built, you can refer to the initial portion of the textual description of its form in Listing 13.15.

LISTING 13.15: The initial portion of the textual description of the form of the MULTIBAR example

```
object Form1: TForm1
  Caption = 'Multipage Toolbar'
  OnCreate = FormCreate
  object TabSet1: TTabSet
    Align = alClient
    Font.Name = 'MS Sans Serif'
    Tabs.Strings = ('')
    TabIndex = 0
    OnChange = TabSet1Change
  end
  object Notebook1: TNotebook
    Align = alTop
    object TPage
      Caption = 'File'
      object SpeedButton13: TSpeedButton
```

LISTING 13.15: The initial portion of the textual description of the form of the
MULTIBAR example (continued)

```
          Left = 5
          Top = 4
          Width = 25
          Height = 25
          Glyph.Data = {...}
        end
        object SpeedButton14: TSpeedButton...
        object SpeedButton15: TSpeedButton...
        object SpeedButton16: TSpeedButton...
        object SpeedButton17: TSpeedButton...
        object SpeedButton18: TSpeedButton...
        object SpeedButton19: TSpeedButton...
        object SpeedButton20: TSpeedButton...
        object SpeedButton21: TSpeedButton...
        object SpeedButton22: TSpeedButton...
        object SpeedButton23: TSpeedButton...
        object SpeedButton24: TSpeedButton...
      end
      object TPage
        Caption = 'Edit'
        object SpeedButton25: TSpeedButton...
        object SpeedButton26: TSpeedButton...
        ...
      end
      object TPage
        Caption = 'Search'
        object SpeedButton37: TSpeedButton...
        ...
      end
      object TPage
        Caption = 'View'
        object SpeedButton49: TSpeedButton...
        ...
      end
      object TPage
        Caption = 'Clock'
        object SpeedButton61: TSpeedButton...
      end
      object TPage
        Caption = 'Help'
        object SpeedButton1: TSpeedButton...
      end
    end
end
```

This example has two problems. The first is that because it has such a large number of bitmaps, it consumes a lot of MS Windows resources. This is indeed a problem that cannot be solved easily. A technique you might use is to create the various buttons at run-time, instead of creating them all at first. However, this will probably make the page-change operation extremely slow.

Another problem, of a completely different kind, is due to the fact that you need to manually select the bitmap for each of the buttons, which can be extremely boring. A solution is to give names to the buttons, so that they can later load a bitmap having the same name. Of course, this can be combined with the idea of creating only a page of buttons at a time, destroying them when a new page is requested. If you follow this approach, another improvement might come from storing the bitmaps as resources inside the executable file, instead of as external BMP files.

Summary

In this chapter, we have seen how Delphi handles form scrolling, and how you can work with it. We have seen how to paint on a scrolling surface and how to track scrolling operations by the user.

In the second part, we focused on other techniques you can use to increase the number of components you can display on a form, using various forms of multiple-page components. We have seen how to connect tabs to notebooks, and also how to use tabs alone or notebooks without tabs.

Delphi components are very flexible. Rather than sticking with a fixed design, you can choose from the many options available. You'll see this theme continued in the next chapter, which is devoted to form splitting and the various ways you can arrange and resize components in a form at run-time.

A third approach to building complex applications is MDI. This will be the topic of Chapter 15.

CHAPTER

FOURTEEN

Splitting Windows

14

- A splitter implemented with Headers

- A splitter based on a Panel

- A splitter line that moves on drag termination

- A File Manager clone with a preview pane

- Direct mouse splitting

An interesting user interface feature that is becoming common is the *splitter*, an element you can drag to resize or move some components in a window. The most typical example is MS Windows 3.1 File Manager's splitter, which separates the directories list box from the files list box. Another interesting example of the use of splitters is in SideKick for Windows, which uses a number of elements in a form instead of an MDI approach.

I decided to focus a whole chapter on this topic, because this is a significant feature of the user interface of many applications, and it involves some interesting programming problems. At the same time, this is a good occasion to start presenting a fairly complex application, which would have required a lot of time to program without Delphi. As our last example in this chapter. we'll build a customized version of File Manager, which, of course, will use a splitter.

Form Splitting Techniques

There are several ways to implement splitters in Delphi, although there is no specific support for them.You can use the following techniques to split forms; that is, to let the user resize some of the components, while the others are arranged automatically:

- A Header component can be used to size components horizontally in a form. The header handles the sizing operations, the mouse, the cursor, and other details automatically, so most of the work is already done. For this reason, it is quite common in Delphi to use a header to implement splitting.

- Any component, but usually a Panel or a GroupBox, can be placed between two other elements that can be resized. Using Delphi's dragging support, this component can be moved, and the change can affect the relative position of other components.

- You can use a component that supports dragging inside itself. For example, the StringGrid and DrawGrid components allow dragging. Using a grid is probably the simplest and most powerful approach to splitting. The drawback is that grids are also the most expensive, in terms of the amount of code included in your executable file.

- You can handle mouse-dragging operations manually, particularly on the form itself. Just leave a blank area between different components, and check when the user drags through this area.

Each of these three approaches will be demonstrated using the same example: a form with three list boxes containing names of animals. The list boxes will support font changing with a mouse double-click.

Splitting with a Header

The use of the Header control is the most common technique used to implement a vertical splitter. You can place a header in the window and align it with the top of the form, then put the components in the remaining area.

For this example, place a list box aligned to the left, a second list box aligned to the right, and a third list box aligned with the client area. You can see the components of the SPLIT1 example, already containing some text, in Figure 14.1.

FIGURE 14.1:

The form of the SPLIT1 example at design-time

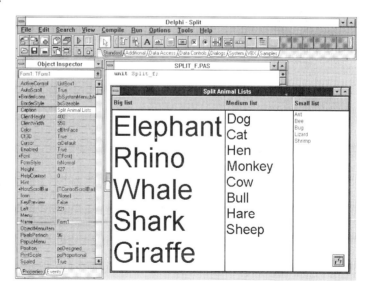

After you've placed these components of the form, enter some text in the list boxes, as well as some text for the titles of the sections of the header (using the Sections property).

NOTE At design-time, to resize the sections of the header, drag with the right mouse button. At run-time, a user will drag the header separators with the left mouse button.

To complete the example, add a default font selection dialog box, and set a proper font size for the three list boxes, as indicated in the description of the form shown in Listing 14.1. This dialog box will appear when the user double-clicks in one of the list boxes, so the user can select a different font for that list box.

LISTING 14.1: The textual description of the SPLIT1 form

```
object Form1: TForm1
  ActiveControl = ListBox1
  Caption = 'Split Animal Lists'
  object Header1: THeader
    Align = alTop
    Font.Color = clBlack
    Font.Height = -13
    Font.Name = 'Arial'
    Font.Style = [fsBold]
    Sections.Sections = (
      #0'263'#0'Big list'
      #0'161'#0'Medium list'
      #0'69'#0'Small list')
    OnSizing = Header1Sizing
    OnSized = Header1Sized
  end
  object ListBox1: TListBox
    Align = alLeft
    Font.Color = clBlack
    Font.Height = -64
    Font.Name = 'Arial'
    ItemHeight = 72
    Items.Strings = (
      'Elephant'
      'Rhino'
      'Whale'
      'Shark'
      'Giraffe')
    OnDblClick = ListBoxDblClick
  end
```

LISTING 14.1: The textual description of the SPLIT1 form (continued)

```
object ListBox2: TListBox
  Align = alLeft
  Font.Color = clBlack
  Font.Height = -32
  Font.Name = 'Arial'
  ItemHeight = 36
  Items.Strings = (
    'Dog'
    'Cat'
    'Hen'
    'Monkey'
    'Cow'
    'Bull'
    'Hare'
    'Sheep')
  OnDblClick = ListBoxDblClick
end
object ListBox3: TListBox
  Align = alClient
  Font.Color = clBlack
  Font.Height = -12
  Font.Name = 'Arial'
  ItemHeight = 15
  Items.Strings = (
    'Ant'
    'Bee'
    'Bug'
    'Lizard'
    'Shrimp')
  OnDblClick = ListBoxDblClick
end
object FontDialog1: TFontDialog
  Font.Color = clWindowText
  Font.Height = -13
  Font.Name = 'System'
end
end
```

Now we need to resize the list boxes each time the user resizes one of the sections of the header. The header has two methods for this: OnSized and OnSizing. The On-Sized method is called when the user has terminated the dragging operation. The OnSizing method is called several times during the operation, once for each mouse movement.

Usually, only the final OnSized event is considered. When this method is called, the program should resize the components. For example, if the user resizes the first section, we can write:

```
ListBox1.Width := AWidth;
```

where AWidth is one of the parameters of the method, indicating the width of the section being resized. The other parameter is ASection, which indicates the number of the section the user is acting on. This is the section to the left of the separator being dragged.

When you drag the header separators, you actually resize only one section. All the other sections are moved but remain the same size. If you have used the alignment values I've suggested, the list boxes behave in the same way. When the first list box is resized, the second one is moved, and the last one (which has the alClient attribute) is resized to fill the remaining portion of the form. In our program, we need only write:

```
procedure TForm1.Header1Sized(Sender: TObject;
  ASection, AWidth: Integer);
begin
  if ASection = 0 then
    ListBox1.Width := AWidth;
  if ASection = 1 then
    ListBox2.Width := AWidth;
end;
```

Setting a Maximum and Minimum Size

By writing this code, we've made the header work as a splitter, but with two limitations:

- The list boxes are resized only when the user ends the sizing operation.
- The list boxes can be reduced or enlarged to any size.

The first problem could be solved by simply copying the above code into the On-Sizing event-response method. However, I've decided not to do this, because if you resize the list boxes too frequently, their repainting operation will cause some flickering on the screen. You might even end up dragging empty list boxes, because the system didn't have time to repaint them during the dragging.

To solve the second problem and make sure that the user cannot make the sections in the header too small, we can write this code for the OnSizing event:

```
procedure TForm1.Header1Sizing(Sender: TObject;
  ASection, AWidth: Integer);
begin
  if AWidth < 40 then
    Header1.SectionWidth [ASection] := 40;
end;
```

You could also add a similar if statement in the Header1Sized method, to prevent the final position from making the list boxes too small. With this code, the dragging operation is not terminated when the user reaches the limit, but the separator will not move beyond the specified width.

This code almost works. However, it causes some flickering on the screen, since the header is trying to reduce the size of the section and your code is enlarging it to 40 pixels. The real problem is that the component repaints the screen before you have a choice to check its size, and eventually change it.

To solve this problem, we can use a technique that is not elegant, but works quite well. When the user tries to make the section too small, we can call the Windows API function ReleaseCapture, which terminates mouse dragging. Since this forced termination skips the sending of the OnSized event, the code should mimic this event:

```
procedure TForm1.Header1Sizing(Sender: TObject;
  ASection, AWidth: Integer);
begin
  if AWidth < 40 then
  begin
    Header1.SectionWidth [ASection] := 40;
    ReleaseCapture;
    Header1Sized (Sender, ASection, 40);
  end;
end;
```

You can add similar code to prevent the user from making the sections too big. The code required for this is more complex, because we need to compute the maximum size each time, considering the size of the form and of the other two list boxes. The other main difference is that you need to consider which section the user is currently dragging, since the fixed section (which is either the first or the second, corresponding to the indexes 0 and 1) should be considered in the computation. You can store the value of the fixed section in a variable, OtherSection:

```
if ASection = 0 then
    OtherSection := 1
  else
    OtherSection := 0;
```

Then you can check whether the current dragging operation has reduced the third section below the limit. In fact, when you increase the size of a section, it is always the last one being reduced. The other sections are eventually moved. If adding the current size of the fixed section, the OtherSection, to the width of the section being resized, AWidth, gives you a value bigger than the size of the width of the client area of the form, minus the 40 pixels we want to leave for the third section, dragging should terminate:

```
if AWidth + Header1.SectionWidth [OtherSection] >
    ClientWidth - 40 then
  begin
    Header1.SectionWidth [ASection] :=
      ClientWidth - 40 - Header1.SectionWidth [OtherSection];
    ReleaseCapture;
    Header1Sized (Sender, ASection,
      ClientWidth - 40 - Header1.SectionWidth [OtherSection]);
  end;
```

If there was a start-dragging event, we could compute the maximum size of the section, which is:

```
ClientWidth - 40 - Header1.SectionWidth [OtherSection]
```

But there isn't such an event, so we must compute this value a number of consecutive times. We can still rewrite the code as:

```
if ASection = 0 then
  MaxWidth := ClientWidth - 40 - Header1.SectionWidth [1]
else
  MaxWidth := ClientWidth - 40 - Header1.SectionWidth [0];
if AWidth > MaxWidth then
begin
  Header1.SectionWidth [ASection] := MaxWidth;
  ReleaseCapture;
  Header1Sized (Sender, ASection, MaxWidth);
end;
```

This is the final version, the one you will find in Listing 14.2, together with the method used to change the font of the list box when the user has double-clicked on it. Notice that there is a single method, using the Sender parameter, for all three list boxes.

LISTING 14.2: The final source code of the SPLIT1 example

```
unit Split_f;

interface

uses
  SysUtils, WinTypes, WinProcs, Messages, Classes, Graphics,
  Controls, Forms, Dialogs, StdCtrls, ExtCtrls;

type
  TForm1 = class(TForm)
    Header1: THeader;
    ListBox1: TListBox;
    ListBox2: TListBox;
    ListBox3: TListBox;
    FontDialog1: TFontDialog;
    procedure Header1Sized(Sender: TObject;
      ASection, AWidth: Integer);
    procedure ListBoxDblClick(Sender: TObject);
    procedure Header1Sizing(Sender: TObject;
      ASection, AWidth: Integer);
  private
    { Private declarations }
  public
    { Public declarations }
  end;

var
  Form1: TForm1;

implementation

{$R *.DFM}

procedure TForm1.Header1Sized(Sender: TObject;
  ASection, AWidth: Integer);
begin
  if ASection = 0 then
    ListBox1.Width := AWidth;
  if ASection = 1 then
    ListBox2.Width := AWidth;
end;
```

LISTING 14.2: The final source code of the SPLIT1 example (continued)

```
procedure TForm1.Header1Sizing(Sender: TObject;
  ASection, AWidth: Integer);
var
  OtherSection, MaxWidth: Integer;
begin
  if AWidth < 40 then
  begin
    Header1.SectionWidth [ASection] := 40;
    ReleaseCapture;
    Header1Sized (Sender, ASection, 40);
  end;
  if ASection = 0 then
    MaxWidth := ClientWidth - 40 -
      Header1.SectionWidth [1]
  else
    MaxWidth := ClientWidth - 40 -
      Header1.SectionWidth [0];
  if AWidth > MaxWidth then
  begin
    Header1.SectionWidth [ASection] := MaxWidth;
    ReleaseCapture;
    Header1Sized (Sender, ASection, MaxWidth);
  end;
end;

procedure TForm1.ListBoxDblClick(Sender: TObject);
begin
  with Sender as TListbox do
  begin
    FontDialog1.Font := Font;
    if FontDialog1.Execute then
      Font := FontDialog1.Font;
  end;
end;

end.
```

Figure 14.2 shows the final version of the SPLIT1 example. This version does not allow a user to reduce any section below 40 pixels. Notice that the first separator cannot be dragged to the right, since the third list box cannot be reduced below the current value.

FIGURE 14.2:
The final version of the SPLIT1 program

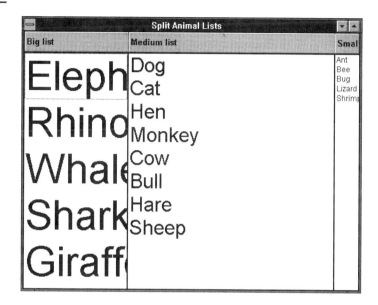

By writing some more code, we can improve the user interface of this program by leaving some pixels between the right border of a list box and left border of the adjacent one. At the same time, we can allow the user to resize the list boxes not only by dragging the separators in the header, but also by dragging the lines separating the various list boxes.

A Header behind the Scenes

Our next version of the SPLIT example will allow the user to drag the separator between list boxes. This can be accomplished in various ways. The first one we'll explore is using a header once again, but this time the header will be placed "behind the scenes." Figure 14.3 shows the output of the SPLIT2 example.

To begin, place a header on the form, and align it with the whole client area. Next, add three list boxes as before, placing them approximately over the three sections of the header. However, do *not* align the three list boxes. The position of the list boxes is not particularly relevant, since we will change it when the application starts (see Listing 14.3 for the changes in the textual description of the form). The

FIGURE 14.3:

The output of the SPLIT2 example, with a header behind the list boxes, but still usable

three list boxes cover all of the header's surface except for its separators, so a user can still drag the sections.

If the separator is placed in the middle of the borders of the two adjacent list boxes, it has a three-dimensional effect and doesn't look like a split bar:

The separator will look better if it is aligned with one of the borders of the list boxes, or at least placed very close to one of the borders, so that the separator is barely visible:

LISTING 14.3: The changes in the textual description of the form of the SPLIT2 example

```
object Form1: TForm1
  ActiveControl = ListBox1
  AutoScroll = False
  BorderStyle = bsDialog
  Caption = 'Split Animal Lists'
  OnCreate = FormCreate
  object Header1: THeader
    Align = alClient
    OnSizing = Header1Sizing
    OnSized = Header1Sized
  end
  object ListBox1: TListBox
    Left = 0
    Top = 0
    Width = 263
    Height = 401
    OnDblClick = ListBoxDblClick
  end
  object ListBox2: TListBox
    Left = 269
    Top = 0
    Width = 141
    Height = 400
    OnDblClick = ListBoxDblClick
  end
  object ListBox3: TListBox
    Left = 416
    Top = 0
    Width = 150
    Height = 401
  end
  object FontDialog1: TFontDialog...
end
```

Now we simply need to move the list boxes so that the separators always remain visible. I've written this code in a specific method, which is called when the form is created, when the header has been resized (OnSized), and eventually also during the dragging operation (OnSizing):

```
procedure TForm1.ResizeListBoxes;
begin
  ListBox1.Width := Header1.SectionWidth [0] - 1;
  ListBox2.Left := Header1.SectionWidth [0] + 3;
  ListBox2.Width := Header1.SectionWidth [1] - 4;
```

```
    ListBox3.Left := Header1.SectionWidth [0] +
      Header1.SectionWidth [1] + 3;
    ListBox3.Width := ClientWidth - ListBox3.Left;
  end;
```

This code leaves one pixel between the border of the list box on the left and the separator, and three pixels between the border of the list box on the right and the separator, so that the separator looks more like a split bar (see the output in Figure 14.3, shown earlier).

The Header1Sizing method is similar to the previous version, and it might call the ResizeListBoxes procedure each time, so that the list boxes are immediately aligned (see Listing 14.4). Although this can cause the negative blinking effect I've described before, if you don't resize the list boxes each time, the user has no hint of the dragging operation, other than the cursor. In the previous version, a user could see the new position of the header sections.

LISTING 14.4: The source code of the form of the SPLIT2 example

```
unit Split_f;

interface

uses
  SysUtils, WinTypes, WinProcs, Messages, Classes, Graphics,
  Controls, Forms, Dialogs, StdCtrls, ExtCtrls;

type
  TForm1 = class(TForm)
    Header1: THeader;
    ListBox1: TListBox;
    ListBox2: TListBox;
    ListBox3: TListBox;
    FontDialog1: TFontDialog;
    procedure Header1Sized(Sender: TObject;
      ASection, AWidth: Integer);
    procedure ListBoxDblClick(Sender: TObject);
    procedure Header1Sizing(Sender: TObject;
      ASection, AWidth: Integer);
```

LISTING 14.4: The source code of the form of the SPLIT2 example (continued)

```
    procedure FormCreate(Sender: TObject);
  private
    { Private declarations }
  public
    procedure ResizeListBoxes;
  end;

var
  Form1: TForm1;

implementation

{$R *.DFM}

procedure TForm1.ResizeListBoxes;
begin
  ListBox1.Width := Header1.SectionWidth [0] - 1;
  ListBox2.Left := Header1.SectionWidth [0] + 3;
  ListBox2.Width := Header1.SectionWidth [1] - 4;
  ListBox3.Left := Header1.SectionWidth [0] +
    Header1.SectionWidth [1] + 3;
  ListBox3.Width := ClientWidth - ListBox3.Left;
end;

procedure TForm1.Header1Sized(Sender: TObject;
  ASection, AWidth: Integer);
begin
  ResizeListBoxes;
end;


procedure TForm1.Header1Sizing(Sender: TObject;
  ASection, AWidth: Integer);
var
  OtherSection, MaxWidth: Integer;
begin
  if AWidth < 40 then
  begin
    Header1.SectionWidth [ASection] := 40;
    ReleaseCapture;
    {ResizeListBoxes;}
  end;
  if ASection = 0 then
    MaxWidth := ClientWidth - 40 - Header1.SectionWidth [1]
  else
    MaxWidth := ClientWidth - 40 - Header1.SectionWidth [0];
  if AWidth > MaxWidth  then
  begin
    Header1.SectionWidth [ASection] := MaxWidth;
    ReleaseCapture;
    {ResizeListBoxes;}
  end;
```

LISTING 14.4: The source code of the form of the SPLIT2 example (continued)

```
    {if you remove this, uncomment the two similar calls above}
    ResizeListBoxes;
end;

procedure TForm1.ListBoxDblClick(Sender: TObject);
begin
  with Sender as TListbox do
  begin
    FontDialog1.Font := Font;
    if FontDialog1.Execute then
      Font := FontDialog1.Font;
  end;
end;

procedure TForm1.FormCreate(Sender: TObject);
begin
  ResizeListBoxes;
end;

end.
```

Splitting with Panels

In our next example, the splitter is based on a Panel component. Although it uses a different approach, the output and the behavior of the resulting program, SPLIT3, is similar to those of the last version, SPLIT2. Compare the output of the new version, shown in Figure 14.4, with the SPLIT2 output in Figure 14.3.

Adding the Panels

To build this third version, place the three list boxes on the form, and then add two thin vertical panels in between (see Figure 14.5). Now align every component, except the third list box, to the left. The third list box, as you can probably guess, is aligned with the client area. Note that you should set the alignment of the components in the proper order, starting from the first list box, moving on to the first panel, then the second list box, the second panel, and finally the third list box. You can see the differences from the last version in the textual description of the new form in Listing 14.5.

FIGURE 14.4:

The output of the SPLIT3 example is similar to that of SPLIT2.

FIGURE 14.5:

The form of the SPLIT3 example at design-time. Notice the panels between the list boxes.

LISTING 14.5: The textual description of the form of the SPLIT3 example (omitting some of the properties in common with the previous version)

```
object Form1: TForm1
  AutoScroll = False
  BorderStyle = bsDialog
  Caption = 'Split Animal Lists'
  object ListBox1: TListBox
    Left = 0
    Top = 0
    Width = 233
    Height = 401
    Align = alLeft
    DragCursor = crHSplit
    OnDblClick = ListBoxDblClick
    OnDragOver = ListBox1DragOver
  end
  object ListBox2: TListBox
    Left = 238
    Top = 0
    Width = 175
    Height = 401
    Align = alLeft
    DragCursor = crHSplit
    OnDblClick = ListBoxDblClick
    OnDragOver = ListBox2DragOver
  end
  object ListBox3: TListBox
    Left = 418
    Top = 0
    Width = 148
    Height = 401
    Align = alClient
    DragCursor = crHSplit
    OnDblClick = ListBoxDblClick
    OnDragOver = ListBox3DragOver
  end
  object Panel1: TPanel
    Left = 233
    Top = 0
    Width = 5
    Height = 401
    Cursor = crHSplit
    Align = alLeft
    BevelOuter = bvNone
    DragCursor = crHSplit
    DragMode = dmAutomatic
    OnDragOver = PanelDragOver
  end
```

LISTING 14.5: The textual description of the form of the SPLIT3 example (continued)

```
object Panel2: TPanel
  Left = 413
  Top = 0
  Width = 5
  Height = 401
  Cursor = crHSplit
  Align = alLeft
  BevelOuter = bvNone
  DragCursor = crHSplit
  DragMode = dmAutomatic
  OnDragOver = PanelDragOver
end
object FontDialog1: TFontDialog...
end
```

This time, there isn't the automatic resizing support offered by the header. Therefore, we need to solve the problem by using the automatic dragging features of any Delphi component. The two panels support automatic dragging—their DragMode property is set to `dmAutomatic`—and they have the special *horizontal-splitting* cursor (`crHSplit`) for both the standard and the custom cursor. The three list boxes use the same cursor for dragging, too.

Each panel accepts the dragging of the panel or panels near its borders, and immediately provides the proper resizing of the list boxes (again causing some repainting problems). As a further enhancement, each list box cannot become less than 40 pixels wide.

For example, only the first panel can be dragged over the first list box, and the cursor horizontal coordinate (X) cannot be less than 40 pixels:

```
procedure TForm1.ListBox1DragOver(Sender, Source: TObject;
  X, Y: Integer; State: TDragState; var Accept: Boolean);
begin
if (Source = Panel1) and (X > 40) then
  begin
    Accept := True;
    ListBox1.Width := X;
  end
  else
    Accept := False;
end;
```

Notice the equality test between the Source parameter and the Panel1 component. When the same panel is dragged over itself (that is, the user is not moving it) Accept should be set to True again, to set the drag cursor instead of the no-drag cursor:

```
procedure TForm1.PanelDragOver(Sender, Source: TObject;
  X, Y: Integer; State: TDragState; var Accept: Boolean);
begin
  if Source = Sender then
    Accept := True
  else
    Accept := False;
end;
```

This time, the program tests whether the component that originated dragging (Source) is the same one that is receiving the drag event (Sender). If this is the case, we are dragging a panel onto itself, and not over another panel. Because we have written the method with this generic code (without references to specific panels), we can use it for both panels.

The first panel can also be dragged onto the second list box. In this case, we should still resize the first list box, enlarging it, but check that the third one doesn't shrink below a certain limit:

```
if (Source = Panel1) and (ListBox3.Width > 40) then
begin
  Accept := True;
  ListBox1.Width := ListBox1.Width + X;
end
```

Now X is relative to the second list box, so we can use it as an increment for the size of the first one. The maximum-width test performed by this code is far from perfect, since it checks to see if the third list box was big enough, not if it still will be more than 40 pixels after the current mouse-move message. The code could test whether the future size of the third list box will be big enough, but in this example, this is probably not necessary. If we end up with a list box that is 30 pixels wide, it isn't a big problem. We could easily fix this by increasing the value we test for (such as using 45 instead of 40, considering an average of 5 pixels for each mouse move message).

> **NOTE**
>
> Actually, no one can say what the movement of the mouse is between two consecutive mouse-move messages. The system cannot send a message for each movement of a single pixel, unless you move the mouse really slowly. The move messages are discrete, not continuous. Their generation depends on system timers and similar hardware-related parameters, but they are added to a message queue. For this reason, an application receives mouse-move messages at a rate that depends on the total workload of the system. The idea of an average of 5 pixels per movement is almost a random guess.

14

The same ListBox2DragOver should also test to see if the second panel is being dragged over the second list box, checking that the list box is not reduced too much. Also, the third list box has an OnDragOver handler, related to the second panel. You can see this code, which is similar to that of the first panel, in Listing 14.6.

LISTING 14.6: The source code of the SPLIT3 example

```
unit Split_f;

interface

uses
  SysUtils, WinTypes, WinProcs, Messages, Classes, Graphics,
  Controls, Forms, Dialogs, StdCtrls, ExtCtrls;

type
  TForm1 = class(TForm)
    ListBox1: TListBox;
    ListBox2: TListBox;
    ListBox3: TListBox;
    FontDialog1: TFontDialog;
    Panel1: TPanel;
    Panel2: TPanel;
    procedure ListBoxDblClick(Sender: TObject);
    procedure ListBox1DragOver(Sender, Source: TObject;
      X, Y: Integer; State: TDragState; var Accept: Boolean);
    procedure PanelDragOver(Sender, Source: TObject;
      X, Y: Integer; State: TDragState; var Accept: Boolean);
    procedure ListBox2DragOver(Sender, Source: TObject;
      X, Y: Integer; State: TDragState; var Accept: Boolean);
    procedure ListBox3DragOver(Sender, Source: TObject;
      X, Y: Integer; State: TDragState; var Accept: Boolean);
```

LISTING 14.6: The source code of the SPLIT3 example (continued)

```
    private
    public
    end;

var
  Form1: TForm1;

implementation

{$R *.DFM}

procedure TForm1.ListBoxDblClick(Sender: TObject);
begin
  with Sender as TListBox do
  begin
    FontDialog1.Font := Font;
    if FontDialog1.Execute then
      Font := FontDialog1.Font;
  end;
end;

procedure TForm1.ListBox1DragOver(Sender, Source: TObject;
  X, Y: Integer; State: TDragState; var Accept: Boolean);
begin
  {if dragging started from the first panel,
  and new size is not too little...}
  if (Source = Panel1) and (X > 40) then
  begin
    Accept := True;
    ListBox1.Width := X;
  end
  else
    Accept := False;
end;

{same code for both panels, used only to set the proper cursor}
procedure TForm1.PanelDragOver(Sender, Source: TObject;
  X, Y: Integer; State: TDragState; var Accept: Boolean);
begin
  if Source = Sender then
    Accept := True
  else
    Accept := False;
end;

procedure TForm1.ListBox2DragOver(Sender, Source: TObject;
  X, Y: Integer; State: TDragState; var Accept: Boolean);
begin
  {if dragging started from the first panel,
  and the size of the third list box is not too little...}
  if (Source = Panel1) and (ListBox3.Width > 40) then
```

LISTING 14.6: The source code of the SPLIT3 example (continued)

```
begin
  Accept := True;
  ListBox1.Width := ListBox1.Width + X;
end
{if dragging started from the second panel,
and new size is not too little...}
else if (Source = Panel2) and (X > 40) then
begin
  Accept := True;
  ListBox2.Width := X;
end
else
  Accept := False;
end;

procedure TForm1.ListBox3DragOver(Sender, Source: TObject;
  X, Y: Integer; State: TDragState; var Accept: Boolean);
begin
  {if dragging started from the second panel,
  and the size of the third list box is not too little...}
  if (Source = Panel2) and (ListBox3.Width > 40) then
  begin
    Accept := True;
    ListBox2.Width := ListBox2.Width + X;
  end
  else
    Accept := False;
end;

end.
```

Drawing a Split Line

In the two preceding examples, we moved or resized the list boxes during the dragging operation, and not at the end. The advantage of this approach is that the user always has a clear picture of what is going on. The disadvantage is that the contents of the list boxes must be repainted several times, often with a nasty flickering.

If you have ever used a splitter in a big application, you have probably dragged a big line indicating the final position of the splitter, without actually moving the components until the end of the dragging operation. This is the approach we'll take in the next version of our example, SPLIT4.

To add a splitter line, we could draw a thick gray line on the list box in the current horizontal position. The problem is that we will need to delete that gray splitter line as soon as the splitter is moved. To accomplish this, the program needs to remember where the line was and be able to restore the previous contents of the list box (its text). A solution is to draw a line using the pmNot pen mode, which reverses the current output. This is useful because, by reversing the output twice, we can easily restore the original drawing. To obtain this effect, for each list box, write:

```
ListBox1.Canvas.Pen.Width := 5;
ListBox1.Canvas.Pen.Mode := pmNot;
```

The form of SPLIT4, shown in Figure 14.6, has the same components as the previous version, but a more complex source code, as you can see in the new code in Listing 14.7. Let's go over the key elements of the source code for this example.

FIGURE 14.6:

The line splitter of the SPLIT4 example

First, notice that there are two custom methods. The DrawDragLine method is used to draw the new line and eventually delete the old one. The other method, DeleteDragLine, is used to delete the current line when dragging ends.

LISTING 14.7: The source code of the SPLIT4 example

```
unit Split_f;

interface

uses
  SysUtils, WinTypes, WinProcs, Messages, Classes, Graphics,
  Controls, Forms, Dialogs, StdCtrls, ExtCtrls;

type
  TForm1 = class(TForm)
    ListBox1: TListBox;
    ListBox2: TListBox;
    ListBox3: TListBox;
    FontDialog1: TFontDialog;
    Panel1: TPanel;
    Panel2: TPanel;
    Shape1: TShape;
    procedure ListBoxDblClick(Sender: TObject);
    procedure ListBox1DragOver(Sender, Source: TObject;
      X, Y: Integer; State: TDragState; var Accept: Boolean);
    procedure PanelDragOver(Sender, Source: TObject;
      X, Y: Integer; State: TDragState; var Accept: Boolean);
    procedure ListBox2DragOver(Sender, Source: TObject;
      X, Y: Integer; State: TDragState; var Accept: Boolean);
    procedure ListBox3DragOver(Sender, Source: TObject;
      X, Y: Integer; State: TDragState; var Accept: Boolean);
    procedure ListBox1DragDrop(Sender, Source: TObject;
      X, Y: Integer);
    procedure ListBox2DragDrop(Sender, Source: TObject;
      X, Y: Integer);
    procedure ListBox3DragDrop(Sender, Source: TObject;
      X, Y: Integer);
    procedure FormCreate(Sender: TObject);
  private
    OldX: Integer;
    OldList: TListBox;
  public
    procedure DrawDragLine (List: TListBox;
      X: Integer; State: TDragState);
    procedure DeleteDragLine (List: TListBox);
  end;

var
  Form1: TForm1;

implementation

{$R *.DFM}

{select a new font for one of the list boxes}
procedure TForm1.ListBoxDblClick(Sender: TObject);
```

14

LISTING 14.7: The source code of the SPLIT4 example (continued)

```
begin
  with Sender as TListbox do
  begin
    FontDialog1.Font := Font;
    if FontDialog1.Execute then
      Font := FontDialog1.Font;
  end;
end;

procedure TForm1.FormCreate(Sender: TObject);
begin
  {initialize variables}
  OldList := nil;
  OldX := -10;

  {initialize line drawing}
  ListBox1.Canvas.Pen.Width := 5;
  ListBox1.Canvas.Pen.Mode := pmNot;
  ListBox2.Canvas.Pen.Width := 5;
  ListBox2.Canvas.Pen.Mode := pmNot;
  ListBox3.Canvas.Pen.Width := 5;
  ListBox3.Canvas.Pen.Mode := pmNot;
end;

procedure TForm1.DrawDragLine (List: TListBox;
  X: Integer; State: TDragState);
begin
  {if there is currently a line...}
  if OldList <> nil then
  begin
    {delete the previous line, re-drawing onto it}
    OldList.Canvas.MoveTo (OldX, 0);
    OldList.Canvas.LineTo (OldX, ClientHeight);
  end;
  {if the user is not leaving the list box, draw the
  new line and store the older values}
  if not (State = dsDragLeave) then
  begin
    List.Canvas.MoveTo (X, 0);
    List.Canvas.LineTo (X, ClientHeight);
    OldX := X;
    OldList := List;
  end
  else
  {if the user is leaving the list box, then do *not* draw
  and set old values to nil/invalid}
  begin
    OldX := -10;
    OldList := nil
  end;
end;
```

LISTING 14.7: The source code of the SPLIT4 example (continued)

```
procedure TForm1.DeleteDragLine (List: TListBox);
begin
  {delete the old line and reset the invalid position}
  if OldList <> nil then
  begin
    OldList.Canvas.MoveTo (OldX, 0);
    OldList.Canvas.LineTo (OldX, ClientHeight);
    OldX := -10;
    OldList := nil;
  end;
end;

procedure TForm1.ListBox1DragOver(Sender, Source: TObject;
  X, Y: Integer; State: TDragState; var Accept: Boolean);
begin
  {default case}
  Accept := False;
  {if dragging started from the first panel}
  if Source = Panel1 then
    {if the new size is not too little}
    if X > 40 then
    begin
      Accept := True;
      DrawDragLine (ListBox1, X, State);
    end
    else
      DeleteDragLine (ListBox1);
end;

procedure TForm1.ListBox1DragDrop(Sender, Source: TObject;
  X, Y: Integer);
begin
  DeleteDragLine (ListBox1);
  ListBox1.Width := X;
end;

{same code for both panels, used only to set the proper cursor}
procedure TForm1.PanelDragOver(Sender, Source: TObject;
  X, Y: Integer; State: TDragState; var Accept: Boolean);
begin
  if Source = Sender then
    Accept := True
  else
    Accept := False;
end;

procedure TForm1.ListBox2DragOver(Sender, Source: TObject;
  X, Y: Integer; State: TDragState; var Accept: Boolean);
```

14

LISTING 14.7: The source code of the SPLIT4 example (continued)

```
begin
  {if dragging is valid, from either panels}
  if ( (Source = Panel1) and (ListBox3.Width - X > 40) ) or
    ( (Source = Panel2) and (X > 40) ) then
  begin
    Accept := True;
    DrawDragLine (ListBox2, X, State);
  end
  else
  begin
    Accept := False;
    DeleteDragLine (ListBox2);
  end;
end;

procedure TForm1.ListBox2DragDrop(Sender, Source: TObject;
  X, Y: Integer);
begin
  DeleteDragLine (ListBox2);
  if Source = Panel1 then
    ListBox1.Width := ListBox1.Width + X
  else
    ListBox2.Width := X;
end;

procedure TForm1.ListBox3DragOver(Sender, Source: TObject;
  X, Y: Integer; State: TDragState; var Accept: Boolean);
begin
  {default case}
  Accept := False;
  {if dragging started from the first panel}
  if Source = Panel2 then
    {if the last list box is not too little}
    if ListBox3.Width - X > 40 then
    begin
      Accept := True;
      DrawDragLine (ListBox3, X, State);
    end
    else
      DeleteDragLine (ListBox3);
end;

procedure TForm1.ListBox3DragDrop(Sender, Source: TObject;
  X, Y: Integer);
begin
  DeleteDragLine (ListBox3);
  ListBox2.Width := ListBox2.Width + X;
end;

end.
```

To draw or delete a line, these functions use the MoveTo and LineTo methods of the canvas of the current list box (passed as parameter) or of the old list box:

```
List.Canvas.MoveTo (X, 0);
List.Canvas.LineTo (X, ClientHeight);
...
OldList.Canvas.MoveTo (OldX, 0);
OldList.Canvas.LineTo (OldX, ClientHeight);
```

Notice that the line-drawing procedure tests the value of the State parameter passed by the dragging event, checked for with dsDragLeave. If the mouse cursor is leaving the list box, the line is not drawn, and the OldList and OldX private fields of the form are set to nil and a random negative value, respectively. Usually, these variables store the position of the last line instead:

```
OldX := X;
OldList := List;
```

Another important part of the SPLIT4 example is the test to see if the OldList object is currently storing a list box or if it has nil. This test is done before any call to a method of the object. If you don't do this, you risk accessing an undefined object, which will raise an exception.

In the code of the three OnDragOver events, you can see something similar to the code in the SPLIT3 example. We check to see if the list box should accept dragging from the current panel (except for ListBox2, which can accept input from both), and then we also test whether the current position is within the permitted range. When the splitter is in the range, the program calls the line drawing (or even better, *moving*) method. When the splitter goes out of the proper area, the program removes the last line, calling DeleteDragLine.

As usual, to test if the position is valid, we check if X is less than 40 or if the last list box has enough space. To make this last check, however, we need to compute the size of the third list box, since it doesn't change continuously during the dragging operation as in the other examples. The simplest way to compute if the third list box is large enough is to test if the increase in width (X) will leave it at more than 40 pixels:

```
ListBox3.Width - X > 40
```

The new width of the list box being dragged is set only when the dragging operation ends, as in:

```
procedure TForm1.ListBox1DragDrop(Sender, Source: TObject;
  X, Y: Integer);
begin
  DeleteDragLine (ListBox1);
  ListBox1.Width := X;
end;
```

As you can see, there is no test of any sort, since dropping can take place only if dragging is allowed. However, in the OnDragDrop method of the second list box, we need to consider which panel originated the dragging:

```
if Source = Panel1 then
  ListBox1.Width := ListBox1.Width + X
else
  ListBox2.Width := X;
```

Although the code of this example is more complex, and it took some time to devise the whole schema, the effect is worth the effort. A particular challenge was handling the case of two consecutive dragging operations on two different list boxes (which takes place only after a fast mouse movement). For this situtation, I developed the idea of the OldList object.

Direct Mouse Splitting

The fifth and final version of this same splitting example is less Delphi-oriented and more Windows-oriented. It uses no components other than the list boxes. Without panels or headers, and without the mouse-dragging support offered by Delphi (which is not available in forms), the form must receive and handle mouse events directly.

The other disadvantage of this approach is that we need to leave some space between the list boxes, to allow the user to operate on the form, and we lose the automatic alignment features. The advantage is that we have a very precise control, although, in this example, I haven't taken advantage of it to implement a splitter line, as in SPLIT4.

NOTE I decided not to include a sixth version that uses the direct mouse splitting method and implements a splitter line, because five implementations of the same example are boring enough. However, it's important to study the advantages and disadvantages of solving a problem in different ways, and you might want to try this approach on your own.

So here we are with three list boxes and a form. You don't see much of the form, just two small vertical areas we will use as a splitter, as shown in Figure 14.7. The form uses the crHSplit cursor that we used in the previous examples. The SPLIT5 version of the form is not much different from the previous one, although now you can see the background of the form between the list boxes. To make the figure more understandable, I've temporarily resized the second list box, to show the form behind it.

FIGURE 14.7:

The form of the SPLIT5 version at design-time

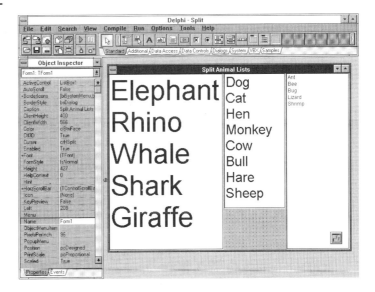

When the user presses the left mouse button on the form (that is, on one of the two vertical lines), the program starts some dragging code, which continues until the user releases the mouse button. During this period of time, any mouse movement has the effect of moving the list boxes, simulating a corresponding movement in the splitter area. Before we discuss the code of this example, however, let's take a moment for an overview of implementing dragging and capturing the mouse input.

Dragging the Mouse

As we discussed in Chapter 9, in MS Windows, there are three basic groups of mouse messages: those related to pressing a button, those related to releasing the button, and those related to moving the mouse. Delphi components also add the notion of the left-button click.

But there is no idea of dragging. So how can you implement it, and how has Borland implemented it in Delphi? The idea behind dragging is quite simple. The program receives a sequence of button-down, mouse-move, and button-up messages. When the button is pressed, dragging begins, although the real actions take place only when the user moves the mouse (without releasing the mouse button) and when dragging terminates (when the button-up message arrives).

The problem with this basic approach is that since a window usually receives mouse events only when the mouse is over its client area, we cannot build a reliable program. For example, what if the mouse button is pressed, the mouse is moved onto another window, and then the button is released? The second window will receive the button-up message.

There are two solutions to this problem. One (seldom used) is mouse clipping. Using a Windows API function (namely `ClipCursor`) you can force the mouse not to leave a certain area of the screen. When you move it outside the specified area, it stumbles against an invisible barrier.

The second, more common, solution is to capture the mouse. When a window captures the mouse, all the subsequent mouse input is sent to that window, as we have already seen in Chapter 10. This is the approach we will use for the SPLIT5 example.

The Dragging Code

The code of SPLIT5 (you can see the full listing in Listing 14.8) is built around three methods: FormMouseDown, FormMouseMove, and FormMouseUp.

LISTING 14.8: The full listing of the SPLIT5 example

```
unit Split_f;

interface

uses
  SysUtils, WinTypes, WinProcs, Messages, Classes, Graphics,
  Controls, Forms, Dialogs, StdCtrls, ExtCtrls;

type
  TForm1 = class(TForm)
    ListBox1: TListBox;
    ListBox2: TListBox;
    ListBox3: TListBox;
    FontDialog1: TFontDialog;
    procedure ListBoxDblClick(Sender: TObject);
    procedure FormMouseDown(Sender: TObject;
      Button: TMouseButton; Shift: TShiftState;
      X, Y: Integer);
    procedure FormMouseMove(Sender: TObject;
      Shift: TShiftState; X, Y: Integer);
    procedure FormMouseUp(Sender: TObject;
      Button: TMouseButton; Shift: TShiftState;
      X, Y: Integer);
  private
    Dragging, FirstSplit: Boolean;
  public

  end;

var
  Form1: TForm1;

implementation

{$R *.DFM}

procedure TForm1.ListBoxDblClick(Sender: TObject);
begin
  with Sender as TListBox do
  begin
    FontDialog1.Font := Font;
    if FontDialog1.Execute then
      Font := FontDialog1.Font;
  end;
end;

procedure TForm1.FormMouseDown(Sender: TObject;
  Button: TMouseButton; Shift: TShiftState; X, Y: Integer);
begin
  if Button = mbLeft then
  begin
    Dragging := True;
```

LISTING 14.8: The full listing of the SPLIT5 example (continued)

```
      SetCapture (Handle);
      if (X <= ListBox2.Left) then
        FirstSplit := True
      else
        FirstSplit := False;
    end;
end;

procedure TForm1.FormMouseMove(Sender: TObject;
  Shift: TShiftState; X, Y: Integer);
begin
  if Dragging then
    if FirstSplit then
      if (X > 40) and
          (X < ClientWidth - ListBox3.Width - 40) then
        begin
          ListBox1.Width := X - 2;
          ListBox2.Left := X + 2;
          ListBox2.Width := ListBox3.Left - ListBox2.Left - 4;
        end
      else {out of range}
        begin
          Dragging := False;
          ReleaseCapture;
        end
    else {second split}
      if (X > ListBox1.Width + 40) and
          (X < ClientWidth - 40) then
        begin
          ListBox2.Width := X - ListBox2.Left - 2;
          ListBox3.Left := X + 2;
          ListBox3.Width := ClientWidth - ListBox3.Left + 1;
        end
      else {out of range}
        begin
          Dragging := False;
          ReleaseCapture;
        end;
end;

procedure TForm1.FormMouseUp(Sender: TObject;
  Button: TMouseButton; Shift: TShiftState; X, Y: Integer);
begin
  if Dragging then
    begin
      ReleaseCapture;
      Dragging := False;
    end;
end;

end.
```

Pressing the left mouse button over the form (that is, over a splitter) starts the process, setting a couple of Boolean fields of the form, named Dragging and FirstSplit. The first variable is used to indicate that dragging is in action, and this variable will be used by the other two methods. The second variable indicates which of the two splitters the user is currently dragging (True indicates the first one; False the second).

```
if (X <= ListBox2.Left) then
  FirstSplit := True
else
  FirstSplit := False;
```

The last, and probably most important, action of this method is the call to the SetCapture API function. When dragging is active, as indicated by the corresponding variable (Dragging), and the user moves the mouse, the program performs a number of actions, but the idea is simple: resize the list boxes, unless we are out of range.

An example of range testing is the following:

```
if FirstSplit then
  if (X > 40) and (X < ClientWidth - ListBox3.Width - 40) then
    ...
```

Notice that this time X is expressed in form coordinates. If we are within the range, the list boxes are moved and arranged properly. In this example, when the first splitter is dragged, the first list box is enlarged and the second is reduced by a corresponding amount. The third list box is not involved. The behavior is different from the previous example, which emulated the behavior of the Header component. When you look at the code that sets the position of the list boxes, remember that some space should be left free to implement the splitter.

In case we move out of the range, the dragging operation terminates, calling the ReleaseCapture API function, and setting the value of the Dragging field to False. The same thing happens when the mouse button is released.

A Custom File Manager

Now that we have explored dragging techniques in some detail, we can use these techniques to build a complex example. Our final example in this chapter is a File Manager clone that has a preview window for the most common file formats. We will build this File Manager in two steps, working first on the form and on limited file handling, and then developing the preview window.

This File Manager won't have all the features we would like included, and it will probably be less usable than the Delphi examples already available with the product. However, you might want to merge the code presented here with some of the code of other File Manager clones, building your own customized version. The key focus of this example is in the preview capabilities, which will be added only in the second version.

Components Used in the File Manager

As you might guess, the FILEMAN1 example uses all the Delphi file-, disk-, and directory-related components of the System page of the Components palette. There are four of these components:

- DirectoryListBox is a graphical and hierarchical list box, an outline, of the directory tree of a certain drive.

- FileListBox is a graphical list box of the files of a certain directory, which match certain properties.

- DriveComboBox is a graphical combo box listing all of the disk drives installed in the system.

- FilterComboBox is a combo box listing the file filters indicated in the Filters property.

You can see all of these components in the form of the FILEMAN1 example in Figure 14.8. One of the most interesting features of these components is that they can be connected using some properties, so that they will automatically work together. Here is a list of the connections:

- The drive combo box has a DirList property that lets you indicate a connected directory list box. When the current drive changes, the value of the Drive property is copied to the corresponding property of the directory outline.

- The directory list box has a FileList property that lets you indicate a connected file list box, so that the Directory properties of the two components are synchronized. The same list box can also be connected to a label using the DirLabel property. Such a label automatically displays the path of the current directory. You can see a label of this kind in the status bar of the FILE-MAN1 form (see Figure 14.8).

- The file list box can be connected to an edit box with the FileEdit property, so that a user can enter the name of a file to select it. (I haven't used this connection in our example here.)

- The filter combo box has a FileList property that lets you indicate the connected file list box. When a new filter is selected, the component notifies the file list box of the new value, setting its Mask property.

14

You make these connections either at design-time or in the code at program startup. I suggest that you make them at design-time, so that the components immediately display live data, as in Figure 14.8. You can see all of the connections of this example in the textual description of the form in Listing 14.9.

FIGURE 14.8:

The form of the FILEMAN1 example at design-time Notice that the file components already display live data.

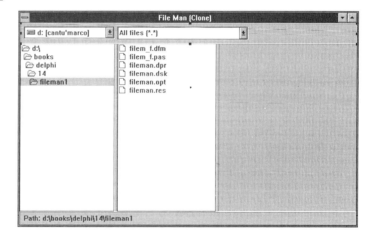

Before reviewing the code, which implements dragging and a few other techniques, let's take a look at some of the important properties of the file list box and filter combo box components.

LISTING 14.9: The textual description of the form of the FILEMAN1 example. Notice the connections among the various file-related components.

```
object Form1: TForm1
  Cursor = crSizeWE
  Caption = 'File Man (Clone)'
  OnMouseDown = FormMouseDown
  OnMouseMove = FormMouseMove
  OnMouseUp = FormMouseUp
  OnResize = FormResize
  object FileListBox1: TFileListBox
    FileType = [ftReadOnly, ftArchive, ftNormal]
    ShowGlyphs = True
    OnDblClick = FileListBox1DblClick
  end
  object DirectoryListBox1: TDirectoryListBox
    DirLabel = PathLabel
    FileList = FileListBox1
  end
  object PreviewPanel: TPanel
    BevelOuter = bvLowered
  end
  object SpeedBar: TPanel
    Align = alTop
    BevelInner = bvLowered
    object DriveComboBox1: TDriveComboBox
      DirList = DirectoryListBox1
    end
    object FilterComboBox1: TFilterComboBox
      FileList = FileListBox1
      Filter = 'All files (*.*)|*.*|Programs (*.exe)|*.exe|Pascal Sources
(*.pas)|*.pas|Delphi Projects (*.dpr)|*.dpr|Images (*.bmp,
*.ico)|*.bmp;*.ico|Sounds (*.wav)|*.wav|All Delphi Files (*.pas, *.dfm,
*.dpr)|*.pas;*.dfm;*.dpr'
    end
  end
  object StatusBar: TPanel
    Align = alBottom
    BevelInner = bvLowered
    object Label1: TLabel
      Caption = 'Path:'
    end
    object PathLabel: TLabel
      Caption = 'd:\books\delphi\14\fileman1'
    end
  end
end
```

The files actually listed by the file list box depend on two properties: Mask, connected to the filter combo box, and FileType, which indicates the type of files being displayed. The FileType property has a value of the TFileType set, which has the following elements:

- `ftReadOnly`, the list box includes files with the read-only attribute.
- `ftHidden`, the list box includes files with the hidden attribute.
- `ftSystem`, the list box includes files with the system attribute.
- `ftVolumeID`, the list box might include the volume name.
- `ftDirectory`, the list box includes directories, shown in square brackets.
- `ftArchive`, the list box includes files with the archive attribute.
- `ftNormal`, the list box includes generic files, with no particular attributes.

In Figure 14.9, you can see a graphical list box, which also displays the directories, some hidden and system files of the root directory, and the volume name. In this example, I've used a set with the following value:

```
[ftReadOnly,ftArchive,ftNormal]
```

FIGURE 14.9:

A file list box with directories, the volume name (`cantu'ma.rco`), and some hidden files, at design-time

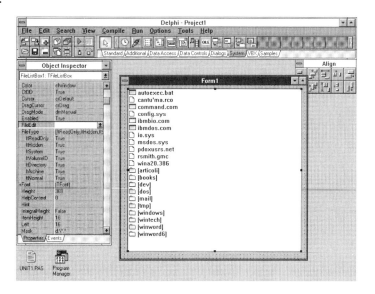

Removing directory names was particularly important, since a user might be tempted to double-click on them to change the current directory (something you would need to implement in the code).

The filter combo box has a Filter property. An important feature of this property, and the corresponding properties of the standard file open and file save dialog boxes, is that you can specify a file type with multiple extensions, as you can see in Figure 14.10.

FIGURE 14.10:

The Filter property editor for the FilterComboBox of the FILEMAN1 example

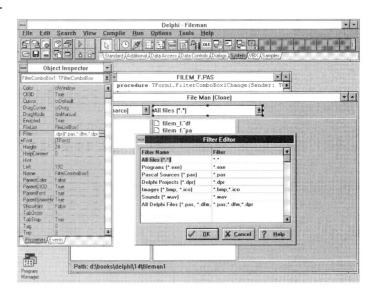

As I've mentioned before, most of this program's code has to do with resizing the components on the form. The code used to accomplish this is similar to the code of the SPLIT5 example. The only differences are that this example includes the status bar and the toolbar, and the window can be resized (the examples in the SPLIT series use a dialog box frame). Notice that the toolbar and the status bar are two panels I've named SpeedBar and StatusBar. This makes the code more readable, since it avoids using identifiers such as Panel2, which let the reader wonder what the panel is for and where it is located in the form.

You can see the implementation of dragging in the source code for this example in Listing 14.10. Let's go over the new portions of code in this listing.

LISTING 14.10: The listing of the FILEMAN1 example, the first version of the customized File Manager

```
unit Filem_f;

interface

uses WinTypes, WinProcs, Classes, Graphics, Forms, Controls,
  FileCtrl, StdCtrls, ExtCtrls, Dialogs, SysUtils;

type
  TForm1 = class(TForm)
    FileListBox1: TFileListBox;
    DirectoryListBox1: TDirectoryListBox;
    PreviewPanel: TPanel;
    SpeedBar: TPanel;
    DriveComboBox1: TDriveComboBox;
    FilterComboBox1: TFilterComboBox;
    StatusBar: TPanel;
    Label1: TLabel;
    PathLabel: TLabel;
    procedure FormMouseDown(Sender: TObject;
      Button: TMouseButton; Shift: TShiftState; X, Y: Integer);
    procedure FormMouseMove(Sender: TObject;
      Shift: TShiftState; X, Y: Integer);
    procedure FormMouseUp(Sender: TObject;
      Button: TMouseButton; Shift: TShiftState; X, Y: Integer);
    procedure FormResize(Sender: TObject);
    procedure FileListBox1DblClick(Sender: TObject);
  private
    { Private declarations }
    Dragging, FirstSplit: Boolean;
  public
    { Public declarations }
  end;

var
  Form1: TForm1;

implementation

{$R *.DFM}

procedure TForm1.FormMouseDown(Sender: TObject;
  Button: TMouseButton; Shift: TShiftState; X, Y: Integer);
begin
  if Button = mbLeft then
  begin
    Dragging := True;
    SetCapture (Handle);
    if (X <= FileListBox1.Left) then
      FirstSplit := True
```

LISTING 14.10: The listing of the FILEMAN1 example (continued)

```
    else
      FirstSplit := False;
  end;
end;

procedure TForm1.FormMouseMove(Sender: TObject;
  Shift: TShiftState; X, Y: Integer);
begin
  if Dragging then
  begin
    if FirstSplit then
      if (X > 20) and
         (X < ClientWidth - PreviewPanel.Width - 20) then
      begin
        DirectoryListBox1.Width := X - 2;
        FileListBox1.Left := X + 2;
        FileListBox1.Width := PreviewPanel.Left -
          FileListBox1.Left - 4;
      end
      else                      {out of range}
      begin
        Dragging := False;
        ReleaseCapture;
      end
    else                        {second split}
      if (X > DirectoryListBox1.Width + 20) and
         (X < ClientWidth - 20) then
      begin
        FileListBox1.Width := X - FileListBox1.Left - 2;
        PreviewPanel.Left := X + 2;
        PreviewPanel.Width := ClientWidth - PreviewPanel.Left;
      end
      else                      {out of range}
      begin
        Dragging := False;
        ReleaseCapture;
      end;
  end;
end;

procedure TForm1.FormMouseUp(Sender: TObject;
  Button: TMouseButton; Shift: TShiftState; X, Y: Integer);
begin
  if Dragging then
  begin
    ReleaseCapture;
    Dragging := False;
  end;
end;
```

LISTING 14.10: The listing of the FILEMAN1 example (continued)

```
procedure TForm1.FormResize(Sender: TObject);
var
  H: Integer;                          {height of lists}
begin
  H := ClientHeight - SpeedBar.Height - StatusBar.Height;
  DirectoryListBox1.Height := H;
  FileListBox1.Height := H;
  PreviewPanel.Height := H;
  PreviewPanel.Width := ClientWidth - PreviewPanel.Left;
end;

procedure TForm1.FileListBox1DblClick(Sender: TObject);
var
  FileExt: string [5];
  FileName: array [0..15] of char;
begin
  FileExt := ExtractFileExt(FileListBox1.Filename);
  StrPCopy (FileName, FileListBox1.Filename);
  if FileExt = '.exe' then
    WinExec (FileName, sw_ShowNormal)
  else
    ShowMessage (FileListBox1.Filename);
end;

end.
```

Changes both in the vertical and horizontal size of the window are handled by the FormResize method. When the vertical size changes, each of the three main elements (the two list boxes and the panel) is set to the height of the client area of the form, minus the two bars:

```
H := ClientHeight - SpeedBar.Height -
  StatusBar.Height;
```

For the horizontal size, the panel on the right is resized to fit in the form:

```
PreviewPanel.Width := ClientWidth - PreviewPanel.Left;
```

With this code, if the user reduces the size of the application too much, the two list boxes remain at the current size, and a horizontal scroll bar automatically appears (see Figure 14.11). This is a nice default behavior of Delphi forms.

FIGURE 14.11:

If you shrink the FILEMAN1 form too much, a scroll bar automatically appears.

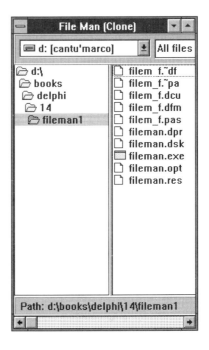

What is the final aim of this version of the example? If the user double-clicks on an executable file in the file list box, that program is executed. This is done with a few lines of code in the FileListBox1DblClick method.

The value of the Filename property of the list, which holds the currently selected name, is copied to a PChar compatible string, Filename, which is used as parameter of the WinExec API function. This is done only if the file extension, retrieved with the ExtractFileExt Delphi function, is .exe. Otherwise, the name of the file is shown in a message box:

```
FileExt := ExtractFileExt(FileListBox1.Filename);
StrPCopy (FileName, FileListBox1.Filename);
if FileExt = '.exe' then
  WinExec (FileName, sw_ShowNormal)
else
  ShowMessage (FileListBox1.Filename);
```

Adding a Preview Pane to the File Manager

On the right side of the form in the FILEMAN1 example there is a useless panel. It is a placeholder for the preview pane we are going to build now, in FILEMAN2. This preview pane can be used for several different types of files: image, text, and sound, plus a hint suggesting how to run the executable programs.

For this reason, the panel has been populated by a number of viewer components, each on a different page of a notebook that fills the entire surface of the panel. The panel itself is almost useless; it just provides the proper three-dimensional effect for the borders.

14

As you can see in the textual description of the form in Listing 14.11, the Notebook component fills the whole client area of the panel, and most of the viewers fill their page of the notebook. This is an advantage because when the form is resized, these components will be adjusted automatically. As an alternative, I could have added some buttons to the various pages, such as a button to shrink or expand the image to fit the whole available area.

LISTING 14.11: The textual description of the form of the FILEMAN2 example (omitting some of the details that are the same as in the FILEMAN1 example)

```
object Form1: TForm1
  Cursor = crSizeWE
  Caption = 'File Man (Clone)'
  OnMouseDown = FormMouseDown
  OnMouseMove = FormMouseMove
  OnMouseUp = FormMouseUp
  OnResize = FormResize
  object FileListBox1: TFileListBox...
  object DirectoryListBox1: TDirectoryListBox...
  object PreviewPanel: TPanel
    BevelOuter = bvLowered
    object Notebook1: TNotebook
      Align = alClient
      PageIndex - 1
      object TPage
        Caption = 'Image'
        object ImagePreview: TImage
          Align = alClient
        end
      end
    end
```

LISTING 14.11 : The textual description of the form of the FILEMAN2 example
(continued)

```
    object TPage
      Caption = 'Text'
      object MemoPreview: TMemo
        Align = alClient
        Lines.Strings = ('MemoPreview')
        ReadOnly = True
        ScrollBars = ssBoth
      end
    end
    object TPage
      Caption = 'Sound'
      object Label2: TLabel
        Align = alTop
        Caption = 'Use the media player panel below to play the current
file'
        Font.Height = -20
        Font.Name = 'Arial'
        WordWrap = True
      end
      object MediaPreview: TMediaPlayer
        Left = 80
        Top = 144
        Width = 113
        Height = 41
        VisibleButtons = [btPlay, btPause, btStop, btPrev]
      end
    end
    object TPage
      Caption = 'Exe'
      object Label3: TLabel
        Align = alTop
        Caption = 'Double click on the executable file in the file list
box to run it'
        Font.Height = -20
        Font.Name = 'Arial'
        WordWrap = True
      end
    end
    object TPage
      Caption = 'None'
    end
  end
end
object SpeedBar: TPanel
  Align = alTop
  BevelInner = bvLowered
  object DriveComboBox1: TDriveComboBox...
  object FilterComboBox1: TFilterComboBox...
end
```

LISTING 14.11: The textual description of the form of the FILEMAN2 example
(continued)

```
object StatusBar: TPanel
  Align = alBottom
  BevelInner = bvLowered
  object Label1: TLabel...
  object PathLabel: TLabel...
end
end
```

14

The notebook has five pages, with descriptive names. These names are not important, because there isn't a tab set attached. The program changes the page depending on the extension of the current file, when the selection in the file list box changes. Here are the names and a short description of the pages (see Listing 14.11 for the details):

- Image contains an Image component, used to view bitmap files and icon files (see Figure 14.12).

FIGURE 14.12:

The FILEMAN2 example with the Image page of the preview notebook active

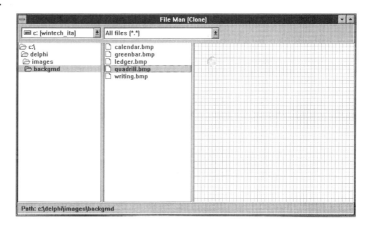

- Text contains a Memo component, used to view any kind of text file, including Windows ini files, Delphi source files, and even old versions of the Delphi source files.

- Sound contains a MediaPlayer component, used to play sound files (wav and mid), and a label with some instructions (see Figure 14.13).

- Exe contains only a label, suggesting that the user double-click on the file in the list box. A button with the same effect—running the file—could be added.

- None is an empty page, used when the file extension is not recognized.

FIGURE 14.13:

The sound page of the notebook of the FILEMAN2 example (the music must be imagined)

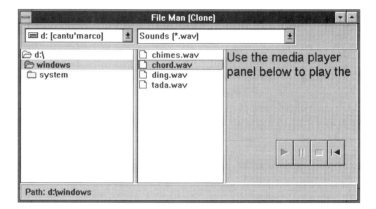

Using a notebook for the preview pane makes this program easily upgradable with new pages that handle other file formats.

TIP

When you work with the form of this program, there are a number of invisible components. For example, if the text page of the notebook is active, the Memo component hides both the notebook and the panel. In this case, the use of the Esc key to navigate the components becomes extremely useful. Each time you press the Esc key, the component hosting the current one will be activated, so you can easily move from the memo to the notebook, from the notebook to the panel, and from the panel to the form.

The code of this example is not very complex. It is the same as the code for the previous version, plus a new method, FileListBox1Change (see Listing 14.12). The code of this procedure is basically a multiple if-then-else statement, checking for the correspondence of the file extension with the predefined values:

```
FileExt := ExtractFileExt(FileListBox1.Filename);
if FileExt = '.exe' then
   ...
else if (FileExt = '.bmp') or (FileExt = '.ico') then
   ...
else if (FileExt = '.txt') or ...
   ...
```

LISTING 14.12: The source code the FILEMAN2 example (omitting some of the details that are the same as in the previous version)

```
unit Filem_f;

interface

uses WinTypes, WinProcs, Classes, Graphics, Forms, Controls,
  FileCtrl, StdCtrls, ExtCtrls, Dialogs, SysUtils, MPlayer;

type
  TForm1 = class(TForm)
    FileListBox1: TFileListBox;
    DirectoryListBox1: TDirectoryListBox;
    PreviewPanel: TPanel;
    SpeedBar: TPanel;
    DriveComboBox1: TDriveComboBox;
    FilterComboBox1: TFilterComboBox;
    StatusBar: TPanel;
    Label1: TLabel;
    PathLabel: TLabel;
    Notebook1: TNotebook;
    ImagePreview: TImage;
    Label3: TLabel;
    MemoPreview: TMemo;
    MediaPreview: TMediaPlayer;
    Label2: TLabel;
    procedure FormMouseDown(Sender: TObject;
      Button: TMouseButton; Shift: TShiftState; X, Y: Integer);
    procedure FormMouseMove(Sender: TObject;
      Shift: TShiftState; X, Y: Integer);
    procedure FormMouseUp(Sender: TObject; Button: TMouseButton;
      Shift: TShiftState; X, Y: Integer);
    procedure FormResize(Sender: TObject);
    procedure FilterComboBox1Change(Sender: TObject);
    procedure FileListBox1DblClick(Sender: TObject);
    procedure FileListBox1Change(Sender: TObject);
```

LISTING 14.12: The source code the FILEMAN2 example (continued)

```
  private
    { Private declarations }
    Dragging, FirstSplit: Boolean;
  end;

var
  Form1: TForm1;

implementation

{$R *.DFM}

{procedures TForm1.FormMouseDown, TForm1.FormMouseMove,
TForm1.FormMouseUp, TForm1.FormResize, and TForm1.FileListBox1DblClick,
are the same as in the previous version, shown in Listing 14.10}

procedure TForm1.FileListBox1Change(Sender: TObject);
var
  FileExt: string [5];
begin
  FileExt := ExtractFileExt(FileListBox1.Filename);
  if FileExt = '.exe' then
    Notebook1.ActivePage := 'Exe'
  else if (FileExt = '.bmp') or (FileExt = '.ico') then
  begin
    Notebook1.ActivePage := 'Image';
    ImagePreview.Picture.LoadFromFile (FileListBox1.Filename);
  end
  else if (FileExt = '.txt') or (FileExt = '.pas') or
    (FileExt = '.ini') or (FileExt = '.dpr') or
    (FileExt = '.bat') or (FileExt = '.dsk') or
    (FileExt = '.rc') or (FileExt = '.~pa') or
    (FileExt = '.×p') then
  begin
    Notebook1.ActivePage := 'Text';
    MemoPreview.Lines.LoadFromFile (FileListBox1.Filename);
  end
  else if (FileExt = '.wav') or (FileExt = '.mid') or
    (FileExt = '.avi') then
  begin
    Notebook1.ActivePage := 'Sound';
    MediaPreview.Filename := FileListBox1.Filename;
    MediaPreview.Open;
  end
  else
    Notebook1.ActivePage := 'None'
end;

end.
```

Each of the branches of this compound statement activates one of the pages of the notebook, indicating its name, and most branches also load a file, as in:

```
Notebook1.ActivePage := 'Image';
ImagePreview.Picture.LoadFromFile (FileListBox1.Filename);
```

The only difference is in the code for the sound files, which just after loading a file calls the Open method to activate it. By the way, I've referred to "sound" files, but, as you can see in the code, video files (avi) are supported, too. You only need to have the proper drivers installed.

The text viewer is the one that can be used with the most file extensions, but you could also add some more extensions:

- .txt, for text files. I have not added other document formats, because in most cases, their content is unreadable.

- .pas, for Pascal source code files.

- .ini, for MS Windows ini files.

- .dpr, for Delphi project files, which are text files with Pascal source code (see Figure 14.14 for an example).

- .bat, for DOS batch files. You could add an option to run these files.

- .dsk, for Delphi desktop information files, which are text files.

FIGURE 14.14:

A Delphi project file loaded in the viewer of the FILEMAN2 example

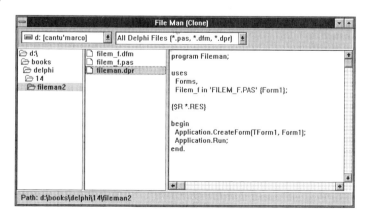

- .rc, for Windows resource files, found in some of the Delphi libraries and source code.
- .pa, for the backup versions of Delphi Pascal files.
- .dp, for the backup versions of Delphi project files.

The preview pane of this example can be useful for browsing through a series of files, even if they have different extensions. Of course, it can handle only the basic formats, not Paintbrush (pcx) files, device-independent bitmaps (dib), or word processor files (doc). Supporting these formats requires coding, and doesn't come for free as in the cases we have seen.

The only real drawback of this immediate preview approach is that long files take a while to load, and if you select an unwanted file, you must wait until it is loaded. This mainly depends on Windows, an operating environment with very limited concurrency. When you are loading a file in Windows, you need to wait until the end of the operation to regain control. A solution might be to check the file size, and for big files, display a warning and wait for a specific action by the user to load the file in the preview pane.

Summary

In this chapter, we have explored several techniques to implement form splitting. These techniques include the use of the Header component, some panels placed between other components, and direct handling of the mouse messages.

Now that you have seen the use of multiple windows, dialog boxes, notebooks, and scrolling, the next step in the development of complex applications is the Windows MDI approach, described in the next chapter.

Besides the Header component, another component we have just mentioned in this chapter is the MediaPlayer. I'll come back to it and provide some more details in Chapter 26.

CHAPTER

FIFTEEN

Creating MDI Applications

- Frame and child windows

- The Window menu

- MDI with multiple child windows

- A child window with a bouncing square

- The MDI Application Expert and template

- An MDI editor

15

So far, we've covered how to handle simple Delphi applications, with a single main form, as well as more complex applications, with a number of different forms and dialog boxes. We also have seen that scrolling, splitting, and layering (that is, using notebooks) are techniques you can use to display a lot of information (and components) in a single form.

Besides using dialog boxes, or secondary forms, and squeezing components into a form, there is a third approach that is common in Windows applications: MDI (Multiple Document Interface). MDI applications are made up of a number of forms that appear inside a single main form.

In this chapter, we'll start with some general and technical information about MDI development in Windows. Then we'll build an MDI program in Delphi step-by-step. We'll also explore using Delphi's MDI Application template to generate the initial code of an MDI application. As the last example in the chapter, we'll build a working editor using MDI.

MDI in Windows: A Technical Overview

In the early days of MS Windows, each application was made up of a number of different windows floating around the screen. This was with the second version of the environment, since the first version of the Microsoft operating system could only *tile* its windows, not overlap them.

A few years later, Microsoft introduced a technique to have a full-blown window (we might call it a *form*) living inside another window, usually called the *frame*. This model is known as Multiple Document Interface (or MDI) because an application generally uses a *child window* for each document. If you use Windows Notepad, you can open only one text document, because Notepad isn't an MDI application. But with your favorite word processor, you can probably open a number of different documents, each in its own child window, because it is an MDI application. All these windows referring to the documents are usually held by a *frame*, or *application*, window, as shown in Figure 15.1.

Although it is quite common to think of MDI as a technique for allowing users to work on a number of documents or files at the same time, this is not always the case.

FIGURE 15.1:

The structure of an MDI application

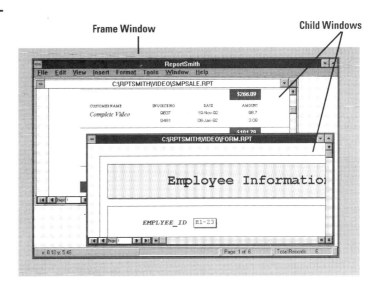

The MS Windows Program Manager and File Manager, for example, use MDI to display system information, not documents. Other applications use MDI to display various views of the same data in different windows.

NOTE   When MS Windows 3.0 was released, Microsoft stressed the use of MDI a lot. By the time Windows 3.1 came out, Microsoft had acknowledged that the implementation of MDI was flawed, and that many users were not comfortable with the interface. With the advent of different approaches to the user interface, and particularly with the release of Windows 95, MDI is becoming less common. However, MDI won't disappear too quickly, because there are simply too many applications following this approach, and the interface has become quite familiar to many users.

This section provides a short overview of MDI, in technical Windows terms. Just forget Delphi for a moment, and I'll try to give you an idea of what MDI really is (not what an MDI application looks like). If you've never built an MDI application, and you want a quick start, you might consider skipping this section, at least the first time you read the book.

You know that the idea behind MDI is to have a child window similar to a main window, but placed inside another window. What you might not know is that to make this work, Windows requires a complex structure. If you simply place a window inside another one, as a child window, a lot of strange things happen.

If you don't believe me, try running the CHILD example. Figure 15.2 shows the output of this application. When you run this program, you'll find that strange things happen when you try to work with the windows. Notice that the active child window does not have an active title bar. Clicking inside the client area of the child window doesn't activate it. Maximizing a child window has a weird effect.

FIGURE 15.2:

The output of the CHILD application. It looks like an MDI application, but doesn't work like one.

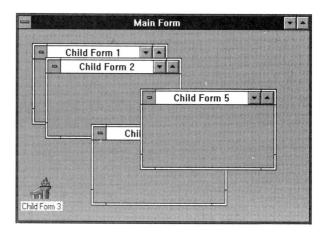

This example defines two forms, a main form and a child form. When the user clicks in the main form, a new child form is created, with the following code:

```
procedure TMainForm.FormClick(Sender: TObject);
var
  NewForm: TChildForm;
begin
  {increase the child window counter}
  Inc (Counter);
  {create a new form and define it as child of the current form}
```

```
  NewForm := TChildForm.Create (self);
  NewForm.Parent := self;
  {add the number to the caption, and move it slightly}
  NewForm.Caption := NewForm.Caption + ' ' + IntToStr (Counter);
  NewForm.Left := Counter * 20;
  NewForm.Top := Counter * 20;
  {show the form}
  NewForm.Show;
end;
```

In this procedure, Counter is an integer, a private field of the form, and TChildForm is the data type of the form defined in a second unit, CHILD_F.PAS. This second form is a plain default form, without any special properties, as is the main form.

The Counter value is used to give a different name to each form, and make sure that they won't all be placed in the same position. But the key element of the program is the assignment to the Parent property of the main form, self. This makes the new form a child of the main window. You can see this with WinSight, as shown in Figure 15.3.

FIGURE 15.3:

The second form of the CHILD example. This form is really a child window, as you can see with WinSight (in the highlighted line).

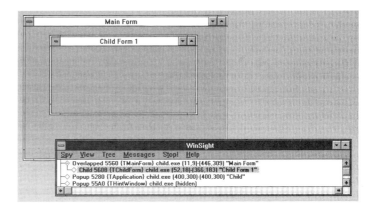

As you can see, this program seems like an MDI application, but it is not. Some of its problems are that the active child doesn't have an active title bar, the child windows are moved to the front only if you select their borders, and the child windows are not maximized properly.

Note that this strange behavior is not Delphi's fault. It is the default (although wrong) MS Windows behavior. This misbehaving application can be corrected by handling a number of Windows messages to make it resemble the default behavior, but there is an easier solution: use the MDI approach. MDI was introduced to fix just these kinds of problems.

Although the MDI structure is not simple, it gives programmers a number of benefits, automatically. For example, Windows handles a list of the child windows in one of the pull-down menus of the application, and there are specific Delphi methods, which activate the corresponding MDI functionality, to tile or cascade the child windows.

The following is the technical structure of an MDI application in Windows:

- The main window of the application acts as a frame, or a container. This window requires a proper menu structure and some specific coding (at least when programming in C).

- A special window, known as the *MDI client*, covers the whole client area of the frame window, providing some special capabilities. For example, the MDI client handles the list of child windows. Although this might seem strange at first, this MDI client is one of the Windows predefined components, just like an edit box or a list box. The MDI client window does not have the typical elements of the interface of a window, such as a caption or border, but it is visible. In fact, you can change the standard system color of the MDI work area using the MS Windows Control Panel.

- A number of child windows, of the same kind or of different kinds. These child windows are not placed in the frame window directly, but each is defined as a child of the MDI client window, which in turn is a child of the frame window. (We might say that the child windows are the nephews of the frame, but this might confuse the matter instead of clearing it up.) See Figure 15.4 for an illustration of the situation.

When you program in C, using the Windows API, some work is usually required to build and maintain this structure, and other coding is needed to handle the menu properly. As you'll see in this chapter, these tasks become much easier with Delphi.

FIGURE 15.4:

The structure of Windows' MDI approach

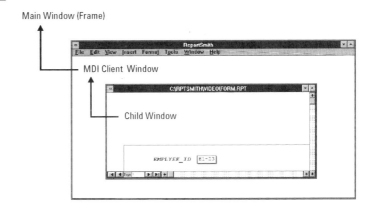

15

Frame and Child Windows in Delphi

Delphi makes the development of MDI applications easy, even without considering the MDI application template. You only need to build at least two forms, one with the FormStyle property set to fsMDIForm, and the other with the same property set to fsMDIChild. That's all, almost.

A First Delphi MDI Demo

Once the two forms have these two values for the Style property, which is set by default to fsNormal, you need to provide a way to create one or more child windows. This can be done by adding a menu with a New menu item, and writing the following code:

```
procedure TMainForm.New1Click(Sender: TObject);
var
  ChildForm: TChildForm;
begin
  ChildForm := TChildForm.Create (Application);
  ChildForm.Show;
end;
```

In the above code, I've named the two forms MainForm and ChildForm. Since you refer to the TChildForm class, the unit defining it should be included in this source code. In the MDIDEMO1 example, this second file is simply CHILD.PAS.

To create an even better program, you can name the pull-down menu containing this item Window, and use it as value of the WindowMenu property of the form. (Of course, you can choose any other name for the menu item, but Window is standard.)

With these simple operations, which might require less than a minute, I have built the first MDI demo program. Listing 15.1 shows the description of the two forms of MDIDEMO1.

LISTING 15.1: The textual description of the two forms of the MDIDEMO1 program

```
object MainForm: TMainForm
  Caption = 'MDI Frame'
  FormStyle = fsMDIForm
  Menu = MainMenu1
  WindowMenu = Window1
  object MainMenu1: TMainMenu
    object Window1: TMenuItem
      Caption = '&Window'
      object New1: TMenuItem
        Caption = '&New'
        OnClick = New1Click
      end
    end
  end
end

object ChildForm: TChildForm
  Caption = 'MDI Child'
  FormStyle = fsMDIChild
  Position = poDefault
end
```

To make this program work properly, we need to take a few more steps. First, notice that only the first form (the main form) should be created automatically at startup. You can set this in the Forms page of the Project Options dialog box. Then, we can add a number to the title of any child window when it is created:

```
procedure TMainForm.New1Click(Sender: TObject);
var
  ChildForm: TChildForm;
```

```
begin
  WindowMenu := Window1;
  Inc (Counter);
  ChildForm := TChildForm.Create (self);
  ChildForm.Caption := ChildForm.Caption + ' ' +
    IntToStr (Counter);
  ChildForm.Show;
end;
```

This first version of the MDIDEMO application performs some of the common tasks of MDI applications. Figure 15.5 shows an example of this program's output. You can open a number of child windows, minimize or maximize each of them, close them, and use the Window pull-down menu to navigate among them.

FIGURE 15.5:

An example of the output of the MDIDEMO1 program

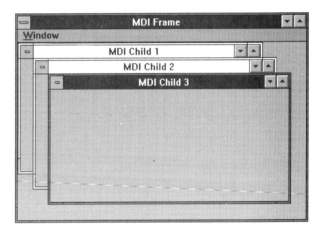

In the Window menu, Delphi has already added the list of child windows, using their names:

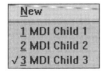

If you create more than nine child windows, a More Windows menu item is added to the pull-down menu:

When you select the More Windows item, you'll see a window with a complete list of the child windows, as shown in Figure 15.6.

Now suppose that we want to close some of these child windows, to unclutter the client area of our program. Double-click on the system menu box of some of the child windows and … they are minimized! What is happening here?

FIGURE 15.6:

The list of child windows in MDIDEMO1

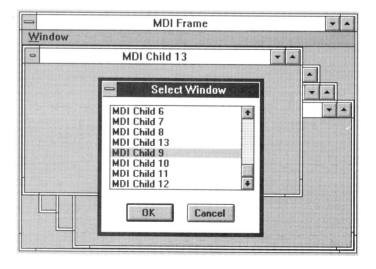

Remember that when you close a window, you generally hide it from view. The closed forms in Delphi still exist, although they are not visible. In the case of child windows, simply hiding them won't work, because the MDI Window menu and the list of windows will still list existing child windows, even if they are hidden. For this reason, Delphi simply minimizes the MDI child windows you try to close. To solve this problem, we need to delete the child windows when they are closed, as we will do in the next version of this example.

MDIDEMO1 has another problem: its Window pull-down menu is somewhat bare. We should add some commands to tile or cascade the child windows, and to arrange their icons. This is standard in any Windows MDI application, and it is simple to implement in Delphi.

Building a Complete Window Menu

Our first task is to define a better menu structure for the example. You can see the structure of the new menu in Listing 15.2.

To handle the menu commands, we can use some of the predefined methods that are available in forms that have the `fsMDIForm` value for the FormStyle property:

- The Cascade method cascades the open MDI child windows. The child forms are arranged starting from the top-left corner of the client area of the frame windows, and moving toward the bottom-left corner. The windows overlap each other. Iconized child windows are also arranged (see ArrangeIcons below).

- The Tile procedure tiles the open MDI child windows. The child forms are arranged so that they do not overlap. The client area of the frame windows is divided into equal portions for the different windows, so that they can all be shown on the screen, no matter how many windows there are. Figure 15.7 shows an example of five child windows tiled on the screen. Iconized child windows are also arranged. The default behavior is horizontal tiling, although if you have several child windows, they will be arranged in several columns. This default can be changed by using the TileMode property.

- The TileMode property determines how the Tile procedure should work. The only two choices are `tbHorizontal`, for horizontal tiling, and `tbVertical`, for vertical tiling. Some applications use two different menu commands for

LISTING 15.2: The menu of MDIDEMO2 (the main difference from the previous version is in the form description)

```
object MainForm: TMainForm
  Caption = 'MDI Frame'
  FormStyle = fsMDIForm
  Menu = MainMenu1
  WindowMenu = Window1
  object MainMenu1: TMainMenu
    object File1: TMenuItem
      Caption = '&File'
      object New1: TMenuItem
        Caption = '&New'
        OnClick = New1Click
      end
      object N1: TMenuItem
        Caption = '-'
      end
      object Exit1: TMenuItem
        Caption = '&Exit'
        OnClick = Exit1Click
      end
    end
    object Window1: TMenuItem
      Caption = '&Window'
      object Cascade1: TMenuItem
        Caption = '&Cascade'
        OnClick = Cascade1Click
      end
      object Tile1: TMenuItem
        Caption = '&Tile'
        OnClick = Tile1Click
      end
      object ArrangeIcons1: TMenuItem
        Caption = '&Arrange Icons'
        OnClick = ArrangeIcons1Click
      end
    end
  end
end
```

the two tiling modes; other applications check whether the Shift key is pressed when the user selects the only Tile menu command.

- The ArrangeIcons procedure arranges all the iconized child windows, starting from the left-bottom of the client area of the frame window, and moving to the right-top. Open forms are not moved.

FIGURE 15.7:

An example of child window tiling in MDIDEMO2

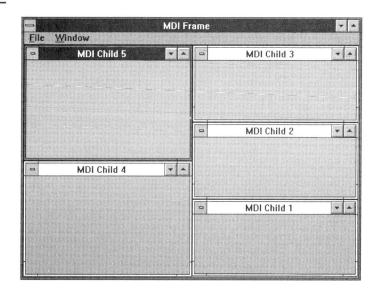

These procedures and properties are useful for handling the Window menu of an MDI application. There are also some other interesting methods and properties related strictly to MDI in Delphi:

- ActiveMDIChild is a run-time and read-only property of the MDI frame form, and holds the active child window. The value can be changed by the user of the program by selecting a new child window or by the program using the Next and Previous procedures.

- The Next procedure activates the child window following the active one in the internal order.

- The Previous procedure activates the child window preceding the active one in the internal order.

- The ClientHandle property holds the Windows handle of the MDI client window, which covers the client area of the main form.

- The MDIChildCount property stores the current number of child windows.

- The MDIChildren property is an array of child windows. You can use this and the MDIChildCount property to cycle among all of the child windows,

15

for example using a `for` loop. This can be useful for finding a particular child window, or to operate on each of them.

Note that the internal order of the child windows is the reverse order of activation. This means that the last child window that has been selected is the active window (the first in the internal list), the second-to-last child window that has been selected is the second, and the first child window that has been selected is the last. This order determines how the windows are arranged on the screen. The first window in the list is the one above all others, while the last window is below all others, and probably hidden away. You can imagine an axis (the Z axis) coming out of the screen towards you. The active window has a higher value for the Z coordinate, and thus covers other windows. For this reason, the MS Windows ordering schema is known as the *Z-order*.

We can now associate some simple code statements to the menu commands, using the specific procedures for MDI frame forms just described. This code is shown in Listing 15.3.

LISTING 15.3: The source code of the main form of MDIDEMO2

```
unit Frame;

interface

uses
  WinTypes, WinProcs, Classes, Graphics, Forms, Controls,
  Child, Menus, SysUtils;

type
  TMainForm = class(TForm)
    MainMenu1: TMainMenu;
    Window1: TMenuItem;
    New1: TMenuItem;
    File1: TMenuItem;
    N1: TMenuItem;
    Exit1: TMenuItem;
    Cascade1: TMenuItem;
    Tile1: TMenuItem;
    ArrangeIcons1: TMenuItem;
    procedure New1Click(Sender: TObject);
    procedure Cascade1Click(Sender: TObject);
    procedure Tile1Click(Sender: TObject);
    procedure ArrangeIcons1Click(Sender: TObject);
    procedure Exit1Click(Sender: TObject);
  private
    { Private declarations }
    Counter: Integer;
```

LISTING 15.3: The source code of the main form of MDIDEMO2 (continued)

```
public
  { Public declarations }
end;

var
  MainForm: TMainForm;

implementation

{$R *.DFM}

procedure TMainForm.New1Click(Sender: TObject);
var
  ChildForm: TChildForm;
begin
  WindowMenu := Window1;
  Inc (Counter);
  ChildForm := TChildForm.Create (self);
  ChildForm.Caption := ChildForm.Caption + ' ' +
    IntToStr (Counter);
  ChildForm.Show;
end;

procedure TMainForm.Cascade1Click(Sender: TObject);
begin
  Cascade;
end;

procedure TMainForm.Tile1Click(Sender: TObject);
begin
  Tile;
end;

procedure TMainForm.ArrangeIcons1Click(Sender: TObject);
begin
  ArrangeIcons;
end;

procedure TMainForm.Exit1Click(Sender: TObject);
begin
  Close;
end;

end.
```

15

To make the list of child windows work properly, we need to add a few lines of code to the OnClose event of the child window, as mentioned earlier:

```
procedure TChildForm.FormClose(Sender: TObject;
  var Action: TCloseAction);
begin
  Action := caFree;
end;
```

This is the only method of the child window class.

Up to now, we have focused on the frame window, but the form used for the child windows has no components and very little code. The frame window usually doesn't change much in the different MDI examples (besides having a toolbar, a status bar, and similar enhancements). Usually, most of the code goes in the child forms. Now it's time to look into a real example of using child windows.

Building a Child Window

In the last two examples, we have seen how to build the structure of an MDI application in Delphi, focusing on the frame window. Thus, we've obtained a program with the typical MDI behavior, but no real functionality.

What can we do with the child form? The answer is anything we can do with a form. We can add a number of components, build editors, add graphics programs, and so on. Any of the programs we have built up to now could be turned into an MDI application (although this wouldn't make much sense for some of them).

Our first example is an MDI version of a simple graphical program (similar to the second version of the SHAPE program we built in Chapter 9), named MDIDEMO3. This program can display a circle in the position where the user clicked one of the mouse buttons. Figure 15.8 shows an example of the output of the MDIDEMO3 example. The program includes a Circle menu, which allows the user to change the color of the surface of the circle, as well as the color and size of its border.

What is interesting here is that to program the child form, we do not need to consider the existence of other forms or of the frame window. We simply write the code of the form, and that's all. The only special care required is for the menus of the two forms.

If we prepare a main menu for the child form, once this is displayed on the screen, it replaces the main menu of the frame window. An MDI child window, in

FIGURE 15.8:

The output of the MDIDEMO3 example, with a child window that displays circles and a flexible menu bar. Notice the different menu bars at startup and when a child window has been created.

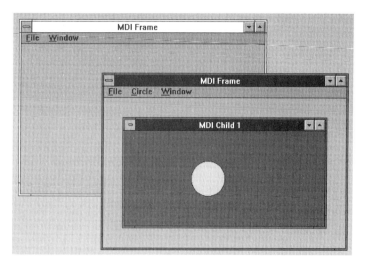

fact, cannot have a menu of its own (unless you mimic it, with a technique similar to the one described for the dialog boxes in Chapter 12). But the fact that a child window can't have any menus should not bother you, because this is the standard behavior of MDI applications. You can use the menu bar of the frame window to display the menus of the child window.

Even better, you can merge the menu bar of the frame window and that of the child form. For example, in this program, the menu of the child form can be placed between the frame window's File and Window pull-down menus. You can accomplish this by using the following group index values:

- File pull-down menu, main menu, main form: 1
- Help pull-down menu, main menu, main form: 3
- Circle pull-down menu, child form: 2

Using these settings for the menu group indexes, the menu bar of the frame window will have either two or three pull-down menus. At startup, the menu bar has two menus. As soon as you create a child window, there are three menus, and when the last child window is closed (destroyed), the Circle pull-down menu disappears. You should spend some time testing this behavior by running the program.

The complete description of the two menu bars of the MDIDEMO3 forms, along with the other relevant properties, is shown in Listing 15.4.

LISTING 15.4: The textual description of the two forms of the MDIDEMO3 example

```
object MainForm: TMainForm
  Caption = 'MDI Frame'
  FormStyle = fsMDIForm
  Menu = MainMenu1
  WindowMenu = Window1
  object MainMenu1: TMainMenu
    object File1: TMenuItem
      Caption = '&File'
      GroupIndex = 1
      object New1: TMenuItem
        Caption = '&New'
        OnClick = New1Click
      end
      object N1: TMenuItem
        Caption = '-'
      end
      object Exit1: TMenuItem
        Caption = '&Exit'
        OnClick = Exit1Click
      end
    end
    object Window1: TMenuItem
      Caption = '&Window'
      GroupIndex = 3
      object Cascade1: TMenuItem
        Caption = '&Cascade'
        OnClick = Cascade1Click
      end
      object Tile1: TMenuItem
        Caption = '&Tile'
        OnClick = Tile1Click
      end
      object ArrangeIcons1: TMenuItem
        Caption = '&Arrange Icons'
        OnClick = ArrangeIcons1Click
      end
    end
  end
end

object ChildForm: TChildForm
  Caption = 'MDI Child'
  Color = clTeal
  FormStyle = fsMDIChild
  Menu = MainMenu1
  Position = poDefault
  OnClose = FormClose
```

LISTING 15.4: The textual description of the two forms of the MDIDEMO3 example (continued)

```
OnCreate = FormCreate
OnMouseDown = FormMouseDown
OnPaint = FormPaint
object MainMenu1: TMainMenu
  object Circle1: TMenuItem
    Caption = '&Circle'
    GroupIndex = 2
    object FillColor1: TMenuItem
      Caption = '&Fill Color...'
      OnClick = FillColor1Click
    end
    object BorderColor1: TMenuItem
      Caption = '&Border Color...'
      OnClick = BorderColor1Click
    end
    object BorderSize1: TMenuItem
      Caption = 'Border &Size...'
      OnClick = BorderSize1Click
    end
    object N1: TMenuItem
      Caption = '-'
    end
    object GetPosition1: TMenuItem
      Caption = '&Get Position'
      OnClick = GetPosition1Click
    end
  end
end
object ColorDialog1: TColorDialog
  Color = clBlack
end
end
```

15

In Listing 15.4, notice that the two forms have some elements with the same names as in the MainMenu1 menu. Using the same names for objects in different forms is not a problem. Each object inside a form is local to the code of the form. Inside the MainForm using the MainMenu1 identifier, you refer to the menu of the main form; inside the code of the other form, you refer to the same name, but to a different local menu object. Notice also that in the form's code, you can refer to the menu (or any other component) of a different form, using a compound identifier, such as Child-Form.MainMenu1. However, this is possible only if the interface of the unit that defines the other form is visible.

The source code of the main form is the same as for the previous version of the program, so it is not repeated for this example. The code of the child window has been customized to handle the painting of the circle and the specific menu commands. See Listing 15.5 for the complete source code of the CHILD.PAS file. It is interesting to notice how the menu commands of the running program pertain to the two forms, and that in the source code, each form handles its own commands, regardless of the existence of other elements.

LISTING 15.5: The source code of the child form of the MDIDEMO3 example

```
unit Child;

interface

uses
  WinTypes, WinProcs, Classes, Graphics, Forms,
  Controls, Menus, Dialogs, SysUtils;

type
  TChildForm = class(TForm)
    MainMenu1: TMainMenu;
    Circle1: TMenuItem;
    FillColor1: TMenuItem;
    BorderColor1: TMenuItem;
    BorderSize1: TMenuItem;
    N1: TMenuItem;
    GetPosition1: TMenuItem;
    ColorDialog1: TColorDialog;
    procedure FormCreate(Sender: TObject);
    procedure FormPaint(Sender: TObject);
    procedure FormMouseDown(Sender: TObject;
      Button: TMouseButton;
      Shift: TShiftState; X, Y: Integer);
    procedure FillColor1Click(Sender: TObject);
    procedure BorderColor1Click(Sender: TObject);
    procedure BorderSize1Click(Sender: TObject);
    procedure GetPosition1Click(Sender: TObject);
    procedure FormClose(Sender: TObject;
      var Action: TCloseAction);
  private
    { Private declarations }
    XCenter, YCenter: Integer;
    BorderSize: Integer;
    BorderColor, Fillcolor: TColor;
  public
    { Public declarations }
  end;
```

LISTING 15.5: The source code of the child form of the MDIDEMO3 example
(continued)

```
var
  ChildForm: TChildForm;

implementation

{$R *.DFM}

procedure TChildForm.FormCreate(Sender: TObject);
begin
  XCenter := - 200;
  YCenter := - 200;
  BorderSize := 1;
  BorderColor := clBlack;
  FillColor := clYellow;
end;

procedure TChildForm.FormPaint(Sender: TObject);
begin
  Canvas.Pen.Width := BorderSize;
  Canvas.Pen.Color := BorderColor;
  Canvas.Brush.Color := FillColor;
  Canvas.Ellipse (XCenter-30, YCenter-30,
    XCenter+30, YCenter+30);
end;

procedure TChildForm.FormMouseDown(Sender: TObject;
  Button: TMouseButton; Shift: TShiftState;
  X, Y: Integer);
begin
  XCenter := X;
  YCenter := Y;
  Repaint;
end;

procedure TChildForm.FillColor1Click(Sender: TObject);
begin
  ColorDialog1.Color := FillColor;
  if ColorDialog1.Execute then
  begin
    FillColor := ColorDialog1.Color;
    Repaint;
  end;
end;

procedure TChildForm.BorderColor1Click(Sender: TObject);
begin
  ColorDialog1.Color := BorderColor;
  if ColorDialog1.Execute then
```

15

LISTING 15.5: The source code of the child form of the MDIDEMO3 example
(continued)

```
begin
    BorderColor := ColorDialog1.Color;
    Repaint;
  end;
end;

procedure TChildForm.BorderSize1Click(Sender: TObject);
var
  InputString: string;
begin
  InputString := IntToStr (BorderSize);
  if InputQuery ('Border', 'Insert width', InputString) then
  begin
    BorderSize := StrToIntDef (InputString, BorderSize);
    Repaint;
  end;
end;

procedure TChildForm.GetPosition1Click(Sender: TObject);
begin
  MessageDlg ('The center of the circle is in the position (' +
    IntToStr (XCenter) + ', ' + IntToStr (YCenter) + ').',
    mtInformation, [mbOk], 0);
end;

procedure TChildForm.FormClose(Sender: TObject; var Action: TCloseAction);
begin
  Action := caFree;
end;

end.
```

The data of the child form, particularly the values of the center of the circle, must be declared using some fields of the form. In this case, in fact, there is a specific memory location for each child window. For example, since each form has a copy of the circle data, you can open two different child windows, each with a circle in a different position and different color, as shown in Figure 15.9.

FIGURE 15.9:

Opening two different child windows of the MDIDEMO3 example

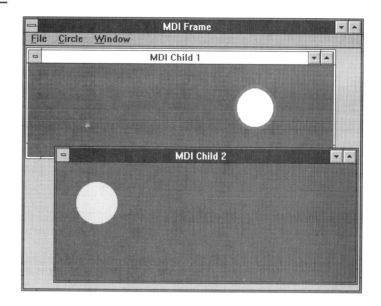

NOTE   Storing the child form's data is simple to implement in Delphi, but not in Windows programming, unless you use the C++ language. Traditional Windows code requires complex schemes to store the data of the child windows of an MDI application. I'll spare you the details, but I thought you should be aware of this great advantage of object-oriented programming in a not truly object-oriented operating environment.

MDI Applications with Different Child Windows

A common approach in complex MDI applications is to include child windows of different kinds (that is, based on different child forms). We can extend the previous example to highlight some problems you may encounter with this approach.

For this example, we need to build a new child form. Any form would do, but I wanted to use this example to show you something new: limited multitasking. Therefore, I decided to use a form that contains a bouncing square.

Adding a Bouncing Shape

The square, a Shape component, moves around the client area of the form at fixed time intervals, using a Timer component, and bounces on the edges of the form, changing its direction.

This turning process is determined by a fairly complex (compared with most of the examples in this book) algorithm. The idea is that the square has its own position and is associated with a Dir (direction) value—another member of the form class—which can assume one of the following values:

```
type
  Directions = (up_right, down_right, down_left, up_left);
```

When the time period elapses, the square is moved in the corresponding direction:

```
procedure TBounceChildForm.Timer1Timer(Sender: TObject);
begin
  case Dir of
    up_right: begin
      Shape1.Left := Shape1.Left + 3;
      Shape1.Top := Shape1.Top - 3;
    end;
    down_right: begin
      Shape1.Left := Shape1.Left + 3;
      Shape1.Top := Shape1.Top + 3;
    end;
    ...
  end;
end;
```

This accounts for the movement. The real problem is to make the square bounce on the edges of the form. In short, each time the square reaches an edge, we must change its direction. To determine when the shape has reached an edge, you can check its top and right values against zero and the bottom and right values against the size of the client area. The bottom and right values are not directly available, but you can compute them by adding the height of the shape to its top value (or the width to the left value):

```
if Shape1.Top <= 0 then ...
if Shape1.Top + Shape1.Height >= ClientHeight then ...
if Shape1.Left <= 0 then ...
if Shape1.Left + Shape1.Width >= ClientWidth ...
```

You might think of making these checks at the end of the case statement increasing the current values, but that would not work. In fact, to make the square move gracefully, you should choose a good (and more complex) pattern. For example, suppose that we want each turn to be at 90 degrees, so that the square doesn't bounce back in the same direction as its approach, as illustrated in Figure 15.10.

15

FIGURE 15.10:

The proper path of the Shape object, which should turn 90 degrees each time it bounces against a border

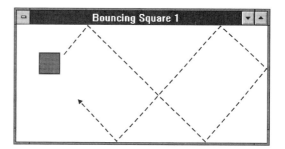

The idea is that if the form is itself a square, the shape should always move clockwise, or always counterclockwise, depending on the initial direction. If the form is a rectangle, the two kinds of turns alternate, as you can see in Figure 15.10. (Of course, you can see this behavior in action by running the MDIDEMO4 program, but if you can't reach your computer right now, the static figure will give you the general idea.)

To obtain this behavior, we need to write some code to change the current direction in each of the different branches of the case statement mentioned before. In fact, the next direction of the square when it has reached a border of the form depends on the current direction. Here is a portion of the code of the OnTimer response function (the complete code is shown in the Listing 15.7, presented in the next section):

```
case Dir of

  up_right: begin
    {move the shape}
    Shape1.Left := Shape1.Left + 3;
    Shape1.Top := Shape1.Top - 3;

    {if it has reached one of the borders,
    make it turn properly}
    if Shape1.Top <= 0 then
      Dir := down_right;
    if Shape1.Left + Shape1.Width >= ClientWidth then
      Dir := up_left;
  end;
  ...
```

The Menu Bar of the New Child Form

Like any child form, the one in our example will have its own menu bar, as you can see in Figure 15.11. This menu is added to, or merged with, the menu bar of the frame window, the main window of this MDI application. The menu structure is quite simple, although it has two different pull-down menus. You can see the definition of the menus, including the value of the group item properties of the pull-down menus, in the overall form description in Listing 15.6. Compare these values with those of the other two forms of the example, shown in the textual description of the MDIDEMO3 example (see Listing 15.4).

FIGURE 15.11:

The Bouncing Square form of the MDIDEMO4 example at design-time

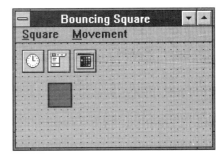

LISTING 15.6: The textual decription of the Bouncing Square form of the MDIDEMO4 example

```
object BounceChildForm: TBounceChildForm
  AutoScroll = False
  Caption = 'Bouncing Square'
  Color = clAqua
  FormStyle = fsMDIChild
  Menu = MainMenu1
  Position = poDefault
  Visible = True
  OnClose = FormClose
  OnCreate = FormCreate
  object Shape1: TShape
    Left = 40
    Top = 48
    Width = 30
    Height = 30
    Brush.Color = clFuchsia
    Pen.Color = clBlue
    Pen.Width = 2
    Shape = stSquare
  end
  object Timer1: TTimer
    Interval = 200
    OnTimer = Timer1Timer
  end
  object MainMenu1: TMainMenu
    object Square1: TMenuItem
      Caption = '&Square'
      GroupIndex = 2
      object FillColor1: TMenuItem
        Caption = '&Fill Color...'
        OnClick = FillColor1Click
      end
      object N1: TMenuItem
        Caption = '-'
      end
      object GetPosition1: TMenuItem
        Caption = '&Get Position'
        OnClick = GetPosition1Click
      end
    end
    object Movement1: TMenuItem
      Caption = '&Movement'
      GroupIndex = 2
      object Start1: TMenuItem
        Caption = '&Start'
        Enabled = False
        OnClick = Start1Click
      end
```

LISTING 15.6: The textual decription of the Bouncing Square form of the
MDIDEMO4 example (continued)

```
      object Stop1: TMenuItem
        Caption = 'S&top'
        OnClick = Stop1Click
      end
    end
  end
  object ColorDialog1: TColorDialog...
end
```

The code to respond to the menu commands is quite simple. Since we use the color
selection dialog box for only one color (the color used to fill the square), we don't
need to store it in a separate variable. Of course, we need to initialize this value,
along with the starting direction, in the FormCreate method. Listing 15.7 shows the
complete listing of the bouncing square form of the MDIDEMO4 example.

LISTING 15.7: The complete listing of the Bouncing Square form of the
MDIDEMO4 example (the file is CHILD2.PAS)

```
unit Child2;

interface

uses
  WinTypes, WinProcs, Classes, Graphics, Forms,
  Controls, Menus, Dialogs, StdCtrls, ExtCtrls,
  SysUtils;

type
  Directions = (up_right, down_right, down_left, up_left);

  TBounceChildForm = class(TForm)
    Timer1: TTimer;
    Shape1: TShape;
    MainMenu1: TMainMenu;
    Square1: TMenuItem;
    FillColor1: TMenuItem;
    N1: TMenuItem;
    GetPosition1: TMenuItem;
    Movement1: TMenuItem;
    Start1: TMenuItem;
    Stop1: TMenuItem;
    ColorDialog1: TColorDialog;
    procedure Timer1Timer(Sender: TObject);
```

LISTING 15.7: The complete listing of the Bouncing Square form of the
MDIDEMO4 example (continued)

```
    procedure FillColor1Click(Sender: TObject);
    procedure FormCreate(Sender: TObject);
    procedure GetPosition1Click(Sender: TObject);
    procedure Start1Click(Sender: TObject);
    procedure Stop1Click(Sender: TObject);
    procedure FormClose(Sender: TObject;
      var Action: TCloseAction);
  private
    { Private declarations }
    Dir : Directions;
  public
    { Public declarations }
  end;

var
  BounceChildForm: TBounceChildForm;

implementation

{$R *.DFM}

procedure TBounceChildForm.Timer1Timer(Sender: TObject);
begin
  case Dir of
    up_right: begin
      Shape1.Left := Shape1.Left + 3;
      Shape1.Top := Shape1.Top - 3;
      if Shape1.Top <= 0 then
        Dir := down_right;
      if Shape1.Left + Shape1.Width >= ClientWidth then
        Dir := up_left;
    end;
    down_right: begin
      Shape1.Left := Shape1.Left + 3;
      Shape1.Top := Shape1.Top + 3;
      if Shape1.Top + Shape1.Height >= ClientHeight then
        Dir := up_right;
      if Shape1.Left + Shape1.Width >= ClientWidth then
        Dir := down_left;
    end;
    down_left: begin
      Shape1.Left := Shape1.Left - 3;
      Shape1.Top := Shape1.Top + 3;
      if Shape1.Top + Shape1.Height >= ClientHeight then
        Dir := up_left;
      if Shape1.Left <= 0 then
        Dir := down_right;
    end;
    up_left: begin
      Shape1.Left := Shape1.Left - 3;
```

15

LISTING 15.7: The complete listing of the Bouncing Square form of the
MDIDEMO4 example (continued)

```
      Shape1.Top := Shape1.Top - 3;
      if Shape1.Top <= 0 then
        Dir := down_left;
      if Shape1.Left <= 0 then
        Dir := up_right;
    end;
  end;
end;

procedure TBounceChildForm.FillColor1Click(Sender: TObject);
begin
  if ColorDialog1.Execute then
    Shape1.Brush.Color := ColorDialog1.Color;
end;

procedure TBounceChildForm.FormCreate(Sender: TObject);
begin
  ColorDialog1.Color := Shape1.Brush.Color;
  Dir := down_left;
end;

procedure TBounceChildForm.GetPosition1Click(Sender: TObject);
begin
  MessageDlg ('The top-left corner of the square was' +
    ' in the position (' + IntToStr (Shape1.Left) +
    ', ' + IntToStr (Shape1.Top) + ').',
    mtInformation, [mbOk], 0);
end;

procedure TBounceChildForm.Start1Click(Sender: TObject);
begin
  Timer1.Enabled := True;
  Start1.Enabled := False;
  Stop1.Enabled := True;
end;

procedure TBounceChildForm.Stop1Click(Sender: TObject);
begin
  Timer1.Enabled := False;
  Start1.Enabled := True;
  Stop1.Enabled := False;
end;

procedure TBounceChildForm.FormClose(Sender: TObject;
  var Action: TCloseAction);
begin
  Action := caFree;
end;

end.
```

The GetPosition method is similar to the one of the other child form. Other commands relate to the Start and Stop menu items on the Movement menu. As the name implies, the code of these methods should start or stop the movement of the shape. This can be accomplished easily by enabling or disabling the timer. Besides this, each of the two procedures disables the corresponding command, and enables the opposite one (it makes no sense to start a moving shape, or stop one that has already been stopped).

Changing the Main Form

Now that the bouncing square form is complete, we need to integrate it into the MDI application. The main form must provide a menu command to create a child form of this new kind and to check the group indexes of the pull-down menus. I've changed the structure of the menu of this form as shown in Listing 15.8.

LISTING 15.8: The new menu of the main form of the MDIDEMO4 example

```
object MainForm: TMainForm
  Caption = 'MDI Frame'
  FormStyle = fsMDIForm
  Menu = MainMenu1
  WindowMenu = Window1
  object MainMenu1: TMainMenu
    object File1: TMenuItem
      Caption = '&File'
      GroupIndex = 1
      object New1: TMenuItem
        Caption = '&New Circle'
        OnClick = New1Click
      end
      object New2: TMenuItem
        Caption = 'New &Bouncing Square'
        OnClick = New2Click
      end
      object CloseAll1: TMenuItem
        Caption = 'Clo&se All'
        OnClick = CloseAll1Click
      end
      object N1: TMenuItem
        Caption = '-'
      end
      object Exit1: TMenuItem
        Caption = '&Exit'
        OnClick = Exit1Click
      end
    end
```

LISTING 15.8: The new menu of the main form of the MDIDEMO4 example
(continued)

```
object Window1: TMenuItem
  Caption = '&Window'
  GroupIndex = 3
  object Cascade1: TMenuItem
    Caption = '&Cascade'
    OnClick = Cascade1Click
  end
  object Tile1: TMenuItem
    Caption = '&Tile Horizontally'
    OnClick = Tile1Click
  end
  object Tile2: TMenuItem
    Caption = 'Tile &Vertically'
    OnClick = Tile2Click
  end
  object ArrangeIcons1: TMenuItem
    Caption = '&Arrange Icons'
    OnClick = ArrangeIcons1Click
  end
  object Count1: TMenuItem
    Caption = 'Count'
    OnClick = Count1Click
  end
end
end
end
```

The File pull-down menu here has a second New menu item, which is used to create a child window of the new kind. The code uses the same child window counter of the other form. As an alternative, you could use two different counters for the two kinds of child windows.

As soon as a form of this kind is displayed on the screen, its menu bar is automatically merged with the main menu bar. When you select a child form of one of the two kinds, the menu bar changes accordingly. Once all the child windows are closed, the original menu bar of the main form is reset. By using the proper menu group indexes, everything is accomplished automatically by Delphi, as you can see in the three windows shown in Figure 15.12.

I've added a few other new menu items in the main form. One menu choice is used to close every child window, a second tiles the child windows horizontally instead of vertically, and another shows some statistics about them. The methods connected

FIGURE 15.12:

The menu bar of the MDIDEMO4 application changes automatically to reflect the currently selected child window or the absence of child windows.

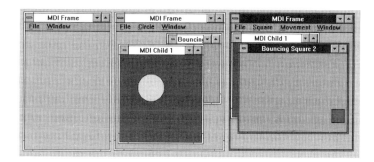

to these menu items use some specific MDI properties of the form, such as the TileMode property, the MDIChildCount property, and the MDIChildren array.

Two of these methods are quite interesting, because they show how to take an action on each of the child windows. For example, the CloseAll1Click procedure has the following code:

```
Total := MDIChildCount - 1;
  for I := 0 to Total do
    MDIChildren [0].Close;
```

To close every child window, you can't refer to the child window by number. Instead, you should always calculate the first one. In fact, as you close windows, their forms are deleted and the structure of the array changes immediately.

Another example is in the method related to the Count command. In this procedure, the array is scanned to count the number of child windows of each kind. This is accomplished using the is RTTI operator:

```
for I := 0 to MDIChildCount - 1 do
  if MDIChildren [I] is TBounceChildForm then
    Inc (NBounce)
  else
    Inc (NCircle);
```

Once these values are computed, they are shown on the screen with the MessageDlg function, as you can see in Figure 15.13. You can see the complete code in Listing 15.9.

FIGURE 15.13:

The output of the Count menu command of the MDIDEMO4 example, indicating the number of child windows of each kind

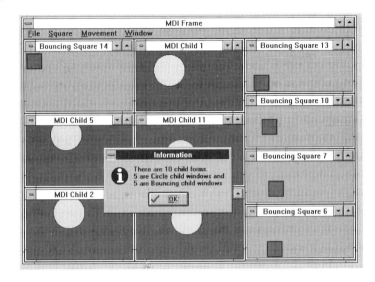

LISTING 15.9: The complete code of the main form in the MDIDEMO4 example

```
unit Frame;

interface

uses
  WinTypes, WinProcs, Classes, Graphics, Forms,
  Controls, Child, Child2, Menus, SysUtils, Dialogs;

type
  TMainForm = class(TForm)
    MainMenu1: TMainMenu;
    Window1: TMenuItem;
    New1: TMenuItem;
    File1: TMenuItem;
    N1: TMenuItem;
    Exit1: TMenuItem;
    Cascade1: TMenuItem;
    Tile1: TMenuItem;
    ArrangeIcons1: TMenuItem;
    New2: TMenuItem;
    Tile2: TMenuItem;
    CloseAll1: TMenuItem;
    Count1: TMenuItem;
    procedure New1Click(Sender: TObject);
    procedure Cascade1Click(Sender: TObject);
```

LISTING 15.9: The complete code of the main form in the MDIDEMO4 example (continued)

```pascal
    procedure Tile1Click(Sender: TObject);
    procedure ArrangeIcons1Click(Sender: TObject);
    procedure Exit1Click(Sender: TObject);
    procedure New2Click(Sender: TObject);
    procedure Tile2Click(Sender: TObject);
    procedure CloseAll1Click(Sender: TObject);
    procedure Count1Click(Sender: TObject);
  private
    { Private declarations }
    Count: Integer;
  public
    { Public declarations }
  end;

var
  MainForm: TMainForm;

implementation

{$R *.DFM}

procedure TMainForm.New1Click(Sender: TObject);
var
  ChildForm: TCircleChildForm;
begin
  Inc (Count);
  ChildForm := TCircleChildForm.Create (self);
  ChildForm.Caption := ChildForm.Caption + ' ' +
    IntToStr (Count);
  ChildForm.Show;
end;

procedure TMainForm.Cascade1Click(Sender: TObject);
begin
  Cascade;
end;

procedure TMainForm.Tile1Click(Sender: TObject);
begin
  TileMode := tbHorizontal;
  Tile;
end;

procedure TMainForm.ArrangeIcons1Click(Sender: TObject);
begin
  ArrangeIcons;
end;
```

15

LISTING 15.9: The complete code of the main form in the MDIDEMO4 example
(continued)

```
procedure TMainForm.Exit1Click(Sender: TObject);
begin
  Close;
end;

procedure TMainForm.New2Click(Sender: TObject);
var
  ChildForm: TBounceChildForm;
begin
  Inc (Count);
  ChildForm := TBounceChildForm.Create (self);
  ChildForm.Caption := ChildForm.Caption + ' ' +
    IntToStr (Count);
  ChildForm.Show;
end;

procedure TMainForm.Tile2Click(Sender: TObject);
begin
  TileMode := tbVertical;
  Tile;
end;

procedure TMainForm.CloseAll1Click(Sender: TObject);
var
  I, Total: Integer;
begin
  Total := MDIChildCount - 1;
  for I := 0 to Total do
    MDIChildren [0].Close;
end;

procedure TMainForm.Count1Click(Sender: TObject);
var
  NBounce, NCircle, I: Integer;
begin
  NBounce := 0;
  NCircle := 0;
  for I := 0 to MDIChildCount - 1 do
    if MDIChildren [I] is TBounceChildForm then
      Inc (NBounce)
    else
      Inc (NCircle);
  MessageDlg ('There are ' + IntToStr(MDIChildCount) +
    ' child forms.' + Chr(13) + IntToStr(NCircle) +
    ' are Circle child windows and' +
    Chr(13) + IntToStr(NBounce) +
    ' are Bouncing child windows',
    mtInformation, [mbOk], 0);
end;

end.
```

A Fast Start with MDI

In this chapter, we have built some MDI applications in Delphi from scratch. Taking this approach allowed us to learn the details of MDI in Windows and of Delphi's support for this approach. However, the "from-scratch" approach is not the best way to follow when you need to build a real MDI application.

Delphi provides an MDI Application template, and you can also use some options of the Application Expert to build the initial code of an MDI application quickly. We'll look at the framework each of these tools produces, and then see how to build an application starting with the code generated by Delphi.

Using the MDI Application Template

One fast-start approach to MDI development in Delphi is the use of the corresponding MDI Application template. Just issue the New Project command, and if the Browse Gallery is enabled, you can move to the Templates page and choose MDI Application, as shown in Figure 15.14. Choose a directory for the project, and Delphi will copy the files you need for a simple MDI application, with a toolbar, a status bar, and a menu, into that directory.

FIGURE 15.14:

The MDI Application template in the Browse Gallery

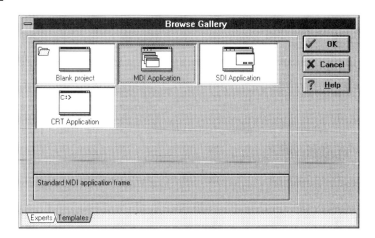

You can see the structure of the form generated by the template in Figure 15.15. I've omitted its textual description because it is quite simple. It contains the elements you see on the screen, including a standard menu bar. The only command we have not used yet is Minimize All, which is on the Window pull-down menu.

The source code of the template does have some interesting elements. This code is shown in Listing 15.10. Let's take a closer look at some of the elements here.

FIGURE 15.15:

The form of the MDI Application template at design-time

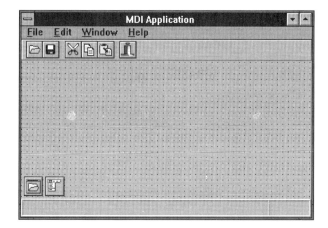

LISTING 15.10: The source code of the MDI Application Template (MDITEMP)

```
unit Main;

interface

uses
  WinTypes, WinProcs, SysUtils, Classes, Graphics, Forms,
  Controls, Menus, StdCtrls, Dialogs, Buttons,
  Messages, ExtCtrls;

type
  TMainForm = class(TForm)
    MainMenu1: TMainMenu;
    {menu items omitted...};
    Panel1: TPanel;
    StatusLine: TPanel;
    Panel2: TPanel;
    OpenDialog: TOpenDialog;
    SpeedPanel: TPanel;
    OpenBtn: TSpeedButton;
```

LISTING 15.10: The source code of the MDI Application Template (continued)

```
      SaveBtn: TSpeedButton;
      CutBtn: TSpeedButton;
      CopyBtn: TSpeedButton;
      PasteBtn: TSpeedButton;
      ExitBtn: TSpeedButton;
      procedure FormCreate(Sender: TObject);
      procedure FileNewItemClick(Sender: TObject);
      procedure WindowCascadeItemClick(Sender: TObject);
      procedure UpdateMenuItems(Sender: TObject);
      procedure WindowTileItemClick(Sender: TObject);
      procedure WindowArrangeItemClick(Sender: TObject);
      procedure FileCloseItemClick(Sender: TObject);
      procedure FileOpenItemClick(Sender: TObject);
      procedure FileExitItemClick(Sender: TObject);
      procedure FileSaveItemClick(Sender: TObject);
      procedure FileSaveAsItemClick(Sender: TObject);
      procedure CutItemClick(Sender: TObject);
      procedure CopyItemClick(Sender: TObject);
      procedure PasteItemClick(Sender: TObject);
      procedure WindowMinimizeItemClick(Sender: TObject);
      procedure FormDestroy(Sender: TObject);
    private
      { Private declarations }
      procedure CreateMDIChild(const Name: string);
      procedure ShowHint(Sender: TObject);
    public
      { Public declarations }
    end;

var
  MainForm: TMainForm;

implementation

{$R *.DFM}

uses ChildWin;

procedure TMainForm.FormCreate(Sender: TObject);
begin
  Application.OnHint := ShowHint;
  Screen.OnActiveFormChange := UpdateMenuItems;
end;

procedure TMainForm.ShowHint(Sender: TObject);
begin
  StatusLine.Caption := Application.Hint;
end;

procedure TMainForm.CreateMDIChild(const Name: string);
var
```

LISTING 15.10: The source code of the MDI Application Template (continued)

```
    Child: TMDIChild;
begin
  { create a new MDI child window }
  Child := TMDIChild.Create(Application);
  Child.Caption := Name;
end;

procedure TMainForm.FileNewItemClick(Sender: TObject);
begin
  CreateMDIChild('NONAME' + IntToStr(MDIChildCount + 1));
end;

procedure TMainForm.FileOpenItemClick(Sender: TObject);
begin
  if OpenDialog.Execute then
    CreateMDIChild(OpenDialog.FileName);
end;

procedure TMainForm.FileCloseItemClick(Sender: TObject);
begin
  if ActiveMDIChild <> nil then
    ActiveMDIChild.Close;
end;

procedure TMainForm.FileSaveItemClick(Sender: TObject);
begin
  { save current file (ActiveMDIChild points to the window) }
end;

procedure TMainForm.FileSaveAsItemClick(Sender: TObject);
begin
  { save current file under new name }
end;

procedure TMainForm.FileExitItemClick(Sender: TObject);
begin
  Close;
end;

procedure TMainForm.CutItemClick(Sender: TObject);
begin
  {cut selection to clipboard}
end;

procedure TMainForm.CopyItemClick(Sender: TObject);
begin
  {copy selection to clipboard}
end;

procedure TMainForm.PasteItemClick(Sender: TObject);
begin
```

LISTING 15.10: The source code of the MDI Application Template (continued)

```
  {paste from clipboard}
end;

procedure TMainForm.WindowCascadeItemClick(Sender: TObject);
begin
  Cascade;
end;

procedure TMainForm.WindowTileItemClick(Sender: TObject);
begin
  Tile;
end;

procedure TMainForm.WindowArrangeItemClick(Sender: TObject);
begin
  ArrangeIcons;
end;

procedure TMainForm.WindowMinimizeItemClick(Sender: TObject);
var
  I: Integer;
begin
  { Must be done backwards through the MDIChildren array }
  for I := MDIChildCount - 1 downto 0 do
    MDIChildren[I].WindowState := wsMinimized;
end;

procedure TMainForm.UpdateMenuItems(Sender: TObject);
begin
  FileCloseItem.Enabled := MDIChildCount > 0;
  FileSaveItem.Enabled := MDIChildCount > 0;
  FileSaveAsItem.Enabled := MDIChildCount > 0;
  CutItem.Enabled := MDIChildCount > 0;
  CopyItem.Enabled := MDIChildCount > 0;
  PasteItem.Enabled := MDIChildCount > 0;
  SaveBtn.Enabled := MDIChildCount > 0;
  CutBtn.Enabled := MDIChildCount > 0;
  CopyBtn.Enabled := MDIChildCount > 0;
  PasteBtn.Enabled := MDIChildCount > 0;
  WindowCascadeItem.Enabled := MDIChildCount > 0;
  WindowTileItem.Enabled := MDIChildCount > 0;
  WindowArrangeItem.Enabled := MDIChildCount > 0;
  WindowMinimizeItem.Enabled := MDIChildCount > 0;
end;

procedure TMainForm.FormDestroy(Sender: TObject);
begin
  Screen.OnActiveFormChange := nil;
end;

end.
```

15

First, notice the code of the FormCreate method. The first statement activates the hints at the application level, as we have seen in the Chapter 11. It works together with the ShowHint procedure, which displays the hints in the StatusLine panel. This panel corresponds to the first portion of the status bar. In the template, Panel1 is the panel in the main form, aligned at the bottom, and it contains two more panels, StatusLine and Panel2. You can see how this looks in the bottom part of Figure 15.15.

The second statement of the FormCreate method is new:

```
Screen.OnActiveFormChange := UpdateMenuItems;
```

What is the Screen object? What is this OnActiveFormChange event? You might remember that I've used the Screen global object in a couple of programs in earlier chapters. This object provides access to the list of fonts installed in the system. The Screen object handles a lot of information related to the output of the application, including the available fonts and a list of the forms in the application.

We will see some more details about the TScreen class in Chapter 19. For the moment, it is enough to know that the OnActivateFormChange event takes place each time the active form of the application changes.

The OnActivateFormChange event refers to the active form or window of the application, not the active application. In other words, this event is not activated when the user changes the active window among all of the Windows applications that are running; the event is activated when the user changes the active form within the current application. It is an application-wide event, not a system-wide one. To execute some code when the active Windows application changes, you can use the OnActivate event of the Application object. Do not confuse this with the OnActivate event of a form, which takes place when the form itself becomes active. You can use the OnActiveFormChange event of the Screen object instead of the OnActivate event of a number of forms, obtaining a similar effect.

As with events of the Application object, events of the Screen object must be set in the code. Notice that this operation is canceled, setting the event to nil, inside the FormDestroy method.

The effect of the UpdateMenuItems procedure is to enable or disable some of the menu items when there are no more child windows. All of the statements of this procedure have the form:

```
FileCloseItem.Enabled := MDIChildCount > 0;
```

Another interesting part of the source code generated by Delphi is the way file opening is handled. There is a CreateMDIChild method, responsible for creating a new child form and giving it a title, using the value of its parameter:

```
Child := TMDIChild.Create(Application);
Child.Caption := Name;
```

This method is called by the procedure related to both the New and Open commands on the File menu. For example, when you open some files, their title is copied into the caption of the child form, as you can see in Figure 15.16. The files are not automatically opened: only the file name is used! We will see how to extend this to actually open files.

FIGURE 15.16:

The output of the MDI template (MDITEMP example) when some files have been opened

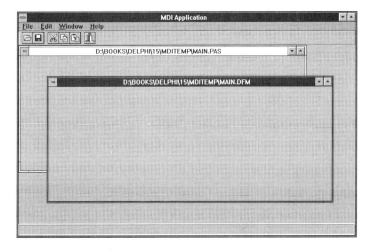

Most of the other methods of this example simply call a single MDI method, or are placeholders for your code (there is only a comment). The only exception is the Window Minimize command handler, which walks through the array of child windows (MDIChildren), setting the state of each to wsMinimized.

Now spend another second looking at the structure and at the code of the child form. There is almost nothing, besides the typical line of code in the FormClose method, to destroy a child form when it is closed.

Developing an MDI Application with the Expert

Another way to let Delphi generate the basic framework of an MDI application is to use the Application Expert. As with the MDI Application template, the Expert is started from the Project Browse Gallery, but this time there are a number of options you can set. Here are my suggestions:

1. Start the Application Expert, and in the first page, select all of the pull-down menus.

2. In the second page, add the support for files with a TXT extension, as you can see in Figure 15.17.

3. The next page allows you to build a toolbar visually. I've decided to add most of the available buttons, including file and clipboard support, to the toolbar. You can see their arrangement in Figure 15.18.

4. Give the application a name, indicate a directory for it (in the companion disk, the name is MDIEXP, and the directory has the same name).

5. Select all of the three check boxes, to have MDI support, add a status bar, and enable hints.

6. Click on the Create button to generate the application.

FIGURE 15.17:

Setting an extension for the file-handling dialog boxes in the Application Expert

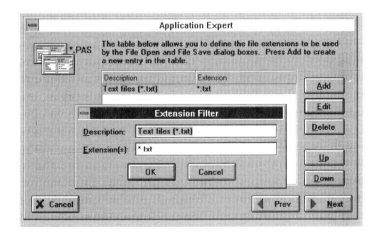

FIGURE 15.18:

The Application Expert allows you to build a toolbar visually.

15

What we obtain is similar to the result of choosing the MDI Application template (described earlier). However, there are some differences you should be aware of.

If you look at the new form at design-time, shown in Figure 15.19, and compare it with the other version (see Figure 15.15), you'll see that they are not exactly alike. The first evident thing is some disorder. The icons of the nonvisual component are scattered around the form. Also notice that the toolbar has the structure we chose with the Expert, with more buttons, and the status bar is a single panel, instead of three.

FIGURE 15.19:

An MDI form generated by the Application Expert. Compare it with the form generated by the MDI Application template (Figure 15.15).

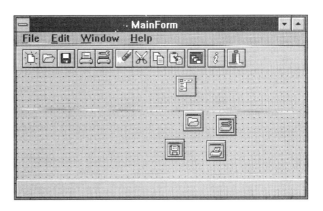

There are some differences in the menus, too (although they are not visible in the figures):

- There is no Minimize All command on the Window menu.

- The Help pull-down menu has some items in addition to About, which is also available in the other version.

- The File menu has Print and Printer Setup commands, and the components of the two corresponding standard dialog boxes have been added to the form.

The code of this version is really simpler than the code generated by the MDI Application template, as you can see in Listing 15.11. The program doesn't handle the status of the menu items, nor does it create a child window (there isn't even the definition of a form for the child window). Also, it has more limited file support. But it has some code that was not available in the previous version, particularly the code for help and printer support.

LISTING 15.11:   The source code of the MDI application generated by the Application Expert

```
unit Main;

interface

uses
  SysUtils, WinTypes, WinProcs, Messages, Classes, Graphics, Controls,
  Forms, Dialogs, StdCtrls, Buttons, ExtCtrls, Menus;

type
  TMainForm = class(TForm)
    MainMenu: TMainMenu;
    {menu items omitted...}
    StatusLine: TPanel;
    OpenDialog: TOpenDialog;
    SaveDialog: TSaveDialog;
    PrintDialog: TPrintDialog;
    PrintSetupDialog: TPrinterSetupDialog;
    SpeedBar: TPanel;
    SpeedButton1: TSpeedButton;   { &New }
    SpeedButton2: TSpeedButton;   { &Open... }
    {other speedbuttons omitted...}
    procedure FormCreate(Sender: TObject);
    procedure ShowHint(Sender: TObject);
    procedure FileNew(Sender: TObject);
    procedure FileOpen(Sender: TObject);
    procedure FileSave(Sender: TObject);
```

LISTING 15.11 : The source code of the MDI application generated by the
Application Expert (continued)

```pascal
    procedure FileSaveAs(Sender: TObject);
    procedure FilePrint(Sender: TObject);
    procedure FilePrintSetup(Sender: TObject);
    procedure FileExit(Sender: TObject);
    procedure EditUndo(Sender: TObject);
    procedure EditCut(Sender: TObject);
    procedure EditCopy(Sender: TObject);
    procedure EditPaste(Sender: TObject);
    procedure WindowTile(Sender: TObject);
    procedure WindowCascade(Sender: TObject);
    procedure WindowArrange(Sender: TObject);
    procedure HelpContents(Sender: TObject);
    procedure HelpSearch(Sender: TObject);
    procedure HelpHowToUse(Sender: TObject);
    procedure HelpAbout(Sender: TObject);
  end;

var
  MainForm: TMainForm;

implementation

{$R *.DFM}

procedure TMainForm.FormCreate(Sender: TObject);
begin
  Application.OnHint := ShowHint;
end;

procedure TMainForm.ShowHint(Sender: TObject);
begin
  StatusLine.Caption := Application.Hint;
end;

procedure TMainForm.FileNew(Sender: TObject);
begin
  { Add code to create a new file }
end;

procedure TMainForm.FileOpen(Sender: TObject);
begin
  if OpenDialog.Execute then
  begin
    { Add code to open OpenDialog.FileName }
  end;
end;

procedure TMainForm.FileSave(Sender: TObject);
begin
  { Add code to save current file under current name }
end;
```

15

LISTING 15.11 : The source code of the MDI application generated by the
Application Expert (continued)

```pascal
procedure TMainForm.FileSaveAs(Sender: TObject);
begin
  if SaveDialog.Execute then
  begin
    { Add code to save current file under SaveDialog.FileName }
  end;
end;

procedure TMainForm.FilePrint(Sender: TObject);
begin
  if PrintDialog.Execute then
  begin
    { Add code to print current file }
  end;
end;

procedure TMainForm.FilePrintSetup(Sender: TObject);
begin
  PrintSetupDialog.Execute;
end;

procedure TMainForm.FileExit(Sender: TObject);
begin
  Close;
end;

procedure TMainForm.EditUndo(Sender: TObject);
begin
  { Add code to perform Edit Undo }
end;

procedure TMainForm.EditCut(Sender: TObject);
begin
  { Add code to perform Edit Cut }
end;

procedure TMainForm.EditCopy(Sender: TObject);
begin
  { Add code to perform Edit Copy }
end;

procedure TMainForm.EditPaste(Sender: TObject);
begin
  { Add code to perform Edit Paste }
end;

procedure TMainForm.WindowTile(Sender: TObject);
begin
  Tile;
end;
```

LISTING 15.11: The source code of the MDI application generated by the
Application Expert (continued)

```
procedure TMainForm.WindowCascade(Sender: TObject);
begin
  Cascade;
end;

procedure TMainForm.WindowArrange(Sender: TObject);
begin
  ArrangeIcons;
end;

procedure TMainForm.HelpContents(Sender: TObject);
begin
  Application.HelpCommand(HELP_CONTENTS, 0);
end;

procedure TMainForm.HelpSearch(Sender: TObject);
const
  EmptyString: PChar = '';
begin
  Application.HelpCommand(HELP_PARTIALKEY, Longint(EmptyString));
end;

procedure TMainForm.HelpHowToUse(Sender: TObject);
begin
  Application.HelpCommand(HELP_HELPONHELP, 0);
end;

procedure TMainForm.HelpAbout(Sender: TObject);
begin
  { Add code to show program's About Box }
end;

end.
```

Weighing the advantages and disadvantages, it is difficult to choose between the
template and Expert approach. My solution is to stick with the template version,
but copy some of the elements of the Expert-generated version into it. This technique is described in the next section.

A Full MDI Editor

To get the best of what is offered by the MDI Application template and the Expert-
generated form (including a custom toolbar), we can use Delphi's copy and paste

capabilities to merge the interesting elements of the two versions.

To begin, copy the source code files of the MDITEMP example, renaming the application file from the standard MDI APP (I've called the file MDINOTES).

The second step is to copy the toolbar of the MDIEXP example to the new program. To do this, delete the old toolbar from the new form first, then open the older project and copy its toolbar. Close that file, open the new project, and paste the toolbar there. The only minor problem is that the new panel will have a default caption, behind the toolbar buttons, that was not present in the original version. Simply delete it, and you'll have the form shown in Figure 15.20.

If you try to compile this program, however, Delphi will give you some error messages. One reason for the errors is that the MDI Application template uses different names for the toolbar buttons than the names the Application Expert gives them. When you solve this problem, you can compile the program, but there are still several things to fix.

FIGURE 15.20:

The form of the MDINOTES program after pasting the toolbar from the MDIEXP example

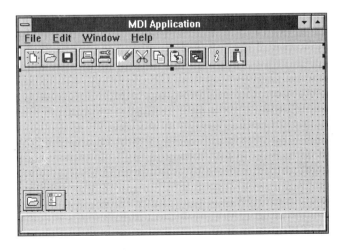

The buttons of the toolbar should be connected to the related menu commands; the Print and Print Setup commands should be added to the File menu, and the Edit menu should have an Undo command. When you add the items, notice that the MDI template uses special names for the menu items, such as FileOpenItem or CutItem. If you are adding just a few menu commands, you should try to make their names consistent with this naming convention (which is not entirely consistent itself, since the name of the pull-down menu is not always added to the name of the item). This completes the modifications for the frame window.

Now we can turn our attention to the child window. To build an MDI text viewer, we need to place a Memo component inside the child form, align it with the client area of the child, remove its text (using the string editor associated with the Lines property), add scroll bars, and remove the border.

The next step is to customize the file-related components and methods. The components should have filters for TXT and other extensions, as you can see in Figure 15.21. It also should have some code to load and save files to and from the Memo components inside the child windows. Another addition is a menu command to change the font of the text. You can see the new or modified methods for this example in Listing 15.12. I've omitted the code that is the same as in Listing 15.10, as well as a couple of simple functions related to the creation of a new file, which are called directly by the code I've changed.

FIGURE 15.21:

The filters of the Open and Save dialog box components

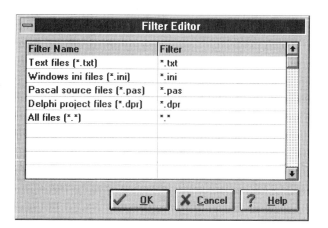

LISTING 15.12: Portions of the source code of the MDINOTES example (omitting
the code that is the same as in Listing 15.10)

```
unit Main;

interface

uses
  WinTypes, WinProcs, SysUtils, Classes, Graphics, Forms,
  Controls, Menus, StdCtrls, Dialogs, Buttons,
  Messages, ExtCtrls;

type
  TMainForm = class(TForm)
    ...
    procedure FileSaveItemClick(Sender: TObject);
    procedure FileSaveAsItemClick(Sender: TObject);
    procedure FontItemClick(Sender: TObject);
  private
    ...
  end;

var
  MainForm: TMainForm;

implementation

{$R *.DFM}

uses ChildWin;

procedure TMainForm.CreateMDIChild(const Name: string);
var
  Child: TMDIChild;
begin
  {create a new MDI child window }
  Child := TMDIChild.Create(Application);
  Child.Caption := Name;
end;

procedure TMainForm.FileNewItemClick(Sender: TObject);
begin
  CreateMDIChild('NONAME' + IntToStr(MDIChildCount + 1));
end;
```

LISTING 15.12 : Portions of the source code of the MDINOTES example (continued)

```
procedure TMainForm.FileOpenItemClick(Sender: TObject);
begin
  if OpenDialog.Execute then
  begin
    CreateMDIChild(OpenDialog.FileName);
    (ActiveMDIChild as TMDIChild).Memo1.
      Lines.LoadFromFile (OpenDialog.FileName);
  end;
end;

procedure TMainForm.FileSaveItemClick(Sender: TObject);
begin
  {check if the caption of the child window begins with NONAME}
  if Pos ('NONAME', (ActiveMDIChild as TMDIChild).Caption) > 0 then
    FileSaveAsItemClick (Sender)
  else
    (ActiveMDIChild as TMDIChild).Memo1.
      Lines.SaveToFile ((ActiveMDIChild as TMDIChild).Caption);
end;

procedure TMainForm.FileSaveAsItemClick(Sender: TObject);
begin
  {check if the caption of the child window begins with NONAME}
  if Pos ('NONAME', (ActiveMDIChild as TMDIChild).Caption) > 0 then
    SaveDialog1.Filename := '*.txt'
  else
    SaveDialog1.Filename :=
      (ActiveMDIChild as TMDIChild).Caption;
  if SaveDialog1.Execute then
  begin
    (ActiveMDIChild as TMDIChild).Memo1.
      Lines.SaveToFile (SaveDialog1.Filename);
    (ActiveMDIChild as TMDIChild).Caption := SaveDialog1.Filename;
  end;
end;

procedure TMainForm.FontItemClick(Sender: TObject);
begin
  FontDialog1.Font := (ActiveMDIChild as TMDIChild).Memo1.Font;
  if FontDialog1.Execute then
    (ActiveMDIChild as TMDIChild).Memo1.Font := FontDialog1.Font;
end;

end.
```

15

You can run this program and see the output shown in Figure 15.22. You can load a number of text files, change the font, modify the text, and save them. (But when the file is saved, the font selection is not stored, only its text.)

FIGURE 15.22:

The MDINOTES program at run-time

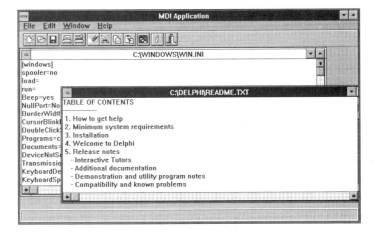

Since we have already done this earlier in the book (in the NOTES2 example of Chapter 6), the important point here is that this version runs inside an MDI application with standard MDI behavior.

This example is far from perfect, however. If you modify a file and close it without saving, the changes are lost. If you open multiple copies of the same file, things get really confused.

The user interface has problems, too. Although I've completed the code of the UpdateMenuItems method to include the new buttons and menu commands, the interface can be improved. For example, when a file has been saved and not modified, the Save button and command should be grayed.

The last problem is that there are two areas of this program that do not work at all: printing and clipboard support. We'll fix these problems and address some other issues when we build another version of the NOTES example later in the book (in Chapters 22 and 24).

Summary

There are many things we could do to further explore MDI support in Windows, but I think that this chapter is enough for an overview. In particular, I've decided not to show you more MDI examples, because this kind of model will be de-emphasized in Windows 95.

With this chapter, we have concluded the specific study of multiple-form applications, which we started in Chapter 12 when we explored secondary forms (modal and modeless) and dialog boxes. We have also seen some examples of notebook-based applications, the use of form-splitting techniques, and in this chapter, MDI.

In some cases, each of these techniques are valid solutions, so you will need to decide which approach to use. I've given equal coverage to each of these techniques, although I have my preferences: few secondary forms, more dialog boxes, a little MDI if it is needed, and notebooks whenever possible.

15

Now we can go back to components, namely VBX components, and then move to one of the hottest topics in Delphi programming: building database applications.

CHAPTER

SIXTEEN

Using VBX Controls

- Differences between VBX controls and Delphi components

- The use of VBX controls in Delphi

- Installation of VBX controls in Delphi

Microsoft's Visual Basic was the first program-development environment to introduce the idea of supplying software components to the mass market. The idea of reusable software components is older, and this idea relates to the theories of object-oriented programming. However, OOP languages never delivered the reusability they promised, probably more because of marketing and standardization problems than for any other reasons.

Although Visual Basic does not fully exploit object-oriented programming, it is able to apply the concept of component through the definition of a standard way to build and distribute new controls that developers can integrate in the environment.

Delphi takes a further step with its own components: it allows you to build components in a truly OOP way. Delphi components have inheritance, something that is lacking in Visual Basic. Delphi's encapsulation of VBX controls even allows you to inherit a new Delphi component from an existing VBX control.

This short chapter shows how VBX controls can be used in Delphi. We'll begin with a definition of VBX, followed by a discussion of the differences between Delphi components and Visual Basic controls. Then we'll look at some examples that use the simple controls included in the Delphi package.

What Is VBX?

The VBX acronym stands for Visual Basic eXtension, but the term is used to denote Visual Basic Custom Controls. VBX is technically a DLL (Dynamic Link Library) which contains the full definition of the controls. These controls are used in Visual Basic almost in the same way that a VCL component is used in Delphi. They include some properties and events, as well as some methods you can call to interact with the components.

Each VBX file can hold one or more components at a time. Your VBX files should be installed in the WINDOWS/SYSTEM directory of the computer you use to develop the program, and also in that same directory of the computer used to run your program.

There have been several slightly different versions of VBX controls, designated as Level 1, 2, and 3. Delphi, (like Visual C++, Borland C++, and other programming environments), supports only Level 1 VBX controls, but this encompasses a large part of the available controls. The later versions are mainly used to connect to databases, and Delphi has its own components for that.

Delphi has a much more powerful, robust, and object-oriented component architecture, so why bother with VBX controls? Simply because Delphi is a new product, which still doesn't have a big market for components, while numerous Visual Basic controls are available to solve a number of problems.

Certainly, Delphi has many standard components, which can meet most of your basic needs. However, if you want to use a specialized tool, you might be able to find many VBX controls that provide that tool, but no VCL component to do the job. A good example is the graphical VBX control included in Delphi, called ChartFX.

> **NOTE** Consider that Microsoft has stated that it won't port the VBX control technology to 32-bit architectures (Windows 95 or Windows NT). Borland has already developed the technology necessary to use 16-bit VBX controls in 32-bit environments (this is a DLL that shipped with Borland C++ 4.5), so it might be possible to use VBX controls in future 32-bit editions of Delphi. Delphi components can be moved to 32-bit platforms. Consider also that many things will change in the future, with the appearance of the new OLE custom control (or OCX) architecture Microsoft is promoting.

16

VBX Controls versus Delphi Components

Before I show you how to use VBX components in Delphi, let's go over some of the technical differences between the two kinds of controls. VBX controls are DLL-based (DLLs will be discussed in Chapter 28). This means that when you use them, you need to distribute their code (the VBX files), along with the application using them. In Delphi, the code of the components is statically linked in the executable file. This single file contains everything.

Someone might claim that the DLL approach is better, because it allows you to share code among different applications, as DLLs usually do. This is true. If two applications use the same control, you need only one copy of it on the hard disk and a single copy in memory. The drawback, however, is that if the two programs use two different versions of the VBX control, a number of compatibility problems might arise.

Another advantage of the Delphi approach is that is tends to be slightly faster (although the executable files tend to be bigger in comparison). You will also have less problems in building an installation program.

The other difference relates to licensees of VBX and Delphi components. When you distribute a VBX file, you might need to pay a royalty, because the VBX control might be used by the client of your application in that user's own development efforts. There are a number of solutions to this problem that could be considered, but I have no intention of discussing them in this book. The point I want to make here is that there are no such problems in Delphi. Components are embedded in the final application, and there is no way to use them for further development without having the original files.

VBX Controls in Delphi

Delphi comes with only four preinstalled VBX controls:

- BiSwitch is a double-state component, with the appearance of a light switch. It can replace a traditional check box, but is not particularly useful.

- BiGauge is a gauge, which is similar in function to the corresponding Delphi component (see the Samples page of the Components palette).

- BiPict is an image viewer, similar to the Delphi Image component.

- ChartFX is an interesting graphical component that you can use to build complex charts.

Figure 16.1 shows examples of each of these VBX controls.

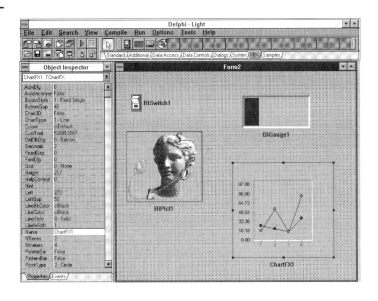

FIGURE 16.1:

Delphi's preinstalled VBX controls, placed in a form

NOTE It is interesting that the three VBX controls written by Borland (as the Bi prefix suggests) were written in Pascal and compiled with Delphi. You can indeed use Delphi to build a VBX control, although building Delphi components is generally recommended.

Using VBX Controls

To place one of Delphi's preinstalled VBX controls into a form, simply drag it there, as you would to place any other component. You can set its properties, handle its events, and work with it almost exactly as you work with other Delphi components.

However, there are indeed some differences in the use of VBX controls, and I've written a small program, named LIGHT, to highlight them. Its form, shown in Figure 16.2, has two VBX controls, plus a few standard Delphi components.

The aim of this program is simple. When you click on the switch, the image to its right should change accordingly, showing a light bulb that is on or off. This involves loading a bitmap from a file and setting a property of the TPic component.

FIGURE 16.2:

The form of the LIGHT example, using two VBX controls

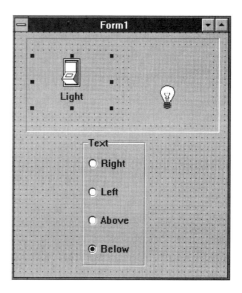

The second thing you can do with this program at run-time is to change the position of the text *Light* by using the radio buttons. To make the example slightly more interesting, I've used the RadioGroup component, instead of a GroupBox, with some RadioButton components. This is probably the first time we've used this component in our examples.

The structure of the form is simple, as you can see in Listing 16.1. The only strange thing is that the VBX controls use numbers for enumeration-based properties, as in:

```
object BiSwitch1: TBiSwitch
   TextPosition = 3
```

When you select the TextPosition property with the Object Inspector, you use numbers again, but there is also a textual description of the value:

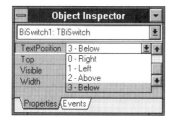

LISTING 16.1: The textual description of the form of the LIGHT example

```
object Form1: TForm1
  Caption = 'Light'
  object Bevel1: TBevel
    Left = 16
    Top = 8
    Width = 273
    Height = 129
  end
  object BiSwitch1: TBiSwitch
    ForeColor = clBlack
    BackColor = clBtnFace
    Caption = 'Light'
    pOn = False
    TextPosition = 3
    TabStop = True
    OnOn = BiSwitch1On
    OnOff = BiSwitch1Off
  end
  object BiPict1: TBiPict
    BorderStyle = 0
    BevelSize = 0
    BevelStyle = 1
    StretchBlt = True
    Picture_Data = {...}
  end
  object RadioGroup1: TRadioGroup
    Caption = 'Text'
    ItemIndex = 3
    Items.Strings = (
      'Right'
      'Left'
      'Above'
      'Below')
    OnClick = RadioGroup1Click
  end
end
```

16

When you need to access this property at run-time, you use a number again. (Of course, you can define some constants with the corresponding values to make the source code more readable.)

In the LIGHT program, however, we have no problem at all. The RadioGroup component has some radio buttons, determined by the string list stored in its Items property. This string list has the same order as the codes of the BiSwitch control's TextPosition property. Since you can access the selected radio button using the

ItemIndex property, this same value can be used for the position of the text. Here is the method connected to the OnClick event of the RadioGroup:

```
procedure TForm1.RadioGroup1Click(Sender: TObject);
begin
  BiSwitch1.TextPosition := RadioGroup1.ItemIndex;
end;
```

Simple, isn't it? Other than this special case, however, using a mnemonic enumeration instead of codes is certainly much simpler.

The other portion of the program—the click on the switch—presented more problems to implement. Figure 16.3 shows the LIGHT program with the switch on and the text in a different position.

FIGURE 16.3:

The LIGHT program with the switch on and a different position for the text.

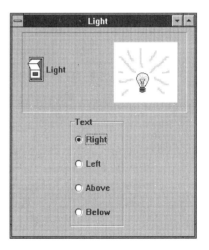

The first thing to note is that this VBX control doesn't have an OnClick event. Instead, it has two different events: OnOn and OnOff. The problem is that to change the bitmap in the BiPic control, you must set its Picture property, which has no relationship with the corresponding property of Delphi's Image component. You can easily spot this by activating the editor of this property from the Object Inspector. The resulting file-open dialog box is different from the default Delphi Picture Editor.

Accessing the property at design-time is easy, because you can use Delphi's Object Inspector. However, at run-time, you need to know what you are doing. Unfortunately, there is no Help information about the Borland VBX controls included in the package. I needed to run the Object Browser to discover that the data type of the property is HPic, a handle to a picture.

But how do you load a file in memory and get an HPic handle to it? Browsing through the BIVBX.INT file included with Delphi (it should be in the DELPHI\DOC directory), you can find a group of functions (not methods of a class) that work with pictures and files. This is a small excerpt of the BIVBX.INT file, with the prototypes of two useful functions:

```
{ pictures }
function VBXCreatePicture(const APic: TVBPicture): HPic;
function VBXGetPicFromFile(var APic: TVBPicture;
  PicFile: PChar): Err;
```

Using these functions, I've written the following code for the OnOn event of the switch:

```
procedure TForm1.BiSwitch1On(Sender: TObject);
var
  MyPic: TVBPicture;
  MyHPic: HPic;
begin
  VBXGetPicFromFile(MyPic, 'LIGHTON.BMP');
  MyHPic := VBXCreatePicture (MyPic);
  BiPict1.Picture := MyHPic;
end;
```

The first statement loads the file, the second gets its handle, and the third stores it in the property. I wrote it in long form (rather than on two lines) to let you see the data types involved. Under the file name LIGHTOFF.BMP, I have also written the code for the method related to the OnOff event, BiSwitch1Off.

The ChartFX VBX Control

Delphi includes just one really powerful VBX control, which is a chart control. This control, named ChartFX, has not been developed by Borland, but by the company Software FX.

This VBX control in documented in the Delphi Help files, but since I'm not used to Visual Basic and its controls, I found it difficult to use compared with Delphi components.

To demonstrate how the ChartFX component works, I've built another simple program, called CHART. There is a chart in the top portion of the screen, with a string grid below. A push button is used to copy the new numeric values of the string grid to the chart. Figure 16.4 shows the CHART form at design-time.

Both the chart and grid components are based on the same 5×4 matrix structure. The chart type can be changed by using the combo box in the bottom-right corner of the form. Not all of the chart types work well, and not all of them use all of the values of the grid. I included all the types to make this example as general as possible, since it is just a test.

You need to set quite a few properties to obtain the final form, as you can see in Listing 16.2. The chart object has a number of properties, and all of them are present in the textual description of the form. Some of them use weird values, such as:

```
Style = 2147480063
```

It is not easy to guess what this value stands for. I suggest that you look at the values of this control's properties in the Object Inspector, instead of trying to understand them in the textual description. I included them to demonstrate some of the advantages of using Delphi's own components instead of VBX controls.

FIGURE 16.4:

The form of the CHART example at design-time

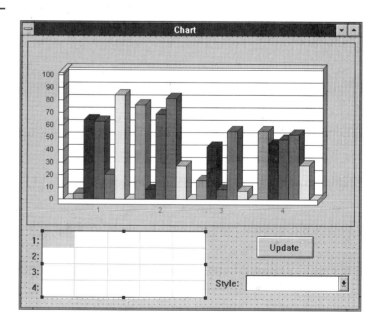

LISTING 16.2: The properties of the components and of the VBX control of the CHART form

```
object Form1: TForm1
  Caption = ' Chart'
  OnCreate = FormCreate
  object Label1: TLabel
    Caption = '1:'
  end
  object Label2: TLabel
    Caption = '2:'
  end
  object Label3: TLabel
    Caption = '3:'
  end
  object Label4: TLabel
    Caption = '4:'
  end
  object Label5: TLabel
    Caption = 'Style:'
  end
  object ChartFX1: TChartFX
    pType = 16642
    Style = 2147480063
    LeftGap = 56
    RightGap = 50
    TopGap = 40
    BottomGap = 40
    Decimals = 0
    PointType = 2
    Scheme = 0
    Stacked = 0
    Grid = 1
    WallWidth = 8
    LineWidth = 1
    LineStyle = 0
    LineColor = clOlive
    LineBkColor = clTeal
    FixedGap = 0
    DblClkDlg = 0
    RigClkDlg = 0
    RGBBarHorz = clFuchsia
    RGBBk = clSilver
    RGB2DBk = clTeal
    RGB3DBk = clWhite
    CustTool = 536813567
    VertGridGap = 1
    about = 'Click on "..."'
    NSeries_Data = {}
    NValues_Data = {...}
    ThisColor_Data = {000000000000}
    ThisBkColor_Data = {}
    AdmDlg_Data = {}
```

16

LISTING 16.2: The properties of the components and of the VBX control of the CHART form (continued)

```
    ViewRot3D_Data = {000036003E00}
    FontDlg_Data = {...}
    TitleDlg_Data = {000000000000000000000000000000000}
    ChartType_Data = {}
    Chart3D_Data = {}
    ToolBar_Data = {}
    PaletteBar_Data = {}
    PatternBar_Data = {}
    ZReserved1 = 'Click on "..."'
    ZReserved2 = 'Click on "..."'
    ZReserved3 = 'Click on "..."'
  end
  object StringGrid1: TStringGrid
    DefaultColWidth = 50
    FixedCols = 0
    FixedRows = 0
    Options = [goFixedVertLine, goFixedHorzLine, goVertLine,
      goHorzLine, goRangeSelect, goEditing]
    RowCount = 4
    ScrollBars = ssNone
    OnGetEditMask = StringGrid1GetEditMask
  end
  object UpdateButton: TButton
    Caption = 'Update'
    OnClick = UpdateButtonClick
  end
  object ComboBox1: TComboBox
    Style = csDropDownList
    Items.Strings = (
      '1 - Lines'
      '2 - Bar'
      '3 - Spline'
      '4 - Mark'
      '5 - Pie'
      '6 - Area'
      '7 - Pareto'
      '8 - Scatter'
      '9 - HiLow')
    OnChange = ComboBox1Change
  end
end
```

The second important component of the CHART example is the string grid, which has standard options, including editing capabilities. To set the grid to accept only numbers, you need to handle its OnGetEditMaskEvent, supplying a mask for numbers only, such as:

```
Value := '!09';
```

This allows you to input one or two numbers (the first number is required and the second is optional). This grid is filled with random values when the form is created, as shown in Figure 16.5. In the same OnCreate method, the grid's elements are copied to the chart by calling the UpdateButtonClick method (that is, by simulating a click on the button). Listing 16.3 shows the complete source code of the CHART example.

The UpdateButtonClick method is probably the core of the example. Before copying new data to the chart, the program must call the OpenData property of the VBX control. At the end, it calls the CloseData method to post the changes. The OpenData property is a sort of array, requiring special codes to access its various items. This code is defined in the ChartFX unit, which is not included by default; you need to add it manually to the uses statement.

16

FIGURE 16.5:

The output of the CHART example at startup depends on the random values of the grid.

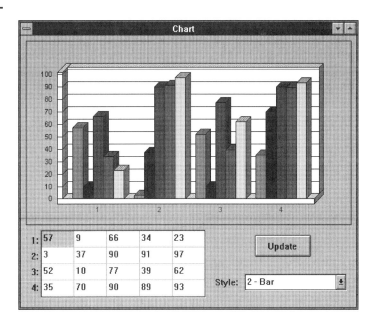

LISTING 16.3: The complete source code of the CHART example

```
unit Chart_f;

interface

uses
  SysUtils, WinTypes, WinProcs, Messages, Classes,
  Graphics, Controls, Forms, Dialogs, VBXCtrl, Chart2FX,
  Grids, StdCtrls, ChartFX;

type
  TForm1 = class(TForm)
    ChartFX1: TChartFX;
    StringGrid1: TStringGrid;
    UpdateButton: TButton;
    ComboBox1: TComboBox;
    procedure StringGrid1GetEditMask(Sender: TObject;
      ACol, ARow: LongInt; var Value: OpenString);
    procedure FormCreate(Sender: TObject);
    procedure UpdateButtonClick(Sender: TObject);
    procedure ComboBox1Change(Sender: TObject);
  private
    { Private declarations }
  public
    { Public declarations }
  end;

var
  Form1: TForm1;

implementation

{$R *.DFM}

procedure TForm1.StringGrid1GetEditMask(Sender: TObject;
  ACol, ARow: LongInt; var Value: OpenString);
begin
  Value := '!09';
end;

procedure TForm1.FormCreate(Sender: TObject);
var
  I, J: Integer;
begin
  {fill the grid with random values}
  Randomize;
  for I := 0 to 4 do
    for J := 0 to 3 do
      StringGrid1.Cells [I, J] :=
        IntToStr (Random (100));

  {update the chart}
  UpdateButtonClick (self);
```

LISTING 16.3: The complete source code of the CHART example (continued)

```
  {select the initial style in the combo box}
  ComboBox1.ItemIndex := ChartFX1.ChartType;
end;

procedure TForm1.UpdateButtonClick(Sender: TObject);
var
  I, J: Integer;
begin
  {open the flow of information}
  ChartFX1.OpenData [COD_VALUES] := MakeLong (5, 4);
  for I := 0 to 4 do
  begin
    {set the current data series}
    ChartFX1.ThisSerie := I;
    for J := 0 to 3 do
      {set one of the values of the series}
      ChartFX1.Value [J] :=
        StrToIntDef (StringGrid1.Cells [I, J], 0);
  end;
  {close the flow of information, posting the new data}
  ChartFX1.CloseData [COD_VALUES] := 0;
end;

procedure TForm1.ComboBox1Change(Sender: TObject);
begin
  {change the type of chart}
  ChartFX1.ChartType := ComboBox1.ItemIndex + 1;
end;

end.
```

16

In between the statements referring to the OpenData and CloseData properties, the program can access an array of values for each series of the chart. To set the current series, use the ThisSerie property. To set the values, use the Value array.

The actual numbers are copied from the grid, and they are converted into strings using the StrToIntDef function. In case of an error, a default value (zero) is used. In Figure 16.6, you can see an example with some strange values and a different type of chart.

The last part of the program relates to the combo box. Its value is initialized in the OnCreate method, and each time the user changes it, the code of the current selection is copied to the Style property of the chart.

FIGURE 16.6:

The CHART program, with a
custom series of values and a new
kind of graph

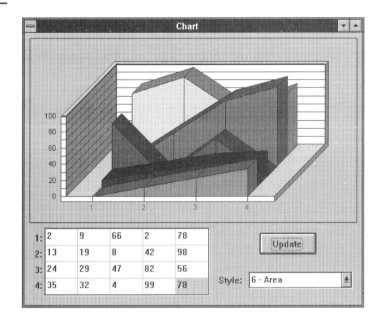

With this limited code, we have built a program that can show a variety of graphs,
based on the data the user inputs. Consider building this program without the support of a component, and you will realize the worth of ChartFX. At the same time,
if I had the choice of using a Delphi component instead of a VBX control, it would
be an easy decision to make. Delphi components are generally much easier to use
once you are familiar with the environment.

You cannot distribute this program without copying the proper VBX file together
with your executable file. And consider writing an installation routine to avoid
overwriting another copy of the same VBX with your older version. You can see
that there is some more work involved. It's worth repeating: VBX controls are great,
but Delphi components are better.

Installing a New VBX Control

Although I've made my point about which type of controls I consider easier to use,
we still must deal with the actual situation. There are indeed many more VBX controls than there are Delphi components, at least for the time being. This means that

you may need to install new VBX controls in Delphi. Here is an overview of the installation process:

1. Select the Install Components command from Delphi's Options menu. This opens the Install Components dialog box. To install new Delphi components (as we will do in Chapter 27), you can click on the Add button. For VBX components, click on the VBX button to see a list of VBX files present in the WINDOW\SYSTEM directory. Figure 16.7 shows both the Install Components and the Install VBX File dialog boxes.

FIGURE 16.7:

The dialog boxes used to install a new VBX control in Delphi

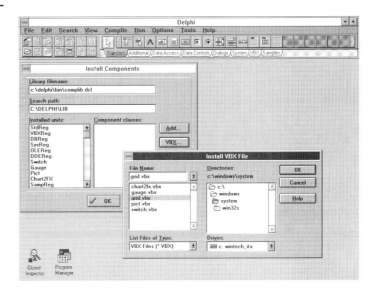

2. Select a VBX file. The next dialog box allows you to specify a file name for the Object Pascal interface to the VBX control. You can also edit the class name. In the example shown in Figure 16.8, I'm changing the grid control's default name, TGrid, to the new name TVBXGrid.

3. After you set the parameters, close the Install VBX File dialog box, and then close the Install Components dialog box. Delphi will rebuild its component library (the VCL) immediately, adding the new VBX control. Of course, this takes some time.

FIGURE 16.8:

After you have selected a VBX control, you can set some of its properties, including a name for the Object Pascal class acting as a wrapper around the control.

4. When the operation is complete, move to the Components palette, and you'll see the new component. Place it in a new form, and use it (assuming you know how or have some documentation). Figure 16.9 shows an example of the VBX grid control added to a form.

The Object Pascal source code file that resulted from the installation contains a definition of the TVBXGrid class wrapping the VBX control. This class has some of the properties of the control itself, as well as some properties that are shared by every Delphi component.

Here's just a single line of the source code file, but it is a very important one:

```
TVBXGrid = class(TVBXControl)
```

The new class is derived by a VCL class, TVBXControl.

FIGURE 16.9:
The new grid VBX control is added to the form. Notice its icon in the Components palette.

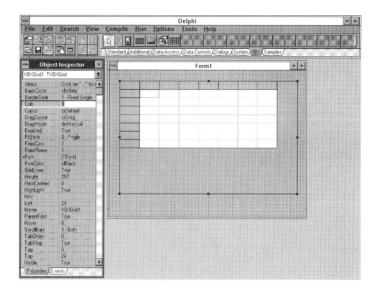

NOTE

The source code in this file is complex and difficult to read. For this reason, I've decided not to place it in a listing here in the book. However, it is on the book's companion disk. Of course, to make any use of it, you need to own the corresponding VBX control.

If you are planning to use VBX controls, follow the procedure outlined here to install them. Then you can study the Object Pascal source code file for each VBX control to see how it is defined.

Summary

In this short chapter, we have focused our attention on a single topic: Delphi's compatibility with VBX controls. You now know the differences between VBX and Delphi components, and I've highlighted the advantages of Delphi's approach.

From the viewpoint of a non-Visual Basic programmer (me), it appears that the structure of the VBX control is weaker than that of the Delphi components, because Delphi (and the VCL) is based on a more powerful language. Also, it is much easier to build new Delphi components than it is to build a VBX control. This is the topic of Chapter 27.

CHAPTER

SEVENTEEN

Building Database Applications

- Delphi's database components

- Manual database application construction

- The use of the Database Form Expert

- Query and table field manipulation

- Forms with more than one database table

17

Database support is one of the key features of the Delphi programming environment. Many programmers spend most of their time writing data-access code, and this should be the most robust portion of a database application.

This chapter provides just an overview of Delphi's extensive support for database programming. You can create even very complex database applications, starting from a blank form or one generated by Delphi's Database Form Expert.

What you won't find here is a discussion of the theory of database design. I'm assuming that you already know the fundamentals of database design and have already designed the structure of a database. I won't delve into database-specific problems; my goal is to help you understand how Delphi supports this kind of programming.

We'll begin with an explanation of how data access works in Delphi, and then review the database components that are available in Delphi. Then we'll move on to some basic examples to see how the components work. After this, we'll delve into some more advanced features, such as getting information about the tables at run-time, creating new tables from Delphi code, using graphics fields, and building forms with more than one table.

> **NOTE**   Besides accessing data in local databases, the Client-Server version (not the Desktop edition) of Delphi can be used to connect to SQL databases on server computers. This topic will be covered in the next chapter.

Data, Files, Databases, and Tables

On a computer, permanent data is always stored in files. This is also true for database data. There are several techniques you can use to accomplish this storage. The two most common approaches are to store a whole database in what appears to the file system as a single file, or to store each table, index, and any other elements of the database in a separate file. In the latter approach, the concept of *database* is not so precise, and a database can be seen as a collection of files, often stored in a single directory.

Delphi can use both approaches; or more precisely, it uses a custom approach that works well with both underlying structures. You always refer to a database with its name or an *alias*, which is a sort of a nickname of a database, but this reference can be to a database file or to a directory containing files with tables. It just depends on the data format you are using. But Delphi is not tied to a specific data format. It can use dBASE or Paradox tables, and access SQL (Structured Query Language) server databases or databases in other formats via the Microsoft ODBC (Open Database Connectivity) standard.

NOTE You can define new aliases for databases by using the Database Engine Configuration utility.

17

Delphi database applications do not have direct access to the data sources they reference. Delphi interfaces with the Borland Database Engine (BDE), which does have direct access to a number of data sources, including dBASE, Paradox, and AS-CII tables (using the appropriate drivers).

The BDE can also interface with Borland's SQL Links, which allows access to a number or local and remote SQL servers. The local server available is InterBase for Windows; remote servers include Oracle, Sybase, Informix, and InterBase. If you need to access a different database or data format, the BDE can interface with ODBC drivers. See Figure 17.1 for an illustration of how database access works in Delphi.

NOTE Although ODBC can provide access to data sources, this is usually the least efficient method. Use ODBC only as a last choice.

The fact that Delphi doesn't support direct data access basically means that you will need to install the DBE along with your applications on your clients' computers. This is not difficult, since Delphi includes a freely distributable DBE installation program. Just remember, without the DBE, your Delphi database applications won't work.

FIGURE 17.1:

The overall picture of data access
in Delphi

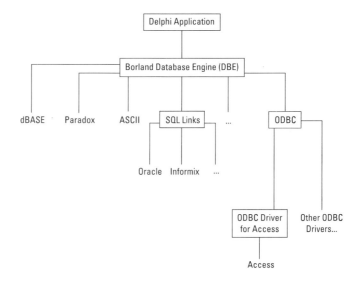

What Is a Table?

In general, we can use the term *database* to refer to a collection of tables. But what exactly is a table? Although most of you probably know the answer, I'll recap the basic information for the database newcomers.

A table in a database can be compared to a file of records in the Pascal language. A table has many records, or *rows*, and many columns, one for each field of the record. You can see the structure of a table, with its key elements labeled, in Figure 17.2. Notice that in a table there are the concepts of *current record* (the record a user is operating in) and *current field* (the active field of the current record).

The structure of a table can be clearly seen when you load it in a table viewer program, such as the Database Desktop included in Delphi. Figure 17.3 shows an example of a database table loaded in the Database Desktop application.

FIGURE 17.2:

The schema of a database table

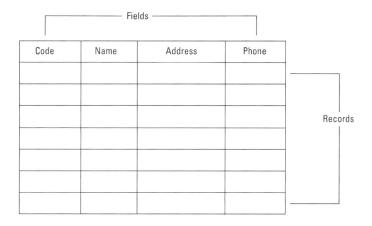

FIGURE 17.3:

A database table in Delphi's Database Desktop application

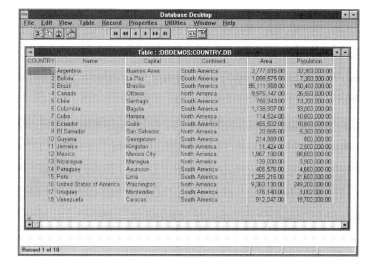

NOTE   The sample table shown in Figure 17.3, COUNTRY.DB, is part of the Delphi examples (in the directory DELPHI\DEMO\DATABASES, also indicated by the DBDEMOS alias, set up by Delphi during the installation). Many of my examples use Delphi databases. This way, instead of needing to build new ones, you already have these files available. In some examples, however, I'll show you how to build new tables from scratch.

Above the table you can see the name of the various fields, such as Name, Capital, Continent, and so on. Below this, there are the actual values of these fields in the various rows of the table. You can also see that there are visual hints indicating the current record and the current field.

Operations on Database Data

Once you have a database table, you can perform a number of actions, such as edit values, insert new records, and delete existing records. You can also perform operations on a window that contains a copy of some of the database data, then later copy that data back into the database. You'll see these two different steps in the code of many of the database application examples.

The problem of synchronizing the values seen by the user with the real data is complicated by the fact that several users might be accessing a database at the same time, from different computers of a network. To avoid conflicts, SQL databases have some form of locking to prevent two users from changing the same database data at the same time. However, you seldom need to deal with this issue directly. The BDE and the databases you connect to shield you from most of the details of database handling and data processing.

Delphi offers a uniform view of database access, but you must be aware of the fact that not all databases support the same features. For example, only the SQL database types have the notion of transaction (a single atomic, indivisible operation on data) and of transaction rollback (the process of ignoring a transaction and returning to the preceding situation).

Delphi Database Components

Delphi includes a number of components related to databases. The Data Access page of the Components palette contains components used to interact with databases. Most of them are nonvisual components, since they encapsulate database connections, tables, queries, and similar elements.

Fortunately, Delphi also provides a number of predefined components you can use to view and edit database data. In the Data Controls page, there are visual components used to view and edit the data in a form. These controls are called *data-aware* components.

To access a database in Delphi, you generally need a data source, described by the DataSource component. The DataSource component, however, does not indicate the data directly; it refers either to a table or to the result of a query. Therefore, you also need a Table or a Query component in the form, as you can see in the scheme shown in Figure 17.4.

What Figure 17.4 does not show is that the DataSource component can be connected to either a table or a query, but not both at the same time. Multiple data-aware components are usually connected to a single data source.

17

FIGURE 17.4:

The role of the DataSource component is to connect the data-aware controls with a table or a query

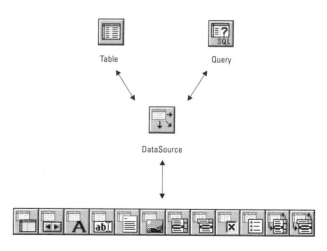

Table   Query

DataSource

Data-Access Components

As soon as you have placed a Table or Query component on the form, you can use the DataSet property of the DataSource component to refer to it:

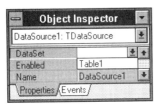

In short, a form must provide a DataSource component and one of the data set components. This is true for all database forms, except in some rare cases. By data set component, I mean either a TTable or a TQuery object, which are both descendents of the TDataSet class.

Tables and Queries

The simplest way to specify data access in Delphi (other than by using the Database Form Expert) is to use the Table component. A Table object simply refers to a database table.

When you use a Table component, you need to indicate the name of the database you want to use in its DatabaseName property. You can enter the name itself, an alias, or the path of the directory with the table files. The Object Inspector lists the available names, which depend on the BDE installation:

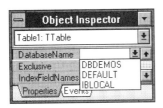

You also need to indicate a proper value in the TableName property. Again this can be an internal name or the name of the file holding the table. The Object Inspector lists the available tables of the current database (or directory):

Two other relevant properties of the Table component are ReadOnly, used to prevent any changes in the data, and Exclusive, used to forbid concurrent access to a networked table from several applications at the same time. There are also the properties related to indexes and master tables. We will focus on these properties again at the end of this chapter, in the MASTDET example.

The other data set available in Delphi is the Query component. A query is usually more complex than a table, because it requires a SQL language string. However, you can customize a query using SQL more easily than you can customize a table (as long as you know at least the basic elements of SQL, of course).

NOTE   SQL is a standard language to write database queries, and generally interact with a database. If you are not fluent in SQL, you can refer to Appendix B for a minimal description of its basic commands. If you remember at least the key elements, however, you can probably read the simple SQL examples in this book without worrying too much about the details. The Client-Server version of Delphi includes a specific tool to create SQL queries, called the Visual Query Builder, which is discussed in Chapter 18.

The Query component also has a DatabaseName property, but it does not have a TableName property. The table is indicated inside the SQL statement, stored in the SQL property. As we will see in an example later in this chapter, this SQL statement can also include parameters, specified with the Parameters property.

You can set the SQL statement both at design-time, by opening the SQL string editor, or at run-time. For example, you can write a simple SQL statement like this:

```
select * from Country
```

where Country is the name of a table, and the star symbol (*) indicates that you want to use all of the fields in the table. If you are fluent in SQL, you will probably use the Query component more often than the Table component.

In a simple example, you can use either a Table or Query component to achieve the same effects. In general, tables tend to be used to browse through most of the fields of a table. Queries are generally used when you have particularly complex restrictive clauses.

Queries are also often used to join two or more tables and see the result as if it were a single table stored in the database. While a Table component refers to a current table of the database, a SQL statement (and therefore a Query component) produces a table as its result. This allows you to browse through a table that is not in the database, but is a result of a join, a selection, or other computations. Of course, these computations take time. Complex operations, such as table joins, might take a lot of time.

Other Data-Access Components

Along with the Table, Query, and DataSource, there are four other components in the Data Access page of the Components palette:

- The Database component is used for transaction control, security, and connection control. It is generally used only to connect to remote databases in client-server applications.

- The StoredProcedure component allows a Delphi application to execute a procedure stored on the server.

- The BatchMove component is used to make batch operations on one or more databases, such as copying, appending, updating, or deleting values.

- The Report component is an interface to Borland's ReportSmith application.

These can be considered to be advanced database components, and some of them are meaningless in a local environment. We will use some of these components in this chapter and the next one, but we won't focus on them in great detail.

Delphi Data-Aware Components

We have seen how it is possible to connect a data source to a database, using either a table or query, but we still do not know how to show the data. For this purpose, Delphi provides many components that resemble the usual Windows controls, but are data-aware. For example, the DBEdit component is similar to the Edit component, and the DBCheckBox component corresponds to the CheckBox component. You can find all of these components in the Data Controls page of the Delphi Components palette:

- DBGrid is a grid, capable of displaying a whole table at once. It allows scrolling and navigation, and you can edit the grid's contents.

- DBNavigator is a collection of buttons used to navigate and perform actions on the database.

- DBLabel is used to display the contents of a field that cannot be modified.

- DBEdit is used to let the user edit a field (change the current value).

- DBMemo is used to let the user see and modify a large text field, eventually stored in a memo or BLOB (which stands for Binary Large OBject) field.

- DBImage is used to show a picture stored in a BLOB field.

- DBListBox and DBComboBox are used to let the user select a single value from a specified set. If this set is the result of another query, which results in data in another table, you can use the DBLookupList or DBLookupCombo component.

- DBCheckBox can be used to show and toggle an option, corresponding to the evaluation of a function.

- DBRadioGroup is used to provide a series of choices, with a number of exclusive selection radio buttons, similar to the ListBox or ComboBox component.

All of these components are connected to a data source using the corresponding property, DataSource. Many of them refer to a specific data field of the source, with the DataField property. Other than these and few other specific properties, the properties of the Data Controls page components are similar to those of the corresponding standard controls. Note however, that the DBEdit component is more like the MaskEdit component than the Edit component.

17

Although we haven't seen many details of the use of the components, this brief overview is enough for the moment. Now let's turn to the job of building database applications. First, we'll see how to create such an application by hand, and then later we'll try using the Database Form Expert.

Building Database Applications by Hand

Now that we know the role of Delphi's various database components, we are ready to start building an application, or actually, a series of simple examples. We will use both tables and queries, and a number of data-aware controls. The first example shows the simplest approach, with the use of a DBGrid component.

A Grid of Countries

Our first database example, called HANDGRID, uses the table shown earlier in Figure 17.3, which lists American countries with their capitals and population. To make things simple, we can use a grid to display all of the data in the table.

To begin, on a new form, place a Table, DataSource, and DBGrid component, as shown in Figure 17.5. Connect the three elements to each other and with the proper database table. To accomplish this, use these properties:

- For the DBGrid component, use DataSource1 as the value of the DataSource property,

- For the DataSource component, use Table1 as the value of the DataSet property.

- For the Table component, use DBDEMOS as the value of the DatabaseName property, and COUNTRY.DB as the value of the TableName property.

These component properties, along with other important ones, such as the ones to set the alignment of the grid, are shown in Listing 17.1.

FIGURE 17.5:

The form of the HANDGRID example at design-time, when the database is not active

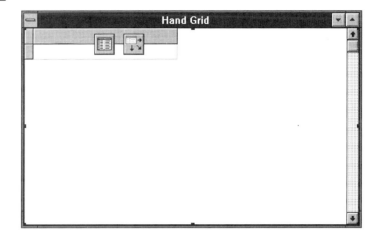

LISTING 17.1: The textual description of the properties of the form of the HANDGRID example and its components

```
object Form1: TForm1
  ActiveControl = DBGrid1
  Caption = 'Hand Grid'
  object DBGrid1: TDBGrid
    Align = alClient
    DataSource = DataSource1
    TitleFont.Color = clWindowText
    TitleFont.Height = -13
    TitleFont.Name = 'System'
    TitleFont.Style = []
  end
  object Table1: TTable
    Active = True
    DatabaseName = 'DBDEMOS'
    TableName = 'COUNTRY.DB'
  end
  object DataSource1: TDataSource
    DataSet = Table1
  end
end
```

If you set the Active property of the table to True, the data will appear in the form at design-time (this technique is usually called *live-data* design). Notice the difference between the new form, shown in Figure 17.6, and the old one (Figure 17.5).

When a grid displays live data, you can even use its scroll bars to navigate through the records and view the other fields. The grid allows you to see all of the data in the table at design-time.

FIGURE 17.6:

The form of the HANDGRID example with live data

Now we can run the program, and it will show the same data we could already see at design-time. The difference now is that we can also edit the values, writing new text in each of the cells. This is possible because the DBGrid component's Options property includes the flag dgEditing and the ReadOnly property is set to False. You are working directly on the database data, so if you make a change, it will become permanent.

Besides changing the current values of a record, this program also allows you to insert or append new records. To insert a new row in a given position, press the Insert key there. To append a new record at the end, just move the cursor below the last element of the grid (go to the last record and press the down arrow key), You can also press the Ctrl and Del keys to delete the current record, after you confirm the action.

Try to use this program for a while (maybe after making a backup copy of the original database), and test how it works when you toggle on and off the various flags of the Options property of the grid.

What about the code of the program? There is none. The Pascal file contains only the usual declarations of the objects used by the form, automatically added by Delphi.

So we have an application with no code at all, which can be used to perform a relevant number of operations on a table. This is really a nice side of Delphi programming.

Navigating through Countries

This example works well, but we want to try using other controls, such as edit boxes, and see just specific information rather than all the data in our database. The next example, called NAVIG1, is similar to the previous one, but it uses some DB-Edit components and a couple of traditional labels, along with the table and the data source. We also need to add a brand new component, the DBNavigator. Figure 17.7 shows the form of the NAVIG1 example.

FIGURE 17.7:
The two DBEdit and the DBNavigator components of the NAVIG1 example, with live data

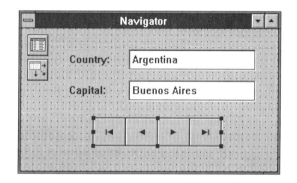

TIP

You can use the standard Windows copy and paste operations to copy components, such as the Table and DataSet components, with all their properties, from one form to another or from one example to another. In this case, the trick is really helpful, because you can copy the two components along with their database connections and all their other properties.

Again, we need to connect the three data-aware controls to the data source, and also indicate a specific field for each of the two edit boxes (Name and Capital are the fields for this example). If you have already connected the data source to the table (or you have copied and pasted the connections using standard Windows techniques) and the edit boxes to the data source, you can simply select a field in the list displayed by the Object Inspector:

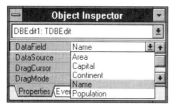

When this connection is made, the values of the first record's fields appear automatically in the two edit boxes (see Figure 17.7). I've also set the ReadOnly property of the two edit boxes to True, so that a user cannot change the current data.

Another step we can take is to disable some of the buttons of the DBNavigator control, by removing some of the elements of the VisibleButtons set. These nine buttons have the following meanings:

nbFirst	Go to the first record
nbPrior	Go to the previous record (of the current one)
nbNext	Go to the next record (of the current one)
nbLast	Go to the last record
nbInsert	Insert a new blank record in the current position
nbDelete	Delete the current record
nbEdit	Allow the editing of the current record
nbPost	Post (store) the changes that occurred in the current edit action
nbCancel	Cancel the changes in the current edit action

You can see the graphical representation of the various buttons of the navigator, along with the descriptions of their actions, in Figure 17.8. The glyphs of some of these buttons are not very intuitive, but they feature automatic fly-over hints, so that a user can see the function of a button just by moving the mouse over it.

FIGURE 17.8:

The meaning of the buttons of the
DBNavigator component.

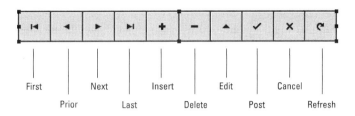

You can turn off the ShowHint property to disable the fly-over hints of the navigator, and also provide a customized description for their text, using the Hints string list. This can be useful when you need to translate an application in another language (or to write it directly in another language, as I often do). The strings you insert are used for the buttons in order: the first string is used for the first button, the second for the second, and so on. If some buttons are not visible, you can provide empty strings (just a blank space), as placeholders.

17

With the properties I've described, the NAVIG1 program is ready. Listing 17.2 shows the textual description of the NAVIG1 example. You can run it and test if it works properly. Try changing some of the properties of the navigator and of the two edit boxes. For example, you might disable the ReadOnly property to allow changes. You can also add new data-aware edit boxes for the other fields of the table.

Notice that when the program is running, at the beginning or when you jump to the first or to the last record of the table, two of the navigator's buttons will be disabled automatically. However, if you move step-by-step to the first or last record, the buttons are disabled only when you try to move before or after those records. Only at this point does the navigator realize that there are no more records in that direction. The same happens when you use the DBGrid's vertical scrollbar.

LISTING 17.2: The textual description of the form of the NAVIG1 example

```
object Navigator: TNavigator
  Caption = 'Navigator'
  object Label1: TLabel
    Caption = 'Country:'
  end
  object Label2: TLabel
    Caption = 'Capital:'
  end
  object DBEdit1: TDBEdit
    DataField = 'Name'
    DataSource = DataSource1
    MaxLength = 24
    ReadOnly = True
  end
  object DBEdit2: TDBEdit
    DataField = 'Capital'
    DataSource = DataSource1
    MaxLength = 24
    ReadOnly = True
  end
  object DBNavigator1: TDBNavigator
    DataSource = DataSource1
    VisibleButtons = [nbFirst, nbPrior, nbNext, nbLast]
  end
  object DataSource1: TDataSource
    DataSet = Table1
  end
  object Table1: TTable
    Active = True
    DatabaseName = 'DBDEMOS'
    TableName = 'COUNTRY.DB'
    TableType = ttDefault
  end
end
```

Using a Query

In the first two examples, we have used a Table component and we have browsed through all of the records in the table.

For our next example, called NAVIG2, we'll delete the Table component and add a Query component instead. We can connect the query to the usual DBDEMO database alias, and enter the text of a simple SQL statement. As we have already seen, we can select all of the fields of all of the records in the table by writing:

```
select * from Country
```

When this query has been entered, you can activate the Query component, using the Active property, and the values of the fields of the first record should appear again in the edit boxes. Of course, this happens only if the SQL statement you have inserted is correct. Otherwise, Delphi will issue an error message, and the query won't be activated.

NOTE   If you want to change the current SQL statement of a query at design-time or at run-time, you need to set the Active property of the component to False first, then change the value, and then set it to True again, reactivating the connection between the data-aware components and the data. Otherwise, you will see no effect (other than an error message!).

Of course, this example is not particularly interesting. Why use the Query component instead of the Table component if this is all we want? We can take advantage of the new component by adding some radio buttons to select different queries at run-time. I decided to add four radio buttons—that is, four different options—as you can see in Figure 17.9.

17

FIGURE 17.9:

The form of the NAVIG2 example, with four radio buttons used to select different SQL statements

The first button is used to select the default SQL statement, and it is checked at startup. The second and third buttons can be used to choose only the records that have a specific value, North America or South America, for their Continent field. To accomplish this, we need to add a where clause to the SQL statement, as we will see shortly. The last radio button allows a user to enter the text of the where statement, writing a custom condition in the edit box next to the radio button.

Letting a user type in a statement is slightly dangerous, since entering the wrong text can cause an error. But Delphi is robust enough to withstand this risk, thanks to its exception handling. You can see the properties of the components of the form in this example in Listing 17.3.

LISTING 17.3: The textual description of the components of the NAVIG2 example

```
object Navigator: TNavigator
  Caption = 'Navigator'
  object Label1: TLabel
    Caption = 'Country:'
  end
  object Label2: TLabel
    Caption = 'Capital:'
  end
  object Bevel1: TBevel
    Left = 16
    Top = 16
    Width = 361
    Height = 161
  end
  object DBEdit1: TDBEdit
    DataField = 'Name'
    DataSource = DataSource1
    MaxLength = 24
    ReadOnly = True
  end
  object DBEdit2: TDBEdit
    DataField = 'Capital'
    DataSource = DataSource1
    MaxLength = 24
    ReadOnly = True
  end
  object DBNavigator1: TDBNavigator
    DataSource = DataSource1
    VisibleButtons = [nbFirst, nbPrior, nbNext, nbLast]
  end
  object GroupBox1: TGroupBox
    Caption = 'Selection'
    object RadioButton1: TRadioButton
      Caption = 'All'
      Checked = True
```

LISTING 17.3: The textual description of the components of the NAVIG2 example
(continued)

```
      OnClick = RadioButton1Click
    end
    object RadioButton2: TRadioButton
      Caption = 'North America'
      OnClick = RadioButton2Click
    end
    object RadioButton3: TRadioButton
      Caption = 'South America'
      OnClick = RadioButton2Click
    end
    object RadioButton4: TRadioButton
      Caption = 'Custom:'
      Enabled = False
      OnClick = RadioButton4Click
    end
    object Edit1: TEdit
      OnChange = Edit1Change
    end
  end
  object DataSource1: TDataSource
    DataSet = Query1
  end
  object Query1: TQuery
    Active = True
    DatabaseName = 'DBDEMOS'
    SQL.Strings = (
      'select * from Country')
  end
end
```

For the first time in this chapter, we need to write some code. The code is necessary to change the value of the SQL property of the Query component when a new radio button is checked. Each time we do this operation, we must remember to call the Close and Open methods of the Query component, or to set the value of the Active property to False and True.

Here is the code associated with the first radio button:

```
procedure TNavigator.RadioButton1Click(Sender: TObject);
begin
  Query1.Active := False;
  Query1.Sql.Clear;
  Query1.Sql.Add('select * from Country');
  Query1.Active := True;
end;
```

Notice that the SQL property is not a string, but has a TStrings type. This can be used to build very long queries (the text limit for an array of strings is high) and to define different portions of the query in different places of the code and merge them. I've chosen to follow a more traditional approach, with a query made of a single line of text.

The second and third radio buttons share the same code, which uses the caption to build the text of the SQL statement:

```
procedure TNavigator.RadioButton2Click(Sender: TObject);
begin
  Query1.Active := False;
  Query1.Sql.Clear;
  Query1.Sql.Add('select * from Country where Continent = ''' +
    (Sender as TRadioButton).Caption + '''');
  Query1.Active := True;
end;
```

You can see the effect of this code in Figure 17.10.

This code defines a SQL statement by adding several substrings. Notice that we need to use double single-quotation marks (that is, two consecutive single quotation marks) to indicate a quotation mark within a Pascal string. For this reason, in

FIGURE 17.10:

Selecting the North American countries in the NAVIG2 example. The first element of the set of records resulting from the query is Canada.

the code above, we happen to have triple and even quadruple quotation marks. In this last case, the four quotation marks in a row, we simply need a string containing a quotation mark, therefore the two external quotation marks indicate the beginning and end of the string, and the two enclosed quotation marks denote the single quotation mark we really need.

For the last radio button, the code is simpler, since we only need to merge the default statement with the text of the edit box:

```
procedure TNavigator.RadioButton4Click(Sender: TObject);
begin
  Query1.Active := False;
  if (Edit1.Text <> '') then
  begin
    Query1.Sql.Clear;
    Query1.Sql.Add('select * from Country where ' + Edit1.Text);
  end;
  Query1.Active := True;
end;
```

17

This code is executed only if the edit box is not empty, hoping that the text is a correct SQL statement (the program doesn't check this assumption). To further improve the program, the last radio button is automatically disabled each time the edit box has no text. This check takes place in the OnChange event of the Edit component :

```
procedure TNavigator.Edit1Change(Sender: TObject);
begin
  RadioButton4.Enabled := Edit1.Text <> '';
end;
```

When you run this program, you can choose any of the four buttons and see immediately the effect on the current record. Notice that the navigator works on the resulting table of the query, so that it correctly considers Canada to be the first North American country (as you saw in Figure 17.10) in alphabetic order, of course.

The Custom edit box can be used in a number of different ways. Figure 17.11 shows two different examples of its use. One example shows a single country of the database selected, and the other shows a population range. If you write something meaningless, or just make a small syntax error, the program will stop with an error message, as shown in Figure 17.12.

FIGURE 17.11:

Two copies of the NAVIG2 example
with a custom where clause. On the
left is the selection of a single
country. On the right is all those
having a large population.

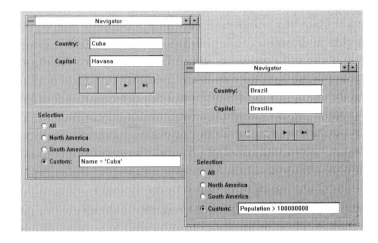

FIGURE 17.12:

The error message displayed by the
NAVIG2 program when the string in
the edit box is not a valid SQL clause

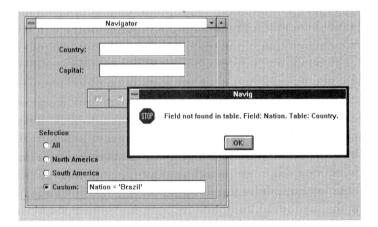

A Query with Parameters

The last version of our navigator example demonstrates the use of query parameters. All of the queries in the previous version were very similar. Instead of building
a new query each time, we can write a query with a parameter, and simply change
the value of the parameter.

If we decide to choose North American or South American countries, for example, we can write the following statement:

```
select * from Country where Continent = :Continent
```

In this SQL clause, `:Continent` is a parameter. We can set its data type and startup value, using the special editor of the Params property of the Query component. You can access this editor from the Object Inspector or through the Define Parameters command on the form's SpeedMenu when the Query component is selected in the form:

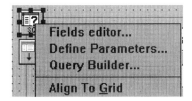

When the Parameters editor is open, as shown in Figure 17.13, you see a list of the parameters defined in the SQL statement of the Query component. For each of these parameters, you can set a data type and provide an initial value.

Using this approach makes the new version of this example extremely simple. Its form, also shown in Figure 17.13, is a reduced version of the previous example's

FIGURE 17.13:

The Parameters editor of a Query component. Behind it is the form of the NAVIG3 example.

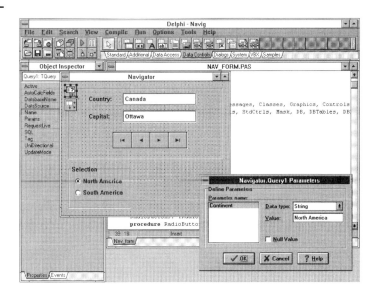

form. Its only significant code is the response method for the OnClick event of both radio buttons. Here is its code:

```
procedure TNavigator.RadioButton2Click(Sender: TObject);
begin
  Query1.Active := False;
  Query1.Params[0].AsString :=
    (Sender as TRadioButton).Caption;
  Query1.Active := True;
end;
```

This method copies the caption of the radio button to the first parameter of the query. The first parameter is number 0, since the Params array is zero-based, and you should access its value as a string. This AsString property is common to parameter and field arrays of the database components. As we will see in more detail later in the chapter, these are arrays of elements that can have different data types, so one of the As conversion properties is always required.

Using the Database Form Expert

We have been able to build some simple examples by placing database components on the main form of the application and then connecting them. Often, this operation requires some time. For this reason, Delphi has a Database Form Expert tool, which provides a fast start in the development of a database application. You had a brief introduction to this tool in Chapter 3, which provided an overview of Delphi's templates and Experts. Now we are ready to use it.

Just to gain some confidence in using this tool, we can try to rebuild the first example in this chapter, HANDGRID, using the Expert. The new example is named EXPGRID.

Create a new, blank project (or select the Database Form Expert as the default project form, as described in Chapter 3), and start the Database Form Expert. In the Expert, select a simple form based on a table, choose the COUNTRY.DB table in the DBDEMOS database, select all the fields, and choose a grid. These steps are shown in Figure 17.14.

Now you can generate the code, remove the older blank form from the project (probably Form1), compile the program, give proper names to the files, and run it.

The result is shown in Figure 17.15. This program is similar to the one we built before, but this time the process was much simpler and faster.

FIGURE 17.14:

The Database Form Expert steps to build the new version of the grid of countries

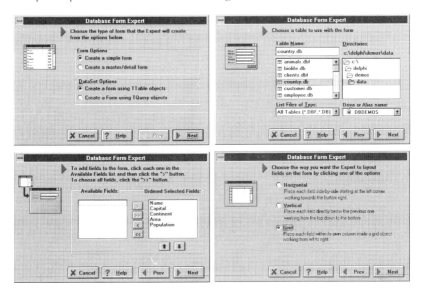

FIGURE 17.15:

The EXPGRID program at run-time

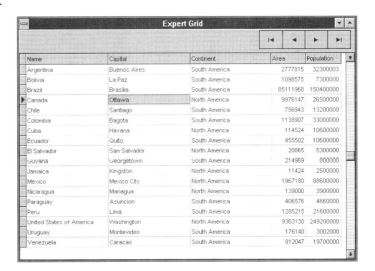

The Expert is even faster when your form is based on labels and edit fields, instead of on a single grid. In this case, placing all of the components on the form, aligning them, and so on, requires more time. But when you use the Database Form Expert, you can simply choose a vertical or a horizontal layout. If you use a vertical layout, you can decide if you want to place the label above or on the left of the corresponding edit field. We will use this approach in an example later in this chapter.

Before we use the Expert to build new examples, let's take a moment to study the code that it has generated for us. The form of the EXPGRID program has six components, as you can partially see in Figure 17.16.

There is a table, connected with the data, a data source associated with the table, a navigator (hosted by two nested panels), and a grid. The two panels (one of which is selected in Figure 17.16) are used to place the navigator near the right border of the form, but not too close to the border (not aligned to the right). The key elements of the textual description of this form are shown in Listing 17.4.

The code generated for this example is simple. The only predefined method corresponds to the OnCreate event of the form; it is used to activate the table:

```
procedure TForm2.FormCreate(Sender: TObject);
begin
  Table1.Open;
end;
```

FIGURE 17.16:

The form of the EXPGRID program at design-time

LISTING 17.4: The textual description of the form of the EXPGRID example

```
object Form2: TForm2
  Caption = 'Expert Grid'
  Font.Height = -11
  Font.Name = 'Arial'
  OnCreate = FormCreate
  object Panel1: TPanel
    Align = alTop
    object Panel2: TPanel
      Align = alRight
      BevelOuter = bvNone
      Caption = 'Panel2'
      object DBNavigator: TDBNavigator
        DataSource = DataSource1
        VisibleButtons = [nbFirst, nbPrior, nbNext, nbLast]
      end
    end
  end
  object DBGrid1: TDBGrid
    Align = alClient
    DataSource = DataSource1
  end
  object DataSource1: TDataSource
    DataSet = Table1
  end
  object Table1: TTable
    DatabaseName = 'DBDEMOS'
    TableName = 'country.db'
  end
end
```

17

Accessing the Fields of a Table or Query

Before we try to build more attractive examples, which include support for images, there are few more technical elements we should explore. Up to now, we have used grids including all of the fields in the source database table. You probably noticed that the Database Form Expert lets you choose the fields you want to use.

Suppose that we have already built the example. How could we remove a field from the grid? How can we add new fields, such as calculated fields? In trying to solve these problems, we face a more general question: How do we access the values—the fields—of the current record from a program? How can we change them, without a direct editing action by the user?

The answer to all of these questions lies in the concept of *field*. Field components (instances of class TField) are nonvisual components that are fundamental for each Delphi database application. Data-aware components are directly connected to these Field objects, which correspond to database fields, as illustrated in Figure 17.17.

FIGURE 17.17:

The relationship between table, field, and data-aware components

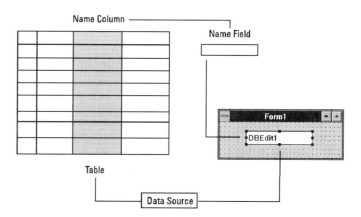

In the examples we have built up to now, TField components were automatically created by Delphi at run-time. This happens each time a DataSet component is active. These fields are stored in the Fields property of tables and queries, which is an array of fields. We can access these values in our program by writing:

```
Table1.Fields[0].AsString
```

As an alternative, the Field components can be created at design-time, using the Fields editor. In this case, you can set a number of properties for these fields. These properties affect the behavior of the data-aware components using them, both for visualization and for editing. When you define new fields at design-time, they are listed in the Object Inspector, just like any other component.

As an example, we can access the Fields editor of the table we generated in the last example. To open the editor for the fields in a table, select the Table object on the form, activate its SpeedMenu, and choose the Fields Editor command.

The Fields editor has two buttons: Add and Define. Using the Add button, you can add any other fields in the database table to the list of fields. Figure 17.18 shows the

Add Fields dialog box displayed when you click on this button. The dialog box lists all the fields that are still available. These are the database table fields that are not already present in the list of fields in the editor.

NOTE There is a drawback to creating fields at design-time. The Table component will require those fields to exist in the database table at run-time, too. For this reason, if you want to let the users open the tables of their choice at run-time, you can't add fields to the Table (or Query) component at design-time. If you change the structure of your table, you'll need to "recalibrate" the fields in the Delphi form. Of course, if you access the fields at run-time, as shown before, there are fewer problems.

17

The Define button in the Fields editor lets you define new calculated fields. Figure 17.19 shows the dialog box that appears when you click on Define. First, enter a descriptive field name, which can include blank spaces. The dialog box generates an internal name—the name of the component—that you can further customize. Next, select a data type for the field. If this is a calculated field, not just a copy of a field redefined to use a new data type, check the Calculated box.

FIGURE 17.18:

The Fields editor with the Add Fields dialog box

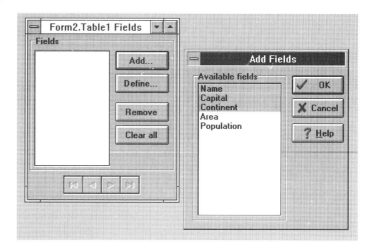

FIGURE 17.19:
The Fields editor with the Define
Field dialog box

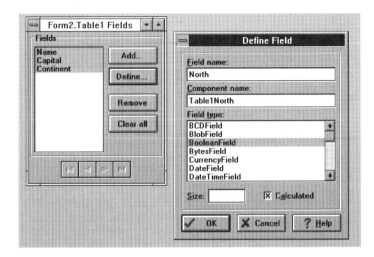

> **NOTE**
>
> A TField component has both a Name property and a FieldName property. The Name property is the usual component name. The FieldName property is the name of the column in the database table, or the name you define for the calculated field. It can be more descriptive and allows blank spaces. The name of the TField component is copied to the DisplayLabel property (which can be changed later) and is used, among other things, to search a field.

All of the fields that you add or define are included in the Fields editor list, which has a nice dragging capability to change the order of the fields. This is particularly important when you define a grid, which arranges its columns using this order.

The list of fields indicates the elements that are available to the data-enabled controls (and in our case, those that are displayed in the grid), and for which there is also a declaration of a TField component (or a component of a subclass of TField) in the form. You can later use this object to access the data of the field, to change several properties, and to compute the calculated fields in the OnCalcFields event of the table.

The TField Components

Before we look at an example, let's go over the use of the TField component, one of the few components not directly available in Delphi Components palette. The importance of this component should not be underestimated. Although it is often used behind the scenes, its role in database applications is fundamental. Even if you do not define specific objects of this kind, you can always access the fields of a table or a query using their Fields property, an array of TField objects. When you use this approach, and also when you handle a Field object directly, you can use a series of As properties to handle the field using a specific data type:

```
AsBoolean: Boolean;
AsDateTime: TDateTime;
AsFloat: Double;
AsInteger: LongInt;
AsString: string;
```

17

This code can be used to assign or read the value of the field. Most of the other properties of the TField component, such as Alignment, DisplayLabel, DisplayWidth, and Visible, reflect elements of the field's user interface and are used in particular with the DBGrid component, since there is no other way to customize the columns of this grid.

When you use a component of a TField subclass, you can also use the Value property directly, and further customize the output for dates, floating-point numbers, and other special data types. Here is a list of the subclasses of TField:

TStringField	Text data of a fixed length (it may be up to 255 characters, but it depends on the database type)
TIntegerField	Whole numbers in the range of long integers (32 bits)
TSmallIntField	Whole numbers in the range of integers (16 bits)
TWordField	Whole positive numbers in the range of words or unsigned integers (16 bits)
TFloatField	Real floating-point numbers
TCurrencyField	Currency values, with the same range of real numbers

TBCDField	Real numbers, with a fixed number of digits after the decimal point
TBooleanField	Field with Boolean value
TDateTimeField	Field with date and time value
TDateField	Field with date value
TTimeField	Field with time value
TBlobField	Field with arbitrary data and no size limit
TBytesField	Field with arbitrary data and no size limit
TVarBytesField	Field with arbitrary data, up to 64K characters
TMemoField	Text of arbitrary length
TGraphicField	Graphic of arbitrary length

The availability of any particular field type depends on the database type or SQL server. For example, InterBase doesn't support BCDs, so you'll never get a BCDField for a table on the InterBase server. The range and precision of floating-point fields and the size of decimal fields also vary among SQL servers.

An Example of a Calculated Field

After this introduction to the use of TField objects, it is time to build a simple example. We can start from the last example we built, EXPGRID, and add a calculated field. The Countries database table we are accessing has both the population and the area of each country, so we can use this data to compute the population density.

To build the new application, named CALC, copy the code of the previous example, or generate a new version with the Database Form Expert (it's so easy and fast). Now select the Table component in the form and open the Fields editor (using the form's SpeedMenu).

In this editor, click on the Add button, and select some of the fields (I've decided to skip only the Continent field). Now click on the Define button and enter a proper name and data type (TFloatField) for the new calculated field, as you can see in Figure 17.20.

FIGURE 17.20:

The definition of a calculated field in the CALC example

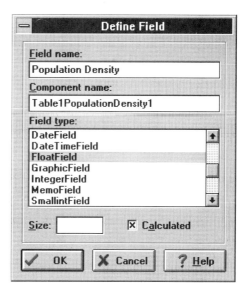

17

Of course, we also need to provide a way to compute the new field. This is accomplished in the OnCalcFields event of the Table component, which has the following code:

```
procedure TForm2.Table1CalcFields(DataSet: TDataSet);
begin
  Table1PopulationDensity.Value :=
    Table1Population.Value / Table1Area.Value;
end;
```

We can write this code, accessing the fields directly, because when you use the Fields editor, some components related to the fields are automatically added to the form:

```
Table1PopulationDensity: TFloatField;
Table1Area: TFloatField;
Table1Population: TFloatField;
Table1Name: TStringField;
Table1Capital: TStringField;
```

Each time you add or remove fields in the Fields editor, you can see the effect of your action immediately in the grid present in the form. Of course, you won't see the values of a calculated field, because they are available only at run-time.

Since we have defined some components for the fields, we can use them to customize some of the visual elements of the grid. For example, I've changed the name of the first column to Country (instead of Name) and set a display format, adding a comma to separate thousands. These changes have an immediate effect on the grid at design-time, as you can see in Figure 17.21.

FIGURE 17.21:

You can set a number of properties of the TField components and see their effect at design-time.

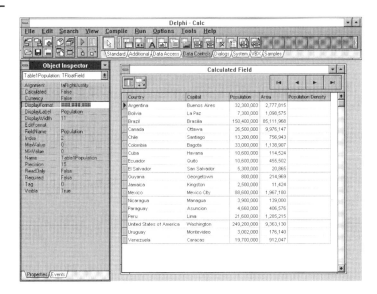

> **NOTE**
>
> The display format I've just mentioned uses the locale information in the WIN.INI file to format the output. The comma is in the format string, but it tells the format code to substitute the proper Thousand-Separator character for the display string. For this reason, the output of the program will automatically adapt itself to different Windows configurations when used outside the United States.

There are several ways that you can customize a form. You can set the alignment, change the name of the grid header, set the output format and precision for

TFloatFields, and set an edit mark for TStringFields. When you use other kinds of fields, there are more customizations available.

You can see the changes I've made to the example by looking at the textual description of its form, in Listing 17.5. The code of this program is quite simple, since it has just the method used to calculate the field, shown above.

LISTING 17.5: The textual description of the form of the CALC example

```
object CalcForm: TCalcForm
  Caption = 'Calculated Field'
  Position = poScreenCenter
  OnCreate = FormCreate
  object Panel1: TPanel
    Align = alTop
    object Panel2: TPanel
      Align = alRight
      BevelOuter = bvNone
      object DBNavigator: TDBNavigator
        DataSource = DataSource1
        VisibleButtons = [nbFirst, nbPrior, nbNext, nbLast]
      end
    end
  end
  object DBGrid1: TDBGrid
    Align = alClient
    DataSource = DataSource1
    TitleFont.Color = clBlack
    TitleFont.Height = -11
    TitleFont.Name = 'Arial'
  end
  object DataSource1: TDataSource
    DataSet = Table1
  end
  object Table1: TTable
    Active = True
    OnCalcFields = Table1CalcFields
    DatabaseName = 'DBDEMOS'
    TableName = 'country.db'
    object Table1Name: TStringField
      DisplayLabel = 'Country'
      DisplayWidth = 22
      FieldName = 'Name'
      Size = 24
    end
    object Table1Capital: TStringField
      DisplayWidth = 16
      FieldName = 'Capital'
      Size = 24
    end
```

17

LISTING 17.5: The textual description of the form of the CALC example (continued)

```
    object Table1Population: TFloatField
      DisplayWidth = 11
      FieldName = 'Population'
      DisplayFormat = '###,###,###'
    end
    object Table1Area: TFloatField
      DisplayWidth = 10
      FieldName = 'Area'
      DisplayFormat = '###,###,###'
    end
    object Table1PopulationDensity: TFloatField
      Calculated = True
      DisplayWidth = 16
      FieldName = 'Population Density'
      DisplayFormat = '###.##'
      Precision = 2
    end
  end
end
```

As a result of this simple code, at run-time the grid will have proper values for the calculated fields, as you can see Figure 17.22. Notice that from the user's point of view, this field is no different than the other ones. However, you should prevent users from inputting values in this column. You could mark the field as read-only, or you could add a second data-entry form to the program, and mark the whole grid as read-only. Having a specific data-entry form is usually the best approach when the user's view of the data is different from the reality (that is, the user sees a table of the database).

Using Fields to Manipulate a Table

The TField components you define, or the elements of the Fields array built automatically by Delphi, can be used to access data and manipulate a table at run-time, through the program. We have seen only a limited example of direct data access; in the previous example, we used the value of two fields to calculate a third one.

FIGURE 17.22:
The output of the CALC example; notice the Population Density calculated column

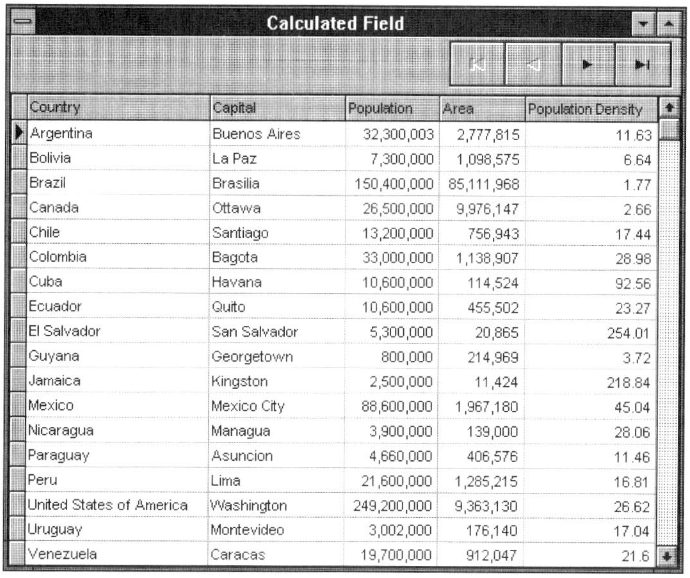

Country	Capital	Population	Area	Population Density
Argentina	Buenos Aires	32,300,003	2,777,815	11.63
Bolivia	La Paz	7,300,000	1,098,575	6.64
Brazil	Brasilia	150,400,000	85,111,968	1.77
Canada	Ottawa	26,500,000	9,976,147	2.66
Chile	Santiago	13,200,000	756,943	17.44
Colombia	Bagota	33,000,000	1,138,907	28.98
Cuba	Havana	10,600,000	114,524	92.56
Ecuador	Quito	10,600,000	455,502	23.27
El Salvador	San Salvador	5,300,000	20,865	254.01
Guyana	Georgetown	800,000	214,969	3.72
Jamaica	Kingston	2,500,000	11,424	218.84
Mexico	Mexico City	88,600,000	1,967,180	45.04
Nicaragua	Managua	3,900,000	139,000	28.06
Paraguay	Asuncion	4,660,000	406,576	11.46
Peru	Lima	21,600,000	1,285,215	16.81
United States of America	Washington	249,200,000	9,363,130	26.62
Uruguay	Montevideo	3,002,000	176,140	17.04
Venezuela	Caracas	19,700,000	912,047	21.6

Now we will build some simple examples that will allow us to use the fields to search elements in a table, operate on the values, and access information about the tables of a database. There are many more possible uses of fields in a table, but this should give you an idea of what can be done.

Looking for Records in a Table

For this example and the following ones, we need a new form, connected to EMPLOYEE.DB, another of the sample Delphi tables. To prepare the form, which has a number of edit fields, you can use the Database Form Expert.

First of all, create a new project. Then start the Expert, choose to create a simple form based on a table (this is the default), select the EMPLOYEE.DB table in the DBDEMOS database, select all of the fields of the table, and choose a vertical layout with labels on the left. The Database Form Expert will create the form, as shown in Figure 17.23.

First, we want to get rid of the DBNavigator in the toolbar to experiment with some manual table navigation. Instead of the Delphi default component, we can add a

FIGURE 17.23:

The form generated by the Database Form Expert, which is the basis for the next example

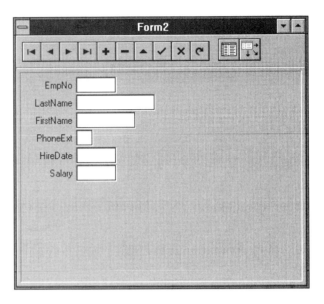

group of six navigational buttons, using the SpeedButton component:

The two buttons on the side are used to move to the first or last record in the table,

and the two in the middle move to the next or previous record. The other two buttons, indicated by a –5 and +5 caption, are used to move by 5 records backward or forward. (I chose the amount of 5 arbitrarily.)

Since there are several SpeedButtons, and we'll add more, I've given each of them a meaningful name, such as SpeedButtonFirst or SpeedButtonNext. Each of these buttons has some code associated with its OnClick event. Basically, these six methods call some navigational procedures of the Table component. Here are the six calls, extracted from the source code of the example, and in the same order as the buttons:

```
Table1.First;
Table1.MoveBy (-5);
```

```
Table1.Prior;
Table1.Next;
Table1.MoveBy (5);
Table1.Last;
```

Moving around in a table is simple. What makes the code complex is handling the Enabled property of the toolbar buttons. Each button used to move toward the end of the table (the last three buttons) should be disabled when we reach the end. The opposite should happen for the three buttons used to move toward the beginning.

We can test if we have reached either extreme of the table by using the BOF (Beginning Of File) and EOF (End Of File) properties of the table. The problem is that there are a number of ways to reach the end of the table and to leave it. For this reason, I've written some procedures to enable and disable the two groups of buttons. Here is one of them:

```
procedure TSearchForm.EnableNextButtons;
begin
  SpeedButtonLast.Enabled := True;
  SpeedButtonNext.Enabled := True;
  SpeedButtonMoveOn.Enabled := True;
end;
```

This procedure is called when the end of file is reached. Here is a procedure that can take place when we click on the Next button:

```
procedure TSearchForm.SpeedButtonNextClick(Sender: TObject);
begin
  Table1.Next;
  EnablePriorButtons;
  if Table1.EOF then
    DisableNextButtons;
end;
```

With this code, we always enable the first three buttons (there isn't much time penalty if they were already enabled) and disable the last three if the EOF property is True. (You can see the rest of the code used to enable and disable the buttons in the complete source code of the example, shown later in the chapter in Listing 17.7.)

Once the navigation SpeedButtons are set, we can improve this example by adding search capabilities. We want to be able to enter a name in an edit box and jump to the corresponding record. This is the reason for the name of the example itself, SEARCH.

Before continuing with the discussion of the example, take a look at its final form in Figure 17.24, and its textual description in Listing 17.6. Notice in particular the structure of the scroll box inside the panel, which hosts the data-aware edit boxes. These components were built by the Database Form Expert, and they work very well, since you can freely resize the form without any problems. When the form becomes too small, scroll bars will appear automatically in the area holding the edit boxes.

FIGURE 17.24:
The form of the SEARCH example at design-time

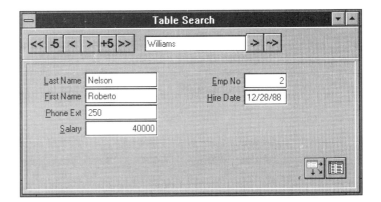

LISTING 17.6: The textual description of the form of the SEARCH example

```
object SearchForm: TSearchForm
  Caption = 'Table Search'
  Position = poScreenCenter
  OnCreate = FormCreate
  object Panel1: TPanel
    Align = alTop
    Font.Height = -16
    Font.Name = 'Arial'
    Font.Style = [fsBold]
    object SpeedButtonFirst: TSpeedButton
      Caption = '<<'
      Enabled = False
      OnClick = SpeedButtonFirstClick
    end
```

LISTING 17.6: The textual description of the form of the SEARCH example
(continued)

```
      object SpeedButtonMoveBack: TSpeedButton
        Caption = '-5'
        Enabled = False
        OnClick = SpeedButtonMoveBackClick
      end
      object SpeedButtonPrior: TSpeedButton
        Caption = '<'
        Enabled = False
        OnClick = SpeedButtonPriorClick
      end
      object SpeedButtonNext: TSpeedButton
        Caption = '>'
        OnClick = SpeedButtonNextClick
      end
      object SpeedButtonMoveOn: TSpeedButton
        Caption = '+5'
        OnClick = SpeedButtonMoveOnClick
      end
      object SpeedButtonLast: TSpeedButton
        Caption = '>>'
        OnClick = SpeedButtonLastClick
      end
      object SpeedButtonGoto: TSpeedButton
        Caption = '->'
        OnClick = SpeedButtonGotoClick
      end
      object SpeedButtonGoNear: TSpeedButton
        Caption = '~>'
        OnClick = SpeedButtonGoNearClick
      end
      object EditName: TEdit
        Font.Color = clBlack
        Font.Height = -11
        Font.Name = 'MS Sans Serif'
        Font.Style = []
        Text = 'Williams'
      end
    end
    object Panel2: TPanel
      Align = alClient
      BevelInner = bvLowered
      BorderWidth = 4
      object ScrollBox: TScrollBox
        HorzScrollBar.Margin = 6
        VertScrollBar.Margin = 6
        Align = alClient
        BorderStyle = bsNone
        object Label1: TLabel
          Alignment = taRightJustify
          AutoSize = False
```

17

LISTING 17.6: The textual description of the form of the SEARCH example
(continued)

```
      Caption = '&Emp No'
      FocusControl = EditEmpNo
    end
    object Label2: TLabel
      Alignment = taRightJustify
      AutoSize = False
      Caption = '&Last Name'
      FocusControl = EditLastName
    end
    object Label3: TLabel
      Alignment = taRightJustify
      AutoSize = False
      Caption = '&First Name'
      FocusControl = EditFirstName
    end
    object Label4: TLabel
      Alignment = taRightJustify
      AutoSize = False
      Caption = '&Phone Ext'
      FocusControl = EditPhoneExt
    end
    object Label5: TLabel
      Alignment = taRightJustify
      AutoSize = False
      Caption = '&Hire Date'
      FocusControl = EditHireDate
    end
    object Label6: TLabel
      Alignment = taRightJustify
      AutoSize = False
      Caption = '&Salary'
      FocusControl = EditSalary
    end
    object EditEmpNo: TDBEdit
      DataField = 'EmpNo'
      DataSource = DataSource1
    end
    object EditLastName: TDBEdit
      DataField = 'LastName'
      DataSource = DataSource1
    end
    object EditFirstName: TDBEdit
      DataField = 'FirstName'
      DataSource = DataSource1
    end
    object EditPhoneExt: TDBEdit
      DataField = 'PhoneExt'
      DataSource = DataSource1
    end
```

LISTING 17.6: The textual description of the form of the SEARCH example
(continued)

```
        object EditHireDate: TDBEdit
          DataField = 'HireDate'
          DataSource = DataSource1
        end
        object EditSalary: TDBEdit
          DataField = 'Salary'
          DataSource = DataSource1
        end
      end
  end
  object DataSource1: TDataSource
    AutoEdit = False
    DataSet = Table1
  end
  object Table1: TTable
    Active = True
    DatabaseName = 'DBDEMOS'
    IndexFieldNames = 'LastName'
    TableName = 'employee.db'
    object Table1Salary: TFloatField
      FieldName = 'Salary'
    end
    object Table1EmpNo: TIntegerField
      FieldName = 'EmpNo'
    end
    object Table1LastName: TStringField
      FieldName = 'LastName'
    end
    object Table1FirstName: TStringField
      FieldName = 'FirstName'
      Size = 15
    end
    object Table1PhoneExt: TStringField
      FieldName = 'PhoneExt'
      Size = 4
    end
    object Table1HireDate: TDateTimeField
      FieldName = 'HireDate'
    end
  end
end
```

17

The searching capabilities are activated by the two new SpeedButtons and the related edit window. The first button is used for an exact match, and the second for a nearest search. In both cases, we want to compare the text in the edit box with the Last Name fields of the Employee table. The Table component has methods to accomplish this, such as GotoKey and GotoNearest, but this component can make searches only on indexed fields.

Adding an Index to a Table

Since the sample Employee table that is shipped with Delphi doesn't have an index on the Last Name, we need to add it. We can restructure the table with the Database Desktop utility included in the Delphi package.

The required steps are simple. Run the Database Desktop, choose the Restructure command from the Utilities menu, and add a key by double-clicking in the Key column in the Field Roster. Figure 17.25 shows this procedure. Adding a key to a Paradox table results in a new index. Therefore, when you click on the Save button, the new secondary index is added to the table. If you don't set the new index in the Employee table using the Database Desktop utility, this sample program (and the next one) will not run and will issue run-time errors.

FIGURE 17.25:

You can add a new index to a table by using the Database Desktop tool included in Delphi.

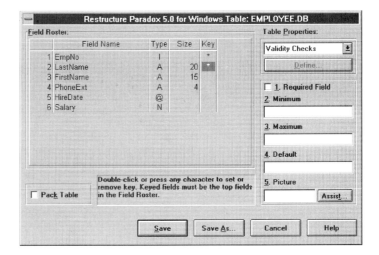

If you already have some background in building databases, you'll probably find the Database Desktop easy to use. This tool is described in the Delphi documentation, so I've decided not to give you a step-by-step description of its capabilities. Its role in Delphi is basically to help you build new tables, structure a database, restructure it (maybe adding new indexes), and copy or merge tables. You can also use it to view existing tables or enter new data, but this can be easily accomplished using a simple program generated by Delphi's Database Form Expert.

Once the index is set up properly, we can activate it in the code used to look up a record using that index:

```
Table1.IndexFieldNames := 'LastName';
```

Even better, we can set this property at design-time. When this is done, we can make the actual search. The simplest of the two is the best-guess search of the Go-toNearest method:

```
Table1.SetKey;
Table1.FieldByName('LastName').AsString := EditName.Text;
Table1.GotoNearest;
```

As you can see in this code, each search on a table is done in three steps:

1. Start up the search state of the table.

2. Set a value for a field. In this example, I've set the value of the LastName field, using it as a string. I've used the FieldByName method instead of a direct access (`Table.Fields[1]`), because the code is more readable, and I was sure to avoid errors.

3. When the search fields are set, you can actually start the process, moving the record pointer to the requested position.

You can see an example of the effect of this search in Figure 17.26. In the code, shown in Listing 17.7, there is one more statement use to enable all of the navigational buttons of the toolbar.

17

FIGURE 17.26:

An example of a best-match search

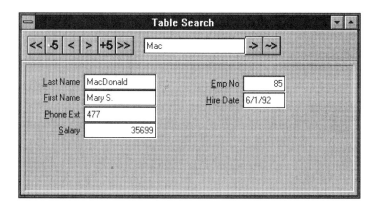

LISTING 17.7: The complete source code of the SEARCH example

```
unit Search_f;

{ WARNING: This program will not run with the default
database samples shipped with Delphi. You need to add a
secondary index to the employee.db table using the
Database Desktop application, as explained in the text}

interface

uses
  SysUtils, WinTypes, WinProcs, Messages, Classes, Graphics,
  Controls, StdCtrls, Forms, DBCtrls, DB, Buttons, DBTables,
  Mask, ExtCtrls, Dialogs;

type
  TSearchForm = class(TForm)
    ScrollBox: TScrollBox;
    {labels omitted...}
    EditEmpNo: TDBEdit;
    EditLastName: TDBEdit;
    EditFirstName: TDBEdit;
    EditPhoneExt: TDBEdit;
    EditHireDate: TDBEdit;
    EditSalary: TDBEdit;
    Panel1: TPanel;
    DataSource1: TDataSource;
    Panel2: TPanel;
    Table1: TTable;
    SpeedButtonFirst: TSpeedButton;
    SpeedButtonPrior: TSpeedButton;
    SpeedButtonNext: TSpeedButton;
```

LISTING 17.7: The complete source code of the SEARCH example (continued)

```
    SpeedButtonLast: TSpeedButton;
    SpeedButtonMoveOn: TSpeedButton;
    SpeedButtonMoveBack: TSpeedButton;
    EditName: TEdit;
    SpeedButtonGoto: TSpeedButton;
    SpeedButtonGoNear: TSpeedButton;
    Table1Salary: TFloatField;
    Table1EmpNo: TIntegerField;
    Table1LastName: TStringField;
    Table1FirstName: TStringField;
    Table1PhoneExt: TStringField;
    Table1HireDate: TDateTimeField;
    procedure FormCreate(Sender: TObject);
    procedure SpeedButtonFirstClick(Sender: TObject);
    procedure SpeedButtonPriorClick(Sender: TObject);
    procedure SpeedButtonNextClick(Sender: TObject);
    procedure SpeedButtonLastClick(Sender: TObject);
    procedure SpeedButtonMoveOnClick(Sender: TObject);
    procedure SpeedButtonMoveBackClick(Sender: TObject);
    procedure SpeedButtonGotoClick(Sender: TObject);
    procedure SpeedButtonGoNearClick(Sender: TObject);
  private
    { private declarations }
  public
    { public declarations }
    procedure EnableNextButtons;
    procedure DisableNextButtons;
    procedure EnablePriorButtons;
    procedure DisablePriorButtons;
    procedure EnableAllButtons;
  end;

var
  SearchForm: TSearchForm;

implementation

{$R *.DFM}

procedure TSearchForm.FormCreate(Sender: TObject);
begin
  Table1.First;
end;

procedure TSearchForm.EnablePriorButtons;
begin
  SpeedButtonFirst.Enabled := True;
  SpeedButtonPrior.Enabled := True;
  SpeedButtonMoveBack.Enabled := True;
end;
```

17

LISTING 17.7: The complete source code of the SEARCH example (continued)

```
procedure TSearchForm.DisablePriorButtons;
begin
  SpeedButtonFirst.Enabled := False;
  SpeedButtonPrior.Enabled := False;
  SpeedButtonMoveBack.Enabled := False;
end;

procedure TSearchForm.EnableNextButtons;
begin
  SpeedButtonLast.Enabled := True;
  SpeedButtonNext.Enabled := True;
  SpeedButtonMoveOn.Enabled := True;
end;

procedure TSearchForm.DisableNextButtons;
begin
  SpeedButtonLast.Enabled := False;
  SpeedButtonNext.Enabled := False;
  SpeedButtonMoveOn.Enabled := False;
end;

procedure TSearchForm.EnableAllButtons;
begin
  EnableNextButtons;
  EnablePriorButtons;
end;

procedure TSearchForm.SpeedButtonFirstClick(
  Sender: TObject);
begin
  Table1.First;
  EnableNextButtons;
  DisablePriorButtons;
end;

procedure TSearchForm.SpeedButtonPriorClick(
  Sender: TObject);
begin
  Table1.Prior;
  EnableNextButtons;
  if Table1.BOF then
    DisablePriorButtons;
end;

procedure TSearchForm.SpeedButtonNextClick(
  Sender: TObject);
begin
  Table1.Next;
  EnablePriorButtons;
  if Table1.EOF then
    DisableNextButtons;
end;
```

LISTING 17.7: The complete source code of the SEARCH example (continued)

```
procedure TSearchForm.SpeedButtonLastClick(
  Sender: TObject);
begin
  Table1.Last;
  EnablePriorButtons;
  DisableNextButtons;
end;

procedure TSearchForm.SpeedButtonMoveOnClick(
  Sender: TObject);
begin
  Table1.MoveBy (5);
  EnablePriorButtons;
  if Table1.EOF then
    DisableNextButtons;
end;

procedure TSearchForm.SpeedButtonMoveBackClick(
  Sender: TObject);
begin
  Table1.MoveBy (-5);
  EnableNextButtons;
  if Table1.BOF then
    DisablePriorButtons;
end;

procedure TSearchForm.SpeedButtonGotoClick(
  Sender: TObject);
begin
  if not Table1.FindKey([EditName.Text]) then
    MessageDlg ('Name not found', mtError, [mbOk], 0)
  else
    EnableAllButtons;
end;

procedure TSearchForm.SpeedButtonGoNearClick(
  Sender: TObject);
begin
  Table1.FindNearest([EditName.Text]);
  EnableAllButtons;
end;

end.
```

17

The code used to call the other search method, using an exact match algorithm, is similar. The differences are in these two statements:

```
Table1.KeyFieldCount := 1;
if not Table1.GotoKey then
  MessageDlg ('Name not found', mtError, [mbOk], 0)
else
  EnableAllButtons;
```

As I've mentioned before, this code requires a proper index for the table. In fact the code does not refer to a specific file, as before, but to the index.

The second difference is that the GotoNearest procedure always succeeds, moving the cursor to the closest match (a closest match always exist, even if it is not very close). On the other hand, the GotoKey method fails if no exact match is available, and you can use the return value of this function to warn the user of the error.

Changing the Data and Computing New Values

So far in our examples, the user can view the current contents of a database table and manually edit the data or insert new records. Now we will see how we can change some data in the table through the program code.

The idea behind this example is quite simple. The Employee table we have been using has a Salary field. A manager of the company could indeed browse through the table and change the salary of a single employee. But what if the manager wants to give a 10 percent salary increase (or decrease) to everyone?

This is the aim of the TOTAL example, which is an extension of the previous program. The toolbar of this new example has two more buttons and a SpinEdit component, as you can see in Figure 17.27. In Listing 17.8, you can see that there are a few differences between the textual description of the form of this example and that of the previous one.

In the textual description of the form, you can also see another change. I opened the Fields editor of the table and removed the Table1Salary field, which was defined as a TFloatField. Then I clicked on the New button and added the same field, with the same name, but using the TCurrencyField data type.

FIGURE 17.27:

The toolbar of the TOTAL example has some more buttons and a SpinEdit component.

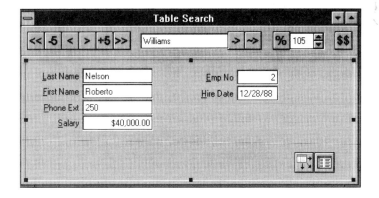

LISTING 17.8: The new elements of the textual description of the form of the TOTAL example

```
object SearchForm: TSearchForm
  object Panel1: TPanel
    object SpeedButtonIncrease: TSpeedButton
      Caption = '%'
      OnClick = SpeedButtonIncreaseClick
    end
    object SpeedButtonTotal: TSpeedButton
      Caption = '$$'
      OnClick = SpeedButtonTotalClick
    end
    object SpinEdit1: TSpinEdit
      Increment = 5
      MaxValue = 200
      MinValue = 50
      Value = 105
    end
  end
  object Table1: TTable
    DatabaseName = 'DBDEMOS'
    TableName = 'employee.db'
    object Table1Salary: TCurrencyField
      FieldName - 'Salary'
      Currency = True
    end
  end
end
```

This is not a calculated field; it's simply a field converted into a new (but equivalent) data type. The reason for this change is that the output of the program changes, as you can see by comparing Figure 17.27 with the output shown in Figure 17.26 for the SEARCH example.

Now we can turn our attention to the code of this new program. First, let's look at the code of the total button, which is the one with the dollar signs ($$) on it. This button lets you compute the sum of the salaries of all the employees, than edit some of the values and compute a new total. Basically, we need to scan the table, reading the value of the Table1Salary field for each record:

```
Total := 0;
Table1.First;
while not Table1.EOF do
begin
  Total := Total + Table1Salary.Value;
  Table1.Next;
end;
MessageDlg ('Sum of new salaries is ' +
  Format ('%m', [Total]), mtInformation, [mbOk], 0);
```

This code uses Table properties we have already seen, such as First, Next, and EOF. One strange thing is the string used as parameter in the MessageDlg function. Instead of writing out the plain number, I've used the code:

```
Format ('%m', [Total])
```

Format is a Delphi system function used to format the output. In this case, I've used the %m flag, which formats the real number passed in the set of parameters (in square brackets) as a currency value. You can see the output of this code in Figure 17.28.

This code works, but it has a number of problems. One problem is that the record pointer is moved to the last record. To avoid this problem, we need to store the current position of the record pointer in the table, and reset it at the end. This can be accomplished using bookmarks. We need to declare a variable of the TBookmark data type, and initialize it while getting the current position from the table:

```
Bookmark := Table1.GetBookmark;
```

FIGURE 17.28:

The output of the TOTAL program, showing the total salaries of the employees

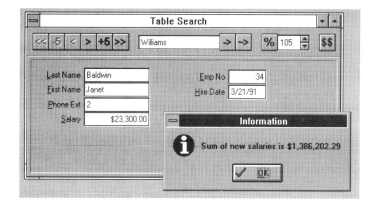

At the end of the code, we can restore the position and delete the bookmark with the following two statements:

```
Table1.GotoBookmark (Bookmark);
Table1.FreeBookmark (Bookmark);
```

Another side effect of the program is that, although we will reset the record pointer to the initial position, we might see the record moving while the algorithm elaborates the data. This can be avoided by disabling the controls connected with the table for the time of the browsing. The table has a DisableControls method we can call before the `while` loop starts, and an EnableControls method we can call at the end, after the record pointer is restored.

Finally, we face some dangers in case of errors in reading the table data, particularly if the program is reading the data from a server using a network (although this is not the current case). If an exception takes place, the controls remain disabled, and the program cannot resume its normal behavior. So, we should use a `try-finally` block. Considering these three changes, you can see how you can rewrite the algorithm above in the first part of Listing 17.9.

I've written this code to show you an example of a loop to browse the contents of a table, but it would be faster to use a SQL query to sum (or batch modify) the data (see Appendix B for an example). SQL statements can be used to query and update local tables, which is usually faster than bringing the data all the way back into the application. When you use a SQL server, the advantage of a SQL call to compute the total is even greater.

LISTING 17.9: The code of the SpeedButtonTotalClick and of the SpeedButton-IncreaseClick methods of the TOTAL example

```
procedure TSearchForm.SpeedButtonTotalClick(
  Sender: TObject);
var
  Bookmark: TBookmark;
  Total: Real;
begin
  {store the current position,
  creating a new bookmark}
  Bookmark := Table1.GetBookmark;
  Table1.DisableControls;
  Total := 0;
  try
    Table1.First;
    while not Table1.EOF do
    begin
      Total := Total + Table1Salary.Value;
      Table1.Next;
    end;
  finally
    {go back to the bookmark and destroy it}
    Table1.GotoBookmark (Bookmark);
    Table1.FreeBookmark (Bookmark);
    Table1.EnableControls;
  end;
  MessageDlg ('Sum of new salaries is ' +
    Format ('%m', [Total]),
    mtInformation, [mbOk], 0);
end;

procedure TSearchForm.SpeedButtonIncreaseClick(
  Sender: TObject);
var
  Bookmark: TBookmark;
  Total: Real;
begin
  {store the current position,
  creating a new bookmark}
  Bookmark := Table1.GetBookmark;
  Table1.DisableControls;
  Total := 0;
  {start edit mode}
  try
    Table1.First;
    while not Table1.EOF do
    begin
      Table1.Edit;
      Table1Salary.Value := Round (Table1Salary.Value
        * SpinEdit1.Value) / 100;
      Total := Total + Table1Salary.Value;
```

LISTING 17.9: The code of the SpeedButtonTotalClick and of the SpeedButton-
IncreaseClick methods of the TOTAL example (continued)

```
    Table1.Next;
  end;
finally
  {go back to the bookmark and destroy it}
  Table1.GotoBookmark (Bookmark);
  Table1.FreeBookmark (Bookmark);
  Table1.EnableControls;
end;
MessageDlg ('Sum of new salaries is ' +
  Format ('%m', [Total]),
  mtInformation, [mbOk], 0);
end;
```

The code of the other method you can see in the listing, which is connected to the
OnClick event of the increase SpeedButton, is similar to the one we have just seen.
This method also scans the table, computing the total of the salaries. It sets a book-
mark, uses a `try-finally` block, and disables the controls, too.

Although there are just two more statements, there is a key difference between the
two. When you increase the salary, you actually change the data of the table. Here
are the two key statements:

```
Table1.Edit;
Table1Salary.Value := Round (Table1Salary.Value
  * SpinEdit1.Value) / 100;
```

The first brings the table into edit mode, so that changes to the fields have an immediate effect. The second statement computes the new salary, by multiplying the
old one by the value of the SpinEdit component (by default, 105), and dividing it
by 100. That's a five percent increase, although the values are rounded to the nearest dollar.

With this program, you can change salaries by any amount—even double the salary
of each employee—with the click of a button, as you can see in Figure 17.29. Note
that when you do this, you permanently alter the contents of the table. There is no
way to restore it at the end, other than trying to make the reverse operation, which
is not always easy, due to the rounding of the dollar values and the approximation
of floating-point computations.

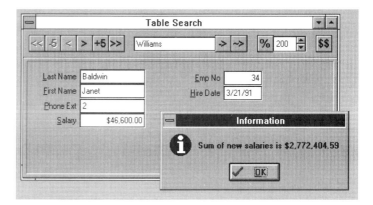

If this table is stored on a SQL server that supports transactions, however, you could start a transaction before the update loop, run through all the updates, then commit the transaction. That would guarantee that either all the salaries get updated or none do. Of course, after the changes are committed, you can't undo them, unless you use the approximate method just described.

Exploring the Tables of a Database

In each of the examples in this chapter, we have always accessed a database table by setting its name at design-time. But what if you do not know which table your program is going to be connected to? At first, you might think that if you do not know the details of the database at design-time, you won't be able to create forms and operate on the table. This is not true.

Setting everything at design-time is certainly easier. Changing almost everything at run-time requires you to write some more code. This is what I've done in the next example, called TABLES, which demonstrates how to access the list of databases available to the BDE, how to access the list of the tables for each database, and how to select which fields to view of a specific table.

Choosing a Database and a Table at Run-time

The first part of the program for this example is quite simple. I've prepared a form with two list boxes (see Listing 17.10). When the program starts, it copies the names of the databases in the first list box, using the following code:

```
procedure TMainForm.FormCreate(Sender: TObject);
var
  DBNames: TStringList;
begin
  DBNames := TStringList.Create;
  Session.GetDatabaseNames (DBNames);
  ListBox1.Items := DBNames;
end;
```

The key element is the call to the GetDatabaseNames procedure of the Session global object. This object of class TSession is automatically defined and initialized by each Delphi database application, but to access its methods, you need to include the DB unit in your code.

17

This procedure fills the string list object you pass to it as parameter, so you need to create it first. After the call, you can use the object as you like. For example, you can copy all of the strings to a list box at once, as you can see in Figure 17.30.

LISTING 17.10: The textual description of the main form of the TABLES example

```
object MainForm: TMainForm
  Caption = 'Tables Browser'
  OnCreate = FormCreate
  object Label1: TLabel
    Caption = 'Databases:'
  end
  object Label2: TLabel
    Caption = 'Tables:'
  end
  object ListBox1: TListBox
    ItemHeight = 16
    OnDblClick = ListBox1DblClick
  end
  object ListBox2: TListBox
    ItemHeight = 16
    OnDblClick = ListBox2DblClick
  end
end
```

FIGURE 17.30:

The main form of the TABLES
example when the program starts

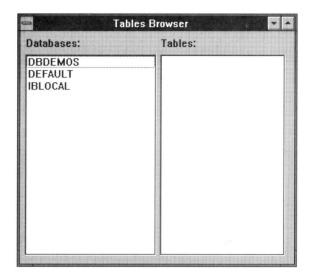

When you click on one of the database names in the first list box, the second one is
filled with the names of the available tables. This time, the code is based on another
method of the Session object, called GetTableNames, which has the following
parameters:

- The name of a database

- A filter string

- Two Boolean values indicating whether to include the table file extensions
  (for local tables only) and whether to include system tables in the list (for
  SQL databases only)

- A list of strings that will be filled with the names of the tables

Here is the code the program executes when the user double-clicks on an item in
the first list box:

```
procedure TMainForm.ListBox1DblClick(Sender: TObject);
var
  CurrentDB: string;
```

```
begin
  CurrentDB := ListBox1.Items [ListBox1.ItemIndex];
  Session.GetTableNames (CurrentDB, '', True, False, ListBox2.Items);
end;
```

You can see the effect of this code in Figure 17.31. As you have seen, the key for this kind of operation is the global Session object, which holds information about the current database activity.

FIGURE 17.31:

When you double-click on a database name, the second list box shows the available tables.

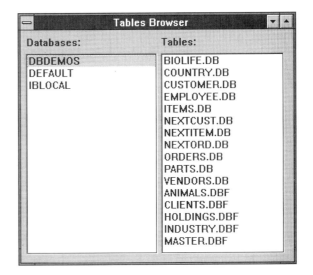

A Table Viewer

The next step in the program is to view the contents of one of the tables the program has listed. To accomplish this, we need to define a second form, based on a DBGrid component. Using a grid, we can easily view all of the fields in a database without needing to create a number of controls at run-time. To avoid cluttering the main form, and to build a more flexible program, I've place the DBGrid component in a second form. You can see this form in Figure 17.32, and look at its details in Listing 17.11.

FIGURE 17.32:

The GridForm of the TABLES
example at design-time

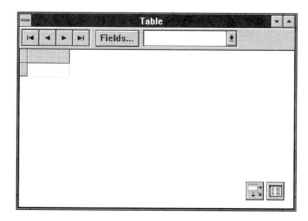

LISTING 17.11: The textual description of the GridForm of the TABLES example

```
object GridForm: TGridForm
  Caption = 'Table'
  OnClose = FormClose
  object DBGrid1: TDBGrid
    Align = alClient
    DataSource = DataSource1
  end
  object Panel1: TPanel
    Align = alTop
    object SpeedButton1: TSpeedButton
      Caption = 'Fields...'
      OnClick = SpeedButton1Click
    end
    object DBNavigator1: TDBNavigator
      DataSource = DataSource1
      VisibleButtons = [nbFirst, nbPrior, nbNext, nbLast]
    end
    object ComboBox1: TComboBox
      Style = csDropDownList
      Sorted = True
      OnChange = ComboBox1Change
    end
  end
  object Table1: TTable
  end
  object DataSource1: TDataSource
    DataSet = Table1
  end
end
```

The basic idea is that each time the user double-clicks on one of the table names in the second list box of the main form, a new secondary form is created, showing the data in the table. A new form is created each time the user views a table's data, so we need to disable the automatic definition of a form at program startup. Keep in mind that this creation is controlled by some of the code of the project files. However, you can change it through the Project Options dialog box. Select the Forms page, and remove the GridForm from the Auto-create forms list, as shown in Figure 17.33. Notice that there is also a third form I've added to the program, which is built at startup.

The advantage of not having a single global object for the second form is that we can create a number of them at run-time. These forms are modeless, which means that we can return to the main form and open another grid without closing the first one.

When the user double-clicks on the second list box in the main form, the code creates a TGridForm object, connects the Table1 component of this form to the proper database and table, and shows the form:

```
procedure TMainForm.ListBox2DblClick(Sender: TObject);
var
  CurrentDB, CurrentTable: string;
  GridForm: TGridForm;
```

FIGURE 17.33:

When you remove its name from the Auto-create forms list, GridForm is not created at startup, but each time the user double-clicks on the Tables list box of the main form.

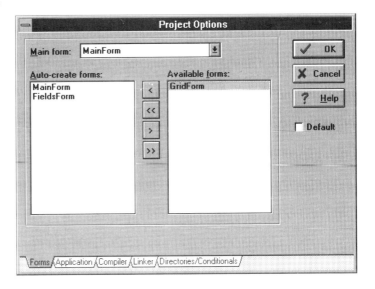

919

```
begin
  CurrentDB := ListBox1.Items [ListBox1.ItemIndex];
  CurrentTable := ListBox2.Items [ListBox2.ItemIndex];

  GridForm := TGridForm.Create (self);

  {connect the table component to the selected
  table and activate it}
  GridForm.Table1.DatabaseName := CurrentDB;
  GridForm.Table1.TableName := CurrentTable;
  try
    GridForm.Table1.Open;
    {set the title and call a custom
    initialization method, then show the form}
    GridForm.Caption := Format ('Table: %s - %s',
      [CurrentDB, CurrentTable]);
    GridForm.FillFieldsCombo;
    GridForm.Show;
  except on Exception do
    GridForm.Close;
  end;

end;
```

This code displays a new form showing the table data, as you can see in Figure 17.34, where two forms of this kind are visible at the same time. Notice that the code simply creates the form and never destroys it. It is the responsibility of a form to delete itself, in its OnClose method:

```
procedure TGridForm.FormClose(Sender: TObject;
  var Action: TCloseAction);
begin
  Action := caFree;
end;
```

At the end of this procedure, the program sets the caption of the form using the name of the table and database, and it also calls a custom method of the form, called FillFieldsCombo. As we will see in a while, this method simply fills a combo box with the names of the fields of the table (this is the reason for the name). Basically, this is an initialization method.

However, this code can't go in the OnCreate event of the form, because the form is created before its Table1 component is properly set up. Instead of trying to find the

FIGURE 17.34:

The TABLES example can be used to open two (or more) table viewers based on a grid.

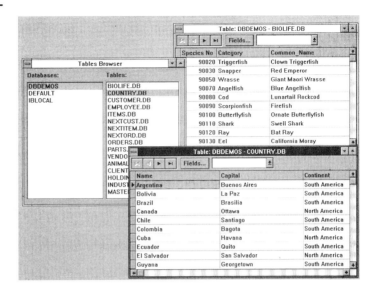

best event to use (OnShow and OnActivate were two good choices), I've just written a custom method called from the main form. The fact that Windows is event-driven should not compel you to write event-response methods only. At times, good old-fashioned methods—not connected to any event or Windows messages, but directly called from another portion of the code—work better and are easier to understand (and debug).

This moves our attention to the code of the DBGrid form. Here is the code of the custom FillFieldsCombo method:

```
procedure TGridForm.FillFieldsCombo;
var
  I: Integer;
begin
  for I := 0 to Table1.FieldCount - 1 do
    ComboBox1.Items.Add (Table1.Fields[I].FieldName);
end;
```

In this procedure, we see how it is possible to access the third element of a database program. After a list of databases and a list of tables within a database, this code lists the fields of a table, storing them in the combo box I've placed in the toolbar of this form.

What is the use of this combo box? Each time a user selects an element, the corresponding field is either shown or hidden depending on its current state:

```
procedure TGridForm.ComboBox1Change(Sender: TObject);
begin
  {toggle the visibility of the field}
  Table1.FieldByName (ComboBox1.Text).Visible :=
    not Table1.FieldByName (ComboBox1.Text).Visible;
end;
```

Notice the use of the FieldByName method to retrieve the field using the current selection of the combo box, and the use of the Visible property. Once a field becomes not visible, it is immediately removed from the grid associated with the table. Therefore, by simply setting this property, the grid changes automatically. You can see an example of the effect of this code in Figure 17.35.

A Field Editor

The combo box we have placed in the toolbar of the GridForm works, but if you need to select several fields in a big table, it is slow and error-prone. As an alternative, I've created a small fields editor form. This is the third form of the TABLES example, named FieldsForm. You can see this third form at design-time in Figure 17.36, and examine its textual description in Listing 17.12.

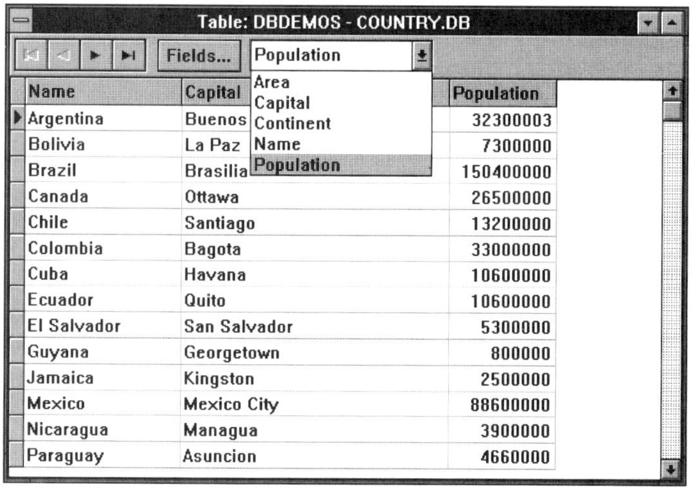

FIGURE 17.35:

You can use the combo box of the GridForm of the TABLES example to hide some fields of the grid.

FIGURE 17.36:

The third form of the TABLES example, FieldsForm, at design-time

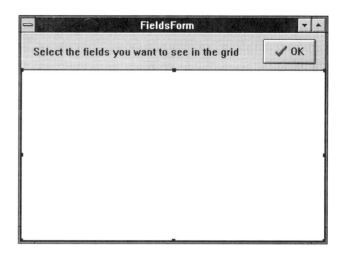

LISTING 17.12: The textual description of the FieldsForm of the TABLES example

```
object FieldsForm: TFieldsForm
  Caption = 'FieldsForm'
  object FieldsList: TListBox
    Align = alClient
    MultiSelect = True
  end
  object Panel1: TPanel
    Align = alTop
    object Label1: TLabel
      Caption = 'Select the fields you want to see in the grid'
    end
    object BitBtn1: TBitBtn
      Kind = bkOK
    end
  end
end
```

This form is displayed as a modal form, so we can use a single global object every time (as you saw in Figure 17.33, this form is created at startup).

This form has no code of its own. When the Fields button of the grid form's toolbar is clicked, the multiple selection list box of the FieldsForm (which is the only relevant component) is filled with the names of the fields of the Table1 component. At the same time, the code selects the list box items corresponding to visible fields, as you can see in Figure 17.37.

The user can toggle the selection of each item in this list box while the modal form is active. When it is closed, the other form retrieves the values of the selected items, and sets the Visible property of the fields accordingly. Here is the complete code of this method:

```
procedure TGridForm.SpeedButton1Click(Sender: TObject);
var
  I: Integer;
begin
  for I := 0 to Table1.FieldCount - 1 do
  begin
    FieldsForm.FieldsList.Items.Add (
      Table1.Fields[I].FieldName);
    if Table1.Fields[I].Visible then
      FieldsForm.FieldsList.Selected [I] := True;
  end;
  FieldsForm.ShowModal;
  for I := 0 to Table1.FieldCount - 1 do
    Table1.Fields[I].Visible :=
      FieldsForm.FieldsList.Selected [I];
  FieldsForm.FieldsList.Clear;
end;
```

FIGURE 17.37:

The list box can be used to select the table fields to show in the grid.

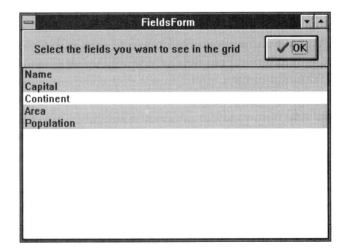

This code ends the description of this complex example, which uses three forms. We have seen that you can write database applications that do most of the work at run-time, although this approach is slightly more complex. Realize that there are many other things we could have done. I've just chosen the basic activities to avoid making the program too complex.

Creating a Graphical Table

When you start a new project, you should sit down first and design the structure of the database tables used by your application. This is not an easy task. Also, in moderately complex programs, a flaw in the database design can lead to incredible problems. If your previous database programming experience is limited, you should consider reading a book on this topic before you start writing a complex database-access application with Delphi.

17

Once you have developed your database, you need to create the tables. There are basically two choices. The simplest method is to use the stand-alone Database Desktop application. The other approach is to write some code in Delphi to create the tables.

To use the Database Desktop, simply run it, select the New Table command from the File menu, and choose a table type in the following dialog box. At this point, the Database Desktop displays a Create Table dialog box, as shown in the example in Figure 17.38, in which you can specify the various fields of the table. For each field, you should enter a name, a type, a size, and whether it is a key field (a required field that has an index connected to it). When you are satisfied with your choices, click on the Save As button and give a name to the new table.

You can even use the Database Desktop to input some values into the table. This makes sense if the table has a number of initial values. If not, an empty table might do. It should be obvious, but when you build a table and create a Delphi application using it, you cannot ship your application without the proper tables, which need to be copied to the proper directories of the other computer. Installation of a database application can be a real headache.

Now suppose that the structure of our table is simple, and that we want to allow the user to create a number of tables of the same kind (or of a similar type). We can use a Delphi application, and create tables in its code. This is the aim of the

FIGURE 17.38:

The Create Paradox 5.0 for Windows Table dialog box of the Database Desktop application

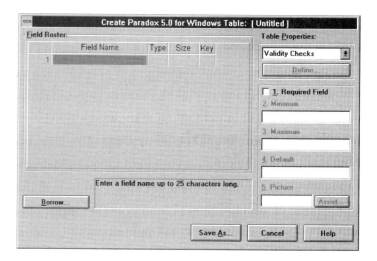

next example, which uses a graphic field, for the first time in the book. It is also the first example that uses the clipboard, a topic discussed in detail in Chapter 24.

> **NOTE**
>
> Graphic, memo, and BLOB fields in Delphi are handled exactly like other fields. Just connect the proper editor or viewer, and most of the work is done behind the scenes by the system. I assume that you have already seen the Delphi graphical example, which shows fish. If not, try to build the FISHFACT example that ships with the package and see how it works.

The name of this example is CREATEG, where G stands for graphics. Its goal is to allow a user to capture images on the screen and store them in a database table. Note that this table will probably become quite big after a while, so if you have limited disk space, beware of using the program. Each time you run CREATEG, it asks you if you want to create a new table or use an existing one. If you want to create a new table, you should provide a table name that doesn't exist so that you won't override existing, valuable data. If you load an existing table, you must use a table with the proper fields: a textual description of the image, the data and time it was saved, and the image itself.

When a suitable table has been created or selected, the program displays its main form, as shown in Figure 17.39. You can now capture an image on the screen, copying it to the clipboard. This step is not made by the program. You can just press the PrintScreen key, or the Alt-PrintScreen key combination, to capture the bitmap of the whole screen or the bitmap of the current active window. Or use another program or technique to copy a bitmap to the clipboard.

After the image has been copied to the clipboard, click on the New button, and the program will ask you for a description of the image, take the system time, copy the bitmap from the clipboard, and insert the new record in the table. If something went wrong, you can use the Delete button to remove the current record. Of course, you can always browse through the records of the table (which are sorted by description). Finally, you can use the check box to stretch the image or view it (or a portion of it) in the default scale.

Of course, there are many ways to improve this program, such as by making the screen capture automatic or by checking the contents of the clipboard. However, the features it does have demonstrate the concepts, and the example is already complex enough.

17

FIGURE 17.39:
The main form of the CREATEG example at run-time. Notice that image stretching is disabled.

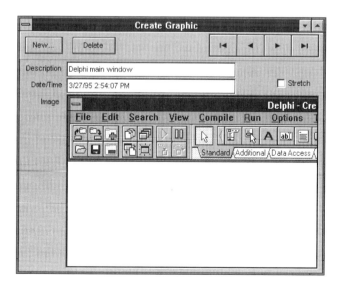

The Form and Its Startup Code

Let's begin by taking a look at the textual description of its main in Listing 17.13. (You can also see this form at run-time in Figure 17.39.) Notice that the form has two Table components. We are going to use the second one, which is not connected to a DataSource component, but referenced inside a search algorithm.

LISTING 17.13: The textual description of the main form of the CREATEG example

```
object GraphForm: TGraphForm
  Caption = 'Create Graphic'
  Position = poScreenCenter
  OnCreate = FormCreate
  object Panel1: TPanel
    Align = alTop
    object NewSpeedButton: TSpeedButton
      Caption = 'New...'
      OnClick = NewSpeedButtonClick
    end
    object DeleteSpeedButton: TSpeedButton
      Caption = 'Delete'
      OnClick = DeleteSpeedButtonClick
    end
    object Panel2: TPanel
      Align = alRight
      BevelOuter = bvNone
      object DBNavigator: TDBNavigator
        DataSource = DataSource1
        VisibleButtons = [nbFirst, nbPrior, nbNext, nbLast]
      end
    end
  end
  object ScrollBox: TScrollBox
    Align = alClient
    BorderStyle = bsNone
    object Label1: TLabel
      Alignment = taRightJustify
      Caption = 'Description'
      FocusControl = EditDescription
    end
    object Label3: TLabel
      Alignment = taRightJustify
      Caption = 'Date/Time'
      FocusControl = EditDate
    end
    object Label4: TLabel
      Alignment = taRightJustify
      Caption = 'Image'
      FocusControl = DBImage
    end
```

LISTING 17.13: The textual description of the main form of the CREATEG example
(continued)

```
    object EditDescription: TDBEdit
      DataField = 'Description'
      DataSource = DataSource1
      MaxLength = 100
    end
    object EditDate: TDBEdit
      DataField = 'Time'
      DataSource = DataSource1
      MaxLength = 100
    end
    object DBImage: TDBImage
      Center = False
      DataField = 'Graphics'
      DataSource = DataSource1
      Stretch = True
    end
    object CheckBox1: TCheckBox
      Caption = 'Stretch'
      State = cbChecked
      OnClick = CheckBox1Click
    end
  end
  object DataSource1: TDataSource
    DataSet = Table1
  end
  object Table1: TTable
    DatabaseName = 'DBDEMOS'
  end
  object Table2: TTable
    DatabaseName = 'DBDEMOS'
  end
end
```

When the program starts, it displays a simple message dialog box, as shown in Figure 17.40. This lets the user choose between creating a new form or using an existing one. The message dialog box has three choices:

```
Code := MessageDlg ('Do you want to create a new table?'
  + Chr(13) + '(choose No to load an existing table' +
  'Cancel to quit)',
  mtConfirmation, mbYesNoCancel, 0);
if Code = idYes then
  CreateNewTable
```

```
else if Code = idNo then
   LoadTable
else
   Application.Terminate;
```

FIGURE 17.40:

The message dialog box shown at
program startup

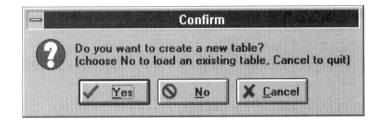

If the user selects the Yes button, the program creates a new table. If the user selects
No, the program loads an existing table. If the user selects Cancel, the application
terminates.

The bulk of the initialization code is in the two custom methods, CreateNewTable
and LoadTable.

Creating a New Table

To create a new table in Delphi, you can call the CreateTable method of a Table component. However, before you do this, you need to set some properties of this
component. You must specify a database name, a table name, the names and types
of the fields, and the name of an index.

The database name is set to the DBDEMOS alias at design-time. You can change it,
but if you do, you need to replace this string with the new one in several places in
the source code. The table name is requested from the user, using the InputQuery
function. Figure 17.41 shows the input query.

When the user has entered a name, we need to verify that a table with the same
name already exists. In fact, the CreateTable method of the TTable class eventually
overrides a table that has the same name as the new one. How do we check if the

FIGURE 17.41:

The input query used to ask the user
to input the name of a new table

name is already in use? We can call a method of the Session global object, as we did
in the last example:

```
TbNames := TStringList.Create;
Session.GetTableNames ('DBDEMOS', '', False, False, TbNames);
if TbNames.IndexOf (TableName) >= 0 then ...
```

The IndexOf method of the string list returns the index of the string, or –1 if the
string does not exist. If the string exists, the program raises an exception, to stop further execution of this method:

```
raise EMyDatabaseError.Create ('Table already exists');
```

EMyDatabaseError is a new exception class I've defined in the code of this program as:

```
type
  EMyDatabaseError =
  class (EDatabaseError)
  end;
```

This kind of exception is checked in the OnCreate method of the form. If an error
occurs in one of the two possible procedures, CreateNewTable or LoadTable, the
program shows an error message and restarts the custom initialization code, asking
again for the user to choose between a new or an existing table:

```
procedure TGraphForm.FormCreate(Sender: TObject);
begin
  try
    {...}
  except
    on E: EMyDatabaseError do
```

```
    begin
      ShowMessage (E.Message);
      FormCreate (self);
    end;
  end;
end;
```

If the table does not exist, we can store its name in the Table1 component, and also set the TableType property with the value ttParadox (or any other table type).

The next step, which is the most complex one, is to define the three fields of the table. We need to use the FieldsDef property (a list of field definitions) of the Table component, and call the Add method three times. The Add method adds a new field to the structure of the table. For example, we can write:

```
Table1.FieldDefs.Add ('Description', ftString, 50, True);
```

Unfortunately, there is a problem with the documentation of this method. Delphi's help documents only three parameters: the name, the type, and the size (required only for some field types). The fourth parameter, which isn't listed in the documentation, indicates if the field is required—if it is a key field. The other two fields are added with similar statements as the one for the index, which is stored in the IndexDefs list:

```
Table1.FieldDefs.Add ('Time', ftDateTime, 0, False);
Table1.FieldDefs.Add ('Graphics', ftGraphic, 0, False);
Table1.IndexDefs.Add('DescrIndex', 'Description',
  [ixPrimary, ixUnique]);
```

Now we can finally call the CreateTable method and open the table. Since the data source and the other data-aware components are already connected, once the table is open, we can start working with it.

NOTE If you still have questions about how this code works, you can refer to the full source code of the example in Listing 17.15, presented later in the chapter.

Choosing a Table with the Proper Fields

The second time you run the program, since you have already built a table with the proper fields, you can load it instead of creating a new one. The loading code is handled by the LoadTable method. This code starts by filling the list box in the a dialog box with the names of the available tables. You can see the simple structure of this dialog box in Listing 17.14.

I thought that simply accessing the dialog box components as usual was enough, but when I tried, I invariably got an error. What's wrong? The problem is that the code we are writing is initialization code, part of the OnCreate method of the main form. If you remember, the code of the typical project file of a Delphi program calls the CreateForm procedure a number of times (once for each form created at startup). One of the effects of the call of this method is that the OnCreate method takes place.

17

For this reason, during the OnCreate event of the main form, the dialog box form has still not been created. Accessing one of its components results in a run-time error. The compiler knows nothing about the order of execution of the events and of the initialization code. To solve the problem, simply disable the automatic creation of TablesForm in the Project Options dialog box (Forms page), and add this statement before accessing any components in the dialog box:

```
TablesForm := TTablesForm.Create (Application);
```

LISTING 17.14: The structure of the dialog box of the CREATEG example

```
object TablesForm: TTablesForm
  BorderStyle = bsDialog
  Caption = 'Tables'
  object ListBox1: TListBox
    ItemHeight = 16
  end
  object BitBtn1: TBitBtn
    Kind = bkOK
  end
  object BitBtn2: TBitBtn
    Kind = bkCancel
  end
end
```

Now we can now move to the core of this procedure. The code retrieves the list of database tables with another call to the GetTableNames of the Session global object, but instead of copying the whole string list to the list box, it performs the following test on each item:

```
(Table2.FieldCount = 3) and
(CompareText (Table2.FieldDefs[0].Name, 'Description') = 0)
and (CompareText (Table2.FieldDefs[1].Name, 'Time') = 0)
and (CompareText (Table2.FieldDefs[2].Name, 'Graphics') = 0)
```

To make the test, the program must open the table first (and close it afterwards). Of course, you should also set the name of the Table2 component, using each of the names of the existing tables at each turn. Notice that I needed to use a new table component, Table2, instead of the already available Table1 component. Table1 is connected to a data source, which in turn is connected to some data-aware components. Opening the Table1 table will immediately cause an error if the fields indicated in the components are not present.

If no table passes the test, an exception is raised. When a table passes the test, it is added to the list box in the dialog box, and a proper flag is set. The dialog box is displayed on the screen, as shown in Figure 17.42. When the dialog box is closed, the list box item selected by the user is copied to the name of the table.

FIGURE 17.42:

The TablesForm dialog box allows a user to choose from only the tables that have the proper fields.

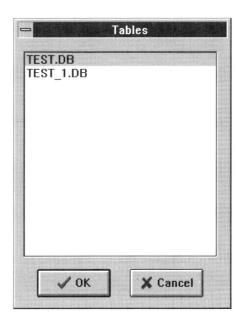

934

Adding or Removing Records

Most of the program code was in the initialization portion. Once a table is open, we can simply insert new records. This happens when the user clicks on the New button in the main form of the program, as shown in Figure 17.43.

The code of this button's OnClick method is quite simple. The procedure asks the user to enter a description (which must be unique), then creates a new record at the end of the table:

```
Table1.Last;
Table1.Insert;
EditDescription.Text := Descr;
EditDate.Text := DateTimeToStr (Now);
DBIMage.PasteFromClipboard;
Table1.Post;
```

17

Notice that the values are copied to the data-aware components, and not directly to the fields. In this case, we can use the PasteFromClipboard method to fill the DBImage component with the bitmap currently in the clipboard. The other two methods of the main form, one to delete the current record and the other to stretch the image (see Figure 17.43), are so simple you can look them up directly in the complete source code, in Listing 17.15.

FIGURE 17.43:

Clicking on the New button in the CREATEG form adds a new record to the current table (notice that the image behind is stretched).

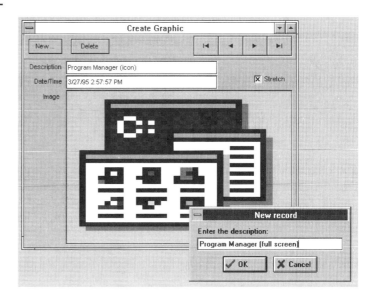

LISTING 17.15: The complete source code of the CREATEG example

```pascal
unit Graph_f;

interface

uses
  SysUtils, WinTypes, WinProcs, Messages, Classes,
  Graphics, Controls, StdCtrls, Forms, DBCtrls, DB,
  DBTables, ExtCtrls, Mask, Buttons, Dialogs, Tables_f;

type
  EMyDatabaseError = class (EDatabaseError) end;
  TGraphForm = class(TForm)
    ScrollBox: TScrollBox;
    Label1: TLabel;
    EditDescription: TDBEdit;
    Label3: TLabel;
    EditDate: TDBEdit;
    Label4: TLabel;
    DBImage: TDBImage;
    DBNavigator: TDBNavigator;
    Panel1: TPanel;
    Panel2: TPanel;
    DataSource1: TDataSource;
    Table1: TTable;
    NewSpeedButton: TSpeedButton;
    DeleteSpeedButton: TSpeedButton;
    Table2: TTable;
    CheckBox1: TCheckBox;
    procedure FormCreate(Sender: TObject);
    procedure NewSpeedButtonClick(Sender: TObject);
    procedure DeleteSpeedButtonClick(Sender: TObject);
    procedure CheckBox1Click(Sender: TObject);
  private
    { private declarations }
  public
    procedure CreateNewTable;
    procedure LoadTable;
  end;

var
  GraphForm: TGraphForm;

implementation

{$R *.DFM}

procedure TGraphForm.FormCreate(Sender: TObject);
var
  Code: Word;
begin
  try
```

LISTING 17.15: The complete source code of the CREATEG example (continued)

```
    Code := MessageDlg ('Do you want to create a new table?'
      + Chr(13) + '(choose No to load an existing table, '
      + Cancel to quit)',
      mtConfirmation, mbYesNoCancel, 0);
    if Code = idYes then
      CreateNewTable
    else if Code = idNo then
      LoadTable
    else
      Application.Terminate;
  except
    on E: EMyDatabaseError do
    begin
      ShowMessage (E.Message);
      FormCreate (self);
    end;
  end;
end;

procedure TGraphForm.CreateNewTable;
var
  TableName: string;
  TbNames: TStringList;
begin
  {request the name of the new table from the user}
  TableName := '';
  if InputQuery ('New Table', 'Enter a new table name:',
    TableName) then
  begin
    {if the table already exists in the DBDEMOS database,
    do not overwrite it}
    TbNames := TStringList.Create;
    Session.GetTableNames ('DBDEMOS', '', False,
      False, TbNames);
    if TbNames.IndexOf (TableName) >= 0 then
      raise EMyDatabaseError.Create (
        'Table already exists');

    {set the name and type of the new table}
    Table1.TableName := TableName;
    Table1.TableType := ttParadox;

    {define the three fields and the index}
    with Table1.FieldDefs do
    begin
      Clear;
      Add ('Description', ftString, 50, True);
      Add ('Time', ftDateTime, 0, False);
      Add ('Graphics', ftGraphic, 0, False);
    end;
```

17

LISTING 17.15: The complete source code of the CREATEG example (continued)

```
    Table1.IndexDefs.Clear;
    Table1.IndexDefs.Add('DescrIndex', 'Description',
      [ixPrimary, ixUnique]);

    {create the table using the above definitions}
    Table1.CreateTable;
    Table1.Open;
  end
  else {if InputQuery}
    {if user selected Cancel instead of
    entering a name for the new table}
    Application.Terminate;
end;

procedure TGraphForm.LoadTable;
var
  TableName: string;
  TbNames: TStringList;
  I: Integer;
  Found: Boolean;                  {available tables exist?}
begin
  {create the form of the dialog box,
  before filling its list box with the table names}
  TablesForm := TTablesForm.Create (Application);

  {retrieve the list of tables from the database}
  Found := False;
  TbNames := TStringList.Create;
  Session.GetTableNames ('DBDEMOS', '', True,
    False, TbNames);

  {check if the table has the proper fields,
  that is, if it was created by this program.
  The code uses a second specific table object}
  for I := 0 to TbNames.Count - 1 do
  begin
    Table2.TableName := TbNames [I];
    Table2.Open;
    if (Table2.FieldCount = 3) and
      (CompareText (Table2.FieldDefs[0].Name,
        'Description') = 0) and
      (CompareText (Table2.FieldDefs[1].Name,
        'Time') = 0)
      and (CompareText (Table2.FieldDefs[2].Name,
        'Graphics') = 0) then
    begin
      {table fields match: add the table to the list}
      TablesForm.ListBox1.Items.Add (Table2.TableName);
      Found := True;
    end;
    Table2.Close;
  end;
```

LISTING 17.15: The complete source code of the CREATEG example (continued)

```
  {if a table was found, show the dialog box}
  if Found then
  begin
    TablesForm.ListBox1.ItemIndex := 0;
    if TablesForm.ShowModal = idOK then
    begin
      {if OK was pressed, open the table}
      Table1.TableName := TablesForm.ListBox1.Items [
        TablesForm.ListBox1.ItemIndex];
      Table1.Open;
    end
    else
      {if Cancel was pressed, close the program}
      Application.Terminate;
  end
  else
    {no proper table was found}
    raise EMyDatabaseError.Create (
      'No table with the proper structure');
end;

procedure TGraphForm.NewSpeedButtonClick(Sender: TObject);
var
  Descr: string;
begin
  if InputQuery ('New record',
    'Enter the description:', Descr) then
  begin
    Table1.Last;
    Table1.Insert;
    EditDescription.Text := Descr;
    EditDate.Text := DateTimeToStr (Now);
    DBImage.PasteFromClipboard;
    Table1.Post;
  end;
end;

procedure TGraphForm.DeleteSpeedButtonClick(Sender: TObject);
begin
  if MessageDlg (
    'Are you sure you want to delete the current record?',
    mtConfirmation, [mbYes, mbNo], 0) = idYes
  then
    Table1.Delete;
end;

procedure TGraphForm.CheckBox1Click(Sender: TObject);
begin
  DBImage.Stretch := CheckBox1.Checked;
end;

end.
```

17

Building a Master Detail Form with the Expert

When you run the Database Form Expert, it asks you if you want to create a form based on a single table or a master detail form. A master detail form involves two tables, with a one-to-many join. You can define this behavior by using a proper SQL statement, or with some properties of the Table component. Either way, you can let the Expert generate the code for you. This is exactly what you'll see in the next example.

Since we're using the sample tables available in Delphi, there are not many choices for building a master detail form. Our example will use the Customer and Order tables, which are also used by some Delphi sample programs.

Here are the steps to build the MASTDET example:

1. Start a new project and run the Database Form Expert.

2. In the first page of the Expert, choose a master detail form and TTable objects.

3. Choose CUSTOMER.DB from DBDEMOS as the master table. Choose some of the fields, and select the horizontal or vertical layout.

4. As the detail table, select ORDERS.DB. Choose some of the fields from this table, and select the default grid layout. You are now on the most important page of the Database Form Expert, shown in Figure 17.44.

5. Select the CustNo index, then select the same field in the two lists of fields.

6. Click on the Add button to define a join.

7. Generate the form (as the main form), and the program is finished. You can run it immediately to see its effect.

Figure 17.45 shows an example of the form at run-time. In the figure, I've increased the size of the form and moved some of the components, but the form's behavior is exactly the same as the one generated by the Expert. Each time you select a new customer, the grid below displays the orders pertaining to that customer.

FIGURE 17.44:

The most important page of the Database Form Expert lets you join two tables.

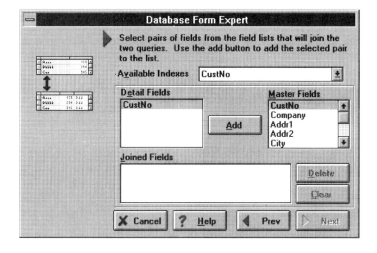

FIGURE 17.45:

The form of the Expert-generated program at run-time, after some minor changes in the layout of the components

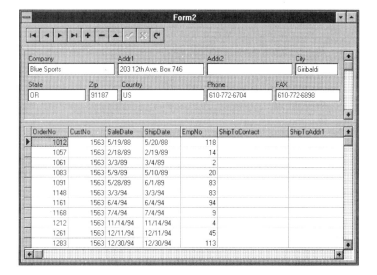

How does this program work? The answer is very simple. If you look at the properties of the two Table components in the Object Inspector, you can see the following values:

```
object Table1: TTable
  DatabaseName = 'DBDEMOS'
  TableName = 'customer.db'
end

object Table2: TTable
  DatabaseName = 'DBDEMOS'
  TableName = 'orders.db'
  IndexFieldNames = 'CustNo'
  MasterFields = 'CustNo'
  MasterSource = DataSource1
end
```

Making a Join with SQL Queries

The previous example used two tables to build the master detail form, because this is exactly what we asked. As an alternative, you can define this type of join using a SQL statement. This is easy, since once again, the Database Form Expert can generate the code for us. Simply run the Expert once more, this time selecting to use a TQuery instead of a TForm.

For this example, I've joined the ORDERS.DB table with ITEMS.DB table, which describes each item in each order. The two tables can be joined using the OrderNo field.

When you generate the code, the program, named ORDERS, behaves exactly like the previous one. This time, however the trick is in the SQL statements of the second query object:

```
Select
  items."OrderNo",
  items."ItemNo",
  items."PartNo",
  items."Qty"
From items
Where
  "items"."OrderNo" =: "OrderNo"
```

As you can see, this SQL statement uses a parameter, :OrderNo. This parameter is connected directly to the first query, because the DataSource property of Query2 is set to DataSource1, which is connected to Query1. In other words, the second query is considered as a data control connected to the first data source. Each time the current record in the first data source changes, the Query2 component is updated, just like any other component connected to DataSource1.

Providing a Closed Selection in a Combo Box

The form of the ORDERS example generated with the Database Form Expert can be improved (you won't find the original version on the companion disk, only the customized one). In the customized version, I've moved some of the editor boxes and labels to place them in two columns, and moved some other elements, but in particular, I've solved a problem that this table had.

In the original version, when you view the records or enter new data, you need to work with the customer number, which is not the most natural way. However, in the database, the names of the customers are stored in a different table, to avoid duplicating the customer data for each order of the same customer. To get around working with customer numbers, I placed a new component in the form, a DBLookupCombo control. This component can be connected to two data sources at the same time, one with the actual data and a second with the display data. Basically, we want to connect it with the CustNo value of DataSource1, the master query, but let it show the information extracted from another table, CUSTOMER.DB.

To accomplish this, I removed the DBEdit component connected to the customer number and replaced in with a DBLookupCombo component and a DBText component. DBText is a sort of label, or text that can't be edited. Then I added a new data source (DataSource3) connected to a table (Table1), which relates to the CUSTOMER.DB file. Figure 17.46 shows the final form at design-time. In the figure, all three data sources are active, and you can see some values from the tables.

For the program to work, you need to set several properties of the DBLookup-Combo1 component. Here is a list of the relevant values:

```
object DBLookupCombo1: TDBLookupCombo
  DataField = 'CustNo'
  DataSource = DataSource1
  LookupSource = DataSource3
```

FIGURE 17.46:

The final form of the ORDERS example at design-time

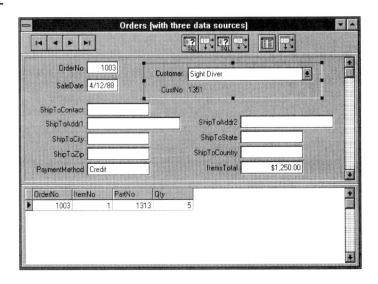

```
      LookupDisplay = 'Company;CustNo'
      LookupField = 'CustNo'
      Options = [loColLines, loTitles]
      DropDownWidth = 250
   end
```

The first two determine the main connection, as usual. The three lookup properties determine the secondary source, the field used for the join (CustNo), and the information to display. In this last property, I entered two values. The first value is the actual field displayed, and the second value is added to the first when the drop-down list connected with the combo box appears.

This list becomes almost a table, as you can see in Figure 17.47. This output is determined by the LookupDisplay property, and also by the Options property (I added a vertical line between columns and the titles of the fields) and the Drop-DownWidth property, which must be large enough to accommodate both fields. What about the code of this program? Well, there is none. Everything works just by setting the correct properties. The three joined data sources do not need custom code.

FIGURE 17.47:

Output of the ORDERS example

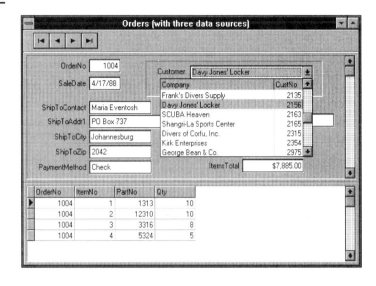

Summary

In this chapter, we have seen a number of examples of the use of database access from Delphi programs. We have reviewed the basics of navigating in a table, entering new values, finding values, and using the grid and navigator components. In the last part of the chapter, we explored some more advanced features, such as building tables at run-time and creating table viewers at run-time to let the user select the fields he or she wants to see. We have seen an example of the use of a graphics field, and some examples of joins.

Is this all one can say about Delphi database programming? Not at all. Delphi database support is very extensive and complete. The purpose of this chapter was to give you an idea of what you can do.

What you didn't find in this chapter was a discussion of database design principles, and I deliberately didn't attempt to design a full-scale database. Database design can be the subject of another book by itself (and, of course, there are many books on this topic that you can refer to).

We will spend some more time on the Windows side of Delphi, and on a number of other topics discussed in some short chapters in the next part of the book. But before moving on to those topics, the next chapter describes some key elements of client/server programming.

CHAPTER

EIGHTEEN

Building Client/Server Applications

- The local InterBase server

- Delphi's InterBase server tools

- Remote SQL server access

- The Visual Query Builder

- Table joins with the Visual Query Builder

18

In Chapter 17, we went through a number of examples of developing database applications. All of those examples accessed data stored in dBASE or Paradox tables; that is, in the usual files. This is certainly good enough for a simple program, but if you need your application to be robust and safe, you might think of moving your data to a SQL server. (See Appendix B for a short overview of SQL.)

The SQL server can reside in a server computer connected to a network, or it can be on the same local machine you are using to develop your programs. Delphi includes the local MS Windows version of Borland's SQL server, InterBase.

In this chapter, we will explore some of the details of using a SQL server. If you do not own the Client-Server edition of Delphi, you might be tempted to skip this chapter. However, some of the tools described here (such as the local InterBase server) are available in every Delphi box.

Accessing a SQL Server

The local SQL server can be used both as a target platform and as a development platform. When you use it as a target platform, you end up installing a copy of the InterBase server, along with your program and the IDAPI libraries your program needs. The lucky owners of the Client-Server edition of Delphi can deploy the local InterBase engine without paying further royalties to Borland.

Realize that the local InterBase server is a single-user implementation, not a full-scale multiuser SQL server. Local InterBase is useful for deploying applications that need to run on stand-alone machines (not networked), without giving up the advantages of SQL queries or writing a separate version of the application to use local tables. Borland also sells full-scale versions of InterBase, which can be used by your Delphi programs that are based on the local version, without any changes.

Often, it is more important to use the local InterBase only as a development platform. Instead of developing the application right on a network, you can build it on a local machine, and then simply change the destination database at the end. This might also be the intermediate step between a local version using files (a prototype of your program) and a fully developed client/server version (your final application).

Developing a Delphi application that accesses a remote server is really not much different from developing a Delphi application that accesses local tables. Once the server database has been set up, and you have defined the proper tables, you use the remote server almost seamlessly from within the development environment.

There are, however, some differences. For example, generally, the user is requested to log in in order to access the database. Another key element of SQL servers is transaction control. Other features include the execution of stored procedures and increased efficiency in using queries rather than tables.

Some of the issues related to these differences can be handled by using some of Delphi's database components. For example, the TDatabase component allows you to customize the database login procedure and to determine how a transaction should interact with another simultaneous transaction accessing the same tables (transaction-isolation level).

Although you are not required to have database components in your Delphi applications, using these components might increase the control you have over the server environment.

Another specific server component is the TStoredProc component. This allows a program to execute a procedure present on the server database, eventually passing some parameters and retrieving a return value.

18

A third useful component for database manipulation is TBatchMove, which allows a program to copy, append, or delete groups of records or an entire table from two different databases. The interesting element is that one of these databases can be a local table and the other a SQL server.

A First InterBase Application

Now let's get to work and build a simple Delphi application using the local Inter-Base engine. We'll create this program using the Database Form Expert, to make it clear that you can use this approach in developing a client/server application. (Everything we have seen in the previous chapter really works as I've described.)

To build this program, create a new Delphi project, then start the Expert. Select a simple form based on a query. Move to the next page and choose the IBLOCAL alias. At this point, The InterBase local server will prompt you with a login dialog box. If you have not worked with the local InterBase server before, the login name will be SYSDBA, as you can see in Figure 18.1. Enter the default password, *masterkey*, and you are ready to go on using the Database Form Expert as usual. For example, you can choose the Country table as the one to access.

FIGURE 18.1:

Logging in to the local InterBase to connect with a SQL server

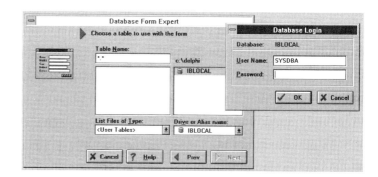

Notice, in this case, tables are not files. The pseudo List Files of Type combo box just lets you choose between User Tables or All Tables, including system tables.

Continue with the Expert, selecting the only two fields in this table and a layout (I chose vertical, with labels on top). Then generate the form.

Customize the form as you like. I activated the table editing (by setting the RequestLive property of the Query component to True), moved some of the components on the screen, and resized the form. I also gave it a new name and caption. An example of the output of the program, named CURRENCY (included on the companion disk), is shown in Figure 18.2.

Each time you run this program, it requests your user name and password. To skip this, you can add a database component to the form, and set the corresponding properties. As an alternative, you might handle the OnLogin event of this component, and enter some values in the LoginParams property. Either way allows you to bypass the login prompt, but is that what you really want to do?

Keep in mind that having a login prompt is one of the key features of database security. You might consider skipping it while you're developing your program, but you'll usually want to require the end users to log in before using the application.

FIGURE 18.2:
The CURRENCY program at run-time (now, what is the last currency rate of my poor lira?)

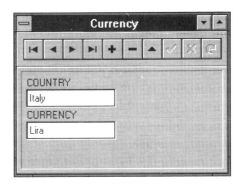

In this example, I used a local SQL database, installed on the same computer I used to develop the Delphi application. This is not the only choice. I could have developed a real client/server application, following the same steps but using a remote server, connected to my computer via a network.

Accessing a Remote Data Source

The only real difference between using a local database and using a remote data source is that you need the Client-Server version of Delphi. With this version, and the investment of the time it might take to install everything properly, the development process is the same for both approaches.

SQL Links is basically an extension of the BDE (Borland Database Engine). As explained in Chapter 17 (and illustrated in Figure 17.1), the BDE can access some data sources, such as Paradox and dBASE tables, directly, or it can interface with ODBC (Open Database Connectivity) drivers or SQL Links.

Since there are a number of layers, you need to take several steps to install and configure everything. You can install the DBE with Delphi or separately, and it can be configured using the DBE Configuration utility. With the configuration utility, you can define aliases, install new ODBC drivers, and set parameters used to connect to the various databases.

The second layer is SQL Links, which also can be configured with the DBE Configuration Utility. After this layer there is the network, which requires the installation of a proper network protocol. The last step is to configure the SQL server.

18

InterBase Server Tools

Delphi includes applications that can be used to set up, configure, and maintain both the local InterBase engine and remote servers.

Server Manager

The Server Manager can be used for administering InterBase local or remote databases and servers. With Server Manager, you can manage database security (authorize new users, change user passwords, and remove user authorizations), back up a database, perform maintenance tasks, and execute other related operations. Figure 18.3 shows an example of using the Server Manager to add a user.

FIGURE 18.3:

The InterBase Server Manager tool, while adding a new user (me!)

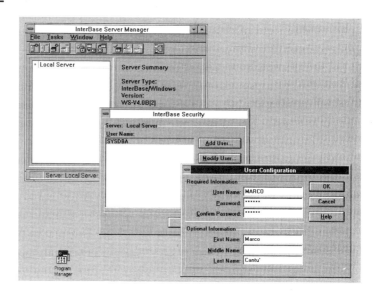

Windows ISQL

The Windows InterBase ISQL (Interactive SQL) application can be used to execute a SQL statement on a local or remote InterBase server. You can start ISQL, connect to an existing database, and enter a SQL statement. For example, you could connect to C:\IBLOCAL\EXAMPLES\EMPLOYEE.GDB, which corresponds to the IBLO-CAL alias, and enter this statement:

```
select First_Name, Last_Name from employee
  where Job_Code = "Eng"
```

This statement outputs the first and last name of all the employees in the Engineering (*Eng*) department, as you can see in Figure 18.4.

FIGURE 18.4:

The result of the execution of a SQL statement in the Windows ISQL application

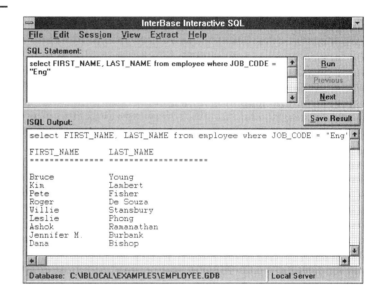

Windows ISQL can be used to view the contents of a database, but its real role is in database setup and maintenance. You can define new tables, add indexes, write procedures (the stored procedures), and so on. This is all done using InterBase SQL, so it is probably not for the casual user.

Database Desktop

Another tool you can use with local and remote InterBase servers is the Database Desktop application. It offers the easiest way to navigate through existing tables or databases, as well as insert and delete records and modify existing values. The Database Desktop can be considered a table configuration tool, while the Server Manager and Windows ISQL can be considered database configuration and definition tools.

You can do everything using SQL, of course, but a table viewer makes a number of operations much simpler. For instance, you can execute the same SQL statement as used in the Windows ISQL example (Figure 18.4) with the Database Desktop, as shown in Figure 18.5.

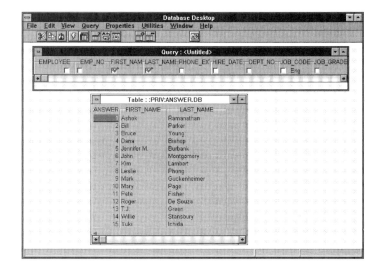

As you can see in the Query window near the top of the screen in the figure, this application supports query by example (QBE). Just add a check mark to two fields, and enter a restrictive clause to select only engineers, by entering *Eng* in the proper column. You might even use this tool to generate a SQL query, producing something like the following:

```
select Distinct First_Name, Last_Name
from Employee
where
(Job_Code = 'Eng')
order by First_Name, Last_Name
```

For more information about the Database Desktop and other Delphi InterBase server tools, refer to the Borland on-line documentation and manuals. Now we will continue with some examples using Delphi—and some code.

Upsizing an Existing Program

The development of a new Delphi database application using a server is similar to the development of an application based on local files. So, what is involved in upsizing an application? To make it work, very little. To take advantage of all the SQL server's features, including transaction processing, just a little more.

The DBNavigator component is already transaction-oriented, so you can easily use it for this purpose. In this section, we'll see what is involved in moving an existing Delphi database application based on a local table to the local InterBase server. This is usually a first step in its move to a remote SQL server. The second step is much simpler.

As an example, let's go through the steps for upsizing the CALC example presented in Chapter 17. The new version will include a viewer of the COUNTRY.DB table with a calculated field, and it will be connected to the local InterBase server. To upsize the program, proceed in two steps:

- Write a program to copy the table from a Paradox file to an InterBase database.
- Update the program to have it use the new table.

Copying a Table

There are basically two ways to copy a Paradox table to a SQL server. One is to use one of the interactive tools, such as the Database Desktop. The other method is to write a program in Delphi, based on the TBatchMove component. I've chosen the second approach. To build the MOVECOUN (for Move Country) example, place two Table components, a BatchMove and a Button in a form, as shown in Figure 18.6.

The first table should be connected with the original Paradox table (COUNTRY.DB) and we can immediately open it (set its Active property to True). The second table should relate to the target database, indicating the name of the new table. I could not choose *Country* as the target name, because there is already a table with this name in the IBLOCAL database. I decided to use *America*, because there are only American countries in the table. Once each table is properly set up, use them for the Source and Destination properties of the BatchMove component.

FIGURE 18.6:

The form of the MOVECOUN
example at design-time

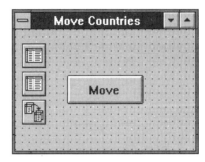

The last step is to choose a proper value for the Move property of the BatchMove component. The default is `batAppend`, which appends records to an existing destination table. But you can set the following:

- `batUpdate`, which updates only matching records.
- `batAppendUpdate`, which does both operations (appends and updates).
- `batCopy`, which creates the destination table, copying the source table "as is."
- `batDelete`, which deletes matching records.

It seems that the `batCopy` parameter might be what we are looking for. Set it, select the BatchMove component, activate the form's SpeedMenu, and choose the Execute command. Delphi will create the new table (after asking for login information).

We have done it, without even compiling the program! As an alternative, we can write one line of code for the OnClick event of the button:

```
BatchMove1.Execute;
```

This is certainly nice, but I would like to show you some more details. For this reason, I used the default `batAppend` mode in the program and created the table in the code, as you can see in Listing 18.1. This method is easy. Before you call the CreateTable method of the Table2 component, you need to copy the structure of the first table to Table2. Here is the whole code:

```
procedure TForm1.ButtonMoveClick(Sender: TObject);
begin
  Table2.FieldDefs := Table1.FieldDefs;
  Table2.IndexDefs.Assign (Table1.IndexDefs);
```

```
      Table2.CreateTable;
      Table2.Open;
      BatchMove1.Execute;
      ButtonMove.Enabled := True;
    end;
```

At the end, the button is disabled, so that the user can make only one copy each time the program is executed. Run the program, click on the button, and fill in the login dialog box. Now you are ready for the second step of the upsizing process.

LISTING 18.1: The textual description of the form of the MOVECOUN example

```
object Form1: TForm1
  Caption = 'Move Countries'
  object ButtonMove: TButton
    Caption = 'Move'
    OnClick = ButtonMoveClick
  end
  object BatchMove1: TBatchMove
    Destination = Table2
    Mode = batCopy
    Source = Table1
  end
  object Table1: TTable
    Active = True
    DatabaseName = 'DBDEMOS'
    TableName = 'COUNTRY.DB'
  end
  object Table2: TTable
    DatabaseName = 'IBLOCAL'
    TableName = 'AMERICA'
  end
end
```

WARNING When you run the MOVECOUN program, you might notice that the SQL operation is quite slow. The program will show a special SQL hourglass, but the screen might not be repainted properly for a while.

Porting the Application

Now that the table has been moved to the InterBase local server, we can turn our attention to improving the CALC application. I've named the new version CALC2.

Open the old application (or a copy), select the Table component, set its Active property to False, and then choose the IBLOCAL database and the America table (which should appear in the list of available tables in the Object Inspector). Activate the table again, and the live data is back, as you can see in Figure 18.7. But now we are accessing a SQL server. When you run the program, the new calculated field will appear, exactly as it did in the previous version. The example works, and it is so simple that performance is not a concern.

FIGURE 18.7:

The live data of the CALC2 example connected to the local InterBase server. Notice the Object Inspector's list of available tables, including America.

The next version of the example, CALC3, uses a Query instead of a Table component. Simply remove the table and add a query. Connect the data source with the query and write the proper SQL statement.

Since we are exploring the development of client/server applications, we will try using another tool included in this version of Delphi: the Visual Query Builder. If you do not have this tool, you can enter the resulting SQL statement in the corresponding property of the Query component.

Using the Visual Query Builder

Running the Visual Query Builder is simple: just select the Query component and activate the local SpeedMenu of the Form Designer by pressing the right mouse button (on the form). Select the Query Builder menu item and fill in the login fields, choosing a database and entering a password. In the following dialog box, choose only the America table. Then close the dialog box. Figure 18.8 shows this process.

FIGURE 18.8:

When the Visual Query Builder starts, you choose the tables you want to use.

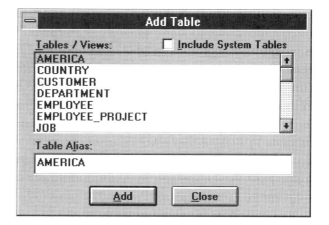

Now we are ready to work. As you can see in Figure 18.9, the Visual Query Builder has a lower area where you build the resulting query and an upper area for the tables you are using. The buttons on the toolbar of the Visual Query Builder and their functions are listed in Table 18.1.

For example, you can drag some fields from the table (operation tables) in the upper portion to the bottom part, adding them to the result. You can also set the sort order of the table resulting from the sort, and set a number of advanced features.

As we will see in an example later in this chapter, when you have more than one table loaded in the Visual Query Builder, you can join them graphically.

FIGURE 18.9:

The main screen of the Visual Query Builder

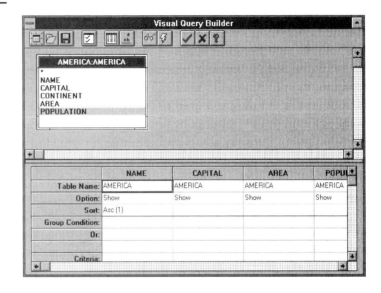

TABLE 18.1: The Visual Query Builder SpeedBar Buttons

Button	Function
	Create a new query.
	Open an existing query, loading it from a file.
	Save the query to file, with a new name.
	Set some options for the query.
	Select the tables for the query.
	Add a column calculated with an expression.
	Show the text of the SQL statement.

TABLE 18.1: The Visual Query Builder SpeedBar Buttons (continued)

Button	Function
⚡	Run the query, showing the result.
✔	Save the query and exit.
✖	Exit without saving the query.

Another thing you can do (and which we'll do right now) is to define calculated fields directly in the query. Click on the Expression button in the toolbar. In the Expression dialog box, give the expression a name (I chose Density), click on the Population field, then on the division sign (/), and then on the Area field.

The expression appears in the Expression box at the bottom of the dialog box, as shown in Figure 18.10. If it's correct, click on the Close button. A new field will be added to the resulting table of the query. Now you can click on the Execute button to see the result, and the calculated field will be there as if it were an original field of the table.

18

FIGURE 18.10:

The Expression dialog box of the Visual Query Builder can be used to define calculated fields.

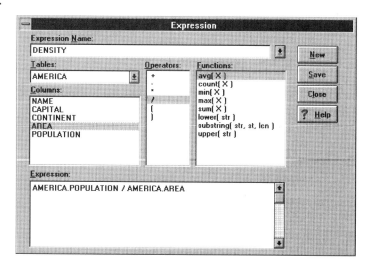

You can also look at the code of the SQL query, which is the following:

```
select America.Name , America.Capital ,
  America.Area , America.Population ,
  ( America.Population / America.Area ) as Density
from America America
order by
  America.Name
```

Click on the SpeedButton with the check mark, and the text of the query will be copied back to the Query component in the form. Now activate it, and you'll see the fields of the form in the grid, including the calculated field, at design-time.

There is still a minor problem, however. The division calculation we have written in the SQL query expression results in a floating-point number with several decimal places. In the expression used to calculate the field in the earlier versions, we called the Round function, which is not available in SQL.

The problem is that the default grid is not wide enough to accommodate the most significant digits, and the values displayed on the screen seem to be wrong. To solve the problem, we simply need to resize the columns of the grid, but this is possible only if you define Field components for the query, using the Fields editor. Open this editor, using the form's SpeedMenu, and add all the fields. (See Chapter 17 for more information about using the Fields editor.) Now, you can resize the grid's columns to obtain the desired effect, as you can see in Figure 18.11.

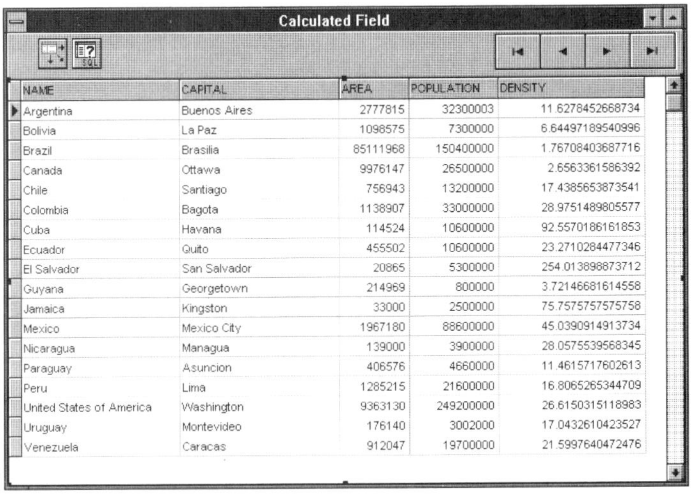

FIGURE 18.11:

The CALC3 form with the SQL calculated field at design-time

NAME	CAPITAL	AREA	POPULATION	DENSITY
Argentina	Buenos Aires	2777815	32300003	11.6278452668734
Bolivia	La Paz	1098575	7300000	6.64497189540996
Brazil	Brasilia	85111968	150400000	1.76708403687716
Canada	Ottawa	9976147	26500000	2.6563361586392
Chile	Santiago	756943	13200000	17.4385653873541
Colombia	Bagota	1138907	33000000	28.9751489805577
Cuba	Havana	114524	10600000	92.5570186161853
Ecuador	Quito	455502	10600000	23.2710284477346
El Salvador	San Salvador	20865	5300000	254.013898873712
Guyana	Georgetown	214969	800000	3.72146681614558
Jamaica	Kingston	33000	2500000	75.7575757575758
Mexico	Mexico City	1967180	88600000	45.0390914913734
Nicaragua	Managua	139000	3900000	28.0575539568345
Paraguay	Asuncion	406576	4660000	11.4615717602613
Peru	Lima	1285215	21600000	16.8065265344709
United States of America	Washington	9363130	249200000	26.6150315118983
Uruguay	Montevideo	176140	3002000	17.0432610423527
Venezuela	Caracas	912047	19700000	21.5997640472476

To have a clearer picture of the steps required to build this program, which has no custom Pascal source code, I've included the description of some of its components' properties in Listing 18.2.

LISTING 18.2: The key portions of the textual description of the form of the CALC3 example

```
object CalcForm: TCalcForm
  ActiveControl = Panel1
  Caption = 'Calculated Field'
  Position = poScreenCenter
  object Panel1: TPanel
    Align = alTop
    object Panel2: TPanel
      Align = alRight
      BevelOuter = bvNone
      object DBNavigator: TDBNavigator
        DataSource = DataSource1
        VisibleButtons = [nbFirst, nbPrior, nbNext, nbLast]
      end
    end
  end
  object DBGrid1: TDBGrid
    Align = alClient
    DataSource = DataSource1
  end
  object DataSource1: TDataSource
    DataSet = Query1
  end
  object Query1: TQuery
    Active = True
    DatabaseName = 'IBLOCAL'
    SQL.Strings = (
      'SELECT AMERICA.NAME , AMERICA.CAPITAL , '
      ' AMERICA.AREA , AMERICA.POPULATION , '
      ' ( AMERICA.POPULATION / AMERICA.AREA )  as DENSITY'
      'FROM AMERICA AMERICA'
      'ORDER BY'
      ' AMERICA.NAME')
    Data = {...}
    object Query1NAME: TStringField
      DisplayWidth = 22
      FieldName = 'NAME'
      Size = 24
    end
    object Query1CAPITAL: TStringField
      DisplayWidth = 15
      FieldName = 'CAPITAL'
      Size = 24
    end
```

18

LISTING 18.2: The key portions of the textual description of the form of the CALC3 example (continued)

```
    object Query1AREA: TFloatField
      DisplayWidth = 10
      FieldName = 'AREA'
    end
    object Query1POPULATION: TFloatField
      DisplayWidth = 14
      FieldName = 'POPULATION'
    end
    object Query1DENSITY: TFloatField
      DisplayWidth = 22
      FieldName = 'DENSITY'
    end
  end
end
```

From Porting to Upsizing

In the CALC3 example, we have obtained two interesting advantages. The first and most evident advantage is that now we can display a calculated field at run-time. This is possible because we do not need compiled Pascal code to make this computation; the server does it, while processing a SQL statement.

This is a key point. We have actually moved some computation from the client application to the server. This means that you can move computations from the client computer to the server computer, which can usually handle the huge amount of data involved in big queries more quickly and efficiently. Although we are currently running both the client and the server code on the same computer, this doesn't modify the general perspective.

This is what real client/server programming means: distribute the workload of an application between a client computer and a server computer. The client should be primarily involved in the user interface, and the server in data processing.

As a consequence of this approach, I would expect this application to run slightly faster than the previous version, although in such a simple case, there probably isn't much difference.

I think this is one of the points that marks the difference between changing an application so that it can connect to a remote database, and upsizing an application, taking advantage of a client/server platform. There are other elements in the picture as well.

The SQL server can be used to improve robustness, data consistency, and speed up the access from multiple users at the same time, just to mention a few ideas. On the whole, moving your data and making the application work with the remote server is just the first step, although a very important one, of the process.

Joining Tables with the Visual Query Builder

In the last section, we saw that owners of the Client-Server version of Delphi can take advantage of a special tool, the Visual Query Builder. We have used it to create a SQL query with a calculated field. Now we will explore another feature of this tool, which is the ability to define table joins graphically.

A Join with Three Tables

The form of the project, named SQLJOIN, includes only three items: a TQuery component, a data source, and a grid aligned to the client area. Basically, we want to display some information about the employees involved in each project, using the data stored in the IBLOCAL database.

The database contains an Employee_Project table, which seems to be exactly what we need. However, this table contains project codes and employee codes. To have some readable information, we need to join this table with the Project table, which contains a description of each project, and the Employee table, which stores information about each employee.

Using the Visual Query Builder, we can express these two joins simply by selecting the three tables and dragging a field onto the corresponding field of the other table. Next, choose some fields for the output. You can see the query I've built with this tool in Figure 18.12.

18

FIGURE 18.12:

The query of the SQLJOIN example in the Visual Query Builder

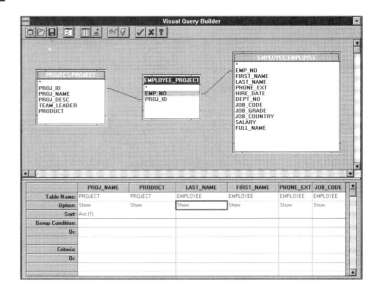

Here are the SQL statements corresponding to this graphical query:

```
select
  Project.Proj_Name , Project.Product ,
  Employee.Last_Name , Employee.First_Name ,
  Employee.Phone_Ext , Employee.Job_Code
from
  Employee Employee , Project Project ,
  Employee_Project Employee_Project
where
  ( Employee_Project.Emp_No = Employee.Emp_No )
  and
  ( Project.Proj_Id = Employee_Project.Proj_Id )
order by
  Project.Proj_Name
```

In the output, we use fields from only two tables. The third table is just used to perform two joins with corresponding codes in the other tables. By setting this query and enabling the Query1 component, we end up with the form shown in Figure 18.13.

The form of the SQLJOIN example at design-time, with live data

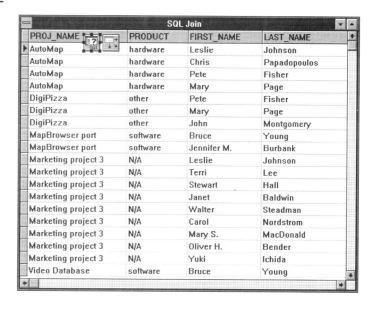

PROJ_NAME	PRODUCT	FIRST_NAME	LAST_NAME
AutoMap	hardware	Leslie	Johnson
AutoMap	hardware	Chris	Papadopoulos
AutoMap	hardware	Pete	Fisher
AutoMap	hardware	Mary	Page
DigiPizza	other	Pete	Fisher
DigiPizza	other	Mary	Page
DigiPizza	other	John	Montgomery
MapBrowser port	software	Bruce	Young
MapBrowser port	software	Jennifer M.	Burbank
Marketing project 3	N/A	Leslie	Johnson
Marketing project 3	N/A	Terri	Lee
Marketing project 3	N/A	Stewart	Hall
Marketing project 3	N/A	Janet	Baldwin
Marketing project 3	N/A	Walter	Steadman
Marketing project 3	N/A	Carol	Nordstrom
Marketing project 3	N/A	Mary S.	MacDonald
Marketing project 3	N/A	Oliver H.	Bender
Marketing project 3	N/A	Yuki	Ichida
Video Database	software	Bruce	Young

WARNING

When you have built a query with the Visual Query Builder, you can indeed see its text in the SQL property of the corresponding TQuery object. However, if you make any change there, you cannot access the query structure in the visual tool any more. To avoid this risk, I suggest that you always save the query to a file before you exit from the Visual Query Builder, so that you can restore the structure later.

In the output of this program, but also in the table at design-time, you can see the reason for the structure of the database, which divides the project information in several tables. You can see that there are employees working on several projects at the same time.

Following the standard database design rules (also called *normalization* rules), no information should be duplicated. For this reason, we cannot store employee data in the project-related tables. At the same time, we cannot store project information in the Employee_Project table, since a project appears several times. The only theoretically sound approach is to divide the data into three tables, as is done in this database. (By the way, if you do not know what I mean by database normalization rules, you should study some database design before delving into the development of complex database applications—with Delphi or any other tool.)

A Join with More Tables

This program is already an interesting example of joining three tables, but there is still some information that is not set properly. For example, the resulting table uses job codes instead of the full job name. We could also add other information that is available in other tables. The improved version (called SQLJOIN2) uses an overly complex SQL statement, built with the Visual Query Builder, as you can see in Figure 18.14.

FIGURE 18.14:

The query of the SQLJOIN2 example in the Visual Query Builder

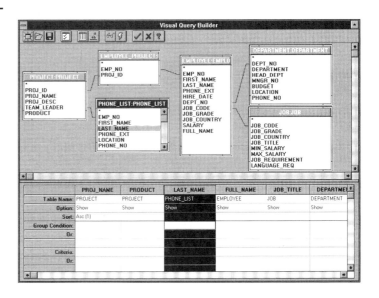

In the query of the SQLJOIN2 example, there is some more information and some more joins. I've added the full job title, replacing the short version, by joining the Job table; the department name by joining the Department table; and the

team leader name by joining a second table with employee information, named Phone_List. This is the resulting SQL statement:

```
select distinct
  Project.Proj_Name , Project.Product ,
  Phone_List.Last_Name , Employee.Full_Name ,
  Job.Job_Title , Department.Department
from
  Department Department ,
  Employee_Project Employee_Project ,
  Employee Employee , Project Project ,
  Phone_List Phone_List , Job Job
where
  ( Employee.Job_Code = Job.Job_Code ) and
  ( Employee.Dept_No = Department.Dept_No ) and
  ( Employee_Project.Emp_No = Employee.Emp_No ) and
  ( Project.Proj_Id = Employee_Project.Proj_Id ) and
  ( Project.Team_Leader = Phone_List.Emp_No )
order by
  Project.Proj_Name
```

The distinct keyword in this statement prevents duplicated records from appearing in the resulting table. Notice that I did not use the Employee table for both the name of the people involved in the project and for the name of the project leader. In fact, this cannot be done directly with the Visual Query Builder. SQL, however, supports such a selection using a subquery, which is a query whose result is used in the main query. You can also use another advanced technique, multiple table aliases.

As an alternative, I could have done two different queries, merging the two results in the Delphi program, using data-aware components. A different solution to this problem, in fact, involves building a master detail query, with master data about the project and detail data about the list of employees working on it. This involves moving back some of the computation to the client side, and having two queries instead of one, but it has some real advantages.

I'll leave building an example that takes the master detail query and detail data approach as an exercise for you to do independently. I suggest that you start using the Database Form Expert for the first version, using the Project_Employee table as master and the Employee table as detail. Remember to use queries, so that you can customize them and join more tables with the proper information.

18

Returning to our SQLJOIN2 example, there is one thing we absolutely must fix. The names of the columns are not easy to understand, particularly the first name column, which stores the name of the team leader. To solve the problem, simply add the components for all of the fields of the query (using the Fields editor), and change their DisplayLabel property. You can see the result of this operation in Figure 18.15. The details are so simple that I haven't listed them here (you can find the source code on the companion disk, which includes the complete form definition).

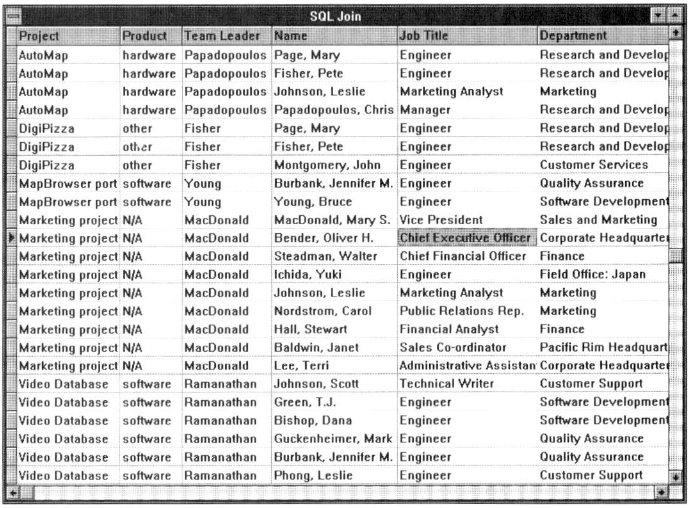

FIGURE 18.15:

The form of the SQLJOIN2 example, at run-time (my preferred job is highlighted)

	SQL Join				
Project	Product	Team Leader	Name	Job Title	Department
AutoMap	hardware	Papadopoulos	Page, Mary	Engineer	Research and Develop
AutoMap	hardware	Papadopoulos	Fisher, Pete	Engineer	Research and Develop
AutoMap	hardware	Papadopoulos	Johnson, Leslie	Marketing Analyst	Marketing
AutoMap	hardware	Papadopoulos	Papadopoulos, Chris	Manager	Research and Develop
DigiPizza	other	Fisher	Page, Mary	Engineer	Research and Develop
DigiPizza	other	Fisher	Fisher, Pete	Engineer	Research and Develop
DigiPizza	other	Fisher	Montgomery, John		Customer Services
MapBrowser port	software	Young	Burbank, Jennifer M.	Engineer	Quality Assurance
MapBrowser port	software	Young	Young, Bruce	Engineer	Software Development
Marketing project	N/A	MacDonald	MacDonald, Mary S.	Vice President	Sales and Marketing
Marketing project	N/A	MacDonald	Bender, Oliver H.	Chief Executive Officer	Corporate Headquarte
Marketing project	N/A	MacDonald	Steadman, Walter	Chief Financial Officer	Finance
Marketing project	N/A	MacDonald	Ichida, Yuki	Engineer	Field Office: Japan
Marketing project	N/A	MacDonald	Johnson, Leslie	Marketing Analyst	Marketing
Marketing project	N/A	MacDonald	Nordstrom, Carol	Public Relations Rep.	Marketing
Marketing project	N/A	MacDonald	Hall, Stewart	Financial Analyst	Finance
Marketing project	N/A	MacDonald	Baldwin, Janet	Sales Co-ordinator	Pacific Rim Headquart
Marketing project	N/A	MacDonald	Lee, Terri	Administrative Assistan	Corporate Headquarte
Video Database	software	Ramanathan	Johnson, Scott	Technical Writer	Customer Support
Video Database	software	Ramanathan	Green, T.J.	Engineer	Software Development
Video Database	software	Ramanathan	Bishop, Dana	Engineer	Software Development
Video Database	software	Ramanathan	Guckenheimer, Mark	Engineer	Quality Assurance
Video Database	software	Ramanathan	Burbank, Jennifer M.	Engineer	Quality Assurance
Video Database	software	Ramanathan	Phong, Leslie	Engineer	Customer Support

Summary

Client/server programming has been a very hot topic for some time now, and terms such as *downsizing*, *upsizing*, and *rightsizing* are becoming increasingly common (whatever they mean, since I've noticed that to different people, these terms mean different things).

In this chapter, we have just seen a few things, scratching the surface of the problems and showing some practical examples. I hope this was enough to make you curious about client/server (which is becoming the buzzword of the year) application development. There is really a lot of work (and a lot of money) involved in this area of programming, which bridges personal computers and bigger machines in a way that has not been possible in the past.

Although it does not contain many more tools than the standard edition, the Client-Server version of Delphi has everything you need to build robust applications for enterprise environments. Furthermore it contains a lot more licensing and redistribution rights than standard Delphi. If you're going to deploy SQL based applications built with Delphi, you need the licensing that's built into the Client/Server edition of Delphi.

With this chapter, the database-specific portion of the book ends, although we will examine another database-related tool, ReportSmith, in Chapter 22. In that chapter, we will add report-printing capability to some of the examples developed in this and the previous chapter. For the moment, we will return to Windows programming, and look into some advanced topics.

18

PART III

Advanced Delphi Programming

CHAPTER

NINETEEN

Discovering the Application Structure

- The roles of the Application object

- Programs without components

- Windows command-line parameters

- A graphical clock application

- Approaches to background processing

- Uses of the Screen object

- How to manipulate Windows initialization files

19

We have seen that Delphi applications are made up of one or more forms. Everything involves forms and components placed inside forms. However, if you just look at the source code of any project file, another element appears: the Application object.

This is a global object, which has the role of the director in an orchestra; but at the same time, it is also a window. The Application object was introduced in Chapter 9. This chapter explores the possible uses of this global object, and of another global object we have already used, the Screen object. In exploring the roles of these objects, many related ideas will emerge, including a broad discussion of Windows messages, timers, and background computing; the use of INI files; and more.

During this exploration, we will focus on another interesting topic: programming without components. It is possible to build a Delphi application without using components.

The central focus of the programs we have built up to now has always been a component placed inside the form, and these components have always received the user input and provided some output. In this chapter, I'll show you something completely different.

Using the Application Object

When you create a new, blank application, Delphi generates some code for the project file:

```
program Project1;

uses
  Forms,
  Unit1 in 'UNIT1.PAS' {Form1};

{$R *.RES}

begin
  Application.CreateForm(TForm1, Form1);
  Application.Run;
end.
```

This code uses a global object, Application, of class TApplication, defined by the VCL. This object is indeed a component, although you cannot set its properties using the Object Inspector. But this is not a real problem, since the application has only a few properties. These properties include the name of the executable file, the title of the application (by default, the name of the executable file without the extension), and a few events. You can also set some of the properties of the global Application object using the Application page of the Project Options dialog box, as shown in Figure 19.1.

We can start understanding the role of the Application object by looking at an example. Just create a new, blank project, compile it (saving the files with the default names, UNIT1.PAS and PROJET1.DPR), and run it. An empty window titled *Form1* appears on the screen.

As soon as you minimize this window, something strange happens. You probably know that when you minimize a window, an icon appears. This icon has the same caption as the original window. In this case, however, the title of the window is *Form1*, while the caption of the icon is *Project1*, which is the name of the executable file.

FIGURE 19.1:

The Application page of the Project Options dialog box can be used to set the name of an application, its icon, and its Help file.

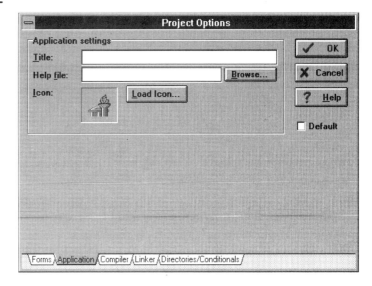

19

Windows' Task Manager lists the
executable file name when a default
Delphi application is running.

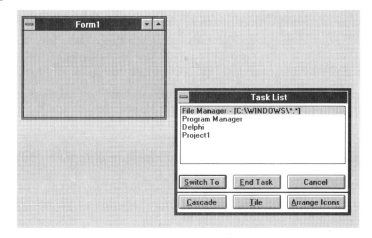

Even stranger is the fact that if you run the MS Windows Task Manager (which, technically speaking, lists the main windows of the system and not the tasks or applications that are running) the name is again *Project1*, as you can see Figure 19.2.

The reason for this behavior is that there are really two windows: one for the application and the other for the form. The application window uses as its title the value of the Title property of the Application object; the form uses the value of its Caption property. Of course, you are free to change the title of the application, so that the two match (as I've already explained in Chapter 9).

Windows uses the application name in its lists of main windows, as in the Task Manager or the switch window that appears when you press the Alt-Tab key combination. Delphi behaves in the same way as the applications it generates (which is obvious since Delphi was built with Delphi itself). When Delphi's main window is visible, you see the name of the project in the title. When you reduce it to an icon, the caption is invariably just *Delphi*.

It is not easy to determine if this is an advantage or a disadvantage. To inexperienced users, seeing two different names can be confusing. However, the application name has the advantage of remaining fixed, while the caption of a program usually changes to reflect the information in the current file or for other reasons.

You probably should use the initial name of the main form as the name of the application, or make sure that the application and form name are the same so that they always match. To accomplish this, you need to change the title of the application each time the caption of the main form changes.

Since Application is a global object, it can be accessed by any unit. As soon as you change the caption of the main form, you can write:

```
Application.Title := Caption;
```

You can also write this code at startup (in the OnCreate event of the main form). As an alternative, you can set the initial application name in the Application page of the Project Options dialog box, together with some other Application object properties.

NOTE
The synchronization of the application and form titles might become less important in Windows 95, where the minimized windows are hosted by the TaskBar, with limited text space. Today, window titles (which are often very long) are probably not suited for Windows 95 TaskBar icons, so it is possible that the use of a shorter name for the minimized window will become common in the new version of the environment.

19

Checking for Multiple Copies of an Application

Probably one of the most common changes in the source code of the project file is to add a check for the existence of a previous copy instance of the application that is already running. Windows programmers probably know that you can test the value of a system parameter, known as HPrevInstance. This is one of the parameters of a typical WinMain function, the entry point of Windows programs written in C.

Delphi programmers can test the value of the HPrevInst global variable, which is set automatically when the program starts, using the corresponding parameter passed by the system to the application. There are four parameters in this group, copied in four Delphi global variables:

- HInstance holds an internal Windows code referring to the current copy, or instance, of an application.

- HPrevInst holds the same code related to the previous running copy of the application. If you are running the first copy, this value is zero.

- CmdLine holds the parameters passed on the command line by the user, such as the name of a file.

- CmdShow holds a display code indicating if the main window of the application should be minimized or maximized at startup.

These four parameters can be important, because they help make your application work seamlessly in the Windows environment.

NOTE

In the 32-bit versions of Windows (Windows 95 and Windows NT) the value of HPrevInst is always zero, since different applications run in different virtual address spaces. Therefore, the code shown in this section will not work in a future version of Delphi for these environments. This doesn't affect a 16-bit Delphi application running in Windows 95.

Testing to See If Another Copy Is Running

If you want to run a single copy of an application, the initialization code of the project source file might be written as follows:

```
begin
  if HPrevInst = 0 then
  begin
    Application.CreateForm(TForm1, Form1);
    Application.Run;
  end
  else
    MessageDlg ('You cannot run another copy ' +
      'of the application!', mtInformation, [mbOK], 0);
end.
```

With this code, the user can start a new copy of the application only if there isn't a previous instance. Otherwise, a message is displayed to the user.

Activating the Previous Instance

To improve the program, you can warn the user that this is the second copy, and then activate the main form of the previous copy of the program. This is the behavior of many Windows programs, from several small applications included in the system to some big commercial applications.

To activate the window of the previous instance of the application, you cannot use the value of the HPrevInst parameter, since this has no direct relationship with the main window. The typical approach, instead, is to call two Windows API functions: FindWindow and SetActiveWindow.

The first function, FindWindow, requires as parameters the name of the window class (in Windows terms) and the caption of the window you are looking for. You can supply only one of these two parameters, which are both very simple. In fact, the internal name WNDCLASS, the structure that defines so-called classes in the system, corresponds to the name of the class in Object Pascal terms (for example, *TForm1*).

The result of the FindWindow function is a handle to the window, exactly the parameter required by the SetActiveWindow function, which activates the window, moving it to the front. So you can write something like:

```
SetActiveWindow (FindWindow ('TForm1', 'One Copy'));
```

To compile this code, you should indicate some units in the uses clause of the project source, as you can see in Listing 19.1 for the ONECOPY1 example. Notice also in this code that I've changed the text of the warning message displayed to the user.

The ONECOPY1 example is a bare program that has a main form with only a single big label. You can see it running in Figure 19.3, where a second copy has been executed. When you click on the OK button in the message box, the first copy is activated and the second terminates its execution.

If you want a program that behaves in the same way as many Windows applications (such as the Clock or File Manager), simply remove the message, and activate the older copy directly.

19

LISTING 19.1: The source code of project file of the ONECOPY1 example

```pascal
program Onecopy;

uses
  Forms, Dialogs, WinProcs, WinTypes,
  One_f in 'ONE_F.PAS' {Form1};

{$R *.RES}

begin
  if HPrevInst = 0 then
  begin
    Application.CreateForm(TForm1, Form1);
    Application.Run;
  end
  else
  begin
    MessageDlg ('You cannot run a second copy ' +
        ' of the application!' + Chr(13) +
        'The form of the older copy will be displayed',
        mtInformation, [mbOk], 0);
    SetActiveWindow (FindWindow ('TForm1', 'One Copy'));
  end
end.
```

FIGURE 19.3:

The output of the first and second copies of the ONECOPY1 example. When you click on the OK button, the first copy is activated again.

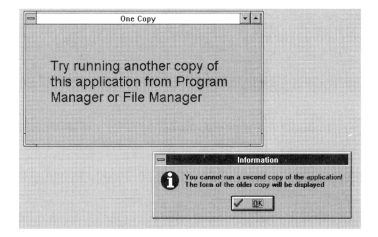

Notice, however, that the program works only if the main window of the previous instance of the application has not been minimized. When the application is minimized, in fact, the form window is hidden and the activation code has no effect. You could use other functions to show the hidden form, but this creates far more problems than it solves. In fact, you might even end up with the form window and the minimized application window on the screen at the same time (horrible and confusing to the user).

After trying a number of ways, I've found a solution that is not elegant but works. Although this code is far from perfect, I've decided to include it in the book, because it shows the use of user-defined Windows messages.

Handling User-Defined Windows Messages

In the ONECOPY2 program, we need to ask the form of another application, the previous instance, to activate itself, even if this form is not be visible. This can be done by sending a user-defined Windows message to the form—a message that the form can handle in a method we write.

When the form is minimized, we can write in the project code:

```
PostMessage (Hwnd, wm_User, 0, 0);
```

The PostMessage API function sends a message to the message queue of the application owning the destination window, indicated as the first parameter (messages are always sent to windows). In the code of the form, you can add a special handling function related to this message:

```
type
  TForm1 = class(TForm)
    Label1: TLabel;
  public
    procedure WMUser (var msg: TMessage); message wm_User;
  end;
```

Now we can write the code of this method, which is simple:

```
procedure TForm1.WMUser (var msg: TMessage);
begin
  Application.Restore;
end;
```

19

Actually, in the project code, we call the `PostMessage` function only if the form is minimized. This can be tested using yet another API function: `IsWindowVisible`.

When you minimize a form in Delphi, it is not minimized—it is hidden, and the minimized application window is displayed instead. You can see the full source code of the project in Listing 19.2.

As an alternative, we could have posted the message in every case, letting the form execute the proper code to activate or restore itself.

If you run the first instance of this program from Delphi, the second instance might not work properly. The `FindWindow` call might end up either returning the handle of the main form of the previous instance or of the form in the Delphi Form Designer, which is simply hidden when the program runs. To test this program, close the design-time form before running it. I'll show you a better version of the program, which does not have this problem, in the next section.

LISTING 19.2: The project code of the ONECOPY2 example

```
program Onecopy;

uses
  Forms, WinProcs, WinTypes, Messages,
  Onecop_f in 'ONECOP_F.PAS' {Form1};

{$R *.RES}

var
  Hwnd: Word;

begin
  if HPrevInst = 0 then
  begin
    Application.CreateForm(TForm1, Form1);
    Application.Run;
  end
  else
  begin
    Hwnd := FindWindow ('TForm1', 'One Copy');
    if (not IsWindowVisible (Hwnd)) then
    begin
      ShowWindow (Hwnd, sw_ShowNormal);
      PostMessage (Hwnd, wm_User, 0, 0);
    end
    else
      SetActiveWindow (Hwnd);
  end
end.
```

Searching the Windows List

The `FindWindow` API function used in the last example is not always reliable. For example, it cannot discriminate between the form of the previous instance of the application and the form used at design-time in the Delphi environment. To make some improvements, I've written a third version of the example, ONECOPY3, which uses a different approach.

When you want to search for a specific main window of the system, you can use the `EnumWindows` API functions. Enumeration functions are quite peculiar in Windows, because they usually require another function as a parameter. To be more precise, they require a pointer to a function. The idea is that this function is applied to each element of the list (in this case, the list of main windows), until the list ends or the function returns True.

We can replace the `FindWindow` call of the last example with:

```
EnumWindows (@EnumWndProc, LongInt (@OldWnd));
```

In this statement, OldWnd is a window handle, passed by pointer, where we will store the result of our search. EnumeWndProc is a function I have written. This function checks the name of each window's class, looking for the string *TForm1*. When this is found, the value of the window instance, retrieved with the `GetWindowWord` API function, is compared with the global `HPrevInst` value:

```
function EnumWndProc(Wnd: HWND; FoundWnd: PHWND): Bool; export;
var
  ClassName: array [0..79] of Char;
  OldInstance: THandle;
begin
  Result := True;
  GetClassName (Wnd, ClassName, SizeOf (ClassName));
  if CompareText (StrPas (ClassName), 'TForm1') = 0 then
  begin
    OldInstance := GetWindowWord(Wnd, GWW_HINSTANCE);
    if OldInstance = HPrevInst then
    begin
      FoundWnd^ := Wnd;
      Result := False;
    end;
  end;
end;
```

19

Notice that we must define the function as `export`, because it is passed as a pointer to another function, and then called by the system. Windows can call directly only functions we mark as exported in the Pascal code.

Programming without Components

As I mentioned at the beginning of this chapter, programming with components is not the only choice of a Delphi developer. In this environment, components certainly have a central role, but it is possible to write applications without any components except forms. (Well, you can also write programs without forms, but this is a very special case.)

Which kind of applications can you write without using components? Windows applications were traditionally written using straight C code, and it is possible to write applications using a similar low-level approach in Delphi, too.

The fact is that my last question was not phrased properly. It should be, "Which kind of applications are easier to write without using components?" I think the answer is that very few applications are easier to write without components and without a visual environment. Both small and big applications benefit from a component approach. Of course, the predefined Delphi components are better suited for some kinds of programs, but by adding the proper custom components to the environment, you can write any type of complex program.

Even if the programs you write have a bare user interface or no user interface at all, like a screen saver or device driver, you can still benefit from some of the objects of the environment, such as streams or lists.

Although you can write Delphi applications without components—ignore the VCL and Delphi visual environment and write C-like code calling API functions—it doesn't make much sense. Even so, we will begin with a couple of short examples, just to show you in practice that this can be done.

> **NOTE**
>
> Another occasion when you are not going to use components, or at least not many, is when you are *writing* a component. This topic is crucial to the development of powerful Delphi applications, particularly in a big organization, and is the subject of Chapter 27.

The Smallest Delphi Program?

As you have seen in the previous examples, you can add some code to the project file of an application. Projects can be handled in Delphi either by using the Project Manager and setting Project Options (this is the recommended way) or by changing the source code file of the project by hand (this is the "hacker" way).

It is possible to write any strange kind of code in the initialization section of the project. Instead of creating a form and running an application, you can produce a beep, display a message box, or run another program. The advantage is that if you do not use forms and the Application object, the size of the executable code shrinks incredibly, because no libraries are included.

Of course, such programs have a very limited use. They can be defined as the smallest programs you can compile with Delphi, but I don't consider them to be real Delphi programs. They are just small Windows applications that have been written and compiled using the Delphi environment.

This is probably the shortest program you can build with Delphi (called BEEP on the companion disk):

```
program Beep;

uses
  WinProcs;

begin
  MessageBeep ($FFFF);
end.
```

The size of the executable file? Less than 3 KB, compared to the typical 200 KB of a simple Delphi executable file. It is useful? Hardly. It just produces a beep and terminates. If you have a sound board installed, you can improve it by using a different parameter to produce one of the predefined Windows sounds instead of a

19

beep (see the description of the MessageBeep API function in Chapter 26).

To create a small program like this, you should remove every form from a project, using the Project Manager window, and change the default uses statement, as shown in the short BEEP program above.

A Note on Link Optimization

The size of the executable file of the BEEP program is 2.8 KB without link optimization, and 2.2 KB with link optimization. Of course, the effect of link optimization is much more important in full-scale Delphi applications.

Note that besides choosing link optimization in the Delphi environment, you can run the DOS command line W8LOSS application, passing a standard executable file as a parameter. In some cases, the effect of this program is to reduce the executable file to 20 percent or less of its original size. (That's why it's called W8LOSS, for weight loss.)

The magic behind link optimization, and the W8LOSS program, is technically called *fix-up chaining*. Fix-up chaining is a feature of the Windows executable file format, which allows the loader to use a single, 8-byte structure to perform a fix-up, instead of using many of these structures. So you save space (fewer fix-ups mean smaller executable files), as well as saving the time to load the program (since there are fewer fix-ups to patch).

Reading the Command Line

The smallest program that is actually meaningful is a simple example of the use of the Windows command-line parameters. Although users seldom write a command line in a graphical user interface, the Windows command-line parameters are important in the system.

Once you have defined an association between a file extension and an application (for example, by using the Windows File Manager), you can simply run a program by selecting an associated file. For example, if you double-click on a bitmap file (with the BMP extension), Paintbrush will generally start and load the bitmap file automatically. In practice, when you double-click an a file that has an association in the File Manager, it runs the corresponding Windows program (for example, Paint-Brush), passing the selected file as a parameter. It is up to the program to open the file passed as a parameter, and a well-behaved Windows application should do so.

The following example, called STRPARAM (for string parameters), demonstrates the use of the command line (or a string command). This program shows the text of the command line, or a notice that there is no text, in a message box.

```
program Strparam;

uses
  Dialogs, SysUtils;

begin
  if StrLen (CmdLine) > 0 then
    ShowMessage (StrPas(CmdLine))
  else
    ShowMessage ('No command line');
end.
```

You can test this program in several ways. If you run it by itself, without a command-line parameter, the "No command line" message is displayed. To provide a command-line parameter, you can use the Parameters option on Delphi's Run menu, as in this example:

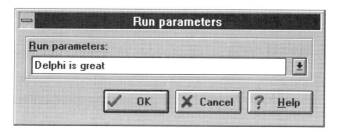

If you now run the program with this command-line parameter, it produces the following output:

Another technique is to open Windows' File Manager, select the directory that contains the executable file of the program, and drag another file over it. The File Manager will have you verify that you want to start the program using that initial file (the dragged file), and then run it. Figure 19.4 shows both the request from the File Manager and the corresponding output.

FIGURE 19.4:

You can provide a command-line parameter to the STRPARAM example by dragging a file over the executable file in Windows File Manager.

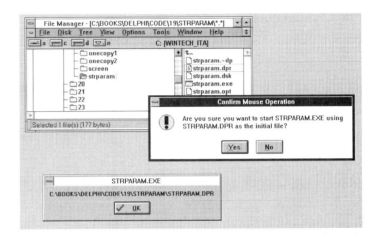

Using the Command Show Parameter

When you start a Windows application, you can actually pass two different parameters: the command string and an integer code. This is quite evident from the parameters of the WinExec API function, which is the simplest way to run an application (an alternative is the ShellExecute function):

```
function WinExec(CmdLine: PChar; CmdShow: Word): Word;
```

The application being executed should use the CmdShow parameter to display itself normally, minimized, maximized, and so on. The most common way to set this parameter is through the Program Items Properties dialog box of Windows' Program Manager, which has a Run Minimized check box, as you can see in Figure 19.5.

You can see the list of values for this parameter in the description of the ShowWindow function in the Windows API Help file included in Delphi. By default, the value is sw_Normal. When you check the Run Minimized box in the Program Manager, the value becomes sw_ShowMinNoActive.

FIGURE 19.5:

The Program Item Properties dialog box of Windows Program Manager can be used to run a program minimized. In the bottom-left is the resulting icon with the special caption.

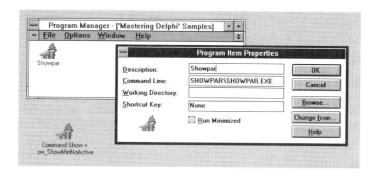

Now we are ready to build our next example, SHOWPAR. Create a new, blank project, with a generic blank form (do not remove the main form, as we did in the two previous examples). Then write the code shown in Listing 19.3 in the project source file.

This program is quite simple. When the CmdShow parameter is sw_ShowMinNoActive, it beeps to warn the user and sets the value of the WindowState property of the form to wsMinimized. As you might remember from Chapter 9, this property determines how the form is displayed at startup, but can also be used to change its display status.

The other feature of the program is that it shows the value of the CmdShow parameter in the caption of the form (as you can see in Figure 19.5, shown earlier). To display the name of the constant instead of a numeric code, I've defined a constant array of strings storing all of the parameter names. With this enhancement, you can use this program to see which value is passed to the application each time it is executed by a shell program, such as the Program Manager, File Manager, or one of the many third-party shells available for the Windows environment.

Events, Messages, and Multitasking in Windows

To understand how Windows applications work, we need to spend a minute discussing how multitasking is supported in this environment. We also need to

LISTING 19.3: The source code of the project file of the SHOWPAR example

```
program Showpar;

uses
  Forms, WinTypes, WinProcs,
  Show_f in 'SHOW_F.PAS' {Form1};

{$R *.RES}

type
  TTenStrings = array [0..9] of string [20];

const
  SwShowNames: TTenStrings = (
    'sw_Hide',
    'sw_ShowNormal',
    'sw_ShowMinimized',
    'sw_ShowMaximized',
    'sw_ShowNoActivate',
    'sw_Show',
    'sw_Minimize',
    'sw_ShowMinNoActive',
    'sw_ShowNA',
    'sw_Restore');

begin
  Application.CreateForm(TForm1, Form1);
  if CmdShow = sw_ShowMinNoActive then
  begin
    {warn the user}
    MessageBeep ($FFFF);
    {minimize the main window}
    Form1.WindowState := wsMinimized;
  end;
  Form1.Caption := 'Command Show = ' +
    SwShowNames [CmdShow];
  Application.Run;
end.
```

understand the role of timers (and the Timer component) and of background, or idle, computing.

In short, we need to delve into the event-driven structure of Windows. I won't discuss this topic in detail, since this is a book about *Delphi* programming, but only provide an overview for the readers who have limited experience in Windows programming. You can find longer and more precise descriptions in several books devoted entirely to Windows.

Event-Driven Programming

The basic idea behind event-driven programming is that some events determine the flow of the application. A program spends most of its time waiting for events, and has code to respond to several of them (not all of them, since a program usually ignores events it is not interested in). For example, when a user clicks one of the mouse buttons, an event occurs. A message describing this external event is sent to the window currently under the mouse cursor. Delphi intercepts the message and calls the method associated with the corresponding event of the component. When the method is finished, the program returns in a waiting state.

Events are serialized; each event is handled only after the previous one is completed. When an application is executing some code (that is, it is not waiting for an event), nothing can stop it—not even Windows. Every other application can have waiting messages, which are stored in a message queue, but cannot receive control of the CPU until the first program has terminated its job.

This is, in short, how multitasking works in any 16-bit version of Windows. Each application runs in turn, but only if it has waiting messages. When an application has responded to a message, it becomes last in the list of programs waiting to handle the next messages.

A problem with Windows 3.1 programming is that an application that is waiting for new messages has no chance to have control again until it receives a message. Also, when an event occurs, a message is sent, but we have no idea of how much time will elapse before the event is handled. Some other applications may need some time to respond to previous messages before this particular event can be handled. Therefore, if you want to write a well-behaved application, you should avoid executing long operations when you respond to a message. However, there are some techniques to divide an algorithm in smaller chunks and execute them one at a time. These techniques include timers and background computing, which are described in the following sections.

The new 32-bit Windows platforms support real multitasking, solving some of the problems mentioned in the previous paragraph.

The simplest events are input events (using the mouse or the keyboard), but in Windows, they account for only a small percentage of the total message flow. Most of the messages are the system's internal messages or messages exchanged between different controls and windows. Even a familiar input operation, such as clicking a

19

mouse button, can result in a huge number of messages, most of which are internal messages.

You can test this yourself by using the WinSight utility included in Delphi. In Win-Sight, choose to view the Message Trace, and select the messages for all of the windows. Select Start, and then perform some normal operations with the mouse. You'll see hundreds of messages in a few minutes, as shown in Figure 19.6. Of course, WinSight is causing Windows to run much slower then usual, because of its monitoring. At normal speed, the flow of messages is much faster.

Windows Message Delivery

Before looking at some real examples, there is another key element of message handling to consider. Windows has two different ways to send a message to a window:

- The PostMessage API function, used to deliver a message to the application's message queue. The message will be handled only when the application has a chance to access its message queue (that is, when it receives control from the system), and only after earlier messages have been processed. This is an asynchronous model, and you do not know when the message will actually be received. This API function was used in the ONECOPY2 example earlier in this chapter (Listing 19.2).

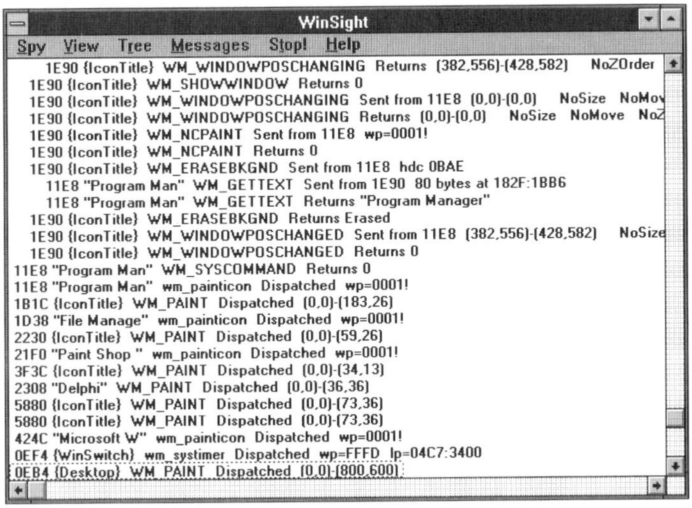

FIGURE 19.6:

An example of a message trace with the WinSight utility

- The `SendMessage` API function, used to execute the message-handler code immediately. `SendMessage` bypasses the message queue and goes straight to its target. This is a synchronous model. This function even has a return value, which can be passed back by the code handling the message.

The difference between these two ways of sending messages is similar to that between mailing a letter, which will reach its destination sooner or later, and sending a fax, which goes straight to the target. Although you will rarely need to use this low-level code in Delphi, you might wonder which one you should use if you do need to write this type of code.

The advantage of using `SendMessage` is obvious: it provides more control over the system. However, you should generally use `PostMessage`, for a very simple reason: when the messages are posted to the queue, each running application has a chance to receive control of the CPU, for basic Windows multitasking. Otherwise, the system will behave less smoothly, and the users will need to wait for their input actions to have any visible effects.

Building a Clock with a Timer

A good example of the problems that arise in an event-driven environment is creating a clock program. A clock should automatically update its output as time passes. A traditional approach might be to check the current time continuously, reading the value stored in the system clock. Although such a program would probably work well, all of the other applications in the system would be out of business, since they would never receive control of the CPU.

19

An alternative is to read the system clock approximately each second, then return the control to the system as soon as possible. But how can the application be awakened when another second has elapsed? This is a typical duty for a timer. A Timer component receives an OnTimer message each time a fixed interval has elapsed.

Behind the Timers: The Clock

Before continuing with the clock program example, let's take a moment to detail some of the aspects of timer behavior in Windows (we have already used this component, but without examining its behavior). Timers are based on an interrupt, driven by the system clock, and timer messages are generated exactly at the specified rate.

The problem is that timer messages, like other messages, are posted to a window and are added to the message queue of the application owning the window. This implies that timer messages are not delivered to the application at the proper rate. If another program takes control of the CPU for a while (for example, during a file-loading operation), timer messages are still generated, but they do not reach the program. Only when the long operation is completed will normal message flow start again.

In this situation, a second problem arises: since timer messages can be very frequent (theoretically, each millisecond; in practice, once each 60 milliseconds at most), they are not accumulated in the message queue. If a second timer message reaches the queue and a previous similar message is still there, the two are merged in a single message. This implies that an application cannot count the number of timer messages received to know how much time has elapsed. The result is that when you receive a timer message, you know for sure that some time has elapsed, but you do not know how much time.

WARNING   Windows imposes another limit on timers. In version 3.1, there is a maximum of 31 timers in the whole system. This means that timers should be used sparingly. Wasting timers in a program can adversely affect, or even prevent, the execution of another application.

How can we use a timer to build a clock? Simply place a Timer and a Panel component in a form, as shown in Figure 19.7. Set the timer interval to 1000 milliseconds (that is, a second), select a suitable font for the panel caption, and align the panel with the client area of the form. The textual description of the form for this example, called CLOCK1, is shown in Listing 19.4,

After you have built this form, simply write the following code to respond to the OnTimer event of the Timer component:

```
procedure TForm1.Timer1Timer(Sender: TObject);
begin
  Panel1.Caption := TimeToStr (Time);
end;
```

FIGURE 19.7:

The simple form of the CLOCK1
example

LISTING 19.4: The textual description of the form of the CLOCK1 example

```
object Form1: TForm1
  ActiveControl = Panel1
  Caption = 'Clock'
  object Panel1: TPanel
    Align = alClient
    Caption = 'Time'
    Font.Color = clBlack
    Font.Height = -64
    Font.Name = 'Arial'
  end
  object Timer1: TTimer
    { the following two properties do not appear in the
    form listing because they have default values:
    Enabled := True;
    Interval := 1000; }
    OnTimer = Timer1Timer
  end
end
```

19

The Time function returns a TDateTime object with the current time, which is converted into a string by the StrToTime function. You can see the result of this code in Figure 19.8.

The output of this program depends on the time-to-string translation performed by the TimeToStr function. This function relies on some constants (remember that you

FIGURE 19.8:

The output of the CLOCK1 example

can change them, they are not real constants) in the SysUtils unit, which have the following default values:

```
Time24Hour: Boolean = False;
TimeSeparator: Char = ':';
TimeLeadZero: Boolean = False;
TimeAMString: string[7] = 'am';
TimePMString: string[7] = 'pm';
```

Their names are intuitive, so I'll spare you a detailed description. Europeans, of course, will probably have WIN.INI settings that are slightly different, such as using a time separator other than the colon or (in some countries) a 24-hour format. In Delphi applications, the settings in WIN.INI are dynamically (and automatically) loaded, to change the default values defined in the SysUtils unit. For a simple test, open the Windows Control Panel, choose the International settings, and select a country different from your own. You'll see some changes in the Time Format area of the dialog box. Accept the new International setting, then run the CLOCK1 example again. You'll find that it automatically uses the new time format.

As you have seen in this example (and as you probably could guess), timers can be used to write time-dependent applications. In Windows, however, you'll need a timer each time an application needs to monitor something. A good example is the Free System Resources (FSR) program presented in Chapter 20.

NOTE   Another use of timers we have seen is to produce animation, as in the WORLD example presented in Chapter 10. However, timers are not the best solution for an animation application, because they have unreliable intervals. For animation, it is much better to use one of the techniques discussed later in this chapter.

At times, an alternative to timers is background computing. We'll investigate this idea a little later in the chapter, after some further refinement of the CLOCK example.

A Full-Scale Graphical Clock

Now that the basic idea is in place, we can think about expanding the CLOCK example by adding a number of new features. Digital clocks are not my favorite. What about a traditional one, with good-looking clock hands?

I know that Windows comes with a clock program, so there is really no need to make a new one. But everyone has his or her own favorite clock style, and there are dozens of Windows clock applications available. So here comes yet another clock for Windows.

The foundation of the new example is the clock program we have already built. The form we need for the clock with hands is even simpler. It has just a timer, and no panel. Most of the code goes inside its OnPaint response method. Since we need to draw three different clock hands, we can add a generic procedure to the TForm1 operation. The procedure that performs this is DrawHand:

```
procedure DrawHand (XCenter, YCenter, Radius,
     BackRadius: Integer; Angle: Real);
```

The DrawHand procedure has five parameters:

- The x coordinate of the center of the clock
- The y coordinate of the center of the clock
- The size of the clock hands (that is, the radius of the clock circle)
- The radius to be used to continue the hand on the opposite side of the center
- The current angle

19

The roles of these five parameters are illustrated in Figure 19.9.

The only way I could work with the analog representation of the clock hands was by using trigonometric functions (cosine and sine). For example, the program draws the line with:

```
Canvas.LineTo (
  XCenter + Round (Radius * Cos (Angle)),
  YCenter + Round (Radius * Sin (Angle)));
```

To make things more complex, instead of starting from the center, the hand can extend in the opposite direction, as you can see in the output shown in Figure 19.10.

As you can see in Listing 19.5, in the FormPaint procedure, the program calculates the center of the form and the radius of the clock, then draws the three clock hands after computing their angle. To accomplish this, it uses Hour, Minute, and Second, which are three private fields I've added to the form. Their value is computed in the OnTimer response function, using the DecodeTime method defined in the Delphi system unit. The OnTimer response procedure then calls the Refresh method to update the image on the screen.

FIGURE 19.9:

A graphical representation of the output of the DrawHand method of the CLOCK2 example

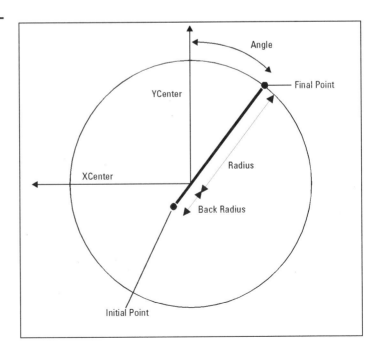

FIGURE 19.10:

The output of the CLOCK2 program. Notice that the seconds hand extends on the other side of the center.

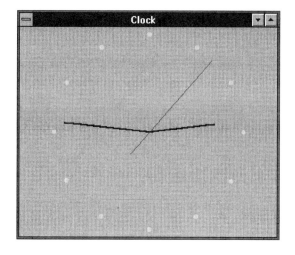

LISTING 19.5: The source code of the CLOCK2 example

```
unit Clock_f;

interface

uses
  SysUtils, WinTypes, WinProcs, Messages, Classes,
  Graphics, Controls, Forms, Dialogs, ExtCtrls;

type
  TForm1 = class(TForm)
    Timer1: TTimer;
    procedure Timer1Timer(Sender: TObject);
    procedure FormPaint(Sender: TObject);
    procedure FormCreate(Sender: TObject);
    procedure FormResize(Sender: TObject);
  private
    Hour, Minute, Second: Word; {current time}
    XCenter, YCenter, Radius: Integer;
  public
    procedure DrawHand (XCenter, YCenter, Radius,
      BackRadius: Integer; Angle: Real);
  end;

var
  Form1: TForm1;

implementation
```

19

LISTING 19.5: The source code of the CLOCK2 example (continued)

```
{$R *.DFM}

procedure TForm1.Timer1Timer(Sender: TObject);
var
  HSec: Word;   {temporary value, not used}
begin
  {get the system time}
  DecodeTime (Time, Hour, Minute, Second, HSec);
  Refresh;
end;

procedure TForm1.FormPaint(Sender: TObject);
var
  Angle: Real;
  I, X, Y, Size: Integer;

begin
  {compute the middle of the form}
  XCenter := ClientWidth div 2;
  YCenter := ClientHeight div 2;
  if XCenter > YCenter then
    Radius := YCenter - 10
  else
    Radius := XCenter - 10;

  {0. Draw the hour marks}
  {Yellow pen and yellow brush}
  Canvas.Pen.Color := clYellow;
  Canvas.Brush.Color := clYellow;
  Size := Radius div 50 + 1;

  for I := 0 to 11 do
  begin
    Angle := 2 * Pi * (I + 9) / 12;
    X := XCenter - Round (Radius * Cos (Angle));
    Y := YCenter - Round (Radius * Sin (Angle));
    Canvas.Ellipse (X - Size, Y - Size, X + Size, Y + Size);
  end;

  {1. Draw the minutes hand}
  {Blue thick pen}
  Canvas.Pen.Width := 2;
  Canvas.Pen.Color := clBlue;
  Angle := 2 * Pi * (Minute+45) / 60;
  DrawHand (XCenter, YCenter,
    Radius * 90 div 100, 0, Angle);

  {2. Draw the hours hand: Percentage of minutes
  added to hour to move the hand smoothly}
  {Same pen as the minutes hand}
  Angle := 2 * Pi * (Hour + 9 + Minute / 60) / 12;
```

LISTING 19.5: The source code of the CLOCK2 example (continued)

```
DrawHand (XCenter, YCenter,
  Radius * 70 div 100, 0, Angle);

{3. Draw the seconds hand: Red thin pen}
Canvas.Pen.Width := 1;
Canvas.Pen.Color := clRed;
Angle := 2 * Pi * (Second+45) / 60;
DrawHand (XCenter, YCenter, Radius,
  Radius * 30 div 100, Angle);
end;

{draw a line using the current pen. The BackRadius
  parameter holds the length of the hand in the
  opposite direction, usually 0}
procedure TForm1.DrawHand (XCenter, YCenter,
  Radius, BackRadius: Integer; Angle: Real);
begin
  Canvas.MoveTo (
    XCenter - Round (BackRadius * Cos (Angle)),
    YCenter - Round (BackRadius * Sin (Angle)));
  Canvas.LineTo (
    XCenter + Round (Radius * Cos (Angle)),
    YCenter + Round (Radius * Sin (Angle)));
end;

procedure TForm1.FormCreate(Sender: TObject);
begin
  {read the time before the form is displayed}
  {Notice that this code 'simulates' a message...}
  Timer1Timer (self);
end;

procedure TForm1.FormResize(Sender: TObject);
begin
  Refresh;
end;

end.
```

19

The FormPaint procedure first computes the center of the form and determines the Radius (another private field of the form) of the clock. It then draws each hand, using code such as:

```
Canvas.Pen.Width := 2;
Canvas.Pen.Color := clBlue;
Angle := 2 * Pi * (Minute + 45) / 60;
DrawHand (XCenter, YCenter,
  Radius * 90 div 100, 0, Angle);
```

This code requires some in-depth explanation. The first two lines are used to set the color and size of the clock hand (in this case, the minutes hand). The third line computes the angle. The complex formula converts the number from 1 to 60 into an angle in radians (hence the use of Pi). During this conversion, we also set the origin of the angle properly, adding three-quarters of a turn (45) to the minutes.

The code used to draw the hours hand is slightly more complex. To make the hand move more smoothly, we can add to the hour the elapsed percentage of the next one (that is, add the current number of minutes divided by 60). The statement to compute the angle of the hours hand becomes:

```
Angle := 2 * Pi * (Hour + 9 + Minute / 60) / 12;
```

Another portion of the painting method draws circular marks corresponding to the hours to improve the readability of the clock. The program computes the position of this mark in a for loop, again based on the sine and cosine functions.

There are two more interesting elements:

- A call to the Refresh procedure is required each time the form is resized, to repaint the whole form, moving the clock to the center of the screen. Figure 19.11 shows the CLOCK2 example with some different forms and clock sizes.

- Notice the strange call to the Timer1Timer method in the OnCreate event. This call is used to paint the clock on the form as soon as it is displayed to the screen.

FIGURE 19.11:

Several instances of the CLOCK2 example with different forms and clock sizes

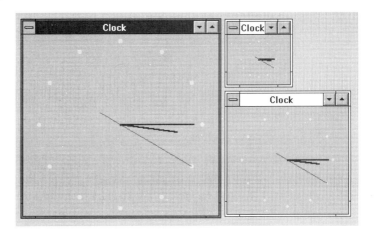

Painting the Seconds Hand with Raster Operations

The CLOCK2 program works, but it is far from satisfactory. The clock image is not steady; it flickers a lot. In fact, each second, the whole surface of the form is erased, then repainted again from scratch. This might seem the only possible behavior, since the seconds hand should move, but it is not. Instead of deleting the whole image, we can delete only the old seconds hand, then repaint it.

The problem now is how to delete the line. You might think of painting a new line with the background color, but this would not work, because you might also delete part of the other two clock hands or part of the hour marks.

Windows Raster Modes

The solution lies in Windows *raster operations* modes, indicated in Delphi by the Mode property of the pen (we used this approach in Chapter 14 for the splitter line example, SPLIT4 in Listing 14.7). Raster operations modes allow you to indicate the behavior of pens (and, in part, also brushes) during drawing functions. These are some examples of raster operations modes:

- pmBlack draws black lines regardless of the pen color you select.
- pmNot reverses the color of the current pixels on the screen, again ignoring the pen color.
- pmCopy is the default mode to copy the color of the pen to the screen.

The output of a number of these modes depends both on the color of the current pixels of the screen and the color of the pen. You can merge the colors, merge the colors inverting one of them, use a color to mask the other, xor the two colors, and perform many, many more operations with the different modes.

The raster operations mode we need to draw the seconds hand of the clock example is pmNotXor. Its result is the inverted color of the exclusive or performed between the two colors. The key feature of this drawing mode is that if you draw the same line twice, it disappears. Also, you can draw in color. This is exactly what we were looking for, since we can use it to delete the old line before drawing a new one.

NOTE   Don't feel bad if you don't quite understand what is going on with the `pmNotXor` mode, including how to `xor` two colors. Our main concern is the *result* of using this mode.

The New Version of the Graphical Clock

How can we change the CLOCK2 program? First of all, each time the timer message arrives, we can store the old value of the seconds and of the minutes in two new private fields of the form: OldMinute and OldSecond. If the value of the minutes has not changed, we use the value of the seconds to delete the old hand and draw the new one:

```
procedure TForm1.Timer1Timer(Sender: TObject);
var
  HSec: Word;   {temporary value, not used}
begin
  {store the old values and get the system time}
  OldMinute := Minute;
  OldSecond := Second;
  DecodeTime (Time, Hour, Minute, Second, HSec);
  {If minutes haven't changed, move the seconds hand
  else redraw the whole clock}
  if Minute = OldMinute then
    DrawSecond
  else
    Refresh;
end;
```

The DrawSecond procedure draws two lines corresponding to the old and the new position of the hand:

```
procedure TForm1.DrawSecond;
var
  Angle, OldAngle: Real;
begin
  {delete the old line, drawing over it again}
  OldAngle := 2 * Pi * (OldSecond+45) / 60;
  DrawHand (XCenter, YCenter, Radius,
    Radius * 30 div 100, OldAngle);

  {draw the new line}
  Angle := 2 * Pi * (Second+45) / 60;
```

```
DrawHand (XCenter, YCenter, Radius,
    Radius * 30 div 100, Angle);
end;
```

For this code to work properly, you need to set the pmNotXor raster mode. However, you can avoid doing this each time the seconds hand is drawn by placing it at the end of the painting code. Here is the final portion of the code of this procedure, with the relevant changes (see the older version in Listing 19.4):

```
{3. Draw the seconds hand}
{Red thin pen, with 'not xor' raster mode}
Canvas.Pen.Width := 1;
Canvas.Pen.Color := clRed;
Canvas.Pen.Mode := pmNotXor;
Angle := 2 * Pi * (Second+45) / 60;
DrawHand (XCenter, YCenter, Radius,
    Radius * 30 div 100, Angle);
```

Avoiding a repetitive call improves the speed of the program. The output of the new version, called CLOCK3, is actually very similar to that of the previous one. But if you look carefully at Figure 19.12, you can see that where the clock hands are overlapped, the raster mode combines the colors of the two hands.

FIGURE 19.12:

The output of the CLOCK3 example, using raster modes (notice the resulting color, or tone of gray in the figure, where the seconds and hours hands overlap)

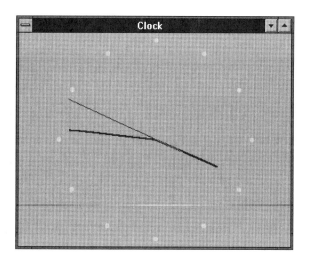

19

Background Computing in Delphi

An alternative to using timers in Delphi is to implement background computing. For example, suppose that you need to implement a time-consuming algorithm. If you write the code as response to a command, Windows will be stopped completely during all the time it takes to process that algorithm. To let the user know that something is being processed, you can activate the hourglass cursor, but this is not a solution.

One solution is to split the algorithm into smaller pieces, and then execute each of them in turn, letting the system and the other applications respond to waiting messages in between processing the pieces. There are actually several ways to implement background computing, as you'll see in the next example. The three most common solutions are the following:

- Add a timer to the program, and execute a step at each timer interval.

- Call the `Application.ProcessMessages` function each time, so that a waiting message can be processed by another application.

- Execute each step of the program when the Application object receives the OnIdle event.

The disadvantage of using a timer is that the execution time has no relationship with the actual workload of the system, and it is very difficult to determine a good timer interval. Both the other two approaches, which are related to the Application object, let the program get more or less system time, depending on the current activity.

The difference between calling ProcessMessages and using OnIdle events is that with ProcessMessages the application has a higher priority than it does with OnIdle. Calling ProcessMessages is a way to let the system perform other operations while your program is computing; using the OnIdle event is a way to implement background processing.

Another way to implement background processing is to post a user-defined message to yourself at the end of each step in your background process:

```
PostMessage (Handle, wm_User, 0, 0);
```

You'll get your message later, so you can execute the next step, then post another message to yourself, continuing until the background processing is done.

To demonstrate some of these choices, I've written an example (what else?), named BACKPROC (for background processing). Figure 19.13 shows the BACKPROC form at design-time. The structure of this form is simple. There are four buttons, four gauges, and four labels. Above these are two other labels and a SpinEdit control. You can see the textual description of the form in Listing 19.6 (omitting descriptions of similar components).

When you click on one of the four buttons, an algorithm is started to compute how many prime numbers there are below the value indicated by the SpinEdit control. The value of SpinEdit1 can be used to slow down or speed up the execution on fast or slow computers. While the prime numbers computation goes on, the gauge beside the selected button is used as a progress indicator (although it is not very precise, because my dumb algorithm is slower when it looks for higher values).

Computing Prime Numbers the Dumb Way

There are a number of very intelligent algorithms you can use to compute prime numbers. I've used none of them, since I needed something slow to demonstrate background computing. For this reason, I've written a simple function to compute prime numbers, which divides a given number by 2, 3, 4, and so on up to the number before the number itself.

19

FIGURE 19.13:
The form of the BACKPROC example at design-time

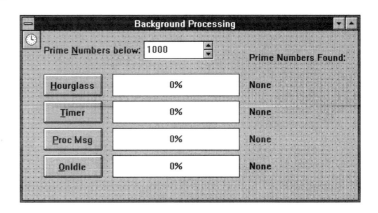

LISTING 19.6: A reduced version of the textual description of the form of the BACKPROC example

```
object Form1: TForm1
  Caption = 'Background Processing'
  object Label1: TLabel
    Caption = 'Prime &Numbers below:'
  end
  object SpinEdit1: TSpinEdit
    Increment = 100
    MaxValue = 20000
    MinValue = 100
    Value = 1000
  end
  object Label2: TLabel
    Caption = 'Prime Numbers Found:'
  end
  object HourButton: TButton
    Caption = '&Hourglass'
    OnClick = HourButtonClick
  end
  object IdleButton: TButton...
  object TimerButton: TButton...
  object ProcButton: TButton...
  object Gauge1: TGauge
    Progress = 0
  end
  object Gauge2: TGauge...
  object Gauge3: TGauge...
  object Gauge4: TGauge...
  object HourLabel: TLabel
    Caption = 'None'
  end
  object TimerLabel: TLabel...
  object ProcLabel: TLabel...
  object IdleLabel: TLabel...
  object Timer1: TTimer
    Enabled = False
    Interval = 50
    OnTimer = Timer1Timer
  end
end
```

NOTE At this point in the description of my prime number function, some of you will already be horrified. In fact, I could have stopped at a value corresponding to the square root of the number. I know it, but I wrote it like this anyway. You don't need to send me e-mail messages telling me how to correct this.

The function looks at the remainder of each integral division, using the mod operator, and if this is zero, the number is not a prime number. When this happens, it stops the loop and returns False:

```
function IsPrime (N: LongInt): Boolean;
var
  Test: LongInt;
begin
  IsPrime := True;
  for Test := 2 to N - 1 do
  begin
    if (N mod Test) = 0 then
    begin
      IsPrime := False;
      break; {jump out of the for loop}
    end;
  end;
end;
```

With this function, we can compute the prime numbers below a certain value with a simple loop:

```
for Number := 2 to Max do
  if IsPrime (Number) then
    Inc (NPrimes);
```

At the end of the loop, the NPrimes variable contains the result. It's simple, but not efficient. This same algorithm is used four times, with some changes in the code of the for loop above.

The Hourglass Approach

The first button, labeled Hourglass, uses the simplest approach. It computes the algorithm, taking the time required and halting the whole system. As a friendly

19

move, it shows the hourglass cursor and updates the progress gauge continuously. Figure 19.14 shows the output of the BACKCOMP example when the Hourglass button is chosen.

FIGURE 19.14:

The output of the BACKCOMP example when the first button is clicked

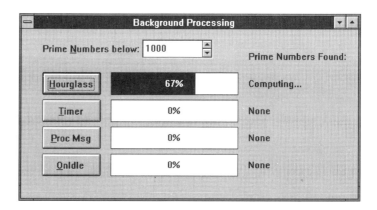

To show the hourglass, this program uses a property of the global Screen object, Cursor:

```
Screen.Cursor := crHourglass;
```

You should be careful to reset the normal cursor at the end, and do it in the `finally` portion of a `try-finally` block. This approach ensures that the cursor is reset properly, even if an exception is raised in the code.

Two other operations are accomplished before starting the actual algorithm: the label at the right is changed to Computing…, and the value of the SpinEdit control is copied to the Max variable. This value will be used a number of times in the following code, so the program reads its value once and stores it. Besides making the code more efficient, this is required by the following versions, which allow the user to perform other operations (including changing the spin edit box value) while the algorithm is being processed.

Each time the loop is executed, the value of the gauge is updated:

```
Gauge1.Progress := Number * 100 div Max;
```

This is probably one of the statements slowing down the algorithm, particularly when its effect is to repaint the control. Strangely enough, checking a hundred or a thousand numbers for prime numbers requires almost the same time. In fact, the gauge is repainted a hundred times with each range, and the difference is limited. When you start checking more than five thousand numbers, the execution gets slower, at least on my computer.

At the end of the execution, the result is copied to the label on the right. I've provided the code of this version mainly to let you know how I changed it in the other versions. Take a look at its code in Listing 19.7 before going on.

LISTING 19.7: The complete source code of the BACKPROC example

```
unit Backp_f;

interface

uses
  SysUtils, WinTypes, WinProcs, Messages, Classes,
  Graphics, Controls, Forms, Dialogs, Gauges, ExtCtrls,
  StdCtrls, Spin;

type
  TForm1 = class(TForm)
    HourButton: TButton;
    IdleButton: TButton;
    TimerButton: TButton;
    ProcButton: TButton;
    Timer1: TTimer;
    Gauge1: TGauge;
    Gauge2: TGauge;
    Gauge3: TGauge;
    Gauge4: TGauge;
    SpinEdit1: TSpinEdit;
    Label1: TLabel;
    HourLabel: TLabel;
    TimerLabel: TLabel;
    ProcLabel: TLabel;
    IdleLabel: TLabel;
    Label2: TLabel;
    procedure HourButtonClick(Sender: TObject);
    procedure TimerButtonClick(Sender: TObject);
    procedure Timer1Timer(Sender: TObject);
    procedure ProcButtonClick(Sender: TObject);
    procedure IdleButtonClick(Sender: TObject);
  private
    TimerNumber, TimerNPrimes, TimerMax: LongInt;
    IdleNumber, IdleNPrimes, IdleMax: LongInt;
```

19

LISTING 19.7: The complete source code of the BACKPROC example (continued)

```
public
  procedure IdleProc (Sender: TObject;
    var Done: Boolean);
  end;

var
  Form1: TForm1;

implementation

{$R *.DFM}

{function local to the unit}
function IsPrime (N: LongInt): Boolean;
var
  Test: LongInt;
begin
  IsPrime := True;
  for Test := 2 to N - 1 do
  begin
    if (N mod Test) = 0 then
    begin
      IsPrime := False;
      break; {jump out of the for loop}
    end;
  end;
end;

procedure TForm1.HourButtonClick(Sender: TObject);
var
  Number, NPrimes, Max: LongInt;
begin
  Screen.Cursor := crHourglass;
  NPrimes := 0;
  Max := SpinEdit1.Value;
  HourLabel.Caption := 'Computing...';
  for Number := 2 to Max do
  begin
    if IsPrime (Number) then
      Inc (NPrimes);
    Gauge1.Progress := Number * 100 div Max;
  end;
  HourLabel.Caption := IntToStr (NPrimes) +
    ' below ' + IntToStr (Max);
  Screen.Cursor := crDefault;
end;

procedure TForm1.TimerButtonClick(Sender: TObject);
begin
  TimerNPrimes := 0;
  TimerMax := SpinEdit1.Value;
  TimerNumber := 2;
```

LISTING 19.7: The complete source code of the BACKPROC example (continued)

```
  Timer1.Enabled := True;
  Gauge2.Progress := 0;
  TimerLabel.Caption := 'Computing...';
end;

procedure TForm1.Timer1Timer(Sender: TObject);
begin
  if TimerNumber < TimerMax then
  begin
    if IsPrime (TimerNumber) then
      Inc (TimerNPrimes);
    Inc (TimerNumber);
  end
  else
  begin
    Timer1.Enabled := False;
    TimerLabel.Caption := IntToStr (TimerNPrimes) +
      ' below ' + IntToStr (TimerMax);
    MessageBeep ($FFFF)
  end;
  Gauge2.Progress := TimerNumber * 100 div TimerMax;
end;

procedure TForm1.ProcButtonClick(Sender: TObject);
var
  Number, NPrimes, Max: LongInt;
begin
  NPrimes := 0;
  Max := SpinEdit1.Value;
  ProcLabel.Caption := 'Computing...';
  Gauge3.Progress := 0;
  for Number := 2 to Max do
  begin
    if IsPrime (Number) then
      Inc (NPrimes);
    Gauge3.Progress := Number * 100 div Max;
    Application.ProcessMessages;
  end;
  ProcLabel.Caption := IntToStr (NPrimes) +
    ' below ' + IntToStr (Max);
  Gauge3.Invalidate;
  MessageBeep ($FFFF)
end;

procedure TForm1.IdleButtonClick(Sender: TObject);
begin
  IdleNPrimes := 0;
  IdleMax := SpinEdit1.Value;
  IdleNumber := 2;
  Application.OnIdle := IdleProc;
  Gauge4.Progress := 0;
  IdleLabel.Caption := 'Computing...';
end;
```

19

LISTING 19.7: The complete source code of the BACKPROC example (continued)

```
procedure TForm1.IdleProc (Sender: TObject;
  var Done: Boolean);
begin
  if IdleNumber < IdleMax then
  begin
    if IsPrime (IdleNumber) then
      Inc (IdleNPrimes);
    Inc (IdleNumber);
    Done := False;
  end
  else
  begin
    IdleLabel.Caption := IntToStr (IdleNPrimes) +
      ' below ' + IntToStr (IdleMax);
    Done := True;
    Gauge4.Refresh;
    MessageBeep ($FFFF);
    Application.OnIdle := nil;
  end;
  Gauge4.Progress := IdleNumber * 100 div IdleMax;
end;

end.
```

Background Processing with Timers

The Timer button in the BACKPROC example starts the worst form of background processing. The use of timers makes this code very slow compared with the other solutions. To make good use of a timer, I've "unfolded" the for loop, using one of its cycles for each timer event. The procedure handling the OnClick event of the button simply sets the initial value of some private variables of the form. I needed to move these variables to the form scope because two different methods need to access them. After this is done, the timer is activated (notice that it is not active at design-time).

The real code is in the Timer1Timer method you can see in Listing 19.7. The for loop is replaced by a plain if statement and a call to the Inc (increase) system procedure:

```
if TimerNumber < TimerMax then
begin
  if IsPrime (TimerNumber) then
```

```
      Inc (TimerNPrimes);
    Inc (TimerNumber);
  end
```

You can compare this code with the original version of the algorithm, based on a for loop and shown in the previous section. The rest of the code is easy to understand. No more changes are made to the cursor, of course, and a simple beep is issued to warn the user at the end.

Notice that while the program is working, the Timer button is not disabled, so the user can restart the algorithm. The user can also click on the Hourglass button, starting the first version of the algorithm, which temporarily stops the timer-based code (as well as any other code in the system).

Processing Messages in the Background

A much easier and better solution is to let the system process some messages in the background while we are computing the prime numbers. This is much simpler because it basically requires adding a single new statement to the original version of the algorithm:

```
Application.ProcessMessages;
```

This statement is written inside the for loop, so that each time, another event in the system has a chance to be handled. This makes the execution smooth. You can do anything in any other window, or on this form, without any real problems—just more slowly. Besides this, I've only added some calls to correct the output of the gauge (without much success). In some rare cases (such as when you drag a window), it is not repainted properly.

As you can see in Figure 19.15, you can click on all of these buttons in the form, computing the prime numbers in parallel. Actually, there is not much multithreading in this program. When you click on the Hourglass button, everything stops. The timer version is much slower. The Idle version is not slow by itself, but it grabs idle time from the system. When the high-priority ProcessMessages version is computing, there is little idle time, but the program tends to be faster. For this reason, the use of the ProcessMessages call is chosen quite often.

19

FIGURE 19.15:

You can start all of the versions of the algorithm at the same time, but they get different priorities.

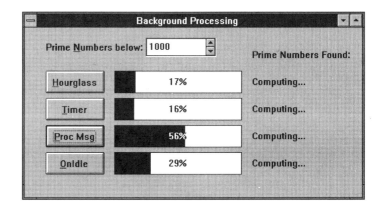

I suggest that you run the program and make these tests yourself. This will help you to understand the relationship between the use of these various approaches to Windows limited multitasking.

Note that you can also restart the Timer version of the algorithm while the program is processing it. The ProcessMessages version, on the other hand, spawns a computation loop of its own, and restarting it may cause some problems. The biggest problem is that each time you start it, a sizable chunk of the stack is used. Starting several versions at the same time may use up all of the program's stack space, something that Windows doesn't like at all (and which could bring the system to a complete stop).

As a general-purpose programming technique, code that uses ProcessMessages must protect against re-entrancy to avoid this kind of stack problem. The best solution is to display a modal status dialog box, so that the main application window (and all its menus) is disabled. In this case, I've just disabled the corresponding button, to let you start up other versions of the algorithm while this is running.

Idle-Time Computing

The solution provided by the bottom button in the BACKPROC example is the only version which really does some processing in background, grabbing idle time from the whole system. As in the timer version, with the OnIdle method, the code is split in two portions. When the OnIdle button is clicked, some initialization code is executed, including setting the OnIdle property (or event handler, if you prefer) of the Application object:

```
Application.OnIdle := IdleProc;
```

Again, this code uses some variables declared in the scope of the form (as private fields), and again it uses a test and an increment instead of a for loop. The core of the IdleProc method is defined as:

```
procedure TForm1.IdleProc (Sender: TObject;
  var Done: Boolean);
```

The second parameter is used to tell the system if further idle-time processing is required or if the algorithm is finished. For this reason, I've set Done to False in the main code and to True at the end. When the algorithm terminates, I also disable the event-response method, to avoid receiving the control when it is not needed:

```
Done := True;
MessageBeep ($FFFF);
Application.OnIdle := nil;
```

Notice that, in this case, we have very limited control over the execution of our code. We do not know how much time it will take. If nothing else is happening on the computer, this version of the code is as fast as the original one; but if you do other operations, such as executing the version based on the call to the ProcessMessages method, it almost stops.

There is no clear winner. For real background computing, using OnIdle is the right choice. If you just want the system to respond while your program is working hard, use ProcessMessages instead.

19

Using the Screen Object

We have explored some of the properties and events of the Application global object. However, there are other documented global objects. One of them is the Screen object. The class of the Screen object, TScreen, can be used to access some information about the screen itself and about the current form of the application. This object also has a list of the available fonts we have already used in some examples (such as FONTGRID in Chapter 10).

Getting Screen Information

Our next example shows some of the operations you can do with the Screen object. Create a form with some labels and two list boxes, as shown in Figure 19.16 and detailed in Listing 19.8.

The first list box is used to provide a list of fonts installed in the system, and the second dynamically shows the active forms of this application. Both list boxes are filled using an array property of the Screen object. However, the second is more complex because it must be updated each time a new form is created, an existing form is destroyed, or the active form of the program changes. Note that the forms the Screen object refers to are the forms of the application, not the windows of the system. To make things interesting, you can create a number of secondary forms by clicking on the New button.

Handling the Forms List

At startup, the OnCreate response method fills the list boxes and computes the size of the screen. You can see this in Listing 19.9, which shows the code of the main form of the SCREEN example. The code used to fill the Forms list box is inside a second procedure, FillFormsList, which is installed as an event handler of the OnActive-FormChange event of the Screen object:

```
Screen.OnActiveFormChange := FillFormsList;
```

FIGURE 19.16:

The form of the SCREEN example at design-time

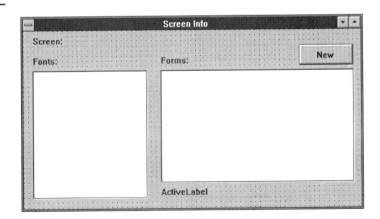

LISTING 19.8: The textual description of the form of the SCREEN example

```
object MainForm: TMainForm
  BorderStyle = bsDialog
  Caption = 'Screen Info'
  OnCreate = FormCreate
  OnClose = FormClose
  object FontsLabel: TLabel
    Caption = 'Fonts:'
  end
  object ScreenLabel: TLabel
    Caption = 'Screen: '
  end
  object FormsLabel: TLabel
    Caption = 'Forms: '
  end
  object ActiveLabel: TLabel
    Caption = 'ActiveLabel'
  end
  object FontsListBox: TListBox
  end
  object FormsListBox: TListBox
    OnClick = FormsListBoxClick
  end
  object NewButton: TButton
    Caption = 'New'
    OnClick = NewButtonClick
  end
end
```

19

WARNING   It is very important that you remove the handler of the OnActive-
FormChange before exiting from the application; that is, before the
main form is destroyed. Otherwise, the code will be executed when
no list box exists, and you'll get a system error—a General Protection
Fault (GPF).

This procedure fills the list box and sets a value for the two labels below and above it, as you can see in Figure 19.17. When you click on the New button, the program creates an instance of the secondary form, gives it a new title, and displays it. The Forms list box is updated automatically because of the handler we have installed. Figure 19.18 shows the output of this program when some secondary windows have been created.

LISTING 19.9: The code of the main form of the SCREEN example

```
unit Screen_f;

interface

uses
  SysUtils, WinTypes, WinProcs, Messages, Classes,
  Graphics, Controls, Forms, Dialogs, StdCtrls,
  Second_f;

type
  TMainForm = class(TForm)
    FontsListBox: TListBox;
    FontsLabel: TLabel;
    ScreenLabel: TLabel;
    FormsLabel: TLabel;
    FormsListBox: TListBox;
    NewButton: TButton;
    ActiveLabel: TLabel;
    procedure FormCreate(Sender: TObject);
    procedure NewButtonClick(Sender: TObject);
    procedure FormClose(Sender: TObject;
      var Action: TCloseAction);
    procedure FormsListBoxClick(Sender: TObject);
  private
    Counter: Integer;        {secondary forms counter}
  public
    procedure FillFormsList (Sender: TObject);
    {handler of a user-defined Windows message}
    procedure ChildClosed (var Message: TMessage);
      message wm_User;
  end;

var
  MainForm: TMainForm;

implementation

{$R *.DFM}

procedure TMainForm.FormCreate(Sender: TObject);
begin
  {compute screen size}
  ScreenLabel.Caption := ScreenLabel.Caption + ' ' +
    IntToStr (Screen.Width) + 'x' + IntToStr (Screen.Height);

  {display fonts and forms data}
  FontsLabel.Caption := 'Fonts: ' + IntToStr (Screen.Fonts.Count);
  FontsListBox.Items := Screen.Fonts;
  FillFormsList (self);

  {set the secondary forms counter to 0}
  Counter := 0;
```

LISTING 19.9: The code of the main form of the SCREEN example (continued)

```
  {activate an event handler of the screen object}
  Screen.OnActiveFormChange := FillFormsList;
end;

procedure TMainForm.FillFormsList (Sender: TObject);
var
  I: Integer;
begin
  FormsLabel.Caption := 'Forms: ' +
    IntToStr (Screen.FormCount);
  FormsListBox.Clear;
  {write class name and form title to the list box}
  for I := 0 to Screen.FormCount - 1 do
    FormsListBox.Items.Add (Screen.Forms[I].ClassName +
      ' - ' + Screen.Forms[I].Caption);
  ActiveLabel.Caption := 'Active Form : ' +
    Screen.ActiveForm.Caption;
end;

procedure TMainForm.ChildClosed (var Message: TMessage);
begin
  {handler of the user message sent by the secondary form}
  FillFormsList (self);
end;

procedure TMainForm.NewButtonClick(Sender: TObject);
var
  NewForm: TSecondForm;
begin
  {create a new form, set its caption, and run it}
  NewForm := TSecondForm.Create (self);
  Inc (Counter);
  NewForm.Caption := 'Second ' + IntToStr (Counter);
  NewForm.Show;
end;

procedure TMainForm.FormClose(Sender: TObject;
  var Action: TCloseAction);
begin
  {VERY IMPORTANT!
    Disable the event handler to avoid a GPFault}
  Screen.OnActiveFormChange := nil;
end;

procedure TMainForm.FormsListBoxClick(Sender: TObject);
begin
  {activate the form the user has clicked onto}
  Screen.Forms [FormsListBox.ItemIndex].BringToFront;
end;

end.
```

19

FIGURE 19.17:

The output of the SCREEN example at startup

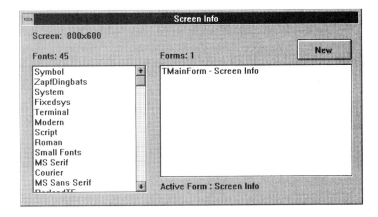

FIGURE 19.18:

The output of the SCREEN example with a number of secondary forms

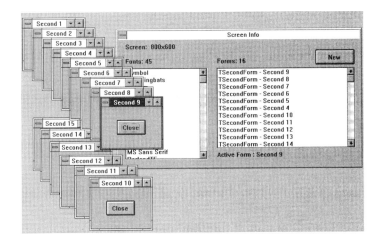

Notice that the program always updates the text of the ActiveLabel below the list box, but this information is almost useless, since the active window is always the first in the list.

The secondary form has a Close button you can select to remove that form. The code handles the OnClose event, setting the Action parameter to caFree, so that the form is actually destroyed when it is closed. However, this code does not work.

Windows moves the focus to a new active form before destroying the old one, so that the list will still contain the name of the form we have closed.

The first idea I had to solve this problem was to call the FillFormsList method directly from the secondary form. This doesn't work, however, because when you make the call, the secondary form still exists. The solution is to use a more Windows-oriented approach: post a message. Since the posted message is queued and not handled immediately, if we send it at the last possible second of life of the secondary form, the main form will receive it when the other is destroyed.

The trick is to post the message in the OnDestroy event handler of the secondary form. To accomplish this, we need to refer to the MainForm object, by adding a proper uses statement in the implementation portion of this unit. I've posted a wm_User, which is handled by a specific message method of the main form (see Listing 19.9). Listing 19.10 shows the source code of the secondary form of the SCREEN example.

LISTING 19.10: The source code of the secondary form of the SCREEN example

```
unit Second_f;

interface

uses
  SysUtils, WinTypes, WinProcs, Messages, Classes,
  Graphics, Controls, Forms, Dialogs, StdCtrls;

type
  TSecondForm = class(TForm)
    CloseButton: TButton;
    procedure CloseButtonClick(Sender: TObject);
    procedure FormClose(Sender: TObject; var Action: TCloseAction);
    procedure FormDestroy(Sender: TObject);
  private
    { Private declarations }
  public
    { Public declarations }
  end;

var
  SecondForm: TSecondForm;

implementation

{$R *.DFM}
```

LISTING 19.10: The source code of the secondary form of the SCREEN example (continued)

```
uses Screen_f;

procedure TSecondForm.CloseButtonClick(Sender: TObject);
begin
  Close;
end;

procedure TSecondForm.FormClose(Sender: TObject;
  var Action: TCloseAction);
begin
  {actually delete the form}
  Action := caFree;
end;

procedure TSecondForm.FormDestroy(Sender: TObject);
begin
  {post a message to the main form, but only if it is
  not closing, to avoid a GPFault}
  if not (csDestroying in MainForm.ComponentState) then
    PostMessage (MainForm.Handle, wm_User, 0, 0);
end;

end.
```

The problem here is that if you close the main window before closing the secondary forms, the main form exists, but its code cannot be executed anymore. To avoid another system error (a General Protection Fault), you need to post the message only if the main form is not closing. But how do you know that? One way is to add a flag to the TMainForm class and change its value when the main form is closing, so that you can test the flag from the code of the secondary window.

This is a good solution—so good that the VCL includes something similar. There is a barely documented ComponentState property, a set which includes a csDestroying flag when the form is closing. Therefore, we can write:

```
if not (csDestroying in MainForm.ComponentState) then
  PostMessage (MainForm.Handle, wm_User, 0, 0);
```

With this code, the second list box always lists all of the forms in the application. Note that you need to disable the automatic creation of the secondary form, by using the Forms page of the Project Options dialog box.

The last functionality I've added to the program is a simple consequence: when you click on an item in the list box, the corresponding form is activated, using the BringToFront method. Nice…well, almost nice. If you click on the list box of an inactive form, the form is activated first, and the list box is rearranged, so you might end up selecting a different form. If you experiment with the program, you'll soon realize what I mean. This minor glitch in the program is an example of the risks you face when you dynamically update some information and let the user work on that element at exactly the same time.

Using INI Files for Status Information

If you want to save any information about the status of an application, in order to restore it the next time the program is executed, you could use a file and store the data in any format you like. Windows, however, has explicit support for initialization files, indicated by the INI extension. Each application can have its own INI file and write strings, numbers, and Boolean values to it. The same values can be easily read.

You can also use the same technique to read system values from the WIN.INI and SYSTEM.INI files, although this is not common; there are Windows API functions to access most of the values of the system initialization files.

Delphi has a class you can use to manipulate INI files, TIniFile. Once you have created an object of this class and connected it to a file, you can read and write information to it. To create the object, you need to call the constructor that passes the name of the file to it, as in:

```
IniFile := TIniFile.Create ('ini_one.ini');
```

There are two choices for the location of the INI file on disk. One option is to store it in the application's directory, providing the full path to the Create constructor. However, if the program is moved to a new directory, it might have problems.

The other, more common, solution is to store the INI files in the Windows directory, the directory used to install Windows. This is done when you provide only a file name, as in the statement above.

19

The Windows directory is usually C:\WINDOWS, but since it might be different, you should use the GetWindowDirectory API function to get it (or let Delphi do this for you). Note that, following the same approach, you can use ParamStr(0) to get the path of the executable file of the application. However, using the Windows directory is generally a better method. Otherwise, you might experience problems when you are running a shared version of Windows, or if the executable file resides in a read-only network directory.

The access to an INI file requires some attention. These files are divided into sections, indicated by a name enclosed in square brackets. Each section has a number of statements of three possible kinds: strings, integers, or Boolean. If you are not aware of the contents of an INI file, you can load it in a text editor, such as the Windows Notepad.

There are three methods of the TIniFile class to read each kind of data: ReadBool, ReadInteger, and ReadString. There are also three methods to write it: WriteBool, WriteInteger, and WriteString. Other methods allow you to read in a whole section or to erase it. In the reading methods, you can specify a default value to be used if the corresponding entry doesn't exist in the INI file.

Our next example, INI_ONE, uses an INI file to store the location, the size, and the status of the main form of the application. The status is the value of the Window-State property: normal, maximized, or minimized. The only real problem in this example is that the value of this property is not always updated by the system, so we need to introduce another test to see if the form was minimized.

The form of the INI_ONE example is just a plain, blank form, without any components. The program handles two events: OnCreate, to create the INI file and read the initial values, and OnClose, to save the status (if the user confirms this operation). You can see the full source code of this example in Listing 19.11. I didn't include a figure showing its output, because showing you an empty form or an icon is not particularly helpful. You should run the program a number of times to investigate its behavior.

LISTING 19.11 : The source code of the INI_ONE example

```
unit Ini_form;

interface

uses
  SysUtils, WinTypes, WinProcs, Messages, Classes,
  Graphics, Controls, Forms, Dialogs, IniFiles;

type
  TForm1 = class(TForm)
    procedure FormCreate(Sender: TObject);
    procedure FormClose(Sender: TObject;
      var Action: TCloseAction);
  private
    IniFile: TIniFile;
  public
    { Public declarations }
  end;

var
  Form1: TForm1;

implementation

{$R *.DFM}

procedure TForm1.FormCreate(Sender: TObject);
var
  Status: Integer;
begin
  IniFile := TIniFile.Create ('ini_one.ini');
  {try to read a value and test if the file exists}
  Status := IniFile.ReadInteger ('MainForm','Status', 0);
  if Status <> 0 then
  begin
    {read position and size, using current values as default}
    Top := IniFile.ReadInteger ('MainForm','Top', Top);
    Left := IniFile.ReadInteger ('MainForm','Left', Left);
    Width := IniFile.ReadInteger ('MainForm','Width', Width);
    Height := IniFile.ReadInteger ('MainForm','Height', Height);

    {set the minimized or maximized status}
    case Status of
      {1: WindowState := wsNormal; {useless: it is the default}
      2: WindowState := wsMinimized;
      3: WindowState := wsMaximized;
    end;
  end;
end;
```

19

LISTING 19.11: The source code of the INI_ONE example (continued)

```
procedure TForm1.FormClose(Sender: TObject; var Action: TCloseAction);
var
  Status: Integer;
begin
  if MessageDlg ('Save the current status of the form?',
    mtConfirmation, [mbYes, mbNo], 0) = IdYes then
  begin
    case WindowState of
      wsNormal: begin
        {save position and size only if the state is normal}
        IniFile.WriteInteger ('MainForm','Top', Top);
        IniFile.WriteInteger ('MainForm','Left', Left);
        IniFile.WriteInteger ('MainForm','Width', Width);
        IniFile.WriteInteger ('MainForm','Height', Height);
        Status := 1;
      end;
      wsMinimized: Status := 2; {useless: it doesn't work}
      wsMaximized: Status := 3;
    end;
    {check if the window is minimized, that is,
    if the form is hidden and not active}
    if not Active then
      Status := 2;
    {write status information}
    IniFile.WriteInteger ('MainForm','Status', Status);
  end;
  {in any case destroy the IniFile object}
  IniFile.Destroy;
end;

end.
```

Summary

In this chapter, we have seen some of the features of the Application global object. We've discussed multitasking, timers, and background computing. We've also discussed the use of the parameters passed from the system to the WinMain function, which are stored in other Delphi global variables. For example, we have seen how to run only a single instance of an application. It was also interesting to write very small examples, without any components.

The examples have demonstrated that you can use Delphi to delve into the intricacies of Windows programming, using very low-level features of the system. This is far from simple, and you won't generally find detailed information about these topics in a typical Delphi book. I've provided just a few hints. For more details, you can refer to Windows programming books, and then try to apply the information to Delphi programming.

The ability to use everything in Windows is a great feature of Delphi. At times, I must admit, using straight C code for some low-level tasks is simpler, mainly because the presence of a hidden window for the application creates some confusing situations. However, I've still found nothing I could not do, and this is not common in a visual programming environment.

We have learned about the Application object, but we have still not explored the whole structure of an application. The next two chapters, which cover topics such as memory and resources, will complete the picture.

19

CHAPTER

TWENTY

Exploring the Behavior of a Program

- Delphi's integrated debugger

- The Object Browser

- Windows message flow

- Windows memory handling

- A resource-monitoring program

- A real Task Manager

20

Once you compile a program in Delphi and run it, you may think you're finished, but not all of your problems may be solved. Programs can have run-time errors, or they may not work as you planned. When this happens, you will need to discover what has gone wrong and how to correct it. Many options and tools are available for exploring the behavior of a Windows application.

Delphi includes an integrated debugger and the Object Browser to let you monitor the result of a compilation process in two different ways. But along with knowing how to use Delphi's tools, to understand what happens in a program, you should also know how it uses memory and how Windows uses the system memory.

This chapter provides an overview of all these topics, demonstrating the key ideas with simple examples. As I've said before, if you want to delve into the details of Windows, you can refer to any of the many good books on the subject. Here you will find only an overview of the ideas every good Delphi programmer should know (at least in my opinion).

The first part of the chapter covers Delphi's debugger and Browser tools. These sections are not tutorials that describe how to activate every feature of these tools; they are technical presentations. The second part of this chapter deals with the key elements of Windows memory handling and internal structure, and describes the memory image of a Delphi application.

Debugging with the Debugger

As I've mentioned a number of times in this book, each time you run a program from the Delphi environment, it is executed in the debugger. This happens unless you have disabled the Integrated Debugger option in the Preferences page of the Environment Options dialog box.

When the program is running in the debugger, you can click on the Pause button on the SpeedBar (if you haven't removed it) to stop the execution. After you stop it, you can execute the program step-by-step, by clicking on the Step Over button. (Or you can start program execution step-by-step from the beginning, instead of running it.)

Consider, however, that Windows applications are message-driven, so there is no way to execute the code of the application step-by-step from the beginning to the end, as you can with a DOS application. For this reason, the most common way to debug a Delphi application, or any other Windows application, is to set some breakpoints in the portions of the code you want to explore.

Debug Information

To debug a Delphi program, you need to add debug information to your compiled code. This is not a problem, because it is Delphi's default behavior. You can turn on of off the generation of debug information in the Delphi compiled units (DCU files) through the Project Options dialog box. As shown in Figure 20.1, the Compiler page includes a Debugging section with three check boxes:

- Debug Information puts information in the compiled unit to map internal addresses to source code line numbers. This increases the size of the DCU file but does not affect the size or speed of the executable program.

- Local Symbols adds the identifiers defined in the implementation part of the unit and in the methods.

- Symbol Info adds the line numbers of all declarations of and references to symbols in a module, to allow the Object Browser to display them.

FIGURE 20.1:

The Compiler page of the Project Options dialog box can be used to include debug information in a compiled unit.

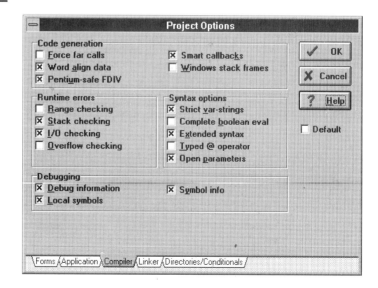

20

1035

All three of these check boxes are checked by default.

These debug information items are used by the integrated debugger. They do not end up in the executable file unless you set the corresponding linker option (in the Linker page of the Project Options dialog box), Include TDW Debug Info.

Adding debug information in the executable file increases the size of your program, and it also allows someone armed with a debugger to understand how your program was written. You need to add debug information to your executable file only if you plan to use an external debugger, such as Borland's Turbo Debugger for Windows (TDW). Do not add debug information to the executable file if you plan to use only the integrated debugger, and remember to remove the debug information from the executable file that you ship. This might seem obvious, but there are commercial products on the market that actually still contain debug information!

On the whole, debugging a Delphi program is not simple. Delphi applications, like all Windows applications, are event-driven. This means that the code statements are not executed in sequence. After the initialization code is executed, the program stops waiting for messages. Everything else happens as a response to an event. To debug a Delphi application, you will often need to place a breakpoint in each handler you want to monitor.

Setting Breakpoints

There are a number of ways to set breakpoints in Delphi. The simplest method is to click in the editor window, to the left of the code (between the text and the border of the window). As soon as you click, an icon appears near the code, and the line is shown in a different color. If you place the breakpoint on an invalid line, a different icon and color are used, to show you that the breakpoint is invalid. Figure 20.2 shows an example with both valid and invalid breakpoints.

Basically, a breakpoint is valid if some code is executed on that line. This excludes procedure and variable declarations, special lines (such as `implementation` and compiler directive lines), and some other cases. Although you can set a breakpoint in an invalid location, when you run the program, Delphi lets you know that it is not correct, as you can see in Figure 20.2.

Once the program execution has reached a line with the breakpoint, the program stops. One common use of breakpoints is simply to let you know that a particular event handler has been executed.

FIGURE 20.2:

Valid and invalid breakpoints in the BREAKP example, and the message displayed by Delphi when it finds invalid breakpoints

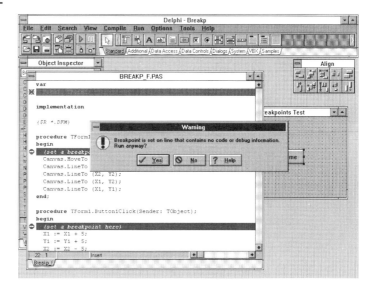

When you have doubts about the flow of execution of a program, because you are not sure when each handler is invoked, you can add a breakpoint at the beginning of each method, as suggested in the BREAKP example. This example draws a series of lines around the border of the form. A button in the middle of the form allows you to move the lines towards the center, but not over the button (see Listing 20.1).

LISTING 20.1: The source code of the BREAKP example

```
unit Breakp_f;

interface

uses
  SysUtils, WinTypes, WinProcs, Messages, Classes,
  Graphics, Controls, Forms, Dialogs, StdCtrls;

type
  TForm1 = class(TForm)
    Button1: TButton;
    procedure FormPaint(Sender: TObject);
    procedure Button1Click(Sender: TObject);
    procedure FormResize(Sender: TObject);
  private
    X1, Y1, X2, Y2: Integer;
```

20

LISTING 20.1: The source code of the BREAKP example (continued)

```
  end;

var
  Form1: TForm1;

implementation

{$R *.DFM}

procedure TForm1.FormPaint(Sender: TObject);
begin
  {set a breakpoint here}
  Canvas.MoveTo (X1, Y1);
  Canvas.LineTo (X2, Y1);
  Canvas.LineTo (X2, Y2);
  Canvas.LineTo (X1, Y2);
  Canvas.LineTo (X1, Y1);
end;

procedure TForm1.Button1Click(Sender: TObject);
begin
  {set a breakpoint here}
  X1 := X1 + 5;
  Y1 := Y1 + 5;
  X2 := X2 - 5;
  Y2 := Y2 - 5;
  if X1 >= Button1.Left then
  begin
    Button1.Enabled := False;
    X1 := Button1.Left;
  end;
  if Y1 >= Button1.Top then
  begin
    Button1.Enabled := False;
    Y1 := Button1.Top;
  end;
  Invalidate;
end;

procedure TForm1.FormResize(Sender: TObject);
begin
  {set a breakpoint here}
  Button1.Enabled := True;
  X1 := 10;
  Y1 := 10;
  X2 := ClientWidth - 10;
  Y2 := ClientHeight - 10;
  Invalidate;
end;

end.
```

When you have set a number of breakpoints (in the position indicated by comment), you can use the Breakpoints command on the View menu to open the Breakpoint List window, which is shown in Figure 20.3.

FIGURE 20.3:

The Breakpoint List window, with its local menu

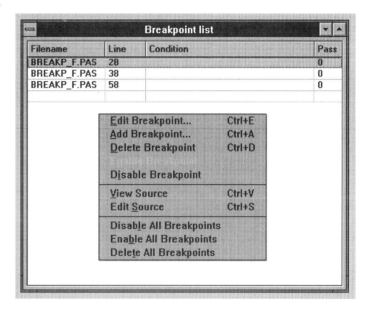

As one of the headings at the top of the Breakpoint List window suggests, you can add a condition to a breakpoint, so that the program halts only when a given condition is met. You'll see an example with a conditional breakpoint a little later in this chapter.

Once the program has stopped, you can continue its execution with the Run command. As I've mentioned before, an alternative is to execute the program step-by-step. The Step Over button on Delphi's SpeedBar allows you to see the execution of statements one after the other. The Trace Into button allows you to trace the methods that are called (that is, to execute the code of the subroutines step-by-step, and the code of the subroutines called by the subroutines, and so on).

The current line of execution is highlighted with a different color, so that you can see what your program is doing. Delphi indicates the line which is about to be

20

executed, or the next line in the program. The effect of the *execution point* (the high-lighted line) is accomplished as soon as you execute another step.

Note that when you trace subroutines and reach a new source code, this file is auto-matically loaded in the editor. While you're tracing a program, you can see the sub-routine calls currently on the stack with the Call Stack command on Delphi's View menu. By adding a breakpoint in the OnClick event of a button, and looking at the stack when the program stops, you get this information:

The Call Stack window shows the names of the methods on the stack and their memory addresses. It is particularly useful when there are a number of nested calls.

Inspecting Values

When a program is stopped in the debugger, you can inspect the value of every identifier (for variables, objects, components, properties, and so on). There are ba-sically two ways to accomplish this: use the Evaluate/Modify dialog box or add a watch to the Watch List window.

As the name suggests, the Evaluate/Modify dialog box is a double-duty tool. You can use it to inspect the value of a given identifier or expression, or to change the value of a variable. The easiest way to open this dialog box is to select the variable in the code editor, and then choose the Evaluate/Modify command from the edi-tor's SpeedMenu. If you want to select a long expression, copy it from the editor and paste it in the dialog box, since long selections are not automatically used.

For example, by setting a breakpoint in the OnResize handler of the BREAKP ex-ample and stepping through the code, you can evaluate and actually change the value of X1, as shown in Figure 20.4. In this dialog box, you can enter complex ex-pressions, as long as there are no function calls involved.

When you want to test the value of a variable over and over, using this dialog box becomes too slow. As an alternative, you can set a watch over any variable, prop-erty, or component. For example, you might set a watch to explore the values involved in the BREAKP example's Button1Click method, which is called each time the user clicks on the button. I've added a number of watches to see the value of the most relevant variables and properties involved in this method, as you can see in Figure 20.5.

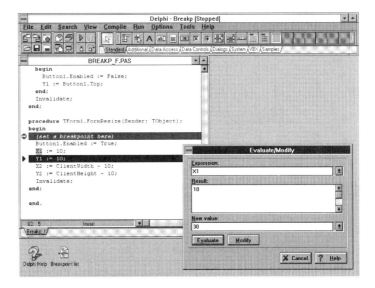

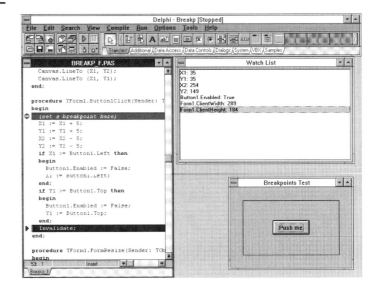

20

You can set watches by using the Add Watch at Cursor command on the editor's SpeedMenu (or just press the Ctrl-F5 key combination). Choose the proper output format, and for the more complex expressions, enter the text. For simple values, you can just give the command when their text is selected in the editor.

You can see the value of a variable only when the program is stopped in the debugger, not when it is running. And you can inspect only the variables in the current scope, of course, because they must exist in order for you to see them!

You can also add watches for (or inspect) components as a whole, but the result is not easy to understand:

```
Watch List
Form1.ClientHeight: 184
Button1: [], 0, Ptr($457F,$BCC), 0, -16, -12, dmManual, Ptr($457F,$1040), False, True, True, True, nil, nil, Ptr(CSeg,$218), nil, nil, nil,
Form1: [], 0, Ptr($457F,$62C), 0, -16, -12, dmManual, Ptr($457F,$D54), False, False, False, True, nil, nil, nil, nil, nil, nil, nil, nil, nil,
```

It is far more common to inspect or watch single properties of a component.

More on Breakpoints

When a program reaches a breakpoint, its stops the execution and shows the current line in the editor. When the editor is activated, however, it might cover some portions of the form of your program. When the code you are going to execute step-by-step involves output, the form appears from behind the editor but disappears again in a while, without letting you view its new contents.

If possible, tile the editor window and the form of your program manually so that they do not overlap (or overlap only partially). With that arrangement, you'll be able to execute a program step-by-step and actually see its output on the screen.

This becomes particularly important for OnPaint handlers. You can try this with the BREAKP example. Open that program again, set a breakpoint in the FormPaint method, and run it. If the editor window and the form overlap, you'll enter an endless series of breakpoints. Each time the form is repainted, the breakpoint stops the program, moving the editor window in front of the form and causing the form to be repainted again, which stops the program on the same breakpoint—over and over again.

The solution is simply to arrange the forms on the screen as shown in Figure 20.6. In this arrangement, you can see the execution of the FormPaint code step-by-step and let the program run without any problems.

FIGURE 20.6:

If the form and the edit window do not overlap, you can easily execute the FormPaint code step-by-step.

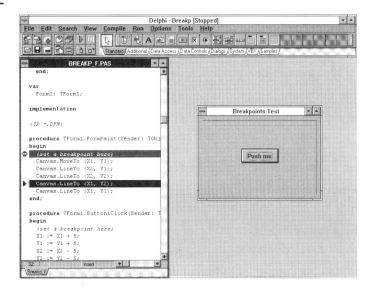

As an alternative, if you only need to know when the OnPaint code is executed, you can disable the breakpoint as it is reached, and later enable it again. In fact, you can add and remove breakpoints easily while the program is running.

WARNING
You shouldn't modify the source code of the program while debugging it. If you do this in Delphi, in fact, you'll notice a strange behavior: the breakpoints you set will correspond to different lines of code than those you see in the editor. The running code and what you see in the editor will not match.

To stop a program on a breakpoint only at certain times, you can use conditional breakpoints. For example, we might want to stop the execution of the Button1Click

20

method (in the BREAKP example) only when the lines have moved near the button. You can set a breakpoint as usual, then open the Breakpoint list, double-click on the breakpoint to open the Edit Breakpoint dialog box, and enter this condition:

```
Button1.Top - Y1 < 10
```

The condition is also added to the Breakpoint List window:

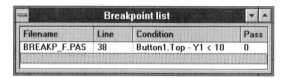

Now you can run the program and click on the button a number of times. Until the condition is not met, the breakpoint is ignored. Only after you click several times will the program actually stop in the debugger.

NOTE There are some special cases in Windows when a message-driven debugger, such as Delphi's integrated debugger, cannot stop at a breakpoint. In these cases, Windows is said to be in *hard mode*. This happens during menu drawing and some kernel operations. When Delphi finds a breakpoint in such a special code areas, it will warn you with a special message.

Tracing through the VCL Source Code

If you own the VCL source code, one of its key uses is in debugging an application. If you want to understand the effects of accessing VCL component properties or calling VCL methods (besides what the documentation tells you), you can include the library source code in your program. Of course, you need to be bold enough and have enough free time to delve into the intricacies of the VCL source code. But when nothing else seems to work, this just might be the ultimate solution.

To include the library source code, simply add the name of the directory with the VCL source code (by default, C:\DELPHI\SOURCE\VCL) in the Search Path combo box of the Directories/Conditional page of the Project Options dialog box. Then rebuild the whole program and start debugging. When you reach statements containing method or property calls, you can trace the program and see the VCL code executed line after line. You can do any common debugging operation with your own code or with the system code.

As an example, Figure 20.7 shows the Call Stack window after tracing the Invalidate call of the OnClick handler of the button. Notice that you can see a lot of activity before the Button1Click method is called (the topmost element in the Call Stack window is the most recent call, and the highlighted method is almost at the top).

FIGURE 20.7:

The Call Stack window when debugging a program that includes the VCL source code

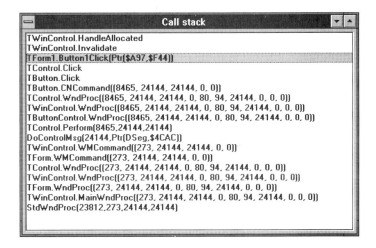

If you compare Figure 20.7 with the contents of the Call Stack window without the VCL source code loaded (shown earlier in the chapter, in the section titled "Setting Breakpoints"), you'll see the different level of detail available. This amount of detail is both an advantage and a disadvantage. It's good because you have all the details you need to get an idea of the status of your program. But how do you pick out the valuable information from all these items?

20

Alternative Debugging Techniques

One common use of breakpoints is to know that a program has reached a certain stage, but there are other ways to get this information besides setting breakpoints. A common technique is to show simple messages (using the ShowMessage procedure) on specific lines for debugging purposes. There are many other manual techniques, such as sending the output to a terminal window, changing the text of a label in a special form, writing to a log file, or adding a line in a list box or a memo field.

All of these alternatives serve a basic purpose: to let you know that a certain statement of the code has been executed, and then to let you watch some values, without actually stopping the program. These approaches avoid the side effects related to stopping and restarting a program (such as the painting problems described earlier), but adding a statement to produce some output is not as easy or fast as setting a breakpoint and removing it.

Debugging with a Terminal Window

Delphi's debugging tools are also much more powerful than the homemade techniques. Being able to step though a program, watching the value of a variable change or tracing through a series of calls, perhaps even those made by the VCL source code, is an invaluable programming aid.

However, homemade debugging techniques have their role, too. As an example, consider debugging the BACKPROC example presented in Chapter 19. This program involves a timer, idle-time computing, and other techniques that would be affected by stopping the program in a debugger. To avoid stopping the program, we could output some debug information to a terminal window. The new version of the program is named BACK2.

The BACK2 version includes the WinCrt unit in its uses statement, and it calls the traditional Pascal Writeln procedure to output a line of text. In the example, I've added one line of this kind to each method of the form class, as in:

```
procedure TForm1.IdleButtonClick(Sender: TObject);
begin
  Writeln ('IdleButtonClick');
  IdleNPrimes := 0;
  IdleMax := SpinEdit1.Value;
  {... same code as before... }
end;
```

The only place where this code wasn't added is in the IsPrime function, because that function is called too often. I've also added a new FormCreate method, related to the OnCreate event, to start up the terminal window (this is done automatically with the first output operation):

```
procedure TForm1.FormCreate(Sender: TObject);
begin
  Writeln ('Form OnCreate event');
end;
```

The reason for this initialization is that the terminal window covers most of the surface of the screen. Now it is displayed at startup, and you can move and resize it before the actual output begins.

> **TIP**
>
> As an alternative, you can display the terminal window calling the InitWinCrt procedure. Before you do this, or make the first output operation, you can also change the value of a number of constants defined by the WinCrt unit. For example, you can change WindowOrg and WindowSize, which specify the position and size of the terminal window, respectively, or ScreenSize, which determines the terminal size, in lines and columns of text.

20

Once everything is properly arranged, just run the program, and you'll see a lot of output in the terminal window. Some of the functions are called for each number to test. In these cases, I've improved the output slightly by adding the current number to the output:

```
procedure TForm1.IdleProc (Sender: TObject; var Done: Boolean);
begin
  Writeln ('IdleProc' + IntToStr (IdleNumber));
```

```
    if IdleNumber < IdleMax then
        ...
    end;
```

You can see an example of a debugging session made with the terminal window in Figure 20.8.

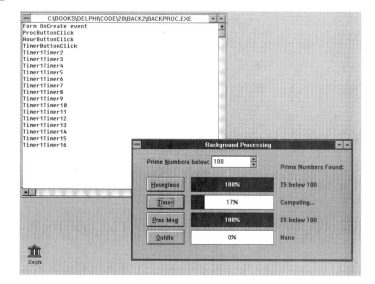

Debug and Release Versions

Adding debugging code to an application is certainly interesting, as the example above demonstrates, but this approach has a serious flaw. In the final version of the program, the one you give to your customers, you need to disable the debugging output, and possibly remove all of the debugging code, to reduce the size of the program.

At first, you might think that this is too big of a problem, and a terminal window is not a professional solution. If you are a C/C++ programmer, however, you might have some ideas on how to do this. The solution to this problem, in fact, lies in a typical C technique known as *conditional compilation*. The idea is simple: you write some lines of code that you want to compile only in certain circumstances and skip on other occasions.

In Delphi, you can use some conditional compiler directives for this:

```
$IFDEF
$IFNDEF
$IFOPT
$ELSE
$ENDIF
```

For example, in our code, we can replace any occurrence of the Writeln procedure with the following:

```
{$IFDEF DEBUG}
  Writeln ('IdleProc' + IntToStr (IdleNumber));
{$ENDIF}
```

This code is included in the compilation only if there is a DEBUG defined before the line, or if the DEBUG symbol has been defined in the Project Options dialog box, as shown in Figure 20.9.

FIGURE 20.9:

The definition of a symbol in the Project Options dialog box

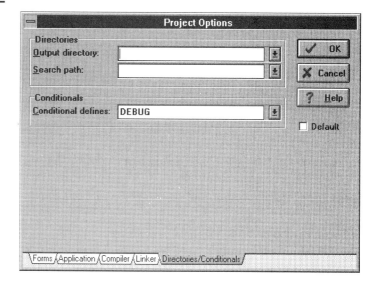

You can even conditionally include the WinCrt unit, by writing this strange-looking `uses` statement:

```
uses
  SysUtils, WinTypes, WinProcs, Messages, Classes,
```

```
Graphics, Controls,
{$IFDEF DEBUG}
WinCrt,
{$ENDIF}
Forms, Dialogs, Gauges, ExtCtrls, StdCtrls, Spin;
```

Now you can compile the program adding the DEBUG symbol (or any other symbol you choose) in the Project Options dialog box, and see the debug output in the terminal window. Then you can remove the symbol definition, choose the Build All command from Delphi's Compile menu, and run it again without the terminal window. The size of the executable file will probably change slightly between the two versions, because some source code is removed. Note that each time you change the symbol definitions in the Project Options dialog box, you need to rebuild the whole program. If you simply run it, the older version will be executed.

WARNING You should use conditional defines for debugging purposes with extreme care. In fact, if you debug a program with this technique, and later change its code (when removing the DEBUG define), you might introduce new bugs or expose bugs that were hidden by the debug process. For this reason, it is generally better to debug the final version of your application carefully, without making any more changes to the source code.

Viewing a Compiled Program with the Object Browser

Another way you can explore a compiled program is with Delphi's Object Browser. The Browser doesn't show the values of the objects and variables of a program; it shows its data types and classes. Once a program is successfully compiled, you can open the Browser and see the whole hierarchy of classes included in your application, as shown in the example in Figure 20.10. The Browse Objects window displays both VCL classes and those defined by your program.

Delphi's Object Browser is similar to the corresponding tool included in many C++ compilers and in previous versions of Borland Pascal. Basically, you can use

FIGURE 20.10:

An example of the output of the Object Browser

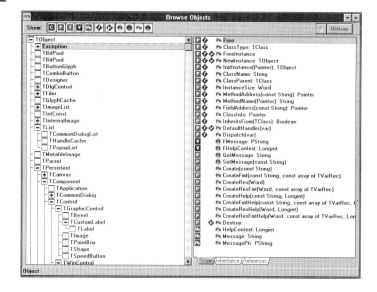

the Browser to see all of the methods, properties, and data fields—both local and inherited—of any class.

If you prefer a partial view, you can choose only a subset of the elements of a class by using the Show buttons at the top of the Browse Objects window. These buttons activate filters for the kind of definition:

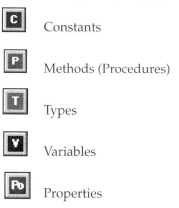

C   Constants

P   Methods (Procedures)

T   Types

V   Variables

Po   Properties

20

These buttons filter the definitions present in the parent class:

 Inherited

 Virtual

And these buttons filter methods, fields, and properties by their visibility:

 Private

 Protected

 Public

 Published

Besides exploring the hierarchy of classes, you can see the elements of each class, and even the details of the definition of each of these elements. You can see when there are references to particular elements in the source code of your application. As with the debugger, if you compile the program including the VCL source files, you can see the references to the VCL source, too, and easily reach the definition of each method, property, or class in the source code. In fact when you select a reference, the Browser opens the corresponding source file in the editor, moving to the proper line.

There are other ways to use this tool. The Browser SpeedMenu offers four choices:

- The Objects command shows the inheritance tree, as in Figure 20.10, with all of the classes of the application.

- The Units command shows the list of units included in the current project.

- The Globals command shows a list of global symbols.

- The Symbol command lets you enter the name of a symbol, and move directly to it.

For example, you can choose the WinProcs unit and see a complete list of the functions of the Windows API, or choose WinTypes to see the definition of all Windows constants.

The Browser is a powerful tool that allows you to explore a complex program, or a not-so-complex program written by another programmer (or by you, but a long time ago), because you can easily jump back and forth from it to the editor. Each time you find a symbol in the editor that you don't recognize, you can select it and use the Browse Symbol at Cursor command on the editor's SpeedMenu to jump to the symbol definition in the Browser. There you can see where the symbol is defined or used, and then jump back to that file in the editor.

The Object Browser lets you explore a program only after you have compiled it, because it uses debugging information generated by the compiler. This means that if you change the source code, and the program doesn't compile any more, you cannot use the Browser to understand what is happening. To avoid this problem, Delphi lets you save the Browser symbols. To do this, select the Desktop and Symbols radio button in the Preferences page of the Environment Options dialog box.

Now each time you compile a program, the information required by the Browser is saved to a file with the DSM extension. With this file, you can use the Object Browser for the program, even if it cannot be built any more due to an error. The Browser can read the DSM file instead of requiring the same information in memory.

The drawback is that DSM files are very big. Therefore, you might turn on this option only when you really need it; that is, when you are developing a complex program.

20

WARNING   Do not save Browser symbols just to look at examples, or your hard disk will soon be filled with almost useless files. If you prefer leaving this option on, you should remember to occasionally search your hard disk for DSM files and delete the old ones.

Exploring the Message Flow

The two tools we have discussed so far in this chapter, the integrated debugger and the Object Browser, provide common ways to explore the source code of a program. In Windows, however, this is often not enough. When you want to understand the details of the interaction between your program and the environment, other Windows-related tools are handy.

One of them is WinSight, a multiple-purpose tool included in Delphi. Others are memory-spying programs. Delphi doesn't included this type of program, but they are available from many sources, including a number of shareware programs, and many samples are included in books and magazine articles.

Using WinSight

We have already seen in previous chapters how the WinSight application can be used to explore an application. Here, I'll provide a short overview, with some new details and tips.

WinSight can be used for three different actions:

- List all of the window classes registered in the system.

- Build a hierarchical graph of the existing windows.

- Display detailed information about the message flow.

These three actions can be activated by the first three commands on WinSight's View menu: Class List, Window Tree, and Message Trace. You can also choose all three views at the same time, placing them in different vertical or horizontal panes, as shown in Figure 20.11.

To become a proficient user of WinSight, and understand all of the information it delivers, you need to have an in-depth knowledge of the structure of Windows and of the Windows applications. Although it might seem beyond the scope of this book, I've decided to give you a brief summary of the information displayed by WinSight, focusing on the information related to Delphi programming.

FIGURE 20.11:

WinSight's three panes: the class list, the window tree, and the message flow

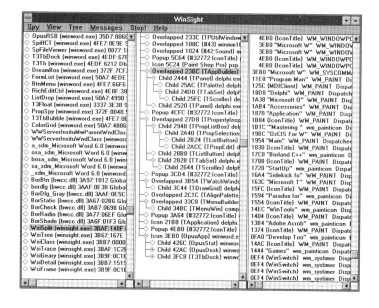

The Class List and the WNDCLASS Structure

The first view of the tool is the class list, which lists all of the *window classes registered* in the system. Some of you might not know what this means.

In short, to create a window of any kind (ranging from the main window of an application to a small control), the Windows environment requires you to specify the class of the window. For this reason, the code of a Windows application written in C often registers a class before creating a window. Every window in the system relates to a class, also known as WNDCLASS from the type name of the data structure used in the registration code (which is TWndClass in Delphi).

But note that *class* as a Windows term has only a limited relationship with the same term in object-oriented programming languages. Windows classes have a fixed number of fields and only one method (called the *window procedure*). This single method is used to respond to all of the messages sent by the system to the windows of that class. For this reason, the typical window procedure is made of a big case

20

statement, with a branch for each message you want to handle. (It is obvious that the object-oriented approach to Windows programming offered by Delphi and some C++ class libraries is far superior to the original C language approach.)

The class list in WinSight shows all of the classes defined in the system, including Windows system classes (some of which are completely undocumented, by the way). Most of the classes are registered by other running Windows applications. If you run a program you have written with Delphi, it registers some window classes, too.

> **NOTE** Borland engineers were smart enough to use an internal class name that is the same as the name of the Object Pascal class, such as TForm1 or TButton. I've mentioned this good choice because other programming environments use unbelievably complex names schemes.

In WinSight's class list pane, you can see the names of these classes, as shown in Figure 20.12. This figure includes the classes of the BREAKP example, presented at the beginning of this chapter. The name of the class is followed by the name of the executable file (or dynamic library) which has registered it, the address of the Windows procedure of that class, and some flags, or class styles. You can see a detailed description of these styles in the Windows API Help file included in Delphi, in the description of the TWndClass structure.

FIGURE 20.12:

The WinSight window indicates the four classes registered by the BREAKP example, and the details of one of them.

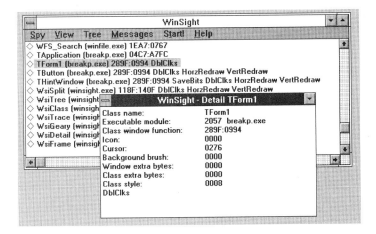

If you double-click on one of the lines in the class list, WinSight opens a Detail window (see Figure 20.12), with some more information, such as the icon and the cursor associated with the window, the brush used to paint its background, and other elements that are seldom of interest. The interesting fact is that Delphi bypassed some of the system information, so what you find here might be different from what you expect.

The Windows Tree: Parents and Children

The Window Tree view in WinSight contains a hierarchical tree of windows. The hierarchical view clarifies the relationship between parent and child windows, which is very important both in Windows and in Delphi (see the Parent and Controls properties).

An important feature of WinSight is that it also lists hidden windows and other windows that aren't visible (for example, windows reduced to a single pixel). You can also see windows completely covered by other windows, such as a panel covered by a notebook, and obtain some details about the internal structure of a program.

Of course, you can get the details of the structure of any Windows application, even the Delphi development environment or WinSight itself, but I'll show you a more interesting example.

In Figure 20.13, you can see the structure of the windows of the COMBOBAR application that we developed in Chapter 11, and also the output of this program, as a reminder. The first and most important thing to notice is that there are a number of components visible in the form (a panel with some speed buttons and other components and a caption covering the client area), and fewer windows in the hierarchy. Is this a flaw of WinSight? Not at all—it is a great technique used by Delphi.

The one component–one window rule, which is a native Windows programming rule, is not applied by Delphi, to our advantage. Windows 3.1 has a limit to the number of windows it can display, and an application with tons of components can severely hamper the behavior of the system. For some components, Delphi simply paints some lines on the screen instead of using a window. For example, speed buttons are painted, while other buttons are real windows. We'll discuss the Windows limits and Delphi's use of windowless components in more detail later in this chapter.

20

FIGURE 20.13:

An example of the windows tree displayed by WinSight for the COMBOBAR application (built in Chapter 11)

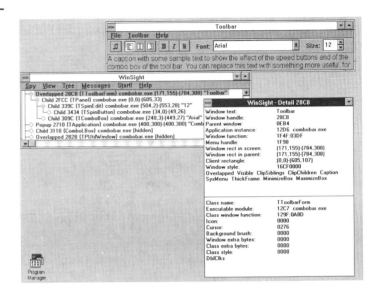

In Figure 20.13, you can see the information displayed by WinSight for each node of the window tree. First comes the kind of window: overlapped, pop-up, or child. Basically, child windows live within a parent window; overlapped and pop-up windows, even if they have a parent, take their pixels from the whole desktop. The different groups of window types also denote a different default behavior determined by the system.

After the kind of window comes the value of the handle, a number in hexadecimal format, such as 28C8. This value is a unique code that refers to the window, which the system uses to denote the window. Since this is the parameter of a number of Window API functions, the handle of a form or of a windowed component is available in Delphi as the Handle property, a run-time and read-only property. The value of the handle is determined by the system when the window is created.

> **NOTE**   Not all Handle properties of Delphi components refer to the handle of a window. There are also icon handles, bitmap handles, menu handles, and so on. Also, not all the other Handle properties are read-only.

Next is the name of the class, the name of the executable file, the position and the size of the window, and its title or caption. In the detailed view, you can also see the handle of the application (the one stored in the HInstance global variable discussed in Chapter 19), the handle of the menu, the window procedure associated with the window, the client rectangle, and the names of the flags that make up the window style. At the end are the details related to the class of the window, which we have already seen in the previous section.

If you are an expert Windows programmer, you might notice that the window procedure of the class and that of the window do not match. Each window uses the window procedure of its own class unless someone has changed this value for the window, a technique known as *subclassing* (although it has little to do with the definition of a subclass in Object Pascal terms).

Subclassing is used extensively in Delphi to let you specify the behavior of an object through event handlers. Windows procedures in Delphi elements are so hidden away in the system that you'll seldom notice them. This approach has many technical advantages. Technically, for all TWinControl and descendent classes, every object instance gets a unique window procedure address to bind to its window handle. Windows calls the window procedure of the window, and that window procedure takes you directly into the associated object instance.

Message Flow and Delphi Events

The main reason I started this analysis of WinSight was to spy (or to examine; *spy* is used in programming jargon, since the original program that allowed this operation was named Spy) the message flow of the Delphi applications. Now, after some digressions, we have reached this point.

To become an expert Delphi programmer, you must learn to study the message flow following an input action by a user. As you know, Delphi programs (like Windows applications in general) are event-driven. Code is executed in response to an event. Windows messages are the key element behind Delphi events, although there isn't a one-to-one correspondence between the two.

In Windows, there are many more messages than there are events in Delphi, but some Delphi events are higher level than Windows messages. For example, in the system, there is a limited support for mouse dragging, while Delphi components offer a full set of mouse-dragging events.

20

Of course, WinSight knows nothing about Delphi events, so that you must figure out the correspondence by yourself (or study the VCL source code, if you have it). WinSight can show you all of the Windows messages that reach a window, indicating the destination window, its title or class, and the parameters in a readable format. You can use the Options command on the Messages menu to filter out some of the messages, and see only the groups you are interested in.

Usually, for Delphi programmers, spying the message flow can be useful when you are faced with some bugs related to the order of windows activation and deactivation, or to receiving and losing the input focus (OnEnter and OnExit events), particularly when message boxes or other model windows are involved. This is quite a common area of problems, and you can often see why things went wrong by looking at the message flow.

You also might want to see the message flow when you want to handle a Windows message directly. You can get more information about when that message arrives and the parameters it carries (other than those parameters listed in the Help file).

A Look at Posted Messages

Another way to see the message flow is to trap some Windows messages directly in a Delphi application. If you limit this analysis to posted messages, excluding sent messages, it becomes almost trivial, since there is a specific event of the TApplication class we can use: the OnMessage event.

This event is intended to give the application a chance to filter all of the messages it receives, and to handle messages for specific windows. For example, you can use it to handle the messages for the window connected with the Application object itself, which has no specific event handlers.

In this example, however, we'll take a look at all of the messages extracted from the message queue of the application (that is, the posted messages). A description of each message is added to a list box covering the form of the example, beside a simple toolbar.

You can see the form of this example at design-time in Figure 20.14, and study the details in Listing 20.2. Notice in particular that I've chosen a fixed font (in this case a Courier font) for the list box, to have formatted output, and some speed buttons with text, to limit the number of windows.

To let you make some real tests, the program has a second form, filled with various kinds of components (chosen at random), used to see the message flow of a standard form. Figure 20.15 shows an example of the output of the MSGFLOW program when the second form is visible. This is the result of selecting the Show button.

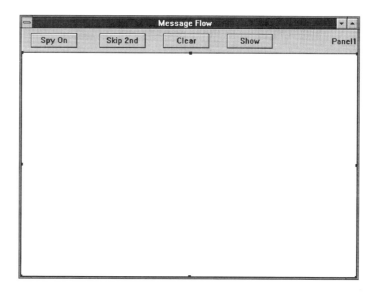

LISTING 20.2: The textual description of the main form of the MSGFLOW example

20

```
object Form1: TForm1
  Caption = 'Message Flow'
  OnCreate = FormCreate
  object ListBox1: TListBox
    Align = alClient
    Font.Color = clWindowText
    Font.Height = -13
    Font.Name = 'Courier New'
    Font.Style = [fsBold]
    ItemHeight = 16
  end
  object Panel1: TPanel
    Align = alTop
    Alignment = taRightJustify
    Caption = 'Panel1'
    TabOrder = 1
```

LISTING 20.2: The textual description of the main form of the MSGFLOW example (continued)

```
    object SpyButton: TSpeedButton
      AllowAllUp = True
      GroupIndex = 1
      Caption = 'Spy On'
      OnClick = SpyButtonClick
    end
    object SkipButton: TSpeedButton
      AllowAllUp = True
      GroupIndex = 2
      Caption = 'Skip 2nd'
      OnClick = SkipButtonClick
    end
    object ClearButton: TSpeedButton
      Caption = 'Clear'
      OnClick = ClearButtonClick
    end
    object ShowButton: TSpeedButton
      Caption = 'Show'
      OnClick = ShowButtonClick
    end
  end
end
```

The basic idea of this example is quite simple. Just define a handler for the OnMessage event of the application, such as:

```
procedure TForm1.HandleMessage (var Msg: TMsg;
  var Handled: Boolean);
```

and install it in the FormCreate event:

```
Application.OnMessage := HandleMessage;
```

In the code of the HandleMessage method, you can add a line to the list box for each message. The goal is to fetch some meaningful information. The parameter of the handler of the OnMessage event, in fact, is of the TMsg type. This is a collection of low-level information about the message, including the handle of the destination window, the code of the message, and some numeric parameters. This is actually the information Windows passes to the application. Instead of using the data directly, I've made it more readable in two ways.

First, the MSGFLOW program displays the caption of the window along with its handle. This caption is retrieved using a Windows API function, GetWindowText,

FIGURE 20.15:

The MSGFLOW program at run-time, with a copy of the second form

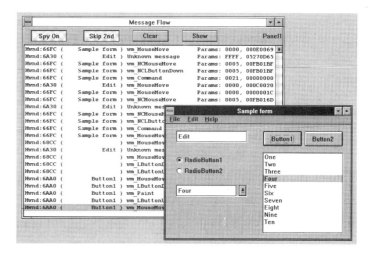

which works for any kind of window or component:

```
GetWindowText (Msg.Hwnd, Caption, Sizeof (Caption));
```

This text is formatted in a 15-character space, using Delphi's Format function:

```
Format ('%15s', [StrPas (Caption)]);
```

The second key improvement is the output of the name of the message, instead of its code. This is not so simple, because message names are not real strings, but names of constants defined in the MESSAGES.PAS system file. Here is an excerpt of this file, with the definition of the first few messages:

```
const
  wm_Null      = $0000;
  wm_Create    = $0001;
  wm_Destroy   = $0002;
  wm_Move      = $0003;
  wm_Size      = $0005;
  wm_Activate  = $0006;
  wm_SetFocus  = $0007;
  wm_KillFocus = $0008;
```

This information is important but not usable in our example. However, we can use this text, with some semiautomatic transformations (using search and replace techniques) in an associative list of strings.

The problem is that we cannot simply define an array, because not all of the possible message numbers actually correspond to a message. As an alternative, you might recall that the TStringList class has both strings and objects. Storing an object in a StringList means storing four bytes, so we might use a trick and add the message number instead of a real object. The code above, becomes:

```
var
  MsgList: TStringList;
...
  MsgList := TStringList.Create;
  MsgList.AddObject ('wm_Null        ', TObject($0000));
  MsgList.AddObject ('wm_Create      ', TObject($0001));
  MsgList.AddObject ('wm_Destroy     ', TObject($0002));
  MsgList.AddObject ('wm_Move        ', TObject($0003));
  MsgList.AddObject ('wm_Size        ', TObject($0005));
  MsgList.AddObject ('wm_Activate    ', TObject($0006));
  MsgList.AddObject ('wm_SetFocus    ', TObject($0007));
  MsgList.AddObject ('wm_KillFocus   ', TObject($0008));
```

This code (it's actually a couple of pages long) has been obtained by replacing the text *wm* with the text *MsgList.AddObject ('wm*, replacing the equal sign with the typecast code, and adding two parentheses at the end. The typecast used from a number to a TObject is really a dirty low-level trick, the kind of thing I usually hate; in this case, I could find no other simple solution to extract the strings from this list using the message number as the key.

NOTE   I've placed the code for this example in a separate source file, MLIST.PAS, on the companion disk. I did not include the listing in the book, because it is a long list of calls, all similar to the ones shown above.

Once this string list is ready, the code used to output the name of a message becomes simple, thanks to the IndexOfObject method:

```
N := MsgList.IndexOfObject (TObject(Msg.Message));
AppendStr (Line, MsgList.Strings [N])
```

You can see the complete Pascal source code of the code associated with the main form of the MSGFLOW example in Listing 20.3. Notice in particular that the description of a message is added to the list only if three conditions are satisfied:

- The Spying Boolean flag is set to True. A user of the program can easily toggle this Boolean value by clicking on the Spy On button, which behaves like a check box.

- The message is not a message for the list box, to avoid a recursive call (since adding a message to the list generates a new message).

- If the Skipping flag is enabled (by clicking on the Skip 2nd button in the toolbar), the message and its destination window should be different from those of the previous message. Mouse-move messages are often sent in series; with this flag only the first message of the series is shown.

LISTING 20.3: The complete source code of the FLOW_F.PAS file of the MSGFLOW example

```
unit Flow_f;

interface

uses
  SysUtils, WinTypes, WinProcs, Messages, Classes, Graphics,
  Controls, Forms, Dialogs, StdCtrls, Buttons, ExtCtrls,
  Mlist,            {define the string list of messages}
  Unit2;            {define the secondary form, TForm2}

type
  TForm1 = class(TForm)
    ListBox1: TListBox;
    Panel1: TPanel;
    SpyButton: TSpeedButton;
    SkipButton: TSpeedButton;
    ClearButton: TSpeedButton;
    ShowButton: TSpeedButton;
    procedure FormCreate(Sender: TObject);
    procedure SpyButtonClick(Sender: TObject);
    procedure SkipButtonClick(Sender: TObject);
    procedure ClearButtonClick(Sender: TObject);
    procedure ShowButtonClick(Sender: TObject);
  private
    Skipping, Spying: Boolean;
    LastMessage: TMsg;
  public
    procedure HandleMessage (var Msg: TMsg;
      var Handled: Boolean);
  end;
```

20

LISTING 20.3: The complete source code of the FLOW_F.PAS file of the MSGFLOW example (continued)

```
var
  Form1: TForm1;

implementation

{$R *.DFM}

procedure TForm1.FormCreate(Sender: TObject);
begin
  {set the OnMessage handler}
  Application.OnMessage := HandleMessage;
  Skipping := False;
  Spying := False;
end;

procedure TForm1.HandleMessage (var Msg: TMsg;
  var Handled: Boolean);
var
  Line: string;
  Caption: array [0..50] of char;
  FormattedCaption: string;
  N: Integer;
begin
  {output the new message only if the spying flag is true,
  the message is not for the list box. If the skipping flag
  is true, ignore a message equal to the previous one}
  if Spying and (Msg.Hwnd <> ListBox1.Handle) and not
    (Skipping and (LastMessage.Message = Msg.Message) and
    (LastMessage.Hwnd = Msg.Hwnd)) then
  begin
    {output the hexadecimal value of the handle}
    Line := 'Hwnd:' + IntToHex (Msg.Hwnd, 4);

    {get the caption from the handle, using an API function}
    GetWindowText (Msg.Hwnd, Caption, Sizeof (Caption));
    if Caption <> '' then
    begin
      {format the caption in 15 characters, after converting it}
      FormattedCaption := Format ('%15s', [StrPas (Caption)]);
      AppendStr (Line, ' (' + FormattedCaption + ' ) ');
    end;
    {access the MsgList object, using the code of the message
    as if it were an object, and reading the corresponding string}
    N := MsgList.IndexOfObject (TObject(Msg.Message));
    if N >= 0 then
      AppendStr (Line, MsgList.Strings [N])
    else
      {if the message is not in the list, use a default one}
      if Msg.Message >= wm_User then
        AppendStr (Line, 'wm_User message      ')
```

LISTING 20.3: The complete source code of the FLOW_F.PAS file of the
MSGFLOW example (continued)

```
      else
        AppendStr (Line, 'Unknown message        ');

    {add the hexadecimal output of the two message parameters}
    AppendStr (Line, 'Params: ' + IntToHex (Msg.wParam, 4) +
      ', ' + IntToHex (Msg.lParam, 8));

    {add the line, selecting it}
    ListBox1.ItemIndex := ListBox1.Items.Add (Line);

    {store the message, to compare it with the next one}
    LastMessage := Msg;
  end;
end;

procedure TForm1.SpyButtonClick(Sender: TObject);
begin
  Spying := SpyButton.Down;
end;

procedure TForm1.SkipButtonClick(Sender: TObject);
begin
  Skipping := SkipButton.Down;
end;

procedure TForm1.ClearButtonClick(Sender: TObject);
begin
  ListBox1.Clear;
end;

procedure TForm1.ShowButtonClick(Sender: TObject);
var
  SecondForm: TForm2;
begin
  {create and show the second form}
  SecondForm := TForm2.Create (Application);
  SecondForm.Show;
end;

end.
```

20

You can see another example of the output of this program in Figure 20.16. In this case, the second form isn't displayed, and the few messages relate to mouse actions on the border of the form (the *nc*, or non-client, messages), and on the panel or its buttons (which are speed buttons, so they are not windows by themselves). Notice

FIGURE 20.16:

An example of the output of MSGFLOW

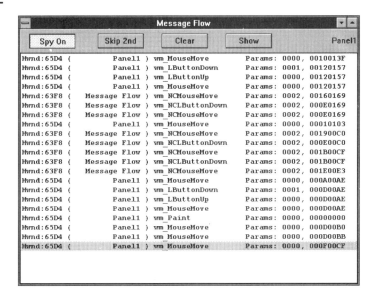

that you can see the caption of the panel window. I haven't removed it to improve the readability of the output of the messages related to this window (so that there wasn't a blank caption in the description of many messages).

The Memory Image of an Application

In Windows, memory is divided in chunks, called *segments*, limited by the system to 64 KB each. Each application has some segments for its compiled code, some segments for its resources, and some for its data.

To get information about the size of the different portions of the memory image of your application, you can use the Information command on Delphi's Compiler menu. The Information dialog box lists the size of the compiled code and of the global data, plus the size of the stack and the local heap, which depend on project settings. Figure 20.17 shows an example of this dialog box.

FIGURE 20.17:

The compilation information about
the MSGFLOW example

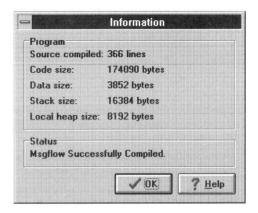

The Code and Resource Segments

The code segments of any programs or DLLs (Dynamic Link Libraries) in Windows are marked as discardable, meaning that the system can simply delete them when memory is low. This is possible because once these code segments have been discarded, they can be loaded again from the executable file. However, only one copy of the code segments of a program is loaded in memory, even if you run the same application a number of times.

Another typical behavior of code segments is that they are not all loaded at program startup. Some of them are loaded in memory later on, when they are required (this optional behavior is indicated as a *load-on-call*, or DEMANDLOAD).

In Delphi, you can change the attributes of code segments by using the $C compiler directive. The default is:

```
{$C MOVEABLE DEMANDLOAD DISCARDABLE}
```

Every unit ends up in a different code segment and can have different attributes, depending on its role. In most cases, however, the default behavior works well enough that you do not need to bother with these issues at all.

Besides the actual compiled code, the executable file also contains the definition of some resources, as icons, bitmaps, cursors, tables of strings, and so on. The segments with resources are similar to code segments, because they are loaded only

20

once, they are discardable, and they are loaded only on request. More precisely, resource segments define read-only data. The use of resources in a Delphi application is the topic of the next chapter.

The Data Segments

The most interesting segments of an application are the data segments, because they have a dynamic life during the execution of an application.

Basically, each Windows application has a single default data segment and an unlimited number of dynamic segments. All data segments are limited to 64 KB.

The default data segment (also known as the *automatic data segment*, or DGroup) contains the global data of an application, plus the area for the stack of the application and the area for a local heap. Figure 20.18 illustrates the structure of the default data segment. The rest of the system's memory is considered a global heap, where each program can allocate many more data segments.

FIGURE 20.18:

The structure of the default data segment of a Windows application

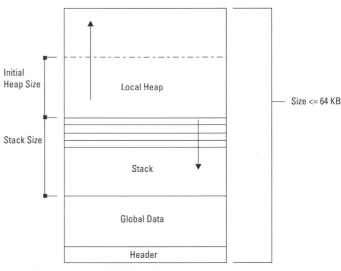

Default Data Segment

The size of the global data area depends on the global variables defined by your program and by the VCL. For a small project, you will end up with few kilobytes in this area. In Delphi, the common way to determine the size of your program's global data is through the Compiler Information dialog box. For example, the MSGFLOW example has 3852 bytes of global data, as you can see in the Information dialog box shown earlier in Figure 20.17. If this size reaches 30 to 35 KB, you can start worrying—and start trying to remove some global variables from your code.

The size of the stack and of the local heap are determined by the Linker page of the Project Options dialog box (or by equivalent compiler directives). The default values are 16,384 bytes (16 KB) for the stack and 8192 bytes (8 KB) for the local heap.

The stack is used for method calls. The local variables of a method and its parameters and return value (if it is a function) are stored on the stack temporarily. Even when you call a DLL, including system libraries, it uses the stack of the caller application. However, it is quite difficult to overcome the limitations of the default size used by Delphi. The real problem is that there is no easy way to know how much of the stack area is effectively used by a program, other than by using specific third-party tools.

The size indicated for the heap is only the initial size. The local heap of a Windows application can grow dynamically until the size of the entire default data segment reaches its limit of 64 KB. This is seldom a problem in Delphi, because the VCL does not use the local heap at all. Some local heap space is used by some Windows API functions and some Windows controls.

The heaps store all the dynamically allocated data, including the image of all Delphi objects. Windows allows you to use two different heaps: the small, but efficient, local heap and the large, but slightly less efficient, global heap. The real problem is that the global heap becomes inefficient when a program allocates a number of very small memory blocks. This can exhaust the global heap manager (which can handle 8192 blocks at most) long before the computer is out of memory.

NOTE   The 8192 selector limit is actually an Intel CPU hardware limit, not a Windows software limit. To overcome this limit, 32-bit operating systems generally increase the size of each memory block to 4 GB, so that each application will typically require only one segment.

To avoid the limits of the local heap and the problems of the global heap, and also allow you to use a uniform notation for every memory block, Delphi uses a powerful memory allocation scheme, known as *subsegment allocation*. Basically, Delphi's heap manager uses the global memory for all allocations. When a program must allocate a big object, it calls the `GlobalAlloc` Windows function directly. When a program allocates smaller objects, a single big block is used for a number of them.

You can even customize the behavior of the subsegment allocation algorithm by changing the value of some global variables defined by the System unit:

- HeapAllocFlags determines the attributes of the new memory block created with the `GlobalAlloc` API function when the heap manager needs more memory.

- HeapLimit indicates the threshold between small blocks allocated as subsegments and large heap blocks allocated by themselves. The default value is 1024 bytes (1 kilobyte).

- HeapBlock defines the size of each block used for subsegment allocation. The default value is 8192 bytes (8 KB).

Generally, there is no reason to change these values, unless you experience particular memory problems. However, it's easy to modify the behavior of the subsegment allocation algorithm if necessary.

Windows System Memory

Besides using some memory in its own data segments, a Windows application uses some system memory, too. Windows libraries, like any other DLL, have their own memory segments, which are limited to 64 KB each, of course. There are three key libraries in Windows: Kernel, User, and GDI (Graphics Device Interface).

Kernel Memory

The Kernel DLL uses a number of small global memory blocks to handle a task database and a module database (these structures are called *databases*, but they are actually linked lists of memory blocks). The module database has an entry for each executable file loaded in the system, including programs, dynamic libraries, system drivers, Visual Basic controls, and many other files in executable format. The module database entries basically store a copy of some header information of the executable file, to speed up loading of segments.

The task database has an entry for each running application, with duplicated entries if a program is running several instances at the same time. The task database entries store low-level system information about the running application, such as its message queue, an area to save the CPU registers for swapping purposes, and so on.

Since kernel memory is made of a number of small chunks allocated in the global heap, it has virtually no limit.

NOTE The task database contains different information than the output of Windows Task Manager, which simply lists the main windows in the system. We will see how to build a real task list later in this chapter.

User and GDI Heaps

The User DLL is based on some heaps that store information about windows and menus. In particular, it uses a heap that has an entry for each window class and each window in the system. This causes one of the biggest problems in Windows 3.1 memory handling. By creating a number of windows, you can rapidly exhaust this system space, bringing the whole system to a halt.

Fortunately, Delphi offers you a number of ways to reduce the number of windows used within an application. As we have already seen, not all Delphi components are actual windows. Using windowless components, you can save some vital memory space in the User heap. Examples of windowless components are the SpeedButton, Image, and Label components, but there are many others. Since all the windowless components are subclasses of TGraphicsControl, you can easily find them by looking at the VCL components hierarchy (see Chapter 6).

The user heap can fill up quite quickly, but it has at least one advantage. When you exit from an application, all the windows it has created are destroyed automatically, freeing this memory space. This doesn't happen in GDI heaps.

20

The GDI DLL stores information about graphic objects, such as pens, brushes, fonts, bitmaps, and so on. Each time you create such an object, you must take care in deleting it. If you don't delete the graphic object, this system memory won't be released, not even after the application terminates.

Even though GDI objects are usually much smaller than the window structures in the User heap, a poorly written program might create and forget to destroy a number of these small GDI objects. If you consider that a form's OnPaint event is called hundreds of times, you can understand that even a small memory leak repeated hundreds of times can be troublesome. Again, when the GDI heap area is filled up, Windows cannot work any more. In this case, even terminating the faulty application won't help. You need to exit from the system.

Free System Resources

The GDI and User heaps are known as system *resources*. This is an unfortunate name, because the term *resources* is also used in Windows to denote graphical portions (and other elements) of a program included in its executable file, as discussed in the previous sections. The two uses of the term *resource* have nothing in common at all.

Windows users are familiar with the use of the term to describe the heaps, because the standard About box of all Windows applications (including the Program Manager) shows the percentage of free system resources. (By the way, we used this same About box in the SHABOUT example in Chapter 12.) You can check the system About box occasionally to make sure you're not running out of system resources.

Another way to check the status of the GDI and User resources is by using one of the many resource-monitoring tools available or to write your own resource-monitoring program. Building a resource-monitoring program in Delphi is simple, because the Windows API includes a function to access this information. The FSR (for free system resources) program is an example. You can see its form in Figure 20.19.

The FSR form has two gauges (with pie charts), two labels to describe them, and a timer. It is much better to update the value of the system resources from time to time (hence the need for a timer) instead of asking the user to click a button or select a menu command to see the new value. Listing 20.4 shows the description of the components used in the example.

FIGURE 20.19:
The form of the FSR example at design-time

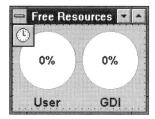

LISTING 20.4: The textual description of the main form of the FSR example

```
object FSRForm: TFSRForm
  BorderIcons = [biSystemMenu, biMinimize]
  BorderStyle = bsSingle
  Caption = 'Free Resources'
  FormStyle = fsStayOnTop
  OnCreate = FormCreate
  object UserLabel: TLabel
    Alignment = taCenter
    Caption = 'User'
    Font.Color = clWindowText
    Font.Height = -15
    Font.Name = 'Arial'
    Font.Style = [fsBold]
  end
  object GdiLabel: TLabel
    Alignment = taCenter
    AutoSize = False
    Caption = 'GDI'
    {... same font of UserLabel ...}
  end
  object UserGauge: TGauge
    Kind = gkPie
    Font.Color = clBlack
    Font.Height = -15
    Font.Name = 'Arial'
    Font.Style = [fsBold]
    BorderStyle = bsNone
    ForeColor = clLime
    Progress = 0
  end
  object GdiGauge: TGauge
    Kind = gkPie
    {... same font of UserGauge ...}
    BorderStyle = bsNone
    ForeColor = clLime
    Progress = 0
  end
end
```

20

LISTING 20.4: The textual description of the main form of the FSR example (continued)

```
  object Timer1: TTimer
    OnTimer = Timer1Timer
  end
end
```

The only method of this form is the handler of the OnTimer event of the Timer component. In this procedure (shown in Listing 20.5), we access the three system values returned by the Windows API function `GetFreeSystemResources`. This function returns the percentage of free space in the two system heaps (using the parameters `gfsr_UserResources` and `gfsr_GdiResources`), or the lowest of the two values (with `gfsr_SystemResources`). Notice that the higher the percentage, the better the situation. You should begin to worry when the free system resources fall below 20 percent.

LISTING 20.5: The source code of the FSR example

```
unit Resform;

interface

uses
  SysUtils, WinTypes, WinProcs, Messages, Classes,
  Graphics, Controls, Forms, Dialogs, ExtCtrls,
  Gauges, StdCtrls;

type
  TFSRForm = class(TForm)
    UserGauge: TGauge;
    GdiGauge: TGauge;
    UserLabel: TLabel;
    GdiLabel: TLabel;
    Timer1: TTimer;
    procedure Timer1Timer(Sender: TObject);
    procedure FormCreate(Sender: TObject);
  private
    { Private declarations }
  public
    { Public declarations }
  end;
```

LISTING 20.5: The source code of the FSR example (continued)

```
var
  FSRForm: TFSRForm;

implementation

{$R *.DFM}

procedure TFSRForm.Timer1Timer(Sender: TObject);
var
  Text: string;
begin
  {set the value of the two gauges and of the caption}
  UserGauge.Progress :=
    GetFreeSystemResources (GFSR_USERRESOURCES);
  GdiGauge.Progress :=
    GetFreeSystemResources (GFSR_GDIRESOURCES);
  FSRForm.Caption := 'FSR = ' + IntToStr (
    GetFreeSystemResources (GFSR_SYSTEMRESOURCES)) + '%';

  {copy the caption to the application title, i.e., the icon}
  Application.Title := FSRForm.Caption;

  {if value is too low, turn color to red}
  if (UserGauge.Progress < 20) then
    UserGauge.ForeColor := clRed
  else
    UserGauge.ForeColor := clLime;
  if (GdiGauge.Progress < 20) then
    GdiGauge.ForeColor := clRed
  else
    GdiGauge.ForeColor := clLime;
end;

procedure TFSRForm.FormCreate(Sender: TObject);
begin
  {set the topmost attribute for the minimized window}
  SetWindowPos (Application.Handle, Hwnd_TopMost,
    0, 0, 0, 0, swp_NoSize or swp_NoMove);
  {update the output ASAP}
  Timer1Timer (self);
end;

end.
```

20

The two specific values for the User heap and the GDI heap are used to set the two gauges. The total value of free system resources is used to change the caption for the form. You can see an example of the output of this program in Figure 20.20.

FIGURE 20.20:

An example of the output of the FSR example

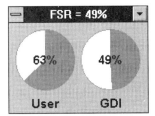

The program also copies the caption to the application title, displayed when the form has been minimized. A user might glance at the icon to get an overall indication, and open the form for the details.

The FSR example uses a topmost form. To make the minimized application topmost, too, I used the SetWindowPos API function, with the handle of the application window as a parameter:

```
SetWindowPos (Application.Handle, Hwnd_TopMost, 0, 0, 0, 0,
  swp_NoSize or swp_NoMove);
```

The form and the icon always remain at the top, although you can easily improve the program by adding a menu command to toggle this attribute on and off (as in the TOP and TOP2 examples in Chapter 9).

When the value of the free system resources becomes too low, the program turns the gauge of the heap that is almost filled to red. You might further improve the program by sounding a beep or by restoring the form to its normal size, to inform the user of the dangerous situation. Another interesting improvement would be to use the icon surface to paint some information. How can we do this in Delphi? I'll show you in the next chapter.

A New Task Manager

Another tool that might be useful to explore the current status of Windows is a real Task Manager. As mentioned earlier, the Windows Task Manager lists the main windows present in the system, and they do not always have a one-to-one correspondence with tasks. An application can have more than a main window, and a program can run without even creating a window (although this is somewhat rare). What is more common is to write a program that does not terminate correctly. It remains in memory even if its main form has been destroyed.

Our next example, called TASKLIST, is an extremely simple example that lists all of the tasks in the system. It has no commands to activate a window or destroy a task, and it doesn't include the graphical output (including the icon of the program) that you might find in similar tools. The TASKLIST application is just a viewer.

The form of the TASKLIST example has a dialog box border and contains a list box with a big font. You can see the output of the program in Figure 20.21. Its code is quite simple, too, and makes extensive use of the functions of the Tool Helper system library.

FIGURE 20.21:
The output of the TASKLIST example

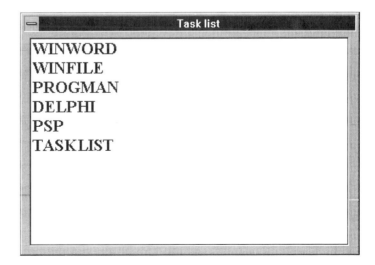

20

The TOOLHELP.DLL has several functions used to explore each of the system Windows structures (the global heap, the task database, the class list, the module database, the stack of an application, and so on). It defines a TTaskEntry data structure, which has a lot of information about a task, extracted by the entries in the task database.

To use this data structure, you need to fill in its dwSize field, which indicates the size of the structure, but is actually used to pass version information. (A future version of the TOOLHELP.DLL might deliver more information, but still recognize the size of the structures defined by older versions.)

Once this is done, you can walk through the system task list by calling the Task-First and TaskNext functions, which both fill the task-entry structure. The TaskNext function is called inside a while loop until it returns False, meaning that the last task in the list has been reached.

The name of the module, present in the TTaskEntry structure, is added to the list box as is. This is probably far from perfect. For example, if you run a DOS session, the module name WINOLDAP is used, as you can see in Figure 20.22. You might also want to remove the TASKLIST itself from the list, since this is not particularly useful information.

FIGURE 20.22:

Another example of the output of the TASKLIST example, when two DOS sessions and several applications are running

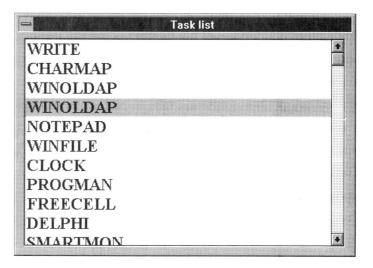

The code of the Activate method (see Listing 20.6) is executed at startup, because of the handler of the form's OnActivate event, and each time the application becomes active, because it is also used as the handler of the OnActivate event of the Application object. Contrary to what the Delphi documentation leads you to believe, in some cases, setting an event handler for the Application object in the OnCreate event of the main form is already too late. This is a good example. The Activate method would not be executed at startup if it were not related to the OnActivate event of the form, or if you didn't call it directly in the FormCreate method.

Summary

In this chapter, we have seen that there are a number of approaches you can use to explore a compiled program or a running application, both by itself and as a whole in the Windows system.

Windows applications do not live in a world by themselves. They have a strong relationship with the system and, usually less directly, with the other applications that are running. The presence of other running Windows applications can affect the performance of your programs, as well as their stability.

In Windows 3.1, there is absolutely no protection between applications. Everyone can access each memory area, regardless of its owner. Every application can use the handle of any window, even if it was created by another program. For this reason, I felt that it was worth spending some time for an overview of Windows memory handling, both at the application level and at the system level.

There is only one concept that we have not discussed yet—the role of resources within an application. I have not mentioned this topic in Chapter 19, which covered the Application object, or in this chapter's discussion of the memory structure of an application for a simple reason: resources are the topic of the next chapter.

20

CHAPTER

TWENTY-ONE

Using Resources

- Delphi's Image editor

- How to load Windows resources

- Icons for minimized forms

- Alternative icons for status changes

- Predefined and custom cursors

- String tables for language translations

As we saw in the previous chapter, the executable files of a Windows application can include special data, known as *resources*. The resources of a Windows program generally include icons, bitmaps, and cursors, which are graphical resources. They can also include lists of strings, templates used to build menus and dialog boxes, and other elements.

Most Delphi applications use resources, since they have at least an icon. And, as we have seen in earlier examples, you can add a bitmap to the resource file of an application, so that you don't need to ship it in a separate file.

This chapter provides an overview of the use of resources in Windows and in Delphi, and includes some interesting examples.

Resources in Windows

In Chapter 20. we discussed the role of resources in Windows from a memory perspective. We have seen that resources are stored in separate blocks in the executable file of an application, that these blocks are loaded in memory on demand and are discardable, and that resource memory segments can be considered as read-only data segments. However, we have still not seen what these resources are. Table 21.1 provides a comprehensive list of Windows resources.

Before looking at special uses of resources in Delphi, let's take a look at the tools you can use to prepare resources. Delphi includes an Image editor for bitmap, icon, and cursor manipulation, but in some cases, you might prefer to use a full resource editor, such as Borland's Resource Workshop (which is not included in Delphi).

Using Resource Editors

You can activate Delphi's Image editor by using one of the default commands on the Tools menu or by adding a new icon to the Delphi group in the Program Manager. The Image editor lets you handle four kinds of files. Three are for specific resources (ICO, CUR, and BMP), and one is for resource files (RES), which can contain all three kinds of graphical resources. A compiled resource file can contain any kind of resources (besides the graphical ones) and is included in Delphi using the $R compiler directives (as discussed later in this chapter).

TABLE 21.1: Types of Windows Resources

Resource	Description
Icons	Small bitmaps, generally 32 × 32 pixels, with a limited set of colors. Used mainly for the minimized windows, but also for other purposes (as in the Program Manager).
Cursors	Small bitmaps, generally 32 × 32, which use only four colors (black, white, transparent, and reverse). Used to indicated the position of the mouse cursor on the screen. Delphi supports a set of predefined cursors, but you can add your own cursors, too.
Menu Templates	Define the structure of a menu. They are not used in Delphi applications.
Dialog Box Templates	Define the structure of a dialog box. They are not used in Delphi applications.
Bitmaps	Define general-purpose bitmaps. Delphi has no direct support for bitmap resources, but you can load a bitmap from the resources instead of from a file.
Fonts	Define new fonts within a single program. Custom font resources are seldom used in Windows. More often, new fonts are installed in the system.
String Tables	Collections of strings, which are placed in resources for flexibility and efficiency, and to solve translation problems. Delphi does not directly support string tables, but they can be useful in some situations.
Accelerator Tables	List the shortcut keys of menu commands. They are not used in Delphi applications.
Version Information	A special resource used to indicate the version and author of a program. This is particularly important for DLLs, in which version handling can become real trouble. Version information has no direct support in Delphi.
Custom Resources	Resources in user-defined formats. Although you'll seldom define your own custom resources, Delphi uses a custom resource format for the binary description of forms.

In the Image editor, you can prepare any kind of icon, cursor, or bitmap. For icons, you can provide a number of images for different screen resolutions, as shown in Figure 21.1. Notice that a single icon can contain all these images, not just one. For cursors, you can set the *hot-spot* position, which is the actual pixel indicated by the cursor.

FIGURE 21.1:

Delphi's Image editor, with the different kinds of images you can define for an icon

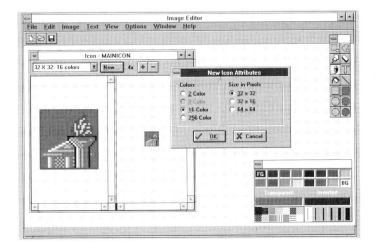

There are basically two ways to use the Image editor:

- Prepare specific files (particularly bitmaps and icons) to be loaded in the Delphi environment.

- Prepare a number of big resource files, and load the resources in the code, using Windows API calls.

When you work with resource files, a tabbed notebook lets you see a list of elements of each group, as in the example shown in Figure 21.2.

The Image editor is a functional tool, but its capabilities are somewhat limited. When you need a full-fledged resource editor, you can use Borland's Resource Workshop (or another resource editor). The Resource Workshop lets you open and edit any resource file. You can also use this tool to extract the resources from a compiled program, a DLL, a VBX, and any other file in executable format (this doesn't mean that it is always legal to do so).

If you open a Delphi application with the Resource Workshop, you will discover that it actually contains a series of resources, besides the icon present in its RES file. By default, a Delphi executable file contains a string table with system messages, captions, and other generic strings (such as the names of the months), binary data describing the form in the custom RCDATA format, some cursors, and one icon.

Figure 21.3 shows the list of resources for the TASKLIST example from Chapter 20. And this is just an example of a simple program. More complex programs may have many more resources, depending on the number of forms, the system units you include, the icons and bitmaps you add to the project, and so on.

FIGURE 21.2:

A list of bitmaps included in a resource file (from the MINES example in Chapter 10)

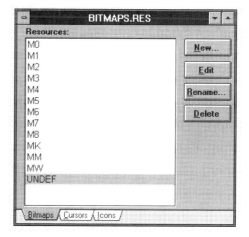

FIGURE 21.3:

The list of resources of a compiled Delphi application in the Resource Workshop (from the TASKLIST example in Chapter 20)

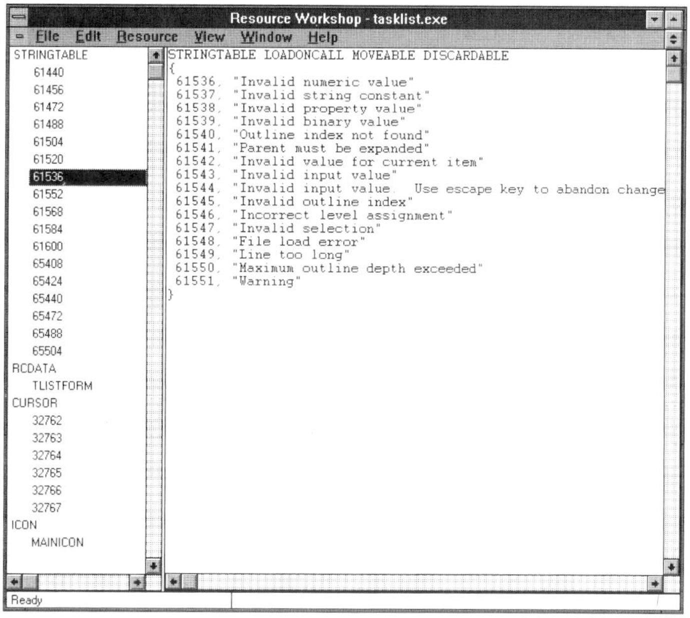

Loading Resources in Delphi

As I've mentioned above, there are basically two ways to define resources and load them in Delphi: by loading them in a property or manually, by defining your own custom resource file.

Loading an Icon or Bitmap in a Property

The simplest approach is to load an icon or a bitmap in a property. For example, you can place an Image component in the background of a dialog box, and load a bitmap into it. Figure 21.4 shows an example of a program, named BACKBMP, that uses a bitmap as a background. In this case, the bitmap is included in the resources of the application. This means that you do not need to ship the original BMP file. (In the example, the original BMP file is in the Delphi Image library, stored by default in the C:\DELPHI\IMAGE subdirectory.)

FIGURE 21.4:

An example of a program (BACKBMP) using a bitmap as background

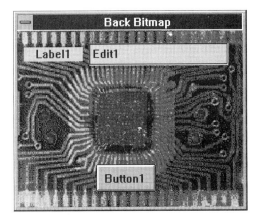

However, in BACKBMP and similar examples, the image is not added to the executable file as a stand-alone bitmap resource. It is included in the binary description of the form. The advantage of this approach is that no one can easily open a resource editor to steal your bitmap. The disadvantage is that it is difficult to make custom operations on that bitmap (such as by loading it separately from the form in which it is defined).

The same happens for the icons you connect to a form or to an application. Icons, however, are placed in the source file in a readable format, to let applications such as the Program Manager extract them and use them as a hint for the user.

The Manual Approach to Loading Resources

The second technique you can use to access resources in Delphi is the manual approach. For this method, you need to define a custom resource file to load any kind of resources. The second step is to include the resource file in the project, with the $R compiler directive.

Contrary to the typical C/C++ approach, Delphi projects can have a number of resource files. Don't customize the default resource file—the one that has the same name as the project—because sometimes Delphi changes that file, and you might lose your customizations. Simply add other RES files to the current directory, and add a compiler directive to load them.

For example, in the MINES example of Chapter 10 (see Figure 21.2 shown earlier), I've added the following code to the implementation portion of the form:

```
{$R BITMAPS.RES}
```

If you open the Pascal source code of the MINES example on the companion disk, or look at its listing in the book (in Chapter 10), you will notice that the statement above follows another similar statement. The code is:

```
{$R *.DFM}
{$R BITMAPS.RES}
```

These two lines look suspiciously similar. The first loads a resource file named as the Pascal file, with the DFM extension. In this compiler directive, in fact, the star doesn't mean "any file," but rather "the file with the same name as the current one." This also shows that Delphi-compiled form files are used by the environment as custom resources.

Once you have defined some resources and included them in your application, you can use the Windows API functions to load resources:

- `LoadAccelerators`
- `LoadBitmap`

- LoadCursor

- LoadIcon

- LoadMenu

- LoadResource

- LoadString

Each of these functions loads the corresponding resource. The exception is Load-Resource, which is used for custom resources. The first parameter of these functions is the handle of the instance of the application, which in Delphi is stored in the HInstance global variable.

The second parameter is the name of the resource. Of course, each application can have a number of icons, bitmaps, and other resources, and you use the name to access each of them. The LoadString function has some other parameters to specify the buffer in which to copy the string and the size of this buffer.

All the other loading functions simply return a handle as the result. You can assign this handle directly to the corresponding VCL object, as in:

```
StrPCopy (Name, 'M' + Code);
Bmp.Handle := LoadBitmap (HInstance, Name);
```

In this code, Name is a character array (a null-terminated string), and Bmp is an object of the class TBitmap. This code is actually extracted from the source of the MINES example I've mentioned before. Study that example and its description in Chapter 10 to see how you can place a number of bitmaps in the resources of an application and the advantages of using this approach.

Since we have placed bitmaps in the resources of this and other applications in previous examples (including the WORLD2 example in Chapter 10, which loaded a series of bitmaps from the resources into an array), we won't build other examples now. Instead, we'll focus on the use of icons, cursors, and string tables.

The Icons for Applications and Forms

21

In Delphi, each form has its own Icon property. You can use this property to specify the icon of the form when it is minimized. When this property is not set, the program uses the value of the Icon property of the Application object by default. You can see and change this default icon through the Application page of the Project Options dialog box.

Icons for Minimized Forms

The most common use of an icon is to provide a bitmap for the minimized form. This icon represents the minimized form, but we have already seen that the application window, not the form window, is used for the minimized application. So it might be surprising to find that if you set both the main form's icon and that of the application, Delphi uses the icon of the form for the minimized window. And when no icon is set in either property, the program uses a white rectangle as the icon. All these cases are demonstrated by a sample program I've written, called ICONS. You can see the form of this example at design-time in Figure 21.5.

The form contains two labels, two panels with two images inside, and four buttons below. It also has a bevel to separate the two areas, and an OpenDialog component. You can see the textual description of this form in Listing 21.1.

FIGURE 21.5:

The form of the ICONS example at design-time

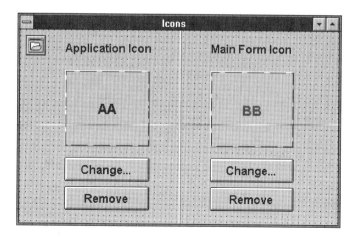

LISTING 21.1: The textual description of the form of the ICONS example

```
object Form1: TForm1
  Caption = 'Icons'
  Font.Color = clWindowText
  Font.Height = -16
  Font.Name = 'Arial'
  Font.Style = [fsBold]
  Icon.Data = {... this is file BB.ICO ...}
  TextHeight = 19
  object Label1: TLabel
    Caption = 'Application Icon'
  end
  object Label2: TLabel
    Caption = 'Main Form Icon'
  end
  object Bevel1: TBevel
    Left = 227
    Top = 0
    Width = 3
    Height = 267
    Style = bsRaised
  end
  object Panel1: TPanel
    object Image1: TImage
      Align = alClient
      Center = True
      Picture.Data = {... this is file AA.ICO ...}
    end
  end
  object Panel2: TPanel
    object Image2: TImage
      Align = alClient
      Center = True
      Picture.Data = {... this is file BB.ICO ...}
    end
  end
  object Button1: TButton
    Caption = 'Change...'
    OnClick = Button1Click
  end
  object Button2: TButton
    Caption = 'Change...'
    OnClick = Button2Click
  end
  object Button3: TButton
    Caption = 'Remove'
    OnClick = Button3Click
  end
  object Button4: TButton
    Caption = 'Remove'
    OnClick = Button4Click
  end
```

LISTING 21.1: The textual description of the form of the ICONS example (continued)

```
object OpenDialog1: TOpenDialog
  Filter = 'Icon (*.ico)|*.ico'
  Options = [ofPathMustExist, ofFileMustExist]
end
end
```

Notice that I've defined the Icon property of the form (using the BB.ICO file), as well as that of the application (using the AA.ICO file), as indicated in the two Image components in Figure 21.5. I prepared the two icon files before using the Image editor.

Each time you click on one of the Change buttons, a new icon is loaded from an external file:

```
procedure TForm1.Button1Click(Sender: TObject);
begin
  with OpenDialog1 do
    if Execute then
    begin
      Application.Icon.LoadFromFile (Filename);
      Image1.Picture.LoadFromFile (Filename);
    end;
end;
```

When one of the two Remove buttons is pressed, the corresponding icon is simply removed:

```
procedure TForm1.Button3Click(Sender: TObject);
begin
  Application.Icon := nil;
  Image1.Picture := nil;
end;
```

You can use this program to see how the two icon properties affect the icon of the minimized application. Some examples are shown in Figure 21.6, including the blank icon used when both properties are set to nil.

If you add the ICONS application to a group in the Program Manager, it will automatically use the application icon, and not the icon of the main form. This is because the icon of the form is hidden inside the custom resources describing the form, while the icon of the application is saved as an icon resource. You can see this by

FIGURE 21.6:

Some of the effects of the ICONS application

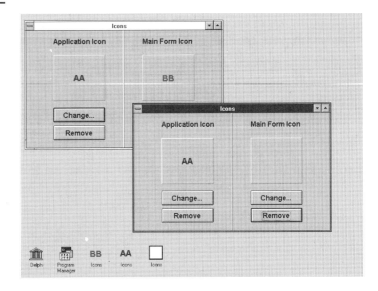

using the Resource Workshop to examine the executable program, or more easily by using Windows Program Manager, as follows:

1. Open the Program Manager.

2. Add an item for the ICONS example.

3. Open its Properties dialog box, click on the Change Icon button, and enter the name of the executable file (if it is not already selected).

You'll see all of the icons present in the program (in this case, the application icon *AA*).

Adding Alternative Icons for Different Conditions

In the ICONS example, you can change the icon of an application by loading it from an external file. This approach has two disadvantages:

- You need to ship the icon files with your program.

- Loading an external file tends to be slightly slower (although, in this case, it won't make much difference).

21

However, there is also an advantage: users can load any icon file they have on their computers.

A technique you may find useful is to add icons to the resources of an application and use them as alternative icons for the program. There are many Windows applications that use different icons to alert the user that the status of the program has changed. For example, mail applications often have an empty mailbox icon and a full mailbox icon. Another common use is in resource-monitoring programs, as in the FSR (free system resources) example we built in Chapter 20.

In the FSR example, the title of the application changes to show the current level of resource usage, and a gauge turns red when the usage reaches a dangerous level. An improvement would be to have the icon change when the color changes. The next example, named FSR2, uses two simple icons representing a green and a red gauge, as you can see in Figure 21.7. These two icons are part of a new resource file, named REDGREEN.RES, created with the Image editor.

The first problem is to figure out how to load the green icon as the icon of the application. Even if the icon is present in the resource file, and the resource file is included in the code, there is no way to use one of these icons as the application icon

FIGURE 21.7:

The two icons used by the FSR2 example

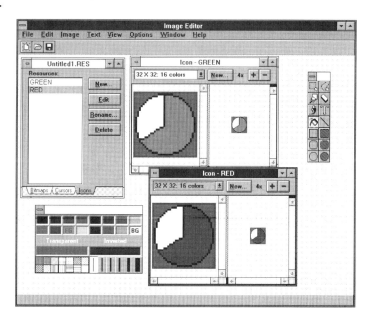

at design-time. To set the icon at design-time, we would need to create an icon file, extracting it from the resource file and copying it to the other file.

The other approach is to do this at run-time. In the FormCreate method, we can write:

```
Application.Icon.Handle :=
    LoadIcon (HInstance, 'GREEN');
```

The only drawback is that the first icon of the program is Delphi's default icon.

The FSR2 example uses the run-time approach. When we add this application to a group in the Program Manager, we can easily change the icon to any one of the three that are available, as you can see in Figure 21.8.

FIGURE 21.8:

The FSR2 example has three icons that can be used by the Program Manager

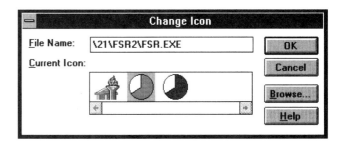

The form of the FSR2 example is the same as the previous version, but its code has a number of changes.

When the free percentage of one of the two heaps goes below the warning threshold (20 percent), the program changes the color of the gauge and also changes the icon of the application, forcing it to repaint with a call to the `InvalidateRect` API function.

This code, and the opposite one restoring the green, is executed only if the color was green. If the gauge was already red, the code is skipped to avoid flickering, and to avoid repeating the warning signal each time.

The structure of this code is quite complex, because it includes three nested `if` statements, as you can see in the complete source code of this application, shown in Listing 21.2. Run the program, load some huge applications, and watch the gauge and the icon turn to red.

LISTING 21.2: The source code of the FSR2 example

```
unit Resform;

interface

uses
  SysUtils, WinTypes, WinProcs, Messages, Classes,
  Graphics, Controls, Forms, Dialogs, ExtCtrls, Gauges,
  StdCtrls;

type
  TFSRForm = class(TForm)
    UserGauge: TGauge;
    GdiGauge: TGauge;
    UserLabel: TLabel;
    GdiLabel: TLabel;
    Timer1: TTimer;
    procedure Timer1Timer(Sender: TObject);
    procedure FormCreate(Sender: TObject);
  private
    UserRed, GdiRed: Boolean;
  public
    { Public declarations }
  end;

var
  FSRForm: TFSRForm;

implementation

{$R *.DFM}
{$R REDGREEN.RES}

procedure TFSRForm.Timer1Timer(Sender: TObject);
var
  Text: string;

begin
  {set the value of the two gauges and of the caption}
  UserGauge.Progress :=
    GetFreeSystemResources (gfsr_UserResources);
  GdiGauge.Progress :=
    GetFreeSystemResources (gfsr_GdiResources);
  FSRForm.Caption := 'FSR = ' + IntToStr (
    GetFreeSystemResources (gfsr_SystemResources)) + '%';

  {copy the caption to the application title, i.e., the icon}
  Application.Title := FSRForm.Caption;

  {if value is too low, turn color to red}
  if (UserGauge.Progress < 20) then
```

LISTING 21.2: The source code of the FSR2 example (continued)

```
begin
  {if it was not already red}
  if not UserRed then
  begin
    {transition from green to red}
    MessageBeep ($FFFF);
    UserGauge.ForeColor := clRed;
    Application.Icon.Handle :=
      LoadIcon (HInstance, 'RED');
    InvalidateRect (Application.Handle, nil, True);
    UserRed := True;
  end
end
else
  {if it was red and now the value is over 20 percent}
  if UserRed then
  begin
    {transition from red to green}
    UserGauge.ForeColor := clLime;
    Application.Icon.Handle :=
      LoadIcon (HInstance, 'GREEN');
    InvalidateRect (Application.Handle, nil, True);
    UserRed := False;
  end;

if (GdiGauge.Progress < 20) then
begin
  {if it was not already red}
  if not GdiRed then
  begin
    {transition from green to red}
    MessageBeep ($FFFF);
    GdiGauge.ForeColor := clRed;
    Application.Icon.Handle :=
      LoadIcon (HInstance, 'RED');
    InvalidateRect (Application.Handle, nil, True);
    GdiRed := True;
  end
end
else
  {if it was red and now the value is over 20 percent}
  if GdiRed then
  begin
    {transition from red to green}
    GdiGauge.ForeColor := clLime;
    Application.Icon.Handle :=
      LoadIcon (HInstance, 'GREEN');
    InvalidateRect (Application.Handle, nil, True);
    GdiRed := False;
  end;
end;
```

LISTING 21.2: The source code of the FSR2 example (continued)

21

```
procedure TFSRForm.FormCreate(Sender: TObject);
begin
  {set the topmost attribute for the minimized window}
  SetWindowPos (Application.Handle, Hwnd_TopMost, 0, 0, 0, 0,
    swp_NoSize or swp_NoMove);
  {update the output ASAP}
  Timer1Timer (self);
  UserRed := False;
  GdiRed := False;
  Application.Icon.Handle :=
    LoadIcon (HInstance, 'GREEN');
end;

end.
```

Painting to an Icon

The FSR2 example is an improvement over the first version, which had a fixed default icon. An alternative solution is to actually paint the output with the current situation in the icon. Instead of painting the two pie gauges, the next version paints two small, rectangular indicators, using green or red as appropriate.

WARNING Painting on an icon is quite common in Windows 3.1, but will be banned in Windows 95. The new version of the operating environment uses icons in many ways, few of which will work correctly if the icon image of the application changes dynamically. Therefore, this technique won't be portable to Windows 95.

Painting on an icon in Delphi brings up a number of problems. You need to handle the OnPaint event of the application, which is not directly available. A good solution is to filter all of the posted messages in the OnMessage handler of the application, and perform the proper painting actions in the case of the wm_Paint message.

The second big problem is that the application window does not have a Canvas property. However, we can create a temporary canvas, and initialize it using some API painting functions. As you might have already guessed, the code of the third version of the free system resources example (FSR3) is quite complex, and it has a number of calls to Windows API functions.

Basically, the FormCreate method sets the new handler for the OnMessage event:

```
Application.OnMessage := AppMessages;
```

This AppMessages method checks for a complex condition to see if the message is wm_Paint, if it is aimed at the application window, and if the application window is minimized. If these three conditions are met, the program executes three key statements to initialize the canvas and set its handle to the return value of the BeginPaint function:

```
HdcPaint := BeginPaint (Application.Handle, Ps);
AppCanvas := TCanvas.Create;
AppCanvas.Handle := HdcPaint;
```

From now on, the program can use the canvas object as usual, setting colors and calling output methods, as you can see in Listing 21.3. Two examples of its output, in normal and critical conditions, are shown in Figure 21.9.

LISTING 21.3: The source code of the FSR3 example

```
unit Resform;

interface

uses
  SysUtils, WinTypes, WinProcs, Messages, Classes,
  Graphics, Controls, Forms, Dialogs, ExtCtrls, Gauges,
  StdCtrls;

type
  TFSRForm = class(TForm)
    UserGauge: TGauge;
    GdiGauge: TGauge;
    UserLabel: TLabel;
    GdiLabel: TLabel;
    Timer1: TTimer;
    procedure Timer1Timer(Sender: TObject);
    procedure FormCreate(Sender: TObject);
    procedure FormClick(Sender: TObject);
  private
    { Private declarations }
  public
    { Public declarations }
    procedure AppMessages (var Msg: TMsg;
      var Handled: Boolean);
  end;
```

LISTING 21.3: The source code of the FSR3 example (continued)

```
var
  FSRForm: TFSRForm;

implementation

{$R *.DFM}

procedure TFSRForm.Timer1Timer(Sender: TObject);
var
  Text: string;

begin
  {set the value of the two gauges and of the caption}
  UserGauge.Progress :=
    GetFreeSystemResources (gfsr_UserResources);
  GdiGauge.Progress :=
    GetFreeSystemResources (gfsr_GdiResources);
  FSRForm.Caption := 'FSR = ' + IntToStr (
    GetFreeSystemResources (gfsr_SystemResources)) + '%';

  {copy the caption to the application title, i.e., the icon}
  Application.Title := FSRForm.Caption;

  {if value is too low, turn color to red}
  if (UserGauge.Progress < 20) then
    UserGauge.ForeColor := clRed
  else
    UserGauge.ForeColor := clLime;
  if (GdiGauge.Progress < 20) then
    GdiGauge.ForeColor := clRed
  else
    GdiGauge.ForeColor := clLime;

  {repaints the icon if the application is minimized}
  if IsIconic (Application.Handle) then
    InvalidateRect (Application.Handle, nil, True);
end;

procedure TFSRForm.FormCreate(Sender: TObject);
begin
  {set the topmost attribute for the minimized window}
  SetWindowPos (Application.Handle, Hwnd_TopMost, 0, 0, 0, 0,
    swp_NoSize or swp_NoMove);
  {update the output ASAP}
  Timer1Timer (self);

  Application.OnMessage := AppMessages;
end;

procedure TFSRForm.AppMessages (var Msg: TMsg;
    var Handled: Boolean);
```

LISTING 21.3: The source code of the FSR3 example (continued)

```
var
  HdcPaint: HDC;
  Ps: TPaintStruct;
  AppCanvas: TCanvas;
begin
  {in case of painting message for the minimized
  application window}
  if (Msg.Message = wm_Paint) and
    (Msg.Hwnd = Application.Handle) and
    IsIconic (Application.Handle) then
  begin
    {create a canvas for the application window}
    HdcPaint := BeginPaint (Application.Handle, Ps);
    AppCanvas := TCanvas.Create;
    AppCanvas.Handle := HdcPaint;

    {paint the first bar}
    AppCanvas.Brush.Color := clWhite;
    AppCanvas.Rectangle (1, 1, 100 div 3, 13);
    if (GetFreeSystemResources (gfsr_UserResources) < 20) then
      AppCanvas.Brush.Color := clRed
    else
      AppCanvas.Brush.Color := clLime;
    AppCanvas.Rectangle (1, 1,
      GetFreeSystemResources (gfsr_UserResources) div 3, 13);

    {paint the second bar}
    AppCanvas.Brush.Color := clWhite;
    AppCanvas.Rectangle (1, 18, 100 div 3, 30);
    if (GetFreeSystemResources (gfsr_GdiResources) < 20) then
      AppCanvas.Brush.Color := clRed
    else
      AppCanvas.Brush.Color := clLime;
    AppCanvas.Rectangle (1, 18,
      GetFreeSystemResources (gfsr_GdiResources) div 3, 30);

    {terminate the painting process}
    EndPaint (Application.Handle, Ps);
    AppCanvas.Free;

    {message is handled}
    Handled := True;
  end;
end;

procedure TFSRForm.FormClick(Sender: TObject);
begin
  MessageDlg ('Free System Resources (FSR)' +
    Chr(13) + 'from the book "Mastering Delphi"' +
    Chr(13) + 'by Marco Cantù',
    mtInformation, [mbOk], 0);
```

LISTING 21.3: The source code of the FSR3 example (continued)

```
{restore the topmost property of the form
and of the application window}
SetWindowPos (Handle, Hwnd_TopMost,
  0, 0, 0, 0, swp_NoSize or swp_NoMove);
SetWindowPos (Application.Handle, Hwnd_TopMost,
  0, 0, 0, 0, swp_NoSize or swp_NoMove);
end;

end.
```

FIGURE 21.9:

Two examples of the painted icon of the FSR3 example (the icons are stretched to be more visible)

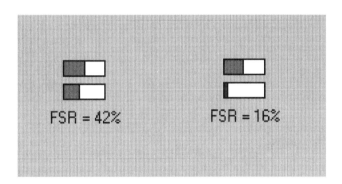

You only need to remember to destroy the items you have initialized by hand, which are the canvas and the device context handle it refers to:

```
EndPaint (Application.Handle, Ps);
AppCanvas.Free;
```

The only other key element is to ask the program to repaint the icon each time the timer elapses and the application in minimized. This code has been added to the Timer1Timer method:

```
if IsIconic (Application.Handle) then
    InvalidateRect (Application.Handle, nil, True);
```

Both `IsIconic` and `InvalidateRect` are two API functions, which have names that describe their meanings quite well.

Last, I've added a sort of About box, which is activated each time a user clicks on the form. The interesting thing to notice here is that by calling the usual MessageDlg function, Delphi disables the Topmost property of the form and of the application, and does not restore them. To take care of this, I've added calls to the `SetWindowPos` function to reset the Topmost attribute (see the TOP2 example in Chapter 9 for a detailed description of this technique).

Although the application is responsible for painting the application, you should set the Icon property of the application properly. In fact, when you drag a minimized window, an icon is required by the system (you cannot paint the icon while you are moving it). In this case, Windows sends a special message, `wm_QueryDragIcon`, to the application, and Delphi returns the icon of the application. To be more precise, Windows later turns this icon into a cursor, which means that it is turned into a black-and-white bitmap. If you drag the icon of any Windows application, it turns to black and white and the cursor seems to disappear; the icon is actually used as a cursor.

NOTE I did not comment these API calls in detail, because they are very complex. If you've never written Windows programs using direct API calls, you might not understand their details. But since Delphi hides these types of details from you 99 percent of the time, and you should use Delphi code whenever possible, it isn't that important if the code of this example is not perfectly clear. The key concepts of Windows painting and device context are discussed in Chapter 9, and you can find further details in Delphi's API Help files.

Now that we have explored the use of icons, including painting on an icon, we can move to a different type of resource: cursors.

Using the Cursor in Delphi

Delphi's support for cursors is extensive, so it takes much less work to customize cursors. Delphi also includes a number of predefined cursors. Some of them are Windows default cursors, and others are added by Delphi. Table 21.2 shows the

Windows predefined cursors, and Table 21.3 shows other standard Delphi cursors. Together, the two tables include all of Delphi's predefined cursors, both borrowed from Windows and new. (Note that the Delphi Help file has information similar to that shown in Tables 21.2 and 21.3, but some of the cursors are missing, and some of the images are not correct.)

TABLE 21.2: Windows Predefined Cursors

Value in Delphi	Cursor
crDefault	⌖
crArrow	⌖
crCross	+
crBeam	I
crHourglass	⌛
crUpArrow	⇧
crSize	✥
crSizeNESW	⤢
crSizeNS	⇕
crSizeNSWE	⤡
crSizeWE	⇔

TABLE 21.3: Delphi Predefined Cursors (Excluding the Windows Predefined Cursors)

Value in Delphi	Cursor
crDrag	
crMultiDrag	
crNoDrop	
crHSplit	
crVSplit	
crSqlWait	

The use of these cursors is straightforward. Simply select the corresponding value for the Cursor or DragCursor property of a component. If you need to set a global cursor for the whole application for a certain amount of time, you can use the Cursor property of the Screen component. This is also the common approach to set the wait cursor (the hourglass) for the application while a long task is executing, as in the BACKPROC example in Chapter 19:

```
Screen.Cursor := crHourglass;
{... time-consuming code ... }
Screen.Cursor := crDefault;
```

Actually a safer way to write this code is:

```
Screen.Cursor := crHourglass;
try
  {... time-consuming code ... }
finally
  Screen.Cursor := crDefault;
```

With this code, if something goes wrong in the execution of the time-consuming code, the default cursor is restored.

The Cursor property of the form and other components and the Cursor property of the Screen object are both of type TCursor. If you look up the definition of this data

21

type in Delphi's help, you are in for a surprise. TCursor is not a class, but simply an integer type.

Technically speaking, this value is an integer referring to an array of cursor handles, stored in the Cursors property (notice the final *s* in *Cursors*) of the Screen object. This array can also be used to add a new cursor to an application, loading it from its resources.

Designing a Custom Cursor

Our next example, named MYCUR, demonstrates how to add a custom cursor to a program, as well as how to use the Cursors property of the Screen object in general. This example uses a new resource file, which contains a new hand cursor, as shown in Figure 21.10. The figure also shows the Hot Spot dialog box for the cursor. When you create a new cursor, always remember to set its hot-spot, the single pixel of the cursor indicating the exact mouse position.

If you are not an artist, you can browse through the collection of cursors available in the Delphi Image Library (located by default in the C:\DELPHI\IMAGES\CUR-SORS directory).

FIGURE 21.10:

Preparing a resource file with a custom cursor with the Image editor

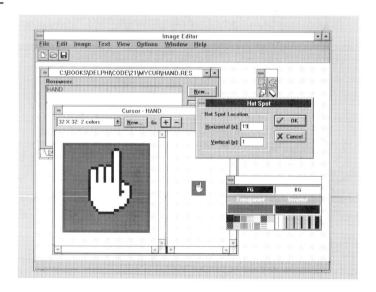

This resource file, named HAND.RES, is included in the source code of the example, which is based on the form shown in Figure 21.11. This form has two panels, a label, and a combo box with a list of available cursors, as you can see in Listing 21.4.

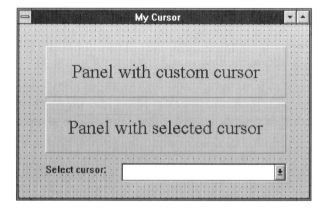

LISTING 21.4: The textual description of the form of the MYCUR example

```
object Form1: TForm1
  Caption = 'My Cursor'
  OnCreate = FormCreate
  object Label1: TLabel
    Caption = 'Select cursor:'
  end
  object Panel1: TPanel
    Caption = 'Panel with custom cursor'
    Font.Height = -27
    Font.Name = 'Times New Roman'
  end
  object Panel2: TPanel
    Caption = 'Panel with selected cursor'
    Font.Height = -27
    Font.Name = 'Times New Roman'
  end
  object ComboBox1: TComboBox
    Style = csDropDownList
    Items.Strings = (
      'crHand (custom cursor)'
      'crDefault'
      'crNone'
      'crArrow'
      'crCross'
```

LISTING 21.4: The textual description of the form of the MYCUR example (continued)

```
        'crIBeam'
        'crSize'
        'crSizeNESW'
        'crSizeNS'
        'crSizeNWSE'
        'crSizeWE'
        'crUpArrow'
        'crHourGlass'
        'crDrag'
        'crNoDrop'
        'crHSplit'
        'crVSplit'
        'crMultiDrag'
        'crSQLWait')
    OnChange = ComboBox1Change
  end
end
```

When the program starts, in the FormCreate method, the custom cursor is loaded from the resources, using the LoadCursor API function:

```
Screen.Cursors [crHand] := LoadCursor (HInstance, 'HAND');
```

This cursor is stored in the Cursors array, using a custom identifier, defined as:

```
const
  crHand = 1;
```

By using positive values, you can avoid overwriting existing cursors, which start from 0 and go backward (we will get to cursor numbering soon). Once the new cursor has been loaded, it can be used like any other cursor:

```
Panel1.Cursor := crHand;
```

Just two lines of code do the trick. The selection of a cursor for the second panel, made with the combo box, is even simpler—a single line of code:

```
procedure TForm1.ComboBox1Change(Sender: TObject);
begin
  {select the cursor corresponding to the selected item}
  Panel2.Cursor := 1 - ComboBox1.ItemIndex;
end;
```

But how can you select an item in a list box as a cursor?

As I mentioned before, the Cursors property of the Screen object is an array that has a cursor handle for each entry. The TCursor type used for the Cursor property is actually an integer. This integer is used by Delphi as the index of the Cursors property to fetch the cursor handle. So when you write:

```
Form1.Cursor := crArrow;
```

The code is actually translated as:

```
Form1.Cursor := -3;
```

This is exactly what we have done for the custom cursor; we've defined a constant and used it as if it were a cursor. With this idea in mind, we can go back to the strange statement above. The trick is that I've added to the combo box some lines in the same order as the corresponding constants. Or better, in the reverse order, because default Delphi cursors have negative values, ranging from 0 up to −17. Since I've added the custom cursor at the beginning of the list, the first item in the list box (with ItemIndex 0) corresponds to cursor 1, the second (with ItemIndex 1) to cursor 0, the third (with ItemIndex 2) to cursor −1, and so on.

WARNING   The Delphi Help file lists the values for all of the cursor constants, but some of them are wrong, and one is missing (at least in the first shipped version). Their order (the reverse order, I mean) is correct, but some numerical values are mistakenly repeated.

A Flexible Cursor

In the MYCUR example discussed in the previous section, you can choose a `crNone` cursor, which isn't listed in the Object Inspector as a proper value for the Cursor property. This is reasonable, because when you select this value, the cursor disappears, at least when you move over the corresponding component.

This is a Windows behavior that allows you to define different cursors for some areas of a form. In fact, if a form or a component does not have a cursor, you can set it manually in a method related to the `wm_SetCursor` message.

The FLEXCUR example shows how this can be done. The form of this application is covered by an empty Image component. This offers us a canvas connected to a memory bitmap, so that the image we build is saved in memory, and the surface of the window can be automatically repainted. You can see the description of this form in Listing 21.5. Notice that the Image component is not aligned with the whole client area, but leaves a thin empty border. We will soon see why this border is needed.

LISTING 21.5: The textual description of the form of the FLEXCUR example

```
object Form1: TForm1
  BorderStyle = bsSingle
  Caption = 'Flex Cursor'
  ClientHeight = 273
  ClientWidth = 427
  Ctl3D = False
  Color = clWhite
  OnCreate = FormCreate
  object Image1: TImage
    Left = 2
    Top = 2
    Width = 423
    Height = 269
    OnMouseDown = Image1MouseDown
    OnMouseMove = Image1MouseMove
  end
end
```

What is the goal of this example, besides demonstrating the use of a flexible cursor? It can be described as a circle painter, with erasing capability. You can click on the Image component to paint a small black circle (but you can easily choose a different color). You can also click on a pixel inside an existing circle to erase it. The difference between the two actions is highlighted by the use of two different cursors; that is, the cursor changes depending on the color of the pixel the mouse is moving over.

To accomplish this, the program sets the cursor of the form to crNone, and has a handler for the Windows wm_SetCursor message (as you can see in Listing 21.6). Inside this handler, we perform two different tests. First, we need to check if the mouse is over the client area or over the borders. This can be done using the Hit-Test parameter to the message, and looking for the htClient value, which means that the cursor is over the client area. (For a list of the HitTest codes, see the Windows API Help file, under the wm_NCHitTest message.)

When the mouse pointer is over non-client areas, the message handler of the parent class is invoked, to have the default behavior for Delphi forms. This call takes place using the inherited keyword.

LISTING 21.6: The full source code of the FLEXCUR example

```
unit Flex_f;

interface

uses
  SysUtils, WinTypes, WinProcs, Messages, Classes,
  Graphics, Controls, Forms, Dialogs, ExtCtrls;

type
  TForm1 = class(TForm)
    Image1: TImage;
    procedure Image1MouseDown(Sender: TObject;
      Button: TMouseButton;
      Shift: TShiftState; X, Y: Integer);
    procedure FormCreate(Sender: TObject);
  public
    procedure WmSetCursor (var Msg: TWMSetCursor);
      message wm_SetCursor;
  end;

var
  Form1: TForm1;

implementation

{$R *.DFM}

procedure TForm1.Image1MouseDown(Sender: TObject;
  Button: TMouseButton;
  Shift: TShiftState; X, Y: Integer);
begin
  if Image1.Canvas.Pixels [X, Y] = clWhite then
  begin
    {paint a black circle}
    Image1.Canvas.Pen.Color := clBlack;
    Image1.Canvas.Brush.Color := clBlack;
    Image1.Canvas.Ellipse (X-15, Y-15, X+15, Y+15);
  end
  else
  begin
    {erases the contiguous black pixels}
    Image1.Canvas.Brush.Color := clWhite;
    Image1.Canvas.FloodFill (X, Y, clWhite, fsBorder);
  end;
end;

procedure TForm1.FormCreate(Sender: TObject);
begin
  Cursor := crNone;
end;
```

LISTING 21.6: The full source code of the FLEXCUR example (continued)

21

```
procedure TForm1.WmSetCursor (var Msg: TWMSetCursor);
var
  CurPos: TPoint;
begin
  {get the position of the cursor,
  and convert it to client coordinates}
  GetCursorPos (CurPos);
  CurPos := Image1.ScreenToClient (CurPos);
  if Msg.HitTest = htClient then
    if Image1.Canvas.Pixels [CurPos.X, CurPos.Y] = clWhite then
      {if the pixel is white}
      SetCursor (Screen.Cursors [crCross])
    else
      {if the pixel is black}
      SetCursor (Screen.Cursors [crSize])
  else
    {if the mouse is outside the client area}
    inherited;
  Msg.Result := 1;
end;

end.
```

If the cursor is over the client area, we need to check the color of the current pixel. Since this message has no coordinate parameters, I've added a call to the `GetCursorPos` API procedure, which returns the value in screen coordinates. The program then transforms the point in coordinates of the Image component, and uses it to check the color of the corresponding pixel, using the Pixels array of the Canvas property of the Image component.

NOTE   The `wm_SetCursor` message reaches a window each time the mouse changes its position over the window. This is what makes the program work. By default, Delphi uses the cursor of the form or component at the mouse position. But you can easily change this default. A simpler approach is to use the OnMouseMove handler, but in this case, the cursor will flicker, because the system will try to use the default cursor (`crNone`) before you change it.

Depending on the result of the color test, the SetCursor function of the Windows API is called, passing as a parameter the handle of the cursor, not its code. To transform the Delphi constant into a handle, use the Cursors property of the Screen:

```
SetCursor (Screen.Cursors [crCross])
```

The program uses a cross cursor for the white surface and the crMove cursor for the black pixels. Here, the move cursor is actually used as a visual hint for the flood-fill operation performed to erase the colored area. This erases not just the single circle, but also the contiguous ones, as you can see in the two consecutive images shown in Figure 21.12.

When the pixel the user has clicked onto is already black, the following FloodFill method is called inside the Image1MouseDown handler in place of the default Ellipse method:

```
Image1.Canvas.FloodFill (X, Y, clWhite, fsBorder);
```

FIGURE 21.12:

The FloodFill method used in the FLEXCUR example erases a group of circles at a time, as you can see by comparing the two images. The bottom screenshot was taken after a single click was made. Notice also the two cursors, added to reproduce run-time behavior.

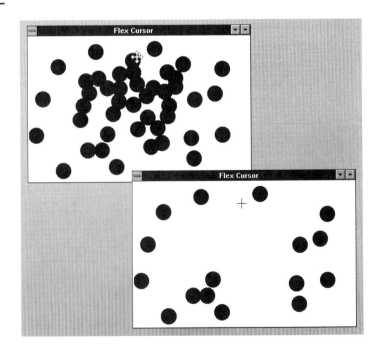

21

The FloodFill method is used, in this case, to fill all of the surface until a white border is found. We could have also used it with the reverse parameters; that is, filling all the contiguous black area:

```
Image1.Canvas.FloodFill (X, Y, clBlack, fsSurface);
```

In both cases, we face the risk of also filling the back border of the form, for a circle too close to it. This is the reason for the two-pixel gap between the form and the Image component.

Going back to the WmSetCursor method, notice the last line, used to set a return value for the message handler:

```
Msg.Result := 1;
```

Return values are seldom used in Windows messages, but when they are needed, if you don't set them properly, you might face real problems. In this case, for example, we need to tell Windows that we have already set the cursor, so the system should not bother setting a default one.

Using String Table Resources

The third kind of resources we will explore in this chapter are string table resources. Although there is almost no support for these resources in Delphi, I thought it was a good idea to show you a simple example of their use, because string tables traditionally play an important role in Windows programming.

There are two main reasons to use string tables instead of hard-coding strings in a program. The first is memory usage. Strings use memory of your application directly, while string tables are loaded in separate, demand-loaded, discardable memory blocks.

The second reason is localization, or translation of a program into another language (such as English to German). When you localize a Windows application written with API calls, you typically translate the text included in the resources and bind the new version to the compiled code.

In Delphi, the process is similar. It involves mainly translating the textual description of form files (DFM). However, the program usually needs to display messages to the user. Instead of hard-coding these messages using Object Pascal strings, you can use string tables. This makes your program as easy to localize as a traditional one that calls only Windows API functions.

This is exactly what happens in the next example, named STRINGT. You can see the form of this application in Figure 21.13. It has two areas, marked by two bevels. One area has a button, and the other has a button and a spin edit control (with its label).

FIGURE 21.13:
The form of the STRINGT example at design-time

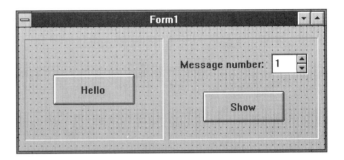

The textual description of this form is extremely simple, because the key to the example is in another file—a resource file. This is a text file with some resource statements, documented in the Windows API Help file. In Listing 21.7, you can see the text of the S_TABLE.RC file (RC is the typical extension of a resource-description file).

LISTING 21.7: The text of the S_TABLE.RC resource file

```
STRINGTABLE
BEGIN
  1, "Hello"
  2, "String Table Test"
  11, "First message"
  12, "Second message"
  13, "Third message"
  14, "Fourth message"
  15, "Fifth message"
  16, "Sixth message"
  17, "Seventh message"
  18, "Eighth message"
  19, "Ninth message"
  20, "Tenth message"
END
```

For the definition of a string table resource, you need the corresponding resource statement (STRINGTABLE) and a list of identifiers followed by strings (the comma separator is optional). Note that the strings must be in C-language format—they must use double quotation marks instead of the Pascal single quotation marks. However, the indicators at the beginning and end of the resource can be either the Pascal ones, shown in the listing, or the C brackets, { and }.

WARNING A string table can have up to 64 thousand strings of 255 characters each. Note, however, that Delphi uses several strings, so you should be careful to avoid duplicate entries. Delphi string identifiers start over 61000; any lower value shouldn't create any problems.

Once you have written this file, you need to compile it into a RES file, the only kind of resource file you can include directly in a Delphi project. This is easier than you might expect, because Delphi includes a full-scale resource compiler, although it is a DOS tool. Simply start a DOS session, move to the subdirectory with the project files, and issue the following command:

```
C:\DELPHI\BIN\BRC -R S_TABLE.RC
```

Of course, if you have installed Delphi in a different directory, your DOS command should be adjusted. BRC is the Borland Resource Compiler, and the R flag serves to compile the resources to a RES file, without trying to link them to an executable file.

Once this resource file has been generated, we can include it in the code, as usual:

```
{$R S_TABLE.RES}
```

Then we can actually start writing the code of our program, using the strings of Listing 21.7. When the Hello button of the form is pressed, you can load the first string and display it. The API function is LoadString, which has as its third parameter a buffer for a zero-terminated string. The return value of the function indicates the number of characters that have been loaded, or 0 in case of an error (for example, if the string has not been found). For this reason, we can test the return value:

```
procedure TForm1.HelloButtonClick(Sender: TObject);
var
  Text: array [0..255] of Char;
  N: Integer;
```

```
begin
  N := LoadString (HInstance, 1, Text, SizeOf (Text));
  if N > 0 then
    ShowMessage (StrPas (Text));
end;
```

This code works, but it is quite complex. As an alternative, we can use Delphi's LoadStr function, which loads a string from the resources directly into a Pascal string. This is the second version of the same method:

```
procedure TForm1.HelloButtonClick(Sender: TObject);
var
  StrMsg: string;
begin
  StrMsg := LoadStr (1);
  if StrMsg <> '' then
    ShowMessage (StrMsg);
end;
```

There is a second function used to load strings in Delphi, FmtLoadStr, which uses the string table string as the format template for the given data parameters. It is a mix of the LoadStr and the Format functions.

We can call LoadStr again to change the title of the window (and of the minimized window), using the second string:

```
procedure TForm1.FormCreate(Sender: TObject);
var
  StrTitle: string;
begin
  StrTitle := LoadStr (2);
  if StrTitle <> '' then
  begin
    Caption := StrTitle;
    Application.Title := StrTitle;
  end;
end;
```

The code of the Show button is only slightly more complex. Instead of displaying a fixed string, it uses the value of the spin edit box to determine the string to use in the range of 10 to 20:

```
procedure TForm1.ShowButtonClick(Sender: TObject);
var
  StrMsg: string;
```

```
begin
  StrMsg := LoadStr (10 + SpinEdit1.Value);
  if StrMsg <> '' then
    ShowMessage (StrMsg);
end;
```

Figure 21.14 shows an example of the output when the Show button is pressed.

FIGURE 21.14:

The output of the STRINGT example when the Show button is pressed

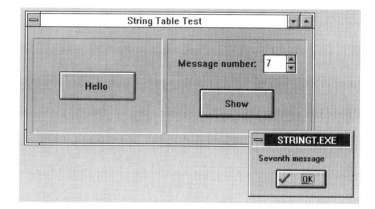

This highlights another traditional use of strings. In the code above, we refer to a group of strings, but it is quite simple to add new entries to the string table, and let the program display the new strings without any change to the source code.

Translating the Strings into Another Language

The program we have written works fine, but its real advantage over a program that uses hard-coded strings is that now we can easily localize the application. Simply give the RC file to a translator and compile the file you receive back with the resource compiler. If the file has a different name, you can replace the file name in the compiler directive used to include the resources and rebuild the program. That's all. (You might even skip this minor name change by using the same name or by merging the resources with the external resource compiler.)

For this localization, I first translated the string into another language (my actual first choice, Italian). You can see the result in Listing 21.8.

LISTING 21.8: The translated version of the resource file, S_TAB_IT.RC

```
STRINGTABLE
BEGIN
   1, "Ciao"
   2, "Prova Tabella Stringhe"
  11, "Primo messaggio"
  12, "Secondo messaggio"
  13, "Terzo messaggio"
  14, "Quarto messaggio"
  15, "Quinto messaggio"
  16, "Sesto messaggio"
  17, "Settimo messaggio"
  18, "Ottavo messaggio"
  19, "Nono messaggio"
  20, "Decimo messaggio"
END
```

Then I recompiled the resource file and changed a line of the source code to:

```
{$R S_TAB_IT.RES}
```

By recompiling and running this program, the title of the form and the messages are now in Italian, as you can see in Figure 21.15. The two figures correspond to the same action, but the output changes.

FIGURE 21.15:

The output of the Italian version of the STRINGT example

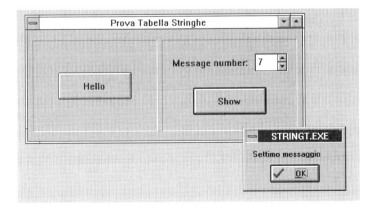

The program, however, is not completely localized. The Delphi portion (the textual description of the form) should be translated, too, to correct the names of the two buttons. To accomplish this, you can load the textual description of the form into the Delphi editor, and translate all of the strings, such as captions and list items. Do not change the internal identifiers, such as the value of the Name property.

I've performed this operation, and saved the new version of the form description in the file STRI_F_I.DFM. This file is loaded with the statement:

```
{$R *.DFM}
```

To fully localize the program, replace this line with:

```
{$R STRI_F_I.DFM}
```

Now both the captions and the messages are in Italian, but we use the same source file for the code of the program. To see the final output, run the Italian version of the executable file, stored on the companion disk as STRING_I.EXE, or rebuild the application following the directions described in the preceding paragraphs.

In a complex program, after this step, you also need to translate the Delphi system strings, such as those you can find in VCL source files (for example, CONST.RC or DBCONSTS.RC). This will complete the program localization.

There is also another approach to creating multilingual programs. You can prepare several different groups of strings, one for each language, using a standard numbering schema. For example, English strings might start from 1, French strings from 10001, German strings from 20001, and so on.

Now each time you need to load a string (say string 235), you can write:

```
MyText := LoadStr (nLanguage * 10000 + 235);
```

In this case, nLanguage is a code corresponding to the language (0 for English, 1 for French, 2 for German, and so on). Then you can add a dialog box to let the user change the language at run-time, setting a new code.

The last thing to consider is that referring to the string by number in the source code is a good way to make it almost unreadable. For this reason, you should define a number of constants corresponding to each string, and use the constant instead of the numeric code.

Summary

In this chapter, we have seen some details about the role, definition, and use of Windows resources. Like many other visual programming environments, Delphi lets you build most of the elements of an application graphically, making use of custom techniques instead of relying on Windows resources.

At times, however, resources have a role. We have seen in previous chapters some examples of loading a bitmap from the resources of an application, and in this chapter, how you can load an icon and a cursor, too.

We have also explored the only kind of non-graphical resources that might be useful in Delphi: string tables. However, building string tables using plain text files is so simple that we can use string tables quite easily even without specific support from the environment.

This chapter ends this section of the book, which has been devoted to the Application object, applications in general, memory, debugging, and resources. With the next chapter, we start exploring other advanced topics that have plenty of specific support in Delphi.

TWENTY-TWO

Adding Printing Capabilities to Delphi Applications

- Standard and custom dialog boxes

- Graphics printing

- Print preview functions

- Text printing

- Database form printing

- The ReportSmith run-time engine and application

Although we have explored many different Delphi programming topics up to now, including some advanced techniques, there are some important topics that have still not been covered. One of these topics is printing, which is the subject of this chapter. Another topic, using files, is covered in the next chapter. Following chapters will explore data exchange between applications.

Some of these capabilities are present even in the most simple real-life programs, such as the ones we've built in previous chapters. Many of the examples in this chapter and the following ones are improved versions of earlier examples, with support for these important capabilities.

This chapter covers two different printing-related topics. The first part discusses form printing, including text and graphics. The second part is about report printing. Delphi provides plenty of support for both of these printing areas, so adding these features to existing programs is easy to do.

Printing a Whole Form

Printing a form in Delphi at run-time is fairly simple. The TForm class has a Print method, which prints the whole form. Calling this method is all that is required. For example, we might add a Print button to a form, and write this code:

```
procedure TForm1.PrintButtonClick (Sender: TObject);
begin
  Print;
end;
```

The effect of this code is to use the current printer, and output a bitmap corresponding to the client area of the form; that is, the form without its border.

To determine the actual output, before you call the Print method, you can set a proper value for the PrintScale property of the form. By default, this property has the value poProportional. This means that the output will conform to the image on the screen, using the PixelPerInch ratio. For example, if the form width is half of the screen, the output will take half of the printed page.

There are two other possible values for this property: poNone and poPrintToFit. With poNone, no scaling is used. Because of the higher pixel-per-inch capability of printers, the resulting image will generally be quite small. If you use the po-PrintToFit parameter, the output will be stretched to fill the whole page, but without changing the horizontal and vertical proportions.

With poPrintToFit as the PrintScale property of the form, you typically get much bigger images. However, since the bitmap corresponding to the form is stretched for the printed image, the output quality decreases as the image size increases. Better print quality is usually obtained with the poNone value.

A Custom Print Dialog Box

Although Delphi has a specific component encapsulating the standard Windows Print dialog box, I've decided not to use it. Instead, I've built a simple custom dialog box, which lets you choose one of the three values of the PrintScale property. You can see the design-time form of this dialog box in Figure 22.1 and its textual description in Listing 22.1.

FIGURE 22.1:

The form of the Print dialog box of the COMBO2 example at design-time

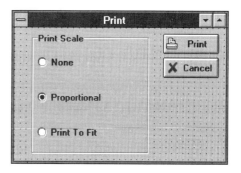

I've added this Print dialog box to an example in Chapter 11, COMBOBAR. The name of the new version is COMBO2. You can see the main form of this example at run-time in Figure 22.2. I've added a Print command to the File menu, and changed the background color of the label that covers the client area of the form (but not its toolbar) to white.

LISTING 22.1: The textual description of the dialog box for the COMBO2 example

```
object PrintDlg: TPrintDlg
  ActiveControl = OKBtn
  BorderStyle = bsDialog
  Caption = 'Print'
  Font.Color = clBlack
  Font.Height = -11
  Font.Name = 'MS Sans Serif'
  Font.Style = [fsBold]
  Position = poScreenCenter
  TextHeight = 13
  object OKBtn: TBitBtn
    Caption = 'Print'
    Default = True
    ModalResult = 1
    Glyph.Data = {... I've loaded the file
      C:\DELPHI\IMAGES\BUTTONS\PRINT.BMP... }
    Margin = 2
    NumGlyphs = 2
    Spacing = -1
    IsControl = True
  end
  object CancelBtn: TBitBtn
    Kind = bkCancel
    Margin = 2
    Spacing = -1
    IsControl = True
  end
  object RadioGroup1: TRadioGroup
    Caption = 'Print Scale'
    ItemIndex = 1
    Items.Strings = (
      'None'
      'Proportional'
      'Print To Fit')
  end
end
```

I choose this example because it has a simple form, and you can change the font of the caption in a number of ways and see the effect both on the screen and on paper. The only problem is that the printed output contains not only the text of the label, but also the image of the toolbar. If you don't want to print the toolbar, you can hide it by using the Visible command on the Toolbar menu or on the toolbar's Speed-Menu (just click the right mouse button over the toolbar to see its local menu). So the program can actually be used to print the text of the caption by itself on a page.

FIGURE 22.2:

The COMBO2 example at run-time

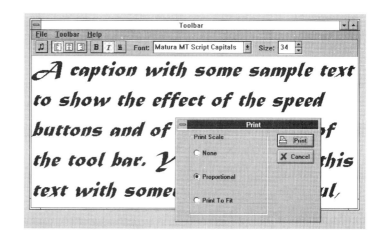

Now add a dialog box with an edit box or memo field to change the text of the caption, and you can print any text. Why buy an expensive word processor?

The code of the example is simple. When the user issues the Print command, the dialog box is displayed. If the user clicks on the Print button (which has a mrOk value for its ModalResult property), the current scaling selection is set, and the form is printed:

```
procedure TToolbarForm.Print1Click(Sender: TObject);
begin
  if PrintDlg.ShowModal = mrOk then
  begin
    case PrintDlg.RadioGroup1.ItemIndex of
      0: PrintScale := poNone;
      1: PrintScale := poProportional;
      2: PrintScale := poPrintToFit;
    end;
    Print;
  end;
end;
```

The dialog box has no code, other than the class definition generated by Delphi. We could add a panel, with a preview of the printed image. In fact, the TForm component also has a GetFormImage method, which returns a bitmap corresponding to the form. This same bitmap is sent to the printer in the code of the Print method.

What is not simple is simulating the print scale, to show the bitmap inside an area corresponding to a page. We'll get to an example (PRINTBMP) that includes a print preview dialog box later in this chapter. You could use that code to improve the COMBO2 example, too.

The Standard Print Dialog Boxes

As an alternative to the custom Print dialog box used in the COMBO2 example, you can use the two standard Windows dialog boxes related to printing and encapsulated in Delphi's PrintDialog and PrinterSetupDialog components.

This is the approach of the next version of our example, named (not surprisingly) COMBO3. This example has the same dialog box as in the previous version, used as a Print Options dialog box, plus two new dialog boxes. To reflect the additions, its File menu has been rearranged, as you can see in Figure 22.3.

FIGURE 22.3:

The File pull-down menu of the COMBO3 example

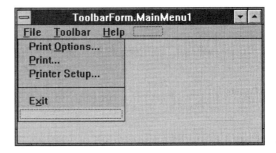

The two new components for the two dialog boxes have no special properties and are used in a simple way. To set up the printer, you just run this dialog box:

```
procedure TToolbarForm.PrinterSetup1Click(Sender: TObject);
begin
  PrinterSetupDialog1.Execute;
end;
```

When you call the Execute method of the PrintDialog component, however, you need to check the return value, to see if the user really wants to print. I've also added the only Print dialog box option that is always available: the selection of the number of copies. The COMBO3 example does not print all the copies. It prints the first one, then asks if the user really wants to print the remaining copies:

```
procedure TToolbarForm.Print1Click(Sender: TObject);
var
  I: Integer;
begin
  if PrintDialog1.Execute then
  begin
    Print;
    if (PrintDialog1.Copies > 1) and
      (MessageDlg ('Do you actually want to print ' +
        IntToStr (PrintDialog1.Copies - 1) + ' more copies?',
        mtConfirmation, [mbYes, mbNo], 0) = mrYes) then
      for I := 1 to PrintDialog1.Copies - 1 do
        Print;
  end;
end;
```

Notice that this dialog box can activate the Printer Setup dialog box, as you can see in Figure 22.4. The Printer Setup command and the corresponding dialog box component could have been omitted, without any real problems. This is the approach taken by many big applications.

FIGURE 22.4:

The standard Print dialog box used by the COMBO3 example

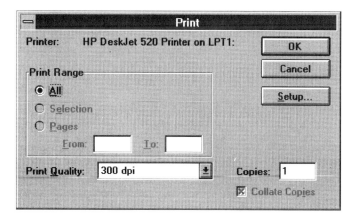

When the user selects the Print Options command, the custom dialog box from the previous version is displayed, the PrintScale property is set, but nothing is printed:

```
procedure TToolbarForm.PrintOptions1Click(Sender: TObject);
begin
  if PrintDlg.ShowModal = mrOk then
    case PrintDlg.RadioGroup1.ItemIndex of
      0: PrintScale := poNone;
      1: PrintScale := poProportional;
      2: PrintScale := poPrintToFit;
    end;
end;
```

This code has one statement less than the previous version, but its result changes radically. I've added an OK button to close this dialog box, and changed the meaning of the Print button. I've also change the label to Print Options to indicate the new meaning of the dialog box. You can see the full source code of this dialog box in Listing 22.2.

LISTING 22.2: The source code of the Print Options dialog box of the COMBO3 example

```
unit Print_f;

interface

uses
  WinTypes, WinProcs, Classes, Graphics, Forms,
  Controls, Buttons, StdCtrls, ExtCtrls;

type
  TPrintDlg = class(TForm)
    OKBtn: TBitBtn;
    CancelBtn: TBitBtn;
    RadioGroup1: TRadioGroup;
    BitBtn1: TBitBtn;
    procedure OKBtnClick(Sender: TObject);
  end;

var
  PrintDlg: TPrintDlg;

implementation

{$R *.DFM}

uses
  Tool_f;
```

22

LISTING 22.2: The source code of the Print Options dialog box of the COMBO3
example (continued)

```
procedure TPrintDlg.OKBtnClick(Sender: TObject);
begin
  case RadioGroup1.ItemIndex of
    0: ToolbarForm.PrintScale := poNone;
    1: ToolbarForm.PrintScale := poProportional;
    2: ToolbarForm.PrintScale := poPrintToFit;
  end;
  ToolbarForm.Print1Click (self);
end;

end.
```

Figure 22.5 shows that you can open the Print Options dialog box, invoke the Print
dialog box, and open the Print Setup dialog box from there. You end up with three
levels of dialog boxes, which can be quite useful, as long as there is a way to reach
each of them directly from the menu. If you don't provide the separate menu items,
the users might not like being forced to navigate through three levels of dialog
boxes to set an option. (By the way, in the COMBO3 example, you can probably
navigate through one or two more levels, depending on the setup options of your
printer driver.)

FIGURE 22.5:

You can use the Print Options dialog
box to open the Print dialog box,
which can be used to access to the
Print Setup dialog box.

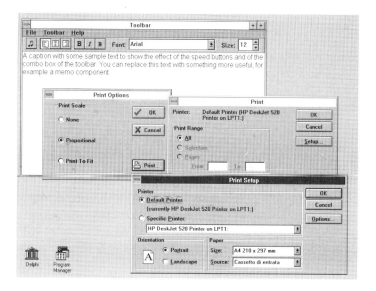

Accessing the Printer Object

Other than for basic operations, such as printing the whole form, to use a printer in a Delphi program, you need to access the global Printer variable. This is an object of class TPrinter, defined in the Printers unit.

The Printer object can be used to access some global properties related to the printer, such as a list of installed drivers or printer fonts. However, its key property is its canvas. You can use the canvas of a printer the same way that you use the canvas of a form. You can output text, graphics, and everything else.

To use this canvas, you need to call the BeginDoc method of the printer to start the printing job, use the canvas methods to produce the output, and then use the End-Doc method to actually send the output to the printer. As an alternative, you can use the Abort method to discard the print job, or use the NewPage method to send the output to the printer and start working on a new page.

Printing Graphics and Print Preview

Our first example of the use of the Printer object is a simple application you can use to print bitmaps. Basically, this is an extension of the TAB1 example presented in Chapter 13. That example used a TabSet component to let the user browse though a series of bitmaps. Of course, to run the new version, called PRINTBMP, and test graphical printing from a Delphi program, your printer must support graphical output.

As shown in Figure 22.6, the form of the PRINTMAP example has a toolbar with four buttons at the top, and a ScrollBox component hosting an Image component in the rest of its area. With this approach, if the image is bigger than the form, you can scroll it without affecting the toolbar. The File menu has a new Print command that will invoke a Print Preview form. You can see the textual description of the Print Preview form in Listing 22.3.

The Print Preview form lets you compare the size of the resulting bitmap with the printed page and scale the bitmap to increase its size. Note that changing the size of the image affects the screen output as well as the printed output. It is not a zoom feature for viewing the image on the screen, but rather a technique for printing

FIGURE 22.6:

The Print Preview form of the
PRINTBMP example at design-time

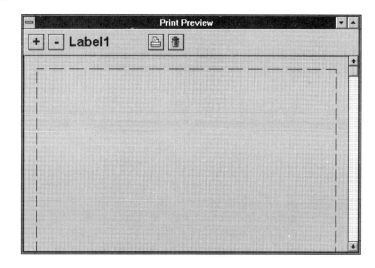

LISTING 22.3: The textual description of the Preview form of the PRINTBMP
example

```
object PreviewForm: TPreviewForm
  Caption = 'Print Preview'
  object Panel1: TPanel
    Align = alTop
    Font.Color = clBlack
    Font.Height = -21
    Font.Name = 'Arial'
    Font.Style = [fsBold]
    object ScalePlusButton: TSpeedButton
      Caption = '+'
      OnClick = ScalePlusButtonClick
    end
    object ScaleMinusButton: TSpeedButton
      Caption = '-'
      OnClick = ScaleMinusButtonClick
    end
    object PrintButton: TSpeedButton
      Glyph.Data = {...}
      NumGlyphs = 2
      OnClick = PrintButtonClick
    end
    object CancelButton: TSpeedButton
      Glyph.Data = {...}
      NumGlyphs = 2
      OnClick = CancelButtonClick
    end
```

LISTING 22.3: The textual description of the Preview form of the PRINTBMP example (continued)

```
    object Label1: TLabel
      Caption = 'Label1'
    end
  end
  object ScrollBox1: TScrollBox
    Align = alClient
    object Image1: TImage
      Left = 20
      Top = 20
      Width = 485
      Height = 330
    end
  end
end
```

larger bitmaps. The example includes the scaling option because bitmaps printed at their standard pixel-per-inch ratio are quite small on the printed page (although more precise).

This example is based on the StretchDraw method of the TCanvas class, which is used both for the preview and for the actual printed output. To use it, you need to define a rectangle, indicating the output area, and the source image. The result is a stretched image that fits the rectangle.

Now let's review some of the code. The main form responds to the Print command by initializing and running the Preview form:

```
procedure TForm1.Print1Click(Sender: TObject);
begin
  {double-check if an image is selected}
  if Image1.Picture.Graphic <> nil then
  begin
    {set a default scale, and start the preview}
    PreviewForm.Scale := 2;
    PreviewForm.SetPage;
    PreviewForm.DrawPreview;
    PreviewForm.ShowModal;
  end;
end;
```

The check at the beginning could have been omitted, since the Preview option is disabled until an image file has been selected, but it ensures that a file is selected (in case you don't make this change to the code to disable the menu option). This code sets a public field of the PreviewForm object, calls two methods I've defined, and finally runs the form as modal. Figure 22.7 shows an example of the Print Preview form.

FIGURE 22.7:

The Print Preview form of the PRINTBMP example, with the main form of the program in the background

As you can see in Listing 22.4, the code of the two methods sets the size of the Image component of the Print Preview form, using the size of the printed page, as in:

```
Image1.Width := Printer.PageWidth div 5;
```

The size of the page is divided by 5 to make it fit into a reasonable area of the screen. You might use a parameter instead of this fixed value to add a zooming feature on the preview page. However, I thought that having a button to increase the size of the printed image and another button to increase it only in the preview was quite confusing, so I decided to skip the zooming capability.

The heart of the code of the Preview form is in the DrawPreview method, which has three different portions. At the beginning, it computes the destination rectangle, leaving a 10-pixel margin, scaling the image, and using the fixed zoom factor of 5 (as you can see in Listing 22.4). The second step is to erase the older image present on the screen, by drawing a white rectangle over it.

LISTING 22.4: The source code of the Preview form of the PRINTBMP example

```
unit Preview;

interface

uses
  SysUtils, WinTypes, WinProcs, Messages, Classes,
  Graphics, Controls, Forms, Dialogs, ExtCtrls,
  Buttons, Printers, StdCtrls;

type
  TPreviewForm = class(TForm)
    Panel1: TPanel;
    ScalePlusButton: TSpeedButton;
    ScaleMinusButton: TSpeedButton;
    PrintButton: TSpeedButton;
    ScrollBox1: TScrollBox;
    Image1: TImage;
    CancelButton: TSpeedButton;
    Label1: TLabel;
    procedure ScalePlusButtonClick(Sender: TObject);
    procedure ScaleMinusButtonClick(Sender: TObject);
    procedure CancelButtonClick(Sender: TObject);
    procedure PrintButtonClick(Sender: TObject);
  public
    Scale: Integer;
    procedure DrawPreview;
    procedure SetPage;
  end;

var
  PreviewForm: TPreviewForm;

implementation

{$R *.DFM}

uses
  Viewer;

procedure TPreviewForm.SetPage;
begin
  {set the image size to be proportional
    with the page size}
  Image1.Width := Printer.PageWidth div 5;
  Image1.Height := Printer.PageHeight div 5;
  {output the scale to the toolbar}
  Label1.Caption := IntToStr (Scale);
end;
```

LISTING 22.4: The source code of the Preview form of the PRINTBMP example (continued)

```pascal
procedure TPreviewForm.ScalePlusButtonClick(
  Sender: TObject);
begin
  {increase the size of the bitmap}
  Scale := Scale * 2;
  Label1.Caption := IntToStr (Scale);
  DrawPreview;
end;

procedure TPreviewForm.DrawPreview;
var
  Rect: TRect;
begin
  {compute the rectangle for the bitmap preview}
  Rect.Top := 10;
  Rect.Left := 10;
  Rect.Right := 10 +
    (Form1.Image1.Picture.Graphic.Width * Scale) div 5;
  Rect.Bottom := 10 +
    (Form1.Image1.Picture.Graphic.Height * Scale) div 5;

  {remove the current image}
  Image1.Canvas.Pen.Mode := pmWhite;
  Image1.Canvas.Rectangle (0, 0,
    Image1.Width, Image1.Height);

  {stretch the bitmap into the rectangle}
  Image1.Canvas.StretchDraw (Rect,
    Form1.Image1.Picture.Graphic);
end;

procedure TPreviewForm.ScaleMinusButtonClick(
  Sender: TObject);
begin
  {decrease the size of the image}
  if Scale > 1 then
  begin
    Scale := Scale div 2;
    Label1.Caption := IntToStr (Scale);
    DrawPreview;
  end;
end;

procedure TPreviewForm.CancelButtonClick(
  Sender: TObject);
begin
  {close (hide) the preview dialog}
  Close;
end;
```

LISTING 22.4: The source code of the Preview form of the PRINTBMP example
(continued)

```
procedure TPreviewForm.PrintButtonClick(
  Sender: TObject);
var
  Rect: TRect;
begin
  {compute the rectangle for the printer}
  Rect.Top := 10;
  Rect.Left := 10;
  Rect.Right := 10 +
    (Form1.Image1.Picture.Graphic.Width * Scale);
  Rect.Bottom := 10 +
    (Form1.Image1.Picture.Graphic.Height * Scale);

  {print the bitmap}
  Printer.BeginDoc;
  Printer.Canvas.StretchDraw (Rect,
    Form1.Image1.Picture.Graphic);
  Printer.EndDoc;
end;

end.
```

The third step is the call to the StretchDraw method of the canvas, using the rectangle calculated before and the image currently active in the Image component of the main form Form1.Image1.Picture.Graphic). To access this information, we need to add a uses clause in the implementation portion of the code.

All this code is executed just to start up the form. The startup code is split into two methods, only because one of them will be called again later. When initialization is completed and the modal form is visible, the user can click on the three toolbar buttons to resize the image, print it, or skip it (throw it in the garbage can, as the bitmap of the button suggests).

The two resize methods are simple, because they just set the new value for the scale and call the DrawPreview procedure to update the image. You can see an example of scaling in Figure 22.8.

The Print method of the Print Preview form is almost a clone of DrawPreview. The only differences are that the destination rectangle is not zoomed by the 5 factor and

FIGURE 22.8:

By scaling the image in the Print Preview form of the PRINTBMP example, you can print a magnified view of a small bitmap.

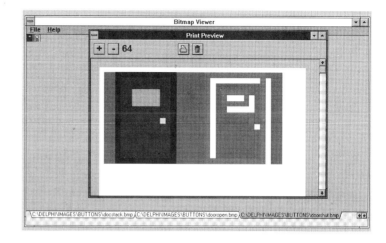

the bitmap is sent to the printer in a new document (a new page):

```
Printer.BeginDoc;
Printer.Canvas.StretchDraw (Rect,
  Form1.Image1.Picture.Graphic);
Printer.EndDoc;
```

Painting to the Printer

Instead of printing a whole form or copying an existing bitmap to the printer canvas, you can actually write standard output code using the canvas of the printer instead of that of a form or a component.

Since the methods you can execute on a printer canvas are the same as those for any other canvas, we can write programs with two output methods—one for the screen and one for the printer—using similar code. Even better, we can write a single output method that can be used for both kinds of output.

As an example of this approach, I've built a new version of the SHAPE4 example of Chapter 9, which stored the description of a list of shapes in memory and later used this description in the OnPaint method. (You might want to review the text describing this example and its listings before you go on reading.)

The new version is named SHAPE6 (because a SHAPE5 example already exists). As usual, the only change in the description of its form is a new Print command in the File menu.

The interesting point is that I have moved the code of the FormPaint example into another method I've defined, called CommonPaint. This new method has two parameters, the canvas and a scale factor:

```
procedure TShapesForm.CommonPaint (
  Canvas1: TCanvas; Scale: Integer);
```

You can see the complete source code of this method in Listing 22.5. Once you have written this code, the FormPrint and Print1 methods are simple. To output the

LISTING 22.5: The source code of the CommonPaint method of the SHAPE6 example

```
procedure TShapesForm.CommonPaint (
  Canvas1: TCanvas; Scale: Integer);
var
  I: Integer;
  CurShape: ShapeData;
begin
  {repaint each shape of the list, using the stored
  values, on the canvas passed as a parameter}
  for I := 0 to ShapesList.Count - 1 do
  begin
    CurShape := ShapesList.Items [I];
    with CurShape do
    begin
      Canvas1.Pen.Color := PenColor;
      Canvas1.Pen.Width := PenSize;
      Canvas1.Brush.Color := BrushColor;
      if Circle then
        Canvas1.Ellipse (
          (X-Size) * Scale, (Y-Size) * Scale,
          (X+Size) * Scale, (Y+Size) * Scale)
      else
        Canvas1.Rectangle (
          (X-Size) * Scale, (Y-Size) * Scale,
          (X+Size) * Scale, (Y+Size) * Scale);
    end;
  end;
end;
```

22

image on the screen, you can call CommonPaint without a scaling factor:

```
procedure TShapesForm.FormPaint(Sender: TObject);
begin
  {repaint the form using the common procedure}
  CommonPaint (Canvas, 1);
end;
```

Painting the Form Contents to the Screen

To paint the contents of the form to the screen instead of the printer, you can reproduce the output on the printer canvas, using a proper scaling factor. Instead of letting the user choose a scale (in a simple Print dialog box with a SpinEdit or a ScrollBar component), I decided to compute it automatically. The idea is to print the shapes of the form as large as possible, by sizing the client area of the form so that it takes up the whole page. The code is probably simpler than the description:

```
procedure TShapesForm.Print1Click(Sender: TObject);
var
  Scale, Scale1: Integer;
begin
  Scale := Printer.PageWidth div ClientWidth;
  Scale1 := Printer.PageHeight div ClientHeight;
  if Scale1 < Scale then
    Scale := Scale1;
  Printer.BeginDoc;
  CommonPaint (Printer.Canvas, Scale);
  Printer.EndDoc;
end;
```

Of course, you need to remember to call the specific commands to start printing and commit the output before and after you call the CommonPaint method.

Printing Text

In the two previous examples, we have used the canvas of the global Printer object to print graphics. At the beginning of the chapter, we saw another example that could be used to print text, but that code was far from adequate. Printing text is an important topic, so it deserves some specific attention.

One approach to printing text from a Delphi program is similar to the one we used in the COMBO2 example. If you prepare the text in a form (or, in general, in a bitmap), you can later print the corresponding image to the screen. This is useful only in a few cases, such as when you have text in a data-entry form, but not in general, because you can print only a limited amount of text and the output quality is usually quite low.

Another approach to printing text is to draw the text, using the TextOut method of the canvas or other text-related drawing functions. This allows you precise control over the position of the text, and you can obtain high-resolution output. The drawback is that there is a lot of work involved, since you must determine the length and position of each line on the page, the height of the font, and many other details. Power never comes free.

The free ticket, however, comes from a third approach. In Delphi, you can associate a file with the printer, then print to the file—send text to the printer—using the standard Writeln procedure. This is much simpler, because the system automatically determines the height of the lines, relieving you of much of the work. The output resolution is good, but the control you have over the output is less precise. Long lines are automatically wrapped to the next line, which is helpful but can produce wildly unformatted output.

We could try to build a full-scale word processor that could produce output both to the screen and to the printer using TextOut calls (using an approach similar to the SHAPE6 example). But I've decided to just update the NOTES2 example from Chapter 8, which already had a menu with the proper printing-related commands in the File menu.

In such a simple example, which uses a single font for the whole text and has no special page-handling capabilities (page numbers, header and footers, and so on), using the Writeln procedure on a file connected with the printer is the easiest approach. We might even extend the example a bit, adding some page-handling capabilities, and still be able to use this approach without any problems.

Technically, the key to this approach in the use of the AssignPrn procedure, which connects a file with the printer. After starting the write process, by calling the Rewrite procedure, you can start using Write and Writeln to output the text.

22

In the new version, named NOTES3, the program simply outputs each of the lines of the Memo component, using a for loop from the first to the last line. In Listing 22.6, you can see the code of the two methods added to the TNoteForm class: Print1Click and PrintSetup1Click.

LISTING 22.6: The source code of the two new methods of the NOTES3 example

```
procedure TNotesForm.PrintSetup1Click(Sender: TObject);
begin
  PrinterSetupDialog1.Execute;
end;

procedure TNotesForm.Print1Click(Sender: TObject);
var
  PrintFile: TextFile;
  I, LinesPerPage: Integer;
begin
  if PrintDialog1.Execute then
  begin
    {assign the printer to a file}
    AssignPrn (PrintFile);
    Rewrite (PrintFile);
    {set the font}
    Printer.Canvas.Font := Memo1.Font;
    {copy all the text of the memo to the printer file}
    for I := 0 to Memo1.Lines.Count - 1 do
      Writeln (PrintFile, Memo1.Lines [I]);
    System.CloseFile (PrintFile);
  end;
end;
```

I could have easily customized this printer function, adding a dialog box to select the range of lines to output, but I decided to use the standard Print dialog box, as you can see in Figure 22.9. The example also uses the standard Printer Setup dialog box and enables only full text printing.

Adding the support for page selection is more complex. First, we must compute the number of lines per page, using the PageHeight property of the printer and the height of the font of the printer canvas. Once this calculation is made, we need to check if each line of text will fit in a printed line or will be wrapped to the next line, or even on the next two lines, and modify the number of lines of the memo field in a given page.

FIGURE 22.9:

The standard Print dialog box used by the NOTES3 example

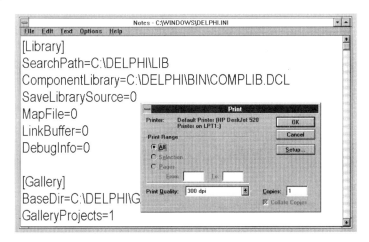

Printing Database Records and Tables

Using Delphi printing capabilities, we can easily provide the output of the database-related forms of our programs. Basically, if a form shows a record of a database table, you can use the Print method of the form to output the data. Of course, if this is your intention, you might as well build the form and arrange the components in such a way that the printed output will look good.

As an alternative, you might develop a print function that temporarily removes the form's toolbar and the status bar, prints the whole surface of the form, and then restores the toolbar and status bar. Even better, you can open up a preview form, copy the bitmap of the form, and print only a portion of that bitmap, excluding the toolbar, status bar, and other extraneous elements.

Of course, this is not the only approach you can use to output records (or full tables, if they fit on the screen) using database-related forms. You can apply any of the techniques described in the previous section to output text. In particular, using the file-printing approach, you can output the name of the field and its value on each line of a page, printing one or all of the records of the table.

Our first example of database-related output is the PRINTNAV application, which is an extension of the NAVIG1 example in Chapter 17. The new form of the example has the elements of the older version, plus three print buttons below the DBNavigator component, as shown in Figure 22.10. As you might remember from Chapter 17, or just guess by looking at the figure, the Table component is connected to the COUNTRY.DB sample table, and the data-aware components are connected to it, via the data source.

FIGURE 22.10:

The form of the PRINTNAV example at design-time

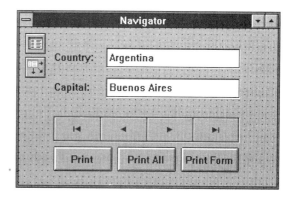

The three buttons perform three different actions involving some type of printer output. The first button simply prints the data of the two visible fields of the current record, using the text of the two labels and two edit boxes:

```
Writeln (PrintFile, Label1.Caption, ' ', DBEdit1.Text);
Writeln (PrintFile, Label2.Caption, ' ', DBEdit2.Text);
```

This code follows the usual assignment of the printer output to the PrintFile file. What is new in this method is that the database access and output operations are executed within a `try-finally` block, to avoid skipping the code that closes the print job in case of an error. You can see the complete source code of this method in Listing 22.7.

The second button, Print All, has a more complex code. It prints the two visible fields for each record of the database, not just of the current one. The program scans the whole table with a code similar to that used in the TOTAL example of Chapter 17. As you can see in the listing, at the beginning it sets a bookmark and disables

LISTING 22.7: The source code of the PRINTNAV example

```
unit Nav_form;

interface

uses
  SysUtils, WinTypes, WinProcs, Messages, Classes, Graphics,
  Controls, Forms, Dialogs, ExtCtrls, DBCtrls, StdCtrls,
  Mask, DB, DBTables, Printers;

type
  TNavigator = class(TForm)
    DataSource1: TDataSource;
    Table1: TTable;
    DBEdit1: TDBEdit;
    DBEdit2: TDBEdit;
    Label1: TLabel;
    Label2: TLabel;
    DBNavigator1: TDBNavigator;
    PrintButton: TButton;
    PrintAllButton: TButton;
    PrintFormButton: TButton;
    procedure PrintButtonClick(Sender: TObject);
    procedure PrintFormButtonClick(Sender: TObject);
    procedure PrintAllButtonClick(Sender: TObject);
  private
    { Private declarations }
  public
    { Public declarations }
  end;

var
  Navigator: TNavigator;

implementation

{$R *.DFM}

procedure TNavigator.PrintButtonClick(Sender: TObject);
var
  PrintFile: TextFile;
begin
  {assign the printer to a file}
  AssignPrn (PrintFile);
  Rewrite (PrintFile);
  try
    {set the font of the form, and output each element}
    Printer.Canvas.Font := Font;
    Writeln (PrintFile, Label1.Caption,
      ' ', DBEdit1.Text);
    Writeln (PrintFile, Label2.Caption,
      ' ', DBEdit2.Text);  finally
```

LISTING 22.7: The source code of the PRINTNAV example (continued)

```
    {close the printing process}
    System.CloseFile (PrintFile);
  end;
end;

procedure TNavigator.PrintFormButtonClick(Sender: TObject);
begin
  Print;
end;

procedure TNavigator.PrintAllButtonClick(Sender: TObject);
var
  Bookmark: TBookmark;
  PrintFile: TextFile;
begin
  {assign the printer to a file}
  AssignPrn (PrintFile);
  Rewrite (PrintFile);
  {set the font of the form, and output each element}
  Printer.Canvas.Font := Font;
  {store the current position, creating a new bookmark}
  Bookmark := Table1.GetBookmark;
  Table1.DisableControls;
  try
    Table1.First;
    while not Table1.EOF do
    begin
      {output the two fields, and a blank line}
      Writeln (PrintFile, 'Country: ',
        Table1.FieldByName ('Name').AsString);
      Writeln (PrintFile, 'Capital: ',
        Table1.FieldByName ('Capital').AsString);
      Writeln (PrintFile);
      Table1.Next;
    end;
  finally
    {go back to the bookmark and destroy it}
    Table1.GotoBookmark (Bookmark);
    Table1.FreeBookmark (Bookmark);
    Table1.EnableControls;
    System.CloseFile (PrintFile);
  end;
end;

end.
```

the controls, then it scans all of the records in a while loop. For each record, the program outputs a caption followed by the text of the field. The program extracts the field with the FieldByName method of the table, and reads its text using the AsString property of the TField class:

```
Writeln (PrintFile, 'Country: ' +
    Table1.FieldByName ('Name').AsString);
```

The Print Form button has the simplest code. As we've seen, to print the output of the form, you simply call its Print method. I've added this last button to the program simply to let you test the three different ways to output the data from a database form. Each of these methods can be improved by adding headers and comments, printing other fields, and so on. This example is intended to give you an idea of the basic code involved.

By expanding on this idea, you can build complex and sophisticated kinds of output, and also create custom reports and different versions of printed output. As an alternative, you can use a specific tool included in Delphi to generate reports: ReportSmith.

Creating Reports

When you want to build a professional report in Delphi, but don't want to build the output line by line, you can take advantage of the Report component, a very simple interface to the ReportSmith engine. This component is not particularly rich. Its properties include the name of the report file you want to print, its directory, plus some other information. You can call its Run method to view the report using the ReportSmith run-time engine and print it.

Just to test the behavior of ReportSmith, I've written a bare program, named PRINTRPT, which loads a report (a file with the RPT extension). When you call the Run method of the Report1 object, the ReportSmith engine is loaded, and you can see the report and print it. This is because the Preview property of the Report component has been set to True. When the Preview property is set to False, the report is printed immediately.

As an alternative, once the report has been loaded in memory with the Run method, you can use the Print method to send a Dynamic Data Exchange (DDE) message to the ReportSmith engine, asking it to actually print the report. Do not call Print before running the report, because it will have no effect.

The PRINTRPT example's form has four components: a file open dialog box to let the user select a report, a Report component, a check box to select the preview mode, and a button to start the operation. You can see its form in Figure 22.11 and the details of these components in Listing 22.8.

FIGURE 22.11:
The form of the PRINTRPT example at design-time

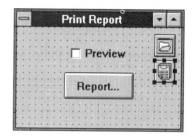

LISTING 22.8: The textual description of the form of the PRINTRPT example

```
object Form1: TForm1
  Caption = 'Print Report'
  object ReportButton: TButton
    Caption = 'Report...'
    OnClick = ReportButtonClick
  end
  object PreviewCheckBox: TCheckBox
    Caption = 'Preview'
  end
  object Report1: TReport
    AutoUnload = True
  end
  object OpenDialog1: TOpenDialog
    Filter = 'Report (*.rpt)|*.rpt'
  end
end
```

When the user clicks on the Report button, the program opens the dialog box so that the user can select a file, and then runs the engine:

```
procedure TForm1.ReportButtonClick(Sender: TObject);
begin
  Report1.Preview := PreviewCheckBox.Checked;
  if OpenDialog1.Execute then
  begin
    Report1.ReportName := OpenDialog1.FileName;
    Report1.Run;
  end;
end;
```

Since I've set the AutoUnload property, when the report terminates, the ReportSmith run-time engine is automatically unloaded from memory. Otherwise, you need to add a specific statement in the OnClose event of the form, calling the CloseApplication method of the Report component.

The effect of this code changes depending on the status of the Preview check box. If the Preview property is set to False, the ReportSmith icon will appear, as you can see in Figure 22.12, and the engine will immediately start printing. Otherwise, the ReportSmith RunTime window will be displayed, as shown in Figure 22.13, in the screen position it was the last time you used it, and you can see the output, which is the preview. Here you can make changes, choose the pages you want to print, and select from many other options.

FIGURE 22.12:

While the ReportSmith engine prints the report, you can see the icon of its window.

FIGURE 22.13:

The preview of the report takes place inside the ReportSmith RunTime window.

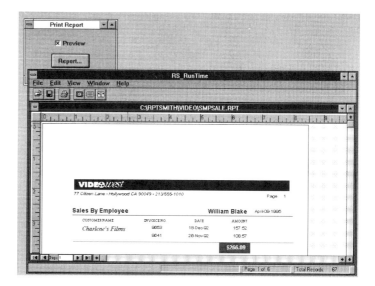

Notice that the connection between Delphi and the ReportSmith run-time engine is somewhat limited. You can indeed execute a number of macro commands, but you actually run an independent application. What you cannot do is see the preview of the report inside a Delphi window. Fortunately, ReportSmith has some DDE support that is encapsulated in some methods of the TReport component type.

Building a Custom Report

Using the PRINTRPT program, you can print (or preview) any existing report, but you cannot create new ones. In other words, if you use this approach in your own applications, the users will not be able to create their own reports, unless they own a copy of ReportSmith. In this case, of course, they will be able to print any existing report file.

Since most of your users won't have ReportSmith, or won't be able to build custom reports, you will need to build one or more reports when you are developing the application, attach them to the Delphi application, and let the user print them with some menu commands.

Building a new report is not really related to Delphi programming. You start ReportSmith (the full version, not the engine) and prepare a report by choosing one of the standard layouts, accessing one or more database tables, and designing a proper layout. For more information about the features of ReportSmith, refer to the manuals or on-line Help files. Here, we will take a look at two examples of reports and their connection with a simple Delphi program.

> **TIP**
>
> Many operations can be done in ReportSmith by selecting an element of the output and clicking the right mouse button to display a local menu. The toolbar has some powerful commands, too.

Our example is a new version of another program presented in Chapter 17, called HANDGRID. The new version, HGRID2, has the same grid as the previous version, plus a menu that lets you print a couple of reports in different ways. See Figure 22.14 for an example of the form at design-time and Listing 22.9 for its textual description.

FIGURE 22.14:

The form of the HGRID2 example at design-time

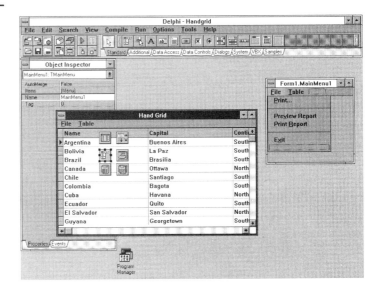

LISTING 22.9: The textual description of the form of the HGRID2 example

```
object Form1: TForm1
  Caption = 'Hand Grid'
  Menu = MainMenu1
  object DBGrid1: TDBGrid
    Align = alClient
    DataSource = DataSource1
  end
  object Table1: TTable
    Active = True
    DatabaseName = 'DBDEMOS'
    TableName = 'COUNTRY.DB'
  end
  object DataSource1: TDataSource
    DataSet = Table1
  end
  object MainMenu1: TMainMenu
    object File1: TMenuItem
      Caption = '&File'
      object Print1: TMenuItem
        Caption = '&Print...'
        OnClick = Print1Click
      end
      object N2: TMenuItem
        Caption = '-'
      end
      object PreviewReport1: TMenuItem
        Caption = 'Pre&view Report'
        OnClick = PreviewReport1Click
      end
      object PrintReport1: TMenuItem
        Caption = 'Print &Report'
        OnClick = PrintReport1Click
      end
      object N1: TMenuItem
        Caption = '-'
      end
      object Exit1: TMenuItem
        Caption = 'E&xit'
        OnClick = Exit1Click
      end
    end
    object Table2: TMenuItem
      Caption = '&Table'
      object PreviewReport2: TMenuItem
        Caption = 'Preview &Report'
        OnClick = Report3Click
      end
    end
  end
end
```

22

LISTING 22.9: The textual description of the form of the HGRID2 example
(continued)

```
  object PrintDialog1: TPrintDialog
  end
  object Report1: TReport
    ReportName = 'country.rpt'
    AutoUnload = True
  end
  object Report2: TReport
    ReportName = 'table.rpt'
    AutoUnload = True
  end
end
```

The structure of the program is simple. There is a DBGrid connected to a table (COUNTRY.DB again). The program has a plain Print command, which uses the standard dialog box just to let the user confirm the action:

```
procedure TForm1.Print1Click(Sender: TObject);
begin
  if PrintDialog1.Execute then
    Print;
end;
```

The other three menu items (two in the File menu and one in the Table menu) are related to two reports. The first report can be either printed directly or opened in preview mode, using the two commands of the File menu. The second report always has the Preview property set to True, and is activated using the only command of the Table menu. All three menu command handlers have the following simple structure:

```
procedure TForm1.PrintReport1Click(Sender: TObject);
begin
  Report1.Preview := False;
  Report1.Run;
end;
```

What changes in the other two cases is the value of the Preview property and the Report component used. The form and the code of this program are simple. All of the work to build the two reports is actually done with ReportSmith. I'll discuss the first report here, and the second one in the next section, because that report uses some advanced features of ReportSmith.

The first report I've built for the HGRID2 example, COUNTRY.RPT, is a plain output of the contents of the database, using a label format. To rebuild it, start ReportSmith, create a new report, choose the label style, and select the proper database table (notice that the BDE aliases are not available here). Next, drag some of the fields to the report page, then add a standard label with the proper check box. You can see a step of the creation of the report in Figure 22.15.

FIGURE 22.15:

Creating a report in ReportSmith is as simple as dragging a few labels.

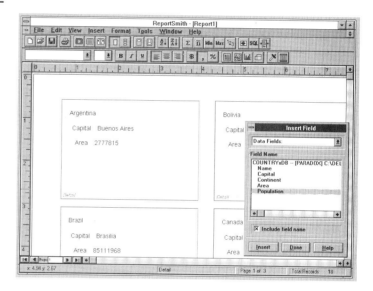

When the report layout is done, save the file, and enter its name in the ReportName property of the Report1 component of the HGRID2 example. Now you can run the program and print or preview the report. It is actually that simple.

WARNING In the report file and in the HGRID2 program, there are some hard-coded directory names, particularly the name of the directory with the database table used by the report. If your installation does not use the default Delphi directories, you might have problems running the program without modification.

Writing a ReportSmith Macro

The second report of the HGRID2 example, TABLE.RPT, is more complex. It uses a columnar report format rather than the label style. Select the table (again COUNTRY.DB), and all of its fields will be arranged in columns. You can resize the columns to make them fit on the page and set a proper format for the numeric output, such as to include thousand separators, as you can see in Figure 22.16.

FIGURE 22.16:

The initial steps of the development of the new report include resizing the columns and choosing proper formats.

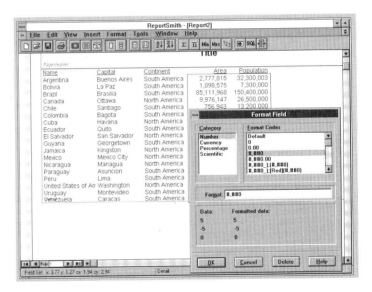

Continue building the report, entering a proper title, sorting it by continent and by name, and grouping the report by continent. Then add a footer to each group of the report. In the footer, place a count of the countries for each continent, the total population, and the total surface of each continent.

Finally, you can move to the tough part: adding a calculated field with the population density, as we did in examples in Chapters 17 and 18. The problem here is that you cannot use a SQL statement with the definition of the calculated field, because this feature is not supported by ReportSmith for Paradox tables.

The only technique available is to define a ReportSmith macro. You can use the Derived fields command on the Tools menu to add a new field name, defined by a

ReportBasic macro. I've used the name Density. Then you can give a name to the macro, as shown in Figure 22.17, and write its code.

FIGURE 22.17:

To define a new derived (or calculated) field, you can use a ReportSmith macro.

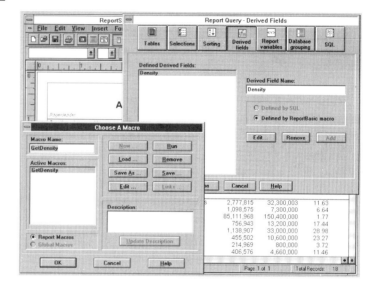

When you click on the New or the Edit button in the Choose a Macro dialog box, the Edit Macro dialog box appears, as shown in Figure 22.18. you can write the text of the macro directly in this macro editor, or you can use the three list boxes at the top to select table fields, commands, functions, and so on. Notice that each of the three list boxes has a combo box above it. Each combo box can be used to select a group of elements for the corresponding list box. For example, the last list box can display four different groups of elements: Basic Functions, Basic Statements, Dialog Box Functions, or Branching & Looping.

Using these lists of available commands and functions can be helpful in writing macros, but you still need to know at least the basics of the language of the ReportSmith macro editor, ReportSmith Basic.

FIGURE 22.18:

The ReportSmith macro editor

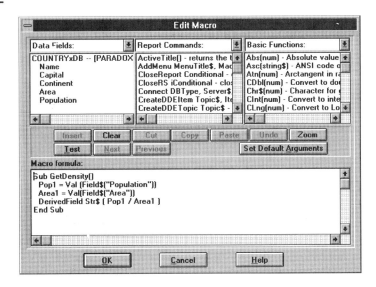

NOTE
When I first realized that I needed to write BASIC language code for this Delphi project, I considered skipping it. After some struggling with the manuals, I came up with the solution for the Density field definition macro, and decided to keep the example in the book. As you have probably guessed, I'm not too fond of BASIC, in any of its incarnations, although it was one of my first programming languages in my early days of computing. But if you want to take advantage of the power of ReportSmith, some background in BASIC will help.

Here is the code of the macro for the new field:

```
Sub GetDensity()
  Pop1 = Val (Field$("Population"))
  Area1 = Val (Field$("Area"))
  DerivedField Str$ ( Pop1 / Area1 )
End Sub
```

This code defines two temporary variables (no declaration is needed in BASIC), and stores the value of two fields. The Field$ function returns the text of the contents of the field for the current record, and the `Val` function extracts the numeric value from the string. The last statement computes the population density and transforms it back into a string, using the `Str$` function. This value is assigned to the `DerivedField` identifier, which automatically refers to the field we are computing with the macro.

You can see the result of this effort in Figure 22.19, which shows the final report displayed by the HGRID2 example in the ReportSmith RunTime window.

FIGURE 22.19:

The TABLE.RPT report shown by the HGRID2 example

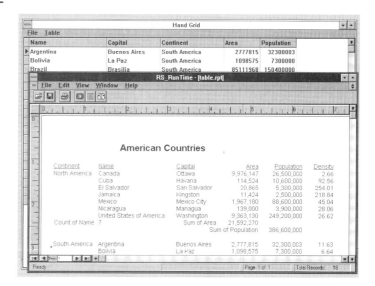

Summary

In this chapter, we have explored Delphi's printing support. We have seen that it is easy to output the image of a form or to connect a text file with the printer and output data. The Canvas component of the Printer object can also be used to build all types of output, even a complex ones.

In Delphi, you work with a canvas to produce both advanced screen output and printer output. This means that you can share the code of these two operations, to produce a WYSIWYG (What You See is What You Get) application, as we saw in the SHAPE6 example.

When you work with database-related forms, you can produce printer output using two completely different approaches. You can drive the printer directly or use the ReportSmith application included in Delphi to build more complex reports. Then you can easily connect these reports to a Delphi application and produce advanced output without a lot of coding effort.

The only drawback (for some of us) is that ReportSmith uses a version of the BASIC language for advanced customization. This might be easy for Delphi programmers with a Visual Basic background, but less simple for the rest of us.

CHAPTER

TWENTY-THREE

23

Adding File Support to Applications

- Text file handling with Object Pascal

- A text case conversion program

- Delphi's file system components

- Delphi's file stream support

- Component persistency

Saving and loading data to files is vital for most of the programs you write. We have already seen several techniques for saving and loading data in Delphi, and also a number of examples that use the standard file open and save dialog boxes. We even created a File Manager clone in Chapter 14.

Although we've covered some aspects of file support, Delphi provides many techniques that you can use to interact with files.

We can broadly define Delphi file support in three different areas:

- Object Pascal language file support is identified by the `file` keyword and by other data types and functions defined in the system unit.

- VCL file support, offered by the TStream and TComponent classes, by the TIniFile class, and by the file loading and storing methods present in several components.

- Database support, particularly for file-based formats, such as dBASE and Paradox tables.

In this chapter, we'll explore the first two approaches in detail. We won't cover database support here, because that was the topic of Chapters 17 and 18.

Files and the Pascal Language

One of the peculiarities of the Pascal language compared with other similar languages is its built-in support for files. As you might recall from Chapter 4 (or from your knowledge of Pascal), the language has a `file` keyword, which is a type of constructor, like `array` or `record`.

You use the `file` keyword to define a new type, and then you can use the new data type to define new variables:

```
type
   IntFile: file of Integers;
var
   IntFile1: IntFile;
```

It is also possible to use the `file` keyword without indicating a data type, by defining an untyped file. As another alternative, you can use the TextFile type defined in the system units to declare files of ASCII text. Each kind of file has its own predefined routines, as we will see later in this chapter.

> **NOTE** The TextFile type is used in Delphi instead of the Text type of earlier versions of Borland Pascal, because Text is a property of some components, notably Edit and Memo.

Once you have defined a file variable, you can assign it to a real file in the file system, with the AssignFile method. The next step is usually to call Reset to open the file for reading at the beginning, Rewrite to open (or create) it for writing, and Append to add new items to the file, without removing the older ones.

Once the input or output operations are done, you should use CloseFile. This last operation should usually be done inside a `finally` block, to avoid having the file left open if the code should generate an exception.

Delphi includes many other file management routines, as you can see in the list in Table 23.1. These routines are not defined in standard Pascal, but have been part of Borland Pascal for a long time. You can find detailed information about these routines in Delphi's Help files. Here I'll show you three simple examples to help clarify how these features can be used.

Handling Text Files

One of the most commonly used file formats is that of text files. As mentioned before, Delphi has some specific support for text files, with the TextFile data type defined by the system unit. We have already used text files in the previous chapter to output text to the printer. In a similar way, we can output text to a real file.

Our first example is an extension of the PRINTNAV application presented in Chapter 22. The new version, named PRINTN2, has the same form with the addition of a new PrintDialog component. The Print to File check box of this dialog box is used to determine whether to output the text to a file or to print it.

The Print button of the form now opens the Print dialog box, as you can see in Figure 23.1, instead of printing immediately. You can test if Print to File is checked by looking at the value of the PrintToFile property of the Print dialog box. In this case,

TABLE 23.1: Delphi's File Management Routines

Append	AssignFile	BlockRead	BlockWrite
ChangeFileExt	CloseFile	DateTimeToFileDate	DeleteFile
DiskFree	DiskSize	Eof	Eoln
Erase	ExpandFileName	ExtractFileExt	ExtractFileName
ExtractFilePath	FileAge	FileClose	FileCreate
FileDateToDateTime	FileExists	FileGetAttr	FileGetDate
FileOpen	FilePos	FileRead	FileSearch
FileSeek	FileSetAttr	FileSetDate	FileSize
FileWrite	FindClose	FindFirst	FindNext
Flush	GetDir	IOResult	MkDir
Read	Readln	Rename	RenameFile
Reset	Rewrite	RmDir	Seek
SeekEof	SeekEoln	SetTextBuf	Truncate
Write	Writeln		

FIGURE 23.1:

The Print dialog box opened by the PRINTN2 example. Notice the Print to File check box.

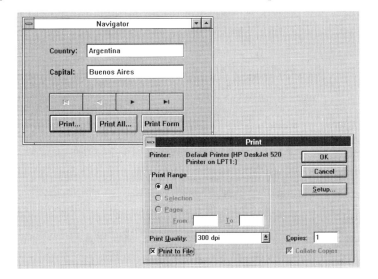

instead of connecting the text file to the printer, the program asks the user to choose a file (using the File Save dialog box) and write the text to it.

The key operation is assigning the text file variable to the actual file:

```
AssignFile (PrintFile, SaveDialog1.FileName);
```

Now you can write to the file, after a call to the Rewrite procedure:

```
Rewrite (PrintFile);
Writeln (PrintFile, Label1.Caption, ' ', DBEdit1.Text);
Writeln (PrintFile, Label2.Caption, ' ', DBEdit2.Text);
CloseFile (PrintFile);
```

To make things safer, you can use a try block for the output operations, and place the CloseFile call in a finally block, so that it is executed even if there is an input/output error. You can see the file version of the PrintButtonClick method in Listing 23.1.

LISTING 23.1: The complete source code of the PRINTN2 example

```
unit Nav_form;

interface

uses
  SysUtils, WinTypes, WinProcs, Messages, Classes, Graphics,
  Controls, Forms, Dialogs, ExtCtrls, DBCtrls, StdCtrls,
  Mask, DB, DBTables, Printers;

type
  TNavigator = class(TForm)
    DataSource1: TDataSource;
    Table1: TTable;
    DBEdit1: TDBEdit;
    DBEdit2: TDBEdit;
    Label1: TLabel;
    Label2: TLabel;
    DBNavigator1: TDBNavigator;
    PrintButton: TButton;
    PrintAllButton: TButton;
    PrintFormButton: TButton;
    PrintDialog1: TPrintDialog;
    SaveDialog1: TSaveDialog;
    procedure PrintButtonClick(Sender: TObject);
    procedure PrintFormButtonClick(Sender: TObject);
    procedure PrintAllButtonClick(Sender: TObject);
  private
    { Private declarations }
```

LISTING 23.1: The complete source code of the PRINTN2 example (continued)

```
  public
    procedure TableToFile (var TFile: TextFile);
  end;

var
  Navigator: TNavigator;

implementation

{$R *.DFM}

procedure TNavigator.PrintButtonClick(Sender: TObject);
var
  PrintFile: TextFile;
begin
  {show the Print dialog box}
  if PrintDialog1.Execute then
    {if the Print to File check box is selected}
    if PrintDialog1.PrintToFile then
    begin
      {choose a file name}
      if SaveDialog1.Execute then
      begin
        {output the text to a file}
        AssignFile (PrintFile, SaveDialog1.FileName);
        try
          Rewrite (PrintFile);
          Writeln (PrintFile, Label1.Caption,
            ' ', DBEdit1.Text);
          Writeln (PrintFile, Label2.Caption,
            ' ', DBEdit2.Text);
        finally
          CloseFile (PrintFile);
        end;
      end;
    end
    else        {Print to File was not checked}
    begin
      {assign the printer to a file}
      AssignPrn (PrintFile);
      Rewrite (PrintFile);
      try
        {set the font and output the record}
        Printer.Canvas.Font := Font;
        Writeln (PrintFile, Label1.Caption,
          ' ', DBEdit1.Text);
        Writeln (PrintFile, Label2.Caption,
          ' ', DBEdit2.Text);
      finally
        {close the printing process}
```

LISTING 23.1: The complete source code of the PRINTN2 example (continued)

```
          CloseFile (PrintFile);
        end;
      end;
end;

procedure TNavigator.PrintFormButtonClick(Sender: TObject);
begin
  {print the whole form}
  Print;
end;

procedure TNavigator.PrintAllButtonClick(Sender: TObject);
var
  File1: TextFile;
begin
  if PrintDialog1.Execute then
    if PrintDialog1.PrintToFile then
    begin
      if SaveDialog1.Execute then
      begin
        {assign the output to a real file}
        AssignFile (File1, SaveDialog1.FileName);
        TableToFile (File1);
      end;
    end
    else
    begin
      {assign the printer to a file}
      AssignPrn (File1);
      {set the font of the form, and output the file}
      Printer.Canvas.Font := Font;
      TableToFile (File1);
    end;
end;

procedure TNavigator.TableToFile (var TFile: TextFile);
var
  Bookmark: TBookmark;
begin
  {store the current position, creating a new bookmark}
  Bookmark := Table1.GetBookmark;
  Table1.DisableControls;
  try
    Rewrite (TFile);
    Table1.First;
    while not Table1.EOF do
    begin
      {output the two fields, and a blank line}
      Writeln (TFile, 'Country: ',
        Table1.FieldByName ('Name').AsString);
      Writeln (TFile, 'Capital: ',
        Table1.FieldByName ('Capital').AsString);
```

23

LISTING 23.1: The complete source code of the PRINTN2 example (continued)

```
      Writeln (TFile);
      Table1.Next;
    end;
  finally
    {go back to the bookmark and destroy it}
    Table1.GotoBookmark (Bookmark);
    Table1.FreeBookmark (Bookmark);
    Table1.EnableControls;
    CloseFile (TFile);
  end;
end;

end.
```

When you look at this portion of the code in the PRINTN2 example, notice that the actual output code is duplicated for printing and file output. Since the other button, Print All, has more complex output operations, it was better to avoid duplicated code.

For this reason, I've written a procedure that outputs the database table to a text file, which can either be connected to the printer or associated with a real file:

```
procedure TableToFile (var TFile: TextFile);
```

In the code of the PrintAllButtonClick method, depending on the status of the Print to File check box, one of the following two source code excerpts is executed:

```
{First: save to file}
AssignFile (File1, SaveDialog1.FileName);
TableToFile (File1);
...
{Second: print}
AssignPrn (File1);
TableToFile (File1);
```

In Figure 23.2, you can see the file generated by a PrintAll operation, loaded in the Delphi editor.

FIGURE 23.2:

One of the text files generated by the PRINTN2 example, loaded in the Delphi editor

```
                        TWO.TXT
Country: Argentina
Capital: Buenos Aires

Country: Bolivia
Capital: La Paz

Country: Brazil
Capital: Brasilia

Country: Canada
Capital: Ottawa

Country: Chile
Capital: Santiago

Country: Colombia
Capital: Bagota

Country: Cuba
Capital: Havana

Country: Ecuador
Capital: Quito

Country: El Salvador
Capital: San Salvador

1: 1                    Insert
Nav_form two.txt
```

A Text File Converter

In the first example of handling files, we produced a text file using the contents of a database table. In our next example, we'll process an existing file, creating a new one with a modified version of the contents. The program, named FILTER, can convert all the characters in a text file to uppercase, capitalize only each initial word of a sentence, or remove the characters of the high portion of the ASCII set.

The form of the program has two edit boxes for the names of the input and output files, and two buttons to select new files using the standard dialog boxes. The lower portion of the form contains a RadioGroup component and a button to apply the current conversion to the selected files. Figure 23.3 shows the main form of the FIL-TER example. You can see the textual description of the components of this form in Listing 23.2.

FIGURE 23.3:

The main form of the FILTER example at design-time

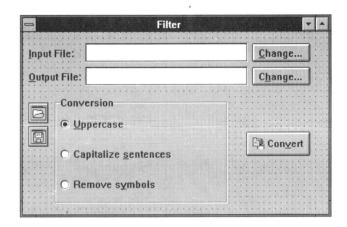

LISTING 23.2: The textual description of the main form of the FILTER example

```
object Form1: TForm1
  Caption = 'Filter'
  object Label1: TLabel
    Caption = '&Input File:'
    FocusControl = Edit1
  end
  object Label2: TLabel
    Caption = '&Output File:'
    FocusControl = Edit2
  end
  object Edit1: TEdit
    TabOrder = 0
  end
  object Edit2: TEdit
    TabOrder = 1
  end
  object Button1: TButton
    Caption = '&Change...'
    TabOrder = 2
    OnClick = Button1Click
  end
  object Button2: TButton
    Caption = 'C&hange...'
    TabOrder = 3
    OnClick = Button2Click
  end
  object RadioGroup1: TRadioGroup
    Caption = 'Conversion'
    ItemIndex = 0
    Items.Strings = (
      '&Uppercase'
```

LISTING 23.2: The textual description of the main form of the FILTER example (continued)

```
      'Capitalize &sentences'
      'Remove s&ymbols')
    TabOrder = 4
  end
  object ConvertBitBtn: TBitBtn
    Caption = 'Con&vert'
    TabOrder = 5
    OnClick = ConvertBitBtnClick
    Glyph.Data = {...}
    NumGlyphs = 2
  end
  object OpenDialog1: TOpenDialog
    Filter = 'Text file (*.txt)|*.txt|Any file (*.*)|*.*'
    Options = [ofPathMustExist, ofFileMustExist]
  end
  object SaveDialog1: TSaveDialog
    Filter = 'Text file (*.txt)|*.txt|Any file (*.*)|*.*'
    Options = [ofOverwritePrompt, ofPathMustExist,
      ofCreatePrompt]
  end
end
```

The user can enter the names of the input and output files in the two edit boxes or click on the Change buttons to open the corresponding file selection dialog box:

```
if OpenDialog1.Execute then
  Edit1.Text := OpenDialog1.Filename;
```

The real code of the example is in the three conversion routines that are called by the handler of the OnClick event of the bitmap button. Let's take a look at one of these conversion routines in detail.

The simplest of the three conversion routines is ConvUpper, which converts any character in the text file to uppercase. Here is its basic code:

```
while not Eof (FileIn) do
begin
  Read (FileIn, Ch);
  Ch := UpCase (Ch);
  Write (FileOut, Ch);
end;
```

It reads each character from the source file until the program reaches the end of the file (Eof). Each single character is converted and copied to the output file. As an alternative, it is possible to read and convert a line—a string—at a time. This will make the program an order of magnitude faster. The approach I've used here is reasonable only for an introductory example.

The actual code of the conversion procedure, however, is more complex. In fact, before calling it, the OnClick event handler of the form's bitmap button shows another form with a gauge, used as progress bar and a button. You can see this secondary form's textual description in Listing 23.3.

LISTING 23.3: The textual description of the secondary form of the FILTER example

```
object ConvertForm: TConvertForm
  BorderStyle = bsDialog
  Caption = 'Converting...'
  object Gauge1: TGauge
    ForeColor = clNavy
    Progress = 0
  end
  object BitBtn1: TBitBtn
    Caption = 'Done'
    Enabled = False
    OnClick = BitBtn1Click
    Kind = bkOK
  end
end
```

At each step of the conversion, a long integer variable with the current position in the file is increased. This variable's value is used to compute the new percentage of work completed, and it is shown in the gauge of the secondary form (see Figure 23.4):

```
Inc (Position);
ConvertForm.Gauge1.Progress :=
  Position * 100 div FileLength;
```

The program also calls the ProcessMessages method of the Application global variable, to let the application update the display and allow the user to drag the window (or even close it). Most of the code related to this form is in the Convert-BitBtnClick method. It disables the Done button of the form, shows it, and enables the button again at the end. The Done button calls the Close method of the secondary form (and this is the only custom code of this source file).

23

FIGURE 23.4:

The progress bar of the secondary form is updated by the conversion procedures to let the user see the percentage of the file already processed.

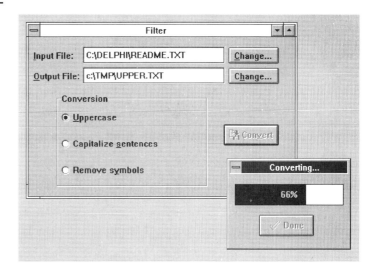

The method associated with the Convert button does most of the work related to handling the files, as you can see in Listing 23.4. This same method opens the input file as a file of bytes the first time, so that it can use the FileSize procedure, which is not available for text files. Then this file is closed and opened again as a text file.

LISTING 23.4: The source code of the main form of the FILTER example

```
unit Filter_f;

interface

uses
  SysUtils, WinTypes, WinProcs, Messages, Classes,
  Graphics, Controls, Forms, Dialogs, StdCtrls,
  ExtCtrls, Buttons, Conv_f;

type
  TForm1 = class(TForm)
    OpenDialog1: TOpenDialog;
    SaveDialog1: TSaveDialog;
    Label1: TLabel;
    Label2: TLabel;
    Edit1: TEdit;
    Edit2: TEdit;
    Button1: TButton;
    Button2: TButton;
```

LISTING 23.4: The source code of the main form of the FILTER example (continued)

```
    RadioGroup1: TRadioGroup;
    ConvertBitBtn: TBitBtn;
    procedure Button1Click(Sender: TObject);
    procedure Button2Click(Sender: TObject);
    procedure ConvertBitBtnClick(Sender: TObject);
  private
    FileIn, FileOut: TextFile;
    FileLength: LongInt;
    procedure ConvUpper;
    procedure ConvCapitalize;
    procedure ConvSymbols;
  end;

var
  Form1: TForm1;

implementation

{$R *.DFM}

function LowCase (C: Char): Char;
begin
  if C in ['A'..'Z'] then
    LowCase := Chr (Ord (C) - Ord ('A') + Ord ('a'))
  else
    LowCase := C;
end;

procedure TForm1.Button1Click(Sender: TObject);
begin
  if OpenDialog1.Execute then
    Edit1.Text := OpenDialog1.Filename;
end;

procedure TForm1.Button2Click(Sender: TObject);
begin
  if SaveDialog1.Execute then
    Edit2.Text := SaveDialog1.Filename;
end;

procedure TForm1.ConvertBitBtnClick(Sender: TObject);
var
  F: file of Byte;
begin
  if (Edit1.Text <> '') and (Edit2.text <> '') then
  begin
    {compute the length of the first file}
    AssignFile (F, Edit1.Text);
    try
      Reset (F);
      FileLength := FileSize (F);
```

LISTING 23.4: The source code of the main form of the FILTER example (continued)

```pascal
    finally
      CloseFile (F);
    end;

    {open the text files}
    AssignFile (FileIn, Edit1.Text);
    try
      AssignFile (FileOut, Edit2.Text);

      {prepare the user interface}
      ConvertForm.Show;
      ConvertForm.BitBtn1.Enabled := False;
      ConvertBitBtn.Enabled := False;
      try
        {move to the beginning of the two files}
        Reset (FileIn);
        Rewrite (FileOut);
        {conversion...}
        case RadioGroup1.ItemIndex of
          0: ConvUpper;
          1: ConvCapitalize;
          2: ConvSymbols;
        end;
      finally
        {close the files and reset the UI}
        CloseFile (FileOut);
        ConvertBitBtn.Enabled := True;
        ConvertForm.BitBtn1.Enabled := True;
      end;
    finally
      CloseFile (FileIn);
    end;
  end
  else
    ShowMessage ('Enter file names');
end;

procedure TForm1.ConvUpper;
var
  Ch: Char;
  Position: LongInt;
begin
  Position := 0;
  while not Eof (FileIn) do
  begin
    Read (FileIn, Ch);
    Ch := UpCase (Ch);
    Write (FileOut, Ch);
    Inc (Position);
    ConvertForm.Gauge1.Progress :=
      Position * 100 div FileLength;
```

LISTING 23.4: The source code of the main form of the FILTER example (continued)

```
    Application.ProcessMessages;
  end;
end;

procedure TForm1.ConvCapitalize;
var
  Ch: Char;
  Period: Boolean;
  Position: LongInt;
begin
  Period := True;
  Position := 0;
  while not Eof (FileIn) do
  begin
    Read (FileIn, Ch);
    case Ch of
      'A'..'Z':
        if Period then
        begin
          Write (FileOut, Ch);
          Period := False;
        end
        else
        begin
          Ch := LowCase (Ch);
          Write (FileOut, Ch);
          Period := False;
        end;
      'a'..'z':
        if Period then
        begin
          Ch := UpCase (ch);
          Write (FileOut, Ch);
          Period := False;
        end
        else
        begin
          Write (FileOut, Ch);
          Period := False;
        end;
      '.', '?', '!':
      begin
        Period := True;
        Write (FileOut, Ch);
      end;
      else
        Write (FileOut, Ch);
    end; {end of case}
    Inc (Position);
    ConvertForm.Gauge1.Progress :=
      Position * 100 div FileLength;
```

LISTING 23.4: The source code of the main form of the FILTER example (continued)

```
    Application.ProcessMessages;
  end; {end of while}
end;

procedure TForm1.ConvSymbols;
var
  Ch: Char;
  Position: LongInt;
begin
  Position := 0;
  while not Eof (FileIn) do
  begin
    Read (FileIn, Ch);
    if Ch < Chr (127) then
      Write (FileOut, Ch);
    Inc (Position);
    ConvertForm.Gauge1.Progress :=
      Position * 100 div FileLength;
    Application.ProcessMessages;
  end;
end;

end.
```

Since the program opens two files and each of these operations can fail, it uses two nested `try` blocks to ensure a high level of protection. As you probably know, it's not unusual for users to enter text that does not correspond to a legal file name.

The other complex piece of code is the procedure used to capitalize the text. It is based on a `case` block with four branches:

- If the letter is uppercase, and it is the first letter after a stop mark (as indicated by the Period Boolean variable), it is left as is; otherwise, it is converted to lowercase. This conversion is not done by a standard procedure, simply because there is none for single characters. It's done with a low-level function I've written (shown at the beginning of Listing 23.4).

- If the letter is lowercase, it is converted only if it was at the beginning of a new sentence. Notice that each time a valid character is found, Period is set to True.

- If the character is a stop mark (full stop, question mark, or exclamation mark), Period is set to True.

- If the character is anything else, it is simply copied to the destination file.

You can see an example of the effect of this code in Figure 23.5, which shows a text file before and after the conversion. This program is far from adequate for professional use, but it is a first step toward building a full-scale letter case conversion program. Its biggest drawbacks are that it turns proper nouns to lowercase, as well as each letter after a full stop (such as the first letter of the extension of a file name!).

FIGURE 23.5:

The result of running the Capitalize conversion of the FILTER example

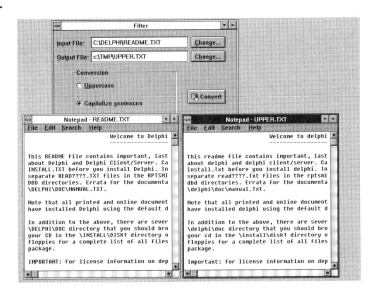

Saving Generic Data

Along with using text files, you can save data to a file using any data type, such as integers, real numbers, records, and other data types besides classes. (We will discuss Delphi's support for saving objects later in the chapter.)

Using a custom file type instead of a text file may be an advantage because it might take less space (the textual version of a number usually takes much more space than its binary value), but this approach won't let the user browse through the files (which might be an advantage, too).

Browsing through the examples in previous chapters, I found one that might benefit from file support—one that is based on a file of integer values rather than on a text file. Our next example, CHART2, builds on the CHART application in Chapter 16. This program used the ChartVBX control to display the data collected in a grid. Since the data is basically a collection of numbers, it makes sense not to save it as text, although the grid contains the strings with the values.

You can see the form of the example (which has basically not changed from the original version) and its new menu in Figure 23.6. The menu bar has a File pull-down menu and a Help menu with the About command. The key element here is given by the three file-related commands. The rest of the code has just a few changes from the older version.

How do you save a series of integers to a file? Simply by reading from or writing them to a file, defined as:

```
SaveFile: file of Integer;
```

As usual, you need to assign the file variable to a real file, operate on it inside a `try` block, and close it in a `finally` block. The program uses a string to hold the name of the current file (CurrentFile) and a flag to know if the data has changed (Modified).

FIGURE 23.6:

The form of the CHART2 example and its menu

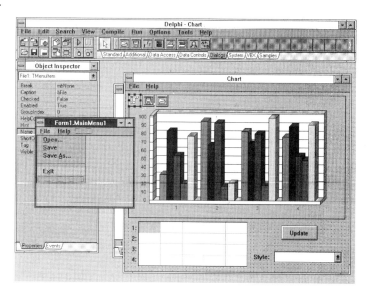

Listing 23.5 contains the full source code of the CHART2 example. Notice that there are several small changes in the old methods (for example, to set the Modified flag properly) and that some of the methods defined by the previous version are called directly by the new procedures.

LISTING 23.5: The complete source code of the CHART2 example

```
unit Chart_f;

interface

uses
  SysUtils, WinTypes, WinProcs, Messages, Classes,
  Graphics, Controls, Forms, Dialogs, VBXCtrl, Chart2fx,
  Grids, StdCtrls, ChartFX, Menus;

type
  TForm1 = class(TForm)
    ChartFX1: TChartFX;
    StringGrid1: TStringGrid;
    UpdateButton: TButton;
    Label1: TLabel;
    Label2: TLabel;
    Label3: TLabel;
    Label4: TLabel;
    Label5: TLabel;
    ComboBox1: TComboBox;
    MainMenu1: TMainMenu;
    File1: TMenuItem;
    Exit1: TMenuItem;
    N1: TMenuItem;
    SaveAs1: TMenuItem;
    Save1: TMenuItem;
    Open1: TMenuItem;
    Help1: TMenuItem;
    About1: TMenuItem;
    SaveDialog1: TSaveDialog;
    OpenDialog1: TOpenDialog;
    procedure StringGrid1GetEditMask(Sender: TObject;
      ACol, ARow: Longint; var Value: OpenString);
    procedure FormCreate(Sender: TObject);
    procedure UpdateButtonClick(Sender: TObject);
    procedure ComboBox1Change(Sender: TObject);
    procedure Exit1Click(Sender: TObject);
    procedure Save1Click(Sender: TObject);
    procedure SaveAs1Click(Sender: TObject);
    procedure Open1Click(Sender: TObject);
    procedure About1Click(Sender: TObject);
  private
    Modified: Boolean;
    CurrentFile: string;
```

LISTING 23.5: The complete source code of the CHART2 example (continued)

```
public
  { Public declarations }
end;

var
  Form1: TForm1;

implementation

{$R *.DFM}

procedure TForm1.StringGrid1GetEditMask(Sender: TObject;
  ACol, ARow: Longint; var Value: OpenString);
begin
  Value := '!09';
end;

procedure TForm1.FormCreate(Sender: TObject);
var
  I, J: Integer;
begin
  {fill the grid with random values}
  Randomize;
  for I := 0 to 4 do
    for J := 0 to 3 do
      StringGrid1.Cells [I, J] :=
        IntToStr (Random (100));
  {update the chart}
  UpdateButtonClick (self);
  {select the initial style in the combo box}
  ComboBox1.ItemIndex := ChartFX1.ChartType;
  Modified := True;
  CurrentFile := '';
end;

procedure TForm1.UpdateButtonClick(Sender: TObject);
var
  I, J: Integer;
begin
  {open the flow of information}
  ChartFX1.OpenData [COD_VALUES] := MakeLong (5, 4);
  for I := 0 to 4 do
  begin
    {set the current data series}
    ChartFX1.ThisSerie := I;
    for J := 0 to 3 do
      {set one of the values of the serie}
      ChartFX1.Value [J] :=
        StrToIntDef (StringGrid1.Cells [I, J], 0);
  end;
```

LISTING 23.5: The complete source code of the CHART2 example (continued)

```
    {close the flow of information, posting the new data}
    ChartFX1.CloseData [COD_VALUES] := 0;
    {set modified flag}
    Modified := True;
end;

procedure TForm1.ComboBox1Change(Sender: TObject);
begin
    {change the type of chart}
    ChartFX1.ChartType := ComboBox1.ItemIndex + 1;
    Modified := True;
end;

procedure TForm1.Exit1Click(Sender: TObject);
begin
    Close;
end;

procedure TForm1.Save1Click(Sender: TObject);
var
    SaveFile: file of Integer;
    I, J, Value: Integer;
begin
    if Modified then
        if CurrentFile = '' then
            {call save as}
            SaveAs1Click (self)
        else
        begin
            {save to the current file}
            AssignFile (SaveFile, CurrentFile);
            try
                Rewrite (SaveFile);
                {write the value of each grid element}
                for I := 0 to 4 do
                    for J := 0 to 3 do
                    begin
                        Value := StrToIntDef (
                            StringGrid1.Cells [I, J], 0);
                        Write (SaveFile, Value);
                    end;
                Value := ComboBox1.ItemIndex;
                Write (SaveFile, Value);
                Modified := False;
            finally
                CloseFile (SaveFile);
            end;
        end;
end;
```

LISTING 23.5: The complete source code of the CHART2 example (continued)

```pascal
procedure TForm1.SaveAs1Click(Sender: TObject);
begin
  if SaveDialog1.Execute then
  begin
    CurrentFile := SaveDialog1.Filename;
    Caption := 'Chart [' + CurrentFile + ']';
    {call save}
    Modified := True;
    Save1Click (self);
  end;
end;

procedure TForm1.Open1Click(Sender: TObject);
var
  LoadFile: file of Integer;
  I, J, Value: Integer;
begin
  if OpenDialog1.Execute then
  begin
    CurrentFile := OpenDialog1.Filename;
    Caption := 'Chart [' + CurrentFile + ']';
    {load from the current file}
    AssignFile (LoadFile, CurrentFile);
    try
      Reset (LoadFile);
      {read the value of each grid element}
      for I := 0 to 4 do
        for J := 0 to 3 do
        begin
          Read (LoadFile, Value);
          StringGrid1.Cells [I, J] := IntToStr(Value);
        end;
      Read (LoadFile, Value);
      ComboBox1.ItemIndex := Value;
      Modified := False;
    finally
      CloseFile (LoadFile);
    end;
    ComboBox1Change (self);
    UpdateButtonClick (self);
  end;
end;

procedure TForm1.About1Click(Sender: TObject);
begin
  MessageDlg ('Chart example with file support' +
    Chr(13) + 'from "Mastering Delphi" by Marco Cantù"',
    mtInformation, [mbOk], 0);
end;

end.
```

As you can see, the Save1Click and SaveAs1Click methods call each other. Save1Click calls the other method to ask for a file name when the file has changed and no file name has been assigned to the CurrentFile variable. This string is also copied to the caption of the form each time it changes (both when you load a file and when you save the current one with a new name). SaveAs1Click, in turn, calls Save1Click to actually save the file once the new file name has been stored.

Both to load and to save the data, the program uses two nested for loops to scan the grid, and then appends the code of the combo box selection at the end of the file. The important thing to notice is that the data should be read in the same order it is written. Another consideration involves the use of the temporary Value variable. The Write and Read procedures require a parameter passed by reference (var), so you cannot pass a property, which doesn't correspond directly to a memory location.

The final items to set are the properties of the SaveDialog and OpenDialog components. They both have a special filter, *Chart files (*.chr)*, and standard options. You can see an example of one of the two standard dialog boxes used by the program in Figure 23.7.

FIGURE 23.7:

Saving a file with a new name in the CHART2 example

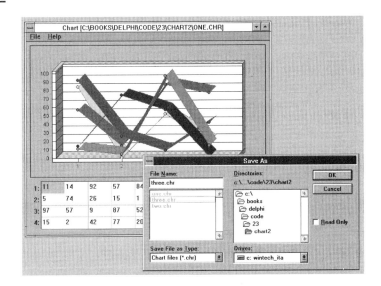

File Support in Delphi Components

Besides the standard Pascal language file support, Delphi includes a number of other choices for handling files. Several components have methods to save or load their contents from a file, such as a text or a bitmap file, and there are other specific classes to handle files.

Many components have the SaveToFile and LoadFromFile methods. In this book, we have used these methods for TBitmap, TPicture, and TStrings (used in TMemo, TListBox, and many other components). They are also available for some data-aware components (TBlobField, TMemoField, and TGraphicField), for other graphic formats (TGraphic, TIcon, and TMetaFile), for OLE (Object Linking and Embedding) containers, and for outlines.

Similar methods are available in TMediaPlayer objects. These methods are named Open and Save, and they have a slightly different syntax and meaning than their LoadFromFile and SaveToFile counterparts. Another file-related class we've already used (in Chapter 19) is TIniFile. This class is a file wrapper specifically intended for Windows initialization files.

The new topics we will cover here are file system components, streaming, and persistency.

File System Components

Delphi file system components are located in the System page of the Components palette:

- TDirectoryListBox
- TDriveComboBox
- TFileListBox
- TFilterComboBox

We have used these components in the TABONLY2 example in Chapter 13 and the File Manager clone example in Chapter 14.

These components are well-known to many Delphi programmers (including those of you who have read the book up to this point). However, what is little known is that the same FileCtrl unit that defines these components also contains three interesting routines:

- DirectoryExists is used to check if a directory exists.
- ForceDirectories can create several directories at once.
- SelectDirectory shows a predefined Delphi dialog box.

Our next example tests the use of these seldom-used routines.

The example, named DIRS, has a simple form with an edit box and three buttons, as you can see in Figure 23.8. There is no textual description of this form, because it is extremely simple. Listing 23.6 shows the source code of the DIRS example. The first two buttons are disabled at design-time, and they are automatically enabled only when there is some text in the edit box (as you can see in the Edit1Change method in Listing 23.6).

FIGURE 23.8:

The output of the DIRS example when the current directory exists

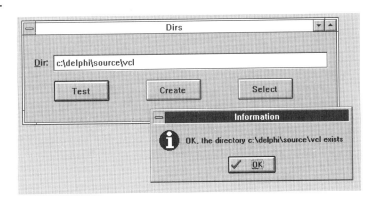

The method associated with the first button tests the existence of the current directory and outputs a corresponding message (see Figure 23.8). The handler of the On-Click event of the second button asks the user to confirm the operation, then creates the directory (or, at least it tries to, because the text might be invalid).

LISTING 23.6: The source code of the DIRS example

```
unit Dirs_f;

interface

uses
  SysUtils, WinTypes, WinProcs, Messages, Classes,
  Graphics, Controls, Forms, Dialogs, StdCtrls,
  FileCtrl;

type
  TForm1 = class(TForm)
    Edit1: TEdit;
    Label1: TLabel;
    TestButton: TButton;
    CreateButton: TButton;
    SelectButton: TButton;
    procedure TestButtonClick(Sender: TObject);
    procedure Edit1Change(Sender: TObject);
    procedure CreateButtonClick(Sender: TObject);
    procedure SelectButtonClick(Sender: TObject);
  private
    { Private declarations }
  public
    { Public declarations }
  end;

var
  Form1: TForm1;

implementation

{$R *.DFM}

procedure TForm1.TestButtonClick(Sender: TObject);
begin
  if DirectoryExists (Edit1.Text) then
    MessageDlg ('OK, the directory ' +
      Edit1.Text + ' exists', mtInformation, [mbOk], 0)
  else
    MessageDlg ('Sorry, the directory ' + Edit1.Text +
      ' doesn''t exist', mtError, [mbOk], 0);
end;

procedure TForm1.Edit1Change(Sender: TObject);
begin
  if Edit1.TExt <> '' then
  begin
    TestButton.Enabled := True;
    CreateButton.Enabled := True;
  end
  else
```

LISTING 23.6: The source code of the DIRS example (continued)

```
  begin
    TestButton.Enabled := False;
    CreateButton.Enabled := False;
  end;
end;

procedure TForm1.CreateButtonClick(Sender: TObject);
begin
  if MessageDlg ('Are you sure you want to create the ' +
      Edit1.Text + ' directory', mtConfirmation,
      [mbYes, mbNo], 0) = mrYes then
    ForceDirectories (Edit1.Text);
end;

procedure TForm1.SelectButtonClick(Sender: TObject);
var
  Text: String;
begin
  if SelectDirectory (Text, [sdAllowCreate,
      sdPerformCreate, sdPrompt], 0) then
    Edit1.Text := Text;
end;

end.
```

The message related to the last button, which is always enabled, simply displays Delphi's Select Directory dialog box, as you can see in Figure 23.9. The three flags passed to the function are used to let the dialog box create a new directory, prompting the user for confirmation.

Streaming Data

Another interesting area is Delphi's support for file streams. The VCL has the abstract TStream class and three subclasses: TFileStream, THandleStream, and TMemoryStream. The parent class, TStream, has just a few properties, but it also has an interesting list of methods you can use to save or load data.

The various methods are described in Delphi's Help file, but it's not so easy to find them. To help you locate the information, you can search the method names in the

FIGURE 23.9:

The Select Directory dialog box is a little-known Delphi system dialog box.

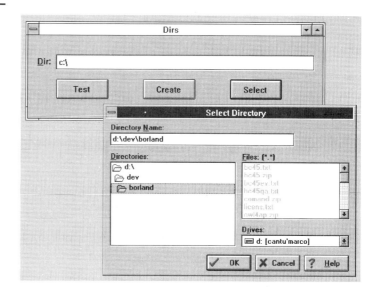

Delphi Help file one by one. The following list of methods of the class might help you locate the information:

```
function Read(var Buffer; Count: LongInt): LongInt;
function Write(const Buffer; Count: LongInt): LongInt;
function Seek(Offset: LongInt; Origin: Word): LongInt;
procedure ReadBuffer(var Buffer; Count: LongInt);
procedure WriteBuffer(const Buffer; Count: LongInt);
function CopyFrom(Source: TStream; Count: LongInt): LongInt;
function ReadComponent(Instance: TComponent): TComponent;
function ReadComponentRes(Instance: TComponent): TComponent;
procedure WriteComponent(Instance: TComponent);
procedure WriteComponentRes(const ResName: string; Instance: TComponent);
procedure ReadResHeader;
```

Most of these functions relate to components, and are used only by component writers, but some of them, such as ReadBuffer and WriteBuffer, can easily be used by anyone.

Creating a TStream instance makes no sense, because this class has no support to actually save data. You can use the two file-based streams to load data from or save it to an actual file. THandleStream is used when you already have the Windows handle to the file. Use TFileStream when you have just a file name. Both classes have special Create methods used to pass file information.

The third stream class is TMemoryStream, which works in memory and not in an actual file. However, this class has special methods to copy its contents to or from another stream, which can be a file stream.

Creating and using a file stream is as simple as creating a file variable:

```
var
  S: TFileStream;
begin
  if OpenDialog1.Execute then
  begin
    S := TFileStream.Create (OpenDialog1.FileName,
      fmOpenRead);
    try
      {... use the stream S ...}
    finally
      S.Free;
    end;
  end;
end;
```

As you can see in this code, the Create method for file streams has two parameters: the name of the file and a flag indicating the requested operation. In this case, the operation is reading the file (fmOpenRead).

Streams can actually replace traditional files, although they might be less intuitive to use at first. A big advantage of streams, for example, is that you can work with memory streams, and then save them to a file, or make the reverse operation. This might be a way to improve the speed of a file-intensive program.

The Idea of Persistency

A particularly interesting element of streams is their ability to stream components. All the VCL component classes are subclasses of TPersistent, a special class used to save objects to streams, and they have methods for saving and loading all of the properties and public fields.

For this reason, all TComponent descendents can actually save themselves to a stream, or they can be created automatically when loaded from a stream. A program can use the WriteComponent and ReadComponent methods of a stream to accomplish this, as we'll see in the next example.

Before the example, however, I would like to give you an idea of how the process works, so you can extend your exploration of this topic. Basically, the streams know nothing about reading or writing components. The methods of the TStream class simply use two other classes: TReader and TWriter, both subclasses of TFiler.

TReader and TWriter objects use the stream they relate to, and they are capable of adding special signatures to it to perform a check on the data format. A TWriter object can save the signature of a component, then save the component, all of its properties, and all of the components it contains. Interestingly enough, it has a method called WriteRootComponent, which writes the component passed as parameter and also each of the components it contains.

Similarly, the TReader class has a ReadRootComponent method, which is capable of creating new objects using the class information stored in the stream. This is possible with one condition: the component name must be registered by the application.

NOTE   A completely different approach (that I'm not going to explore in detail) is to save whole forms with their components as Windows resources, the typical format used by Delphi. In fact, DFM files are just RES files, including custom resources. There are specific methods to save and load components to and from resource files.

After this general introduction, here comes the example, named CREF2. As the 2 in the name suggests, this is the second version of an older example, CLASSREF, of Chapter 5. With the original example, a user could create a number of components of three different kinds inside a form. Now, with the new version, a user can also save these components to a file or load them from an existing file. The program is not a general-purpose Delphi application; it can work only with files created by Delphi. In the next chapter, we'll build a new version that lets the user copy or paste components to the clipboard (and from there to virtually any other Delphi tool).

The form of the CREF2 example is quite simple. It has a panel with some radio buttons, as you can see in Figure 23.10 and in the textual description shown in Listing 23.7.

FIGURE 23.10:

The form of the CREF2 example at design-time

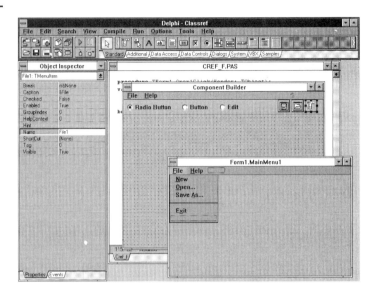

LISTING 23.7: The textual description of the form of the CREF2 example

```
object Form1: TForm1
  Caption = 'Component Builder'
  Menu = MainMenu1
  OnCreate = FormCreate
  OnMouseDown = FormMouseDown
  object Panel1: TPanel
    Align = alTop
    object RadioRadioButton: TRadioButton
      Caption = 'Radio Button'
      Checked = True
      OnClick = RadioButtonRadioClick
    end
    object ButtonRadioButton: TRadioButton
      Caption = 'Button'
      OnClick = RadioButtonButtonClick
    end
    object EditRadioButton: TRadioButton
      Caption = 'Edit'
      OnClick = RadioButtonEditClick
    end
  end
  object MainMenu1: TMainMenu
    object File1: TMenuItem
      Caption = '&File'
```

LISTING 23.7: The textual description of the form of the CREF2 example (continued)

```
              object New1: TMenuItem
                Caption = '&New'
                OnClick = New1Click
              end
              object Open1: TMenuItem
                Caption = '&Open...'
                OnClick = Open1Click
              end
              object SaveAs1: TMenuItem
                Caption = 'Save &As...'
                OnClick = SaveAs1Click
              end
              object N1: TMenuItem
                Caption = '-'
              end
              object Exit1: TMenuItem
                Caption = 'E&xit'
                OnClick = Exit1Click
              end
            end
            object Help1: TMenuItem
              Caption = '&Help'
              object About1: TMenuItem
                Caption = '&About...'
                OnClick = About1Click
              end
            end
          end
          object OpenDialog1: TOpenDialog
            Filter = 'Components file (*cmp)|*.cmp|Any file (*.*)|*.*'
            Options = [ofPathMustExist, ofFileMustExist]
          end
          object SaveDialog1: TSaveDialog
            Filter = 'Components file (*cmp)|*.cmp|Any file (*.*)|*.*'
            Options = [ofOverwritePrompt, ofPathMustExist,
              ofCreatePrompt]
          end
        end
```

As in the older version, the example uses class references to determine the kind of component to create each time a user clicks in the client area of the form. This portion of the code is similar to the original version. What's new is the code of the method related to the menu commands, New, Open, SaveAs, Exit, and About. You can see this new code in Listing 23.8.

LISTING 23.8: The source code of the CREF2 example

```
unit Cref_f;

interface

uses
  SysUtils, WinTypes, WinProcs, Messages, Classes,
  Graphics, Controls, Forms, Dialogs, StdCtrls,
  ExtCtrls, Menus;

type
  CRefType = class of TControl;
  TForm1 = class(TForm)
    MainMenu1: TMainMenu;
    File1: TMenuItem;
    Exit1: TMenuItem;
    N1: TMenuItem;
    SaveAs1: TMenuItem;
    Open1: TMenuItem;
    New1: TMenuItem;
    Help1: TMenuItem;
    About1: TMenuItem;
    Panel1: TPanel;
    RadioRadioButton: TRadioButton;
    ButtonRadioButton: TRadioButton;
    EditRadioButton: TRadioButton;
    OpenDialog1: TOpenDialog;
    SaveDialog1: TSaveDialog;
    procedure RadioButtonRadioClick(Sender: TObject);
    procedure RadioButtonButtonClick(Sender: TObject);
    procedure RadioButtonEditClick(Sender: TObject);
    procedure FormCreate(Sender: TObject);
    procedure FormMouseDown(Sender: TObject;
      Button: TMouseButton; Shift: TShiftState;
      X, Y: Integer);
    procedure New1Click(Sender: TObject);
    procedure Open1Click(Sender: TObject);
    procedure SaveAs1Click(Sender: TObject);
    procedure About1Click(Sender: TObject);
    procedure Exit1Click(Sender: TObject);
  private
    ClassRef: CRefType;
    Counter: Integer;
  end;

var
  Form1: TForm1;

implementation

{$R *.DFM}
```

LISTING 23.8: The source code of the CREF2 example (continued)

```
procedure TForm1.RadioButtonRadioClick(Sender: TObject);
begin
  ClassRef := TRadioButton;
end;

procedure TForm1.RadioButtonButtonClick(Sender: TObject);
begin
  ClassRef := TButton;
end;

procedure TForm1.RadioButtonEditClick(Sender: TObject);
begin
  ClassRef := TEdit;
end;

procedure TForm1.FormCreate(Sender: TObject);
begin
  ClassRef := TRadioButton;
  Counter := 0;
end;

procedure TForm1.FormMouseDown(Sender: TObject;
  Button: TMouseButton; Shift: TShiftState;
  X, Y: Integer);
var
  MyObj: TControl;
  MyName: String;
begin
  {create an object using the current class reference}
  MyObj := ClassRef.Create (self);
  MyObj.Parent := self;
  MyObj.Left := X;
  MyObj.Top := Y;
  Inc (Counter);
  {define the name using the class name, without the
  initial T, and the number of the Counter}
  MyName := ClassRef.ClassName + IntToStr (Counter);
  Delete (MyName, 1, 1);
  MyObj.Name := MyName;
  MyObj.Visible := True;
end;

procedure TForm1.New1Click(Sender: TObject);
var
  I: Integer;
begin
  {delete all existing components, except the panel}
  for I := ControlCount - 1 downto 0 do
    if Controls[I].ClassName <> 'TPanel' then
      Controls[I].Free;
  Counter := 0;
end;
```

23

LISTING 23.8: The source code of the CREF2 example (continued)

```
procedure TForm1.Open1Click(Sender: TObject);
var
  S: TFileStream;
  New: TComponent;
begin
  if OpenDialog1.Execute then
  begin
    {remove existing controls}
    New1Click (self);

    {open the stream}
    S := TFileStream.Create (OpenDialog1.FileName,
      fmOpenRead);
    try
      while S.Position < S.Size do
      begin
        {read a component and add it to the form}
        New := S.ReadComponent (nil);
        InsertControl (New as TControl);
        Inc (Counter);
      end;
    finally
      S.Free;
    end;
  end;
end;

procedure TForm1.SaveAs1Click(Sender: TObject);
var
  S: TFileStream;
  I: Integer;
begin
  if SaveDialog1.Execute then
  begin
    {open or create the stream file}
    S := TFileStream.Create (SaveDialog1.FileName,
      fmOpenWrite or fmCreate);
    try
      {save each component except the panel}
      for I := 0 to ControlCount - 1 do
        if Controls[I].ClassName <> 'TPanel' then
          S.WriteComponent (Controls[I]);
    finally
      S.Free;
    end;
  end;
end;

procedure TForm1.About1Click(Sender: TObject);
begin
  MessageDlg ('CREF2 Example: Save components to file' +
```

LISTING 23.8: The source code of the CREF2 example (continued)

```
    Chr(13) + 'From "Mastering Delphi", by Marco Cantù',
    mtInformation, [mbOk], 0);
end;

procedure TForm1.Exit1Click(Sender: TObject);
begin
  Close;
end;

initialization
  {register the classes of the components; this code is
  required by the stream loader}
  RegisterClasses ([TRadioButton, TEdit, TButton]);
end.
```

The New command handler deletes all of the existing components, except for the panel used as the toolbar. To accomplish this, it scans the Controls array of the form in reverse order (downto). In fact, each time a new component is removed, the Controls property changes. Using the reverse order, the changes are limited to the controls that have an order above the value of the loop counter (I), so they have no influence on the following operations. Notice that this method resets the value of the component's Counter, too.

The SaveAs command handler uses a standard loop to save each of the components to a stream, as described earlier. Again, the code skips the TPanel component. The program uses a try-finally block to be able to close the stream even if an error occurs. In Figure 23.11, you can see an example of the use of this program, as well as a view of the resulting file loaded in a text editor.

The Load1Click method is not much different. This time, the program loops until it reaches the end of the stream. In the loop, it calls the ReadComponent method, passing a nil parameter to indicate that it needs to create a new component. As an alternative, you can assign the value read from the stream to an existing component (which must be of the proper type).

To make the stream reading operation work, I've added to the initialization section of the unit a call to the system procedure RegisterClasses, which creates a list of class names and class references, used by the stream reader. This means that the program is capable of reading only files with the components registered with

FIGURE 23.11:

You can use the CREF2 example to save only the files that the program can read.

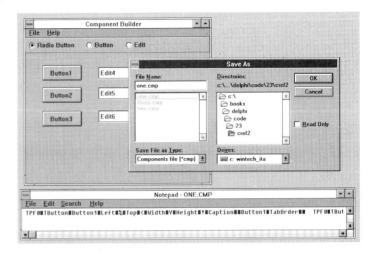

these functions. If you want to extend the program with new components, you can add their names to this list.

Each time a new component is loaded, it is added to the form list of controls, using the InsertControl method (which requires a parameter of TControl type, of course), and the counter is increased, to avoid creating duplicate names later on, when you add new components to the form.

Summary

Using files is a key element of most applications, and you'll find plenty of file support available in Delphi. Several components have specific methods to save their contents (usually text of bitmaps) to a file, and there are several specific classes related to files, such as the stream classes of the TIniFile class.

You can always use traditional Pascal language file handling support, which is a key feature of the language. However, the nice idea in Delphi is that each component is persistent—it can save itself to a stream, or a file. This leads to a number of interesting options for writing Delphi add-on tools (something that is beyond the scope of this book).

Files are used to save data for a later use, but they can also be used as a means of data exchange between different applications, provided that they can read and write the same file format. However, there are several other techniques you can use to exchange data between programs in Windows, including the clipboard, DDE, and OLE. These three techniques are the subject of the next two chapters.

23

CHAPTER

TWENTY-FOUR

Exchanging Data

24

- How the Windows clipboard works

- How to add Clipboard support to your programs

- An overview of DDE

- How to add DDE support to your programs

- Simple server and client applications

- An automatic server and graphical DDE client

Windows users frequently run several applications at a time. Every application usually has its own window, and each application window seems to be separate from the other application windows. However, from a technical point of view, this is far from true. In practice, users benefit from the various forms of data exchange between applications available in Windows.

The three main approaches for data exchange are the use of the clipboard, DDE, and OLE. These three approaches have many differences, both from the user's standpoint and from the programmer's standpoint.

The focus of this chapter is on the use of the clipboard and DDE. As you'll see, these data-exchange techniques sometimes work together, and it is not always easy to draw a clear line to separate them.

What Is the Clipboard?

Basically, the Windows clipboard is a storage area for a single unit of information. This information can be a portion of text, a bitmap, some data in a proprietary format, an OLE object, and so on.

Since there is a specific format for data, each time an application copies data to the clipboard, it also must specify a clipboard format. This can be one of the standard formats or a new clipboard format defined by the application using the `Register-ClipboardFormat` API function.

Actually, the situation is even more complex. The one unit of information in the clipboard can be available in several different formats at the same time. An application can copy data in a custom format *and* in a standard format. The application accessing this data can use the custom format if it knows how to handle it. If not, it can take the copy in the standard format, usually losing some of the information.

As an example, consider the case of passing data from your favorite word processor to Windows Notepad. The word processor copies the data with font and text format information, but Notepad cannot access that information; it can only retrieve the basic text, which the word processor copied to the clipboard as a second version of the data in plain text format.

To have an idea of the contents of the clipboard, you can use the Clipboard Viewer application, which shows the data in one of the standard formats and also lists all of the currently available formats, as you can see in Figure 24.1. Windows for Workgroups 3.11 includes a more powerful Clipboard Viewer, which can better handle saved clipboard files and includes network support. If you are new to clipboard programming, the Clipboard Viewer (whichever version you have) can help you understand what happens in the clipboard.

FIGURE 24.1:

Windows 3.1 Clipboard Viewer, with a list of available formats. Notice that inside the clipboard there is a bitmap with an image of the screen containing the Clipboard Viewer itself, with a Delphi component inside.

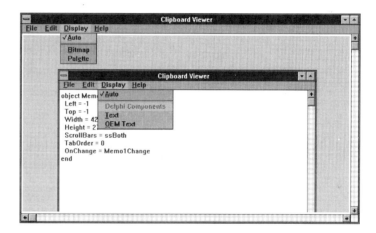

The clipboard offers *user-driven data exchange*. The user must copy (or cut) data to the clipboard from the source application, move to the destination program, and paste the data there. The user has control over the whole operation.

A drawback of this approach is that if the original data changes, the user needs to repeat the whole process again. DDE and OLE were developed to overcome this limitation. In two completely different ways, these techniques can connect the data to the source application.

Another key element is that the clipboard supports a single-copy/multiple-paste operation. This means that when you copy new data to the clipboard, the previous content is lost, but the paste operation is nondestructive. Once you have pasted some data to an application, it is still available in the clipboard for another paste operation.

As you know, the clipboard-related commands are located in the Edit pull-down menu of an application. These commands are named Cut, Copy, and Paste, and have new shortcut keys (Ctrl-X, Ctrl-C, and Ctrl-V, respectively), replacing the older Ctrl-Ins, Ctrl-Del, and Shift-Ins. The same Edit menu often hosts other clipboard-related commands, such as Paste Link and Paste Special, which are actually DDE and OLE commands.

The Clipboard in Delphi

In Delphi, clipboard support comes in two different forms:

- Some components have specific clipboard-related methods. For example, TMemo, TEdit, and TDBImage, among other components, have the CopyToClipboard, CutToClipboard, and PasteFromClipboard methods.
- There is a specific global Clipboard object of the TClipboard class, which has a number of specific clipboard-related features. For full clipboard support, the use of the Clipboard object, defined in the Clipbrd unit, is required.

A program can use the Clipboard object to see if a certain format is available (using the HasFormat method), to list all the available formats, and to place data in the clipboard (when this function isn't handled directly by other components).

The Clipboard object can also be used to open the clipboard and copy data in different formats. This is the only case in which you need to open and close the clipboard in Delphi—something that is always required using the Windows API.

Copying and Pasting Text

Our first example of the use of the clipboard is a new version of the NOTES program. After adding printing support, which we did in Chapter 22, we can now build the final version, NOTES4. There isn't much to do to add clipboard support to this program.

Simply enable the Cut, Copy, and Paste commands, set their shortcut keys properly, and write the following three simple methods:

```
procedure TNotesForm.Copy1Click(Sender: TObject);
begin
  Memo1.CopyToClipboard;
end;
```

```
procedure TNotesForm.Cut1Click(Sender: TObject);
begin
  Memo1.CutToClipboard;
end;

procedure TNotesForm.Paste1Click(Sender: TObject);
begin
  Memo1.PasteFromClipboard;
end;
```

Figure 24.2 shows the Edit menu in the Menu Designer.

24

FIGURE 24.2:

The Edit menu of the NOTES4 example in the Menu Designer

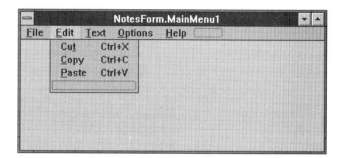

Now you can run the program and work with the clipboard. Notice that the first two commands, Cut and Copy, operate on the text selected inside the Memo component. Paste can either replace the current selection (if any) or add the text at the insertion point.

The program works, but these three commands don't always work. When there is no selection, there is nothing to copy or cut; and when the clipboard doesn't hold data in text format, there is nothing you can paste. The solution is to enable only the menu items that have an effect, by testing the current selection and the current contents of the clipboard.

But where do we write this code? We can't put the test after when one of these menu items is selected, because it is too late. It can't be when responding to a user action in the Memo component, because we won't know if another application has changed the contents of the clipboard.

The location for the test is in the OnClick event of the Edit pull-down menu itself. By adding an Edit1Click method to the form, with the code shown in Listing 24.1, the program behaves as it should. You can test it by running the program. Figure 24.3 shows an example of the program when no text is selected but the clipboard has data in text format.

LISTING 24.1: The source code of the Edit1Click method of the NOTES4 example, used to disable the unavailable items of the Edit menu

```
procedure TNotesForm.Edit1Click(Sender: TObject);
begin
  {if some text is selected in the memo,
  enable the cut and copy commands}
  if Memo1.SelLength > 0 then
  begin
    Copy1.Enabled := True;
    Cut1.Enabled := True;
  end
  else
  begin
    Copy1.Enabled := False;
    Cut1.Enabled := False;
  end;
  {if the clipboard contains some text,
  enable the Paste command}
  if Clipboard.HasFormat (CF_TEXT) then
    Paste1.Enabled := True
  else
    Paste1.Enabled := False;
end;
```

In Listing 24.1 you can see a first example of the use of the global Clipboard object. To compile this code, remember to include the Clipbrd unit in the uses statement of the unit. The HasFormat method used here is documented in the Delphi Help file with five different formats:

CF_TEXT

CF_BITMAP

CF_METAFILE

CF_PICTURE

CF_OBJECT

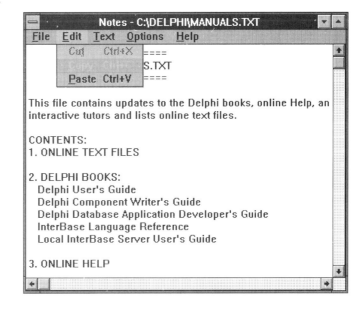

FIGURE 24.3:

The NOTES4 program, when no text is selected but the clipboard has text data

These are the formats typically used by Delphi and by VCL components. The Windows API, however, defines many more formats:

CF_BITMAP	CF_OWNERDISPLAY
CF_DIB	CF_PALETTE
CF_DIF	CF_PENDATA
CF_DSPBITMAP	CF_RIFF
CF_DSPMETAFILEPICT	CF_SYLK
CF_DSPTEXT	CF_TEXT
CF_METAFILEPICT	CF_TIFF
CF_OEMTEXT	CF_WAVE

You can use these Windows formats without any particular problems, although there isn't specific support in Delphi to retrieve these types of data.

In this example, we have used two methods of the TMemo class to perform the clipboard operations, but we could have accomplished the same effect with some of the text-related features of the TClipboard class, the AsText property (used to copy or paste Pascal strings of 255 characters or less), and the SetTextBuf and GetTextBuf methods (used for PChar strings, with no limit besides memory constraints).

The TClipboard class has specific support only for text. When you want to work with other elements, you need to use the Assign method or work with handles.

Copying and Pasting Bitmaps

The most common technique for copying or pasting a bitmap in Delphi is to use the Assign method of the TClipboard and TBitmap classes. As a slightly more advanced example of the use of the clipboard, I've made a new version of the PRINTBMP example in Chapter 22, which was an improved version of the TAB2 example in Chapter 13.

The new example can show bitmaps from a selected file or from the clipboard, if available, and print them (with the Preview dialog box). The structure of the form is always the same, with a TabSet component in the bottom part and an Image component above. The menu, however, is slightly more complex, as you can see in the textual description of the form of Listing 24.2.

LISTING 24.2: The textual description of the form of the COPYBMP example

```
object Form1: TForm1
  Caption = 'Bitmap Viewer'
  Menu = MainMenu1
  object Image1: TImage
    Align = alClient
  end
  object TabSet1: TTabSet
    Align = alBottom
    OnChange = TabSet1Change
  end
  object OpenDialog1: TOpenDialog
    Filter = 'Bitmaps (*.bmp)|*.bmp'
    Options = [ofHideReadOnly, ofAllowMultiSelect,
      ofFileMustExist]
  end
  object MainMenu1: TMainMenu
    object File1: TMenuItem
      Caption = '&File'
      OnClick = File1Click
      object Open1: TMenuItem
        Caption = '&Open...'
        OnClick = Open1Click
      end
```

LISTING 24.2: The textual description of the form of the COPYBMP example (continued)

```
            object Print1: TMenuItem
              Caption = 'Print...'
              OnClick = Print1Click
            end
            object N1: TMenuItem
              Caption = '-'
            end
            object Exit1: TMenuItem
              Caption = 'E&xit'
              OnClick = Exit1Click
            end
          end
          object Edit1: TMenuItem
            Caption = '&Edit'
            OnClick = Edit1Click
            object Cut1: TMenuItem
              Caption = 'Cu&t'
              OnClick = Cut1Click
              ShortCutText = 'Ctrl+X'
            end
            object Copy1: TMenuItem
              Caption = '&Copy'
              OnClick = Copy1Click
              ShortCutText = 'Ctrl+C'
            end
            object Paste1: TMenuItem
              Caption = '&Paste'
              OnClick = Paste1Click
              ShortCutText = 'Ctrl+V'
            end
            object N2: TMenuItem
              Caption = '-'
            end
            object Delete1: TMenuItem
              Caption = '&Delete'
              OnClick = Delete1Click
            end
          end
          object Help1: TMenuItem
            Caption = '&Help'
            object About1: TMenuItem
              Caption = '&About...'
              OnClick - About1Click
            end
          end
        end
      end
end
```

When you select the Paste command of COPYBMP example, a new tab named Clipboard is added to the tab set (unless it is already present), as you can see in Figure 24.4. Then the number of the new tab is used to change the active tab:

```
TabNum := TabSet1.Tabs.Add ('Clipboard');
TabSet1.TabIndex := TabNum;
```

FIGURE 24.4:

The Clipboard page of the tab set of the COPYBMP example shows the current contents of the clipboard if it is a bitmap. Notice that there is a *recursive* image, again.

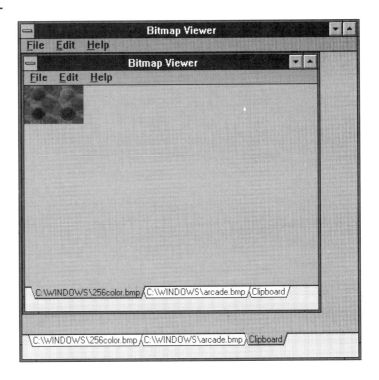

Changing the tab activates the TabSet1Change method, which can load the bitmap from the current file or paste it from the clipboard, as you can see in Listing 24.3. Notice that if the Picture property of the Image component is still not initialized, you must create the bitmap before calling the Assign method:

```
Image1.Picture.Graphic.Assign (Clipboard);
```

LISTING 24.3: The source code of the COPYBMP example

```
unit Viewer;

interface

uses
  WinTypes, WinProcs, Classes, Graphics, Forms,
  Controls, StdCtrls, Tabs, Menus, Dialogs, ExtCtrls,
  Printers, Preview, Clipbrd;

type
  TForm1 = class(TForm)
    Image1: TImage;
    TabSet1: TTabSet;
    OpenDialog1: TOpenDialog;
    MainMenu1: TMainMenu;
    File1: TMenuItem;
    Open1: TMenuItem;
    Exit1: TMenuItem;
    Help1: TMenuItem;
    About1: TMenuItem;
    Print1: TMenuItem;
    Edit1: TMenuItem;
    Paste1: TMenuItem;
    Copy1: TMenuItem;
    Cut1: TMenuItem;
    Delete1: TMenuItem;
    procedure Open1Click(Sender: TObject);
    procedure TabSet1Change(Sender: TObject;
      NewTab: Integer; var AllowChange: Boolean);
    procedure Exit1Click(Sender: TObject);
    procedure About1Click(Sender: TObject);
    procedure Print1Click(Sender: TObject);
    procedure Edit1Click(Sender: TObject);
    procedure Paste1Click(Sender: TObject);
    procedure Copy1Click(Sender: TObject);
    procedure Cut1Click(Sender: TObject);
    procedure Delete1Click(Sender: TObject);
    procedure File1Click(Sender: TObject);
  private
    { Private declarations }
  public
    { Public declarations }
  end;

var
  Form1: TForm1;

implementation

{$R *.DFM}
```

24

LISTING 24.3: The source code of the COPYBMP example (continued)

```
procedure TForm1.Open1Click(Sender: TObject);
begin
  {multiple selection open dialog}
  if OpenDialog1.Execute then
    {add the new selection ot the tabs}
    TabSet1.Tabs.AddStrings (OpenDialog1.Files);
end;

procedure TForm1.TabSet1Change(Sender: TObject; NewTab: Integer;
  var AllowChange: Boolean);
begin
  Image1.Visible := True;
  if TabSet1.Tabs [NewTab] <> 'Clipboard' then
    {load the file indicated in the tab}
    Image1.Picture.LoadFromFile (TabSet1.Tabs [NewTab])
  else
    if Clipboard.HasFormat (CF_BITMAP) then
    begin
      {if the tab is 'Clipboard' and a bitmap
      is available in the clipboard}
      if Image1.Picture.Graphic = nil then
        Image1.Picture.Graphic := TBitmap.Create;
      Image1.Picture.Graphic.Assign (Clipboard);
    end
    else
    begin
      {else remove the clipboard tab}
      TabSet1.Tabs.Delete (NewTab);
      if TabSet1.Tabs.Count = 0 then
        Image1.Visible := False;
    end;
end;

procedure TForm1.Exit1Click(Sender: TObject);
begin
  Close;
end;

procedure TForm1.About1Click(Sender: TObject);
begin
  MessageDlg ('Bitmap Viewer with Tabs,' +
    ' from "Mastering Delphi"',
    mtInformation, [mbOk], 0);
end;

procedure TForm1.Print1Click(Sender: TObject);
begin
  {double-check if an image is selected}
  if Image1.Picture.Graphic <> nil then
  begin
    {set a default scale, and start the preview}
    PreviewForm.Scale := 2;
```

LISTING 24.3: The source code of the COPYBMP example (continued)

```
      PreviewForm.SetPage;
      PreviewForm.DrawPreview;
      PreviewForm.ShowModal;
    end;
end;

procedure TForm1.Edit1Click(Sender: TObject);
begin
  if Clipboard.HasFormat (CF_BITMAP) then
    Paste1.Enabled := True
  else
    Paste1.Enabled := False;
  if TabSet1.Tabs.Count > 0 then
  begin
    Cut1.Enabled := True;
    Copy1.Enabled := True;
    Delete1.Enabled := True;
  end
  else
  begin
    Cut1.Enabled := False;
    Copy1.Enabled := False;
    Delete1.Enabled := False;
  end;
end;

procedure TForm1.Paste1Click(Sender: TObject);
var
  TabNum: Integer;
begin
  if TabSet1.Tabs.IndexOf ('Clipboard') < 0 then
    {create a new page for the clipboard}
    TabNum := TabSet1.Tabs.Add ('Clipboard')
  else
    {locate the page}
    TabNum := TabSet1.Tabs.IndexOf ('Clipboard');
  {go to the clipboard page}
  TabSet1.TabIndex := TabNum;
end;

procedure TForm1.Copy1Click(Sender: TObject);
begin
  Clipboard.Assign (Image1.Picture.Graphic);
end;

procedure TForm1.Cut1Click(Sender: TObject);
begin
  Copy1Click (self);
  Delete1Click (self);
end;
```

LISTING 24.3: The source code of the COPYBMP example (continued)

```
procedure TForm1.Delete1Click(Sender: TObject);
begin
  if TabSet1.TabIndex >= 0 then
    TabSet1.Tabs.Delete (TabSet1.TabIndex);
  if TabSet1.Tabs.Count = 0 then
    Image1.Visible := False;
end;

procedure TForm1.File1Click(Sender: TObject);
begin
  if TabSet1.Tabs.Count > 0 then
    Print1.Enabled := True
  else
    Print1.Enabled := False;
end;

end.
```

If you forget to create the new bitmap and no graphic is associated with the picture, the Assign operation will fail (raising an exception). This is because the Assign method isn't a constructor; it is a method of an object, and if the object has not been created, you'll get a GPF error when you try to call one of its methods.

> **NOTE** The Assign method doesn't make a copy of the actual bitmap. Its effect it to let two bitmap objects refer to the same bitmap memory image, and refer to the same bitmap handle.

Notice that the code of the example pastes the bitmap from the clipboard each time you change the tab. The program, in fact, stores only one image at a time, and has no way to store the clipboard bitmap. However, as soon as the clipboard content changes, and the bitmap format is no longer available, the Clipboard tab is automatically deleted the first time it is selected by the user:

```
TabSet1.Tabs.Delete (NewTab);
if TabSet1.Tabs.Count = 0 then
  Image1.Visible := False;
```

If no more tabs are left, the Image component is hidden. The image can also be removed by using two menu commands: Delete and Cut. Delete simply removes the current tab. Cut makes the same operation after making a copy of the bitmap to the clipboard. In practice, the Cut1Click method does nothing besides calling the Copy1Click and the Delete1Click methods. The Copy1Click method is responsible for copying the current image to the clipboard:

```
Clipboard.Assign (Image1.Picture.Graphic);
```

The rest of the code has to do with opening new files and adding them to the tabs (instead of replacing the current tabs, as the older versions of the example did), and enabling and disabling menu items in the File1Click and Edit1Click methods. It also includes the printer code we added in Chapter 23.

24

Copying Delphi Components to the Clipboard

Along with using text and bitmaps, you can copy any kind of data to the clipboard, including custom data. Delphi does so when it copies components. Actually, when Delphi copies a component to the clipboard, it copies both the custom definition (binary code) and the textual description, which is readable with any text editor, as we saw in Chapter 2.

The specific commands to copy or paste components to the clipboard are the Get-Component and SetComponent methods of the TClipboard class. These methods might be useful for programmers writing Delphi add-on tools, but they are really not as helpful as they might seem at first, as we will see later.

We can use these methods to extend the CREF2 example presented in the previous chapter (the new example is CREF3). The form of the example remains the same, with the addition of a new pull-down menu with the Copy and Paste commands. When a user copies a component to the clipboard, the program shows a list of components in a dialog box, as shown in Figure 24.5, so that the user can choose the component to paste.

The dialog box includes just a default list box, a label, and two standard bitmap buttons inside a new form, named ListForm. All of the code is in the Copy1Click of the main form, as you can see in Listing 24.4. The ItemIndex property of the list box—the position of the selected element—is used as a counter of the Controls array. The

FIGURE 24.5:

The Paste command of the CREF3 example opens a dialog box with a list of available components.

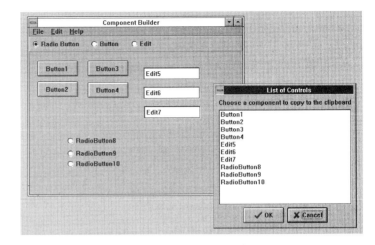

trick here is to add a value of 1 to the ItemIndex to consider the presence of the panel, which is always the first control of the array.

LISTING 24.4: The source code of the Copy1Click, Paste1Click, and Edit1Click methods of the CREF3 form

```
procedure TForm1.Copy1Click(Sender: TObject);
var
  I, Index: Integer;
begin
  {fill the list of the dialog box}
  ListForm.Listbox1.Clear;
  for I := 0 to ControlCount - 1 do
    if Controls[I].ClassName <> 'TPanel' then
      ListForm.Listbox1.Items.Add (Controls[I].Name);
  if ListForm.ShowModal = mrOk then
  begin
    Index := ListForm.Listbox1.ItemIndex + 1;
    {copy the component and change its name}
    Clipboard.SetComponent (Controls[Index]);
    Controls[Index].Name :=
      Controls[Index].Name + 'C';
    Controls[Index].Width :=
      Controls[Index].Width + 10;
  end;
end;
```

LISTING 24.4: The source code of the Copy1Click, Paste1Click, and Edit1Click
methods of the CREF3 form (continued)

```
procedure TForm1.Paste1Click(Sender: TObject);
var
  New: TComponent;
begin
  {retrieve the component, moving it slightly}
  New := Clipboard.GetComponent (self, self);
  (New as TControl).Left :=
    (New as TControl).Left + 50;
  (New as TControl).Top :=
    (New as TControl).Top + 50;
  Inc (Counter);
  New.Name := New.Name + 'P' + IntToStr (Counter);
  (New as TControl).Width :=
    (New as TControl).Width + 10;
end;

procedure TForm1.Edit1Click(Sender: TObject);
var
  Format: Word;
begin
  Format := RegisterClipboardFormat (
    'Delphi Component');
  if Clipboard.HasFormat (Format) then
    Paste1.Enabled := True
  else
    Paste1.Enabled := False;
  if ControlCount > 1 then
    Copy1.Enabled := True
  else
    Copy1.Enabled := False;
end;
```

Notice that once the component is copied, its name is changed to avoid any problem in case the copy is pasted back to the same form, as shown in Figure 24.6. This happens each time; therefore, if you copy the same component several times, many C's are added to the name. An alternative would be to set the Name property to an empty string, and give a reasonable value to the Caption property, but I preferred to adjust the names in both methods to try to give each component a unique identifier.

The Paste1Click method simply pastes the current component on the clipboard, changing its position, name, and width (to accommodate the longer name), as you can see in Figure 24.7. The most complex piece of code is in the Edit1Click method.

FIGURE 24.6:

When you copy a component with the CREF3 example, the name of the original object is changed.

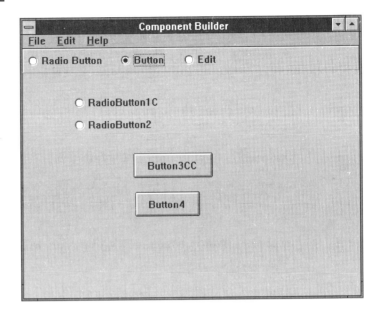

FIGURE 24.7:

The names and positions of two components copied and pasted in the same form, and the information given by the Clipboard Viewer

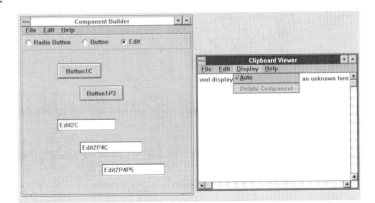

To determine whether to enable the Copy menu item, we need to check if there is a component in the clipboard. By using the Clipboard Viewer (as in Figure 24.7), you can see the name of the clipboard format.

To check if this format is on the clipboard, we can call the `RegisterClipboardFormat` function of the Windows API, passing as a parameter the name of the format. The return value is a system-wide format code. This means that if two applications use the same format name, they end up with the same format code.

The CREF3 programs works, although it can be improved in a number of ways. For example, if you paste the same component twice, the older object is covered. But the major problem I discovered is that the format used by this clipboard method is not the same format used internally by Delphi's form editor.

Besides the fact that it also copies the textual description of the component, the form editor uses a different format, namely *Delphi Components*. This format is not compatible with the *Delphi Component* (without the *s*) format used by the SetComponent method of the TClipboard class. Therefore, this program is probably not a good example of how to develop add-on tools for Delphi.

24

Copying Custom Data to the Clipboard

Our next example adds clipboard support to a program with a generic custom data type. To accomplish this, we can use the SetAsHandle and GetAsHandle methods of the TClipboard class, which call the `SetClipboardData` and `GetClipboardData` functions of the Windows API. These methods refer to a handle to a Windows global memory block, allocated via the `GlobalAlloc` function. For an advanced use of the clipboard, we need to learn how to handle Windows memory blocks, something that will be useful for DDE, too.

Note that in the first shipped version of Delphi, the documentation of the SetAsHandle method does not include a parameter for the handle, which is obviously an error. The correct syntax for the SetAsHandle method is:

```
procedure SetAsHandle(Format: Word; Value: THandle);
```

The real work of this example is to prepare a memory block with the information in a custom format. To accomplish this, we need to call some Windows API functions (which is the easy part) and then fill the memory block with the data. The most common approach for this is to use a pointer to scan the memory area. So this is another first—the first example in the book that uses pointers (this is the advanced section, isn't it?).

This example is a new version of the CHART2 example in Chapter 23, This version, named CHART3, has a new Edit menu, with the usual three functions connected to Copy, Paste, and the selection of the Edit pull-down menu itself. Other than the changes in the menu, the form of the application is exactly the same as in the previous version. The most interesting part of the program is probably the Copy1Click method.

As I mentioned, you can allocate a memory block in Windows using the GlobalAlloc function, which requires as a parameter a flag indicating the type of memory, and the size of the block. The return value is a handle to the memory block, which can be passed to the GlobalLock API function to have a pointer to the first location of the memory block:

```
HMem := GlobalAlloc (ghnd, 25 * SizeOf (Integer));
PInt := GlobalLock (HMem);
```

Note that in Delphi you can skip these two steps and simply get the pointer. This happens each time you create an object. However, in this case, we actually need to bypass Delphi memory management, because we need a standard memory block for the clipboard. When we pass this block to the clipboard, it becomes the owner of the block, and we have no more rights to it.

Once we have a valid PInt pointer, we can scan the memory block and fill it with values. This is generally done using pointers to integers, that is considering the block of memory as if it were an array of integers we can scan with the pointers. In our case, we end up calling these two statements over and over (inside a loop):

```
PInt^ := Value;
Inc (PInt);
```

The first stores a value in the memory location referred to by the pointer, and the second moves the pointer to the next memory slot. When the memory block is ready, we can simply call:

```
Clipboard.SetAsHandle (ClipForm, HMem);
```

NOTE The Windows Help file points out that you need to call the `Global-Unlock` API function each time the `GlobalLock` function has been called, to release the memory block properly. This was true for older versions of the operating environment (the real mode support under Windows 3.0), but now you can usually ignore this advice. Windows memory management has changed a lot in version 3.1, but this is not always reflected properly by the API documentation.

24

If you look at the source code of the Copy1Click method in Listing 24.5, you can see that the code has another feature. The program copies the current information to the clipboard in two different formats: a custom format and a textual format (a string).

LISTING 24.5: The source code of the new methods of the CHART3 example

```
procedure TForm1.Copy1Click(Sender: TObject);
var
  ClipForm, HMem: Word;
  Text: String;
  PInt: ^Integer;
  I, J, Value: Integer;
begin
  {register a custom clipboard format}
  ClipForm := RegisterClipboardFormat (
    'Chart_Data');

  {allocate a memory block and
  retrieve a pointer to it}
  HMem := GlobalAlloc (ghnd,
    25 * Sizeof (Integer));
  PInt := GlobalLock (HMem);
  Text := '';

  {build the data, in both versions}
  for I := 0 to 4 do
    for J := 0 to 3 do
    begin
      {add the number for each cell of the grid}
      Value := StrToIntDef (
        StringGrid1.Cells [I, J], 0);
      PInt^ := Value;
      Inc (PInt);
      AppendStr (Text,
        StringGrid1.Cells [I, J] + ';');
    end;
```

LISTING 24.5: The source code of the new methods of the CHART3 example
(continued)

```
{add the code of the combo box}
Value := ComboBox1.ItemIndex;
PInt^ := Value;
AppendStr (Text, 'Style:' +
  IntToStr (ComboBox1.ItemIndex));

{open the clipboard, to copy multiple
versions of the data}
Clipboard.Open;
Clipboard.SetAsHandle (ClipForm, HMem);
Clipboard.AsText := Text;
Clipboard.Close;
end;

procedure TForm1.Edit1Click(Sender: TObject);
var
  ClipForm: Word;
begin
  {if the proper format is available,
  enable Paste}
  ClipForm := RegisterClipboardFormat (
    'Chart_Data');
  if Clipboard.HasFormat (ClipForm) then
    Paste1.Enabled := True
  else
    Paste1.Enabled := False;
end;

procedure TForm1.Paste1Click(Sender: TObject);
var
  HMem, ClipForm: Word;
  PInt: ^Integer;
  I, J, Value: Integer;
begin
  {get the memory block from the clipboard}
  ClipForm := RegisterClipboardFormat (
    'Chart_Data');
  HMem := Clipboard.GetAsHandle (ClipForm);
  PInt := GlobalLock (HMem);

  {read each number}
  for I := 0 to 4 do
    for J := 0 to 3 do
      begin
        Value := PInt^;
        StringGrid1.Cells [I, J] :=
          IntToStr(Value);
        Inc (PInt);
      end;
```

LISTING 24.5: The source code of the new methods of the CHART3 example (continued)

```
{read the graph type}
Value := PInt^;
ComboBox1.ItemIndex := Value;

{update everything}
ComboBox1Change (self);
UpdateButtonClick (self);
end;
```

To copy two versions of the data to the clipboard, you need to hold its control for the time required for all operations, using the Open and Close methods of the TClipboard class. Without them, the next item you copy to the clipboard will hide the existing one. Instead, using these methods, you can copy several versions of the data, as you can see in Figure 24.8 in the Clipboard Viewer and in the Notepad where I've copied the data.

FIGURE 24.8:

The CHART3 data can be pasted to a text editor, because the program copies data to the clipboard using two different formats.

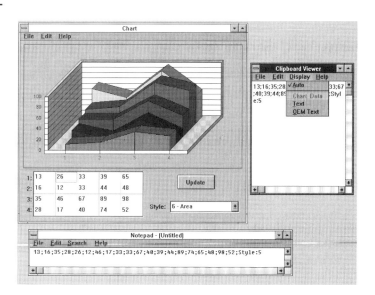

Notice also that I've declared a custom clipboard format, Chart_Data, which is tested in the Edit1Click method, to see if some proper information is available. The program could be improved to accept textual data input (from the clipboard), too. However, scanning the string to see if the data has a valid format and extracting the proper information is somewhat too complex for this example. For this reason, only a Chart_Data memory block can be pasted back, as you can see in the code of the Paste1Click method.

The Paste command handler performs basically the reverse operation of the Copy handler. It scans the memory block, again using a pointer to an integer, and retrieves the data. In particular, the program retrieves the handle to the memory block from the clipboard, then uses the GlobalLock function to access it:

```
HMem := Clipboard.GetAsHandle (ClipForm);
PInt := GlobalLock (HMem);
```

Notice that you are not allowed to store the memory handler the clipboard passes to you. You need to read it immediately (as I've done in the CHART3 program), or make a copy in a new memory block. In fact, the next time some information is copied to the clipboard, the memory block will be deleted by the clipboard itself.

Dynamic Data Exchange: A Technical Overview

As stated at the beginning of this chapter, the use of the clipboard is basically user-driven. If you want to allow an application to move data to another application automatically, without a specific action by the user, the standard approach is to use Windows DDE.

DDE allows two applications to establish a connection and use this connection to pass data. There are different situations DDE can handle, such as sending data on request and performing a continuous update of a data item that changes over time.

The first version of DDE was primarily used as an add-on to MS Excel spreadsheets. It was a message-based protocol, which means that applications sent special Windows messages to each other to exchange information. The protocol was basically a set of rules to use to be able to communicate with applications written by other programmers.

Things have changed over time. DDE has become an integral part of Windows. A new version, named DDEML (DDE Management Library), was added to Windows 3.1. DDEML has a sort of repository where information about the current DDE activities is stored. Instead of communicating directly with another application, DDEML works as an intermediary between the two connected programs, solving problems that arise. This makes DDE far more reliable.

DDE Conversations

24

DDE is used to let two applications communicate in a *conversation*. One of the two applications involved in the conversation is indicated as the server, and the second as the client. The server is basically the information provider; the client is the application that drives the process.

Each application can act as a server to multiple clients, or as a client for multiple servers, and also as a client and a server at the same time. You can see a graphical example of some DDE conversations in Figure 24.9.

FIGURE 24.9:

Examples of DDE conversations

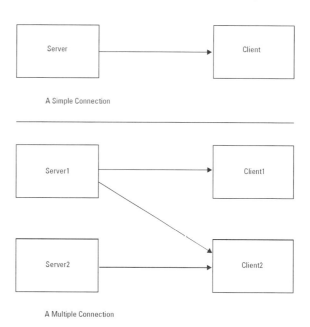

A Simple Connection

A Multiple Connection

Roles of the Server and Client

What actual roles do the server and client play? What can happen when a DDE conversation is active between two applications? The role of the server is basically to send data to the client. The role of the client is to start the conversation, request the data from the server, send unsolicited data to the server (*poke*), or ask the server to execute commands (*execute*).

The central element is certainly sending data. Once a conversation is active, the client can ask for data from the server (*request*) or start an *advise loop*. Starting an advise loop means that the client can ask the server to be notified of any change to a certain piece of data. The server will forward either a notification or a new copy of the data each time it changes.

To determine which server you can connect to, and which is the subject of the exchange, DDE uses three elements:

- *Service* is basically the name of the DDE server application. It can be the name of the executable file (without the extension), but it can also a different name determined by the server itself.

- *Topic* is the global theme of a conversation. It can be a data file, a window of the server, or anything else. A DDE conversation is established between a client and a server about a certain topic.

- *Item* is an identifier of a specific data element. It can be a field of a database, a cell of a spreadsheet, or a stock in an exchange market. Within a single conversation, a client and a server can exchange data about multiple items.

A Simple Example of DDE

After this general introduction, it is time to return to Delphi and explore its DDE support. The System page of the Components palette contains four DDE-related components:

- DdeServerConv handles a description of the conversation (including the name of the topic) from the server side, supporting execute operations.

- DdeClientConv handles a conversation from the client side, indicating the current server and topic, and is required to start a conversation.

- DdeServerItem refers to a data item within a conversation for the server. This is the data that is usually sent to the client, or received from it in the case of a poke operation. The name of this component indicates the DDE item.

- DdeClientItem refers to data received by the server (or sent to it with the poke operation). It refers to the DDE item of the server, and relates to a conversation.

24

To build a server or a client, you can simply place some of these components in two different forms of two different applications, and write a few lines of code. Of course, the aim of DDE is to communicate with applications written by other programmers. However, since I don't know which DDE-enabled programs you have on your computer, our examples here include both of the applications, the server and the client.

Building a Simple Server

Our first program for this example is probably the simplest possible server, which will soon be connected to the simplest possible client. Then the application will evolve into a more complex one.

The form of the first server (FIRSTSER) example, has an edit box and a DdeServerItem component, as shown in Figure 24.10. The service name will be the name of the application, without the .EXE extension. This form doesn't include a DdeServerConv component, which is required only to provide a custom name to the topic and handle execute commands. If you do not use a DdeServerConv component, the topic name will be the title of the form hosting the DdeServerItem.

You can see the textual description of the form in Listing 24.6. Its code simply copies the contents of the edit box to the DdeServerItem's Text property each time the Edit component changes:

```
procedure TForm1.Edit1Change(Sender: TObject);
begin
  DdeServerItem1.Text := Edit1.Text;
end;
```

You can run this server application, but it will be far more interesting after we build the client applicaton.

The simple form of the FIRSTSER example

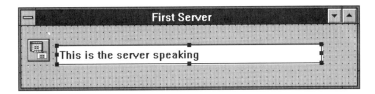

LISTING 24.6: The textual description of the form of the FIRSTSER example

```
object Form1: TForm1
  Caption = 'First Server'
  object Edit1: TEdit
    Text = 'This is the server speaking'
    OnChange = Edit1Change
  end
  object DdeServerItem1: TDdeServerItem
  end
end
```

Building a Simple Client

The first client application, FIRSTCLI, is just slightly more complex than the first server program. As you can see in Figure 24.11, the form has both a DdeClientConv and a DdeClientItem component, plus an edit box and a button.

DdeClientItem1 is connected to the conversation component, using the DdeConv property, as you can see in Listing 24.7, but there is no design-time connection from DdeClientConv1 to the server. The connection is initialized when the button is pressed:

```
procedure TForm1.Button1Click(Sender: TObject);
begin
  if DdeClientConv1.SetLink ('firstser', 'First Server') then
  begin
    ShowMessage ('Connected');
    DdeClientItem1.DdeItem := 'DdeServerItem1';
  end
  else
    ShowMessage ('Error');
end;
```

FIGURE 24.11:

The form of the FIRSTCLI example

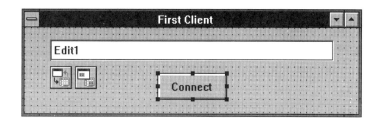

24

LISTING 24.7: The textual description of the form of the FIRSTCLI example

```
object Form1: TForm1
  Caption = 'First Client'
  object Edit1: TEdit
    Text = 'Edit1'
  end
  object Button1: TButton
    Caption = 'Connect'
    OnClick = Button1Click
  end
  object DdeClientConv1: TDdeClientConv
  end
  object DdeClientItem1: TDdeClientItem
    DdeConv = DdeClientConv1
    OnChange = DdeClientItem1Change
  end
end
```

The program calls the SetLink method, passing as parameters the service (the name of the server) and the topic (the title of the form). If the connection is successful, besides showing a message, the application sets the DdeItem property of the client item to the server item.

When the connection is set and the link is active, the server application starts sending data to the client each time the data on the server changes. The client application can simply copy the data it receives to its own edit box:

```
procedure TForm1.DdeClientItem1Change(Sender: TObject);
begin
  Edit1.Text := DdeClientItem1.Text;
end;
```

When the connection and the link are established (when both the client and server programs are running and the client user clicks on the Connect button), everything the user types in the server edit box is copied to the client edit box. Figure 24.12 shows an example of a server edit box change and the corresponding change in the client edit box. (Of course, you should run both of these programs yourself to fully appreciate their capabilities.)

Notice that the DDE link is between the DdeServerItem component of the server application and the DdeClientItem component of the client application. Each time the Text property of the server item changes, this change is automatically reflected in the Text property of the client item. However, since we have established a custom link between the text of the two Text properties of the DDE items, and the corresponding properties of the two Edit components, in practice we have connected the two edit boxes via DDE.

> **NOTE**   What we have built in these DDE applications in Delphi is a DDE advise loop (also known as hot-link) using the DDEML library. Writing the same code in C takes a while, because DDEML is not exactly the simplest Windows API. Delphi's support for advise loops makes this program simpler than a DDE conversation based on a request by the client, which is based on the RequestData method of the DdeClientConv component.

FIGURE 24.12:

When the connection and the link are established, everything you type in the server edit box is copied to the client edit box.

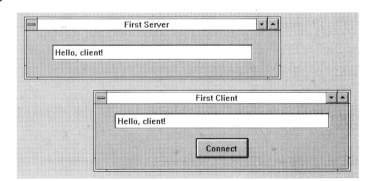

Design-Time DDE Connections

In this DDE example, we made the connection at run-time. However, in Delphi it is also possible to make DDE connections at design-time. To test this, run the server application, open the client project, select the Conversation component, and open the property editor of the DdeService or DdeTopic property. In the following dialog box, enter the required information, as shown in the example in Figure 24.13.

FIGURE 24.13:

The property editor of the DdeService and DdeTopic properties of the DdeClientConv component

Now you can select the client item, select the proper conversation, and enter the name of the DdeItem property, and the connection is established. Make a change in the server, and the new text appears in the Object Inspector, as you can see in Figure 24.14.

Once you have set the connection and the link at design-time, you can actually remove the Connect button and its code. Simply running the client program sets up the DDE connection, and the application will work immediately (as long as the server is running). In general, I prefer the run-time connection approach, which doesn't require the user to start the two applications in a fixed order.

This example could be extended to support poke operations and macro execution, direct requests for data from the client, and provide some information about the current links. However, the result of such efforts would be similar to the examples available in Delphi itself, so I decided to work in a different direction.

FIGURE 24.14:

If the server is running (see the bottom-right corner) when you set the connection and the link, the Text property of the client item is automatically updated with the server text.

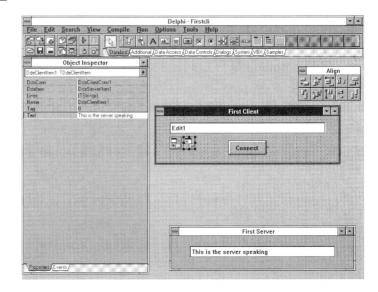

Copying and Pasting DDE Links

Our next step will be to add the DDE version of copy and paste support to the DDE program, by changing it a bit and opening up its interaction with other applications besides those I've written.

Copying Link Data to the Clipboard

As when we started, the first step in building a new version of the DDE example is to build a server. The form of the new paste server program (PASTESER) has three edit boxes, connected with three DdeServerItem components, and three buttons. This version also has a DdeServerConv component. You can see the structure of the form in Figure 24.15 and its textual description in Listing 24.8.

FIGURE 24.15:

The form of the PASTESER example

LISTING 24.8: The textual description of the form of the PASTESER example

24

```
object Form1: TForm1
  Caption = 'Paste Server'
  OnCreate = FormCreate
  object Edit1: TEdit
    Text = 'First line'
    OnChange = Edit1Change
  end
  object CopyButton1: TButton
    Caption = 'Copy'
    OnClick = CopyButton1Click
  end
  object Edit2: TEdit
    Text = 'Second line'
    OnChange = Edit2Change
  end
  object CopyButton2: TButton
    Caption = 'Copy'
    OnClick = CopyButton2Click
  end
  object Edit3: TEdit
    Text = 'Third line'
    OnChange = Edit3Change
  end
  object CopyButton3: TButton
    Caption = 'Copy'
    OnClick = CopyButton3Click
  end
  object DdeServerItem1: TDdeServerItem
    ServerConv = DdeServerConv1
  end
  object DdeServerConv1: TDdeServerConv
  end
  object DdeServerItem2: TDdeServerItem
    ServerConv = DdeServerConv1
  end
  object DdeServerItem3: TDdeServerItem
    ServerConv = DdeServerConv1
  end
end
```

The code of this program is still quite simple, and also somewhat repetitive. When the form is first created, the text of the edit boxes is copied to the corresponding server items:

```
procedure TForm1.FormCreate(Sender: TObject);
begin
  DdeServerItem1.Text := Edit1.Text;
  DdeServerItem2.Text := Edit2.Text;
  DdeServerItem3.Text := Edit3.Text;
end;
```

This text is copied again each time one of the edit boxes changes. Here is one of the three methods:

```
procedure TForm1.Edit2Change(Sender: TObject);
begin
  DdeServerItem2.Text := Edit2.Text;
end;
```

The new code is in the OnClick handlers of the three buttons. When the user clicks on a button, the text in the edit box and the link are both copied to the clipboard:

```
procedure TForm1.CopyButton1Click(Sender: TObject);
begin
  Clipboard.Open;
  Clipboard.AsText := DdeServerItem1.Text;
  DdeServerItem1.CopyToClipboard;
  Clipboard.Close;
end;
```

The copy operation of the server item copies information about the link. This information is not the actual data, but rather the text. For this reason, both copies are needed. If you make only the link, many third-party applications won't recognize this data, because you don't specify anything about the format.

With this code, you can copy the text of one of the edit boxes from this program and paste it in almost any DDE client. For example, Microsoft Word for Windows, both versions 2 and 6, can either Paste or Paste Link this data. Simply run the PASTESER program, copy one of the messages, open a Word document, and choose the Paste Special command on the Edit menu. In the Paste Special dialog box, check the Paste Link radio button to establish a connection, as shown in Figure 24.16.

Now the text is inserted, but when you move to the server and change the text, it will change in Word for Windows as well. This should not surprise you, since the

FIGURE 24.16:

The Paste Special dialog box in Microsoft Word can be used to establish a link with the server we have written.

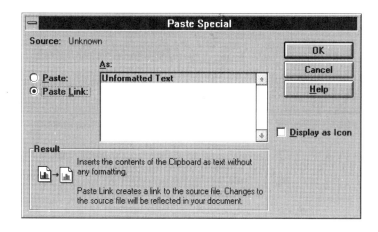

aim of DDE is to allow communication between applications written by different programmers. You should be able to obtain this same effect with many Windows applications, using menu commands named something like Paste Special or Paste Link.

You can see an example of the effect I can obtain in Word in Figure 24.17. I've pasted the contents of each of the server's three edit boxes, making a connection, but I've also pasted them without a connection (with the usual Paste command). Only the copy that has an active link changes while I type in the server edit boxes. Note that if you close the server, the link is temporarily broken, but you can later restore it. Usually, DDE client applications have a specific Links command in the Edit menu to support restoring a broken link.

Pasting the Data to the Client

Now that the server works, even with third-party applications, we can build a new client capable of pasting the data. If we had just a single source of data, we could set the link at design-time.

If we paste some data from the server while it is running, then open the DDE client application in Delphi, we can establish a connection through the DDE Info dialog box. Select the DdeClientConv component and open the editor of the DdeService property. The Paste Link button should be enabled, and you can click on it to establish a connection with the server, as you can see in Figure 24.18.

FIGURE 24.17:

Word links the text changes as I type in the server edit boxes—not a bad result for four lines of Delphi code.

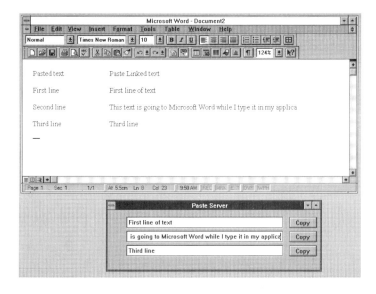

FIGURE 24.18:

When a DDE link is present in the clipboard, you can use the Paste Link button of the DDE Info property editor to establish a connection.

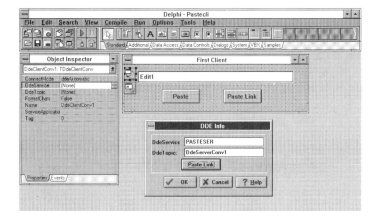

In Figure 24.18, you can also see the form of the PASTECLI example at design-time. Its structure is basically the same as the FIRSTCLI example, except that there are now two buttons instead of one. Again, the Edit component is connected with the client item:

```
procedure TForm1.DdeClientItem1Change(Sender: TObject);
begin
  Edit1.Text := DdeClientItem1.Text;
end;
```

The new Paste button simply copies the text in the clipboard and disables the DDE connection:

```
procedure TForm1.PasteButtonClick(Sender: TObject);
begin
  if Clipboard.HasFormat (CF_TEXT) then
  begin
    Edit1.Text := Clipboard.AsText;
    DdeClientConv1.CloseLink;
  end
  else
    {nothing to do}
    MessageBeep ($FFFF);
end;
```

The problems started to emerge when I wrote the code of the OnClick event of the Paste Link button. How do you know if link information is available? How do you retrieve it? As it turns out, both of these operations are directly supported by Delphi, although they are not documented in detail.

Browsing through the source code, I found that Delphi's Ddeman unit defines a global object, ddeMgr, of class TDdeMgr. This object handles the connection between the application and the DDEML library, and it has a number of private methods. However, it also has three properties: DdeInstId indicates an identifier given to the program by the DDEML library, AppName is the server name, and Link-ClipFmt is the clipboard format used for DDE link data.

This is the information we need for our Paste Link code. We can test if there is DDE link data in the clipboard by writing:

```
Clipboard.HasFormat (ddeMgr.LinkClipFmt)
```

The second problem is even easier to solve. The same Delphi unit has a ready-to-use function to retrieve the DDE link data from the clipboard. Here is its definition:

```
function GetPasteLinkInfo (var Service: String;
  var Topic: String; var Item: String): Boolean;
```

Its parameters, which are used only as return values, are quite intuitive, and the return value informs us whether the function was successful. Now we can write the PasteLink1Click method of the PASETCLI example:

```
procedure TForm1.PasteLinkButtonClick(Sender: TObject);
var
  Service, Topic, Item: String;
begin
  if Clipboard.HasFormat (ddeMgr.LinkClipFmt) then
  begin
    GetPasteLinkInfo(Service, Topic, Item);
    DdeClientConv1.SetLink (Service, Topic);
    DdeClientItem1.DdeItem := Item;
  end
  else
    {nothing to do}
    MessageBeep ($FFFF);
end;
```

By setting these values, the connection is automatically established, because the default value of the ConnectMode property of the client Conversation component is ddeAutomatic. When you run the PASTESER and the PASTECLI examples at the same time, you can make a traditional copy of the text in one of the server's three edit boxes, or establish a link. You can see an example in Figure 24.19.

This example demonstrates the difference between the traditional use of the clipboard and the use of DDE. When a DDE connection is started, the data is copied

FIGURE 24.19:

Copying data and connections between PASTESER and PASTECLI

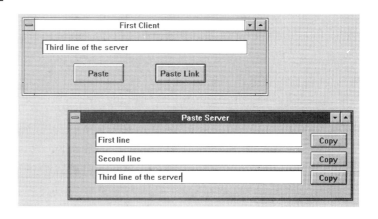

without any action by the user. Using the clipboard, the user needs to copy and paste the data over and over.

Most applications use the clipboard (and the typical Copy and Paste commands) to start a DDE connection and also to copy OLE objects (the topic of the next chapter).

DDE Communication with the Program Manager

24

Another typical use of DDE is to give commands to programs. You can create a new group in the Program Manager or create new program items. This is particularly useful if you need to write an installation program. Delphi supplies an example of this use, so we won't build a new one here.

Basically, to communicate with the Program Manager, you need to place a client conversation component in a form, and set both its DdeService and DdeTopic properties to PROGMAN. To add a new group, you can execute a macro containing the proper command:

```
DdeClientConv1.ExecuteMacro (
  '[CreateGroup ("New Group")]',
  False));
```

> **NOTE** The text and syntax of a macro depends on the server, and should be documented by the server. The Program Manager macros are documented in the Windows API Help file.

Adding a new item requires a more complex DDE macro command. The AddItem Program Manager macro has four parameters:

- The complete path, including the name of the executable file
- The title you want to give to the item
- The working directory
- The number of the icon to use, among those included in the executable file

In the following sample statement, notice the use of C string, indicated by double quotation marks, inside the Pascal string used as a parameter:

```
DdeClientConv1.ExecuteMacro (
  '[AddItem ("C:\DEV\TEST.EXE","Test Program","C:\DEV"',1)]',
  False));
```

DDE with Timers and Graphics

Most of the DDE examples in Delphi use text as a data-exchange element. This is because Delphi has specific support for text items. It is possible to use Delphi DDE support and call some functions of the DDEML API, to extend it. Generally, it is easier to convert data to text and use DDE support than to try to use Delphi undocumented features and direct API calls.

To test Delphi's DDE capabilities beyond handling text items, I've built an example that involves graphics, although the data exchange takes place with a string. This example is different from the previous ones for two reasons. First, the server data is automatically updated, using a timer. Second the client shows a graphical version of the data.

The Automatic Server

The server, named DATASERV, has the usual simple form, with the addition of a read-only Memo component and a timer, as you can see in Figure 24.20. The textual description of this form is in Listing 24.9.

When the form is created, it starts the random number generation and calls the Randomize procedure. This is required, because each time the timer interval elapses, the values of the five lines of the memo are changed by adding a random value between –10 and 10 (adding or subtracting a number from 1 to 10). At the end of the handler, the text of the memo is copied to the DdeServerItem:

```
procedure TForm1.Timer1Timer(Sender: TObject);
var
  I, Value: Integer;
begin
  for I := 0 to 4 do
```

FIGURE 24.20:

The form of the DATASER example

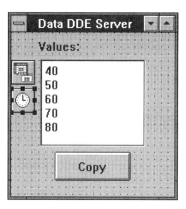

24

LISTING 24.9: The textual description of the form of the DATASER example

```
object Form1: TForm1
  Caption = 'Data DDE Server'
  OnCreate = FormCreate
  object Label1: TLabel
    Caption = 'Values:'
  end
  object Memo1: TMemo
    TabStop = False
    Enabled = False
    Lines.Strings = (
      '40'
      '50'
      '60'
      '70'
      '80')
    ReadOnly = True
  end
  object CopyButton: TButton
    Caption = 'Copy'
    OnClick = CopyButtonClick
  end
  object Timer1: TTimer
    OnTimer = Timer1Timer
  end
  object DdeServerItem1: TDdeServerItem
  end
end
```

```
begin
  Value := StrToIntDef (Memo1.Lines [I], 50);
  Value := Value + Random (21) - 10;
  Memo1.Lines [I] := IntToStr (Value);
end;
DdeServerItem1.Lines := Memo1.Lines;
end;
```

The other method is a copy-to-clipboard operation you should already be familar with. Besides copying the data, we also copy the DDE link:

```
procedure TForm1.CopyButtonClick(Sender: TObject);
begin
  Clipboard.Open;
  Clipboard.AsText := Memo1.Text;
  DdeServerItem1.CopyToClipboard;
  Clipboard.Close;
end;
```

When we copy from this server and paste the result in any application, the data will change automatically, without any user action. You can see an example, once more using Microsoft Word, in Figure 24.21. Run this program to appreciate its effect.

FIGURE 24.21:

You can copy the DATASERV data to WinWord, and it will automatically change at each timer interval

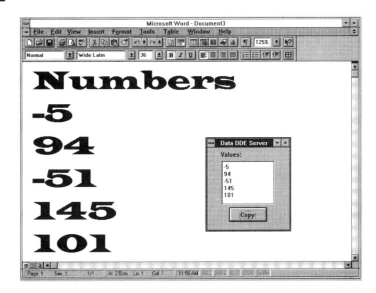

A Graphical DDE Client

Showing the numbers that change automatically in a third-party application is certainly interesting, but this is just text. The client application that works with this server will show the data graphically.

The form of the VIEWDATA client contains just the two typical DDE client conversation and DDE client item components, without any special property set. Since the form is so bare, you might expect the code to be complex, and it really is.

When the form is created, the DDE connection is established:

```
procedure TForm1.FormCreate(Sender: TObject);
begin
  if DdeClientConv1.SetLink ('dataserv', 'Data DDE Server') then
    DdeClientItem1.DdeItem := 'DdeServerItem1'
  else
    ShowMessage ('Start the server before the client');
end;
```

Instead of simply showing a message, you might try to actually run the server, using the WinExec API. However, this can get complicated if it doesn't reside in the same directory or in one of the directories of the system path.

Each time the DDE item data changes, the new values are extracted from the string and copied to an array of integers, defined as:

```
Values: array [0..4] of Integer;
```

At first, I thought that the lines of the server item were copied to the lines of the client item, so that this code simply needed to extract and convert each string. But the program ended up with a single string holding all of the numbers.

After some trials, I found my error. The FormatChars property of the DdeClientConv component should be set to True, to avoid skipping the new-line characters. When you have set this property, simply write:

```
procedure TForm1.DdeClientItem1Change(Sender: TObject);
var
  I: Integer;
begin
  {extract the numbers}
  for I := 0 to 4 do
    if I < DdeClientItem1.Lines.Count then
```

```
        Values [I] := StrToIntDef (DdeClientItem1.Lines[I], 50);
    Invalidate;
  end;
```

The if statement might seem redundant, but it is not. This method is also called at startup, when the values are still not there.

Now for the real code. The last line of the OnChange event handler of the DdeClientItem component, above, calls Invalidate to repaint the form.

The FormPaint method (see Listing 24.10) is quite complex. Its aim is to draw five vertical bars, in the range –100 to 200, equally spaced in the form. At the beginning, the program computes some internal values. The width of each bar, DX, is computed by dividing the width of the client area of the form by 11, because there are five bars and six empty spaces around them. The DY value serves as unit of measure for a value of a hundred (of the data), and to draw the reference line. You can see the effect, with some hints, in the graph shown in Figure 24.22.

LISTING 24.10: The FormPaint method of the VIEWDATA example

```
procedure TForm1.FormPaint(Sender: TObject);
var
  I, DX, DY: Integer;
  Scale: Real;
begin
  {DX is the width of each band}
  DX := ClientWidth div 11;
  {DY is the height corresponding to a value of 100}
  DY := ClientHeight div 3;
  Scale := DY / 100;

  {draw axis, at Y=0}
  Canvas.Pen.Width := 3;
  Canvas.MoveTo (0, DY * 2);
  Canvas.LineTo (ClientWidth, DY * 2);

  {draw 100 mark}
  Canvas.Pen.Width := 1;
  Canvas.MoveTo (0, DY);
  Canvas.LineTo (ClientWidth, DY);

  for I := 0 to 4 do
  begin
    {green for positive values,
    red for negative values}
    if Values [I] > 0 then
      Canvas.Brush.Color := clGreen
```

LISTING 24.10: The FormPaint method of the VIEWDATA example (continued)

```
    else
      Canvas.Brush.Color := clRed;
    {draw the bar}
    Canvas.Rectangle (DX * (2 * I + 1),
      DY * 2 - Round (Values [I] * Scale),
      DX * (2 * I + 2),
      DY * 2);
  end;
end;
```

24.

FIGURE 24.22:

The axis of the VIEWDATA output

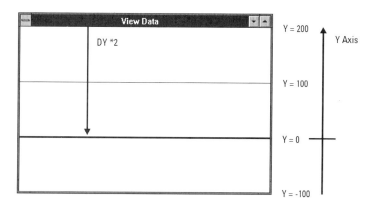

For each value of the array, the program draws a rectangle, at a fixed horizontal position, which depends on its number. The vertical position range starts at the origin (DY*2) and reaches the value of the element, reduced to the proper scale. If the number becomes negative, there is no problem, since the parameters of the Rectangle method are considered as the sides of the rectangle, and the order is not important.

You can see the result of this painting code in Figure 24.23, where two copies of the program are running to show that the image is automatically scaled to the form size.

The bars of the VIEWDATA example change automatically over the time, without any user action, both on the client program and on the server application.

FIGURE 24.23:

Two examples of the output of the
VIEWDATA program

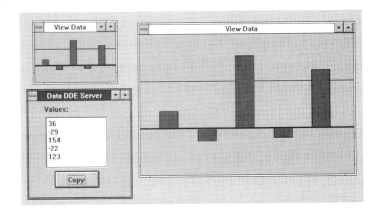

Summary

In this chapter, we have seen how you can add clipboard and DDE support to existing or new programs, and we have seen the similarities and differences between the two techniques.

The use of the clipboard is very common in Windows applications, and those you write should be no exception. Adding clipboard support is generally quite simple (even when you write Windows programs using the API).

DDE support can be a real enhancement to your program. Letting a user copy and paste links, and not only data, between two programs you have written is certainly interesting. Even better, with DDE links, users of your programs can exchange data with other widely used Windows applications.

DDE support in Delphi is simple, particularly if you compare it with the code behind the scenes. The only drawbacks are that it is not very well documented and that not all of the DDE features are easily available. Delphi's support, however, is probably good enough for most programmers.

Now it is time to look to the third Windows data-exchange technique, OLE. This is the subject of the next chapter.

CHAPTER

TWENTY-FIVE

The Power of OLE

- A simple OLE container

- Support for inserting new embedded or linked objects

- OLE objects loaded from files and saved to files

- Link-handling support

- Menu bar merging and toolbar replacement for in-place editing

- A form with multiple OLE containers

For several reasons, OLE can be considered as an extension of the other data-exchange techniques we discussed in the previous chapter, the clipboard and DDE. OLE was developed later, it used DDE connections behind the scenes in the first version, and is often activated using Copy and Paste menu commands. As with DDE, OLE connections can originate from the clipboard.

OLE merits an entire chapter because it comes in several flavors, involves client and server applications, exists in two main versions, offers features similar to DDE execute (indicated as OLE automation), and is becoming one of the key elements of Microsoft software strategy.

Although this chapter begins with a short introduction to OLE and its terminology, you won't find details about the many aspects of OLE—there are whole books devoted to that topic. I assume that you have some experience with OLE applications. Our focus here is on Delphi OLE support, which is limited to client applications—or *container* applications, to use OLE jargon. With Delphi, you can call any API functions, so you can create any Windows application, including OLE servers. However, to build a server, you need to work with plain API calls, without any help from the environment. The same holds true for OLE automation.

There is nothing preventing Borland, or you, from writing other OLE components for Delphi, and some third-party developers are doing just this. Borland has promised full OLE support in the next version of Delphi.

What Is OLE?

OLE has two different faces: embedding and linking. One way to see object embedding is as a smart version of the copy and paste operations made with the clipboard. The key difference is that when you copy an OLE object from a server application and paste it in a container application, you can automatically activate the server from within the container to edit the data. Of course, there is much more than this. You can create new OLE objects in an application, you do not need to run the server by itself (some OLE servers are built-in DLLs, so they cannot be executed at all), and you can benefit from the compound document model (saving to disk an OLE object inside another OLE object).

One way to see object linking is as a smart version of DDE advise loops. You generally activate object linking by using the clipboard and making a paste-link operation.

However, the server application doesn't need to be open to change its data. From the OLE container application, you can activate the server and work on the original data. Again, there is much more than this. Object linking has a number of advanced features you won't find in DDE, and it is generally quite easy for users to work with linked objects.

When you have a linked object, if you open the server, it always works in a separate window. When you have an embedded object, however, if the server is an OLE 2.0 server, the container can support visual editing, which means that you can work on the server inside the container's main window. The two windows, their menus, and their toolbars are merged automatically, allowing the user to work within a single window on a number of different object types—with a number of different OLE servers—without leaving the application.

Another key difference between embedding and linking is that the data of an embedded object is stored and managed by the container application. The container saves the embedded object in its own files. A linked object physically resides in a separate file, which is handled by the server exclusively, even if the link refers only to a small portion of the file.

In both cases, the container application doesn't know how to handle the object and its data—not even how to display it—without the help of the server. The server application has a lot of work to do, even when you are not editing the data. Container applications often make a copy of the image of an OLE object and use the bitmap to represent the data, which speeds up some operations with the object. The drawback of this approach is that many commercial OLE applications end up with bloated files (because two copies of the same data are saved).

If you add this to the relative slowness of OLE and the amount of work necessary to develop OLE servers, you can understand why the use of this powerful approach is still somewhat limited. Things might change as new tools are developed to make OLE programming easier, and as OLE faces some competition from OpenDoc and other alternative approaches in the future.

The Flavors of OLE

OLE comes in several flavors, and there are currently Windows applications using compatible but different versions of OLE. The first version, included in Windows 3.1, has been replaced by version 2.0, which has several more features: in-place or visual

25

editing, better support for object storage, support for automation, and support for the development of OLE controls.

You can freely mix applications using the two versions of OLE without any problems. Of course, if you write an OLE 2.0 container in Delphi, when you use an older server, the new capabilities won't be available.

There are also two kinds of OLE servers:

- Full servers are stand-alone applications, which have file support and are available for any possible use of OLE.

- Mini servers are servers in DLLs, which cannot be executed by themselves and don't have their own storage. Mini servers support only embedding, not linking.

On the other side, containers can support OLE in various degrees. Without considering the different versions, there are several techniques for placing an object in a container:

- You can insert a new object, using a specific menu command to create an embedded object.

- You can paste an object from the clipboard, creating a new embedded object.

- You can paste-link an object from the clipboard, creating a new linked object.

- You can create a new object from a file generated by a server. This can result in either an embedded object or a linked object.

- You can drag an object from a server to a container, if the two applications support this feature.

- You can create an object inside another object (only with OLE 2), if the server can also be a container.

Once the object is inside the container, you can then make some operations on it, using the server's available *verbs,* or actions. Usually the *edit verb* is the default action, which is the action usually performed with a double-click on the object. For other objects, play is defined as the default action. You can typically see the list of actions supported by the current container object when it is not active (when you are not editing it) by using the Object menu item, generally in the Edit pull-down menu. The Object menu item generally has a submenu that lists its verbs.

OLE Behind the Scenes

We object-oriented programmers (Delphi programmers are legitimately included in this group) think in terms of a variable corresponding to a specific data type. The data type has some method we can apply to the objects. Objects have unique values for properties and data, but we access the object by using its public interface, and often know nothing about the details of the implementation.

In OLE, objects are similar. We know very little about their implementation (that is, the code of the server application), and can use only their public interface. Being based on the C language, this public interface is basically an array of function pointers—procedural types in Object Pascal terms. Most of these functions are internal to OLE. They are used to ask the server to draw an object, print it, activate its menus, agree on the toolbar arrangement, and so on. Few of the functions correspond to the verbs, or to the actions a user can perform on the object, with the help of the server.

As an Object Pascal object, an OLE object contains data and not code. In an OOP language, the methods of the object are available using the type information. In OLE, every object has a connection (through a unique ID) to a description of the server, which is stored in a central repository, the registration database. This database, actually the REG.DAT file in Windows 3.1, can be browsed using a little-known Windows application, called REGEDIT, for Registration Editor. To view detailed information, run this tool with the /v parameter on its command line.

The Registration Editor has, among many other things, an indication of where the server resides on the computer, and it can activate this application or library by running it or by activating it. In any case, to work on the object in the container, the server application must be loaded in memory.

Once this has happened, the container and the server start to communicate and exchange data. For this purpose, the two applications access some OLE DLLs, but these DLLs keep in contact using the DDEML (the DDE Management Library, mentioned in the previous chapter).

That's enough for a minimal overview of technical OLE details. Now we will move on to the real topic of this chapter: writing OLE containers in Delphi.

25

OLE Support in Delphi

OLE support in Delphi comes through the TOleContainer component. This component is defined in the ToCtrl unit, together with some useful OLE helper procedures and functions. This component, as well as all of the OLE support in Delphi, is documented in detail in the Help file and in Delphi's *User's Guide*. You can refer to those sources for a general description of the component and other OLE information. Here, we will look at an OLE example built step-by-step, with a final effect similar to the OLE examples available in Delphi.

Building the Minimum OLE Container

To create a simple OLE container application in Delphi, place an OLE container component in a form and select its ObjClass property. You'll see the Insert Object dialog box, which allows you to choose a server application, as shown in Figure 25.1. The list of servers that appears in this dialog box depends on the OLE applications installed on your system and stored in the registration database.

FIGURE 25.1:

The dialog box that appears when you choose the ObjClass property allows you to select an OLE server installed on your system.

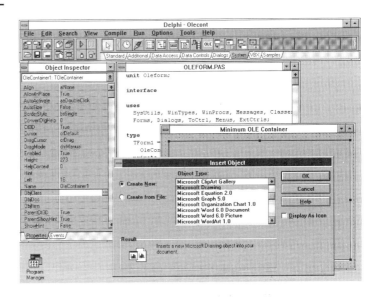

The OLE object inserted in the container in indicated by three properties: ObjClass, ObjDoc, and ObjItem. The first indicates the server and is always required. The other two indicate a document, a file, and a data-item within the document, such as a spreadsheet cell or the portions of a drawing. These two properties are required only for linked OLE objects, not for embedded OLE objects. (If you study these properties carefully, you'll notice that they look suspiciously similar to the three elements of a DDE connection: service, topic, and item.)

Once you have selected a server for an embedded object, that application will open in a separate window and let you edit the data of the object. When you close the server application, you can update the object in the container and see it at design-time in the form of the Delphi application you are developing, as shown in Figure 25.2.

25

FIGURE 25.2:

The Microsoft Drawing OLE object inside the form of the OLECONT1 example at design-time

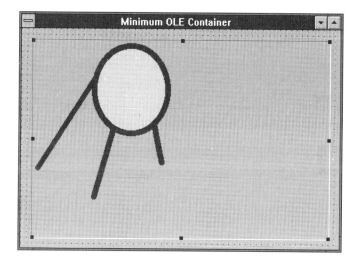

I haven't made any other relevant changes to this program, named OLECONT1. I've just removed the border of the OLE container component. You can see the textual description of this form in Listing 25.1.

As you can see in the listing, Delphi adds two properties: InitInfo and Data. InitInfo holds system information about the embedded object. This is not exactly a property, but actually the data referred to by the PInitInfo property, which is a pointer. We

LISTING 25.1: The textual description of the form of the OLECONT1 example

```
object Form1: TForm1
  Caption = 'Minimum OLE Container'
  object OleContainer1: TOleContainer
    BorderStyle = bsNone
    ObjClass = 'Microsoft Drawing'
    InitInfo = (
      'FLink 1'
      'Where 3'
      'Iconic 0'
      'Left 16'
      'Top 16'
      'Right 216'
      'Bottom 240')
    Data = {... omitted ...}
  end
end
```

will use this property later in this chapter. The Data property (omitted in the listing) is the actual data of the OLE object.

Using this approach, the data of the object is actually stored inside the form, and then in the executable file of the program. This can certainly increase the size of the program a lot, depending on the server and the amount of data. Another problem is that you can run this program only on a computer that has the required server installed. Otherwise, you'll get a run-time error. This is also true for the sample program. You can run OLECONT1 only if the Microsoft Drawing server is installed on your computer. If you don't have that application, edit the program to select a different server.

When you run the OLECONT1 example, you can simply double-click on the OLE container component, and the server will show the data in its own window, where you can edit it, as shown in Figure 25.3. The editing of the object starts when you double-click on the object because of the value of the AutoActivate property, which is aaDoubleClick by default. Other alternatives are aaGetFocus and aaManual. When the value is aaManual, you can use the Active property to start the server. Note that you cannot always use the same property to end editing; if the server has its own window, the user generally closes it.

The OLE1 example at run-time, with the server open

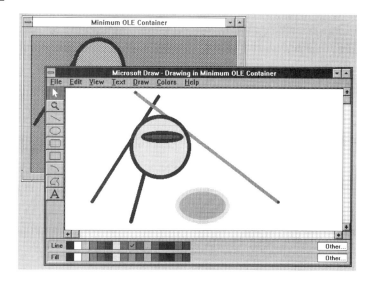

25

Notice that the behavior of this program is similar to that of an OLE application, since it doesn't support visual editing. To accomplish this in a Delphi application, you can add a menu bar to the form, as we'll do in the next section.

The Minimal Menu of an OLE Container

To build a better version of the sample OLE container application, OLECONT2, I've created a new form, which includes an OLE container component, a menu, and a panel. Figure 25.4 shows the form of the OLECONT2 example at design-time, and Listing 25.2 shows the textual description.

In this version, the container does not have a predefined OLE object. A new OLE object will be created with the New command on the File menu, one of the few menu items of the application that is enabled.

The other important menu item is the Object command on the Edit menu, which is connected to the OLE container. You make this connection by setting the value of the form's ObjectMenuItem property to Object1. The Object menu item will be enabled automatically when the OLE container is selected (but not active) and has an object inside. In this case, the text of the menu item changes to reflect the type of

FIGURE 25.4:

The form of the OLECONT2
example at design-time

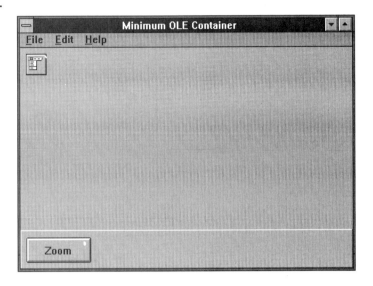

LISTING 25.2: The textual description of the form of the OLECONT2 example

```
object Form1: TForm1
  Caption = 'Minimum OLE Container'
  Menu = MainMenu1
  ObjectMenuItem = Object1
  object OleContainer1: TOleContainer
    Align = alClient
    BorderStyle = bsNone
    Ctl3D = False
    ParentCtl3D = False
  end
  object Panel1: TPanel
    Align = alBottom
    Locked = True
    object ZoomButton: TButton
      Caption = 'Zoom...'
      OnClick = ZoomButtonClick
    end
  end
  object MainMenu1: TMainMenu
    object File1: TMenuItem
      Caption = '&File'
      object New1: TMenuItem
        Caption = '&New...'
        OnClick = New1Click
      end
```

LISTING 25.2: The textual description of the form of the OLECONT2 example (continued)

```
      object Open1: TMenuItem
        Caption = '&Open...'
        Enabled = False
      end
      object SaveAs1: TMenuItem
        Caption = 'Save &As...'
        Enabled = False
      end
      object N2: TMenuItem
        Caption = '-'
      end
      object Exit1: TMenuItem
        Caption = 'E&xit'
        OnClick = Exit1Click
      end
    end
    object Edit1: TMenuItem
      Caption = '&Edit'
      GroupIndex = 1
      object Cut1: TMenuItem
        Caption = 'Cu&t'
        Enabled = False
        ShortCutText = 'Ctrl+X'
      end
      object Copy1: TMenuItem
        Caption = '&Copy'
        Enabled = False
        ShortCutText = 'Ctrl+C'
      end
      object Paste1: TMenuItem
        Caption = '&Paste'
        Enabled = False
        ShortCutText = 'Ctrl+V'
      end
      object PasteSpecial1: TMenuItem
        Caption = 'Paste &Special...'
        Enabled = False
      end
      object N3: TMenuItem
        Caption = '-'
      end
      object Links1: TMenuItem
        Caption = 'Lin&ks...'
        Enabled = False
      end
      object Object1: TMenuItem
        Caption = '&Object'
        Enabled = False
      end
    end
  end
```

25

LISTING 25.2: The textual description of the form of the OLECONT2 example
(continued)

```
    object Help1: TMenuItem
      Caption = '&Help'
      GroupIndex = 5
      object About1: TMenuItem
        Caption = '&About...'
        OnClick = About1Click
      end
    end
  end
end
```

the OLE object, and a second-level pull-down menu lists the verbs of the OLE object, which are the actions you can perform on it, as you can see in Figure 25.5.

FIGURE 25.5:

The Object menu item when an OLE
container component is selected

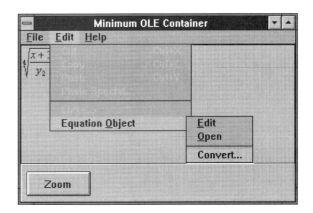

Another important feature of the menus of an OLE container application that supports in-place editing is menu merging. When the OLE object is activated in-place, some of the pull-down menus of its menu bar are added to the menu bar of the container. At the same time, some of the corresponding pull-down menus of the container should disappear.

OLE menu merging is handled almost automatically by Delphi. You only need to set the proper indexes for the menu items of the container, using the GroupIndex property. Basically, the menu items with an odd index are replaced by the corresponding elements of the active OLE object.

In short, the File (0) and Window (4) pull-down menus are those of the container. The Edit (1), View (3), and Help (5) pull-down menus (or groups of pull-down menus with those indexes) are those of the OLE server. A sixth group, named Object and indicated with the index 2, can be used by the container to display another pull-down menu between the Edit and View groups, even when the OLE object is active.

In our example, the GroupIndex properties are 0 for File, 1 for Edit, and 5 for Help, as you can see in Listing 25.2. Figure 25.6 shows an example of menu merging, using the same OLE object as in Figure 25.5. This time, however, the OLE object is active.

25

FIGURE 25.6:

The menu merging of an active OLE object. Notice that the OLE object uses in-place editing.

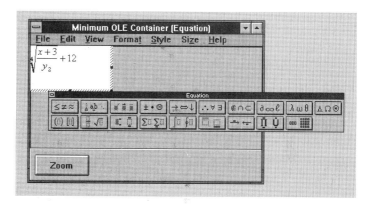

The only menu item we need to code is the New command, used to insert a new OLE object in the container. The code of the corresponding method is based on the InsertOleObjectDlg Delphi function, which displays the standard Insert OLE Object dialog box, shown in Figure 25.7.

The result of the function is stored in the TInitInfo pointer passed as a third parameter. As you can see in the code below, this pointer is used to initialize the OLE

FIGURE 25.7:

The standard Insert Object dialog box allows a user to create a new object or load one from a file.

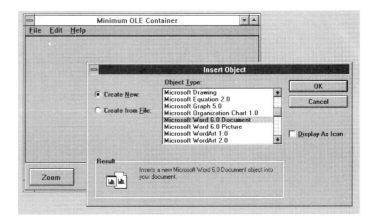

container component, and then its memory is released:

```
procedure TForm1.New1Click(Sender: TObject);
var
  InitInfo: Pointer;
begin
  if InsertOleObjectDlg (self, 0, InitInfo) then
  begin
    OleContainer1.PInitInfo := InitInfo;
    ReleaseOleInitInfo (InitInfo);
  end;
end;
```

The InsertOleObjectDlg function also has a return value, indicating, as usual, if the user pressed the OK or Cancel button. These three lines of code are enough to let a user insert a new embedded OLE object, insert an embedded object from a file, and create a link with an object in a file.

The other functionality of the OLECONT2 example relates to its simple toolbar, placed at the bottom of the form, and the Zoom button, which is the only button of this toolbar. The presence of the toolbar provides ways to deactivate the TOleContainer component, to activate it without editing the object, and so on. Just click on the button and on the container to switch the focus between the two components.

To keep this toolbar visible while in-place editing takes place, the panel should have the Locked property set to True. This allows the panel to remain present in the application, and not to be replaced by a toolbar of the server, as we will see in the next example.

The Zoom button in the form displays a Zoom dialog box, as shown in Figure 25.8. The structure of this secondary form is simple, as you can see in its textual description shown in Listing 25.3. When a user clicks on the Zoom button, the current zoom factor of the OLE container component is selected in the list box, and then the dialog box is displayed as modal. If the user selects the OK button, the selection of the list box is copied back to the Zoom property:

```
procedure TForm1.ZoomButtonClick(Sender: TObject);
begin
  ZoomForm.Listbox1.ItemIndex := Ord (OleContainer1.Zoom);
  if ZoomForm.ShowModal = mrOk then
    OleContainer1.Zoom := TZoomFactor (
      ZoomForm.Listbox1.ItemIndex);
end;
```

25

FIGURE 25.8:

The Zoom dialog box of the OLECONT2 example

The trick here is in the two type conversions between the index of the list box, an integer, and the Zoom property, a TZoomFactor enumeration.

LISTING 25.3: The textual description of the ZoomForm of the OLECONT2 example

```
object ZoomForm: TZoomForm
  BorderStyle = bsDialog
  Caption = 'Zoom'
  object ListBox1: TListBox
    Items.Strings = (
      '25%'
      '50%'
      '100%'
      '150%'
      '200%')
  end
  object BitBtn1: TBitBtn
    Kind = bkOK
  end
  object BitBtn2: TBitBtn
    Kind = bkCancel
  end
end
```

NOTE   The Zoom property has an effect only when the object is not active. If you enlarge the view of an object, its resolution decreases. When in-place editing starts, a part of the image of the object might be visible behind the editing area. This is not a very pleasant effect.

Visual Editing and Toolbars

If you use the OLECONT2 example, activate an OLE object in-place (this depends on the level of the server you are using), and the server has toolbars, the result is generally awkward. You can see an example of this negative effect in Figure 25.9.

To solve the problem, we can add a toolbar to the example. Add a panel to the form, align it to the top, and that area will be used by servers to display their own toolbars. A Delphi form, in fact, considers any components aligned to a side, with the exception of locked panels, as areas for the server's toolbars.

This approach works with servers that have just a toolbar, those that have a toolbar and a status bar, and even servers with vertical toolbars. However, it doesn't work

FIGURE 25.9:

FIGURE 25.9:
In OLECONT2 the toolbars of the server overlap the edit area, causing an awkward effect

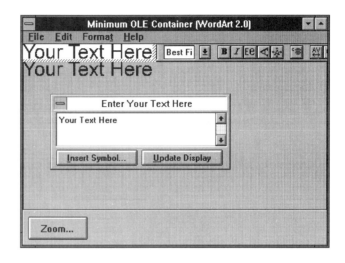

very well with some of the newer applications that have multiple toolbars under the caption, such as version 6 of MS Word for Windows.

In the OLECONT3 example, I've added a real toolbar to the form, with some speed buttons, and a message area to the status bar. You can see the textual description of these two components in Listing 25.4. Notice that the status bar uses a strange approach, so that the message area can resize itself automatically to always leave enough space for the button.

LISTING 25.4: The textual description of the toolbar and of the status bar of the OLECONT3 example

```
object Panel1: TPanel
  Align = alBottom
  Locked = True
  object StatusPanel: TPanel
    Align = alClient
    Alignment = taLeftJustify
    BevelOuter = bvLowered
    Caption = 'Ready'
  end
  object Panel2: TPanel
    Align = alLeft
    BevelOuter = bvNone
```

LISTING 25.4: The textual description of the toolbar and of the status bar of the OLECONT3 example (continued)

```
    object ZoomButton: TButton
      Caption = 'Zoom...'
      OnClick = ZoomButtonClick
    end
  end
end

object ToolbarPanel: TPanel
  Align = alTop
  object NewSpeedButton: TSpeedButton
    Glyph.Data = {...}
    OnClick = New1Click
  end
  object CutSpeedButton: TSpeedButton
    Enabled = False
    Glyph.Data = {...}
  end
  object CopySpeedButton: TSpeedButton
    Enabled = False
    Glyph.Data = {...}
  end
  object PasteSpeedButton: TSpeedButton
    Enabled = False
    Glyph.Data = {...}
  end
  object AboutSpeedButton: TSpeedButton
    Glyph.Data = {...}
    OnClick = About1Click
  end
end
```

The new form of the program, at run-time, shows the toolbar and the new status bar, as you can see in the upper window in Figure 25.10. When in-place editing starts in a server application that has a toolbar, that server's toolbar replaces the form's toolbar, as you can see in the second part of Figure 25.10 (which shows what happens after activating the OLE object in the upper window). Compare the bottom window in Figure 25.10 with the one shown in Figure 25.9, which displayed the previous version of the example, in a similar situation and using the same server.

The other feature of the example is the status bar. Some OLE servers, besides showing messages in their own status bar, can notify the container of the request to display a message. In Delphi, this is the OnStatusLineEvent of the OLE container

FIGURE 25.10:

The toolbar of the OLECONT3 example (above) and the toolbar of the server, replacing it (below)

component. By adding a handler to this event, with the following code, the container can display server messages:

```
procedure TForm1.OleContainer1StatusLineEvent(
  Sender: TObject; Msg: String);
begin
  StatusPanel.Caption := Msg;
end;
```

You can see an example of a status bar message sent by the server to the container in Figure 25.11.

Creating OLE Objects at Run-Time

In the examples, we have been able to create new OLE objects at run-time using the InsertOleObjectDlg function. However, there are other ways to create OLE objects.

FIGURE 25.11:

Status messages sent by the server, for example to describe a menu selection, can be displayed by the container in its own status bar.

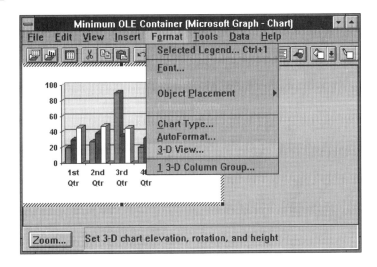

One way is to use a similar function, PasteSpecialDlg. A third way to create OLE object is by dragging, but this is not explored in the book, because the use of dragging between applications is not common for Windows 3.1 users (although it will probably become a key point of Windows 95).

Creating new OLE objects is not as simple as the Delphi interface might lead you to believe, but for Delphi programmers, there are no special problems.

In the fourth version of our example, named OLECONT4, I've added Paste Special support and some other clipboard support to the OLE container. Another addition to the example is its handling of OLE links. This is another operation available with a standard dialog box, wrapped in a Delphi function.

The OLE Standard Dialog Boxes

There are several standard dialog boxes in OLE. Some of them are directly available in Delphi using some special functions:

- InsertOleObjectDlg
- LinksDlg
- PasteSpecialDlg

- LinksDlgEnabled

- PasteSpecialEnabled

The first three functions display three standard dialog boxes, and the last two can be used to check if displaying the corresponding dialog boxes makes sense. They can be used in the code to write an `if` statement just before the call, or to enable the corresponding menu item, as I've done in the following example.

The OLECONT4 example uses essentially the same form as the previous version, with a few changes in the toolbar, such as removing the Cut button, enabling Copy and Paste, and adding some hints. However, the real difference it that the new version has more code, including the following methods:

- A method related to the OnClick event of the Edit pull-down menu, used to enable some of the menu items, which you can see in Listing 25.5

- Links1Click and PasteSpecial1Click methods

- Methods to initialize some data structures required to handle the paste special operation

- A method to copy the object to the clipboard, which has a second check on the existence of the object, because the method can be invoked by the toolbar button, too

LISTING 25.5: The source code of the OLECONT4 example

```
unit Oleform;

interface

uses
  SysUtils, WinTypes, WinProcs, Messages, Classes,
  Graphics, Controls, Forms, Dialogs, ToCtrl,
  Menus, ExtCtrls, StdCtrls, Buttons, BOleDefs;

type
  TForm1 = class(TForm)
    OleContainer1: TOleContainer;
    MainMenu1: TMainMenu;
    File1: TMenuItem;
    Exit1: TMenuItem;
    SaveAs1: TMenuItem;
    Open1: TMenuItem;
    New1: TMenuItem;
```

LISTING 25.5: The source code of the OLECONT4 example (continued)

```
    Help1: TMenuItem;
    About1: TMenuItem;
    Edit1: TMenuItem;
    Object1: TMenuItem;
    Links1: TMenuItem;
    PasteSpecial1: TMenuItem;
    Paste1: TMenuItem;
    Copy1: TMenuItem;
    Cut1: TMenuItem;
    Panel1: TPanel;
    ToolbarPanel: TPanel;
    NewSpeedButton: TSpeedButton;
    CutSpeedButton: TSpeedButton;
    CopySpeedButton: TSpeedButton;
    PasteSpeedButton: TSpeedButton;
    AboutSpeedButton: TSpeedButton;
    StatusPanel: TPanel;
    Panel2: TPanel;
    ZoomButton: TButton;
    procedure Exit1Click(Sender: TObject);
    procedure New1Click(Sender: TObject);
    procedure About1Click(Sender: TObject);
    procedure ZoomButtonClick(Sender: TObject);
    procedure OleContainer1StatusLineEvent(
      Sender: TObject; Msg: String);
    procedure Edit1Click(Sender: TObject);
    procedure FormCreate(Sender: TObject);
    procedure PasteSpecial1Click(Sender: TObject);
    procedure Links1Click(Sender: TObject);
    procedure Copy1Click(Sender: TObject);
  private
    OleFormats: array [0..1] of BOleFormat;
    procedure DefineOleFormat (var OleFmt: BOleFormat;
      ClipFmt: Word; AllowLink: Boolean);
  end;

var
  Form1: TForm1;

implementation

{$R *.DFM}

uses
  Zoom_f;

procedure TForm1.Exit1Click(Sender: TObject);
begin
  Close;
end;
```

LISTING 25.5: The source code of the OLECONT4 example (continued)

```
procedure TForm1.New1Click(Sender: TObject);
var
  InitInfo: Pointer;
begin
  {create a new OLE object, choosing a server}
  if InsertOleObjectDlg (self, 0, InitInfo) then
  begin
    OleContainer1.PInitInfo := InitInfo;
    ReleaseOleInitInfo (InitInfo);
  end;
end;

procedure TForm1.About1Click(Sender: TObject);
begin
  MessageDlg ('Sample OLE container' +
    Chr (13) + 'From the book "Mastering Delphi"',
    mtInformation, [mbOk], 0);
end;

procedure TForm1.ZoomButtonClick(Sender: TObject);
begin
  {display the Zoom form}
  ZoomForm.Listbox1.ItemIndex :=
    Ord (OleContainer1.Zoom);
  if ZoomForm.ShowModal = mrOk then
    OleContainer1.Zoom := TZoomFactor (
      ZoomForm.Listbox1.ItemIndex);
end;

procedure TForm1.OleContainer1StatusLineEvent(
  Sender: TObject; Msg: String);
begin
  {copy the server message to the status line}
  StatusPanel.Caption := Msg;
end;

procedure TForm1.Edit1Click(Sender: TObject);
begin
  {enable/disable some menu items of the pull-down}
  if PasteSpecialEnabled (self, OleFormats) then
    PasteSpecial1.Enabled := True
  else
    PasteSpecial1.Enabled := False;
  if LinksDlgEnabled (self) then
    Links1.Enabled := True
  else
    Links1.Enabled := False;
  if OleContainer1.OleObjAllocated then
    Copy1.Enabled := True
  else
    Copy1.Enabled := False;
end;
```

25

LISTING 25.5: The source code of the OLECONT4 example (continued)

```
procedure TForm1.DefineOleFormat (var OleFmt: BOleFormat;
  ClipFmt: Word; AllowLink: Boolean);
begin
  {store standard values, using the supplied parameters}
  {this function is called twice by the FormCreate method}
  OleFmt.fmtId := ClipFmt;
  OleFmt.fmtMedium := BOleMediumCalc (ClipFmt);
  OleFmt.fmtIsLinkable := AllowLink;
  StrPCopy (OleFmt.fmtName, '%s');
  StrPCopy (OleFmt.fmtResultName, '%s');
end;

procedure TForm1.FormCreate(Sender: TObject);
var
  EmbedCF, LinkCF: Word;
begin
  {define two clipboard formats}
  EmbedCF := RegisterClipboardFormat ('Embedded Object');
  LinkCF := RegisterClipboardFormat ('Link Source');

  {define two OleFormats, storing them in the array}
  DefineOleFormat (OleFormats [0], EmbedCF, False);
  DefineOleFormat (OleFormats [1], LinkCF, True);
end;

procedure TForm1.PasteSpecial1Click(Sender: TObject);
var
  ClipFmt, Handle: Word;             {temporary values}
  InitInfo: Pointer;
begin
  if PasteSpecialEnabled (self, OleFormats) then
    {show the standard Paste Special dialog box}
    if PasteSpecialDlg (Self, OleFormats, 0, ClipFmt,
      Handle, initInfo) then
    begin
      OleContainer1.PInitInfo := InitInfo;
      ReleaseOleInitInfo (InitInfo);
    end;
end;

procedure TForm1.Links1Click(Sender: TObject);
begin
  {show the Links dialog box}
  LinksDlg (self, 0);
end;

procedure TForm1.Copy1Click(Sender: TObject);
begin
  {copy the OLE object to the clipboard,
  removing the existing content}
```

LISTING 25.5: The source code of the OLECONT4 example (continued)

```
  if OleContainer1.OleObjAllocated then
    OleContainer1.CopyToClipboard (True); end;
end.
```

In short, to handle the paste operation, you need to register two specific clipboard formats, *Embedded Object* and *Link Source*, and then define a BOleFormat structure for each of them. These structures are inserted in an array (private data of the form), and used by the PasteSpecialEnabled and PasteSpecialDlg functions. As you can see in the code, the initialization of these data structures takes place at startup, in the FormCreate method.

The Paste Special dialog box, shown in Figure 25.12, allows you to embed or link the object currently in the clipboard, depending on the capabilities of the server and as long as the object is a portion of an actual file (a required condition to establish a link). Using these standard dialog boxes, the simple example we are building becomes a complex one, which supports linking and embedding in a number of different ways.

FIGURE 25.12:

The Paste Special dialog box of the OLECONT4 example

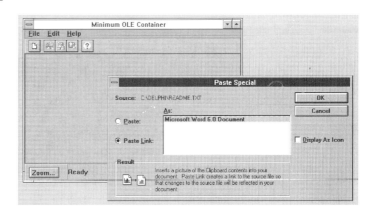

Another plus is offered by the Links dialog box, shown in Figure 25.13, which can be used to change some of the properties of the current links. In our example, there

FIGURE 25.13:

The Links dialog box of the
OLECONT4 example

can be one link at most, since there is only one OLE container component. The dialog box allows you to choose between automatic and manual updates. If you set manual updating, you can use this same dialog box to perform the updates. The Links dialog box also has options for opening the source, changing the source, and breaking the link (transforming the object in an embedded object).

Loading and Saving Objects in Files

The last minor enhancement in the series of OLE container examples involves adding support for files. This is actually one of the simplest additions we can make, because the OLE container component already has file support. I decided to add this code only because we'll use a different approach to file saving in the next OLE examples, and you'll be able to compare the two techniques.

The new example, OLECONT5, has just a few more lines of code, as you can see in Listing 25.6. Its form has two standard dialog components (OpenDialog1 and SaveDialog1), two new speed buttons in the toolbar, and a few other changes.

LISTING 25.6: The new source code of the OLECONT5 example

```
procedure TForm1.Open1Click(Sender: TObject);
begin
  if OpenDialog1.Execute then
  begin
    OleContainer1.LoadFromFile (OpenDialog1.Filename);
    OleContainer1.Invalidate;
  end;
end;

procedure TForm1.SaveAs1Click(Sender: TObject);
begin
  if OleContainer1.OleObjAllocated then
    if SaveDialog1.Execute then
      OleContainer1.SaveToFile (SaveDialog1.Filename);
end;

procedure TForm1.File1Click(Sender: TObject);
begin
  if OleContainer1.OleObjAllocated then
    SaveAs1.Enabled := True
  else
    SaveAs1.Enabled := False;
end;
```

25

You can see an example of the program at run-time in Figure 25.14. The figure shows the program while loading an object stored in a file. Notice, in the listing, that at the end of this operation, you need to update the user interface of the component, because this operation (strangely enough) doesn't take place automatically.

To sum things up, our OLE container application now includes support for inserting new embedded or linked objects, pasting objects from the clipboard, copying objects to the clipboard, loading objects from files, and saving objects to files. We have added link-handling support, a menu bar that is merged with that of the active server application (in case of in-place editing), and a toolbar that also can be replaced by the server application's toolbar during in-place editing. The status bar of the program is fixed, but it can display messages from the server.

That's a lot of OLE capabilities, although still not complete. The program doesn't support OLE object drag-and-drop, lacks a dialog box to display information about the current object, and cannot adjust the size of its toolbar per the server's request. The first and second of these shortcomings can be easily remedied; the third is more difficult to achieve.

FIGURE 25.14:
The OLECONT5 example can be
used to save and load OLE objects
to files.

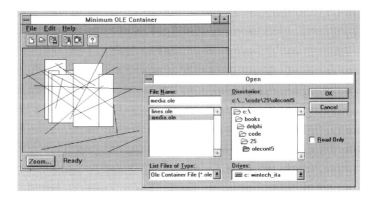

Multiple OLE Containers

All of the versions of the OLECONT example could display only one OLE object at
a time, because there was only one fixed OLE container component. Our next example, named MULTIOLE, shows how to use multiple OLE container components
in the same form.

> **NOTE**
>
> At first, I thought of using the MDI approach to build this example, but
> then I realized that there is already an example of this kind in the
> Delphi package, described with some detail in Delphi's *User's Guide*.
> That is why I decided to write a different one, capable of displaying
> multiple OLE objects in a single form. You can compare the approach
> in this example with the MDI approach in Delphi's example.

The MULTIOLE example can actually display both shapes (only squares) and OLE
containers. Components of the two kinds are created when the user double-clicks
on the surface of the form, in the position of the click event. The choice between the
two components depends on the status of the two speed buttons of the toolbar,
which behave like radio buttons. You can see the form of the example in Figure 25.15
and its textual description in Listing 25.7.

FIGURE 25.15:

The form of the MULTIOLE example at design-time

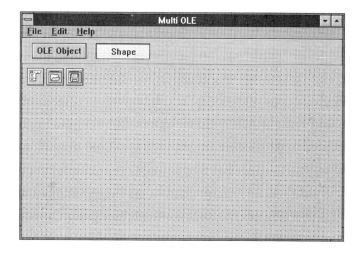

25

LISTING 25.7: The textual description of the form of the MULTIOLE example

```
object Form1: TForm1
  Caption = 'Multi OLE'
  Menu = MainMenu1
  ObjectMenuItem = Object1
  OnCreate = FormCreate
  OnDblClick = FormDblClick
  OnDragDrop = FormDragDrop
  OnDragOver = FormDragOver
  OnMouseDown = FormMouseDown
  object Panel1: TPanel
    Align = alTop
    object SpeedButton1: TSpeedButton
      GroupIndex = 1
      Caption = 'OLE Object'
      OnClick = SpeedButton1Click
    end
    object SpeedButton2: TSpeedButton
      GroupIndex = 1
      Down = True
      Caption = 'Shape'
      OnClick = SpeedButton2Click
    end
  end
  object MainMenu1: TMainMenu
    object File1: TMenuItem
      Caption = '&File'
      OnClick = File1Click
      object Open1: TMenuItem
        Caption = '&Open...'
```

LISTING 25.7: The textual description of the form of the MULTIOLE example
(continued)

```
        OnClick = Open1Click
      end
      object Save1: TMenuItem
        Caption = '&Save as...'
        OnClick = Save1Click
      end
      object N1: TMenuItem
        Caption = '-'
      end
      object Exit1: TMenuItem
        Caption = 'E&xit'
        OnClick = Exit1Click
      end
    end
    object Edit1: TMenuItem
      Caption = '&Edit'
      GroupIndex = 1
      OnClick = Edit1Click
      object Links1: TMenuItem
        Caption = '&Links...'
        OnClick = Links1Click
      end
      object List1: TMenuItem
        Caption = 'Li&st...'
        OnClick = List1Click
      end
      object Object1: TMenuItem
        Caption = '&Object'
        Enabled = False
      end
    end
    object Help1: TMenuItem
      Caption = '&Help'
      GroupIndex = 5
      object About1: TMenuItem
        Caption = '&About...'
        OnClick = About1Click
      end
    end
  end
  object OpenDialog1: TOpenDialog
    Filter = 'Multi OLE file (*.mof)|*.mof'
    Options = [ofPathMustExist, ofFileMustExist]
  end
  object SaveDialog1: TSaveDialog
    Filter = 'Multi OLE file (*.mof)|*.mof'
    Options = [ofOverwritePrompt, ofPathMustExist,
      ofCreatePrompt]
  end
end
```

The example also has other capabilities. You can drag each component, shape, or OLE container; click on an OLE container to activate it; and save all of the components to a stream (a file). You can use the Tab key to select an OLE container, and then use its Object menu. Alternatively, you can use the usual Links dialog box or a special List dialog box, which lists the names of all of the components in the form.

The source code of this example is quite complex, but some portions were borrowed from older examples. In particular, there are many similarities to the CREF3 example of Chapter 23, including the file streams and the dynamic creation of components. You can see the complete source code of the MULTIOLE example in Listing 25.8.

LISTING 25.8: The complete source code of the MULTIOLE example

25

```
unit Multio_f;

interface

uses
  SysUtils, WinTypes, WinProcs, Messages, Classes,
  Graphics, Controls, Forms, Dialogs, Toctrl, Buttons,
  ExtCtrls, Menus, List_f;

type
  TForm1 = class(TForm)
    Panel1: TPanel;
    SpeedButton1: TSpeedButton;
    SpeedButton2: TSpeedButton;
    MainMenu1: TMainMenu;
    File1: TMenuItem;
    Open1: TMenuItem;
    Save1: TMenuItem;
    N1: TMenuItem;
    Exit1: TMenuItem;
    Edit1: TMenuItem;
    Links1: TMenuItem;
    List1: TMenuItem;
    help1: TMenuItem;
    About1: TMenuItem;
    Object1: TMenuItem;
    OpenDialog1: TOpenDialog;
    SaveDialog1: TSaveDialog;
    procedure FormCreate(Sender: TObject);
    procedure FormMouseDown(Sender: TObject;
      Button: TMouseButton; Shift: TShiftState;
      X, Y: Integer);
    procedure SpeedButton1Click(Sender: TObject);
```

LISTING 25.8: The complete source code of the MULTIOLE example (continued)

```
      procedure SpeedButton2Click(Sender: TObject);
      procedure FormDblClick(Sender: TObject);
      procedure FormDragOver(Sender, Source: TObject;
        X, Y: Integer; State: TDragState;
        var Accept: Boolean);
      procedure FormDragDrop(Sender, Source: TObject;
        X, Y: Integer);
      procedure File1Click(Sender: TObject);
      procedure Exit1Click(Sender: TObject);
      procedure Links1Click(Sender: TObject);
      procedure Edit1Click(Sender: TObject);
      procedure List1Click(Sender: TObject);
      procedure Save1Click(Sender: TObject);
      procedure About1Click(Sender: TObject);
      procedure Open1Click(Sender: TObject);
    private
      OleObj: Boolean;                  {Ole or Shape}
      X1, Y1: Integer;               {mouse position}
      OleCount, ShapeCount: Integer;{number of controls}
    public
      procedure OleContainerDragDrop(
        Sender, Source: TObject; X, Y: Integer);
      procedure OleContainerDragOver(
        Sender, Source: TObject; X, Y: Integer;
        State: TDragState; var Accept: Boolean);
    end;

var
  Form1: TForm1;

implementation

{$R *.DFM}

procedure TForm1.FormCreate(Sender: TObject);
begin
  {initial value}
  OleObj := False;
end;

procedure TForm1.FormMouseDown(Sender: TObject;
  Button: TMouseButton; Shift: TShiftState;
  X, Y: Integer);
begin
  {store the position of the mouse down event,
  used later in the FormDblClick method}
  X1 := X;
  Y1 := Y;
end;
```

LISTING 25.8: The complete source code of the MULTIOLE example (continued)

```
procedure TForm1.SpeedButton1Click(Sender: TObject);
begin
  OleObj := True;
end;

procedure TForm1.SpeedButton2Click(Sender: TObject);
begin
  OleObj := False;
end;

procedure TForm1.FormDblClick(Sender: TObject);
var
  InitInfo: Pointer;
  OleCont: TOleContainer;
  Shape: TShape;
begin
  if OleObj then
  begin
    {create a new OLE container, asking the user
    to select the server or a file for the link}
    if InsertOleObjectDlg (self, 0, InitInfo) then
    begin
      OleCont := TOleContainer.Create (self);
      OleCont.Parent := self;
      {generate a unique name}
      Inc (OleCount);
      OleCont.Name := 'OleContainer' +
        IntToStr (OleCount);
      {set the position}
      OleCont.Top := Y1;
      OleCont.Left := X1;
      OleCont.AutoSize := True;
      {enable dragging}
      OleCont.DragMode := dmAutomatic;
      {enable click to activate OLE object}
      OleCont.OnDragDrop := OleContainerDragDrop;
      OleCont.OnDragOver := OleContainerDragOver;
      {define the OLE object}
      OleCont.PInitInfo := InitInfo;
      ReleaseOleInitInfo (InitInfo);
    end;
  end
  else
  begin
    {create a new shape}
    Shape := TShape.Create (self);
    Shape.Parent := self;
    {define a unique name and set the position}
    Inc (ShapeCount);
    Shape.Name := 'Shape' + IntToStr (ShapeCount);
    Shape.Left := X1;
```

LISTING 25.8: The complete source code of the MULTIOLE example (continued)

```
    Shape.Top := Y1;
    {activate dragging}
    Shape.DragMode := dmAutomatic;
  end;
end;

procedure TForm1.FormDragOver(
  Sender, Source: TObject; X, Y: Integer;
  State: TDragState; var Accept: Boolean);
begin
  {dragging of OLE containers and shapes is allowed}
  if (Source is TOleContainer) or
      (Source is TShape) then
    Accept := True;
end;

procedure TForm1.FormDragDrop(
  Sender, Source: TObject; X, Y: Integer);
var
  Rect: TRect;
begin
  {change the position}
  (Source as TControl).Left := X;
  (Source as TControl).Top := Y;
  {if it is an OLE container, change the PartRect, the
  rectangle used for in-place activation}
  if Source is TOleContainer then
  begin
    Rect.Left := X;
    Rect.Top := Y;
    Rect.Right := X + TOleContainer(Source).Width;
    Rect.Bottom := Y + TOleContainer(Source).Height;
    TOleContainer(Source).PartRect := Rect;
  end;
end;

procedure TForm1.File1Click(Sender: TObject);
begin
  {enable Save, if the form is not empty}
  if ControlCount > 1 then
    Save1.Enabled := True
  else
    Save1.Enabled := False;
end;

procedure TForm1.Exit1Click(Sender: TObject);
begin
  Close;
end;
```

LISTING 25.8: The complete source code of the MULTIOLE example (continued)

```pascal
procedure TForm1.Links1Click(Sender: TObject);
begin
  {show the standard Links dialog box}
  LinksDlg (self, 0);
end;

procedure TForm1.Edit1Click(Sender: TObject);
begin
  {eventually enable the List and Links commands}
  if ControlCount > 1 then
    List1.Enabled := True
  else
    List1.Enabled := False;
  if LinksDlgEnabled (self) then
    Links1.Enabled := True
  else
    Links1.Enabled := False;
end;

procedure TForm1.List1Click(Sender: TObject);
var
  I: Integer;
begin
  {fill and show the List dialog box}
  ListForm.Listbox1.Clear;
  for I := 0 to ControlCount - 1 do
    if not (Controls [I] is TPanel) then
      ListForm.Listbox1.Items.Add (Controls [I].Name);
  ListForm.ShowModal;
end;

procedure TForm1.OleContainerDragDrop(
  Sender, Source: TObject; X, Y: Integer);
begin
  {allow dragging over the same component
  an operation which is considered a click}
  if Sender = Source then
    (Sender as TOleContainer).Active := True;
end;

procedure TForm1.OleContainerDragOver(
  Sender, Source: TObject; X, Y: Integer;
  State: TDragState; var Accept: Boolean);
begin
  {if dragging onto itself, that is clicking,
  activate the OLE object, starting the server}
  if Sender = Source then
    Accept := True;
end;
```

25

LISTING 25.8: The complete source code of the MULTIOLE example (continued)

```
procedure TForm1.Save1Click(Sender: TObject);
var
  S: TFileStream;
  I: Integer;
begin
  if SaveDialog1.Execute then
  begin
    {open or eventually create the stream file}
    S := TFileStream.Create (SaveDialog1.FileName,
      fmOpenWrite or fmCreate);
    try
      {save each component except the panel}
      for I := 0 to ControlCount - 1 do
        if Controls[I].ClassName <> 'TPanel' then
          S.WriteComponent (Controls[I]);
    finally
      S.Free;
    end;
  end;
end;

procedure TForm1.About1Click(Sender: TObject);
begin
  MessageDlg ('Multiple Ole Container example' +
    Chr (13) + 'From "Mastering Delphi" by Marco Cantù',
    mtInformation, [mbOk], 0);
end;

procedure TForm1.Open1Click(Sender: TObject);
var
  S: TFileStream;
  New: TComponent;
  I: Integer;
begin
  if OpenDialog1.Execute then
  begin
    {remove existing controls, except the panel}
    for I := ControlCount - 1 downto 0 do
      if not (Controls[I] is TPanel) then
        Controls[I].Free;

    {open the stream}
    S := TFileStream.Create (OpenDialog1.FileName,
      fmOpenRead);
    try
      while S.Position < S.Size do
      begin
        {read a component and add it to the form}
        New := S.ReadComponent (nil);
        InsertControl (New as TControl);
        {increase the component count}
```

LISTING 25.8: The complete source code of the MULTIOLE example (continued)

```
        if New is TShape then
          Inc (ShapeCount)
        else
        begin
          Inc (OleCount);
          {set the dragging methods}
          (New as TOleContainer).OnDragDrop :=
            OleContainerDragDrop;
          (New as TOleContainer).OnDragOver :=
            OleContainerDragOver;
        end;
      end;
    finally
      S.Free;
    end;
  end;
end;

initialization
  {register the classes of the components; this code is
  required by the stream loader}
  RegisterClasses ([TShape, TOleContainer]);
end.
```

25

Creating OLE Containers at Run-Time

One of the key elements of the source code is the FormDblClick method, which is used to create new components when the user double-clicks on the surface of the form. You can see the effect of executing this code several times in Figure 25.16.

The FormDblClick has two distinct parts: the creation of a shape and the creation of an OLE container. The choice between the two depends on the currently selected speed button. I suggest that you look first at the second part of the code, used to create shapes, because it is simpler.

The code creates a new component, sets its Parent property, and gives it a unique name. Then it sets the position of the shape, using two values stored when the user clicked the mouse button, and activates dragging, setting the DragMode property. For dragging to work, we need to handle a couple of methods of the form, as we will see later.

FIGURE 25.16:

With the MULTIOLE example, you can create several OLE containers, as well as shapes

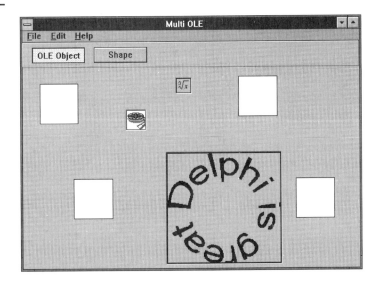

To create a new OLE container, the code performs similar operations. First it calls the InsertOLEObjectDlg function, to let the user select a server for an embedded object or a file to define an OLE link. Again, the code sets the DragMode property to dmAutomatic to enable dragging, but a problem occurs.

If you double-click on an OLE container, this operation is ignored, because the mouse clicks are trapped by the dragging code. Instead of customizing the dragging code, I've decided to start the editing of the OLE container when the user clicks on it; that is, when the dragging operation terminates on the same component that started it. To accomplish this, the program dynamically defines a handler for the OnDragDrop and OnDragOver events of the OLE container component.

Dragging Components and Activating OLE Containers

The program has four dragging-related methods: two connected to the form and used for real dragging operations and two used to activate the OLE containers.

As you can see in the listing, the form accepts dragging from TOleContainer and TShape components, and basically changes the position of the component to the point where the drop event took place. Using the coordinates passed by the Form-DragDrop method to set the Left and Top properties of the component is not a perfect solution. You should also consider the relative position from the mouse to the top-left corner of the components when the dragging operation started.

Besides this minor glitch, the first version of the program I wrote had a very bad effect. Although I could move the OLE containers, when I activated them, in-place editing took place in the older position. First, I struggled with the InitInfo pointers and fields (and the undocumented BOleInitInfo structure) with no success. Then, using the Object Browser and the Inspect dialog box of the integrated debugger, I found what I was looking for: the (undocumented) PartRect property of the OLE container component.

This property, a rectangle, stores the position used by the in-place editing code. Changing its value to reflect the new position of the component saved the day, and made the example work properly.

The other two dragging-related methods are much simpler. The key code is in two lines of the OleContainerDragOver procedure:

```
if Sender = Source then
  Accept := True;
```

You should remember that these two methods are connected to the OLE container components at run-time, when the components are created. The result it that a click on a component activates it, as you can see in Figure 25.17.

The Edit and File Menus

The rest of the code of the example refers to menu commands. Both the File and Edit pull-down menus have an OnClick event, used to enable or disable some menu items, as usual.

The Edit menu has an Object item, used as value of the ObjectMenuItem property of the form. The Edit menu also has a Links item, used to display the standard Links dialog box. As you can see in Figure 25.18, the program can have multiple links at the same time, since there is no limit to the number of OLE container components of the form. This program does not include Paste Special support; the only way to create a link is to create a new OLE object from a file, in the Insert New Object dialog box.

FIGURE 25.17:

In-place activation of an OLE
container of the MULTIOLE example

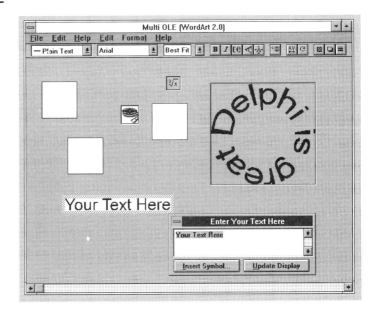

FIGURE 25.18:

The Links dialog box with multiple
links

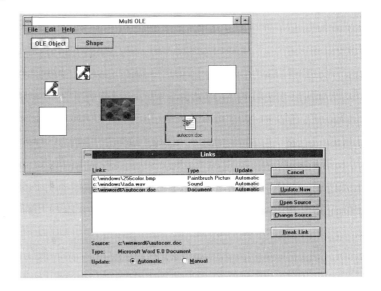

The List item on the Edit menu shows a dialog box, built with a very simple form. As you can see in Figure 25.19, this dialog box lists all the current components by their names.

FIGURE 25.19:

FIGURE 25.19:

The List dialog box of the MULTIOLE example

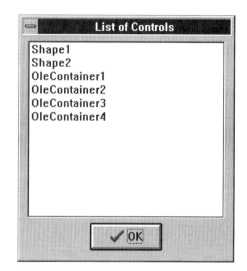

The last two interesting menu commands are Save As and Open on the File menu. As I mentioned, the code of these commands is almost the same of that of the CREF3 example of Chapter 23. Also, in the MULTIOLE example, I've used a stream to write (or read) the components.

The TOleContainer class actually has two specific SaveToStream and LoadFromStream methods. (These methods were not in the original Help file, but they are mentioned in the *User's Guide*.) However, in this case, I wanted to save not only the OLE object data, but also the position and other properties of the component. However, the methods are not saved, so the program must manually restore the value of the two dragging events.

Realize that if you add some big OLE objects to the form, such as a Paintbrush image or any other large file, the files saved by the program will be that big. Files of several hundred kilobytes are nothing strange. Remember also that to load and re-create the new components properly, you need to call the RegisterClasses procedure, as described in Chapter 23.

Summary

Chapter 24, which discussed the clipboard and DDE, and this chapter about OLE have covered the data-exchange capabilities of Windows applications. Certainly, OLE is the most important of the three technologies, and the one with the brightest future, at least according to Microsoft. The company has a clear intention of promoting OLE support, particularly in Windows 95, and making the whole Windows platform OLE-centric.

For this reason, OLE is a central element for program development, and Delphi has the capabilities to let developers interact with every aspect of OLE. In the first version, Delphi's automatic support for OLE is limited to containers. To build OLE server or automation capabilities into your Delphi applications immediately, you can shop around for third-party add-on components for Delphi, or dust off your OLE programming guide and write your own Delphi code to call the OLE API functions directly. Or, you can look forward to the next version of Delphi, which Borland has said will offer much more extensive OLE support in its built-in components.

Now we'll take a break with a more relaxing topic (multimedia applications) in the next chapter, and then we will be ready for the last part of the book, which covers building components and libraries.

CHAPTER

TWENTY-SIX

Multimedia Fun

- Windows default sounds, from beeps to music

- The Media Player component—playing sounds and running videos

- Applications for CD drives

26

After a chapter about the printer and one about the file system, in this chapter I want to focus on other devices that might be attached to your PC, such as a sound board or a CD-ROM reader. Besides being physically connected to your computer, these devices should be properly installed in Windows.

Windows has an entire specific API to handle external devices, including video, output, MIDI, and CD. This API is known as the Multimedia API, and Delphi provides a specific Help file describing it (MMSYSTEM.HLP, by default in the C:\DELPHI\BIN directory). Delphi also includes an easy-to-use component, the Media Player, to handle most multimedia devices.

Before discussing this component, which is the key element of the chapter, we'll look at some simpler ways to produce sound in Windows, in addition to the simple beeps we have used up to now.

Windows Default Sounds

Every time I wanted to warn the user of an error or a specific event, I used to call a Windows API function, `MessageBeep`, passing to it the $FFFF parameter, which corresponds to the –1 value indicated in the Help file. Since the data type of a parameter is declared as a word, using –1 in Delphi will produce a compiler error.

However, the `MessageBeep` function can also have other parameters. Here they are listed with the corresponding Windows sounds they produce:

mb_IconAsterisk	Asterisk sound
mb_IconExclamation	Exclamation sound
mb_IconHand	Critical Stop sound
mb_IconQuestion	Question sound
mb_Ok	Default Beep sound

Each message box flag corresponds to a sound file (with a WAV extension), as indicated by the WIN.INI file. You can change the association between system events and sound files using the Control Panel (see Figure 26.1), which lists the sounds under the names shown in the right column above.

FIGURE 26.1:

Setting Windows default sounds
with the Control Panel

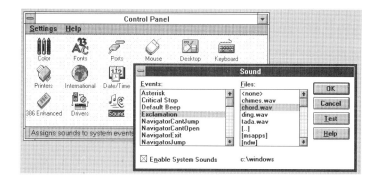

Notice that these flags are actually also the possible values of the MessageBox API function, encapsulated in the MessageBox method of the TApplication class. It is common to produce the corresponding sound when the message box is displayed. This feature is not directly available in the Delphi MessageDlg function, but we can extend it easily by building a SoundMessageDlg function, as demonstrated by the following example.

Every Box Has a Beep

To show you the capabilities of the MessageBeep API function, I've prepared a simple example, BEEPS. You can see, in the form of this example in Figure 26.2, that the program allows a user to choose one of the five valid flags of the MessageBeep function. The details of the form are in Listing 26.1.

The program plays the sound corresponding to the current selection when the user presses the Beep Sound button. (The other buttons have different behaviors, as we will see in a while.) The handler of this button's OnClick event first determines the flag corresponding to the selected button of the radio group, using a case statement, and then plays the sound. You can see its code in Listing 26.2.

FIGURE 26.2:

The form of the BEEPS example

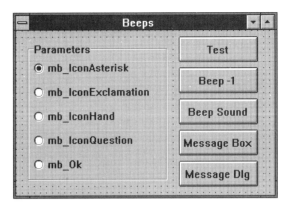

LISTING 26.1: The textual description of the form of the BEEPS example

```
object Form1: TForm1
  Caption = 'Beeps'
  object RadioGroup1: TRadioGroup
    Caption = 'Parameters'
    ItemIndex = 0
    Items.Strings = (
      'mb_IconAsterisk'
      'mb_IconExclamation'
      'mb_IconHand'
      'mb_IconQuestion'
      'mb_Ok')
  end
  object BeepButton: TButton
    Caption = 'Beep Sound'
    OnClick = BeepButtonClick
  end
  object BoxButton: TButton
    Caption = 'Message Box'
    OnClick = BoxButtonClick
  end
  object BeepOneButton: TButton
    Caption = 'Beep -1'
    OnClick = BeepOneButtonClick
  end
  object MessDlgButton: TButton
    Caption = 'Message Dlg'
    OnClick = MessDlgButtonClick
  end
  object TestButton: TButton
    Caption = 'Test'
    OnClick = TestButtonClick
  end
end
```

LISTING 26.2: The source code of the BEEPS example

```
unit Beeps_f;

interface

uses
  SysUtils, WinTypes, WinProcs, Messages, Classes,
  Graphics, Controls, Forms, Dialogs, StdCtrls,
  MmSystem;

type
  TForm1 = class(TForm)
    BeepButton: TButton;
    BoxButton: TButton;
    RadioGroup1: TRadioGroup;
    BeepOneButton: TButton;
    MessDlgButton: TButton;
    TestButton: TButton;
    procedure BeepButtonClick(Sender: TObject);
    procedure BeepOneButtonClick(Sender: TObject);
    procedure BoxButtonClick(Sender: TObject);
    procedure MessDlgButtonClick(Sender: TObject);
    procedure TestButtonClick(Sender: TObject);
  private
    { Private declarations }
  public
    { Public declarations }
  end;

function SoundMessageDlg (const Msg: string;
  AType: TMsgDlgType; AButtons: TMsgDlgButtons;
  HelpCtx: LongInt): Word;

var
  Form1: TForm1;

implementation

{$R *.DFM}

procedure TForm1.BeepButtonClick(Sender: TObject);
var
  Flag: Word;
begin
  case RadioGroup1.ItemIndex of
    0: Flag := mb_IconAsterisk;
    1: Flag := mb_IconExclamation;
    2: Flag := mb_IconHand;
    3: Flag := mb_IconQuestion;
    4: Flag := mb_Ok;
  end;
  MessageBeep (Flag);
end;
```

26

LISTING 26.2: The source code of the BEEPS example (continued)

```
procedure TForm1.BeepOneButtonClick(Sender: TObject);
begin
  MessageBeep ($FFFF);
end;

procedure TForm1.BoxButtonClick(Sender: TObject);
var
  Flag: Word;
  Text: array [0..100] of Char;
begin
  case RadioGroup1.ItemIndex of
    0: Flag := mb_IconAsterisk;
    1: Flag := mb_IconExclamation;
    2: Flag := mb_IconHand;
    3: Flag := mb_IconQuestion;
    4: Flag := mb_Ok;
  end;
  MessageBeep (Flag);
  StrPCopy (Text,
    RadioGroup1.Items [RadioGroup1.ItemIndex]);
  Application.MessageBox (Text, 'Sound', Flag);
end;

function SoundMessageDlg (const Msg: string;
  AType: TMsgDlgType; AButtons: TMsgDlgButtons;
  HelpCtx: LongInt): Word;
var
  Flag: Word;
begin
  case AType of
    mtWarning: Flag := mb_IconAsterisk;
    mtError: Flag := mb_IconHand;
    mtInformation: Flag := mb_IconExclamation;
    mtConfirmation: Flag := mb_IconQuestion;
  else
    Flag := mb_Ok;
  end;
  MessageBeep(Flag);
  SoundMessageDlg :=
    MessageDlg (Msg, AType, AButtons, HelpCtx);
end;

procedure TForm1.MessDlgButtonClick(Sender: TObject);
var
  DlgType: TMsgDlgType;
begin
  case RadioGroup1.ItemIndex of
    0: DlgType := mtWarning;
    1: DlgType := mtInformation;
    2: DlgType := mtError;
    3: DlgType := mtConfirmation;
```

LISTING 26.2: The source code of the BEEPS example (continued)

```
    4: DlgType := mtCustom;
  end;
  SoundMessageDlg (
    RadioGroup1.Items [RadioGroup1.ItemIndex],
    DlgType, [mbOK], 0);
end;

procedure TForm1.TestButtonClick(Sender: TObject);
begin
  if WaveOutGetNumDevs > 0 then
    SoundMessageDlg ('Sound is supported',
      mtInformation, [mbOk], 0)
  else
    SoundMessageDlg ('Sound is NOT supported',
      mtError, [mbOk], 0);
end;

end.
```

26

To compare the sound with the default beep, press the second button of the column. To test whether a sound driver is installed in your system (with or without a sound card, since it is possible to have a sound driver for the PC speaker), press the first button, which uses a multimedia function, WaveOutGetNumDevs, to perform the test. Notice that to compile this function, you need to add the MmSystem unit in the uses statement. If your computer has no proper sound driver installed, you will hear only standard beeps, whichever flag is selected.

The last two buttons have a different aim. The first of the two displays a message box, playing the corresponding sound (see Figure 26.3). The Message Box button uses the traditional Windows approach. It calls the MessageBeep function and the MessageBox method of the Application object soon afterward. The effect is that the sound is played when the message box is displayed. In fact, playing a sound doesn't stop other Windows operations. (Well, this actually depends on the sound driver, so this is only the suggested behavior.)

If you press the last button, the program calls the SoundMessageDlg function, which is not a Delphi function. It's one I've added to the program, but you can use it in your applications. The only suggestion I have is to choose a shorter name if you want to use it frequently. SoundMessageDlg plays a sound, depending on the type parameter, and then displays the Delphi standard message box (see Figure 26.4). It

FIGURE 26.3:

The output of the MessageBox call, accompanied by sound

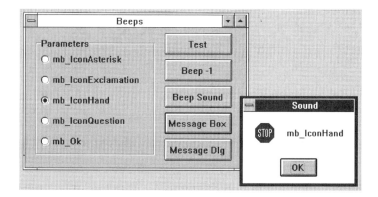

FIGURE 26.4:

The SoundMessageDlg function plays a system sound and shows a Delphi message box.

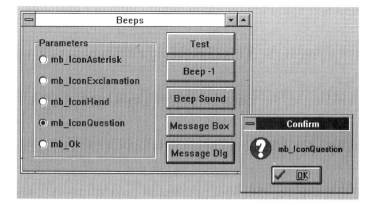

is a simple function, but your programs can really benefit from its use. Notice that the code of the TestButtonClick method uses this function, too.

From Beeps to Music

When you use the MessageBeep function, your choice of sounds is limited to the default system sounds. Another Windows API function, SndPlaySound, can be used to play a system sound, as well as any other waveform file (WAV).

Again, I've built a simple example to show you this approach. The example is indicated as EXTBEEP, Extended Beep, and has the simple form shown in Figure 26.5.

FIGURE 26.5:

The form of the EXTBEEP example

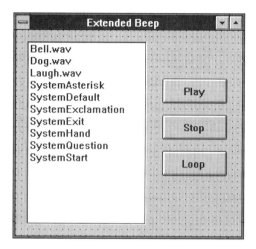

The list box of this example lists the names of the system sounds and some WAV files, available in the current directory (that is, the directory of the example). When the user presses the Play button, the SndPlaySound function (defined in the MmSystem unit) is called:

```
procedure TForm1.PlayButtonClick(Sender: TObject);
var
  Text: array [0..100] of Char;
begin
  with ListBox1 do
    StrPCopy (Text, Items [ItemIndex]);
  SndPlaySound (Text, snd_Async);
end;
```

This code can be used to play both system sounds and WAV files. If the list box item has no corresponding file or system sound, the program plays the system default sound. The second parameter indicates that the function should return immediately and let the sound play asynchronously.

The typical alternative is the snd_Sync parameter. If you use it, the function doesn't return until the sound has been completely played. In the first case, asynchronous play, you can stop a long sound by calling the same function again, without the first parameter:

```
procedure TForm1.StopButtonClick(Sender: TObject);
begin
  SndPlaySound (nil, 0);
end;
```

This is the code executed by the EXTBEEP example when the user presses the Stop button. This button is particularly useful for stopping the repeated execution of the sound started by the Loop button with the code:

```
procedure TForm1.LoopButtonClick(Sender: TObject);
var
  Text: array [0..100] of Char;
begin
  with ListBox1 do
    StrPCopy (Text, Items [ItemIndex]);
  SndPlaySound (Text, snd_Async or snd_Loop);
end;
```

The only other method of the example, FormCreate, selects an item of the list box at startup, to avoid run-time errors if the user presses the button before selecting an item of the list box:

```
procedure TForm1.FormCreate(Sender: TObject);
begin
  ListBox1.ItemIndex := 0;
end;
```

Again, test this example by running it, and eventually add names of new WAV files. I suggest you also test new values for the function's second parameter. You can find the complete list in the Multimedia Windows Help file by searching for the name of the function. Notice, however, that this help is not indexed with the other Delphi Help files, which means that a Topic Search operation won't find it. Instead, you need to open this Help file manually.

The Media Player Component

By browsing through the other API functions described by the Windows Multimedia Help file, you can learn many other techniques for playing sounds and controlling other devices. Instead of delving into this topic directly, I prefer to move back to Delphi and use the Media Player component.

The Delphi TMediaPlayer class encapsulates most of the capabilities of the Windows Media Control Interface (MCI), a high-level interface for controlling internal and external media devices.

As you probably remember, we already used the Media Player component in the FILEMAN2 example of Chapter 14, to play WAV files. This is exactly what we're going to do again in the next example. Before we move to the examples, however, let me give you a couple of general notes about the component.

First of all, consider the DeviceType property of the TMediaPlayer component. Its value can be `dtAutoSelect`, indicating that the type of the device depends on the file extension of the current file (the FileName property). As an alternative, you can indicate a specific device type, such as `dtAVIVideo`, `dtCDAudio`, `dtWaveAudio`, or many others. This is the only approach you can use for devices that do not relate to a file as the reader of an audio CD.

26

Once the device type, and eventually the file, has been chosen, you can open the device (or set AutoOpen to True), and the buttons of the Media Player component will be enabled. Notice that the component has a number of buttons, not all of which are meaningful for each media type.

There are actually three properties referring to the buttons: VisibleButtons, EnabledButtons, and ColoredButtons. The first determines which of the buttons are present in the control, the second which buttons are enabled, and the third which buttons have colored marks. By using the first two of these properties, you can permanently hide or temporarily disable some of the buttons.

My last comment concerns the component's events. The OnClick event is different from usual because it contains a parameter indicating which button was pressed and a second you can use to disable the default action connected to the button. The OnNotify event later informs the component of the success of the action generated by the button. Another event, OnPostClick, is sent either when the action starts or when it ends, depending on the value of the Wait property. This property determines whether or not the operation on the device should be synchronous.

Playing Sound Files

The first example of the use of the media player is very simple. As you can see in Figure 26.6, the form of the MMSOUND example has some labels describing the current status, a button to select a new file, and an OpenDialog component. You can see the detailed description of the form in Listing 26.3.

FIGURE 26.6:

The form of the MMSOUND example at design-time

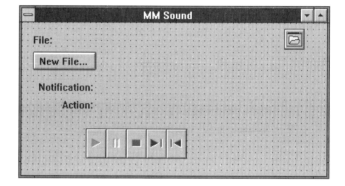

LISTING 26.3: The textual description of the form of the MMSOUND example

```
object Form1: TForm1
  Caption = 'MM Sound'
  object Label1: TLabel
    Caption = 'File:'
  end
  object FileLabel: TLabel...
  object Label2: TLabel
    Caption = 'Notification:'
  end
  object NotifLabel: TLabel...
  object Label3: TLabel
    Caption = 'Action:'
  end
  object ActionLabel: TLabel...
  object MediaPlayer1: TMediaPlayer
    VisibleButtons = [btPlay, btPause, btStop,
      btNext, btPrev]
    OnClick = MediaPlayer1Click
    OnNotify = MediaPlayer1Notify
  end
```

LISTING 26.3: The textual description of the form of the MMSOUND example (continued)

```
object NewButton: TButton
  Caption = 'New File...'
  OnClick = NewButtonClick
end
object OpenDialog1: TOpenDialog
  Filter = 'Wavetable files (*.wav)¦*.wav¦
    Midi files (*.mid)¦*.mid'
end
end
```

NOTE At first I wanted to name the example SOUND, not MMSOUND, but this name is in conflict with that of a system library, preventing the program from loading. Delphi even refuses to generate a program with this name, claiming that it is already running.

26

When a user opens a new file, a wave table, or a midi file, the program enables the media player, and you can play the sound and use the other buttons, too. The messages of the labels are automatically updated to reflect the current status, as you can see in Figure 26.7.

FIGURE 26.7:
A notification message displayed by the MMSOUND example

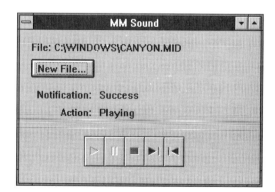

The code of the example is simple, so you can probably read it and understand it with no problem (see Listing 26.4). Notice only that you need to set the Notify property to True every time the OnNotify event handler is called in order to receive further notifications.

LISTING 26.4: The source code of the MMSOUND example

```
unit Sound_f;

interface

uses
  SysUtils, WinTypes, WinProcs, Messages, Classes,
  Graphics, Controls, Forms, Dialogs, StdCtrls, MPlayer;

type
  TForm1 = class(TForm)
    MediaPlayer1: TMediaPlayer;
    FileLabel: TLabel;
    Label2: TLabel;
    Label3: TLabel;
    ActionLabel: TLabel;
    NewButton: TButton;
    OpenDialog1: TOpenDialog;
    Label1: TLabel;
    NotifLabel: TLabel;
    procedure NewButtonClick(Sender: TObject);
    procedure MediaPlayer1Notify(Sender: TObject);
    procedure MediaPlayer1Click(Sender: TObject;
      Button: TMPBtnType; var DoDefault: Boolean);
  private
    { Private declarations }
  public
    { Public declarations }
  end;

var
  Form1: TForm1;

implementation

{$R *.DFM}

procedure TForm1.NewButtonClick(Sender: TObject);
var
  Volume: LongInt;
begin
  if OpenDialog1.Execute then
  begin
    FileLabel.Caption := OpenDialog1.Filename;
    MediaPlayer1.Filename := OpenDialog1.Filename;
```

LISTING 26.4: The source code of the MMSOUND example (continued)

```
    MediaPlayer1.Open;
    MediaPlayer1.Notify := True;
  end;
end;

procedure TForm1.MediaPlayer1Notify(Sender: TObject);
begin
  case MediaPlayer1.NotifyValue of
    nvSuccessful : NotifLabel.Caption := 'Success';
    nvSuperseded : NotifLabel.Caption := 'Superseded';
    nvAborted    : NotifLabel.Caption := 'Aborted';
    nvFailure    : NotifLabel.Caption := 'Failure';
  end;
  MediaPlayer1.Notify := True;
end;

procedure TForm1.MediaPlayer1Click(Sender: TObject;
  Button: TMPBtnType; var DoDefault: Boolean);
begin
  case Button of
    btPlay: ActionLabel.Caption := 'Playing';
    btPause: ActionLabel.Caption := 'Paused';
    btStop: ActionLabel.Caption := 'Stopped';
    btNext: ActionLabel.Caption := 'Next';
    btPrev: ActionLabel.Caption := 'Previous';
  end;
end;

end.
```

26

Running Videos

Up to now, we have always worked with sound. Of course, you could run the previous example only if you had a sound driver installed in your system. Now it is time to move to another kind of device, video. You indeed have a video on your system, but to play video files (such as AVI files), you need a specific driver, such as Microsoft Video for Windows.

If your computer can display videos, writing a Delphi application to do this is almost trivial: place a Media Player component in a form, select an AVI file in the File-Name property, set the AutoOpen property to True, and run the program. As soon as you press the Play button, the system opens a second window and shows the video in it, as you can see in Figure 26.8.

FIGURE 26.8:

By default, an AVI file is displayed
in its own window.

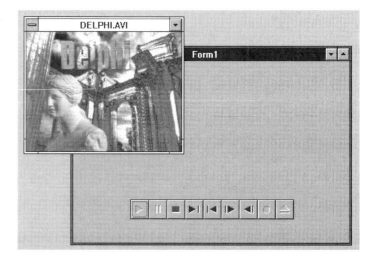

In this case, I've chosen the DELPHI.AVI present on the Delphi CD-ROM in the VIDEOS directory. Instead of playing the file in its own window, we can add a panel (or any other windowed component) to the form and use the name of this panel as the value of the media player's Display property. As an alternative, we can set the Display property, and also the DisplayRect property, to indicate which portions of the output window the video should cover.

> **NOTE** The following two examples, MMVIDEO and MMVIDEO2, require the DELPHI.AVI file to run. You can either copy this file from the Delphi CD to the C:\DELPHI directory and run the program as is or change the file name property. You can set it to the DELPHI.AVI file directly on the CD (but only if your CD-ROM drive is fast enough) or else choose any other AVI file from either your hard disk or another CD-ROM.

For example, the MMVIDEO example has the output shown in Figure 26.9. Notice that this is a steady image, obtained by stepping through the video with the last two buttons (Step and Back). This program has no code at all. To create it, you need only set some properties, as indicated in the text above and detailed in Listing 26.5.

FIGURE 26.9:

The output of an AVI file into a panel. Compare this figure with the previous one.

LISTING 26.5: The textual description of the form of the MMVIDEO example, which has no code

```
object Form1: TForm1
  Caption = 'MM Video'
  object MediaPlayer1: TMediaPlayer
    VisibleButtons = [btPlay, btPause, btStop,
      btNext, btPrev, btStep, btBack]
    AutoOpen = True
    Display = Panel1
    FileName = 'C:\DELPHI\DELPHI.AVI'
  end
  object Panel1: TPanel
    Left = 14
    Top = 8
    Width = 234
    Height = 169
  end
end
```

A Video in a Form

The Media Player component has some limits regarding the window it can use to produce the output. You can use many components, but not all of them. A strange thing you can try is to use the same Media Player component as the video's output window.

This works, but there are two problems. First, the TMediaPlayer cannot be aligned, and it cannot be sized at will. If you try to use big buttons, at run-time their size will be automatically reduced. The second problem is that if you press the Pause button, you'll see the button in front of the video, while the other buttons are still covered. I suggest you try this approach, anyway, for fun.

One thing you cannot do directly is display the video in a form. Instead of trying other approaches, I've followed this one: place a panel in a form, align it with the client area, and set the Visible property of the Media Player component to False. Now choose a file, and set other properties as shown in Listing 26.6.

LISTING 26.6: The textual description of the form of the MMVIDEO2 example

```
object Form1: TForm1
  Caption = 'MMV (Stopped)'
  object MediaPlayer1: TMediaPlayer
    VisibleButtons = [btPlay, btPause, btStop]
    AutoOpen = True
    Display = Panel1
    FileName = 'C:\DELPHI\DELPHI.AVI'
    Visible = False
    OnNotify = MediaPlayer1Notify
  end
  object Panel1: TPanel
    Hint = 'Click to play video'
    Align = alClient
    BevelOuter = bvNone
    Ctl3D = False
    ShowHint = True
    OnClick = Panel1Click
  end
end
```

Of course, you have to write some code to start and stop the video. As the Hint property of the Panel1 component suggests (see Listing 26.6), these actions take place when the user clicks on the panel. The same action is used to play the file or to stop it if it is already playing:

```
procedure TForm1.Panel1Click(Sender: TObject);
begin
  if Playing then
  begin
    MediaPlayer1.Stop;
    Playing := False;
```

```
      Caption := 'MM Video (Stopped)';
      Panel1.Hint := 'Click to play video';
    end
    else
    begin
      MediaPlayer1.DisplayRect := Panel1.BoundsRect;
      MediaPlayer1.Play;
      Playing := True;
      Caption := 'MMV (Playing)';
      Panel1.Hint := 'Click to stop video';
    end;
  end;
```

In this code, Playing is a private field of the form. Notice that the program shows the video using the full size of the panel—that is, the full client area of the form, which is always completely covered by the panel. The best way to look at the video is to use the original size, but with this program you can actually stretch it, and even change its proportions, as you can see in Figure 26.10 (which also shows the hint).

26

FIGURE 26.10:

A stretched video, with very poor resolution, and the hint indicating the current effect of a click

Of course, the file can also stop when it reaches the end or an error occurs. In both cases, we receive a notification event:

```
procedure TForm1.MediaPlayer1Notify(Sender: TObject);
begin
  Playing := False;
  Caption := 'MMV (Stopped)';
  Panel1.Hint := 'Click to play video';
end;
```

An alternative approach is to add a second panel, behaving as a toolbar and having some buttons to mimic a Media Player component. (You can also place the Media Player component directly into the toolbar and avoid writing most of the code.)

Working with a CD Drive

In addition to audio and video files, the MCI interface is generally used to operate external devices. The examples are many, but the most common MCI device connected to a PC is probably a CD-ROM drive. Most CD-ROM drives can also read normal audio CD disks, sending the output to an external speaker.

You can use the MCI interface, and the Media Player component, to write applications that handle such a device. Basically, you need to set the DeviceType property to dtCDAudio, make sure no file is selected in the FileName property, and be ready with a CD player.

Indeed, just by placing a Media Player component in a form, setting the above properties, and compiling and running the program, you end up with a fully functional audio CD player. When you start customizing the player, though, not everything is as simple as it seems at first sight.

I've built an example using some of the capabilities of this component related to audio CD. You can see the form of the CDPLAYER example in Figure 26.11 and its textual description in Listing 26.7.

FIGURE 26.11:
The form of the CDPLAYER example at design-time

LISTING 26.7: The textual description of the form of the CDPLAYER example

```
object Form1: TForm1
  Caption = 'Cd Player'
  OnClose = FormClose
  OnCreate = FormCreate
  object Bevel2: TBevel...
  object Bevel1: TBevel...
  object TracksLabel: TLabel
    Caption = 'Tracks'
  end
  object CurPosLabel: TLabel
    Caption = 'CurPosLabel'
  end
  object Label1: TLabel
    Caption = 'Disk'
  end
  object TrackNumberLabel: TLabel
    Caption = 'TrackNumberLabel'
  end
  object Label3: TLabel
    Caption = 'New track:'
  end
  object MediaPlayer1: TMediaPlayer
    VisibleButtons = [btPlay, btPause, btStop,
      btNext, btPrev]
    DeviceType = dtCDAudio
    OnPostClick = MediaPlayer1PostClick
  end
  object NewButton: TButton
    Caption = 'New'
    OnClick = NewButtonClick
  end
  object SpinEdit1: TSpinEdit
    MaxValue = 10
    MinValue = 1
    Value = 1
  end
  object GoButton: TButton
    Caption = 'Go'
    OnClick = GoButtonClick
  end
  object Timer1: TTimer
    Enabled = False
    OnTimer = Timer1Timer
  end
end
```

26

The idea is to inform the user of the number of tracks on a disk, the current track, and the current position within a track. I also tried to add the length of a track and similar information, but it was far more complex than I was expecting, so I finally gave up. Most of the problems arise from the way the Windows multimedia subsystem handles time information.

For example, if you set the tfTMSF value (Track, Minute, Second, Frame) for the Time Format property, when you access the Position property, the result indicates the four elements of the format above. Extracting the values is not too complex if you use the proper functions of the MmSystem unit, such as:

```
CurrentTrack := Mci_TMSF_Track (Position);
```

The value for the current track and position are computed this way each time the timer interval elapses (see Listing 26.8 for the complete code and Figure 26.12 for a sample output). This is not good, because if you want to play an audio CD while using other programs, a timer accessing the media player information often slows down the system too much. Of course, this mainly depends on the hardware you are working with.

LISTING 26.8: The source code of the CDPLAYER example

```
unit Player_f;

interface

uses
  SysUtils, WinTypes, WinProcs, Messages, Classes,
  Graphics, Controls, Forms, Dialogs, MPlayer,
  ExtCtrls, StdCtrls, MmSystem, Spin;

type
  TForm1 = class(TForm)
    MediaPlayer1: TMediaPlayer;
    TracksLabel: TLabel;
    CurPosLabel: TLabel;
    Label1: TLabel;
    Timer1: TTimer;
    Bevel1: TBevel;
    Bevel2: TBevel;
    TrackNumberLabel: TLabel;
    NewButton: TButton;
    Label3: TLabel;
    SpinEdit1: TSpinEdit;
    GoButton: TButton;
    procedure FormCreate(Sender: TObject);
```

LISTING 26.8: The source code of the CDPLAYER example (continued)

```
    procedure Timer1Timer(Sender: TObject);
    procedure FormClose(Sender: TObject;
      var Action: TCloseAction);
    procedure MediaPlayer1PostClick(
      Sender: TObject; Button: TMPBtnType);
    procedure NewButtonClick(Sender: TObject);
    procedure GoButtonClick(Sender: TObject);
  private
    { Private declarations }
  public
    procedure CheckDisk;
    procedure CheckPosition;
  end;

var
  Form1: TForm1;

implementation

{$R *.DFM}

procedure TForm1.FormCreate(Sender: TObject);
begin
  MediaPlayer1.Open;
  CheckDisk;
  CheckPosition;
  MediaPlayer1.TimeFormat := tfTMSF;
end;

procedure TForm1.CheckDisk;
var
  NTracks: Integer;
begin
  NTracks := MediaPlayer1.Tracks;
  TracksLabel.Caption := 'Tracks: ' +
    IntToStr (NTracks);
  SpinEdit1.MaxValue := NTracks;
end;

procedure TForm1.Timer1Timer(Sender: TObject);
begin
  CheckPosition;
end;

procedure TForm1.CheckPosition;
var
  CtPos: LongInt;
begin
  CtPos := MediaPlayer1.Position;
  CurPosLabel.Caption := 'Position: ' +
    IntToStr (Mci_TMSF_Minute (CtPos)) + ':' +
```

LISTING 26.8: The source code of the CDPLAYER example (continued)

```
    IntToStr (Mci_TMSF_Second (CtPos));
  TrackNumberLabel.Caption := 'Current track: ' +
    IntToStr (Mci_TMSF_Track (CtPos));
end;

procedure TForm1.FormClose(Sender: TObject;
  var Action: TCloseAction);
begin
  MediaPlayer1.Stop;
end;

procedure TForm1.MediaPlayer1PostClick(
  Sender: TObject; Button: TMPBtnType);
begin
  if MediaPlayer1.Mode = mpPlaying then
    Timer1.Enabled := True
  else
    Timer1.Enabled := False;
  CheckPosition;
end;

procedure TForm1.NewButtonClick(Sender: TObject);
begin
  CheckDisk;
  CheckPosition;
end;

procedure TForm1.GoButtonClick(Sender: TObject);
begin
  MediaPlayer1.Position :=
    MediaPlayer1.TrackPosition[SpinEdit1.Value];
  CheckPosition;
end;

end.
```

Besides advising the user of what is going on, the form has two buttons the user can press (aside from the media player buttons). The New button computes the number of tracks and similar information when the user changes the CD. The Go button jumps to the track selected in the SpinEdit component. This task is accomplished with the code:

```
MediaPlayer1.Position :=
    MediaPlayer1.TrackPosition[SpinEdit1.Value];
```

The CDPLAYER example running

In fact, the TrackPosition property indicates the starting position of each track. After this code I added the statement:

```
MediaPlayer1.Play;
```

With this call, the program indeed starts playing the current track automatically, as soon as it moves to it. The real problem is that the status and user interface of the Media Player component are not always updated properly. If you change the Position property, the player generally is correctly stopped, and the enabled buttons change accordingly. However, if you start it again with the Play procedure, at times nothing changes in the component's user interface, which is certainly peculiar behavior. The problem here is that many CD-ROM and MCI device drivers do not implement the whole API, as they should. The nice thing about MCI is that it is a very flexible device control API. That's also MCI's biggest problem—it's so flexible that drivers from different vendors for the same kind of device can vary in behavior quite a bit.

A good extension of this program would be to connect it to a CD database with the title of each CD you own and the title of each track. (I would have done it if it hadn't been for the time it would have taken to enter the title and track of each of my disks.)

Summary

In this chapter, we have seen some audio capabilities we can add to Delphi applications in general and have looked at the Media Player component. We have seen how to add sound effects to underline user actions, although this should generally be a program option that a user can turn off (besides disabling sounds in Windows).

We have also seen three examples of the use of the media player, with sound files, video files, and an external device (an audio CD). As the hardware becomes more powerful and CD-ROM players faster, video will become an important feature of many applications. I suggest you not underestimate this area of programming just because you are writing *serious* business programs.

This chapter ends the part of the book devoted to advanced Windows programming topics. One of the most interesting areas of Delphi development awaits you in the next chapter: building Delphi components.

PART IV

Creating Components
and Libraries

CHAPTER

TWENTY-SEVEN

Creating Components

- How to extend the VCL library

- How to customize existing components

- A tabbed list box

- How to build graphical components

- How to define custom events

- Clock components

- Array properties

- A dialog box in a component

27

Delphi offers two main approaches to programming: using components and writing components. While most Delphi programmers are probably component users, many of them need to write simple components or customize existing ones.

One of the most interesting aspects of Delphi is that writing components is simple. For this reason, although this book is for Delphi programmers, not for Delphi tool writers, this chapter covers the topic of writing components.

In this chapter, I'll give you an overview of Delphi component writing and a number of simple examples. There is no space for the source code and description of very complex components, but I hope the ideas in this chapter can help you write any kind of component.

Extending the VCL

When you write a new component, you basically extend the VCL. To do this, you use many features of the Object Pascal language that component users seldom need. I've presented an overall description of the language in Chapters 4 and 5, so I'm not going to underline language concepts here. Instead, I'll focus on some Object Pascal constructs specific to components, such as the definition of properties, that I didn't cover before.

Chapter 6 presented an overview of the VCL, together with some hierarchy graphs and a discussion of the role of properties, methods, and events. If you skipped that chapter or do not feel confident with the basic ideas about VCL, read it before going on with this chapter.

Delphi Components Are Classes

Delphi components are classes, and the VCL library is the collection of all the classes defining Delphi components. Each time you add a new component to Delphi, you actually extend the VCL with a new class.

Technically, the code of the components installed in Delphi is stored in the COMPLIB.DCL file, a component library file. When you install a new component, you extend the VCL by actually adding new components to the component library.

This new class will be derived from one of the existing component-related classes. You can inherit a new component from an existing component to add new capabilities, or inherit from an abstract component class—one that does not correspond to a usable component. The VCL hierarchy includes many of these intermediate classes to let you choose a default behavior for your new component and to change its properties.

In fact, when you subclass a component with a specific property, you cannot remove it in the inherited component; you can only add new properties. If you have a property you do not want, you should choose a higher-level class in the VCL hierarchy.

Static Linking Components

Another very important element in understanding Delphi components is their linking. (I discussed this topic in Chapter 16, where I compared Delphi components to VBX controls.) Although we won't focus on dynamic linking in Windows until the next chapter, the basic idea is that the code of a Delphi component ends up inside the executable code of a compiled Delphi application.

When you have written a component (or bought it), you have to install it in Delphi. Installing a component means adding its code to a component library (by default, the file COMPLIB.DCL in the DELPHI\BIN directory).

Once your component's code is part of the library and its icon has been added to the Components palette, you can use it in any Delphi project. When you compile the project, the required code is copied from the library to the application's executable file. This means that to run the program, a user doesn't need to have the component, unlike what happens with VBX controls.

Rules for Writing Components

Some general rules govern the writing of components. You can find a detailed description of most of them in the Delphi *Component Writer's Guide.*

> **NOTE** The *Component Writer's Guide* is certainly required reading for Delphi component writers, but the information in this manual is somewhat limited. For this reason, it is important to delve into the details of component creation using Delphi's *Component Writer's Help,* an on-line reference with many details about components that are not available in the basic Delphi help because they are interesting for component writers, not for component users. The VCL source code and the VCL reference manual (both not present in the basic Delphi box) are other important references for component writers.

Here is my own summary of rules for component writers:

- Study the Object Pascal language with care, particularly inheritance, method overriding, the difference between public and published sections, and the definition of properties and events.

- Study the structure of the VCL hierarchy and have a graph with the classes at hand (see Chapter 6).

- Be ready to write *real* code and forget the Delphi visual programming environment. Writing components generally means writing code without a related form.

- Follow the Borland naming conventions. There are many of them for components, as we will see, and following these rules makes it easier for other programmers to interact and further extend your component.

- Keep components simple, mimic other components, and avoid dependencies. These three rules basically mean that a user of the components you write should be able to use them as easily as Delphi preinstalled components. If you try to use the same properties, methods, and event names whenever possible, it helps. If users can avoid learning complex rules about the use of the component (that is, if the dependencies between methods or properties are limited) and can simply access properties with readable names, they'll be happy.

- Use exceptions. When something goes wrong, the component should raise an exception. When you are allocating resources of any kind, you must protect them with `try-finally` blocks, as well as with destructors.

- Test a component in a sample form before installing it in the system. Installing a component with bad errors can blow up Delphi, and reinstalling a component over and over takes more time than compiling new text programs.

- To complete a component, add a bitmap to it for the Components palette, and if you want to sell it, also add a Help file.

Introducing Some Simple Components

Before going on with the theory and looking at complete examples of components, I would like to show you a couple of simple, almost useless, components. The aim of this section, which skips most of the details, is to give you an idea of how easy it is to write new components.

The Fonts Combo Box

Many applications have a toolbar with a combo box you can use to select a font. A similar example, COMBOBAR, was shown in Chapter 11. Now, if you happen to use a similar customized combo box, why not make it a component? It would probably take less than a minute.

Close any project in the Delphi environment and start the Component Expert, by choosing the New Component command on the File menu. In the Expert's window, enter a name for the class of the new component and choose a parent class (see Figure 27.1). Also select the page of the Components palette where you want to add the new component.

When you press the OK button, the Expert generates a simple Pascal source file, with the structure of your component. One of the key elements is the class

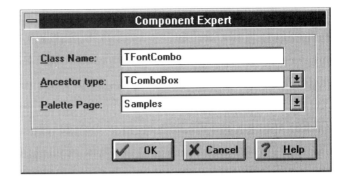

definition, which begins by indicating the parent class:

```
type
  TFontCombo = class(TComboBox)
    ...
  end;
```

The rest of the code is in the Register procedure:

```
procedure Register;
begin
  RegisterComponents('Samples', [TFontCombo]);
end;
```

You can see that the Components Expert does its work, but it is not a lot of work. Now you can start writing code. That's all it takes to build a component. Of course, in this example the code is very simple. We need only copy all the system fonts to the Items property of the combo box at startup.

To accomplish this, we can override the Create method:

```
public
  { Public declarations }
  constructor Create (AOwner: TComponent); override;
```

Now we can write some code in this method (in the implementation portion of the unit), such as:

```
constructor TFontCombo.Create (AOwner: TComponent);
begin
  inherited Create (AOwner);
```

```
    Style := csDropDownList;
    Items := Screen.Fonts;
  end;
```

Notice that before writing any custom code, we perform a default initialization, calling the Create method of the parent class.

If we tried to add this component to the component library, the operation would succeed but the component would not be usable. The problem here is that we cannot access the combo box's Items property, which refers to an element of the Windows related-component, before the component is completely built. However, the component cannot be built until all its key properties (such as Parent) have been set up.

Instead of assigning the new strings in the Create constructor, we can perform this operation in the CreateWnd procedure, which is called to create the window control. Again, we execute the default behavior, and then we can write our custom code:

```
procedure TFontCombo.CreateWnd;
begin
  inherited CreateWnd;
  Items := Screen.Fonts;
end;
```

We could also skip the Create constructor and write all the code here, but I prefer using both startup methods to let you see the difference between them. In Listing 27.1 you can see the complete source code of the TFontCombo constructor.

LISTING 27.1: The complete source code of the TFontCombo component

```
unit Fontcomb;

interface

uses
  SysUtils, WinTypes, WinProcs, Messages, Classes,
  Graphics, Controls, Forms, Dialogs, StdCtrls;

type
  TFontCombo = class(TComboBox)
  private
    { Private declarations }
  protected
    { Protected declarations }
  public
    constructor Create (AOwner: TComponent); override;
    procedure CreateWnd; override;
```

LISTING 27.1: The complete source code of the TFontCombo component (continued)

```
  published
    property Style default csDropDownList;
  end;

procedure Register;

implementation

constructor TFontCombo.Create (AOwner: TComponent);
begin
  inherited Create (AOwner);
  Style := csDropDownList;
end;

procedure TFontCombo.CreateWnd;
begin
  inherited CreateWnd;
  Items := Screen.Fonts;
end;

procedure Register;
begin
  RegisterComponents('Samples', [TFontCombo]);
end;

end.
```

Notice that besides giving a new value to the component's Style property, in the Create method, I've redefined this property by setting a value with the `default` keyword. We have to do both operations because giving a property a default value has no effect on its initial value. The only reason to use a property's default value is that properties having a value corresponding to the default value are not streamed with the form definition.

Now we have to install the component in the system library. Invoke the Install Components command on the Delphi Options menu and select the file that defines the new component, as shown in Figure 27.2. (Of course, save the file with a proper name first.)

When you have added a new file, it is added to the Installed Units list box and its path becomes part of the Search Path edit box. In my case, the text of this box becomes

```
  C:\DELPHI\LIB;c:\books\delphi\code\27\fontbox
```

FIGURE 27.2:

The selection of a file defining a new component

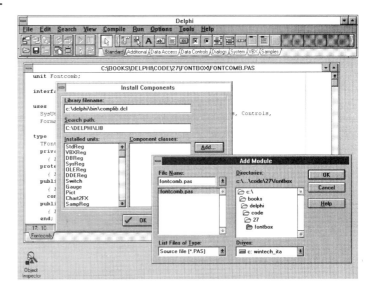

Once you press the OK button in the Install Components dialog box, Delphi updates the component library, compiling the new component. If you open this dialog box again later on, you'll see the name of the unit defining the new component, as well as the list of the components it defines (in this case, only one). You can see this situation in Figure 27.3.

NOTE In this and the following examples in this chapter, I'll always make changes to the COMPLIB.DCL component library, but nothing prevents you from make a copy of this library and working on that copy. Delphi, in fact, allows you to switch between multiple component libraries and choose the one you want to use each time (for each project).

The other effect of the compilation of the new component is that a bitmap for it is added to the Samples page of the Components palette, as indicated by the Register function. The bitmap used will be the same as the parent class because we haven't provided a custom bitmap (we will do this in future examples). Notice that the new

FIGURE 27.3:

After the compilation of the library with the new source files, you can see the names of the components defined by each unit.

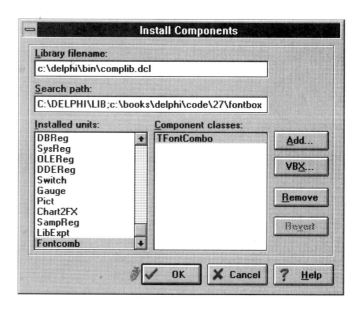

component will use as a hint the name of the class without the initial *T*, as you can see here:

Using the Fonts Combo Box

Now you can create a new Delphi program to test the fonts combo box. Move to the palette, select the component, and add it to a new form. A traditional combo box will appear. However, if you select the Items Property Editor, you'll see its default contents (as shown in Figure 27.4).

To build a simple text example, I've added a Memo component to the form and selected some text inside it (actually, it is the text of the Pascal file defining the new component). You can see the textual description of the form, including the new component, in Listing 27.2.

FIGURE 27.4:

As soon as you place a new TFontCombo component on the form, its Items property receives the names of the fonts installed in the system.

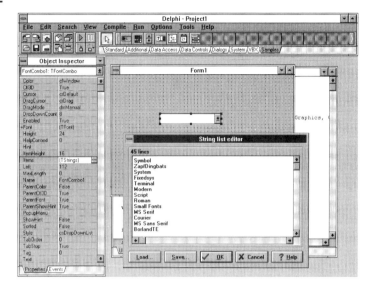

LISTING 27.2: The textual description of the form of the FONTBOX example

```
object Form1: TForm1
  Caption = 'Form1'
  OnCreate = FormCreate
  object Memo1: TMemo
    Lines.Strings = (
      'unit Fontcomb;'
      ''
      'interface'
      ''
      ...)
  end
  object FontCombo1: TFontCombo
    Items.Strings = (
      'Algerian'
      'Arial'
      'Arial Narrow'
      ...)
    Sorted = True
    OnChange = FontCombo1Change
  end
end
```

27

The program has little code. When a user selects a new font in the combo box, the new value is used for the name of the memo's font:

```
procedure TForm1.FontCombo1Change(Sender: TObject);
begin
  Memo1.Font.Name :=
    FontCombo1.Items [FontCombo1.ItemIndex];
end;
```

At the beginning, the reverse action is performed; the name of the memo's font is selected in the combo box:

```
procedure TForm1.FormCreate(Sender: TObject);
begin
  with FontCombo1 do
    ItemIndex := Items.IndexOf (Memo1.Font.Name);
end;
```

The aim of this simple program (see Figure 27.5 for its output) is only to test the behavior of the new component we have built. The component is not very useful—we could have written a couple of lines of code in any example to obtain the same effect—but looking at a couple of simple components is useful to give you an idea of what is involved in component building.

FIGURE 27.5:

The output of the FONTBOX example

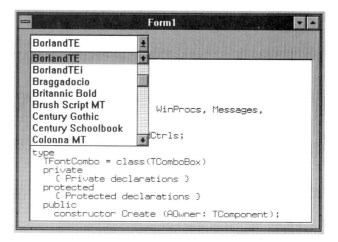

A Tabbed List Box

The Delphi TListBox component misses a feature that is generally useful in Windows list boxes: the use of tabs. Tabs can be used to output text in a list box on multiple columns, so we can build a new, simple component extending the standard Delphi list boxes with this new feature. Since tabbed columns are difficult to maintain, as we will see later in this chapter, the Borland choice is not casual. Instead of correcting the behavior of the list boxes, Borland programmers have chosen a radical solution, the Grid family of components.

From a technical point of view, a list box can have tabs if it has the `lbs_UseTabStops` window style. This style is set in the control wrapped by the TListBox component when it is created. Luckily, we can use a hook to change the control creation. We saw in the earlier example that the window connected to the component is created in a second step, with the CreateWnd method. When this method is executed, we have a choice of looking at the parameters of the Windows API `CreateWindow` function and changing some values before the actual window creation takes place. This method is CreateParams, and its parameter is a reference of type TCreateParams.

27

NOTE
Windows programmers might already know that the TCreateParams type is a record with fields corresponding to each parameter of the `CreateWindow` API function. A pointer to this parameter is passed to the window being created in the `wm_Create` message.

The CreateParams method is used in Delphi components to change some of the standard values used in component creation. For example, we can write:

```
procedure TTabList.CreateParams (var Params: TCreateParams);
begin
  inherited CreateParams (Params);
  Params.Style := Params.Style or lbs_UseTabStops;
end;
```

This code reads the default parameters, calling the method of the parent class, and then adds the `lbs_UseTabStops` flag to the window style.

Now we can use this list box and use tabs inside it to output the text in multiple columns. However, we can do something more. We can add a property to set the position of these tabs, but since this is quite complex, for the moment I'll skip it. In fact, this addition requires the use of an array property, which I'll show you later on in this chapter, when I finish this example.

For the moment, I've stayed with the simpler example. I've opened the Component Expert and chosen a name for the class of the new component, TTabList; a parent component, TListBox; and a page in the palette, Samples. In the automatically generated Pascal file, I've deleted some useless declarations and written the method above, including the declaration inside the class. You can see the result in Listing 27.3.

LISTING 27.3: The source code of the TTabList component

```
unit Tablist;

interface

uses
  SysUtils, WinTypes, WinProcs, Messages, Classes,
  Graphics, Controls, Forms, Dialogs, StdCtrls;

type
  TTabList = class(TListBox)
  public
    procedure CreateParams (
      var Params: TCreateParams); override;
  end;

procedure Register;

implementation

procedure TTabList.CreateParams (var Params: TCreateParams);
begin
  inherited CreateParams (Params);
  Params.Style := Params.Style or lbs_UseTabStops;
end;

procedure Register;
begin
  RegisterComponents('Samples', [TTabList]);
end;

end.
```

The code of this example is another demonstration that writing a component can be an easy task. Again, I've written a program to test the new component, the TAB-TEST example.

Testing the Tab List Component

To test the TTabList component, I've added it and a normal list box to the same form, side by side. The form also has three edit boxes and a button.

After adding these components to the form, I wrote the new items for both list boxes, using the same lines of text, which include tabs. In Figure 27.6, you can see the text I used for both list boxes, which includes some tabs. In the background of the figure, you can already see how this text is displayed by the two list boxes.

FIGURE 27.6:

The form of the TABTEST example at design-time

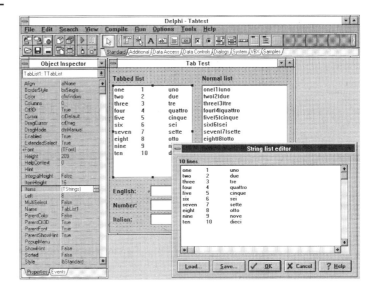

27

> **TIP** To add tabs in the String List Property Editor, simply press the Ctrl-Tab keys instead of the Tab key alone.

The final description of the form is shown in Listing 27.4. When you run this program, besides looking at the differences between the two list boxes, you can actually add new entries. The text of the three edit boxes is used to form a string, with two tabs between the three parts. This string is added to both list boxes, with the code:

```
procedure TForm1.AddButtonClick(Sender: TObject);
var
  NewItem: String;
begin
  if Edit1.Text <> '' then
  begin
    NewItem := Edit1.Text + #9 + Edit2.Text +
      #9 + Edit3.Text;
    TabList1.Items.Add (NewItem);
    ListBox1.Items.Add (NewItem);
  end;
end;
```

LISTING 27.4: The textual description of the form of the TABTEST example

```
object Form1: TForm1
  Caption = 'Tab Test'
  object Label1: TLabel
    Caption = 'Tabbed list'
  end
  object Label2: TLabel
    Caption = 'Normal list'
  end
  object Label3: TLabel
    Caption = 'English:'
  end
  object Label4: TLabel
    Caption = 'Number:'
  end
  object Label5: TLabel
    Caption = 'Italian:'
  end
  object TabList1: TTabList
    ItemHeight = 16
    Items.Strings = (
      'one'#9'1'#9'uno'
      'two'#9'2'#9'due'
      'three'#9'3'#9'tre'
      'four'#9'4'#9'quattro'
      'five'#9'5'#9'cinque'
      'six'#9'6'#9'sei'
      'seven'#9'7'#9'sette'
      'eight'#9'8'#9'otto'
```

LISTING 27.4: The textual description of the form of the TABTEST example (continued)

```
      'nine'#9'9'#9'nove'
      'ten'#9'10'#9'dieci')
  end
  object ListBox1: TListBox
    ItemHeight = 16
    Items.Strings = {...same as above...}
  end
  object Edit1: TEdit...
  object Edit2: TEdit...
  object Edit3: TEdit...
  object AddButton: TButton
    Caption = 'Add'
    OnClick = AddButtonClick
  end
end
```

You can see an example of the effect of this code in Figure 27.7, where I've added the number 20 to the list of English and Italian numbers.

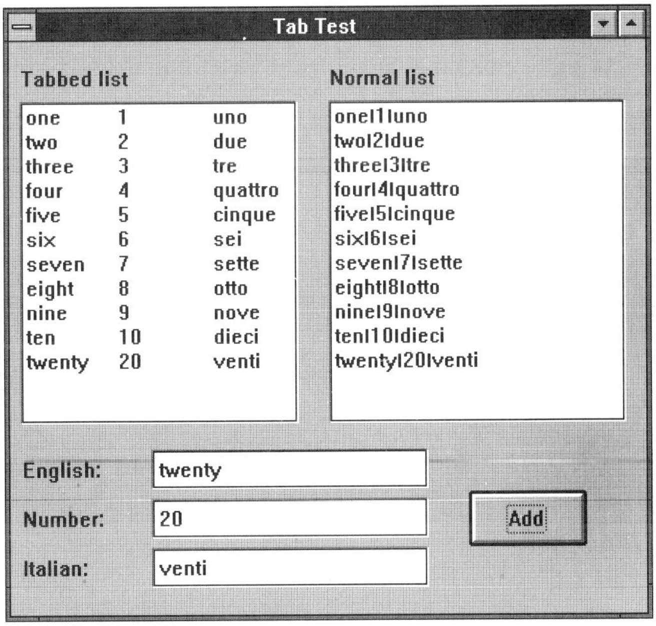

FIGURE 27.7:

The TABTEST example shows the difference between a standard Delphi list box and the tab list component.

Building Brand-New Components

The simple components we have built were just extensions of existing ones, with limited changes. This is what you'll probably do most of the time. At other times, however, you'll define brand-new components or components derived from generic classes, such as the TCustomXXX classes. When you write a brand-new component, you can subclass one of the higher-level classes:

- TWinControl is the parent class of components based on a window. In this case, the control can receive the input focus and get Windows messages from the system. You can also use its handle when calling API functions.

- TGraphicControl is the parent class of visible components that have no Windows handle, thus saving some Windows resources. These components cannot receive the input focus.

- TComponent is the parent class of all components and can be used as a direct parent class for nonvisual components.

In the rest of the chapter, we will build some components using various approaches, looking at the differences among them.

NOTE When you derive a new component from these high-level classes, it already has some properties that are common to all components. Refer to the graph in Chapter 6 (Figure 6.7) to see the properties defined in some of the high-level VCL classes.

A Graphical Component Built Step-by-Step

The graphical component I want to build is an arrow component. Arrows are often useful in graphical programs and other applications. You can use such a component to indicate a flow of information, an action, and many other elements.

Instead of showing you the final version of the component, which is quite complex, I've built it in consecutive steps. To avoid rebuilding the component library each time, I've tested this component in a program that creates it at run-time. I'll install the component in Delphi only at the end of the process.

Defining an Enumerated Property

After generating the new component with the Component Expert, choosing TGraphicControl as the parent class, we can start to customize its source code. The arrow can point in four different directions: up, down, left, and right. To express these choices, I've defined an enumerated type:

```
TArrowDirection = (adUp, adDown, adLeft, adRight);
```

This enumerated type defines a private data member of the component and a parameter of a procedure used to change it:

```
TArrow = class(TGraphicControl)
  private
    FDirection: TArrowDirection;
    procedure SetDirection (Value: TArrowDirection);
  ...
```

Now that we have private data and a method to set it, we can define a corresponding property as follows:

```
published
  property Direction: TArrowDirection
    read FDirection write SetDirection default adRight;
```

The property, which is of the same TArrowDirection data type, is read directly from the FDirection data and is written using the SetDirection procedure. The default value is adRight.

Notice several things here. First of all, look at the naming conventions:

- The private data is indicated with an *F* (field) in front of it, followed by the name of the property.

- The property has a plain, readable name.

- The function used to change the value of the property has the word *Set* at the beginning.

- An eventual function used to read the property would be named GetDirection.

These are just naming conventions. The compiler doesn't enforce them; they are only a general indication to make programs more readable. Probably such a standard approach can be used to write tools to generate the basic code of new properties. I wouldn't be surprised to see such a tool (a Property Expert) in the next version of Delphi.

Another important element refers to the definition of a property since this is the first property we define. The simplest way to define a property is to indicate a direct access to a field of the component (which should be a private field):

```
property NewProperty read FNewProperty write FNewProperty;
```

This direct access is seldom used because in general, when you change the value of a property, you need to repaint the component and cause other side effects. Each of these cases requires a procedure. For the arrow component, the code of the SetDirection method is:

```
procedure TArrow.SetDirection (Value: TArrowDirection);
begin
  if FDirection <> Value then
  begin
    FDirection := Value;
    Invalidate;
  end;
end;
```

Notice that the side effect takes place only if the property is really changing its value. Otherwise, the code is skipped and the method ends immediately. This code structure is very common, and we will use it for most of the Set procedures of properties.

The last thing we have to remember is to write a constructor to set the default value of the property in the code:

```
constructor TArrow.Create (AOwner: TComponent);
begin
  inherited Create (AOwner);
  FDirection := adRight;
end;
```

This constructor is defined in the public section of the type definition of the new component.

Drawing the Arrow Component

What is quite complex in this example is drawing the arrow. I've overridden the Paint method, in the protected section of the type definition, and used the Canvas property (automatically available for each TGraphicControl component). With a series of MoveTo and LineTo calls, you can draw the arrow in the different directions, as indicated in Figure 27.8 for the adUp direction.

FIGURE 27.8:

The code used to draw the adUp arrow and the resulting effect

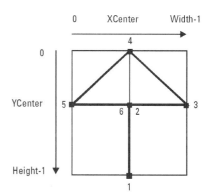

```
1) MoveTo (XCenter, Height-1);
2) LineTo (XCenter, YCenter);
3) LineTo (Width 1, YCenter);
4) LineTo (XCenter, 0);
5) LineTo (0, YCenter);
6) LineTo (XCenter, YCenter);
```

The code computes the center of the component area and uses it to determine the position of the arrow and the division between its two parts (the line and the triangle). Notice that the drawing fills the whole surface of the component.

You can see the code of the Paint method in Listing 27.5, together with the rest of the code of the first version of the arrow component.

Testing the Arrow

Now, instead of installing this component in the palette, we can write a test program to see whether it works properly. We cannot place the new component in the form of this example, ARROW1, because it is still not installed in the Delphi component library. Instead, we can create it at run-time. (By the way, notice that ARROW1 is the name of the directory, where you can find the code of the component, while the actual name of the project file is ATEST.)

LISTING 27.5: The first version of the arrow component, in the file ARROW1.PAS

```pascal
unit Arrow1;

interface

uses
  SysUtils, WinTypes, WinProcs, Messages, Classes,
  Graphics, Controls, Forms, Dialogs;

type
  TArrowDirection = (adUp, adDown, adLeft, adRight);
  TArrow = class(TGraphicControl)
  private
    FDirection: TArrowDirection;
    procedure SetDirection (Value: TArrowDirection);
  protected
    procedure Paint; override;
  public
    constructor Create (AOwner: TComponent); override;
  published
    property Direction: TArrowDirection
      read FDirection write SetDirection
      default adRight;
  end;

procedure Register;

implementation

constructor TArrow.Create (AOwner: TComponent);
begin
  inherited Create (AOwner);
  FDirection := adRight;
end;

procedure TArrow.SetDirection (
  Value: TArrowDirection);
begin
  if FDirection <> Value then
  begin
    FDirection := Value;
    Invalidate;
  end;
end;

procedure TArrow.Paint;
var
  XCenter, YCenter: Integer;
begin
  {compute the center}
  YCenter := (Height - 1) div 2;
  XCenter := (Width - 1) div 2;
```

LISTING 27.5: The first version of the arrow component, in the file ARROW1.PAS (continued)

```
{draw the line and the arrow}
case FDirection of
  adUp:
    with Canvas do
    begin
      MoveTo (XCenter, Height-1);
      LineTo (XCenter, YCenter);
      LineTo (Width-1, YCenter);
      LineTo (XCenter, 0);
      LineTo (0, YCenter);
      LineTo (XCenter, YCenter);
    end;
  adDown:
    with Canvas do
    begin
      MoveTo (XCenter, 0);
      LineTo (XCenter, YCenter);
      LineTo (Width - 1, YCenter);
      LineTo (XCenter, Height - 1);
      LineTo (0, YCenter);
      LineTo (XCenter, YCenter);
  end;
  adLeft:
    with Canvas do
    begin
      MoveTo (Width - 1, YCenter);
      LineTo (XCenter, YCenter);
      LineTo (XCenter, Height - 1);
      LineTo (0, YCenter);
      LineTo (XCenter, 0);
      LineTo (XCenter, YCenter);
    end;
  adRight:
    with Canvas do
    begin
      MoveTo (0, YCenter);
      LineTo (XCenter, YCenter);
      LineTo (XCenter, Height - 1);
      LineTo (Width - 1, YCenter);
      LineTo (XCenter, 0);
      LineTo (XCenter, YCenter);
    end;
  end;
end;

procedure Register;
begin
  RegisterComponents('Samples', [TArrow]);
end;

end.
```

27

The form has other components, which set some of the arrow's properties. As you can see in Figure 27.9, the form contains two spin edit components to set the width and height of the arrow, a button to accept these changes (*Size*), and a second button to turn the arrow (*Turn*), changing its Direction property.

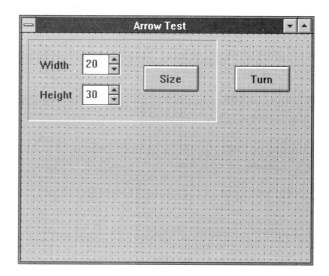

There is no textual description of this form because it is very simple. When the form is built, it creates a new arrow component:

```
procedure TForm1.FormCreate(Sender: TObject);
begin
  A := TArrow.Create (self);
  A.Parent := self;
  A.Left := 150;
  A.Top := 150;
  A.Width := 20;
  A.Height := 30;
end;
```

In this code, *A* is a private field of the form, declared with the component type:

```
private:
  A: TArrow;
```

You can see the effect of this code in the top portion of Figure 27.10. In the second part of the same figure, you can see the effect of some changes on the arrow component.

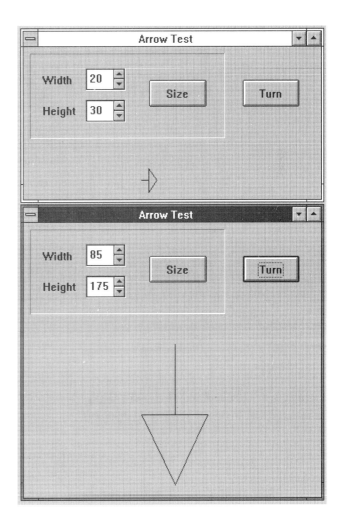

The arrow component changes when one of the two buttons is pressed. The Size button uses the values of the two spin edits to change the component's height and size:

```
procedure TForm1.SizeButtonClick(Sender: TObject);
begin
  A.Width := SpinEdit1.Value;
  A.Height := SpinEdit2.Value;
end;
```

The other button, Turn, changes the direction of the arrow. It reads the current value of the Direction property we have defined and increases its value by calling the system Succ procedure. In case the highest value of the set has been reached (High (TArrowDirection)), the lowest value is taken (Low (TArrowDirection)). This is the code of the Turn button's OnClick event handler:

```
procedure TForm1.TurnButtonClick(Sender: TObject);
begin
  if A.Direction = High (TArrowDirection) then
    A.Direction := Low (TArrowDirection)
  else
    A.Direction := Succ (A.Direction);
end;
```

As you can see in Figure 27.10 and test yourself by running the program, the new component works. The problem is that its capabilities are very limited. We have no way to change the size of the arrow point or to act on the colors used and the size of the lines. We will address these problems in the next versions.

The Point of the Arrow, Plus a Pen and a Brush

To determine the aspect of the point of the arrow, I've added two properties to the component, ArrowHeight and Filled:

```
property ArrowHeight: Integer
  read FArrowHeight write SetArrowHeight default 10;
property Filled: Boolean
  read FFilled write SetFilled default False;
```

The first property determines the size of the arrow's point, the second whether or not it should be colored. The color used for the point is determined by the current brush of the canvas, so we should add one more property to change the brush.

While we are at it, why not add another property for the pen? We have a lot of work to do for the new version of the component.

First of all, we have to implement the two properties above, ArrowHeight and Filled. Both have a corresponding private field in the class, as well as a private access function, as indicated in the definition of the property. Their code is simple. The biggest effect of these new properties, in fact, is on the Paint method, which should consider the size of the arrow's point and its color. Here is an excerpt of Paint:

```
adUp:
  with Canvas do
  begin
    MoveTo (XCenter, Height-1);
    LineTo (XCenter, FArrowHeight);
    LineTo (Width-1, FArrowHeight);
    LineTo (XCenter, 0);
    LineTo (0, FArrowHeight);
    LineTo (XCenter, FArrowHeight);
    if FFilled then
      FloodFill (XCenter, FArrowHeight div 2,
        Pen.Color, fsBorder);
  end;
```

You can see a graph with the effect of this code in Figure 27.11 and compare it with the older version in Figure 27.8. To fill a surface with FloodFill, you have to use the first two parameters to indicate a point inside it. I've chosen a point approximately

FIGURE 27.11:

A schema of the new version of the Paint code for the up arrow

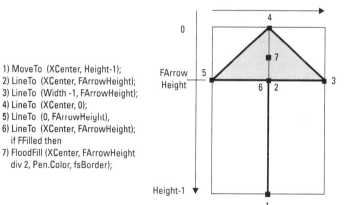

```
1) MoveTo (XCenter, Height-1);
2) LineTo (XCenter, FArrowHeight);
3) LineTo (Width -1, FArrowHeight);
4) LineTo (XCenter, 0);
5) LineTo (0, FArrowHeight);
6) LineTo (XCenter, FArrowHeight);
   if FFilled then
7) FloodFill (XCenter, FArrowHeight
   div 2, Pen.Color, fsBorder);
```

in the center of the arrow point, but any other point within the boundaries of the arrow point would do. The FloodFill method can be used with two different approaches. In this case, I've passed the `fsBorder` flag to fill all of the area included within a line of the pen color. As an alternative, I could have filled all of the area of a given color. (See Delphi Help about this method for the details.)

The other two new properties are defined as follows:

```
property Pen: TPen read FPen write SetPen;
property Brush: TBrush read FBrush write SetBrush;
```

These properties refer to VCL classes (or VCL objects, to use a standard term), so handling them is slightly different. Each of them again has a private field in the form, and a set method, with similar code:

```
procedure TArrow.SetPen (Value: TPen);
begin
  FPen.Assign(Value);
  Invalidate;
end;
```

The problem, however, is that at design-time or run-time, the value of one of the fields of the pen might change without changing the whole pen. Pens, brushes, and other classes have a specific event for this, OnChange. If you assign a method to the OnChange event of these components, the method will be called each time one of the parameters or properties of the class changes.

In the arrow component, I've added this code to the Create method:

```
FPen.OnChange := RepaintRequest;
FBrush.OnChange := RepaintRequest;
```

The RepaintRequest handler is declared in the private section of the component as:

```
procedure RepaintRequest (Sender: TObject);
```

Its effect, as the name suggests, is to repaint the component, calling the Invalidate method. You can see the code of this method, together with the rest of the source code of the second version of the component, in Listing 27.6.

LISTING 27.6: The source code of the second version of the arrow component, ARROW2.PAS

```pascal
unit Arrow2;

interface

uses
  SysUtils, WinTypes, WinProcs, Messages,
  Classes, Graphics, Controls, Forms, Dialogs;

type
  TArrowDirection = (adUp, adDown, adLeft, adRight);
  TArrow = class(TGraphicControl)
  private
    FDirection: TArrowDirection;
    FArrowHeight: Integer;
    FFilled: Boolean;
    FPen: TPen;
    FBrush: TBrush;
    procedure SetDirection (Value: TArrowDirection);
    procedure SetArrowHeight (Value: Integer);
    procedure SetFilled (Value: Boolean);
    procedure SetPen (Value: TPen);
    procedure SetBrush (Value: TBrush);
    procedure RepaintRequest (Sender: TObject);
  protected
    procedure Paint; override;
  public
    constructor Create (AOwner: TComponent); override;
    destructor Destroy; override;
  published
    property Direction: TArrowDirection
      read FDirection write SetDirection
      default adRight;
    property ArrowHeight: Integer
      read FArrowHeight write SetArrowHeight
      default 10;
    property Filled: Boolean
      read FFilled write SetFilled default False;
    property Pen: TPen
      read FPen write SetPen;
    property Brush: TBrush
      read FBrush write SetBrush;
  end;

procedure Register;

implementation

constructor TArrow.Create (AOwner: TComponent);
begin
  {call the parent constructor}
```

LISTING 27.6: The source code of the second version of the arrow component, ARROW2.PAS (continued)

```
  inherited Create (AOwner);
  {set the default values}
  FDirection := adRight;
  FArrowHeight := 10;
  FFilled := False;
  {create the pen and the brush}
  FPen := TPen.Create;
  FBrush := TBrush.Create;
  {set a handler for the OnChange event}
  FPen.OnChange := RepaintRequest;
  FBrush.OnChange := RepaintRequest;
end;

destructor TArrow.Destroy;
begin
  {delete the two objects}
  FPen.Free;
  FBrush.Free;
  {call the parent destructor}
  inherited Destroy;
end;

procedure TArrow.SetDirection (
  Value: TArrowDirection);
begin
  if FDirection <> Value then
  begin
    FDirection := Value;
    Invalidate;
  end;
end;

procedure TArrow.SetArrowHeight (
  Value: Integer);
begin
  if FArrowHeight <> Value then
  begin
    FArrowHeight := Value;
    Invalidate;
  end;
end;

procedure TArrow.SetFilled (
  Value: Boolean);
begin
  if FFilled <> Value then
  begin
    FFilled := Value;
    Invalidate;
  end;
end;
```

LISTING 27.6: The source code of the second version of the arrow component, ARROW2.PAS (continued)

```pascal
procedure TArrow.SetPen (Value: TPen);
begin
  FPen.Assign(Value);
  Invalidate;
end;

procedure TArrow.SetBrush (Value: TBrush);
begin
  FBrush.Assign(Value);
  Invalidate;
end;

procedure TArrow.RepaintRequest (
  Sender: TObject);
begin
  Invalidate;
end;

procedure TArrow.Paint;
var
  XCenter, YCenter: Integer;
begin
  YCenter := (Height - 1) div 2;
  XCenter := (Width - 1) div 2;

  {use the current pen and brush}
  Canvas.Pen := FPen;
  Canvas.Brush := FBrush;

  {draw the line and the arrow, eventually
  filling the point with the brush color}
  case FDirection of
    adUp:
      with Canvas do
      begin
        MoveTo (XCenter, Height-1);
        LineTo (XCenter, FArrowHeight);
        LineTo (Width-1, FArrowHeight);
        LineTo (XCenter, 0);
        LineTo (0, FArrowHeight);
        LineTo (XCenter, FArrowHeight);
        if FFilled then
          FloodFill (XCenter, FArrowHeight div 2,
            Pen.Color, fsBorder);
      end;
    adDown:
      with Canvas do
      begin
        MoveTo (XCenter, 0);
        LineTo (XCenter,
          Height - 1 - FArrowHeight);
```

LISTING 27.6: The source code of the second version of the arrow component, ARROW2.PAS (continued)

```pascal
          LineTo (Width - 1,
            Height - 1 - FArrowHeight);
          LineTo (XCenter, Height - 1);
          LineTo (0,
            Height - 1 - FArrowHeight);
          LineTo (XCenter,
            Height - 1 - FArrowHeight);
          if FFilled then
            FloodFill (XCenter,
              Height - FArrowHeight div 2,
              Pen.Color, fsBorder);
        end;
      adLeft:
        with Canvas do
        begin
          MoveTo (Width - 1, YCenter);
          LineTo (FArrowHeight, YCenter);
          LineTo (FArrowHeight, Height - 1);
          LineTo (0, YCenter);
          LineTo (FArrowHeight, 0);
          LineTo (FArrowHeight, YCenter);
          if FFilled then
            FloodFill (FArrowHeight div 2, YCenter,
              Pen.Color, fsBorder);
        end;
      adRight:
        with Canvas do
        begin
          MoveTo (0, YCenter);
          LineTo (Width - 1 - FArrowHeight,
            YCenter);
          LineTo (Width - 1 - FArrowHeight,
            Height - 1);
          LineTo (Width - 1, YCenter);
          LineTo (Width - 1 - FArrowHeight, 0);
          LineTo (Width - 1 - FArrowHeight,
            YCenter);
          if FFilled then
            FloodFill (Width - FArrowHeight div 2,
              YCenter, Pen.Color, fsBorder);
        end;
    end;
end;

procedure Register;
begin
  RegisterComponents('Samples', [TArrow]);
end;

end.
```

Notice that FPen and FBrush are two objects, and as with any other objects that are not components, they must be initialized. These two lines have been added to the Create method:

```
FPen := TPen.Create;
FBrush := TBrush.Create;
```

Then I added a Destroy destructor to the component and wrote its code as:

```
destructor TArrow.Destroy;
begin
  FPen.Free;
  FBrush.Free;
  inherited Destroy;
end;
```

This is probably the first time we have effectively used a destructor in a real example. Writing components really requires the use of many features of the Object Pascal language seldom used in other cases.

Testing the Second Version of the Arrow

27

To test the new version of the arrow component, still without installing it in Delphi, I've extended the last test example. The new version has a form with some additional components, as you can see in Figure 27.12. Again, the form is quite simple, so there is no listing with the textual description. Some special values have been set only for the ScrollBar component:

```
object ScrollBar1: TScrollBar
  Max = 50
  Min = 1
  Position = 1
  OnChange = ScrollBar1Change
end
```

The code of the example is simply an extension of the previous version. As you can see in Listing 27.7, the value of the new spin edit control is used when the user presses the Size button, the buttons related to the color of the pen and the brush use the ColorDialog component, and a change in the check box or in the scroll bar automatically determines a change in the properties of the component, as well as of its user interface. Figure 27.13 shows an example of the output of this test program.

FIGURE 27.12:

The form of the ARROW2 test
example at design-time

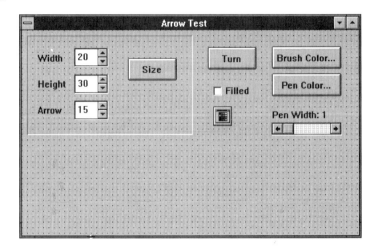

LISTING 27.7: The source code of the ARROW2 example

```
unit At_f;

interface

uses
  SysUtils, WinTypes, WinProcs, Messages, Classes,
  Graphics, Controls, Forms, Dialogs, Arrow2, StdCtrls,
  Spin, ExtCtrls;

type
  TForm1 = class(TForm)
    SpinEdit1: TSpinEdit;
    SpinEdit2: TSpinEdit;
    SizeButton: TButton;
    SpinEdit3: TSpinEdit;
    TurnButton: TButton;
    FilledCheckBox: TCheckBox;
    Label1: TLabel;
    Label2: TLabel;
    Label3: TLabel;
    Bevel1: TBevel;
    BrushButton: TButton;
    PenButton: TButton;
    ScrollBar1: TScrollBar;
    PenLabel: TLabel;
    ColorDialog1: TColorDialog;
    procedure FormCreate(Sender: TObject);
    procedure FormDestroy(Sender: TObject);
```

LISTING 27.7: The source code of the ARROW2 example (continued)

```
    procedure SizeButtonClick(Sender: TObject);
    procedure TurnButtonClick(Sender: TObject);
    procedure FilledCheckBoxClick(Sender: TObject);
    procedure BrushButtonClick(Sender: TObject);
    procedure PenButtonClick(Sender: TObject);
    procedure ScrollBar1Change(Sender: TObject);
  private
    A: TArrow;
  public
    { Public declarations }
  end;

var
  Form1: TForm1;

implementation

{$R *.DFM}

procedure TForm1.FormCreate(Sender: TObject);
begin
  A := TArrow.Create (self);
  A.Parent := self;
  A.Left := 200;
  A.Top := 200;
  A.Width := 20;
  A.Height := 30;
  A.ArrowHeight := 15;
end;

procedure TForm1.FormDestroy(Sender: TObject);
begin
  A.Free;
end;

procedure TForm1.SizeButtonClick(
  Sender: TObject);
begin
  A.Width := SpinEdit1.Value;
  A.Height := SpinEdit2.Value;
  A.ArrowHeight := SpinEdit3.Value;
end;

procedure TForm1.TurnButtonClick(
  Sender: TObject);
begin
  if A.Direction = High (TArrowDirection) then
    A.Direction := Low (TArrowDirection)
  else
    A.Direction := Succ (A.Direction);
end;
```

27

LISTING 27.7: The source code of the ARROW2 example (continued)

```
procedure TForm1.FilledCheckBoxClick(
  Sender: TObject);
begin
  A.Filled := not A.Filled;
end;

procedure TForm1.BrushButtonClick(
  Sender: TObject);
begin
  ColorDialog1.Color := A.Brush.Color;
  if ColorDialog1.Execute then
    A.Brush.Color := ColorDialog1.Color;
end;

procedure TForm1.PenButtonClick(
  Sender: TObject);
begin
  ColorDialog1.Color := A.Pen.Color;
  if ColorDialog1.Execute then
    A.Pen.Color := ColorDialog1.Color;
end;

procedure TForm1.ScrollBar1Change(
  Sender: TObject);
begin
  PenLabel.Caption := 'Pen Width: ' +
    IntToStr (ScrollBar1.Position);
  A.Pen.Width := ScrollBar1.Position;
end;

end.
```

Defining a New Custom Event

To end the development of the arrow component, I want to add a custom event. Most of the time, new components use the event of the parent classes. For example, in the third version of Arrow, I've made available some standard events simply by redeclaring them in the published section:

```
published
  property OnClick;
  property OnDragDrop;
  property OnDragOver;
```

FIGURE 27.13:

An example of the output of the ARROW2 test program

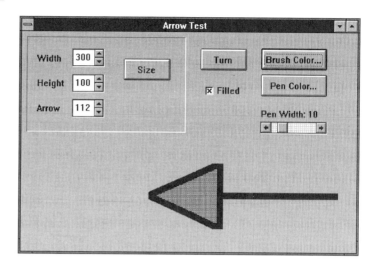

FIGURE 27.13:

An example of the output of the ARROW2 test program

```
property OnEndDrag;
property OnMouseDown;
property OnMouseMove;
property OnMouseUp;
```

Simply by means of this declaration, the above events will be available in the Object Inspector when we install the component. What is more interesting, of course, is to see how you can add a custom event, although this operation is not often performed. Most of the components will work well enough if you simply redefine some custom events, eventually changing their behavior.

To define a brand-new event, you first need to add a field to the class, defining the type of the handler. This field is actually a method pointer. Here is the definition I've added in the private section of the TArrow class:

```
FArrowDblClick: TNotifyEvent;
```

Around this field I've defined a very simple published property, with direct access to the data:

```
property OnArrowDblClick: TNotifyEvent
    read FArrowDblClick write FArrowDblClick;
```

Notice again the standard naming convention, with properties starting with *On*. The handler associated with the property is executed in the ArrowDblClick dynamic method, but only if it exists:

```
if Assigned (FArrowDblClick) then
  FArrowDblClick (self);
```

Notice (by looking at Listing 27.8) that this method is defined in the protected section of the type definition to allow future subclasses both to call and to change it.

LISTING 27.8:   The third type definition of the Arrow component and the code of the new methods

```
unit Arrow3;

{...}

type
  TArrowDirection = (adUp, adDown, adLeft, adRight);
  TArrow = class(TGraphicControl)
  private
    FDirection: TArrowDirection;
    FArrowHeight: Integer;
    FFilled: Boolean;
    FPen: TPen;
    FBrush: TBrush;
    FArrowDblClick: TNotifyEvent;
    procedure SetDirection (
      Value: TArrowDirection);
    procedure SetArrowHeight (Value: Integer);
    procedure SetFilled (Value: Boolean);
    procedure SetPen (Value: TPen);
    procedure SetBrush (Value: TBrush);
    procedure RepaintRequest (Sender: TObject);
    procedure WMLButtonDlbClk (
      var Msg: TWMLButtonDblClk);
      message wm_LButtonDblClk;
  protected
    procedure Paint; override;
    procedure ArrowDblClick; dynamic;
  public
    constructor Create (AOwner: TComponent); override;
    destructor Destroy; override;
  published
    property Direction: TArrowDirection
      read FDirection write SetDirection
      default adRight;
    property ArrowHeight: Integer
      read FArrowHeight write SetArrowHeight
      default 10;
    property Filled: Boolean
      read FFilled write SetFilled
      default False;
```

LISTING 27.8: The third type definition of the Arrow component and the code of
the new methods (continued)

```
    property Pen: TPen
      read FPen write SetPen;
    property Brush: TBrush
      read FBrush write SetBrush;
    property OnClick;
    property OnDragDrop;
    property OnDragOver;
    property OnEndDrag;
    property OnMouseDown;
    property OnMouseMove;
    property OnMouseUp;
    property OnArrowDblClick: TNotifyEvent
      read FArrowDblClick write FArrowDblClick;
  end;

{...}

procedure TArrow.WMLButtonDlbClk (
  var Msg: TWMLButtonDblClk);
var
  ArrowPoints: array [0..2] of TPoint;
  XCenter, YCenter: Integer;
  HRegion: HRgn;
begin
  {perform default handling}
  inherited;

  {compute the points}
  YCenter := (Height - 1) div 2;
  XCenter := (Width - 1) div 2;
  case FDirection of
    adUp:
    begin
      ArrowPoints [0] :=
        Point (0, FArrowHeight);
      ArrowPoints [1] :=
        Point (XCenter, 0);
      ArrowPoints [2] :=
        Point (Width-1, FArrowHeight);
    end;
    adDown:
    begin
      ArrowPoints [0] := Point (
        XCenter, Height - 1);
      ArrowPoints [1] := Point (
        0, Height - 1 - FArrowHeight);
      ArrowPoints [2] := Point (
        Width - 1,
        Height - 1 - FArrowHeight);
    end;
```

27

LISTING 27.8: The third type definition of the Arrow component and the code of the new methods (continued)

```
    adLeft:
    begin
      ArrowPoints [0] :=
        Point (FArrowHeight, Height - 1);
      ArrowPoints [1] :=
        Point (0, YCenter);
      ArrowPoints [2] :=
        Point (FArrowHeight, 0);
    end;
    adRight:
    begin
      ArrowPoints [0] := Point (
        Width - 1 - FArrowHeight,
        Height - 1);
      ArrowPoints [1] := Point (
        Width - 1 - FArrowHeight, 0);
      ArrowPoints [2] := Point (
        Width - 1, YCenter);
    end;
  end;

  {check whether the click took place
  in the arrow-point region}
  HRegion := CreatePolygonRgn (
    ArrowPoints, 3, WINDING);
  if PtInRegion (HRegion,
      Msg.XPos, Msg.YPos) then
    ArrowDblClick;
  DeleteObject (HRegion);
end;

procedure TArrow.ArrowDblClick;
begin
  {call the handler, if available}
  if Assigned (FArrowDblClick) then
    FArrowDblClick (self);
end;
```

Basically, the ArrowDblClick method is called by the handler of the wm_LButtonDblClk Windows message, but this should happen only if the double-click took place inside the arrow's point. To test this condition, we can use some region functions of the Windows API.

A *region* is an area of the screen enclosed by any shape. For example, we can build a polygonal region using the three vertexes of the arrow-point triangle. The only problem is that to fill the surface property, we must define an array of TPoints in a clockwise direction (see the description of the `CreatePolygonalRgn` in the Windows API Help for the details of this strange approach).

Once we have defined a region, we can test whether the current point where the double-click took place is inside the region by using the `PtInRegion` API call. You can see the complete source code of this procedure in Listing 27.8, together with the type definition of the TArrow class. The methods already present in the previous version have not changed, so I've omitted them from this listing.

Testing the OnArrowDblClick Event

Now that we have defined the complete version of the component, we can make a last test on the new event before installing it in Delphi.

The third version of the test program, saved in the ARROW3 subdirectory, has the same form as the previous version. Its code, though, has a new method, ArrowDoubleClick. This procedure is declared in the public portion of the form and is defined as follows:

```
procedure TForm1.ArrowDoubleClick (Sender: TObject);
begin
  ShowMessage ('You have double clicked ' +
    'on the point of the arrow');
end;
```

It is a handler of the same type as that required by the arrow component's OnArrowDblClick event, so we can set it with the new line at the end of the form's Create method:

```
procedure TForm1.FormCreate(Sender: TObject);
begin
  A := TArrow.Create (self);
  A.Parent := self;
  A.Left := 200;
  A.Top := 200;
  A.Width := 20;
  A.Height := 30;
  A.ArrowHeight := 15;
  A.OnArrowDblClick := ArrowDoubleClick;
end;
```

27

The result of this code? If you run the program and double-click inside the triangular point of the arrow, a message is displayed, as shown in Figure 27.14. If, instead, you double-click on the component but outside the arrow point, nothing happens.

FIGURE 27.14:

The output message displayed by the ARROW3 example when a user clicks on the arrow's point

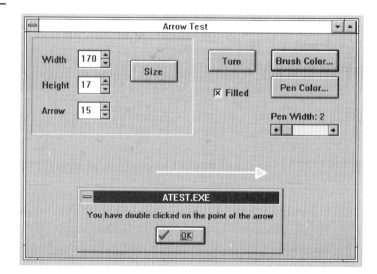

Adding a Bitmap for the Components Palette

Now that we have written the component's code, before installing it we have to take a further step: we must define a bitmap for the Components palette. The first two components we defined in this chapter had no specific bitmap, so they used those of their parent class. In this case, since there is no parent class having a bitmap, we'll get a default Delphi bitmap.

Luckily, defining a new bitmap is easy, once you know the rules. First of all, open the Image editor, start a new project, and select the DCR (Delphi Component Resource) project type, as shown in Figure 27.15.

FIGURE 27.15:

The definition of a new DCR project with the Image editor

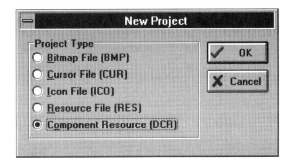

TIP

DCR files are nothing less than standard RES files with a different extension. So if you prefer, you can prepare them with any resource editor, including the Borland Resource Workshop, which is certainly a more powerful tool than the Delphi Image editor.

Add a new bitmap to the project, choosing a size of 24 x 24 pixels. Now you are ready to draw the bitmap. The only precaution you have to take is to choose the typical dark yellow color (clOlive in Delphi terms) for the background, because this is the color the Components palette replaces with the default grays for the selected or unselected component. In Figure 27.16, you can see the bitmap I've prepared for the arrow component.

The other important rule refers to naming. In this case, the rules do not just define a naming convention; they are enforced by the system:

- The name of the bitmap resource must match the name of the component, including the initial *T*. In this case, the name is TARROW.

- The name of the DCR file must match the name of the compiled unit that defines the component, which is the same as the name of the file defining it. In this case, the file name is ARROW3.DCR. The file must be saved in the same directory as the component.

Notice that the source code does *not* include the resource. The component's bitmap is used by the Delphi environment, and in particular the Components palette, not

FIGURE 27.16:

The bitmap representing the arrow component

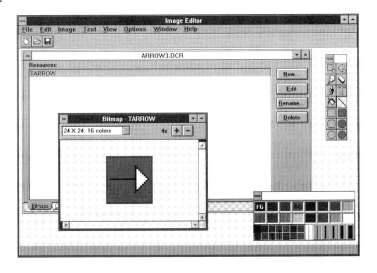

by the final program. For this reason, the component's bitmaps are not linked in the VCL, and, of course, are not part of the compiled applications.

When the bitmap for the component is ready, you can install it in Delphi using the usual approach. Choose the Install Components command, select the new file, AR-ROW3.PAS, and press the OK button. The component is added to the VCL, and its bitmap appears on the palette, after the other components we defined:

The Final Test of the Arrow Component

Now that the component is installed, we can write a small example to test it. This time, we will be able to use the component like any standard component, setting properties and events with the Object Inspector.

This second test, after we have written the program, is very important. Often, when you create the component at run-time, some elements may be different from what you would expect. Also, by testing various values for the properties, you can find errors the first kind of test did not show. Actually, when testing the component to build this example, I found two errors in the code I had written.

First of all, the component has no default size, so when you place it in a form, its size will be a single pixel. Second, when you select most of the alternative pen styles, the filling algorithm doesn't work anymore, as you can see in Figure 27.17.

FIGURE 27.17:

If you try to use a dotted pen in the ARROW3 component, a problem in the filling code emerges at design-time.

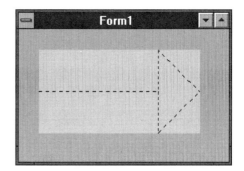

Since these problems are fairly common, I've left the ARROW3 code as it was (that is, with bugs) and made the changes in a new version, ARROW4. You can install one of the two versions at a time in Delphi to test them; when you install a version, you have to remove the other one because you cannot have two components—two classes in the components library—with the same name.

Correcting Bugs in the Arrow Component

The first change in the arrow component is adding the default values for the Width and Height properties, both in the description of these properties and in the Create method:

```
property Width default 50;
property Height default 20;
```

The above is simply a redeclaration of the properties, already defined by a parent class, with a new default value. Actually, providing a default value for the height and width is not common in Delphi, but I thought it was a good idea anyway. In fact, if the programmer doesn't change these standard values, they won't show up in the textual description of the form.

The other changes are related to the FloodFill method. If you use FloodFill, the region should have a continuous border. Dashed lines don't make continuous borders, so FloodFill *leaks* outside the proper area. It is time for a complete rewrite of the component's Paint method, using the PolyLine and Polygon methods of the TCanvas class instead of FloodFill. The difference between PolyLine and Polygon is that the first draws a line and the second fills the resulting polygon with the current brush. Polygon fills its interior using pure vectors. It doesn't matter what is on the screen; the polygon will be filled properly. So in this case Polygon is a better choice than FloodFill.

We have already seen how to build a polygon with an array of points to test whether the click was on the arrow point. A similar code can be used now. The only problem is that the PolyLine procedure doesn't automatically close the polygon. To draw a triangle, it requires a fourth point in the same position as the first one. You can see the new Paint function in Listing 27.9, together with the complete source code of the final version of the arrow component.

LISTING 27.9: The final version of the Arrow component, in file ARROW4.PAS

```
unit Arrow4;

interface

uses
  SysUtils, WinTypes, WinProcs, Messages, Classes,
  Graphics, Controls, Forms, Dialogs;

type
  TArrowDirection = (adUp, adDown, adLeft, adRight);
  TArrow = class(TGraphicControl)
  private
    FDirection: TArrowDirection;
    FArrowHeight: Integer;
    FFilled: Boolean;
    FPen: TPen;
    FBrush: TBrush;
    FArrowDblClick: TNotifyEvent;
    procedure SetDirection (Value: TArrowDirection);
```

LISTING 27.9: The final version of the Arrow component, in file ARROW4.PAS (continued)

```
    procedure SetArrowHeight (Value: Integer);
    procedure SetFilled (Value: Boolean);
    procedure SetPen (Value: TPen);
    procedure SetBrush (Value: TBrush);
    procedure RepaintRequest (Sender: TObject);
    procedure WMLButtonDlbClk (var Msg: TWMLButtonDblClk);
      message wm_LButtonDblClk;
  protected
    procedure Paint; override;
    procedure ArrowDblClick; dynamic;
  public
    constructor Create (AOwner: TComponent); override;
    destructor Destroy; override;
  published
    property Width default 50;
    property Height default 20;
    property Direction: TArrowDirection
      read FDirection write SetDirection
      default adRight;
    property ArrowHeight: Integer
      read FArrowHeight write SetArrowHeight
      default 10;
    property Filled: Boolean
      read FFilled write SetFilled default False;
    property Pen: TPen
      read FPen write SetPen;
    property Brush: TBrush
      read FBrush write SetBrush;
    property OnClick;
    property OnDragDrop;
    property OnDragOver;
    property OnEndDrag;
    property OnMouseDown;
    property OnMouseMove;
    property OnMouseUp;
    property OnArrowDblClick: TNotifyEvent
      read FArrowDblClick write FArrowDblClick;
  end;

procedure Register;

implementation

constructor TArrow.Create (AOwner: TComponent);
begin
  {call the parent constructor}
  inherited Create (AOwner);
  {set the default values}
  FDirection := adRight;
  Width := 50;
```

LISTING 27.9: The final version of the Arrow component, in file ARROW4.PAS (continued)

```
  Height := 20;
  FArrowHeight := 10;
  FFilled := False;
  {create the pen and the brush}
  FPen := TPen.Create;
  FBrush := TBrush.Create;
  {set a handler for the OnChange event}

  FPen.OnChange := RepaintRequest;
  FBrush.OnChange := RepaintRequest;
end;

destructor TArrow.Destroy;
begin
  {delete the two objects}
  FPen.Free;
  FBrush.Free;
  {call the parent destructor}
  inherited Destroy;
end;

procedure TArrow.SetDirection (
  Value: TArrowDirection);
begin
  if FDirection <> Value then
  begin
    FDirection := Value;
    Invalidate;
  end;
end;

procedure TArrow.SetArrowHeight (Value: Integer);
begin
  if FArrowHeight <> Value then
  begin
    FArrowHeight := Value;
    Invalidate;
  end;
end;

procedure TArrow.SetFilled (Value: Boolean);
begin
  if FFilled <> Value then
  begin
    FFilled := Value;
    Invalidate;
  end;
end;
```

LISTING 27.9: The final version of the Arrow component, in file ARROW4.PAS (continued)

```pascal
procedure TArrow.SetPen (Value: TPen);
begin
  FPen.Assign(Value);
  Invalidate;
end;

procedure TArrow.SetBrush (Value: TBrush);
begin
  FBrush.Assign(Value);
  Invalidate;
end;

procedure TArrow.RepaintRequest (
  Sender: TObject);
begin
  Invalidate;
end;

procedure TArrow.Paint;
var
  XCenter, YCenter: Integer;
  ArrowPoints: array [0..3] of TPoint;
begin
  YCenter := (Height - 1) div 2;
  XCenter := (Width - 1) div 2;

  {use the current pen and brush}
  Canvas.Pen := FPen;
  Canvas.Brush := FBrush;

  {draw a line and compute the triangle
  for the arrow point}
  case FDirection of
    adUp:
    begin
      Canvas.MoveTo (XCenter, Height-1);
      Canvas.LineTo (XCenter, FArrowHeight);
      ArrowPoints [0] :=
        Point (0, FArrowHeight);
      ArrowPoints [1] :=
        Point (XCenter, 0);
      ArrowPoints [2] :=
        Point (Width-1, FArrowHeight);
      ArrowPoints [3] :=
        Point (0, FArrowHeight);
    end;
    adDown:
    begin
      Canvas.MoveTo (XCenter, 0);
      Canvas.LineTo (XCenter,
        Height - 1 - FArrowHeight);
```

27

LISTING 27.9: The final version of the Arrow component, in file ARROW4.PAS (continued)

```
      ArrowPoints [0] := Point (
        XCenter, Height - 1);
      ArrowPoints [1] := Point (
        0, Height - 1 - FArrowHeight);
      ArrowPoints [2] := Point (
        Width - 1, Height - 1 - FArrowHeight);
      ArrowPoints [3] := Point (
        XCenter, Height - 1);
    end;
    adLeft:
    begin
      Canvas.MoveTo (Width - 1, YCenter);
      Canvas.LineTo (FArrowHeight, YCenter);
      ArrowPoints [0] :=
        Point (FArrowHeight, Height - 1);
      ArrowPoints [1] :=
        Point (0, YCenter);
      ArrowPoints [2] :=
        Point (FArrowHeight, 0);
      ArrowPoints [3] :=
        Point (FArrowHeight, Height - 1);
    end;
    adRight:
    begin
      Canvas.MoveTo (0, YCenter);
      Canvas.LineTo (Width - 1 - FArrowHeight,
        YCenter);
      ArrowPoints [0] := Point (
        Width - 1 - FArrowHeight, Height - 1);
      ArrowPoints [1] := Point (
        Width - 1 - FArrowHeight, 0);
      ArrowPoints [2] := Point (
        Width - 1, YCenter);
      ArrowPoints [3] := Point (
        Width - 1 - FArrowHeight, Height - 1);
    end;
  end;

  {draw the arrow point, eventually filling it}
  if FFilled then
    Canvas.Polygon (ArrowPoints)
  else
    Canvas.PolyLine (ArrowPoints);
end;

procedure TArrow.WMLButtonDlbClk (
  var Msg: TWMLButtonDblClk);
var
  ArrowPoints: array [0..2] of TPoint;
  XCenter, YCenter: Integer;
  HRegion: HRgn;
```

LISTING 27.9: The final version of the Arrow component, in file ARROW4.PAS
(continued)

```
begin
  {perform default handling}
  inherited;

  {compute the points}
  YCenter := (Height - 1) div 2;
  XCenter := (Width - 1) div 2;
  case FDirection of
    adUp:
    begin
      ArrowPoints [0] :=
        Point (0, FArrowHeight);
      ArrowPoints [1] :=
        Point (XCenter, 0);
      ArrowPoints [2] :=
        Point (Width-1, FArrowHeight);
    end;
    adDown:
    begin
      ArrowPoints [0] := Point (
        XCenter, Height - 1);
      ArrowPoints [1] := Point (
        0, Height - 1 - FArrowHeight);
      ArrowPoints [2] := Point (
        Width - 1, Height - 1 - FArrowHeight);
    end;
    adLeft:
    begin
      ArrowPoints [0] :=
        Point (FArrowHeight, Height - 1);
      ArrowPoints [1] :=
        Point (0, YCenter);
      ArrowPoints [2] :=
        Point (FArrowHeight, 0);
    end;
    adRight:
    begin
      ArrowPoints [0] := Point (
        Width - 1 - FArrowHeight, Height - 1);
      ArrowPoints [1] := Point (
        Width - 1 - FArrowHeight, 0);
      ArrowPoints [2] := Point (
        Width - 1, YCenter);
    end;
  end;

  {check whether the click took place
  in the arrow-point region}
  HRegion := CreatePolygonRgn (
    ArrowPoints, 3, WINDING);
```

27

LISTING 27.9: The final version of the Arrow component, in file ARROW4.PAS (continued)

```
  if PtInRegion (HRegion,
      Msg.XPos, Msg.YPos) then
    ArrowDblClick;
  DeleteObject (HRegion);
end;

procedure TArrow.ArrowDblClick;
begin
  {call the handler, if available}
  if Assigned (FArrowDblClick) then
    FArrowDblClick (self);
end;

procedure Register;
begin
  RegisterComponents('Samples', [TArrow]);
end;

end.
```

Arrows and Shapes

Now that everything should work fine, we can test this component in an example. The form of this example, TARROW (which stands for Test Arrow), is in Figure 27.18. As you can see, it has four arrows, four shapes, and a timer. The textual description of this form, including the instances of our new component, is in Listing 27.10.

LISTING 27.10: The textual description of the form of the TARROW example

```
object Form1: TForm1
  Caption = 'Test Arrow'
  OnCreate = FormCreate
  object Arrow1: TArrow
    Left = 96
    Top = 32
    Width = 241
    Height = 41
    ArrowHeight = 30
    Filled = True
    OnArrowDblClick = ArrowDoubleClick
  end
  object Arrow4: TArrow
    {some properties have been removed...}
    Direction = adUp
```

LISTING 27.10: The textual description of the form of the TARROW example
(continued)

```
    OnArrowDblClick = ArrowDoubleClick
  end
object Arrow2: TArrow
  Direction = adDown
  OnArrowDblClick = ArrowDoubleClick
  end
object Arrow3: TArrow
  Direction = adLeft
  OnArrowDblClick = ArrowDoubleClick
  end

  object Shape2: TShape...
  object Shape3: TShape...
  object Shape4: TShape...
  object Shape1: TShape...
  object Timer1: TTimer
    OnTimer = Timer1Timer
  end
end
```

27

FIGURE 27.18:

The form of the TARROW example
at design-time

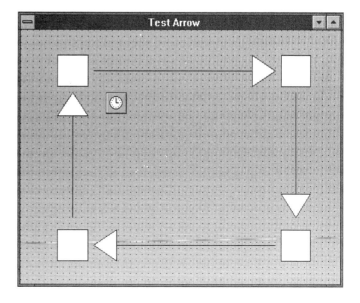

The aim of the example is to see a colored element move around the surface of the form. The color, indicating a hypothetical active element of a process, is moved from a square to the following arrow, then to the next square, and so on.

This is the reason for having a timer. When the form is created, it stores the four shapes and the four arrows in an array of graphical components, defined as:

```
private
  Graph: array [1..8] of TGraphicControl;
```

Here is the code of the Create method:

```
procedure TForm1.FormCreate(Sender: TObject);
var
  I: Integer;
begin
  Active := 1;
  Shape1.Brush.Color := clYellow;
  for I := 1 to 4 do
  begin
    Graph [I * 2 - 1] :=
      (FindComponent ('Shape' + IntToStr (I))
      as TGraphicControl);
    Graph [I * 2] :=
      (FindComponent ('Arrow' + IntToStr (I))
      as TGraphicControl);
  end;
end;
```

Well, I've managed to show you something new about the use of components in Delphi even in this example. The FindComponent method simply returns a component with the given name of the form, scanning the form's Components array.

When this array has been built, you can change the color of the active element quite easily (as you can see in Figure 27.19). Remember that you also need to restore the color of the element that was active before:

```
procedure TForm1.Timer1Timer(Sender: TObject);
begin
  if Graph [Active] is TArrow then
    TArrow (Graph [Active]).Brush.Color := clWhite
  else
    TShape (Graph [Active]).Brush.Color := clWhite;
  Active := Active mod 8 + 1;
```

```
      if Graph [Active] is TArrow then
        TArrow (Graph [Active]).Brush.Color := clRed
      else
        TShape (Graph [Active]).Brush.Color := clYellow;
    end;
```

FIGURE 27.19:

The output of the TARROW example

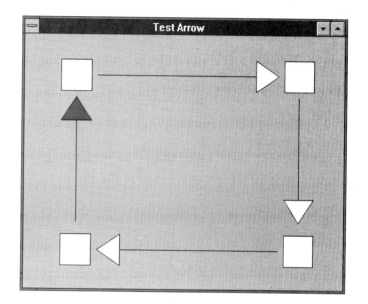

That's all. Well, almost all. In fact, why not show a message when the user double-clicks exactly on the arrow point of the active arrow? The following method is connected to all four arrow components, using the Object Inspector:

```
procedure TForm1.ArrowDoubleClick(Sender: TObject);
begin
  if (Sender as TArrow).Brush.Color = clRed then
    ShowMessage ('Click on active arrow');
end;
```

This example, which might be the output of a simulation program, ends the part of the chapter devoted to the step-by-step development of the arrow component. Now it is time to move to another component, a digital clock.

> **NOTE**
>
> An interesting exercise (left to the readers) is to rewrite the Arrow paint method to use only one set of points and use GDI coordinate transformations to orient those points to suit the direction. The new version should have the same performance but require less machine code. In this particular example the gain is limited, but coordinate transforms can pay off in more complicated cases.

The Clock Components

The new component I want to focus on is a clock. I'll actually build two components: a digital clock and an analog clock. I'll pack both components in a single source file. This example has some interesting features. First of all, it uses other components, including a timer; second, it shows the live-data approach; third, it shows how to place two components in a single source file.

The Digital Clock

First of all, we will focus on the digital clock. Since I have to provide some text output, I thought of subclassing the TLabel component. However, in this case, a user can change the label's caption—that is, its text. To avoid this problem, I simply used the TCustomLabel component as the parent class, which has the same capabilities but fewer published properties. In other words, a TCustomLabel subclass, as with similar components, can decide which properties should be available and which should remain hidden.

Besides re-declaring some of the properties of the parent class, TDigClock has one of its own, Active. This property indicates whether or not the clock is working. As you might have guessed, the clock has a Timer component inside to make it work. However, the timer is not made public through a property since I don't want programmers to access all its properties. Instead, I made available the Enabled property of the timer, wrapping it inside the Active property of the digital clock. Here is the portion of the type definition related to these elements:

```
type
  TDigClock = class (TCustomLabel)
```

```
private
  FTimer: TTimer;
  function GetActive: Boolean;
  procedure SetActive (Value: Boolean);
published
  property Active: Boolean
    read GetActive write SetActive;
end;
```

Notice that we need a method both to write and to read the value of the Active property because it is not local data but refers to a member of the embedded component, the timer.

The other problems of the example relate to the use of the timer. We have to override both the constructor and the destructor of the class and provide a function to connect to the OnTimer event:

```
protected
  procedure UpdateClock (Sender: TObject);
public
  constructor Create (AOwner: TComponent); override;
  destructor Destroy; override;
```

The Create method calls the corresponding method of the base class and starts the timer:

```
FTimer := TTimer.Create (AOwner);
FTimer.OnTimer := UpdateClock;
```

In some circumstances, one more line is required to register the data type of the Timer component used by the clock, before the object is created:

```
RegisterClasses ([TTimer]);
```

The opposite of Create, the Destroy method, frees the timer. The key piece of the component's code is the UpdateClock procedure, which is just one statement:

```
Caption := TimeToStr (Time);
```

It uses Caption, which is a property not accessible outside the component itself.

The Analog Clock

The code of the analog clock can be built starting from the code of the digital clock but cannot be derived from it. It makes no sense to say the analog clock is a label.

Instead, I've inherited the TAnalogClock component from the TGraphicComponent class.

As a result, some of the code of the digital clock has been duplicated. Also, the new clock has a timer, an Active property, and so on. However, it has much more code because it has to draw the hands of the clock, eventually including the seconds hand and the marks for the hours. Certain properties determine the presence of these optional elements, while other properties determine the color of the various elements. Actually, just two colors are available, one for the hand of the seconds and the other for all the other elements, but you can easily extend the example to include more finely tuned properties.

Most of the code of this component has actually been borrowed from the CLOCK2 and CLOCK3 examples of Chapter 19. However, I could not use the last optimized version, CLOCK3, as it was. At design-time, the graphical component can produce output only in a Paint method, probably because it is not a window by itself. Trying to draw the seconds hand with the xor pen mode, as I did in CLOCK3, failed. Of course, everything worked fine at run-time, but I liked the idea of showing a working analog clock at design-time.

So I decided to build a non-optimized version of the component, which has some flickering when the seconds hand is present. To reduce this problem, I tried to speed up the Paint method, limiting the changes on pens, drawing pixels instead of circles for the hour marks, and so on.

You can see the final code of the TAnalogClock component, together with TDigitalClock, in Listing 27.11. I won't provide a detailed description of this component's code because reading the discussion of the CLOCK3 example and the component above should have provided you with all the elements for understanding its source code.

LISTING 27.11: The DIGCLOCK.PAS file with the code of the TDigClock and TAnalogClock components

```
unit Digclock;

interface

uses
  SysUtils, WinTypes, WinProcs, Messages, Classes, Graphics,
  Controls, Forms, Dialogs, StdCtrls, ExtCtrls, Menus;
```

LISTING 27.11: The DIGCLOCK.PAS file with the code of the TDigClock and
TAnalogClock components (continued)

```
type
  TDigClock = class (TCustomLabel)
  private
    FTimer: TTimer;
    function GetActive: Boolean;
    procedure SetActive (Value: Boolean);
  protected
    procedure UpdateClock (Sender: TObject);
  public
    constructor Create (AOwner: TComponent); override;
    destructor Destroy; override;
  published
    property Align;
    property Alignment;
    property Color;
    property Font;
    property ParentColor;
    property ParentFont;
    property ParentShowHint;
    property PopupMenu;
    property ShowHint;
    property Transparent;
    property Visible;
    property Active: Boolean
      read GetActive write SetActive;
  end;

  TAnalogClock = class (TGraphicControl)
  private
    FTimer: TTimer;
    FSeconds: Boolean;
    FHourMarks: Boolean;
    FColorHands: TColor;
    FColorSeconds: TColor;
    Hour, Minute, Second: Word; {current time}
    OldMinute: Word;
    function GetActive: Boolean;
    procedure SetActive (Value: Boolean);
    procedure SetSeconds (Value: Boolean);
    procedure SetHourMarks (Value: Boolean);
    procedure SetColorHands (Value: TColor);
    procedure DrawHand (XCenter, YCenter, Radius,
      BackRadius: Integer; Angle: Real);
  protected
    procedure UpdateClock (Sender: TObject);
    procedure Paint; override;
  public
    constructor Create (AOwner: TComponent); override;
    destructor Destroy; override;
  published
```

27

LISTING 27.11: The DIGCLOCK.PAS file with the code of the TDigClock and
TAnalogClock components (continued)

```
    property Align;
    property Color;
    property ParentColor;
    property ParentShowHint;
    property PopupMenu;
    property ShowHint;
    property Visible;
    property Active: Boolean
      read GetActive write SetActive;
    property Seconds: Boolean
      read FSeconds write SetSeconds default True;
    property HourMarks: Boolean
      read FHourMarks write SetHourMarks default True;
    property ColorHands: TColor
      read FColorHands write SetColorHands default clBlue;
    property ColorSeconds: TColor
      read FColorSeconds write FColorSeconds default clRed;
  end;

procedure Register;

implementation

{digital clock}

constructor TDigClock.Create (AOwner: TComponent);
begin
  inherited Create (AOwner);
  RegisterClasses ([TTimer]);
  FTimer := TTimer.Create (AOwner);
  FTimer.OnTimer := UpdateClock;
  FTimer.Enabled := True;
end;

destructor TDigClock.Destroy;
begin
  FTimer.Free;
  inherited Destroy;
end;

procedure TDigClock.UpdateClock (Sender: TObject);
begin
  Caption := TimeToStr (Time);
end;

function TDigClock.GetActive: Boolean;
begin
  Result := FTimer.Enabled;
end;
```

LISTING 27.11: The DIGCLOCK.PAS file with the code of the TDigClock and TAnalogClock components (continued)

```pascal
procedure TDigClock.SetActive (Value: Boolean);
begin
  FTimer.Enabled := Value;
end;

{analog clock}

constructor TAnalogClock.Create (AOwner: TComponent);
begin
  inherited Create (AOwner);
  RegisterClasses ([TTimer]);
  FTimer := TTimer.Create (AOwner);
  FTimer.OnTimer := UpdateClock;
  FTimer.Enabled := True;
  {set default values}
  Width := 100;
  Height := 100;
  FSeconds := True;
  FHourMarks := True;
  FColorSeconds := clRed;
  FColorHands := clBlue;
  {get the current time before
  the clock is first painted}
  UpdateClock (self);
end;

destructor TAnalogClock.Destroy;
begin
  FTimer.Free;
  inherited Destroy;
end;

procedure TAnalogClock.UpdateClock (Sender: TObject);
var
  HSec: Word;   {temporary value, not used}
begin
  OldMinute := Minute;
  DecodeTime (Time, Hour, Minute, Second, HSec);
  if FSeconds or not (Minute = OldMinute) then
    Invalidate;
end;

procedure TAnalogClock.Paint;
{see the CLOCK2 and CLOCK3 examples of Chapter 19}
var
  Angle: Real;
  I, X, Y, Radius, XCenter, YCenter: Integer;
begin
  {compute the middle of the component}
  XCenter := Width div 2;
  YCenter := Height div 2;
```

LISTING 27.11: The DIGCLOCK.PAS file with the code of the TDigClock and TAnalogClock components (continued)

```
  if XCenter > YCenter then
    Radius := YCenter - 1
  else
    Radius := XCenter - 1;

  {draw hour marks}
  if FHourMarks then
  begin
    for I := 0 to 11 do
    begin
      Angle := 2 * Pi * (I + 9) / 12;
      X := XCenter - Round (Radius * Cos (Angle));
      Y := YCenter - Round (Radius * Sin (Angle));
      Canvas.Pixels [X, Y] := FColorHands;
      Canvas.Pixels [X+1, Y] := FColorHands;
      Canvas.Pixels [X, Y+1] := FColorHands;
      Canvas.Pixels [X+1, Y+1] := FColorHands;
    end;
  end;

  {draw the minutes hand}
  Canvas.Pen.Color := FColorHands;
  Angle := 2 * Pi * (Minute + 45) / 60;
  DrawHand (XCenter, YCenter,
    Radius * 90 div 100, 0, Angle);

  {draw the hours hand}
  Angle := 2 * Pi * (Hour + 9 + Minute / 60) / 12;
  DrawHand (XCenter, YCenter,
    Radius * 70 div 100, 0, Angle);

  if FSeconds then
  begin
    {draw the seconds hand}
    Canvas.Pen.Color := FColorSeconds;
    Angle := 2 * Pi * (Second + 45) / 60;
    DrawHand (XCenter, YCenter, Radius,
      Radius * 30 div 100, Angle);
  end;
end;

{draw a line using the current pen. BackRadius holds the
length of the hand in the opposite direction, usually 0}
procedure TAnalogClock.DrawHand (XCenter, YCenter,
  Radius, BackRadius: Integer; Angle: Real);
begin
  Canvas.MoveTo (
    XCenter - Round (BackRadius * Cos (Angle)),
    YCenter - Round (BackRadius * Sin (Angle)));
```

LISTING 27.11: The DIGCLOCK.PAS file with the code of the TDigClock and
TAnalogClock components (continued)

```
  Canvas.LineTo (
    XCenter + Round (Radius * Cos (Angle)),
    YCenter + Round (Radius * Sin (Angle)));
end;

function TAnalogClock.GetActive: Boolean;
begin
  Result := FTimer.Enabled;
end;

procedure TAnalogClock.SetActive (Value: Boolean);
begin
  FTimer.Enabled := Value;
end;

procedure TAnalogClock.SetSeconds (Value: Boolean);
begin
  if not (FSeconds = Value) then
  begin
    FSeconds := Value;
    Invalidate;
  end;
end;

procedure TAnalogClock.SetHourMarks (Value: Boolean);
begin
  if not (FHourMarks = Value) then
  begin
    FHourMarks := Value;
    Invalidate;
  end;
end;

procedure TAnalogClock.SetColorHands (Value: TColor);
begin
  if not (FColorHands = Value) then
  begin
    FColorHands := Value;
    Invalidate;
  end;
end;

procedure Register;
begin
  RegisterComponents('Samples', [TDigClock, TAnalogClock]);
end;

end.
```

27

If you want to optimize the repaint operations of this component, you should change the last part of the TAnalogClock.UpdateClock method from this code:

```
if FSeconds or not (Minute = OldMinute) then
  Invalidate;
```

To something like:

```
if Minute = OldMinute then
  begin
  if FSeconds then
    InvalidateSeconds;
  end
else
    Invalidate;
```

What is not easy is writing the InvalidateSeconds method. You have to invalidate both the area of the hand's previous position and the area of the new position. If you invalidate rectangular areas, you have to consider that its top-left and bottom-right corners change depending on the hand's position. You can get the position of the two extreme points of the hand, see which has the lower and higher X and Y values, and use the result to build the rectangle.

Then, of course, you are still invalidating too much. Instead of a rectangle, it might be better to build a region just around the hand; although computing requires some time, you'll actually save most of the paint time and reduce flickering to a minimum.

If you try to do this—an interesting exercise—remember also that you should invalidate a portion of the area of the parent component. You should use the parent's handle as the first parameter of the InvalidateRect or InvalidateRgn call. Then, remember to define the rectangle or region in the coordinates of the parent form, adding the value of the component's Top and Left properties to each vertical and horizontal coordinate, respectively.

Another alternative you might consider is to use an off-screen bitmap, so that you'll copy only the final bitmap to the screen, avoiding the flickering.

What might be really interesting instead is to correct the component to make it more flexible. Basically, we should look at the Paint method and move all the constants to properties. Here is a list of suggestions:

- A property for the color of each element

- A property for the length of each hand (in both directions)
- A property for the hour marks (none; only 4; 12, as it is now; 60) and their style

A First Test

Now that we have two new components, we need to test them. I actually built a test program while I was developing these components, not after, in a process similar to that of the arrow example. However, for these new components, I decided to show you only their final code and the final version of the test program, which is very simple.

The form of the DIGTEST example (present in the DIGCLOCK subdirectory) is empty, and all its code is in the FormCreate and FormDestroy methods. You can see this code in Listing 27.12. (By the way, the name of the example indicates that I first wrote it for the digital clock component only and then decided to add the new analog clock, but the name of the directory has not changed.)

LISTING 27.12:   The FormCreate and FormDestroy methods of the DIGTEST example

27

```
procedure TForm1.FormCreate(Sender: TObject);
begin
  Clock1 := TDigClock.Create (self);
  Clock1.Parent := self;
  Clock1.Left := 10;
  Clock1.Top := 10;

  Clock2 := TAnalogClock.Create (self);
  Clock2.Parent := self;
  Clock2.Left := 10;
  Clock2.Top := 50;
  Clock2.HourMarks := False;

  Clock3 := TAnalogClock.Create (self);
  Clock3.Parent := self;
  Clock3.Left := 150;
  Clock3.Top := 50;
  Clock3.Seconds := False;
  Clock3.ColorHandles := clRed;
end;

procedure TForm1.FormDestroy(Sender: TObject);
begin
  Clock1.Free;
  Clock2.Free;
  Clock3.Free;
end;
```

The three clock components used in this program are defined in the form as follows:

```
private
    Clock1: TDigClock;
    Clock2, Clock3: TAnalogClock;
```

When you run this program, you can only see the clocks on the screen; you have no way to change their properties. The output of the example is shown in Figure 27.20.

FIGURE 27.20:

The output of the DIGTEST example, with the two clock components

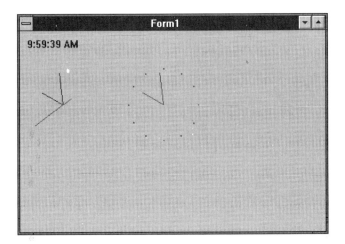

Installing the Clock Components

Since the components seem to work in the test program, it is time to install them in the Delphi VCL. You should know the process by now, so I won't describe it again. However, notice that for the bitmaps, you have to write a single DCR file, named after the source code file. The single DCR file should contain two bitmaps, one for each component, having the names of the classes.

WARNING

If you install these components and have already installed the other components mentioned in this book or other components you own, you might have reached the limit of the path string in the Install Components dialog box. When you use this dialog box and press the Add button to add new component source files, the path of each of these files is added to the Search Path edit box. If you use long paths, such as for the examples in this book, this edit box will soon reach its maximum number of characters. When this happens, no warning message is issued, the path is truncated, and the next compilation of the library will fail. To avoid this problem, I suggest you copy the source or compiled code of all the components you want to install in one directory or a few directories.

Now that the components are installed in the components library and on the palette, you can see an example of the live-data Delphi approach. As soon as you place a digital or an analog clock on a form, it starts working, as you can see in Figure 27.21.

27

FIGURE 27.21:

Two clocks at design-time. Notice their properties and their bitmaps in the Components palette.

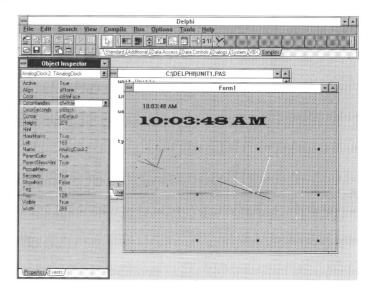

Now you can create any example that uses clocks you like. You can place a graphical clock on a toolbar or a digital clock on a status bar or simply use one of them in a form.

Defining an Array Property

Now that we have built some interesting components, the arrow and the two clocks, we can move back to an example introduced at the beginning of the chapter, the tabbed list box. We can now complete this example using, for the first time, an array property.

There is actually nothing strange about the definition of an array property, but this is not well documented in detail, so I decided to provide a specific example. When implementing this example, we will face another strange issue, dialog box units.

The New Tabbed List

The new version of the tabbed list box has a new property, which sets the position of the tabs. This is the definition of the array property:

```
property TabStops [Index: Integer]: Integer
   read GetTabStops write SetTabStops;
```

This property cannot be added to the published portion of the unit because its type is not an object data type. However, we can declare it in the public portion, making it a run-time property. Although it is not necessary, I've added an array field to the component to store the current values:

```
private
   FTabStops: TTabsArray;
```

In this declaration, I used a specific data type I defined before:

```
type
   TTabsArray = array [0..10] of Integer;
```

But what is really important is the definition of the two access methods for the property, which have a different structure than usual. In fact, this time both the Get function and the Set procedure have one more parameter, the index used to access the property:

```
function GetTabStops (Index: Integer): Integer;
procedure SetTabStops (Index, Value: Integer);
```

The code of these two methods is simple, as you can see in Listing 27.13. Other methods are much more complex. The overridden CreateWnd method initializes the array, with fixed values:

```
for I := Low (FTabStops) to High (FTabStops) do
  FTabStops [I] := I * 100;
```

LISTING 27.13: The final source code of the TTabbedList component

```
unit Tablist;

interface

uses
  SysUtils, WinTypes, WinProcs, Messages, Classes,
  Graphics, Controls, Forms, Dialogs, StdCtrls;

type
  TTabsArray = array [0..10] of Integer;

  TTabList = class(TListBox)
  private
    FTabStops: TTabsArray;
    function GetTabStops (Index: Integer): Integer;
    procedure SetTabStops (Index, Value: Integer);
  protected
    procedure UpdateTabStops;
  public
    procedure CreateParams (
      var Params: TCreateParams); override;
    procedure CreateWnd; override;
    property TabStops [Index: Integer]: Integer
      read GetTabStops write SetTabStops;
  end;

procedure Register;

implementation

procedure TTabList.CreateParams (
  var Params: TCreateParams);
begin
  inherited CreateParams (Params);
  Params.Style := Params.Style or lbs_UseTabStops;
end;
```

LISTING 27.13: The final source code of the TTabbedList component (continued)

```
procedure TTabList.CreateWnd;
var
  I: Integer;
begin
  inherited CreateWnd;
  for I := Low (FTabStops) to High (FTabStops) do
    FTabStops [I] := I * 100;
  UpdateTabStops;
end;

procedure TTabList.SetTabStops (
  Index, Value: Integer);
begin
  if FTabStops [Index] <> Value then
  begin
    FTabStops [Index] := Value;
    UpdateTabStops;
    Invalidate;
  end;
end;

function TTabList.GetTabStops (Index: Integer): Integer;
begin
  Result := FTabStops [Index];
end;

procedure TTabList.UpdateTabStops;
var
  I: Integer;
  HUnits: Integer;
  ConvertedTabs: TTabsArray;
begin
  {determine the horizontal dialog box units
  used by the list box, which depend on
  its current font}
  Canvas.Font := Font;
  HUnits := Canvas.TextWidth (
    'ABCDEFGHIJKLMNOPQRSTUVWXYZabcdefghijklmnopqrstuvwxyz')
    div 52;

  {convert the array of tab values}
  for I := Low (ConvertedTabs) to High (ConvertedTabs) do
    ConvertedTabs [I] := FTabStops [I] * 4 div HUnits;

  {activate the tab stops in the list box,
  sending a Windows list box message}
  SendMessage (Handle, lb_SetTabStops,
    1 + High (ConvertedTabs) – Low (ConvertedTabs),
    LongInt (@ConvertedTabs));
end;
```

LISTING 27.13: The final source code of the TTabbedList component (continued)

```
procedure Register;
begin
  RegisterComponents('Samples', [TTabList]);
end;

end.
```

Next, the CreateWnd method calls UpdateTabStops. The same happens each time the user changes one of the tabs with the SetTabStop method. The UpdateTabStops method is actually the key element of this component.

Basically, it sets the tab stops in the list box control encapsulated in the component. To accomplish this, a program has to send an `lb_SetTabStops` message to the list box, passing as parameters the number of tabs you want to set and a pointer to an array of integers, with these tab values:

```
SendMessage (Handle, lb_SetTabStops,
  1 + High (ConvertedTabs) - Low (ConvertedTabs),
  LongInt (@ConvertedTabs));
```

Using Dialog Box Units

In the code above, ConvertedTabs is another TTabsArray variable. You cannot pass the FTabStops array directly because the list box uses different units. In fact, the list box tabs are expressed in dialog box units, even if you place the list box in a generic window (or any kind of form or container component). However, I don't want to force programmers to use these units; I want to let them work in pixels. For this reason, I've added some conversion code to the UpdateTabStops method.

First of all, what are dialog box units? *Dialog box units* are based on the dialog's font because the controls of a dialog box (such as list boxes, labels, and edit boxes) base their size on the current font. (Consider that Windows' font handling for components is less flexible than the one offered by Delphi.) Dialog box units are computed by taking the average character width and height and dividing them by 4 and 8, respectively.

Now, how do you make this a conversion to dialog box units? The Windows API function `GetDialogBaseUnits` returns the base value of the dialog box units (the x in the low word and the *y* in the high word), so you might be tempted to write:

```
XDialog := XPixels * 4 div LoWord (GetDialogBaseUnits);
```

However, this function is not reliable. It works only for dialog boxes (or list boxes) using the system font. As an alternative, you can compute the average width of the font in your code. You should use only the same code Windows itself uses, which is based on the GetTextExtent API function. In Delphi, we can use the TextWidth method of the TCanvas class instead.

The Windows rule is that you have to take the 26 uppercase and 26 lowercase characters, get their widths, and compute the average by dividing by 52:

```
HUnits := Canvas.TextWidth (
  'ABCDEFGHIJKLMNOPQRSTUVWXYZabcdefghijklmnopqrstuvwxyz')
  div 52;
```

Of course, you should set the font first, as you can see in Listing 27.13. When you have the base dialog box unit, you can easily compute the new value for each of the tabs and set them in the Windows list box control.

Installing the Component

You can install the component as usual, eventually providing a new bitmap, instead of using the one in the list box. In addition to solving the problem mentioned earlier (the length of the path), you should remove the older tabbed list box component before installing the new one.

Up to now, we have always installed components from source code files and have made them available to other applications. In fact, as soon as you add a component you have defined to a form, its source file is included in the list of units of the uses statement. You add only the compiled unit to the VCL, as an alternative, but for static linking purposes, you need to supply the source file with the interface of the unit defining the component.

Remember that if you want to build the compiled unit of a component, among other approaches, you can open its Pascal file as a project file (with the Delphi Open Project command). When you have done this, you can both check the syntax of the component and compile it into the DCU format.

By the way, particularly to solve the path-length bug but also for version-handling issues, I've copied the final version of all the components defined in this chapter in a LIB directory of the chapter (that is, 27\LIB).

A Header and a Tabbed List Box

Before moving to a new component, I want to test the tabbed list box with the most typical example: adding a header above it to let an application's user move the tabs at run-time. The form of this example, TABTEST2, is similar to the one of the previous version, TABTEST1. You can see the new form, with the header and the tab aligned at the top of the form, in Figure 27.22.

FIGURE 27.22:

The form of the TABTEST2 example at design-time

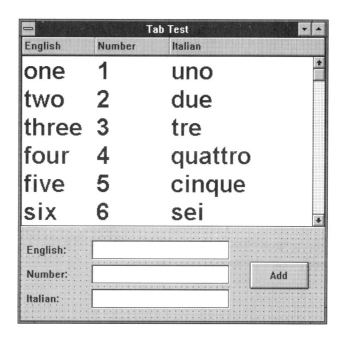

The values of the tabs in the list box are set at the beginning, in the FormCreate method, and then again each time one of the header separators is moved, in the Header1Sized method. Both procedures are based on a similar array, which computes the tabs by adding the size of each header to those of the preceding headers. In fact, tabs have an absolute value, while the position of the header component's separators is indicated as the width of the section, so it is relative to the previous one. Here is the code common to both methods:

```
for I := 0 to Header1.Sections.Count - 1 do
begin
  TabList1.TabStops [I] :=
    Header1.SectionWidth [I] + Last;
  Last := Header1.SectionWidth [I];
end;
```

The FormCreate method has another for loop to set the other tabs to a high value (the actual number used is not important) so that they won't interfere:

```
for I := Header1.Sections.Count to 10 do
  TabList1.TabStops [I] := 1000;
```

When you use this code, the list box tabs are automatically resized with the header sections, giving you a nice effect. As you can see in Figure 27.23, this works with any font, not only the system font. The real code is not in this example, anyway, but in the tabbed list box component it uses. That's the power of Delphi components.

Notice that we might further extend this example by preparing a single component, featuring a *tabbed list box with a header.* This will indeed be a useful component.

FIGURE 27.23:

The output of the TABTEST2 example

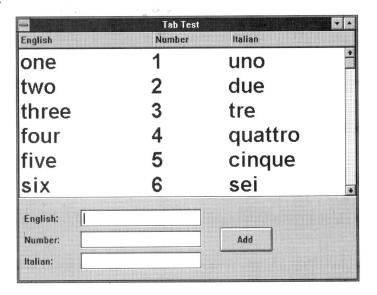

On the down side, notice that the tabs of the list box are indeed tabs. This means that if you move the second column too close to the first, some of the tabs will be lost, depending on the length of the words in the first column. You can see an example of this behavior, which is not a bug but is *as designed,* in Figure 27.24. For example, you might compute the size of a tab by checking the length of each of the strings in the first column with the current font.

FIGURE 27.24:

The behavior of the tabbed list box when tabs are too short

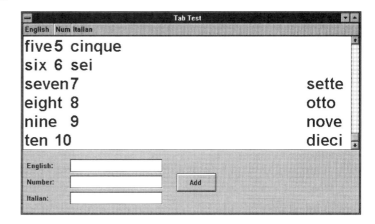

Forms Are Components, Too

The last component in the chapter will be completely different from the ones we have seen up to now. Now that I have built controls (such as the tabbed list box) and many graphic components (that is, windowless components) I'm going to build a nonvisual component.

The basic idea is that forms are components. When you have built a form that might be particularly useful in a number of projects, you can add it as a template to the Delphi Browse Gallery or make a component out of it. The second approach is more complex than the first one, but it makes using the new form easier and allows you to distribute the form placed inside a component without its source code, which is not possible with templates.

As an example, I'll build a component based on a custom dialog box, trying to mimic as much as possible the standard Delphi dialog box components.

A Dialog Box in a Component

The first step in building a dialog box in a component is to write the code of the dialog box itself, using the standard Delphi approach. Just define a new form and work on it as usual. When a component is based on a form, you can almost visually design the component. Of course, once the dialog box has been built, you have to define a component around it by writing code.

The standard dialog box I want to build is based on a list box. It is common to let a user choose a value from a list of strings. I've customized this common behavior in a dialog box first and then used it to build a component.

You can see the simple ListBoxForm form I built in Figure 27.25 and its textual description in Listing 27.14. I've provided this listing to underline the fact that we are building a form as usual.

FIGURE 27.25:

The dialog box I'm going to place in a component

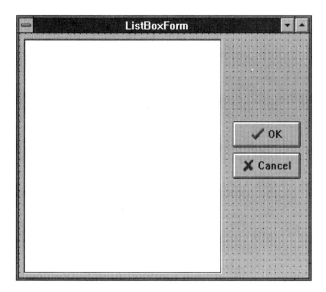

LISTING 27.14: The textual description of the form encapsulated in the component

```
object ListBoxForm: TListBoxForm
  BorderStyle = bsDialog
  Caption = 'ListBoxForm'
  object ListBox1: TListBox
    ItemHeight = 16
    TabOrder = 0
    OnDblClick = ListBox1DblClick
  end
  object BitBtn1: TBitBtn
    TabOrder = 1
    Kind = bkOK
  end
  object BitBtn2: TBitBtn
    TabOrder = 2
    Kind = bkCancel
  end
end
```

The only method of this dialog box relates to the double-click event of the list box, which closes the dialog box as though the OK button had been pressed:

```
procedure TListBoxForm.ListBox1DblClick(Sender: TObject);
begin
  ModalResult := mrOk;
end;
```

Once this form works, we can start arranging its source code, adding the definition of a component, removing the declaration of the form variable, and moving the form's type definition to the implementation portion.

The most important of these operations is the definition of the TListBoxDialog component, a nonvisual component:

```
TListBoxDialog = class (TComponent)
```

What determines that this component is nonvisual is that its immediate ancestor class is TComponent. As you can see in Listing 27.15, the component has three published properties and a public one. These are the three published properties:

- Lines is a TStrings object, accessed with its own methods, which use the Assign procedure when writing to the private field. This object is initialized in the Create method and destroyed in the Destroy procedure.

27

- Selected is an integer that directly accesses the corresponding private field. It stores the selected element of the list of strings.

- Title is a string used to change the title of the dialog box (it might have been a write-only property).

LISTING 27.15: The source code of the ListDial component

```
unit Listdial;

interface

uses
  SysUtils, WinTypes, WinProcs, Messages, Classes,
  Graphics, Controls, Forms, Dialogs, StdCtrls,
  Buttons;

type
  TListBoxDialog = class (TComponent)
  private
    FLines: TStrings;
    FSelected: Integer;
    FTitle: string;
    function GetSelItem: string;
    procedure SetLines (Value: TStrings);
    function GetLines: TStrings;
  public
    constructor Create(AOwner: TComponent);
      override;
    destructor Destroy; override;
    function Execute: Boolean;
    property SelItem: string
      read GetSelItem;
  published
    property Lines: TStrings
      read GetLines write SetLines;
    property Selected: Integer
      read FSelected write FSelected;
    property Title: string
      read FTitle write FTitle;
  end;

procedure Register;

implementation

{$R *.DFM}

type
  TListBoxForm = class(TForm)
    ListBox1: TListBox;
```

LISTING 27.15: The source code of the ListDial component (continued)

```
    BitBtn1: TBitBtn;
    BitBtn2: TBitBtn;
    procedure ListBox1DblClick(Sender: TObject);
  private
    { Private declarations }
  public
    { Public declarations }
  end;

constructor TListBoxDialog.Create(
  AOwner: TComponent);
begin
  inherited Create (AOwner);
  FLines := TStringList.Create;
  FTitle := 'Choose a string';
end;

destructor TListBoxDialog.Destroy;
begin
  FLines.Free;
  inherited Destroy;
end;

function TListBoxDialog.GetSelItem: string;
begin
  if Selected >= 0 then
    Result := FLines [Selected]
  else
    Result := '';
end;

function TListBoxDialog.GetLines: TStrings;
begin
  Result := FLines;
end;

procedure TListBoxDialog.SetLines (Value: TStrings);
begin
  FLines.Assign (Value);
end;

function TListBoxDialog.Execute: Boolean;
var
  ListBoxForm: TListBoxForm;
begin
  if FLines.Count = 0 then
    raise EStringListError.Create (
      'No items in the list');
  ListBoxForm := TListBoxForm.Create (self);
  try
    ListBoxForm.ListBox1.Items := FLines;
```

LISTING 27.15: The source code of the ListDial component (continued)

```
    ListBoxForm.ListBox1.ItemIndex := FSelected;
    ListBoxForm.Caption := FTitle;
    if ListBoxForm.ShowModal = mrOk then
    begin
      Result := True;
      Selected := ListBoxForm.ListBox1.ItemIndex;
    end
    else
      Result := False;
  finally
    ListBoxForm.Destroy;
  end;
end;

procedure TListBoxForm.ListBox1DblClick(
  Sender: TObject);
begin
  ModalResult := mrOk;
end;

procedure Register;
begin
  RegisterComponents('Dialogs', [TListBoxDialog]);
end;

end.
```

The public property is SelItem, a read-only property that automatically retrieves the selected element of the list of strings. Notice that this property has no storage and no data: it simply accesses other properties, providing a virtual representation of data.

Most of the code of this example is in the Execute method, a function that returns True or False depending on the modal result of the dialog box. This is consistent with the Execute method of most standard Delphi dialog box components. The Execute function creates the form dynamically, sets some of its values using the component's properties, shows the dialog box, and if the result is okay, updates the current selection.

Notice that the code is executed in a `try-finally` block, so if a run-time error occurs when the dialog box is displayed, the form will be destroyed. I've also used exceptions to raise an error if the list is empty when a user runs it. This error is by design, and using an exception is a good technique to enforce it.

Of course, since we are manually writing the code of the component, without the help of the Component Expert, we have to remember to write the Register procedure. This is one of the changes to the typical structure of a form's code, as you can see in Listing 27.15. Notice that the form's code is so messed up now that the environment cannot recognize it. If you include this unit in a normal project, Delphi won't be able to load it. The Delphi project manager, in fact, has requirements on the source code. However, you can still compile the project with the command-line compiler.

Using the Nonvisual Component

Now that the component is ready, you must provide a bitmap. For nonvisual components, bitmaps are very important because they are used not only for the Components palette but also when you place the component on a form.

So you can prepare the bitmap, install the component, and write a simple project to test it. You can see the form of my simple test program, LDTEST (notice the new component) in Figure 27.26. Next to it are a button and an edit box.

After preparing this form, I added some elements to the list. Notice that you can edit the Lines property using a standard TStrings editor (again, see Figure 27.26).

FIGURE 27.26:

The form of the LDTEST example, with the editor of the ListDial component's Lines property

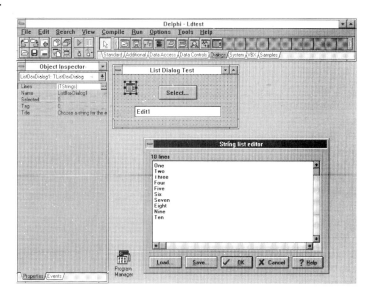

These values are also saved in the textual description of the form (see Listing 27.16).

LISTING 27.16: The textual description of the form of the LDTEST example

```
object Form1: TForm1
  Caption = 'List Dialog Test'
  object Button1: TButton
    Caption = 'Select...'
    OnClick = Button1Click
  end
  object Edit1: TEdit
    Text = 'Edit1'
  end
  object ListBoxDialog1: TListBoxDialog
    Lines.Strings = (
      'One'
      'Two'
      'Three'
      'Four'
      'Five'
      'Six'
      'Seven'
      'Eight'
      'Nine'
      'Ten')
    Selected = 0
    Title = 'Choose a string for the edit box'
  end
end
```

Now you can write a few lines of code, corresponding to the click on the button:

```
procedure TForm1.Button1Click(Sender: TObject);
begin
  if ListBoxDialog1.Execute then
    Edit1.Text := ListBoxDialog1.SelItem;
end;
```

That's all you need to run the dialog box we have placed in the component, as you can see in Figure 27.27. I think this is an interesting approach to the development of some common dialog boxes.

FIGURE 27.27:

The LDTEST example can show the dialog box we encapsulated in the ListDial component.

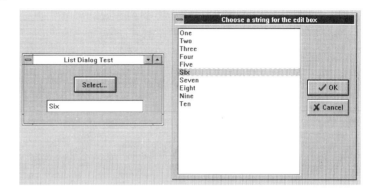

Summary

This chapter has been devoted to the definition of Delphi components. We have seen how to define various types of properties, how to add events, and how to define methods. We have seen different examples of components, including simple changes to existing ones, new graphical components, and, in the final section, a dialog box inside a component.

While building these components, we have faced some new Windows programming challenges. In general, it is not uncommon to have to use the Windows API directly when writing new components.

However, building components in Delphi is not an activity for a few experts, as it probably is in the Visual Basic approach, but is something any good Delphi programmer should learn to do. I haven't provided information specifically for programmers developing components a business might need, such as writing Help files for the components or customizing the property editors; instead I've focused on simple components you might develop for your own applications or for some of your colleagues.

Notice again that Delphi components are based on a traditional compile-and-link approach, which has nothing to do with Windows' dynamic linking. Writing and using DDLs, however, is another interesting approach to component software development in general, particularly when you need to build projects using several Windows programming environments at a time. Writing DLLs is the topic of the next chapter.

CHAPTER

TWENTY-EIGHT

Dynamic Link Libraries

- **DLLs in Windows**

- **How to use a C++ DLL in Delphi**

- **How to use a Delphi form in Paradox**

- **A DLL of icons**

- **How to call DLL functions at run-time**

28

Windows executable files come in two flavors: programs and dynamic link libraries (DLLs). When you write a Delphi application, you typically generate a program file, an EXE. However, Delphi applications often use calls to functions stored in DLLs. While Delphi itself relies more on static linking than on dynamic linking for its own components and code, each time you call a Windows API function directly, you actually call a DLL.

Although it is not very common, besides generating programs, Delphi can generate new dynamic link libraries. There is no specific support for DLL generation in the environment, but this operation is so simple it is not a problem. However, some problems arise from the nature of DLLs. Writing a DLL in Windows is not always as simple as it seems, and debugging programs with multiple executable files (the main program and one or more DLLs) is often a headache.

This chapter, the last in the book, covers the basics of DLL programming from the Delphi point of view. As usual, I'll show you some examples of what you can place in a Delphi DLL, or in a DLL in general. However, I'll also show you a couple of examples using other programming languages and environments, simply because one of the key reasons for writing a DLL in Delphi is to be able to call the DLL from a program written with another development environment and a different programming language.

The Role of DLLs in Windows

Before delving into the development of DLLs, both in Delphi and in other programming languages, I'll give you a short technical overview of DLLs in Windows, highlighting the key elements.

We will start by looking at dynamic linking, at the way Windows uses DLLs, and at the differences between DLLs and executable files, ending with some general rules to follow when writing DLLs.

What Is Dynamic Linking?

First of all, you need to understand the difference between static and dynamic linking of functions or procedures. When a subroutine is not directly available in a source file, the compiler adds it to an internal table, which includes all external symbols. Of course, the compiler must have seen the declaration of the subroutine and know about its parameters and type, or it will issue an error.

After compilation, for a normal—*static*—subroutine, the linker fetches the subroutine's compiled code from a Delphi compiled unit (or static library) and adds it to the executable. The resulting EXE file includes all the code of the program and of the units involved. Actually, the Delphi linker is smart enough to include only the minimum amount of code of the units included in the program, not all of it.

In the case of dynamic linking, the linker simply uses the information of the `external` declaration of the subroutine to add some internal tables to the executable file. When the executable file is loaded in memory, it loads all the DLLs it requires first (unless they are already in memory); then the program starts. During this loading process, the program's internal tables are filled with the addresses of the functions in memory since each DLL has been loaded and is now available. If for some reason the DLL is not found, the program won't start.

Each time the program reaches an external call, the call is sent to the DLL. Notice that this scheme does not involve two different applications. The DLL is seen as part of the current program, and (as we will see later in this chapter) all the parameter passing takes place on the stack as for any static function call.

You can see a sketch of how the program calls function in the case of static or dynamic linking in Figure 28.1. Notice that I've omitted a portion of the process—that is, the compilation of the DLL—because I wanted to focus on the two different linking mechanisms.

28

NOTE The term *dynamic linking*, as used when referring to DLLs, has nothing to do with the late-binding feature of the object-oriented programming language. Virtual or dynamic methods in Object Pascal have nothing to do with DLLs. Unfortunately, the same term is used for both kinds of procedures and functions, which causes a lot of confusion. When I speak of dynamic binding in this chapter, I am referring not to polymorphism but to DLLs.

There is also another approach to the use of DLLs, even more dynamic than the one we have seen. In fact, at run-time, you can load a DLL in memory, search for a

FIGURE 28.1:

Static and dynamic binding in Windows

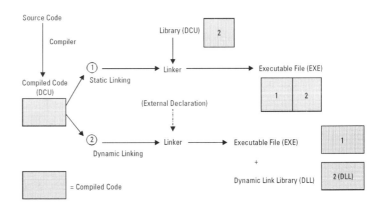

function (provided you know its name), and call it. This approach requires much more complex coding and is generally slower, but you don't need to have the DLL available to start the program.

What Are DLLs For?

Now that you have a general idea of how DLLs work, we can focus on the reasons for their use. Here are some of the reasons to use dynamic link libraries in Windows:

- If the same code is used by different programs, it is loaded in memory only once, thus sparing some system memory. This advantage is based on the fact that a DLL cannot be loaded twice in memory. Once it is there, it is used by any following program that needs it. The system implements a usage-count mechanism, so when the last program requiring the DLL terminates, the DLL is unloaded from memory.

- You can provide a different version of a DLL, replacing the current one. If the subroutines in the DLL have the same parameters, you can run the program with the new version of the DLL without having to recompile it. If the DLL has new subroutines, it doesn't matter at all. Problems might arise only if a procedure of the older version of the DLL is missing in the new one.

- You can use a DLL as a central repository of information that each of the programs using it can access. For example, a DLL can provide an interface to a device and take care of disciplining its use by different applications. This approach won't work in Windows NT but will work in Windows 95.

These generic advantages apply in several cases. If you have some complex algorithms of some complex windows that several applications require, you can store them in a DLL and then include them in different programs. This will let you save some memory when you run all the programs at the same time, but unless the size of this program portion is very big, the work of moving to the DLL approach might not be worth the memory you save.

The second advantage is interesting for complex applications, too. If you have a very big program that requires frequent updates and bug fixes, dividing it into many executables and several DLLs allows you to distribute to your clients only the DLL that has been fixed, not a single big executable.

This makes sense in particular for Windows system libraries. If Borland makes a new version of the Database Engine libraries and writes new SQL Links to access other SQL server databases, you probably won't need to recompile your application to take advantage of the changes.

Another common technique is to prepare DLLs with resources. You can build a version of the DLL with strings for each language and then change the language at runtime, or you can prepare a library of icons and bitmaps and then use them in different applications.

Another key advantage, as I already mentioned, is that DLLs are language independent. Actually, DLL functions and procedures use something between the C and Pascal languages since their parameters are based on C plus some Windows additions and their parameter passing is that of Pascal.

In any case, any Windows programming environment, including most macro languages of end-user applications, allows a programmer to call a subroutine stored in a DLL. This means you can build a DLL in Delphi and call it from C++, Visual Basic, Paradox, dBASE, Excel, WordPerfect, and many other Windows applications.

28

The System DLLs

The three key advantages of DLLs I've highlighted are all used by the Windows system DLLs. For this reason, it is worth examining them.

First of all, Windows has many system DLLs. There are the three central blocks of Windows—Kernel, User, and GDI—which are DLLs, although their files have an EXE extension. (You can find these files in the WINDOW\SYSTEM directory.) Other DLLs come in the form of extension DLLs (such as the DLL for common dialog boxes, the DLL for DDEML, the OLE DLLs, and so on), device drivers, fonts, VBX controls, and others.

In the case of Windows itself, using DLLs is extremely important. We might say DLLs are one of the key technical foundations of the Microsoft operating environment. Since each application uses the system DLLs for anything from creating windows to producing output, every program is linked to those DLLs. Now imagine how much memory you computer would need if each application had to include the code of the system libraries. The fact that each application uses the same code, which is loaded in memory only once, is vital.

Another central element is the possibility of having different versions of the same library. This serves different needs. First of all, consider device drivers. When you change your printer, you do not need to rebuild your application, not even to buy a new version of the Windows GDI library, which manages the printer output. You need only a specific driver, which is a DLL called by the GDI, to access your printer. Each printer has its own driver, or DLL, making the system extremely flexible.

From a different point of view, version handling is important for the system itself. If you have an application compiled for Windows 3.0, you should be able to run it on Windows 3.1, Windows for Workgroups 3.11, and even Windows 95. Each version of Windows has different system files, but since each new version contains the older API functions, the old code still works, although it cannot take advantage of the new features.

Actually, this is not entirely true. The old program cannot use the new API functions, but if an existing function's code changes, the program will end up using the new code. Consider as an obvious example the user interface of the windows. If you build an application for Windows 3.1, you can run it on Windows 95, and it will really have a different user interface. You have not recompiled your program; it uses the features of the new system libraries, which are linked dynamically to it.

The system DLLs are also used as system information archives. For example, the User module has a list of all the windows in the system (as I mentioned in Chapter 20), and any application can directly access this list. The same holds for the GDI system library.

Differences between DLLs and EXEs

Now that you know the basic elements of dynamic linking and some reasons to use it, we can focus on the difference between a normal executable file (an EXE file) and a file with a dynamic link library (a DLL file). Basically, the internal structure of the file is the same; the key difference is the file extension.

Each DLL can have multiple code and data segments, and even resource segments, like any executable. It is when a DLL is loaded in memory that things change.

As I mentioned earlier, a DLL can be loaded in memory only once. There can be only one instance (that is, one default data segment) for a DLL. An executable file, on the other hand, can have multiple instances (each with its own default data segment), even if its code is still loaded in memory only once. For the DLLs, a proper usage-count mechanism ensures that the code and data segments of a library are not un-loaded too early.

Another important difference is that a library has an entry in the module database but not in the task database (for definitions of these terms, see Chapter 20). A library, even when loaded in memory, is not a running program. It is only a collection of procedures and functions that other programs can call. These procedures and functions have some memory they can use (a local heap), but they use the stack of the calling program. So another key difference between a program and a library is that a library has no stack. It uses the stack of the program calling it.

As a program, however, a library has an instance handle. In fact, the instance handle in Windows refers to the default data segment of an application, and a DLL has this data segment, even if it has no stack area. The instance handle of a DLL is very important when you load a DLL dynamically, using the LoadLibrary API function.

28

Rules for DLL Writers

What I've described so far can be summarized in some rules DLL programmers. A DLL function or procedure to be called by external programs must follow these guidelines:

- It has to be declared as `far` and `export` and has to be listed in the DLL's `exports` clause. This makes the routine visible to the outside world.

- It should use the Pascal calling convention (which is easy in Delphi).

- It must use `far` pointers, which is the default in Delphi.

- It should not store in global variables data passed by calling applications since different programs will end up using the same memory address. (Remember, there is only one DLL default memory segment for all the programs calling it.)

- It should allocate Windows global memory with care. When you call the Windows API function `GlobalAlloc` directly, you have to take care using the `gmem_Share` flag (or use the Delphi HeapAllocFlags system variable) to let the DLL own the memory. Otherwise, the memory will be owned by the calling application and automatically disposed of when this program terminates. This is not a big problem, in any case, because if you allocate memory using Delphi standard methods (such as GetMem or New), the memory is automatically allocated with the `gmem_DDE_Share flag`, which gives ownership of the memory to the DLL, not to the calling application.

I'll give you more details on these rules when we start writing some examples.

Using Existing DLLs

Before writing DLLs in Delphi, what about using them? Well, we have done that in a number of examples in the book, when calling Windows API functions. As you might remember, all the API functions are declared in the system WinProcs unit. In the interface portion of the unit, functions are declared, such as:

```
function Ellipse(DC: HDC; X1, Y1, X2, Y2: Integer): Bool;
function EmptyClipboard: Bool;
```

```
function EnableMenuItem(Menu: HMenu; IDEnableItem: Word;
  Enable: Word): Bool;
function EnableWindow(Wnd: HWnd; Enable: Bool): Bool;
procedure EndDialog(Dlg: HWnd; Result: Integer);
```

Then, in the implementation portion, instead of providing their code, the unit refers to the external definition in a DLL:

```
function Ellipse;              external 'GDI' index 24;
function EmptyClipboard;       external 'USER' index 139;
function EnableMenuItem;       external 'USER' index 155;
function EnableWindow;         external 'USER' index 34;
procedure EndDialog;           external 'USER' index 88;
```

The external definition of these functions refers to the name of the DLL they use. This is the internal name of the module, which often, but not always, matches the file name without the extension. For example, even if the file name of one of the system DLLs is KRNL386.EXE, its module name is invariably KERNEL.

To call a function from a DLL, you can simply provide these declarations and external definitions, as shown above, or you can merge them in a single declaration. This is what I've done on a couple of occasions—for example, in the SHABOUT example in Chapter 12, which called an undocumented Windows API function. An undocumented function is basically a function available in a Windows DLL but not listed in WinProcs (or in the corresponding C header files distributed by Microsoft). Here is an excerpt of the code of that example:

28

```
function ShellAbout (
  HwndOwner: Hwnd;
  AppName, MoreInfo: PChar;
  Icon: HIcon): Bool;
  far; external 'SHELL' index 22;
```

The index that is present both in my code and in the system code is the number of the function's entry in a table of the DLL. You can access DLL functions by either name or number. Accessing by number is slightly faster and solves many problems related to the different name-generation approaches different systems use. Most of the time, however, you can simply declare a function with the proper name and omit the number, as I'll show you in the next section.

Once the function is properly defined, you can call it in the code of your Delphi application as though it were a normal function. There is nothing special about this; it is just a function call.

Calling a C++ DLL

As a further example of how to call a DLL, I've decided to write a new, very simple DLL in C++, with some useless functions, and show you how to call it from a Delphi application. I won't comment the C++ code in detail (it is basically C code, anyway) but will focus instead on the calls between the two languages. This is important because it is common in Delphi to use a DLL written in C or C++.

The C++ DLL

In Listing 28.1, you can see the source code of the C++ file used to build the CPPDLL library. Needless to say, this is actually Borland C++ code, compiled with version 4.5 of the compiler, but most of the things I discuss here will also work with any other compiler.

LISTING 28.1: The C++ source code of the CDLL library (the file name is CPPDLL.CPP)

```
#include <windows.h>
#include <bwcc.h>

int FAR PASCAL LibMain (
  HINSTANCE, WORD, WORD, LPSTR)
{
  return 1;
}

void FAR PASCAL _export Beep ()
{
  MessageBeep (-1);
}

extern "C"
int FAR PASCAL _export Double (int n)
{
  return n * 2;
}

extern "C"
void FAR PASCAL _export ShowMessage (HWND hwnd, LPSTR text)
{
  BWCCMessageBox (hwnd, text,
    "Message", MB_OK | MB_ICONINFORMATION);
}
```

This code is very simple, but it contains one useful element: a function wrapping the call to the message box of the Borland Windows Custom Controls library (BWCC). We could have called this library directly from Delphi, but I have just used it to illustrate parameter passing.

Notice that all the functions are defined as FAR PASCAL _export to indicate that they are far functions, functions called by another module; that they should use the Pascal calling convention; and that they should be exported to be made available to other programs. Two of these C++ functions also use the C naming convention (indicated by the extern "C" statement), but one doesn't. We will see what changes when we call these functions from a Delphi application.

The file in Listing 28.1 is the only source file of the CPPDLL project (the corresponding IDE file is available on the companion disk). You can see the target options of the example in Figure 28.2.

FIGURE 28.2:

The target options of the CPPDLL Borland C++ library

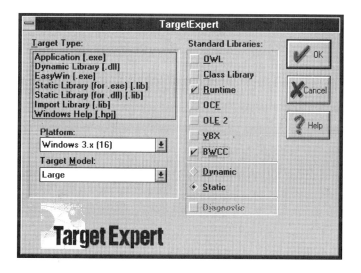

28

Declaring the DLL Functions in Delphi

Now that I've written this DLL in C++, we can write a Delphi example to call it. The example, named CALLCPP and stored in the same directory as the C++ DLL

(28\CPPDLL) on the companion disk, is simple. As you can see in Figure 28.3, its form has three buttons, to call each function of the DLL, plus a spin edit and an edit box to provide some input values for the parameters.

FIGURE 28.3:

The form of the CALLCPP example

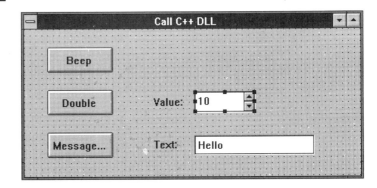

The first thing you have to do to write this program is provide a proper definition of the functions. For the first function we can write:

```
procedure Beep;
   far; external 'CPPDLL' index 2;
```

Notice that since it has no return value (it is a C++ void function), I've indicated it as a procedure, the Pascal version of a function without a return value.

Since this is a function using C++ naming conventions (unlike the other two functions of the DLL, which use C naming), you need to provide the index. Otherwise, the Delphi program will compile, but as soon as you press the button and call the function, a Windows error message with the text *Undefined Dynalink* appears. This immediately terminates the application.

But how do I know the index is really 2? Well, you can guess that this is the second function of the C++ code, not because of the LibMain function but because of another system function automatically added by the Borland C++ compiler. Aside from guessing, you can use a tool available in Delphi to test the index of the DLL function. This is very important if you want to link a Delphi program to a DLL you have not written.

The tool is TDUMP, a command-line tool. Open a DOS window, move to the directory containing the DLL, and write something like:

```
\DELPHI\BIN\TDUMP CPPDLL.DLL | MORE
```

The output consists of several pages, so you should send it to a file or to the MORE DOS utility to show it page by page. In the third page (more or less) of the output, you can see the Resident Name Table of the DLL, with the following description:

```
Resident Name Table           offset: 00E0h
  Module Name: 'CPPDLL'
  Name: WEP                    Entry: 0001
  Name: beep()                 Entry: 0002
  Name: DOUBLE                 Entry: 0003
  Name: SHOWMESSAGE            Entry: 0004
```

Notice not only the index number of the entries (this is what we were looking for) but also the internal names of the functions. The first of the functions we have written, Beep, has a strange internal name because it uses C++ name managing. The name you see, in fact, is not the real internal function name but a more readable version. To obtain the real function name, you have to call TDUMP with the -m parameter. This is the result:

```
  Name: @BEEP$QV              Entry: 0002
```

The other functions do not change, which is the reason we must provide an index for this function. The alternative, using the internal name as the function name, is not possible in this case because @BEEP$QV is not a legal identifier for the name of a Pascal procedure. What you can do is add a name directive to the external declaration by writing:

```
procedure Beep;
  far; external 'CPPDLL' name '@BEEP$QV';
```

Now we can move to the other two functions, which are much simpler to code because they haven't got the problem just described. For the second function, you can simply write:

```
function Double (N: Integer): Integer;
  far; external 'CPPDLL';
```

For the third function, I could use a similar approach. However, in Delphi, a Show-Message procedure already exists to avoid hiding this system procedure and confusing programmers. I've simply renamed it, using the index to establish the connection:

```
procedure ShowBWCCMessage (Handle: Hwnd; Text: PChar);
   far; external 'CPPDLL' index 4;
```

You can use this approach to give the name you want to any function stored in a DLL. Now that we have seen the definitions, you can look at the full source code of the CALLDLL example in Listing 28.2.

LISTING 28.2: The source code of the CALLDLL example

```
unit Callc_f;

interface

uses
  SysUtils, WinTypes, WinProcs, Messages,
  Classes, Graphics, Controls, Forms, Dialogs,
  StdCtrls, Spin;

type
  TForm1 = class(TForm)
    BeepButton: TButton;
    DoubleButton: TButton;
    MessageButton: TButton;
    SpinEdit1: TSpinEdit;
    Label1: TLabel;
    Label2: TLabel;
    Edit1: TEdit;
    procedure BeepButtonClick(Sender: TObject);
    procedure DoubleButtonClick(Sender: TObject);
    procedure MessageButtonClick(Sender: TObject);
  end;

var
  Form1: TForm1;

implementation

{$R *.DFM}

{definition of the functions of the DLL}
procedure Beep;
  far; external 'CPPDLL' index 2;
function Double (N: Integer): Integer;
  far; external 'CPPDLL';
procedure ShowBWCCMessage (Handle: Hwnd; Text: PChar);
  far; external 'CPPDLL' index 4;
```

LISTING 28.2: The source code of the CALLDLL example (continued)

```
procedure TForm1.BeepButtonClick(Sender: TObject);
begin
  Beep;
end;

procedure TForm1.DoubleButtonClick(Sender: TObject);
begin
  SpinEdit1.Value := Double (SpinEdit1.Value);
end;

procedure TForm1.MessageButtonClick(Sender: TObject);
var
  Text: array [0..255] of Char;
begin
  StrPCopy (Text, Edit1.Text);
  ShowBWCCMessage (Handle, Text);
end;

end.
```

The output of the program is very simple. When you press the Beep button, the system beeps; when you press the Message button, a BWCC-style message box appears (see Figure 28.4); and when you press the Double button, the value of the spin edit changes. Pressing this button a number of times in a row causes the integer value to overflow eventually, giving incorrect results.

28

FIGURE 28.4:

The output of the CALLDLL example, when the ShowMessage DLL function is called

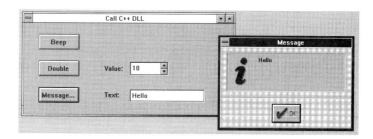

Creating a DLL in Delphi

Besides using DLLs written with other environments, you can use Delphi to build DLLs that can be used in Delphi itself or with any other tool. Note that Delphi is probably the only visual programming tool that can build DLLs. This is because Delphi is based on a real compiler, something other visual programming environments are not.

However, in general, I would discourage you from building DLLs in Delphi to be used in other Delphi projects unless the application you are building is huge and you want to use this technique to split the work among several programmers. Before building DLLs, consider whether working with static libraries (that is, compiled units), form templates, and components instead would be satisfactory.

By building DLLs you might think you are sparing some memory, but you'll probably end up requiring more. In fact, each Delphi executable includes the same runtime library code and probably also a lot of standard VCL code. If you build an EXE and a DLL, this code will be duplicated, so even if two applications share the DLL, you might end up needing more memory than when using static linking.

Static linking is also more selective, and it allows you to add to the program only the code you really use (at least in an ideal situation). When you load a DLL, you load it all, at least in theory, since some code modules might actually remain on the disk and be loaded on request. As you might guess, it is not easy to give a definitive statement, because there are many parameters. My suggestion to not write Delphi DLLs for a Delphi program is just a general guideline. Later in the chapter, I'll show you some cases in which it makes sense to do so.

Routines, Methods, Objects, and DLLs

Another reason not to use DLLs when they are not required is that DLLs typically export routines, functions, and procedures, not methods, objects, or components. When you work with Delphi visual tools, turning your code into a DLL is generally more complex than turning it into a component. You do not need to write more code. You need a paradigm shift, thinking in terms of functions and procedures instead of classes and methods.

When you build complex Delphi applications, you can also use object-oriented programming to define your application's structure. If you later divide it into DLLs, you lose this advantage.

What you can use Delphi DLLs for is to write algorithms and access resources and other elements that can be based on Pascal more than on Object Pascal. When you have code of this kind, you can consider placing it in a DLL. In this case, if you use no VCL code, the memory overhead is minimal, too.

Aside from these special cases, the main reason to write DLLs in Delphi is to provide portions of applications for programmers working with other environments.

A First Simple Delphi DLL

Before studying a real example, a form in a DLL, I'll show you a very simple DLL built in Delphi. This is more or less a new version of the DLL we already built in C++. The primary focus of this example will be the syntax you use to define a DLL in Delphi.

To start, create a new project, as usual, and then remove the form (using the Project Manager) and open the source code of the project. Since I've saved the project with the name FIRSTDLL, the source code is now the following:

```
program Firstdll;

uses
  Forms;

{$R *.RES}

begin
  Application.Run;
end.
```

The key element of building a DLL instead of a normal application is to replace the keyword program at the beginning of the code with the keyword library:

```
library Firstdll;
```

Then you can add one or more functions, marked with the export keyword, and list all these functions in a new exports statement:

```
procedure Beep; export;
begin
  MessageBeep ($FFFF);
end;

exports
  Beep;
```

Eventually, you can assign a given index to the exported procedure or function by writing:

```
exports
  Beep index 2;
```

You can also remove the inclusion of resources, change the initialization code (or simply delete it), and correct the uses statement. You can see the final code of the DLL in Listing 28.3.

By Using Delphi, you can build the DLL with the Build All or Compile command on the Run menu. You can also issue the Run command, but Delphi will complain that it cannot run a DLL, as you can see in Figure 28.5.

LISTING 28.3: The source code of FIRSTDLL

```
library Firstdll;

uses
  WinProcs;

procedure Beep; export;
begin
  MessageBeep ($FFFF);
end;

function Double (N: Integer): Integer; export;
begin
  Double := N * 2;
end;

exports
  Beep, Double;

begin
end.
```

The error message Delphi displays
when you try to run a DLL

Since we have not included any VCL code, the resulting DLL is extremely small, actually below 2K. If you now add the Dialogs unit to the uses statement and add a line to the Beep procedure, as follows:

```
procedure Beep; export;
begin
  MessageBeep ($FFFF);
  ShowMessage ('Beep');
end;
```

the total size of the DLL will become slightly less than 222K, just for a call. The difference is that now a lot of code from the VCL is included in the DLL executable file.

Of course, if you add a second call to another VCL function, the size of the DLL won't double again. It will remain almost the same. Once the core of the VCL code is included in a DLL, you pay a very small penalty by using more VCL features. For this reason, it might make sense to put a number of forms into a single DLL so that the VCL code overhead is shared among them.

How can you use this library? Well, you can call it from within another Delphi project or from other environments. As a sample, I've built a new version of the CALLCPP example, named CALLFRST, that defines the two external functions as:

```
{functions of the Delphi DLL}
procedure Beep; far; external 'FIRSTDLL';
function Double (N: Integer): Integer;
  far; external 'FIRSTDLL';
```

This is similar to the preceding code. This time, we have no problems with function names, and we refer to a different library, of course. Besides this change and the removal of the third button, the code of the example remains the same, so I've skipped its description. You can find all the code on the companion disk.

28

It is useful to build libraries of small functions if the same functions have to be called from different environments or if they are subject to change, because you can provide different versions of these libraries for different users (as happens with device drivers). At the same time, the overhead is very limited because DLLs that do not use the VCL are extremely small. As you may remember from Chapter 19, the same size reduction took place in Delphi applications using no components at all.

Placing a Form in a DLL

What is much more interesting, particularly if you work in different development environments, is placing a complete form built with Delphi in a DLL. This can be a dialog box or any other kind of form.

To build the FORMDLL example, I've started with a very old form, the main form of the SCROLLC example in Chapter 7. You can see the new version of the form, with two new bitmap buttons, in Figure 28.6. The only other change I made was to set the BorderStyle property of the form to bsDialog.

FIGURE 28.6:

The new version of the SCROLLC form, with two bitmap buttons

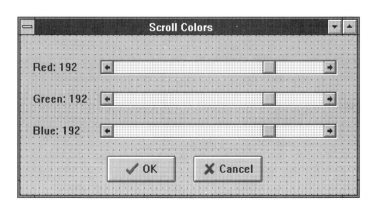

The source code of the form, its type definition and its code, has no other changes. I've only added a new function to the unit, defined as:

```
function GetColor (Col: LongInt): LongInt; export;
```

The color passed as a parameter is used as the initial color, and the return value is the final color (which is the same as the initial color if the user pressed the Cancel button). You can see the source code of this function, together with the rest of the code of the unit, in Listing 28.4.

LISTING 28.4: The source code of the SCROLL_F unit

```
unit Scroll_f;

interface

uses
  SysUtils, WinTypes, WinProcs, Messages,
  Classes, Graphics, Controls, Forms, Dialogs,
  StdCtrls, Buttons;

type
  TFormScroll = class(TForm)
    ScrollBarRed: TScrollBar;
    ScrollBarGreen: TScrollBar;
    ScrollBarBlue: TScrollBar;
    LabelRed: TLabel;
    LabelGreen: TLabel;
    LabelBlue: TLabel;
    BitBtn1: TBitBtn;
    BitBtn2: TBitBtn;
    procedure ScrollBarRedScroll(
      Sender: TObject; ScrollCode: TScrollCode;
      var ScrollPos: Integer);
    procedure ScrollBarGreenScroll(
      Sender: TObject; ScrollCode: TScrollCode;
      var ScrollPos: Integer);
    procedure ScrollBarBlueScroll(
      Sender: TObject; ScrollCode: TScrollCode;
      var ScrollPos: Integer);
  end;

var
  FormScroll: TFormScroll;

function GetColor (Col: LongInt): LongInt; export;

implementation

{$R *.DFM}

procedure TFormScroll.ScrollBarRedScroll(Sender: TObject;
  ScrollCode: TScrollCode; var ScrollPos: Integer);
```

28

LISTING 28.4: The source code of the SCROLL_F unit (continued)

```
begin
  LabelRed.Caption := 'Red: ' + IntToStr(ScrollPos);
  FormScroll.Color := RGB (ScrollBarRed.Position,
    ScrollBarGreen.Position, ScrollBarBlue.Position);
end;

procedure TFormScroll.ScrollBarGreenScroll(Sender: TObject;
  ScrollCode: TScrollCode; var ScrollPos: Integer);
begin
  LabelGreen.Caption := 'Green: ' + IntToStr(ScrollPos);
  FormScroll.Color := RGB (ScrollBarRed.Position,
    ScrollBarGreen.Position, ScrollBarBlue.Position);
end;

procedure TFormScroll.ScrollBarBlueScroll(Sender: TObject;
  ScrollCode: TScrollCode; var ScrollPos: Integer);
begin
  LabelBlue.Caption := 'Blue: ' + IntToStr(ScrollPos);
  FormScroll.Color := RGB (ScrollBarRed.Position,
    ScrollBarGreen.Position, ScrollBarBlue.Position);
end;

{interface function}
function GetColor (Col: LongInt): LongInt;
begin
  FormScroll := TFormScroll.Create (Application);
  {initialize the data}
  FormScroll.Color := Col;
  FormScroll.ScrollBarRed.Position :=
    GetRValue (ColorToRGB (Col));
  FormScroll.ScrollBarGreen.Position :=
    GetGValue (ColorToRGB (Col));
  FormScroll.ScrollBarBlue.Position :=
    GetBValue (ColorToRGB (Col));
  try
    {show the form}
    if FormScroll.ShowModal = mrOK then
      Result := ColorToRGB (FormScroll.Color)
    else
      Result := Col;
  finally
    FormScroll.Free;
  end;
end;

end.
```

When you want to place a Delphi component (such as a form) in a DLL, you cannot make the component available to DLL users; you can only provide some functions that create, initialize, or run the component or access its properties and data. The simplest approach is to have a single function that sets the data, runs the component, and returns the result, as in the current example. However, for complex cases, you might have to provide complex data structures as parameters. For actual examples, you can look at the Windows API functions for the common dialog boxes (such as `GetOpenFileName` or `ChooseColor`) in the Help file.

Another important element is the structure of the code of the GetColor function in Listing 28.4. The code creates the form at the beginning, then sets some initial values, and then runs the form in a protected block (`try-finally`). By checking the return value of the ShowModal method, it determines the result of the function.

Notice also that I've passed as a parameter a long integer, which stands for the Windows COLORREF data type. Using TColor, a Delphi type, might have caused problems with non-Delphi applications, even though a TColor is very similar to a COLORREF. When you write a DLL, use Windows native data types.

Now that we have written the unit's code, we can move to the project code. Starting from a standard Delphi project, the code becomes:

```
library Scrollc;

uses
  Scroll_f in 'SCROLL_F.PAS' {FormScroll};

exports
  GetColor index 1;

begin
  {DLL initialization code}
end.
```

28

Calling the DLL Form from Delphi

We can now test the form we have placed in the DLL in a Delphi program. I consider this just a test because, as I've already mentioned, in a similar case this approach makes no sense.

On the companion disk, the test example, USECOL, is in the same directory (FORMDLL). The reason for this approach is that the DLL must reside in the same directory as the program that uses it, in a directory of the PATH, or in a Windows system directory. Using the current directory is the ideal solution for a simple test as well as for many complex applications.

The USECOL example is simple. Its form contains only a button. When the user presses the button, the DLL function is called. Here is the definition of this function and the code of the Button1Click method:

```
function GetColor (Col: LongInt): LongInt;
  far; external 'SCROLLC';

procedure TForm1.Button1Click(Sender: TObject);
var
  Col: LongInt;
begin
  Col := ColorToRGB (Color);
  Color := GetColor (Col)
end;
```

When you run this program (see Figure 28.7), the dialog box is displayed, using the current background color of the main window. If you change the color and press the OK button, the new color is activated in the main form.

FIGURE 28.7:

The execution of the USECOL test program when it calls the dialog box we have placed in a DLL

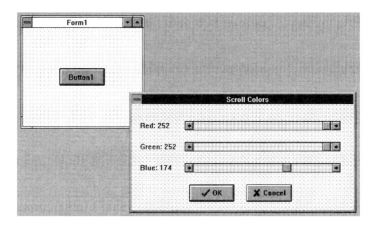

Calling a Delphi DLL from Other Languages

What is interesting in this example is that we can run this dialog box from other programming languages. Calling this DLL from C or C++ is easy. You need to declare the function as:

```
extern COLORREF GetColor (COLORREF);
```

Then you can call it as usual:

```
MyColor = GetColor (OldColor);
```

To link this application, you need to generate an import library (by running the IMPLIB utility on the DLL) and add it to the project.

Since I've already used Borland C++ in this chapter, instead of completing this example, I want to write a similar one with Paradox.

To start, create a new Paradox form and place in it a button and an ellipse, as shown in Figure 28.8. The button is named MyButton and the ellipse MyEllipse. Then choose a color for the ellipse and for the form.

28

FIGURE 28.8:

The Paradox form used in the example that calls the Delphi DLL

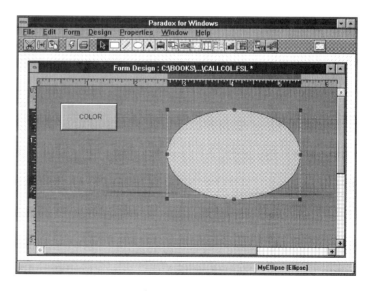

Now, define the button's pushButton method and write the following code:

```
uses ScrollC
  GetColor (AColor CLONG) CLONG
enduses

method pushButton(var eventInfo Event)
var
  MyColor LongInt
endvar
  MyColor = MyEllipse.Color
  MyColor = GetColor (MyColor)
  MyEllipse.Color = MyColor
endmethod
```

The first three lines declare the GetColor function of the DLL. To avoid problems, I've copied the DLL file in the WINDOWS\SYSTEM directory so any application can access it. The CLONG type is the definition of the Windows long integer type.

The rest of the code simply calls the function, passing to it the color of the ellipse and using the return value as the new color for the shape. You can see the result of this program in Figure 28.9. The PDOXCALL directory on the companion disk contains the CALLCOL.FSL file for this example. Of course, you need to have Paradox to run it.

FIGURE 28.9:

The output of the Paradox form using the Delphi dialog box

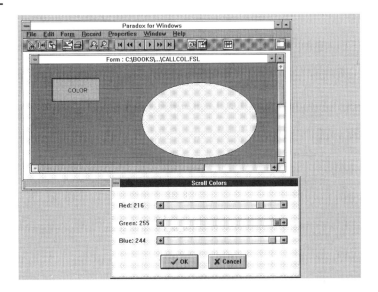

A DLL of Icons

Dynamic link libraries in Windows have many other uses. As an example, we'll build a DLL of icons and then load icons from it dynamically in a program.

This will be the first time we access a DLL from an application at run-time, without any compile-time link, as usually happens. As a consequence, the program will run even if the DLL is not available.

To build a DLL of icons, or other Windows resources, you need only prepare a resource file and link it with a library. For example, I've prepared a file with three resources, named *Icon_A, Icon_B,* and *Icon_C,* representing the corresponding letters, as you can see in Figure 28.10.

Once the resource file is ready (in this case, it is named ICONS.RES), you can write the simple source code of the DLL:

```
library Iconsdll;

uses
  SysUtils;

{$R ICONS.RES}

begin
end.
```

28

Actually, the uses statement is redundant, but if you remove it, Delphi complains that it is missing each time you load the file in the editor. However, the code will compile even without that line. Build this program, and the ICONSDLL.DLL library will be ready to use.

Consider this DLL as a collection of icons and other resources, such as standard strings for error messages or bitmaps with company logos, used by several applications at the same time. In fact, if two applications will use this DLL, only one copy of the resources will be in memory. However, if the same resource file is included in several programs, it will be duplicated.

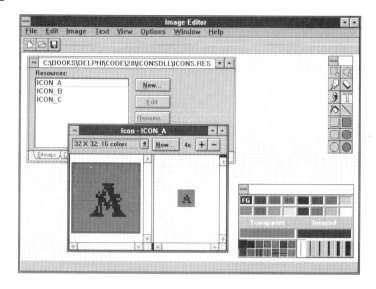

Loading the Icons from the DLL

Now that we have built the DLL, we have to load it in a program. For this purpose, I've built a simple example, USEICONS (saved in the ICONSDLL directory), which allows users to enter the name of the icon they want to see.

The form of this application is shown in Figure 28.11. It contains a label, an edit box, a button, a bevel, and an image, all using standard properties.

When the form is created, it tries to open the DLL, calling the LoadLibrary API function:

```
procedure TForm1.FormCreate(Sender: TObject);
begin
  HInst := LoadLibrary ('Iconsdll.dll');
  if HInst <= 32 then
    LoadButton.Enabled := False;
end;
```

LoadLibrary returns the handle of the instance of the library. If this value is below 32, it is an error code. In this case, the program disables the button, so the library won't be accessed. The application's handle is saved in a private field of the form, HInst.

28

FIGURE 28.11:

The form of the USEICONS example at design-time

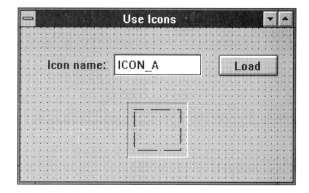

This value, in fact, is used in the LoadButtonClick method to load an icon from the DLL. The icon is indicated by name, using the text of the Edit component. Once the icon's handle has been loaded, it is used to set the new image:

```
procedure TForm1.LoadButtonClick(Sender: TObject);
var
  HIcon: THandle;
  IconName: array [0..20] of Char;
begin
  StrPCopy (IconName, Edit1.Text);
  HIcon := LoadIcon (HInst, IconName);
  if HIcon = 0 then
    ShowMessage ('Icon not found')
  else
    Image1.Picture.Icon.Handle := HIcon;
end;
```

Of course, there's a good chance the icon won't be found. In this case, the user sees an error message, and the image does not change (as you can see in Figure 28.12).

The last part of the program is very important, too. When you load a library manually by using LoadLibrary, you must remember to free it by using the FreeLibrary call:

```
procedure TForm1.FormDestroy(Sender: TObject);
begin
  FreeLibrary (HInst);
end;
```

FIGURE 28.12:

The output of the USEICONS
program in the case of an error

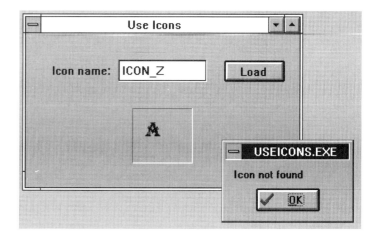

If you forget to do this, the library will remain in memory until you exit Windows,
and you won't even be able to recompile it.

Calling a DLL Function at Run-Time

Now that we know how to access a DLL at run-time, we might want to use this approach to access a function. Since this is quite uncommon, I've built just a very simple example that doesn't make much sense. Let me show you the example first, and then I'll describe when this approach might be interesting.

The example is named DYNACALL and uses the FIRSTDLL library we built earlier in this chapter. Instead of declaring the Beep function and using it as a plain Delphi function, this example obtains the same effect with much more code.

The form of this example simply contains a button. When this button is pressed, the only method of the program is executed. First of all, it calls the LoadLibrary function, as you can see in Listing 28.5. Then, if the handle of the instance is valid, it calls the GetProcAddress API function. This function searches the DLL, looking for the name of the function passed as a parameter. If it finds a match, it returns a pointer to the requested procedure.

LISTING 28.5: The source code of the DYNACALL example

```
unit Dyna_f;

interface

uses
  SysUtils, WinTypes, WinProcs, Messages, Classes,
  Graphics, Controls, Forms, Dialogs, StdCtrls;

type
  TForm1 = class(TForm)
    Button1: TButton;
    procedure Button1Click(Sender: TObject);
  end;

var
  Form1: TForm1;

implementation

{$R *.DFM}

type
  Proc = procedure;

procedure TForm1.Button1Click(Sender: TObject);
var
  HInst: THandle;
  FPointer: TFarProc;
  MyProc: Proc;
begin
  HInst := LoadLibrary ('Firstdll.dll');
  if HInst > 32 then
  begin
    FPointer := GetProcAddress (HInst, 'Beep');
    if FPointer <> nil then
    begin
      MyProc := Proc (FPointer);
      MyProc;
    end;
  end;
end;

end.
```

28

How do you call a procedure in Delphi, once you have a pointer to it? One solution is to convert the pointer to a procedural type and then call the procedure using the procedural type variable. This is the solution the DYNACALL example uses.

Notice that the procedural type you define must be compatible with the definition of the procedure of the DLL function you access. This is the Achilles' heel of this method: there is no check on the parameters.

What is the advantage of this approach? In theory, you can use it to access any function of any DLL at any time. In practice, it is useful when you have different DLLs with compatible functions (or a single DLL with several compatible functions) and you want to be able to access these functions at run-time.

With this code, the compiler and the linker ignore the existence of the DLL. When the program is loaded, the DLL is useless, too. We might mimic the last example, the icon loaded, and let the user enter the name of the DLL to use—or even the name of the function to use, provided it is compatible with a given procedural type. In some cases, this is a great advantage. A user might make a DLL switch while running the program that uses the DLL, something the other approach does not allow.

Note that this approach to loading DLL functions is common in macro languages and is used by most visual programming environments. Also, the Paradox code we saw earlier in this chapter probably uses this approach to call the external DLL function.

Only a system based on a compiler and a linker, such as Delphi, can use the other approach, which is generally more reliable and also a little bit faster.

I think the dynamic loading approach the DYNALINK example uses is generally not useful. However, when you really need it, it can be extremely powerful.

Summary

This chapter about DLL programming ends the book. We have seen how you can use application DLLs created in C++ or other languages and how to create DLLs using Delphi itself. Although I haven't underlined this, Delphi DLLs are as fast, reliable, and usable in other programming environments as C or C++ DLLs. There is no real difference.

To understand DLL programming, we have examined a number of general ideas about DLLs in Windows. Although not a lot them were strictly required in the simple examples we have built, they provide some hints on future development of Delphi DLLs.

However, I do discourage you from building DLLs for Delphi projects. The alternatives, such as compiled units, template forms, and components, are generally more powerful and easier to use. They are more closely related to the Delphi environment and approach, too.

Delphi and Windows share many elements but also have different "views" of programming. When possible, follow the Delphi object-oriented approach over the Windows one, and you'll probably benefit a lot.

Delphi is a great programming environment: now that you can master Delphi, enjoy it.

28

APPENDICES

APPENDIX

A

A Short Overview of OOP Concepts

- The OOP concept of class

- Inheritance and class definitions

- Object polymorphism

- Types of OOP languages

A

The Delphi language, Object Pascal, is an object-oriented programming (OOP) language. Chapter 5 describes the object-oriented features of the language, but it doesn't include much information about OOP in general. This appendix provides an overview of the key elements of OOP.

Abstraction in Programming Languages

The foundation of OOP lies in the idea of abstraction. Programming languages were invented and are used to describe a process at a higher level than the CPU machine code. Traditionally, the abstraction offered by programming languages could be divided into two categories, related to the representation of data and control structures.

The fundamental idea of abstraction in the representation of data is the concept of the data type. Historically, the first generation of programming languages introduced the concept of type, and the second generation (including the original Pascal language) added the idea of user-defined data types, such as records and arrays.

Later on, the idea of the data type evolved into the concept of the *abstract data type,* a type associating the representation of data with the operations used to manipulate it. In an abstract data type, the representation of the data is usually hidden to its users. In these languages, a new data type is perceived as an extension of the type system provided by the language. Classes, as defined by OOP languages, can be considered an extension of the concept of abstract data types.

On the side of control structures, the first programming languages introduced statements for jumps, broaches, and loops. Then came the idea of subroutines (in the form of procedures and functions). With the advent of subroutines, many programming theories were developed, including *functional top-down decomposition.* The abstraction of subroutines is illustrated by the fact that you can call them knowing *what* they do, but you don't need to know *how* they do it. Similarly to abstract data types, new subroutines can be considered extensions of the programming language.

Classes

The first key element of OOP is the concept of class. A class can be defined as the abstract description of a group of objects, each with a specific state but all capable of performing the same operations.

For instance, a bottle is an object that has a state (it can be empty or full and can have different contents, often indicated by a label) and that allows some operations, such as filling it, pouring it, opening it, closing it, changing its contents, and so on. Of course, some operations depend on the state—pouring from an empty bottle doesn't make much sense.

In different words, a class is a type definition that has some fields (the data representing the status of an object of that class) and some methods (the operations), which generally depend on the object's status. Note that in OOP, the term *class* refers to the data type and the term *object* to an instance of the data type, a variable. Unfortunately, some OOP languages (including older versions of Object Pascal) use different terminology.

Within a program, classes have two main purposes:

- Classes define the abstraction they relate to. You can use them to define real-world entities, no matter how complex they are. If the entity is very complex, you can use classes to describe some of its subelements (or subsystems). As I mentioned, you can view classes as extensions of the data types of the program. In the same way, you can consider the new Delphi components you write as extensions of the original VCL shipped with Delphi.

- Classes are the basis of the modularity of a program. In Object Pascal, you can place each new class (defining a form or another element) in its own unit, dividing even a big application into small, manageable pieces. The way Delphi handles the source code of forms naturally leads to this kind of approach. According to the idea of modularity, each class should hide, or encapsulate, some of its elements.

Being based on classes is not the only requirement for a language to be defined as object-oriented. Two other key features are inheritance and polymorphism.

Inheritance

By using inheritance, you can build a new class by defining it in terms of another existing class, instead of by building the class from scratch. A subclass inherits both fields and methods from its parent class.

In the example of the bottle given in the previous section, you can inherit, from the generic bottle, plastic bottles, glass bottles, or specific ones (such as beer or wine bottles). Each bottle has its own form, is handled in a different way, and might have a liquid inside. However, all the bottles share some common characteristics, properties, and methods.

Inheritance is a very powerful language construct, but it is not always easy to understand and use. Here are some guidelines and tips:

- In theory, inheritance represents *specialization*. You can consider a subclass as a special case of the parent class. This is often expressed using an *"is a"* relationship (as in "a plastic bottle *is a* bottle").

- At times, inheritance is used to express *generalization.* If you have a class for managers, one for secretaries, and one for accountants, you can come up with a generic employee class you can use as the parent class for each other class. You can use this parent class to share the common elements, as well as some common code.

- In practice, inheritance is a way to avoid code duplication. Instead of using copy-and-paste techniques to build two similar classes, it is much easier to use one as the parent class of the second. Besides saving some code, you can save some debugging time and handle future changes more easily because there is only one version of the code.

- Another reason to use inheritance is that the compiler *does* understand it. A parent class and a subclass have some form of type compatibility, as described in the next section.

Polymorphism

The other key feature of OOP languages (besides classes and inheritance) is polymorphism, which literally indicates the ability of an object to take many forms. In other words, polymorphism allows you to refer to objects of different classes by means of the same program variable. It also allows you to perform operations on that variable in different ways, according to the data type, the class, and the object currently associated with that variable at the moment.

For example, I can declare a generic variable of the bottle class (say, MyBottle) and then assign to it objects of the TWineBottle or TBeerBottle class. (The *T* in front of the name is a common Borland notation.) Now suppose every class has an Open procedure, each with a different implementation. This method must use dynamic binding. In Object Pascal, this means declaring it in the parent class as `virtual` or `dynamic` (as discussed in Chapter 5) and redefining it with the `override` keyword.

When you apply the Open method to MyBottle, what happens? The Open procedure of the current type of the object is called. If MyBottle is currently a TWineBottle object, the cork is extracted using a proper opener. Opening a beer bottle involves a different action and a different tool.

You can use inheritance and polymorphism together to build programs based on class hierarchies. Writing hierarchy-based code is probably the ultimate OOP approach.

A Definition of OOP

Now that we know what classes, inheritance, and polymorphism are, we can say an OOP language is a language that has at least these three key capabilities. To be more precise, there are three degrees of *object-orientedness*:

- Object-based languages support objects—that is, elements with a set and a state.

- Class-based languages have both objects and classes. Every object is an instance of a class, which defines the operations and the representation of the data.

- Object-oriented languages also have inheritance and polymorphism, two elements that are often related.

There are other more complex and complete definitions of OOP, but each author tends to gear them toward the language he or she prefers, giving a biased opinion.

OOP Languages

There are many OOP languages. Some consider Simula67 the first one, but Small-talk was the first language to provide a complete implementation of the OOP concepts. Then came hybrid languages (that is, OOP languages built on existing languages), such as C++, Objective-C, CLOS (an LISP derivative), and Object Pascal. Other important, and more theoretically sound, OOP languages include Eiffel and Sather. But new OOP languages appear frequently.

You can use two key categories to group OOP languages:

- *Pure versus hybrid:* Pure OOP languages are languages that do not allow other programming models. You cannot write a function by itself if it is not part of a class. You cannot declare a global variable. Examples of pure OOP languages are Smalltalk and Eiffel. With hybrid languages, you can do whatever you want, including forgetting to apply OOP principles completely. Examples of hybrid OOP languages are all those compatible with an existing one, such as C++ or Object Pascal.

- *Static versus dynamic:* Static languages are based on the notion of the data type and perform much compile-time type-checking. Dynamic languages have a weaker type notion and perform most of the checks at run-time. Dynamic languages, such as Smalltalk, are generally interpreted. Static languages, such as Object Pascal, are always compiled.

Object-Oriented Analysis and Design

You can use an OOP language in many ways, particularly when it is an extension of an existing language. However, to exploit the full power of OOP languages, particularly in complex projects, you should probably analyze and design the program following object-oriented principles.

There are several methodologies of object-oriented analysis (OOA) and many object-oriented design (OOD) approaches. Refer to the literature on these specific subjects for information.

Summary

Do not underestimate the role of OOP in Delphi. If you are not familiar with OOP, spend some time learning it, besides delving into Delphi elements and features. A clear comprehension of OOP concepts will allow you to better understand Delphi's inner structure and to write better programs.

Templates, classes, and components are great tools for reusability, but without proper design, applications bigger than the sample programs in this book can get messy. To gain the benefits of OOP (reusability, easy maintenance, and so on), you must know what you are doing, not only how to use an OOP tool.

APPENDIX

B

An Introduction to SQL

- A definition of SQL

- The Select statement and its clauses

- The distinct keyword for eliminating duplicates

- Multiple table joins

- Other SQL statements

B

When you use the TQuery component in a Delphi database application, you need to write a SQL statement for its SQL property, as we saw in Chapter 17. If you own the Client-Server version of Delphi, you can use the Visual Query Builder tool instead of writing a SQL statement from scratch.

In both cases, you need to understand the SQL language. In Chapters 17 and 18, we use some simple SQL statements without describing them in detail. This appendix serves as an introduction to the basics of SQL programming for programmers who have never used SQL.

You can test these SQL statements using the Database Desktop tool. All the SQL statements in this appendix work with the Database Desktop, provided you have selected the proper alias (DBDEMO) with the Alias command of the SQL menu.

What Is SQL?

Before looking at SQL statements and how SQL works, we should have a definition of what SQL is. The SQL acronym stands for Structured Query Language, but this term is often pronounced according to its former name, SEQUEL (for Structured English QUEry Language). SQL is the standard language used to construct and access relational database management systems (RDBMS) of different kinds and on many hardware platforms. Although it is a standard language, there are differences among the SQL dialects implemented in SQL databases.

Here, I'll refer just to a few elements of the language, which, as far as I know, should be common to each SQL dialect. Note that although the name refers to queries, you can use SQL for many other operations besides queries, such as for deleting or updating a database.

The Select Statement

The most important SQL statement is probably the Select statement, which is built around three clauses:

- The `select` clause indicates a list of fields you want in the result of the query; by using the asterisk symbol (*) instead of a list of fields, you can select all of them.

- The from clause indicates the tables you want to consider to build the query.

- The where clause indicates some selection criteria. If the where clause is missing, all the fields are selected.

For example, if you want to select all the rows (or records) of the COUNTRY.DB table (as in the NAVIG2 example in Chapter 17), you can write:

```
select * from Country
```

To specify the rows (or records) you want to consider in the result, you can write:

```
select Name, Capital
  from Country
```

The Where Clause

If you want only some of the rows instead of all of them, you can add a where clause:

```
select Name, Capital
  from Country
  where Population > 20000000
```

This returns only the countries that have more than 20 million inhabitants. In the where clause, you can write several different expressions, including an expression to look for a single element, as in:

```
select *
  from Country
  where Name = "Argentina"
```

Of course, you can also write multiple conditions at the same time. You can merge two conditions with and to indicate that they must be met at the same time, or use or to indicate the record should meet one of the conditions:

```
select *
  from Country
  where Continent - "South America"
  and Population < 10000000

select Name, Capital
  from Country
  where Name <= "Brazil"
  or Capital >= "Ottawa"
```

B

The first statement selects the South American countries with fewer than 10 million inhabitants. The second statement selects the countries that have a name preceding *Brazil* in an alphabetical order and those that have a capital with a name following *Ottawa*.

Avoiding Duplicates

Now suppose you want to have a list of continents for the countries. You can write:

```
select Continent from Country
```

However, like any Select statement in general, this returns the same continent several times. To avoid duplicate elements in the result, you can add one more SQL keyword, `distinct`, which forces duplicate removal:

```
select distinct Continent
    from Country
```

Making a Join

In most cases, SQL statements refer to two or more tables. When you work with two tables, you can join them or use the result of a table to express the condition used in the second one.

When you work on two or more source tables, you'll generally join them. In SQL, there is no specific statement or clause to express a join (although this is possible in the SQL dialect of some RDBMS, including InterBase).

You can simply work on two tables and join them properly using the where clause to match the value of two fields. For example, we can join the Orders and Customer tables to find the date of each order and the company involved by writing:

```
select Orders.OrderNo, Orders.SaleDate,
    Customer.Company, Customer.Contact
  from Orders, Customer
  where Orders.CustNo = Customer.CustNo
```

In exactly the same way, you can join three tables using two conditions. In this case, we also want to know the name of the employee who processed the order:

```
select Orders.OrderNo, Orders.SaleDate,
    Customer.Company, Customer.Contact,
    Employee.LastName
  from Orders, Customer, Employee
  where Orders.CustNo = Customer.CustNo
    and Orders.EmpNo = Employee.EmpNo
```

With the following SQL statement, we retrieve the amount paid by each customer who ordered something by *Johnson:*

```
select Orders.AmountPaid, Customer.Company
  from Orders, Customer, Employee
  where Orders.CustNo = Customer.CustNo
    and Orders.EmpNo = Employee.EmpNo
    and Employee.LastName = "Johnson"
```

More Select Clauses

Besides select, from, and where, you can use other clauses in a Select statement. You can use an ordering clause or a grouping clause, and you can make some computations on tables or groups in a SQL statement.

Choosing an Order

Another SQL clause is order by (two separate words), which determines the order of the values in the resulting query:

```
select *
  from Country
  where Population > 10000000
  order by Continent, Name
```

This statement returns a table with countries ordered by continent first and then by name.

B

Computing Values

In the select clause, instead of a field of a table, you can have the result of a computation. For example, you can compute the number of employees with this statement:

```
select count (*)
  from Employee
```

For a more complex example, you can compute the number of orders taken by an employee, the total amount, and the average:

```
select Sum (Orders.AmountPaid),
    Count (Orders.AmountPaid), Avg (Orders.AmountPaid)
  from Orders, Employee
  where Orders.EmpNo = Employee.EmpNo
    and Employee.LastName = "Johnson"
```

Defining Groups

Besides making a computation on the result of a query, you can compute a value for each group of elements, as indicated by the group by clause.

```
select Employee.LastName, Sum(Orders.AmountPaid)
  from Orders, Employee
  where Orders.EmpNo = Employee.EmpNo
  group by Employee.LastName
```

The result is a list of employees, each with the total amount of the orders that employee has taken.

Beyond Select

Select statements are just a part of SQL, although a very important one and also the main topic of this appendix. However there are other SQL statements you should be aware of. Here are the most important ones:

- Use Insert to add data to a table. Generally, it is also possible to insert the result of a sub-table into a table, although the Database Desktop doesn't allow this.

- Use Update to update the values of a table.

- Delete removes some of the rows of a table.

- Create Table defines a new table.

- Alter Table restructures an existing table, adding or removing columns.

- Drop Table removes a table.

- Create Index builds a new index for a table.

- Drop Index removes an existing index.

Summary

This appendix has presented a very concise exploration of SQL, aimed at beginners. If you want to become a fluent SQL programmer, I suggest that you refer to books on database theories in general, because a good understanding of the basic database concepts is required to write complex SQL statements. Do not overlook how writing the same SQL statement in different ways can affect performance, because this is another important topic, mostly related to the SQL servers you work with.

B

INDEX

Page numbers in *italics* refer to figures; page numbers in **bold** refer to significant discussions of the topic.

B

O

X

Z

FOR EVERY COMPUTER QUESTION, THERE IS A SYBEX BOOK THAT HAS THE ANSWER

Each computer user learns in a different way. Some need thorough, methodical explanations, while others are too busy for details. At Sybex we bring nearly 20 years of experience to developing the book that's right for you. Whatever your needs, we can help you get the most from your software and hardware, at a pace that's comfortable for you.

We start beginners out right. You will learn by seeing and doing with our **Quick & Easy** series: friendly, colorful guidebooks with screen-by-screen illustrations. For hardware novices, the **Your First** series offers valuable purchasing advice and installation support.

Often recognized for excellence in national book reviews, our **Mastering** titles are designed for the intermediate to advanced user, without leaving the beginner behind. A **Mastering** book provides the most detailed reference available. Add our pocket-sized **Instant Reference** titles for a complete guidance system. Programmers will find that the new **Developer's Handbook** series provides a more advanced perspective on developing innovative and original code.

With the breathtaking advances common in computing today comes an ever increasing demand to remain technologically up-to-date. In many of our books, we provide the added value of software, on disks or CDs. Sybex remains your source for information on software development, operating systems, networking, and every kind of desktop application. We even have books for kids. Sybex can help smooth your travels on the **Internet** and provide **Strategies and Secrets** to your favorite computer games.

As you read this book, take note of its quality. Sybex publishes books written by experts—authors chosen for their extensive topical knowledge. In fact, many are professionals working in the computer software field. In addition, each manuscript is thoroughly reviewed by our technical, editorial, and production personnel for accuracy and ease-of-use before you ever see it—our guarantee that you'll buy a quality Sybex book every time.

To manage your hardware headaches and optimize your software potential, ask for a Sybex book.

FOR MORE INFORMATION, PLEASE CONTACT:

Sybex Inc.
2021 Challenger Drive
Alameda, CA 94501
Tel: (510) 523-8233 • (800) 227-2346
Fax: (510) 523-2373

Sybex is committed to using natural resources wisely to preserve and improve our environment. As a leader in the computer books publishing industry, we are aware that over 40% of America's solid waste is paper. This is why we have been printing our books on recycled paper since 1982.

This year our use of recycled paper will result in the saving of more than 153,000 trees. We will lower air pollution effluents by 54,000 pounds, save 6,300,000 gallons of water, and reduce landfill by 27,000 cubic yards.

In choosing a Sybex book you are not only making a choice for the best in skills and information, you are also choosing to enhance the quality of life for all of us.

[1739-2] Mastering Delphi

GET A FREE CATALOG JUST FOR EXPRESSING YOUR OPINION.

Help us improve our books and get a **FREE** full-color catalog in the bargain. Please complete this form, pull out this page and send it in today. The address is on the reverse side.

Name _____   Company _____

Address _____   City _____ State ____ Zip _____

Phone ( )_____

1. How would you rate the overall quality of this book?

❑ Excellent
❑ Very Good
❑ Good
❑ Fair
❑ Below Average
❑ Poor

2. What were the things you liked most about the book? (Check all that apply)

❑ Pace
❑ Format
❑ Writing Style
❑ Examples
❑ Table of Contents
❑ Index
❑ Price
❑ Illustrations
❑ Type Style
❑ Cover
❑ Depth of Coverage
❑ Fast Track Notes

3. What were the things you liked *least* about the book? (Check all that apply)

❑ Pace
❑ Format
❑ Writing Style
❑ Examples
❑ Table of Contents
❑ Index
❑ Price
❑ Illustrations
❑ Type Style
❑ Cover
❑ Depth of Coverage
❑ Fast Track Notes

4. Where did you buy this book?

❑ Bookstore chain
❑ Small independent bookstore
❑ Computer store
❑ Wholesale club
❑ College bookstore
❑ Technical bookstore
❑ Other _____

5. How did you decide to buy this particular book?

❑ Recommended by friend
❑ Recommended by store personnel
❑ Author's reputation
❑ Sybex's reputation
❑ Read book review in _____
❑ Other _____

6. How did you pay for this book?

❑ Used own funds
❑ Reimbursed by company
❑ Received book as a gift

7. What is your level of experience with the subject covered in this book?

❑ Beginner
❑ Intermediate
❑ Advanced

8. How long have you been using a computer?

years _____
months _____

9. Where do you most often use your computer?

❑ Home
❑ Work

❑ Both
❑ Other _____

10. What kind of computer equipment do you have? (Check all that apply)

❑ PC Compatible Desktop Computer
❑ PC Compatible Laptop Computer
❑ Apple/Mac Computer
❑ Apple/Mac Laptop Computer
❑ CD ROM
❑ Fax Modem
❑ Data Modem
❑ Scanner
❑ Sound Card
❑ Other _____

11. What other kinds of software packages do you ordinarily use?

❑ Accounting
❑ Databases
❑ Networks
❑ Apple/Mac
❑ Desktop Publishing
❑ Spreadsheets
❑ CAD
❑ Games
❑ Word Processing
❑ Communications
❑ Money Management
❑ Other _____

12. What operating systems do you ordinarily use?

❑ DOS
❑ OS/2
❑ Windows
❑ Apple/Mac
❑ Windows NT
❑ Other _____

13. On what computer-related subject(s) would you like to see more books?

_____

_____

_____

_____

14. Do you have any other comments about this book? (Please feel free to use a separate piece of paper if you need more room)

_____

_____

_____

_____

- - - - - - - - - - - - - - - PLEASE FOLD, SEAL, AND MAIL TO SYBEX - - - - - - - - - - - -

SYBEX INC.
Department M
2021 Challenger Drive
Alameda, CA
94501

Mastering Delphi Companion CD-ROM

The contents of the companion CD are listed below. You can use a special program on the CD, CDVIEW.EXE, to browse through the CD. See the introduction of this book for information about how the examples are organized on the CD and requirements for running some of the executable files.

BOOKCODE	Source code of samples and executable files
01-28	Samples for Chapters 1 through 28, each in its own subdirectory
COMPONEN	Third-party Delphi components
ABC	Advanced business components
ANIMATE	TAnimated component
BORBTN	BWCC style button components
ESCHALON	Eschalon Power Controls and Setup
INFOPOWE	InfoPower demonstration
INSTALL2	Freeware TInstall component
KINGCAL	King Calendar demonstration
LENHAM	Lenham components
MAGICDEM	Demo of Magic Panel, enhanced TPanel
MBHINT	Multiple-line Hint component
MOBIUS	mobius DrawKit demo
OLEAUTO	TOLEAutomationClient sample
OPAQUE	oxButton and oxDockBar fromOpaque Software
PERSEUS	Demonstration of Perseus components
REPORT	ReportPrinter component
REPORTER	Reporter control
SHORELIN	Trial version of VisualPROS Component Pack
TBLINFO	TblInfo Dlg component
TCONSOL	Text Console component
TPOWER	Trial-run version of Orpheus
TQBE3	TQBE (query by example) component
MAGAZINE	Electronic versions of Delphi-specific magazines
DELPHIMA	Delphi Magazine, in Adobe Acrobat format
INFORMAN	Delphi Informant, in Adobe Acrobat format
UNOFFIC	Unofficial Delphi Newsletter
TOOLS	Delphi-related tools that are not components
BDEPRINT	BDE (Borland Database Engine) Structure Printer
DELPHIR	A resource editor for Delphi
FORM3D	3-D form code and example
OBJREF	A complete list of object classes inVCL
STERP	PASTERP, a script language for Delphi